T0180896

Lecture Notes in Computer Science 12841

More information about this subseries at http://www.springer.com/series/7410

Jung Hee Cheon · Jean-Pierre Tillich (Eds.)

Post-Quantum Cryptography

12th International Workshop, PQCrypto 2021
Daejeon, South Korea, July 20–22, 2021
Proceedings

 Springer

Editors
Jung Hee Cheon ⓘ
Seoul National University
Seoul, Korea (Republic of)

Jean-Pierre Tillich ⓘ
Inria
Paris, France

ISSN 0302-9743 ISSN 1611-3349 (electronic)
Lecture Notes in Computer Science
ISBN 978-3-030-81292-8 ISBN 978-3-030-81293-5 (eBook)
https://doi.org/10.1007/978-3-030-81293-5

LNCS Sublibrary: SL4 – Security and Cryptology

This Springer imprint is published by the registered company Springer Nature Switzerland AG
The registered company address is: Gewerbestrasse 11, 6330 Cham, Switzerland

Preface

PQCrypto 2021, the 12th International Conference on Post-Quantum Cryptography, was held in Daejeon, South Korea, during July 20–22, 2021. The aim of the PQCrypto conference series is to serve as a forum for researchers to present results and exchange ideas on cryptography in an era with large-scale quantum computers. Following the same model as its predecessors, PQCrypto 2021 adopted a two-stage submission process in which authors registered their paper one week before the final submission deadline. The conference received 65 submissions. Each paper (that had not been withdrawn by the authors) was reviewed in private by at least three Program Committee members. The private review phase was followed by an intensive discussion phase, conducted online. At the end of this process, the Program Committee selected 25 papers for inclusion in the technical program and publication in these proceedings. The accepted papers cover a broad spectrum of research within the conference's scope, including code-, hash-, isogeny-, and lattice-based cryptography, multivariate cryptography, and quantum cryptanalysis.

Along with the 25 contributed technical presentations, the program featured outstanding two invited talks - by Dustin Moody on "The Homestretch: the Beginning of the End of the NIST PQC 3rd Round" and by Damien Stehlé on "An Overview of Intractability Assumptions on Module Lattices"- and a special presentation on NIST's post-quantum cryptography standardization.

The PC selected a paper to receive the Best Paper Award: "Decoding supercodes of Gabidulin codes and applications to cryptanalysis" by Maxime Bombar and Alain Couvreur.

Organizing and running this year's edition of the PQCrypto conference series was a team effort, and we are indebted to everyone who helped make PQCrypto 2021 a success. In particular, we would like thank all members of the Program Committee and the external reviewers who were vital for compiling the technical program. Evaluating and discussing the submissions was a labor-intense task, and we truly appreciate the work that went into this. In the name of the community, let us say that we are all indebted to Dooho Choi from ETRI and Kwangjo Kim from KAIST for organizing this meeting. We also thank Neelakandan Paramasivam, Maree Shirota, Selma Somogy, and their colleagues at Springer for handling the publication of these conference proceedings.

June 2021

Jung Hee Cheon
Jean-Pierre Tillich

Organization

General Chairs

Dooho Choi   ETRI, South Korea
Kwangjo Kim   KAIST, South Korea

Program Committee Chairs

Jung Hee Cheon   Seoul National University, South Korea
Jean-Pierre Tillich   Inria, France

Program Committee

Magali Bardet   University of Rouen Normandy, France
Daniel J. Bernstein   University of Illinois at Chicago, USA and
     Ruhr University Bochum, Germany
Olivier Blazy   Université de Limoges, France
André Chailloux   Inria, France
Chen-Mou Cheng   Kanazawa University, Japan
Jintai Ding   University of Cincinnati, USA
Leo Ducas   CWI, Netherlands
Scott Fluhrer   Cisco Systems, USA
Philippe Gaborit   University of Limoges, France
Tommaso Gagliardoni   Kudelski Security, Switzerland
Steven Galbraith   The University of Auckland, New Zealand
Tim Güneysu   Ruhr-Universität Bochum and DFKI,
     Germany
Dong-Guk Han   Kookmin University, South Korea
David Jao   University of Waterloo and evolutionQ,
     Canada
Thomas Johansson   Lund University, Sweden
Howon Kim   Pusan National University, South Korea
Jon-Lark Kim   Sogang University, South Korea
Kwangjo Kim   Korea Advanced Institute of Science and
     Technology, South Korea
Elena Kirshanova   I.Kant Baltic Federal University, Russia
     and Ruhr University Bochum, Germany
Tanja Lange   Eindhoven University of Technology,
     Netherlands

Changmin Lee	KIAS, South Korea
Christian Majenz	QuSoft and CWI, Netherlands
Alexander May	Ruhr-Universität Bochum, Germany
Rafael Misoczki	Google, USA
Michele Mosca	University of Waterloo, Canada
Khoa Nguyen	Nanyang Technological University, Singapore
Ray Perlner	NIST, USA
Christophe Petit	Université libre de Bruxelles, Belgium
Rachel Player	Royal Holloway, University of London, UK
Thomas Prest	PQShield Ltd., UK
Thomas Pöppelmann	Infineon, Germany
Nicolas Sendrier	Inria, France
Jae Hong Seo	Hanyang University, South Korea
Benjamin Smith	Inria and École Polytechnique, France
Daniel Smith-Tone	NIST, USA
Yongsoo Song	Seoul National University, South Korea
Damien Stehlé	ENS de Lyon, France
Rainer Steinwandt	The University of Alabama in Huntsville, USA
Tsuyoshi Takagi	The University of Tokyo, Japan
Keita Xagawa	NTT, Japan
Bo-Yin Yang	Academia Sinica, Taiwan
Aaram Yun	Ewha Womans University, South Korea
Zhenfei Zhang	Algorand, USA

Additional Reviewers

Nicolas Aragon	Boris Fouotsa
Florian Bache	Aymeric Genêt
Nina Bindel	Erin Hales
Xavier Bonnetain	Adrien Hauteville
Maxime Bros	Daniel Heinz
Jonathan Chang	Julius Hermelink
Ilaria Chillotti	Kathrin Hövelmanns
Anamaria Costache	Andreas Hülsing
Benjamin Curtis	Yasuhiko Ikematsu
Delpech de Saint-Guilhem Cyprien	Junki Kang
Thomas Debris-Alazard	Jiseung Kim
Rafaël Del Pino	Miran Kim
Julien Devevey	Stefan Kolbl
Samuel Dobson	Péter Kutas
Jelle Don	Yi-Fu Lai

Contents

Code-Based Cryptography

Decoding Supercodes of Gabidulin Codes and Applications
to Cryptanalysis 3
   Maxime Bombar and Alain Couvreur

LESS-FM: Fine-Tuning Signatures from the Code Equivalence Problem 23
   Alessandro Barenghi, Jean-François Biasse, Edoardo Persichetti,
   and Paolo Santini

Classical and Quantum Algorithms for Generic Syndrome Decoding
Problems and Applications to the Lee Metric 44
   André Chailloux, Thomas Debris-Alazard, and Simona Etinski

Multivariate Cryptography

Improving Thomae-Wolf Algorithm for Solving Underdetermined
Multivariate Quadratic Polynomial Problem 65
   Hiroki Furue, Shuhei Nakamura, and Tsuyoshi Takagi

New Practical Multivariate Signatures from a Nonlinear Modifier 79
   Daniel Smith-Tone

On the Effect of Projection on Rank Attacks in Multivariate Cryptography 98
   Morten Øygarden, Daniel Smith-Tone, and Javier Verbel

Quantum Algorithms

Quantum Key Search for Ternary LWE 117
   Iggy van Hoof, Elena Kirshanova, and Alexander May

A Fusion Algorithm for Solving the Hidden Shift Problem in Finite
Abelian Groups 133
   Wouter Castryck, Ann Dooms, Carlo Emerencia, and Alexander Lemmens

The "Quantum Annoying" Property of Password-Authenticated Key
Exchange Protocols 154
   Edward Eaton and Douglas Stebila

Implementation and Side Channel Attack

Differential Power Analysis of the Picnic Signature Scheme 177
  Tim Gellersen, Okan Seker, and Thomas Eisenbarth

Implementation of Lattice Trapdoors on Modules and Applications 195
  Pauline Bert, Gautier Eberhart, Lucas Prabel, Adeline Roux-Langlois,
  and Mohamed Sabt

Verifying Post-Quantum Signatures in 8 kB of RAM 215
  Ruben Gonzalez, Andreas Hülsing, Matthias J. Kannwischer,
  Juliane Krämer, Tanja Lange, Marc Stöttinger, Elisabeth Waitz,
  Thom Wiggers, and Bo-Yin Yang

Fast NEON-Based Multiplication for Lattice-Based NIST Post-quantum
Cryptography Finalists 234
  Duc Tri Nguyen and Kris Gaj

Isogeny

CSI-RAShi: Distributed Key Generation for CSIDH 257
  Ward Beullens, Lucas Disson, Robi Pedersen, and Frederik Vercauteren

SimS: A Simplification of SiGamal 277
  Tako Boris Fouotsa and Christophe Petit

Memory Optimization Techniques for Computing Discrete Logarithms
in Compressed SIKE 296
  Aaron Hutchinson, Koray Karabina, and Geovandro Pereira

Lattice-Based Cryptography

Generating Cryptographically-Strong Random Lattice Bases
and Recognizing Rotations of $\mathbb{Z}^n$ 319
  Tamar Lichter Blanks and Stephen D. Miller

Zero-Knowledge Proofs for Committed Symmetric Boolean Functions 339
  San Ling, Khoa Nguyen, Duong Hieu Phan, Hanh Tang,
  and Huaxiong Wang

Short Identity-Based Signatures with Tight Security from Lattices 360
  Jiaxin Pan and Benedikt Wagner

On Removing Rejection Conditions in Practical Lattice-Based Signatures 380
  Rouzbeh Behnia, Yilei Chen, and Daniel Masny

Secure Hybrid Encryption in the Standard Model from Hard Learning
Problems 399
    Xavier Boyen, Malika Izabachène, and Qinyi Li

Cryptanalysis

Attacks on Beyond-Birthday-Bound MACs in the Quantum Setting 421
    Tingting Guo, Peng Wang, Lei Hu, and Dingfeng Ye

An Algebraic Approach to the Rank Support Learning Problem 442
    Magali Bardet and Pierre Briaud

Quantum Indistinguishability for Public Key Encryption 463
    Tommaso Gagliardoni, Juliane Krämer, and Patrick Struck

A Practical Adaptive Key Recovery Attack on the LGM (GSW-like)
Cryptosystem 483
    Prastudy Fauzi, Martha Norberg Hovd, and Håvard Raddum

Author Index 499

Code-Based Cryptography

Decoding Supercodes of Gabidulin Codes and Applications to Cryptanalysis

Maxime Bombar[1,2]([✉]) and Alain Couvreur[1,2]

[1] LIX, CNRS UMR 7161, École Polytechnique, Institut Polytechnique de Paris,
1 rue Honoré d'Estienne d'Orves, 91120 Palaiseau Cedex, France
[2] Inria Saclay, Palaiseau, France
{maxime.bombar,alain.couvreur}@inria.fr

Abstract. This article discusses the decoding of Gabidulin codes and shows how to extend the usual decoder to any supercode of a Gabidulin code at the cost of a significant decrease of the decoding radius. Using this decoder, we provide polynomial time attacks on the rank metric encryption schemes RAMESSES and LIGA.

Keywords: Code–based cryptography · Gabidulin codes · Decoding · Rank metric · Cryptanalysis

Introduction

It is well–known that error correcting codes lie among the possible candidates for post quantum cryptographic primitives. For codes endowed with the Hamming metric the story begins in 1978 with McEliece's proposal [14]. The security of this scheme relies on two difficult problems: the hardness of distinguishing classical Goppa codes from arbitrary codes and the hardness of the syndrome decoding problem. To instantiate McEliece scheme, the only requirement is to have a family of codes whose structure can be hidden and benefiting from an efficient decoder. In particular, this paradigm does not require the use of codes endowed with the Hamming metric. Hence other metrics may be considered such as the rank metric, as proposed by Gabidulin, Paramonov and Tretjakov in [8].

Besides McEliece's paradigm, another approach to perform encryption with error correcting codes consists in using codes whose structure is no longer hidden but where encryption is performed so that decryption without the knowledge of the secret key would require to decode the public code far beyond the decoding radius. This principle has been first instantiated in Hamming metric by Augot and Finiasz in [3] using Reed–Solomon codes. Later, a rank metric counterpart is designed by Faure and Loidreau in [7]. Both proposals have been subject to attacks, by Coron [6] for the Hamming metric proposal and by Gaborit, Otmani and Talé–Kalachi [9] for the rank metric one. More recently, two independent and different repairs of Faure–Loidreau scheme resisting to the attack of Gaborit, Otmani and Talé–Kalachi appeared. The first one, due to Renner, Puchinger and Wachter–Zeh and is called LIGA [16,19]. The second one, due to Lavauzelle, Loidreau and Pham is called RAMESSES [12].

© Springer Nature Switzerland AG 2021
J. H. Cheon and J.-P. Tillich (Eds.): PQCrypto 2021, LNCS 12841, pp. 3–22, 2021.
https://doi.org/10.1007/978-3-030-81293-5_1

Our Contribution. In the present article, we show how to extend the decoding of a Gabidulin code to a supercode at the cost of a significant decrease of the decoding radius. With this decoder in hand we perform a polynomial time message recovery attack on RAMESSES and LIGA.

1   Notation and Prerequisites

In this article, we work over a finite field $\mathbb{F}_q$ and we frequently consider two nested extensions denoted $\mathbb{F}_{q^m}$ and $\mathbb{F}_{q^{mu}}$. Rank metric codes will be subspaces $\mathscr{C} \subseteq \mathbb{F}_{q^m}^n$, the code length and dimension are respectively denoted as n and k.

Vectors are represented by lower case bold face letters such as $\boldsymbol{a}, \boldsymbol{c}, \boldsymbol{e}$ and matrices by upper case letters $\boldsymbol{A}, \boldsymbol{G}, \boldsymbol{M}$. The space of $m \times n$ matrices with entries in a field $\mathbb{K}$ is denoted by $\mathcal{M}_{m,n}(\mathbb{K})$. When $m = n$ we denote it by $\mathcal{M}_n(\mathbb{K})$ and the group of non-singular matrices is denoted by $\mathrm{GL}_n(\mathbb{K})$. Given a matrix $\boldsymbol{M} \in \mathcal{M}_{m,n}(\mathbb{F}_q)$ its rank is denoted by $\mathbf{rank_q}(\boldsymbol{M})$. Similarly, given a vector $\boldsymbol{c} \in \mathbb{F}_{q^m}^n$, the $\mathbb{F}_q$*-rank* or *rank* of $\boldsymbol{c}$ is defined as the dimension of the subspace of $\mathbb{F}_{q^m}$ spanned by the entries of $\boldsymbol{c}$. Namely,

$$\mathbf{rank_q}(\boldsymbol{c}) \overset{\text{def}}{=} \dim_{\mathbb{F}_q}\left(\mathbf{Span}_{\mathbb{F}_q}\{c_1, \ldots, c_n\}\right).$$

We will consider two notions of *support* in the rank metric. Inspired by the Hamming metric, the most natural one which we will denote by the *column support* of a vector $\boldsymbol{c} \in \mathbb{F}_{q^m}^n$ is the linear subspace spanned by its coordinates:

$$\mathrm{Supp}(\boldsymbol{c}) \overset{\text{def}}{=} \mathbf{Span}_{\mathbb{F}_q}\{c_1, \ldots, c_n\}.$$

Given $\boldsymbol{c} = (c_1, \ldots, c_n) \in \mathbb{F}_{q^m}^n$, and $j \in \{0, \ldots, m-1\}$, we denote

$$\boldsymbol{c}^{[j]} \overset{\text{def}}{=} (c_1^{q^j}, \ldots, c_n^{q^j}).$$

Similarly, for a code $\mathscr{C} \subseteq \mathbb{F}_{q^m}^n$, we denote $\mathscr{C}^{[j]} \overset{\text{def}}{=} \left\{\boldsymbol{c}^{[j]} \mid \boldsymbol{c} \in \mathscr{C}\right\}$.. Let $n \leqslant m$, $k \leqslant n$ and $\boldsymbol{g} \in \mathbb{F}_{q^m}^n$ with $\mathbf{rank_q}(\boldsymbol{g}) = \mathbf{n}$, the *Gabidulin code of dimension* k *supported by* $\boldsymbol{g}$ is defined as

$$\mathscr{G}_k(\boldsymbol{g}) \overset{\text{def}}{=} \mathbf{Span}_{\mathbb{F}_{q^m}}\left\{\boldsymbol{g}^{[i]} \mid 0 \leqslant i \leqslant k-1\right\}.$$

A q*-polynomial* is a polynomial $P \in \mathbb{F}_{q^m}[X]$ whose monomials are only q-th powers of X, *i.e.* a polynomial of the form $P(X) = p_0 X + p_1 X^q + \cdots + p_r X^{q^r}$.

Assuming that $p_r \neq 0$ then the integer r is called the q*-degree* of P. Such a polynomial induces an $\mathbb{F}_q$-linear map $P : \mathbb{F}_{q^m} \to \mathbb{F}_{q^m}$ and we call the *rank* of the q-polynomial, the rank of the induced map. A well-known fact on q-polynomials is that the $\mathbb{F}_q$ – dimension of the kernel of the induced endomorphism is bounded from above by their q-degree. Conversely, any $\mathbb{F}_q$ – linear endomorphism of $\mathbb{F}_{q^m}$ is uniquely represented by a q – polynomial of degree $< m$. Denote by $\mathcal{L}$ the space of q-polynomials, this space equipped with the composition law is a non commutative ring which is left and right Euclidean [11, Section 1.6] and the two–sided ideal $(X^{q^m} - X)$ is the kernel of the canonical map

$$\mathcal{L} \longrightarrow \mathrm{Hom}_{\mathbb{F}_q}(\mathbb{F}_{q^m}, \mathbb{F}_{q^m})$$

inducing an isomorphism : $\mathcal{L}/(X^{q^m} - X) \simeq \mathrm{Hom}_{\mathbb{F}_q}(\mathbb{F}_{q^m}, \mathbb{F}_{q^m})$. Finally, given a positive integer $k < m$, we denote by $\mathcal{L}_{<k}$ (resp. $\mathcal{L}_{\leqslant k}$) the space of q–polynomials of q–degree less than (resp. less than or equal to) k. The Gabidulin code $\mathscr{G}_k(\boldsymbol{g})$ is canonically isomorphic to $\mathcal{L}_{<k}$ under the isomorphism:

$$\begin{cases} \mathcal{L}_{<k} \longrightarrow & \mathscr{G}_k(\boldsymbol{g}) \\ P \longmapsto & (P(g_1), \dots, P(g_n)). \end{cases}$$

The above map is actually an isometry: it is rank preserving. In this article, we will extensively use this isometry and Gabidulin codes will be represented either as an evaluation code or as a space of q–polynomials of bounded degree $\mathcal{L}_{<k}$, when one representation is more suitable than the other.

Another notion which is very useful in the sequel is the notion of *adjoint* of a class of q–polynomial $P = \sum_{i=0}^{m-1} p_i X^{q^i}$ in $\mathcal{L}/(X^{q^m} - X)$, which is defined as

$$P^{\vee}(X) \stackrel{\mathrm{def}}{=} \sum_{i=0}^{m-1} X^{q^{m-i}} p_i = \sum_{i=0}^{m-1} p_i^{q^{m-i}} X^{q^{m-i}}. \tag{1}$$

Regarding P as an $\mathbb{F}_q$–linear endomorphism of $\mathbb{F}_{q^m}$, the notion of adjoint is nothing but the usual notion of *adjoint* or *transposed* endomorphism with respect to the inner product $\begin{cases} \mathbb{F}_{q^m} \times \mathbb{F}_{q^m} \longrightarrow & \mathbb{F}_q \\ (x, y) \longmapsto & \mathrm{Tr}_{\mathbb{F}_{q^m}/\mathbb{F}_q}(xy) \end{cases}$ (see [2, Section 2.4]) In particular, for any $P \in \mathcal{L}/(X^{q^m} - X)$, we have $\mathbf{rank_q(P)} = \mathbf{rank_q(P^{\vee})}$.

2 Two Rank Metric Proposals with Short Keys

2.1 LIGA encryption scheme

In this section, we recall Faure–Loidreau cryptosystem [7] and the repaired version [19] recently extended to proposal LIGA [16].

Parameters. Let q, m, n, k, u, w be positive integers such that q is a prime power, $u < k < n$ and

$$n - k > w > \lfloor \tfrac{n-k}{2} \rfloor.$$

In the following, we consider the three finite fields $\mathbb{F}_q \subseteq \mathbb{F}_{q^m} \subseteq \mathbb{F}_{q^{mu}}$.

Let $t_{pub} \stackrel{\mathrm{def}}{=} \lfloor \frac{n-k-w}{2} \rfloor$ be the public $\mathbb{F}_q$–rank of the error in the ciphertext, and let $\boldsymbol{G}$ be a generator matrix of a public Gabidulin code of length n and dimension k over $\mathbb{F}_{q^m}$.

Key Generation. Alice picks uniformly at random a vector $\boldsymbol{x} \in \mathbb{F}_{q^{mu}}^k$ whose last u entries form an $\mathbb{F}_{q^m}$–basis of $\mathbb{F}_{q^{mu}}$, and a vector $\boldsymbol{z} \in \mathbb{F}_{q^{mu}}^n$ of $\mathbb{F}_q$–rank w. In order to do that, she chooses a full-rank vector $\boldsymbol{s} \in \mathbb{F}_{q^{mu}}^w$ and a non-singular matrix $\boldsymbol{P} \in \mathrm{GL}_n(\mathbb{F}_q)$ and sets

$$\boldsymbol{z} = (\boldsymbol{s} \mid \boldsymbol{0}) \cdot \boldsymbol{P}^{-1}.$$

The *private key* is then $(\boldsymbol{x}, \boldsymbol{z}, \boldsymbol{P})$ and the *public key* is the *vector*

$$\boldsymbol{k}_{pub} \overset{\text{def}}{=} \boldsymbol{x} \cdot \boldsymbol{G} + \boldsymbol{z} \in \mathbb{F}_{q^{mu}}^n.$$

The key generation is summarised by Algorithm 1.

Algorithm 1: Original Faure–Loidreau Key Generation

Input: Parameters $q, \boldsymbol{G}, m, n, k, u, w$.
Output: Private key **sk**, and public key **pk**
1   $\boldsymbol{x} \xleftarrow{\$} \{\boldsymbol{a} \in \mathbb{F}_{q^{mu}}^k \mid \dim(\mathbf{Span}_{\mathbb{F}_{q^m}}\{a_{k-u+1}, \ldots, a_k\}) = u\}$
2   $\boldsymbol{s} \xleftarrow{\$} \{\boldsymbol{a} \in \mathbb{F}_{q^{mu}}^w \mid \mathbf{rank_q}(\boldsymbol{a}) = \mathbf{w}\}$
3   $\boldsymbol{P} \xleftarrow{\$} \mathrm{GL}_n(\mathbb{F}_q)$
4   $\boldsymbol{z} \leftarrow (\boldsymbol{s} \mid \boldsymbol{0}) \cdot \boldsymbol{P}^{-1}$
5   $\boldsymbol{k}_{pub} \leftarrow \boldsymbol{x} \cdot \boldsymbol{G} + \boldsymbol{z}$
6   $\mathbf{sk} \leftarrow (\boldsymbol{x}, \boldsymbol{z}, \boldsymbol{P})$
7   $\mathbf{pk} \leftarrow \boldsymbol{k}_{pub}$
8   **return** (**sk**, **pk**)

Encryption. Let $\boldsymbol{m} = (m_1, \ldots, m_{k-u}, 0, \ldots, 0) \in \mathbb{F}_{q^m}^k$ be the plaintext. Note that the last u entries are chosen to be zero in order to be able to decrypt. The encryption of $\boldsymbol{m}$ works as follows:

1. Pick $\alpha \in \mathbb{F}_{q^{mu}}$ at random.
2. Pick $\boldsymbol{e} \in \mathbb{F}_{q^m}^n$ such that $\mathbf{rank_q}(\boldsymbol{e}) \leqslant \mathbf{t_{pub}}$ at random.

The ciphertext is then $\boldsymbol{c} \in \mathbb{F}_{q^m}^n$:

$$\boldsymbol{c} = \boldsymbol{m} \cdot \boldsymbol{G} + \mathrm{Tr}_{q^{mu}/q^m}(\alpha \boldsymbol{k}_{pub}) + \boldsymbol{e}.$$

As shown in (2) below, the public key acts on the one hand as a one-time pad on the message $\boldsymbol{m}$, and on the other hand adds a random error of large weight. The ciphertext can indeed be seen as a codeword of the Gabidulin code corrupted by a two-part errors formed by the private key $\boldsymbol{z}$ and the random error vector $\boldsymbol{e}$:

$$\boldsymbol{c} = (\boldsymbol{m} + \mathrm{Tr}_{q^{mu}/q^m}(\alpha \boldsymbol{x})) \cdot \boldsymbol{G} + (\mathrm{Tr}_{q^{mu}/q^m}(\alpha \boldsymbol{z}) + \boldsymbol{e}). \tag{2}$$

With very high probability, the error in the *ciphertext* is of rank-weight $w + t_{pub}$. See [16] for a detailed discussion about the parameters in order to avoid so-called weak keys.

Decryption. The *receiver* first computes

$$\boldsymbol{c} \cdot \boldsymbol{P} = (\boldsymbol{m} + \mathrm{Tr}_{q^{mu}/q^m}(\alpha \boldsymbol{x})) \cdot \boldsymbol{GP} + (\mathrm{Tr}_{q^{mu}/q^m}(\alpha \boldsymbol{s}) \mid 0) + \boldsymbol{eP}.$$

whose last $n - w$ entries are given by

$$\boldsymbol{c}' = (\boldsymbol{m} + \mathrm{Tr}_{q^{mu}/q^m}(\alpha \boldsymbol{x})) \cdot \boldsymbol{G}' + \boldsymbol{e}',$$

where $\boldsymbol{G}'$ is the generator matrix of a Gabidulin code of length $n - w$ and dimension k and $\boldsymbol{e}'$ is an error vector of rank-weight at most $t_{pub} = \lfloor \frac{n-w-k}{2} \rfloor$. By decoding in this new Gabidulin code, the *receiver* obtains the vector

$$\boldsymbol{m}' = \boldsymbol{m} + \mathrm{Tr}_{q^{mu}/q^m}(\alpha \boldsymbol{x}).$$

Since by construction $\boldsymbol{m}$ is chosen such that its last u components are 0 and the last u components of $\boldsymbol{x}$ form a basis of $\mathbb{F}_{q^{mu}}/\mathbb{F}_{q^m}$, the *receiver* can deduce the plaintext $\boldsymbol{m}$ from the knowledge of $\boldsymbol{m}'$ and $\boldsymbol{x}$. This encryption scheme has no decryption failure.

A Key Recovery Attack. In [9], Gaborit, Otmani and Talé–Kalachi showed that a valid private key for this system could be efficiently computed from $\boldsymbol{k}_{pub}$, and later in [16,19], Renner, Puchinger and Wachter–Zeh introduced a coding-theoretic interpretation of the public key as a corrupted codeword of an u–interleaved Gabidulin code. They derived an equally powerful key recovery attack, and proved that the failure conditions of both attacks were equivalent.

Based on this interpretation, Renner et al. proposed to change the key generation algorithm to resist previous attacks. More precisely, they proved that if ζ denotes the dimension of the $\mathbb{F}_{q^m}$–support of $\boldsymbol{z}$, all then known attacks were inefficient when $\zeta < \frac{w}{n-k-w}$. The new key generation can be summarised in Algorithm 2.

2.2 Ramesses

In this section, we present the proposal RAMESSES [12] which is another repair of the Faure–Loidreau scheme. We chose to describe the scheme in a rather different manner which turns out to be completely equivalent to the original proposal. The connection between this point of view and that of the original article is detailed in Appendix A. Our presentation rests only on q–polynomials. As explained in Sect. 1, the space $\mathcal{L}_{<k}$ will be regarded as a Gabidulin code of dimension k. We also fix an $\mathbb{F}_q$–basis $\mathscr{B}$ of $\mathbb{F}_{q^m}$, which permits to have an $m \times m$ matrix representation of q–polynomials (modulo $(X^{q^m} - X)$) and conversely provides a description of any $m \times m$ matrix with entries in $\mathbb{F}_q$ as a q–polynomial of q–degree less than m.

Parameters. The public parameters are integers $1 \leqslant w, k, \ell, t \leqslant m$ and should satisfy

$$t \leqslant \frac{n - k - \ell - w}{2}. \tag{3}$$

Algorithm 2: LIGA Key Generation

Input: Parameters $q, G, m, n, k, u, w, \zeta$.
Output: Private key **sk**, and public key **pk**

1   $\gamma \xleftarrow{\$} \{a \in \mathbb{F}_{q^{mu}}^{u} \mid \mathbf{rank_{q^m}}(a) = \mathbf{u}\}$

2   $x \xleftarrow{\$} \{a \in \mathbb{F}_{q^{mu}}^{k} \mid \dim(\mathbf{Span}_{\mathbb{F}_{q^m}}\{a_{k-u+1}, \ldots, a_k\}) = u\}$

3   $\mathcal{A} \xleftarrow{\$} \{$subspaces $\mathcal{U} \subseteq \mathbb{F}_{q^m}^{w} \mid \dim \mathcal{U} = \zeta, \; \mathcal{U}$ has a basis of full-$\mathbb{F}_q$-rank elements$\}$

4   $\begin{pmatrix} s_1 \\ \vdots \\ s_u \end{pmatrix} \xleftarrow{\$} \left\{ \begin{pmatrix} s'_1 \\ \vdots \\ s'_u \end{pmatrix} \middle| \langle s'_1, \ldots, s'_u \rangle_{\mathbb{F}_{q^m}} = \mathcal{A}, \; \mathbf{rank_q}(s'_i) = \mathbf{w} \; \forall \mathbf{i} \right\}$

5   $s \leftarrow \sum_{i=1}^{u} s_i \gamma_i^{*}$

6   $P \xleftarrow{\$} \mathrm{GL}_n(\mathbb{F}_q)$

7   $z \leftarrow (s \mid 0) \cdot P^{-1}$

8   $k_{pub} \leftarrow xG + z$

9   sk$\leftarrow (x, z, P)$

10   pk$\leftarrow k_{pub}$

11   **return (sk, pk)**

Key Generation. Alice picks a uniformly random q–polynomial K_{sec} of rank w. The public key is the affine space:

$$\mathscr{C}_{\mathrm{pub}} \overset{\mathrm{def}}{=} K_{\mathrm{sec}} + \mathcal{L}_{<k}.$$

Encryption. The plaintext m is a t–dimensional $\mathbb{F}_q$–subspace of $\mathbb{F}_{q^m}$. It is encrypted as follows:

– Pick a uniformly random $T \in \mathcal{L}$ of q–degree ℓ
– Pick a uniformly random $E \in \mathcal{L}_{<m}$ whose matrix representation admits m as its row space, equivalently E is such that m is the image of $E^{\vee}$.
– Pick a uniformly random $C \in \mathcal{L}_{<k}$
– Pick a uniformly random $C_0 \in \mathcal{L}_{<k}$, yielding a uniformly random

$$C' = C_0 + K_{\mathrm{sec}} \in \mathscr{C}_{\mathrm{pub}}.$$

The ciphertext is

$$Y \overset{\mathrm{def}}{=} C + C' \circ T + E. \tag{4}$$

Note that, this cipher text satisfies

$$Y = C_1 + K_{\mathrm{sec}} \circ T + E, \tag{5}$$

where $C_1 = C + C_0 \circ T \in \mathcal{L}_{<k} + \mathcal{L}_{<k} \circ T \subseteq \mathcal{L}_{<k+\ell}$. This C_1 is *a priori* unknown by anyone.

Decryption. The owner of K_{sec} knows a q–polynomial $V \in \mathcal{L}_{\leqslant w}$ such that $V \circ K_{\mathrm{sec}} \equiv 0 \mod (X^{q^m} - X)$. Hence she can compute

$$V \circ Y \equiv V \circ C_1 + V \circ E \mod (X^{q^m} - X).$$

Now, $V \circ C_1 \in \mathcal{L}_{<k+\ell+w}$, *i.e.* lies in a Gabidulin code, while $\mathbf{rank_q}(\mathbf{V} \circ \mathbf{E}) \leqslant \mathbf{rank_q}(\mathbf{E}) = \mathbf{t}$. Hence, thanks to (3), one can deduce $V \circ E$ and as soon as $\mathbf{rank_q}(\mathbf{V} \circ \mathbf{E}) = \mathbf{t}$, the row space of the matrix representation of E is that of $V \circ E$ which can be recovered.

3   Decoding of Gabidulin Codes on the Right

In this section, we assume that $n = m$, *i.e.* $\boldsymbol{g} \overset{\text{def}}{=} (g_1, \ldots, g_n)$ forms a basis of the extension field $\mathbb{F}_{q^m}/\mathbb{F}_q$. Let $\mathscr{C}$ be a Gabidulin code of dimension k and support $\boldsymbol{g}$. Suppose we receive a vector $\boldsymbol{y} = \boldsymbol{c} + \boldsymbol{e}$ where $\boldsymbol{c} \in \mathscr{C}$ and $\boldsymbol{e}$ has rank $t \leqslant \lfloor \frac{n-k}{2} \rfloor$. There exist three q–polynomials $C \in \mathcal{L}_{<k}$ and $Y, E \in \mathcal{L}_{<m}$ with $\mathbf{rank_q}(\mathbf{E}) = \mathbf{t}$ such that

$$Y = C + E \tag{6}$$

and the polynomial Y can be deduced from the knowledge of $\boldsymbol{y}$ and the basis $\boldsymbol{g}$ by interpolation (see for instance [18, Chapter 3]).

Remark 1. Note that the requirement $n = m$ is necessary. Indeed, if $n < m$ the choice of the interpolating polynomial $Y \in \mathcal{L}_{<m}$ is not unique and a wrong choice for Y yields an $E = Y - C$ of too large rank. It is not clear to us how to weaken this condition.

In a nutshell, our approach can be explained as follows. Starting from the decoding problem (6) and applying the adjunction operator we have to solve the problem

$$Y^{\vee} = C^{\vee} + E^{\vee},$$

where $\mathbf{rank_q}\mathbf{E}^{\vee} = \mathbf{rank_q}\mathbf{E} \leqslant \lfloor \frac{n-k}{2} \rfloor$ and $C^{\vee}$ is contained in a code which is equivalent to a Gabidulin code. Hence, $C^{\vee}$ can be recovered by applying the decoding algorithm of [13]. In Appendix B, we give further details on how to implement in practice such a decoder. We believe that this algorithm might be folklore, but we weren't able to find it in the literature.

4   Decoding Supercodes of Gabidulin Codes

A common feature of the cryptanalyses to follow can be understood as the decoding of a supercode of a Gabidulin code. Consider a code (represented as a subspace of $\mathcal{L}_{<m}$)

$$\mathscr{C} \overset{\text{def}}{=} \mathcal{L}_{<k} \oplus \mathscr{T},$$

where $\mathscr{T} \subseteq \mathcal{L}_{<m}$, the code $\mathscr{C}$ benefits from a decoding algorithm in a similar manner to that of [13]. Indeed, given a received word $Y = C + E$ where $C \in \mathscr{C}$ and $E \in \mathcal{L}_{<m}$ with $\mathbf{rank_q}\mathbf{E} = \mathbf{t}$, one can look for the left annihilator of E. Let $\Lambda \in \mathcal{L}_{\leqslant t}$ be the left annihilator of E. We have to solve

$$\Lambda \circ Y \equiv \Lambda \circ C \mod (X^{q^m} - X),$$

where the unknowns are Λ, C. Then, similarly to the decoding of Gabidulin codes, one may linearise the system. For this sake, recall that $C = C_0 + T$ for $C_0 \in \mathcal{L}_{<k}$ and $T \in \mathcal{T}$. Therefore, we are looking for the solutions of a system

$$\Lambda \circ Y \equiv N \quad \mathrm{mod}\ (X^{q^m} - X) \tag{7}$$

where $N \in (\mathcal{L}_{\leqslant t} \circ \mathcal{L}_{<k}) + \mathcal{L}_{\leqslant t} \circ \mathcal{T} = \mathcal{L}_{<k+t} + \mathcal{L}_{\leqslant t} \circ \mathcal{T}$.

Lemma 1. *Under the assumption that* $(\mathcal{L}_{<k+t} + \mathcal{L}_{\leqslant t} \circ \mathcal{T}) \cap (\mathcal{L}_{\leqslant t} \circ E) = \{0\}$, *any nonzero solution* (Λ, N) *of the system (7) satisfies* $\Lambda \circ E = 0$.

Proof. Let (Λ, N) be such a nonzero solution. Then,

$$\Lambda \circ Y - \Lambda \circ C \equiv \Lambda \circ E \quad \mathrm{mod}\ (X^{q^m} - X).$$

Since $\Lambda \circ Y \equiv N \mod (X^{q^m} - X)$, the left–hand side is contained in $(\mathcal{L}_{<k+t} + \mathcal{L}_{\leqslant t} \circ \mathcal{T})$ while the right–hand one is contained in $\mathcal{L}_{\leqslant t} \circ E$. Therefore, by assumption, both sides are zero. This yields the result. □

Under the hypotheses of Lemma 1, decoding can be performed as follows.

1. Solve System (7).
2. Take a nonzero solution (Λ, N) of the system. Compute the right kernel of Λ. This kernel contains the image of E and hence the support of the error.
3. Knowing the support of E, one can recover it by solving a linear system. See for instance [10, Section 3] or [1, Section 1.4].

Remark 2. Note that for the decoding of Gabidulin codes, once a solution (Λ, N) is computed, one can recover C by left Euclidean division of N by Λ. In the present situation, this calculation is no longer efficient. Indeed, the proof of Lemma 1 permits only to assert that $N \equiv \Lambda \circ C \mod (X^{q^m} - X)$. In the Gabidulin case, the fact that $\deg_q C < k$ permits to assert that $\deg_q \Lambda \circ C < m$ and hence that $N = \Lambda \circ C$. This is no longer true in our setting since, there is *a priori* no upper bound on the q–degree of C. For this reason, we need to use the knowledge of the support of the error to decode.

For the decoding to succeed, the condition $(\mathcal{L}_{<k+t} + \mathcal{L}_{\leqslant t} \circ \mathcal{T}) \cap (\mathcal{L}_{\leqslant t} \circ E) = \{0\}$ needs to be satisfied. In the case of Gabidulin codes (*i.e.* $\mathcal{T} = \{0\}$), this is guaranteed by a minimum distance argument entailing that $\mathcal{L}_{<k+t} \cap \mathcal{L}_{\leqslant t} \circ E$ is zero as soon as $t \leqslant \frac{n-k}{2}$. In our situation, estimating the minimum distance of $\mathcal{L}_{<k+t} + \mathcal{L}_{\leqslant t} \circ \mathcal{T}$ is difficult. However, one can expect that in the typical case, the intersection $(\mathcal{L}_{<k+t} + \mathcal{L}_{\leqslant t} \circ \mathcal{T}) \cap (\mathcal{L}_{\leqslant t} \circ E)$ is 0 when the sums of the dimensions of the codes is less than that of the ambient space. Therefore, one can reasonably expect to correct almost any error of rank t as soon as

$$k + 2t + \dim(\mathcal{L}_{\leqslant t} \circ \mathcal{T}) \leqslant n. \tag{8}$$

In the case $\mathcal{T} = \{0\}$, we find back the decoding radius of Gabidulin codes.

The right–hand side version. In the spirit of Sect. 3, a similar approach using right–hand side decoding shows that decoding is also possible when

$$k + 2t + \dim(\mathscr{T} \circ \mathcal{L}_{\leqslant t}) \leqslant n. \tag{9}$$

5 Applications to Cryptanalysis

5.1 RAMESSES

Using the notation of Sect. 2.2, suppose we have a ciphertext as in (5):

$$Y = C + E \quad \text{with} \quad C = C_1 + K_{\text{sec}} \circ T,$$

where $C_1 \in \mathcal{L}_{<k+\ell}$, $T \in \mathcal{L}_\ell$ and $E \in \mathcal{L}_{<m}$ of rank t. Recall that the plaintext is the row space of E (equivalently, the image of $E^{\vee}$). We perform the right–hand side version of the decoding algorithm of Sect. 4. Here the code $\mathscr{T}$ is $K_{\text{sec}} \circ \mathcal{L}_{\leqslant \ell}$ and the supercode $\mathscr{C}$ is $\mathcal{L}_{<k+\ell} + \mathscr{T}$.

We compute the solutions (Λ, N) of the system

$$Y \circ \Lambda \equiv N \quad \mod (X^{q^m} - X),$$

where

$$N \in \mathscr{C} \circ \mathcal{L}_{\leqslant t} = \mathcal{L}_{<k+\ell+t} + K_{\text{sec}} \circ \mathcal{L}_{\leqslant \ell+t}.$$

According to Lemma (1) and (9), the algorithm will very likely return pairs of the form $(\Lambda, C \circ \Lambda)$ with $E \circ \Lambda = 0$ as soon as

$$k+\ell+2t+\dim(\mathscr{T}\circ\mathcal{L}_{\leqslant t}) = k+\ell+2t+\dim(K_{\text{sec}}\circ\mathcal{L}_{\leqslant t+\ell}) = k+3t+2\ell+1 \leqslant n. \tag{10}$$

Once such a Λ is obtained, one recovers E and the image of $E^{\vee}$ yields the plaintext.

A comparison of (10) with the proposed parameters for RAMESSES in [12, Section 4] is given in Table 1. As observed, inequality (10) is satisfied for any proposed parameter set.

Table 1. This table compares the values of the formula (10) with the parameters proposed for RAMESSES. The first three rows are parameters for RAMESSES as a KEM and the last one are parameters for RAMESSES as a PKE. Note that for any proposed parameter set, we have $m = n$.

$m\ (=n)$	k	w	ℓ	t	Security (bits)	$k + 3t + 2\ell + 1$
64	32	19	3	5	141	54
80	40	23	3	7	202	68
96	48	27	3	9	265	82
164	116	27	3	9	256	150

5.2   A Message Recovery Attack Against LIGA Cryptosystem

In this section, we show that it is possible to recover the plaintext from a cipher-text. Notice that LIGA cryptosystem has been proven IND-CCA2 in [16], under some computational assumption, namely the Restricted Gabidulin Code Decision Problem ([16], Problem 4). We are not disproving this claim here, however our attack can be precisely used as a distinguisher, and hence this problem is not as hard as supposed.

Recall that G is a generator matrix of a public Gabidulin code $\mathscr{G}_k(g)$, the public key is a noisy vector $k_{pub} = x \cdot G + z$ and the encryption of a message m is $c = m \cdot G + \mathrm{Tr}_{q^{mu}/q^m}(\alpha k_{pub}) + e$ for some uniformly random element $\alpha \in \mathbb{F}_{q^{mu}}$ and a uniformly random error e of small rank weight $t_{pub} = \lfloor \frac{n-k-w}{2} \rfloor$ both chosen by Alice. See Sect. 2.1 for further details.

The attack works in two parts. First, we introduce a supercode of the public Gabidulin code, in which we are able to decode the ciphertext and get rid of the small error. Then, we recover the plaintext.

Step 1: Get Rid of the Small Error. Let $\zeta \overset{\text{def}}{=} \mathrm{rank}_{q^m}(z)$, so that $z = \sum_{i=1}^{\zeta} \mu_i z_i$ where the μ_i's $\in \mathbb{F}_{q^{mu}}$ and the z_i's $\in \mathbb{F}_{q^m}^n$ are both linearly independent over $\mathbb{F}_{q^m}$. The ciphertext can now be written as

$$c = m \cdot G + \sum_{i=1}^{\zeta} \mathrm{Tr}_{q^{mu}/q^m}(\alpha \mu_i) z_i + e \tag{11}$$

Let

$$\mathscr{C} \overset{\text{def}}{=} \mathscr{G}_k(g) + \mathbf{Span}_{\mathbb{F}_{q^m}}\{z_1, \dots, z_\zeta\} \subseteq \mathbb{F}_{q^m}^n. \tag{12}$$

The ciphertext can be seen as a codeword of $\mathscr{C}$ corrupted by a small rank weight error e. Moreover, $\mathscr{C}$ can be computed from public data as suggested by the following statement.

Theorem 1. *Let $\mathscr{C}$ be the code defined in (12) and $\mathscr{C}_{pub}$ be the code generated by $\mathscr{G}_k(g)$ and $\mathrm{Tr}_{q^{mu}/q^m}(\gamma_i k_{pub})$ for $i \in \{1, \dots, \zeta\}$, where the γ_i's denote ζ elements of $\mathbb{F}_{q^{mu}}$ linearly independent over $\mathbb{F}_{q^m}$. Then, for a uniformly random choice of $(\gamma_1, \dots, \gamma_\zeta)$,*

$$\mathbb{P}(\mathscr{C} = \mathscr{C}_{pub}) = 1 - e^{O\left(\frac{1}{q^m}\right)}.$$

The proof of Theorem 1 rests on the following technical lemma.

Lemma 2. *Let F be a linear subspace of dimension m in a linear space E of dimension n over a finite field $\mathbb{F}_q$. Then, $\#\{G \mid F \oplus G = E\} = q^{m(n-m)}$.*

Proof. Let $\mathrm{Stab}(F)$ denote the stabiliser of F under the action of $\mathrm{GL}(E)$. It is isomorphic to the group of the matrices of the form $\begin{pmatrix} A & B \\ 0 & C \end{pmatrix}$ with $A \in \mathrm{GL}_m(\mathbb{F}_q)$, $C \in \mathrm{GL}_{n-m}(\mathbb{F}_q)$ and $B \in \mathcal{M}_{m,n-m}(\mathbb{F}_q)$, *i.e.*

$$\mathrm{Stab}(F) \cong (\mathrm{GL}_m(\mathbb{F}_q) \times \mathrm{GL}_{n-m}(\mathbb{F}_q)) \ltimes \mathcal{M}_{m,n-m}(\mathbb{F}_q).$$

This group acts transitively on the complement spaces of F. Indeed, let G and G' be such that $F \oplus G = F \oplus G' = E$. Let $(f_1, \ldots, f_m)$ be a basis of F and $(g_1, \ldots, g_{n-m})$ (respectively $(g_1', \ldots, g_{n-m}')$) be a basis of G (resp. G'). Then the linear map that stabilises F and maps g_i onto g_i' is an element of $\mathrm{Stab}(F)$ that maps G onto G'. The stabiliser of a complement G under this action is simply $\mathrm{GL}_m(\mathbb{F}_q) \times \mathrm{GL}_{n-m}(\mathbb{F}_q)$. Hence,

$$\#\{G \mid F \oplus G = E\} = \frac{(\#\mathrm{GL}_m(\mathbb{F}_q)) \times (\#\mathrm{GL}_{n-m}(\mathbb{F}_q)) \times q^{m(n-m)}}{(\#\mathrm{GL}_m(\mathbb{F}_q)) \times (\#\mathrm{GL}_{n-m}(\mathbb{F}_q))} = q^{m(n-m)}.$$

□

Proof of Theorem 1. We wish to estimate the probability that $\mathscr{C} = \mathscr{C}_{\mathrm{pub}}$. Note first that inclusion $\supseteq$ is always satisfied. This can be checked by an elementary calculation.

Therefore, the following equality of events holds:

$$(\mathscr{C} = \mathscr{C}_{\mathrm{pub}}) = (\mathscr{C} \subseteq \mathscr{C}_{\mathrm{pub}}),$$

and we are reduced to study the probability that $\mathscr{C} \subseteq \mathscr{C}_{\mathrm{pub}}$.

Let $c \in \mathscr{C}$. There exists $\boldsymbol{m} \in \mathbb{F}_{q^m}^k$ and $\lambda_1, \ldots, \lambda_\zeta \in \mathbb{F}_{q^m}$ such that

$$c = \boldsymbol{m}\boldsymbol{G} + \sum_{i=1}^{\zeta} \lambda_i \boldsymbol{z}_i.$$

If we can find $\alpha \stackrel{\mathrm{def}}{=} (\alpha_1, \ldots, \alpha_\zeta) \in \mathbb{F}_{\mathbf{q^m}}^\zeta$ such that $c - \sum_{i=1}^{\zeta} \alpha_i \mathrm{Tr}_{q^{mu}/q^m}(\gamma_i \boldsymbol{k}_{pub}) \in \mathscr{G}_k(\boldsymbol{g})$, then we are done.

$$c - \sum_{i=1}^{\zeta} \alpha_i \mathrm{Tr}_{q^{mu}/q^m}(\gamma_i \boldsymbol{k}_{pub}) =$$
$$\left(\boldsymbol{m} - \sum_{i=1}^{\zeta} \alpha_i \mathrm{Tr}_{q^{mu}/q^m}(\gamma_i \boldsymbol{x}) \right) \boldsymbol{G} + \sum_{i=1}^{\zeta} \left(\lambda_i - \sum_{j=1}^{\zeta} \alpha_j \mathrm{Tr}_{q^{mu}/q^m}(\gamma_j \mu_i) \right) \boldsymbol{z}_i.$$

It suffices to choose α such that $\lambda_i - \sum_{j=1}^{\zeta} \alpha_j \mathrm{Tr}_{q^{mu}/q^m}(\gamma_j \mu_i) = 0$ for $i \in \{1, \ldots, \zeta\}$, *i.e.*

$$(\lambda_1, \ldots, \lambda_\zeta) = (\alpha_1, \ldots, \alpha_\zeta) \begin{pmatrix} \mathrm{Tr}_{q^{mu}/q^m}(\gamma_1 \mu_1) & \cdots & \mathrm{Tr}_{q^{mu}/q^m}(\gamma_1 \mu_\zeta) \\ \vdots & \ddots & \vdots \\ \mathrm{Tr}_{q^{mu}/q^m}(\gamma_\zeta \mu_1) & \cdots & \mathrm{Tr}_{q^{mu}/q^m}(\gamma_\zeta \mu_\zeta) \end{pmatrix}.$$

Let $\boldsymbol{M}$ denote this last matrix. The previous remark implies $\mathbb{P}(\mathscr{C} \subseteq \mathscr{C}_{\mathrm{pub}}) \geqslant \mathbb{P}(\boldsymbol{M}$ is non singular $)$, therefore it suffices to prove that $\boldsymbol{M}$ is non singular with overwhelming probability over the choice of $\gamma_1, \ldots, \gamma_\zeta$.

Let
$$\Gamma \overset{\text{def}}{=} \mathbf{Span}(\gamma_1, \ldots, \gamma_\zeta) \quad \text{and} \quad \mathcal{M} \overset{\text{def}}{=} \mathbf{Span}(\mu_1, \ldots, \mu_\zeta).$$
Then, M is singular if and only if $\Gamma \cap \mathcal{M}^\perp \neq \{0\}$. Since Γ and $\mathcal{M}$ have the same dimension ζ over $\mathbb{F}_{q^m}$, $\Gamma \cap \mathcal{M}^\perp = \{0\}$ if and only if $\Gamma \oplus \mathcal{M}^\perp = \mathbb{F}_{q^{mu}}$. Therefore,

$$\mathbb{P}(M \text{ is non singular }) = \frac{\#\{\Gamma \mid \mathcal{M}^\perp \oplus \Gamma = \mathbb{F}_{q^{mu}}\}}{\#\{\Gamma \mid \dim_{\mathbb{F}_{q^m}}(\Gamma) = \zeta\}}.$$

Recall the Gaussian binomial coefficient $\begin{bmatrix} u \\ \zeta \end{bmatrix}_{q^m}$ denotes the number of $\mathbb{F}_{q^m}-$linear subspaces of dimension ζ in an $\mathbb{F}_{q^m}-$vector space of dimension u. Applying Lemma 2, we have

$$\mathbb{P}(M \text{ is non singular}) = \frac{q^{m\zeta(u-\zeta)}}{\begin{bmatrix} u \\ \zeta \end{bmatrix}_{q^m}} \geqslant \left(1 - \frac{1}{q^m}\right)^{\frac{q^m}{q^m - 1}},$$

where the inequality on the right–hand side can be found for instance in [5, Appendix A]. This yields Theorem 1.   □

Set $\mathscr{T} \overset{\text{def}}{=} \bigoplus_{i=1}^{\zeta} \mathbf{Span}_{\mathbb{F}_{q^m}} \left\{ \mathrm{Tr}_{q^{mu}/q^m}(\gamma_i \boldsymbol{k}_{pub}) \right\}$. By interpolation, it can be regarded as a subspace of $\mathcal{L}_{<m}$, and $\mathscr{C}_{pub} = \mathcal{L}_{<k} \oplus \mathscr{T}$. In order to remove the error $\boldsymbol{e}$ we just need to decode in this public supercode. Notice that

$$\dim(\mathcal{L}_{\leqslant t} \circ \mathscr{T}) \leqslant \zeta(t + 1).$$

Therefore, using the algorithm of Sect. 4, one can expect to decode in $\mathscr{C}_{pub}$ whenever

$$k + 2t + \zeta(t + 1) \leqslant n. \tag{13}$$

Table 2 compares (13) with the proposed parameters for LIGA in [16, Section 7]. As observed, Inequality (13) is satisfied for any proposed parameter set. Moreover, if one tries to increase ζ in order to avoid this attack, one also needs to increase w to resist the key recovery attack from [9], which decreases $t \overset{\text{def}}{=} \lfloor \frac{n-k-w}{2} \rfloor$ that must be greater than 1.

Table 2. This table compares the values of the formula (13) with the parameters proposed for LIGA.

Name	n	k	t	ζ	Security (bits)	$k + 2t + \zeta(t + 1)$
LIGA-128	92	53	6	2	128	79
LIGA-192	120	69	8	2	192	103
LIGA-256	148	85	10	2	256	127

Step 1 is summed up in Proposition 1.

Proposition 1. *If $c = m \cdot G + \mathrm{Tr}_{q^{mu}/q^m}(\alpha k_{pub}) + e$ is the encryption of a plaintext m, then we can recover the support of the error e and the corrupted codeword $m \cdot G + \mathrm{Tr}_{q^{mu}/q^m}(\alpha k_{pub})$ in polynomial time using only the knowledge of the public key.*

Step 2: Remove the z Dependency. From now on, since we got rid of the small error term e, we can do as if the ciphertext was

$$c' \overset{\text{def}}{=} m \cdot G + \mathrm{Tr}_{q^{mu}/q^m}(\alpha k_{pub}) \tag{14}$$
$$= (m + \mathrm{Tr}_{q^{mu}/q^m}(\alpha x)) \cdot G + \mathrm{Tr}_{q^{mu}/q^m}(\alpha z).$$

This is a codeword of a Gabidulin code $\mathscr{G} \overset{\text{def}}{=} \mathscr{G}_k(g)$, corrupted by an error of rank $w > \lfloor \frac{n-k}{2} \rfloor$. Hence, we cannot decode in $\mathscr{G}$ to recover the plaintext. However, thanks to the knowledge of the public key, one can easily recover the affine space

$$A \overset{\text{def}}{=} \{\beta \in \mathbb{F}_{q^{mu}} \mid c' - \mathrm{Tr}_{q^{mu}/q^m}(\beta k_{pub}) \in \mathscr{G}\}$$

using linear algebra.

Lemma 3. *Let $\beta \in \mathbb{F}_{q^{mu}}$. Then $c' - \mathrm{Tr}_{q^{mu}/q^m}(\beta k_{pub}) \in \mathscr{G}$ if and only if $\mathrm{Tr}_{q^{mu}/q^m}((\alpha - \beta)z) = 0$.*

Proof. Note that for any $\lambda \in \mathbb{F}_{q^{mu}}$,

$$\mathrm{rank}_q(\mathrm{Tr}_{q^{mu}/q^m}(\lambda z)) \leqslant \mathrm{rank}_q(z) = w < n - k.$$

Indeed, let $\mathscr{B}$ be a basis of the extension field $\mathbb{F}_{q^{mu}}/\mathbb{F}_q$. Then, if $\lambda \neq 0$, the extension of λz in $\mathscr{B}$ is the extension of z in the basis $\lambda\mathscr{B}$. Therefore,

$$\mathrm{RowSupp}(\lambda z) = \mathrm{RowSupp}(z)$$

and the trace cannot increase the rank.
Let $\beta \in \mathbb{F}_{q^{mu}}$. Then

$$c' - \mathrm{Tr}_{q^{mu}/q^m}(\beta k_{pub}) = (m + \mathrm{Tr}_{q^{mu}/q^m}((\alpha - \beta)x))G + \mathrm{Tr}_{q^{mu}/q^m}((\alpha - \beta)z).$$

Therefore, $\beta \in A$ if and only if $\mathrm{Tr}_{q^{mu}/q^m}((\alpha - \beta)z) \in \mathscr{G}$. Since it has rank weight less than the minimum distance of $\mathscr{G}$, it follows that $\mathrm{Tr}_{q^{mu}/q^m}((\alpha - \beta)z) = 0$. $\square$

Lemma 4. *Let $\mathscr{E} \overset{\text{def}}{=} \bigcap_{i=1}^{\varsigma} \langle \mu_i \rangle^{\perp}$. Then A is the affine space $\alpha + \mathscr{E}$.*

Proof. $\beta \in A$ if and only if

$$\mathrm{Tr}_{q^{mu}/q^m}((\alpha - \beta)z) = \sum_{i=1}^{\varsigma} \mathrm{Tr}_{q^{mu}/q^m}((\alpha - \beta)\mu_i)z_i = 0.$$

By the linear independence of the z_i's, it follows that $\mathrm{Tr}_{q^{mu}/q^m}((\alpha - \beta)\mu_i) = 0$ for all i, i.e. $A = \alpha + \bigcap_{i=1}^{\varsigma} \langle \mu_i \rangle^{\perp}$. $\square$

We are now able to remove the z dependency in the ciphertext. Indeed, let $\mathscr{F} \overset{\text{def}}{=} \{\mathrm{Tr}_{q^{mu}/q^m}(\gamma x) \mid \gamma \in \mathscr{E}\}$. The knowledge of A gives finally access to the affine space $m + \mathscr{F}$.

Step 3: Recover the Plaintext. Denote by $f \overset{\text{def}}{=} \dim_{\mathbb{F}_{q^m}} \mathscr{F}$. Since $\mathscr{F}$ is the image of $\mathscr{E}$ by a surjective map, we have $f \leqslant \dim \mathscr{E} = u - \zeta \leqslant u - 1$. Let s be some random element of $m + \mathscr{F}$. Notice that from a description of the affine space $m + \mathscr{F}$ it is possible to recover a basis $(e_1, \dots, e_f)$ of $\mathscr{F}$. Then, s can be decomposed as

$$s \overset{\text{def}}{=} m + \sum_{i=1}^{f} \lambda_i e_i$$

for some unknown coefficients $\lambda_i \in \mathbb{F}_{q^m}$. Furthermore, recall that the last u positions of m are 0. Then, m is a solution of the following linear system of $k + f$ unknowns and $u + k$ equations:

$$\begin{cases} m + \sum_{i=1}^{f} \lambda_i e_i = s \\ m_{k-u+1} = \dots = m_k = 0 \end{cases} \tag{15}$$

Finally, the following lemma shows that m can be recovered from *any* solution of (15).

Lemma 5. *Let (m', λ') be another solution of (15). Then $m' = m$.*

Proof. Since $m - m' = \sum_{i=1}^{f} (\lambda_i' - \lambda_i) e_i \in \mathscr{F}$, it is of the form $\mathrm{Tr}_{q^{mu}/q^m}(\gamma x)$ for some $\gamma \in \mathscr{E}$. Moreover, its last u positions are 0. Recall that $(x_{k-u+1}, \dots, x_k)$ is a basis of $\mathbb{F}_{q^{mu}}/\mathbb{F}_{q^m}$. Then, the last u positions of $\mathrm{Tr}_{q^{mu}/q^m}(\gamma x)$ are the coefficients of γ in the dual basis $\{x_{k-u+1}^*, \dots, x_k^*\}$. Hence, $\gamma = 0$ and $m = m'$. ☐

Summary of the Attack

- Decode in a public supercode of a Gabidulin code to get rid of the small error e and recover $c' = mG + \mathrm{Tr}_{q^{mu}/q^m}(\alpha k_{pub})$.
- Using linear algebra, deduce the affine space

$$A = \{\beta \in \mathbb{F}_{q^{mu}} \mid c' - \mathrm{Tr}_{q^{mu}/q^m}(\beta k_{pub}) \in \mathscr{G}\}.$$

- Recover the affine space $m + \mathscr{F}$ where $\mathscr{F} = \{\mathrm{Tr}_{q^{mu}/q^m}(\gamma x) \mid \alpha + \gamma \in A\}$.
- Deduce a basis of $\mathscr{F}$.
- Solve linear system (15) to recover the plaintext m.

Implementation. Tests have been done using SageMath v9.2 [17] on an Intel® Core i5-10310U CPU. We are able to recover the plaintext on the three LIGA proposals. The average running times are listed in Table 3. Our implementation is available on Github https://github.com/mbombar/Attack_on_LIGA.

Table 3. Average running times for the attack on LIGA.

Name	Parameters (q, n, m, k, w, u, ζ)	Claimed security level	Average running time
LIGA-128	$(2, 92, 92, 53, 27, 5, 2)$	128 bits	8 min
LIGA-192	$(2, 120, 120, 69, 35, 5, 2)$	192 bits	27 min
LIGA-256	$(2, 148, 148, 85, 43, 5, 2)$	256 bits	92 min

Acknowledgements. The second author is partially funded by the ANR project 17-CE39-0007 *CBCrypt*.

A   Further Details About RAMESSES' Specifications

As explained in Sect. 2.2, our presentation of RAMESSES may seem to differ from the original proposal [12]. Indeed in Sect. 2.2, we present the scheme using only q–polynomials, while the original publication prefers using matrices and vectors. The purpose of the present appendix is to prove that our way to present RAMESSES is equivalent to that of [12].

Caution. In the present article we use q to denote the cardinality of the ground field $\mathbb{F}_q$. In [12] the ground field is always supposed to be $\mathbb{F}_2$ and q refers to some power of 2, *i.e.* $q = 2^n$ for some positive n. Moreover, the exponent of q is denoted n while it is denoted m in the present article. This might be confusing while reading both papers in parallel.

The other notations w, k, ℓ, t are the same in the two articles. Finally, in [12] a public $\mathbb{F}_q$–basis $\boldsymbol{g} = (g_1, \ldots, g_m)$ of $\mathbb{F}_{q^m}$ is fixed once for all. Our presentation does not require such a setting.

A.1   Key Generation

Recall that [12] fixes a vector $\boldsymbol{g} \in \mathbb{F}_{q^m}^m$ of rank m (*i.e.* an $\mathbb{F}_q$–basis of $\mathbb{F}_{q^m}$). This data together with a parity–check matrix $\boldsymbol{H}$ of the Gabidulin code $\mathscr{G}_k(\boldsymbol{g})$ are public.

Original presentation The key generation consists in picking a uniformly random $\boldsymbol{k}_{\mathrm{priv}} \in \mathbb{F}_{q^m}^m$ of weight w and the public key is its syndrome $\boldsymbol{k}_{pub} \stackrel{\text{def}}{=} \boldsymbol{H}\boldsymbol{k}_{\mathrm{priv}}^{\top}$ with respect to the public Gabidulin code.

Our presentation Since the code $\mathscr{G}_k(\boldsymbol{g})$ is public, any of its elements may be associated to an element of $\mathcal{L}_{<k}$. The transition from codewords to q–polynomials is nothing but interpolation. Similarly, the choice of a vector $\boldsymbol{k}_{\mathrm{priv}} \in \mathbb{F}_{q^m}^m$ of rank w is (again by interpolation) equivalent to that of a q–polynomial K of rank w. Finally, publishing its syndrome $\boldsymbol{H}\boldsymbol{k}_{\mathrm{priv}}^{\top}$ is equivalent to publish the coset $\boldsymbol{k}_{\mathrm{priv}} + \mathscr{G}_k(\boldsymbol{g})$, which in our setting is nothing but publishing the affine space $K_{\mathrm{sec}} + \mathcal{L}_{<k}$.

A.2 Encryption

Original presentation The plain text is encoded into a matrix $P \in \mathbb{F}_q^{m \times m}$ in row echelon form and of rank t.

– Compute $y \in \mathbb{F}_{q^m}^m$ such that $Hy^\top = k_{pub}$
– Pick a uniformly random $T \in \mathbb{F}_q^{m \times m}$ of g–degree ℓ *i.e.* representing a q–polynomial of q–degree ℓ in the basis g;
– Pick a uniformly random $S \in \mathrm{GL}_m(\mathbb{F}_q)$.

The ciphertext is
$$u^\top \stackrel{\mathrm{def}}{=} H(yT + gSP)^\top.$$

Our presentation. The vector u is a syndrome of any word of the form:
$$yT + gSP + c,$$

where c ranges over $\mathscr{G}_k(g)$. From a q–polynomial point of view, such a word corresponds to:
$$(K_{\mathrm{sec}} + C_0) \circ T + G \circ S \circ P + C,$$

where

– C, C_0 are arbitrary elements of $\mathcal{L}_{<k}$;
– $T \in \mathcal{L}_\ell$ is the interpolating polynomial of T;
– and G, S, P are the respective interpolating polynomials of g, S, P.

Note that, since g has rank m and S is supposed to be nonsingular, then their interpolating polynomials are invertible in $\mathcal{L}/(X^{q^m} - X)$. Hence, setting $E \stackrel{\mathrm{def}}{=} G \circ S \circ P$, we get a q–polynomial whose matrix representation in basis g has the same row space as the matrix representation of P. Thus, we get the ciphertext description in (4).

A.3 Decryption

Original presentation. Start by computing $x \in \mathbb{F}_{q^m}^n$ such that $Hx^\top = u^\top$. Next, knowing k_{priv}, one can compute an annihilator polynomial $V_{k_{\mathrm{priv}}} \in \mathcal{L}_w$ of the support of k_{priv}. Then, compute $z \stackrel{\mathrm{def}}{=} V_{k_{\mathrm{priv}}}(x) = (V_{k_{\mathrm{priv}}}(x_1), \ldots, V_{k_{\mathrm{priv}}}(x_m))$ and decode z as a corrupted codeword of $\mathscr{G}_{k+\ell+w}(g)$. If succeeds, it returns an error vector a. If its rank equals t, then the row echelon form of $\mathrm{Ext}_g(a)$ yields P.

Our presentation. Similarly, the approach is based on applying $V_{k_{\mathrm{priv}}}$ and performing Gabidulin codes decoding. Indeed, starting from ciphertext (4), we apply $V = V_{k_{\mathrm{priv}}}$ and get
$$V \circ Y \equiv V \circ C_1 + V \circ E$$

and a decoding procedure returns $V \circ E$. If this q–polynomial has rank t, then the row echelon form of its matrix representation yields the plaintext P.

B   Detailed Presentation of the Right–Hand Side Version of the Decoding of Gabidulin Codes

In this appendix, we provide a detailed and self–contained version of the alternative decoder for Gabidulin codes presented in Sect. 3.

Starting from the decoding problem $Y = C + E$, the decoding problem can be thought as finding the q–polynomial C, given Y. Using the analogy with Reed–Solomon codes, Loidreau introduced in [13] a Welch–Berlekamp like algorithm to decode Gabidulin codes that consists in finding the unique q–polynomial V of q–degree less than or equal to t such that V vanishes on the column support of e, which is equivalent to $V \circ E = 0$, $i.e.$ V is a left annihilator of the error. Using a linearisation technique, this leads to the resolution of a linear system that can be efficiently solved provided that t is less than half the minimum distance. It then suffices to compute a left Euclidean division to recover C and therefore the codeword c.

The core of the algorithm to follow consists in searching a right–hand side annihilator of E instead of a left–hand side one. Due to the non commutativity of the ring $\mathcal{L}$, working on the right–hand side is not directly equivalent to working on the left–hand side.

We begin to state the existence of a right–hand side annihilator.

Proposition 2. *Let E be a q–polynomial of rank t. Then there exists a unique monic q–polynomial V with $\deg_q(V) \leqslant t$ such that $E \circ V = 0$ modulo $(X^{q^m} - X)$.*

Proof. Let $Q \overset{\text{def}}{=} \sum_{i=0}^{t} a_i X^{q^i}$ be the unique monic q–polynomial of q–degree less than or equal to t that vanishes exactly on $\text{Im}(E^{\vee})$, $i.e.$ $\text{Im}(E^{\vee}) = \text{Ker} Q$. Such a q–polynomial is guaranteed to exist (see for instance [4] or [15].) It follows that $\text{Ker}(E) = \text{Im}(Q^{\vee})$. Moreover,

$$Q^{\vee} = \sum_{i=0}^{t} a_i^{q^{m-i}} X^{q^{m-i}} = \left(\sum_{i=0}^{t} a_{t-i}^{q^{m-t+i}} X^{q^i} \right) \circ X^{q^{m-t}}.$$

Let V be the leftmost factor of $Q^{\vee}$ in the above decomposition. It is a q–polynomial of q–degree t, and $E \circ Q^{\vee} = 0$ leads to $E \circ V \circ X^{q^{m-t}} = 0$. Since $X^{q^{m-t}}$ is invertible in $\mathcal{L}/(X^{q^m} - X)$, we get $E \circ V = 0 \mod (X^{q^m} - X)$.   □

The goal is to compute this right–hand side annihilator V. It satisfies

$$Y \circ V = C \circ V + E \circ V \equiv C \circ V \mod (X^{q^m} - X). \tag{16}$$

Equation (16) leads to a non linear system of n equations whose variables are the $t + k + 1$ unknown coefficients of C and V.

$$\begin{cases} (Y \circ V)(g_i) = C \circ V(g_i) \\ \deg_q V \leqslant t \\ \deg_q C \leqslant k - 1. \end{cases} \tag{17}$$

Due to the non linearity, it is not clear how this can efficiently be solved. That is why we consider instead the following linearised system

$$\begin{cases} (Y \circ V)(g_i) = N(g_i) \\ \deg_q V \leqslant t \\ \deg_q N \leqslant k + t - 1, \end{cases} \tag{18}$$

whose unknowns are the $k + 2t + 1$ coefficients of N and V. The latter is *a priori* more general than the former. But we can link the set of solutions of the two systems. This is specified in the following two propositions.

Proposition 3. *Any solution (V, C) of (17) gives a solution $(V, N = C \circ V)$ of (18).*

Proof. This is the direct analogue of [[13], Proposition 1]. □

Proposition 4. *Assume that E is of rank $t \leqslant \lfloor \frac{n-k}{2} \rfloor$. If (V, N) is a nonzero solution of (18) then $N = C \circ V$ where $C = Y - E$ is the interpolating q-polynomial of the codeword.*

Proof. Let $(V, N) \neq (0, 0)$ be a solution of (18), and let C be the q-polynomial of q-degree strictly less than k that interpolates the codeword. Let $R \overset{\text{def}}{=} N - C \circ V$. It is a q-polynomial, of q-degree at most $k - 1 + t$. Assume that $R \neq 0$. Then,

$$(Y - C) \circ V = Y \circ V - C \circ V = N - C \circ V \equiv R \mod (X^{q^m} - X)$$

i.e.

$$E \circ V \equiv R \mod (X^{q^m} - X). \tag{19}$$

Hence, $\mathbf{rank_q(R)} \leqslant \mathbf{rank_q(E)} \leqslant \mathbf{t}$. Since $R \neq 0$, $\deg_q R \geqslant \dim \mathrm{Ker} R$. Therefore, by the rank–nullity theorem,

$$n = \dim \mathrm{Ker} R + \mathbf{rank_q(R)} \leqslant \deg_q \mathbf{R} + \mathbf{rank_q(R)} \leqslant \mathbf{k} - \mathbf{1} + \mathbf{2t} \leqslant \mathbf{n} - \mathbf{1} < \mathbf{n}$$

which is a contradiction. Therefore, R must be zero, *i.e.* $N = C \circ V$. □

Thenceforth, whenever $t \leqslant \lfloor \frac{n-k}{2} \rfloor$, any non zero solution of (18) allows to recover the codeword by simply computing a right–hand side Euclidean division, which can be done efficiently (see [15]). The decoding process boils down to solving the system of equations (18). However, despite the transformation, the system is only semi-linear over $\mathbb{F}_{q^m}$. To address this issue, we will again use the adjoint of a (class of) q-polynomial. Let $y_i{}^\vee \overset{\text{def}}{=} Y^\vee(g_i)$, for all $i = 1, \ldots, n$. Using the anticommutativity of the adjoint operator, system (18) is equivalent to

$$V^\vee(y_i{}^\vee) = N^\vee(g_i) \text{ for } i = 1, \ldots, n. \tag{20}$$

which is now an $\mathbb{F}_{q^m}$-linear system of n equations whose unknowns are the coefficients of $V^\vee$ and $N^\vee$, that are in explicit one-to-one correspondence with the coefficients of V and N.

Algorithm 3: Right–hand side variant of Welch–Berlekamp

Input: q a prime power, k, n, m integers, $\boldsymbol{g} = (g_1, \ldots, g_n)$ a basis of $\mathbb{F}_{q^m}/\mathbb{F}_q$, $\mathscr{C}$ a Gabidulin code of dimension k and support $\boldsymbol{g}$, $t \leqslant \lfloor \frac{n-k}{2} \rfloor$ an integer, $\boldsymbol{y} \in \mathbb{F}_{q^m}^n$.

Output: $c \in \mathscr{C}$ such that $\boldsymbol{y} = \boldsymbol{c} + \boldsymbol{e}$ for some $\boldsymbol{e} \in \mathbb{F}_{q^m}^n$ with $\mathbf{rank_q}(\boldsymbol{e}) \leqslant \mathbf{t}$.

1 Find Y the q–polynomial of q–degree strictly less than n such that $Y(g_i) = y_i$

2 Compute $\overset{\vee}{Y}$ and evaluate in $\boldsymbol{g}$ to get $\boldsymbol{y}^\vee \overset{\text{def}}{=} \overset{\vee}{Y}(\boldsymbol{g}) \in \mathbb{F}_{q^m}^n$

3 Find a non zero solution (V_0, N_0) of the linear system (20)

4 Compute $V \overset{\text{def}}{=} \overset{\vee}{V_0}$ and $N \overset{\text{def}}{=} \overset{\vee}{N_0}$

5 Recover C by computing the right–hand side Euclidean division of N by V

6 **return** $c \overset{\text{def}}{=} C(\boldsymbol{g})$

An implementation of this algorithm using SageMath v9.2 [17] can be found on Github: https://github.com/mbombar/Attack_on_LIGA.

References

1. Aragon, N., Gaborit, P., Hauteville, A., Tillich, J.P.: Improvement of generic attacks on the rank syndrome decoding problem, October 2017. https://hal.archives-ouvertes.fr/hal-01618464, working paper or preprint
2. Augot, D., Couvreur, A., Lavauzelle, J., Neri, A.: Rank-metric codes over arbitrary Galois extensions and rank analogues of Reed-Muller codes, June 2020. https://hal.archives-ouvertes.fr/hal-02882019, 26 pages, 1 figure. https://hal.archives-ouvertes.fr/hal-02882019
3. Augot, D., Finiasz, M.: A public key encryption scheme based on the polynomial reconstruction problem. In: Biham, E. (ed.) EUROCRYPT 2003. LNCS, vol. 2656, pp. 229–240. Springer, Heidelberg (2003). https://doi.org/10.1007/3-540-39200-9_14
4. Berlekamp, E.R.: Algebraic Coding Theory (Revised Edition), World Scientific (2015). https://doi.org/10.1142/9407
5. Coggia, D., Couvreur, A.: On the security of a Loidreau's rank metric code based encryption scheme. In: WCC 2019 - Workshop on Coding Theory and Cryptography. Saint Jacut de la mer, France, March 2019. https://hal.archives-ouvertes.fr/hal-02064465
6. Coron, J.: Cryptanalysis of the repaired public-key encryption scheme based on the polynomial reconstruction problem. IACR Cryptology ePrint Archive 2003, 219 (2003). http://eprint.iacr.org/2003/219
7. Faure, C., Loidreau, P.: A new public-key cryptosystem based on the problem of reconstructing p-polynomials. In: Coding and Cryptography, International Workshop, WCC 2005, Bergen, Norway, 14–18 March 2005. Revised Selected Papers, pp. 304–315 (2005)
8. Gabidulin, E.M., Paramonov, A.V., Tretjakov, O.V.: Ideals over a non-commutative ring and their application in cryptology. In: Davies, D.W. (ed.) EUROCRYPT 1991. LNCS, vol. 547, pp. 482–489. Springer, Heidelberg (1991). https://doi.org/10.1007/3-540-46416-6_41

9. Gaborit, P., Otmani, A., Talé-Kalachi, H.: Polynomial-time key recovery attack on the Faure-Loidreau scheme based on Gabidulin codes. Des. Codes Cryptogr. **86**(7), 1391–1403 (2018)

10. Gaborit, P., Ruatta, O., Schrek, J.: On the complexity of the rank syndrome decoding problem. CoRR abs/1301.1026 (2013). http://arxiv.org/abs/1301.1026

11. Goss, D.: Basic Structures of Function Field arithmetic, Ergebnisse der Mathematik und ihrer Grenzgebiete (3), vol. 35. Springer-Verlag, Berlin (1996).[Results in Mathematics and Related Areas (3)]

12. Lavauzelle, J., Loidreau, P., Pham, B.D.: RAMESSES, a rank metric encryption scheme with short keys, January 2020. https://hal.archives-ouvertes.fr/hal-02426624, working paper or preprint. Available online at ArXiv:1911.13119

13. Loidreau, P.: A Welch-Berlekamp like algorithm for decoding Gabidulin codes. In: Ytrehus, Ø. (ed.) Coding and Cryptography, pp. 36–45. Springer, Berlin Heidelberg (2006)

14. McEliece, R.J.: A public-key system based on algebraic coding theory, pp. 114–116. Jet Propulsion Lab (1978), dSN Progress Report 44

15. Ore, O.: On a special class of polynomials. Trans. Amer. Math. Soc. **35**(3), 559–584 (1933)

16. Renner, J., Puchinger, S., Wachter-Zeh, A.: LIGA: A cryptosystem based on the hardness of rank-metric list and interleaved decoding (2020), available online at ArXiv:1812.04892

17. Stein, W., et al.: Sage Mathematics Software (Version 9.2). The Sage Development Team (2020), http://www.sagemath.org

18. Wachter-Zeh, A.: Decoding of block and convolutional codes in rank metric. theses, Université Rennes 1, October 2013. https://tel.archives-ouvertes.fr/tel-01056746

19. Wachter-Zeh, A., Puchinger, S., Renner, J.: Repairing the Faure-Loidreau public-key cryptosystem. In: Proceedings of IEEE International Symposium Information Theory - ISIT, pp. 2426–2430 (2018). https://doi.org/10.1109/ISIT.2018.8437561

LESS-FM: Fine-Tuning Signatures from the Code Equivalence Problem

Alessandro Barenghi[1], Jean-François Biasse[2], Edoardo Persichetti[3(✉)],
and Paolo Santini[4]

[1] Politecnico di Milano, Milan, Italy
[2] University of South Florida, Tampa, USA
[3] Florida Atlantic University, Boca Raton, USA
epersichetti@fau.edu
[4] Universitá Politecnica delle Marche, Ancona, Italy

Abstract. Code-based cryptographic schemes are highly regarded among the quantum-safe alternatives to current standards. Yet, designing code-based signatures using traditional methods has always been a challenging task, and current proposals are still far from the target set by other post-quantum primitives (e.g. lattice-based). In this paper, we revisit a recent work using an innovative approach for signing, based on the hardness of the code equivalence problem. We introduce some optimizations and provide a security analysis for all variants considered. We then show that the new parameters produce instances of practical interest.

1 Introduction

Digital signature schemes are a fundamental primitive in modern times as they offer a way to achieve authentication, one of the most important cryptographic goals. Since their inception, signature schemes have traditionally been designed using classical number theory problems like integer factorization and computing discrete logarithms. In [11], Biasse, Micheli, Persichetti and Santini described LESS, a Zero-Knowledge protocol and signature scheme whose security provably relies on the hardness of the Code Equivalence problem (CE). Unlike signatures based on factoring or discrete logarithms, there does not seem to be efficient quantum attacks against LESS. The LESS signature scheme differs from the other proposals for quantum-safe signatures based on coding theory, because it does not rely on the hardness of the Syndrome Decoding Problem (SDP). Note that the CE problem can be solved using decoding algorithms in the Hamming metric, such as ISD (e.g. [9,17]); however, it yields more efficient choices of parameters, overall, than schemes based directly on SDP. It is worth noting also that the graph isomorphism problem provably reduces to (permutation) CE. Prior to the appearance of an efficient algorithm for the resolution of the

J.-F. Biasse is supported by NIST grant 60NANB17D184 and NSF grant 183980. Edoardo Persichetti is supported by NSF grant 1906360.

© Springer Nature Switzerland AG 2021
J. H. Cheon and J.-P. Tillich (Eds.): PQCrypto 2021, LNCS 12841, pp. 23–43, 2021.
https://doi.org/10.1007/978-3-030-81293-5_2

former [4], this could have documented hardness of CE. However, an efficient solution to the graph isomorphism problem does not give any information on the hardness of CE. Finally, we point out that if CE is NP-hard, then the polynomial hierarchy collapses, thus making CE unlikely to be NP-hard.

Interestingly, CE can be framed as a *cryptographic group action* [2] (also described by Couveignes as a hard homogeneous space [12]). Such a framework can be used to highlight similarities between LESS and other ZK protocols and signature schemes such as SeaSign [13]. This can facilitate the adaptation of optimizations from other schemes based on group actions to the case of LESS. The main roadblock to the conversion of other existing schemes is that the group action induced by CE is non-commutative. In particular, this seems to prevent a CE-based key agreement protocol *à la* Diffie-Hellman.

Our Contribution. In this paper, we build on the original description of LESS [11]. Our main contribution, is to leverage the cryptographic group action framework to introduce a number of significant optimizations. We present two techniques. The first is a generalization of the underlying identification scheme that makes use of multi-bit challenges, by changing the role of the selected challenge bits. This results in a tradeoff, with a reduction in signature size, at the expense of an increase in public key size. The second technique, instead, exploits the imbalance between the cost of different responses corresponding to the chosen challenge bits. Choosing the challenge string to have a fixed, low Hamming weight ends up in much shorter signatures, as well as providing constant-time verification. We show that the two techniques can be combined, providing a flexible and practical scheme. We give an explicit proof for the EUF-CMA security property of the original LESS scheme, with minor tweaks. This proof serves as a basis for the security of the variant schemes. Note that the multi-bit variants rely on a new problem which we call Multiple Codes Linear Equivalence (MCLE, Problem 2), and for which we give a tight reduction to the Code Equivalence problem. Finally, we present multiple sets of parameters for a concrete instantiation of our scheme, and make practical considerations, including a comparison with the existing code-based alternatives.

The paper is organized as follows. We begin by recalling some useful background notions in Sect. 2. The LESS signature scheme, and the underlying group action, are presented in Sect. 3. In Sect. 4, we describe the various optimizations for the scheme. Finally, in Sect. 5, we briefly summarize the different attacks techniques against the code equivalence problem, and then provide a discussion on parameter choices, including the comparison with other code-based signature schemes.

2   Background

We will use the following notation throughout the paper: a for scalars, A for sets, $\boldsymbol{a}$ for vectors, $\boldsymbol{A}$ for matrices, a for functions, $\mathcal{A}$ for algorithms. We denote with $\boldsymbol{I}_n$ the $n \times n$ identity matrix, with $[a; b]$ the set of integers $\{a, a+1, \ldots, b\}$, and with $\xleftarrow{\$} A$ the action of sampling uniformly at random from A. We denote with $\mathbb{Z}_q$ the ring of integers modulo q, and with $\mathbb{F}_q$ the finite field of order q. The multiplicative group of $\mathbb{F}_q$ is indicated as $\mathbb{F}_q^*$. We denote with $\mathsf{Aut}(\mathbb{F}_q)$ the group of automorphisms of the field $\mathbb{F}_q$. The sets of vectors and matrices with elements in $\mathbb{Z}_q$ (resp. $\mathbb{F}_q$) are denoted by $\mathbb{Z}_q^n$ and $\mathbb{Z}_q^{m \times n}$ (resp. $\mathbb{F}_q^n$ and $\mathbb{F}_q^{m \times n}$). We also write $\mathbb{Z}_{q,w}^n$ (resp. $\mathbb{F}_{q,w}^n$) to indicate the set of vectors with components in $\mathbb{Z}_q$ (resp. $\mathbb{F}_q$) with length n and Hamming weight w. We write $\mathsf{GL}_k(q)$ for the set of invertible $k \times k$ matrices with elements in $\mathbb{F}_q$, or simply GL_k when the finite field is implicit. Let S_n be the set of permutations over n elements. For a vector $\boldsymbol{x} = (x_1, \cdots, x_n) \in \mathbb{F}_q^n$ and a permutation $\pi \in \mathsf{S}_n$, we write the action of π on $\boldsymbol{x}$ as $\pi(\boldsymbol{x}) = (x_{\pi(1)}, \cdots, x_{\pi(n)})$. A permutation can equivalently be described as an $n \times n$ matrix with exactly one 1 per row and column. Analogously, for *linear isometries*, i.e. transformations $\mu = (\boldsymbol{v}; \pi) \in \mathbb{F}_q^{*n} \rtimes \mathsf{S}_n$, we write the action on a vector $\boldsymbol{x}$ as $\mu(\boldsymbol{x}) = (v_1 x_{\pi(1)}, \cdots, v_n x_{\pi(n)})$. Then, we can also describe these in matrix form as a product $\boldsymbol{Q} = \boldsymbol{DP}$ where $\boldsymbol{P}$ is an $n \times n$ permutation matrix and $\boldsymbol{D} = \{d_{ij}\}$ is an $n \times n$ diagonal matrix with entries in $\mathbb{F}_q^*$. We denote with M_n the set of such matrices, usually known as *monomial* matrices.

2.1 Code Equivalence

An $[n, k]$-*linear code* $\mathfrak{C}$ of length n and dimension k over $\mathbb{F}_q$ is a k-dimensional vector subspace of $\mathbb{F}_q^n$. It can be represented by a matrix $\boldsymbol{G} \in \mathbb{F}_q^{k \times n}$, called *generator matrix*, whose rows form a basis for the vector space, i.e., $\mathfrak{C} = \{\boldsymbol{uG}, \ \boldsymbol{u} \in \mathbb{F}_q^k\}$. Alternatively, a linear code can be represented as the kernel of a matrix $\boldsymbol{H} \in \mathbb{F}_q^{(n-k) \times n}$, known as *parity-check matrix*, i.e. $\mathfrak{C} = \{\boldsymbol{x} \in \mathbb{F}_q^n : \boldsymbol{Hx}^T = 0\}$. For both representations, there exists a standard choice, called *systematic form*, which corresponds, respectively, to $\boldsymbol{G} = (\boldsymbol{I}_k \mid \boldsymbol{M})$ and $\boldsymbol{H} = (-\boldsymbol{M}^T \mid \boldsymbol{I}_{n-k})$. Generator (resp. parity-check) matrices in systematic form are obtained by calculating the row-reduced echelon form starting from any other generator (resp. parity-check) matrix. We denote such a procedure by sf. The parity-check matrix is important also as it is a generator for the *dual code*, defined as the set of words that are orthogonal to the code, i.e. $\mathfrak{C}^\perp = \{\boldsymbol{y} \in \mathbb{F}_q^n : \forall \boldsymbol{x} \in \mathfrak{C}, \ \boldsymbol{x} \cdot \boldsymbol{y}^T = 0\}$. A code $\mathfrak{C}$ is called *self-orthogonal* or *weakly self-dual* if $\mathfrak{C} \subseteq \mathfrak{C}^\perp$, and simply *self-dual* if $\mathfrak{C} = \mathfrak{C}^\perp$. The concept of *equivalence* between two codes, in its most general formulation, is defined as follows.

Definition 1 (Code Equivalence). *We say that two linear codes $\mathfrak{C}$ and $\mathfrak{C}'$ are equivalent, and write $\mathfrak{C} \sim \mathfrak{C}'$, if there exists a field automorphism $\alpha \in \mathsf{Aut}(\mathbb{F}_q)$ and a linear isometry $\mu = (\boldsymbol{v}; \pi) \in \mathbb{F}_q^{*n} \rtimes \mathsf{S}_n$ that maps $\mathfrak{C}$ into $\mathfrak{C}'$, i.e. such that $\mathfrak{C}' = \mu(\alpha(\mathfrak{C})) = \{\boldsymbol{y} \in \mathbb{F}_q^n : \boldsymbol{y} = \mu(\alpha(\boldsymbol{x})), \ \boldsymbol{x} \in \mathfrak{C}\}$.*

Clearly, if $\mathfrak{C}$ and $\mathfrak{C}'$ are two codes with generator matrices $\boldsymbol{G}$ and $\boldsymbol{G}'$, respectively, it holds that

$$\mathfrak{C} \sim \mathfrak{C}' \iff \exists(\boldsymbol{S}; (\alpha, \boldsymbol{Q})) \in \mathsf{GL}_k \rtimes (\mathsf{Aut}(\mathbb{F}_q) \times \mathsf{M}_n) \text{ s.t. } \boldsymbol{G}' = \boldsymbol{S}\alpha(\boldsymbol{GQ}).$$

The notion we just presented is usually known as *semilinear equivalence* and it is the most generic. If the field automorphism is the trivial one (i.e. $\alpha = id$), then the notion is simply known as *linear equivalence*. If, furthermore, the monomial matrix is a permutation (i.e. $Q = DP$ with $D = I_n$), then the notion is known as *permutation equivalence*. Note that, in this work, we always work with prime fields $\mathbb{F}_q$, and therefore the last two notions are the only ones of interest to us. Finally, we state the following computational problem.

Problem 1 (Code Equivalence). *Let $G, G' \in \mathbb{F}_q^{k \times n}$ be two generator matrices for two linearly equivalent codes $\mathfrak{C}$ and $\mathfrak{C}'$. Find a field automorphism $\alpha \in \mathsf{Aut}(\mathbb{F}_q)$ and two matrices $S \in \mathsf{GL}_k$ and $Q \in \mathsf{M}_n$ such that $G' = S\alpha(GQ)$.*

Note that this problem is traditionally formulated as a decisional problem in literature, yet for our purposes it is more natural to present here the search version. We normally refer, respectively, to *semilinear, linear* or *permutation equivalence problem*, according to what is the notion of code equivalence considered. Alternatively, we refer simply to the *code equivalence problem* where such distinction is not important.

3 Code-Based Group Actions and Applications

We begin by describing the group action associated to code equivalence. To do this we consider the set $X \subseteq \mathbb{F}_q^{k \times n}$ comprised of all full-rank $k \times n$ matrices, i.e. the set of generator matrices of $[n, k]$-linear codes, and $G = \mathsf{GL}_k \rtimes (\mathsf{Aut}(\mathbb{F}_q) \times \mathsf{M}_n)$. Note that this group is isomorphic to the group $(\mathsf{GL}_k \times (\mathbb{F}_q^*)^n) \rtimes (\mathsf{Aut}(\mathbb{F}_q) \times \mathsf{S}_n)$ if we decompose each monomial matrix $Q \in \mathsf{M}_n$ into the product $D \cdot P \in (\mathbb{F}_q^*)^n \rtimes \mathsf{M}_n$; then the group operation $\circ$ is defined as

$$((S, D); (\alpha, P)) \circ ((S', D'); (\alpha', P')) = ((S\alpha(S'), D \cdot \alpha(D'P)); (\alpha\alpha', PP')).$$

The group action is given by

$$\begin{aligned} \star : \quad X \times G \quad &\to \quad X \\ (G, (S; (\alpha, Q))) &\to S\alpha(GQ) \end{aligned}$$

It is easy to see that the action is well-formed, with the identity element being $(I_k; (id, I_n))$. Furthermore, it possesses some essential properties that are of cryptographic interest. First of all, the action satisfies all the basic requirements such as efficient membership testing, sampling, computation etc., to which the authors in [2] assign the nomenclature of *effective*. The action is also *one-way*, based on the hardness of the code equivalence problem. In fact, given G and $S\alpha(GQ)$, it should be infeasible to recover S, α and Q in polynomial time, else this would provide a solver for the problem. Unfortunately, our group action does not satisfy some useful additional properties (as formalized in [2]). For instance, it is not *transitive*, meaning that it is not possible to connect every element of X (i.e. every generator matrix) via a group element. Most importantly, the action is not commutative, which is a considerable obstacle in the design of cryptographic protocols. Nevertheless, it is possible to employ the group action for this purpose successfully, as we will see. Note that the above formulation includes some trivial instances, e.g. those such that $Q = vI_n$, for $v \in \mathbb{F}_q^*$, in which case the action returns just a different generator matrix for the same code. Thus, in practice, it makes sense to consider a simplified version of the group action, where X contains only the (full-rank) generator matrices in systematic form, and $G = \mathsf{Aut}(\mathbb{F}_q) \times \mathsf{M}_n$.

The work of [11] introduces a 3-pass identification scheme, with soundness error $1/2$, which defines a zero-knowledge proof of knowledge of an isometry between codes, and is based precisely on code equivalence. The authors suggest that such a scheme can be turned into a signature scheme by applying the Fiat-Shamir transformation, without however providing full details. We give here an explicit description of such a scheme, with the addition of some minor tweaks[1].

Table 1. The LESS signature scheme.

Setup	Input parameters $q, n, k, \lambda \in \mathbb{N}$, then set $t = \lambda$. Choose matrix $G \in \mathbb{F}_q^{k \times n}$ and hash function $\mathsf{H} : \{0,1\}^* \to \{0,1\}^\lambda$. Set $Q_0 = I_n$ and $G_0 = \mathsf{sf}(G)$.
Private Key	Monomial matrix $Q_1 \in \mathsf{M}_n$.
Public Key	Generator matrix $G_1 = \mathsf{sf}(GQ_1)$.

SIGNER   VERIFIER

For $i = 0 \ldots t - 1$, choose $\tilde{Q}_i \xleftarrow{\$} \mathsf{M}_n$
and set $\tilde{G}_i = \mathsf{sf}(G\tilde{Q}_i)$.
Set $h = \mathsf{H}(\tilde{G}_0, \ldots, \tilde{G}_{t-1}, m)$.
Parse $h = h_0, \ldots h_{t-1}$, for $h_i \in \{0, 1\}$.
For $i = 0 \ldots t-1$, compute $\mu_i = Q_{h_i}^{-1} \tilde{Q}_i$.
Set $\sigma = (\mu_0, \ldots \mu_{t-1}, h)$.

$$\xrightarrow{(m,\sigma)}$$

Parse $h = h_0, \ldots h_{t-1}$, for $h_i \in \{0, 1\}$.
For $i = 0 \ldots t - 1$, compute $\hat{G}_i = \mathsf{sf}(G_{h_i} \mu_i)$.
Accept if $\mathsf{H}(\hat{G}_0, \ldots, \hat{G}_{t-1}, m) = h$.

---

[1] For example the original scheme did not use public keys in systematic form.

It is immediate to verify the correctness of the scheme, which follows from the argument given in [11, Section 4]. In particular, when $h_i = 0$, we have $\mu_i = \tilde{Q}_i$ and so $G_i = \mathsf{sf}(G_0\mu_i) = \mathsf{sf}(G\tilde{Q}_i) = \tilde{G}_i$; on the other hand, when $h_i = 1$, we have $\mu_i = Q_1^{-1}\tilde{Q}_i$ and so again $G_i = \mathsf{sf}(G_1\mu_i) = \mathsf{sf}(GQ_1Q_1^{-1}\tilde{Q}_i) = \tilde{G}_i$.

A proof of EUF-CMA security for LESS is given in Appendix B.

4   Optimizations

In this section we discuss possible strategies for optimization. We start by noticing that, for the original LESS scheme (Table 1), we have the following features:

- the public key size is $k(n-k)\lceil \log_2(q) \rceil$ bits;
- the number of rounds t is equal to the desired security level λ;
- consequently, the average signature size in bits is given by

$$t\left(1 + \frac{l_{\mathsf{Seed}} + n\lceil \log_2(n) \rceil + n\lceil \log_2(q) \rceil}{2}\right).$$

In the formula above, l_{Seed} stands for the binary length of the seed used as randomness. Note that, when using permutations instead of monomial transformations, the signature size gets reduced as the factor $n\lceil \log_2(q) \rceil$ is removed.

4.1   Multi-bit Challenges

A first natural observation is that signature size can be reduced by decreasing the number of rounds that are necessary to reach the desired preimage security level. This, obviously, requires the soundness error in the underlying ZK identification scheme to decrease proportionally. Such a scenario can be realized, for instance, by increasing the number of challenge bits in each round, as described in Seasign [13]. Each challenge bit becomes an ℓ-bit challenge string, which can be interpreted as an integer between 0 and $2^\ell - 1$, i.e. as an element of $\mathbb{Z}_{2^\ell}$, using the well-known correspondence $\mathbb{Z}_2^\ell = \mathbb{Z}_{2^\ell}$. Accordingly, the scheme is modified to feature $r = 2^\ell$ independent public keys; each challenge string is then used to select one of the keys, for which a response is produced (using the corresponding private key). To keep notation simple, we exploit the bijection mentioned above, and interchangeably use the same symbol to denote an ℓ-bit string (as part of a hash output) or an integer in $[0; 2^\ell - 1]$ (for example, when used as an index). A pictorial representation of this variant is given in Table 2, below, where we call the scheme LESS-M (for Multi-bit).

Table 2. The LESS-M signature scheme.

Setup	Input parameters $q, n, k, \ell, \lambda \in \mathbb{N}$, then set $r = 2^\ell$ and $t = \lambda/\ell$. Choose matrix $G \in \mathbb{F}_q^{k \times n}$ and hash function $\mathsf{H} : \{0,1\}^* \to \{0,1\}^\lambda$.
Private Key	Monomial matrices $Q_0 \ldots Q_{r-1} \in \mathsf{M}_n$.
Public Key	Generator matrices $G_0 \ldots G_{r-1}$, where $G_i = \mathsf{sf}(GQ_i)$ for $i = 0 \ldots r-1$.

SIGNER	VERIFIER

SIGNER

For $i = 0 \ldots t-1$, choose $\tilde{Q}_i \xleftarrow{\$} \mathsf{M}_n$
and set $\tilde{G}_i = \mathsf{sf}(G\tilde{Q}_i)$.
Set $h = \mathsf{H}(\tilde{G}_0, \ldots, \tilde{G}_{t-1}, m)$.
Parse $h = h_0, \ldots h_{t-1}$, for $h_i \in \mathbb{Z}_2^\ell$.
For $i = 0 \ldots t-1$, compute $\mu_i = Q_{h_i}^{-1}\tilde{Q}_i$.
Set $\sigma = (\mu_0, \ldots \mu_{t-1}, h)$.

$$\xrightarrow{\ (m,\sigma)\ }$$

VERIFIER

Parse $h = h_0, \ldots h_{t-1}$, for $h_i \in \mathbb{Z}_2^\ell$.
For $i = 0 \ldots t-1$, compute $\hat{G}_i = \mathsf{sf}(G_{h_i}\mu_i)$.
Accept if $\mathsf{H}(\hat{G}_0, \ldots, \hat{G}_{t-1}, m) = h$.

Note that this variant is more natural than what it may seem at a first glance. In fact, the original LESS signature scheme of Table 1 can be seen as a particular case of the LESS-M scheme, where $\ell = 1$ and $Q_0 = I_n$. The main difference is in the security notion underlying the scheme. The security assumption in this case becomes the following.

Problem 2 (Multiple Codes Linear Equivalence). *Consider a collection of linearly equivalent $[n, k]$-linear codes $\mathfrak{C}_0 \ldots \mathfrak{C}_{r-1}$, admitting generator matrices $G_0, \ldots, G_{r-1}$ of the form $S_0GQ_0, \ldots, S_{r-1}GQ_{r-1}$. Find matrices $S^* \in \mathsf{GL}_k$ and $Q^* \in \mathsf{M}_n$ such that $G_{j'} = S^*G_jQ^*$, for some $j \neq j'$.*

This problem is still hard, and directly connected to the hardness of the linear code equivalence problem. A reduction is given in Appendix C, together with a proof of EUF-CMA security for LESS-M.

4.2   Fixed-Weight Challenges

In this variant, the key intuition is that different responses, corresponding to different challenge bits, have a very unbalanced impact on the size of the signature. In particular, for the original LESS (Table 1), in the case $h_i = 0$ the response μ_i consists of the purely random monomial matrix $\tilde{Q}_i$, and therefore the signer can transmit just the seed used to generate such random object. This, of course, is much more compact than the monomial matrix $Q_1^{-1}\tilde{Q}_i$ which needs to be transmitted, in full, when $h_i = 1$. It makes sense, therefore, to try and minimize the amount of bits h_i that are equal to 1, in the challenge string h output by H.

In our case, a natural way to implement this idea is to switch the output distribution of H, to return a vector of fixed Hamming weight. In other words, we need to pick H to be a *weight-restricted* hash function, whose range is the set $\mathbb{Z}_{2,\omega}^t$. The modified protocol is described in Table 3 below, where we call the scheme LESS-F (for Fixed-weight).

Table 3. The LESS-F signature scheme.

Setup	Input parameters $q, n, k, \lambda, t, \omega \in \mathbb{N}$. Choose matrix $\boldsymbol{G} \in \mathbb{F}_q^{k \times n}$ and w.r. hash function $\mathsf{H} : \{0,1\}^* \to \mathbb{Z}_{2,\omega}^t$. Set $\boldsymbol{Q}_0 = \boldsymbol{I}_n$ and $\boldsymbol{G}_0 = \mathsf{sf}(\boldsymbol{G})$.
Private Key	Monomial matrix $\boldsymbol{Q}_1 \in \mathsf{M}_n$.
Public Key	Generator matrix $\boldsymbol{G}_1 = \mathsf{sf}(\boldsymbol{G}\boldsymbol{Q}_1)$.

SIGNER   VERIFIER

For $i = 0 \ldots t - 1$, choose $\tilde{\boldsymbol{Q}}_i \xleftarrow{\$} \mathsf{M}_n$
and set $\tilde{\boldsymbol{G}}_i = \mathsf{sf}(\boldsymbol{G}\tilde{\boldsymbol{Q}}_i)$.
Set $h = \mathsf{H}(\tilde{\boldsymbol{G}}_0, \ldots, \tilde{\boldsymbol{G}}_{t-1}, \boldsymbol{m})$.
Parse $h = h_0, \ldots h_{t-1}$, for $h_i \in \{0, 1\}$.
For $i = 0 \ldots t-1$, compute $\mu_i = \boldsymbol{Q}_{h_i}^{-1}\tilde{\boldsymbol{Q}}_i$.
Set $\sigma = (\mu_0, \ldots \mu_{t-1}, h)$.

$$\xrightarrow{(\boldsymbol{m}, \sigma)}$$

Parse $h = h_0, \ldots h_{t-1}$, for $h_i \in \{0, 1\}$.
For $i = 0 \ldots t - 1$, compute $\hat{\boldsymbol{G}}_i = \mathsf{sf}(\boldsymbol{G}_{h_i}\mu_i)$.
Accept if $\mathsf{H}(\hat{\boldsymbol{G}}_0, \ldots, \hat{\boldsymbol{G}}_{t-1}, \boldsymbol{m}) = h$.

Note that this idea is not new in the context of identification and signature schemes. In fact, as reported in [18], the suggestion to use a fixed-weight challenge vector is already present in the original Fiat-Shamir work [16]. More recently, some signature schemes appeared that also make use of a similar approach, albeit in a different context. For instance, Picnic, which earned much praise during the NIST post-quantum standardization process [1], uses a pre-processing stage and a cut-and-choose procedure to achieve the desired security level. This technique was later revisited and generalized by Beullens [10], who presents an application to multivariate schemes, as well as PKP. In all cases, it is evident how picking the challenge vector from a carefully crafted distribution beats the simple parallel repetition of the protocol.

A necessary condition to avoid losing security during the process is that the final preimage security level of the protocol remain equal to the original goal of $2^{-\lambda}$. This was naturally obtained via parallel repetition. In our case, simply constraining the challenge vector to a target Hamming weight would be guaranteed to lose security bits. Indeed, this happens even in the most basic scenario, i.e. if we restrict to the expected value $\omega = t/2$; for instance, when $\lambda = 128$, sampling h among the vectors of weight 64 only leads to approximately

124 preimage security bits. To understand this, recall that *preimage security* corresponds, essentially, to the difficulty of guessing the entire challenge vector. In the case of parallel repetition, since each instance is independent from the others, this is equivalent to correctly picking the challenge in each round, which leads to a probability of ε^t, where ε is the soundness error (in our case $1/2$). However, if the challenge is sampled among vectors of fixed Hamming weight, the difficulty of guessing is the reciprocal of

$$\left| \mathbb{Z}_{2,\omega}^t \right| = \binom{t}{\omega}.$$

From this, it follows that, in order to safely switch to constrained-weight challenge vectors, it is necessary to ensure that $\log_2 \binom{t}{\omega} \geq \lambda$. This leads to an increase in the overall length of the challenge vector, yet yields consistently smaller signatures. A discussion on the EUF-CMA security of LESS-F, and relative proof, are given in Appendix D.

4.3 Combining the Approaches

In this section we explain how to combine the approaches illustrated in the previous sections. The result is depicted in Table 4, below, where we call the scheme LESS-FM (as it is a combination of the two techniques). Note that this formulation is the most generic, as it includes the previous ones as particular cases. The quantity to consider for preimage security is

Table 4. The LESS-FM signature scheme.

Setup	Input parameters $q, n, k, \ell, \lambda, t, \omega \in \mathbb{N}$, then set $r = 2^\ell$. Choose matrix $\boldsymbol{G} \in \mathbb{F}_q^{k \times n}$ and w.r. hash function $\mathsf{H} : \{0,1\}^* \to \mathbb{Z}_{2^\ell,\omega}^t$. Set $\boldsymbol{Q}_0 = \boldsymbol{I}_n$ and $\boldsymbol{G}_0 = \mathsf{sf}(\boldsymbol{G})$.
Private Key	Monomial matrices $\boldsymbol{Q}_1 \ldots \boldsymbol{Q}_{r-1} \in \mathsf{M}_n$.
Public Key	Generator matrices $\boldsymbol{G}_1 \ldots \boldsymbol{G}_{r-1}$, where $\boldsymbol{G}_i = \mathsf{sf}(\boldsymbol{G}\boldsymbol{Q}_i)$ for $i = 1 \ldots r - 1$.

SIGNER   **VERIFIER**

For $i = 0 \ldots t - 1$, choose $\tilde{\boldsymbol{Q}}_i \overset{\$}{\leftarrow} \mathsf{M}_n$
and set $\tilde{\boldsymbol{G}}_i = \mathsf{sf}(\boldsymbol{G}\tilde{\boldsymbol{Q}}_i)$.
Set $h = \mathsf{H}(\tilde{\boldsymbol{G}}_0, \ldots, \tilde{\boldsymbol{G}}_{t-1}, \boldsymbol{m})$.
Parse $h = h_0, \ldots h_{t-1}$, for $h_i \in \{0,1\}^\ell$.
For $i = 0 \ldots t-1$, compute $\mu_i = \boldsymbol{Q}_{h_i}^{-1} \tilde{\boldsymbol{Q}}_i$.
Set $\sigma = (\mu_0, \ldots \mu_{t-1}, h)$.

$$\xrightarrow{\quad (\boldsymbol{m},\sigma) \quad}$$

Parse $h = h_0, \ldots h_{t-1}$, for $h_i \in \{0,1\}^\ell$.
For $i = 0 \ldots t - 1$, compute $\hat{\boldsymbol{G}}_i = \mathsf{sf}(\boldsymbol{G}_{h_i} \mu_i)$.
Accept if $\mathsf{H}(\hat{\boldsymbol{G}}_0, \ldots, \hat{\boldsymbol{G}}_{t-1}, \boldsymbol{m}) = h$.

$$\left| \mathbb{Z}_{2^\ell, \omega}^t \right| = \binom{t}{\omega} (2^\ell - 1)^\omega .$$

Optimal parameter choices for all variants will be discussed in the next section.

Before selecting parameters, we present a brief summary of the complexities of the main known techniques to solve code equivalence. For more details about attacks and complexity estimates, we refer the interested reader to the full version of this paper [6].

Table 5. Summary of techniques to solve the code equivalence problem.

Type	Algorithm	Complexity	Notes
Permutation	Leon [17]	$O(C_{ISD}(q, k, d_{GV}) \cdot 2\log(N_w))$	Best with small finite fields and large hulls
	Beullens [9]	$O\left(\dfrac{2L \cdot C_{ISD}(q,n,k,w)}{N_w \left(1 - 2^{L \log_2(1 - L/N_w)}\right)} \right)$	Best with large finite fields and hulls. May fail when L is too small
	SSA [19]	$O\left(n^3 + n^2 q^{d_h} \log n\right)$	Efficient with small, non-trivial hulls
	BOS [5]	$\begin{cases} O\left(n^{2.373} C_{WGI}(n)\right) & \text{if } d_h = 0 \\ O\left(n^{2.373 + d_h + 1} C_{WGI}(n)\right) & \text{if } d_h > 0 \end{cases}$	Efficient with trivial hulls
Linear	Leon [17]	$O(C_{ISD}(q, n, k, d_{GV}) \cdot 2\log(N_w))$	Best with small finite fields and large hulls
	Beullens [9]	$O\left(\dfrac{2L \cdot C_{ISD}(q,n,k,w)}{N_w \left(1 - 2^{L \log_2(1 - L/N_w)}\right)} \right)$	Best with large finite fields and hulls. May fail when L is too small
	SSA [19]	$\begin{cases} O\left(n^3 + n^2 q^{d_h} \log n\right) & \text{if } q < 5 \\ O\left(n^3 + n^2 q^{k} \log n\right) & \text{if } q \geq 5 \end{cases}$	Efficient if $q < 5$ and the hull is trivial

In Table 5, N_w is the number of codewords of weight w, L is the number of codewords employed for the attack, d_h is the dimension of the hull of the code, d_{GV} is the Gilbert-Varshamov distance, and C_{ISD} and C_{WGI} stand for the costs of Information-Set Decoding and Weighted Graph Isomorphism, respectively.

Note that the algorithms to solve the code equivalence problem essentially do not change with the equivalence type. In fact, apart from some small choices in setting the attack options (for instance, the value of w and L in Beullens' algorithm), we have that the complexities for the linear case are identical to those of the permutation case. Then, one may be led into thinking that the two problems are equally hard; yet, this claim is fundamentally false. To be clear, the permutation equivalence problem is actually easy in many cases. Using either SSA or BOS, one can comfortably solve random instances since, with very high probability, they have a hull with very small dimension. Yet, these algorithms fail in successfully solving the problem when the hull dimension increases, which is the case, for example, of (weakly) self-dual codes. In such cases, the problem becomes harder and one must rely on algorithms such as those of Leon and Beullens, whose running time is exponential. So we can conclude that the permutation equivalence is hard only for some very specific instances.

The situation is quite the opposite, when dealing with the linear equivalence problem. Indeed, in this case, SSA is efficient only for random codes defined over finite fields with $q \le 5$, and becomes exponentially hard if the field size grows, regardless of the code properties. Hence, for large q, it is fair to say that no polynomial-time solver is currently known. This seems to suggest that, for large finite fields, the linear equivalence problem is a much harder problem, in general, compared to permutation equivalence.

5 Concrete Parameter Sets and Implementation Strategies

Selecting optimal parameters for LESS-FM involves a multi-target optimization where the considered figures of merit are: i) the desired security level, ii) the size of the keypair and of the transmitted signature message, and iii) the computational load required. In this work, we propose parameter sets which are targeted to a computational effort of 2^{128} classical gates, as is standard in literature. This will also facilitate a comparison with other existing signature schemes. Nevertheless, we also ensured that our parameters achieve at least 64 quantum security bits, according to the best known quantum algorithm techniques, an analysis of which is also reported in the full version of this work [6].

Table 6 gives a synthetic view of public key and signature sizes as a function of the LESS variant parameters. To achieve the reported storage complexity, the LESS keypairs are stored representing the field elements of $\mathbb{F}_q$ as $Q = \lceil \log_2(q) \rceil$ integers, and linearizing on the storage the non-trivial portion of the $\mathbf{G}_i$ matrices of the public keys performing bitpacking. This yields a public key size of $(2^\ell - 1)k(n - k)Q$ (considering one can always set $\mathbf{Q}_0 = \mathbf{I}_n$ and $\mathbf{G}_0 = \mathsf{sf}(\mathbf{G})$). Concerning the storage of the monomial matrices composing the private key, they can be represented as an length-n vector of pairs storing the index of the permuted element, and the value of its multiplicative coefficient on $\mathbb{F}_q$.

Table 6. Overview of the number of rounds and public key/signature sizes in bits as a function of the LESS variant parameters, with $N = \lceil \log_2(n) \rceil$ and $Q = \lceil \log_2(q) \rceil$.

Version	Type	Num. of rounds	$|\mathsf{pk}|$	$|\sigma|$
–	Perm	λ	$k(n-k)Q$	$\lambda \left(1 + \frac{\lambda + nN}{2}\right)$
	Mono	λ	$k(n-k)Q$	$\lambda \left(1 + \frac{\lambda + nN + nQ}{2}\right)$
M	Perm	$\lceil \frac{\lambda}{\ell} \rceil$	$(2^\ell - 1)k(n-k)Q$	$\lceil \frac{\lambda}{r} \rceil \left(2\ell + \frac{nN}{2}\right)$
	Mono	$\lceil \frac{\lambda}{\ell} \rceil$	$(2^\ell - 1)k(n-k)Q$	$\lceil \frac{\lambda}{r} \rceil \left(2r + \frac{nN + nQ}{2}\right)$
F	Perm	t s.t. $\binom{t}{\omega} > 2^\lambda$	$k(n-k)Q$	$t + (t - \omega)\lambda + \omega nN$
	Mono	t s.t. $\binom{t}{\omega} > 2^\lambda$	$k(n-k)Q$	$t + (t - \omega)\lambda + \omega n (N + Q)$
FM	Perm	t s.t. $\binom{t}{\omega}(2^\ell - 1)^\omega > 2^\lambda$	$(2^\ell - 1)k(n-k)Q$	$\ell t + (t - \omega)\lambda + \omega nN$
	Mono	t s.t. $\binom{t}{\omega}(2^\ell - 1)^\omega > 2^\lambda$	$(2^\ell - 1)k(n-k)Q$	$\ell t + (t - \omega)\lambda + \omega n (N + Q)$

Note that, while a compact representation of the permutation alone is possible over $\lceil \log_2(n!) \rceil$ bits, this saves a relatively small amount of space (about 4.5% when minimizing both the public key and signature, where such an effect is most evident), at the cost of performing the relatively demanding computation of permutation unranking, to bring the permutation in a usable representation. Finally, as noted, we achieve a significant reduction in signature size by sending the seeds employed to generate the ephemeral random monomial matrices $\tilde{\mathbf{Q}}_i$ instead of the monomial matrices themselves. We also note that, from a computational standpoint, it is more efficient to store the inverses of the monomial matrices in the private key, moving their computation to the key generation process. This results in an overall improvement in the computation time in all the cases where long-term keys for the signatures are employed.

Table 7 reports the result of the optimization of the LESS-FM parameters when targeting the minimization of i) the public key size, ii) the signature size or iii) the sum of the aforementioned quantities. The rationale behind these criteria is to highlight the flexibility of LESS-FM in application scenarios where i) the space for public key storage is constrained (e.g. microcontrollers with tight Flash memory limits), ii) digital certificates, which employ a concatenation of public keys and signatures, and iii) application scenarios where a large amount of signed messages are exchanged between two endpoints employing long-term keypairs.

Table 7. Parameter sets for LESS-FM, for a security level of $\lambda = 128$ classical bits.

Optimization criterion	LESS	Type	n	k	q	ℓ	t	ω	pk (kB)	sig (kB)	pk + sig (kB)
Min. pk size	F	Mono	198	94	251	1	283	28	9.77	15.2	24.97
Min. sig size	FM	Perm	235	108	251	4	66	19	205.74	5.25	210.99
Min. pk + sig size	F	Perm	230	115	127	1	233	31	11.57	10.39	21.96
Beullens [9]	–	Mono	250	125	53	1	128	–	11	28	39

Despite our conservative quantification of the computational effort required by the most effective cryptanalytic approaches, LESS can be instantiated with parameters pushing the size of the public key below 10 kB, or keep the sum of the public key and signature below 22 kB. Our balanced optimization criterion, combined with the use of fixed-weight challenges allows us to reduce to less than half the signature size, with respect to the parameter sets proposed by Beullens in [9], while retaining the same public key size. Finally, we are able, at the cost of a larger public key size, to achieve a minimum signature size of 5.25 kB, reducing the signature size by close to 3× with respect to the other parameter sets.

Table 8 reports a comparison of the data sizes achieved by LESS variants with other code-based signature schemes.

Considering the algorithms employing Fiat-Shamir, we see that LESS consistently outperforms the traditional schemes based on the Hamming metric (such as Stern, Veron and CVE), even when compared to 80-bit security versions, while its characteristics are orthogonal to those of cRVDC (which is rank-based). Indeed, despite a much larger public key, LESS achieves more compact

Table 8. Size comparison of with other code-based signature schemes.

Scheme	Security level	pk (kB)	sig (kB)	pk + sig (kB)	Security assumption
Stern [15]	80	18.48	113.5	131.98	Low-weight Hamming
Veron [15]	80	18.52	109.05	127.57	Low-weight Hamming
CVE [15]	80	5.31	66.44	71.75	Low-weight Hamming
Wave [14]	128	3205	1.04	3206.04	High-weight Hamming
cRVDC [8]	125	0.15	22.48	22.63	Low-weight Rank
Durandal - I [3]	128	15.24	4.06	19.3	Low-weight Rank
Durandal - II [3]	128	18.60	5.01	23.61	Low-weight Rank
LESS-F min. pk size	128	9.77	15.2	24.97	Linear Equivalence
LESS-FM min. sig size	128	205.74	5.25	210.99	Perm Equivalence
LESS-F min. pk + sig size	128	11.57	10.39	21.96	Perm Equivalence

signatures, and therefore compares favourably in scenarios ii) and iii). Finally, we consider two recent signature algorithms (namely, Wave and Durandal). We observe that LESS also provides favourable figures with respect to Wave, as it features a public key which is smaller by two orders of magnitude, albeit at the cost of an increase of an order of magnitude in signature size. This provides a practical advantage in scenarios where a public key/signature pair is transferred at each communication, such as in the TLS authentication phase, which transmits X.509 certificates. In this regard, the performance of LESS is very similar to that of Durandal, which is an adaptation of the Schnorr's paradigm to the rank metric. It is then worth noting that the closest competition for LESS, in terms of performance, is represented by rank metric schemes, an area which is somewhat further away from traditional coding theory (while strongly related to multivariate cryptography), and, in the case of Durandal, relying on younger, ad-hoc computational assumptions.

Acknowledgments. The authors would like to thank Ward Beullens and Robert Ransom for fruitful discussions about LESS optimizations.

A   Cryptographic Group Actions

At a high level, a *group action* is an operator involving a group, for which an identity exists, and that satisfies the *compatibility* property, as follows.

Definition 2. *Let X be a set and $(G, \circ)$ be a group. A group action is a mapping*

$$\star : X \times G \to X$$
$$(x, g) \to x \star g$$

such that, for all $x \in X$ and $g_1, g_2 \in G$, it holds that $(x \star g_1) \star g_2 = x \star (g_1 \circ g_2)$.

A group action is usually called *cryptographic* if it satisfies some additional properties that make it interesting in a cryptographic context. In the first place, besides efficient sampling, computation, and membership testing, a cryptographic group action should certainly be *one-way*, i.e. given randomly chosen

$x_1, x_2 \in X$, it should be hard to find $g \in G$ such that $x_1 \star g = x_2$ (if such a g exists). Other desirable properties include, for instance, *pseudorandomness* of the output, as well as more traditional ones such as commutativity, transitivity etc. Due to space constraints, we refer the reader to [2] for an extensive treatment of cryptographic group actions and their properties.

B   EUF-CMA Security of LESS

In here, we show that the LESS signature scheme is EUF-CMA secure. We begin with the following trivial result.

Lemma 1. *Let* M_n *be the set of monomial matrices as defined in Sect. 2. Then for any* $\boldsymbol{A} \in \mathsf{M}_n$ *and* $\boldsymbol{B} \xleftarrow{\$} \mathsf{M}_n$, $\boldsymbol{A}^{-1}\boldsymbol{B}$ *is uniformly distributed over* M_n.

Next, we recall the Forking Lemma, which is the traditional tool required for proofs of this kind. We use the formulation of Bellare-Neven (see [7]).

Lemma 2. *Fix an integer* $Q \geq 1$ *and a set* H *of size* $|H| \geq 2$. *Let* $\mathcal{A}$ *be a randomized algorithm that takes as input elements* $h_1, \dots, h_Q \in H$ *and outputs a pair* (J, σ) *where* $1 \leq J \leq Q$ *with probability* P. *Consider the following experiment:*

1. *Choose* $h_1, \dots, h_Q$ *uniformly at random from* H.
2. $\mathcal{A}(h_1, \dots, h_Q)$ *outputs* (I, σ) *with* $I \geq 1$.
3. *Choose* $h_I', \dots, h_Q'$ *uniformly at random from* H.
4. $\mathcal{A}(h_1, \dots, h_{I-1}, h_I', \dots, h_Q')$ *outputs* (I', σ').

Then the probability that $I' = I$ *and* $h_I' \neq h_I$ *is at least*

$$P\left(\frac{P}{Q} - \frac{1}{|H|}\right).$$

The main result is given below.

Theorem 1. *The LESS signature scheme described in Table 1 is existentially unforgeable under adaptive chosen-message attacks, in the random oracle model, under the hardness of the linear code equivalence problem.*

Proof. Let $\mathcal{A}$ be a polynomial-time EUF-CMA adversary for LESS. $\mathcal{A}$ takes as input a verification key vk, then performs a polynomial number of signing queries, say q_s, and a polynomial number of random oracle queries, say q_r. Eventually, $\mathcal{A}$ outputs a forgery $(\boldsymbol{m}^*, \sigma^*)$, with a certain probability of success p. We now show how to construct an adversary $\mathcal{A}'$ that is able to solve the linear code equivalence problem. $\mathcal{A}'$ will interact with $\mathcal{A}$ and use it as a subroutine, playing the role of the challenger in the EUF-CMA game and simulating correct executions of the LESS protocol, without obviously having access to the private key.

To begin with, $\mathcal{A}'$ is given an instance $(\boldsymbol{G}, \boldsymbol{G}' = \boldsymbol{SGQ})$ of Problem 1, which he sets up as public key in the simulated LESS protocol. $\mathcal{A}'$ will answer signing queries and random oracle queries as described below; to ensure consistency of the simulation, the queries will be tracked with the help of a table T, initially empty, where the calls to the random oracle will be stored as they are answered, in the form of pairs $(input, output)$.

Setup. Set $G_0 = G$ and $G_1 = G'$.

Random Oracle Queries. In a random oracle query, $\mathcal{A}$ submits an input x of the form $(\hat{G}_0, \ldots, \hat{G}_{t-1}, m)$ and expects to receive a λ-bit string h. $\mathcal{A}'$ proceeds as follows:

1. Look up x in T. If $(x, h) \in$ T for some h, return h and halt.
2. Generate uniformly at random a λ-bit string h.
3. Add (x, h) to T.
4. Return h.

Signing Queries. In a signing query, $\mathcal{A}$ submits a message m and expects to receive a valid signature σ for it. $\mathcal{A}'$ proceeds as follows:

1. Generate uniformly at random a λ-bit string h.
2. Generate uniformly at random matrices $\hat{Q}_0, \ldots, \hat{Q}_{t-1}$.
3. Set $\mu_i = \hat{Q}_i$.
4. Return signature $\sigma = (\mu_0, \ldots \mu_{t-1}, h)$.

After that, $\mathcal{A}'$ adjusts his registry of queries by recording the query corresponding to h in table T. More specifically, $\mathcal{A}'$ will parse $h = h_0, \ldots h_{t-1}$, where $h_i \in \{0,1\}$, then compute $\hat{G}_i = \mathsf{sf}(G_{h_i}\mu_i)$ and finally set h to be the response to the random oracle query with input $(\hat{G}_0, \ldots, \hat{G}_{t-1}, m)$. Note that, due to Lemma 1, signatures produced in this way are indistinguishable from authentic signatures, since they follow the exact same distribution.

The simulation halts if, during a signing query, the input to the random oracle had already been queried before, in which case the signing query outputs $\perp$ instead. Note that this can only happen with negligible probability; more precisely, the probability is at most q'/K^t, where $q' = q_s + q_r$ is the total number of queries performed, and K is an upper bound on the probability of finding a collision, i.e. sampling two monomial matrices that lead to linearly equivalent codes (see Proposition 1 of Appendix E)[2].

Once $\mathcal{A}$ has finished performing queries, it will output a forgery (m, σ), where $\sigma = (\mu_0, \ldots \mu_{t-1}, h_0, \ldots h_{t-1})$, that successfully passes verification. At this point, $\mathcal{A}'$ rewinds his tape and plays the simulation again, in the exact same way, except that one of the random oracle queries is answered differently. By the Forking Lemma, $\mathcal{A}$ will now output, with non-negligible probability, a forgery

---

[2] If two monomials Q and Q' are such that the codes generated by GQ and GQ' are equivalent, then there exists $S \in \mathsf{GL}_k$ such that $G = SGQ'Q^{-1}$, implying that QQ'^{-1} is an automorphism for the code generated by G.

$(\boldsymbol{m}', \sigma')$, where $\sigma' = (\mu'_0, \ldots \mu'_{t-1}, h'_0, \ldots h'_{t-1})$, for the same message $\boldsymbol{m}' = \boldsymbol{m}$ and the same random oracle input $(\hat{\boldsymbol{G}}_0, \ldots, \hat{\boldsymbol{G}}_{t-1}, \boldsymbol{m})$, such that $\sigma' \neq \sigma$. Let l be the index such that $h'_l \neq h_l$; then $\mathsf{sf}(\boldsymbol{G}_{h'_l}\mu'_l) = \mathsf{sf}(\boldsymbol{G}_{h_l}\mu_l)$, which means that the monomial matrix $\mu'_l \mu_l^{-1}$ is a solution to the linear code equivalence problem as desired.   □

C   EUF-CMA Security of LESS-M

We begin showing that the Multiple Codes Linear Equivalence Problem (Problem 2) reduces tightly to the Linear Equivalence Problem (Problem 1).

Theorem 2. *Given an algorithm to solve Problem 2, that runs in time T and succeeds with probability ε, it is possible to solve Problem 1, in time approximately equal to $T + O(rn^3)$, with probability of success equal to $\varepsilon/2$.*

Proof. Let $\mathcal{A}$ be an adversary for Problem 2. We now show how to construct an adversary $\mathcal{A}'$ that is able to solve the linear code equivalence problem. $\mathcal{A}'$ will interact with $\mathcal{A}$ and use it as a subroutine. To begin, $\mathcal{A}'$ is given an instance $(\boldsymbol{G}, \boldsymbol{G}' = \boldsymbol{SGQ})$ of Problem 1. It will then proceed to generate $r = 2^\ell$ equivalent codes, in the following way. First, $\mathcal{A}'$ samples uniformly at random matrices $\boldsymbol{S}_0, \ldots, \boldsymbol{S}_{r-1}$ and $\boldsymbol{Q}_0, \ldots, \boldsymbol{Q}_{r-1}$. Then, it computes half of the codes starting from $\boldsymbol{G}$, and half starting from $\boldsymbol{G}'$; wlog, we can imagine that $\boldsymbol{G}_i$ is generated as $\boldsymbol{S}_i \boldsymbol{G} \boldsymbol{Q}_i$ when $i \in [0; r/2 - 1]$, and as $\boldsymbol{S}_i \boldsymbol{G}' \boldsymbol{Q}_i$ when $i \in [r/2; r - 1]$ (and then reordered). It is clear that this computation can be done in polynomial time, at most $O(rn^3)$, and that there is no way to distinguish how an individual matrix was generated (i.e. from $\boldsymbol{G}$ rather than from $\boldsymbol{G}'$). At this point $\mathcal{A}'$ runs $\mathcal{A}$ on input $\boldsymbol{G}_0, \ldots, \boldsymbol{G}_{r-1}$, and $\mathcal{A}$ will output, with probability ε, a response $(\boldsymbol{S}^*, \boldsymbol{Q}^*)$ such that $\boldsymbol{G}_{j'} = \boldsymbol{S}^* \boldsymbol{G}_j \boldsymbol{Q}^*$. Now, if one of the two matrices was of the first type, and the other of the second type, $\mathcal{A}'$ is able to win. For instance, if $\boldsymbol{G}_j = \boldsymbol{S}_j \boldsymbol{G} \boldsymbol{Q}_j$ and $\boldsymbol{G}_{j'} = \boldsymbol{S}_{j'} \boldsymbol{G}' \boldsymbol{Q}_{j'}$, then it must be $\boldsymbol{Q}^* = \boldsymbol{Q}_j^{-1} \boldsymbol{Q} \boldsymbol{Q}_{j'}$, which immediately reveals[3] $\boldsymbol{Q}$. Since this happens with probability $1/2$, we get the thesis.   □

We now state the security result.

Theorem 3. *The LESS-M signature scheme described in Table 2 is existentially unforgeable under adaptive chosen-message attacks, in the random oracle model, under the hardness of the multiple codes linear equivalence problem.*

Proof. (Sketch) The proof is nearly identical to the proof of Theorem 1, above. Indeed, let $\mathcal{A}$ be a polynomial-time EUF-CMA adversary for LESS-M. In this case $\mathcal{A}$ will serve as subroutine for an adversary $\mathcal{A}'$ against Problem 2. To begin with, $\mathcal{A}'$ is given an instance $(\boldsymbol{G}_0, \ldots, \boldsymbol{G}_{r-1})$ of Problem 2, which he sets up as public key in the simulated LESS-M protocol. As before, $\mathcal{A}'$ will answer signing queries and random oracle queries with the help of an auxiliary table T. For random oracle queries, the input is still of the form $(\hat{\boldsymbol{G}}_0, \ldots, \hat{\boldsymbol{G}}_{t-1}, \boldsymbol{m})$, with the

---

[3] If needed, $\boldsymbol{S}$ can then be found in polynomial time also.

only difference being that before we had $t = \lambda$, whereas now we have $t = \lambda/\ell$. Queries are answered in the exact same way as above, by selecting a uniform random λ-string h and updating the table. For signing queries, the procedure is also very similar. Once again, a signature is created using uniformly-sampled matrices $\hat{Q}_0, \ldots, \hat{Q}_{t-1}$ (with $t = \lambda/\ell$). Now, when $\mathcal{A}'$ adjusts his registry of queries, he will parse $h = h_0, \ldots h_{t-1}$, where $h_i \in \mathbb{Z}_2^\ell$, then proceed as before, computing $\hat{G}_i = \mathsf{sf}(G_{h_i}\mu_i)$ and matching h with the random oracle query with input $(\hat{G}_0, \ldots, \hat{G}_{t-1}, m)$. It is easy to see that signatures produced in this way are still indistinguishable from authentic signatures.

The rest of the proof proceeds exactly as before, with $\mathcal{A}'$ rewinding the tape, repeating the simulation and invoking the Forking Lemma to obtain two valid forged signatures $\sigma' \neq \sigma$ for the same message. Again, if l is the index such that $h_l' \neq h_l$, then $\mathsf{sf}(G_{h_l'}\mu_l') = \mathsf{sf}(G_{h_l}\mu_l)$ and therefore $\mu_l'\mu_l^{-1}$ is a solution to the multiple codes linear equivalence problem as desired (with $j' = h_l' \neq h_l = j$ as per the formulation of Problem 2).   □

D   EUF-CMA Security of LESS-F

In this section we discuss the EUF-CMA security of LESS-F. We have the following result.

Theorem 4. *The LESS-F signature scheme described in Table 3 is existentially unforgeable under adaptive chosen-message attacks, in the random oracle model, under the hardness of the linear code equivalence problem.*

Proof. (Sketch) The proof is essentially identical to the proof of Theorem 1. If $\mathcal{A}$ is a polynomial-time EUF-CMA adversary for LESS-F, it will be used as subroutine by an adversary $\mathcal{A}'$ against Problem 1. The setup is the same, including the use of the auxiliary table T. Indeed the only difference between the two proofs is in the output of the hash function H. This means that the random string h, generated to answer both random oracle and signing queries, is sampled uniformly from $\mathbb{Z}_{2,\omega}^t$ rather than from $\{0,1\}^\lambda$. The remainder of the proof proceeds unchanged.   □

Note that the aforementioned difference is relevant exclusively in the statement of the Forking Lemma. In fact, the (inverse of the) size of H appears in the Lemma's statement as a negative term (and should therefore be negligible). In the original LESS scheme (as is customary) one has $H = \{0,1\}^\lambda$, so $|H| = 2^\lambda$ and thus the term appearing in the Lemma is $1/2^\lambda$. Accordingly, with this variant, we have $H = \mathbb{Z}_{2,\omega}^t$, so $|H| = \binom{t}{\omega}$, which is precisely why we require $\log_2\binom{t}{\omega} \geq \lambda$.

E   The Automorphism Group of a Random Code

We now derive an estimate on the size of the automorphism group of a random linear code, and use it to derive an upper bound on the probability that applying a random monomial (or permutation) returns an equivalent code. We anticipate the main result, and then proceed by proving it.

Proposition 1. *Let* $\mathfrak{C} \subseteq \mathbb{F}_q^n$ *be a random linear code with dimension* k. *Let* d_{GV} *denote the GV distance of* $\mathfrak{C}$, *and* $N_{d_{GV}} = \left\lceil \binom{n}{d_{GV}}(q-1)^{d_{GV}-2}q^{k-n+1} \right\rceil$. *Let* $d_{GV}^{\perp}$ *be the GV distance of* $\mathfrak{C}^{\perp}$, *and* $N_{d_{GV}}^{\perp} = \left\lceil \binom{n}{d_{GV}^{\perp}}(q-1)^{d_{GV}^{\perp}-2}q^{-k+1} \right\rceil$. *The probability that* $\pi \xleftarrow{\$} S_n$ *is in the permutations automorphism group of* $\mathfrak{C}$, *i.e.,* $\pi(\mathfrak{C}) = \mathfrak{C}$, *is not greater than*

$$(q-1)\min\left\{ \frac{N_{d_{GV}}!}{\binom{n}{d_{GV}!}}, \frac{N_{d_{GV}}^{\perp}!}{\binom{n}{d_{GV}^{\perp}!}} \right\},$$

while the probability that $\mu \xleftarrow{\$} M_n$ *is in the monomials automorphism group of* $\mathfrak{C}$, *i.e.,* $\mu(\mathfrak{C}) = \mathfrak{C}$, *is not greater than*

$$\min\left\{ \frac{N_{d_{GV}}!(q-1)^{-d_{GV}+1}}{\binom{n}{d_{GV}!}}, \frac{N_{d_{GV}}^{\perp}!(q-1)^{-d_{GV}^{\perp}+1}}{\binom{n}{d_{GV}^{\perp}!}} \right\}.$$

We prove the above result explicitly for the case of permutations. In the case of monomials, the proof can be easily adapted; due to space constraints, such a proof will be presented explicitly only in the full version of this paper.

E.1 Proof for the Permutations Automorphism Group

To derive a bound on the size of the automorphism group of a code, we will consider the action of permutations on the set of minimum weight codewords. To this end, we first derive some preliminary results.

Lemma 3. *Let* $a, b \in \mathbb{F}_q^n$ *with the same Hamming weight* d *and same entries multisets. Let* $\mathsf{Mors}_{S_n}(a, b) = \{\pi \in S_n \mid \pi(a) = b\}$. *Then, the cardinality of* $\mathsf{Mors}_{S_n}(a, b)$ *is not greater than* $w!(n - w)!$.

Proof. Let $E = \{i \in [0; n-1] \mid a_i = 0\}$. For a permutation π, we can have $\pi(i) = j$ if and only if $a_i = b_j$. Let m_x, for $x \in \mathbb{F}_q$, be the number of entries with value equal to x in both a and b; since a and b have Hamming weight w, it holds that $m_0 = n - w$ and $\sum_{x \in \mathbb{F}_q^*} m_x = w$. Then, we have

$$|\mathsf{Mors}_{S_n}(a, b)| = \prod_{x \in \mathbb{F}_q} m_x! = (n-w)! \prod_{x \in \mathbb{F}_q^*} m_x!.$$

It is immediately seen that $\prod_{x \in \mathbb{F}_{q^*}} m_x! \leq \left(\sum_{x \in \mathbb{F}_q^*} m_x \right)! = w!$, so that as an upper bound on the size of $\mathsf{Mors}_{S_n}(a, b)$ we can use $(n - w!)w!$. □

Lemma 4. *Let* $A \subseteq \mathbb{F}_q^n$, *with cardinality* M, *such that all the contained vectors have Hamming weight* w. *Let* $\mathsf{Auts}_{S_n}(A) = \{\pi \in S_n \mid \pi(a) \in A, \ \forall a \in A\}$; *then, the size of* $\mathsf{Auts}_{S_n}(A)$ *is not greater than* $M!w!(n - w)!$.

Proof. If $\pi \in \mathsf{Auts}_n(A)$, then for each $a \in A$, either $\pi(a) = a$ or there exists $a' \in A$, $a' \neq a$, such that $\pi(a) = a'$. Let us define some order for the elements of A and write $A = \{a^1, a^2, \cdots, a^M\}$. For each $\pi \in \mathsf{Auts}_n(A)$, there exists one and only one bijection $f : \{1, \cdots, M\} \mapsto \{1, \cdots, M\}$ such that $f(i) = j$ if and only if $\pi(a^i) = a^j$. On the contrary, for a fixed bijection f, we may have more than one valid permutation, i.e., a permutation that places i in position j if and only if $f(i) = j$. It is easily seen that, for a bijection f, the set of all valid permutations is obtained as follows $\mathsf{Aut}_{\mathsf{S}_n}^{(f)}(A) = \bigcap_{i=1}^M \mathsf{Mors}_n(a^i, a^{f(i)})$. Each bijection f can be seen as an element of the symmetric group on M elements (which we denote as S_M), so that the number of possible bijections is given by $M!$. Notice that, if $\pi \in \mathsf{Aut}_{\mathsf{S}_n}^{(f)}(A)$, then it is also in $\mathsf{Auts}_n(A)$: hence, $\mathsf{Auts}_n(A)$ corresponds to the union of all sets $\mathsf{Aut}_{\mathsf{S}_n}^{(f)}(A)$, that is

$$\mathsf{Auts}_n(A) = \bigcup_{f \in \mathsf{S}_M} \mathsf{Aut}_{\mathsf{S}_n}^{(f)}(A) = \bigcup_{f \in \mathsf{S}_M} \left(\bigcap_{i=1}^M \mathsf{Mors}_n\left(a^i, a^{f(i)}\right) \right).$$

We are now able to derive an upper bound on the size of $\mathsf{Auts}_n(A)$, as follows

$$|\mathsf{Auts}_n(A)| = \left| \bigcup_{f \in \mathsf{S}_M} \left(\bigcap_{i=1}^M \mathsf{Mors}_n\left(a^i, a^{f(i)}\right) \right) \right| \leq |\mathsf{S}_M| \cdot \left| \bigcap_{i=1}^M \mathsf{Mors}_n\left(a^i, a^{f(i)}\right) \right|$$

$$= M! \cdot \left| \bigcap_{i=1}^M \mathsf{Mors}_n\left(a^i, a^{f(i)}\right) \right| \leq M! w! (n - w!),$$

where the last inequality comes from Lemma 3.   □

Using the previous results, we prove the following theorem.

Theorem 5. *Let $\mathfrak{C} \subseteq \mathbb{F}_q^n$ be a linear code with minimum distance d. Let $T_q(c) = \{bc \mid b \in \mathbb{F}_q^*\}$, and let $V \subset \mathbb{F}_q$ be the set of N_d codewords such that*

i) if $c \in \mathfrak{C}$ has weight d, then $T_q(c)$ and V have only one element in common;
ii) all codewords in V have weight d.

Let $\mathsf{Auts}_n(\mathfrak{C})$ be the permutations automorphism group of $\mathfrak{C}$. Then, the cardinality of $\mathsf{Auts}_n(\mathfrak{C})$ is not greater than $(N_d)!(q-1)d!(n-d)!$.

Proof. Without loss of generality, we can define V such that all of its codewords have the first entry that is equal to 1. Now, let $\pi \in \mathsf{Auts}_n(\mathfrak{C})$; then, π must map the set of codewords of $\mathfrak{C}$ with weight d into itself. Since this set is obtained as $V_q = \bigcup_{c \in V} T_q(c)$, we have that the image of V_q under the permutation π is equal to itself. Hence, for each $c \in \mathfrak{C}$ with weight d, there must be $c' \in V$ such that $\pi(c) \in T_q(c')$. Note that this also guarantees that, for each $\hat{c} \in T_q(c)$, one also has $\pi(\hat{c}) \in T_q(c')$. To put it differently, for each $c \in V$ there must exist i) another codeword $c' \in V$, and ii) a non null element $b \in \mathbb{F}_q^*$, such that $\pi(c) = bc'$. Hence, we have

$$\mathsf{Aut}_{\mathsf{S}_n}(V_q) = \bigcup_{f \in S_{N_d}} \bigcup_{b \in \mathbb{F}_q^*} \left(\bigcap_{i=1}^{N_d} \mathsf{Mors}_n\left(c^i, bc^{f(i)}\right) \right).$$

This allows us to derive a bound on the size of $\mathsf{Aut}_{\mathsf{S}_n}(V_q)$, using the union bound for two times

$$|\mathsf{Aut}_{\mathsf{S}_n}(V)| = \left| \bigcup_{f \in S_{N_d}} \bigcup_{b \in \mathbb{F}_q^*} \left(\bigcap_{i=1}^{N_d} \mathsf{Mors}_n\left(c^i, bc^{f(i)}\right) \right) \right|$$

$$\leq |\mathsf{S}_{N_d}| \cdot |\mathbb{F}_q^*| \cdot \left| \bigcap_{i=1}^{N_d} \mathsf{Mors}_n\left(c^i, bc^{f(i)}\right) \right| \leq N_d!(q-1)d!(n-d)!.$$

Finally, we consider that if $\pi \in \mathsf{Aut}_{\mathsf{S}_n}(\mathfrak{C})$, then it must necessarily be $\pi \in \mathsf{Aut}_{\mathsf{S}_n}(V_q)$: hence, it must be $\mathsf{Aut}_{\mathsf{S}_n}(\mathfrak{C}) \subseteq \mathsf{Aut}_{\mathsf{S}_n}(V_q)$. So, we can use the bound on the cardinality of $\mathsf{Aut}_{\mathsf{S}_n}(V_q)$ as an upper bound for the size of $\mathsf{Aut}_{\mathsf{S}_n}(\mathfrak{C})$.   □

The above results allow to prove the bound on the permutations automorphism group stated in Proposition 1. To estimate the minimum distance of a code, we use the well known Gilbert-Varshamov bound, and estimate the number of weight w codewords (without counting scalar multiples) as $\lceil \binom{n}{w}(q-1)^{w-2}q^{k-n+1} \rceil$. We then divide the upper bound on the size of the automorphism group resulting from Lemma 5 by the cardinality of S_n (that is, $n!$). Finally, we consider that the automorphism group of a code coincides with that of its dual: we repeat the reasoning for the dual code and, take the minimum between the two obtained probabilities (i.e., the one for the code and that for its dual).

References

1. 2007. https://csrc.nist.gov/Projects/Post-Quantum-Cryptography
2. Alamati, N., De Feo, L., Montgomery, H., Patranabis, S.: Cryptographic group actions and applications. In: Moriai, S., Wang, H. (eds.) ASIACRYPT 2020. LNCS, vol. 12492, pp. 411–439. Springer, Cham (2020). https://doi.org/10.1007/978-3-030-64834-3_14
3. Aragon, N., Blazy, O., Gaborit, P., Hauteville, A., Zémor, G.: Durandal: a rank metric based signature scheme. In: Ishai, Y., Rijmen, V. (eds.) EUROCRYPT 2019. LNCS, vol. 11478, pp. 728–758. Springer, Cham (2019). https://doi.org/10.1007/978-3-030-17659-4_25
4. Babai, L.: Graph isomorphism in quasipolynomial time. In: Proceedings of the Forty-Eighth Annual ACM Symposium on Theory of Computing, pp. 684–697 (2016)
5. Bardet, M., Otmani, A., Saeed-Taha, M.: Permutation code equivalence is not harder than graph isomorphism when hulls are trivial. In: IEEE ISIT 2019, pp. 2464–2468 (2019)

6. Barenghi, A., Biasse, J.-F., Persichetti, E., Santini, P.: LESS-FM: fine-tuning signatures from the code equivalence problem. Cryptology ePrint Archive, Report 2021/396 (2021). https://eprint.iacr.org/2021/396
7. Bellare, M., Neven, G.: Multi-signatures in the plain public-key model and a general forking lemma. In: CCS, pp. 390–399 (2006)
8. Bellini, E., Caullery, F., Gaborit, P., Manzano, M., Mateu, V.: Improved Veron identification and signature schemes in the rank metric. In: ISIT, Paris, France, pp. 1872–1876 (2019)
9. Beullens, W.: Not enough less: An improved algorithm for solving code equivalence problems over f_q. Cryptology ePrint Archive, Report 2020/801
10. Beullens, W.: Sigma protocols for MQ, PKP and SIS, and fishy signature schemes. In: Canteaut, A., Ishai, Y. (eds.) EUROCRYPT 2020. LNCS, vol. 12107, pp. 183–211. Springer, Cham (2020). https://doi.org/10.1007/978-3-030-45727-3_7
11. Biasse, J.-F., Micheli, G., Persichetti, E., Santini, P.: LESS is more: code-based signatures without syndromes. In: Nitaj, A., Youssef, A. (eds.) AFRICACRYPT 2020. LNCS, vol. 12174, pp. 45–65. Springer, Cham (2020). https://doi.org/10.1007/978-3-030-51938-4_3
12. Couveignes, J.M.: Hard homogeneous spaces. IACR Cryptol. ePrint Arch. 2006:291 (2006)
13. De Feo, L., Galbraith, S.D.: SeaSign: compact isogeny signatures from class group actions. In: Ishai, Y., Rijmen, V. (eds.) EUROCRYPT 2019. LNCS, vol. 11478, pp. 759–789. Springer, Cham (2019). https://doi.org/10.1007/978-3-030-17659-4_26
14. Debris-Alazard, T., Sendrier, N., Tillich, J.-P.: Wave: a new family of trapdoor one-way preimage sampleable functions based on codes. In: Galbraith, S.D., Moriai, S. (eds.) ASIACRYPT 2019. LNCS, vol. 11921, pp. 21–51. Springer, Cham (2019). https://doi.org/10.1007/978-3-030-34578-5_2
15. El Yousfi Alaoui, S.M., Cayrel, P.-L., El Bansarkhani, R., Hoffmann, G.: Code-based identification and signature schemes in software. In: Cuzzocrea, A., Kittl, C., Simos, D.E., Weippl, E., Xu, L. (eds.) CD-ARES 2013. LNCS, vol. 8128, pp. 122–136. Springer, Heidelberg (2013). https://doi.org/10.1007/978-3-642-40588-4_9
16. Fiat, A., Shamir, A.: How to prove yourself: practical solutions to identification and signature problems. In: Odlyzko, A.M. (ed.) CRYPTO 1986. LNCS, vol. 263, pp. 186–194. Springer, Heidelberg (1987). https://doi.org/10.1007/3-540-47721-7_12
17. Leon, J.: Computing automorphism groups of error-correcting codes. IEEE Trans. Inf. Theory 28(3), 496–511 (1982)
18. Ransom, R.: Constant-time verification for cut-and-choose-based signatures. Cryptology ePrint Archive, Report 2020/1184 (2020)
19. Sendrier, N.: The support splitting algorithm. IEEE Trans. Inf. Theory 46, 1193–1203 (2000)

Classical and Quantum Algorithms
for Generic Syndrome Decoding Problems
and Applications to the Lee Metric

André Chailloux[1], Thomas Debris-Alazard[2(✉)], and Simona Etinski[1]

[1] Inria de Paris, EPI COSMIQ, Paris, France
{andre.chailloux,simona.etinski}@inria.fr
[2] Inria Saclay, Palaiseau, France
thomas.debris@inria.fr

Abstract. The security of code-based cryptography usually relies on the hardness of the Syndrome Decoding (SD) problem for the Hamming weight. The best generic algorithms are all improvements of an old algorithm by Prange, and they are known under the name of Information Set Decoding (ISD) algorithms. This work aims to extend ISD algorithms' scope by changing the underlying weight function and alphabet size of SD. More precisely, we show how to use Wagner's algorithm in the ISD framework to solve SD for a wide range of weight functions. We also calculate the asymptotic complexities of ISD algorithms, both for the classical and quantum case. We then apply our results to the Lee metric, which is currently receiving a significant amount of attention. By providing the parameters of SD for the Lee weight for which decoding seems to be the hardest, our study could have several applications for designing code-based cryptosystems and their security analysis, especially against quantum adversaries.

1   Introduction

Code-based cryptography is one of the leading proposals for post-quantum cryptography. It traditionally relies on the hardness of the Syndrome Decoding problem. For fixed q, n, k, w, the problem is defined as follows: starting from a parity-check matrix $\mathbf{H} \in \mathbb{F}_q^{n \times (n-k)}$ and a syndrome $\mathbf{s} \in \mathbb{F}_q^{n-k}$ the goal is to find $\mathbf{e} \in \mathbb{F}_q^n$ such that $\mathbf{He} = \mathbf{s}$ and $\mathbf{e}$ has the Hamming weight[1] w. This problem has been studied for a long time and mostly for the alphabet size $q = 2$. Despite many efforts, the best algorithms for solving this problem [Pra62, Ste88, Dum91, MMT11, BJMM12, MO15] require an exponential running time and they are all refinements of the original Prange's algorithm [Pra62]. They are commonly known under one name: Information Set Decoding (ISD).

It is notoriously difficult to put the syndrome decoding problem into practice. For example, constructing an efficient signature scheme in code-based cryptography often requires to use pseudo-random functions, and some other

---

[1] The Hamming weight of a vector $\mathbf{e} = (e_1, \dots, e_n)$ is $|\mathbf{e}|_{\mathrm{H}} \overset{\text{def}}{=} |\{i : e_i \neq 0\}|$.

© Springer Nature Switzerland AG 2021
J. H. Cheon and J.-P. Tillich (Eds.): PQCrypto 2021, LNCS 12841, pp. 44–62, 2021.
https://doi.org/10.1007/978-3-030-81293-5_3

cryptographic assumptions. A generalized version of the problem promises to be harder and to offer a more exploitable structure that leads to creating more efficient constructions. Some proposals, like DURANDAL [ABG+19] change the Hamming weight with the rank metric which allows the designers to do a Schnorr-Lyubashevski type signature. Another proposal, the WAVE signature scheme [DST19], uses the Hamming weight with $q = 3$ but considers the case of large weight w, which allows the construction of a trapdoor one-way preimage sampleable function which would not be possible with $q = 2$ or with $q = 3$ in small weight.

These examples already show the usefulness of going beyond the $q = 2$ and the Hamming weight setting. We are however still at an early stage of using these variants for cryptographic schemes and it is therefore important to study their hardness at the same time, especially against quantum computers since a big appeal of code-based cryptography is its post-quantum security.

Lee's metric is an appealing metric for code-based cryptography. SD with Lee's metric seems to be harder than in Hamming's metric while preserving many of its properties. It has already been used profitably as a replacement for SD in the Hamming metric [HW19] and should have potentially many more applications in this setting. For specific parameters and alphabet size, there has been a study of its classical security in [WKH+21].

Our work. In this work, we perform a generic analysis of different ISD algorithms. Our analysis works for any weight function $wt : \mathbb{F}_q^n \to \mathbb{R}_+$ satisfying $wt(\mathbf{e}) \overset{\text{def}}{=} \sum_{i=1}^n wt'(e_i)$ for some function $wt' : \mathbb{F}_q^n \to \mathbb{R}_+$ and $wt'(0) = 0$. However, we primarily focus on the analysis of Lee weight, where $|\mathbf{x}|_{\text{L}} \overset{\text{def}}{=} \sum_{i=1}^n \min(x_i, q - x_i)$. for which we perform a complete analysis. This framework can also be used to study the security of the Restricted Syndrome Decoding problem [BBC+20a]. Nevertheless, it does not work for the rank metric norm where we do not know how to construct ISD algorithms better than Prange's algorithm[2].

But what kind of ISD algorithms do we study here? We study of course Prange and Dumer but also ISD algorithms based on Wagner's algorithm [Wag02]. These were studied in [BCDL19] when analyzing the ternary case in large Hamming weight, and in the classical regime. Starting from [BCDL19] we broaden the analysis to the higher alphabet sizes, usage of a different weight function, and the study of both classical and quantum algorithms. This is the first time such a generic analysis of quantum ISD algorithms was done since the work of [KT17] that studied only the standard $q = 2$ and Hamming weight case.

In order to perform such a generic analysis, we need a way of computing sphere surface areas for our weight function, *i.e.* sizes of sets of the form $\{\mathbf{e} \in \mathbb{F}_q^n : wt(\mathbf{e}) = p\}$. To do this we start with the approach presented in [Ast84], applied to the Lee weight case, and we derived a convex optimization method for calculating the asymptotic sphere surface area independently of the metric. We thus provide a simple approach for analyzing Syndrome Decoding problems in a vector space endowed with an arbitrary metric, and weight functions derived from it.

---

[2] Best decoding algorithms [BBB+20,BBC+20b] are based on Gröbner basis.

Our approach aims to be as generic as possible so we can't use representations [BJMM12] or nearest neighbor methods [MO15]. Indeed, one needs to precisely tailor these methods for each weight function without necessarily giving better results while our method is generic and requires only to compute the volumes of spheres associated to the weight function. For example, for ternary SD at WAVE parameters, Wagner's (smoothed) algorithm is essentially as powerful as representations even though representations these do better for other parameters [BCDL19] .

Notations

Throughout the paper, we use $[n] \overset{\text{def}}{=} \{1, \ldots, n\}$ and given a finite set $\mathscr{E}$, we denote by $|\mathscr{E}|$ its size. We consider a weight function $wt : \mathbb{F}_q^n \to \mathbb{R}_+$ which satisfies the following:

$$\forall \mathbf{e} = (e_i) \in \mathbb{F}_q^n, \ wt(\mathbf{e}) = \sum_i wt'(e_i) \text{ where } wt' : \mathbb{F}_q \to \mathbb{R}_+ \text{ and } wt'(0) = 0 \ (1)$$

This weight function is usually - but not always - obtained as $wt(\mathbf{x}) = d(\mathbf{x}, 0)$ where d is a distance. We will sometimes use the terminology of distance instead of weight when this is the case. When q and wt are fixed and explicit, we define the surface area of weight w in dimension n as $S_w^n \overset{\text{def}}{=} |\{\mathbf{e} \in \mathbb{F}_q^n, wt(\mathbf{e}) = w\}|.$[3]

2 Syndrome Decoding Problems

We fix an alphabet size q and a weight function wt. The Syndrome Decoding problem is defined as follows:

Problem 1. Syndrome Decoding $SD(n, k \le n, w)$

- Input: A matrix $\mathbf{H} \in \mathbb{F}_q^{(n-k) \times n}$, a column vector (the syndrome) $\mathbf{s} \in \mathbb{F}_q^{n-k}$.
- Goal: Find a column vector $\mathbf{e} \in \mathbb{F}_q^n$ s.t. $\mathbf{H}\mathbf{e} = \mathbf{s}$ and $wt(\mathbf{e}) = w$.

The decision version of this problem is NP-complete for $q = 2$ with the Hamming weight function [BMvT78] and also with Lee's metric [WKH+21].

In what follows we study algorithms to solve SD with the following distribution of inputs: pick a random matrix $\mathbf{H} \in \mathbb{F}_q^{(n-k) \times n}$ of rank $n - k$, pick a random $\mathbf{e} \in \mathbb{F}_q^n$ with $wt(\mathbf{e}) = w$, and output $(\mathbf{H}, \mathbf{s} = \mathbf{H}\mathbf{e})$. Note that the problem always has at least one solution for this distribution and that SD for this distribution is believed to be hard, even against quantum computers. We will only consider a prime q to avoid attacks that would use sub-fields of the alphabet field $\mathbb{F}_q$.

Another problem of interest is the following, which we call Checkable Multiple Syndrome Decoding. We are interested in this problem because in our framework, it is used as a building block for solving the generic SD problem.

---

[3] In coding theory, it is often standard to consider the volume of balls of radius w by replacing $wt(\mathbf{e}) = w$ with $wt(\mathbf{e}) \le w$. This is fine when we study small weight but cannot be used when we deal with large weights, where the volume of the ball and the surface area are very different.

Problem 2. Checkable Multiple Syndrome Decoding CMSD(n, m, w, Y, Z)

- Input: A matrix $\mathbf{H} \in \mathbb{F}_q^{m \times n}$, a syndrome $\mathbf{s} \in \mathbb{F}_q^m$
- Goal: output the description of a function $f : [Y] \rightarrow \mathbb{F}_q^n$ such that f is efficiently computable, and $|\{\mathbf{e} : \mathbf{e} \in \mathrm{Im}(f), \mathbf{He} = \mathbf{s} \text{ and } wt(\mathbf{e}) = w\}| = Z$.

This problem is a bit funny looking at first sight. It is very similar to asking for Z solutions of the syndrome decoding problem. Indeed, from a description f, one can output Z solutions to SD in time Y by enumerating all the $f(1), \ldots, f(Y)$. Reciprocally, if one can find Z solution $\mathbf{e}_1, \ldots, \mathbf{e}_Z$ to SD(n, m, w) in time $T \geq Z$ then one can solve CMSD(n, m, w, Z, Z) by defining $f(i) = \mathbf{e}_i$.

In the quantum setting, we want to have access to the function f but without paying for a time cost of Z for writing down these solutions. That will allow us to search over solutions more efficiently, using Grover's algorithm, and also justifies the slightly odd definition. Another remark is that while f should be efficiently computable, it doesn't need have an efficient description. Typically, f can store some large precomputed databases, but computing $f(x)$ will only query the database a small number of times.

3   Information Set Decoding Algorithms for Any Metric

We present Information Set Decoding algorithms for SD, which consist of a partial Gaussian elimination followed by solving an instance of CMSD. The description here is essentially the one from [BCDL19] with the difference that here we use the CMSD problem.

3.1   Information Set Decoding Framework

Fix $\mathbf{H} \in \mathbb{F}_q^{(n-k) \times n}$ of rank $(n - k)$ and $\mathbf{s} \in \mathbb{F}_q^{n-k}$. Recall that we want to find $\mathbf{e} \in \mathbb{F}_q^n$ such that $wt(\mathbf{e}) = w$ and $\mathbf{He} = \mathbf{s}$. Let us introduce ℓ, p, Y, and Z, four parameters of the system that we consider fixed for now. In this framework, an algorithm for solving SD(n, k, w) consists of four steps: a permutation step, a partial Gaussian Elimination step, a CMSD step, and a test step.

1. *Permutation step.* Pick a random permutation π. Let $\mathbf{H}_\pi$ be the matrix $\mathbf{H}$ with the columns permuted according to π. We now want to solve SD(n, k, w) on inputs $\mathbf{H}_\pi$ and $\mathbf{s}$.
2. *Partial Gaussian Elimination step.* If the top left square submatrix of $\mathbf{H}_\pi$ of size $n - k - \ell$ is not of full rank, go back to step 1 and choose another random permutation π. That happens with constant probability[4]. If the submatrix is of full rank, perform Gaussian elimination on the rows of $\mathbf{H}_\pi$ using the first $n - k - \ell$ columns. Let now $\mathbf{S} \in \mathbb{F}_q^{(n-k) \times (n-k)}$ be the invertible matrix

---

[4] For $q = 2$, this happens with probability at least 0.288 and this probability increases as q increases (see [Coo00], for example).

corresponding to this operation. There are two matrices, $\mathbf{H}' \in \mathbb{F}_q^{(n-k-\ell) \times (k+\ell)}$ and $\mathbf{H}'' \in \mathbb{F}_q^{\ell \times (k+\ell)}$, such that:

$$\mathbf{SH}_\pi = \begin{pmatrix} \mathbf{1}_{n-k-\ell} & \mathbf{H}' \\ \mathbf{0} & \mathbf{H}'' \end{pmatrix}.$$

A vector $\mathbf{e} \in \mathbb{F}_q^n$ can be written as $\mathbf{e} = \begin{pmatrix} \mathbf{e}' \\ \mathbf{e}'' \end{pmatrix}$, where $\mathbf{e}' \in \mathbb{F}_q^{n-k-\ell}$ and $\mathbf{e}'' \in \mathbb{F}_q^{k+\ell}$. One can write $\mathbf{Ss} = \begin{pmatrix} \mathbf{s}' \\ \mathbf{s}'' \end{pmatrix}$ with $\mathbf{s}' \in \mathbb{F}_q^{n-k-\ell}$ and $\mathbf{s}'' \in \mathbb{F}_q^{\ell}$.

$$\mathbf{H}_\pi \mathbf{e} = \mathbf{s} \iff \mathbf{SH}_\pi \mathbf{e} = \mathbf{Ss}$$

$$\iff \begin{pmatrix} \mathbf{1}_{n-k-\ell} & \mathbf{H}' \\ \mathbf{0} & \mathbf{H}'' \end{pmatrix} \begin{pmatrix} \mathbf{e}' \\ \mathbf{e}'' \end{pmatrix} = \begin{pmatrix} \mathbf{s}' \\ \mathbf{s}'' \end{pmatrix}$$

$$\iff \begin{cases} \mathbf{e}' + \mathbf{H}' \mathbf{e}'' = \mathbf{s}' \\ \mathbf{H}'' \mathbf{e}'' = \mathbf{s}'' \end{cases} \tag{2}$$

To solve the problem, we try to find a solution $\begin{pmatrix} \mathbf{e}' \\ \mathbf{e}'' \end{pmatrix}$ to the above system such that $wt\,(\mathbf{e}'') = p$ and $wt\,(\mathbf{e}') = w - p$.

3. *The CMSD step.* Solve $\mathrm{CMSD}(k+\ell, \ell, p, Y, Z)$ on input $(\mathbf{H}'', \mathbf{s}'')$, and let f be the output function.

4. *The test step.* For each $i \in [Y]$, let $\mathbf{e}_i'' = f(i)$ and let $\mathbf{e}_i' = \mathbf{s}' - \mathbf{H}' \mathbf{e}_i''$. For each i such that $\mathbf{H}'' \mathbf{e}'' = \mathbf{s}''$, Eq. (2) ensures that $\mathbf{H}_\pi \begin{pmatrix} \mathbf{e}_i' \\ \mathbf{e}_i'' \end{pmatrix} = \mathbf{s}$. If $wt\,(\mathbf{e}_i'') = p$ and $wt\,(\mathbf{e}_i') = w - p$, $\mathbf{e}_i = \begin{pmatrix} \mathbf{e}_i' \\ \mathbf{e}_i'' \end{pmatrix}$ is therefore a solution to $\mathrm{SD}(n, k, w)$ on inputs $\mathbf{H}_\pi$ and $\mathbf{s}$. The solution to $\mathrm{SD}(n, k, w)$ can then be turned into a solution of the initial problem by permuting the indices, as detailed in Eq. (3) below. If we do not find any solution after checking all $i \in [Y]$, we go back to step 1.

At the end of the protocol, we have a vector $\mathbf{e}$ such that $\mathbf{H}_\pi \mathbf{e} = \mathbf{s}$ and $wt\,(\mathbf{e}) = w$. Let $\mathbf{e}_{\pi^{-1}}$ be the vector $\mathbf{e}$ with the permuted coordinates according to π^{-1}. Hence,

$$\mathbf{H} \mathbf{e}_{\pi^{-1}} = \mathbf{H}_\pi \mathbf{e} = \mathbf{s} \quad \text{and} \quad wt\,(\mathbf{e}_{\pi^{-1}}) = wt\,(\mathbf{e}) = w. \tag{3}$$

Therefore, $\mathbf{e}_{\pi^{-1}}$ is a solution to the problem.

3.2 Information Set Decoding: Complexity Analysis (Classical and Quantum)

We fix q, and a weight function wt. Recall that for any n, w, the surface area of a sphere (according to wt) in $\mathbb{F}_q^n$ of radius w is defined as:

$$S_w^n = |\{\mathbf{e} \in \mathbb{F}_q^n : wt\,(\mathbf{e}) = w\}|.$$

With this definition, we can now present the complexity analysis of the above algorithm for solving $\mathrm{SD}(n, k, w)$, for fixed algorithm parameters ℓ, p, Y, Z.

Lemma 1. *Let P_1 be the probability that at step 4, for a fixed i, $wt\,(\mathbf{e}'_i) = w - p$. We have:*

$$P_1 = \frac{S_{w-p}^{n-k-\ell}}{\max\{1, \min\{S_w^n q^{-\ell}, q^{n-k-\ell}\}\}}.$$

Proof. This lemma can be seen as a generalization of Proposition 2 of [BCDL19] (where a max was omitted) for any weight function. We give the proof of this Lemma in Appendix B. □

We now present our generic formula for the running time of the Information Set Decoding algorithm presented above.

Proposition 1. *Fix parameters ℓ, p, Y, Z of the information set decoding algorithm. The classical running time T_{ISD} of the algorithm is:*

$$T_{\mathrm{ISD}} = O\left(\max\left\{1, \frac{1}{P_1 Z}\right\} \cdot (\mathrm{poly}(n) + T_{\mathrm{CMSD}} + \mathrm{poly}(n)Y)\right),$$

where P_1 is the probability from the above lemma and T_{CMSD} is the running time of step 3 i.e. of solving $\mathrm{CMSD}(k + \ell, \ell, p, Y, Z)$.

Proof. Steps 1 and 2 take $\mathrm{poly}(n)$ time, step 3 takes time T_{CMSD} and step 4 takes $\mathrm{poly}(n)$ time for each $i \in [Y]$, hence the right part of the expression. How many times do we loop over this process? Step 2 succeeds with constant probability and step 4 finds a solution with probability $1 - (1 - P_1)^Z$ so we have to loop over the steps $O\left(\frac{1}{1-(1-P_1)^Z}\right) = O\left(\max\left\{1, \frac{1}{P_1 Z}\right\}\right)$ times, hence the result. □

The quantum setting. Our formulation allows for a simple extension to the quantum setting (see Appendix A for brief quantum preliminaries). We consider the algorithm we described with the following two changes: (1) in step 4, we use Grover's algorithm to check whether there is an i such that $f(i)$ will give us a solution; (2) each time we run one loop of the algorithm i.e. that we start from step 1, the algorithm will find a solution with probability $p = \Omega(\min\{1, P_1 Z\})$. This loop can be done coherently with a quantum algorithm that doesn't do intermediate measurements and that outputs a solution with probability p. We then use amplitude amplification in order to find a solution by repeating the loop $O(\frac{1}{\sqrt{p}})$ times.

Proposition 2. *Fix parameters ℓ, p, Y, Z of the information set decoding algorithm. The quantum running time T_{ISD}^Q of the algorithm is*

$$T_{\mathrm{ISD}}^Q = O\left(\sqrt{\max\left\{\frac{1}{Z P_1}, 1\right\}} \cdot \left(\mathrm{poly}(n) + T_{\mathrm{CMSD}} + \mathrm{poly}(n)\sqrt{Y}\right)\right),$$

where P_1 is the probability from Lemma 1 and T_{CMSD} is the running time of step 3 i.e. of solving $\mathrm{CMSD}(k + \ell, \ell, p, Y, Z)$.

Proof. Again, Steps 1 and 2 take poly(n) time, and step 3 takes time T_{CMSD}. In step 4, we run Grover's algorithm so this whole step takes time poly(n)$O(\sqrt{Y})$. This can be done because the function that on input i determines whether $wt(\mathbf{e}'_i) = w - p$ runs in polynomial time (since f runs in polynomial time). As we described above, we repeat the loop $O\left(\sqrt{\max\left\{\frac{1}{ZP_1}, 1\right\}}\right)$ times which gives us the result.   □

The full ISD algorithm. In order to find the best ISD algorithm for solving $SD(n, k, w)$, we optimize the above over parameters p, ℓ, Y, Z. Actually, in many cases, we don't have full control over Y and Z and they will be predetermined from other values. For instance, in Wagner's algorithm we present next, there will be an extra parameter a (the number of levels) after which Y and Z will be fixed so we will optimize over p, ℓ and a here.

4   Wagner's Algorithm for Solving CMSD

In this section, we present our analysis of Wagner's algorithm for solving $\mathrm{CMSD}(N, m_0 N, \omega_0 N, Y, Z)$. Notice that we changed the variable names so that our statements can be made independently of the previous section and not to confuse the variables between those two sections. Also, we will present asymptotic values as N goes to $+\infty$.

Wagner's algorithm [Wag02] was used for solving Generalized Birthday Problems and is well suited for this problem. Because of length requirements, we will put our analysis in Appendix C. We only present here the results we obtain.

4.1   Complexity Analysis of Wagner's Algorithm

We construct two variants of Wagner's algorithm. The first variant is closely related to the original Wagner's algorithm [Wag02] and will be used to solve CMSD with a running time $T = Y$ and with $Z \leq Y$.

Proposition 3. *Fix parameters m_0, ω_0 as well as a number of levels a. Let $s_{\omega_0} = \lim_{n\to\infty} \frac{1}{n}\log_q(S^n_{n\omega_0})$, $u = \min\{\frac{s_{\omega_0}}{2^a}, m_0/a\}$ and $x = m_0 - (a - 1)u$. Our first variant of Wagner's algorithm on a levels solves the $\mathrm{CMSD}(N, m_0 N, \omega_0 N, Y, Z)$ problem in time T_{CMSD} where*

$$Z = q^{N(2u-x+o(1))}, \quad T_{\mathrm{CMSD}} = q^{N(u+o(1))}, \quad Y = T_{\mathrm{CMSD}}$$

and the $o(1)$ hides an expression that goes to 0 as N goes to $+\infty$.

Note that Y, Z are determined by m_0, ω_0, a and cannot be chosen arbitrarily.

We now present the complexity of our second variant. Here, we unbalance Wagner's algorithm to have $T = \sqrt{Y}$.

Proposition 4. *Fix parameters m_0, ω_0 as well as a number of levels a. Let $s_{\omega_0} = \lim_{n \to \infty} \frac{1}{n} \log_q(S^n_{n\omega_0})$, $u' = \min\{\frac{s_{\omega_0}}{2^a+1}, m_0/a\}$ and $x = m_0 - (a-1)u$. The variant 2 of Wagner's algorithm on a levels solves the* $\mathrm{CMSD}(N, m_0 N, \omega_0 N, Y, Z)$ *problem in time T_{CMSD} where*

$$Z = q^{N(3u' - x + o(1))}, \quad T_{\mathrm{CMSD}} = q^{N(u' + o(1))}, \quad Y = q^{N(2u' + o(1))}$$

and the $o(1)$ hides an expression that goes to 0 as N goes to $+\infty$.

Putting everything together. In our ISD algorithm, we need to solve an instance of $\mathrm{CMSD}(k + \ell, \ell, p, Y, Z)$. This means we can use the above propositions by defining $N = k + \ell, m_0 = \frac{\ell}{\ell + \ell}, \omega_0 = \frac{p}{k + \ell}$. We can then plug in Proposition 3 into Proposition 1 for the classical case and plug Proposition 4 into Proposition 2 for the quantum case, and we optimize also over the number of levels a.

For parameters k, ℓ and a note that Y and Z are fixed. Therefore, with these formulas we optimize in our ISD algorithm over k, ℓ and a from which we can extract Y and Z.

5 Application to Lee's Distance

We apply our results to Lee's metric. We first show how to compute the surface areas of spheres in this metric and then present the classical and quantum time analysis.

5.1 Computing Surface Area of a Sphere

Here we primarily rely on the combinatorial approach presented in [Ast84]. Some of the other approaches are presented in more recent papers as, for example, [GS91, BB19, WKH+21]. We decided to rely on the approach presented in [Ast84] as it enables us to derive a generic method for calculating the asymptotic value of the sphere surface area independently of the weight function and the alphabet size.

Proposition 5. *Fix a parameter q, and a weight function wt' satisfying Eq. (1). Let $C \stackrel{def}{=} \{\mathbf{c} = (c_0, \cdots, c_{q-1}) : i \in \{0, 1, ..., q - 1\}, c_i \in \mathbb{N}, \sum_{i=0}^{q-1} c_i = n, \sum_{i=0}^{q-1} c_i wt'(i) = w\}$. The sphere surface area, and its corresponding asymptotic value when n grows are given by the following expressions:*

$$S_w^n = \sum_{\mathbf{c} \in C} \binom{n}{\mathbf{c}}.^{(7)} \tag{4}$$

$^{(7)}$ $\binom{n}{\mathbf{c}}$ *denotes a multinomial coefficient.*

$$s_\omega = \lim_{n \to +\infty} \max_{\mathbf{c} \in C} \left(\sum_{i=0}^{q-1} -\frac{c_i}{n} \log_q \frac{c_i}{n} \right). \tag{5}$$

Proof. This proposition can be considered as the generalization of the combinatorial approach presented in [Ast84] for any weight function, and for arbitrary alphabet size. We give the proof of this proposition in Appendix D.   □

We compute the the asymptotic value of the sphere surface area s_ω by reducing Eq. (5) to the following convex optimization problem:

Problem 3. Let $\boldsymbol{\lambda} = (\lambda_0, \lambda_1, ..., \lambda_{q-1})$, and $\lambda_i \in \mathbb{R}_+$ for each $i \in \{0, 1, ..., q-1\}$.

 - Maximize: $-\sum_{i=0}^{q-1} \lambda_i \log_q \lambda_i$,
 - Subject to: $\sum_{i=0}^{q-1} \lambda_i = 1$, $\sum_{i=0}^{q-1} \lambda_i wt'(i) = \omega$.

It can be easily verified that when replacing the optimization variable λ_i with c_i/n from (5), the optimization problem remains convex. If we denote by $\tilde{\boldsymbol{\lambda}} = (\tilde{\lambda}_0, \tilde{\lambda}_1, ..., \tilde{\lambda}_{q-1})$ the solution of Problem 3, the asymptotic value of the sphere surface area is given by: $s_\omega = -\sum_{i=0}^{q-1} \tilde{\lambda}_i \log_q \tilde{\lambda}_i$.

We not only compute the surface areas but also the typical weight pattern of words of Lee weight w, *i.e.* the $\mathbf{c} \in C$ that maximizes the quantity in Eq. (5). This is necessary if we want to use this problem in Stern's signature scheme.

5.2   Results for Lee's Metric

We use our framework to compare SD with Hamming and Lee weight. For $q = 2$ and $q = 3$, the weight functions are the same by their definitions. However for $q > 3$ our numerical results show that the asymptotic complexities of the problem differ in these two cases, and that the problem is harder in Lee weight case (Fig. 1 and 2).

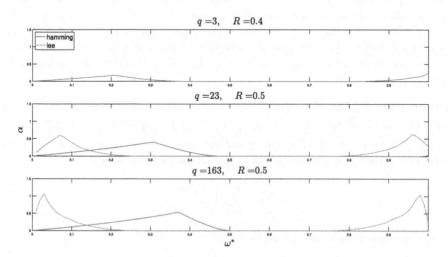

Fig. 1. Comparison of the Hamming and Lee SD problem: for a fixed q and R, the exponents α s.t. $Time = 2^{\alpha n}$ are given as a function of ω^*, where $\omega^* = \omega$ in the Hamming weight case, and $\omega^* = \omega \lfloor q/2 \rfloor$ in the Lee weight case.

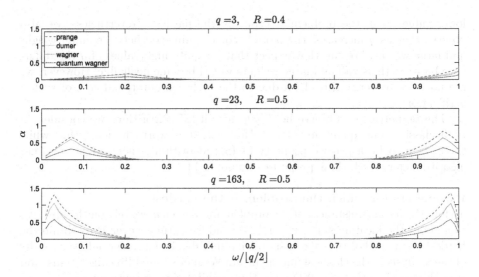

Fig. 2. Hardness of the Lee SD problem: The exponents α of the binary asymptotic complexity, $Time = 2^{\alpha n}$, of four ISD algorithms in Lee weight setting.

The following plot illustrates some of the numerical results we obtain for the Lee weight for different algorithms[5].

What we observe is that for any fixed q and R, the asymptotic complexity of our algorithms, as a function of ω^*, has 2 local maxima: at some values $\omega_-^* \in [0, x)$ and $\omega_+^* \in (x, \lfloor \frac{q}{2} \rfloor]$, with $x = \frac{q^2-1}{4q}$[6]. Moreover, these local maxima always satisfy:

$$\omega_-^* = \omega \in [0, x) \text{ st. } s_\omega = (1 - R).^{(10)}$$

$$\omega_+^* = \begin{cases} \omega \in (x, \lfloor \frac{q}{2} \rfloor] \text{ st. } s_\omega = (1 - R)^{(10)} \text{ if such an } \omega \text{ exists} \\ \lfloor \frac{q}{2} \rfloor \text{ otherwise.} \end{cases}$$

[10] In that case, we have $S_w^n = q^{n-k}$, which is the case where we have on average 1 solution to the SD problem on random inputs $\mathbf{H}, \mathbf{s}$.

This characterization of the local maxima is particularly useful when aiming to obtain the hardest instances of a problem. Namely, for a fixed q, it allows us to find the R that yields the hardest problem, and then to check only the 2 corresponding weights, ω_- and ω_+, so that we obtain the hardest instance. This makes our calculations more efficient, which becomes increasingly important as the value of q increases, and the convex optimization part of the calculations becomes costly due to the number of constraints in Problem 3.

It is also important to note here that many of previous papers only consider the case ω_-^* and miss out on very interesting parameter ranges where, for the

---

[5] The code that gives all our results is available at https://github.com/setinski/Information-Set-Decoding-Analysis.

[6] This value corresponds to the average Lee weight of a uniform vector.

lower values of q, the problem is typically the hardest. Nevertheless, we also observe that as q increases, the plots become symmetric between small weight and large weight. We can thus expect that for quite high values of q the difference between the small and large weights would become negligible. However, we are not able to verify this claim due to the high computational cost of such a verification.

The properties we observe here hold for all ISD algorithms we consider, in both classical and quantum setting. However, it is worth noticing that while these seem to be a generic property of ISD algorithms, there might be other algorithms for which these properties do not hold.

Parameters for which the problem is the hardest

To find the hardest instances of the problem for a given q, we rely on the observation about the local maxima, ω_-^* and ω_+^*, and we optimize over R to obtain the hardest instance. For the sake of simplicity, in Table 1 we present only the results of the analysis of the classical and quantum Wagner's based ISD algorithms, and remark that the other two ISD algorithms exhibit similar behavior.

Table 1. Hardest instances of Lee SD problem: the asymptotic complexity exponents α and $\hat{\alpha}$ correspond to the binary asymptotic complexity, $Time = 2^{\alpha n}$, and q-ary asymptotic complexity, $Time = q^{\hat{\alpha} n}$, respectively.

q	Classical Wagner ISD complexity				Quantum Wagner ISD complexity			
	R	$\omega/\lfloor q/2 \rfloor$	α	$\hat{\alpha}$	R	$\omega/\lfloor q/2 \rfloor$	α	$\hat{\alpha}$
3	0.370	1.000	0.269	0.170	0.369	1.000	0.148	0.093
5	0.572	1.000	0.357	0.154	0.569	1.000	0.206	0.089
13	0.480	0.957	0.522	0.141	0.501	0.962	0.283	0.076
43	0.454	0.954	0.794	0.146	0.472	0.959	0.429	0.079
163	0.442	0.967	1.117	0.152	0.464	0.971	0.607	0.083
331	0.438	0.974	1.291	0.154	0.464	0.978	0.703	0.084

It can be readily verified that the complexity of a problem, expressed as $2^{n(\alpha+o(1))}$, becomes higher as q increases. This is expected since the size of the inputs also increase, and we don't get this extra difficulty for free. If, for example, we want to use this problem in Stern's signature scheme, where the signature size essentially scales with the size of q-ary vectors of size n or $n-k$, this increase of the input size becomes relevant. Therefore, we propose the scaling where the complexity is of the form $q^{n(\hat{\alpha}+o(1))}$ instead of $2^{n(\alpha+o(1))}$, and we refer to them as q-ary asymptotic complexity and binary asymptotic complexity, respectively. Observing the q-ary complexity, the problem now is the hardest for $q = 3$. Intricately, the q-ary complexity diminishes and then increases again at some point as q increases. Hence, it would be interesting to see what would be the asymptotic q-ary complexity when both q and n grows beyond bounds. We can also observe that while for $q = 3$ and $q = 5$ the optimal values were for $\omega^* = 1$, this property doesn't hold for larger q. Nevertheless, it still remains in the range close to 1 (typically, in the range $(0.95, 1]$). We can see, as well, that the hardest instances of the problem occur at the mid-range code rates and, typically, in the range $(0.35, 0.6)$.

Cost of Our Quantum Algorithm to Attack Wave
Wave [DST19] is a code-based signature whose security relies on SD. For λ bits of classical security in Wave, parameters of SD are: $n = 66.34\lambda$, $w = 0.9396n$, $k = 0.66n$ and $q = 3$. For these parameters, the cost of our quantum algorithm is $2^{0.0097n(1+o(1))}$. Therefore, for 128 bits of classical security, Wave has 82 bits of quantum security according to our analyse.

Acknowledgments. The authors want to thank Nicolas Sendrier and Anthony Leverrier for helpful discussions. S.E. has received funding from the European Union's Horizon 2020 research and innovation program under the Marie Skłodowska-Curie grant agreement No 754362.

A   Quantum preliminaries

We refer to [NC00] for a basic introduction to quantum computing. We use the gate model where the running time of a quantum algorithm is the number of gates in its corresponding circuit description. We will be in the QRAM model where we assume the operation $U_{QRAM} : |i\rangle|y\rangle|b_1, \ldots, b_n\rangle \rightarrow |i\rangle|y + x_i\rangle|b_1, \ldots, b_n\rangle$ can be done in time $polylog(n)$, when each b_i is a single bit.

Grover's algorithm. [Gro96] For a function $f : \{0,1\}^n \rightarrow \{0,1\}$ which has an efficient classical description, Grover's algorithm can find x such $f(x) = 1$ in time $O(poly(n)2^{n/2})$ if such an x exists and output "no solution" otherwise.

Amplitude amplification. [BH97] Fix a function $f : \{0,1\}^n \rightarrow \{0,1\}$ which has an efficient classical description and consider a quantum algorithm $\mathscr{A}$ that outputs x such that $f(x) = 1$ with probability p and that doesn't perform intermediate quantum measurements. Using amplitude amplification, one can find x such that $f(x) = 1$ by making $O(\frac{1}{\sqrt{p}})$ calls to $\mathscr{A}$. If we start from a classical algorithm $\mathscr{A}$, there are generic ways to run $\mathscr{A}$ coherently as a quantum algorithm that doesn't have intermediate quantum measurements and that behaves exactly like $\mathscr{A}$.

B   Proof of Lemma 1

The proof goes as follows. Let $S = \{\mathbf{e} : wt(\mathbf{e}) = w \land \mathbf{H}_\pi \mathbf{e} = \mathbf{s}\}$ be the set of solutions to our syndrome decoding problem on input $\mathbf{H}_\pi, \mathbf{s}$ and let $S_2 = \{\mathbf{e} =$

$\begin{pmatrix} \mathbf{e}' \\ \mathbf{e}'' \end{pmatrix}$: $wt(\mathbf{e}) = w \wedge \mathbf{H}''\mathbf{e}'' = \mathbf{s}''\}$ where $\mathbf{H}''$ is the matrix from step 2. By definition, $S \subseteq S_2$. We have that S has average size $\max\{1, S_w^n q^{-(n-k)}\}$ and S_2 has average size $\max\{S_w^n q^{-\ell}, 1\}$.

Fix i, and $\mathbf{e}_i'' = f(i)$ satisfying $\mathbf{H}''\mathbf{e}_i'' = \mathbf{s}''$ and $wt(\mathbf{e}_i'') = p$. $T_i = \left\{ \mathbf{e}_i = \begin{pmatrix} \mathbf{e}_i' \\ \mathbf{e}_i'' \end{pmatrix} : wt(\mathbf{e}_i) = w \right\}$. T_i is of average size $S_{w-p}^{n-k-\ell}$. Step 4 will find a solution if $T_i \cap S \neq \emptyset$. Since $T_i \subseteq S_2$ and is uniformly distributed in this set, this happens with probability

$$P_1 = \frac{|T_i||S|}{|S_2|} = \frac{S_{w-p}^{n-k-\ell} \cdot \max\{1, S_w^n q^{-(n-k)}\}}{\max\{S_w^n q^{-\ell}, 1\}} = \frac{S_{w-p}^{n-k-\ell}}{\max\{1, \min\{S_w^n q^{-\ell}, q^{n-k-\ell}\}\}}.$$

C   Analysis of Wagner's algorithms

In this section, we present Wagner's algorithm. We first present the list-merging procedure that we will use throughout this section.

C.1   The list merging procedure

We start from 2 lists L_1, L_2 of vectors in $\mathbb{F}_q^n$, and we present the list merge on $J \subseteq [n]$ and $\mathbf{t} \in \mathbb{F}_q^{|J|}$. We write the list merge operator $\bowtie$ as follows:

$$L = L_1 \bowtie_J^{\mathbf{t}} L_2 = \{\mathbf{x} = \mathbf{y} + \mathbf{z} : \mathbf{y} \in L_1, \mathbf{z} \in L_2, \mathbf{x}_{|J} + \mathbf{y}_{|J} = \mathbf{t}\}$$

where $\mathbf{y}_{|J} \stackrel{\text{def}}{=} (y_j)_{j \in J}$. Computing L from L_1 and L_2 can be done in time $\tilde{O}(\max\{|L_1|, |L_2|, |L|\})$. If the elements in L_1, L_2 are random vectors of $\mathbb{F}_q^n$, we have on average $|L| = \frac{|L_1||L_2|}{q^{|J|}}$. We now show how to perform this list-merge.

List merge algorithm. Computing $L = L_1 \bowtie_J^{\mathbf{t}} L_2$ is done as follows:

- Start from an empty list L. Sort the elements of L_1 according to the lexicographic order on the J coordinates.
- For each $\mathbf{y} \in L_2$, search for elements $\mathbf{x} \in L_1$ such that $\mathbf{x}_{|J} = \mathbf{y}_{|J} + \mathbf{t}_{|J}$. Since L_1 is sorted on the J coordinates, each time this can be done in time $O(\log(|L_2|))$ using dichotomic search. For each solution found, add $\mathbf{x} + \mathbf{y}$ in L. If there are s_i such solutions for a fixed i, this algorithm takes $O(s_i \log(|L_2|))$ time to find them all.

The total size of L is then $\sum_i s_i$. This algorithm takes time $\tilde{O}(|L_1|)$ to sort L_1, then the second step takes time $\tilde{O}(\max\{|L_2|, \sum_i s_i \log(|L_2|)\})$ which concludes the claim of the list-merge running time.

We now present 2 variants of Wagner's algorithm for solving CMSD($N, N\ell_0$, $N\omega_0, Y, Z$) on input $(\mathbf{H}, \mathbf{s})$. The first one will be useful for the classical ISD algorithm and the other one for the quantum setting.

C.2   Variant 1 of Wagner's algorithm

We fix a number of levels a and we assume $2^a | n$. For each $i \in [2^a]$, we define

$$\mathscr{I}_i \stackrel{\text{def}}{=} \{ \mathbf{b} \in \mathbb{F}_q^n : \mathbf{b} = (0^{(i-1)n/2^a}, \mathbf{b}_i, 0^{(2^a-i)n/2^a}) \text{ with } \mathbf{b}_i \in \mathbb{F}_q^{n/2^a} \wedge wt(\mathbf{b}_i) = N\omega_0/2^a \},$$

$$L_i^f \stackrel{\text{def}}{=} \{ \mathbf{H} \cdot \mathbf{b}_i \}_{\mathbf{b}_i \in \mathscr{I}_i}.$$

We start the algorithm by constructing 2^a lists $L_i \subseteq L_i^f$ of the same size[7]. We put these lists on the bottom floor. Then, we take these lists into pairs $L_{2i-1,2i}$ for $i \in [2^{a-1}]$ and perform a list-merge $\bowtie_{J_1}^{t_1^i}$. Then, with the 2^{a-1} created lists, we again take pairs of them and perform $\bowtie_{J_2}^{t_2^i}$ for $i \in [2^{a-2}]$. We continue doing this and at the top of the tree, we have 2 lists on which we perform a list merge $\bowtie_{J_a}^{t_a^1 = s_{|J_a}}$. The J_i are chosen such that they form a partition of $[n]$ and the t_j^i are randomly with the constraint that for each level $j \in [a]$, $\sum_i(t_j^i)_{|J_j} = s_{J_j}$. The final list created like this contains therefore only solutions to the problem. In particular, elements of the top list are of the form $\mathbf{H} \cdot \mathbf{b}_i$ with $wt(\mathbf{b}_i) = N\omega_0$ which comes from the property of the weight function we use (Eq. 1) and the choice of $\mathscr{I}_i$. This means that in order to find the number of solutions outputted by the algorithm, we just need to compute the size of the final lists. We choose the size of each J_j such that the lists remain of the same size, except for J_a on which we have no control since $\sum_j |J_j| = n$ from the partition constraint. An example of Wagner's algorithm on 3 levels is presented below (Fig. 3).

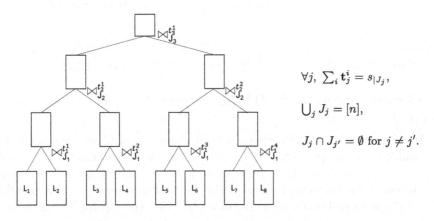

$$\forall j, \ \sum_i \mathbf{t}_j^i = s_{|J_j},$$

$$\bigcup_j J_j = [n],$$

$$J_j \cap J_{j'} = \emptyset \text{ for } j \neq j'.$$

Fig. 3. Variant 1 of Wagner's algorithm for $a = 3$.

---

[7] There are previous description where we actually have $L_i = L_i^f$. The inclusion will allow better parameters.

We take all our bottom lists L_i to be random subsets of size q^{Nu} of L_i^{f8}. We also choose the J_j such that $|J_1| = \cdots = |J_{a-1}| = u$ and $|J_a| = x$. From our list-merge procedure, all the lists up to the floor where we have 2 lists are of size q^u. The final list has size q^{2u-x}. All the elements in the final list are solution so we can construct q^{2u-x} solutions. For the running time, all the list merges take time q^u except the last one that takes time q^{2u-x} hence $T = \max\{q^u; q^{2u-x}\}$. We have an algorithm that finds $S = q^u$ solutions in time T. We can from there construct a function f as required for CMSD problem using the procedure described in Sect. 2.

C.3   Variant 2: Unbalanced Wagner.

We present here a variant of Wagner's algorithm that we will use for our quantum algorithm. Here, all the bottom lists will have the same size except the rightmost list which will be quadratically larger than the others (we also change the definition of L_i^f accordingly). In order to construct the function f required by the CMSD problem, we never construct the rightmost lists of each step. Since we will compute and sort the other lists, we will be able to construct an efficient function f that for each point of the bottom right list, will find it's corresponding element in the top list (if it exists).

Here, we modify our sets. For $i \in [2^a - 1]$, we define

$$\mathscr{I}_i \stackrel{\text{def}}{=} \{\mathbf{b} \in \mathbb{F}_q^n : \mathbf{b} = (\mathbf{0}^{(i-1)n/(2^a+1)}, \mathbf{b}_i, \mathbf{0}^{((2^a+1)-i)n/(2^a+1)})$$
$$\text{with } \mathbf{b}_i \in \mathbb{F}_q^{n/(2^a+1)} \wedge wt\,(\mathbf{b}_i) = N\omega_0/(2^a + 1)\},$$

and

$$\mathscr{I}_{2^a} \stackrel{\text{def}}{=} \{\mathbf{b} \in \mathbb{F}_q^n : \mathbf{b} = (\mathbf{0}^{(2^a-1)n/(2^a+1)}, \mathbf{b}_i) \text{ with } \mathbf{b}_i \in \mathbb{F}_q^{2n/(2^a+1)} \wedge wt\,(\mathbf{b}_i) = 2N\omega_0/(2^a+1)\}.$$

As before, we also define $L_i^f \stackrel{\text{def}}{=} \{\mathbf{H} \cdot \mathbf{b}_i\}_{\mathbf{b}_i \in \mathscr{I}_i}$. For $i \in [2^a-1]$, we have $|L_i^f| = \frac{s_{\omega_0}}{2^a+1}$ and $|L_{2^a}^f| = \frac{2s_{\omega_0}}{2^a+1}$.

We choose each L_i so that they are random subsets of L_i^f of size $q^{u'}$, except L_{2^a} which is of size $q^{2u'}$. For $j \in [a-1]$, we choose j such that $|J_j| = u'$ and $|J_a| = x$. At each floor, the new lists are of size $q^{u'}$ after a list merge except the rightmost list which is of size $q^{2u'}$. For the final top-merge, we have one list of size $q^{u'}$ and one list of size $q^{2u'}$. Since $|J_a| = q^x$, the top list L^{top} is of size $q^{3u'-x}$.

With this variant, we want to solve $\mathrm{CMSD}(N, l_0 N, \omega_0 N, Y, Z)$ for $Y = q^{2Nu'}$ and $Z = q^{N(3u'-x)}$. Let us now construct the function f required for this problem. Let $\mathbf{y}_{2^a}^1, \ldots, \mathbf{y}_{2^a}^Y$ the elements of L_{2^a}.

---

[8] Notice that $\lim_{n \to \infty} \frac{1}{N} \log_q |L_i^f| = \lim_{N \to \infty} \frac{1}{N} \log_q S_{N\omega_0/2^a}^{N/2^a} = \frac{1}{2^a} s_{\omega_0}$, so we can choose asymptotically any $u \leq \frac{s_{\omega_0}}{2^a}$.

For a fixed k, if there exists $\exists \mathbf{y}'_1, \ldots, \mathbf{y}'_{2^a-1}$ such that each $\mathbf{y}'_i \in L_i$ and $\sum_i \mathbf{y}'_i + \mathbf{y}^k_{2^a} = \mathbf{s}$ (*i.e.* $\in L^{top}$), we get for $i \in [2^a - 1]$ the associated $\mathbf{b}_i$ such that $\mathbf{Hb}_i = \mathbf{y}'_i$, and $\mathbf{Hb}_{2^a} = \mathbf{y}^k_{2^a}$. Let $\mathbf{e}_k = \sum_i \mathbf{b}_i$ in this case, and if there are several such vectors, we take the first one according to the lexicographical order. If this equality holds then $\mathbf{He}_k = \mathbf{s}$. We define f as follows

$$f(k) = \begin{cases} \mathbf{e}_k \text{ defined above, if such a vector exists,} \\ \mathbf{0}, \text{ otherwise.} \end{cases}$$

We now show how to construct f: we construct all the lists for each floor except the right-most list. Then, we sort these lists in lexicographical order according on the indices of the according J_j. Then from an input k, we start from $\mathbf{y}^k_{2^a}$ and we try if it can be summed with an element $\mathbf{y}'$ of the left neighboring list so that the sum appears in the list on top (again, if we have several, we take any one, say the first one in lexicographical order). This can bee done efficiently with dichotomic search in logarithmic time in the list size. We repeat this process until we fail (then we output $\mathbf{0}$) or we arrive at the top list, and we output the corresponding $\mathbf{e}_k$.

So constructing and sorting the lists to compute f take time $q^{N(u'+o(1))}$ (omitting the constant multiplicative term 2^a), but computing f afterwards take polynomial time. The number of k such that $f(k)$ outputs a good solution is actually the size of L^{top} *i.e.* $q^{N(3u'-x)}$ and since $f : [Y] \to \mathbb{F}^n_q$, this proves our proposition.

D   Computing surface areas

Let us first take a multiset of size n where elements are taken from $\{0, \cdots, q-1\}$, and each element is repeated c_i times, $i \in \{0, 1, ..., q-1\}$. The number of permutations of such a multiset is given by the multinomial coefficient, defined as: $\binom{n}{c_0,c_1,\ldots,c_{q-1}} \overset{\text{def}}{=} \frac{n!}{c_0!c_1!\ldots c_{q-1}!}$. This number corresponds to the number of vectors consisting of c_0 zeros, c_1 ones, ..., c_q values of q.

Let us further recall that $C \overset{\text{def}}{=} \{\mathbf{c} = (c_0, \cdots, c_{q-1}) : i \in \{0, 1, ..., q-1\}, c_i \in \mathbb{N}, \sum_{i=0}^{q-1} c_i = n, \sum_{i=0}^{q-1} c_i wt'(i) = w\}$. By the definition of the sphere surface area, we thus have: $S^n_w = \sum_{\mathbf{c} \in C} \binom{n}{\mathbf{c}}$.

Given the classical combinatorial result for the number of multinomial coefficients for a fixed n and q, the size of a set C, and thus the number of the elements in the sum, is upper bounded by $\binom{n+q-1}{q-1}$. The upper and lower bounds of S^n_w are thus given by: $\max_{\mathbf{c} \in C} \binom{n}{\mathbf{c}} \leq S^n_w \leq \binom{n+q-1}{q-1} \max_{\mathbf{c} \in C} \binom{n}{\mathbf{c}}$.

Following the same line of reasoning as in [Ast84], i.e. by taking log_q of each part of the equation above, multiplying them by $\frac{1}{n}$, where $n \to +\infty$, and using a Stirling's approximation we finally obtain Eq. (5) (Fig. 4).

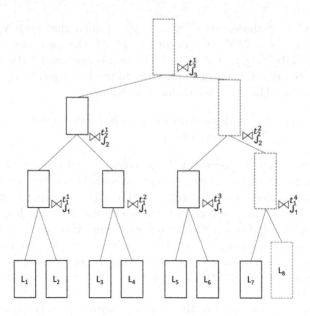

Fig. 4. Variant 2 of Wagner's algorithm for $a = 3$.

E   Convex optimization problem

It can be shown that Problem 3 belongs to the subclass of the convex optimization problems, namely the class of conic optimization problems [BV14]. As such it is susceptible to solving via MOSEK solver [ApS21], so we utilize MOSEK as a primary computational tool. Nevertheless, to be solved via MOSEK, Problem 3 needs to be transformed so that it aligns with the standard form of conic optimization problems, as presented in the following problem.

Problem 4. Let $\lambda \stackrel{\text{def}}{=} (\lambda_0, \lambda_1, ..., \lambda_{q-1}) \in \mathbb{R}_+^q$ and $\tau \stackrel{\text{def}}{=} (\tau_0, \tau_1, ..., \tau_{q-1}) \in \mathbb{R}_+^q$.

– Maximize: $\sum_{i=0}^{q-1} \tau_i$,
– Subject to: $\sum_{i=0}^{q-1} \lambda_i = 1$, $\sum_{i=0}^{q-1} \lambda_i \, wt'(i) = \omega$, $(1, \lambda, \tau) \in K_{exp}$.

where the constraint $(1, \lambda, \tau) \in K_{exp}$ means that $\tau_i \leq -\lambda_i \log_q \lambda_i$, for each $i \in \{0, 1, ..., q-1\}$. It can be easily verified that Problems 3 and 4 are equivalent, hence finding a solution of either of the two yields the asymptotic value of the sphere surface area.

References

[ABG+19] Aragon, N., Blazy, O., Gaborit, P., Hauteville, A., Zémor, G.: Durandal: a rank metric based signature scheme. In: Ishai, Y., Rijmen, V. (eds.) EUROCRYPT 2019. LNCS, vol. 11478, pp. 728–758. Springer, Cham (2019). https://doi.org/10.1007/978-3-030-17659-4_25

[ApS21] MOSEK ApS. MOSEK Fusion API for C++. Version Release 9.2.38 (2021)

[Ast84] Astola, J.: On the asymptotic behaviour of lee-codes. Discret. Appl. Math. **8**(1), 13–23 (1984)

[BB19] Bhattacharya, S., Banerjee, A.: A method to find the volume of a sphere in the lee metric, and its applications. In: 2019 IEEE International Symposium on Information Theory (ISIT), pp. 872–876 (2019)

[BBB+20] Bardet, M., et al.: An algebraic attack on rank metric code-based cryptosystems. In: Canteaut, A., Ishai, Y. (eds.) EUROCRYPT 2020. LNCS, vol. 12107, pp. 64–93. Springer, Cham (2020). https://doi.org/10.1007/978-3-030-45727-3_3

[BBC+20a] Baldi, M., et al.: A new path to code-based signatures via identification schemes with restricted errors. CoRR (2020)

[BBC+20b] Bardet, M., et al.: Improvements of algebraic attacks for solving the rank decoding and MinRank problems. In: Moriai, S., Wang, H. (eds.) ASIACRYPT 2020. LNCS, vol. 12491, pp. 507–536. Springer, Cham (2020). https://doi.org/10.1007/978-3-030-64837-4_17

[BCDL19] Bricout, R., Chailloux, A., Debris-Alazard, T., Lequesne, M.: Ternary syndrome decoding with large weight. In: Paterson, K.G., Stebila, D. (eds.) SAC 2019. LNCS, vol. 11959, pp. 437–466. Springer, Cham (2020). https://doi.org/10.1007/978-3-030-38471-5_18

[BH97] Brassard, G., Høyer, P.: An exact quantum polynomial-time algorithm for simon's problem. In: Fifth Israel Symposium on Theory of Computing and Systems, ISTCS 1997, Ramat-Gan, Israel, 17–19 June 1997, Proceedings, pp. 12–23. IEEE Computer Society (1997)

[BJMM12] Becker, A., Joux, A., May, A., Meurer, A.: Decoding random binary linear codes in $2^{n/20}$: How $1 + 1 = 0$ improves information set decoding. In: Pointcheval, D., Johansson, T. (eds.) EUROCRYPT 2012. LNCS, vol. 7237, pp. 520–536. Springer, Heidelberg (2012). https://doi.org/10.1007/978-3-642-29011-4_31

[BMvT78] Berlekamp, E., McEliece, R., van Tilborg, H.: On the inherent intractability of certain coding problems. IEEE Trans. Inform. Theory **24**(3), 384–386 (1978)

[BV14] Boyd, S., Boyd, S.P., Vandenberghe, L.: Convex Optimization. Cambridge University Press, Cambridge (2014)

[Coo00] Cooper, C.: On the distribution of rank of a random matrix over a finite field. Random Struct. Algorithms **17**, 197–212 (2000)

[DST19] Debris-Alazard, T., Sendrier, N., Tillich, J.-P.: Wave: a new family of trapdoor one-way preimage sampleable functions based on codes. In: Galbraith, S.D., Moriai, S. (eds.) ASIACRYPT 2019. LNCS, vol. 11921, pp. 21–51. Springer, Cham (2019). https://doi.org/10.1007/978-3-030-34578-5_2

[Dum91] Dumer, I.: On minimum distance decoding of linear codes. In: Proceedings 5th Joint Soviet-Swedish International Workshop Information Theory, pp. 50–52, Moscow (1991)

[Gro96] Grover, L.K.: A fast quantum mechanical algorithm for database search. In: Miller, G.L. (ed.) Proceedings of the Twenty-Eighth Annual ACM Symposium on the Theory of Computing, Philadelphia, Pennsylvania, USA, 22–24 May 1996, pP. 212–219. ACM (1996)

[GS91] Gardy, D., Solé, P.: Saddle point techniques in asymptotic coding theory. In: Cohen, G., Lobstein, A., Zémor, G., Litsyn, S. (eds.) Algebraic Coding 1991. LNCS, vol. 573, pp. 75–81. Springer, Heidelberg (1992). https://doi.org/10.1007/BFb0034343

[HW19] Horlemann-Trautmann, A.L., Weger, V.: Information set decoding in the lee metric with applications to cryptography. CoRR, abs/1903.07692 (2019)

[KT17] Kachigar, G., Tillich, J.-P.: Quantum information set decoding algorithms. In: Lange, T., Takagi, T. (eds.) PQCrypto 2017. LNCS, vol. 10346, pp. 69–89. Springer, Cham (2017). https://doi.org/10.1007/978-3-319-59879-6_5

[MMT11] May, A., Meurer, A., Thomae, E.: Decoding Random Linear Codes in $\tilde{\mathcal{O}}(2^{0.054n})$. In: Lee, D.H., Wang, X. (eds.) ASIACRYPT 2011. LNCS, vol. 7073, pp. 107–124. Springer, Heidelberg (2011). https://doi.org/10.1007/978-3-642-25385-0_6

[MO15] May, A., Ozerov, I.: On computing nearest neighbors with applications to decoding of binary linear codes. In: Oswald, E., Fischlin, M. (eds.) EUROCRYPT 2015. LNCS, vol. 9056, pp. 203–228. Springer, Heidelberg (2015). https://doi.org/10.1007/978-3-662-46800-5_9

[NC00] Nielsen, M.A., Chuang, I.: Quantum Computation and Quantum Information. Cambridge University Press, Cambridge (2000)

[Pra62] Prange, E.: The use of information sets in decoding cyclic codes. IRE Trans. Inf. Theory 8(5), 5–9 (1962)

[Ste88] Stern, J.: A method for finding codewords of small weight. In: Cohen, G., Wolfmann, J. (eds.) Coding Theory 1988. LNCS, vol. 388, pp. 106–113. Springer, Heidelberg (1989). https://doi.org/10.1007/BFb0019850

[Wag02] Wagner, D.: A generalized birthday problem. In: Yung, M. (ed.) CRYPTO 2002. LNCS, vol. 2442, pp. 288–304. Springer, Heidelberg (2002). https://doi.org/10.1007/3-540-45708-9_19

[WKH+21] Weger, V., Battaglioni, M., Santini, P., Horlemann-Trautmann, A.L., Persichetti, E.: On the hardness of the lee syndrome decoding problem. arXiv quant-ph 2002.12785 (2021)

Multivariate Cryptography

Multivariate Cryptography

Improving Thomae-Wolf Algorithm for Solving Underdetermined Multivariate Quadratic Polynomial Problem

Hiroki Furue[1]([⊠]), Shuhei Nakamura[2], and Tsuyoshi Takagi[1]

[1] Department of Mathematical Informatics, The University of Tokyo, Tokyo, Japan
{furue-hiroki261,takagi}@g.ecc.u-tokyo.ac.jp
[2] Department of Basic Sciences, Nihon University, Tokyo, Japan
nakamura.shuhei@nihon-u.ac.jp

Abstract. The multivariate quadratic polynomial problem ($\mathcal{MQ}$ problem) is a fundamental computational problem in post-quantum cryptography. We denote by $MQ(q, n, m)$ the $\mathcal{MQ}$ problem of m quadratic equations in n variables over finite field $\mathbb{F}_q$. At PKC 2012, an efficient algorithm for solving the underdetermined $MQ(2^r, n, m)$ for $n > m$ was proposed by Thomae and Wolf (TW algorithm). Specifically, by eliminating the cross-product terms in α quadratic polynomials through linearization, $MQ(2^r, n, m)$ can be reduced to $MQ(2^r, m - k - \alpha, m - \alpha)$, where k is the number of variables fixed in the hybrid approach after the TW algorithm is applied. Then, the algorithm yields the smallest $\mathcal{MQ}$ problem for the largest linearization factor $\alpha = \lfloor \frac{n}{m} \rfloor - 1$ among possible α, where $\lfloor \cdot \rfloor$ is the floor function.

In this study, we propose an algorithm that improves the linearization factor α by combining the hybrid approach and the TW algorithm. In particular, the proposed algorithm can reduce $MQ(2^r, n, m)$ to $MQ(2^r, m - k - \alpha_k, m - \alpha_k)$ with linearization factor $\alpha_k = \lfloor \frac{n-k}{m-k} \rfloor - 1$. Because $\alpha_k \geq \alpha$, the proposed algorithm is more efficient than the TW algorithm for some parameter sets. Furthermore, for the binary field case $r = 1$, we provide a non-trivial improved algorithm and obtain a larger linearization factor $\beta_k = \lfloor \frac{n-1}{m-k-1} \rfloor - 1$ for suitable k.

Keywords: Post-quantum cryptography $\cdot$ Multivariate public key cryptography $\cdot$ $\mathcal{MQ}$ problem, hybrid approach, underdetermined system.

1 Introduction

Multivariate public key cryptography, which is based on the difficulty of solving a system of multivariate quadratic polynomial equations over a finite field (the multivariate quadratic polynomial ($\mathcal{MQ}$) problem), has been regarded as a strong candidate for post-quantum cryptography (PQC). The $\mathcal{MQ}$ problem

© Springer Nature Switzerland AG 2021
J. H. Cheon and J.-P. Tillich (Eds.): PQCrypto 2021, LNCS 12841, pp. 65–78, 2021.
https://doi.org/10.1007/978-3-030-81293-5_4

is NP-complete [14] and is thus likely to be secure in the post-quantum era. In fact, multivariate signature schemes such as Rainbow [11] and GeMSS [7] have been selected in the third round of the NIST PQC standardization project [17]. The security of these schemes is based on the difficulty of solving the underdetermined $\mathcal{MQ}$ problem, where the number of variables is larger than the number of equations.

To solve the underdetermined $\mathcal{MQ}$ problem of m equations in n variables $(n > m)$, a natural approach is to fix $n - m$ variables and apply an $\mathcal{MQ}$ solver, such as F4 [12], F5 [13], or XL [10], on the resulting system with m equations and variables. Furthermore, the hybrid approach [5,19] can often be used to solve the underdetermined $\mathcal{MQ}$ problem efficiently. After $n - m$ variables are fixed, k additional variables are guessed, and an $\mathcal{MQ}$ solver is applied to the resulting system of m equations in $m - k$ variables. We stress that the above two approaches do not exploit the additional $n - m$ variables to solve the problem.

There are several algorithms that use the additional $n - m$ variables of the underdetermined $\mathcal{MQ}$ problem. In 1999, Kipnis et al. [16] showed that if $n \geq m(m + 1)$ over $\mathbb{F}_2$, then this problem can be solved in polynomial time. Specifically, for the $\mathcal{MQ}$ problem $\mathcal{P}(\mathbf{x}) = \mathbf{0}$, a linear map $\mathcal{S}$ is obtained such that all polynomials of $\mathcal{P} \circ \mathcal{S}$ have the following form:

$$\sum_{i=1}^{m} a_i^{(\ell)} x_i^2 + \sum_{i=1}^{m} x_i L_i^{(\ell)}(x_{m+1}, \ldots, x_n) + Q^{(\ell)}(x_{m+1}, \ldots, x_n), \qquad (1)$$

where $a_i^{(\ell)} \in \mathbb{F}_q$, and $L_i^{(\ell)}$ and $Q^{(\ell)}$ denote linear and quadratic functions of $x_{m+1}, \ldots, x_n$, respectively. Using this form, the system can be regarded as linear. Furthermore, Courtois et al. [9] and Cheng et al. [8] proposed polynomial-time algorithms for $n \geq 2^{m/7}(m + 1)$ and $n \geq m(m + 1)/2$, respectively. However, the settings discussed in the above studies are excessively underdetermined and thus not practical from the perspective of cryptanalysis.

In 2012, Thomae and Wolf [18] proposed an algorithm applicable to general underdetermined systems over $\mathbb{F}_{2^r}$ by extending the result obtained by Kipnis et al. [16]. Given the $\mathcal{MQ}$ problem $\mathcal{P}(\mathbf{x}) = \mathbf{0}$ of m equations in n variables, a linear map $\mathcal{S}$ is first generated such that only the first α polynomials of $\mathcal{P} \circ \mathcal{S}$ have the form in equation (1) for some non-negative integer α. Subsequently, the first α polynomials are linearized by some manipulations such as determining the values of $x_{m+1}, \ldots, x_n$, and α variables are eliminated from the remaining $m - \alpha$ equations. Consequently, a smaller $\mathcal{MQ}$ problem of $m - \alpha$ variables and equations is obtained. Then, the largest possible α yields the smallest $\mathcal{MQ}$ problem, and α is set to $\lfloor \frac{n}{m} \rfloor - 1$ in the algorithm. In the present study, such an α is called a *linearization factor*, and the objective is to increase it as much as possible so that a smaller $\mathcal{MQ}$ problem may be obtained.

Contribution. In this study, we propose a new algorithm that reduces the size of the underdetermined $\mathcal{MQ}$ problem in $\mathbb{F}_{2^r}$ by combining the Thomae–Wolf (TW) algorithm and the hybrid approach. The proposed algorithm fixes k

variables, and a system of $m - \alpha_k$ equations in $m - k - \alpha_k$ variables is obtained, where α_k is the linearization factor of the proposed algorithm.

A linear map $\mathcal{S}$ is first generated such that the first α_k polynomials of $\mathcal{P} \circ \mathcal{S}$ take the following form instead of that in Eq. (1), which is used in the TW algorithm:

$$\sum_{i=1}^{m-k} a_i^{(\ell)} x_i^2 + \sum_{i=1}^{m-k} x_i L_i^{(\ell)}(x_{m-k+1}, \dots, x_n) + Q^{(\ell)}(x_{m-k+1}, \dots, x_n), \quad (2)$$

where $a_i^{(\ell)}$, $L_i^{(\ell)}$, and $Q^{(\ell)}$ are as in Eq. (1). It should be noted that the restriction of the linearization factor α_k for obtaining Eq. (2) is weaker than that for Eq. (1). Subsequently, we represent $n - m$ variables $x_{m+1}, \dots, x_n$ as linear functions of k variables $x_{m-k+1}, \dots, x_m$, which are guessed as in the hybrid approach. Then, the first α_k polynomials are linearized as in the TW algorithm, and a system of $m - \alpha_k$ equations in $m - k - \alpha_k$ variables is obtained. As a result, by the weaker restriction of α_k, the proposed algorithm can take $\alpha_k = \lfloor \frac{n-k}{m-k} \rfloor - 1$ as the largest value, which is larger than or equal to that of the TW algorithm. Therefore, we can obtain a smaller $\mathcal{MQ}$ problem for some parameters. We stress that the proposed algorithm is exactly the same as the TW algorithm if $k = 0$.

Furthermore, we improve the proposed algorithm in the binary field case by using $x_i^2 = x_i$ for any variable x_i. In this algorithm, the linearization factor β_k can be set to $\lfloor \frac{n-1}{m-k-1} \rfloor - 1$, which is larger than or equal to that for $\mathbb{F}_{2^r}$. This algorithm with $k = 0$ achieves a non-trivial improvement over the TW algorithm on the $\mathcal{MQ}$ problem over the binary field.

2 Multivariate Quadratic Polynomial Problem

Herein, we introduce the $\mathcal{MQ}$ problem and a direct approach to its solution.

Let $\mathbb{F}_q$ be the finite field with q elements, and let n and m be two positive integers. For a system of quadratic polynomials $\mathcal{P} = (p_1(x_1, \dots, x_n), \dots, p_m(x_1, \dots, x_n))$ in n variables over $\mathbb{F}_q$, the problem of finding a solution $\mathbf{x} \in \mathbb{F}_q^n$ to $\mathcal{P}(\mathbf{x}) = \mathbf{0}$ is called the $\mathcal{MQ}$ problem and is denoted by $MQ(q, n, m)$. If $n > m$, then the system is called *underdetermined*, whereas if $n < m$, it is called *overdetermined*. Garey and Johnson [14] proved that this problem is NP-complete; thus, it is considered to have the potential to resist quantum computer attacks.

2.1 Hybrid Approach

Given a quadratic polynomial system $\mathcal{P} = (p_1, \dots, p_m)$ in n variables over $\mathbb{F}_q$, we consider the system $\mathcal{P}(\mathbf{x}) = \mathbf{0}$. Herein, we assume that the number of variables n is smaller than or equal to the number of equations m, as, if $n > m$, $n - m$ variables can be randomly specified so that, with high probability, the existence of a solution is not affected.

A quadratic system can be solved using the XL [10] algorithm or Gröbner basis [6] techniques, such as the F4 [12] and F5 [13] algorithms. Furthermore, we introduce the hybrid approach [5,19], which combines an exhaustive search with an $\mathcal{MQ}$ solver, such as XL, F4, or F5. In this approach, for $0 \leq k \leq n-1$, k variables are randomly guessed before an $\mathcal{MQ}$ solver is applied to the system in the remaining $n-k$ variables; this is repeated until a solution is obtained. Using the complexity of Wiedemann XL [20], the complexity of the hybrid approach is estimated as

$$O\left(q^k \cdot 3 \cdot \binom{n-k}{2} \cdot \binom{n-k+d_{reg}}{d_{reg}}^2\right), \tag{3}$$

where we guess k variables. In the above equation, d_{reg} is the degree of regularity of the system [1]. The degree of regularity d_{reg} for a certain class of polynomial systems called *semi-regular systems* [1,2,4] is estimated by the degree of the first non-positive term of the series $(1-z^2)^m / (1-z)^n$ [4]. Empirically, randomly selected polynomial systems are semi-regular with very high probability; therefore, this formula can be used to estimate the degree of regularity.

Furthermore, Eq. (3) is modified in the binary field as follows when k variables are guessed:

$$O\left(2^k \cdot 3 \cdot \binom{n-k}{2} \cdot \left(\sum_{i=0}^{d_{reg}} \binom{n-k}{i}\right)^2\right).$$

Subsequently, the degree of regularity d_{reg} for semi-regular systems over $\mathbb{F}_2$ is estimated by the degree of the first non-positive term of $(1+z)^n / (1+z^2)^m$ [4].

3   Thomae–Wolf Algorithm

Herein, we introduce an algorithm that reduces the complexity of solving the underdetermined $\mathcal{MQ}$ problem over a finite field of even characteristic proposed by Thomae and Wolf [18]. After describing the TW algorithm, we discuss the complexity reduction.

3.1   Description

Given an underdetermined system $\mathcal{P}$ of m quadratic equations in n variables ($n > m$) over the finite field $\mathbb{F}_{2^r}$, we consider solving the equation $\mathcal{P}(\mathbf{x}) = \mathbf{0}$, where $\mathbf{x} = (x_1, \ldots, x_n)$.

The TW algorithm reduces an underdetermined $MQ(2^r, n, m)$ to an $MQ(2^r, m - \alpha, m - \alpha)$, where α is called *linearization factor*. This algorithm primarily consists of four steps as follows: First, a linear map S is generated to remove some terms of $x_i x_j$ ($1 \leq i < j \leq m$) from the first α equations; second, the values of the additional variables $x_{m+1}, \ldots, x_n$ are determined; third, α variables are eliminated from the resulting system by linearizing the first α equations and then solving the resulting system. The first and second steps imply that the linearization factor α is bounded from above. This algorithm uses the bound $\lfloor \frac{n}{m} \rfloor - 1$ as the optimal value of α (see Sect. 3.2 for more details).

To describe the TW algorithm, we introduce some notations. Let S be a linear map, and s_{ij} $(1 \leq i, j \leq n)$ be a coefficient of S such that the i-th element of $S(\mathbf{x})$ is equal to $\sum_{j=1}^{m} s_{ij} x_j$. For a quadratic map $P = (p_1(\mathbf{x}), \ldots, p_m(\mathbf{x}))$, let $a_{ij}^{(\ell)}, b_i^{(\ell)}, c^{(\ell)} \in \mathbb{F}_q$ $(1 \leq i \leq j \leq n, 1 \leq \ell \leq m)$ be coefficients such that

$$p_\ell(\mathbf{x}) = \sum_{i \leq j} a_{ij}^{(\ell)} x_i x_j + \sum_i b_i^{(\ell)} x_i + c^{(\ell)}.$$

Furthermore, let $\mathcal{F}$ be a quadratic map constructed by composing P and S, that is, $\mathcal{F} = P \circ S$. As in the case of P, for $\mathcal{F} = (f_1(\mathbf{x}), \ldots, f_m(\mathbf{x}))$, let $\bar{a}_{ij}^{(\ell)}, \bar{b}_i^{(\ell)}, \bar{c}^{(\ell)} \in \mathbb{F}_q$ $(1 \leq i \leq j \leq n, 1 \leq \ell \leq m)$ be coefficients such that

$$f_\ell(\mathbf{x}) = \sum_{i \leq j} \bar{a}_{ij}^{(\ell)} x_i x_j + \sum_i \bar{b}_i^{(\ell)} x_i + \bar{c}^{(\ell)}.$$

Then, using $\mathcal{F} = P \circ S$, we have

$$\bar{a}_{ij}^{(\ell)} = \begin{cases} \sum_{t \leq u} a_{tu}^{(\ell)} (s_{ti} s_{uj} + s_{tj} s_{ui}) & (i \neq j) \\ \sum_{t \leq u} a_{tu}^{(\ell)} s_{ti} s_{ui} & (i = j). \end{cases} \tag{4}$$

This equation for $i \neq j$ indicates that $\bar{a}_{ij}^{(\ell)}$ is in a bilinear form with two sets of variables S_i and S_j, where $S_i = (s_{1i}, \ldots, s_{ni})$, that is, the i-th column of S.

In the first step of the TW algorithm, for $\alpha \in \{0, \ldots, m\}$, a linear map S satisfying the following condition is required:

$$\bar{a}_{ij}^{(\ell)} = 0 \quad (1 \leq i < j \leq m, 1 \leq \ell \leq \alpha). \tag{5}$$

Then, the quadratic polynomials f_ℓ $(1 \leq \ell \leq \alpha)$ of $\mathcal{F} = P \circ S$ are of the following form:

$$f_\ell = \sum_{i=1}^{m} \bar{a}_{ii}^{(\ell)} x_i^2 + \sum_{i=1}^{m} x_i L_i^{(\ell)}(x_{m+1}, \ldots, x_n) + Q^{(\ell)}(x_{m+1}, \ldots, x_n),$$

where $L_i^{(\ell)}$ and $Q^{(\ell)}$ denote linear and quadratic functions of $x_{m+1}, \ldots, x_n$, respectively. Equation (5) is bilinear in two sets of variables: S_i and S_j (see Eq. (4)). Hence, when $S_1, \ldots, S_{j-1}$ are fixed, the j-th column S_j is obtained by solving linear system $\bar{a}_{ij}^{(\ell)} = 0$ $(1 \leq i < j, 1 \leq \ell \leq \alpha)$. Therefore, by fixing the first column S_1, we can determine $S_2, \ldots, S_m$ satisfying the condition (5) by solving the linear system for each column. Moreover, regarding the invertibility of S, it is shown in [18] that the linear map S is restricted to the following form:

$$S = \begin{pmatrix} I_{m \times m} & 0_{m \times (n-m)} \\ *_{(n-m) \times m} & I_{(n-m) \times (n-m)} \end{pmatrix}. \tag{6}$$

In the second step, the system of linear equations $L_i^{(\ell)} = 0$ $(1 \leq i \leq m, 1 \leq \ell \leq \alpha)$ is solved to determine the values of $x_{m+1}, \ldots, x_n$. By substituting the obtained values for $x_{m+1}, \ldots, x_n$ in $\mathcal{F}(\mathbf{x}) = \mathbf{0}$, the first α equations are converted as follows:

$$\sum_{i=1}^{m} \bar{a}_{ii}^{(\ell)} x_i^2 + c'^{(\ell)} = 0 \quad (1 \leq \ell \leq \alpha),$$

where $c'^{(\ell)} \in \mathbb{F}_q$.

In the third step, the first α equations of $\mathcal{F}(\mathbf{x}) = \mathbf{0}$ are raised to the 2^{r-1}-th power and take the following form:

$$\sum_{i=1}^{m} (\bar{a}_{ii}^{(\ell)})^{2^{r-1}} x_i + c''^{(\ell)} = 0 \quad (1 \leq \ell \leq \alpha). \tag{7}$$

Using this equation to eliminate α variables in the remaining $m - \alpha$ equations of $\mathcal{F}(\mathbf{x}) = \mathbf{0}$, we obtain the $\mathcal{MQ}$ problem of $m - \alpha$ variables and equations.

Finally, in the fourth step, $MQ(2^r, m - \alpha, m - \alpha)$ is solved using an $\mathcal{MQ}$ solver or the hybrid approach.

3.2   Choice of Linearization Factor

In the TW algorithm, the size of the $\mathcal{MQ}$ problem is reduced by transforming α equations of the system into the form of equation (7). Herein, we discuss the optimal choice of the linearization factor α and the complexity of the TW algorithm.

The linearization factor α is set so that the TW algorithm may solve with high probability every system of linear equations. In the first step of the TW algorithm, the linear system $\bar{a}_{ji}^{(\ell)} = 0$ $(1 \leq j \leq i - 1, 1 \leq \ell \leq \alpha)$ is solved to determine the i-th column of $\mathcal{S}$ $(2 \leq i \leq m)$. Then, these linear systems consist of $\alpha(i - 1)$ equations in $n - m$ variables from Eq. (6). In the second step, the linear system $L_i^{(\ell)} = 0$ $(1 \leq i \leq m, 1 \leq \ell \leq \alpha)$, comprising αm equations in $n - m$ variables, is solved to determine the values of $x_{m+1}, \ldots, x_n$. To obtain the solutions of these linear systems, the number of variables must be larger than or equal to the number of equations in each system. Therefore, the linearization factor α is restricted as follows:

$$n - m \geq \alpha m \quad \therefore \alpha \leq \frac{n}{m} - 1.$$

Then, to obtain the smallest $\mathcal{MQ}$ problem, the optimal value of α is $\lfloor \frac{n}{m} \rfloor - 1$.

In conclusion, given the $\mathcal{MQ}$ problem of m equations in n variables, with $n > m$, over finite fields of even characteristic, the complexity of solving the system can be reduced to

$$O\left(q^k \cdot 3 \cdot \binom{m - k - (\lfloor \frac{n}{m} \rfloor - 1)}{2} \cdot \binom{m - k - (\lfloor \frac{n}{m} \rfloor - 1) + d_{reg}}{d_{reg}}^2 \right), \tag{8}$$

when k variables are guessed, by Eq. (3).

If the linearization factor α is larger, then the complexity (8) becomes smaller. In the next section, we propose a new algorithm that enables us to increase α.

4   Proposed Algorithm

Herein, we propose a new algorithm that solves the underdetermined $\mathcal{MQ}$ problem over finite fields of even characteristic by combining the idea of the TW algorithm [18] and the hybrid approach [5,19].

4.1   Description

Let $\mathcal{P}$ be an underdetermined system of m quadratic polynomials in n variables $(n > m)$ over the finite field $\mathbb{F}_{2^r}$, and we consider solving the equation $\mathcal{P}(\mathbf{x}) = \mathbf{0}$. Furthermore, let k be the number of randomly fixed variables, as in the hybrid approach; moreover, let α_k be the linearization factor, as in the TW algorithm in Sect. 3.

The proposed algorithm, by combining the guessing of k variables with the TW algorithm, provides a larger linearization factor. It comprises five steps: eliminating some cross-product terms, determining $n - m$ additional variables, guessing k variables, eliminating α_k variables, and solving the resulting system. We describe each step in more detail in the following.

First, a linear map $\mathcal{S}$ of n variables is obtained such that some coefficients of the quadratic terms of $\mathcal{F} = \mathcal{P} \circ \mathcal{S}$ are zero, as in the TW algorithm. However, we change the number of coefficients set to zero in α_k polynomials of $\mathcal{F}$. In the proposed algorithm, $\mathcal{F}$ satisfies the following condition:

$$\bar{a}_{ij}^{(\ell)} = 0 \quad (1 \leq i < j \leq m - k, 1 \leq \ell \leq \alpha_k).$$

Here, we use the same notation for $\mathcal{F}$ as in Sect. 3.1. Then, the quadratic polynomials f_k $(1 \leq k \leq \alpha_k)$ of $\mathcal{F} = \mathcal{P} \circ \mathcal{S}$ have the following form:

$$f_\ell = \sum_{i=1}^{m-k} \bar{a}_{ii}^{(\ell)} x_i^2 + \sum_{i=1}^{m-k} x_i L_i^{(\ell)}(x_{m-k+1}, \ldots, x_n) + Q^{(\ell)}(x_{m-k+1}, \ldots, x_n), \quad (9)$$

where $L_i^{(\ell)}$ and $Q^{(\ell)}$ denote linear and quadratic functions of $x_{m-k+1}, \ldots, x_n$, respectively. In this step, such a $\mathcal{S}$ is determined as in the TW algorithm. By fixing the first column $\mathcal{S}_1$, we can determine $\mathcal{S}_2, \ldots, \mathcal{S}_{m-k}$ satisfying condition (9) by solving the linear system for each column. Furthermore, $\mathcal{S}$ is restricted to the form

$$\mathcal{S} = \begin{pmatrix} I_{(m-k) \times (m-k)} & 0_{(m-k) \times (n-(m-k))} \\ *_{(n-(m-k)) \times (m-k)} & I_{(n-(m-k)) \times (n-(m-k))} \end{pmatrix},$$

by the same discussion as in Sect. 3.1.

In the second step, the system of linear equations $L_i^{(\ell)} = 0$ $(1 \leq i \leq m-k, 1 \leq \ell \leq \alpha_k)$ is solved only for variables $x_{m+1}, \ldots, x_n$. We then obtain

$$x_i = L_i'(x_{m-k+1}, \ldots, x_m) \quad (m + 1 \leq i \leq n), \quad (10)$$

where L_i' denote linear functions of $x_{m-k+1}, \ldots, x_m$.

In the third step, the values of k variables $x_{m-k+1}, \ldots, x_m$ are guessed, as in the hybrid approach. Then, the values of $n - m$ variables $x_{m+1}, \ldots, x_n$ are also determined using Eq. (10). Thus, the first α_k equations of $\mathcal{F}(\mathbf{x}) = \mathbf{0}$ have the following form:

$$\sum_{i=1}^{m-k} \bar{a}_{ii}^{(\ell)} x_i^2 + c'^{(\ell)} = 0 \quad (1 \le \ell \le \alpha_k). \tag{11}$$

In the fourth step, using the same method as in the TW algorithm, we eliminate α_k variables in the remaining $m - \alpha_k$ equations of $\mathcal{F}(\mathbf{x}) = \mathbf{0}$. Finally, in the fifth step, $MQ(q, m - k - \alpha_k, m - \alpha_k)$ is solved using an $\mathcal{MQ}$ solver or the hybrid approach. It should be noted that if a solution cannot be obtained, the algorithm returns to the third step.

4.2 Choice of Linearization Factor

Herein, we discuss the choice of the linearization factor α_k and the complexity of the proposed algorithm in a manner similar to that in Sect. 3.2 for the TW algorithm.

In the first step of the proposed algorithm, a system of $\alpha_k(i - 1)$ linear equations in $n - (m - k)$ variables is solved to determine the i-th column of S ($2 \le i \le m - k$). Furthermore, in the second step, to represent $n - m$ variables $x_{m+1}, \ldots, x_n$ by linear functions of k variables $x_{m-k+1}, \ldots, x_m$, a system of $\alpha_k(m - k)$ linear equations in $n - m$ variables is solved. As a result, α_k must satisfy the following condition:

$$\begin{cases} n - (m - k) \ge \alpha_k(i - 1) & (2 \le i \le m - k), \\ n - m \ge \alpha_k(m - k) \end{cases}$$

$$\therefore \alpha_k \le \frac{n - m}{m - k} = \frac{n - k}{m - k} - 1.$$

Then, to obtain the smallest $\mathcal{MQ}$ problem, the optimal value of α_k is $\lfloor \frac{n-k}{m-k} \rfloor - 1$. If $k = 0$, then the proposed and the TW algorithm have the same linearization factor. Accordingly, the proposed algorithm can be considered a natural extension of the TW algorithm.

We have that α_k is larger than or equal to the linearization factor α of the TW algorithm, and therefore, as mentioned in the last paragraph of Sect. 3.2, we succeeded in improving the TW algorithm.

In terms of complexity, the first four steps are explicitly executed in polynomial time, and the fifth step, in which $MQ(q, m - k - \alpha_k, m - \alpha_k)$ is solved, is dominant. As a result, by using Wiedemann XL in the fifth step, the complexity of solving the underdetermined $\mathcal{MQ}$ problem of m equations in n variables ($n > m$) using the proposed algorithm with k fixed variables is estimated by

$$O\left(q^k \cdot 3 \cdot \binom{m - k - (\lfloor \frac{n-k}{m-k} \rfloor - 1)}{2} \cdot \binom{m - k - (\lfloor \frac{n-k}{m-k} \rfloor - 1) + d_{reg}}{d_{reg}}^2 \right). \tag{12}$$

As discussed earlier, if $k = 0$, then Eq. (12) is equivalent to Eq. (8).

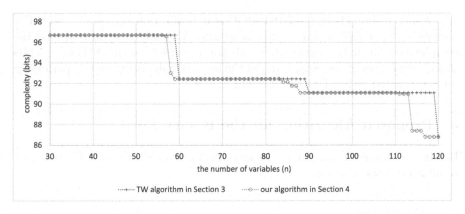

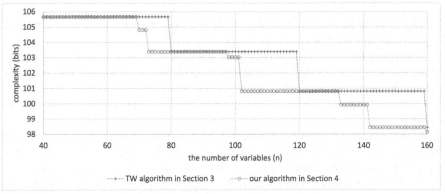

Fig. 1. Complexity comparison between the proposed algorithm in Sect. 4 and the TW algorithm [18] in Sect. 3 on a system of 30 equations ($m = 30$) over $\mathbb{F}_{2^8}$ (above), and a system of 40 equations ($m = 40$) over $\mathbb{F}_{2^4}$ (below)

4.3 Comparison

Figure 1 shows a comparison of the bit complexity of the proposed algorithm in Sect. 4 and the TW algorithm in Sect. 3 on $MQ(2^8, n, 30)$ ($30 \leq n \leq 120$) and $MQ(2^4, n, 40)$ ($40 \leq n \leq 160$). In these comparisons, we selected 30 and 40 as the number of equations because solving $MQ(2^8, 30, 30)$ and $MQ(2^4, 40, 40)$ requires approximately 2^{100} operations.

In particular, it is seen that when n is slightly smaller than ℓm ($\ell \in \mathbb{N}$), the proposed algorithm performs better than the TW algorithm. Furthermore, the proposed algorithm enables us to use the fewest additional variables for solving underdetermined systems among existing algorithms. By comparing the results in Fig. 1, it is seen that the proposed algorithm is more effective in $\mathbb{F}_{2^4}$ than in $\mathbb{F}_{2^8}$. This is because, in a small finite field, the number k of fixed variables can be larger from the complexity perspective.

For the third-round parameter set $(q, v_1, o_1, o_2) = (256, 96, 36, 64)$ of Rainbow at security level V (the number of variables and equations are 196 and

100, respectively) [11] in the NIST PQC standardization project [17], the TW algorithm is not valid because the linearization factor α is equal to 0, and the complexity of the hybrid approach on this parameter set is estimated as 278.5 bits by Eq. (8). However, the complexity of the proposed algorithm on this parameter set is estimated as 274.7 bits by Eq. (12).

5   Proposed Algorithm for the Binary Field

Herein, we propose a variant of the algorithm proposed in Sect. 4 for underdetermined quadratic systems over $\mathbb{F}_2$.

5.1   Description

Our objective is to improve the algorithm proposed in Sect. 4 for the finite field $\mathbb{F}_2$. Here, we use the linearization factor β_k.

The algorithm for $\mathbb{F}_2$ comprises four steps: eliminating some cross-product terms, guessing k variables, eliminating β_k variables, and solving the resulting system. Namely, the algorithm for $\mathbb{F}_2$ is constructed by omitting the second step of the algorithm in Sect. 4. In the following, we explain the reason for this omission.

In the second step of the algorithm in Sect. 4, the values of $x_{m+1}, \ldots, x_n$ are obtained as linear functions of $x_{m-k+1}, \ldots, x_m$ so that polynomials in the form of Eq. (11) can be obtained after k variables are fixed. However, in $\mathbb{F}_2$, we have $x_i^2 = x_i$ for any variable. Therefore, in the algorithm for $\mathbb{F}_2$, after k variables are guessed, the first β_k equations of $\mathcal{F}(\mathbf{x}) = \mathbf{0}$ are of the form

$$\sum_{i=1}^{m-k} \bar{a}_{ii}^{(\ell)} x_i + c'^{(\ell)} = 0 \quad (1 \leq \ell \leq \beta_k),$$

without selecting suitable values for $x_{m+1}, \ldots, x_n$. As a result, without executing the second step of the algorithm in Sect. 4, we can obtain β_k linear equations after guessing k variables in the binary field.

5.2   Choice of Linearization Factor

Herein, we discuss the choice of the linearization factor β_k and the complexity of the algorithm for the binary field.

In the first step of the algorithm for $\mathbb{F}_2$, a system of $\beta_k(i-1)$ linear equations in $n-(m-k)$ variables ($2 \leq i \leq m-k$) is solved, as in the case of the algorithm in Sect. 4. The linearization factor β_k is restricted only by these conditions. As a result, as in Sect. 4.2, β_k is restricted as follows:

$$n - (m - k) \geq \beta_k(i - 1) \quad (2 \leq i \leq m - k),$$

$$\therefore \beta_k \leq \frac{n - (m - k)}{(m - k) - 1} = \frac{n - 1}{m - k - 1} - 1.$$

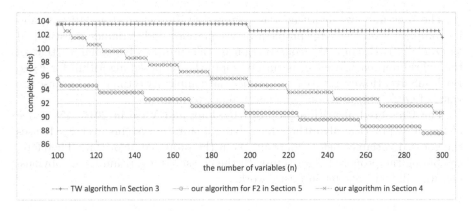

Fig. 2. Complexity comparison between the proposed algorithm for $\mathbb{F}_2$ in Sect. 5 and the TW algorithm [18] in Sect. 3 on a system of 100 equations ($m = 100$) over $\mathbb{F}_2$

Then, to obtain the smallest $\mathcal{MQ}$ problem, the optimal value of β_k is $\lfloor \frac{n-1}{m-k-1} \rfloor -$ 1. We have that β_k is larger than or equal to the linearization factor of the algorithm in Sect. 4.

As in the algorithm proposed in Sect. 4, the algorithm proposed for $\mathbb{F}_2$ is executed in polynomial time, except for solving quadratic systems directly. Therefore, the complexity of solving $MQ(2, n, m)$ ($n > m$) using the proposed algorithm for $\mathbb{F}_2$ with k fixed variables is estimated by

$$ O\left(2^k \cdot 3 \cdot \binom{m - k - (\lfloor \frac{n-1}{m-k-1} \rfloor - 1)}{2} \cdot \left(\sum_{i=0}^{d_{reg}} \binom{m - k - (\lfloor \frac{n-1}{m-k-1} \rfloor - 1)}{i} \right)^2 \right). \quad (13) $$

Unlike Eq. (12), if $k = 0$, Eq. (13) is different from the complexity of the TW algorithm. This is because, in the proposed algorithm for $\mathbb{F}_2$, it is not necessary to determine the values of $n - m$ variables $x_{m+1}, \ldots, x_n$.

5.3 Comparison

Figure 2 shows a comparison of the bit complexity of the proposed algorithm for $\mathbb{F}_2$ in Sect. 5 and the TW algorithm [18] in Sect. 3 on $MQ(2, n, 100)$ ($100 \le n \le 300$); the complexity corresponding to $\alpha_k = \lfloor \frac{n-k}{m-k} \rfloor - 1$ in the proposed algorithm for $\mathbb{F}_{2^r}$ in Sect. 4 is used for reference. Here, we select 100 as the number of equations because solving $MQ(2, 100, 100)$ requires approximately 2^{100} operations. A comparison with Fig. 1 indicates that the proposed algorithm for $\mathbb{F}_2$ further reduces complexity compared with the TW algorithm. It should be noted that the proposed algorithm in $\mathbb{F}_2$ is effective for not only underdetermined but also determined systems ($n = m$).

Remark 1. Two algorithms are primarily used for the $\mathcal{MQ}$ problem over the binary field: *BooleanSolve* [3] and *Crossbred* [15]. In this remark, we discuss whether the proposed algorithm can be combined with these algorithms for $\mathbb{F}_2$.

The BooleanSolve algorithm was proposed by Bardet et al. in 2012 [3], and its complexity on the $\mathcal{MQ}$ problem of n equations and variables is estimated as $O(2^{0.792n})$. Because the construction of this protocol is similar to that of the hybrid approach, we can naturally apply the proposed algorithm for $\mathbb{F}_2$ to BooleanSolve. However, we cannot reduce the complexity estimation because the value of $O(2^{0.792n})$ is estimated when n tends to infinity.

The Crossbred algorithm proposed by Joux and Vitse in 2017 [15] is one of the most practical algorithms for solving quadratic systems over $\mathbb{F}_2$. It uses the guessed variables before guessing, as in the proposed algorithm. Therefore, combining the proposed algorithm with the crossbred algorithm is not obvious, and we will focus on this in future work.

6   Conclusion

It is important in post-quantum cryptography to investigate the complexity of solving the $\mathcal{MQ}$ problem. In this study, we revisited the TW algorithm proposed by Thomae and Wolf at PKC 2012, which reduces the underdetermined $MQ(2^r, n, m)$ with $n > m$ to $MQ(2^r, m-k-\alpha, m-\alpha)$, where k is the number of variables fixed in the hybrid approach, and the linearization factor α is optimal for $\lfloor \frac{n}{m} \rfloor - 1$.

We proposed a new algorithm that reduces the size of the underdetermined $\mathcal{MQ}$ problem by combining the idea of the TW algorithm and the hybrid approach. The proposed algorithm reduces $MQ(2^r, n, m)$ to $MQ(2^r, m-k-\alpha_k, m-\alpha_k)$, with linearization factor $\alpha_k = \lfloor \frac{n-k}{m-k} \rfloor - 1$ when k variables are randomly guessed. Because $\alpha_k \geq \alpha$, the proposed algorithm is more efficient than the TW algorithm for some parameter sets. Furthermore, the proposed algorithm exhibited improved performance for the binary field case, obtaining a larger linearization factor $\beta_k = \lfloor \frac{n-1}{m-k-1} \rfloor - 1$ for suitable k.

In future work, we will consider the application of the proposed algorithm for $\mathbb{F}_2$ to the Crossbred algorithm, which solves the $\mathcal{MQ}$ problem over $\mathbb{F}_2$.

Acknowledgments. This work was supported by JST CREST Grant Number JPMJCR14D6 and JSPS KAKENHI Grant Number 21J20391 and 20K19802.

References

1. Bardet, M.: Étude des systèms algébriques surdéterminés. Applications aux codes correcteurs et à la cryptographie. PhD thesis, Université Pierre et Marie Curie-Paris VI (2004)
2. Bardet, M., Faugère, J.-C., Salvy, B.: Complexity of Gröbner basis computation for semi-regular overdetermined sequences over $\mathbb{F}_2$ with solutions in $\mathbb{F}_2$. Research Report, RR-5049, INRIA (2003). https://hal.inria.fr/inria-00071534
3. Bardet, M., Faugère, J.-C., Salvy, B., Spaenlehauer, P.-J.: On the complexity of solving quadratic boolean systems. J. Complex. **29**(1), 53–75 (2013)

4. Bardet, M., Faugère, J.-C., Salvy, B., Yang, B.-Y.: Asymptotic behavior of the index of regularity of quadratic semi-regular polynomial systems. In: MEGA 2005 (2005). https://hal.archives-ouvertes.fr/hal-01486845

5. Bettale, L., Faugère, J.-C., Perret, L.: Hybrid approach for solving multivariate systems over finite fields. J. Math. Cryptol. **3**, 177–197 (2009)

6. Buchberger, B.: Ein algorithmus zum auffinden der basiselemente des restklassenringes nach einem nulldimensionalen polynomideal. PhD thesis, Universität Innsbruck (1965)

7. Casanova, A., Faugère, J.-C., Macario-Rat, G., Patarin, J., Perret, L., Ryckeghem, J.: GeMSS signature schemes proposal for NIST PQC project (round 3 version) (2020). https://csrc.nist.gov/projects/post-quantum-cryptography/round-3-submissions

8. Cheng, C.-M., Hashimoto, Y., Miura, H., Takagi, T.: A Polynomial-Time Algorithm for Solving a Class of Underdetermined Multivariate Quadratic Equations over Fields of Odd Characteristics. In: Mosca, M. (ed.) PQCrypto 2014. LNCS, vol. 8772, pp. 40–58. Springer, Cham (2014). https://doi.org/10.1007/978-3-319-11659-4_3

9. Courtois, N., Goubin, L., Meier, W., Tacier, J.-D.: Solving Underdefined Systems of Multivariate Quadratic Equations. In: Naccache, D., Paillier, P. (eds.) PKC 2002. LNCS, vol. 2274, pp. 211–227. Springer, Heidelberg (2002). https://doi.org/10.1007/3-540-45664-3_15

10. Courtois, N., Klimov, A., Patarin, J., Shamir, A.: Efficient Algorithms for Solving Overdefined Systems of Multivariate Polynomial Equations. In: Preneel, B. (ed.) EUROCRYPT 2000. LNCS, vol. 1807, pp. 392–407. Springer, Heidelberg (2000). https://doi.org/10.1007/3-540-45539-6_27

11. Ding, J., Chen, M.-S., Kannwischer, M., Patarin, J., Petzoldt, A., Schmidt, D., Yang, B.-Y.: Rainbow signature schemes proposal for NIST PQC project (round 3 version) (2020). https://csrc.nist.gov/projects/post-quantum-cryptography/round-3-submissions

12. Faugère, J.-C.: A new efficient algorithm for computing Gröbner bases (F4). J. Pure Appl. Algebra **139**(1–3), 61–88 (1999)

13. Faugère, J.-C.: A new efficient algorithm for computing Gröbner bases without reduction to zero (F5). In: ISSAC 2002, pp. 75–83. ACM (2002)

14. Garey, M.-R., Johnson, D.-S.: Computers and intractability: a guide to the theory of NP-completeness. W.H. Freeman (1979)

15. Joux, A., Vitse, V.: A Crossbred Algorithm for Solving Boolean Polynomial Systems. In: Kaczorowski, J., Pieprzyk, J., Pomykała, J. (eds.) NuTMiC 2017. LNCS, vol. 10737, pp. 3–21. Springer, Cham (2018). https://doi.org/10.1007/978-3-319-76620-1_1

16. Kipnis, A., Patarin, J., Goubin, L.: Unbalanced Oil and Vinegar Signature Schemes. In: Stern, J. (ed.) EUROCRYPT 1999. LNCS, vol. 1592, pp. 206–222. Springer, Heidelberg (1999). https://doi.org/10.1007/3-540-48910-X_15

17. NIST: Post-quantum cryptography CSRC. https://csrc.nist.gov/Projects/post-quantum-cryptography/post-quantum-cryptography-standardization

18. Thomae, E., Wolf, C.: Solving Underdetermined Systems of Multivariate Quadratic Equations Revisited. In: Fischlin, M., Buchmann, J., Manulis, M. (eds.) PKC 2012. LNCS, vol. 7293, pp. 156–171. Springer, Heidelberg (2012). https://doi.org/10.1007/978-3-642-30057-8_10

19. Yang, B.-Y., Chen, J.-M., Courtois, N.T.: On Asymptotic Security Estimates in XL and Gröbner Bases-Related Algebraic Cryptanalysis. In: Lopez, J., Qing, S., Okamoto, E. (eds.) ICICS 2004. LNCS, vol. 3269, pp. 401–413. Springer, Heidelberg (2004). https://doi.org/10.1007/978-3-540-30191-2_31
20. Yang, B.-Y., Chen, O.C.-H., Bernstein, D.J., Chen, J.-M.: Analysis of QUAD. In: Biryukov, A. (ed.) FSE 2007. LNCS, vol. 4593, pp. 290–308. Springer, Heidelberg (2007). https://doi.org/10.1007/978-3-540-74619-5_19

New Practical Multivariate Signatures from a Nonlinear Modifier

Daniel Smith-Tone[1,2]([✉])

[1] National Institute of Standards and Technology, Gaithersburg, USA
daniel.smith@nist.gov
[2] University of Louisville, Louisville, USA

Abstract. Multivariate cryptography is dominated by schemes supporting various tweaks, or "modifiers," designed to patch certain algebraic
weaknesses they would otherwise exhibit. Typically these modifiers are linear in nature—either requiring an extra composition with an affine map, or
being evaluated by a legitimate user via an affine projection. This description applies to the minus, plus, vinegar and internal perturbation modifiers, to name a few. Though it is well-known that combinations of various
modifiers can offer security against certain classes of attacks, cryptanalysts
have produced ever more sophisticated attacks against various combinations of these linear modifiers.

In this article, we introduce a more fundamentally nonlinear modifier,
called Q, that is inspired from relinearization. The effect of the Q modifier
on multivariate digital signature schemes is to maintain inversion efficiency
at the cost of slightly slower verification and larger public keys, while altering the algebraic properties of the public key. Thus the Q modifier is ideal
for applications of digital signature schemes requiring very fast signing and
verification without key transport. As an application of this modifier, we
propose new multivariate digital signature schemes with fast signing and
verification that are resistant to all known attacks.

Keywords: Post-quantum · Digital signature · Multivariate

1 Introduction

The National Institute of Standards and Technology (NIST) is currently engaged
in a process to establish new cryptographic standards [19] that offer security
against adversaries with access to large scale quantum computing technology.
This process aims to "Shor"-up NIST's public key suite of algorithms as a
response to the exponential speed-ups offered by Shor's quantum algorithms
[33] for solving the problems on which the current public key infrastructure is
based. NIST's process is currently in the third round [26] and consists of 9 public
key encryption or key-establishment algorithms and 6 digital signature schemes,
see [20].

While the majority of the diverse array of key-establishment candidates target general use applications and offer good performance in many metrics, the

J. H. Cheon and J.-P. Tillich (Eds.): PQCrypto 2021, LNCS 12841, pp. 79–97, 2021.
https://doi.org/10.1007/978-3-030-81293-5_5

situation for digital signatures is very different. First, applications of digital signatures are extremely diverse and often different applications require dramatically different performance characteristics; moreover, many "niche" applications are actually quite pervasive. Secondly, there are very few candidates that are general purpose or that offer acceptable performance for some applications. The situation is of sufficient concern that NIST has asked for public feedback on the issue of signature scheme diversity on the NIST Post-Quantum Cryptography (PQC) Forum [11].

Part of this concern arises from the recent cryptanalyses [4,30,38] of two of the non-lattice-based digital signature schemes that made it to the third round of NIST's post-quantum standardization process. These candidate algorithms, Rainbow [21] and GeMSS [1], are both multivariate signature schemes with long histories. If neither scheme can be repaired in such a way that public confidence in the approach is restored, then there can be no Federal Information Processing Standard-compliant (FIPS-compliant) alternative to the lattice signatures CRYSTALS-Dilithium [43] and Falcon [40] for applications requiring signatures significantly shorter than a kilobyte in length.

Not only are the above cryptanalyses concerning, also the recent advances in generic techniques have contributed to apprehension about the security of multivariate signature schemes in general. In particular, the most effective attack [4] on the NIST round 3 finalist Rainbow is made efficient by the support minors method of solving the MinRank problem, see [2]. This advance alone changes the complexity of rank attacks on schemes like Rainbow and GeMSS by orders of magnitude *in the exponent*.

In addition, the cryptanalysis of GeMSS in [38] bypasses the combination of the vinegar and minus modifiers, one of the last remaining combinations of modifiers for multivariate systems that was believed to offer security for the so-called "big field" schemes— schemes requiring the multiplicative structure of an extension field. This advance invites the question of whether big field schemes are at all viable or whether secure multivariate digital signatures require a structure like that of Unbalanced Oil-Vinegar (UOV), see [23].

In this article we suggest a very strange answer to the above question. We propose that a big field scheme may be secure by turning it into an odd form of a UOV scheme by way of a new nonlinear modifier. This modifier, called Q, transforms any quadratic map into a UOV map in a way that preserves the structure of the original map in the sense that with secret information, the legitimate user can use the inversion procedure for the original central map to find a preimage.

As an application of this modifier, we construct multivariate digital signatures by applying the Q modifier to C^* and show that the resulting scheme, QC^*, is secure against all known attacks. We also select a "small field" cryptosystem, the Step-wise Triangular System (STS) multivariate encryption scheme, and use the Q modifier to create QSTS. Thus, we use the Q modifier to convert two insecure encryption schemes into secure digital signature schemes, which is quite humorous.

This article is organized as follows. In the next section, we introduce some of the multivariate cryptosystems we have discussed above and which we will be modifying. In Sect. 3, we present and discuss the common modifiers of multivariate schemes and their security properties. We then introduce the new Q modifier in the subsequent section. Next, we present a few new schemes based on the Q modifier, illustrating the breadth of possible schemes it can produce. In Sect. 6, we present a thorough analysis of the security of these schemes. We next propose parameters for the focus of future study and application of these schemes in Sect. 7. Finally, we conclude, discussing the possible directions to which this work leads.

2   Multivariate Signature Schemes

Multivariate cryptosystems can broadly be categorized as "big field" or "small field" schemes. Big field schemes rely on the multiplicative structure of an extension field to provide a nonlinear efficiently invertible function. In contrast, small field schemes accomplish this task directly by selecting nonlinear functions with some special structure embedded. In both cases, the structure that allows for efficient inversion is hidden with the application of some morphism of polynomials.

2.1   Unbalanced Oil-Vinegar (UOV)

The unbalanced oil-vinegar (UOV) signature scheme [23] is the oldest small field scheme still considered secure. Like most small field schemes, UOV relies on the sequential derivation of preimage variables for the inversion of the private key.

Given the finite field $\mathbb{F}_q$, one selects integers $v \approx 2o$ or $v \approx 3o$ and constructs the vector space $O \oplus V \approx \mathbb{F}_q^{o+v}$, where $O \approx \mathbb{F}_q^o$ is called the oil subspace and $V \approx \mathbb{F}_q^v$ is known as the vinegar subspace. The private key then consists of a random linear map $L : \mathbb{F}_q^{o+v} \to \mathbb{F}_q^{o+v}$, and a random quadratic function F that is affine on cosets of O. Specifically, the map F is defined coordinate-wise by

$$F_\ell(x_1, x_2, \ldots, x_{o+v}) = \sum_{i=o+1}^{o+v} \sum_{j=1}^{o+v} a_{ij\ell} x_i x_j.$$

Each coordinate of F can be written as a quadratic form of the shape presented in Fig. 1. Given any constant vector $\begin{bmatrix} c_{o+1} \cdots c_{o+v} \end{bmatrix} \in V$, we have that $F(\cdot, \ldots, \cdot, c_{o+1}, \ldots, c_{o+v})$ is an affine function on O. The public key is then the composition $P = F \circ L$.

A preimage for any element in the codomain of P can be efficiently found by a legitimate user by randomly selecting an element $\mathbf{c}$ of V, inverting the affine map $F(\cdot, \mathbf{c})$ and finally inverting L. Verification is accomplished by merely evaluating the public key at a given signature.

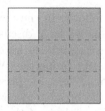

Fig. 1. The shape of the matrix representations of each central quadratic form of unbalanced oil-vinegar (UOV) is $v = 2o$. The shaded regions represent possibly nonzero values while unshaded areas have coefficients of zero.

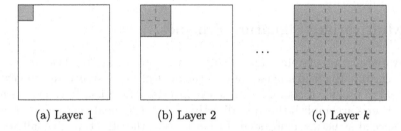

(a) Layer 1   (b) Layer 2   (c) Layer k

Fig. 2. The shape of the matrix representations of quadratic forms from each layer of the central map of a generic STS system. The shaded regions represent possibly nonzero values while unshaded areas have coefficients of zero.

2.2 Step-Wise Triangular System (STS)

The main line of what we would today call step-wise triangular schemes originated in Shamir's birational permutation scheme over large rings in [32]. A very similar idea emerged which was called the sequential solution method (SSM) in [42]. These ideas were extended to construct the RSE system of [22] and were further adapted in [18] where the authors made it clear that these schemes were broken. This more general scheme was named triangle-plus-minus (TPM), which was further generalized into what we now call step-wise triangular schemes (STS) in [44]. There have since been numerous variations on the theme including [17,37,41]. They are all very similar and the simplest exposition to provide a good understanding of all of them is to present the generic STS constructions of [44].

Unlike UOV, the STS-style schemes are designed for encryption. Also unlike UOV, STS cryptosystems have a special differentiation in the structure of equations as well as the structure of the space of variables. As such, STS schemes require affine maps mixing both the inputs and outputs of the secret central map F. Thus a public key looks like $P = T \circ F \circ U$. The critical structure in the STS family is the structure of the central map.

The central map of a generic STS instance is defined by selecting integers $0 = u_0 < u_1 < \ldots < u_k = n$, and random quadratic maps $\mathbf{y}_i = \psi_i(\mathbf{x}_i)$, where $\mathbf{x}_i = (x_1, \ldots, x_{u_i})$ and $dim(\mathbf{y}_i) = u_i - u_{i-1}$ for $i = \{1, \ldots, k\}$. The central map is then the direct sum $\bigoplus_{i=1}^{k} \psi_i$, see Fig. 2 for a visualization.

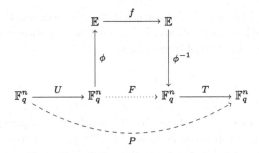

Fig. 3. The structure of a C^* scheme. The map ϕ is a $\mathbb{F}_q$-vector space isomorphism, F is a vector-valued function on $\mathbb{F}_q^n$, and f is an univariate function over $\mathbb{E}$.

Again, the technique for inversion of the secret map F is sequential. One first parses the output vector $\mathbf{y}$ into the component vectors $\mathbf{y}_i$ for each of the k layers. Then sequentially, the quadratic equations $\psi_i(\mathbf{x}_i) = \mathbf{y}_i$ are solved using the coordinates previously solved for $\mathbf{x}_{i-1}$ as a prefix of $\mathbf{x}_i$.

All of these constructions are vulnerable to generic combinatorial rank attacks as shown in [44]. In fact, all such schemes are vulnerable to both the MinRank attack—finding a low rank non-zero linear combination of the public quadratic forms— and the dual rank attack—finding a small subspace that is in the kernel of a large subspace of the quadratic forms.

2.3 C^*

The progenitor of all "big field" schemes is commonly known as C^*, or the Matsumoto-Imai scheme, see [25]. This scheme exploits the fact that an extension field $\mathbb{E}$ of $\mathbb{F}_q$ is an $\mathbb{F}_q$-algebra to produce two versions of a function—a vector-valued version which is quadratic over the base field, and a monomial function whose input and output lie in the extension field. Specifically, the C^* central map is the univariate function $f : \mathbb{E} \to \mathbb{E}$ defined by

$$f(X) = X^{q^\theta + 1},$$

where $|\mathbb{E} : \mathbb{F}_q| = n$ and $(q^\theta + 1, q^n - 1) = 1$. The final condition ensures that the power map is invertible in $\mathbb{E}^*$. To complete the construction, one composes invertible affine maps to produce the public key $P(\mathbf{x}) = T \circ F \circ U$, see Fig. 3. The C^* scheme can be considered a sort of multivariate version of RSA; in fact, the design of C^* intends for the inversion of F to be accomplished in exactly the same way as RSA, that is, by exponentiation by the multiplicative inverse of the encryption exponent modulo the size of the unit group.

C^* was broken by Patarin in [27] by way of linearization equations. Patarin discovered that there is a bilinear relationship between the plaintext $\mathbf{x}$ and ciphertext $\mathbf{y}$. In all but a few pathological cases, an adversary can interpolate this bilinear function by generating many plaintext-ciphertext pairs. Once recovered, these linearization equations provide an even faster method of decryption than using the private key. Indeed later derivatives of C^* derive linearization equations from the private key as a fast method of inversion, see [7–9].

3 Modifiers

The cryptanalysis of the C^* scheme by Patarin in [27] inspired the creation of modifiers to make certain attacks infeasible. There are two categories of such alterations: one can modify the central map in some specific way preserving efficient invertibility; or one can make one or both affine transformations non-invertible. Of course, various modifications can be taken together as well. We present here some prominent modifiers.

Shortly after the cryptanalysis of C^*, Patarin introduced in [29] three modifiers aiming to enhance the security of C^*. These three modifiers include the minus $(-)$ modifier (the removal of public equations), the plus $(+)$ modifier (the addition of random equations in the central map that can be ignored on inversion) and the projection (p) modifier (the assignment of one or more input variables to constant values before the publication of the key).

The purpose of the minus modifier is clear. The idea is to remove some public equations and thereby change the algebraic structure of the central map. This method is equivalent to making the output transformation T singular. An immediate consequence in the case of C^* is that the minus modified scheme, C^*-, no longer has linearization equations. Still, C^*- was proven weak by an attack [14] exploiting a symmetric relation satisfied by the public key.

The projection modifier is the analogous modification on the input space. Instead of making the output transformation T singular, the input transformation U is made singular. Interestingly, this modification does not prevent the linearization equations attack if applied to C^*. The only cryptosystem proposed that is essentially of the pC^* form is SQUARE, see [10], which was broken by an attack analogous to that on C^*-, see [5].

The plus modifier is in some sense the opposite of the minus modifier. Additional random equations are added to the central map and then mixed via the output transformation. In the case of C^*, the plus modifier does not enhance security. The MinRank attack of [3] with a target rank of 2 recovers an equivalent C^* key. Still, this modifier has found use in numerous schemes, most recently including the, so named, PCBM scheme, see [36].

In [28], the vinegar (v) modifier (the addition of variables in the central map, the values of which can be randomly assigned upon inversion) is introduced in the QUARTZ scheme. QUARTZ is a parametrization of Hidden Field Equations with the vinegar and minus modifiers (HFEv-), the same construction as used in GeMSS, see [1]. Thus, the attack of [38] breaks the vinegar modification, even in conjunction with the minus modifier, if the central map is of low rank.

In [13], the internal perturbation (ip) modifier (the addition of a random summand with a small support) is used to produce the Perturbed Matsumoto-Imai (PMI) cryptosystem. The random summand introduced by the internal perturbation modifier has such small support that its value can be guessed and subtracted from the output of the central map before inversion. This modifier applied to C^* was also broken, see [16].

All of these modifiers share the property that they either constitute a linear action on the public key or can be removed by a linear action on the public key. More specifically, the projection and minus modifiers are obviously linear projections and are dual to each other, while the vinegar and plus modifiers can both be removed via the application of the appropriate linear projection on the input or output space. Even the internal perturbation modifier can be removed via a projection, though the resulting scheme is the same as the original with an application of the projection modifier.

4   The Q Modifier

In this section we introduce a new generic modifier for multivariate schemes, named Q, that is inspired by relinearization, see [24]. As we will see, the Q modifier is not linear in the sense that each of the modifiers in the previous section are. Q is not a linear function on a public key nor can it be removed by a linear function on the public key.

First let us recall the relinearization technique first introduced in [24]. The idea of the technique is to symbolically solve a system of nonlinear equations by iteratively linearizing the system and recalling relations between the variables. Specifically, given a multivariate system in the variables $x_1, \ldots, x_n$, the relinearization technique assigns a new variable y_{ij} to each monomial of the form $x_i x_j$, attempts to solve the resulting linear system, and recalls the relations of the form $y_{ij} y_{k\ell} = y_{ik} y_{j\ell}$, among others. While relinearization did not provide the originally promised performance in solving overdefined systems, it did inspire the development of XL, see [12], and offers a new technique for modifying quadratic systems.

We begin the description in as general a context as possible and then discuss the specifications required to apply Q in special contexts. First, let $F : \mathbb{F}_q^m \to \mathbb{F}_q^m$ be an arbitrary homogenous quadratic function in the variable $\mathbf{x} = [x_1 \ldots x_m]$. We select a short vector of auxiliary variables $\mathbf{w} = [w_1, \ldots, w_\ell]$ and form products between these variables and terms of F (at this point, in an arbitrary way) to create a cubic map $\widetilde{F} : \mathbb{F}_q^{m+\ell} \to \mathbb{F}_q^m$. We then consider the general monomial of the form $x_i x_j w_k$. Such a monomial must always contain exactly one variable from $\mathbf{w}$. We define a vector $\mathbf{z}$ of $m\ell$ new variables $z_{ik} = x_i w_k$. Thus we have the relations

$$x_i x_j w_k = x_i z_{jk} = x_j z_{ik}. \tag{1}$$

We replace $\widetilde{F}$ with a new function $\widehat{F} : \mathbb{F}_q^{(\ell+1)m} \to \mathbb{F}_q^m$ in a two step process. First, we use relations of the form of Equation (1) to replace every cubic monomial in $\mathbf{x}$ with a monomial bilinear in $\mathbf{x}$ and $\mathbf{z}$ randomly. Second, we introduce new quadratic summands of the form $\alpha x_i z_{jk} - \alpha x_j z_{ik}$ and $\alpha z_{ij} z_{rs} - \alpha z_{is} z_{rj}$ for randomly selected $\alpha \in \mathbb{F}_q$. These summands must equal zero by the definition of the variables in $\mathbf{z}$. The function $\widehat{F}$ is now a new quadratic function.

We illustrate with a small example. For space, we only use two equations in three variables. Suppose that $\begin{bmatrix} y_1 & y_2 \end{bmatrix} = F(x_1, x_2, x_3)$ over $\mathbb{F}_7$ is given by

$$y_1 = 2x_1x_2 + 3x_1x_3 + x_2x_3$$
$$y_2 = x_1^2 + 5x_1x_3 + 2x_2x_3.$$

We multiply by the variables w_1 and w_2 in an arbitrary way producing $\widetilde{F}$ defined by

$$y_1 = 2x_1x_2w_2 + 3x_1x_3w_1 + 3x_1x_3w_2 + x_2x_3w_1$$
$$y_2 = x_1^2w_1 + x_1^2w_2 + 5x_1x_3w_2 + 2x_2x_3w_1.$$

Next we substitute for x_iw_j and add cancelling terms (in parentheses below) in the new variables $z_{11}, z_{12}, \ldots, z_{32}$ to produce $\widehat{F}$ of the form

$$y_1 = 2x_2z_{12} + 3x_1z_{31} + 3x_1z_{32} + x_3z_{21} + (4z_{12}z_{31} + 3z_{11}z_{32} + x_1z_{22} + 6x_2z_{12})$$
$$y_2 = x_1z_{11} + x_1z_{12} + 5x_3z_{12} + 2x_2z_{31} + (x_3z_{12} + 6x_1z_{32} + 4z_{22}z_{11} + 3z_{12}z_{21}).$$

There are three things to notice. First, the resulting function $\widehat{F}$ is a UOV map. The map is clearly linear in $\mathbf{x}$ and quadratic in $\mathbf{z}$. Therefore, we can find a preimage under $\widehat{F}$ by using the inversion procedure for UOV. Consequently, we can see that the Q modifier embeds some distribution of quadratic maps into a subspace of the space of UOV keys necessarily having less entropy.

Second—and this is a key point—if there is an assignment of the ℓ variables $\mathbf{w}$ that makes $\widetilde{F}(\cdot, \mathbf{w})$ an efficient to invert quadratic system, then we have a second way to invert $\widehat{F}$. Specifically, the user assigns values to $\mathbf{w}$, solves for $\mathbf{x}$ such that $\widetilde{F}(\mathbf{x}, \mathbf{w}) = \mathbf{y}$, and computes $\mathbf{z} = \mathbf{x} \otimes \mathbf{w}$. We note here that quadratic terms in $\mathbf{z}$ never need to be computed unlike in the case of inversion as a UOV map. Thus, for functions $\widetilde{F}(\cdot, \mathbf{w})$ with sufficiently efficient inversion, the inversion of the maps transformed by Q is more efficient than UOV inversion.

Finally, since the original monomials are gone, there exists no linear projection on the input nor the output that transforms $\widehat{F}$ into a linear function of F. In fact, the Q transformation is a quadratic substitution, hence the name. Therefore attacks exploiting projections away from a modifier are ineffective against Q.

Thus, the Q modifier is particularly useful in cases in which we have families of efficiently invertible quadratic maps that can be parametrized by an additional auxiliary set of variables. In such a case for any fixed $\mathbf{w}$, the function $\widetilde{F}(\cdot, \mathbf{w})$ is efficiently invertible. Then we may use the inversion procedure for $\widetilde{F}(\cdot, \mathbf{w})$ to find preimages of $\widehat{F}$ with greater efficiency than the UOV inversion procedure. We present some explicit examples of constructing such parametrized families $\widetilde{F}$ in Sect. 5.

5   New Schemes

We can now explain the most complicated part of the Q modifier, the task of creating the parametrized family of efficiently invertible functions $\widetilde{F}(\mathbf{x}, \mathbf{w})$ from an efficiently invertible function F. The key is to use the structure that makes F efficiently invertible.

5.1 QC^*

Let $F(\mathbf{x}) = \phi^{-1} \circ f \circ \phi(\mathbf{x})$ where $f(X) = X^{q^\theta+1}$ is a C^* central map. We may select a linear transformation $B : \mathbb{F}_q^\ell \to \mathbb{F}_q^m$ and construct the function

$$\widetilde{F}(\mathbf{x}, \mathbf{w}) = \phi^{-1}\left(\phi(B(\mathbf{w}))f(\phi(\mathbf{x}))\right).$$

For any fixed nonzero $\mathbf{w}$, the quantity $a_\mathbf{w} = \phi(B(\mathbf{w}))$ is just some constant in $\mathbb{E}$, therefore the family of functions is simply the small field representations of the functions $a_\mathbf{w} X^{q^\theta+1}$, a collection of C^* maps with coefficients other than 1. Every such function has linearization equations which are trivial for the user to derive and use for extremely efficient inversion, see [7–9, 27].

In fact, when ℓ is very small, linearization equations can be derived for all nonzero values of $\mathbf{w}$ and inversion is accomplished with a very small number of multiplications. Specifically, let $\mathbf{L}_i^\mathbf{w}$ be the ith linearization equation corresponding to $a_\mathbf{w} X^{q^\theta+1}$. Then we may invert $P(\tilde{\mathbf{x}}) = T \circ \widehat{F}(U\tilde{\mathbf{x}}) = \mathbf{y}$ by first computing a left kernel element $\mathbf{u}$ of the block matrix

$$\left[\mathbf{L}_1^\mathbf{w}\mathbf{T}^{-\top}\mathbf{y}^\top \cdots \mathbf{L}_m^\mathbf{w}\mathbf{T}^{-\top}\mathbf{y}^\top\right],$$

appending $\mathbf{u} \otimes \mathbf{w}$, and multiplying on the right by $\mathbf{U}^{-1}$. Since $\mathbf{L}_i^\mathbf{w}\mathbf{T}^{-\top}$ are all precomputed as part of the private key, inversion only involves computing $m+1$ matrix vector products, an $m\ell$ dimensional Kronecker product and solving a linear system.

Thus, the complexity of inversion is $m^3+m^\omega+m^2(\ell+1)^2+m\ell$, multiplications in $\mathbb{F}_q$ where $2 \leq \omega \leq 3$ is the linear algebra constant. For comparison, the complexity of inverting UOV$(m,m\ell)$ using the structure of equivalent keys, see [45], is $\frac{1}{2}m^3\ell^2 + m^3\ell + m^\omega + \frac{3}{2}m^2\ell$ multiplications in $\mathbb{F}_q$.

5.2   QSTS

Let $F(\mathbf{x})$ be a step-wise triangular function with m steps of size 1. For any vector $\mathbf{w}$ we can construct the function $\widetilde{F}(\mathbf{x}, \mathbf{w})$ from F by randomly multiplying each term by a linear form in $\mathbf{w}$. For all constant nonzero assignments $\mathbf{w} = \mathbf{c}$ the resulting function of $\mathbf{x}$, $\widetilde{F}(\mathbf{x}, \mathbf{c})$ is still a triangular map, so inversion can proceed as normal.

Inversion of the public key is straightforward. Given $\mathbf{y} = P(\tilde{\mathbf{x}}) = T \circ \widehat{F}(U'\tilde{\mathbf{x}}, U''\tilde{\mathbf{x}})$, the user simply inverts T, finds the preimage $\mathbf{u}$ under $\widetilde{F}(\cdot, \mathbf{w})$, appends $\mathbf{u} \otimes \mathbf{w}$ and inverts the input transformation $U = U' \oplus U''$.

Since the inversion process for $\widetilde{F}(\cdot, \mathbf{w})$ is inversion of a triangular map, it is very efficient. In total, inversion requires $m^3 + 2\binom{m+2}{3} + m^2(\ell+1)^2 + m\ell$ multiplications in $\mathbb{F}_q$.

6   Security Analysis

In this section we consider the security of the schemes introduced in the previous section as well as some general considerations for the security of Q modified schemes. Attacks on the UOV structure are well known and easy to avoid. Thus, we consider four main attack avenues.

6.1   Q Kernel Attacks

In the case of using the Q modifier generically, there exists an injection $M :$ $\mathbb{F}_q^m \to \mathbb{F}_q^{m(\ell+1)}$ such that $\mathbf{M} \mathbf{P}_i \mathbf{M}^\top = \mathbf{0}_{m \times m}$ for all $1 \leq i \leq m$. Notice also, though, since monomials of the form $z_{ik} z_{jk}$ do not occur in $\widehat{F}$ that there also exist injections $M' : \mathbb{F}_q^\ell \to \mathbb{F}_q^{m(\ell+1)}$ such that $\mathbf{M}' \mathbf{P}_i \mathbf{M}'^\top = \mathbf{0}_{\ell \times \ell}$ for all $1 \leq i \leq m$. Thus, we either have a system of m^3 homogeneous quadratic equations in the $m^2(\ell+1)$ unknown coefficients of $\mathbf{M}$ or a system of $m\ell^2$ homogeneous quadratic equations in the $m\ell(\ell+1)$ unknown coefficients of $\mathbf{M}'$.

Such systems can be solved via Gröbner basis methods. Given a hybrid approach, see [46], of guessing k variables and resolving the system, we either obtain a system of m^3 equations in $m^2(\ell+1) - k$ variables or a system of $m\ell^2$ equations in $m\ell(\ell+1) - k$ variables. Let d_{sr} and d'_{sr} represent the semi-regular degrees of such systems. For sufficiently large q, these values are given by the degree of the first nonpositive coefficient in the series expansions of

$$ S(t) = \frac{(1-t^2)^{m^3}}{(1-t)^{m^2(\ell+1)-k}}, \ S'(t) = \frac{(1-t^2)^{m\ell^2}}{(1-t)^{m\ell(\ell+1)-k}}. $$

Assuming that such systems are semi-regular, we find a complexity

$$ \mathcal{O}\left(q^k \binom{m^2(\ell+1) - k + d_{sr}}{d_{sr}}^\omega\right), \text{ or } \mathcal{O}\left(q^k \binom{m\ell(\ell+1) - k + d'_{sr}}{d'_{sr}}^\omega\right). $$

6.2   Direct Attacks

Direct attacks try to invert the public key directly as a quadratic function. Typically this process involves using some polynomial system solver based on either XL, see [12], or F4, see [15].

Since the public key of a Q modified scheme is underdetermined, we can employ the reduction procedure from [39] to convert the public key into a system of $m - \ell - 1$ equations in $m - \ell - 1$ variables. We can then take a hybrid approach and guess the values of k variables. The semi-regular degree for systems of $m - \ell - 1$ equations in $m - \ell - 1 - k$ variables is the degree d_{sr} of the first nonpositive coefficient in the series

$$S(t) = \frac{(1 - t^2)^{m-\ell-1}}{(1 - t)^{m-\ell-1-k}}.$$

Under the assumption that the system derived from the public key is semi-regular, the complexity of the direct attack is

$$\mathcal{O}\left(q^k \binom{m - \ell - 1 - k + d_{sr}}{d_{sr}}^{\omega}\right).$$

6.3 Rank Attacks

The STS cryptosystem is vulnerable to every type of rank attack, as shown in [44]. The Q modification, because it introduces terms involving all variables, in general makes all of the maps full rank when the field is large enough. Thus QSTS has no rank defect.

The C^* scheme does have a rank defect with respect to the extension field $\mathbb{E}$. We note, however, that due to the addition of the cancelling terms of the form $x_i z_{jk} - x_j z_{ik}$ and $z_{ij} z_{rs} - z_{is} z_{rj}$ that there is no longer an $\mathbb{E}$ combination of the public quadratic forms with low rank. In particular, there exists no linear injection $M : \mathbb{F}_q^m \to \mathbb{F}_q^{m(\ell+1)}$ such that $P \circ M$ is a C^* public key; thus, QC^* is safe from rank attack.

6.4 Differential Attacks

The C^* scheme and higher degree analogues are also vulnerable to differential attacks directly as shown, for example, in [35]. Therefore, we need to verify that the Q transformation prevents such an attack. As outlined in [34], the only maps that satisfy a differential symmetry on an $\mathbb{E}$-algebra are componentwise multiples of C^* monomial maps. Thus the attack is only possible if there exists a linear injection M such that $P \circ M$ is componentwise C^*. Due to the quadratic substitution, there exists no such injection.

6.5 Chosen Message Attacks

Recall that in the case of QC^* it is desirable to store linearization equations for efficient inversion. As a result, the private key of QC^* is quite large. It may be tempting for an implementer to select a few possible values of $\mathbf{w}$ and store only the corresponding linearization equations. There is a cost to such a choice, however.

We present a chosen message attack in the extreme case that a lazy implementer fixes $\mathbf{w}$ to a constant. The idea is very simple. The adversary collects $\mathcal{O}(m)$ signatures and notes that the linear span of the signatures is m-dimensional. At this point, the adversary may calculate a linear embedding

$\rho : \mathbb{F}_q^m \to \mathbb{F}_q^{(\ell+1)m}$ by simply row reducing the matrix of basis vectors of this m-dimensional space. Composing this map with the public key recovers an instance of the underlying scheme, for example, C^*. In fact, the row reduction reveals the constant value selected for $\mathbf{w}$ when factored through the input transformation.

If the lazy implementer instead allows $\mathbf{w}$ to attain k values where k is small, then the chosen message attack reveals at most k distinct m-dimensional subspaces of the signature space. In a similar manner to the above case, the basis matrix reveals the distinct values of $\mathbf{w}$ factored through the transformation. As k increases toward q^ℓ, we begin to have enough subspaces that there are nontrivial intersections among these m-dimensional subspaces.

Thus, using more values of $\mathbf{w}$ makes the scheme more resistant to this style of chosen message attack. Of course, QC^* and QSTS only offer universal unforgeability, anyway. Thus any realistic implementation will require not only a large number of supported values of $\mathbf{w}$, but also an EUF-CMA transformation such as the SSH transform of [31].

7   Parameters and Performance

Selecting parameters to achieve security against the attacks from Sect. 6, we find that the limiting attack is the direct attack. With the complexity estimate then given in Sect. 6, we find that the optimal attack classically uses a hybrid approach with $k = 3$ in the case of $q = 2^8$ for all realistic parameters.

Using a linear algebra exponent of $\omega = 2.8$, we find that $m = 44$ and $\ell = 3$ are sufficient to achieve 151-bit security, which is comfortably NIST Level I. For a fair comparison, we implemented simple proof of concept implementations of QC^*, QSTS and UOV with the same parameters in the MAGMA Computer Algebra System[1] see [6]. We observed that at the precision of measurement we were able to make that the performance of the Q modified schemes was extremely consistent between the variants and was better than that of our implementation of UOV. The results are presented in Table 1. Please note that these implementations are not at all optimized.

Table 1. The parameters and performance of QC^* and QSTS in comparision to UOV. The Q schemes performance data were essentially identical and are presented under the row labelled Q-schemes.

	q	m	ℓ	# Eqs	# Vars	sig. (B)	PK (B)	sign (ms)	ver. (ms)
Q-schemes	2^8	44	3	44	176	176	677600	0.6	2.9
UOV	2^8	N/A	N/A	44	176	176	677600	3.7	2.9

---

[1] Any mention of commercial products does not indicate endorsement by NIST.

8 Conclusion

Digital signature schemes based on systems of nonlinear multivariate equations have been around for a long time. The break-and-patch evolution of the discipline as well as the multitude of attack paths available has always made multivariate cryptography a somewhat risky venture. The appeal of some of the performance characteristics of these schemes (e.g., very short signatures, very fast verification) has helped to keep alive the hope that multivariate schemes will find a permanent home in our future standards.

Recent advances in cryptanalytic techniques, however, have further shaken public confidence in certain multivariate approaches. Most multivariate schemes rely on a low rank property at some point in the inversion process. The new support minors method introduced in [2] is a dramatic improvement in generic technique and led to a significant attack against Rainbow, see [4]. Another recent advance, see [38], shows that the combination of vinegar and minus modifiers are not sufficient alone to secure big field schemes. As a result, there are no remaining multivariate candidates in NIST's post-quantum standardization process that have not suffered some significant attack.

In this work we present the Q modifier and show that it is qualitatively different from the modifiers that have been studied for a couple of decades. Q is inherently nonlinear and creates a new map divorced from the algebraic properties of the original map. Still, the new map, which is of UOV form, is related via a hidden quadratic relationship to the original map, so that inversion can still be accomplished with the original structure.

The fact that the Q modifier is generic suggests that it may be a promising direction requiring further study. In particular, it is possible to eliminate the UOV structure of the resulting scheme by appending a 1 at the end of the vector $\mathbf{w}$ defined in Sect. 4. The consequence of this change is that one may include terms quadratic in $\mathbf{x}$ in the central map. Thus, depending on the structure of the map, there may exist a linear projection onto the prototype function for the scheme. This alteration seems risky for systems with a rank defect, but is a topic worthy of further research in the general case.

A Toy Example

In this section we present a toy example of QSTS. We illustrate the selection of F, $\widetilde{F}$ and $\widehat{F}$ and then present a valid public key. Finally, we demonstrate inversion of the public key.

We randomly select a function F of STS shape over $\mathrm{GF}(7)$:

$$y_1 = 5x_1^2$$
$$y_2 = 6x_1^2 + 4x_1x_2$$
$$y_3 = 6x_1^2 + 3x_1x_2 + 5x_2^2 + 3x_1x_3 + x_3^2$$
$$y_4 = 5x_1^2 + 5x_1x_2 + 6x_1x_3 + x_2x_3 + x_1x_4 + 6x_2x_4 + 6x_3x_4 + x_4^2$$

We then construct the parametric family of STS functions, $\widetilde{F}$, by randomly multiplying monomials in F by random linear forms in the variables w_1, w_2:

$$y_1 = 3x_1^2 w_1 + 3x_1^2 w_2$$
$$y_2 = 2x_1^2 w_1 + 4x_1 x_2 w_1 + 5x_2^2 w_2$$
$$y_3 = 6x_1 x_2 w_1 + 5x_2^2 w_1 + 5x_1 x_3 w_1 + 5x_3^2 w_1$$
$$\qquad + x_1^2 w_2 + 6x_1 x_2 w_2 + 6x_2^2 w_2 + 3x_1 x_3 w_2$$
$$y_4 = 2x_1^2 w_1 + 6x_1 x_3 w_1 + x_2 x_3 w_1 + 6x_1 x_4 w_1 + 5x_2 x_4 w_1 + x_3 x_4 w_1 + 2x_1^2 w_2$$
$$\qquad + 6x_1 x_2 w_2 + 5x_1 x_3 w_2 + x_2 x_3 w_2 + 5x_1 x_4 w_2 + 2x_2 x_4 w_2 + 5x_4^2 w_2$$

Next, we do the final step of performing random replacements $x_i w_j = z_{ij}$ and adding random summands of the forms $a x_i z_{jk} - a x_j z_{ik}$ and $a z_{ij} z_{rs} - a z_{is} z_{rj}$ to obtain $\widehat{F}$. In matrix form we have:

$$\widehat{\mathbf{F}}_1 = \begin{bmatrix}
0 & 0 & 0 & 0 & 5 & 5 & 3 & 0 & 3 & 6 & 2 & 4 \\
0 & 0 & 0 & 0 & 4 & 0 & 0 & 0 & 1 & 0 & 1 & 1 \\
0 & 0 & 0 & 0 & 4 & 1 & 6 & 0 & 0 & 0 & 6 & 1 \\
0 & 0 & 0 & 0 & 5 & 3 & 6 & 6 & 1 & 6 & 0 & 0 \\
5 & 4 & 4 & 5 & 0 & 0 & 0 & 6 & 0 & 2 & 0 & 4 \\
5 & 0 & 1 & 3 & 0 & 0 & 1 & 0 & 5 & 0 & 3 & 0 \\
3 & 0 & 6 & 6 & 0 & 1 & 0 & 0 & 0 & 4 & 0 & 3 \\
0 & 0 & 0 & 6 & 6 & 0 & 0 & 0 & 3 & 0 & 4 & 0 \\
3 & 1 & 0 & 1 & 0 & 5 & 0 & 3 & 0 & 0 & 0 & 6 \\
6 & 0 & 0 & 6 & 2 & 0 & 4 & 0 & 0 & 0 & 1 & 0 \\
2 & 1 & 6 & 0 & 0 & 3 & 0 & 4 & 0 & 1 & 0 & 0 \\
4 & 1 & 1 & 0 & 4 & 0 & 3 & 0 & 6 & 0 & 0 & 0
\end{bmatrix}, \quad
\widehat{\mathbf{F}}_2 = \begin{bmatrix}
0 & 0 & 0 & 0 & 1 & 6 & 3 & 0 & 5 & 6 & 5 & 6 \\
0 & 0 & 0 & 0 & 6 & 0 & 0 & 0 & 5 & 3 & 3 & 0 \\
0 & 0 & 0 & 0 & 2 & 1 & 2 & 4 & 0 & 0 & 2 & 4 \\
0 & 0 & 0 & 0 & 2 & 1 & 4 & 0 & 5 & 3 & 0 & 0 \\
1 & 6 & 2 & 2 & 0 & 0 & 0 & 2 & 0 & 0 & 0 & 6 \\
6 & 0 & 1 & 1 & 0 & 0 & 5 & 0 & 0 & 0 & 1 & 0 \\
3 & 0 & 2 & 4 & 0 & 5 & 0 & 0 & 0 & 0 & 0 & 1 \\
0 & 0 & 4 & 0 & 2 & 0 & 0 & 0 & 0 & 0 & 6 & 0 \\
5 & 5 & 0 & 5 & 0 & 0 & 0 & 0 & 0 & 0 & 0 & 2 \\
6 & 3 & 0 & 3 & 0 & 0 & 0 & 0 & 0 & 0 & 5 & 0 \\
5 & 3 & 2 & 0 & 0 & 1 & 0 & 6 & 0 & 5 & 0 & 0 \\
6 & 0 & 4 & 0 & 6 & 0 & 1 & 0 & 2 & 0 & 0 & 0
\end{bmatrix},$$

$$\widehat{\mathbf{F}}_3 = \begin{bmatrix}
0 & 0 & 0 & 0 & 0 & 4 & 4 & 1 & 0 & 0 & 6 & 1 \\
0 & 0 & 0 & 0 & 6 & 2 & 6 & 3 & 2 & 1 & 2 & 6 \\
0 & 0 & 0 & 0 & 6 & 5 & 5 & 6 & 6 & 0 & 2 & 1 \\
0 & 0 & 0 & 0 & 1 & 6 & 5 & 1 & 5 & 6 & 0 & 0 \\
0 & 6 & 6 & 1 & 0 & 0 & 0 & 5 & 0 & 4 & 0 & 1 \\
4 & 2 & 5 & 6 & 0 & 0 & 2 & 0 & 3 & 0 & 6 & 0 \\
4 & 6 & 5 & 5 & 0 & 2 & 0 & 0 & 0 & 2 & 0 & 0 \\
1 & 3 & 6 & 1 & 5 & 0 & 0 & 0 & 5 & 0 & 0 & 0 \\
0 & 2 & 6 & 5 & 0 & 3 & 0 & 5 & 0 & 0 & 0 & 3 \\
0 & 1 & 0 & 6 & 4 & 0 & 2 & 0 & 0 & 0 & 4 & 0 \\
6 & 2 & 2 & 0 & 0 & 6 & 0 & 0 & 0 & 4 & 0 & 0 \\
1 & 6 & 1 & 0 & 1 & 0 & 0 & 0 & 3 & 0 & 0 & 0
\end{bmatrix}, \quad
\widehat{\mathbf{F}}_4 = \begin{bmatrix}
0 & 0 & 0 & 0 & 1 & 1 & 4 & 2 & 5 & 0 & 5 & 4 \\
0 & 0 & 0 & 0 & 3 & 1 & 0 & 0 & 2 & 4 & 2 & 1 \\
0 & 0 & 0 & 0 & 5 & 6 & 2 & 0 & 0 & 0 & 3 & 3 \\
0 & 0 & 0 & 0 & 5 & 2 & 4 & 0 & 1 & 4 & 0 & 6 \\
1 & 3 & 5 & 5 & 0 & 0 & 0 & 0 & 0 & 1 & 0 & 3 \\
1 & 1 & 6 & 2 & 0 & 0 & 0 & 0 & 6 & 0 & 4 & 0 \\
4 & 0 & 2 & 4 & 0 & 0 & 0 & 0 & 0 & 0 & 0 & 4 \\
2 & 0 & 0 & 0 & 0 & 0 & 0 & 0 & 0 & 0 & 3 & 0 \\
5 & 2 & 0 & 1 & 0 & 6 & 0 & 0 & 0 & 0 & 0 & 4 \\
0 & 4 & 0 & 4 & 1 & 0 & 0 & 0 & 0 & 0 & 3 & 0 \\
5 & 2 & 3 & 0 & 0 & 4 & 0 & 3 & 0 & 3 & 0 & 0 \\
4 & 1 & 3 & 6 & 3 & 0 & 4 & 0 & 4 & 0 & 0 & 0
\end{bmatrix}$$

$$U = \begin{bmatrix}
1 & 4 & 0 & 2 & 0 & 6 & 4 & 1 & 3 & 6 & 1 & 5 \\
2 & 4 & 1 & 5 & 2 & 2 & 2 & 3 & 5 & 1 & 1 & 5 \\
6 & 2 & 4 & 1 & 4 & 3 & 0 & 0 & 1 & 6 & 3 & 5 \\
5 & 1 & 1 & 1 & 0 & 4 & 0 & 0 & 0 & 3 & 0 & 5 \\
3 & 6 & 4 & 1 & 6 & 5 & 2 & 5 & 4 & 4 & 3 & 5 \\
1 & 6 & 3 & 5 & 1 & 1 & 5 & 3 & 6 & 3 & 1 & 6 \\
4 & 1 & 2 & 4 & 3 & 5 & 0 & 4 & 3 & 4 & 3 & 6 \\
1 & 6 & 5 & 4 & 0 & 0 & 2 & 4 & 3 & 3 & 1 & 2 \\
3 & 4 & 6 & 4 & 5 & 1 & 5 & 0 & 4 & 4 & 6 & 4 \\
4 & 1 & 5 & 6 & 3 & 6 & 4 & 6 & 4 & 1 & 0 & 1 \\
0 & 3 & 2 & 0 & 3 & 5 & 0 & 5 & 5 & 6 & 1 & 6 \\
3 & 1 & 0 & 4 & 0 & 3 & 4 & 3 & 5 & 5 & 3 & 5
\end{bmatrix}, \text{ and } T = \begin{bmatrix}
3 & 5 & 6 & 4 \\
3 & 0 & 2 & 1 \\
1 & 5 & 0 & 0 \\
5 & 3 & 1 & 6
\end{bmatrix}.$$

$$P_1 = \begin{bmatrix}
4 & 5 & 3 & 3 & 6 & 2 & 3 & 2 & 4 & 4 & 3 & 0 \\
5 & 2 & 0 & 1 & 5 & 5 & 4 & 1 & 0 & 1 & 2 & 6 \\
3 & 0 & 6 & 3 & 6 & 1 & 3 & 2 & 4 & 5 & 0 & 4 \\
3 & 1 & 3 & 3 & 2 & 3 & 0 & 1 & 5 & 1 & 2 & 6 \\
6 & 5 & 6 & 2 & 4 & 0 & 4 & 3 & 0 & 6 & 6 & 6 \\
2 & 5 & 1 & 3 & 0 & 3 & 1 & 2 & 4 & 5 & 3 & 4 \\
3 & 4 & 3 & 0 & 4 & 1 & 1 & 5 & 6 & 2 & 6 & 3 \\
2 & 1 & 2 & 1 & 3 & 2 & 5 & 4 & 1 & 2 & 0 & 1 \\
4 & 0 & 4 & 5 & 0 & 4 & 6 & 1 & 3 & 4 & 2 & 0 \\
4 & 1 & 5 & 1 & 6 & 5 & 2 & 2 & 4 & 5 & 3 & 0 \\
3 & 2 & 0 & 2 & 6 & 3 & 6 & 0 & 2 & 3 & 0 & 5 \\
0 & 6 & 4 & 6 & 6 & 4 & 3 & 1 & 0 & 0 & 5 & 6
\end{bmatrix}, P_2 = \begin{bmatrix}
3 & 3 & 1 & 6 & 3 & 6 & 5 & 2 & 2 & 0 & 1 & 6 \\
3 & 3 & 3 & 6 & 1 & 2 & 4 & 0 & 0 & 0 & 6 & 3 \\
1 & 3 & 4 & 6 & 1 & 4 & 5 & 1 & 1 & 4 & 3 & 0 \\
6 & 6 & 6 & 0 & 1 & 2 & 1 & 3 & 2 & 6 & 6 & 3 \\
3 & 1 & 1 & 1 & 3 & 0 & 0 & 3 & 3 & 4 & 2 & 5 \\
6 & 2 & 4 & 2 & 0 & 2 & 1 & 1 & 0 & 1 & 0 & 4 \\
5 & 4 & 5 & 1 & 0 & 1 & 0 & 0 & 4 & 4 & 0 & 6 \\
2 & 0 & 1 & 3 & 3 & 1 & 0 & 3 & 1 & 4 & 1 & 5 \\
2 & 0 & 1 & 2 & 3 & 0 & 4 & 1 & 0 & 0 & 0 & 0 \\
0 & 0 & 4 & 6 & 4 & 1 & 4 & 4 & 0 & 5 & 5 & 2 \\
1 & 6 & 3 & 6 & 2 & 0 & 0 & 1 & 0 & 5 & 4 & 1 \\
6 & 3 & 0 & 3 & 5 & 4 & 6 & 5 & 0 & 2 & 1 & 3
\end{bmatrix},$$

$$P_3 = \begin{bmatrix}
4 & 0 & 3 & 1 & 2 & 4 & 5 & 2 & 4 & 0 & 1 & 2 \\
0 & 3 & 1 & 6 & 5 & 0 & 1 & 3 & 0 & 3 & 1 & 4 \\
3 & 1 & 2 & 4 & 6 & 4 & 2 & 3 & 3 & 2 & 1 & 1 \\
1 & 6 & 4 & 6 & 1 & 4 & 3 & 3 & 3 & 6 & 5 & 1 \\
2 & 5 & 6 & 1 & 3 & 1 & 2 & 6 & 6 & 0 & 4 & 0 \\
4 & 0 & 4 & 4 & 1 & 6 & 5 & 6 & 0 & 0 & 0 & 1 \\
5 & 1 & 2 & 3 & 2 & 5 & 2 & 5 & 2 & 5 & 3 & 4 \\
2 & 3 & 3 & 3 & 6 & 6 & 5 & 1 & 0 & 2 & 1 & 6 \\
4 & 0 & 3 & 3 & 6 & 0 & 2 & 0 & 1 & 0 & 4 & 4 \\
0 & 3 & 2 & 6 & 0 & 0 & 5 & 2 & 0 & 1 & 5 & 6 \\
1 & 1 & 1 & 5 & 4 & 0 & 3 & 1 & 4 & 5 & 0 & 2 \\
2 & 4 & 1 & 1 & 0 & 1 & 4 & 6 & 4 & 6 & 2 & 2
\end{bmatrix}, P_4 = \begin{bmatrix}
5 & 2 & 4 & 3 & 4 & 6 & 5 & 6 & 4 & 1 & 0 & 0 \\
2 & 5 & 5 & 5 & 3 & 4 & 3 & 5 & 0 & 4 & 5 & 2 \\
4 & 5 & 6 & 5 & 0 & 0 & 6 & 6 & 4 & 2 & 6 & 4 \\
3 & 5 & 5 & 5 & 4 & 6 & 2 & 3 & 6 & 2 & 4 & 4 \\
4 & 3 & 0 & 4 & 3 & 1 & 2 & 1 & 0 & 5 & 0 & 2 \\
6 & 4 & 0 & 6 & 1 & 2 & 3 & 0 & 5 & 2 & 2 & 3 \\
5 & 3 & 6 & 2 & 2 & 3 & 1 & 6 & 2 & 1 & 0 & 1 \\
6 & 5 & 6 & 3 & 1 & 0 & 6 & 2 & 3 & 6 & 1 & 0 \\
4 & 0 & 4 & 6 & 0 & 5 & 2 & 3 & 6 & 6 & 4 & 5 \\
1 & 4 & 2 & 2 & 5 & 2 & 1 & 6 & 6 & 5 & 5 & 1 \\
0 & 5 & 6 & 4 & 0 & 2 & 0 & 1 & 4 & 5 & 4 & 2 \\
0 & 2 & 4 & 4 & 2 & 3 & 1 & 0 & 5 & 1 & 2 & 3
\end{bmatrix}.$$

Finally, we choose input and output transformations U and T and derive the above public key.

We now demonstrate the inversion process for the public key. Given the ciphertext

$$\mathbf{y} = \begin{bmatrix} 3 & 2 & 2 & 5 \end{bmatrix},$$

we first randomly select the nonzero vector of auxiliary variables

$$\mathbf{w} = \begin{bmatrix} 6 & 3 \end{bmatrix}.$$

Then evaluating $\widetilde{F}$ at $\mathbf{w}$ we obtain the STS central map $\widetilde{F}(\cdot, \mathbf{w})$:

$$y_1 = 6x_1^2,$$
$$y_2 = 6x_1^2 + 3x_1x_2,$$
$$y_3 = 3x_1^2 + 5x_1x_2 + 6x_2^2 + 4x_1x_3 + 2x_3^2,$$
$$y_4 = 4x_1^2 + 4x_1x_2 + 2x_1x_3 + 2x_2x_3 + 2x_1x_4 + x_2x_4 + 6x_3x_4 + x_4^2.$$

We then compute $\mathbf{yT}^{-1} = \begin{bmatrix} 5 & 2 & 2 & 3 \end{bmatrix}$ and find the preimage under the above STS map:

$$\mathbf{u} = \begin{bmatrix} 3 & 2 & 5 & 6 \end{bmatrix}.$$

Next, we append

$$\mathbf{u} \otimes \mathbf{w} = \begin{bmatrix} 4 & 2 & 5 & 6 & 2 & 1 & 1 & 4 \end{bmatrix}$$

to $\mathbf{u}$. Finally we compute the plaintext

$$\mathbf{x} = (\mathbf{u} \oplus (\mathbf{u} \otimes \mathbf{w}))\, U^{-1} = \begin{bmatrix} 1 & 5 & 4 & 2 & 0 & 3 & 2 & 1 & 5 & 6 & 1 & 4 \end{bmatrix}.$$

We check that, indeed, $P(\mathbf{x}) = \mathbf{y}$.

References

1. Casanova, A., Faugère, J.-C., Macario-Rat, G., Patarin, J., Perret, L., Ryckeghem, J.: GeMSS: a great multivariate short signature. Technical report, National Institute of Standards and Technology. https://csrc.nist.gov/CSRC/media/Projects/post-quantum-cryptography/documents/round-3/submissions/GeMSS-Round3.zip
2. Bardet, M., et al.: Improvements of algebraic attacks for solving the rank decoding and MinRank problems. In: Moriai, S., Wang, H. (eds.) ASIACRYPT 2020. LNCS, vol. 12491, pp. 507–536. Springer, Cham (2020). https://doi.org/10.1007/978-3-030-64837-4_17
3. Bettale, L., Faugère, J.-C., Perret, L.: Cryptanalysis of HFE, multi-HFE and variants for odd and even characteristic. Des. Codes Cryptography **69**(1), 1–52 (2013)
4. Beullens, W.: Improved cryptanalysis of UOV and rainbow. IACR Cryptol. ePrint Arch. 2020:1343 (2020)
5. Billet, O., Macario-Rat, G.: Cryptanalysis of the square cryptosystems. In: Matsui, M. (ed.) ASIACRYPT 2009. LNCS, vol. 5912, pp. 451–468. Springer, Heidelberg (2009). https://doi.org/10.1007/978-3-642-10366-7_27
6. Bosma, W., Cannon, J., Playout, C.: The magma algebra system i: the user language. J. Symb. Comput. **24**(3–4), 235–265 (1997)
7. Cartor, R., Smith-Tone, D.: EFLASH: a new multivariate encryption scheme. In: Cid, C., Jacobson, M.J., Jr. (eds.) SAC 2018. LNCS, vol. 11349, pp. 281–299. Springer, Cham (2018). https://doi.org/10.1007/978-3-030-10970-7_13

8. Cartor, R., Smith-Tone, D.: All in the c* family. Des. Codes Cryptogr. **88**(6), 1023–1036 (2020)

9. Chen, M.-S., Yang, B.-Y., Smith-Tone, D.: Pflash - secure asymmetric signatures on smart cards. Lightweight Cryptography Workshop 2015 (2015). http://csrc.nist.gov/groups/ST/lwc-workshop2015/papers/session3-smith-tone-paper.pdf

10. Clough, C., Baena, J., Ding, J., Yang, B.-Y., Chen, M.: Square, a new multivariate encryption scheme. In: Fischlin, M. (ed.) CT-RSA 2009. LNCS, vol. 5473, pp. 252–264. Springer, Heidelberg (2009). https://doi.org/10.1007/978-3-642-00862-7_17

11. International Community. Nist pqc-forum (email forum). Google Groups (2021). https://groups.google.com/a/list.nist.gov/g/pqc-forum

12. Courtois, N., Klimov, A., Patarin, J., Shamir, A.: Efficient algorithms for solving overdefined systems of multivariate polynomial equations. In: Preneel, B. (ed.) EUROCRYPT 2000. LNCS, vol. 1807, pp. 392–407. Springer, Heidelberg (2000). https://doi.org/10.1007/3-540-45539-6_27

13. Ding, J.: A new variant of the Matsumoto-Imai cryptosystem through perturbation. In: Bao, F., Deng, R., Zhou, J. (eds.) PKC 2004. LNCS, vol. 2947, pp. 305–318. Springer, Heidelberg (2004). https://doi.org/10.1007/978-3-540-24632-9_22

14. Dubois, V., Fouque, P.-A., Shamir, A., Stern, J.: Practical cryptanalysis of SFLASH. In: Menezes, A. (ed.) CRYPTO 2007. LNCS, vol. 4622, pp. 1–12. Springer, Heidelberg (2007). https://doi.org/10.1007/978-3-540-74143-5_1

15. Faugere, J.C.: A new efficient algorithm for computing grobner bases (f4). J. Pure Appl. Algebra **139**, 61–88 (1999)

16. Fouque, P.-A., Granboulan, L., Stern, J.: Differential cryptanalysis for multivariate schemes. In: Cramer, R. (ed.) EUROCRYPT 2005. LNCS, vol. 3494, pp. 341–353. Springer, Heidelberg (2005). https://doi.org/10.1007/11426639_20

17. Gotaishi, M., Tsujii, S.: Hidden pair of bijection signature scheme. Cryptology ePrint Archive, Report 2011/353 (2011). http://eprint.iacr.org/

18. Goubin, L., Courtois, N.T.: Cryptanalysis of the TTM cryptosystem. In: Okamoto, T. (ed.) ASIACRYPT 2000. LNCS, vol. 1976, pp. 44–57. Springer, Heidelberg (2000). https://doi.org/10.1007/3-540-44448-3_4

19. Cryptographic Technology Group. Submission requirements and evaluation criteria for the post-quantum cryptography standardization process. NIST CSRC (2016). http://csrc.nist.gov/groups/ST/post-quantum-crypto/documents/call-for-proposals-final-dec-2016.pdf

20. NIST Cryptographic Technology Group. Post quantum cryptography standardization (website) (2021). https://csrc.nist.gov/projects/post-quantum-cryptography/post-quantum-cryptography-standardization

21. Ding, J., et al.: Rainbow. Technical report, National Institute of Standards and Technology (2020). https://csrc.nist.gov/CSRC/media/Projects/post-quantum-cryptography/documents/round-3/submissions/Rainbow-Round3.zip

22. Kasahara, M., Sakai, R.: A construction of public-key cryptosystem based on singular simultaneous equations. IEICE Trans. **88**–**A**(1), 74–80 (2005)

23. Kipnis, A., Patarin, J., Goubin, L.: Unbalanced oil and vinegar signature schemes. In: Stern, J. (ed.) EUROCRYPT 1999. LNCS, vol. 1592, pp. 206–222. Springer, Heidelberg (1999). https://doi.org/10.1007/3-540-48910-X_15

24. Kipnis, A., Shamir, A.: Cryptanalysis of the HFE public key cryptosystem by relinearization. In: Wiener, M. (ed.) CRYPTO 1999. LNCS, vol. 1666, pp. 19–30. Springer, Heidelberg (1999). https://doi.org/10.1007/3-540-48405-1_2

25. Matsumoto, T., Imai, H.: Public quadratic polynomial-tuples for efficient signature-verification and message-encryption. In: Barstow, D., et al. (eds.) EUROCRYPT 1988. LNCS, vol. 330, pp. 419–453. Springer, Heidelberg (1988). https://doi.org/10.1007/3-540-45961-8_39

26. National Institute of Standards and Technology: NISTIR 8309: Status Report on the Second Round of the NIST Post-Quantum Cryptography Standardization Process. NIST (2020). https://doi.org/10.6028/NIST.IR.8309

27. Patarin, J.: Cryptanalysis of the Matsumoto and Imai public key scheme of Eurocrypt'88. In: Coppersmith, D. (ed.) CRYPTO 1995. LNCS, vol. 963, pp. 248–261. Springer, Heidelberg (1995). https://doi.org/10.1007/3-540-44750-4_20

28. Patarin, J., Courtois, N., Goubin, L.: QUARTZ, 128-Bit long digital signatures. In: Naccache, D. (ed.) CT-RSA 2001. LNCS, vol. 2020, pp. 282–297. Springer, Heidelberg (2001). https://doi.org/10.1007/3-540-45353-9_21

29. Patarin, J., Goubin, L., Courtois, N.: [C_* and HM: variations around two schemes of T. Matsumoto and H. Imai]. In: Ohta, K., Pei, D. (eds.) ASIACRYPT 1998. LNCS, vol. 1514, pp. 35–50. Springer, Heidelberg (1998). https://doi.org/10.1007/3-540-49649-1_4

30. Perlner, R.A., Smith-Tone, D.: Rainbow band separation is better than we thought. IACR Cryptol. ePrint Arch. 2020:702 (2020)

31. Sakumoto, K., Shirai, T., Hiwatari, H.: On provable security of UOV and HFE signature schemes against chosen-message attack. In: Yang, B.-Y. (ed.) PQCrypto 2011. LNCS, vol. 7071, pp. 68–82. Springer, Heidelberg (2011). https://doi.org/10.1007/978-3-642-25405-5_5

32. Shamir, A.: Efficient signature schemes based on birational permutations. In: Stinson, D.R. (ed.) CRYPTO 1993. LNCS, vol. 773, pp. 1–12. Springer, Heidelberg (1994). https://doi.org/10.1007/3-540-48329-2_1

33. Shor, P.W.: Polynomial-time algorithms for prime factorization and discrete logarithms on a quantum computer. SIAM J. Sci. Stat. Comput. **26**, 1484 (1997)

34. Smith-Tone, D.: On the differential security of multivariate public key cryptosystems. In: Yang, B.-Y. (ed.) PQCrypto 2011. LNCS, vol. 7071, pp. 130–142. Springer, Heidelberg (2011). https://doi.org/10.1007/978-3-642-25405-5_9

35. Smith-Tone, D.: Practical cryptanalysis of k-ary C^*. In: Ding, J., Tillich, J.-P. (eds.) PQCrypto 2020. LNCS, vol. 12100, pp. 360–380. Springer, Cham (2020). https://doi.org/10.1007/978-3-030-44223-1_20

36. Smith-Tone, D., Tone, C.: A multivariate cryptosystem inspired by random linear codes. Finite Fields Their Appl. **69**, 101778 (2021)

37. Tadaki, K., Tsujii, S.: Two-sided multiplications are reduced to one-sided multiplication in linear piece in hand matrix methods. In: Proceedings of the International Symposium on Information Theory and its Applications, ISITA 2010, Taichung, Taiwan, 17–20 October 2010, pp. 900–904. IEEE (2010)

38. Tao, C., Petzoldt, A., Ding, J.: Improved key recovery of the hfev- signature scheme. IACR Cryptol. ePrint Arch. 2020:1424 (2020)

39. Thomae, E., Wolf, C.: Solving underdetermined systems of multivariate quadratic equations revisited. In: Fischlin, M., Buchmann, J., Manulis, M. (eds.) PKC 2012. LNCS, vol. 7293, pp. 156–171. Springer, Heidelberg (2012). https://doi.org/10.1007/978-3-642-30057-8_10

40. Prest, T., et al.: FALCON: fast-fourier lattice-based compact signatures over NTRU. Technical report, National Institute of Standards and Technology (2020). https://csrc.nist.gov/CSRC/media/Projects/post-quantum-cryptography/documents/round-3/submissions/Falcon-Round3.zip

41. Tsujii, S., Gotaishi, M., Tadaki, K., Fujita, R.: Proposal of a signature scheme based on STS trapdoor. In: Sendrier, N. (ed.) PQCrypto 2010. LNCS, vol. 6061, pp. 201–217. Springer, Heidelberg (2010). https://doi.org/10.1007/978-3-642-12929-2_15

42. Tsujii, S., Itoh, T., Fujioka, A., Kurosawa, K., Matsumoto, T.: A public-key cryptosystem based on the difficulty of solving a system of nonlinear equations. Syst. Comput. Jpn. **19**(2), 10–18 (1988)

43. Lyubashevsky, V., et al.: CRYSTALS-Dilithium. Technical report, National Institute of Standards and Technology (2020). https://csrc.nist.gov/CSRC/media/Projects/post-quantum-cryptography/documents/round-3/submissions/Dilithium-Round3.zip

44. Wolf, C., Braeken, A., Preneel, B.: Efficient cryptanalysis of RSE(2)PKC and RSSE(2)PKC. In: Blundo, C., Cimato, S. (eds.) SCN 2004. LNCS, vol. 3352, pp. 294–309. Springer, Heidelberg (2005). https://doi.org/10.1007/978-3-540-30598-9_21

45. Wolf, C., Preneel, B.: Equivalent keys in multivariate quadratic public key systems. J. Math. Cryptol. **4**(4), 375–415 (2011)

46. Yang, B.-Y., Chen, J.-M., Courtois, N.T.: On asymptotic security estimates in XL and Gröbner bases-related algebraic cryptanalysis. In: Lopez, J., Qing, S., Okamoto, E. (eds.) ICICS 2004. LNCS, vol. 3269, pp. 401–413. Springer, Heidelberg (2004). https://doi.org/10.1007/978-3-540-30191-2_31

On the Effect of Projection on Rank Attacks in Multivariate Cryptography

Morten Øygarden[1](✉), Daniel Smith-Tone[2,3], and Javier Verbel[4]

[1] Simula UiB, Bergen, Norway
morten.oygarden@simula.no
[2] National Institute of Standards and Technology, Gaithersburg, USA
daniel.smith@nist.gov
[3] University of Louisville, Louisville, USA
[4] Cryptography Research Centre, Technology Innovation Institute, Abu Dhabi, UAE
javier.verbel@tii.ae

Abstract. The multivariate scheme HFEv- used to be considered a promising candidate for a post-quantum signature system. First suggested in the early 2000s, a version of the scheme made it to the third round of the ongoing NIST post-quantum standardization process. In late 2020, the system suffered from an efficient rank attack due to Tao, Petzoldt, and Ding. In this paper, we inspect how this recent rank attack is affected by the projection modification. This modification was introduced to secure the signature scheme PFLASH against its predecessor's attacks. We prove upper bounds for the rank of projected HFEv- (pHFEv-) and PFLASH under the new attack, which are tight for the experiments we have performed. We conclude that projection could be a useful tool in protecting against this recent cryptanalysis.

Keywords: Post-quantum cryptography · Multivariate cryptography · Minrank

1 Introduction

Multivariate cryptography has received increased attention over the last years, due to its potential of providing quantum–safe public key cryptosystems. Signature schemes based on these ideas seemed particularly promising, with one finalist, Rainbow [12], and one alternate candidate, GeMSS [8], reaching the third and current round of the NIST post–quantum standardization process. Recently, new attacks have been presented against both of these candidates [3,24]. The rank attack against GeMSS seems particularly effective, breaking all the suggested parameters for this scheme.

A similar story took place over a decade ago, when the signature scheme SFLASH was broken [14]. In the aftermath, it was discovered that this attack can be avoided by projecting the input space [13], and the amended scheme, PFLASH

J. H. Cheon and J.-P. Tillich (Eds.): PQCrypto 2021, LNCS 12841, pp. 98–113, 2021.
https://doi.org/10.1007/978-3-030-81293-5_6

[9], has withstood cryptanalysis up until this point. In this article, we study the effect of projection on the new rank attack from [24], with a particular interest in the setting of HFEv- (the core of the GeMSS scheme), and PFLASH. After briefly describing the schemes and the attack, we prove that the attack also applies to PFLASH, breaking all of the proposed parameters. We then provide upper bounds for the rank in both the setting of HFEv- and PFLASH. We test the validity of these results through experiments, before concluding with a discussion on possible secure parameters and the impact these changes have on signing time.

Notation. For readability, we use the following notational conventions throughout the article. $\mathbb{F}_q^{n_1 \times n_2}$ will denote the space of matrices of size $n_1 \times n_2$ over $\mathbb{F}_q$, and matrices will be written in **bold**. Row (resp. column) entries in matrices will be written as an integer modulo n_1 (resp. n_2). For two matrices $\mathbf{A}$ and $\mathbf{B}$, we let $\mathbf{A}|\mathbf{B}$ denote their horizontal concatenation, and $\mathbf{A} \oplus \mathbf{B} = \begin{bmatrix} \mathbf{A} & \mathbf{0} \\ \mathbf{0} & \mathbf{B} \end{bmatrix}$ is the direct sum. Maps over $\mathbb{F}_q$ will be written using capital letters, while maps over extension fields, $\mathbb{F}_{q^n}$, will be written with lowercase letters.

2   Big Field Cryptosystems

We start by describing a general big field cryptosystem, with the vinegar, minus and projection modifiers. Let q be the power of a prime, n a positive integer, and fix an isomorphism $\phi : \mathbb{F}_q^n \to \mathbb{F}_{q^n}$. Define $\psi = \phi \times \mathrm{id}_v : \mathbb{F}_q^{n+v} \to \mathbb{F}_{q^n} \times \mathbb{F}_q^v$, where $\psi = \phi$ if $v = 0$. A quadratic central map is chosen of the form $F = \phi^{-1} \circ f \circ \psi : \mathbb{F}_q^{n+v} \to \mathbb{F}_q^n$, where f is specifically chosen in a way such that it is efficient to find preimages of it. Choose a linear map $U = (S \oplus \mathrm{id}_v) \circ U' : \mathbb{F}_q^{n+v-p} \to \mathbb{F}_q^{n+v}$, where both $S : \mathbb{F}_q^{n-p} \to \mathbb{F}_q^n$ and $U' : \mathbb{F}_q^{n+v-p} \to \mathbb{F}_q^{n+v-p}$ are linear maps of full rank. Let $T : \mathbb{F}_q^n \to \mathbb{F}_q^{n-a}$ be a linear map of full rank. Then the public key is created as the composition $P = T \circ F \circ U : \mathbb{F}_q^{n+v-p} \to \mathbb{F}_q^{n-a}$. Figure 1 gives an overview of the construction. We will say that the scheme uses the minus modification if $a > 0$, the vinegar modification if $v > 0$, and the projection modification if $p > 0$.

HFEv-. The signature scheme HFEv- is based on the HFE central map proposed in [21]. It inspired two submissions to the NIST post–quantum standardization process: GeMSS [8] and Gui [11], where the former advanced to the third

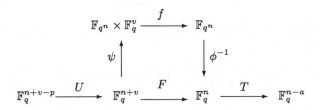

Fig. 1. Diagram of a general big field scheme with minus, vinegar and projection modifiers.

round as an alternate candidate. Fix a positive integer D, and denote the vinegar variables by $\mathbf{x_v} = (x_{n+1}, \ldots, x_{n+v})$. The central map is constructed from a polynomial f of the form

$$f_{hfe}(X, \mathbf{x_v}) = \sum_{\substack{i,j \in \mathbb{N} \\ q^i + q^j \leq D}} \alpha_{i,j} X^{q^i + q^j} + \sum_{\substack{i \in \mathbb{N} \\ q^i \leq D}} \beta_i(\mathbf{x_v}) X^{q^i} + \gamma(\mathbf{x_v}),$$

where $\alpha_{i,j} \in \mathbb{F}_{q^n}$, the β_i's are linear maps $\mathbb{F}_q^v \to \mathbb{F}_{q^n}$, and γ is a quadratic map $\mathbb{F}_q^v \to \mathbb{F}_{q^n}$. The rank attack introduced in [24], which we will recall in the next section, breaks GeMSS with the proposed parameters for the third round of the NIST Standardization process [8].

PFLASH. The signature scheme PFLASH [9,13] is based on the C^* cryptosystem [18], and it uses the projection and minus modifiers. Since there are no vinegar modifiers, we will simply write $U = S$ for the input map. For an integer $0 < \theta < n - 1$, the central map is based on the monomial $f_{C^*} = X^{1+q^\theta}$, which is a bijection when $\gcd(q^\theta + 1, q^n - 1) = 1$. In this case, f_{C^*} can be inverted by exponentiation. With the secret key, one can also compute bilinear relations of inputs and outputs of the central map [20], which can be used to find preimages of the public key, as used in [7]. We also refer to [6] for more information on the security of PFLASH.

3   New Rank Attack

In this section, we briefly recall the new rank attack against HFEv-, that was introduced in [24]. More information about the underlying constructions can also be found in [2]. For simplicity, we consider $\mathbb{F}_q$ to be a field of odd characteristic in this section, but note that the results generalize to even fields as well (see e.g., Sect. 6.3 in [2]). In particular, the results in later sections will also hold in the binary case. Recall that $\mathbf{x_v} = (x_{n+1}, \ldots, x_{n+v})$ denotes the vinegar variables, and that all matrix entries are counted modulo n. For $X \in \mathbb{F}_{q^n}[X]$ we will write $\underline{X} = (X, X^q, \ldots, X^{q^{n-1}})$.

Proposition 1 ([24]). *Let f_{hfe} be an HFEv- polynomial over $\mathbb{F}_{q^n}$. Then,*

$$f_{hfe}(\underline{X}, \mathbf{x_v}) = (\underline{X}, \mathbf{x_v}) \begin{bmatrix} \mathbf{A} & \mathbf{B} \\ \mathbf{B}^\top & \mathbf{D} \end{bmatrix} (\underline{X}, \mathbf{x_v})^\top,$$

where $\mathbf{A} = [\alpha_{i,j}] \in \mathbb{F}_{q^n}^{n \times n}$, $\mathbf{B} = [\beta_{i,j}] \in \mathbb{F}_{q^n}^{n \times v}$ and $\mathbf{D} = [\delta_{i,j}] \in \mathbb{F}_{q^n}^{v \times v}$. Also, for each $0 \leq k < n$

$$(f_{hfe}(\underline{X}, \mathbf{x_v}))^{q^k} = (\underline{X}, \mathbf{x_v}) \mathbf{F}^{*k} (\underline{X}, \mathbf{x_v})^\top,$$

where $\mathbf{F}^{*k} \in \mathbb{F}_{q^n}^{(n+v) \times (n+v)}$ *and its* (i,j)-*coordinate is given by*

$$
\begin{cases}
\alpha_{i-k,j-k}^{q^k} & if\ 0 \le i,j < n-1 \\
\beta_{i-n,j-k}^{q^k} & if\ n \le i < n+v\ and\ 0 \le j < n \\
\beta_{i-k,j-n}^{q^k} & if\ n \le j < n+v\ and\ 0 \le i < n \\
\delta_{i-n,j-n}^{q^k} & otherwise.
\end{cases}
$$

Let $\mathbf{M} \in \mathbb{F}_{q^n}^{n \times n}$ be an invertible matrix associated with a vector basis of $\mathbb{F}_{q^n}$ over $\mathbb{F}_q$ (see Proposition 2 [2]), and let us consider an HFEv- public key $(P_1, \ldots, P_{n-a}) = T \circ F \circ U$. If $\mathbf{P}_i$ is the symmetric matrix such that $P_i(\mathbf{x}) = \mathbf{x} \mathbf{P}_i \mathbf{x}^\top$, then we have

$$
(\mathbf{x}\mathbf{P}_1\mathbf{x}^\top, \ldots, \mathbf{x}\mathbf{P}_{n-a}\mathbf{x}^\top) = (\mathbf{x}\mathbf{W}\mathbf{F}^{*0}\mathbf{W}^\top\mathbf{x}^\top, \ldots, \mathbf{x}\mathbf{W}\mathbf{F}^{*(n-1)}\mathbf{W}^\top\mathbf{x}^\top)\mathbf{M}^{-1}\mathbf{T},
$$

where $\mathbf{W} = \mathbf{U}\tilde{\mathbf{M}}$ and $\tilde{\mathbf{M}} = \mathbf{M} \oplus \mathbf{I}_v$. By symmetry we have the following matrix equation

$$
(\mathbf{P}_1 | \cdots | \mathbf{P}_{n-a}) = \left(\mathbf{W}\mathbf{F}^{*0}\mathbf{W}^\top | \cdots | \mathbf{W}\mathbf{F}^{*(n-1)}\mathbf{W}^\top\right)\left(\mathbf{M}^{-1}\mathbf{T} \otimes \mathbf{I}_{n+v}\right). \qquad (1)
$$

For any vector $\mathbf{u} \in \mathbb{F}_{q^n}^{n+v}$, we define

$$
\mathbf{u}\mathbf{F}^* := \begin{bmatrix} \mathbf{u}\mathbf{F}^{*0} \\ \vdots \\ \mathbf{u}\mathbf{F}^{*(n-1)} \end{bmatrix} \in \mathbb{F}_{q^n}^{n \times (n+v)}, \text{ and } \mathbf{u}\mathbf{P}^* := \begin{bmatrix} \mathbf{u}\mathbf{P}_1 \\ \vdots \\ \mathbf{u}\mathbf{P}_{n-a} \end{bmatrix} \in \mathbb{F}_{q^n}^{(n-a) \times (n+v)}.
$$

Notice that if the central map of the given public key $(P_1, \ldots, P_{n-a})$ has univariate degree at most D, then

$$
\mathrm{rank}\,(\mathbf{e}\mathbf{F}^*) \le \lceil \log_q(D) \rceil,
$$

where $\mathbf{e} \in \mathbb{F}_{q^n}^{n+v}$ is any vector of weight one. Since $p = 0$, $\mathbf{W}$ is nonsingular, and by Eq. (1), we have

$$
\mathrm{rank}\,(\mathbf{u}\mathbf{P}^*) \le \lceil \log_q(D) \rceil,
$$

where $\mathbf{u} = \mathbf{e}\mathbf{W}^{-1}$. In [24] the authors find such a vector $\mathbf{u}$ by solving an instance of the MinRank problem with $n + v$ matrices in $\mathbb{F}_q^{(n-a) \times (n+v)}$ and target rank $\lceil \log_q(D) \rceil$. Furthermore, [24] shows how this vector $\mathbf{u}$ can be used to recover an equivalent key for $(P_1, \ldots, P_{n-a})$. That is, to find linear maps T', U' and a HFEv- central map F' of degree at most D, such that

$$
(P_1, \ldots, P_{n-a}) = T' \circ F' \circ U'.
$$

The complexity of this attack is dominated by performing the MinRank step to recover $\mathbf{u}$. This computation in turn relies heavily on the rank of $\mathbf{u}\mathbf{P}^*$, which will be our primary focus in the next sections.

4   Effect of Projection on the New Rank Attack

We now turn our attention to how the projection modification affects the recently introduced rank attack that was described in the previous section. The first thing to notice is that the invertibility of the input transformation S is required to justify the rank bound. Thus, one may wonder whether the projection modifier masks the rank property just as it was shown to protect PFLASH from the attack on SFLASH, see [14, 22].

Despite the similarities between the HFE and C^* central maps, we find that there are subtle differences in how projection affects the different schemes. As a result, we consider the two settings separately in the following subsections.

4.1   Projection and the HFE Central Map

We adopt an approach dual to that of [25], where removing equations was shown to be equivalent to increasing the degree of the central map. Specifically, we prove that projection is equivalent to increasing the degree of the central map. Thus pHFEv- with degree bound D and projection p is an instance of HFEv- with degree bound $q^p D$.

For any $\mathbb{F}_q$-subspace K of $\mathbb{F}_{q^n}$ there exists a linear polynomial of the form

$$\min_K(X) = \prod_{\alpha \in K} (X - \alpha),$$

having K as its kernel. This polynomial is also known as the minimal polynomial of K, see [10]. We start by showing the following result.

Lemma 1. *There is a bijective correspondence between k-dimensional subspaces of $\mathbb{F}_{q^n}$ and $(n - k)$-dimensional subspaces of $\mathbb{F}_{q^n}$ given by*

$$W \mapsto Im(\min_W(X)).$$

Proof. Let $\mathcal{V}_k$ be the collection of k-dimensional subspaces of $\mathbb{F}_{q^n}$. Define the map $\psi_k : \mathcal{V}_k \to \mathcal{V}_{n-k}$ by $\psi(W) = Im(\min_W(X)) = W'$. Note that since $\min_W(X)$ has kernel of dimension k, and is $\mathbb{F}_q$–linear, the space W' will have dimension $n - k$, and ψ_k is thus well–defined. Moreover, $\min_{W'}(\min_W(X)) = 0$, and by degree considerations we have, more exactly, $\min_{W'}(\min_W(X)) = X^{q^n} - X$.

Suppose that

$$\min_W(X) = \sum_{i=0}^{k} \alpha_i X^{q^i} \quad \text{and} \quad \min_{W'}(X) = \sum_{i=0}^{n-k} \beta_i X^{q^i}.$$

Then we observe that the composition is

$$\min_{W'} \circ \min_W(X) = \sum_{i=0}^{n-k} \sum_{j=0}^{k} \alpha_j^{q^i} \beta_i X^{q^{i+j}}$$

$$= \sum_{r=0}^{n} \left(\sum_{\substack{0 \leq i \leq n-k \\ 0 \leq j \leq k, \ j+i=r}} \alpha_j^{q^i} \beta_i \right) X^{q^r} = X^{q^n} - X. \tag{2}$$

Recalling that $\alpha_k = \beta_{n-k} = 1$, we find that this relation produces a system of n bilinear equations in the $k-1$ coefficients α_j and the $n-k-1$ coefficients β_i. Now fix a space W' in the image of ψ_k, and let β_i be the fixed, associated constants of $\min_{W'}(X)$. Ordering the equations from $r = n-1$ to $r = 0$, we may sequentially solve for α_j. In fact, other than the Frobenius powers applied to the α_j values, the system is triangular, and hence uniquely solvable (see Appendix A for a small toy example of this). Thus, ψ_k is injective. Since the action of taking the orthogonal complement twice yields the original space, the number of subspaces of dimension k and of dimension $n-k$ are equal. It follows that ψ_k is also surjective, and hence a bijection.

Now let S be a linear map[1] $\mathbb{F}_q^n \to \mathbb{F}_q^n$ with kernel of dimension p. Using Lemma 1, we choose π to be the unique minimal polynomial such that $\phi^{-1}(Im(\pi)) = Im(S)$. Note that π has degree q^p. Then we have an exact sequence

$$\mathbb{F}_q^n \xrightarrow{\phi^{-1} \circ \pi \circ \phi} Im(S) \to 0.$$

Since $\mathbb{F}_q$-vector spaces are free (and therefore projective) $\mathbb{F}_q$-modules, there exists an S' such that the following diagram commutes:

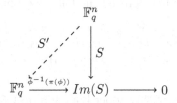

If S' is singular, then its rank is at least $n-p$, and its kernel is then contained in the kernel of S. If necessary, we can replace S' with a nonsingular linear map by redefining its value on $ker(S')$ to map into $ker(\phi^{-1} \circ \pi \circ \phi)$. We may then without loss of generality choose S' to be of full rank. Thus, we obtain the matrix equation $\mathbf{S} = \mathbf{S}'\mathbf{Q}$, where $\mathbf{x}\mathbf{Q} = \phi^{-1} \circ \pi \circ \phi(\mathbf{x})$.

We may now apply this result in the case of an HFEv- scheme. In this case, we have the public key

$$[\mathbf{P}_1| \cdots |\mathbf{P}_{n-a}] = \left[\mathbf{U}\widetilde{\mathbf{M}}\mathbf{F}^{*0}\widetilde{\mathbf{M}}^\top\mathbf{U}^\top| \cdots |\mathbf{U}\widetilde{\mathbf{M}}\mathbf{F}^{*(n-1)}\widetilde{\mathbf{M}}^\top\mathbf{U}^\top\right](\mathbf{M}^{-1}\mathbf{T} \otimes \mathbf{I}_n),$$

where $\widetilde{\mathbf{M}} = \mathbf{M} \oplus \mathbf{I}_v$ and $\mathbf{U} = \mathbf{U}'(\mathbf{S} \oplus \mathbf{I}_v)^2$. We observe that

$$\widetilde{\mathbf{U}}\widetilde{\mathbf{M}}\mathbf{F}^{*i}\widetilde{\mathbf{M}}^\top\widetilde{\mathbf{U}}^\top = \mathbf{U}'(\mathbf{S} \oplus \mathbf{I}_v)\widetilde{\mathbf{M}}\mathbf{F}^{*i}\widetilde{\mathbf{M}}^\top(\mathbf{S}^\top \oplus \mathbf{I}_v)\mathbf{U}'^\top$$

$$= \mathbf{U}'(\mathbf{S}'\mathbf{Q} \oplus \mathbf{I}_v)\widetilde{\mathbf{M}}\mathbf{F}^{*i}\widetilde{\mathbf{M}}^\top(\mathbf{Q}^\top\mathbf{S}'^\top \oplus \mathbf{I}_v)\mathbf{U}'^\top$$

$$= \mathbf{U}'(\mathbf{S}'\mathbf{Q}\mathbf{M} \oplus \mathbf{I}_v)\mathbf{F}^{*i}(\mathbf{M}^\top\mathbf{Q}^\top\mathbf{S}'^\top \oplus \mathbf{I}_v)\mathbf{U}'^\top$$

---

[1] This is a slight abuse of notation from the S defined in Sect. 2, which had $\mathbb{F}_q^{n-p}$ as its domain. This is easily remedied by composing with a projection along the $n-p$ first coordinates.

[2] Following our slight abuse of notation when compared with Sect. 2: U' will now be an invertible linear map $\mathbb{F}_q^{n+v} \to \mathbb{F}_q^{n+v}$.

We may further rewrite the last expression to obtain

$$\mathbf{U}'(\mathbf{S}'\mathbf{M} \oplus \mathbf{I}_v)(\mathbf{M}^{-1}\mathbf{Q}\mathbf{M} \oplus \mathbf{I}_v)\mathbf{F}^{*i}(\mathbf{M}^\top\mathbf{Q}^\top\mathbf{M}^{-\top} \oplus \mathbf{I}_v)(\mathbf{M}^\top\mathbf{S}'^\top \oplus \mathbf{I}_v)\mathbf{U}'^\top$$

We finally note that

$$\mathbf{X}(\mathbf{M}^{-1}\mathbf{Q}\mathbf{M} \oplus \mathbf{I}_v)\mathbf{F}^{*i}(\mathbf{M}^\top\mathbf{Q}^\top\mathbf{M}^{-\top} \oplus \mathbf{I}_v)\mathbf{X}^\top = \mathbf{X}\mathbf{G}^{*i}\mathbf{X}^\top,$$

where $\mathbf{X} = \begin{bmatrix} X \ X^q \cdots X^{q^{n-1}} \ x_1 \cdots x_v \end{bmatrix}$ and where

$$G(X, x_1, \ldots, x_v) = F(\pi(X), x_1, \ldots, x_v).$$

Thus the public key can also be expressed as

$$[\mathbf{P}_1| \cdots |\mathbf{P}_{n-a}] = \left[\mathbf{U}''\widetilde{\mathbf{M}}\mathbf{G}^{*0}\widetilde{\mathbf{M}}^\top\mathbf{U}''^\top| \cdots |\mathbf{U}''\widetilde{\mathbf{M}}\mathbf{G}^{*(n-1)}\widetilde{\mathbf{M}}^\top\mathbf{U}''^\top\right] (\mathbf{M}^{-1}\mathbf{T} \otimes \mathbf{I}_n),$$

where $\mathbf{U}''$ is the nonsingular map $\mathbf{U}'(\mathbf{S}' \oplus \mathbf{I}_v)$. Thus, the pHFEv-$(n, D, a, v, p)$ public key is also an HFEv-$(n, q^p D, a, v)$ public key.

This allows us to follow the same reasoning used in the attack of HFEv- with degree $D = q^{p+d}$, and we have proved the following upper bound.

Proposition 2. *Let* $(\mathbf{P}_1, \ldots, \mathbf{P}_{n-a})$ *be the symmetric matrices of the public key of an instance of pHFEv-(n, D, a, v, p), where p is the projection corank. Then there is a non–zero tuple $\mathbf{u} \in \mathbb{F}_{q^n}^{n-p}$ such that $\mathbf{u}\mathbf{P}^*$ has rank at most $p + d$, where $d = \lceil \log_q D \rceil$.*

We will test the tightness of this upper bound in Sect. 5.

4.2 Projection and the C^* Central Map

Define the symmetric matrix $\mathbf{F}_{C^*}^{*i}$, associated with $f_{C^*}^{q^i}$, in a manner similar to Proposition 1. Describing $\mathbf{F}_{C^*}^{*i}$ is simpler than what was done in Proposition 1, seeing that it is 1 at the entries $(i, \theta+i)$ and $(\theta+i, i)$, and 0 elsewhere (recall that entries are counted modulo n). While we may apply the theory from Sect. 4.1, the problem is that we no longer have a bound D on the non–zero part of $\mathbf{F}_{C^*}^{*0}$. Following the same reasoning as before would have yielded an upper bound of $2 + 2p$ for the rank, but it is possible to do better.

We define $\mathbf{v} = (v_0, \ldots, v_{n-1}) = \mathbf{u}\mathbf{S}\mathbf{M} \in \mathbb{F}_{q^n}^n$, and examine what rank the matrix $\mathbf{v}\mathbf{F}_{C^*}^*$ can take. Note that the entry v_i, for $i \in \mathbb{Z}_n$, will contribute to the two entries in positions

$$e_1(i) = (i, i + \theta) \quad \text{and} \quad e_2(i) = (i - \theta, i - \theta), \tag{3}$$

in the matrix $\mathbf{v}\mathbf{F}_{C^*}^*$. Fix an integer i_0, and consider the pair v_{i_0} and $v_{i_0+\theta}$. They will now contribute to four entries in $\mathbf{v}\mathbf{F}_{C^*}^*$, but two of them, $e_1(i_0) = (i_0, i_0 + \theta)$ and $e_2(i_0 + \theta) = (i_0, i_0)$, appear in the same row. It follows that the pair v_{i_0} and $v_{i_0+\theta}$ can only make a contribution of at most three to the rank of $\mathbf{v}\mathbf{F}^*$. This is the key observation for the following result.

Lemma 2. *Let $I = \{i_0, \ldots, i_{k-1}\}$ be a set of k integers in $\mathbb{Z}_n$, such that $i_{j+1} = i_j + \theta$, for $0 \leq j < k - 1$. Consider the vector $\mathbf{v}_I = (v_0, \ldots, v_{n-1})$, where $v_j \in \mathbb{F}_{q^n} \setminus \{0\}$ if $j \in I$, and $v_j = 0$ otherwise. Then $\mathbf{v}_I \mathbf{F}_{C^*}^*$ has rank at most $k + 1$.*

Proof. For $l = 1, 2$, let $E_l(x)$ be the $n \times n$ matrix that is 1 at entry $e_l(x)$ (as defined in (3)), and 0 elsewhere. Then we can write $\mathbf{v}_I \mathbf{F}_{C^*}^*$ as the sum

$$\mathbf{v}_I \mathbf{F}_{C^*}^* = \sum_{j=0}^{k-1} (E_1(i_j) + E_2(i_j)).$$

From the discussion prior to the lemma, we know that $E_1(i_{j_0}) + E_2(i_{j_0+1})$ has rank 1, for $0 \leq j_0 < k - 1$. Hence, $\mathbf{v}_I \mathbf{F}_{C^*}^*$ can be written as the sum of $2k - (k-1)$ matrices of rank 1, which proves the upper bound.

The next step is to look at which of these vectors $\mathbf{v}_I$ we can find in the image of **SM**. This leads to the following upper bound.

Proposition 3. *Let $(\mathbf{P}_1, \ldots, \mathbf{P}_{n-a})$ be the symmetric matrices of the public key of an instance of PFLASH with projection p. Then there is a non–zero tuple $\mathbf{u} \in \mathbb{F}_{q^n}^{n-p}$ such that $\mathbf{u}\mathbf{P}^*$ has rank at most $2 + p$.*

Proof. Let I be as defined in Lemma 2, and consider an associated vector $\mathbf{v}_I$, with the difference that $v_j \in \mathbb{F}_{q^n}$ if $j \in I$ (i.e., allowing 0 in these entries as well). **SM** has cokernel of dimension p, so choosing I of order $p + 1$ will guarantee that there is a non–trivial way to choose the entries in $\mathbf{v}_I$ such that it lies in the image of **SM**. This can seen by performing Gaussian elimination on **SM**, where the entries corresponding to I are being eliminated last. If all v_j for $j \in I$ are non–zero, we are done by Lemma 2. Otherwise, suppose one of them is zero, say $v_{i_l} = 0$. Then we may split I into the two (potentially empty) sets $I_1 = \{i_0, \ldots, i_{l-1}\}$, and $I_2 = \{i_{l+1}, \ldots, i_p\}$. Upon considering the two associated vectors $\mathbf{v}_{I_1}$ and $\mathbf{v}_{I_2}$, we may write $\mathbf{v}_I \mathbf{F}_{C^*}^* = \mathbf{v}_{I_1} \mathbf{F}_{C^*}^* + \mathbf{v}_{I_2} \mathbf{F}_{C^*}^*$. Using Lemma 2 on $\mathbf{v}_{I_1} \mathbf{F}_{C^*}^*$ and $\mathbf{v}_{I_2} \mathbf{F}_{C^*}^*$, along with the fact that $|I_1| + |I_2| = p$ ensures that the rank of $\mathbf{v}_I \mathbf{F}_{C^*}^*$ sums up to at most $p + 2$.

Finally, the cases where several entries v_j, $j \in I$ are zero, are dealt with by induction on this argument.

This upper bound is tight for the experiments we have run for PFLASH; more information can be found in Sect. 5. For now, we note that the integer set I used in the proof of Proposition 3 is not unique, and we can even consider a more general class of sets, than what was discussed in Lemma 2. Indeed, from the entries in (3), we note that the pair v_{i_0} and $v_{i_0+2\theta}$ will in particular contribute to the entries $e_1(i_0) = (i_0, i_0 + \theta)$ and $e_2(i_0 + 2\theta) = (i_0 + \theta, i_0 + \theta)$, each of which lies in the same column. Note that Lemma 2, and the proof of Proposition 3, could easily have been adopted to sets I where the consecutive indices have relative distance 2θ, as opposed to θ. Furthermore, we can use combinations of θ and 2θ for distance, as shown in the following result, which is a direct generalization of Lemma 2. The proof is identical to that of the aforementioned lemma.

Lemma 3. *Let $I = \{i_0, \ldots, i_{k-1}\}$ be a set of k integers in $\mathbb{Z}_n$, such that for $0 \leq j < k - 1$, the difference $i_{j+1} - i_j$ is congruent to either θ or 2θ mod n. Consider the vector $\mathbf{v}_I = (v_0, \ldots, v_{n-1})$, where $v_j \in \mathbb{F}_{q^n} \setminus 0$ if $j \in I$, and $v_j = 0$ otherwise. Then $\mathbf{v}_I \mathbf{F}_{C^*}^*$ has rank at most $k + 1$.*

Number of Solutions for the MinRank Step. Recall that [24] suggests setting $u_0 = 1$, in order to avoid finding multiples of the same solution to the MinRank–step of the attack. Let I a set of the form described in Lemma 3. Note that any such I of order $p + 1$ could have been used to prove Proposition 3. Hence, we expect each choice of I to, in general, correspond to a unique solution u of the MinRank problem of rank $p + 2$. If $\gcd(n, \theta) = 1$, and $2(p + 1) < n$, there are $n2^p$ ways to construct I (2^p combinations of distances θ and 2θ, with n rotations).

We ran a few toy examples to test this theory, by running the MinRank–step for the parameters $q = 2$, $n = 13$, $\theta = 3$, and $p = 1, 2$ and 3. In each test we found all possible solutions $\mathbf{u}$, and inspected the corresponding $\mathbf{v} = \mathbf{uSM}$. In each test the number of solutions were indeed $n2^p$, and the $\mathbf{v}$-vectors corresponded to all the different choices for I.

Weak Choices of n and θ. In special cases, it would be possible to derive a lower upper bound than what was presented in Proposition 3. This can, for instance, happen if the set I from Lemma 3 of order $k \geq 1$ is a loop, in the sense that $i_{k-1} - i_0 \equiv \theta$ or 2θ mod n. This is possible if the following equation has a solution:

$$x\theta + y2\theta \equiv 0 \quad \text{mod } n, \quad x, y \in \mathbb{Z}_{\geq 0}, \text{ and } x + y = k - 1. \tag{4}$$

Solutions for this condition, with low values of k, can be found when the least common multiple of n and θ is small, or equivalently, when $\gcd(n, \theta)$ is large. Indeed, we can observe this effect in the last two rows of the right side of Table 1: in both tests we have $n = 14$ and $p = 4$, but they differ by $\theta = 5$ and 6. In the first case, we have $\gcd(14, 5) = 1$, and we find no solutions $\mathbf{u}$ such that $\mathbf{uP}^*$ has rank 5. In the second case we have $\gcd(14, 6) = 2$, and $x = 1$, $y = 3$ is a solution of (4), with $k = 5$. The resulting effect is that we are able to find solutions of $\mathbf{u}$ such that $\mathbf{uP}^*$ is of rank 5. We include the condition $\gcd(n, \theta) = 1$ in our other PFLASH experiments in order to exclude weak cases like these.

5   Experiments

In the previous section we proved an upper bound on the rank of $\mathbf{uP}^*$, for both pHFEv-, and PFLASH; we will now examine this bound through experiments.

All tests have been performed as follows. After creating the public key P, we construct $\mathbf{uP}^*$ with the indeterminate vector $\mathbf{u}$, where $u_0 = 1$. For rank r, we follow the minors modelling [17], by computing the $(r + 1) \times (r + 1)$ minors of $\mathbf{uP}^*$, and solving the associated polynomial system using the implementation of F_4 [15] in the MAGMA Computer Algebra System[3], see [4]. For efficiency, we did not always include all the minors when computing the Gröbner basis. We chose the rank r to be one less than, or equal, to the upper bound determined in Propositions 2 and 3 for pHFE- and PFLASH, respectively. Red marks that the polynomial system from the minors modelling at this rank was inconsistent, whereas blue indicates that we were able to find solutions. The results are presented in Table 1.

Table 1. Experimentally found rank of $\mathbf{uP}^*$ for various parameters of pHFE- (left) and PFLASH (right). The number X indicates that there are no $\mathbf{u}$ such that $\mathbf{uP}^*$ has rank $\leq X$. The number X means that we were able to find a solution $\mathbf{u}$ yielding $\mathbf{uP}^*$ of rank $\leq X$. See Sect. 4.2 for a discussion on †.

q	n	a	p	D	Upper Bound	Rank of uP*
2	13	0	1	5	4	3, 4
2	13	0	2	5	5	4, 5
2	13	0	3	5	6	5
2	15	0	4	5	7	6
2	13	0	0	9	4	3, 4
2	13	4	1	9	5	4, 5
2	13	4	2	9	6	5, 6
2	17	6	1	9	5	4, 5
2	13	4	0	17	5	4, 5
2	13	4	1	17	6	5, 6
2	13	0	2	17	7	6

q	n	a	p	θ	Upper Bound	Rank of uP*
2	21	0	1	13	3	2, 3
2	21	0	2	13	4	3, 4
4	31	0	1	7	3	2
4	13	0	3	5	5	4, 5
4	25	8	0	11	2	1, 2
4	25	8	1	11	3	2, 3
4	17	5	3	7	5	4, 5
2	15	1	4	7	6	5, 6
2	15	0	5	7	7	6
4	14	4	4	5	6	5
4	14	4	4	6	6†	5

We note that in all our experiments, the upper bound seems to be tight. The notable exception is the last row on the right side of Table 1, where $\gcd(n, \theta) \neq 1$, as discussed in Sect. 4.2. The tests include cases where f_{C^*} is not a permutation, i.e., $\gcd(q^n - 1, q^\theta + 1) \neq 1$, and this does not seem to have an effect on this attack. Finally, the target r and the dimension of $\mathbf{uP}^*$ cannot be too close, in order to ensure that the solutions we find are truly a result of the extension field structure of the scheme. We have chosen to keep $(n - a) > r + 3$ in our experiments. Indeed, in an earlier experiment with pHFE- of parameters $q = 2$, $n = 13$, $a = 4$, $p = 2$ and $D = 17$, we found a unique solution to u at $r = 6$, even though our upper bound is seven here. Upon further inspection, this solution was in the subfield $\mathbb{F}_q$ (as opposed to being in $\mathbb{F}_{q^n}$ proper, which is the case for the other tests), and we have not been able to find such solutions when rerunning the case. Hence, we conclude that this was a "false positive" caused by the small parameters of the test.

6 Complexity

In this section we compute the complexity of signing for pHFEv- and PFLASH. The inversion methods are quite disparate, so, again, we separate the exposition.

---

[3] Any mention of commercial products does not indicate endorsement by NIST.

6.1 PHFEv- Signing

For this subsection we consider the base field $q = 2$. This is what was used in the GeMSS submission, which is what we will use as a baseline for comparing pHFEv-. The most complex step of the inversion of an HFEv- public key lies in the application of the Berlekamp algorithm, see [1], for inverting the central map. In the case of pHFEv-, there is a tension between the complexity of inverting the degree D polynomial and the number, 2^p, of times that the polynomial must be inverted.

As shown in Sect. 4, an instance of pHFEv-(n, D, a, v, p) is also an instance of HFEv-$(n, 2^p D, a, v)$. Thus, we may always invert pHFEv-(n, D, a, v, p) by using the inversion procedure for HFEv-$(n, 2^p D, a, v)$. On the other hand, we may invert the instance of pHFEv- by inverting the central map of degree D, until the preimage lies in the image of the input projection. For each preimage, the probability that it lies in the image of a corank p projection is 2^{-p}. To see which is the better of the two methods, we begin by making the analysis in [8] for the complexity of inversion more tight.

As noted in [8, Theorem 1], the complexity of Berlekamp applied to a polynomial of degree D is $\mathcal{O}\left(M_{2^n}(D)(n + \log_2 D)\log_2 D\right)$, where $M_{2^n}(D)$ is the number of operations in the field $\mathbb{F}_{2^n}$ required to multiply two polynomials of degree D. The well-known formula, see [5], for this quantity

$$M_{2^n}(D) = \mathcal{O}\left(D \log_2 D \log_2 \log_2 D\right)$$

produces a complexity of

$$\mathcal{O}\left(D(\log_2 D)^2 (n + \log_2 D) \log_2 \log_2 D\right).$$

The above quantity only provides the algebraic complexity of polynomial inversion over $\mathbb{F}_{2^n}$. Since each multiplication in $\mathbb{F}_{2^n}$ requires $2n^2 + n$ bit operations, we have that inverting the central map has a bit complexity of

$$\mathcal{O}\left((2n^2 + n)D \log_2(D)^2 (n + \log_2 D) \log_2 \log_2 D\right).$$

Since we are considering values of $\log_2 D$ that are far less than n, we may further simplify to obtain the approximate bit complexity

$$Cn^3 D \log_2(D)^2 \log_2 \log_2 D,$$

for some constant C. We note that $\log_2 \log_2 D$ may be as large as three or four, for the values of D needed to secure against [24]. It is thus a nontrivial factor in this expression.

Since the complexity of inverting pHFEv-(n, D, a, v, p) is 2^p times the complexity of inverting HFEv-(n, D, a, v), it is a factor of

$$\frac{(p + \log_2 D)^2 \log_2(p + \log_2 D)}{\log_2(D)^2 \log_2 \log_2 D}$$

faster than inverting the scheme as an instance of HFEv-$(n, 2^p D, a, v)$.

Thus, securing the parameters of GeMSS while maintaining the array of parameters merely requires applying the projection modifier with a sufficiently large corank p to secure the scheme from the attack of [24]. We should note that projection does have the negative effect of increasing the signature failure rate by a factor of approximately e^{2^p}, but the rate is still $\exp(2^p - 2^{a+v})$ which is negligible for any realistic parameters.

Parameters for pHFEv-. Let $d = \lceil \log_2 D \rceil$. Similar to [24], we use the support minors equations to derive a bilinear system in $n_x + n_y$ variables, where $n_x = n+v$ and $n_y = \binom{n'}{d+p}$, and $n' = \left\lceil \frac{(n+v)(d+p+1)}{n-a} \right\rceil + d + p + 1$. Such a bilinear system is expected to be solved at degree 3. The overall complexity of solving this system is then given by $\mathcal{O}\left((n_x n_y^2 + n_x^2 n_y)^\omega\right)$, where ω is the linear algebra constant.

In Appendix B, Table 2, we consider the third round parameters of GeMSS, and compute the size of the projection that is needed to achieve the required security level.

6.2   PFLASH Signing

For PFLASH, we recommend using the private key to derive the linearization equations proven to exist by Patarin in [20]. With these equations the legitimate user can find a preimage of the public key in one step instead of inverting the input and output transformations and using exponentiation to invert the central map.

As shown in Sect. 4, the rank of $\mathbf{uP}^*$ is $p + 2$. The parameters suggested in [9] had $p = 1$, which makes them vulnerable to the rank attack we have studied. It is, once again, possible to protect against this by increasing the projection. However, the signing time will now be multiplied by a factor q^p, which favours the use of a small ground field, maybe even $q = 2$. In this setting, direct methods may also become an issue. Particularly a generalized version of the analysis presented in [19], perhaps using some of the notions from [26] should be considered. This is, however, beyond the scope of this article, and we leave it as an open question to determine if and how secure and efficient parameters for PFLASH may be chosen.

7   Conclusion

We have studied how projection affects the new rank attack from [24]. For the pHFEv- and PFLASH systems we have derived an upper bound on how the rank grows with the projection p, which in turn can be used to estimate the complexity of the attack as a whole. These bounds were furthermore observed to be tight in experiments.

While projection is a cheap modification for encryption systems, it does increase the signing time for signature schemes, typically by a factor of q for each dimension. Nevertheless, in the HFEv- setting, we note that projecting is a useful alternative to simply increasing the degree D. PFLASH can also be made secure against rank attacks by increasing p, but we believe more analysis on direct attacks are needed before we can suggest potential parameters.

A   Toy Example of Composing Minimal Polynomials

We provide a small toy example of the bilinear system from the proof of Lemma 1. Consider $n = 5$ and $k = 2$. Then, by Equation (2), and recalling $\alpha_2 = \beta_3 = 1$, we have

$$\min_{W'} \circ \min_W(X) = X^{q^5} - X$$

$$= \alpha_0 \beta_0 X + (\beta_0 \alpha_1 + \beta_1 \alpha_0^q) X^q + (\beta_0 + \beta_1 \alpha_1^q + \beta_2 \alpha_0^{q^2}) X^{q^2}$$

$$+ (\beta_1 + \beta_2 \alpha_1^{q^2} + \alpha_0^{q^3}) X^{q^3} + (\alpha_1^{q^3} + \beta_2) X^{q^4} + X^{q^5}.$$

If the β_j's are known constants, we note that α_1 is uniquely determined by the equation $\alpha_1^{q^3} + \beta_2 = 0$. Subsequently, α_0 will be uniquely determined by $\alpha_0^{q^3} + \beta_2 \alpha_1^{q^2} + \beta_1 = 0$.

B   GeMSS Minrank Complexity

In Table 2, we consider the third round parameters of GeMSS, and compute the size of the projection that is needed to achieve the required security level. We do this for two values of ω: $\omega_1 = 2.37$ is the best known asymptotic bound [16], and $\omega_2 = 2.81$ is the more realistic value from Strassen's algorithm [23].

Table 2. Complexity of the MinRank attack from [24] against the GeMSS parameters with projection. The value p_1 (resp. p_2) is the minimum projection needed to achieve security with ω_1 (resp. ω_2), and C_{ω_1} (resp. C_{ω_2}) denotes $\log_2$ of the resulting complexity.

Scheme	(n, v, D, a)	p_1	C_{ω_1}	p_2	C_{ω_2}
GeMSS128	$(174, 12, 513, 12)$	2	136	0	139
BlueGeMSS128	$(175, 14, 129, 13)$	4	140	1	128
RedGeMSS128	$(177, 15, 17, 15)$	6	131	4	128
WhiteGeMSS128	$(175, 12, 513, 12)$	2	136	0	139
CyanGeMSS128	$(177, 13, 129, 14)$	4	140	1	128
MagentaGeMSS128	$(178, 15, 17, 15)$	6	131	4	128
GeMSS192	$(265, 20, 513, 22)$	7	192	5	201
BlueGeMSS192	$(265, 23, 129, 22)$	9	192	7	201
RedGeMSS192	$(266, 25, 17, 23)$	12	192	10	205
WhiteGeMSS192	$(268, 21, 513, 21)$	7	192	5	201
CyanGeMSS192	$(270, 22, 129, 23)$	9	192	7	201
MagentaGeMSS192	$(271, 24, 17, 24)$	12	192	10	205
GeMSS256	$(354, 33, 513, 30)$	14	263	10	267
BlueGeMSS256	$(358, 32, 129, 34)$	16	267	11	256
RedGeMSS256	$(358, 35, 17, 34)$	18	258	14	256
WhiteGeMSS256	$(364, 29, 513, 31)$	14	263	10	263
CyanGeMSS256	$(364, 32, 129, 31)$	16	263	12	263
MagentaGeMSS256	$(366, 33, 17, 33)$	19	263	15	267

References

1. Berlekamp, E.R.: Factoring polynomials over large finite fields. Math. Comput. **24**(111), 713–735 (1970)
2. Bettale, L., Faugère, J.-C., Perret, L.: Cryptanalysis of HFE, multi-HFE and variants for odd and even characteristic. Des. Codes Cryptogr. **69**(1), 1–52 (2013)
3. Beullens, W.: Improved Cryptanalysis of UOV and Rainbow. Cryptology ePrint Archive, Report 2020/1343 (2020). https://eprint.iacr.org/2020/1343
4. Bosma, W., Cannon, J., Playoust, C.: The magma algebra system i: the user language. J. Symb. Comput. **24**(3–4), 235–265 (1997)
5. Cantor, D., Kaltofen, E.: On fast multiplication of polynomials over arbitrary algebras. Acta Informatica **28**, 693–701 (1991)
6. Cartor, R., Smith-Tone, D.: An updated security analysis of PFLASH. In: Lange, T., Takagi, T. (eds.) PQCrypto 2017. LNCS, vol. 10346, pp. 241–254. Springer, Cham (2017). https://doi.org/10.1007/978-3-319-59879-6_14
7. Cartor, R., Smith-Tone, D.: EFLASH: a new multivariate encryption scheme. In: Cid, C., Jacobson, M.J., Jr. (eds.) SAC 2018. LNCS, vol. 11349, pp. 281–299. Springer, Cham (2018). https://doi.org/10.1007/978-3-030-10970-7_13

8. Casanova, A., Faugère, J.-C., Macario-Rat, G., Patarin, J., Perret, L., Ryckeghem, J.: GeMSS: a great multivariate short signature (Round 3 submission). Technical report, National Institute of Standards and Technology (2020). https://csrc.nist.gov/projects/post-quantum-cryptography/round-3-submissions

9. Chen, M.-S., Yang, B.-Y., Smith-Tone, D.: PFLASH-secure asymmetric signatures on smart cards. In: Lightweight Cryptography Workshop (2015)

10. Daniels, T., Smith-Tone, D.: Differential properties of the *HFE* cryptosystem. In: Mosca, M. (ed.) PQCrypto 2014. LNCS, vol. 8772, pp. 59–75. Springer, Cham (2014). https://doi.org/10.1007/978-3-319-11659-4_4

11. Ding, J., Chen, M.-S., Petzoldt, A., Schmidt, D., Yang, B.-Y.: GUI. Technical report, National Institute of Standards and Technology (2017). https://csrc.nist.gov/Projects/post-quantum-cryptography/Round-1-Submissions

12. Ding, J., et al.: Rainbow (round 3 submission). Technical report, National Institute of Standards and Technology (2020). https://csrc.nist.gov/Projects/post-quantum-cryptography/round-3-submissions

13. Ding, J., Dubois, V., Yang, B.-Y., Chen, O.C.-H., Cheng, C.-M.: Could SFLASH be Repaired? In: Aceto, L., et al. (eds.) ICALP 2008. LNCS, vol. 5126, pp. 691–701. Springer, Heidelberg (2008). https://doi.org/10.1007/978-3-540-70583-3_56

14. Dubois, V., Fouque, P.-A., Shamir, A., Stern, J.: Practical cryptanalysis of SFLASH. In: Menezes, A. (ed.) CRYPTO 2007. LNCS, vol. 4622, pp. 1–12. Springer, Heidelberg (2007). https://doi.org/10.1007/978-3-540-74143-5_1

15. Faugère, J.-C.: A new efficient algorithm for computing Gröbner bases (F4). J. Pure and Appl. Algebra **139**(1–3), 61–88 (1999)

16. Le Gall, F.: Powers of tensors and fast matrix multiplication. In: Proceedings of the 39th International Symposium on Symbolic and Algebraic Computation, pp. 296–303 (2014)

17. Faugère, J.-C., Levy-dit-Vehel, F., Perret, L.: Cryptanalysis of MinRank. In: Wagner, D. (ed.) CRYPTO 2008. LNCS, vol. 5157, pp. 280–296. Springer, Heidelberg (2008). https://doi.org/10.1007/978-3-540-85174-5_16

18. Matsumoto, T., Imai, H.: Public quadratic polynomial-tuples for efficient signature-verification and message-encryption. In: Barstow, D., et al. (eds.) EUROCRYPT 1988. LNCS, vol. 330, pp. 419–453. Springer, Heidelberg (1988). https://doi.org/10.1007/3-540-45961-8_39

19. Øygarden, M., Felke, P., Raddum, H., Cid, C.: Cryptanalysis of the multivariate encryption scheme EFLASH. In: Jarecki, S. (ed.) CT-RSA 2020. LNCS, vol. 12006, pp. 85–105. Springer, Cham (2020). https://doi.org/10.1007/978-3-030-40186-3_5

20. Patarin, J.: Cryptanalysis of the Matsumoto and Imai public key scheme of Eurocrypt'88. In: Coppersmith, D. (ed.) CRYPTO 1995. LNCS, vol. 963, pp. 248–261. Springer, Heidelberg (1995). https://doi.org/10.1007/3-540-44750-4_20

21. Patarin, J.: Hidden Fields Equations (HFE) and Isomorphisms of Polynomials (IP): two new families of asymmetric algorithms. In: Maurer, U. (ed.) EUROCRYPT 1996. LNCS, vol. 1070, pp. 33–48. Springer, Heidelberg (1996). https://doi.org/10.1007/3-540-68339-9_4

22. Smith-Tone, D.: Properties of the discrete differential with cryptographic applications. In: Sendrier, N. (ed.) PQCrypto 2010. LNCS, vol. 6061, pp. 1–12. Springer, Heidelberg (2010). https://doi.org/10.1007/978-3-642-12929-2_1

23. Strassen, V.: Gaussian elimination is not optimal. Numerische mathematik **13**(4), 354–356 (1969)

24. Tao, C., Petzoldt, A., Ding, J.: Improved Key Recovery of the HFEv- Signature Scheme. Cryptology ePrint Archive, Report 2020/1424 (2020). https://eprint.iacr.org/2020/1424

25. Vates, J., Smith-Tone, D.: Key recovery attack for all parameters of HFE-. In: Lange, T., Takagi, T. (eds.) PQCrypto 2017. LNCS, vol. 10346, pp. 272–288. Springer, Cham (2017). https://doi.org/10.1007/978-3-319-59879-6_16
26. Øygarden, M., Felke, P., Raddum, H.: Analysis of Multivariate Encryption Schemes: Application to Dob. Cryptology ePrint Archive, Report 2020/1442 (2020). https://eprint.iacr.org/2020/1442

Quantum Algorithms

Quantum Key Search for Ternary LWE

Iggy van Hoof[1], Elena Kirshanova[1,2(✉)] (iD), and Alexander May[1] (iD)

[1] Horst Görtz Institute for IT-Security, Ruhr University Bochum, Bochum, Germany
{iggy.hoof,elena.kirshanova,alex.may}@rub.de
[2] Immanuel Kant Baltic Federal University, Kaliningrad, Russia

Abstract. Ternary LWE, i.e., LWE with coefficients of the secret and the error vectors taken from $\{-1, 0, 1\}$, is a popular choice among NTRU-type cryptosystems and some signatures schemes like BLISS and GLP.

In this work we consider *quantum* combinatorial attacks on ternary LWE. Our algorithms are based on the quantum walk framework of Magniez-Nayak-Roland-Santha. At the heart of our algorithms is a combinatorial tool called *the representation technique* that appears in algorithms for the subset sum problem. This technique can also be applied to ternary LWE resulting in faster attacks. The focus of this work is quantum speed-ups for such representation-based attacks on LWE.

When expressed in terms of the search space $\mathcal{S}$ for LWE keys, the asymptotic complexity of the representation attack drops from $\mathcal{S}^{0.24}$ (classical) down to $\mathcal{S}^{0.19}$ (quantum). This translates into noticeable attack's speed-ups for concrete NTRU instantiations like NTRU-HRSS [CHES'17] and NTRU Prime [SAC'17].

Our algorithms do not undermine current security claims for NTRU or other ternary LWE based schemes, yet they can lay ground for improvements of the combinatorial subroutines inside hybrid attacks on LWE.

Keywords: Small secret LWE · Representations · Quantum random walk

1 Introduction

The Learning with Errors problem (LWE) [Reg03] asks to find the secret vector $s \in \mathbb{Z}_q^n$, given $(A, b = As + e \mod q) \in \mathbb{Z}_q^{m \times n} \times \mathbb{Z}_q^m$, where the A is a matrix with entries taken uniformly at random from $\mathbb{Z}_q$ and e is a short "error" vector. Being an average-case hard problem, LWE is at least as hard as some worst-case problems on lattices [Reg03,SSTX09,LPR10]. That allowed LWE to serve as a foundation to numerous cryptographic schemes [BDK+18,PFH+19,Lyu12,BCLv17], some of which chose to use the secret s and the error e with bounded ℓ_∞−norm.

I. van Hoof and A. May—Funded by DFG under Germany's Excellence Strategy - EXC 2092 CASA - 390781972.

E. Kirshanova—Supported by the "5-100" Russian academic excellence project and the "Young Russian Mathematics" grant.

J. H. Cheon and J.-P. Tillich (Eds.): PQCrypto 2021, LNCS 12841, pp. 117–132, 2021.
https://doi.org/10.1007/978-3-030-81293-5_7

This allows for more efficient constructions and shorter keys. Examples include the famous NTRU cryptosystems [HRSS17, BCLv17] and some efficient signature schemes like [DDLL13, GLP12]. These schemes rely on the hardness of LWE with *ternary* secret and the error, i.e., $s_i, e_i \in \{-1, 0, 1\}$.

The fact that s and e are small does not significantly undermine the security of LWE: there exists a reduction from "standard" LWE to binary secret LWE [BLP+13], yet this reduction loses a $\log(n)$-factor in the secret dimension. On the other hand, there exist attacks that exploit the fact that the secret is small [BG14, KF15], thus impacting, although mildly, the concrete security of such schemes.

Small-secret LWE opens up a path for combinatorial attacks.[1] In this direction, the most prominent attacks were proposed by Odlyzko [HPS98, HGSW03] and Howgrave-Graham [How07], where the authors give a Meet-in-the-Middle attack on NTRU keys. Recently, May in [May21] noticed that these MitM attacks can be significantly improved using the so-called representation technique that originates from attacks on subset sum [HJ10, BCJ11, BBSS20]. In this work, we investigate how the MitM algorithm MEET-LWE from [May21] can be sped up on a quantum computer.

Our Contributions. Building upon the work of May [May21], we

- instantiate representation-based combinatorial algorithms for ternary LWE in the quantum walk framework setting from [MNRS11], thereby using techniques from [BJLM13, HM18],
- study the impact of our quantum algorithms on concrete parameters of NTRU [HRSS17, BCLv17], BLISS(I+II) [DDLL13], and GLP [GLP12], all of which rely on ternary LWE,
- obtain time-memory tradeoffs for our quantum walk based algorithms and show concrete bit complexities of the above schemes when we only have polynomial classical and polynomial quantum memory.

Our quantum walk-based algorithm, called QMEET-LWE, provides (in its optimized instantiation QREP-1) the following asymptotic improvements: for search space size S for ternary LWE key, we improve from roughly $S^{0.24}$ (classically) downto roughly $S^{0.19}$ (quantumly). This translates into considerable speed-ups (by factors in the range $2^{50} - 2^{130}$) for concrete security estimates. We provide such estimates for NTRU-HRSS [HRSS17], NTRU-Prime [BCLv17], signatures BLISS(I+II) [DDLL13], and GLP [GLP12] parameters. For our low-memory quantum algorithms the concrete savings are even larger.

Our estimates are currently inferior to the best quantum lattice-based estimates, thus our analysis does not invalidate the aforementioned schemes' security claims. However, our quantum algorithm, yet being heuristic, relies on *different* rather mild assumptions than the numerous heuristics for lattice-based attacks. Further, we believe that our quantum LWE Key search algorithm QMEET-LWE

---

[1] By 'combinatorial' here we exclude BKW-like algorithms [KF15, GJS15], since these apply only to LWE with $m \gg n$, which is not the case for NTRU-type schemes.

might be used as an improved building block inside more involved algorithms, e.g. for potentially speeding up the so-called Lattice Hybrid attack [How07].

2   Preliminaries

2.1   LWE-keys

In this work, we only consider ternary LWE keys, defined as follows.

Definition 1 (Ternary LWE Key). *An LWE Key consists of three public parameters q, $A \in \mathbb{Z}_q^{m \times n}$, $b \in \mathbb{Z}_q^m$, and two secret parameters $s \in \mathbb{Z}_q^n$ and (error) $e \in \mathbb{Z}_q^m$ that satisfy the identity $As = b + e \mod q$. We call s and e ternary keys if $||s||_\infty = ||e||_\infty = 1$. We denote by $\mathcal{T}^n$ the set of n-dimensional ternary keys.*

Throughout the paper, we only consider ternary keys s, e as well as square A with $m = n$. Practical implications of LWE-based cryptosystems of the NTRU-type [HPS98, GLP12, DDLL13, BCLv17] also limit the number of non-zero entries in the secrets.

Definition 2 (Weight). *Let $s = (s_1, ..., s_n)$ be a vector in $\mathbb{F}^n$. The weight w of this vector s is defined as its Hamming Weight $w = \Sigma_{s_i \neq 0} 1$. Relative to n we also define the relative weight $\omega = w/n$ where $0 \leq \omega \leq 1$. The set of ternary weight-w keys with an even number $w/2$ of ± 1-entries each is denoted by $\mathcal{T}^n(w/2)$. For ease of notation, in the following we omit any roundings.*

   Current security analysis suggests an optimal relative weight in the range $\omega \in [\frac{1}{3}, \frac{2}{3}]$ [HRSS17, BCLv17] with $\omega = \frac{3}{8}$ and $\omega = \frac{1}{2}$ being prominent choices for NTRU-type schemes.
   We approximate the search space $\mathcal{S}$ for ternary key using the following standard formula that holds up to a small polynomial factor of $\frac{1}{\sqrt{n}}$. In general, we omit small polynomial factors throughout this paper.

Lemma 1 (Multinomial approximation). *Let $D = \{d_1, ..., d_k\} \subset \mathbb{Z}_q$ be a digit set of cardinality k. The number of vectors $s \in \mathbb{Z}_q^n \cap D^n$ having exactly $c_i n$ many d_i-entries with $\sum_{i=1}^k c_i = 1$, is*

$$\binom{n}{c_1 n, ..., c_k n} \approx 2^{H(c_1, ..., c_k)n} \text{ with entropy } H(c_1, ..., c_k) = \sum_{i=1}^k c_i \log_2 \left(\frac{1}{c_i}\right).$$

For multinomial coefficients $\binom{n}{c_1 n, ..., c_k n}$ we write $\binom{n}{c_1 n, ..., c_{k-1} n, \cdot}$, where $\cdot$ represents the last term $c_k n = n - c_1 n - ... - c_{k-1} n$. Analogous, we write $H(c_1, ..., c_k)$ more compactly as $H(c_1, ..., c_{k-1}, \cdot)$.

2.2   Quantum Walk

To translate the classical MEET-LWE algorithm to the quantum setting, we utilize the quantum walk framework by Magniez-Nayak-Roland-Santha [MNRS11].

Classical Random Walks. Classical random walks search for a marked vertex in some graph in 3 steps:

1. **Set up** a single explicit vertex v in set up time T_S.
2. **Update** v by walking to a random adjacent vertex $1/\delta$ times, where a single update takes time T_U.
3. **Check** whether the resulting vertex is marked in checking time T_C. If not marked, go back to 2.

Here, the spectral gap δ of the graph tells us how many steps we need to perform, until we can arrive at some (almost) uniformly random vertex that we check. Thus, if an ε-fraction of vertices is marked, we have total time complexity

$$T_{\text{RW}} = T_S + \frac{1}{\varepsilon}\left(T_C + \frac{1}{\delta}T_U\right).$$

Quantum Walks. Rather than walking to a random adjacent vertex, we can walk to a superposition of all adjacent vertices. We need to repeat this only $1/\sqrt{\delta}$ times. And rather than checking whether a vertex is marked, we can change the phase of states with a marked vertex. Repeating this $1/\sqrt{\varepsilon}$ times we measure a marked node within quantum time complexity

$$T_{\text{QW}} = T_S + \frac{1}{\sqrt{\varepsilon}}\left(T_C + \frac{1}{\sqrt{\delta}}\cdot T_U\right). \tag{1}$$

Johnson graphs are useful to minimize update costs.

Definition 3 (Johnson graph). *Let L be a set of size N. For some $r \leq N$, the Johnson graph $J(N, r)$ is an undirected graph $G_J = (V_J, E_J)$ with $|V_J| = \binom{N}{r}$ vertices representing the size-r subsets of L. We have $\{v, v'\} \in E_J$ iff $v, v' \in V_J$ represent subsets S, S' that differ by a single element, i.e. $|S \cap S'| = r - 1$.*

We may combine several Johnson graphs via Cartesian products.

Definition 4. *Given graphs $G_1 = (V_1, E_1), G_2 = (V_2, E_2)$ we define the Cartesian product $G_1 \times G_2 = (V, E)$ as:*

$$V = V_1 \times V_2 = \{v_1 v_2 | v_1 \in V_1, v_2 \in V_2\} \text{ and}$$
$$E = \{v_1 v_2, v_1' v_2' | (v_1 = v_1', (v_2, v_2') \in E_2) \text{ or } ((v_1, v_1') \in E_1, v_2 = v_2')\}.$$

In the Cartesian product of m Johnson graphs two vertices are adjacent iff all m subsets represented by their vertices are equal, except for a single pair of subsets that differs by one element. The spectral gap of the Cartesian product of m Johnson graphs $J^m(N, r) = \bigtimes_{i=1}^{m} J(N, r)$ can be approximated with the following formula due to Kachigar and Tillich [KT17]:

$$\delta(J^m(N, r)) \geq \frac{1}{m}\delta(J(N, r)) = \Omega\left(\frac{1}{r}\right) \text{ for fixed } m. \tag{2}$$

Heuristics on Quantum Random Walks. While classical subroutines may not terminate in expected runtimes, quantum subroutines, such as update costs, must terminate within a given fixed time. This problem has been addressed in [Amb07, Sect. 6] (see also Sect. 5 of [BBSS20]). It has been shown that terminating updates within a polynomial factor of their expected runtime, will not significantly impact final quantum states. Ignoring polynomial factors, this allows us to work in the following *solely using expected costs*.

3   Quantum Meet-LWE - High Level Idea

3.1   Classical Meet-LWE

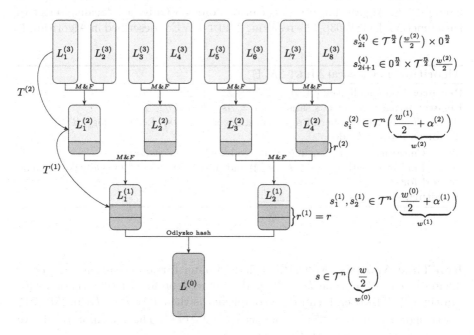

Fig. 1. The classical MEET-LWE algorithm

Let us describe the high-level idea of May's classical MEET-LWE algorithm, see also Fig. 1. Let s be a ternary weight-w LWE secret key with even number of ± 1. Let $w^{(0)} = w/2$, then $s \in \mathcal{T}^n(w^{(0)})$. We write $s = s_1^{(1)} + s_2^{(1)}$ with $s_1^{(1)}, s_2^{(1)} \in T^n(w^{(1)})$, where $w^{(1)} \geq w^{(0)}/2$.

We rewrite the LWE identity $As = b + e \bmod q$ as

$$As_1^{(1)} + e_1 = b - As_1^{(1)} + e_2 \bmod q \text{ for some } e_1, e_2 \in \{0, 1\}^n. \tag{3}$$

In a nutshell, MEET-LWE constructs candidate solutions $s_1^{(1)}, s_2^{(1)}$ that fulfill Eq. (3) on r coordinates. Let $R^{(1)}$ be the number of representations to write s as a sum $s_1^{(1)} + s_2^{(1)}$. Let us set $r = \lfloor \log_q(R^{(1)}) \rfloor$, and fix a random target $t \in \mathbb{Z}_q^r$. We denote by $\pi_r : \mathbb{Z}_q^n \to \mathbb{Z}_q^r$ the projection to the first r coordinates. Then on expectation at least one representation of s satisfies

$$\pi_r(As_1^{(1)} + e_1) = t = \pi_r(b - As_1^{(1)} + e_2) \bmod q. \tag{4}$$

Notice that Equation (4) can be checked if we know $\pi_r(e) \in T^r$, which in turn gives us $\pi_r(e_1)$, $\pi_r(e_2)$. Thus, MEET-LWE involves a guessing step that guesses r coordinates of e.

Eventually, once all candidates $s_1^{(1)} \in L_1^{(1)}$ and $s_2^{(1)} \in L_2^{(1)}$ satisfying Eq. (4) have been constructed, we have to find a pair (s_1, s_2) such that $A(s_1 + s_2) - b \bmod q \in T^n$. Algorithmically, this can be done via Odlyzko's locality sensitive hash function [HGSW03]. The resulting MEET-LWE is described in Algorithm 1.

Algorithm 1. Classical MEET-LWE

Require: LWE public key $(A, b) \in \mathbb{Z}_q^{n \times n} \times \mathbb{Z}_q^n$, weight $w \in \mathbb{N}$
Ensure: ternary weight-w s satisfying $e = As - b \bmod q \in T^n$
1: Let $R^{(1)}$ be the number of representations $s = s_1 + s_2$. Let $r = \lfloor \log_q(R^{(1)}) \rfloor$.
2: **for** all $\pi_r(e) \in T^r$ **do**
3:     Construct $L_1^{(1)}, L_2^{(1)}$ using some tree-based list construction.
4:     Find s_1, s_2 with $s_1 + s_2 \in T^n(w/2)$ and $A(s_1 + s_2) - b \in T^n$ via Odlyzko hashing.
5: **end for**
6: **return** $s = s_1 + s_2$

Run Time Analysis. MEET-LWE has an outer **for**-loop that guesses r coordinates of $e \in T^n$ in time $T_g = 3^r$, and an inner loop for list construction with run time T_ℓ. The overall run time complexity is then $T = T_g + T_\ell$. In [May21], it was shown that $T_\ell = 2^{\Theta(n)}$ whereas $T_g = 2^{\mathcal{O}(\frac{n}{\log n})}$. Thus, asymptotically we may omit the guessing cost T_g.

In the following, we describe how to compute T_ℓ, since this is crucial for the analysis of our MEET-LWE's quantum walk version. The classical run time analysis follows the typical *Match-and-Filter* approach, denoted $M\&F$ in Fig. 1, within the representation technique. Namely, on each level $0 \le j < 3$ of the search tree we filter out all vectors $s_i^{(j)}$ that do not have the correct weight distribution $T^n(w^{(j)})$.

Let $L^{(j)}$ be the expected list size on level j. We show how to compute these values in the next sections. The time to compute each level-3 list is $T^{(3)} = L^{(3)}$.

Define $r^{(3)} = 0$. Then the *Match-and-Filter* approach constructs every level-j list for $j = 1, 2$ in time

$$T^{(j)} = \frac{(L^{(j+1)})^2}{q^{r^{(j)} - r^{(j+1)}}}.$$

Once we have the level-1 lists $L_1^{(1)}, L_2^{(1)}$ we construct the solution via Odlyzko's approximate matching. Since we already exactly matched elements on $r^{(1)} = \lfloor \log_q R^{(1)} \rfloor$ elements, it remains to approximately match on $n - r^{(1)}$ coordinates. This can be done in time

$$T^{(0)} = \frac{(L^{(1)})^2}{2^{n - r^{(1)}}}.$$

The list construction time T_ℓ and memory complexity M is then in total

$$T_\ell = \max\{T^{(0)}, \ldots, T^{(3)}\} \text{ and } M = \max\{L^{(1)}, \ldots, L^{(3)}\}.$$

3.2   Quantum Meet-LWE (QMEET-LWE)

To translate MEET-LWE to a quantum random walk QMEET-LWE we use the same techniques that have been introduced in the context of the subset sum problem [HJ10, BCJ11, BBSS20].

Assume that we have a level-d search tree, see Fig. 1 for an example with $d = 3$. Let $L^{(d)}$ be the size of our level-d list. For a quantum walk, in the setup phase we choose random subsets $U_i^{(d)} \subseteq L_i^{(d)}$ ($i = 1, \ldots, 2^d$), each having $U^{(d)} := (L^{(d)})^\gamma$, $\gamma < 1$ elements. One then simply runs MEET-LWE with the new depth-d lists $U_i^{(d)}$.

Recall that the parameter choice for $L_i^{(d)}$ guarantees on expectation a representation $s = s_1^{(d)} \ldots + s_{2^d}^{(d)}$ that survives all Match-and-Filter steps up to the root list $L^{(0)}$. However, by construction we have $s_i \in U_i^{(d)}$ for all $i = 1, \ldots, 2^d$ only with probability

$$\epsilon = \left(\frac{U^{(d)}}{L^{(d)}} \right)^{2^d} = (L^{(d)})^{(\gamma - 1)2^d}. \tag{5}$$

Let us define $N = L^{(d)}, r = U^{(d)}$. For all lists $L_i^{(d)}$, $i = 1, \ldots, 2^d$, we define their corresponding Johnson graph $J_i(N, r)$. We then perform our random walk on the graph

$$J(N, r) = J_1(N, r) \times \ldots \times J_{2^d}(N, r).$$

Using Eq. 2, the spectral gap of $J(N, r)$ is

$$\delta(J(N, r)) = \Omega\left(\frac{1}{r} \right) = \Omega\left(\frac{1}{U^{(d)}} \right). \tag{6}$$

Let $v \in J(N, r)$ be a node defined by the Cartesian product of the size-r subsets $U_1^{(d)} \times \ldots \times U_{2^d}^{(d)}$. Then we label v with $U_1^{(d)} \times \ldots \times U_{2^d}^{(d)}$. Every node

v contains the complete classical MEET-LWE search tree from Sect. 3.1 build with its label as level-d lists.

We call v *marked* if its corresponding level-0 list $U^{(0)}$ is non-empty, i.e. it contains a representation of s that survived all Match-and-Filter steps and Odlyzko's hash function. Notice that $\Pr[v \text{ is marked}] = \epsilon$. Checking whether a node is marked can be done in time $\mathcal{O}(1)$ and, thus, is asymptotically neglected.

Walking to a neighbor node in $J(N, r)$ implies by the definition of a Johnson graph that we exchange exactly one element in one of the depth-d lists $L_i^{(d)}$. We will detail the *update costs* of updating a MEET-LWE tree by such an exchange in the following section.

4   QREP-0: A First Implementation of QMEET-LWE

Let us instantiate the quantum random walk QMEET-LWE from Sect. 3.2, which in turn uses a variant of the classical MEET-LWE from Sect. 3.1. The latter is first instantiated by chosing tree depth $d = 2$ with optimization parameter $\alpha^{(1)} = 0$. This easiest representation setting is called REP-0 in [May21].

QMEET-LWE's *Setup Cost* T_S. Using $\alpha^{(1)} = 0$, the MEET-LWE level-2 list sizes are $L^{(2)} = \binom{n/2}{w/8, w/8, \cdot}$. For the quantum walk, we choose parameter $\gamma = \frac{4}{5}$. We see in the following that this choice balances quantum walk costs. Thus, we obtain in QMEET-LWE level-2 lists of size

$$U^{(2)} = (L^{(2)})^\gamma = \binom{n/2}{w/8, w/8, \cdot}^\gamma \approx 2^{\frac{2}{5} H(\omega/4, \omega/4, \cdot)n}.$$

We structure the level-2 lists of size $U^{(2)}$ as follows

$$U_1^{(2)} = \{(\pi_r(As_1^{(2)} + e_1), s_1^{(2)}) \mid s_1^{(2)} \in 0^{n/2} \times T^{n/2}(w/8)\},$$
$$U_2^{(2)} = \{(\pi_r(As_2^{(2)} + e_1) \bmod q, s_2^{(2)}) \mid s_2^{(2)} \in T^{n/2}(w/8) \times 0^{n/2}\},$$
$$U_3^{(2)} = \{(\pi_r(b - As_3^{(2)} + e_2), s_3^{(2)}) \mid s_3^{(2)} \in 0^{n/2} \times T^{n/2}(w/8)\},$$
$$U_4^{(2)} = \{(\pi_r(b - As_4^{(2)} + e_2) \bmod q, s_4^{(2)}) \mid s_4^{(2)} \in T^{n/2}(w/8) \times 0^{n/2}\}.$$

On level 1, we obtain $R^{(1)} = \binom{w/2}{w/4}^2 \approx 2^{\omega n}$ representations of $s \in T^n(w/2)$ as sums of the form $s_1^{(1)} + s_2^{(1)}$ with $s_i^{(1)} \in T^n(w/4)$. Let $r = \lfloor \log_q R^{(1)} \rfloor$, and let $t \in T^r$ be our random target vector. Moreover, let ℓ denote Odlyzko's locality sensitive hash function. Then level-1 lists are defined as

$$U_1^{(1)} = \{(\ell(As_1^{(1)}), s_1^{(1)}) \mid (x, s_1^{(1)}) \in U_1^{(2)}, (t - x, s_2^{(2)}) \in U_2^{(2)}, s_1^{(1)} = s_1^{(2)} + s_2^{(2)}\},$$
$$U_2^{(1)} = \{(\ell(b - As_2^{(1)}), s_2^{(1)}) \mid (x, s_3^{(2)}) \in U_3^{(2)}, (t - x, s_4^{(2)}) \in U_4^{(2)}, s_2^{(1)} = s_3^{(2)} + s_4^{(2)}\}.$$

The expected size of level-1 lists is

$$U^{(1)} = \frac{(U^{(2)})^2}{R^{(1)}} \approx 2^{(\frac{4}{5} H(\omega/4, \omega/4, \cdot) - \omega)n}.$$

Finally for layer 0 we obtain the list

$$U_1^{(0)} = \{s = s_1^{(1)} + s_2^{(1)} \in T(w/2) \mid (x, s_1^{(1)}) \in U_1^{(1)}, (x, s_2^{(1)}) \in U_2^{(1)}, As_1^{(1)} = b - As_2^{(1)}\}.$$

The expected size of this list is $U^{(0)} \leq \frac{(U^{(1)})^2}{2^{n-r}} \approx 2^{(\frac{8}{5}H(w/4,w/4,\cdot)-2w-1)n+r}$. In summary, the expected setup cost of QMEET-LWE is

$$T_S = \max\{U^{(2)}, U^{(1)}, U^{(0)}\} = U^{(2)} \text{ for all } w \in \left[\frac{1}{3}, \frac{2}{3}\right]. \tag{7}$$

A node in our Johnson graph is marked if $U^{(0)}$ contains at least one element, which can be checked in time $T_C = \mathcal{O}(1)$.

QMEET-LWE's *Update Cost* T_U. The update algorithm requires us to insert into and delete an element from one of the $U_i^{(2)}$. For example, say we want to exchange an element $s_2^{(2)}$ in $U_2^{(2)}$. The update of $U_2^{(2)}$ can be done in time $\mathcal{O}(1)$.

The update impacts the list $U_1^{(1)}$ below if there are matching $s_1^{(2)}$'s such that $\pi_r(A(s_1^{(2)} + s_2^{(2)}) + e_1) \bmod q = t$. The expected number of those elements is $U^{(2)}/R$, both for deletion and insertion. For the bottom list $U_1^{(0)}$, we expect $U^{(1)}/2^{n-r}$ deletions/insertions for each of the $U^{(2)}/R$ elements. In total, the expected update cost is

$$T_U = \max\left\{1, \frac{U^{(2)}}{R}, \frac{U^{(1)}U^{(2)}}{2^{n-r}R}\right\} = 1 \text{ for all } w \in \left[\frac{1}{3}, \frac{2}{3}\right]. \tag{8}$$

QMEET-LWE *Random Walk Cost.* Plugging Eqs. (2), (5), (7) and (8) into Eq. (1), we obtain a quantum walk runtime of

$$T_\ell \leq T_S + \frac{1}{\sqrt{\varepsilon}}\left(\frac{1}{\sqrt{\delta}} \cdot T_U + T_C\right) = |U^{(2)}| + \left(\frac{L^{(2)}}{U^{(2)}}\right)^2\left(\sqrt{U^{(2)}} \cdot 1 + 1\right)$$

$$= (L^{(2)})^{\frac{4}{5}} + (L^{(2)})^{2-\frac{6}{5}}.$$

Thus, our choice $\gamma = \frac{4}{5}$ balances the setup time T_S with the cost of the random walk until we hit a marked node. Neglecting low order terms, we achieve QMEET-LWE run time

$$(L^{(2)})^{\frac{4}{5}} = \left(\frac{n/2}{w/8, w/8, \cdot}\right)^{\frac{4}{5}} \approx 2^{\frac{2}{5}H(w/4,w/4,\cdot)n}. \tag{9}$$

In Sect. 6, we provide QMEET-LWE's asymptotic costs T_ℓ and non-asymptotic costs $T_g \cdot T_\ell$.

5   QREP-1: Optimized QMEET-LWE

We now optimize the parameters $\alpha^{(i)}$ as well as the tree depth d in QMEET-LWE, and, therefore, also in MEET-LWE. We advise the reader to follow Fig. 1.

As depicted in Fig. 1, we first describe QMEET-LWE in depth $d = 3$, and then provide the necessary adjustments for depth $d = 4$.

As shown in [May21], for MEET-LWE we obtain level-j, $j = 1, 2$, list sizes $L^{(j)} = S^{(j)}/R^{(j)}$ where

$$S^{(j)} = \binom{n}{w^{(j)}, w^{(j)}, \cdot} \text{ and } R^{(j)} = \binom{w^{(j-1)}}{w^{(j-1)}/2}^2 \binom{n - 2w^{(j-1)}}{\alpha_j, \alpha_j, \cdot}.$$

Further, we have level-3 list size $L^{(3)} = \binom{n/2}{w^{(2)}/2, w^{(2)}, \cdot} \approx \sqrt{S^{(2)}}$. We let $r = \lfloor \log_q R^{(1)} \rfloor$.

QMEET-LWE's *Setup Cost T_S*. We choose $\gamma = \frac{8}{9}$ for depth $d = 3$. This yields for QMEET-LWE level-3 list sizes

$$U^{(3)} = (L^{(3)})^\gamma = \binom{n/2}{w^{(2)}/2, w^{(2)}/2, \cdot}^{\frac{8}{9}} \approx 2^{\frac{4}{9} H(\omega^{(2)}/2, \omega^{(2)}/2, \cdot)}.$$

Analogously to Sect. 3.1 and Sect. 4, we obtain in the Match-and-Filter construction expected costs

$$U^{(2)} \leq \frac{(U^{(3)})^2}{R^{(2)}}, U^{(1)} \leq \frac{(U^{(2)})^2 R^{(2)}}{R^{(1)}} \leq \frac{(U^{(3)})^4}{R^{(1)} R^{(2)}}, U^{(0)} \leq \frac{(U^{(1)})^2}{2^{n-r}} \leq \frac{(U^{(3)})^8}{2^{n-r}(R^{(1)} R^{(2)})^2}.$$

Thus, the setup cost can be bounded as

$$T_S \leq \max \left\{ U^{(3)}, \frac{(U^{(3)})^2}{R^{(2)}}, \frac{(U^{(3)})^4}{R^{(1)} R^{(2)}}, \frac{(U^{(3)})^8}{2^{n-r}(R^{(1)} R^{(2)})^2} \right\}.$$

An analysis similar to Sect. 4 yields an update cost of

$$T_U \leq \max \left\{ 1, \frac{U^{(3)}}{R^{(2)}}, \frac{(U^{(3)})^3}{R^{(1)} R^{(2)}}, \frac{(U^{(3)})^7}{2^{n-r}(R^{(1)} R^{(2)})^2} \right\}.$$

QMEET-LWE *Random Walk Cost*. Notice that if we estimate T_S, T_U via their upper bounds, then we obtain the relation $T_S = U^{(3)} T_U$. This helps us to estimate the random walk cost as

$$T_\ell \leq T_S + \frac{1}{\sqrt{\varepsilon}} \left(\frac{1}{\sqrt{\delta}} \cdot T_U + T_C \right) = U^{(3)} T_U + \left(\frac{L^{(3)}}{U^{(3)}} \right)^4 \left(\sqrt{U^{(2)}} \cdot T_U + 1 \right)$$

$$= (L^{(3)})^{\frac{8}{9}} T_U + (L^{(3)})^{4 - \frac{28}{9}} T_U = 2(L^{(3)})^{\frac{8}{9}} T_U. \tag{10}$$

Thus, again our choice of $\gamma = \frac{8}{9}$ balances setup costs with the cost to find a marked node.

QMEET-LWE *level-4 cost*. If we use QMEET-LWE with depth $d = 4$, then a similar analysis yields quantum random walk cost

$$T_\ell \leq (L^{(4)})^{\frac{16}{17}} \cdot T_U \text{ with } L^{(4)} = \binom{n/2}{w^{(3)}/2, w^{(3)}/2, \cdot} \tag{11}$$

and

$$T_U \leq \max \left\{ 1, \frac{U^{(4)}}{R^{(3)}}, \frac{(U^{(4)})^3}{R^{(2)}R^{(3)}}, \frac{(U^{(4)})^7}{R^{(1)}R^{(2)}(R^{(3)})^2}, \frac{(U^{(3)})^{15}}{2^{n-r}(R^{(1)}R^{(2)})^2(R^{(3)})^4} \right\}.$$

Notice that the exponent γ converges to 1 for increasing depth. Thus, QMEET-LWE degrades to MEET-LWE.

6 Quantum Complexity Estimates

Asymptotics. Recall that QMEET-LWE's run time is $T = T_g \cdot T_\ell$, where T_g is the time to guess r coordinates of e, and T_ℓ is the quantum walk time. As mentioned in Sect. 3.1 asymptotically the guessing cost T_g can be neglected.

Thus, here we simply use the formulas for T_ℓ derived for our QREP-0 instantiation in Sect. 4, Eq. (9) and for our QREP-1 instantiation in Sect. 5 for depth 3 in Eq. (10) and for depth 4 in Eq. (11).

The results are given in Table 1 as a function of ω, and asymptotically in n. Here we compare our quantum complexities with a classical instantiation of MEET-LWE with optimized α_i as in Sect. 5, called CREP-1. Let $\mathcal{S}$ denote the size of the search space for the secret LWE key s, and T the complexity of our algorithms for recovering s. Then we give in Talbe 1 the values $\log_{\mathcal{S}} T$. We obtained optimal values for QREP-1 in depth 4 using Eq. (11). The optimization parameters $\zeta_i := \frac{\alpha_i}{n}$ are also provided in Table 1.

Table 1. Improvement in the exponent of the search space of QREP-1.

ω	QREP-0	CREP-1	QREP-1	ζ_1	ζ_2	ζ_3
0.3	0.257	0.238	**0.191**	0.030	0.017	0.005
0.375	0.266	0.243	**0.184**	0.029	0.017	0.005
0.441	0.274	0.237	**0.182**	0.027	0.017	0.005
0.5	0.283	0.235	**0.182**	0.025	0.017	0.005
0.62	0.305	0.243	**0.188**	0.021	0.017	0.005
0.667	0.316	0.244	**0.193**	0.019	0.017	0.005

Notice that whereas MEET-LWE achieves complexities slight below $\mathcal{S}^{\frac{1}{4}}$ its quantum random walk version QMEET-LWE improves these complexity below $\mathcal{S}^{\frac{1}{5}}$. The improvement in the exponent is in the range of 20–25%.

Non-asymptotical Results on Real-World Cryptosystems. For estimating the quantum costs of attacks on real-world cryptosystems we have to take the guessing costs T_g into account. Quantumly, we use amplitude amplification [Gro96,BHMT02] to find r coordinates of a random e in time $T_g = 3^{\frac{r}{2}}$ (Table 2).

Table 2. Bit complexities of QREP-0 in comparison to CREP-0.

	(n, q, w)	CREP-0	QREP-0+GROVER
NTRU-Enc	$(509, 2048, 254)$	$248 = 212 + 36$	$230 = 212 + 18$
	$(677, 2048, 254)$	$377 = 341 + 36$	$254 = 236 + 18$
	$(821, 4096, 510)$	$555 = 488 + 67$	$425 = 391 + 34$
	$(701, 8192, 468)$	$491 = 434 + 57$	$377 = 348 + 29$
NTRU-Prime	$(653, 4621, 288)$	$383 = 346 + 37$	$271 = 252 + 19$
	$(761, 4591, 286)$	$420 = 384 + 36$	$284 = 265 + 19$
	$(857, 5167, 322)$	$479 = 439 + 40$	$322 = 302 + 20$
BLISS I+II	$(512, 12289, 154)$	$257 = 240 + 18$	$174 = 165 + 9$
GLP I	$(512, 8383489, 342)$	$338 = 214 + 24$	$264 = 252 + 12$

QREP-0. Table 3 provides the cost of our QREP-0 attack from Sect. 4 in comparison to the corresponding classical attack CREP-0 for NTRU-type encryption schemes NTRU-HPS [HRSS17] and NTRUPrime [BCLv17], and for signatures BLISS [DDLL13] and GLP [GLP12].

The costs in Table 3 are in bit complexity format in the form $\log_2 T = \log_2 T_\ell + \log_2 T_g$.

Table 3. Bit complexities of QREP-0 in comparison to CREP-0.

	(n, q, w)	CREP-0	QREP-0+GROVER
NTRU-Enc	$(509, 2048, 254)$	$248 = 212 + 36$	$230 = 212 + 18$
	$(677, 2048, 254)$	$377 = 341 + 36$	$254 = 236 + 18$
	$(821, 4096, 510)$	$555 = 488 + 67$	$425 = 391 + 34$
	$(701, 8192, 468)$	$491 = 434 + 57$	$377 = 348 + 29$
NTRU-Prime	$(653, 4621, 288)$	$383 = 346 + 37$	$271 = 252 + 19$
	$(761, 4591, 286)$	$420 = 384 + 36$	$284 = 265 + 19$
	$(857, 5167, 322)$	$479 = 439 + 40$	$322 = 302 + 20$
BLISS I+II	$(512, 12289, 154)$	$257 = 240 + 18$	$174 = 165 + 9$
GLP I	$(512, 8383489, 342)$	$338 = 214 + 24$	$264 = 252 + 12$

Notice that QREP-0 gives large savings compared to CREP-0, often by more than 100 bits. In bit complexity, we save typically around 30%.

QREP-1. For QREP-1 we achieved best results for depth-4 trees (except for BLISS), similar to CREP-1. The results are provided in Table 4, where we also give the optimization parameters $[\alpha_1, \alpha_2, \alpha_3]$.

Table 4. Improvements from QREP-1 in comparison to cREP-1.

	(n, q, w)	cREP-1	$[\alpha]_i$	REP-1+GROVER	$[\alpha]_i$
NTRU-Enc	$(509, 2048, 254)$	$267 = 193 + 74$	$[34, 15, 4]$	$188 = 155 + 33$	$[22, 11, 3]$
	$(677, 2048, 254)$	$313 = 235 + 78$	$[28, 12, 3]$	$223 = 191 + 32$	$[16, 8, 2]$
	$(821, 4096, 510)$	$449 = 336 + 113$	$[44, 20, 4]$	$320 = 268 + 52$	$[32, 16, 4]$
	$(701, 8192, 468)$	$387 = 295 + 92$	$[41, 20, 8]$	$278 = 235 + 43$	$[29, 15, 4]$
NTRU-Prime	$(653, 4621, 288)$	$309 = 236 + 73$	$[28, 12, 2]$	$225 = 190 + 35$	$[24, 12, 3]$
	$(761, 4591, 286)$	$344 = 265 + 79$	$[32, 14, 3]$	$245 = 206 + 39$	$[30, 15, 4]$
	$(857, 5167, 322)$	$383 = 294 + 89$	$[37, 15, 2]$	$274 = 236 + 38$	$[23, 10, 2]$
BLISS I+II	$(512, 12289, 154)$	$206 = 168 + 38$	$[15, 4]$	$149 = 133 + 16$	$[9, 3]$
GLP I	$(512, 8383489, 342)$	$250 = 210 + 40$	$[36, 15, 5]$	$193 = 175 + 18$	$[20, 11, 3]$

We obtain large savings of around 100 bits for the encryption schemes, and over 50 bits for the signature schemes. Although our results are still relatively far from the bit complexities offered by quantum lattice-based attacks (by around a factor of 2, see the estimator from [ACD+18]), our QMEET-LWE might serve as a useful quantum building block to speed up more advanced algorithms.

7   Time-Memory Tradeoffs

If we have a fixed (but still exponential in n) number of qubits, which is smaller than what the optimal runtime needs, we can still instantiate and run the quantum walk but with smaller $U^{(i)}$'s. This will have the following effect on the runtime: the complexity of the setup phase will become smaller, but ε, the probability that a vertex contains a solution, will also decrease. Since the optimal runtime already balances the costs in Eq. 1, lowering the memory will necessarily incur larger runtime. For instance, Fig. 2 shows time-memory tradeoffs for the NTRU-Enc parameter set $(509, 2048, 254)$.

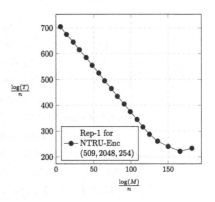

Fig. 2. Time-memory tradeoffs

Turning to the realm of polynomial memory, [May21] shows how to phrase the problem of finding s_1, s_2 that satisfy the MiTM Eq. (3) as a claw-finding problem. Namely, he defines two functions $f_1 : s_1 \mapsto \pi_r(\ell(As_1))$ and $f_2 : s_2 \mapsto \pi_r(\ell(b - As_2))$, where π_r is the projection function defined in Sect. 3.1 and ℓ is Odlyzko's hash function [HGSW03]. The domain of f_1, f_2 is the search space for s_1, s_2 of size $\mathcal{S}$, and the range can be (almost) objectively mapped to a set of ternary vectors of the same size as the domain if we choose $r = \lceil \log_3(\mathcal{S}) \rceil$.

A claw for f_1, f_2 is a pair (s_1, s_2) that gives the correct $s = s_1 + s_2$. Thus the number of claws is the number of representations.

To find a claw classically we use collision-finding algorithms [Niv04, Pol75]. Assuming f_1, f_2 behave like random functions, thus expecting S collisions between them, out of which R collisions are good, we find a good collision in expected time $T_{\text{class}} = \sqrt{S} \cdot S/R$, where $\sqrt{S}$ is the expected time to find any collision. For NTRU, BLISS, and GLP the concrete complexities under this polynomial memory attack are given in Table 5.

Quantumly, the claw-finding problem has been studied in [BDH+05, Tan07]. Most of these works apply quantum random walk technique, resulting in large quantum memory requirement. The work of Buhrman et al. [BDH+05] uses Grover's algorithms allowing for polynomial memory regime. In this regime, the algorithm simply creates a superposition over all (s_1, s_2) and applies Grover's algorithm to find a good pair. The checking function for Grover's routine verifies if $(As_1 - (b - As_2))$ is ternary and the corresponding (s_1, s_2) have the right weight. Since we expect R good pairs in the search space of size S^2, Grover's algorithm outputs a solution in expected time $T_{\text{quant}} = S/\sqrt{R}$. This is a algorithm uses only polynomial classical and quantum memory. The concrete runtimes for NTRU, BLISS, and GLP are given in Table 5.

Table 5. Bit complexities for classical and quantum claw-finding algorithms from Sect. 7 with polynomial classical and quantum memory.

	(n, q, w)	Classical	Quantum
NTRU-Enc	$(509, 2048, 254)$	491	401
	$(677, 2048, 254)$	581	463
	$(821, 4096, 510)$	856	708
	$(701, 8192, 468)$	751	620
NTRU-Prime	$(653, 4621, 288)$	600	486
	$(761, 4591, 286)$	654	521
	$(857, 5167, 322)$	736	586
BLISS I+II	$(512, 12289, 308)$	396	309
GLP I	$(512, 8383489, 342)$	548	453

References

[ACD+18] Albrecht, M.R., Curtis, B.R., Deo, A., Davidson, A., Player, R., Postlethwaite, E.W., Virdia, F., Wunderer, T.: Estimate All the LWE, NTRU Schemes! In: Catalano, D., De Prisco, R. (eds.) SCN 2018. LNCS, vol. 11035, pp. 351–367. Springer, Cham (2018). https://doi.org/10.1007/978-3-319-98113-0_19

[Amb07] Ambainis, A.: Quantum walk algorithm for element distinctness. SIAM J. Comput. **37**(1), 210–239 (2007)

[BBSS20]   Bonnetain, X., Bricout, R., Schrottenloher, A., Shen, Y.: improved classical and quantum algorithms for subset-sum. In: Moriai, S., Wang, H. (eds.) ASIACRYPT 2020. LNCS, vol. 12492, pp. 633–666. Springer, Cham (2020). https://doi.org/10.1007/978-3-030-64834-3_22

[BCJ11]   Becker, A., Coron, J.-S., Joux, A.: Improved generic algorithms for hard knapsacks. In: Paterson, K.G. (ed.) EUROCRYPT 2011. LNCS, vol. 6632, pp. 364–385. Springer, Heidelberg (2011). https://doi.org/10.1007/978-3-642-20465-4_21

[BCLv17]   Bernstein, D.J., Chuengsatiansup, C., Lange, T., van Vredendaal, C.: NTRU prime: reducing attack surface at low cost. In: Adams, C., Camenisch, J. (eds.) SAC 2017. LNCS, vol. 10719, pp. 235–260. Springer, Cham (2018). https://doi.org/10.1007/978-3-319-72565-9_12

[BDH+05]   Buhrman, H., et al.: Quantum algorithms for element distinctness. SIAM J. Comput. **34**(6), 1324–1330 (2005)

[BDK+18]   Bos, W.J., et al.: Crystals - kyber: a CCA-secure module-lattice-based kem. In: EuroS&P, pp. 353–367 (2018)

[BG14]   Bai, S., Galbraith, S.D.: Lattice decoding attacks on binary LWE. In: Susilo, W., Mu, Y. (eds.) ACISP 2014. LNCS, vol. 8544, pp. 322–337. Springer, Cham (2014). https://doi.org/10.1007/978-3-319-08344-5_21

[BHMT02]   Brassard, G., Høyer, P., Mosca, M., Tapp, A.: Quantum amplitude amplification and estimation. Quantum Comput. Inf. **305**, 53–74 (2002). https://doi.org/10.1090/conm/305

[BJLM13]   Bernstein, D.J., Jeffery, S., Lange, T., Meurer, A.: Quantum algorithms for the subset-sum problem. In: Gaborit, P. (ed.) PQCrypto 2013. LNCS, vol. 7932, pp. 16–33. Springer, Heidelberg (2013). https://doi.org/10.1007/978-3-642-38616-9_2

[BLP+13]   Brakerski, Z., Langlois, A., Peikert, C., Regev, O., Stehlé, D.: Classical hardness of learning with errors. In: Boneh, D., Roughgarden, T., Feigenbaum, J. (eds.) 45th ACM STOC. ACM Press, pp. 575–584 (2013)

[DDLL13]   Ducas, L., Durmus, A., Lepoint, T., Lyubashevsky, V.: Lattice Signatures and Bimodal Gaussians. In: Canetti, R., Garay, J.A. (eds.) CRYPTO 2013. LNCS, vol. 8042, pp. 40–56. Springer, Heidelberg (2013). https://doi.org/10.1007/978-3-642-40041-4_3

[GJS15]   Guo, Q., Johansson, T., Stankovski, P.: Coded-BKW: solving LWE using lattice codes. In: Gennaro, R., Robshaw, M. (eds.) CRYPTO 2015. LNCS, vol. 9215, pp. 23–42. Springer, Heidelberg (2015). https://doi.org/10.1007/978-3-662-47989-6_2

[GLP12]   Güneysu, T., Lyubashevsky, V., Pöppelmann, T.: Practical lattice-based cryptography: a signature scheme for embedded systems. In: Prouff, E., Schaumont, P. (eds.) CHES 2012. LNCS, vol. 7428, pp. 530–547. Springer, Heidelberg (2012). https://doi.org/10.1007/978-3-642-33027-8_31

[Gro96]   Grover, L.K.: A fast quantum mechanical algorithm for database search. In: 28th ACM STOC, pp. 212–219. ACM Press (1996)

[HGSW03]   Howgrave-Graham, N., Silverman, J.H., Whyte, W.: A meet-in-the-middle attack on an NTRU private key, Technical report, NTRU Cryptosystems, June 2003. Report (2003)

[HJ10]   Howgrave-Graham, N., Joux, A.: New generic algorithms for hard knapsacks. In: Gilbert, H. (ed.) EUROCRYPT 2010. LNCS, vol. 6110, pp. 235–256. Springer, Heidelberg (2010). https://doi.org/10.1007/978-3-642-13190-5_12

[HM18]   Helm, A., May, A.: Subset sum quantumly in 1.17^n .In: 13th Conference on the Theory of Quantum Computation, Communication and Cryptography (TQC 2018), Leibniz International Proceedings in Informatics (LIPIcs), vol. 111, Schloss Dagstuhl-Leibniz-Zentrum fuer Informatik, pp. 5:1–5:15 (2018)

[How07]   Howgrave-Graham, N.: A hybrid lattice-reduction and meet-in-the-middle attack against NTRU. In: Menezes, A. (ed.) CRYPTO 2007. LNCS, vol. 4622, pp. 150–169. Springer, Heidelberg (2007). https://doi.org/10.1007/978-3-540-74143-5_9

[HPS98]   Hoffstein, J., Pipher, J., Silverman, J.H.: NTRU: a ring-based public key cryptosystem. In: Buhler, J.P. (ed.) International Algorithmic Number Theory Symposium, Springer, vol. 1423, pp. 267–288. Springer, Berlin, Heidelberg (1998). https://doi.org/10.1007/BFb0054868

[HRSS17]   Hülsing, A., Rijneveld, J., Schanck, J., Schwabe, P.: High-speed key encapsulation from NTRU. In: Fischer, W., Homma, N. (eds.) CHES 2017. LNCS, vol. 10529, pp. 232–252. Springer, Cham (2017). https://doi.org/10.1007/978-3-319-66787-4_12

[KF15]   Kirchner, P., Fouque, P.-A.: An improved BKW algorithm for LWE with applications to cryptography and lattices. In: Gennaro, R., Robshaw, M. (eds.) CRYPTO 2015. LNCS, vol. 9215, pp. 43–62. Springer, Heidelberg (2015). https://doi.org/10.1007/978-3-662-47989-6_3

[KT17]   Kachigar, G., Tillich, J.-P.: Quantum information set decoding algorithms. In: Lange, T., Takagi, T. (eds.) PQCrypto 2017. LNCS, vol. 10346, pp. 69–89. Springer, Cham (2017). https://doi.org/10.1007/978-3-319-59879-6_5

[LPR10]   Lyubashevsky, V., Peikert, C., Regev, O.: On ideal lattices and learning with errors over rings. In: Gilbert, H. (ed.) EUROCRYPT 2010. LNCS, vol. 6110, pp. 1–23. Springer, Heidelberg (2010). https://doi.org/10.1007/978-3-642-13190-5_1

[Lyu12]   Lyubashevsky, V.: Lattice signatures without trapdoors. In: Pointcheval, D., Johansson, T. (eds.) EUROCRYPT 2012. LNCS, vol. 7237, pp. 738–755. Springer, Heidelberg (2012). https://doi.org/10.1007/978-3-642-29011-4_43

[May21]   May, A.: How to meet ternary lwe keys, Cryptology ePrint Archive, Report 2021/216 (2021). https://eprint.iacr.org/2021/216

[MNRS11]   Magniez, F., Nayak, A., Roland, J., Santha, M.: Search via quantum walk. SIAM J. Comput. **40**(1), 142–164 (2011)

[Niv04]   Nivasch, G.: Cycle detection using a stack. Inf. Process. Lett. **90**, 135–140 (2004)

[PFH+19]   Prest, T., et al.: Falcon, Technical report, National Institute of Standards and Technology (2019). https://csrc.nist.gov/projects/post-quantum-cryptography/round-2-submissions

[Pol75]   Pollard, J.M.: A Monte Carlo method for factorization. BIT Numer. Math. **15**, 331–334 (1975)

[Reg03]   Regev, O.: New lattice based cryptographic constructions. In: 35th ACM STOC, pp. 407–416. ACM Press (2003)

[SSTX09]   Stehlé, D., Steinfeld, R., Tanaka, K., Xagawa, K.: Efficient public key encryption based on ideal lattices. In: Matsui, M. (ed.) ASIACRYPT 2009. LNCS, vol. 5912, pp. 617–635. Springer, Heidelberg (2009). https://doi.org/10.1007/978-3-642-10366-7_36

[Tan07]   Tani, S.: In improved claw finding algorithm using quantum walk. Math. Found. Comput. Sci. **2007**, 536–547 (2007)

A Fusion Algorithm for Solving the Hidden Shift Problem in Finite Abelian Groups

Wouter Castryck[1,3]([✉]), Ann Dooms[2], Carlo Emerencia[2],
and Alexander Lemmens[1]

[1] imec-COSIC, Department of Electrical Engineering, KU Leuven, Leuven, Belgium
wouter.castryck@esat.kuleuven.be
[2] DIMA, Department of Mathematics and Data Science, VUB, Ixelles, Belgium
[3] Department of Mathematics: Algebra and Geometry, Ghent University,
Ghent, Belgium

Abstract. It follows from a result by Friedl, Ivanyos, Magniez, Santha and Sen from 2014 that, for any fixed integer $m > 0$ (thought of as being small), there exists a quantum algorithm for solving the hidden shift problem in an arbitrary finite abelian group $(G, +)$ with time complexity

$$\text{poly}(\log|G|) \cdot 2^{O(\sqrt{\log|mG|})}.$$

As discussed in the current paper, this can be viewed as a modest statement of Pohlig–Hellman type for hard homogeneous spaces. Our main contribution is a somewhat simpler algorithm achieving the same runtime for $m = 2^t p$, with t any non-negative integer and p any prime number, where additionally the memory requirements are mostly in terms of quantum random access classical memory; indeed, the amount of qubits that need to be stored is $\text{poly}(\log|G|)$. Our central tool is an extension of Peikert's adaptation of Kuperberg's collimation sieve to arbitrary finite abelian groups. This allows for a reduction, in said time, to the hidden shift problem in the quotient $G/2^t pG$, which can then be tackled in polynomial time, by combining methods by Friedl et al. for p-torsion groups and by Bonnetain and Naya-Plasencia for 2^t-torsion groups.

Keywords: Hidden shift · Collimation sieve · Hard homogeneous space

1 Introduction

In 1994 Simon's algorithm [25] laid the basis for Shor's celebrated polynomial-time quantum algorithm [24] for factoring integers and computing discrete logarithms. It is now a standard fact that Shor's algorithm is essentially equivalent to solving the *hidden subgroup problem* in finite abelian groups, which led to investigating this problem for non-abelian groups as well.

© Springer Nature Switzerland AG 2021
J. H. Cheon and J.-P. Tillich (Eds.): PQCrypto 2021, LNCS 12841, pp. 133–153, 2021.
https://doi.org/10.1007/978-3-030-81293-5_8

One of the most famous results in that direction is that of Kuperberg [15] from 2003, who showed that for any finite abelian group G, the hidden subgroup problem in the associated generalized dihedral group $\mathrm{Dih}(G)$ can be tackled in quantum sub-exponential time, namely using

$$2^{O(\sqrt{\log |G|})} \tag{1}$$

operations, i.e., queries and gates. In fact, a more natural description of Kuperberg's algorithm is that it solves the *hidden shift problem* in G (also called the *hidden translation problem*), which can be seen to be equivalent to the hidden subgroup problem in $\mathrm{Dih}(G)$; see [15, §6]. Formally, we define:

Definition 1.1. (Abelian hidden shift problem). *Given a finite abelian group* $(G, +)$*, a set* X*, and oracle access to injective functions* $f_1, f_2 : G \to X$ *for which there exists an* $s \in G$ *such that* $f_1(g) = f_2(g + s)$ *for all* $g \in G$*, find* s*.*

The literature contains versions with non-injective f_1, f_2, see e.g. [12], but these will not be considered here.

Kuperberg's result increased the interest in the hidden shift problem as a stand-alone problem. It gained relevance for public-key cryptography when Childs, Jao and Soukharev [8] tied it to the vectorization problem in hard homogeneous spaces such as CRS [10,23] and CSIDH [4], which is a candidate post-quantum replacement for the discrete logarithm problem. Note that the hidden shift problem also naturally appears as the security primitive of certain symmetric cryptosystems, see e.g. [1].

Unfortunately, Kuperberg's algorithm requires storage of a similar amount of qubits as (1). This was mitigated by Regev [21], who showed how to obtain polynomial space complexity at the expense of a small increase of the runtime. While Regev restricted his attention to cyclic 2-groups, the method generalizes to arbitrary finite abelian groups by recycling parts of Kuperberg's discussion [15, Alg. 5.1, Thm. 7.1]. A detailed elaboration of this can be found in [8, App. A]. In a 2011 follow-up paper [16], Kuperberg described the *collimation sieve*, which reachieves a time and space complexity of (1), but with an important bonus: the main space requirements are in terms of quantum random access *classical* memory (QRACM, also known as QROM), which is cheaper than quantum memory (we refer to [7, App. A.1] and the references therein for details). The amount of qubits that need to be stored in the collimation sieve remains polynomial. Kuperberg provided the details for cyclic 2-groups, while pointing out that the general case again follows along the lines of [15, Alg. 5.1, Thm. 7.1]; see [18, §2.6.3] for some further particulars. Recently, Peikert [19] worked out a "most-significant bits first" variant of the collimation sieve for finite cyclic groups.

There exist, however, special families of groups in which the hidden shift problem becomes much easier. The basic example is where $G \cong \mathbb{Z}_2^r$ for some $r \geq 1$. Indeed, for such groups the associated generalized dihedral group is abelian, allowing Shor's algorithm, which boils down to Simon's method in this case, to recover s in polynomial time. This example can be generalized. For instance, a version of Simon that works for $G \cong \mathbb{Z}_p^r$ for any fixed prime p can be found in a paper by Friedl, Ivanyos, Magniez, Santha and Sen [13, Thm. 3.5]. In a different direction, this was generalized to $G \cong \mathbb{Z}_{2^t}^r$ for any fixed integer $t \geq 1$ by Bonnetain and Naya-Plasencia [2], who did so by incorporating ingredients from Kuperberg's first algorithm.

Contributions. On an algorithmic level, the contributions of this paper are:

(*i*) We extend the method of Bonnetain–Naya-Plasencia from groups of the form $\mathbb{Z}_{2^t}^r$ to arbitrary 2^t-torsion groups, i.e., to groups of the form $\bigoplus_{i=1}^r \mathbb{Z}_{2^{t_i}}$ with $t_i \leq t$ for all i. Moreover, we show how to combine this with the method of Friedl et al., in order to obtain a polynomial-time quantum algorithm for tackling the hidden shift problem in finite abelian $2^t p$-torsion groups.

(*ii*) We work out the details of a collimation sieve for arbitrary finite abelian groups; our method builds on Peikert's "most-significant bits first" variant.

(*iii*) We merge the algorithms from (*i*) and (*ii*). When solving the hidden shift problem in an arbitary finite abelian group G, one can use collimation to produce phase vectors that only involve $2^t p$-torsion characters. At that point, one can switch to the polynomial-time algorithm from (*i*) for finding $s \bmod 2^t pG$. Then a run of algorithm (*ii*) on $2^t pG$ allows one to conclude.

Altogether, this leads to the following theorem:

Theorem 1.2. *For any fixed prime number p and non-negative integer t, there exists a quantum algorithm for solving the hidden shift problem in any finite abelian group $(G, +)$, with time, query and QRACM complexity*

$$\mathrm{poly}(\log |G|) \cdot 2^{O(\sqrt{\log |2^t pG|})}$$

and requiring storage of $\mathrm{poly}(\log |G|)$ qubits.

We note that the runtime part of this statement is not new, although this is somewhat hidden in the quantum physics literature and does not seem well-known among cryptographers. Indeed, an application of [13, Prop. 4.13] to the chain $G \geq 2G \geq \cdots \geq 2^t G \geq 2^t pG \geq \{0\}$, in combination with [13, Prop. 2.2], leads to an algorithm with the same time complexity. In fact, by modifying the chain, one obtains the same result for any positive integer m, rather than just m's of the form $2^t p$. However, our method is somewhat simpler and keeps the key advantage of the collimation sieve, namely that the main memory requirements are in terms of QRACM; only a polynomial number of qubits is needed.

As a consequence, if our finite abelian group G has a large $2^t p$-torsion subgroup for certain small p and t, or more generally a large m-torsion subgroup for a certain small m, then one can essentially discard this subgroup when assessing the hardness of the hidden shift problem. As discussed more extensively in Sect. 2, this observation can be viewed as a modest result of Pohlig–Hellman [20] type for the vectorization problem in arbitrary hard homogeneous spaces. In the specific case of CRS and CSIDH, it was already shown in [5, §5.1] how to get rid of part of the 2-torsion, using very different (classical) methods.

Paper Organization. The implications of Theorem 1.2 and alike for the vectorization problem are discussed more elaborately in Sect. 2. In Sect. 3 we describe our polynomial-time quantum algorithm for solving the hidden shift problem in $2^t p$-torsion groups. Section 4 presents a detailed version of the collimation sieve that works for arbitrary finite abelian groups. Then in Sect. 5 we show how to incorporate the first algorithm in this extended collimation sieve, leading to Theorem 1.2. Finally, in Sect. 6 we give some concluding remarks.

Prerequisites. All algorithms below rely on the *standard approach* for hidden shift finding which, at the cost of calls to f_1, f_2 and a quantum Fourier transform, produces length-two phase vectors, i.e. qubits of the form

$$\Psi(\chi) = \frac{1}{\sqrt{2}}|0\rangle + \frac{1}{\sqrt{2}}\chi(s)|1\rangle, \tag{2}$$

with χ a *known* but uniformly random element of the character group $G^\vee = \{\text{homomorphisms } G \rightarrow \mathbb{C}^*\}$; see e.g. [21, §2.2] for more details. We will treat the standard approach as an oracle in its own right. Beyond this, our discussion is more or less stand-alone, but concise, so some familiarity with prior hidden-shift algorithms is convenient. We refer the reader to [3, 7, 19] for recent accounts.

2 Consequences for the Vectorization Problem

The *vectorization problem* is a generalization of the discrete logarithm problem that was formally introduced by Couveignes [10]. Here, we assume that our finite abelian group G acts freely and transitively on the set X, which means that we are given a map

$$G \times X \rightarrow X : (s, x) \mapsto s \star x$$

such that $0 \star x = x$, $(s_1 + s_2) \star x = s_1 \star (s_2 \star x)$ and $G \rightarrow X : s \mapsto s \star x$ is a bijection for all $s_1, s_2 \in G, x \in X$. Then the vectorization problem is about extracting s from any given pair $x, s \star x$. By considering the maps

$$f_1 : G \rightarrow X : a \mapsto a \star (s \star x), \qquad f_2 : G \rightarrow X : a \mapsto a \star x$$

one sees that this indeed concerns an instance of the hidden shift problem.

An efficient solution to the vectorization problem clearly breaks the Diffie–Hellman style key exchange protocol depicted in Fig. 1. Note that key recovery actually amounts to finding $(s_1 + s_2) \star x$ when given a triple $x, s_1 \star x, s_2 \star x$. This is called the *parallelization problem* which, a priori, could be easier than vectorization, but in the presence of quantum computers, both problems are in fact equivalent [14]. If the vectorization problem and the parallelization problem are hard, then X is called a *hard homogeneous G-space*. In view of Kuperberg's algorithm, we know that quantum computers can solve these problems in time (1). Therefore, the best one can hope is that quantum adversaries cannot do significantly better than this.

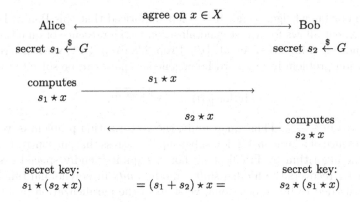

Fig. 1. Diffie–Hellman key exchange in a hard homogeneous G-space X

Example 2.1. Textbook Diffie–Hellman, based on exponentiation in a finite cyclic group H, arises by letting

$$G = \mathbb{Z}_{|H|}^*, \qquad X = \{\text{ generators of } H \}.$$

In this context, the vectorization problem, resp. the parallelization problem, becomes the discrete logarithm problem, resp. the computational Diffie–Hellman problem. Quantum computers break these problems using Shor's algorithm, therefore we focus on classical adversaries, to which both problems are still believed to be equivalent [17]. Then by the well-known Pohlig–Hellman reduction [20], the discrete logarithm problem in H is essentially as hard as that in its largest prime order subgroup. In particular, the discrete logarithm problem is weakened by the presence of many small prime factors in $|H|$. In contrast, assuming that $|H|$ is a large prime, we are unaware of classical exploits of the structure of the acting group $G = \mathbb{Z}_{|H|}^*$.

Example 2.2. The only known instantiation believed to be secure against quantum adversaries is due to Couveignes [10] and Rostovtsev–Stolbunov [23, 27], the fastest version of their construction being CSIDH [4]. Here, $G = \mathrm{Cl}(\mathcal{O})$ is the ideal-class group of an order $\mathcal{O}$ in an imaginary quadratic number field, and

$$X = \{\text{ elliptic curves } E/\mathbb{F}_q \text{ with Frobenius trace } t \text{ and } \mathrm{End}_{\mathbb{F}_q}(E) \cong \mathcal{O} \} / \cong_{\mathbb{F}_q},$$

with $\mathbb{F}_q$ a finite field and t an integer such that X is non-empty. The action is isogeny-wise; see the cited references for details. Using the Tate pairing on elliptic curves it is possible, in *classical* polynomial time, to recover the hidden shift s modulo a certain subgroup H satisfying $2G \le H \le G$; concretely H arises as the joint kernel of the quadratic characters of G that have a polynomially small modulus [5, §5.1]. This can be used to reduce the hidden shift problem in G to that in H, which can be viewed as a modest statement of Pohlig–Hellman type, in the sense that the vectorization problem can be weakened by the presence of a large 2-torsion subgroup.

Up to our knowledge, so far, it was left unnoticed that this Pohlig–Hellman type statement allows for a vast generalization in the presence of quantum computers: indeed, from Friedl et al. [13, Prop. 2.2, Prop. 4.13] we learn that the vectorization problem in any hard homogeneous space can be solved in time

$$\text{poly}(\log |G|) \cdot 2^{O(\sqrt{\log |mG|})},$$

for any fixed $m \in \mathbb{Z}_{>0}$. Thus, quantumly, the vectorization problem is weakened by the presence of a large m-torsion subgroup. We stress that, in contrast with [5], neither the algorithm by Friedl et al. nor our qubit-friendly special case from Theorem 1.2 recovers the hidden shift s modulo mG in polynomial time, which would be needed to break decisional versions of the parallelization problem.

Example 2.3 (continuation of Example 2.2). For $m = 2$ we do not learn much new. In the specific case of CSIDH, one always has $H = 2G$; for CRS it may happen that $H > 2G$, and then the remaining gap can be bridged by our algorithm from Theorem 1.2. Beyond $m = 2$ we obtain further potential security losses; see Example 5.1 for a concrete example. Luckily, class groups of imaginary quadratic orders seem well-protected against these. Indeed, Gerth's extension [11] of the Cohen–Lenstra heuristic [9, §9] predicts that $2G$ has a strong tendency to be cyclic, i.e., it is likely that for all primes p the p-torsion part of $2G$ has rank 0 or 1. More precisely, the "probability" that the p-rank equals r is

$$\approx p^{-r^2} \cdot \prod_{k=1}^{r} (1 - p^{-k})^{-2} \cdot \prod_{k=1}^{\infty} (1 - p^{-k}),$$

which decays very quickly with r. E.g., this yields a chance of about $5.2 \cdot 10^{-31}$ that $2G$ contains a 3-torsion subgroup of rank at least 10. Nevertheless, some extra care may be desirable when setting up CRS or CSIDH using a class group whose structure is unknown.

We end by emphasizing that this section discusses an exploit of the structure of the *acting* group, rather than of a group that is acted upon, as is the case for standard Pohlig–Hellman. We also stress that the full Pohlig–Hellman reduction is a much stronger type of exploit, capable of tackling certain families of large cyclic groups like

$$\prod_{\text{primes } p \leq \log N} \mathbb{Z}_p,$$

which is of size $\approx N$ for any choice of N, in polynomial time. Our reduction cannot achieve this. We note that breaking the vectorization problem for large cyclic groups would be a spectacular result, with dramatic consequences for lattice-based cryptography [22]. As explained in [26, §12], naively porting the standard Pohlig–Hellman algorithm to the group action setting fails for fundamental reasons.

3   Polynomial-Time Hidden Shifts in $2^t p$-torsion Groups

Fix a prime number p and a positive integer t. In this section, we describe a polynomial-time quantum algorithm for solving the hidden shift problem in a finite abelian group $(G, +)$ where every element g satisfies $2^t p g = 0$. This part is heavily inspired by Bonnetain–Naya-Plasencia [2], Csáji [6] and Friedl et al. [13]. We remark that [13] contains results for more general abelian groups of low exponent, but these do not use the standard approach to hidden shift finding, which seems to make them incompatible with the collimation sieve. Without loss of generality we can assume that $p > 2$ and that $G = \mathbb{Z}_p^m \times \mathbb{Z}_{2^{t_1}} \times \cdots \times \mathbb{Z}_{2^{t_n}}$ for certain integers $m, n \geq 0$ and $t = t_1 \geq t_2 \geq \ldots \geq t_n \geq 1$.

Step 3.1. We describe a routine for producing length-two phase vectors $\Psi(\chi)$ such that $\chi^p = 1$. Following Kuperberg [15, §3], two phase vectors $\Psi(\chi_1)$ and $\Psi(\chi_2)$ as in (2) can be combined to yield $\Psi(\chi_1\chi_2)$ or $\Psi(\chi_1\chi_2^{-1})$, each with probability $1/2$. More generally, any $k \geq 2$ phase vectors $\Psi(\chi_1), \ldots, \Psi(\chi_k)$ can be merged into a phase vector of the form

$$\Psi(\chi_1^{\pm 1} \cdots \chi_k^{\pm 1}). \tag{3}$$

We call a phase vector $\Psi(\chi)$ ℓ-*divisible* if $\chi^{2^{t-\ell}p} = 1$. Our routine merges fresh, 0-divisible phase vectors into 1-divisible ones, 1-divisible phase vectors into 2-divisible ones, and so on, until we find t-divisible phase vectors as requested.

For each ℓ, we let r_ℓ denote the largest integer such that $t_1, \ldots, t_{r_\ell} \geq t - \ell$. Consider $r_\ell + 1$ phase vectors $\Psi(\chi_i)$ that are ℓ-divisible. Each χ_i is of the form

$$\chi_i : (g_1, \ldots, g_m, h_1, \ldots, h_n) \mapsto e^{2\pi i \left(\frac{a_{i,1}g_1 + \ldots + a_{i,m}g_m}{p} + \frac{b_{i,1}h_1}{2^{t_1}} + \ldots + \frac{b_{i,n}h_n}{2^{t_n}} \right)}$$

for certain $a_{i,j} \in \mathbb{Z}_p$ and $b_{i,j} \in \mathbb{Z}_{2^{t_j}}$. For all $j \leq r_\ell$ it holds that $2^{\ell+t_j-t}|b_{i,j}$, in view of the ℓ-divisibility. By defining $c_{i,j} = b_{i,j}/2^{\ell+t_j-t} \bmod 2$, we obtain $r_\ell + 1$ vectors $(c_{i,1}, \ldots, c_{i,r_\ell})$ that are necessarily $\mathbb{Z}_2$-linearly dependent. So we can find integers $d_1, \ldots, d_{r_\ell+1} \in \{0,1\}$ such that $d_1 c_{1,j} + \ldots + d_{r_\ell+1}c_{r_\ell+1,j} \equiv 0 \bmod 2$ for $j = 1, \ldots, r_\ell$. We then merge those $\Psi(\chi_i)$'s for which $d_i = 1$, in order to end up with a qubit $\Psi(\chi)$ which, when writing

$$\chi : (g_1, \ldots, g_m, h_1, \ldots, h_n) \mapsto e^{2\pi i \left(\frac{a_{\chi,1}g_1 + \ldots + a_{\chi,m}g_m}{p} + \frac{b_{\chi,1}h_1}{2^{t_1}} + \ldots + \frac{b_{\chi,n}h_n}{2^{t_n}} \right)},$$

has the property that all ratios $b_{\chi,j}/2^{\ell+t_j-t}$ are even. Note that the unpredictable signs in (3) have no influence on this. We conclude that $\Psi(\chi)$ is $(\ell+1)$-divisible.

By pipelining this for $\ell = 0, \ldots, t-1$, we obtain our desired routine. Each output requires at most $(r_0+1)\cdots(r_{t-1}+1)$ fresh phase vectors as input. Note, by the way, that the phase vectors $\Psi(\chi_i)$ for which $d_i = 0$ can be recycled.

Step 3.2. Next, we describe how to use phase vectors $\Psi(\chi)$ with $\chi^p = 1$ for computing the first m components of the hidden shift $s = (s_1, \ldots, s_m, s'_1, \ldots, s'_n)$. We apply the Hadamard transform, yielding $(1 + \chi(s))/2 \, |0\rangle + (1 - \chi(s))/2 \, |1\rangle$, and we measure. Each time we measure 1, we learn that the coefficient $1 - \chi(s)$ cannot be zero, hence $\chi(s) \neq 1$. Since $\chi^p = 1$ we can write

$$\chi : (g_1, \ldots, g_m, h_1, \ldots, h_n) \mapsto e^{\frac{2\pi i}{p}(a_{\chi,1}g_1 + \ldots + a_{\chi,m}g_m)}$$

and thus we see that $a_{\chi,1}s_1 + \ldots + a_{\chi,m}s_m \neq 0$ in $\mathbb{Z}_p$. This implies $(a_{\chi,1}s_1 + \ldots + a_{\chi,m}s_m)^{p-1} = 1$, which gives a linear equation in the monomial expressions of degree $p-1$ in $s_1, \ldots, s_m$. If we never measure 1, then we know that $(s_1, \ldots, s_m) = (0, \ldots, 0)$. In the other case, from [13] we learn that the expected number of tries needed to end up with a full-rank system of linear equations is bounded by

$$p\binom{m+p-2}{p-1} = O(m^{p-1}).$$

This allows us to find the exact values of the degree $p-1$ monomials in $s_1, \ldots, s_m$, from which it is easy to determine the vector $(s_1, \ldots, s_m)$ up to multiplication by an unknown scalar. We are left with $p-1$ options, which can be tested one by one, for instance by transforming $\Psi(\chi)$ into

$$\frac{1}{\sqrt{2}}|0\rangle + \frac{1}{\sqrt{2}}\chi(\tilde{s})^{-1}\chi(s)|1\rangle,$$

for some concrete guess $\tilde{s}$, before feeding it to the Hadamard transform (indeed, if we then measure 1, we know that the $\mathbb{Z}_p^m$-part of the guess is wrong), or simply by proceeding with Step 3.3 by trial and error. An alternative option is to equip G with a dummy $\mathbb{Z}_p$-factor, where the hidden shift has known component $s_0 = 1$.

Step 3.3. Once we know $s_1, \ldots, s_m$, we define

$$f_1'(h_1, \ldots, h_n) = f_1(0, \ldots, 0, h_1, \ldots, h_n),$$
$$f_2'(h_1, \ldots, h_n) = f_2(s_1, \ldots, s_m, h_1, \ldots, h_n).$$

For all $h_1, \ldots, h_n$ we have $f_1'(h_1, \ldots, h_n) = f_2'(h_1 + s_1', \ldots, h_n + s_n')$. Thus we face an instance of the hidden shift problem in $\mathbb{Z}_{2^{t_1}} \times \cdots \times \mathbb{Z}_{2^{t_n}}$. We again use our routine from Step 3.1, but this time, instead of creating t-divisible phase vectors, we make them $(t-1)$-divisible, so that they are of the form $\Psi(\chi)$ where $\chi^2 = 1$. We can use this to find the parity of $s_1', \ldots, s_n'$ in the same way as above, with the bonus that *every* measurement now produces an exact linear equation in the s_i' (in other words, we basically run Simon's algorithm at this stage). This can be used to reduce to the hidden shift problem in a 2^{t-1}-torsion subgroup; an iterative application eventually retrieves all of s.

Complexity. The procedure is summarized in Algorithm 1. Overall we need $O(m^{p-1}r_0 \cdots r_{t-1}) = \text{poly}(\log|G|)$ phase vectors $\Psi(\chi)$ to find s; recall that we view p and t as constants. The corresponding calls to the standard approach dominate the runtime of our algorithm.

Algorithm 1: Finding hidden shifts in finite abelian $2^t p$-torsion groups

Input : $G = \mathbb{Z}_p^m \times \mathbb{Z}_{2^{t_1}} \times \cdots \times \mathbb{Z}_{2^{t_n}}$, with p odd, $t = t_1 \geq t_2 \geq \cdots \geq t_n \geq 1$
Access to phase vectors $\frac{1}{\sqrt{2}}(|0\rangle + \chi(s)|1\rangle)$ for known but uniformly
random $\chi \in G^\vee$ and unknown but fixed $s \in G$

Output: s

1 **for** ℓ *from* 0 *to* t **do**
2   Determine r_ℓ maximal such that $t_{r_\ell} \geq t - \ell$
3 **end**
4 **if** $m > 0$ **then**
5   Call for $(r_0 + 1)(r_1 + 1) \cdots (r_{t-1} + 1)$ phase vectors
6   **for** j *from* 0 *to* $t - 1$ **do**
7   Divide the phase vectors into groups of size $r_j + 1$
8   Create a $(j + 1)$-divisible phase vector from every such group
9   **end**
10   Repeat Steps 5–10 until we can apply Friedl et al. to obtain $s \bmod pG$
11   Apply **Algorithm 1** on $pG \cong \mathbb{Z}_{2^{t_1}} \times \cdots \times \mathbb{Z}_{2^{t_n}}$
12 **else**
13   Call for $(r_0 + 1)(r_1 + 1) \cdots (r_{t-2} + 1)$ phase vectors
14   **for** j *from* 0 *to* $t - 2$ **do**
15   Divide the phase vectors into groups of size $r_j + 1$
16   Create a $(j + 1)$-divisible phase vector from every such group
17   **end**
18   Apply Simon's algorithm to obtain $s \bmod 2G$
19   Apply **Algorithm 1** on $2G \cong \mathbb{Z}_{2^{t_1-1}} \times \cdots \times \mathbb{Z}_{2^{t_n-1}}$
20 **end**

---

4 Collimation for Products of Cyclic Groups

We now describe our version of the collimation sieve for arbitrary finite abelian groups G, obtained by extending Peikert's method from [19]. We start from a chain of strict inclusions $\{1\} = G_0 \leq G_1 \leq \ldots \leq G_M = G^\vee$, where the groups G_i are such that all quotients G_i/G_{i-1} are cyclic, say isomorphic to $\mathbb{Z}_{k_i}$. Throughout, we fix quotient homomorphisms $q_i : G_i \to \mathbb{Z}_{k_i}$ with kernel G_{i-1}. We use these to define a set of subsets of $G^\vee$, which play the role of the intervals in Peikert's algorithm:

$$\mathcal{A} = \{\chi \cdot q_i^{-1}(I) \mid \chi \in G^\vee, i \in \{1, \ldots, M\}, I \text{ is an interval in } \mathbb{Z}_{k_i}\}.$$

Here, by an interval in $\mathbb{Z}_{k_i}$ we mean the reduction mod k_i of a set of the form $\{a, a + 1, \ldots, b\} \subseteq \mathbb{Z}$. Sets of the form $\chi \cdot q_i^{-1}(I)$ are said to be *at level* i. Note that if I is a singleton, then such a set is also at level $i - 1$, since it can be rewritten as $\chi' \cdot q_{i-1}^{-1}(\{0, \ldots, k_{i-1} - 1\})$ for an appropriate $\chi' \in G^\vee$.

The algorithm revolves around handling phase vectors of arbitrary length L, by which we mean quantum states of the form

$$\Psi = \frac{1}{\sqrt{L}} \sum_{j=0}^{L-1} \chi_j(s)|j\rangle.$$

To each such phase vector we attach a support set $A_\Psi \in \mathcal{A}$ that contains all the χ_j appearing in it. The *density* of Ψ is then said to be $\delta(\Psi) = L/|A_\Psi|$. For example, considering fresh length-two phase vectors $\Psi(\chi)$ yielded by the standard approach, and taking $A_{\Psi(\chi)} = G^\vee$, we find the tiny density $2/|G^\vee| = 2/|G|$.

Collimation is a combination-and-measurement process with the goal of producing phase vectors with an increased density. Concretely, two phase vectors

$$\Psi_1 = \frac{1}{\sqrt{L_1}} \sum_{j_1=0}^{L_1-1} \chi_{j_1}(s)|j_1\rangle \quad \text{and} \quad \Psi_2 = \frac{1}{\sqrt{L_2}} \sum_{j_2=0}^{L_2-1} \chi_{j_2}(s)|j_2\rangle$$

with support sets A_{Ψ_1}, A_{Ψ_2} are tensored together, to get

$$\frac{1}{\sqrt{L_1 L_2}} \sum_{j_1=0}^{L_1-1} \sum_{j_2=0}^{L_2-1} (\chi_{j_1} \chi_{j_2})(s)|j_1\rangle|j_2\rangle.$$

We then take a partition of $A_{\Psi_1} + A_{\Psi_2} = \bigsqcup_{\ell=1}^{r} A_\ell$ into many disjoint elements of $\mathcal{A}$. For any j_1, j_2 we define ℓ_{j_1,j_2} to be the unique index ℓ such that $\chi_{j_1}\chi_{j_2} \in A_\ell$. We then compute the ℓ_{j_1,j_2} for all j_1, j_2 in our quantum state:

$$\frac{1}{\sqrt{L_1 L_2}} \sum_{j_1=0}^{L_1-1} \sum_{j_2=0}^{L_2-1} (\chi_{j_1} \chi_{j_2})(s)|j_1, j_2\rangle|\ell_{j_1,j_2}\rangle. \tag{4}$$

Upon measurement of the last register we find a value ℓ, collapsing the state to

$$\frac{1}{\sqrt{L_3}} \sum_{\chi_{j_1}\chi_{j_2} \in A_\ell} (\chi_{j_1} \chi_{j_2})(s)|j_1, j_2\rangle.$$

We then classically compute a list of all (j_1, j_2) satisfying $\chi_{j_1}\chi_{j_2} \in A_\ell$ and compute a bijection from this list to $\{0, \ldots, L_3 - 1\}$, to find a length L_3 phase vector with support set $A_{\Psi_3} = A_\ell$.[1]

In practice, we only combine support sets at the same level i. Thus, after taking out some global phase if needed, we can assume $A_{\Psi_1} = q_i^{-1}(\{0, \ldots, a_1\})$ and $A_{\Psi_2} = q_i^{-1}(\{0, \ldots, a_2\})$, so that $A_{\Psi_1} + A_{\Psi_2} = q_i^{-1}(\{0, \ldots, a_1 + a_2\})$. We then use partitions of the form

$$A_{\Psi_1} + A_{\Psi_2} = \bigsqcup_{\ell=1}^{r} q_i^{-1}(\{b_\ell, \ldots, b_{\ell+1}\}) \qquad (b_1 = 0, b_{r+1} = a_1 + a_2).$$

When the intervals $\{b_\ell, \ldots, b_{\ell+1}\}$ become singletons, one can partition further into sets at level $i - 1$ if wanted, and even beyond; in the end, we will want L_1, L_2 and the size of the partition to be of a comparable size (denoted by L).

---

[1] Note that a support set A_Ψ is not intrinsic to its phase vector Ψ: in principle, it could be any set in $\mathcal{A}$ containing all the χ_j occurring in Ψ. It could therefore be useful to shrink this set after a collimation step, making it as small as possible.

The *quality* of a collimation step combining Ψ_1 and Ψ_2 into Ψ_3 is defined as

$$Q = \delta(\Psi_3)/\sqrt{\delta(\Psi_1)\delta(\Psi_2)}.$$

The number of collimation steps required to obtain phase vectors of density > 1 has a major influence on the time complexity and is determined largely by the quality of the collimation steps. To be more precise, if Q is the average quality of the collimation steps and F is the factor by which the density has to increase, then the number of collimation steps is in $2^{O(\log_Q F)}$. We are interested in the geometric average of the quality, which is $\exp(\mathbb{E}\log Q)$. In Appendix A we prove a lower bound on the expected value of the logarithm of the quality of a collimation step. When applied to Ψ_1 and Ψ_2 from above, it gives

$$\exp(\mathbb{E}\log Q) \geq \sqrt{L_1 L_2}\frac{\sqrt{(a_1+1)(a_2+1)}}{\min(a_1+a_2+1, k_i)}.$$

Since we want this number to be as large as possible, we want the phase vector lengths L_1, L_2 to be as large as possible. The factor $\sqrt{(a_1+1)(a_2+1)}/\min(a_1+a_2+1, k_i)$ is seen to be upper-bounded by 1. If a_1 and a_2 are of similar sizes then this factor is approximately $\frac{a_1+a_2+2}{2\min(a_1+a_2+1,k_i)}$, which is larger than $1/2$. If a_1 and a_2 are of very different sizes then the factor can get close to zero, so we typically want to collimate phase vectors with similar-sized support sets.

Our Algorithm. To find our hidden shift s, we repeatedly call for length-two phase vectors $\Psi(\chi)$ using the standard approach. These can be combined into phase vectors of some power-of-2 length L, by taking tensor products. We then:

Step 4.1. Recursively collimate these low density phase vectors, forming higher density phase vectors, until that density exceeds 1;

Step 4.2. Thin out and regularize the resulting states;

Step 4.3. Either directly apply a Fourier transform, or tensor some of the regular states together and then apply a Fourier transform, so as to learn $q(s)$ for some non-trivial quotient homomorphism q from G;

Step 4.4. Reduce to the hidden shift problem in the subgroup $G' = \ker q$, by choosing $s' \in G$ such that $q(s') = q(s)$, and noticing that the functions

$$f_1' : G' \to X : g \mapsto f_1(g), \qquad f_2' : G' \to X : g \mapsto f_2(g+s')$$

hide the shift $s' - s \in G'$.

We then repeat until all of s is found. We discuss Steps 4.2–4.3 in more detail:

Step 4.2. In view of the *coupon collector's problem*, when the density of a length L phase vector Ψ exceeds 1 by a big enough factor, it is likely that every $\chi \in A_\Psi$ will occur in Ψ. Write $A = A_\Psi$. The idea will be to choose some function $f : \{0, \ldots, L-1\} \to \{1, \ldots, \ell\} \cup \{0\}$ such that for each $i = 1, \ldots, \ell$ and $\chi \in A$

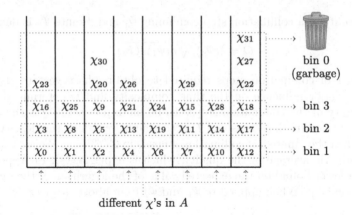

different χ's in A

Fig. 2. Example construction of the function f from Step 4.2, with $|A| = 8$ and $L = 32$ (with $\ell = 3$), where $f(j) = i$ is illustrated by χ_j being deposited in bin i.

there is exactly one $j \in \{0, \ldots, L-1\}$ such that $\chi_j = \chi$ and $f(j) = i$; see Fig. 2 for an illustration. We then compute

$$\frac{1}{\sqrt{L}} \sum_{j=0}^{L-1} \chi_j(s)|j\rangle|f(j)\rangle$$

and measure $f(j)$. If we measure 0, the process fails and we have to somehow recycle the phase vector and return to Step 4.1, or throw it away. Otherwise if $i = f(j) > 0$, we know that each $\chi \in A$ occurs exactly once in the resulting expression:

$$\frac{1}{\sqrt{|A|}} \sum_{f(j)=i} \chi_j(s)|j\rangle.$$

We then compute a bijection from $\{j \mid f(j) = i\}$ to A and apply this using QRACM to obtain $(1/\sqrt{|A|}) \sum_{\chi \in A} \chi(s)|\chi\rangle$.[2]

Step 4.3. By multiplying Ψ with a global phase if needed, we can assume that $1 \in A$. If A is a subgroup of $G^\vee$ then the inverse Fourier transform yields $|q(s)\rangle$, where q is the quotient morphism $G \to B := G/\ker A$, with $\ker A$ denoting the joint kernel of the χ's in A.[3] So upon measurement we know $q(s)$. More generally, if A *contains* a non-trivial subgroup H of $G^\vee$ such that $H \in \mathcal{A}$, then A will be a union of cosets of H. Through measurement we can collapse Ψ to a phase vector

---

[2] Remark that, in practice, we can be more lax and allow for incomplete phase vectors, choosing f so that for each $i = 1, \ldots, \ell$ and $\chi \in A$ there is at most one $j \in \{0, \ldots, L-1\}$ such that $\chi_j = \chi$. Then some $\chi \in A$ could be missing in the resulting state, but this is tolerable to some extent. For simplicity, we stick to the complete case.

[3] Note that $A \cong B^\vee$ because each $\chi \in A$ is of the form $\chi' \circ q$ for some $\chi' \in B^\vee$.

Ψ' supported on one such coset. Again after taking out a global phase if needed, we will have $A_{\Psi'} = H$ and we can act as above.

Otherwise A is at level 1, i.e., it is an interval $I = \{0, \ldots, a_1 - 1\}$ in $G_1 \cong \mathbb{Z}_{k_1}$. We can write our state Ψ as

$$\frac{1}{\sqrt{a_1}} \sum_{j_1=0}^{a_1-1} e^{\frac{2\pi i}{k_1} q(s) j_1} |j_1\rangle,$$

where $q : G \to \mathbb{Z}_{k_1}$ is a surjective homomorphism with kernel $\ker G_1$. Our goal is to find $q(s)$. For this we follow Peikert, who aims at finding phase vectors

$$\frac{1}{\sqrt{a_2}} \sum_{j_2=0}^{a_2-1} e^{\frac{2\pi i}{k_1} q(s) j_2 a_1} |j_2\rangle, \tag{5}$$

leading to a tensor product

$$\frac{1}{\sqrt{a_1}} \sum_{j_1=0}^{a_1-1} e^{\frac{2\pi i}{k_1} q(s) j_1} |j_1\rangle \otimes \frac{1}{\sqrt{a_2}} \sum_{j_2=0}^{a_2-1} e^{\frac{2\pi i}{k_1} q(s) j_2 a_1} |j_2\rangle \; = \; \frac{1}{\sqrt{a_1 a_2}} \sum_{j=0}^{a_1 a_2-1} e^{\frac{2\pi i}{k_1} q(s) j} |j\rangle.$$

Similarly, if we can tensor with a phase vector

$$\frac{1}{\sqrt{a_3}} \sum_{j_3=0}^{a_3-1} e^{\frac{2\pi i}{k_1} q(s) j_3 a_1 a_2} |j_3\rangle \qquad \text{to obtain} \qquad \frac{1}{\sqrt{a_1 a_2 a_3}} \sum_{j=0}^{a_1 a_2 a_3-1} e^{\frac{2\pi i}{k_1} q(s) j} |j\rangle,$$

and so on, we eventually find a phase vector

$$\frac{1}{\sqrt{a_1 \cdots a_r}} \sum_{j=0}^{a_1 \cdots a_r-1} e^{\frac{2\pi i}{k_1} q(s) j} |j\rangle$$

with $a_1 \cdots a_r \geq k_1$. Then one measures $\lfloor j/k_1 \rfloor$ so as to obtain either

$$\frac{1}{\sqrt{k_1}} \sum_{j=0}^{k_1-1} e^{\frac{2\pi i}{k_1} q(s) j} |j\rangle \qquad \text{or} \qquad \frac{1}{\sqrt{t}} \sum_{j=0}^{t-1} e^{\frac{2\pi i}{k_1} q(s) j} |j\rangle,$$

for some $t < k_1$. We end up with the first superposition if we measure $\lfloor j/k_1 \rfloor$ to be smaller than $\lfloor a_1 \cdots a_r/k_1 \rfloor$ and with the second if $\lfloor j/k_1 \rfloor$ is measured to equal $\lfloor a_1 \cdots a_r/k_1 \rfloor$.[4] In the first case we take the inverse Fourier transform to retrieve $q(s)$. In the second case we recycle the resulting state, tensoring it with a new vector, and once it is longer than k_1 try again.

We now explain how to produce a vector of the form (5); all subsequent steps are analogous. If a_1 happens to be coprime to k_1 then every phase vector supported on G_1 can be written as

$$\frac{1}{\sqrt{L}} \sum_{j=0}^{L-1} e^{\frac{2\pi i}{k_1} q(s) b_j a_1} |j\rangle. \tag{6}$$

---

[4] Unless $k_1 \mid a_1 \cdots a_r$ in which case we always get the first superposition.

Algorithm 2: Finding hidden shifts in finite abelian groups

Input : Finite abelian group G, length parameter L, density parameter δ
    Access to phase vectors $\frac{1}{\sqrt{2}}(|0\rangle + \chi(s)|1\rangle)$ for known but uniformly
    random $\chi \in G^\vee$ and unknown but fixed $s \in G$

Output: s

1 Create chain of subgroups $\{1\} = G_0 \leq G_1 \leq G_2 \leq \cdots \leq G_M = G^\vee$ such that
   the groups G_i/G_{i-1} are cyclic; this gives rise to a type $\mathcal{A}$ of support sets

2 **recursively** *(depth-first):*

3   Create phase vectors Ψ of length $\approx L$ by tensoring $\lceil \log_2(L) \rceil$ fresh
       length-two phase vectors; endow with support set $A_\Psi := G^\vee$

4   Increase density by collimating phase vectors Ψ_1, Ψ_2 with support sets

$$A_{\Psi_1}, A_{\Psi_2} \text{ of size } \approx |G^\vee|/(L/2)^i$$

    into a length $\approx L$ phase vector Ψ_3 with support set

$$A_{\Psi_3} \text{ of size } \approx |G^\vee|/(L/2)^{i+1}$$

5 **until** *we obtain a phase vector Ψ with density $\geq 1 + \delta$;*

6 Thin out and regularize Ψ

7 If needed, remove global phase so that $1 \in A_\Psi$

8 **if** *A_Ψ contains a non-trivial subgroup $H \leq G^\vee$ contained in $\mathcal{A}$* **then**

9   Recover s modulo $G' = \ker H$ by applying a quantum Fourier transform

10   Run **Algorithm 2** on G'

11 **else**

12   Repeat Steps 2–7 to obtain phase vectors with "dilated" support sets inside
       G_1 *(Peikert's method)*

13   Take tensor products and shorten if needed, to find complete phase vector
       with support set G_1

14   Recover s modulo $G' = \ker G_1$ by applying a quantum Fourier transform

15   Run **Algorithm 2** on G'

16 **end**

The reason is that every $\chi_j \in G_1$ is of the form $g \mapsto \exp(\frac{2\pi i}{k_1} q(g) c_j)$ for some integer c_j. By adding an appropriate multiple of k_1 to c_j, we can always assume that c_j is a multiple of a_1; this uses that $\gcd(a_1, k_1) = 1$. Then, in complete analogy with standard collimation, through a process of combination and measurement one can turn phase vectors of the form (6) into phase vectors of the desired form (5). When a_1 is not coprime to k_1, then we slightly shorten Ψ, replacing a_1 with the greatest integer smaller than a_1 that is coprime to k_1.

Special Cases. If $G = \mathbb{Z}_{2^n}$ and we start from the chain $1 = G_0 \leq G_1 \leq \cdots \leq G_n = G^\vee$ where each quotient G_i/G_{i-1} has order 2, then one checks that $\mathcal{A} = \bigcup_{i=0}^{n} \{$ cosets of G_i in $G^\vee \}$. We stop collimating as soon as $|A_\Psi|$ is sufficiently smaller than L, in which case A_Ψ is a coset of G_i for some $i < \log L$. As explained in Steps 4.2 and 4.3 we recover s modulo $\ker G_i = \{ a \in \mathbb{Z}_{2^n} \mid a \bmod 2^i = 0 \}$. Thus we recover Kuperberg's original "least-significant bits" version of the collimation sieve. On the other hand, starting from the trivial chain $1 = G_0 \leq G_1 = G^\vee$, we consider $G^\vee$ itself as a cyclic group, without exploiting its subgroup structure. Now $\mathcal{A}$ consists of intervals in $G^\vee$ and we recover Peikert's "most-significant bits" method. See the preamble of [19, §3] for a related discussion.

Complexity. Summarizing pseudocode can be found in Algorithm 2. The asymptotic complexity of our algorithm, as well as its analysis, is very similar to that of Peikert's, leading to the statement of Theorem 1.2 in which $|2^t pG|$ is replaced by $|G|$. We omit the details, instead referring to [19], as well as to the next section, which contains a related analysis.

5   Merging both Algorithms

We now describe our fusion algorithm, resulting in Theorem 1.2. The idea is to apply collimation, as outlined in the previous section, but in our chain of inclusions $\{1\} = G_0 \leq G_1 \leq \ldots \leq G_M = G^\vee$ we now let

$$G_1 = G^\vee[2^t p] = \{\, \chi \in G^\vee \mid \chi^{2^t p} = 1 \,\}$$

be the $2^t p$-torsion subgroup of $G^\vee$, rather than a cyclic group. The goal is to produce length-two phase vectors $\Psi(\chi)$ with $\chi \in G_1$, which can then be used as input to our algorithm from Sect. 3, ran on the $2^t p$-torsion group

$$G/\ker G_1 = G/2^t pG$$

(of which G_1 can be viewed as the dual), which will allow us to find $s \bmod 2^t pG$.

Concretely, we stop collimating as soon as the density exceeds some small multiple of $2/|G_1|$. Consider a resulting phase vector Ψ. By measuring to which coset of G_1 the χ's in A_Ψ belong, it collapses to a phase vector

$$\frac{1}{\sqrt{L}} \sum_{j=0}^{L-1} \chi_j(s)|j\rangle$$

where all χ_j's belong to the same coset of G_1. By taking out a global phase if needed we can assume that this coset is G_1 itself. We expect $L \geq 2$, because the measurement decreases the numerator and the denominator of $\delta(\Psi)$ by a similar factor. If $L = 2$ then we succeeded, while if $L = 1$ then we failed. If $L > 2$ then measuring $\lfloor j/2 \rfloor$ typically yields a state with only two terms, as wanted. This procedure is summarized in Algorithm 3.

Our algorithm then proceeds using $t + 2$ collimation rounds:

Round 1. In a first collimation round, we produce length-two phase vectors $\Psi(\chi)$ with $\chi \in G_1$ and feed them as input to Step 3.1, in order to obtain phase vectors $\Psi(\chi)$ with $\chi^p = 1$. These can then be used as input to Step 3.2, allowing us to find $s \bmod pG$.

Rounds 2 to $t+1$. Knowing $s \bmod pG$, we can reduce to a hidden shift problem in the subgroup pG. We then proceed as in Step 3.3. That is, we again use

---

Algorithm 3: Producing length-two phase vectors supported on the $2^t p$-torsion characters of a finite abelian group

---

Input   : Finite abelian group G, length parameter L, density parameter δ
Access to phase vectors $\frac{1}{\sqrt{2}}(|0\rangle + \chi(s)|1\rangle)$ for known but uniformly random $\chi \in G^{\vee}$ and unknown but fixed $s \in G$

Output: Phase vector $\frac{1}{\sqrt{2}}(|0\rangle + \chi'(s)|1\rangle)$ for known random $\chi' \in G^{\vee}[2^t p]$

1 Create chain of subgroups $\{1\} = G_0 \leq G_1 = G^{\vee}[2^t p] \leq G_2 \leq \cdots \leq G_M = G^{\vee}$
   such that G_i/G_{i-1} is cyclic for $i \geq 2$; this invokes a type $\mathcal{A}$ of support sets
2 **repeat**
3   Produce length $\approx L$ phase vector Ψ of density $\approx 2/|G_1|$ using collimation;
        this is done in full analogy with Steps 2–5 of **Algorithm 2**
4   Restrict the support of Ψ to a single coset of G_1 through measurement
5   Shorten Ψ if needed, so that it has length ≤ 2
6 **until** *length of Ψ equals* 2;
7 Take out global phase to rewrite Ψ as $\Psi(\chi')$ for some $\chi' \in G_1$

Algorithm 4: Finding hidden shifts in finite abelian groups containing a large $2^t p$-torsion subgroup

---

Input   : Finite abelian group G, length parameter L, density parameter δ
Access to phase vectors $\frac{1}{\sqrt{2}}(|0\rangle + \chi(s)|1\rangle)$ for known but uniformly random $\chi \in G^{\vee}$ and unknown but fixed $s \in G$

Output: s

1 Run **Algorithm 1** on $G/2^t pG$, where access to length-two phase vectors is now provided by **Algorithm 3** ran on G, rather than the standard approach
2 Run **Algorithm 2** on $2^t pG$

---

collimation to produce input for Step 3.1, but as explained in Step 3.3, we now construct $(t-1)$-divisible phase vectors, which can be used to determine $s \bmod 2pG$ by means of Simon's algorithm. We then reiterate, until we find $s \bmod 2^t pG$.

Round $t+2$. We are left with solving a hidden shift problem in $2^t pG$, for which we do a complete run of the collimation algorithm from Sect. 4. Note: only at this stage, we perform Steps 4.2 (thin out and regularize) and 4.3 (Fourier transform).

Complexity. Our fusion algorithm is summarized in Algorithm 4. As for the complexity, let us focus on the renewed trade-off between the number of calls to the standard approach and the amount of QRACM needed, when compared to [19]. From Sect. 3 we know that, for rounds 1 to $t+1$, the required amount of length-two phase vectors $\Psi(\chi)$ with $\chi \in G_1$ is poly$(\log |G|)$. This means that for the collimation part, the number of fresh length-two phase vectors we need to call for using the standard approach is

$$\text{poly}(\log |G|) \cdot \log L \cdot 2^{O(\log_Q(\delta_{\text{end}}/\delta_{\text{start}}))}.$$

Here $\delta_{\text{start}} = L/|G^\vee| = L/|G|$ is the density of the phase vectors we feed to the collimation phase and $\delta_{\text{end}} = 2/|G_1|$ is the targeted density. The factor $\log L$ comes from the number of length-two phase vectors we need to tensor together to make a phase vector of length L, and Q denotes the average quality of a collimation step, which in view of our discussion from Sect. 4 we estimate as $L/2$. This gives

$$\text{poly}(\log|G|) \cdot \log L \cdot 2^{O(\log_{L/2}(|G|/|G_1|))} \tag{7}$$

oracle queries. One sees: the larger the initial phase vector length L, the smaller the number of oracle queries and collimation steps.

However, larger values of L lead to an increase of the resources needed for every collimation step. The dominating cost is in terms of QRACM, which is about importing classical information into a quantum state, or uncomputing it away. Concretely, this is used in all transitions of the form

$$\sum_{j=0}^{r-1} |j\rangle \quad \rightarrow \quad \sum_{j=0}^{r-1} |j, c_j\rangle$$

and vice versa, for some set of classically stored values $c_0, \ldots, c_{r-1}$. Following [7, App. A.1] we estimate the corresponding gate cost as $O(rw)$, with w the number of bits of each c_j. The main such cost lies in handling (4), leading to the estimate

$$O(L^2 \log L). \tag{8}$$

The optimal balance between (7) and (8) is found by taking $\log L$ on the order of $\sqrt{\log(|G|/|G_1|)} = \sqrt{\log|2^t pG|}$. Together with the fact that round $t + 2$ is ran on the group $2^t pG$, this gives the estimates in Theorem 1.2.

Example 5.1 Let $G = \mathbb{Z}_{2^n} \times \mathbb{Z}_3^m$ where $n, m \in \mathbb{Z}_{>0}$. If we consider the subgroup chain $1 \leq G_1 \leq G_2 \leq \ldots \leq G_{n+1} = G^\vee$ where $G_1 \cong \mathbb{Z}_3^m$ and $G_i \cong \mathbb{Z}_3^m \times \mathbb{Z}_{2^{i-1}}, 2 \leq i \leq n+1$, then – as discussed at the end of Sect. 4 – our algorithm collimates on the least-significant bits of the $\mathbb{Z}_{2^n}$-component of s, going down the chain until, after one or two measurements, we obtain a length-two phase vector supported on G_1. Each such run takes about $2^{O(\sqrt{n})}$ operations; this ignores the small overhead caused by working in a bigger ambient group. As discussed in Sect. 3, once we have about $3m(m+1)/2$ such phase vectors, we can apply the algorithm of Friedl et al. to retrieve the hidden shift s modulo $\ker G_1$, i.e., to find its $(\mathbb{Z}_3)^m$-component. We then rerun the collimation process on the remaining $\mathbb{Z}_{2^n}$-part in order to conclude. Hence, the total complexity of our algorithm amounts to $m^2 2^{O(\sqrt{n})}$. This should be compared to

$$2^{O(\sqrt{n + m \log 3})},$$

which is the cost of applying Kuperberg's collimation algorithm directly to all of G.

6 Conclusion

The hidden shift problem plays a central role in the quantum cryptanalysis of several candidate symmetric and public-key cryptosystems. For general finite abelian groups, the best result we have is an algorithm with sub-exponential runtime due to Kuperberg. For special families we have polynomial-time solutions, e.g., for groups of type $\mathbb{Z}_p^n$ for any fixed prime p due to Friedl et al., and for groups of type $\mathbb{Z}_{2^t}^n$ for a fixed integer $t \geq 1$ due to Bonnetain and Naya-Plasencia.

In this paper, we merge the two latter solutions into one polynomial-time quantum algorithm for arbitrary finite abelian $2^t p$-torsion groups, and we modify Peikert's "least-significant bits first" variant of Kuperberg's most recent sub-exponential time algorithm, called the *collimation sieve*, to a version that works for any finite abelian group $(G, +)$. Finally, we fuse both results into a single quantum algorithm for solving the hidden shift problem in G in time

$$\mathrm{poly}(\log |G|) \cdot 2^{O(\sqrt{\log |2^t pG|})},$$

while keeping the key advantage of the collimation sieve, namely that the main memory requirements are in terms of quantum random access classical memory; only a polynomial number of qubits is needed. This can be seen as a memory-friendly special case of a result due to Friedl et al. Such results entail a security issue for hard homogeneous spaces when a large low-torsion subgroup is present, which can be viewed as a modest result of Pohlig–Hellman type.

Possible tracks for future research include:

1. Making a more detailed complexity analysis, where the goal is to acquire a better understanding of the hidden constants (including how they depend on p and t, as in [13, Prop. 4.13]). This should allow for a better security analysis of concrete hard homogeneous spaces. To achieve this, it may be helpful to reformulate our algorithm as a sequence of routines solving k-list type problems, as was done in [21].
2. Further reducing the time and memory requirements of our algorithm, e.g., by devising an optimal strategy in choosing our subgroups G_i, or by decreasing the QRACM requirements by storing the characters χ in an extra register as in [7, p. 10–11];
3. Generalizing our results to other torsion, where the ultimate target is to replace $2^t p$ by any fixed m; for this, it would suffice to find a way of incorporating the collimation sieve into the work of [13].

Acknowledgments. This work was supported by the Research Council KU Leuven grant C14/18/067, by CyberSecurity Research Flanders with reference number VR20192203, and by the Research Foundation Flanders (FWO) through the WOG Coding Theory and Cryptography. We thank the anonymous referees and shepherd for pointing us to a number of missing references, and for various other suggestions for improvement.

A   Expected Quality of a Collimation Step

Proposition A.1. *When Ψ_1 and Ψ_2 are given, we have*

$$\mathbb{E}\left(\frac{1}{\delta(\Psi_3)}\right) \leq \frac{|A_{\Psi_1} + A_{\Psi_2}|}{L_1 L_2},$$

regardless of how $A_{\Psi_1} + A_{\Psi_2}$ is subdivided, with equality holding as long as every set A_i in the subdivision contains at least one character $\chi_{j_1}\chi_{j_2}$ occurring in $\Psi_1 \otimes \Psi_2$. Using this the expected value of the logarithm of the density can be bounded as $\mathbb{E}\log\delta(\Psi_3) \geq \log(L_1 L_2/|A_{\Psi_1} + A_{\Psi_2}|)$. If Q is the quality of the collimation step then the expected value of the logarithm is bounded as

$$\mathbb{E}\log Q \geq \log\left(\sqrt{L_1 L_2}\frac{\sqrt{|A_{\Psi_1}||A_{\Psi_2}|}}{|A_{\Psi_1} + A_{\Psi_2}|}\right).$$

Proof. We have

$$\mathbb{E}\left(\frac{1}{\delta(\Psi_3)}\right) = \mathbb{E}\left(\frac{|A_{\Psi_3}|}{L_3}\right) = \sum_{i=1}^{p}\mathbb{P}(A_{\Psi_3} = A_i)\frac{|A_i|}{|\{(j_1,j_2)|\chi_{j_1}\chi_{j_2} \in A_i\}|} =$$

$$\sum_{i=1}^{p}\frac{|\{(j_1,j_2)|\chi_{j_1}\chi_{j_2} \in A_i\}|}{L_1 L_2}\frac{|A_i|}{|\{(j_1,j_2)|\chi_{j_1}\chi_{j_2} \in A_i\}|} = \sum_{i=1}^{p}\frac{|A_i|}{L_1 L_2} = \frac{|A_{\Psi_1} + A_{\Psi_2}|}{L_1 L_2}.$$

Note that if $\mathbb{P}(A_{\Psi_3} = A_i) = 0$ then we simply omit that term from the sum. In this case we only have an upper bound on the expected value of one over the density, rather than an equality. This proves the first statement.

To obtain the second statement we use the result from probability theory that

$$\mathbb{E}\left(-\log\left(\frac{1}{X}\right)\right) \geq -\log\mathbb{E}\frac{1}{X},$$

for any random variable X that only assumes positive values. This follows from Jensen's inequality and the fact that $-\log x$ is a convex function on $\mathbb{R}_{>0}$. This can be rewritten as $\mathbb{E}\log X \geq -\log\mathbb{E}X^{-1}$. The second statement follows from this result by applying it to $X = \delta(\Psi_3)$. The third statement follows from the second and the definition of the quality Q. $\qquad\square$

References

1. Berger, T.P., Francq, J., Minier, M., Thomas, G.: Extended generalized Feistel networks using matrix representation to propose a new lightweight block cipher: Lilliput. IEEE Trans. Comput. **65**(7), 2074–2089 (2016)
2. Bonnetain, X., Naya-Plasencia, M.: Hidden shift quantum cryptanalysis and implications. In: Peyrin, T., Galbraith, S. (eds.) ASIACRYPT 2018, Part I. LNCS, vol. 11272, pp. 560–592. Springer, Cham (2018). https://doi.org/10.1007/978-3-030-03326-2_19

3. Bonnetain, X., Schrottenloher, A.: Quantum security analysis of CSIDH. In: Canteaut, A., Ishai, Y. (eds.) EUROCRYPT 2020, Part II. LNCS, vol. 12106, pp. 493–522. Springer, Cham (2020). https://doi.org/10.1007/978-3-030-45724-2_17

4. Castryck, W., Lange, T., Martindale, C., Panny, L., Renes, J.: CSIDH: an efficient post-quantum commutative group action. In: Peyrin, T., Galbraith, S. (eds.) ASIACRYPT 2018, Part III. LNCS, vol. 11274, pp. 395–427. Springer, Cham (2018). https://doi.org/10.1007/978-3-030-03332-3_15

5. Castryck, W., Sotáková, J., Vercauteren, F.: Breaking the decisional Diffie-Hellman problem for class group actions using genus theory. In: Micciancio, D., Ristenpart, T. (eds.) CRYPTO 2020. LNCS, vol. 12171, pp. 92–120. Springer, Cham (2020). https://doi.org/10.1007/978-3-030-56880-1_4

6. Csáji, G.: A new quantum algorithm for the hidden shift problem in $\mathbb{Z}_{2^t}^n$, preprint available at https://arxiv.org/abs/2102.04171 (2021)

7. Chávez-Saab, J., Chi-Domínguez, J.-J., Jaques, S., Rodríguez-Henríquez, F.: The SQALE of CSIDH: Square-root Vélu quantum-resistant isogeny action with low exponents, preprint available at https://eprint.iacr.org/2020/1520 (2020)

8. Childs, A.M., Jao, D., Soukharev, V.: Constructing elliptic curve isogenies in quantum subexponential time. J. Math. Cryptol. 8(1), 1–29 (2014)

9. Cohen, H., Lenstra, H.W.: Heuristics on class groups of number fields. In: Jager, H. (ed.) Number Theory Noordwijkerhout 1983. LNM, vol. 1068, pp. 33–62. Springer, Heidelberg (1984). https://doi.org/10.1007/BFb0099440

10. Couveignes, J.-M.: Hard homogeneous spaces (unpublished). https://eprint.iacr.org/2006/291

11. Gerth, F., III.: The 4-class ranks of quadratic fields. Invent. Math. 77, 489–515 (1984)

12. van Dam, W., Hallgren, S., Ip, L.: Quantum algorithms for some hidden shift problems. SIAM J. Comput. 36(3), 763–778 (2006)

13. Friedl, K., Ivanyos, G., Magniez, F., Santha, M., Sen, P.: Hidden translation and translating coset in quantum computing. SIAM J. Comput. 43(1), 1–24 (2014)

14. Galbraith, S.D., Panny, L., Smith, B., Vercauteren, F.: Quantum equivalence of the DLP and CDHP for group actions. Math. Cryptol. 1(1), 40–44 (2021)

15. Kuperberg, G.: A subexponential time quantum algorithm for the dihedral hidden subgroup problem. SIAM J. Comput. 35(1), 170–188 (2005)

16. Kuperberg, G.: Another subexponential-time quantum algorithm for the dihedral hidden subgroup problem. In: Proceedings of TQC 2013, Leibniz International Proceedings in Informatics, vol. 22, pp. 20–34 (2013)

17. Maurer, U.M., Wolf, S.: The Diffie-Hellman protocol. Des. Codes Crypt. 19, 147–171 (2000)

18. Panny, L.: Cryptography on isogeny graphs. Ph.D. thesis, TU Eindhoven (2021)

19. Peikert, C.: He gives C-sieves on the CSIDH. In: Canteaut, A., Ishai, Y. (eds.) EUROCRYPT 2020, Part II. LNCS, vol. 12106, pp. 463–492. Springer, Cham (2020). https://doi.org/10.1007/978-3-030-45724-2_16

20. Pohlig, S., Hellman, M.: An improved algorithm for computing logarithms over $GF(p)$ and its cryptographic significance. IEEE Trans. Inf. Theory 24(1), 106–110 (1978)

21. Regev, O.: A subexponential time algorithm for the dihedral hidden subgroup problem with polynomial space (unpublished). https://arxiv.org/abs/quant-ph/0406151

22. Regev, O.: Quantum computation and lattice problems. SIAM J. Comput. 33(3), 738–760 (2004)

23. Rostovtsev, A., Stolbunov, A.: Public-key cryptosystem based on isogenies (unpublished). https://eprint.iacr.org/2006/145.pdf
24. Shor, P.W.: Polynomial-time algorithms for prime factorization and discrete logarithms on a quantum computer. SIAM J. Comput. **26**(5), 1484–1509 (1997)
25. Simon, D.R.: On the power of quantum computation. SIAM J. Comput. **26**(5), 1474–1483 (1997). A preliminary version appeared in Proc. of the 35th Annual Symposium on Foundations of Computer Science, pp. 116–123 (1994)
26. Smith, B.: Pre- and post-quantum Diffie–Hellman from groups, actions, and isogenies. In: Budaghyan, L., Rodríguez-Henríquez, F. (eds.) WAIFI 2018. LNCS, vol. 11321, pp. 3–40. Springer, Cham (2018). https://doi.org/10.1007/978-3-030-05153-2_1
27. Stolbunov, A.: Constructing public-key cryptographic schemes based on class group action on a set of isogenous elliptic curves. Adv. Math. Commun. **4**(2), 215–235 (2010)

The "Quantum Annoying" Property of Password-Authenticated Key Exchange Protocols

Edward Eaton[1,2]($\boxtimes$) and Douglas Stebila[1]

[1] University of Waterloo, Waterloo, Canada
eeaton@uwaterloo.ca
[2] ISARA Corporation, Waterloo, Canada

Abstract. During the Crypto Forum Research Group (CFRG)'s standardization of password-authenticated key exchange (PAKE) protocols, a novel property emerged: a PAKE scheme is said to be "quantum-annoying" if a quantum computer *can* compromise the security of the scheme, but only by solving one discrete logarithm for each guess of a password. Considering that early quantum computers will likely take quite long to solve even a single discrete logarithm, a quantum-annoying PAKE, combined with a large password space, could delay the need for a post-quantum replacement by years, or even decades.

In this paper, we make the first steps towards formalizing the quantum-annoying property. We consider a classical adversary in an extension of the generic group model in which the adversary has access to an oracle that solves discrete logarithms. While this idealized model does not fully capture the range of operations available to an adversary with a general-purpose quantum computer, this model does allow us to quantify security in terms of the number of discrete logarithms solved. We apply this approach to the CPace protocol, a balanced PAKE advancing through the CFRG standardization process, and show that the $\text{CPace}_{\text{base}}$ variant is secure in the generic group model with a discrete logarithm oracle.

Keywords: Password-authenticated key exchange · Post-quantum · Quantum-annoying · Generic group model

1 Introduction

Password-authenticated key exchange protocols, or PAKEs, are used in scenarios where public key infrastructure is unavailable, such as client-to-server authentication. Without public keys, authentication comes from a password provided by the user. This puts the security of PAKEs in an interesting place. These passwords are assumed to have low entropy, so it is possible for a malicious adversary to perform brute-force searches over the password space. The challenge in designing PAKEs is to obtain the maximum amount of security possible, despite

© Springer Nature Switzerland AG 2021
J. H. Cheon and J.-P. Tillich (Eds.): PQCrypto 2021, LNCS 12841, pp. 154–173, 2021.
https://doi.org/10.1007/978-3-030-81293-5_9

the fact that authentication comes from low-entropy passwords. One important property of PAKEs is resistance against offline dictionary attacks: if a passive adversary observes an honest session, they still should not have enough information to break security via a brute-force search through the password space. Moreover, for an online adversary sending messages to a target session, each interaction should allow for only a single guess of the password. Thus, despite relying on low-entropy secrets, a secure PAKE can only be compromised with many online interactions, which would hopefully be noticed and stopped by a participant.

In 2019, the Crypto Forum Research Group (CFRG) issued a call for candidate password-authenticated key exchange protocols to be recommended for use in IETF protocols [14]. Both balanced PAKEs (where both parties share a password) and augmented PAKEs (where one party only has information derived from the password) were considered. Four balanced and four augmented PAKEs were considered, and in early 2020 the balanced PAKE CPace and the augmented PAKE OPAQUE were selected as recommended for usage in IETF protocols [13].

As PAKEs inherently can only be as secure the as the entropy of the password space allows, extremely detailed and fine-grained security analysis of each scheme was a focus of the selection process. In discussing potential security properties, Thomas proposed the notion of a PAKE being "quantum annoying" [15]. If a scheme is quantum annoying, then being able to solve discrete logarithms does not immediately provide the ability to compromise a system; instead, each discrete logarithm an adversary solves only allows them to eliminate a single possible password. Essentially, the adversary must guess a password, solve a discrete logarithm based on their guess, and then check to see if they were correct. This property became a topic of frequent discussion throughout the process.

CPace tries to be quantum annoying by having the base used for the Diffie–Hellman key exchange be a group element derived from the password: the parties exchange $U = g_{pw}^u$ and $V = g_{pw}^v$, and the shared secret is (roughly speaking) g_{pw}^{uv}. Seeing U and V does not yield any information about the password, since in a prime order group for every pw' there exists a u' such that $g_{pw}^u = g_{pw'}^{u'}$. For a quantum adversary to check a password against a transcript, it could pick a password guess pw, compute $u = \mathsf{DLOG}(g_{pw}, U)$, then check if V^u matches the session key. CPace would be quantum annoying if this is the best way to check passwords. (The other PAKE recommended by CFRG, OPAQUE, is not known to be quantum annoying.)

Current estimates for how long quantum computers will take to solve a cryptographically relevant discrete logarithm problem vary depending on factors such as the error rate and the number of coherent qubits available. In a recent analysis, Gheorghiu and Mosca [7] estimated that, to solve a discrete logarithm on the NIST P-256 elliptic curve, it would take one day on a quantum computer with 2^{26} physical qubits, or a 6 min on a 2^{34}-physical-qubit quantum computer. With early quantum computers taking hours or days, and even mature ones taking minutes for a single discrete logarithm, brute-forcing passwords in a quantum-annoying scheme is probably infeasible for all but the most dedicated and resourceful adversary. For well-chosen passwords from high entropy spaces, considerable quantum resources would be needed to compromise a single password. In such a scenario it would of course be best to replace PAKEs with a suitable post-quantum primitive, but quantum annoyingness is still appealing.

However, there has thus far been little formal discussion or analysis of this property. The perceived quantum annoyingness of each PAKE candidate was evaluated as part of the recommendation process, but no proof for any scheme was provided. In fact, there have been few efforts to even provide a formal definition. Quantum security models are notoriously tricky to define and use in security proofs, especially when trying to consider the cost of using Shor's algorithm [11]. Clarifying what quantum annoyingness really means and establishing how the property can be assessed for a real scheme has thus remained an open problem.

Our Contributions. In this work, we take the first steps towards putting the quantum annoying property on solid theoretical foundations. There are many difficulties in working within a fully quantum security model. Besides the typical challenges in proving security in the quantum random oracle model [4], it is not even clear what problem we could reduce to, or how that reduction would work, since we are considering an adversary that can solve discrete logarithms.

Modelling Quantum-Annoying via the Generic Group Model with a Discrete Logarithm Oracle. Instead, we consider a classical adversary in the generic group model [10,12] who has access to a discrete logarithm oracle. This allows us to consider how 'quantum annoying' a scheme is by considering how many queries to the discrete logarithm oracle are needed in order to compromise security.

Part of the challenge in working with a discrete logarithm oracle is that the adversary can freely mix together group elements to prepare an oracle query of their choosing. For example, say we do not want the adversary to learn the discrete logarithm between group elements A and C. If the adversary queries the oracle to get the discrete logarithm between A and B, and then between B and C, they can calculate the target discrete logarithm without ever having queried it. One of the main technical difficulties we overcome in our proof is to construct a system that allows us to carefully account for exactly how much information the adversary has been able to extract from their discrete logarithm queries. We show that no matter how the adversary prepares their queries to the oracle, the information they get can be modelled as a linear system. In this view, questions about whether the adversary is 'aware' of the discrete logarithm between any two group elements can be reduced to questions on whether certain vectors appear in the rowspan of a matrix. The probability of certain events can in turn be reduced to question about the rank of this matrix. To our knowledge, this is the first time a generic group model proof has been extended with a discrete logarithm oracle, and we think that the resulting system has an interesting structure that illuminates questions about how solutions to discrete logarithms help (or don't) with the calculation of additional discrete logarithms.

Admittedly, a classical adversary in the generic group model with a discrete logarithm oracle is not a perfect model of a quantum adversary. An innovative quantum adversary could try to invent some new quantum algorithm inspired by Shor's algorithm which does not directly take discrete logarithms. Nonetheless, our approach allows for at least some formal assessment of quantum annoyingness.

Security Analysis of CPace. To make use of our techniques, we focus on the protocol CPace, which was selected by the CFRG as the balanced PAKE recommendation for use in IETF protocols. We prove that $CPace_{base}$, an abstraction of the protocol that focuses on the most essential parts, is secure in a variant of the BPR model [2].

Our analysis proceeds as follows. First, we design in Sect. 3.1 a cryptographic problem called $CPace_{core}$ which in some sense captures the cryptographic core of $CPace_{base}$. Next, we calculate the probability that an adversary can solve in the $CPace_{core}$ problem in the generic group model with a discrete logarithm oracle; the success probability is measured in terms of the number of online interactions with a protocol participant and the number of group operations and discrete logarithms performed. An outline of the proof is provided in Sect. 3.2 and the full proof is given in Sect. 3.3. In the full version of the paper [5], we show that $CPace_{base}$ is a secure PAKE in our variant of the BPR model.

As a preview of our theorem, the probability that an adversary manages to win the game is dominated by a term $(q_C + q_D)/N$ term, where q_C is the number of online interactions, q_D is the number of discrete log oracle queries, and N is the size of the password space. This lines up exactly with the intuitive guarantees we would expect a quantum annoying system to have: guess a password and try using it in an active session, or guess a password and take a discrete logarithm based on it to see if it was the password used in a passively-observed session.

2   Background

2.1   The CPace Protocol

CPace is a balanced PAKE with a simple and effective design, based on earlier protocols SPEKE [9] and PACE [3,6]. It can (optionally) be used as a subroutine for the augmented PAKE, AuCPace [8]. The fundamental structure is for the parties, sharing a password, to hash that password to a group element G and then perform a Diffie–Hellman-like key exchange with G acting as the generator. We describe it in full in Fig. 1.

We will focus on $CPace_{base}$, a theoretical variant introduced by Abdalla, Haase, and Hesse [1] that distills CPace to its most essential elements. The changes between $CPace_{base}$ and the full CPace protocol are that $CPace_{base}$ uses a (multiplicatively written) group with prime order p (instead of composite order), and assumes that the random oracle H_1 maps onto the group. This variant allows us to focus on the parts of the protocol relevant to an adversary capable of solving discrete logarithms. Aspects of the security related to the process of

Client C		Server S
Input: sid, S		Input: sid, C
$G \leftarrow H_1(\text{sid}\|pw_{C,S}\|\text{oc}(C,S))$		$G \leftarrow H_1(\text{sid}\|pw_{C,S}\|\text{oc}(C,S))$
$u \leftarrow^\$ \mathbb{Z}_p$		$v \leftarrow^\$ \mathbb{Z}_p$
$U \leftarrow G^u$	$\xrightarrow{\quad U \quad}$	$V \leftarrow G^v$
$K \leftarrow V^u$	$\xleftarrow{\quad V \quad}$	$K' \leftarrow U^v$
Abort if $K = I_{\mathcal{G}}$		Abort if $K' = I_{\mathcal{G}}$
$\text{sk} \leftarrow H_2(\text{sid}\|K\|\text{oc}(U,V))$		$\text{sk}' \leftarrow H_2(\text{sid}\|K'\|\text{oc}(U,V))$
Output sk		Output sk$'$

Fig. 1. The CPace$_{\text{base}}$ protocol.

hashing a password to a group element have been extensively covered in analysis by Abdalla et al. [1], who also give a security proof for CPace$_{\text{base}}$ in the universal composability framework. While their proof does not have any consideration of quantum annoyingness (i.e., without considering an adversary who can compute discrete logarithms), one benefit of their proof is that it does not rely on the stronger generic group model we use here.

In a CPace$_{\text{base}}$ session, the client C and server S both have a copy of the shared password $pw_{C,S}$. They receive as input a session identifier sid, and the identifier of their peer. The session identifier is assumed to come from a higher-level protocol; in some contexts, the initiator is meant to choose an sid and provide it with the first message. We will assume that the mechanism that distributes the sid to protocol participants always distributes unique values; see the full version [5] for details. The parties hash the session identifier, password, and a channel identifier (which is the ordered concatenation $\text{oc}(C,S)$ of the identities of the parties sorted by a canonical ordered) to obtain a group element G, which they then use as the base in a Diffie–Hellman key exchange.

2.2   The Generic Group Model

The generic group model [10,12] is a cryptographic model that idealizes groups, similar to how the random oracle model idealizes hash functions. In the random oracle model, the adversary must ask the challenger to answer all hash function queries; in the generic group model; the adversary must ask the challenger to carry out all group operations using oracle queries. Group elements are represented as random strings in $\{0,1\}^n$; these representations give the adversary no information about the structure of the group, except what they can learn by querying for it.

The generic group model was first used to provide a lower bound on the number of queries needed to solve the Diffie–Hellman problem [12] and establish bounds on reducing the discrete logarithm to the Diffie–Hellman problem [10].

As an idealization, proofs in the generic group model justify the security of these problems against an adversary who attacks in generically, regardless of the group. In the real world schemes can fall prey to better attacks, such as the number field sieve attacking the discrete logarithm problem over finite fields. However, analyzing a cryptographic scheme in the generic group model can provide some understanding of security where there otherwise may be none available.

More recently, the generic group model has been used by Yun to consider the security of the multiple discrete logarithm problem [16]. Yun showed that solving n distinct discrete logarithm problems requires at least $O(\sqrt{np})$ group operations, which matched known generic algorithms. The question of how much harder it is to solve n instances of the discrete logarithm problem on a quantum computer, which is relevant to the quantum annoying property, remains open.

3   Generic Group Model Proof of CPace$_{\text{core}}$

We now define the CPace$_{\text{core}}$ game, and prove an upper-bound on winning this game in the generic group model. The CPace$_{\text{core}}$ game is highly customized to go hand-in-hand with the task of proving security of the CPace$_{\text{base}}$ protocol, but the basic idea of adding a discrete logarithm oracle to the generic group model as a way to capture quantum-annoyingness may have applications beyond this specific scenario.[1]

3.1   CPace$_{\text{core}}$ Game Definition

Overview. The game takes place over a collection of instances, each indexed by an integer i. For each instance i, there are N generators $g_{i,j}$. One of these generators is picked at random (represented by a target index t_i), and a Diffie–Hellman session is initiated, picking random integers $u_i, v_i \leftarrow_\$ \mathbb{Z}_p$, and calculating $U_i \leftarrow g_{i,t_i}^{u_i}$, $V_i \leftarrow g_{i,t_i}^{v_i}$. All of this is set up by calls to a NewInstance oracle. We keep track of a counter variable ctr that is incremented every time NewInstance is called to keep track of the number of instances. When NewInstance is called, the adversary can optionally provide an index $\ell \leq$ ctr. This indicates that they want the new instance to be *linked* to a previous instances; linked instances use the same target index t_i. (When we interface with a PAKE adversary, this will represent sessions being instantiated with the same password.) Note that even though the index is repeated, the set of generators is distinct.

---

[1] We initially started out with a much simpler game in generic group model with a discrete logarithm oracle, and planned to put most of the complexity into the AKE proof. However, as developed the AKE proof, we frequently encountered steps where the only way we could see to proceed was to extend the generic group model game. Interestingly, the proof of the generic group model game often did not change very much as a result: the core idea of the proof—maintaining a linear system and checking for certain events based on the rank of a consistency matrix—was robust for the many features we added to the CPace$_{\text{core}}$ problem.

At the beginning of the game, a challenge bit s is drawn uniformly. Eventually the adversary may call a Challenge oracle with an instance i, a group element W, and a bit b indicating if they want to challenge the U half or the V half. If the challenge bit $s = 0$, then we provide $H(i, W^{u_i}, \text{OC}(U_i, W))$ or $H(i, W^{v_i}, \text{OC}(V_i, W))$ depending on which half the adversary chose to challenge. If the challenge bit $s = 1$, then the response they receive is drawn uniformly from $\mathcal{C}$ instead. The adversary is allowed to query Challenge twice per instance, once each for the U and V halves. The main challenge of the adversary is to determine the challenge bit s by trying to figure out the Diffie–Hellman completion without knowing which target index was used.

The interface with the Challenge oracle may seem somewhat arbitrary at first, with two Diffie–Hellman halves provided, and then the adversary allowed to use them separately when querying the Challenge oracle. When we interface with a real PAKE adversary in our proof of CPace$_\text{base}$, this simply reflects the fact that some sessions may have one or both endpoints not controlled by the adversary.

The adversary has access to a few other sources of information. The group operation ($\cdot$) and DLOG oracles are how the adversary can find new information about group elements and the relationships between them. The GetGen oracle gives the adversary a representation of a generator for an instance and index, and the GetTarget oracle tells the adversary the target index for an instance i. In order to not make the game trivial, when GetTarget is called, we change the behaviour of the oracle H, so that whatever information the adversary was provided before is made to be consistent with H.

Details. For a positive integer m, $[m]$ represents the integers 1 through m. If $m = 0$ it represents the empty set. Define the set $\mathcal{G} \subseteq \{0, 1\}^n$ to be the representation of group elements provided to an adversary, for some suitably large n. Define $\mathcal{C} = \{0, 1\}^\lambda$ to be a set of confirmation values.

Parameters of the game are N, the size of the generator space; and p, the (prime) size of the group. The state of the game is maintained by a non-negative integer ctr and a bit s, with ctr initially set to 0 and s sampled uniformly from $\{0, 1\}$. The adversary is given (a representation of) a generator $\mathfrak{g}$ of $\mathcal{G}$, as well as the identity element. The adversary has access to the following oracles:

- $\cdot : \mathcal{G} \times \mathcal{G} \to \mathcal{G}$: The group operation oracle.
- $\text{DLOG} : \mathcal{G} \times \mathcal{G} \to \mathbb{Z}_p$: A discrete logarithm oracle.
- $H : [\text{ctr}] \times \mathcal{G} \times \mathcal{G} \times \mathcal{G} \to \mathcal{C}$: A confirmation value oracle. This acts as a random oracle, taking in a counter, a Diffie–Hellman completion K, and the ordered concatenation of two group elements, and returns a uniformly random group element.
- GetGen : $[\text{ctr}] \times [N] \to \mathcal{G}$: On input (i, j), returns $g_{i,j}$.
- NewInstance : $[\text{ctr}] \cup \{\bot\} \to \mathcal{G} \times \mathcal{G}$: This oracle creates a new instance of the problem. If the input is $\bot$, a new instance independent from all previous instances is generated:
  1. Increment ctr.
  2. Sample fresh generators $g_{\text{ctr},j} \leftarrow^\$ \mathcal{G}$ for $j \in [N]$.

3. Sample a uniform target index $t_{\text{ctr}} \leftarrow_{\$} [N]$.
4. Sample uniform $u_{\text{ctr}}, v_{\text{ctr}} \leftarrow_{\$} \mathbb{Z}_p$ and compute $U_{\text{ctr}} \leftarrow g_{\text{ctr}, t_{\text{ctr}}}^{u_{\text{ctr}}}$, $V_{\text{ctr}} \leftarrow g_{\text{ctr}, t_{\text{ctr}}}^{v_{\text{ctr}}}$.
5. Return $U_{\text{ctr}}, V_{\text{ctr}}$.

If the input is $\ell \leq \text{ctr}$, the instance has the same target index as instance ℓ. The same steps are repeated but the same target index as that of session ℓ is used: step 3 is replaced by $t_{\text{ctr}} \leftarrow t_\ell$. This instance is said to be *linked* to instance ℓ, as well as all other instances that instance ℓ is linked to.

- Challenge : $[\text{ctr}] \times \{0,1\} \times \mathcal{G} \to \mathcal{C}$: On input $(i, b, W_{i,b})$, if $b = 0$ we calculate $K \leftarrow W_{i,0}^{u_i}$, and if $b = 1$, $K \leftarrow W_{i,1}^{v_i}$. If K is equal to the identity element, return $\bot$. Otherwise if the challenge bit $s = 0$ or GetTarget has been called on this or a linked instance, then return $H(i, K, \text{OC}(U_i, W_{i,b}))$ or $H(i, K, \text{OC}(V_i, W_{i,b}))$ depending on b. If $s = 1$ and GetTarget has not been called on a linked instance, return a randomly sampled $h_i \leftarrow_{\$} \mathcal{C}$. This oracle can only be called twice per instance i, once with $b = 0$ and once with $b = 1$.
- GetTarget : $[\text{ctr}] \to [N]$: Returns the target index t_i for instance i. If $s = 1$, then for each instance linked to instance i, we reprogram H to behave correctly: modify H so that $H(i, W_{i,0}^{u_i}, \text{OC}(U_i, W_{i,0})) = h_{i,0}$, and $H(i, W_{i,1}^{v_i}, \text{OC}(V_i, W_{i,1})) = h_{i,1}$, where $h_{i,b}$ is the value that was previously provided for the challenge. If Challenge has not yet been called for one of the linked instances, then eventually is, H will skip the check for the value of s and always return the output determined by H.

The adversary wins if any of three conditions is met:

1. The adversary queries $H(i, W_{i,0}^{u_i}, \text{OC}(U_i, W_{i,0}))$ after making a Challenge $(i, 0, W_{i,0})$ query, but before making a GetTarget query on a linked instance.
2. The adversary queries $H(i, W_{i,1}^{v_i}, \text{OC}(V_i, W_{i,1}))$ after making a Challenge $(i, 1, W_{i,1})$ query, but before making a GetTarget query on a linked instance.
3. At the end of the game, the adversary guesses s correctly.

We want to determine the probability of the adversary's success in terms of the number of queries they make. We count the number of queries as follows:

- $q_{\mathcal{G}}$, the number of queries to the group operation oracle.
- q_D, the number of queries to the discrete logarithm oracle.
- q_N, the number of queries to NewInstance (i.e., the total number of instances).
- q_C, the number of queries to Challenge where the adversary did *not* submit $(i, 0, V_i)$ or $(i, 1, U_i)$. In other words, the number of instances for which the adversary actively participated in the Diffie–Hellman session, rather than passively observed one.
- q_G, the number of queries to GetGen.

While there are two conditions under which the adversary wins, in truth, they are one and the same. The only way to find information on the challenge bit s is to detect if the output of H is correct or not for a given instance. If a GetTarget query is made, then the output of H changes to no longer depend on s for that or any linked instance, and so the relevant query must be made prior to a GetTarget query. Thus the advantage of the adversary is entirely quantified by their ability to query $\mathsf{Challenge}(i, b, W_{i,b})$ and then either $H(i, W_{i,0}^{u_i}, \mathsf{OC}(U_i, W_{i,0}))$ or $H(i, W_{i,1}^{v_i}, \mathsf{OC}(U_i, W_{i,1}))$ before ever making a $\mathsf{GetTarget}(i)$ query.

The heart of the proof comes from the fact that even though $\mathsf{NewInstance}$ gives the adversary $U_i = g_{i,t_i}^{u_i}$ and $V_i = g_{i,t_i}^{v_i}$, it does not actually leak any information about what index t_i was used for instance i. We can write the elements of G in terms of the generator provided to the adversary, $\mathfrak{g}$. The N generators for instance i can be rewritten as $g_{i,1} = \mathfrak{g}^{p_{i,1}}, g_{i,2} = \mathfrak{g}^{p_{i,2}}, \ldots, g_{i,N} = \mathfrak{g}^{p_{i,N}}$. In this view, choosing a random generator corresponds to setting $U_i = \mathfrak{g}^{p_{i,t_i} \cdot u_i}$, for a random u_i and t_i. But note that *each* generator and corresponding p_{i,t_i} value is equally possible, as $p_{i,t_i} \cdot u_i = p_{i,j} \cdot (p_{i,j}^{-1} p_{i,t_i} u_i)$. Thus the only way for the adversary to proceed is to guess the generator, compute the $W_{i,0}^{u_i}$ value and query it to H. However each guess requires the adversary to know the discrete logarithm of either U_i, V_i, or $W_{i,b}$ with respect to the generator $g_{i,j}$. This requires either a discrete logarithm query to be made, or for the $W_{i,b}$ value to have been crafted so that $\mathsf{DLOG}(g_{i,t_i}, W_{i,b})$ is known to the adversary. We will therefore establish that each query to DLOG and each customised query to $\mathsf{Challenge}$ essentially provides one guess for the target index t_i, so in expectation an adversary must make roughly N such queries.

Other than this, there are small terms in the upper bound that are related to the adversary finding collisions in the generators (and thus being able to make a single DLOG query relevant to multiple instances) and the adversary calculating discrete logarithms by making group operation, rather than DLOG, queries, both of which are divided by the group order p, which is cryptographically large.

Theorem 1. *Let $\mathcal{A}$ be an adversary in the $\mathsf{CPace_{core}}$ game. The probability that $\mathcal{A}$ wins the game is at most $\frac{1}{2} + \frac{q_D + q_C}{N} + O(q_G^2/p) + O(q_D q_G^2/p)$.*

3.2 Proof Outline

As is typical for generic group model proofs, we will maintain a table T that translates between the (additive) secret representation of elements as numbers in $\mathbb{Z}_p$ and the (multiplicative) public representation provided to the adversary, which are random unique elements of $\{0,1\}^n$. The secret representation of the identity element is 0, and the secret representation of the generator $\mathfrak{g}$ is 1.

For an instance i and bit b, let $W_{i,b}$ be the group element that the adversary submitted to the $\mathsf{Challenge}$ oracle for the bit b, and let $w_{i,b}$ be $\mathsf{DLOG}(g_{i,t_i}, W_{i,b})$. To provide an upper bound on the adversary's ability to guess s, we need to determine their ability to query $g_{i,t_i}^{u_i w_{i,0}}$ or $g_{i,t_i}^{v_i w_{i,1}}$ to H. Except where it is relevant, for ease of notation, we will focus on the $b = 0$ case for the adversary's challenge queries, with the understanding that an implicit 'and similarly for $b = 1$' follows.

If $\mathfrak{g}^{p_{i,t_i}} = g_{i,t_i}$, then this would mean that the adversary would be unable to make a relevant query until the secret representation $p_{i,t_i} u_i w_{i,0}$ of $g_{i,t_i}^{u_i w_{i,0}}$ is added to T. However, rather than maintaining a specific $p_{i,j} \in \mathbb{Z}_p$ as the secret representation of $g_{i,j}$, we will instead maintain a variable $X_{i,j}$. For example, say the adversary queries $g_{1,1} \cdot \mathfrak{g}$ to the group operation oracle. With a specific $p_{1,1}$ in mind such that $g_{1,1} = \mathfrak{g}^{p_{1,1}}$, the secret representation of such an element would be $p_{1,1} + 1$. Instead, we write the secret representation as the linear combination $X_{1,1} + 1$, and, if we have not seen this linear combination before, choose a new public representation for it and return that to the adversary.

Similarly, the adversary may query $g_{1,1} \cdot g_{1,1}$ to the group operation oracle. We would record $2X_{1,1}$ in the table, and assuming that this term has not appeared before, give it a random unused representation. Other generators have corresponding variables $X_{i,j}$. By making group operation oracle queries combining these terms, arbitrary linear combinations of these variables can be added into the table T. This allows us to precisely quantify the information that the adversary has obtained through the discrete logarithm oracle, which in turn will allow us to precisely calculate the probability that the adversary is capable of causing certain events to happen, like making relevant queries to H.

On the other hand, the discrete logarithm oracle informs the adversary of the relationship between those linear combinations. For example, if the adversary has used the group operation oracle to figure out the representation of $\mathfrak{g}^c$ and $\mathfrak{g}^d$, and queries these to the discrete logarithm oracle, they must be provided with $c^{-1}d \bmod p$. Of course such a query provides no additional information to the adversary as they could compute it themselves. Useful queries to the discrete logarithm oracle involve group elements given to the adversary from the NewInstance or GetGen oracles. If the query $\mathsf{DLOG}(\mathfrak{g}, g_{i,j})$ is made, then a value for the corresponding $X_{i,j}$ must be decided and provided as a response.

In order to query H with the completion of the Diffie–Hellman-like session, at least one of $\mathsf{DLOG}(g_{i,t_i}, U_i)$, $\mathsf{DLOG}(g_{i,t_i}, V_i)$, $\mathsf{DLOG}(g_{i,t_i}, W_{i,b})$ must be defined. If all are undefined, the completion is undefined as well, and not possible to query. In our table T, the secret representation of U_i should be $u_i X_{i,t_i}$. However, we will instead choose a constant $\mu_i \in \mathbb{Z}_p$ and set that to be the secret representation of U_i (the secret representation of V_i will be ν_i). This means that until the adversary makes a DLOG query that causes X_{i,t_i} to become defined, u_i will not be defined.

When the adversary makes a Challenge query for an instance i, they choose a bit b and submit a group element $W_{i,b}$. In our table T, $W_{i,b}$ will have a secret representation of some linear combination of the $X_{i,j}$ variables, plus a possible constant. We must also consider the adversary's ability to cause $\mathsf{DLOG}(g_{i,t_i}, W_{i,b})$ to become defined. Essentially, the adversary will get one guess per challenge query. The adversary can select an index j and hope that $j = t_i$. Then they can construct the challenge so that they know the $w_{i,b}$ such that $W_{i,b} = g_{i,t_i}^{w_{i,b}}$, in which case the discrete logarithm is defined and the adversary can complete the challenge. We will establish however, that the adversary will only get one such guess out of the Challenge queries that they craft themselves to try and make the discrete logarithm defined.

So, the overall idea of the proof is that queries to the group operation oracle populate the table T with linear expressions and the discrete logarithm oracle enforces linear relationships between those expressions. With enough queries to the discrete logarithm oracle, the adversary can force enough relations between the various $X_{i,j}$ values that each one is entirely decided. But unless the value of X_{i,t_i} has been defined by making the proper queries to the discrete logarithm oracle, or the adversary manages to guess t_i when making a challenge oracle query, there is no way for the adversary to query $g_{i,t_i}^{u_i w_{i,b}}$ to H, as that value is undefined, and thus has not been given a public representation.

Each query to the DLOG oracle imposes at most one linear constraint on the $X_{i,j}$ variables. Since any given j is not more likely than any other from the adversary's perspective, we need to consider the expected number of linear constraints that need to be put on the X variables before X_{i,t_i} is defined. We will show that the probability X_{i,t_i} is defined after q_D queries to the discrete logarithm oracle is at most q_D/N, which corresponds exactly to picking one session and performing a brute force search of computing the discrete logarithm of $g_{i,1}, g_{i,2} \ldots$. (Viewed as a PAKE, this matches the quantum annoying property exactly: the adversary guesses the password, computes the generator that corresponds to that password, and finds the discrete logarithm with respect to that generator to make a guess towards the secret key.)

The remaining terms in the theorem's bound, $O((q_D q_\mathcal{G}^2 + q_\mathcal{G}^2)/p)$ come from the adversary's ability to distinguish that the oracle has been managed with unknown $X_{i,j}$ variables, rather than 'real' secret representations. The $O(q_G^2/p)$ term comes from the fact that we will provide each generator with a unique representation, while in the real world, we would expect there to eventually be collisions in the representation of the generators.

The numerator in the other term, $q_D q_\mathcal{G}^2$, is asymptotically the same as the number of queries to the group operation oracle required to calculate a discrete logarithm (e.g., using the baby-step giant-step algorithm). So in our model, if the adversary uses the group operation oracle to calculate a discrete logarithm, rather than the provided discrete logarithm oracle, then they may notice that the discrete logarithm oracle is not behaving entirely faithfully. This happens because, when calls to the discrete logarithm oracle are made, the values of the $X_{i,j}$ can become defined. If enough group elements have been added to the table T, then it is possible that when an $X_{i,j}$ becomes defined, two of the linear polynomials in T will take on the same value in $\mathbb{Z}_p$, even though the adversary was given different representations in the generic group. However for large p, roughly $\sqrt{p}$ values need to be added to the table T in order to expect a collision to occur (the birthday paradox has come into effect).

Hence, as long as fewer than $O((q_G + q_D q_\mathcal{G}^2)/p)$ queries to the group operation oracle happen, the discrete logarithm and group operation oracles will be managed in such a way that the adversary is unlikely to notice any difference.

3.3 Proof of Theorem 1

We now get into the specifics of the proof: how is the table T managed, what exactly are the linear relations imposed by the discrete logarithm oracle, and proofs of the bounds. Algorithms 1 through 6 provide a reference for how all of the algorithms are simulated.

Algorithm 1. Simulating New Instance queries in GGM

Input: Integer $\ell \leq$ ctr or $\perp$

1: Increment ctr.
2: **if** input was integer ℓ **then** set the target index $t_{\text{ctr}} \leftarrow t_\ell$. Mark instance ctr as linked to instance ℓ, as wall as all instances ctr is linked to, and vice versa.
3: **else** Sample a uniform $t_{\text{ctr}} \leftarrow\!\!\$\ [N]$.
4: Sample uniform $\mu_{\text{ctr}}, \nu_{\text{ctr}} \leftarrow\!\!\$\ \mathbb{Z}_p^2$, compute $U_{\text{ctr}} \leftarrow \mathfrak{g}^{\mu_{\text{ctr}}}$, $V_{\text{ctr}} \leftarrow \mathfrak{g}^{\nu_{\text{ctr}}}$.
5: Return U_{ctr}, V_{ctr}.

Algorithm 2. Simulating DLOG queries in GGM

Input: Query $(g_a, g_b) \in \mathcal{G} \times \mathcal{G}$, table T, matrix D and row $\vec{r}$.

1: Use table T to look up secret representations $g_a \hookrightarrow a_0 + a_1 X_1 + \cdots + a_N X_N$ and $g_b \hookrightarrow b_0 + b_1 X_1 + \cdots + b_N X_N$. If either secret representation doesn't appear in T, then return $\perp$.
2: Select a random $\vec{s}$ such that $D\vec{s} = \vec{r}$.
3: Compute $\delta = (\vec{a} \cdot \vec{s})^{-1}(\vec{b}\vec{s})$.
4: Compute the row $[\delta \cdot a_1 - b_1, \delta \cdot a_2 - b_2, \ldots, \delta \cdot a_N - b_N]$ and the value $b_0 - \delta a_0$.
5: Append the row to D and the value to $\vec{r}$.
6: Return δ, D, $\vec{r}$.

The main technical points of the proof consist of: how group operation oracle queries add entries to T, how the NewInstance, GetGen, and Challenge oracles allow the adversary to begin interacting with the group, how discrete logarithm oracle queries are answered, and how we guarantee that responses to the oracles are consistent with each other and with past responses. With this in hand we show bound the probability that the discrete logarithm between g_{i,t_i} and U_i, V_i, or $W_{i,b}$ is defined after q_D queries to the discrete logarithm oracle and q_C modified queries to the Challenge oracle.

The Group Operation Oracle and the Table T. The table T is used to convert between the public representations provided to the adversary and the secret representation of the element in the additive group $\mathbb{Z}_p$. To begin with, the table has just 2 elements in it: a generator $\mathfrak{g}$ and the identity element. The public representation of each of these elements is chosen at random from $\{0, 1\}^n$. Note that it is common in generic group model proofs to choose n large enough so that we do not need to worry about collisions in our representations, or the adversary 'guessing' a group element that has not been added to T. Since new public representations are added to T by queries to the group operation and GetGen oracles, choosing $n \gg \log_2(q_\mathcal{G} + q_G)$ is sufficient. It is also easy to check and see if a representation has already been used and, if so, re-sample. Since it is easy to choose a large enough n, and it impacts no other parts of the proof, we omit a term that considers the probability of picking the same representation twice.

The secret representation of $\mathfrak{g}$ is naturally 1, the identity element 0, and the secret representation of each $g_{i,j}$ from GetGen is represented by a variable

---

Algorithm 3. Simulating Challenge queries in GGM

Input: Instance $i \in [\text{ctr}]$, bit $b \in \{0, 1\}$, group element $W_{i,b} \in \mathcal{G}$.

1: **if** Query starting with i and b has been made before **then** return $\bot$
2: **if** Instance i or a linked instance has had a GetTarget query issued **then**
3:     **if** b = 0 **then** Return $H(i, W_{i,b}^{u_i}, oc(U_i, W_{i,b}))$
4:     **else** Return $H(i, W_{i,b}^{v_i}, oc(V_i, W_{i,b}))$.
5: **else** Sample a uniform $h_{i,b} \leftarrow_\$ \mathcal{C}$ and return.

Algorithm 4. Simulating GetTarget queries in the GGM

Input: Instance $i \in [\text{ctr}]$.

1: **if** GetTarget has never been called before on i or a linked instance **then**
2:     **for** Each instance j linked to instance i (including i) **do**
3:         Mark that instance has had a GetTarget query called on a linked instance
4:         Query $\mathsf{DLOG}(g_{j,t_j}, U_j)$ and $\mathsf{DLOG}(g_{j,t_j}, V_j)$ to cause X_{j,t_j}, v_{j,t_j} to become
         defined (if not already defined). Calculate $u_j \leftarrow X_{j,t_j}^{-1} \mu_j$, $v_j \leftarrow X_{j,t_j}^{-1} \nu_j$.
5:         **if** Challenge$(j, 0, W_{j,0})$ has been called **then**
6:             **if** $H(i, W_{j,0}^{u_j}, oc(U_j, W_{j,0}))$ has been called **then** adversary has won game
7:             **else**
8:                 Program oracle H so that $H(i, W_{j,0}^{u_j}, oc(U_j, W_{j,0}))$ returns $h_{j,0}$, the
                 response to the Challenge query.
9:         **if** Challenge$(j, 1, W_{j,1})$ has been called **then**
10:            **if** $H(i, W_{j,1}^{v_j}, oc(V_j, W_{j,1}))$ has been called **then** adversary has won game
11:            **else**
12:                Program oracle H so that $H(i, W_{j,1}^{v_j}, oc(V_j, W_{j,1}))$ returns $h_{j,1}$, the
                 response to the Challenge query.
13: Return t_i

$X_{i,j}$. When the group operation oracle is queried on elements g_a and g_b, the public representations are queried in the table to find the corresponding secret representation. If no such representation exists, then the query is considered invalid, and returned as such[2]. Otherwise, the secret representation of g_a and g_b will be two linear combinations of the $X_{i,j}$ variables as well as a possible constant, which we can write as $g_a \hookrightarrow a_0 + \sum_{i \in [q_N]} \sum_{j \in [N]} a_{i,j} X_{i,j} = a_0 + \vec{a} \cdot \vec{X}$ and $g_b \hookrightarrow b_0 + \sum_{i \in [q_N]} \sum_{j \in [N]} b_{i,j} X_{i,j} = b_0 + \vec{a} \cdot \vec{X}$, with $a_{i,j}, b_{i,j} \in \mathbb{Z}_p$. We can then compute the secret representation of $g_a \cdot g_b \hookrightarrow (a_0 + b_0) + \sum_{i,j} (a_{i,j} + b_{i,j}) X_{i,j}$. Once the secret representation has been computed, we can check to see if this new linear combination already exists in the table. If it does, then use the already existing representation of the group element. If not, then we can generate a new random public representation for this new linear combination and provide it to the adversary.

---

[2] This is correct behaviour so long as the representation does not later become valid. Since representations are randomly chosen, the probability that this happens is negligible in n, the bit length of the representations. As discussed, we assume n is chosen to make this probability negligible.

Algorithm 5. Simulating group operation oracle queries in GGM

Input: Query $(g_a, g_b) \in \mathcal{G} \times \mathcal{G}$, table T, matrix D and row $\vec{r}$.
Output: Response g_c, updated table T.

1: Use table T to look up secret representations $g_a \hookrightarrow a_0 + a_1 X_1 + \cdots + a_N X_N$ and $g_b \hookrightarrow b_0 + b_1 X_1 + \cdots + b_N X_N$. If either secret representation doesn't appear in T, then return $\perp$.
2: Compute $a_0 + b_0 + \sum_{i,j}(a_{i,j} + b_{i,j})X_{i,j}$. Look up this secret representation in the table T. If it exists, return the corresponding public representation (no updates to T necessary). Otherwise, proceed.
3: **for** each secret representation $F(\vec{X})$ in table T **do**
4:     Compute row $\vec{g} = [c_{1,1} - f_{1,1}, c_{1,2} - f_{1,2}, \ldots, c_{q_N,N} - f_{q_N,N}]$ and value $e = f_0 - c_0$.
5:     Check and see if $\vec{g}$ is linearly independent from the rows of D. If it is, then proceed to the next secret representation in the table.
6:     Otherwise, there exists a linear combination of rows that adds up to $\vec{g}$, i.e., a row vector $\vec{h}$ such that $\vec{h} \cdot D = \vec{g}$. Compute such a $\vec{h}$.
7:     If $\vec{h} \cdot \vec{r} = -e$, then return the public representation of $F(X)$. Otherwise, proceed to the next secret representation.
8: Sample a new public representation g_c for $C(X)$. Add $C(X), g_c$ to the table T and return g_c.

Algorithm 6. Simulating GetGen queries in GGM

Input: Instance $i \in [\text{ctr}]$, index $j \in [N]$, table T
1: **if** $X_{i,j}$ already appears in the table T **then** return the corresponding public representation $g_{i,j}$.
2: **else** Sample a new public representation $g_{i,j}$ and add $X_{i,j}, g_{i,j}$ to the table T and return $g_{i,j}$.

This simple check will only work until the adversary begins to make discrete logarithm oracle queries. As queries to the discrete logarithm oracle impose linear relationships between the $X_{i,j}$ variables, we need to check if that linear combination *modulo the relations defined* already exists in the table. We will discuss more on this point when we explain how linear relationships between the $X_{i,j}$ variables are defined by queries to the discrete logarithm oracle. As a preview, these linear relations will be encoded into a matrix D. To check and see if two secret representations $\vec{a}$ and $\vec{b}$ actually encode the same group element, we see if $\vec{a} - \vec{b}$ is linearly independent from the rows of D. If it is, then its value is not dependent on the linear relations that have been defined, and we can conclude that these represent distinct group elements.

Note as well that the group operation oracle can be extended to allow for inverses to be calculated as well. This simply means calculating $-a_0 - \sum_{i \in [q_N]} \sum_{j \in [N]} a_{i,j} X_{i,j}$ and otherwise performing the same sequence of steps.

Oracles NewInstance, GetGen, *and* Challenge. The game begins with the adversary only aware of a single generator element and the identity element. In order to begin meaningfully interacting with the game, NewInstance must be called.

When this happens, we increment ctr, and if the instance is not linked to another instance, then we sample a new target index t_{ctr} from $[N]$.

Rather than earnestly generating a Diffie–Hellman-like instance from $g_{\mathsf{ctr},t_{\mathsf{ctr}}}$, we instead sample values $\mu_{\mathsf{ctr}}, \nu_{\mathsf{ctr}} \leftarrow_{\$} \mathbb{Z}_p$. We will set $U_{\mathsf{ctr}} \leftarrow \mathfrak{g}^{\mu_{\mathsf{ctr}}}$, $V_{\mathsf{ctr}} \leftarrow \mathfrak{g}^{\nu_{\mathsf{ctr}}}$. We calculate the public representation of these elements (which may be entirely new, requiring new entries into T), and return the public representation to the adversary.

We do this, rather than sending honestly generated U_i and V_i values in order to allow the discrete logarithm between g_{i,t_i} and U_i or V_i to remain undefined. Note that this does not affect the distribution of U_i or V_i. Since u_i and v_i are chosen uniformly at random, choosing the products μ_{ctr} and ν_{ctr} uniformly matches the distribution exactly. But until X_{i,t_i} becomes defined, the discrete logarithm between g_{i,t_i} and U_i and V_i is similarly undefined.

After having created an instance, the adversary can access generators through the GetGen oracle. When GetGen(i,j), where $i \leq \mathsf{ctr}$, is called, we sample a new public representation and add it and $X_{i,j}$ to T. We always sample unique representations, and this does create a small incongruity with the real game. In the real game, after sampling roughly $\sqrt{p}$ generators, an adversary would expect to see repetition in the public representations. But we will always provide unique representations, no matter how many times the oracle is called. This results in a $O(\mathfrak{g}^2/p)$ term in the theorem statement, representing the adversary's ability to cause a collision in the generators.

The challenge oracle is how the adversary is able to gain an advantage in winning the game. When Challenge$(i, 0, W_{i,0})$ is called, we are expected to respond with either a random $h_i \leftarrow_{\$} \mathcal{C}$ or $H(i, W_{i,0}^{u_i}, oc(U_i, W_{i,0}))$. We will always respond with a random h_i, so long as GetTarget(i) has not been called on a related instance i. This is indistinguishable as long as the adversary does not query $W_{i,0}^{u_i}$ without having previously made a GetTarget(i) query. If such a query is made, we consider them to have won.

The Discrete Logarithm Oracle and the Linear Relationship Matrix D. For queries to the discrete logarithm oracle, we need to define what linear relations are imposed, and how future oracle responses are managed for consistency. When group elements with secret representations α and $\beta \in \mathbb{Z}_p$ are queried, the response should be a value $\delta \in \mathbb{Z}_p$ such that $\alpha \cdot \delta \equiv \beta \pmod{p}$. So when a group element with secret representation $\alpha = a_0 + \sum a_{i,j} X_{i,j}$ and $\beta = b_0 + \sum X_{i,j}$ are queried, by returning a value $\delta \in \mathbb{Z}_p$ we are declaring that $\delta(a_0 + \sum_{i,j} a_{i,j} X_{i,j}) = b_0 + \sum_{i,j} b_{i,j} X_{i,j}$, or equivalently,

$$\sum_{i,j} (\delta a_{i,j} - b_{i,j}) X_{i,j} = b_0 - \delta \cdot a_0. \tag{1}$$

When a discrete logarithm oracle query is made, we thus need to choose a value δ consistent with all previous δ values provided. To do this we maintain a matrix D and a vector $\vec{r}$ that encodes all previous responses. That is, when a linear equation (1) is defined, we append the row

$$[\delta \cdot a_{1,1} - b_{1,1} \quad \delta \cdot a_{1,2} - b_{1,2} \quad \cdots \quad \delta \cdot a_{q_N,N} - b_{q_N,N}] \tag{2}$$

to D and extend $\vec{r}$ by the entry $b_0 - \delta \cdot a_0$. Thus the set of responses provided to the adversary so far imposes the linear constraints $D\vec{X} = \vec{r}$, where $\vec{X} = [X_{1,1}, X_{1,2}, \ldots, X_{1,N}, X_{2,1}, \ldots, X_{q_N,N}]^T$.

With this linear system in place, when a new query comes in, we can pick an arbitrary $\vec{s}$ such that $D\vec{s} = \vec{r}$, i.e., an arbitrary solution. This can be done by, for example, finding one solution and then choosing an arbitrary point in the kernel of D. Then to respond to the query $(a_0 + \vec{a} \cdot \vec{X}, b_0 + \vec{b} \cdot \vec{X}$, we can replace the $X_{i,j}$ values with the random $s_{i,j}$ values, and respond with $\delta = (a_0 + \vec{a} \cdot \vec{s})^{-1}(b_0 + \vec{b} \cdot \vec{s})$. We then add the row from (2) to D and append $b_0 - \delta \cdot a_0$ to $\vec{r}$. Our new answer is guaranteed to be consistent with all previous responses as it is consistent with $\vec{s}$, which was chosen from the solution space.

This also allows us to tell if a given $a_0 + \vec{a} \cdot \vec{X}$ has a value determined by D and $\vec{r}$, and if so, what that value is. If we can construct a linear combination of the rows of D that add up to $\vec{a}$, then the value of the linear combination is determined. Let $\vec{w}$ be the linear combination of rows, so that $\vec{w}^T D = \vec{a}^T$. Then the matrix D is telling us that $\vec{a} \cdot \vec{X} = (\vec{w}^T D)\vec{X} = \vec{w}^T(D\vec{X}) = \vec{w}^T\vec{r} = \vec{w} \cdot \vec{r}$. Thus the value (in $\mathbb{Z}_p$) of $a_0 + \vec{a} \cdot \vec{X}$ is $a_0 + \vec{w} \cdot \vec{r}$, where $\vec{w}$ is the linear combination of the rows of D that add up to $\vec{a}$. If there is no such linear combination, i.e., $\vec{a}$ is not in the rowspace of D, then the value of $a_0 + \vec{a} \cdot \vec{X}$ is not yet determined by D and $\vec{r}$. When D and $\vec{r}$ do determine a secret representations value in $\mathbb{Z}_p$, we will write it as $\cong$. So if $\vec{w}^T D = \vec{a}^T$, then $a_0 + \vec{a} \cdot \vec{X} \cong a_0 + \vec{w} \cdot \vec{r}$.

Now we may discuss how we check if a linear combination modulo the linear constraints has already appeared in the table T. When a group operation oracle query is made that will add the secret representation $a_0 + \vec{a} \cdot \vec{X}$ to the table T, we consider the difference $\vec{a} - \vec{b}$ between $\vec{a}$ and the coefficients of every other linear combination of $X_{i,j}$ values in the table T, $\vec{b}$. For each difference $\vec{a} - \vec{b}$ we need to check to see if the linear relations set forth by D mean that the new group element $a_0 + \vec{a} \cdot \vec{X}$ is actually the same as $b_0 + \vec{b} \cdot \vec{X}$.

To do this, we check to see if the rank of the matrix D is increased by appending $\vec{a} - \vec{b}$ as a row. If the rank does increase, this tells us that the relation between $\vec{a}$ and $\vec{b}$ is not defined by D. But if the rank does not increase, then the relation is defined. This means we can find the value $c \in \mathbb{Z}_p$ such that $\vec{a} - \vec{b} \cong c$.

If $c = b_0 - a_0$, then we know that these two group elements with secret representations $a_0 + \vec{a} \cdot \vec{X}$ and $b_0 + \vec{b} \cdot \vec{X}$ must be the same given the relations provided to the adversary by the discrete logarithm oracle. In this case, a new entry does not need to be added to the table T, and instead the public representation for the element already provided can be given. If $c \neq b_0 - a_0$, then the matrix D is telling us that $\vec{a}$ and $\vec{b}$ differ by a constant factor, but they are not the same element, and so the next $\vec{b}$ can be checked.

One counterintuitive aspect is that the group operation oracle is being simulated in a very expensive way. Each time a query is made, the simulator checks against each previous query made, resulting in quadratic expense. But this is not relevant to the bounds in the proof. We are not reducing CPace$_{\text{core}}$ to another problem, but providing an information-theoretic bound in terms of the number of oracle calls being made. Thus, it does not matter how efficient the simulator is, only that it counts the number of queries to the various oracle properly.

At this point, we have guarantees that (i) when a response to a discrete logarithm query is provided, it is consistent with all previous responses to the discrete logarithm oracle, and (ii) when a response to a group operation query is provided, it is consistent with all previous responses to both the group operation oracle and the discrete logarithm oracle. The remaining question is whether responses to the discrete logarithm oracle are consistent with the previous responses to the group operation oracle. In fact, they are not guaranteed to be so. Consider the case where the adversary enumerates through the entire group to get the representation of $\mathfrak{g}, \mathfrak{g}^2, \mathfrak{g}^3, \ldots, \mathfrak{g}^{p-1}$. These will all be given different public representations, but the representations will also be different from those given to all of the generators returned from GetGen. If a discrete logarithm query of the form $(\mathfrak{g}, g_{i,j})$ is made, a specific $p_{i,j} \in \mathbb{Z}_p$ will be provided. But we will have already given g^{p_i} a different representation than $g_{i,j}$, causing an inconsistency.

Since the discrete logarithm oracle responds with random answers from the solution space, these inconsistencies require the adversary to make an enormous number of group operation oracle queries to happen: it is only if $O(\sqrt{p})$ queries to the group operation oracle occur that we must worry about this inconsistency. We provide a full justification for this claim after briefly discussing the adversary's success probability.

We now return to the analysis of this game: what is the probability that the adversary succeeds after making discrete logarithm queries, and what is the difference between managing the group operation and discrete logarithm oracles in this way and a 'proper' way?

As discussed, the adversary must have done one of two things in order to possibly win. For a session i not linked to a session where a GetTarget query has been made, they must either know the discrete logarithm between g_{i,t_i} and either U_i, V_i, or $W_{i,b}$. We need to characterize when it is possible for an adversary to learn this based on the matrix D, and then provide an upper bound on the adversary's success probability in triggering that event.

Lemma 1. *Let $\vec{e}_{i,t_i}$ be the standard basis vector in $\mathbb{Z}^{q_N \cdot N}$ with a 1 in position (i, t_i) and 0 everywhere else. Let $\vec{w}$ be the vector representation of $W_{i,b}$, the row vector whose entries are the coefficients of the $X_{i,j}$ variables in the corresponding secret representation. Let D be the matrix of linear relations defined by the queries to the discrete logarithm oracle. Then the discrete logarithm between g_{i,t_i} and U_i, V_i, or $W_{i,b}$ is only defined if $\vec{e}_{i,t_i}$ appears in the rowspan of $\left[\frac{D}{\vec{w}} \right]$.*

Proof. Recall that the secret representation of g_{i,t_i} is X_{i,t_i}, and for U_i and V_i it is a randomly chosen pair $\mu_i, \nu_i \leftarrow_\$ \mathbb{Z}_p^2$. For the discrete logarithm between these two to be defined, the value X_{i,t_i} must be forced to have a specific value from the linear constraints of D. If it is not entirely constrained, then it can still take on any value in $\mathbb{Z}_p$. For it to take on a specific value, it must be the case that there is a linear combination of the rows of D that add up to $\vec{e}_{i,t_i}$.

Similarly, for $W_{i,b}$ we consider its vector representation $\vec{w}$. For the discrete logarithm to be defined, we must be able to rewrite this vector as a multiple of

X_{i,t_i}. We can assume that X_{i,t_i} is undefined, since it being defined was already covered by the previous case. So, it must be possible, modulo the linear relations defined, to rewrite $\vec{w}$ as a multiple of $\vec{e}_{i,t_i}$. But 'zeroing out' the other entries of $\vec{v}$ like this means that $\vec{e}_{i,t_i}$ is in the rowspan of $\left[\frac{D}{\vec{w}}\right]$, as expected.   □

Corollary 1. *Let W be the matrix whose rows consist of the vectorizations of each $W_{i,b}$ submitted to the* Challenge *oracle not equal to U_i or V_i. Then the instances i for which $W_{i,b}^{u_i}$ can be queried to H are restricted to those where $\vec{e}_{i,t_i}$ appears in $\left[\frac{D}{V}\right]$.*

This corollary allows us to calculate the overall probability of having the relevant discrete logarithms defined, and thus the probability of querying a Diffie-Hellman completion and winning the game. The rank of the matrix $\left[\frac{D}{W}\right]$ is at most the number of rows of D plus the number of rows of W, which is $q_D + q_C$, the number of Challenge queries where a customised $W_{i,b}$ was submitted. The rank also limits the number of basis vectors that can appear in the row span to the same number, so at most $q_D + q_C$ basis vectors can appear there.

This is how we can bound the probability that the adversary can submit the relevant group element to H. To do this, they need to have an instance i for which no GetTarget query has been made for any linked instance, and $\vec{e}_{i,t_i}$ is in the rowspan of $\left[\frac{D}{W}\right]$. Since no GetTarget query has been made for this instance, the distribution of which $\vec{e}_{i,j}$ basis vectors appear in the rowspan is independent of t_i. Thus the adversary has $q_D + q_C$ chances for a target basis vector to appear in the rowspan. So the overall probability that one appears can be upper-bounded as $(q_N + q_C)/N$.

Next we consider the question of whether the adversary can detect that we are not managing the group operation and discrete logarithm oracles perfectly. As mentioned, we do not ensure that responses to the DLOG oracle are perfectly consistent with all previous group operation oracle queries. With enough entries in T it is possible for the adversary to notice a discrepancy in how queries were handled. For example, say the adversary has queried for group elements with secret representation X_1 and d, and in the process of making discrete logarithm queries, the value of X_1 is set to be d. Since that happens after having queried X_1 and d, the two group elements will be given different public representations.

To determine the probability that any inconsistency occurs, we consider each pair of linear combinations in the table T, $(a_0 + \vec{a} \cdot \vec{X}, b_0 + \vec{b} \cdot \vec{X})$. For a given pair, we want to check to see if a new linear constraint added to D has made these two previously distinct elements take on the same value. This occurs if, before the discrete logarithm oracle query, $\vec{a} - \vec{b}$ was linearly independent from the rows of D, but after updating to D', it is now linearly *dependent*, and furthermore we have that $\vec{a} - \vec{b} \cong b_0 - a_0$.

For every pair of elements, the probability that this happens is at most $1/p$. To see this we will discuss the geometric structure of how linear constraints are added to D and what two intersecting elements means in this geometry.

Each row of D and $\vec{r}$ adds a linear constraint to the system. If the first row of D is $\vec{d}$ and the first entry of $\vec{r}$ is r then the solution space is constrained so that $\vec{d} \cdot \vec{X} = r$. We can view this as an affine hyperplane, an $(n-1)$-dimensional subspace of $\mathbb{Z}_n$. When a new row is added, this corresponds to adding another affine hyperplane. The solution space is the intersection of all hyperplanes.

The process of adding a new row to D is to select a random point in the solution space, and then construct a response to the adversary's query. The adversary's query can be seen as determining the direction of the affine hyperspace (i.e., the linear subspace that goes through zero), but the response is determined by choosing a random point in the solution space and offsetting the submitted linear subspace so that it goes through that random point, constructing an affine space.

Meanwhile, pairs in our table T collide if $\vec{a} - \vec{b}$ is linearly independent before a row is added, but linearly dependent after. The vector $\vec{a} - \vec{b}$ and value $b_0 - a_0$ also can be viewed as a hyperplane H. So the geometric interpretation of the linear relations $(D, \vec{r})$ forcing $(\vec{a} - \vec{b}) \cdot \vec{X}$ to be equal to $b_0 - a_0$ is that the solution space S is contained entirely within the hyperplane H.

This case occurs if, before a new hyperplane is added to the linear constraints, the solution space is not entirely within the hyperplane H, but, after the discrete logarithm oracle query, it is. As discussed, the process of adding a new hyperplane involves picking a random point in the solution space and making sure the new hyperplane goes through that point. For the resulting solution space to be entirely within H, it must be the case that the random point that is chosen is also within H. So the question becomes, how many points in the solution space S are also in H? Since it is not the case that S is entirely contained within H, it cannot be all of them. Since S is generated by the intersection of a series of affine hyperplanes, the intersection between that and H must be either empty, or is at most a fraction $1/p$ of the space S, as desired. This is because the intersection of such hyperplanes is an affine subspace with smaller dimension. Our base field is $\mathbb{Z}_p$, and so the subspace must have a size a power of p.

So each time a new linear constraint is added to D and $\vec{r}$, for every two entries in the table T there is at most a $1/p$ chance that these two entries now represent the same group element, modulo these constraints. Since this happens for each pair in the table, we can upper bound the overall probability of any collision happening as $O(q_\mathcal{G}^2/p)$, and the probability of a collision happening on any of the q_D queries to the discrete logarithm oracle as $O(q_D q_\mathcal{G}^2/p)$.

Thus the probability that the adversary notices the oracles misbehaving is at most $O(q_D q_\mathcal{G}^2/p)$, the probability that it is noticed that generators are always unique is at most $O(q_\mathcal{G}^2/p)$, and the probability that they win assuming they do not notice misbehaviour is at most $(q_D + q_C)/N$. So the overall probability of winning is at most $(q_D + q_C)/N + O((q_D q_\mathcal{G}^2 + q_\mathcal{G}^2)/p)$.

Acknowledgement. E.E. was supported by a Natural Sciences and Engineering Research Council of Canada (NSERC) Alexander Graham Bell Canada Graduate Scholarship. D.S. was supported by NSERC Discovery grant RGPIN-2016-05146 and a Discovery Accelerator Supplement.

References

1. Abdalla, M., Haase, B., Hesse, J.: Security analysis of CPace. Cryptology ePrint Archive, Report 2021/114, January 2021. https://eprint.iacr.org/2021/114
2. Bellare, M., Pointcheval, D., Rogaway, P.: Authenticated key exchange secure against dictionary attacks. In: Preneel, B. (ed.) EUROCRYPT 2000. LNCS, vol. 1807, pp. 139–155. Springer, Heidelberg (2000). https://doi.org/10.1007/3-540-45539-6_11
3. Bender, J., Fischlin, M., Kügler, D.: Security analysis of the PACE key-agreement protocol. In: Samarati, P., Yung, M., Martinelli, F., Ardagna, C.A. (eds.) ISC 2009. LNCS, vol. 5735, pp. 33–48. Springer, Heidelberg (2009). https://doi.org/10.1007/978-3-642-04474-8_3
4. Boneh, D., Dagdelen, Ö., Fischlin, M., Lehmann, A., Schaffner, C., Zhandry, M.: Random oracles in a quantum world. In: Lee, D.H., Wang, X. (eds.) ASIACRYPT 2011. LNCS, vol. 7073, pp. 41–69. Springer, Heidelberg (2011). https://doi.org/10.1007/978-3-642-25385-0_3
5. Eaton, T., Stebila, D.: The "quantum annoying" property of password-authenticated key exchange protocols. Cryptology ePrint Archive, May 2021
6. Federal Office for Information Security (BSI). Advanced security mechanism for machine readable travel documents (extended access control (EAC), password authenticated connection establishment (PACE), and restricted identification (RI)), 2008. SI-TR-03110, Version 2.0. https://www.bsi.bund.de/EN/Service-Navi/Publications/TechnicalGuidelines/TR03110/BSITR03110.html
7. Gheorghiu, V., Mosca, M.: Benchmarking the quantum cryptanalysis of symmetric, public-key and hash-based cryptographic schemes (2019). arXiv:1902.02332
8. Haase, B., Labrique, B.: AuCPace: efficient verifier-based PAKE protocol tailored for the IIoT. IACR TCHES 2019(2), 1–48 (2019). https://tches.iacr.org/index.php/TCHES/article/view/7384. https://doi.org/10.13154/tches.v2019.i2.1-48
9. Jablon, D.P.: Strong password-only authenticated key exchange. Comput. Commun. Rev. 26(5), 5–26 (1996). https://doi.org/10.1145/242896.242897
10. Maurer, U.M., Wolf, S.: Lower bounds on generic algorithms in groups. In: Nyberg, K. (ed.) EUROCRYPT 1998. LNCS, vol. 1403, pp. 72–84. Springer, Heidelberg (1998). https://doi.org/10.1007/BFb0054118
11. Shor, P.W.: Polynomial-time algorithms for prime factorization and discrete logarithms on a quantum computer. SIAM J. Comput. 26(5), 1484–1509 (1997). https://doi.org/10.1137/S0097539795293172
12. Shoup, V.: Lower bounds for discrete logarithms and related problems. In: Fumy, W. (ed.) EUROCRYPT 1997. LNCS, vol. 1233, pp. 256–266. Springer, Heidelberg (1997). https://doi.org/10.1007/3-540-69053-0_18
13. Smyshlyaev, S., Sullivan, N., Melnikov, A.: [CFRG] Results of the PAKE selection process. CFRG Mailing List, March 2020. https://mailarchive.ietf.org/arch/msg/cfrg/LKbwodpa5yXo6VuNDU66vt_Aca8/
14. Sullivan, N., Smyshlyaev, S., Paterson, K., Melnikov, A.: Proposed PAKE selection process. CFRG Mailing List, May 2019. https://mailarchive.ietf.org/arch/msg/cfrg/-J43ZsPw2J5MBC-k8y6-kJJtZk/
15. Thomas, S.: Re: [CFRG] proposed PAKE selection process. CFRG Mailing list, June 2019. https://mailarchive.ietf.org/arch/msg/cfrg/dtf91cmavpzT47U3AVxrVGNB5UM/
16. Yun, A.: Generic hardness of the multiple discrete logarithm problem. In: Oswald, E., Fischlin, M. (eds.) EUROCRYPT 2015, Part II. LNCS, vol. 9057, pp. 817–836. Springer, Heidelberg (2015). https://doi.org/10.1007/978-3-662-46803-6_27

Implementation and Side Channel Attack

Differential Power Analysis of the Picnic Signature Scheme

Tim Gellersen, Okan Seker$^{(\boxtimes)}$, and Thomas Eisenbarth

University of Lübeck, Lübeck, Germany
tim.gellersen@student.uni-luebeck.de,
{okan.seker,thomas.eisenbarth}@uni-luebeck.de

Abstract. This work introduces the first differential side-channel analysis of the Picnic Signature Scheme, an alternate candidate in the ongoing
competition for post-quantum cryptography by the National Institute of
Standards and Technology (NIST). We present a successful side-channel
analysis of the underlying multiparty implementation of the LowMC
block cipher (MPC-LowMC) and show how side-channel information can
be used to recover the entire secret key by exploiting two different parts of
the algorithm. LowMC key recovery then allows to forge signatures for the
calling Picnic post-quantum signature scheme. We target the NIST reference implementation executed on a FRDM-K66F development board.
Key recovery succeeds with fewer than 1000 LowMC traces, which can
be obtained from fewer than 30 observed Picnic signatures.

Keywords: Picnic Signature Scheme · LowMC · Multiparty
computation · Power analysis · DPA · MPC-in-the-Head

1 Introduction

Public key cryptography is an indispensable component of secure communication. Quantum computers could break most of the widely used public key cryptographic schemes, due to Shor's algorithm [40]. Due to massive investments into
their development in recent decades, the existence of usable quantum computers might become reality in the near future. Even if general-purpose quantum
computers that are able to process enough bits to break the current public key
schemes never become reality, expanding the narrow portfolio of deployable public key schemes is advantageous. NIST has started a competition to standardize
quantum-resistant public-key cryptographic algorithms in 2017 and is currently
in the third round of the standardization process. The security of cryptographic
systems does not only require resistance to purely computational cryptanalysis. For practical implementations, resistance to other attacks such as physical
attacks is also relevant, as highlighted in the status report on the second round
by NIST [4].

Physical attacks are divided into two main classes: active *fault injection
attacks* and passive *side-channel attacks*. Fault injection attacks manipulate

© Springer Nature Switzerland AG 2021
J. H. Cheon and J.-P. Tillich (Eds.): PQCrypto 2021, LNCS 12841, pp. 177–194, 2021.
https://doi.org/10.1007/978-3-030-81293-5_10

the (secret) state of a cryptographic scheme, while it is performing an encryption/decryption or signing operation. Afterwards, the attacker tries to extract information about the scheme's secret key, from the faulted output of the scheme [9,11]. On the other hand, side-channel attacks exploit the physical information given by the device on which the implementation of the algorithm is running such as timing information [30], cache behavior [43,44], emitted sound [22], power consumption [29] or electromagnetic emanation [20]. These attacks have been successfully implemented in the last decades on various targets that run unprotected cryptographic implementations. The impact of side-channel analysis is shown in the literature and ranges from high-speed CPU's [21] to virtual machines in cloud systems [25]. Furthermore, system-on-chip embedded platforms [32] and even white-box implementations [13] are vulnerable to these kind of attacks.

Prior work has already shown, that post-quantum cryptographic schemes on embedded systems are vulnerable to side-channel attacks [42]. In 2018, Park et al. [34] presented that correlation power analysis can be applied to signature schemes based on multivariate quadratic equations namely; UOV [28] and Rainbow [17]. Side-channel properties of hash based signatures have also been analysed [14,19]. More recent work by Aranha et al. [7] analyses the security of Fiat-Shamir based signature schemes against fault attacks. Ravi et al. [36] investigate the security of Dilithium [18] (a lattice-based scheme in the competition) against Side-channel attacks and successfully extract the secret from LWE instance. Zhang et al. [45] analyse SIKE [8] and propose a theoretical DPA attack on the scheme. Furthermore, practical fault attacks are shown effective against lattice-based key-encapsulation mechanisms such as Kyber [12] and NewHope [6] by Pessl et al. [35].

In this work we focus on the base Picnic signature scheme presented in CCS 2017 [15]. The foundation of the scheme builds on a symmetric key primitive, MPC-in-the-head (MPCitH) paradigm introduced by Ishai et al. [26], for constructing zero-knowledge (ZK) proof systems. The base scheme has been built on zero knowledge for Boolean circuits (ZKBoo) by Giacomelli et al. [23] and ZKB++ by Chase et al. [15] and has been improved over the years through several iterations such as Picnic2 and Picnic3. The new versions of the signature rely on MPCitH paradigm with preprocessing introduced by Katz et al. [27] and produce shorter signatures. Moreover the scheme has different versions such as BBQ [37], Banquet [10] and Limbo [38], which use AES instead of LowMC. Also a side-channel secure implementation of Picnic has been proposed at CCS 2020 [39]. Note that the attack presented here was already described theoretically in [39] to motivate the need for a countermeasure. In this work we describe the attacks in detail with its practical setup and a detailed description how to reconstruct the secret key.

Our Contribution: We present the first successful side-channel analysis of the Picnic signature scheme, by analysing its core component; MPC-LowMC. We explore the security features of MPC-LowMC and its direct effects on the security of the whole signature scheme. We show how to recover the secret key from

MPC-LowMC using two different attacks: an attack on the secret sharing process and an attack on the Multiparty Computation of the Sbox layer. To demonstrate the practicality of the attack, we apply it to the reference implementation of Picnic [3], run on a FRDM-K66F development board while monitoring electromagnetic emanation. The first attack is able to recover Picnic's secret key using less then 5000 power traces, which corresponds to around 30 observed Picnic signatures. The second attack can be used to leak 30 bits of secret key related information from each round of the MPC-LowMC cipher. However, this step can be repeated in the deeper rounds to form a system of linear equations, whose solution is the 128-bit secret key of the Picnic scheme. Whether the information obtained in the first step leads to linear independent equations or not depends on the randomised matrices that are used by MPC-LowMC. In practice, we were able to solve the system of linear equations by combining the information obtained from the first five rounds of the MPC-LowMC cipher. For longer key sizes, like 196 or 256 bits, we can adaptively use more rounds, to receive 220 or 280 linear equations.

2   Preliminaries

In this section, we provide the definitions used in this paper. We start with differential power analysis (DPA) which is introduced by Kocher et al. [31].

In order to implement DPA, an adversary first selects an intermediate variable which is a function $f(p_i, k^*)$ of a secret value (k^*) and a known value (e.g. plaintext p_i). In the next step, the adversary chooses a function ϕ that models how a register value influences the power consumption. Common models are the Hamming weight or a single bit [33] of the register. We refer to this function as the *key hypothesis*. In the second step the adversary collects a large number of side-channel traces to implement a statistical analysis.

In our analysis we use correlation as our statistical tool. For each key candidate $k^* \in \mathcal{K}^1$, where $\mathcal{K}$ denotes the key space, we form the following set:

$$(\phi(f(p_1, k^*)), \dots, \phi(f(p_N, k^*))),$$

where N is the number of traces and p_i for $1 \leq i \leq N$ is the known input. This set is then applied to the statistical tool (e.g. Pearson's correlation coefficient [16]) together with the side-channel measurements. The statistical analysis results in an observable peak for the correct key hypothesis, while wrong keys reside within a threshold.

LowMc Block Cipher: In order to present our target implementation, we first need to introduce the underlying scheme. LowMC [5] is a flexible block cipher with low AND depth. Thus it is a suitable cipher for Secure Multiparty Computation (MPC), Zero-Knowledge Proofs (ZK) and Fully Homomorphic Encryption (FHE). An overview of the structure of the scheme with the parameters (n, k, r)

---

[1] $|\mathcal{K}|$ is small enough to process the analysis and generally it ranges from 2^1 to 2^8.

where n, k and r denote block length, key size and number of rounds respectively, can be found in Algorithm 1 in Appendix B. The details of the ith round are as follows:

1. **SboxLayer:** The round function consists of multiple parallel instances of the same 3×3 bit Sbox as shown in Eq. (1). However, only a part of the state is processed by the Sbox layer. The remaining bits stay unchanged.

$$Sbox(a, b, c) = (a \oplus bc, a \oplus b \oplus ac, a \oplus b \oplus c \oplus ab). \tag{1}$$

2. **LinearLayer:** The state is multiplied with a random and invertible matrix LM_i, where $LM_i \in \mathbb{F}_2^{n \times n}$.
3. **ConstantAddition:** A constant vector RC_i is added to the state, where $RC_i \in \mathbb{F}_2^n$.
4. **KeyAddition:** The round key k_i is added to the state, where k_i is obtained by the multiplication of the key matrix KM_i where $KM_i \in \mathbb{F}_2^{n \times k}$ and k_s is the master-secret key .

ZKBoo decomposition and Picnic Signature Scheme: Zero knowledge for Boolean circuits (ZKBoo) is a protocol introduced by Giacomelli et al. [23], that can prove the knowledge of a preimage of a one-way function f, such that $f(x) = y$, without leaking any information on x. The main idea of ZKBoo is to use the MPC-in-the-head paradigm introduced in [26].

In the ZKBoo scheme, the verifier and the prover both know the output y. However, the prover is the only one knowing x, such that $y = f(x)$. The prover then calculates $f(x)$ using a n-privacy circuit decomposition of f, i.e. at least $n + 1$ shares are required to reconstruct x. The scheme can be summarized as follows: The prover runs the MPC-Circuit multiple times and commits to each of the generated views, before sending the committed values to the verifier. The verifier then chooses a *challenge* and requests the prover to open the commitment of some (less or equal to n) shares from each execution and checks the revealed values for consistency. As at most n shares of each run are opened, the verifier does not learn anything about x.

The Picnic scheme is introduced by Chase et al. [15], uses ZKB++ (which is an improved version of ZKBoo) to create signatures. They chose the LowMC cipher as the one-way function f, because it only requires a low amount of AND gates, greatly reducing the complexity of the (2,3)-circuit decomposition (2-Privacy, 3 Player). An overview of the Picnic signature scheme can be seen in Fig. 1. As seen in the figure, the MPC-LowMC circuit is the foundation of the scheme. Next, we describe our attacks on the MPC-LowMC part of the scheme. The aim of the attacks is to recover the secret key k_s which is also the secret key used in Picnic.

3   DPA on LowMC and The Extensions to Picnic

Figure 1 depicts the signing process of Picnic. Our goal is to apply a DPA attack on MPC-LowMC to gain information about intermediate state values which then

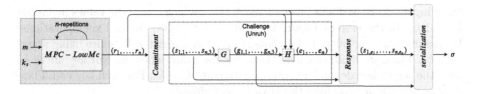

Fig. 1. Overview of the Picnic signature scheme where m is constant plaintext that is used in LowMC such that $\mathsf{LowMC}(m, k_s) = y$, $sk = ((y, m), k_s)$ is the secret key and $pk = (y, m)$ is the public key. The figure is adapted from [7].

will be used to recover the secret key. As our target, we focus on the reference implementation given by the authors [3] which uses the Unruh transformation with security parameters L1. However, our attacks are independent of the actual transformation (Fiat-Shamir or Unruh Transformation) and can be adapted to the different security parameters. The first attack targets the initial sharing of the secret key before its use in the MPC-LowMC implementation while the second attack targets an intermediate state in the shared Sbox implementation of MPC-LowMC.

Attacker Model: We model an adversary who has physical access to a target device, running the Picnic signature scheme. In particular, the attacker is able to measure the side-channel information, such as power or electromagnetic emanation, during the signing of any message. Afterwards the adversary can obtain the valid signature and verify the signature, thus having access to the opened values. In other words, while the implementation follows the MPC paradigm, the adversary learns two out of three shares from the signature and can, with a correct guess of the constant secret, correctly predict the third share. The side-channel leakage of the unknown third share is then used to verify the correctness of the guessed secret, as usual. Please note that the signed message does not affect our model, since the message does not change the computation performed by LowMC, which is based on a fixed (and public) input m and a secret key k_s.

3.1 Attack on the Secret Sharing Process

Our first attack targets the initial secret sharing process of the secret key k_s of the MPC-LowMC reference implementation. As shown in Fig. 3, the secret sharing process is located before the actual MPC-LowMC part starts. Our analysis targets the secret sharing of the secret key k_s, which is simply stored in the implementation and freshly shared for each call to MPC-LowMC. First, two n bit keys (or key shares) for two players k_0 and k_1 are generated randomly. Using the random key shares, the key share for the last player k_2 is calculated as:

$$k_2 = k_s \oplus k_0 \oplus k_1.$$

During the challenge/opening phase of the *Picnic* scheme, the key shares of two of the three players are revealed and become part of the signature. In the following analysis, we focus on challenge 0 (C_0), which reveal the values including k_0 and k_1. In the case of Picnic, k_2 is the result of two chained xor-operations. We assume that the output of $k_s \oplus k_0$ is saved in a register R before being xored with k_1. Thus, we build our hypothesis for the point where we xor key share k_1 with the secret key dependent intermdiate state $k_s \oplus k_0$. For each key candidate $k^* \in \mathcal{K}$ we produce the hypothesis value as follows:

$$H_{k^*} = \text{HW}(k_1 \oplus R), \text{ such that } R = k^* \oplus k_0, \tag{2}$$

where HW is the Hamming weight function (i.e. $\phi := \text{HW}$). Using the hypothesis values H_{k^*} for all $k^* \in \mathcal{K}$ (where $\mathcal{K}$ denotes the key space), we can implement a statistical analysis and the best key candidate reveals k_s. While exploiting the leakage of a linear XOR operation is not ideal in terms of distinguishability (wrong keys also show high correlation in this attack), we show that for the target implementation the attack still succeeds with a low number of traces.

It is known that secret sharing of sensitive inputs to an MPC circuit should not be observable by a side channel adversary. An easy fix for this leakage exists by keeping the secret k_s in shared representation in memory. A refreshing of the shared representation before each MPC-LowMC call is implicitly part of the Picnic protocol already and would thus not incur further overhead.

3.2 Attack on the Substitution Layer

Our second attack targets the MPC-LowMC Sbox. We denote the MPC-LowMC players as $\mathcal{P}_0$, $\mathcal{P}_1$, and $\mathcal{P}_2$ and their states as p_0, p_1, and p_2, respectively. We further denote a (*theoretical*) unshared version (player $\mathcal{P}$) of the state as p, i.e. $p = p_0 \oplus p_1 \oplus p_2$.

We analyse the state values of LowMC(m, k_s) with MPC-LowMC(m, k_s), where m is the constant (and predefined) plaintext and k_s is the secret key. MPC-LowMC starts by initializing the state of $\mathcal{P}_i$ with k_i such that $k_s = k_0 \oplus k_1 \oplus k_2$. As shown in Algorithm 1, the plaintext is xored with the key value. In the MPC setting, this step is only performed for the first player's state. In the unmasked LowMC version we set the $\mathcal{P}$ state to the value $KM_0 \cdot k_s \oplus m$. In summary, the initial states of the MPC-LowMC variant and the (imaginary) LowMC variant (p) are as follows:

$$p_i \leftarrow KM_0 \cdot k_i \oplus \delta_i \cdot m \text{ for } i = \{0, 1, 2\} \text{ and } p \leftarrow KM_0 \cdot k_s \oplus m$$

where $\delta_i = 1$ if $i = 0$ and $\delta_i = 0$ if $i \neq 0$. The state of $\mathcal{P}$ always equals the xor of all other players' corresponding states, i.e. p equals to $p_0 \oplus p_1 \oplus p_2$ at any given time. In the context of the attack on a single Sbox, the state values p_i corresponds to three bit vector (a_i, b_i, c_i). Similarly, the unshared states p denotes three bit vector (a, b, c) such that $a = a_0 \oplus a_1 \oplus a_2$, $b = b_0 \oplus b_1 \oplus b_2$ and $c = c_0 \oplus c_1 \oplus c_2$. Using this notation we can introduce the Sbox operation within SboxLayer as;

$$Sbox(a, b, c) = (a \oplus bc, a \oplus b \oplus ac, a \oplus b \oplus c \oplus ab). \tag{3}$$

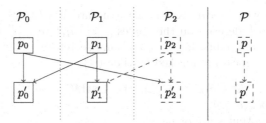

Fig. 2. SboxLayer calculation for MPC-LowMC (left) and LowMC (right). Dashed boxes and arrows represent the values that are *not* opened during the challenge C_0 and p_i (resp. p_i') represents the state of $\mathcal{P}_i$ before (resp. after) the Sbox operation

In the MPC-LowMC setting, the Sbox is defined according to the linear decomposition of the binary multiplication gate. That means that the players need to communicate their bits according to the definition in ZKBoo [15]. Assume that the values ab, bc and ac are calculated in the MPC setting and the state values for $\mathcal{P}_i$ are denoted by $[ab]_i$, $[bc]_i$ and $[ac]_i$ respectively (for example $ab = [ab]_0 \oplus [ab]_1 \oplus [ab]_2$). Each player calculates the following equations in order to generate the shared representations of the state values:

$$[bc]_i = b_i c_i \oplus b_j c_i \oplus b_i c_j \oplus r_i^{bc} \oplus r_j^{bc}$$
$$[ac]_i = a_i c_i \oplus a_j c_i \oplus a_i c_j \oplus r_i^{ac} \oplus r_j^{ac} \qquad (4)$$
$$[ab]_i = a_i b_i \oplus a_j b_i \oplus a_i b_j \oplus r_i^{ab} \oplus r_j^{ab}$$

where $j = i + 1 \bmod 3$ and r_i^{ab} (resp. r_i^{ac} and r_i^{bc}) represents the random bit generated by the ith player while calculating the output share of $[bc]_i$ (resp. $[ac]_i$ and $[ab]_i$).

In Picnic, n runs of the *MPC-LowMC* are pre-computed and in the challenge response phase, two players' keys and random tapes are opened. For example, for the challenge C_0 the values a_i, b_i, c_i, and $r_i = (r_i^{ab}, r_i^{ac}, r_i^{bc})$ for $i = 0, 1$ are opened. A visualization of challenge C_0 and which values are revealed is shown in Fig. 2.

Setup and Hypothesis: Similar to the previous attack, we focus on the challenge C_0. Adapting the attack to other challenges C_1 and C_2 is possible in the natural way. As described in the *Attacker Model* we assume a scenario where an adversary can access the values the state values p_0 and p_1. We also assume a leakage model where an implementation leaks weak and noisy information about each intermediate variable, separately and independently in observable measurement traces. Our claim is that the MPCitH measurements have a weak and noisy dependence on p_2, which can be exploited due the revealed shares p_0 and p_1.

We define a state-guess p^* of $\mathcal{P}$ of the input for the Sbox. The aim of the DPA attack is to get knowledge of the state of $\mathcal{P}_2$. As mentioned before, we cannot directly recover it with a first order DPA attack (due to the circuit decomposition), as we would need to guess the actual state as well as the random value/mask. However, we can exploit the structure of MPCitH. Remark that in the following attack description the values $p_i = (a_i, b_i, c_i)$, $p'_i = (a'_i, b'_i, c'_i)$ and $r_i = (r_i^{ab}, r_i^{bc}, r_i^{ac})$ are public for $i = \{0, 1\}$ and secret for $i = 2$ The values that depend on the key guess are marked by tilde ($\sim$).

1. For each $p^*(:= (\tilde{a}, \tilde{b}, \tilde{c})) \in \mathcal{K}$ (in the LowMC case $\mathcal{K} := \mathbb{F}_2^3$) compute $(\tilde{a}', \tilde{b}', \tilde{c}') = Sbox(\tilde{a}, \tilde{b}, \tilde{c})$.
2. Compute the output state of $\mathcal{P}_2$ as:

$$(\tilde{a}'_2, \tilde{b}'_2, \tilde{c}'_2) = (\tilde{a}' \oplus a_0 \oplus a_1, \tilde{b}' \oplus b_0 \oplus b_1, \tilde{c}' \oplus c_0 \oplus c_1)$$

3. DPA: perform a statistical analysis using $\phi(\tilde{p}'_2)$ with the side-channel leakage of the device.

For each state guess p^*, we are not considering the random bits used in LowMC-MPC, instead we use the knowledge of revealed values to correctly guess the final share p_2. A more compact description of the attack can be found in Algorithm 2.

4   Practical Setup and Experimental Results

Next, we experimentally evaluate our attacks on the reference implementation of Picnic, ported to the FRDM-K66F development board [1]. The board features an NXP MK66FN2M0VMD18 Cortex-M4F MCU with 2MB flash and 256 KB SRAM, which we clocked at to 120 MHz. To measure the dynamic power consumption during Picnic, we collected 20,000 traces using a Langer EM Probe [2] placed 1 mm above the C37 $0.1\,\mu$F blocking capacitor of the FRDM-K66F board. Measurements were taken using a Tektronix MSO6 at 312.5 MHz sampling rate. Since the relevant part of the signature generation are the calls to LowMC, we placed a trigger before the start of the LowMC calls.

Recall that in each MPC-round the prover chooses a random challenge and depending on the challenge the prover opens a subset of the views for verification. In our test environment, we decrease the number of MPC-Rounds to 50 from 219 and also fixed the challenge to ease analysis. As in Picnic there exists 3 possible challenge and 219 MPC-rounds, which means that the number of traces per challenge is $\sim$73. Thus, our setup lower-bounds the information observed by a real-world adversary.

An example trace starting with the secret sharing until the end of the first SboxLayer can be seen in Fig. 3, which contains the relevant initial operations as well as operations from the first round of MPC-LowMC. The 10 shared Sbox computations are on the right side, while the secret sharing happens early, as indicated on the left side of the plot. We applied a minimal pre-processing step, of cutting the necessary part for each attack.

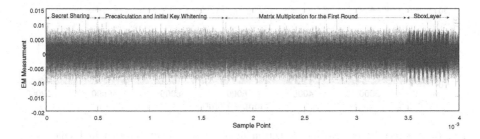

Fig. 3. An annotated example EM trace for one round of LowMC.

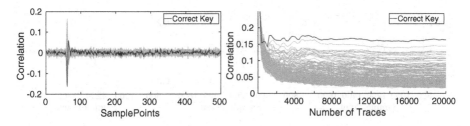

Fig. 4. Left side: DPA using 5000 sample points and 20,000 traces. Right side: The change of absolute values of DPA results with respect to number of traces. Although we can see a positive peak in the first figure, the second figure shows that the correct key is distinguishable with less that 2000 traces.

4.1 Results of the Attack on the Secret Sharing Process

The resulting correlation for the key hypothesis with 5,000 sample points and 20,000 traces can be seen on the left hand side of Fig. 4 which shows the correlation values for the first byte of the secret key. The right side of Fig. 4 shows the change in correlation results for each key guess with respect to the number of traces. In our analysis we choose the key space as $\mathbb{F}_2^8$ (however the space can be defined as $\mathbb{F}_2$ or $\mathbb{F}_2^{32}$). As a result, we see 9 clusters for the different key guesses based on the *Hamming weight* values. We can clearly distinguish the correct secret key with 2000 traces.

4.2 The Practical Results of Attack on the Substitution Layer

In order to validate the leakage model, we use a simple t-test setup. In this analysis we collect traces of Picnic signature generation. The analysis uses the side-channel information of the unopened view and the two opened shares of a multiplication gadget. We target a single bit (e.g. a' in Eq. (1)) inside the SboxLayer. We classify the traces into two groups depending on the value of $a'_0 \oplus a'_1$. The result of the t-test in Fig. 5 shows the clear dependence between the unrevealed share a'_2 and the observable measurement traces, as the t-value clearly exceeds 4.5.

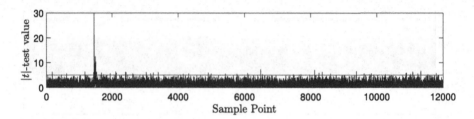

Fig. 5. A t-test based leakage detection of a single output bit (a') in Picnic using the classification based on $i = a'_0 \oplus a'_1$. The details of the experimental setup and formulation can found in Appendix A.

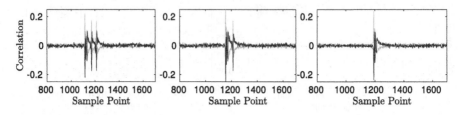

Fig. 6. DPA with 20,000 traces on the 10^{th}th Sbox using first, second and third bit.

In order to experimentally verify this leakage, we applied the attack (as described in Sect. 3.2) to the first five rounds of MPC-LowMC. Due to the SboxLayer structure of LowMC, only the first 30 bits of state are processed by Sbox operations, therefore we can only recover 30 bits of state-information of the first round key.

In Fig. 6, we present the DPA of the 3 output bits of the 10th Sbox of the first round using 20,000 traces. We see that the two lines corresponding to the key guesses are the inverse of each other. As a result of our measurement setup, the negatives peaks correspond to the device's current and therefore give us the correct bits. As this behavior is the same for all leaking key bits, prior knowledge of the negative correlation is not necessary.

The Sbox structure of LowMC has some characteristics (seen in Equation (1)), such as first input bit a is xored with the first, the second and the third output bit. Therefore, when we build our hypothesis on the first bit of the Sbox output (i.e. $a \oplus bc$), the guessed value is highly correlated with the second and the third output bit. Thus, we see three peaks in the first figure. Similarly, in the second one (where we guess the $a \oplus b \oplus ac$) we see two peaks and in the last one we can see only one peak. In Fig. 7, we can see the distinguishability of the three bits of the 10th Sbox. We can see that no more than 1,000 traces are needed to clearly identify the correct key. The attack uses the opened state values of the two players, such as $\mathcal{P}_0$ and $\mathcal{P}_1$. Therefore the attack can be implemented independently to the deeper rounds to recover key-related information. The attacks on the deeper rounds can be seen in Appendix C. As the scheme uses a constant plaintext for all challenges, the unshared state $\mathcal{P}$ is constant for every run.

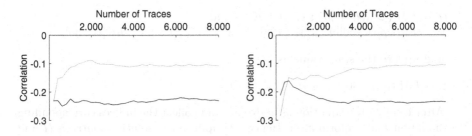

Fig. 7. The change of *minimum* values of DPA results with respect to number of traces. Clearly, the correct key (which has the highest-negative value) is distinguishable even after 2,000 traces.

That means, our attack can be applied to every round to receive 30 bits of key-related information.

4.3 Algebraic Key Recovery

In the previous part, we have described how to gain key-related information using side-channel analysis. In this section, we introduce how to combine this information from different rounds and extract the master key k_s. We form a system of linear equations $\mathcal{U}k_s = \mathcal{V}$ where k_s is the n-bit master key, $\mathcal{U}$ is a $30 \cdot t \times n$ matrix (t is the number of analysed rounds) and $\mathcal{V}$ is a $30 \cdot t$-bit recovered-state. To produce such a system we consider attacks on individual round and find equations like $\mathcal{U}_i k_s = \mathcal{V}_i$. In the following, the notation $\mathcal{U}[i : j]$ is used to denote the rows of a matrix between i^{th} and j^{th} index. The ith round state before and after SboxLayer is denoted by p_i and p'_i respectively. Remark that, due to the structure of LowMc only first 30-bit of the state is processed by the SboxLayer, i.e. $p'_i[1 : 30] = Sbox(p_i)[1 : 30]$ and $p'_i[31 : 128] = p_i[31 : 128]$. We start with the initial step or *zero round attack*.

Zero Round Attack: As described in Sect. 3.2, we can recover 30-bit state information that correspond to first 30-bit of $KM_0 \times k_s$. Therefore, the equations can be initialized as $\mathcal{U}[1 : 30] \leftarrow KM_0[1 : 30]$ and $\mathcal{V}[1 : 30] \leftarrow k_0[1 : 30]$.

i^{th}-*Round Attack:* Using the above analysis we can repeat the same procedure for the deeper rounds. We reformulate the state values with initial values $\mathcal{U}_0 = KM_0$ and $t_0 = m$

$$
\begin{aligned}
p_{i+1} &= LM_i(Sbox(p_i)) \oplus RC_i \oplus KM_i k_s \\
&= LM_i(p'_i[1 : 30] \,\|\, p_i[31 : 128]) \oplus RC_i \oplus KM_i k_s \\
&= LM_i(p'_i[1 : 30] \,\|\, (\mathcal{U}_{i-1} k_s \oplus t_{i-1})[31 : 128]) \oplus RC_i \oplus KM_i k_s \\
&= LM_i(p'_i[1 : 30] \,\|\, t_{i-1}[31 : 128]) \oplus LM_i(\mathcal{Z} \,\|\, ((\mathcal{U}_{i-1} k_s)[31 : 128])) \\
&\quad \oplus RC_i \oplus KM_i k_s
\end{aligned}
$$

where $\mathcal{Z}$ is a 30×128 zero matrix and $t_0 = m$. Using this state representation we can define the system of linear equations $\mathcal{U}_i k_s = \mathcal{V}_i$ as:

- $\mathcal{U}_i = LM_i(\mathcal{Z}||(\mathcal{U}_{i-1})[31:128]) \oplus KM_i$ and
- $\mathcal{V}_i = LM_i(p'_i[1:30]||t_{i-1}[31:128])[1:30] \oplus p_{i+1}[1:30] \oplus RC_i[1:30]$.

and update the state value as:

- $t_i = LM_i(p'_i[1:30]||t_{i-1}[31:128]) \oplus RC_i$

After forming the equation as above, we can collect the indices corresponding to the 30-bit state information. Hence, we update the solution matrices $\mathcal{U}$ and $\mathcal{V}$ as follows:

$$\mathcal{U}[30i+1:30(i+1)] \leftarrow \mathcal{U}_i[1:30] \text{ and } \mathcal{V}[30i+1:30(i+1)] \leftarrow \mathcal{V}_i[1:30]$$

This calculation holds for any round, thus we can generate equations for 30 rows of $\mathcal{U}_i$ with the solution in $\mathcal{V}_i$. After collecting enough equations, we can solve the system $\mathcal{U}k_s = \mathcal{V}$ with a simple Gaussian elimination and recover the secret key. As we gain 30 equations per observed round, 5 rounds suffice to make the search space small enough to recover the key quickly. The algorithm can be found in Appendix B.

Remark that, the attack can work with less number of rounds. For example an attack on three rounds will produce 90 independent linear equations and a solution space with 2^{128-90} possible solution which can be still exploitable.

5   Conclusion

In this work, we presented the first side-channel analysis of the Picnic signature scheme, a family of digital signature schemes secure against attacks by quantum computers and currently considered an alternate candidate in round three of the NIST PQC standardization process. We showed that the core part of the scheme, MPC-LowMC is vulnerable to side-channel attacks. By exploiting the features of the known shares for side-channel analysis, we were able to recover 30 bits of each round state of LowMC. We showed how key leakage from several rounds can be combined in an algebraic key recovery by solving a system of linear equations that reveals the secret key. Our analysis shows that we can recover the secret key with less than 2,000 traces for a specific challenge, depending on the attack.

We further showed how the attack, which only targets the secret sharing part, can be extended to completely recover the secret key of Picnic. As one Picnic signature contains at least 219 calls to MPC-LowMC, as little as 30 signatures suffice to recover the secret key even if we only use traces for one particular unknown party. These results highlight the need for side-channel protection for Picnic. When compared to classic block cipher protection, the MPC-in-the-head approach rather makes the attack easier, as known inputs are available for all rounds of computation.

Acknowledgment. This work has been supported by the German Federal Ministry of Education and Research (BMBF) under the project PQC4MED (FKZ 16KIS1045).

A   Leakage Assessment

The test vector leakage assessment (TVLA) leakage detection method by Goodwill et al. [24] is recognised as a pass-fail test to decide if an implementation can be consider as secure or not. The test detects leakages at a given orders using two different method: the non-specific and the specific method. The first one, analyses two different set of traces, one generated by processing a fixed input and one generated by processing a random input. The latter one employs only the traces with a random input and used a function of inputs to sort the traces. The main favour of the second method is that it can lead to an actual attack. After collecting and sorting the traces, the means (μ_0, μ_1) and standard deviations (σ_0, σ_1) for two sets are calculated in both variants. Welch's t-test is computed as

$$t = \frac{\mu_f - \mu_r}{\sqrt{(\sigma_f^2/n_f) + (\sigma_r^2/n_r)}},$$

where n_0 and n_1 denote the number of traces for the two distinguished sets, respectively. Typically, it is assumed that leakage is present if a threshold of $t \geq 4.5$ or 5 is exceeded [41].

B   Additional Algorithms

Algorithm 1. LowMC Encryption Scheme

Input: Key matrices $KM_{i \in [1,r]} \in \mathbb{F}_2^{n \times k}$, Linear matrices $LM_{i \in [1,r]} \in \mathbb{F}_2^{n \times n}$, Round
   constants $RC_{i \in [1,r]} \in \mathbb{F}_2^n$, a plaintext $p \in \mathbb{F}_2^n$ and a secret-key $k_s \in \mathbb{F}_2^k$
Output: Ciphertext $s \in \mathbb{F}_2^n$ such that $s = \mathsf{LowMC}(p, k_s)$.
1: $s \leftarrow (KM_0 \cdot k_s) \oplus p$ ▷ Initial Key Addition
2: **for** $1 \leq i \leq r$ **do**
3:      $s \leftarrow Sbox(s)$ ▷ SboxLayer
4:      $s \leftarrow LM_i \cdot s$ ▷ LinearLayer
5:      $s \leftarrow RC_i \oplus s$ ▷ ConstantAddition
6:      $s \leftarrow (KM_i \cdot k_s) \oplus s$ ▷ KeyAddition
7: **return** s

Algorithm 2. DPA Attack on the State of LowMC.

Input: The set of revealed (public) values $p_i = (a_i, b_i, c_i)$, $p'_i = (a'_i, b'_i, c'_i)$ and a side-
   channel trace T.
Output: Best state candidate k^*.
1: **for all** $p^* \in \mathcal{K}$ **do**
2:      $(\tilde{a}', \tilde{b}', \tilde{c}') \leftarrow Sbox(\tilde{a}, \tilde{b}, \tilde{c})$
3:      $(\tilde{a}'_2, \tilde{b}'_2, \tilde{c}'_2) = (\tilde{a}' \oplus a_0 \oplus a_1, \tilde{b}' \oplus b_0 \oplus b_1, \tilde{c}' \oplus c_0 \oplus c_1)$
4:      $R \leftarrow \mathrm{corr}(\phi(p'_{2H}), T)$
5: **return** best state candidate p^*

Algorithm 3. Algebraic Key Recovery

Input: The state values recovered using DPA, $p_i[1:30]$ for $i = 0, \ldots, n$.
Output: k_s
1: $\mathcal{U}_0 = KM_0$ and $t_0 = m$
2: $\mathcal{U}[1:30] \leftarrow \mathcal{U}_0[1:30]$ and $\mathcal{V}[1:30] \leftarrow k_0[1:30]$
3: **for** Round $i = 1$ to n **do**
4:      $\mathcal{U}_i = LM_i(\mathcal{Z}||(\mathcal{U}_{i-1})[31:128]) \oplus KM_i$
5:      $\mathcal{V}_i = LM_i(p_i'[1:30]||t_{i-1}[31:128]) \oplus p_{i+1}[1:30] \oplus RC_i[1:30]$
6:      $t_i = LM_i(p_i'[1:30]||t_{i-1}[31:128]) \oplus RC_i$
7:      $\mathcal{U}[30i+1:30(i+1)] = \mathcal{U}_i[1:30]$ ▷ Update the coefficient Matrix
8:      $\mathcal{V}[30i+1:30(i+1)] = \mathcal{V}_i[1:30]$ ▷ Update the solution Matrix
9: **Return** Solution of $\mathcal{U} \cdot k_s = \mathcal{V}$

C   Differential Power Analysis Results on Rounds 2–5

The attack results for rounds 2–5 can be found in Figs. 8, 9, 10 and 11 respectively.

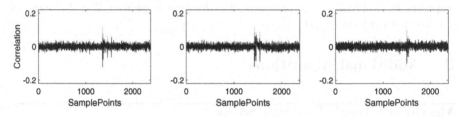

Fig. 8. DPA of the second round using uses 6,200 traces. The negative peaks correspond to first, second and third bit input-state of the 10th Sbox.

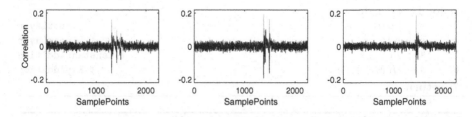

Fig. 9. DPA of the third round using uses 6,200 traces. The negative peaks correspond to first, second and third bit input-state of the 10th Sbox.

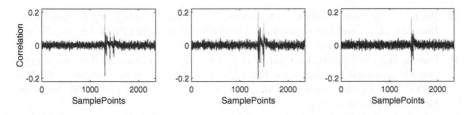

Fig. 10. DPA of the fourth round using uses 6,200 traces. The negative peaks correspond to first, second and third bit input-state of the 10th Sbox.

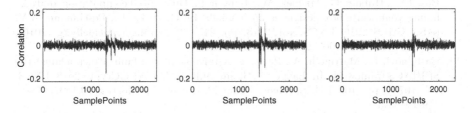

Fig. 11. DPA of the fifth round using uses 6,200 traces. The negative peaks correspond to first, second and third bit input-state of the 10th Sbox.

References

1. FRDM-K66F: Freedom Development Platform for Kinetis. https://www.nxp.com/downloads/en/schematics/FRDM-K66F-SCH.pdf
2. LF-U 2.5, H-Field Probe 100 kHz–50 MHz. https://www.langer-emv.de/en/product/lf-passive-100-khz-50-mhz/36/lf-u-2-5-h-field-probe-100-khz-up-to-50-mhz/5
3. Picnic: Post Quantum Signatures. https://github.com/microsoft/Picnic
4. Alagic, G., et al.: Status Report on the Second Round of the NIST, Post-Quantum Cryptography Standardization Process (2020). https://nvlpubs.nist.gov/nistpubs/ir/2020/NIST.IR.8309.pdf
5. Albrecht, M.R., Rechberger, C., Schneider, T., Tiessen, T., Zohner, M.: Ciphers for MPC and FHE. In: Oswald, E., Fischlin, M. (eds.) EUROCRYPT 2015. LNCS, vol. 9056, pp. 430–454. Springer, Heidelberg (2015). https://doi.org/10.1007/978-3-662-46800-5_17
6. Alkim, E., Ducas, L., Pöppelmann, T., Schwabe, P.: Post-quantum key exchange-a new hope. In: 25th {USENIX} Security Symposium ({USENIX} Security 16), pp. 327–343 (2016)
7. Aranha, D.F., Orlandi, C., Takahashi, A., Zaverucha, G.: Security of hedged Fiat-Shamir signatures under fault attacks. In: Canteaut, A., Ishai, Y. (eds.) EUROCRYPT 2020. LNCS, vol. 12105, pp. 644–674. Springer, Cham (2020). https://doi.org/10.1007/978-3-030-45721-1_23
8. Azarderakhsh, R., et al.: Supersingular isogeny key encapsulation. Submission to the NIST Post-Quantum Standardization project (2017)
9. Bar-El, H., Choukri, H., Naccache, D., Tunstall, M., Whelan, C.: The sorcerer's apprentice guide to fault attacks. Proc. IEEE **94**(2), 370–382 (2006)

10. Baum, C., de Saint Guilhem, C.D., Kales, D., Orsini, E., Scholl, P., Zaverucha, G.: Banquet: short and fast signatures from AES. Cryptology ePrint Archive, Report 2021/068 (2021). https://eprint.iacr.org/2021/068

11. Boneh, D., DeMillo, R.A., Lipton, R.J.: On the importance of checking cryptographic protocols for faults. In: Fumy, W. (ed.) Advances in Cryptology EURO-CRYPT'97. Lecture Notes in Computer Science, vol. 1233, pp. 37–51. Springer, Berlin Heidelberg (1997)

12. Bos, J., et al.: CRYSTALS - kyber: A CCA-secure module-lattice-based KEM. In: 2018 IEEE European Symposium on Security and Privacy (EuroSP), pp. 353–367 (2018)

13. Bos, J.W., Hubain, C., Michiels, W., Teuwen, P.: Differential computation analysis: hiding your white-box designs is not enough. In: Gierlichs, B., Poschmann, A.Y. (eds.) CHES 2016. LNCS, vol. 9813, pp. 215–236. Springer, Heidelberg (2016). https://doi.org/10.1007/978-3-662-53140-2_11

14. Castelnovi, L., Martinelli, A., Prest, T.: Grafting trees: a fault attack against the SPHINCS framework. In: Lange, T., Steinwandt, R. (eds.) PQCrypto 2018. LNCS, vol. 10786, pp. 165–184. Springer, Cham (2018). https://doi.org/10.1007/978-3-319-79063-3_8

15. Chase, M., et al.: Post-quantum zero-knowledge and signatures from symmetric-key primitives. In: Proceedings of the 2017 ACM SIGSAC Conference on Computer and Communications Security, pp. 1825–1842 (2017)

16. Coron, J.S., Kocher, P., Naccache, D.: Statistics and secret leakage. In: Frankel, Y. (ed.) Financ. Crypt., pp. 157–173. Springer, Berlin Heidelberg, Berlin, Heidelberg (2001)

17. Ding, J., Schmidt, D.: Rainbow, a new multivariable polynomial signature scheme. In: Ioannidis, J., Keromytis, A., Yung, M. (eds.) ACNS 2005. LNCS, vol. 3531, pp. 164–175. Springer, Heidelberg (2005). https://doi.org/10.1007/11496137_12

18. Ducas, L., Kiltz, E., Lepoint, T., Lyubashevsky, V., Schwabe, P., Seiler, G., Stehlé, D.: CRYSTALS-Dilithium: A lattice-based digital signature scheme. IACR Trans. Crypt. Hardware Embedded Syst. 2018(1), 238–268 (2018). https://doi.org/10.13154/tches.v2018.i1.238-268, https://tches.iacr.org/index.php/TCHES/article/view/839

19. Eisenbarth, T., von Maurich, I., Ye, X.: Faster hash-based signatures with bounded leakage. In: Lange, T., Lauter, K., Lisoněk, P. (eds.) SAC 2013. LNCS, vol. 8282, pp. 223–243. Springer, Heidelberg (2014). https://doi.org/10.1007/978-3-662-43414-7_12

20. Gandolfi, K., Mourtel, C., Olivier, F.: Electromagnetic analysis: concrete results. In: Koç, Ç.K., Naccache, D., Paar, C. (eds.) CHES 2001. LNCS, vol. 2162, pp. 251–261. Springer, Heidelberg (2001). https://doi.org/10.1007/3-540-44709-1_21

21. Genkin, D., Pachmanov, L., Pipman, I., Tromer, E.: Stealing keys from PCs using a radio: cheap electromagnetic attacks on windowed exponentiation. In: Güneysu, T., Handschuh, H. (eds.) CHES 2015. LNCS, vol. 9293, pp. 207–228. Springer, Heidelberg (2015). https://doi.org/10.1007/978-3-662-48324-4_11

22. Genkin, D., Shamir, A., Tromer, E.: RSA key extraction via low-bandwidth acoustic cryptanalysis. In: Garay, J.A., Gennaro, R. (eds.) CRYPTO 2014. LNCS, vol. 8616, pp. 444–461. Springer, Heidelberg (2014). https://doi.org/10.1007/978-3-662-44371-2_25

23. Giacomelli, I., Madsen, J., Orlandi, C.: ZKBoo: faster zero-knowledge for Boolean circuits. In: 25th USENIX Security Symposium (USENIX Security 16), pp. 1069–1083. USENIX Association, Austin (2016)

24. Goodwill, G., et al.: A testing methodology for side-channel resistance validation. nIST non-invasive attack testing workshop (2011). https://csrc.nist.gov/csrc/media/events/non-invasive-attack-testing-workshop/documents/08_goodwill.pdf

25. Inci, M.S., Gulmezoglu, B., Irazoqui, G., Eisenbarth, T., Sunar, B.: Cache attacks enable bulk key recovery on the cloud. In: International Conference on Cryptographic Hardware and Embedded Systems, pp. 368–388. Springer (2016)

26. Ishai, Y., Kushilevitz, E., Ostrovsky, R., Sahai, A.: Zero-knowledge from secure multiparty computation. In: STOC 2007, pp. 21–30. Association for Computing Machinery (2007)

27. Katz, J., Kolesnikov, V., Wang, X.: Improved non-interactive zero knowledge with applications to post-quantum signatures. In: CCS 2018. Association for Computing Machinery (2018)

28. Kipnis, A., Patarin, J., Goubin, L.: Unbalanced oil and vinegar signature schemes. In: Stern, J. (ed.) EUROCRYPT 1999. LNCS, vol. 1592, pp. 206–222. Springer, Heidelberg (1999). https://doi.org/10.1007/3-540-48910-X_15

29. Kocher, P., Jaffe, J., Jun, B., Rohatgi, P.: Introduction to differential power analysis. J. Crypt. Eng. 1(1), 5–27 (2011)

30. Kocher, P.C.: Timing attacks on implementations of Diffie-Hellman, RSA, DSS, and other systems. In: Koblitz, N. (ed.) CRYPTO 1996. LNCS, vol. 1109, pp. 104–113. Springer, Heidelberg (1996). https://doi.org/10.1007/3-540-68697-5_9

31. Kocher, P., Jaffe, J., Jun, B.: Differential power analysis. In: Wiener, M. (ed.) CRYPTO 1999. LNCS, vol. 1666, pp. 388–397. Springer, Heidelberg (1999). https://doi.org/10.1007/3-540-48405-1_25

32. Longo, J., De Mulder, E., Page, D., Tunstall, M.: SoC It to EM: electromagnetic side-channel attacks on a complex system-on-chip. In: Güneysu, T., Handschuh, H. (eds.) CHES 2015. LNCS, vol. 9293, pp. 620–640. Springer, Heidelberg (2015). https://doi.org/10.1007/978-3-662-48324-4_31

33. Mangard, S., Oswald, E., Popp, T.: Power Analysis Attacks: Revealing the Secrets of Smart Cards (Advances in Information Security). Springer, Berlin (2007)

34. Park, A., Shim, K.A., Koo, N., Han, D.G.: Side-channel attacks on post-quantum signature schemes based on multivariate quadratic equations. IACR Trans. Crypt. Hardware Embedded Syst. **2018**, 500–523 (2018). https://doi.org/10.13154/tches.v2018.i3.500-523

35. Pessl, P., Prokop, L.: Fault attacks on CCA-secure lattice KEMs. IACR Trans. Crypt. Hardware Embedded Syst. **2021**(2), 37–60 (2021). https://doi.org/10.46586/tches.v2021.i2.37-60, https://tches.iacr.org/index.php/TCHES/article/view/8787

36. Ravi, P., Jhanwar, M.P., Howe, J., Chattopadhyay, A., Bhasin, S.: Side-channel assisted existential forgery attack on dilithium - a NIST PQC candidate. Cryptology ePrint Archive, Report 2018/821 (2018). https://eprint.iacr.org/2018/821

37. de Saint Guilhem, C.D., De Meyer, L., Orsini, E., Smart, N.P.: BBQ: using AES in picnic signatures. In: Paterson, K.G., Stebila, D. (eds.) Selected Areas in Cryptography - SAC 2019, pp. 669–692. Springer International Publishing, Cham (2020)

38. de Saint Guilhem, C.D., Orsini, E., Tanguy, T.: Limbo: efficient zero-knowledge MPCitH-based arguments. Cryptology ePrint Archive, Report 2021/215 (2021). https://eprint.iacr.org/2021/215

39. Seker, O., Berndt, S., Wilke, L., Eisenbarth, T.: SNI-in-the-head: protecting MPC-in-the-head protocols against side-channel analysis. In: Proceedings of the 2020 ACM SIGSAC Conference on Computer and Communications Security, CCS 2020, pp. 1033–1049. Association for Computing Machinery, New York (2020)

40. Shor, P.W.: Polynomial time algorithms for prime factorization and discrete logarithms on a quantum computer. SIAM J. Sci. Statist. Comput. **26**, 1484 (1997)
41. Standaert, F.-X.: How (Not) to use Welch's t-test in side-channel security evaluations. In: Bilgin, B., Fischer, J.-B. (eds.) CARDIS 2018. LNCS, vol. 11389, pp. 65–79. Springer, Cham (2019). https://doi.org/10.1007/978-3-030-15462-2_5
42. Taha, M., Eisenbarth, T.: Implementation attacks on post-quantum cryptographic schemes. IACR Cryptology ePrint Archive 2015, p. 1083 (2015)
43. Tromer, E., Osvik, D.A., Shamir, A.: Efficient cache attacks on AES, and countermeasures. J. Cryptol. **23**(1), 37–71 (2010)
44. Yarom, Y., Falkner, K.: FLUSH+RELOAD: a high resolution, low noise, L3 cache side-channel attack. In: 23rd USENIX Security Symposium (USENIX Security 14), pp. 719–732. USENIX Association, San Diego (2014). https://www.usenix.org/conference/usenixsecurity14/technical-sessions/presentation/yarom
45. Zhang, F., Yang, B., Dong, X., Guilley, S., Liu, Z., He, W., Zhang, F., Ren, K.: Side-channel analysis and countermeasure design on arm-based quantum-resistant SIKE. IEEE Trans. Comput. **69**(11), 1681–1693 (2020). https://doi.org/10.1109/TC.2020.3020407

Implementation of Lattice Trapdoors on Modules and Applications

Pauline Bert, Gautier Eberhart, Lucas Prabel[(⊠)], Adeline Roux-Langlois, and Mohamed Sabt

Univ Rennes, CNRS, IRISA, Rennes, France
`lucas.prabel@irisa.fr`

Abstract. We develop and implement efficient Gaussian preimage sampling techniques on module lattices, which rely on the works of Micciancio and Peikert in 2012, and Micciancio and Genise in 2018. The main advantage of our implementation is its modularity, which makes it practical to use for signature schemes, but also for more advanced constructions using trapdoors such as identity-based encryption. In particular, it is easy to use in the ring or module setting, and to modify the arithmetic on $\mathcal{R}_q$ (as different schemes have different conditions on q).

Relying on these tools, we also present two instantiations and implementations of proven trapdoor-based signature schemes in the module setting: GPV in the random oracle model and a variant of it in the standard model presented in Bert *et al.* in 2018. For that last scheme, we address a security issue and correct obsolescence problems in their implementation by building ours from scratch. To the best of our knowledge, this is the first efficient implementation of a lattice-based signature scheme in the standard model. Relying on that last signature, we also present the implementation of a standard model IBE in the module setting. We show that while the resulting schemes may not be competitive with the most efficient NIST candidates, they are practical and run on a standard laptop in acceptable time, which paves the way for practical advanced trapdoor-based constructions.

Keywords: Lattice-based cryptography · Trapdoors · Gaussian preimage sampling · Module lattices · Signature scheme · Identity-based encryption

1 Introduction

Lattice-based cryptography is a viable candidate for possibly replacing number theoretic cryptography in the future. Hardness assumptions on lattices are conjecturally quantum resistant, whereas the discrete logarithm and factorization problems are known to be solvable in polynomial time in a quantum setting [Sho94]. Worst-case to average-case reductions from fundamental lattice problems (relaxations of NP-hard problems) also provide strong theoretical security guarantees for lattice-based primitives.

© Springer Nature Switzerland AG 2021
J. H. Cheon and J.-P. Tillich (Eds.): PQCrypto 2021, LNCS 12841, pp. 195–214, 2021.
https://doi.org/10.1007/978-3-030-81293-5_11

Although such constructions were quite inefficient in the early years of the field, the introduction of ideal lattices (or the ring setting) [PR06, SST+09, LPR10], module lattices [LS15] and NTRU lattices [HPS98, SS13] led to constructions relying on lattices that possess a polynomial structure, effectively speeding up computations and reducing storage costs. On the practical side, much work has been put into improving the efficiency of polynomial multiplication [Sei18, AHH+19], Gaussian sampling over the integers [Kar16, MW17], and Gaussian preimage sampling [MP12, GM18]. Some schemes now have an efficiency comparable to their classical counterparts, but quasilinear in the security parameter, providing much better scalability and long-term security.

The NIST's post-quantum cryptography standardization process, which aims to select public-key encryption (PKE) schemes, key encapsulation mechanisms (KEM), and signatures, is now in its third round. In the PKE/KEM category, 3 out of 4 candidates are lattice-based, and 2 out of 3 for signatures, proving that cryptography based on lattices can be competitive in practice. Additionally, there are many advanced cryptographic constructions built on lattices, such as identity-based encryption [GPV08, ABB10b, BFRS18], attribute-based encryption [GVW13], group signature [LLL+13] or Fully Homomorphic Encryption.

Lattice-Based Signatures. The first direct constructions for proven lattice-based signatures were given in 2008. Gentry, Peikert, and Vaikuntanathan [GPV08] proposed a hash-and-sign signature scheme and proved its security in the Random Oracle Model (ROM). Lyubashevsky and Micciancio [LM08] constructed a one-time signature scheme in the standard model, and combined it with a tree structure to obtain an unrestricted signature scheme.

The GPV signature scheme [GPV08] was the first of a family of proven trapdoor-based signature schemes. The idea behind it is the following: the public key is a matrix $A \in \mathbb{Z}_q^{n \times m}$ that defines the q-ary lattice $\Lambda_q^\perp(A) = \{ x \in \mathbb{Z}^m \mid Ax = 0 \bmod q \}$, and the secret key is a trapdoor for A which is a short basis $T \in \mathbb{Z}^{m \times m}$ of this lattice. To sign a message $M \in \{0, 1\}^*$, the signer first hashes it to a vector $u = \mathcal{H}(M) \in \mathbb{Z}_q^n$, and then computes a small preimage of u under the function $f_A : x \longmapsto Ax$. This operation, known as Gaussian preimage sampling, is made possible by knowledge of the trapdoor: using T, one can sample a vector $\nu \in \mathbb{Z}^m$ following a narrow discrete Gaussian distribution and is such that $A\nu = u \bmod q$. Verification simply consists in checking that $A\nu = \mathcal{H}(M) \bmod q$ and that ν is sufficiently short. This scheme admits strong EU-CMA security in the ROM, under the hardness of the SIS problem.

This construction as such was never instantiated in practice because of its inefficiency, but several later improvements led to instantiations and implementations. First, Micciancio and Peikert [MP12] proposed a new notion of trapdoor, which was an improvement on short bases, and efficient associated algorithms in the case where the modulus q is a power of two. In [BB13], the authors implemented these techniques in both the unstructured and the ring settings. Then, Genise and Micciancio [GM18], using the same trapdoors, gave more efficient presampling algorithms in the ring setting and for an arbitrary modulus, which were later implemented in [GPR+18, GPR+19]. Finally, a notion of approximate trapdoors was introduced in [CGM19], enabling the inversion of the one-way function f_A approximately rather than exactly, and leading to smaller parameters in concrete instantiations of signature schemes.

Even with these tools, lattice-based hash-and-sign signatures remain costly in practice, the primary bottlenecks being the generation of the trapdoor and Gaussian preimage sampling. Falcon [FHK+17], a lattice-based NIST candidate, is based on the same paradigm but still efficient in practice. It instantiates the GPV framework over NTRU lattices [SS13], using a Gaussian preimage sampler called fast Fourier sampling, itself derived from the Fast Fourier Orthogonalization algorithm [DP16]. Apart from being used to build signature schemes, lattice trapdoors have shown their utility by enabling many advanced constructions such as identity or attribute-based encryption [GPV08, ABB10b, GVW13] and group signature [LLL+13].

There are several direct constructions of lattice-based signatures in the standard model [CHK+10, Boy10, MP12], which are often similar to identity-based encryption schemes [CHK+10, ABB10b]. In these schemes, a message M is encoded into a lattice $\Lambda_q^{\perp}(A_M)$, where A_M is a matrix that depends on the public key and M. Signing M then consists in sampling Gaussian preimages on $\Lambda_q^{\perp}(A_M)$, similarly to [GPV08]. In [Boy10], $A_M = [A \mid A_0 + \sum_i M_i A_i]$, where the M_i are the bits of M, and the A_i are part of the public key. This results in very large public keys. In [BFRS18], $A_M = A + [0 \mid H(M)G]$, where H is a function with a strong injectivity property and G the very structured gadget matrix of [MP12]. This yields much lighter public keys, and combines particularly well with the trapdoors from [MP12]. As far as we know, [BFRS18] provides the previously only implementation of a lattice-based standard model signature.

The concept of Identity Based Encryption (IBE) was defined by Shamir in [Sha84]. The first IBE constructions were based respectively on bilinear maps and on quadratic residue assumptions. The first supposedly post-quantum IBE scheme was introduced in [GPV08] and was based on hard lattice problems. It was then followed by many improvements [CHK+10, ABB10a, DLP14, Yam16]. Note that both [DLP14] and more recently [ZMS+21] provide an implementation of an IBE scheme based on NTRU lattices. We notice that a disadvantage of these schemes is that they additionally need the NTRU assumption.

Gaussian Preimage Sampling. Gaussian preimage sampling is a crucial operation and often the main bottleneck in trapdoor-based schemes, whether it be signature or more advanced constructions. It consists in sampling a vector from a discrete Gaussian distribution on the set $\Lambda_q^u(A) = \{ x \in \mathbb{Z}^m \mid Ax = u \bmod q \}$, given $A \in \mathbb{Z}_q^{n \times m}$, $u \in \mathbb{Z}^n$, and a trapdoor T for the matrix A. The result is then a preimage of u under the function $f_A : x \longmapsto Ax$, hence the name.

In early constructions, the trapdoor $T \in \mathbb{Z}^{m \times m}$ was a short basis of $\Lambda_q^{\perp}(A)$, and one would accomplish this task by using Klein's sampler [Kle00, GPV08], with the cost of having to compute the Gram-Schmidt orthogonalization of T. Since the introduction of the trapdoors from [MP12], a more efficient method has been combining two complementary operations: G-sampling and perturbation sampling. The problem of efficient G-sampling, which consists in sampling from a spherical Gaussian on a very structured fixed lattice, was solved for a power-of-two modulus in [MP12] and for an arbitrary modulus in [GM18]. Perturbation sampling, whose goal is to produce vectors following a discrete Gaussian on $\mathbb{Z}^m$ with a covariance that depends on T, was made efficient in the ring setting in [GM18], but resorts to the generic Klein sampler in the unstructured setting.

Alternatively, fast Fourier sampling [DP16, FHK+17] follows the same ideas as the generic Klein sampler, but uses the so-called Fast Fourier Orthogonalization, linear algebra that preserves the underlying structure of the matrices in the ring setting, making it much faster in this case.

The Module Setting. The ring setting and ideal lattices [PR06, SST+09, LPR10], usually based on rings of the form $\mathcal{R}_q = \mathbb{Z}_q[X]/\langle X^n + 1 \rangle$, are often the first choice for efficient lattice-based constructions. Module lattices [LS15], based on modules of the form $\mathcal{R}_q^d$, lie somewhere between ideal lattices and unstructured ones. Constructions in the module setting are (almost) as efficient as ring-based ones, and have other advantages for practical schemes.

Typically, module schemes fix a modulus q and a degree n for all parameter sets, and the security parameter is the rank d of the module. This leads to a more flexible choice of parameters, and potentially easier optimisation (since one only has to optimize arithmetic in the base ring $\mathcal{R}_q$ to obtain a faster arithmetic for all parameter sets). Additionally, fundamental problems on module lattices might not suffer from the same structural weaknesses as on ideal lattices (see [PHS19]). As an example of the interest of module lattices, we note that several NIST candidates at the post-quantum cryptography standardization process rely on them [DKL+18, DKR+18], and that a recent result [CPS+19] proposes a module variant of the Falcon signature scheme [FHK+17].

Our Contribution. Our main contribution is the development and the implementation of efficient Gaussian preimage sampling techniques on module lattices. The main advantages of our implementation are its constant-timeness and its modularity, making it practical for both signature schemes and more advanced constructions using trapdoors. For instance, it can be used on rings or modules, with a different arithmetic over $\mathcal{R}_q$ depending on the choice of the parameter q. Relying on this, we also present two instantiations and constant-time implementations of proven signature schemes in the module setting (GPV in the ROM and one of its variant in the standard model) and the instantiation and implementation of a standard model IBE in the module setting. To the best of our knowledge, this is the first implementation of a secure lattice-based signature scheme in the standard model. Our resulting C implementation is public and open-source, available at https://github.com/lucasprabel/module_gaussian_lattice.

Preimage Sampling. As mentioned above, Gaussian preimage sampling is a very important operation in trapdoor-based schemes, and to the best of our knowledge no methods adapted to module lattices existed previously. We develop efficient algorithms for trapdoor generation and Gaussian preimage sampling in the module setting, by generalizing existing tools in the unstructured and ring settings [MP12, GM18]. Even if most of this adaptation is quite direct, it has to be done carefully to correctly work over modules. In particular, the perturbation sampling step does not directly adapt, and we resort to our own algorithm, using some subroutines from [GM18]. We also provide a detailed description of those algorithms and of the conditions needed to choose their parameters. This can be used as a building block for advanced trapdoor-based constructions, such as identity-based encryption, attribute-based encryption, or group signature.

Our implementation requires no external dependencies, and is easy to modify if needed. In particular, it is very modular and relies on several basic blocks that can be swapped out, as represented in Fig. 1: the arithmetic over $\mathbb{Z}_q$ and $\mathcal{R}_q$, a pseudorandom number generator, and a (constant-time) sampler of discrete Gaussian distributions over $\mathbb{Z}$. For instance, we do not use the same arithmetic over $\mathcal{R}_q$ in our two signature schemes, as they need the ring $\mathcal{R}_q$ to have a different structure.

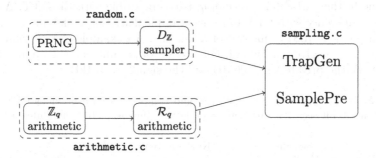

Fig. 1. Basic structure of our implementation and relationships between the blocks.

Table 1. Overview of the performances of our trapdoor tools and cost of sampling scalar Gaussians for $n = 256$ and $d = 4$.

Phase	TrapGen	SamplePre		
		Perturb. sampling	G-sampling	Global
Running time	36.56 ms	5.48 ms	8.28 ms	14.87 ms
Sampling $D_{\mathbb{Z}}$	74%	60%	84%	70%

In Table 1 we give an overview of the running times of our trapdoor algorithms on an Intel i7-8650U CPU running at 1.90 GHz. In particular, we highlight the proportion of time spent sampling Gaussians over $\mathbb{Z}$, and notice that having an efficient sampler is very important, since it makes up the largest part of the running times.

Applications. As an application, we propose an implementation of two trapdoor-based signature schemes and of an identity-based encryption scheme. The GPV signature is the simplest trapdoor-based scheme one can think of, since key generation is exactly the trapdoor generation algorithm, and signing essentially consists in Gaussian preimage sampling. As such, it makes for a natural way of evaluating trapdoor tools and techniques. Our second signature scheme, proven secure in the standard model, is a variation on GPV, and has been constructed by adapting the scheme from [BFRS18] to the module setting. The original construction was using an encoding function which should satisfy a strong injectivity property but does not in practice. We propose a construction for this encoding using a result of [LS18], which allows us to find invertible elements in R_q, and which needs a specific q as a consequence. Relying on this signature scheme, we also implement the standard model IBE scheme from [BFRS18], which was inspired by the IBE [ABB10a], in the module setting.

Our GPV implementation relies on our trapdoor tools, as well as a Number Theoretic Transform for fast multiplication in R_q, adapted from CRYSTALS-Kyber [DKL+18]. In our standard model schemes, the particular structure of the ring, due to the particular choice of q, is incompatible with the NTT. As such, the main difference with GPV in terms of implementation is the use of a partial NTT inspired by [LS18], instead of a full one. An example of performances of our signatures is given in Table 2. For this set of parameters, the public key has size 508kB, the private key 5.06MB and the signature 131kB.

Table 2. Performances of our signatures and comparison with previous GPV implementation (96-bit security parameter sets, lattice dimension 1024, modulus $q \approx 2^{30}$).

Scheme	KeyGen	Sign	Verify
GPV ([GPR+19])	5.86 ms	32.42 ms	0.28 ms
GPV (this work)	8.94 ms	13.08 ms	0.29 ms
BFRS (this work)	9.46 ms	15.66 ms	1.19 ms

Comparison with Previous Works. From a theoretical point of view, the adaptation of the algorithms from [MP12, GM18] to the module setting is quite direct but has to be done carefully, in particular concerning the perturbation sampling algorithm which is an important step in those algorithms. This algorithm over rings is iteratively sampling vectors with a covariance matrix of dimension 2×2 over $\mathcal{R}$, whereas in our case, the matrix has size $2d \times 2d$, where d is the module rank. As a consequence, we have to decompose the covariance matrix into blocks of different sizes at each iteration instead of simply updating ring elements.

We chose to only compare our GPV implementation with the recent work of Gür *et al.* [GPR+19], as it already outperforms previous implementations of Gaussian preimage sampling [BB13, GPR+18] Again, we stress that one of the main advantages of our implementation compared to [GPR+19] is its modularity rather than its performance.

We provide a new encoding function for the signature and the IBE schemes which allows to correct a security issue in the corresponding schemes in [BFRS18]. Our implementation does not rely on the BFRS one and then does not use the NFLlib library. We do not compare the original implementation of the BFRS scheme [BFRS18] with our corrected version, as the former's limited security would make the comparison irrelevant.

We also present a public and open-source implementation of a standard model IBE scheme in the module setting, relying on our standard model signature scheme, which represents also a contribution, given the low number of existing IBE implementations. In particular, our construction does not rely on the NTRU assumption as both implementations in [DLP14, ZMS+21].

Organization of the Paper. This article focuses mainly on our implementation contribution, which we believe is the major contribution of the paper, but we also describe the Gaussian preimage sampling techniques on module lattices in Sect. 3. In Sect. 4, we explain our applications with two proven trapdoor-based signature schemes and a standard model IBE in the module setting. The theoretical part which led us to these implementations is presented and detailed in a rigorous way in the appendices of the full version of the paper.

Conclusion and Open Problems. Our results show that while the resulting schemes are not competitive with the most efficient NIST candidates (in particular the keys are quite large and probably not fit for embedded platforms), they are practical and run on a standard laptop in acceptable time (see Table 2), paving the way for practical advanced trapdoor-based constructions. Besides, the standard model security of our second scheme comes at a low additional cost compared to the ROM GPV signature.

We believe that our schemes performances can still be improved. In particular, the modularity of our implementation makes it easy to modify if needed. For instance, the use of another Gaussian sampler over integers could reduce our timings. Our results seem to confirm that using NTRU lattices provides much better results even if it requires an additionally NTRU assumption. Finally, an interesting open problem would be to study the impact of approximate trapdoors [CGM19] on IBE schemes, and possibly on more advanced schemes.

2 Preliminaries

Notations. We denote (column) vectors by bold lowercase letters, and matrices by bold uppercase letters. The norm $\|\cdot\|$ denotes the euclidean norm, and the norm of a vector over $\mathbb{Z}_q$ is the norm of the corresponding vector over $\mathbb{Z}$ with entries in $\{-\lfloor q/2 \rfloor, \ldots, \lfloor q/2 \rfloor\}$. A symmetric matrix $M \in \mathbb{R}^{n \times n}$ is said to be positive definite (resp. positive semidefinite) if for all nonzero $x \in \mathbb{R}^n$ we have $x^T M x > 0$ (resp. $x^T M x \geq 0$), in which case we write $M \succ 0$ (resp. $M \succeq 0$).

Lattices and Discrete Gaussian Distributions. Given a set of linearly independent vectors $\boldsymbol{B} = \{\boldsymbol{b}_1, \ldots, \boldsymbol{b}_k\} \subset \mathbb{R}^m$, the lattice with basis $\boldsymbol{B}$ is the set $\{\sum_{i=1}^{k} \lambda_i \boldsymbol{b}_i, \lambda_i \in \mathbb{Z}\}$, and its rank is k. For $\boldsymbol{A} \in \mathbb{Z}_q^{n \times m}$ and $\boldsymbol{u} \in \mathbb{Z}_q^n$, we define the following m-dimensional q-ary lattice and its coset $\Lambda_q^{\perp}(\boldsymbol{A}) = \{\boldsymbol{x} \in \mathbb{Z}^m \mid \boldsymbol{A}\boldsymbol{x} = \boldsymbol{0} \bmod q\}$ and $\Lambda_q^u(\boldsymbol{A}) = \{\boldsymbol{x} \in \mathbb{Z}^m \mid \boldsymbol{A}\boldsymbol{x} = \boldsymbol{u} \bmod q\}$.

Module lattices are particular lattices that have a polynomial structure. We consider the ones that are based on the rings $\mathcal{R} = \mathbb{Z}[X]/\langle X^n + 1\rangle$ and $\mathcal{R}_q = \mathbb{Z}_q[X]/\langle X^n + 1\rangle$, where n is a power of two and q is prime. They are sublattices of the full lattice $\mathcal{R}^m$, itself isomorphic to the integer lattice $\mathbb{Z}^{nm}$.

The discrete Gaussian distribution of center $\boldsymbol{c} \in \mathbb{R}^n$ and parameter $\sigma > 0$ over a full-rank lattice $\Lambda \subset \mathbb{Z}^n$ is denoted $D_{\Lambda,\sigma,\boldsymbol{c}}$. It is the probability distribution over Λ such that each $\boldsymbol{x} \in \Lambda$ is assigned a probability proportional to $\rho_{\sigma,\boldsymbol{c}}(\boldsymbol{x}) = \exp(-\frac{\pi\|\boldsymbol{x}-\boldsymbol{c}\|^2}{\sigma^2})$. For a positive definite matrix $\boldsymbol{\Sigma} \in \mathbb{R}^{n \times n}$, we also define the (skewed) density $\rho_{\boldsymbol{c},\sqrt{\boldsymbol{\Sigma}}}(\boldsymbol{x}) = \exp(-\pi(\boldsymbol{x}-\boldsymbol{c})^T\boldsymbol{\Sigma}^{-1}(\boldsymbol{x}-\boldsymbol{c}))$, and the corresponding discrete Gaussian distribution of center $\boldsymbol{c}$ and covariance $\boldsymbol{\Sigma}$ denoted $D_{\Lambda,\sqrt{\boldsymbol{\Sigma}},\boldsymbol{c}}$.

Smoothing Parameter. The smoothing parameter $\eta_\varepsilon(\Lambda)$ of a lattice Λ was introduced in [MR07]. We use the following lemma to find a lower bound for it.

Lemma 1 ([GPV08, Lemma 3.1]). *Let $\Lambda \subset \mathbb{R}^n$ be a lattice with basis $\boldsymbol{B}$, and $\tilde{\boldsymbol{B}}$ the Gram-Schmidt orthogonalization of $\boldsymbol{B}$. Then, for any $\varepsilon > 0$, we have $\eta_\varepsilon(\Lambda) \leq \|\tilde{\boldsymbol{B}}\| \cdot \sqrt{\ln(2n(1 + 1/\varepsilon))/\pi}$.*

Gaussian Tailcut. We denote by t the tailcut of the discrete Gaussian of parameter σ. It is a positive number such that samples from $D_{\mathbb{Z},\sigma}$ land outside of $[-t\sigma, t\sigma]$ only with negligible probability. We choose it using the fact that $\Pr_{x \leftarrow D_{\mathbb{Z},\sigma}}[|x| > t\sigma] \leq \mathrm{erfc}(t/\sqrt{2})$, where $\mathrm{erfc}(x) = 1 - \frac{2}{\pi}\int_0^x \exp^{-u^2} du$. This generalizes to higher dimensions using the following lemma.

Lemma 2 ([MR07, Lemma 4.4]). *For any n-dimensional lattice Λ, vector $\boldsymbol{c} \in \mathbb{R}^n$, reals $0 < \varepsilon < 1$ and $\sigma \geq \eta_\varepsilon(\Lambda)$, if x is distributed according to $D_{\Lambda,\sigma,\boldsymbol{c}}$, then we have $\Pr[\|\boldsymbol{x} - \boldsymbol{c}\| > \sigma\sqrt{n}] \leq \frac{1+\varepsilon}{1-\varepsilon} \cdot 2^{-n}$.*

Module Hardness Assumptions. As in most practical lattice-based constructions [ABB+19, ADP+16, BFRS18, DKL+18, FHK+17], we consider rings of the form $\mathcal{R} = \mathbb{Z}[X]/\langle X^n + 1\rangle$ and $\mathcal{R}_q = \mathbb{Z}_q[X]/\langle X^n + 1\rangle$, where n is a power of two and q a prime modulus. The polynomial $X^n + 1$ is the cyclotomic polynomial of order $2n$, and $\mathcal{R}$ is the corresponding cyclotomic ring.

The module variants generalizing Ring-SIS and Ring-LWE were introduced in [LS15]. The parameter d corresponds to the rank of the module, and nd is the dimension of the corresponding module lattice ($d = 1$ gives the ring problem). Their difficulty is proven by worst-case to average-case reductions from hard problems on module lattices [LS15].

Definition 1 (Module-SIS$_{n,d,m,q,\beta}$). *Given a uniformly random $\boldsymbol{A} \in \mathcal{R}_q^{d \times m}$, find a vector $\boldsymbol{x} \in \mathcal{R}^m$ such that $\boldsymbol{A}\boldsymbol{x} = \boldsymbol{0} \bmod q$, and $0 < \|\boldsymbol{x}\| \leq \beta$.*

Definition 2 (Decision Module-LWE$_{n,d,q,\sigma}$). *Given a uniform $\boldsymbol{A} \in \mathcal{R}_q^{m \times d}$ and the vector $\boldsymbol{b} = \boldsymbol{As} + \boldsymbol{e} \bmod q$, where $\boldsymbol{s} \leftarrow \mathcal{U}(\mathcal{R}_q^d)$ and $\boldsymbol{e} \leftarrow D_{\mathcal{R}^m,\sigma}$, distinguish the distribution of $(\boldsymbol{A}, \boldsymbol{b})$ from the uniform distribution over $\mathcal{R}_q^{m \times d} \times \mathcal{R}_q^m$.*

3   Gaussian Preimage Sampling on Module Lattices

Efficient trapdoor-based schemes, including the two signatures and the IBE we implement, are based on the notion of trapdoor from [MP12]. These trapdoors are an improvement on the short bases of [GPV08], as they are more compact and enjoy faster algorithms, both asymptotically and in practice. They were generalized to ideal lattices in [LCC14], and an efficient instantiation of the associated algorithms was given in [GM18]. To the best of our knowledge, neither the trapdoors nor their algorithms had been adapted yet to the module setting.

In the full version of this article, we generalize in detail these constructions to module lattices, following the ideas from [MP12], by accomplishing two goals:

- We derive an algorithm TrapGen from [MP12, Section 5.2], which is described in the full version of the paper. It generates a uniform matrix $\boldsymbol{A} \in \mathcal{R}_q^{d \times m}$ along with its trapdoor $\boldsymbol{T} \in \mathcal{R}^{2d \times dk}$, where $k = \lceil \log_b q \rceil$ and $m = d(k+2)$. The trapdoor $\boldsymbol{T}$ is sampled from a Gaussian distribution of parameter σ. The matrix $\boldsymbol{A}$ defines hard module SIS and ISIS problems.
- We give an algorithm SamplePre, described in the full version of the paper, that uses $\boldsymbol{T} \in \mathcal{R}^{2d \times dk}$ to perform efficient Gaussian preimage sampling with parameter ζ, effectively solving the module SIS and ISIS problems.

Gaussian preimage sampling consists in sampling from a spherical discrete Gaussian distribution on cosets of the lattice $\Lambda_q^{\perp}(\boldsymbol{A})$ (that is, the sets $\Lambda_q^{u}(\boldsymbol{A})$ for $\boldsymbol{u} \in \mathcal{R}^d$) using $\boldsymbol{T}$. The standard deviation ζ of this distribution should be small (so that it is hard to sample from it without knowing $\boldsymbol{T}$), and the produced vectors should not leak any information about $\boldsymbol{T}$. To this end, we follow the method introduced in [MP12] where sampling from $D_{\Lambda_q^{u}(\boldsymbol{A}),\zeta}$ is divided into two complementary phases:

- *G-sampling* of parameter α (described in Section A.2 of the full version of the paper), which ensures that our samples actually lie in the good coset.
- *Perturbation sampling* with parameters ζ and α (described in Sect. 3.1), which conceals the information about $\boldsymbol{T}$ in the output distribution.

Most of these steps are direct adaptations of the original results, except the last one that we now explain more in detail.

3.1   Perturbation Sampling

Perturbation sampling aims at sampling vectors following the Gaussian distribution over $\mathcal{R}^m$ of covariance $\boldsymbol{\Sigma}_p = \zeta^2 \boldsymbol{I} - \alpha^2 \begin{bmatrix} \boldsymbol{T} \\ \boldsymbol{I} \end{bmatrix} \begin{bmatrix} \boldsymbol{T}^T & \boldsymbol{I} \end{bmatrix}$. In a way, this covariance matrix is complementary to the one of $\left[\begin{smallmatrix}T\\I\end{smallmatrix}\right]z$, where z is the output of the G-sampling. This is so that when we sum the perturbation p and $\left[\begin{smallmatrix}T\\I\end{smallmatrix}\right]z$, the final covariance matrix $\Sigma_p + \alpha^2 \left[\begin{smallmatrix}T\\I\end{smallmatrix}\right][T^T\ I] = \zeta^2 I$ does not leak any information about the trapdoor T.

Internally, perturbation sampling takes place in the ring $\mathcal{P} = \mathbb{R}[X]/\langle X^n + 1\rangle$ rather than the usual ring $\mathcal{R}$. As in most discrete Gaussian sampling algorithms, computations are done with real numbers even if the end result is composed of integers only. Since $\mathcal{R}$ can naturally be embedded in $\mathcal{P}$, we can consider T and covariance matrices to have entries in $\mathcal{P}$.

Genise and Micciancio made this operation efficient in the ring setting [GM18]. In particular, they describe an algorithm SampleFz which takes as input a covariance polynomial f and a center c, and returns a sample from the corresponding Gaussian distribution over $\mathcal{R}$. Their method cannot be applied directly to the module setting because of the additional rank module parameter d. Instead of having to sample vectors with a covariance matrix of dimension 2×2 over $\mathcal{R}$ and with a center $(c_0, c_1) \in \mathcal{R}^2$ as in [GM18], we have to work with a covariance matrix $\Sigma \in \mathcal{P}^{2d \times 2d}$ and a center $c \in \mathcal{P}^{2d}$. However, by using [GM18, Lemma 4.3] and the SampleFz algorithm, we wisely decompose the covariance matrices into blocks of different sizes at each iteration and update our center, allowing us to iteratively sample the perturbations $p_i \in \mathcal{R}$.

An Efficient Algorithm for Sampling Perturbations. We now give a description of the algorithm SamplePerturb which, given the trapdoor T and the Gaussian parameters ζ and α, returns a vector p sampled from the centered discrete Gaussian over $\mathcal{R}^m$ of covariance $\Sigma_p = \zeta^2 I - \alpha^2 \left[\begin{smallmatrix}T\\I\end{smallmatrix}\right][T^T\ I]$. This algorithm does not explicitly use $\Sigma_p \in \mathcal{P}^{m \times m}$, but only a much smaller matrix $\Sigma \in \mathcal{P}^{2d \times 2d}$, which can be computed in advance. It uses the algorithm SampleFz [GM18, Section 4] to sample from discrete Gaussians over $\mathcal{R}$.

Algorithm 1 SamplePerturb(T, ζ, α) for sampling a perturbation vector

1: **function** SamplePerturb($T \in \mathcal{P}^{2d \times dk}, \zeta > 0, \alpha > 0$)
2:    $p_s \leftarrow D_{\mathcal{R}^{dk}, \zeta^2 - \alpha^2}$ $\triangleright\ p_s \in \mathcal{R}^{dk}$
3:    $c \leftarrow -\frac{\alpha^2}{\zeta^2 - \alpha^2} T p_s$ $\triangleright\ c \in \mathcal{P}^{2d}$
4:    $\Sigma \leftarrow \zeta^2 I - (\alpha^{-2} - \zeta^{-2})^{-1} T T^T$ $\triangleright\ \Sigma \in \mathcal{P}^{2d \times 2d}$
5:    **for** $i = 2d - 1 \ldots 0$ **do**
6:       $\Sigma = \begin{bmatrix} A & B \\ B^T & f \end{bmatrix}$ $\triangleright\ A \in \mathcal{P}^{i \times i}, B \in \mathcal{P}^{i \times 1}, f \in \mathcal{P}$
7:       $c = (c', c_i)$ $\triangleright\ c' \in \mathcal{P}^i, c_i \in \mathcal{P}$
8:       $p_i \leftarrow D_{\mathcal{R}, \sqrt{f}, c_i}$ $\triangleright\ p_i \in \mathcal{R}$
9:       $c \leftarrow c' + f^{-1} B(p_i - c_i)$ $\triangleright\ c \in \mathcal{P}^i$
10:     $\Sigma \leftarrow A - f^{-1} B B^T$ $\triangleright\ \Sigma \in \mathcal{P}^{i \times i}$
11:   $p \leftarrow (p_0, \ldots, p_{2d-1}, p_s)$ $\triangleright\ p \in \mathcal{R}^m$
12:   **return** p

Note that in lines 6 and 7 of Algorithm 1, no computation is actually performed: different parts of the variables Σ and c are just given names, for a clearer understanding.

Algorithm 1 has a complexity of $\Theta(d^2 n \log n)$ scalar operations, if we ignore the updates to Σ (which only depend on T and can actually be precomputed in $\Theta(d^3 n \log n)$ in the trapdoor generation). This stems from the fact that multiplication in $\mathcal{P}$ and SampleFz both take $\Theta(n \log n)$ time.

The correctness of this algorithm is proven by the following Theorem.

Theorem 1. *Let $T \in \mathcal{P}^{2d \times dk}$, $\zeta, \alpha > 0$, and $\Sigma_p = \zeta^2 I - \alpha^2 \begin{bmatrix} T \\ I \end{bmatrix} \begin{bmatrix} T^T & I \end{bmatrix} \in \mathcal{P}^{m \times m}$ be the derived perturbation covariance matrix.*

If $\Sigma_p \succeq \eta_\varepsilon^2(\mathbb{Z}^{nm})$, then SamplePerturb$(T, \zeta, \alpha)$ returns a vector $p \in \mathcal{R}^m$ whose distribution is statistically indistinguishable from $D_{\mathcal{R}^m, \sqrt{\Sigma_p}}$.

We provide more details about this algorithm (in particular how transposition over $\mathcal{P}$ is defined) and a proof of correctness in Appendix A.3 of the full version of this paper.

3.2 Implementation

To generate our specific discrete Gaussian distributions, we make use of the following building blocks: the AES-based pseudorandom number generator from [MN17] (implemented using AES-NI instructions for x86 architectures), and a sampler of discrete Gaussians over $\mathbb{Z}$ similar to Karney's sampler [Kar16]. We chose this sampler as it can generate samples in constant time, independently of the center, Gaussian parameter, and output value. All of the computations that deal with non-integers are carried out with floating-point operations that do not involve subnormal numbers.

Our implementation of trapdoor generation and G-sampling are quite direct from the description of the algorithms, and do not have any peculiarities. As such, we will focus our explanations on the techniques used to optimize SamplePerturb.

To obtain an efficient arithmetic in $\mathcal{P} = \mathbb{R}[X]/\langle X^n + 1 \rangle$ we used the Chinese Remainder Transform (CRT, as defined in [LPR13]), as in several other works [DP16, GM18, GPR+18]. It is a kind of fast Fourier transform that evaluates a polynomial $f \in \mathcal{P}$ at the complex primitive $2n^{\text{th}}$ roots of unity, the n points of the form $\omega_i = e^{\frac{ki\pi}{n}}$ for $i \in \{1, 3, \ldots, 2n - 1\}$, in time $\Theta(n \log n)$. As explained in [GM18, Section 4.1], this CRT transform combines especially well with the algorithm SampleFz whose recursive structure is similar to that of an FFT.

Also, the matrix Σ is not actually updated during a run of SamplePerturb. Instead, we precompute (during the trapdoor generation) all of the $2d$ values that it would take during the execution of the algorithm, and store them in a single $2d \times 2d$ triangular matrix by "stacking" them. This is possible because at each iteration of the loop, Σ is an $i \times i$ matrix of which we only use the last line and column. This comes with an additional storage cost of $d(2d + 1)$ elements from $\mathcal{P}$ in the secret key, and Table 3 quantifies the time gains in practice.

Our implementation is constant-time, assuming the compiler produces constant-time code for reduction modulo q and basic operations such as integer division and multiplication. Indeed, our algorithms do not require branching nor memory access that depend on secret values. In particular, our sampler of discrete Gaussians over $\mathbb{Z}$'s running time is independent of both the input parameters and the output value.

3.3   Performances

We now present running times for our trapdoor generation and preimage sampling algorithms, and the cost of their different components. Our experimentations were carried out with $n = 256$, $k = \lceil \log_b q \rceil = 30$ (the values used in our signature schemes in Sects. 4), and values of d up to 10. We ran them on an Intel i7-8650U CPU running at 1.90 GHz.

In Table 3, we see how the trapdoor generation is divided into three main operations: sampling from $D_{\mathbb{Z},\sigma}$ for the construction of $\boldsymbol{T}$, the precomputations concerning the covariance matrices (see Sect. 3.2), and arithmetic, which is mainly computing the matrix product.

Table 4 concerns the algorithm SamplePre. We also measured that sampling from discrete Gaussians over $\mathbb{Z}$ constitutes 57–64% of the perturbation sampling (decreasing with d) and about 85% of the G-sampling, for a total of 67–72% of the whole presampling. Gaussian sampling over $\mathbb{Z}$ makes up most of the running times of both TrapGen and SamplePre. As such, it is important for efficiency to use a fast sampler of discrete Gaussians over $\mathbb{Z}$ as a building block. We remind the reader that in our implementation, this sampler can easily be swapped out for another if needed.

Table 3. Running time of the TrapGen algorithm.

d	4	6	8	10
$D_{\mathbb{Z},\sigma}$ sampling	27.17 ms (74%)	56.37 ms (72%)	100.22 ms (67%)	159.10 ms (64%)
Σ computations	7.03 ms (19%)	17.11 ms (22%)	39.40 ms (26%)	71.92 ms (29%)
Arithmetic	2.34 ms (6%)	1.11 ms (1%)	2.60 ms (2%)	5.25 ms (2%)
Total	36.56 ms	78.52 ms	149.57 ms	248.09 ms

Table 4. Running time of the SamplePre algorithm.

d	4	6	8	10
Perturb. sampling	4.73 ms (36%)	6.63 ms (38%)	9.43 ms (38%)	12.03 ms (39%)
G-sampling	7.48 ms (57%)	9.83 ms (56%)	13.29 ms (54%)	16.43 ms (53%)
Arithmetic	0.82 ms (6%)	1.20 ms (7%)	1.98 ms (8%)	2.64 ms (8%)
Total	13.28 ms	17.66 ms	24.70 ms	31.10 ms

4   Applications

4.1   The GPV Signature Scheme on Modules

A direct application of our Gaussian preimage sampling techniques on module lattices is the GPV signature [GPV08] in the module setting. It was originally formulated on unstructured lattices, and has previously been implemented using improved trapdoors and algorithms [MP12, GM18] in the ring setting [BB13, GPR+18, GPR+19].

You can refer to the full version of this article to see a description of how we instantiate it in the module setting, using the Gaussian preimage sampling tools from [MP12, GM18] that we extended to module lattices. Our goal here is not to obtain a competitive signature scheme, but rather to show the relevance of the tools we developed.

Estimating Security and Choosing Parameters. In Table 5, we propose four parameter sets and corresponding security estimates, taking the prime modulus $q = 1073738753$ of bitsize $k = 30$. The sets I and IV corresponds to the ring setting, where n is a power of two and $d = 1$. The sets II and III are intermediate using the module setting. We describe how we chose those parameters, estimating the difficulty of the underlying lattice problems in the full version of the paper.

Table 5. Suggested parameter sets for our instantiation of the GPV signature.

Parameter set	I	II	III	IV
nd	1024	1280	1536	2048
n	1024	256	512	2048
k	30	30	30	30
d	1	5	3	1
σ	7.00	5.55	6.15	6.85
α	48.34	54.35	60.50	67.40
ζ	83832	83290	112522	160778
BKZ blocksize b to break LWE	367	478	614	896
Classical security	107	139	179	262
Quantum security	97	126	163	237
BKZ blocksize b to break SIS	364	482	583	792
Classical security	106	140	170	231
Quantum security	96	127	154	210

Performance and Comparison with Previous Work. We now present in Table 6 the running times for our implementation of the GPV signature scheme. While it is practical and runs on a standard laptop in acceptable time, the comparison with lattice-based NIST candidates given in Table 12, Appendix E of the full version of the paper shows that it is not competitive.

Table 6. Performances of our GPV signature.

Parameter set	KeyGen	Sign	Verify
I	7.48 ms	11.47 ms	0.73 ms
II	51.34 ms	15.25 ms	1 ms
III	36.49 ms	17.45 ms	1.12 ms
IV	15.55 ms	22.64 ms	1.48 ms

Comparison Between Rings and Modules. As already explained, one goal of using a module variant instead of a ring variant is to be more flexible in the parameters. The comparison between the different levels of security shows that the running time for signing and verifying is increasing with nd, and then that having intermediate levels allow to be faster to sign and verify.

On the other hand, the KeyGen algorithm does not depend only on nd but is slower for larger d. We give a more concrete example of this in Table 7. When nd is constant, so is the estimated security provided. With a higher n and a lower d ($d = 1$ being the ring setting), the underlying lattices have a stronger structure and the signature is more efficient. With a lower n and a higher d (the extreme being $n = 1$ in the unstructured setting), the lattices have less structure, leading to increased flexibility at the cost of efficiency.

Table 7. Cost of KeyGen, Sign and Verify depending of the parameter d for $nd = 1024$.

(n, d)	KeyGen	Sign	Verify
$(1024, 1)$	$7.62 + 1.32 = 8.94$ ms	13.08 ms	0.79 ms
$(512, 2)$	$15.32 + 2.81 = 18.13$ ms	13.20 ms	0.79 ms
$(256, 4)$	$29.53 + 7.03 = 36.56$ ms	13.36 ms	0.74 ms

Comparison with [GPR+19]. In Table 8, we compare our timings with the work of [GPR+19]. Their parameter set where $(n, k) = (1024, 27)$ is compared with ours where $(nd, k) = (1024, 30)$, which provide approximately the same security.

Table 8. Comparison of GPV implementations.

Implementation		KeyGen	Sign	Verify
[GPR+19]	$n = 1024$	5.86 ms	32.42 ms	0.28 ms
This work	$(n, d) = (1024, 1)$	$7.62 + 1.32 = 8.94$ ms	13.08 ms	0.79 ms

4.2   A Standard Model Signature Scheme on Modules

The second application of our tools that we present is an implementation of a signature scheme that is proven secure in the standard model, as opposed to the GPV signature and the NIST schemes.

This scheme is the signature from [BFRS18], which is a variant of GPV, adapted to the module setting. For the security proof to hold, the encoding must fulfil a strong injectivity property. However, the original encoding described in [BFRS18] did not meet these requirements, leading to a limited security. We propose a modified version of this scheme: we translated it to the module setting, and instantiated it with a correct encoding.

We give a complete description of our scheme and state its correctness and security in the full version of the paper, in Appendix C.

Encoding Messages with Full-Rank Differences. We first describe the notion of an encoding with full-rank differences (FRD) needed in our scheme. Note that this definition of FRD differs from the one used in [ABB10b], which does not use the MP12 trapdoors, and therefore does not need the $H(m)$ to be invertible.

Definition 3 (Adapted from [ABB10b]). *An encoding with full-rank differences from the set $\mathcal{M}$ to a ring $\mathcal{R}$ is a map $H : \mathcal{M} \longrightarrow \mathcal{R}$ such that:*

- *for any $m \in \mathcal{M}$, $H(m)$ is invertible,*
- *for any $m_1, m_2 \in \mathcal{M}$ such that $m_1 \neq m_2$, $H(m_1) - H(m_2)$ is invertible,*
- *H is computable in polynomial time.*

Before constructing an FRD encoding in the module setting (that is, taking values in $\mathcal{R}_q^{d \times d}$), we first construct one in the ring setting (taking values in $\mathcal{R}_q$). Our construction is based on the following result of [LS18], which allows us to find invertible elements in $\mathcal{R}_q$.

Theorem 2 ([LS18, Corollary 1.2]). *Let $n \geq r > 1$ be powers of 2, and q a prime such that $q \equiv 2r + 1 \pmod{4r}$. Then the cyclotomic polynomial $X^n + 1$ factors in $\mathbb{Z}_q[X]$ as $X^n + 1 = \prod_{i=1}^{r} \left(X^{n/r} - s_i \right)$, for some distinct $s_i \in \mathbb{Z}_q^*$ such that the $\left(X^{n/r} - s_i \right)$ are irreducible in $\mathbb{Z}_q[X]$. Moreover, any $f \in \mathcal{R}_q$ such that $0 < \|f\|_\infty < q^{1/r}/\sqrt{r}$ or $0 < \|f\| < q^{1/r}$ is invertible.*

This result can be used to build two different types of FRD encodings. One could encode messages as polynomials of l_∞-norm smaller than $\frac{q^{1/r}}{2\sqrt{r}}$ with an injective map and obtain an FRD this way. But we decided to use the "low-degree" FRD described in Proposition 1 as opposed to a "small-norm" one, as it results in a slightly more efficient implementation.

Proposition 1. *Let $n \geq r > 1$ be powers of 2, q a prime such that $q \equiv 2r + 1$ (mod $4r$), and $\mathcal{M} = \mathbb{Z}_q^{n/r} \setminus \{0\}$ the set of messages. Then the following map $H : \mathcal{M} \longrightarrow \mathcal{R}_q$ is an FRD encoding.*

$$(m_0, \ldots, m_{n/r-1}) \longmapsto \sum_{i=0}^{n/r} m_i X^i$$

The proof of this proposition is given in the full version of the paper.

FRD on Modules. We build an FRD encoding in the module setting using an existing FRD encoding in the ring setting $H_R : \mathcal{M} \longrightarrow \mathcal{R}_q$ by constructing:

$$H_M : \mathcal{M} \longrightarrow \mathcal{R}_q^{d \times d}$$

$$m \longmapsto H_R(m) \cdot \boldsymbol{I}_d = \begin{bmatrix} H_R(m) & & \\ & \ddots & \\ & & H_R(m) \end{bmatrix},$$

where $\boldsymbol{I}_d \in \mathcal{R}_q^{d \times d}$ is the identity matrix.

Lemma 3. *If H_R is an FRD (in the ring setting) from $\mathcal{M}$ to $\mathcal{R}_q$, then H_M as constructed above is an FRD (in the module setting) from $\mathcal{M}$ to $\mathcal{R}_q^{d \times d}$.*

Implementation and Performance. The main point that differs from our ROM scheme in the implementation is the arithmetic over $\mathcal{R}_q$. While without having $q \equiv 1 \pmod{2n}$ one cannot use the NTT, we can still make use of the structure of our ring to speed up the multiplication of polynomials. Described at a high level, what we perform is a "partial NTT". To multiply polynomials, we first reduce them modulo all the $X^{n/r} - s_i$ in $\Theta(n \log r)$ operations. Then, we multiply them in the smaller rings $\mathbb{Z}_q[X]/\langle X^{n/r} - s_i \rangle$ by using the Karatsuba multiplication algorithm, and reducing them both modulo q and modulo the $X^{n/r} - s_i$. The result can then be mapped back to the ring $\mathcal{R}_q$ in time $\Theta(n \log r)$ using an inverse transform. These ideas were formulated in [LS18].

In Table 9, we present the performance of our implementation of this standard model scheme, and in particular highlight the additional cost compared to our ROM scheme of Sect. 4.1.

Table 9. Performances of our standard model signature.

Parameter set	KeyGen	Sign	Verify
I	9.46 ms (+27%)	15.66 ms (+37%)	1.19 ms (+63%)
II	73.41 ms (+43%)	21.92 ms (+44%)	2.23 ms (+123%)
III	51.79 ms (+42%)	29.11 ms (+66%)	2.37 ms (+112%)

We do not give a comparison with the implementation of [BFRS18] as it would not be relevant, given the limited security provided by their instantiation of the FRD encoding.

4.3 An Identity-Based Encryption Scheme on Modules

Finally, we built a more advanced construction based on our tools: a standard model identity-based encryption scheme.

We give a complete description of our IBE in the full version of our paper.

Implementation and Performance. As in our standard model signature scheme, we make use of our ring to speed up the multiplication of polynomials by performing a partial NTT. We make use of the same encoding as in the previous section, which imposes the condition $q \equiv 2r + 1 \pmod{4r}$ on the modulus, to map identities in $\mathcal{M} = \mathbb{Z}_q^{n/r} \setminus \{0\}$ to invertible elements in $\mathcal{R}_q^{d \times d}$. In Table 10, we present the performance of our implementation of this standard model IBE scheme.

Table 10. Timings of the different operations of our scheme: Setup, Extract, Encrpt, and Decrypt

Parameter Set	Setup	Extract	Encrypt	Decrypt
I	9.82 ms	16.54 ms	4.87 ms	0.99 ms
II	44.91 ms	18.09 ms	5.48 ms	1.04 ms

In Table 11, we give timings for the different operations of some IBE schemes. Our timings could seem worse than the ones in [BFRS18] but the two implementations cannot be compared as the latter's limited security would make the comparison irrelevant. A part of the difference comes from the arithmetic we need to use in order to build a proper FRD encoding. Moreover, in contrast to [DLP14], we did not use NTRU lattices, which explains the differences in the timings.

Table 11. Timings of the different operations for some IBE schemes.

Scheme	(λ, n)	Setup	Extract	Encrypt	Decrypt
BF-128 [Fou13]	$(128, -)$	–	0.55 ms	7.51 ms	5.05 ms
DLP-14 [MSO17]	$(80, 512)$	4.034 ms	3.8 ms	0.91 ms	0.62 ms

Acknowledgements. This work was supported by the European Union PROMETHEUS project (Horizon 2020 Research and Innovation Program, grant 780701). Lucas Prabel is funded by the Direction Générale de l'Armement (Pôle de Recherche CYBER).

References

[ABB+19] Alkim, E., Barreto, P.S.L.M., Bindel, N., Longa, P., Ricardini, J.E.: The lattice-based digital signature scheme qtesla. IACR Cryptology ePrint Archive 2019:85 (2019)

[ABB10a] Agrawal, S., Boneh, D., Boyen, X.: Efficient lattice (H)IBE in the standard model. In: Gilbert, H. (ed.) EUROCRYPT 2010. LNCS, vol. 6110, pp. 553–572. Springer, Heidelberg (2010). https://doi.org/10.1007/978-3-642-13190-5_28

[ABB10b] Agrawal, S., Boneh, D., Boyen, X.: Lattice basis delegation in fixed dimension and shorter-ciphertext hierarchical IBE. In: Rabin, T. (ed.) CRYPTO 2010. LNCS, vol. 6223, pp. 98–115. Springer, Heidelberg (2010). https://doi.org/10.1007/978-3-642-14623-7_6

[ADP+16] Alkim, E., Ducas, L., Pöppelmann, T., Schwabe, P.: Post-quantum key exchange - a new hope. In: USENIX Security Symposium, pp. 327–343. USENIX Association (2016)

[AHH+19] Albrecht, M.R., Hanser, C., Höller, A., Pöppelmann, T., Virdia, F., Wallner, A.: Implementing RLWE-based schemes using an RSA co-processor. IACR TCHES **2019**(1), 169–208 (2019)

[BB13] El Bansarkhani, R., Buchmann, J.: Improvement and efficient implementation of a lattice-based signature scheme. In: Lange, T., Lauter, K., Lisoněk, P. (eds.) SAC 2013. LNCS, vol. 8282, pp. 48–67. Springer, Heidelberg (2014). https://doi.org/10.1007/978-3-662-43414-7_3

[BFRS18] Bert, P., Fouque, P.-A., Roux-Langlois, A., Sabt, M.: Practical implementation of ring-SIS/LWE based signature and IBE. In: Lange, T., Steinwandt, R. (eds.) PQCrypto 2018. LNCS, vol. 10786, pp. 271–291. Springer, Cham (2018). https://doi.org/10.1007/978-3-319-79063-3_13

[Boy10] Boyen, X.: Lattice mixing and vanishing trapdoors: a framework for fully secure short signatures and more. In: Nguyen, P.Q., Pointcheval, D. (eds.) PKC 2010. LNCS, vol. 6056, pp. 499–517. Springer, Heidelberg (2010). https://doi.org/10.1007/978-3-642-13013-7_29

[CGM19] Chen, Y., Genise, N., Mukherjee, P.: Approximate trapdoors for lattices and smaller hash-and-sign signatures. In: Galbraith, S.D., Moriai, S. (eds.) ASIACRYPT 2019. LNCS, vol. 11923, pp. 3–32. Springer, Cham (2019). https://doi.org/10.1007/978-3-030-34618-8_1

[CHK+10] Cash, D., Hofheinz, D., Kiltz, E., Peikert, C.: Bonsai trees, or how to delegate a lattice basis. In: Gilbert, H. (ed.) EUROCRYPT 2010. LNCS, vol. 6110, pp. 523–552. Springer, Heidelberg (2010). https://doi.org/10.1007/978-3-642-13190-5_27

[CPS+19] Chuengsatiansup, C., Prest, T., Stehlé, D., Wallet, A., Xagawa, K.: Modfalcon: compact signatures based on module NTRU lattices. IACR Cryptol. ePrint Arch. 2019:1456 (2019)

[DKL+18] Ducas, L., et al.: Crystals-dilithium: a lattice-based digital signature scheme. TCHES **2018**(1), 238–268 (2018)

[DKR+18] D'Anvers, J.-P., Karmakar, A., Sinha Roy, S., Vercauteren, F.: Saber: module-LWR based key exchange, CPA-secure encryption and CCA-secure KEM. In: Joux, A., Nitaj, A., Rachidi, T. (eds.) AFRICACRYPT 2018. LNCS, vol. 10831, pp. 282–305. Springer, Cham (2018). https://doi.org/10.1007/978-3-319-89339-6_16

[DLP14] Ducas, L., Lyubashevsky, V., Prest, T.: Efficient identity-based encryption over NTRU lattices. In: Sarkar, P., Iwata, T. (eds.) ASIACRYPT 2014. LNCS, vol. 8874, pp. 22–41. Springer, Heidelberg (2014). https://doi.org/10.1007/978-3-662-45608-8_2

[DP16] Ducas, L., Prest, T.: Fast fourier orthogonalization. In: ISSAC, pp. 191–198. ACM (2016)

[FHK+17] Fouque, P.-A., et al.: Falcon: fast-fourier lattice-based compact signatures over NTRU (2017). https://falcon-sign.info/falcon.pdf

[Fou13] Fouotsa, E.: Calcul des couplages et arithmetique des courbes elliptiques pour la cryptographie. Ph.D. thesis, Rennes 1 (2013)

[GM18] Genise, N., Micciancio, D.: Faster Gaussian sampling for trapdoor lattices with arbitrary modulus. In: Nielsen, J.B., Rijmen, V. (eds.) EUROCRYPT 2018. LNCS, vol. 10820, pp. 174–203. Springer, Cham (2018). https://doi.org/10.1007/978-3-319-78381-9_7

[GPR+18] Gür, K.D., Polyakov, Y., Rohloff, K., Ryan, G.W., Savas, E.: Implementation and evaluation of improved gaussian sampling for lattice trapdoors. In: WAHC@CCS, pp. 61–71. ACM (2018)

[GPR+19] Gür, K.D., Polyakov, Y., Rohloff, K., Ryan, G.W., Sajjadpour, H., Savas, E.: Practical applications of improved gaussian sampling for trapdoor lattices. IEEE Trans. Comput. 68(4), 570–584 (2019)

[GPV08] Gentry, C., Peikert, C., Vaikuntanathan, V.: Trapdoors for hard lattices and new cryptographic constructions. In: STOC, pp. 197–206. ACM (2008)

[GVW13] Gorbunov, S., Vaikuntanathan, V., Wee, H.: Attribute-based encryption for circuits. In: STOC, pp. 545–554. ACM (2013)

[HPS98] Hoffstein, J., Pipher, J., Silverman, J.H.: NTRU: a ring-based public key cryptosystem. In: Buhler, J.P. (ed.) ANTS 1998. LNCS, vol. 1423, pp. 267–288. Springer, Heidelberg (1998). https://doi.org/10.1007/BFb0054868

[Kar16] Karney, C.F.F.: Sampling exactly from the normal distribution. ACM Trans. Math. Softw. 42(1), 3:1-3:14 (2016)

[Kle00] Klein, P.N.: Finding the closest lattice vector when it's unusually close. In: SODA, pp. 937–941. ACM/SIAM (2000)

[LCC14] Lai, R.W.F., Cheung, H.K.F., Chow, S.S.M.: Trapdoors for ideal lattices with applications. In: Lin, D., Yung, M., Zhou, J. (eds.) Inscrypt 2014. LNCS, vol. 8957, pp. 239–256. Springer, Cham (2015). https://doi.org/10.1007/978-3-319-16745-9_14

[LLL+13] Laguillaumie, F., Langlois, A., Libert, B., Stehlé, D.: Lattice-based group signatures with logarithmic signature size. In: Sako, K., Sarkar, P. (eds.) ASIACRYPT 2013. LNCS, vol. 8270, pp. 41–61. Springer, Heidelberg (2013). https://doi.org/10.1007/978-3-642-42045-0_3

[LM08] Lyubashevsky, V., Micciancio, D.: Asymptotically efficient lattice-based digital signatures. In: Canetti, R. (ed.) TCC 2008. LNCS, vol. 4948, pp. 37–54. Springer, Heidelberg (2008). https://doi.org/10.1007/978-3-540-78524-8_3

[LPR10] Lyubashevsky, V., Peikert, C., Regev, O.: On ideal lattices and learning with errors over rings. In: Gilbert, H. (ed.) EUROCRYPT 2010. LNCS, vol. 6110, pp. 1–23. Springer, Heidelberg (2010). https://doi.org/10.1007/978-3-642-13190-5_1

[LPR13] Lyubashevsky, V., Peikert, C., Regev, O.: A toolkit for ring-LWE cryptography. In: Johansson, T., Nguyen, P.Q. (eds.) EUROCRYPT 2013. LNCS, vol. 7881, pp. 35–54. Springer, Heidelberg (2013). https://doi.org/10.1007/978-3-642-38348-9_3

[LS15] Langlois, A., Stehlé, D.: Worst-case to average-case reductions for module lattices. Des. Codes Cryptogr. 75(3), 565–599 (2014). https://doi.org/10.1007/s10623-014-9938-4

[LS18]   Lyubashevsky, V., Seiler, G.: Short, invertible elements in partially splitting cyclotomic rings and applications to lattice-based zero-knowledge proofs. In: Nielsen, J.B., Rijmen, V. (eds.) EUROCRYPT 2018. LNCS, vol. 10820, pp. 204–224. Springer, Cham (2018). https://doi.org/10.1007/978-3-319-78381-9_8

[MN17]   Mennink, B., Neves, S.: Optimal PRFs from blockcipher designs. IACR ToSC **2017**(3), 228–252 (2017)

[MP12]   Micciancio, D., Peikert, C.: Trapdoors for lattices: simpler, tighter, faster, smaller. In: Pointcheval, D., Johansson, T. (eds.) EUROCRYPT 2012. LNCS, vol. 7237, pp. 700–718. Springer, Heidelberg (2012). https://doi.org/10.1007/978-3-642-29011-4_41

[MR07]   Micciancio, D., Regev, O.: Worst-case to average-case reductions based on gaussian measures. SIAM J. Comput. **37**(1), 267–302 (2007)

[MSO17] McCarthy, S., Smyth, N., O'Sullivan, E.: A practical implementation of identity-based encryption over NTRU lattices. In: O'Neill, M. (ed.) IMACC 2017. LNCS, vol. 10655, pp. 227–246. Springer, Cham (2017). https://doi.org/10.1007/978-3-319-71045-7_12

[MW17]   Micciancio, D., Walter, M.: Gaussian sampling over the integers: efficient, generic, constant-time. In: Katz, J., Shacham, H. (eds.) CRYPTO 2017. LNCS, vol. 10402, pp. 455–485. Springer, Cham (2017). https://doi.org/10.1007/978-3-319-63715-0_16

[PHS19] Pellet-Mary, A., Hanrot, G., Stehlé, D.: Approx-svp in ideal lattices with pre-processing. IACR Cryptology ePrint Archive 2019:215 (2019)

[PR06]   Peikert, C., Rosen, A.: Efficient collision-resistant hashing from worst-case assumptions on cyclic lattices. In: Halevi, S., Rabin, T. (eds.) TCC 2006. LNCS, vol. 3876, pp. 145–166. Springer, Heidelberg (2006). https://doi.org/10.1007/11681878_8

[Sei18] Seiler, G.: Faster AVX2 optimized NTT multiplication for ringlwe lattice cryptography. IACR Cryptology ePrint Archive 2018:39 (2018)

[Sha84] Shamir, A.: Identity-based cryptosystems and signature schemes. In: Blakley, G.R., Chaum, D. (eds.) CRYPTO 1984. LNCS, vol. 196, pp. 47–53. Springer, Heidelberg (1985). https://doi.org/10.1007/3-540-39568-7_5

[Sho94] Shor, P.W.: Polynomial time algorithms for discrete logarithms and factoring on a quantum computer. In: Adleman, L.M., Huang, M.-D. (eds.) ANTS 1994. LNCS, vol. 877, pp. 289–289. Springer, Heidelberg (1994). https://doi.org/10.1007/3-540-58691-1_68

[SS13]   Stehlé, D., Steinfeld, R.: Making ntruencrypt and ntrusign as secure as standard worst-case problems over ideal lattices. IACR Cryptology ePrint Archive 2013:4 (2013)

[SST+09] Stehlé, D., Steinfeld, R., Tanaka, K., Xagawa, K.: Efficient public key encryption based on ideal lattices. In: Matsui, M. (ed.) ASIACRYPT 2009. LNCS, vol. 5912, pp. 617–635. Springer, Heidelberg (2009). https://doi.org/10.1007/978-3-642-10366-7_36

[Yam16] Yamada, S.: Adaptively secure identity-based encryption from lattices with asymptotically shorter public parameters. In: Fischlin, M., Coron, J.-S. (eds.) EUROCRYPT 2016. LNCS, vol. 9666, pp. 32–62. Springer, Heidelberg (2016). https://doi.org/10.1007/978-3-662-49896-5_2

[ZMS+21] Zhao, R.K., McCarthy, S., Steinfeld, R., Sakzad, A., O'Neill, M.: Quantum-safe hibe: does it cost a latte? Cryptology ePrint Archive, Report 2021/222 (2021)

Verifying Post-Quantum Signatures
in 8 kB of RAM

Ruben Gonzalez[1]([✉]), Andreas Hülsing[2]([✉]), Matthias J. Kannwischer[3]([✉]),
Juliane Krämer[4]([✉]), Tanja Lange[2]([✉]), Marc Stöttinger[5]([✉]),
Elisabeth Waitz[6]([✉]), Thom Wiggers[7]([✉]), and Bo-Yin Yang[8]([✉])

[1] Hochschule Bonn-Rhein-Sieg, Bonn, Germany
[2] Eindhoven University of Technology, Eindhoven, The Netherlands
[3] Max Planck Institute for Security and Privacy, Bochum, Germany
[4] Technische Universität Darmstadt, Darmstadt, Germany
[5] Hessen3C, Wiesbaden, Germany
[6] Elektrobit Automotive GmbH, Erlangen, Germany
[7] Radboud University, Nijmegen, The Netherlands
[8] Academica Sinica, Taipei, Taiwan
streaming-pq-sigs@kannwischer.eu

Abstract. In this paper, we study implementations of post-quantum signature schemes on resource-constrained devices. We focus on verification of signatures and cover NIST PQC round-3 candidates Dilithium, Falcon, Rainbow, GeMSS, and SPHINCS$^+$. We assume an ARM Cortex-M3 with 8 kB of memory and 8 kB of flash for code; a practical and widely deployed setup in, for example, the automotive sector. This amount of memory is insufficient for most schemes. Rainbow and GeMSS public keys are too big; SPHINCS$^+$ signatures do not fit in this memory. To make signature verification work for these schemes, we stream in public keys and signatures. Due to the memory requirements for efficient Dilithium implementations, we stream in the public key to cache more intermediate results. We discuss the suitability of the signature schemes for streaming, adapt existing implementations, and compare performance.

Keywords: NISTPQC · Cortex-M3 · Signature Verification · Streaming · Post-Quantum Signatures · Memory-Constrained Devices

1 Introduction

The generally larger keys and signatures of post-quantum signature schemes have enormous impact on cryptography on constrained devices. This is especially important when the payload of the signed message is much smaller than the signature, due to additional transmission overhead required for the signature. Such short messages are for example used in the real-world use case of feature activation in the automotive domain. Feature activation is the remote activation of features that are already implemented in the soft- and hardware of the car. For example, an additional infotainment package. Usually, a short activation code is protected with a signature to prevent unauthorized activation of the feature.

© Springer Nature Switzerland AG 2021
J. H. Cheon and J.-P. Tillich (Eds.): PQCrypto 2021, LNCS 12841, pp. 215–233, 2021.
https://doi.org/10.1007/978-3-030-81293-5_12

In the automotive sector, it is very common to perform all cryptographic operations on a dedicated hardware security module (HSM) that resembles a Cortex-M3 processor with a clock frequency of 100 MHz and limited memory resources, e.g., [13]. Typically, the HSM is in the same package as the main processor with its own memory and is connected via an internal bus with a bus speed of about 20 Mbit/s. A fair estimate for available memory for signature verification on the HSM is under 18 kB of RAM and 10 kB of flash. However, we aim for a lower memory usage of 8 kB of RAM and flash to allow additional space for other applications and an operating system.

In this scenario signatures are verified in the very constrained environment of an HSM. It may not be able to store large public keys or keep large signatures in memory. Sometimes even the main processor does not have sufficient memory resources. Then the public key or signature must be provided to the HSM by another device in the vehicle network, like the head unit. In this case, the public key or signature must be streamed in portions over the in-vehicle network to the destination processor. A typical streaming rate over the CAN bus of an in-vehicle network is about 500 kbit/s, considering a low error transmission rate. Appendix A provides more details on the use case.

Contribution In this work, we address the challenge of performing signature verification of post-quantum signature schemes with a large public key or signature in a highly memory-constrained environment. Our approach is to stream the public key or the signature.[1] We show that this way signature verification can be done keeping only small data packets in constrained memory. When streaming the public key, the device needs to securely store a hash value of the public key to verify the authenticity of the streamed public key. During signature verification, the public key is incrementally hashed, matching the data flow of the streamed public key. We implemented and benchmarked the proposed public key and signature streaming approach for four different signature schemes (Dilithium, SPHINCS+, Rainbow, and GeMSS). Although for Dilithium streaming the public key is not strictly necessary, the saved bytes allow us to keep more intermediate results in memory. This results in a speed-up.

For comparison, we also implemented the lattice-based scheme Falcon for which streaming small data packets is not necessary in our scenario as the entire public key and signature fit into RAM. The source code is published and available at https://git.fslab.de/pqc/streaming-pq-sigs. We demonstrate that the proposed streaming approach is very well suited for constrained devices with a maximum utilization of 8 kB RAM and 8 kB Flash.

Related Work To the best of our knowledge, this is the first work that addresses signature verification by streaming in the public key or signature. For

---

[1] Appendix B sketches an alternative scheme that relies on symmetric cryptography with device-specific keys. This would fit even more constrained environments, but comes at the expense of the downsides of symmetric key management.

signature schemes, streaming approaches have been investigated in [14] but the focus of that work was on signature generation (for stateless hash-based signatures). The encryption scheme Classic McEliece was studied for constrained device, solving the issue of public keys being larger than the available RAM by either streaming [29,30] or placing them in additional Flash [7,10].

2   Analyzed Post-Quantum Signature Schemes

We now briefly discuss the different signature schemes that we considered. Our exposition is focused on signature verification due to limited space. For all schemes we selected parameters that meet at least NIST security level 1. Where possible we prioritized verification speed over signature speed as we assume that signatures are created on devices that are significantly more powerful than the ones we consider for signature verification.

2.1   Hash-Based Schemes

For hash-based signature schemes security solely relies on the security properties of the cryptographic hash function(s) used. Hash-based signatures can be split into stateful and stateless schemes. Stateful schemes require that a user keeps a state with the secret key. The stateful schemes LMS and XMSS are already specified as RFCs [15,20] and standardized by NIST [8]. As these schemes have sufficiently small signatures and keys, we do not consider them in this work.

SPHINCS$^+$ SPHINCS$^+$ is the last remaining stateless hash-based signature scheme in the NIST competition [3]. In the following we give a rough overview of SPHINCS$^+$ signature verification and motivate our parameter choice. For a high-level description of SPHINCS$^+$ see Appendix C.

SPHINCS$^+$ signature verification consists of four components. First, the message compression, second message mapping functions, third computing hash chains, and fourth verifying authentication paths in binary hash trees. The message mapping functions take negligible time compared to the other operations and also only minimally increase space. Hence, they are ignored in our exposition. Message compression consumes an n-bit randomizer value from the signature in addition to the message which can in theory be streamed in chunks of the internal block size of the used hash function. The resulting message digest is mapped to a set of indices used later to decide the ordering of hash values in the authentication path verifications. Hash chain computation consumes one n-bit hash value from the signature and iterates the hash function a few times on the given value. The results of 67 hash chain computations are compressed using one hash function call. Hence, results have to be kept in memory until one block for the hash function is full. Finally, authentication path computation takes the n-bit result of a previous computation and consumes one authentication path node per tree level. In theory, these computations can be done one-by-one which would allow streaming each n-bit node separately.

SPHINCS$^+$ is defined as a signature framework with a magnitude of different instantiations and parameter sets. SPHINCS$^+$ defines parameters for three different hash functions: SHA-3, SHA-256, and Haraka. We chose a SHA-256 parameter set due to its performance, well understood security, and widely deployed hardware support. Moreover, SPHINCS$^+$ defines *simple* and *robust* parameters. We chose *simple* as it matches the security assumptions of the schemes that we compare to and has better performance. Lastly, the SPHINCS$^+$ specification [1] proposes *fast* and *small* parameters, the former optimized for signing speed, the latter for signature size. However, the small parameters have better verification speed. We chose to implement `sphincs-sha256-128s-simple` and `sphincs-sha256-128f-simple` to allow for a comparison and show what is possible when reduced signing speed is not an issue. For these SPHINCS$^+$ parameters, signing speed on a general purpose CPU is about a factor 16 slower for the s-parameters [3]. All internal hash values in SPHINCS$^+$ have $n = 16$ bytes for the parameters we use. Public keys are $2n = 32$ bytes. Hence, they can easily be stored on the device without any compression.

2.2 Multivariate-Based Schemes

Multivariate signature schemes are based on the hardens of finding solutions to systems of equations in many variables over finite fields, where the degree of the equations is at least two. The first multivariate signature scheme was designed by Matsumoto and Imai [19] and broken by Patarin [22]. Patarin with several coauthors went on to design modified schemes [17,23,26] which form the basis of modern multivariate signature schemes.

To fix notation, let the system of equations be given by m equations in n variables over a finite field $\mathbb{F}_q$. Most systems use multivariate quadratic (MQ) equations, i.e. equations of total degree two. Then the m polynomials have the form

$$f_k(x_1, x_2, \ldots, x_n) = \sum_{1 \leq i \leq j \leq n} a_{i,j}^{(k)} x_i x_j + \sum_{1 \leq i \leq n} b_i^{(k)} x_i + c^{(k)} \qquad (1)$$

with coefficients $a_{i,j}^{(k)}, b_i^{(k)}, c^{(k)} \in \mathbb{F}_q$.

Let M be a message and let $H : \{0,1\}^* \times \{0,1\}^r \to \mathbb{F}_q^m$ be a hash function. A signature on M is a vector $(X_1, X_2, \ldots, X_n) \in \mathbb{F}_q^n$ and a string $R \in \{0,1\}^r$ satisfying for all $1 \leq k \leq m$ that $f_k(X_1, X_2, \ldots, X_n) = h_k$ for $H(M, R) = (h_1, h_2, \ldots, h_m)$. The inclusion of R is necessary because not every system has a solution.

Verification is conceptually easy – simply test that all signature equations hold. Signing depends on the type of construction and what information the signer has to permit finding a solution to the system, but this is outside the scope of this paper.

General considerations for streaming MQ systems lead to short signatures but the public keys need to contain the coefficients of (1) and are thus very large, in the range of a few hundred kB. The public keys can be streamed in blocks of rows or columns, depending on how the public key is represented. At most m elements of $\mathbb{F}_q$ are needed to hold the partial results of evaluating $f_k(X_1, X_2, \ldots, X_n), 1 \leq k \leq m$ in addition to the n elements for the signature and the m elements for the hash.

Rainbow Rainbow [9] is a finalist in round 3 of the NIST competition. Rainbow uses two layers of the Oil and Vinegar (OV) scheme [24]. For Rainbow the finite field is $\mathbb{F}_{2^4}$, so signatures require $\lceil m/2 \rceil$ bytes, leading to 66 bytes in NIST security level 1. We implement `rainbowI-classic` rather than one of the "circumzenithal" or "compressed" variants. Public keys are 158 kB for `rainbowI-classic`.

In Rainbow, the coefficients b and c are all zero. During verification, we load in columns $a_{i,j}^{(*)}$ corresponding to coefficients of each monomial $x_i x_j$, $i \leq j$. If $0 \neq x_i x_j = k \in \mathbb{F}_{16}$, we accumulate $a_{i,j}$ into a column $\mathbf{A}_k$, If $x_i = 0$, we skip all columns involving x_i. The final result is $\sum_{k \in \mathbb{F}_{16}^*} k \mathbf{A}_k$.

GeMSS GeMSS [6] is an alternate in round 3 of the NIST competition. GeMSS is based on the HFEv− scheme [25]. For GeMSS the finite field is $\mathbb{F}_2$, so signatures are very small, starting at 258 bits for category I, but to achieve security the public key needs to be very large, starting at 350 kB for category I.

It bears mentioning that GeMSS is special among multivariates in that it employs the Patarin-Feistel structure to achieve very short signatures, wherein a public key is used *four* times during the verification. With pubkey f being m equations in n variables, to verify the signature of the message $\mathbf{M}$, we do:

1. write the signature as $(\mathbf{S}_4, \mathbf{X}_4, \mathbf{X}_3, \mathbf{X}_2, \mathbf{X}_1)$ where $\mathbf{S}_i$ are size m and the $\mathbf{X}_i$ are size $n - m$ (so the actual length of the signature is $4n - 3m$).
2. At stage i, which goes from 4 to 1, we set $\mathbf{S}_{i-1} = f(\mathbf{S}_i \| \mathbf{X}_i) \oplus \mathbf{D}_i$, where $\mathbf{D}_i$ is the first m bits of $(\text{SHA} - 3)^i(\mathbf{M})$.
3. The signature is valid if $\mathbf{S}_0$ is the zero vector.

There are three types of GeMSS parameters. "RedGeMSS" uses very aggressive parameters; "BlueGeMSS" uses more conservative parameters. Just "GeMSS" falls in the middle, and this is what we choose to implement. The parameter set targeting NIST security level 1 is `gemss-128` and has 350 kB public keys.

2.3 Lattice-Based Schemes

Lattice-based cryptographic schemes are promising post-quantum replacements for currently used public-key cryptography since they are asymptotically efficient, have provable security guarantees, and are very versatile, i.e., they offer far more functionality than plain encryption or signature schemes.

Lattice-based signature schemes are constructed using one of two techniques, either the GPV framework that is based on the hash-and-sign paradigm [11], or the Fiat-Shamir transformation [18]. The security of lattice-based signature schemes can be proven based on hard lattice problems (usually the LWE problem, the SIS problem, and variants thereof) or the NTRU assumption.

220   R. Gonzalez et al.

Dilithium Dilithium is a NIST round 3 finalist [2]. Signature verification for Dilithium works as follows: The public key $pk = (\rho, \mathbf{t_1})$ consists of a uniform random 256-bit seed ρ, which expands to the matrix of polynomials $\mathbf{A}$, and $\mathbf{t_1}$. For MLWE samples $\mathbf{t} = \mathbf{As} + \mathbf{e}$, $\mathbf{t_1}$ is the first output of the Power2Round procedure [2, Figure 3], and $(\mathbf{t_1}, \mathbf{t_0}) = \text{Power2Round}_q(\mathbf{t}, d)$ is the straightforward bit-wise way to break up an element $r = r_1 \cdot 2^d + r_0$, where $r_0 = r \mod 2^d$ and $r_1 = (r - r_0)/2^d$ with $-2^d/2 \leq r_0 < 2^d/2$. Hence, the coefficients of $\mathbf{t_0}$ are the d lower order bits and the coefficients of $\mathbf{t_1}$ — the second part of the public key — are the $\lceil \log q \rceil - d$ higher order bits of the coefficients of $\mathbf{t}$. To verify a signature $(\mathbf{z}, \mathbf{h}, c)$ for a message M, one computes $\mathbf{w'} = \mathbf{Az} - c \cdot \mathbf{t_1} \cdot 2^d$, uses the hint vector $\mathbf{h}$ to recover $\mathbf{w'_1} = \text{UseHint}(\mathbf{h}, \mathbf{w'})$, and finally verifies that $c = h(h(h(\rho\|\mathbf{t_1})\|M)\|\mathbf{w'_1})$. For the details, we refer to [2].

All Dilithium parameter sets use $q = 2^{23} - 2^{13} + 1$ and $d = 13$. Hence, while the coefficients of $\mathbf{t}$ need 23 bits, the coefficients of the public key $\mathbf{t_1}$ need only 10 bits. We use the smallest instance of Dilithium, which is NIST level 2 parameter set `dilithium2`. The public key size of `dilithium2` in total is 1 312 bytes and a signature needs 2 420 bytes.

Falcon Falcon, too, is a NIST round 3 finalist [28]. Falcon's signature verification works as follows: A signature for message M, consisting of the tuple (r, s), can be verified given the public key $h = gf^{-1} \pmod{q}$, where $f, g \in \mathbb{Z}_q[x]/(\phi)$ for a modulus q and a cyclotomic polynomial $\phi \in \mathbb{Z}[x]$ of degree n. Firstly r and M are concatenated and hashed into a polynomial c and s is decompressed using a unary code into s_2. Then, $s_1 = c - s_2 h$ is computed and it is verified that (s_1, s_2) has a small enough norm ($\leq \lfloor \beta^2 \rfloor$). Coefficients are compressed one-by-one and hence can be decompressed individually. The embedding norm that is computed in [28, Algorithm 16, line 6] can be computed in linear time and only requires two coefficients at a time. However, the preceding polynomial multiplication requires all coefficients of one operand to be present, preventing coefficient-by-coefficient streaming for both the signature and the public key at the same time. If, however, only the signature or the public key is streamed, the polynomial multiplication could be performed. We use `falcon-512`, targeting NIST level I, which uses dimension $n = 512$ and $q = 12289 \approx 2^{14}$, hence each coefficient of the public key needs 14 bits.

3 Implementation

The following section describes the implementations of the signature schemes for the use case of feature activation described in Sect. 1. The signature verification is performed on a Cortex-M3. The consumption for program flash should be limited to 8 kB. The RAM usage should not exceed 8 kB. The bus speed for streaming is assumed to run at either 500 kbit/s or 20 Mbit/s.

3.1 Streaming Interface

Signed messages and public keys are streamed into the embedded Cortex-M3 device. To avoid performance overhead, our streaming implementation follows a very simple protocol. In a first step, the length of the signed message is transmitted to the embedded device. Then the embedded device initializes streaming by supplying a chunk size to the sender and additionally supplies if signed message or public key is to be streamed first. After every chunk, the embedded device can request a new chunk or return a verification result. The chunk size may be altered between chunks, but the public key and the signed message are always streamed in-order. The result is a one-bit message, signaling if the verification succeeded or failed, followed by the message in case the verification succeeded.

3.2 Public Key Verification

As the public key is being streamed in from an untrusted source, it is imperative to validate that the key is actually authentic. We assume that a hash of the public key is stored inside the HSM in some integrity-protected area. While the public key is being streamed in, we incrementally compute a hash of it that we eventually compare with the known hash. We use the same hash function as used by the studied scheme, i.e., SHA-256 for `sphincs-sha256` and `rainbowI-classic`, SHAKE-128 for `gemss-128` and SHAKE-256 for `dilithium2` and `falcon-512`. We keep the hash state in memory, occupying additional 200 bytes for SHAKE-128 and 32 bytes for SHA-256. We use the incremental SHA-256 and SHAKE implementations from pqm4 [16].

In the case of `gemss-128`, the public key is needed multiple times; once in every of the four evaluations of the public map. Note that the integrity needs to be verified each time.

3.3 Implementation Details

In the following, we describe the modifications to existing implementations of the five studied schemes needed to use them with the given platform constraints. Table 1 lists the public key, signature sizes, and the time needed for streaming them into the device at 500 kbit/s and 20 Mbit/s.

SPHINCS$^+$ Our SPHINCS$^+$ implementation is based on the round-3 reference implementation [1]. Preceding work [16] shows that computation time for SPHINCS$^+$ verification on single-core embedded devices is almost exclusively spent in the underlying hash function. We did therefore not investigate further optimization possibilities. Aligning the implementation to a streaming API is fairly straightforward as SPHINCS$^+$ signatures get processed in-order. For both `sphincs-sha256-128f-simple` and `sphincs-sha256-128s-simple` a public key is 32 bytes and hence does not require streaming.

For `sphincs-sha256-128f-simple`, a signature is 17 088 bytes. The selected SPHINCS$^+$ parameter sets use $n = 16$ byte and so a streaming chunk size of 16

Table 1. Communication overhead in bytes and milliseconds at 500 kbit/s and 20 Mbit/s. GeMSS requires to stream in the public key nb_ite times (4 for `gemss-128`). All other schemes require streaming in the public key and signed message once.

	streaming data			streaming time	
	$|pk|$	$|sig|$	total	500 kbit/s	20 Mbit/s
sphincs-s[a]	32	7856	7888	126.2 ms	3.2 ms
sphincs-f[b]	32	17088	17120	273.9 ms	6.9 ms
rainbowI-classic	161600	66	161666	2586.7 ms	64.7 ms
gemss-128	352188	33	1408785[c]	22540.6 ms	563.5 ms
dilithium2	1312	2420	3732	59.7 ms	1.5 ms
falcon-512	897	690	1587	25.4 ms	0.6 ms

[a] `-sha256-128s-simple`   [b] `-sha256-128f-simple`   [c] $4 \cdot |pk| + |sig|$

bytes is possible. However, such a small chunk is undesirable due to overhead in terms of memory and computation. The leading 16 bytes of the signature make up the randomizer value, followed by the 3696 byte FORS signature, consisting of 33 authentication paths, and the 13376 bytes for 22 MSS signatures. Our implementation first processes a 3712 byte chunk containing the randomizer value and FORS signature. This is used to compute the message digest and then the FORS root, evaluating the 33 authentication paths. Then, the computed FORS root is verified using the MSS signatures. The overall 22 MSS signatures, each consisting of a WOTS+ signature and an authentication path, are processed in three chunks. Given the memory constraints, the largest available chunk size is 4864 bytes containing 8 MSS signatures. MSS signature streaming is therefore done in two 4864 byte chunks and one final 3648 byte chunk. Starting from the FORS root, this data is used to successively reconstruct all the MSS tree roots from the respectively previous root: first computing 67 hash chains using the WOTS+ signature, compressing their end nodes in a single hash, and then evaluating an authentication path. The last (or "highest") MSS tree root is then compared to the root node in the public key. For this to work, the reserved chunk buffer needs to be 4864 bytes large.

For `sphincs-sha256-128s-simple`, streaming works analogously. The signature size is 7856 bytes and only seven - slightly larger - MSS signatures are used within the scheme. This makes it possible to stream in all 7 MSS signatures in a single 4928 bytes chunk. Streaming therefore consists of one FORS+randomizer-value (2928 bytes) and one MSS (4928 bytes) chunk.

Rainbow The round-3 submission of Rainbow [9] contains an implementation targeting the Cortex-M4. As it relies only on instructions also available on the Cortex-M3, it is also functional on the Cortex-M3. However, due to the large public key (162 kB), we adapt the implementation for streaming. Rainbow signatures consist of an ℓ bit (128 for `rainbowI-classic`) salt and n (100) variables x_i in a small finite field ($\mathbb{F}_{16}$ for `rainbowI-classic`). Two $\mathbb{F}_{16}$ elements are packed into one byte in the signature and public key. We first unpack the elements of the signature and store one x_i in the lower four bits of a byte. This doubles memory usage from 50 to 100 bytes, but makes look-ups for individual elements easier. After the signature and corresponding x_i are stored in memory, the public key is streamed in. The public key consists of the Macaulay matrix $p_{i,j}^{(k)}$ representing the public map consisting of m (64) equations of the form

$$p^{(k)}(x_1, \ldots, x_n) = \sum_{i=1}^{n} \sum_{j=i}^{n} p_{i,j}^{(k)} x_i x_j$$

with the x_i, x_j corresponding to the variables from the signature. For computational efficiency the public key is represented in the column-major form. The public key's first 32 byte chunk therefore has the form $[p_{1,1}^{(1)}|p_{1,1}^{(2)}|\ldots|p_{1,1}^{(m)}]$ and the contained coefficients should be multiplied by x_1^2. Subsequent 32 byte chunks have the same form ($[p_{1,2}^{(1)}|\ldots|p_{1,2}^{(m)}]$ should be multiplied by $x_1 \cdot x_2$ and so forth.). To increase performance, Rainbow implementations delay multiplications. Before the actual multiplication step, coefficient sums are accumulated. Every incoming 32 byte chunk is added to one of 15 accumulators a_k based on the 15 possible values of $y_{i,j} = x_i \cdot x_j$ with $y_{i,j} > 0$. If $y_{i,j}$ is zero, the chunk is discarded. Once all chunks are consumed, every accumulator is multiplied by its corresponding factor $\tilde{a}_k = [k \cdot a_k^{(1)}|k \cdot a_k^{(2)}|\ldots]$ and added summed up the final result.

One can exploit that if an element x_i is zero, all monomials $x_i x_j$ will be zero and the corresponding columns of the public key will not contribute to the result. As every 16th x_i is expected to be zero, this results in a significant speed-up. As Rainbow is using $\mathbb{F}_{16}$ arithmetic, additions are XOR. For multiplications, we use the bitsliced implementation from the Rainbow Cortex-M4 implementation [9].

The smallest reasonable chunk size for Rainbow is a single column of the Macaulay matrix, i.e., 32 bytes. However, as larger chunk sizes result in lower overhead, we use the largest chunk size which fits in our available memory. Due to the low memory footprint of the Rainbow implementation, we can afford to use chunks of 214 columns, i.e., 6 848 bytes. As there are 5 050 ($n \cdot (n+1)/2$) columns, the last chunk is only 128 columns, i.e., 4 096 bytes.

GeMSS To the best of our knowledge, there are no GeMSS implementations available targeting microcontrollers and we, hence, write our own. We base our GeMSS implementation on the reference implementation accompanying the specification [6]. The biggest challenge is that the entirety of the 352 kB public key is needed in each of the evaluations of the public map **p**. Due to the iterative construction of the HFEv- scheme, there appears to be no better approach than streaming in the public key in each iteration, i.e., nb_ite (4 for gemss-128) times.

Each application of the public map p requires the computation of

$$p_i = \sum_{i=0}^{n+v} \sum_{j=i}^{n+v} x_i x_j a_{i,j} + a_0.$$

Each column of the Macaulay matrix needs to be multiplied by a product of two variables and then added to the accumulator. The field used by GeMSS is

$\mathbb{F}_2$ and, hence, field multiplication is logical AND and field addition is XOR which allows straightforward bitslicing of operations. Unfortunately, since the number of equations (m) is not a multiple of 8 ($m = 162$ for gemss-128), one cannot simply store the Macaulay matrix in column-major form since this would result in the columns not being aligned to byte boundaries. Therefore, GeMSS stores the first $8 \cdot \lfloor m/8 \rfloor$ (160) equations in a column-major form making up the first $\lfloor m/8 \rfloor \cdot (((n+v) \cdot (n+v+1))/2+1)$ (347 840) bytes of the public key with $n+v$ ($n = 174, v = 12$) being the number of variables. The last 2 equations are stored row-wise occupying the last $2 \cdot (((n + v) \cdot (n + v + 1))/2 + 1)/8$ (4348) bytes.

We split the computation in two parts: The first $8 \cdot \lfloor m/8 \rfloor$ equations and the last ($m \mod 8$) equations. For the former, the most important optimization comes from the observation that if either of the two variables x_i or x_j is zero, the corresponding column does not impact the result. Similar to the Rainbow implementation, in the case x_i is zero, the entire inner loop and, hence, $n+v-i$ columns of the public key can be skipped. As half of the x_i are expected to be zero, this results in a vast performance gain. For the last ($m \mod 8$), we first compute the monomials $x_i x_j$ and store them in a vector, then we add this vector to each row of the public key. Lastly, we compute the parity of each row. The smallest reasonable chunk size for the first part of the computation is one column of the public key (20 bytes), while it is one row (2174 bytes) for the second part. However, we use 4 560 byte-chunks (285 columns) to achieve lowest overhead with 8 kB RAM.

Dilithium Our Dilithium implementation is based on previous work targeting the Cortex-M3 and Cortex-M4 [12]. However, this work predates the round 3 Dilithium submission [2] which introduced some algorithm tweaks and parameter changes. Most notably for the performance of dilithium2 verification, the matrix dimension of $\mathbf{A}$ changed from $(k, \ell) = (4, 3)$ to $(4, 4)$. Therefore, we adapt the existing Cortex-M3 implementation to the new parameters.

For dilithium2, the implementation of [12] requires 9 kB of stack in addition to the 2.4 kB signature and 1.3 kB public key in memory. We apply a couple of tricks to fit it within 8 kB: We compute one polynomial of $\mathbf{w}'$ at a time, which allows us to stream in the public key $\mathbf{t}_1$. Usually, one computes $\mathbf{w}' = \mathbf{A}\mathbf{z} - c \cdot \mathbf{t}_1 \cdot 2^d$ as $\text{NTT}^{-1}(\hat{\mathbf{A}} \cdot \text{NTT}(\mathbf{z}) - \text{NTT}(c) \cdot \text{NTT}(\mathbf{t}_1 \cdot 2^d))$. Hence, it is desirable for performance to keep $\text{NTT}(\mathbf{z})$ and $\text{NTT}(c)$ in memory. However, that already occupies 5 kB. We instead keep the compressed forms of $\mathbf{z}$ and c in memory, occupying only $\ell \cdot 576 = 2304$ and 32 bytes, respectively, and recompute the NTT operations.

Previous implementations of Dilithium use 3 temporary polynomials to compute $\text{NTT}^{-1}(\hat{\mathbf{A}} \cdot \text{NTT}(\mathbf{z}) - \text{NTT}(c) \cdot \text{NTT}(\mathbf{t}_1 \cdot 2^d))$, one for the accumulator and two temporary ones for the inputs. We instead compute $\text{NTT}^{-1}(-\text{NTT}(c) \cdot \text{NTT}(\mathbf{t}_1 \cdot 2^d) + \hat{\mathbf{A}} \cdot \text{NTT}(\mathbf{z}))$, which can be computed in 2 polynomials by sampling $\hat{\mathbf{A}}$ coefficient-wise, as was also proposed for Kyber [5].

The total memory consumption comprises the 2 420-byte signature, 2 polynomials of 1 024 bytes each, 3 Keccak states of 200 bytes each, and about 600 bytes of other buffers, i.e., approximately 5 670 bytes in total. To improve speed, one can cache as much of NTT($\mathbf{z}$) and NTT($\mathbf{c}$) as possible. We cache NTT($\mathbf{c}$) and 3 polynomials of NTT($\mathbf{z}$) while still remaining below 8 kB of stack.

Falcon We used a Cortex-M4 optimized implementation which is also part of Falcon's round-3 submission [27,28]. It is compatible with Cortex-M3 processors, but relies on emulated floating point arithmetic. This leads to data-dependent runtimes, which is unproblematic for verification, but may be an issue when considering signing as well. On the Cortex-M3, the implementation submitted to NIST uses around 500 bytes of stack space, public keys of circa 900 bytes, signatures of around 800 bytes, and a 4 kB scratch buffer. The overall memory footprint is about 6.5 kB. Hence, streaming in the data in small packets is not necessary. Our implementation copies the whole public key and signature to RAM before running the unmodified Falcon verification algorithm.

4 Results

We chose an ARM Cortex-M3 board with 128 kB RAM and 1 MB Flash, an STM32 Nucleo-F207ZG, as the platform for the implementation of our case study. This board meets most of the specifications of an environment with limited resources of a typical automotive HSM embedded in MCUs. The only mismatch is the non-volatile memory (NVM). A typical limited HSM has much less NVM.

We clock the Cortex-M3 at 30 MHz (rather than the maximum frequency of 120 MHz) to have no Flash wait states. In a practical deployment in an HSM one would use fast ROM instead of Flash and, hence, our cycle counts are close to what we would expect in an automotive HSM.

We base our benchmarking setup on the pqm3[2] framework and adapt it to support our streaming API. For counting clock cycles, we use the SysTick counter. We stream in the signed message and public key using USART, but disregard the cycles spent waiting for serial communication. We stream in the signed message and public key using USART using a baud rate of 57 600 bps, which is much slower than what we would expect in a practical HSM. We use arm-none-eabi-gcc version 10.2.0 with -O3. We use a random 33-byte message which resembles the short messages needed for feature activation.

Table 2 presents the speed results for our implementations. The studied signature schemes rely on either SHA-256 (rainbowI-classic, sphincs-sha256) or SHA-3/SHAKE (dilithium2, falcon-512, and gemss-128). In a typical HSM-enabled device SHA-256 would be available in hardware and SHA-3/SHAKE will also be available in the future. However, on the Nucleo-F207ZG no hardware accelerators are available. Hence, we resort to software implementations instead. For SHA-256 we use the optimized C implementation from SUPERCOP.[3] For SHA-3/SHAKE, we rely on the ARMv7-M implementation from the XKCP.[4]

---

[2] https://github.com/mupq/pqm3
[3] https://bench.cr.yp.to/supercop.html
[4] https://github.com/XKCP/XKCP

Table 2. Cycle count for signature verification for a 33-byte message. Average over 1 000 signature verifications. Hashing cycles needed for verification of the streamed in public key (hashing and comparing to embedded hash) are reported separately. We also report the verification time on a practical HSM running at 100 MHz and also the total time including the streaming at 20 Mbit/s.

	w/o pk vrf.	w/ pk verification			w/ streaming
		pk vrf.	total	time[e]	20 Mbit/s
sphincs-s[a]	8 741k	0	8 741k	87.4 ms	90.6 ms
sphincs-f[b]	26 186k	0	26 186k	261.9 ms	268.7 ms
rainbowI-classic	333k	6 850k[d]	7 182k	71.8 ms	136.5 ms
gemss-128	1 619k	109 938k[c]	111 557k	1 115.6 ms	1 679.1 ms
dilithium2	1 990k	133k[c]	2 123k	21.2 ms	21.8 ms
falcon-512	581k	91k[c]	672k	6.7 ms	8.2 ms

[a] -sha256-128s-simple   [b] -sha256-128f-simple   [c] SHA-3/SHAKE
[d] SHA-256   [e] At 100 MHz (no wait states)

While GeMSS and Rainbow only compute a (randomized) hash of the message, SPHINCS[+], Dilithium, and Falcon use hashing as a core building block of the verification. Consequently, the amount of hashing in multivariate cryptography is minimal (2% for rainbowI-classic, 4% for gemss-128), while it makes up large parts for lattice-based (65% for dilithium2, 36% for falcon-512) and hash-based signatures (90% for sphincs-sha256-128s-simple and 88% for sphincs-sha256-128f-simple). Clearly lattice-based and hash-based schemes would benefit more from hardware accelerated hashing.

Additionally, we need to verify the authenticity of the streamed in public key. We report the time needed for public key verification separately. For hash-based signatures this operation comes virtually for free as the public key itself can be stored in the device, so that no hashing is required. For multivariate cryptography, the public key verification becomes the most dominant operation due to the large public keys and fast arithmetic. This is particularly pronounced for GeMSS as the public key is the largest and needs to be verified 4 times.

Table 3 presents the memory requirements of our implementations.

Table 3. Memory and code-size requirements in bytes for our implementations. Memory includes stack needed for computations, global variables stored in the .bss section and the buffer required for streaming. Code-size excludes platform and framework code as well as code for SHA-256 and SHA-3.

	memory				code
	total	buffer	.bss	stack	.text
sphincs-s[a]	6 904	4 928	780	1 196	2 724
sphincs-f[b]	7 536	4 864	780	1 892	2 586
rainbowI-classic	8 168	6 848	724	596	2 194
gemss-128	8 176	4 560	496	3 120	4 740
dilithium2	8 048	40	6 352	1 656	7 940
falcon-512	6 552	897	5 255	400	5 784

[a] -sha256-128s-simple   [b] -sha256-128f-simple

Acknowledgments. Part of this work was done during the Lorentz Center Workshop "Post-Quantum Cryptography for Embedded Systems", Oct. 2020. This work was carried out while the third and fifth author were visiting Academia Sinica. This work has been supported by the European Commission through the ERC Starting Grant 805031 (EPOQUE) and by the German Federal Ministry of Education and Research (BMBF) under the project QuantumRISC. Part of Marc Stöttinger's contribution to this work was done while he was employed at Continental AG. This work was supported by Taiwan Ministry of Science and Technology Grant 109-2221-E-001-009-MY3, Sinica Investigator Award AS-IA-109-M01, Executive Yuan Data Safety and Talent Cultivation Project (AS-KPQ-109-DSTCP). This work has been supported by the Netherlands Organisation for Scientific Research (NWO) under grant 628.001.028 (FASOR) aand by the Deutsche Forschungsgemeinschaft (DFG, German Research Foundation) under Germany's Excellence Strategy—EXC 2092 CASA—390781972 "Cyber Security in the Age of Large-Scale Adversaries".

References

1. Aumasson, J.P., Bernstein, D.J., Beullens, W., Dobraunig, C., Eichlseder, M., Fluhrer, S., Gazdag, S.L., Hülsing, A., Kampanakis, P., Kölbl, S., Lange, T., Lauridsen, M.M., Mendel, F., Niederhagen, R., Rechberger, C., Rijneveld, J., Schwabe, P., Westerbaan, B.: SPHINCS+. Submission to the NIST Post-Quantum Cryptography Standardization Project (2020), available at https://sphincs.org/

2. Bai, S., Lyubashevsky, V., Ducas, L., Kiltz, E., Lepoint, T., Schwabe, P., Seiler, G., Stehlé, D.: CRYSTALS-DILITHIUM. Submission to the NIST Post-Quantum Cryptography Standardization Project (2020), available at https://pq-crystals.org/dilithium/

3. Bernstein, D.J., Hülsing, A., Kölbl, S., Niederhagen, R., Rijneveld, J., Schwabe, P.: The SPHINCS$^+$ Signature Framework. ACM CCS. ACM (2019). https://doi.org/10.1145/3319535.3363229

4. Bernstein, D.J., Hopwood, D., Hülsing, A., Lange, T., Niederhagen, R., Papachristodoulou, L., Schneider, M., Schwabe, P., Wilcox-O'Hearn, Z.: SPHINCS: Practical Stateless Hash-Based Signatures. In: Oswald, E., Fischlin, M. (eds.) EUROCRYPT, Lecture Notes in Computer Science, vol. 9056, pp. 368–397. Springer (2015), https://eprint.iacr.org/2014/795

5. Botros, L., Kannwischer, M.J., Schwabe, P.: Memory-efficient high-speed implementation of Kyber on Cortex-M4. In: Buchmann, J., Nitaj, A., Rachidi, T. (eds.) Progress in Cryptology – Africacrypt 2019. Lecture Notes in Computer Science, vol. 11627, pp. 209–228. Springer (2019), https://eprint.iacr.org/2019/489

6. Casanova, A., Faugère, J.C., Macario-Rat, G., Patarin, J., Perret, L., Ryckeghem, J.: GeMSS. Submission to the NIST Post-Quantum Cryptography Standardization Project (2020), available at https://www-polsys.lip6.fr/Links/NIST/GeMSS.html

7. Chen, M.S., Chou, T.: Classic McEliece on the ARM Cortex-M4. Cryptology ePrint Archive, Report 2021/492 (2021), https://eprint.iacr.org/2021/492

8. Cooper, D., Apon, D., Dang, Q., Davidson, M., Dworkin, M., Miller, C.: NIST Special Publication 800-208: Recommendation for stateful hash-based signature schemes (2020). https://doi.org/10.6028/NIST.SP.800-208

9. Ding, J., Chen, M.S., Kannwischer, M., Patarin, J., Petzoldt, A., Schmidt, D., Yang, B.Y.: Rainbow. Submission to the NIST Post-Quantum Cryptography Standardization Project (2020), available at https://www.pqcrainbow.org/

10. Eisenbarth, T., Güneysu, T., Heyse, S., Paar, C.: MicroEliece: McEliece for embedded devices. In: Clavier, C., Gaj, K. (eds.) CHES. pp. 49–64. Springer (2009). https://doi.org/10.1007/978-3-642-04138-9_4

11. Gentry, C., Peikert, C., Vaikuntanathan, V.: Trapdoors for hard lattices and new cryptographic constructions. In: ACM STOC. p. 197–206. STOC '08, ACM (2008). https://doi.org/10.1145/1374376.1374407

12. Greconici, D.O.C., Kannwischer, M.J., Sprenkels, D.: Compact Dilithium implementations on Cortex-M3 and Cortex-M4. IACR TCHES 2021(1), 1–24 (2020), https://eprint.iacr.org/2020/1278

13. Henniger, O., Ruddle, A., Seudié, H., Weyl, B., Wolf, M., Wollinger, T.: Securing vehicular on-board IT systems: The EVITA project. In: 25th Joint VDI/VW Automotive Security Conference (Oct 2009), https://evita-project.org/Publications/HRSW09.pdf

14. Hülsing, A., Rijneveld, J., Schwabe, P.: ARMed SPHINCS – Computing a 41KB signature in 16KB of RAM. In: Persiano, G., Yang, B.-Y. (eds.) Public Key Cryptography – PKC 2016. Lecture Notes in Computer Science, vol. 9614, p. 446–470. Springer (2016). https://eprint.iacr.org/2015/1042

15. Hülsing, A., Butin, D., Gazdag, S.L., Rijneveld, J., Mohaisen, A.: XMSS: eXtended Merkle Signature Scheme. RFC 8391 (May 2018). https://doi.org/10.17487/RFC8391

16. Kannwischer, M.J., Rijneveld, J., Schwabe, P., Stoffelen, K.: pqm4: Testing and benchmarking NIST PQC on ARM Cortex-M4. Workshop Record of the Second NIST PQC Standardization Conference (2019), https://eprint.iacr.org/2019/844

17. Kipnis, A., Patarin, J., Goubin, L.: Unbalanced oil and vinegar signature schemes. In: EUROCRYPT. Lecture Notes in Computer Science, vol. 1592, pp. 206–222. Springer (1999). https://doi.org/10.1007/3-540-48910-X_15

18. Lyubashevsky, V.: Fiat-Shamir with aborts: Applications to lattice and factoring-based signatures. In: ASIACRYPT. pp. 598–616. Springer (2009). https://doi.org/10.1007/978-3-642-10366-7_35

19. Matsumoto, T., Imai, H.: Public quadratic polynominal-tuples for efficient signature-verification and message-encryption. In: EUROCRYPT. Lecture Notes in Computer Science, vol. 330, pp. 419–453. Springer (1988). https://doi.org/10.1007/3-540-45961-8_39

20. McGrew, D., Curcio, M., Fluhrer, S.: Leighton-Micali Hash-Based Signatures. RFC 8554 (Apr 2019). https://doi.org/10.17487/RFC8554

21. Merkle, R.: A certified digital signature. In: CRYPTO. Lecture Notes in Computer Science, vol. 435, pp. 218–238. Springer (1990). https://doi.org/10.1007/0-387-34805-0_21

22. Patarin, J.: Cryptanalysis of the Matsumoto and Imai public key scheme of Eurocrypt'88. In: CRYPTO. Lecture Notes in Computer Science, vol. 963, pp. 248–261. Springer (1995). https://doi.org/10.1007/3-540-44750-4_20

23. Patarin, J.: Hidden fields equations (HFE) and isomorphisms of polynomials (IP): two new families of asymmetric algorithms. In: EUROCRYPT. Lecture Notes in Computer Science, vol. 1070, pp. 33–48. Springer (1996). https://doi.org/10.1007/3-540-68339-9_4

24. Patarin, J.: The oil and vinegar signature scheme. In: Dagstuhl Workshop on Cryptography (Sep 1997)

25. Patarin, J., Courtois, N.T., Goubin, L.: Quartz, 128-bit long digital signatures. In: CT-RSA. Lecture Notes in Computer Science, vol. 2020, pp. 282–297. Springer (2001). https://doi.org/10.1007/3-540-45353-9_21

26. Patarin, J., Goubin, L., Courtois, N.T.: C^*_{-+} and HM: variations around two schemes of T. Matsumoto and H. Imai. In: ASIACRYPT. Lecture Notes in Computer Science, vol. 1514, pp. 35–49. Springer (1998). https://doi.org/10.1007/3-540-49649-1_4

27. Pornin, T.: New efficient, constant-time implementations of Falcon. Cryptology ePrint Archive, Report 2019/893 (2019), https://eprint.iacr.org/2019/893

28. Prest, T., Fouque, P.A., Hoffstein, J., Kirchner, P., Lyubashevsky, V., Pornin, T., Ricosset, T., Seiler, G., Whyte, W., Zhang, Z.: FALCON. Submission to the NIST Post-Quantum Cryptography Standardization Project (2020), available at https://falcon-sign.info/

29. Roth, J., Karatsiolis, E.G., Krämer, J.: Classic McEliece implementation with low memory footprint. In: CARDIS. Lecture Notes in Computer Science, vol. 12609, pp. 34–49. Springer (2020). https://doi.org/10.1007/978-3-030-68487-7_3

30. Strenzke, F.: How to implement the public key operations in code-based cryptography on memory-constrained devices. Cryptology ePrint Archive, Report 2010/465 (2010), https://eprint.iacr.org/2010/465

A   Feature Activation

Feature Activation is intended to activate additional functionality on an embedded device that is already deployed and active in the running environment. It differs from a software update because all software and required hardware for the feature's functionality is already included in the device, but not activated.

The feature is activated by an authentic message from an authorized instance. The activation of the feature is device specific, therefore the activation messages must not be portable to other devices. The protocol 1 describes the actual feature activation process between an embedded device on which the feature is to be activated and an authorized instance, e.g., a back-end system. To authenticate the feature activation request, a signature is part of the message sent from the authorization instance to the embedded device. Nowadays, this signature is implemented, for example, by an ECC signature, which is not a post-quantum algorithm. In the scenario shown, the overall protocol does not take into account any resource constraints on the device, so that, for example, the ECC signature and the public key are stored entirely on the device.

The protocol 1 can be roughly paraphrased as follows: The user, e.g. the car owner, creates a request to activate a desired feature for a specific vehicle (identified by a vehicle identification number - VIN). This can be done through an online platform. The authorization instance, which can be represented by a back-end, validates the feature request for the feature policies it stores for the requested vehicle, and requests and verifies the user's authentication. Upon successful authorization, the authorization instance generates a device-specific feature activation request A_{msg} for the device that is part of the vehicle and implements the requested feature. Furthermore, the authorization instance generates a signature T_1 for the message A_{msg} using its private key pr_{AE}. When the device successfully verifies the signature T_1, it updates its feature policies, activates the requested feature, and stores the feature policy hash. Finally, the

User	Authorization Entity: AE	Device: D
$\xrightarrow{\text{Req. feature activation}}$	Validate feature activation request	
$\xleftarrow{\text{Req. authentication}}$		
$\xrightarrow{\text{Authenticate}}$	Verify authentication	
	Generate A_{msg}	
	$T_1 : Sign_{pr_{AE}}(A_{msg})$ $\xrightarrow{\text{Send } \{A_{msg}|T_1\}}$	Verify T_1 using pb_{AE}
		Update feature policies
		Activate feature
		Secure hash of the feature policies
	Update feature polices of D $\xleftarrow{\text{Send } \{A_{rec}\}}$	Generate A_{rec}

Protocol 1: Protocol for feature activation

embedded device confirms the feature activation status in a message A_{rec} to the authorization instance. The authorization instance itself also updates and stores the feature policy for the specific device.

B   Alternative Implementation

For embedded applications it is sometimes attractive to use symmetric cryptography in place of public-key cryptography. Not only is symmetric cryptography a lot faster, it also benefits from already-present hardware acceleration and key sizes are significantly smaller. Of course, the secret keys in symmetric devices are extremely sensitive. We need that a secret key extracted from a particular deployed device does not compromise the entire scheme. This implies the need to provision each device with its own individualised key. However, when deploying hundreds or thousands of devices this means we have a potentially significant key management problem. Fortunately, the many-to-one architecture in this automotive application implies we only need a single key between each device and the back-end. Furthermore, each deployed device has public identifiers, like the vehicle VIN or a serial number. This allows us to only let the manufacturer store a single key for all deployed devices.

We use these properties to construct an efficient key distribution scheme. Let each device have a unique identifing number n. This could for example be the concatenation of the vehicle VIN and the device's serial number. We let the manufacturer generate a main secret key K_m. Then, we provision at time of manufacturing each device with the following key K_d, such that

$$K_d = \text{KDF}(K_m, n).$$

Here, KDF is an appropriate key-derivation function.

Then, whenever the device needs to use their key K_d in communication with the manufacturer, they send over their identifier n along with the message. For example, if they need to send an authenticated message m, they might send $\{n, m, \text{MAC}_{K_d}(n, m)\}$. The manufacturer can then easily compute K_d based on n and the main secret K_m, and verify the message. As the device does not have access to K_m, they can only have produced this MAC if they were provisioned with K_d at time of manufacture.

Of course, this entire scheme falls down when K_m is compromised. As such, special care needs to be taken to protect it. Although the private keys used in public-key cryptography also need to be protected, we can use revocation mechanisms to recover from a compromise. This is not possible with symmetric cryptography.

C Hash-Based Signatures

Hash-based signature schemes are signature schemes for which security solely relies on the security properties of the cryptographic hash function(s) used. In contrast to other proposals for digital signature schemes it does not require an additional complexity theoretic hardness assumption. Given that the security of cryptographic hash functions is well understood and even more, we know that generic attacks using quantum computers cannot significantly harm the security of cryptographic hash functions, hash-based signatures present a conservative choice for post-quantum secure digital signatures. The description in this section is simplified, and we refer to the official specification [1] for a detailed exposition.

One-Time Signature Schemes (OTS) Hash-based signatures built on the concept of a one-time signature scheme (OTS). This is a signature scheme where a key pair may only be used to sign one message. If two messages are signed with the same secret key, the scheme becomes insecure. Such OTS can be constructed from cryptographic hash functions. The very generic concept is that the secret key consists of random values while the public key contains their hash values. A signature consists of a subset of the values in the secret key, selected by the message. A signature is verified by hashing the values in the signature and comparing the resulting hash values to the respective values in the public key. The OTS commonly used today is the Winternitz OTS (WOTS) or variations thereof which generalizes the above concept to hash chains. WOTS has the important property that a signature is verified by computing a candidate public key by hashing the values in the signature several times (depending on the message) and comparing the result to the public key.

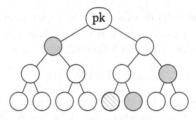

Fig. 1. The authentication path of the fifth leaf (Source [3])

Merkle Signature Schemes (MSS) Given a OTS, a many-time signature scheme can be constructed following the concept of Merkle Signature Schemes (MSS) [21]. For these, a number (a power of 2) of OTS key pairs is generated and their public keys are authenticated using a binary hash tree, called a Merkle tree. The hashes of the public keys form the leaves of the tree. Inner nodes are the hash of the concatenation of their two child nodes. The root node becomes the MSS public key. Assuming WOTS is used as OTS, a signature consists of the leaf index, a WOTS signature and the so-called authentication path (cf. Figure 1). The authentication path contains the sibling nodes on the path from the used leaf to the root. Verification uses the WOTS signature (and the message) to compute a candidate public key and from that the corresponding leaf. This leaf is then used together with the authentication path to compute a root node: Starting with the leaf, the current buffer is concatenated with the next authentication path node and hashed to obtain the next buffer value. The order of concatenation is determined by the leaf index in the MSS signature. The final buffer value is then compared to the root node in the public key.

In general, this leads a so-called stateful scheme as a signer has to remember which OTS key pairs she already used. This concept is the general idea underlying the schemes described in recent RFCs [15,20] LMS and XMSS.

SPHINCS+ The limitation of having to keep a state as signer can be overcome in practice using the SPHINCS construction [4] (previous theoretically efficient proposals by Goldreich go back to the last century but were only of theoretical interest). SPHINCS+ [3] essentially instantiates the SPHINCS construction. The first idea in SPHINCS uses a few-time signature scheme (FTS) - a signature scheme where a key pair can be used to sign a small number of messages without keeping a state before the scheme gets insecure. SPHINCS+ uses a huge number of FTS key-pairs (in the order of 2^{64} depending on the parameters). For every new message, a random FTS key is picked to sign. By making the number of FTS keys large enough, the probability that one key gets used to sign more than a few messages can be made vanishingly small. The public keys of all these FTS key pairs are authenticated using a certfication tree of MSS key pairs called the hypertree. The hyper tree is essentially a PKI. To the top MSS key works as a root CA and the bottom layer MSS keys certify FTS public keys. The whole structure is deterministically generated using pseudorandom generators. That way, it is not necessary to store which OTS keys where used for an MSS key because the message that a specfic OTS key will be used to sign is predetermined.

The FTS in SPHINCS$^+$ is FORS. A FORS secret key consists of several sets of random values the values in each set are authenticated via a Merkle tree. These trees have the hashes of the secret values as leaves. The public key is the hash of the concatenation of all root nodes of these Merkle trees. A signature consists of one secret key value from each set (determined by the message) and the respective authentication path. Verfication works by computing the leaves from the signature values and afterwards computing candidate root nodes as for MSS. This can be done per tree. Afterwards, the roots are used to compute a candidate public key.

A SPHINCS$^+$ signature consists of a randomizer R that is hashed with the message to obtain the message digest, a FORS signature, and the MSS signatures on the path from the FORS keypair to the top tree. Verification computes a message digest using the message and R. The message digest is split into the index of the FORS signature and the indices of the Secret key values in the FORS signature. With this, the FORS signature is used to compute a candidate public key. This candidate FORS public key is used as message to compute a candidate MSS root node with the first MSS signature which is used as message for the next signature, and so on. The final MSS root node is compared to the root node in the public key.

Fast NEON-Based Multiplication for Lattice-Based NIST Post-quantum Cryptography Finalists

Duc Tri Nguyen[(✉)] and Kris Gaj

George Mason University, Fairfax, VA 22030, USA
{dnguye69,kgaj}@gmu.edu

Abstract. This paper focuses on high-speed NEON-based constant-time implementations of multiplication of large polynomials in the NIST PQC KEM Finalists: NTRU, Saber, and CRYSTALS-Kyber. We use the Number Theoretic Transform (NTT)-based multiplication in Kyber, the Toom-Cook algorithm in NTRU, and both types of multiplication in Saber. Following these algorithms and using Apple M1, we improve the decapsulation performance of the NTRU, Kyber, and Saber-based KEMs at the security level 3 by the factors of 8.4, 3.0, and 1.6, respectively, compared to the reference implementations. On Cortex-A72, we achieve the speed-ups by factors varying between 5.7 and 7.5× for the Forward/Inverse NTT in Kyber, and between 6.0 and 7.8× for Toom-Cook in NTRU, over the best existing implementations in pure C. For Saber, when using NEON instructions on Cortex-A72, the implementation based on NTT outperforms the implementation based on the Toom-Cook algorithm by 14% in the case of the `MatrixVectorMul` function but is slower by 21% in the case of the `InnerProduct` function. Taking into account that in Saber, keys are not available in the NTT domain, the overall performance of the NTT-based version is very close to the performance of the Toom-Cook version. The differences for the entire decapsulation at the three major security levels (1, 3, and 5) are −4, −2, and +2%, respectively. Our benchmarking results demonstrate that our NEON-based implementations run on an Apple M1 ARM processor are comparable to those obtained using the best AVX2-based implementations run on an AMD EPYC 7742 processor. Our work is the first NEON-based ARMv8 implementation of each of the three NIST PQC KEM finalists.

Keywords: ARMv8 · NEON · Karatsuba · Toom-Cook · Number theoretic transform · NTRU · Saber · Kyber · Latice · Post-quantum cryptography

1 Introduction

In July 2020, NIST announced the Round 3 finalists of the Post-Quantum Cryptography Standardization process. The main selection criteria were security, key

© Springer Nature Switzerland AG 2021
J. H. Cheon and J.-P. Tillich (Eds.): PQCrypto 2021, LNCS 12841, pp. 234–254, 2021.
https://doi.org/10.1007/978-3-030-81293-5_13

and ciphertext sizes, and performance in software. CRYSTALS-Kyber, NTRU, and Saber are three lattice-based finalists in the category of encryption/Key Encapsulation Mechanism (KEM).

There exist constant-time software implementations of all these algorithms on various platforms, including Cortex-M4, RISC-V, and Intel and AMD processors supporting Advanced Vector Extensions 2 (AVX2, also known as Haswell New Instructions). However, there is still a lack of high-performance software implementations for mobile devices, which is an area dominated by ARM.

The popularity of ARM is undeniable, with billions of devices connected to the Internet[1]. As a result, there is clearly a need to maintain the secure communication among these devices in the age of quantum computers. Without high-speed implementations, the deployment and adoption of emerging PQC standards may be slowed down. Our goal is to fill the gap between low-power embedded processors and power-hungry x86-64 platforms. To do that, we have developed the first optimized constant-time ARMv8 implementations of three lattice-based KEM finalists: Kyber, NTRU, and Saber. We assumed the parameter sets supported by all schemes at the beginning of Round 3. The differences among the implemented algorithms in terms of security, decryption failure rate, and resistance to side-channel attacks is out of scope for this paper.

In short, we have implemented the Toom-Cook multiplication for NTRU, NTT-based multiplication for Kyber, and both Toom-Cook and NTT-based multiplications for Saber. We achieved significant speed-ups as compared to the corresponding reference implementations. We have benchmarked our implementations on the best ARMv8 CPU on the market and compared them against the best implementations targeting a high-performance x86-64 CPU.

Contributions. Our work is the first optimized ARMv8 `NEON` implementation of the PQC KEM finalists. Our results obtained using Apple M1 are slightly worse than the results achieved using the corresponding AVX2-based implementations, but overall, the speeds of encapsulation and decapsulation are comparable. The lack of an instruction equivalent to the AVX2 instruction `vmulhw` is responsible for a larger number of clock cycles required to implement NTT using ARMv8. We improve the performance of NTRU-HPS677 by proposing a new Toom-Cook implementation setting.

Source Code is publicly available at: https://github.com/GMUCERG/PQC_NEON.

2   Previous Work

The paper by Streit et al. [23] was the first work about the NEON-based ARMv8 implementation of New Hope Simple. This work, published before the NIST PQC Competition, proposed a "merged NTT layers" structure. Scott [20] and

---
[1] https://www.tomshardware.com/news/arm-6-7-billion-chips-per-quarter.

Westerbaan [26] proposed lazy reduction as a part of their NTT implementation. Seiler [21] proposed an FFT trick, which has been widely adopted in the following work. Zhou et al. [27] proposed fast implementations of NTT and applied them to Kyber.

In the area of low-power implementations, most previous works targeted Cortex-M4 [16]. In particular, Botros et al. [7] and Alkim et al. [2] developed ARM Cortex-M4 implementations of Kyber. Karmakar et al. [18] reported results for Saber. Chung et al. [8] proposed an NTT-based implementation for an NTT-unfriendly ring, targeting Cortex-M4 and AVX2. We adapted this method to our NTT-based implementation of Saber. From the high-performance perspective, Gupta et al. [14] proposed GPU implementation of Kyber; Roy et al. [22] developed $4 \times Saber$ by utilizing 256-bit AVX2 vectors; Danba et al. [11] developed a high-speed implementation of NTRU using AVX2. Finally, Hoang et al. [15] implemented a fast NTT-function using ARMv8 Scalable Vector Extension (SVE).

3   Background

NTRU, Saber, and Kyber use variants of the Fujisaki-Okamoto (FO) transform [12] to define the Chosen Ciphertext Attack (CCA)-secure KEMs based on the underlying public-key encryption (PKE) schemes. Therefore, speeding up the implementation of PKE also significantly speeds up the implementation of the entire KEM scheme.

The parameters of Kyber, Saber, and NTRU are summarized in Table 1. Saber uses two power of two moduli, p and q, across all security levels. NTRU has different moduli for each security level. NTRU-HRSS701 shares similar attributes with NTRU-HPS and has parameters listed in the second line for security level 1.

The symbols ↑ and ↓ indicate the increase or decrease of the CCA-secure KEM ciphertext ($|ct|$) size, as compared with the public-key size ($|pk|$) (both in bytes (B)).

Table 1. Parameters of Kyber, Saber, and NTRU

	Polynomial	n			$p\ [, q]$			$|pk|$ (B)			$|ct| - |pk|$ (B)		
		1	3	5	1	3	5	1	3	5	1	3	5
Kyber	$x^n + 1$	256			3329			800	1184	1568	↓ 32	↓ 96	0
Saber	$x^n + 1$	256			$2^{13}, 2^{10}$			672	992	1312	↑ 64	↑ 96	↑ 160
NTRU-HPS	$\Phi_1 = x - 1$	677	821	–	2^{11}	2^{12}	–	931	1230	–	0	0	–
NTRU-HRSS	$\Phi_n = \frac{x^n - 1}{x - 1}$	701	–		2^{13}	–		1138	–				

3.1 NTRU

The Round 3 submission of NTRU [1] is a merger of the specifications for NTRU-HPS and NTRU-HRSS. The NTRU KEM uses polynomial $\Phi_1 = x - 1$ for *implicit rejection*. It rejects an invalid ciphertext and returns a pseudorandom key, avoiding the need for re-encryption, which is required in Saber and Kyber.

The advantage of NTRU is fast Encapsulation (only 1 multiplication) but the downside is the use of time-consuming inversions in key generation.

3.2 Saber

Saber [1] relies on the hardness of the Module Learning With Rounding problem (M-LWR). Similarly to NTRU, the Saber parameter p is a power of two. This feature supports inexpensive reduction mod p. However, such parameter p prevents the best time complexity multiplication algorithm (NTT) to be applied *directly*. Among the three investigated algorithms, Saber has the smallest public keys and ciphertext sizes, $|pk|$ and $|ct|$, as shown in Table 1.

3.3 Kyber

The security of Kyber [3] is based on the hardness of the learning with errors problem in module lattices, so-called M-LWE. Similar to Saber and NTRU, the KEM construction is based on CPA public-key encryption scheme with a slightly tweaked FO transform [12]. Improving performance of public-key encryption helps speed up KEM as well. Kyber public and private keys are assumed to be already in NTT domain. This feature clearly differentiates Kyber from Saber and NTRU. The multiplication in the NTT domain has the best time complexity of $O(n \log n)$.

3.4 Polynomial Multiplication

In this section, we introduce polynomial multiplication algorithms, arranged from the worst to the best in terms of time complexity. The goal is to compute the product of two polynomials in Eq. 1 as fast as possible.

$$C(x) = A(x) \times B(x) = \sum_{i=0}^{n-1} a_i x^i \times \sum_{i=0}^{n-1} b_i x^i \tag{1}$$

$$Schoolbook \quad \longrightarrow Toom - Cook \longrightarrow NTT$$

$$O(n^2) \qquad\qquad O(n^{\frac{\log(2k-1)}{\log k}}) \qquad\qquad O(n \log n)$$

Schoolbook Multiplication is the simplest form of multiplication. The algorithm consists of two loops with the $O(n)$ space and $O(n^2)$ time complexity, as shown in Eq. 2.

$$C(x) = \sum_{k=0}^{2n-2} c_k x^k = \sum_{i=0}^{n-1}\sum_{j=0}^{n-1} a_i b_j x^{(i+j)} \tag{2}$$

Toom-Cook and Karatsuba are multiplication algorithms that differ greatly in terms of computational cost versus the most straightforward schoolbook method when the degree n is large. Karatsuba [17] is a special case of Toom-Cook (Toom-k) [9,25]. Generally, both algorithms consist of five steps: splitting, evaluation, point-wise multiplication, interpolation, and recomposition. An overview of polynomial multiplication using Toom-k is shown in Algorithm 1. Splitting and recomposition are often merged into evaluation and interpolation, respectively.

Examples of these steps in Toom-4 are shown in Eqs. 3, 4, 5, and 6, respectively. In the splitting step, Toom-k splits the polynomial A(x) of the degree $n-1$ (containing n coefficients) into k polynomials with the degree $n/k - 1$ and n/k coefficients each. These polynomials become coefficients of another polynomial denoted as $\mathcal{A}(\mathcal{X})$. Then, $\mathcal{A}(\mathcal{X})$ is evaluated for $2k - 1$ different values of $\mathcal{X} = x^{n/k}$. Below, we split $A(x)$ and evaluate $\mathcal{A}(\mathcal{X})$ as an example.

$$A(x) = x^{\frac{3n}{4}} \sum_{i=\frac{3n}{4}}^{n-1} a_i x^{(i-\frac{3n}{4})} + \cdots + x^{\frac{n}{4}} \sum_{i=\frac{n}{4}}^{\frac{2n}{4}-1} a_i x^{(i-\frac{n}{4})} + \sum_{i=0}^{\frac{n}{4}-1} a_i x^i$$

$$= \alpha_3 \cdot x^{\frac{3n}{4}} + \alpha_2 \cdot x^{\frac{2n}{4}} + \alpha_1 \cdot x^{\frac{n}{4}} + \alpha_0$$

$$\implies \mathcal{A}(\mathcal{X}) = \alpha_3 \cdot \mathcal{X}^3 + \alpha_2 \cdot \mathcal{X}^2 + \alpha_1 \cdot \mathcal{X} + \alpha_0, \quad \text{where} \quad \mathcal{X} = x^{\frac{n}{4}}. \tag{3}$$

Toom-k evaluates $\mathcal{A}(\mathcal{X})$ and $\mathcal{B}(\mathcal{X})$ in at least $2k - 1$ points $[p_0, p_1, \ldots p_{2k-2}]$, starting with two trivial points $\{0, \infty\}$, and extending them with $\{\pm 1, \pm\frac{1}{2}, \pm 2, \ldots\}$ for the ease of computations. Karatsuba, Toom-3, and Toom-4 evaluate in $\{0, 1, \infty\}$, $\{0, \pm 1, -2, \infty\}$ and $\{0, \pm 1, \pm\frac{1}{2}, 2, \infty\}$, respectively.

$$\begin{bmatrix} \mathcal{A}(0) \\ \mathcal{A}(1) \\ \mathcal{A}(-1) \\ \mathcal{A}(\frac{1}{2}) \\ \mathcal{A}(-\frac{1}{2}) \\ \mathcal{A}(2) \\ \mathcal{A}(\infty) \end{bmatrix} = \begin{bmatrix} 0 & 0 & 0 & 1 \\ 1 & 1 & 1 & 1 \\ -1 & 1 & -1 & 1 \\ \frac{1}{8} & \frac{1}{4} & \frac{1}{2} & 1 \\ -\frac{1}{8} & \frac{1}{4} & -\frac{1}{2} & 1 \\ 8 & 4 & 2 & 1 \\ 1 & 0 & 0 & 0 \end{bmatrix} \cdot \begin{bmatrix} \alpha_3 \\ \alpha_2 \\ \alpha_1 \\ \alpha_0 \end{bmatrix} \quad (4) \qquad \begin{bmatrix} \mathcal{C}(0) \\ \mathcal{C}(1) \\ \mathcal{C}(-1) \\ \mathcal{C}(\frac{1}{2}) \\ \mathcal{C}(-\frac{1}{2}) \\ \mathcal{C}(2) \\ \mathcal{C}(\infty) \end{bmatrix} = \begin{bmatrix} \mathcal{A}(0) \\ \mathcal{A}(1) \\ \mathcal{A}(-1) \\ \mathcal{A}(\frac{1}{2}) \\ \mathcal{A}(-\frac{1}{2}) \\ \mathcal{A}(2) \\ \mathcal{A}(\infty) \end{bmatrix} \cdot \begin{bmatrix} \mathcal{B}(0) \\ \mathcal{B}(1) \\ \mathcal{B}(-1) \\ \mathcal{B}(\frac{1}{2}) \\ \mathcal{B}(-\frac{1}{2}) \\ \mathcal{B}(2) \\ \mathcal{B}(\infty) \end{bmatrix} \quad (5)$$

The pointwise multiplication computes $\mathcal{C}(p_i) = \mathcal{A}(p_i) * \mathcal{B}(p_i)$ for all values of p_i in $2k - 1$ evaluation points. If the sizes of polynomials are small, then these multiplications can be performed directly using the Schoolbook algorithm.

Otherwise, additional layers of Toom-k should be applied to further reduce the cost of multiplication.

The inverse operation for evaluation is interpolation. Given evaluation points $C(p_i)$ for $i \in [0, \ldots 2k-2]$, the optimal interpolation presented by Borato et al. [6] yields the shortest inversion-sequence for up to Toom-5.

We adopt the following formulas for the Toom-4 interpolation, based on the thesis of F. Mansouri [19], with slight modifications:

$$\begin{bmatrix} \theta_0 \\ \theta_1 \\ \theta_2 \\ \theta_3 \\ \theta_4 \\ \theta_5 \\ \theta_6 \end{bmatrix} = \begin{bmatrix} 0 & 0 & 0 & 0 & 0 & 0 & 1 \\ 1 & 1 & 1 & 1 & 1 & 1 & 1 \\ 1 & -1 & 1 & -1 & 1 & -1 & 1 \\ \frac{1}{64} & \frac{1}{32} & \frac{1}{16} & \frac{1}{8} & \frac{1}{4} & \frac{1}{2} & 1 \\ \frac{1}{64} & -\frac{1}{32} & \frac{1}{16} & -\frac{1}{8} & \frac{1}{4} & -\frac{1}{2} & 1 \\ 64 & 32 & 16 & 8 & 4 & 2 & 1 \\ 1 & 0 & 0 & 0 & 0 & 0 & 0 \end{bmatrix}^{-1} \cdot \begin{bmatrix} C(0) \\ C(1) \\ C(-1) \\ C(\frac{1}{2}) \\ C(-\frac{1}{2}) \\ C(2) \\ C(\infty) \end{bmatrix} \quad \text{where} \quad C(\mathcal{X}) = \sum_{i=0}^{6} \theta_i \mathcal{X}^i \quad (6)$$

In summary, the overview of a polynomial multiplication using Toom-k is shown in Algorithm 1, where splitting and recomposition are merged into evaluation and interpolation.

Algorithm 1: Toom-k: Product of two polynomials $A(x)$ and $B(x)$

Input: Two polynomials $A(x)$ and $B(x)$
Output: $C(x) = A(x) \times B(x)$

1 $[\mathcal{A}_0(\mathcal{X}), \ldots \mathcal{A}_{2k-2}(\mathcal{X})] \leftarrow$ **Evaluation** of $A(x)$
2 $[\mathcal{B}_0(\mathcal{X}), \ldots \mathcal{B}_{2k-2}(\mathcal{X})] \leftarrow$ **Evaluation** of $B(x)$
3 **for** $i \leftarrow 0$ **to** $2k - 2$ **do**
4 $\quad \mathcal{C}_i(x) = \mathcal{A}_i(\mathcal{X}) * \mathcal{B}_i(\mathcal{X})$
5 $C(x) \leftarrow$ **Interpolation** of $[\mathcal{C}_0(\mathcal{X}), \ldots \mathcal{C}_{2k-2}(\mathcal{X})]$

Toom-k has a complexity $O(n^{\frac{\log(2k-1)}{\log k}})$. As a result, Toom-3 has a complexity of $O(n^{\frac{\log 5}{\log 3}}) = O(n^{\log_3 5}) \approx O(n^{1.46})$, and Toom-4 has a complexity of $O(n^{\frac{\log 7}{\log 4}}) = O(n^{\log_4 7}) \approx O(n^{1.40})$.

Number Theoretic Transform (NTT) is a transformation used as a basis for a polynomial multiplication algorithm with the time complexity of $O(n \log n)$ [10]. This algorithm performs multiplication in the ring $\mathcal{R}_q = \mathbf{Z}_q[X]/(X^n + 1)$, where degree n is a power of 2. The modulus $q \equiv 1 \bmod 2n$ for complete NTT, and $q \equiv 1 \bmod n$ for incomplete NTT, respectively. Multiplication algorithms based on NTT compute pointwise multiplication of vectors with elements of degree 0 in the case of Saber, and of degree 1 in the case of Kyber.

Complete $\mathcal{NTT}$ is similar to traditional $\mathcal{FFT}$ but uses the root of unity in the discrete field rather than in real numbers. $\mathcal{NTT}$ and $\mathcal{NTT}^{-1}$ are forward and inverse operations, where $\mathcal{NTT}^{-1}(\mathcal{NTT}(f)) = f$ for all $f \in \mathcal{R}_q$. $C_i = \mathcal{A}_i * \mathcal{B}_i$ denote pointwise multiplication for all $i \in [0, \ldots n-1]$. The algorithm used to multiply two polynomials is shown in Eq. 7.

$$C(x) = A(x) \times B(x) = \mathcal{NTT}^{-1}(\mathcal{C}) = \mathcal{NTT}^{-1}(\mathcal{A} * \mathcal{B})$$
$$= \mathcal{NTT}^{-1}(\mathcal{NTT}(A) * \mathcal{NTT}(B)) \tag{7}$$

In Incomplete $\mathcal{NTT}$, the idea is to pre-process polynomial before converting it to the NTT domain. In Kyber, the Incomplete NTT has $q \equiv 1 \bmod n$ [27]. The two polynomials $A(x), B(x)$, and the result $C(x)$ are split to polynomials with odd and even indices, as shown in Eq. 8. $\mathcal{A}$, $\mathcal{B}$, $\mathcal{C}$ and A, B, C indicate polynomials in the NTT domain and time domain, respectively. An example shown in this section is Incomplete $\mathcal{NTT}$ used in Kyber.

$$C(x) = A(x) \times B(x) = (A_{even}(x^2) + x \cdot A_{odd}(x^2)) \times (B_{even}(x^2) + x \cdot B_{odd}(x^2))$$
$$= (A_{odd} \times (x^2 \cdot B_{odd}) + A_{even} \times B_{even}) + x \cdot (A_{even} \times B_{odd} + A_{odd} \times B_{even})$$
$$= C_{even}(x^2) + x \cdot C_{odd}(x^2) \in \mathbf{Z}_q[x]/(x^n + 1). \tag{8}$$

The pre-processed polynomials are converted to the NTT domain in Eq. 9. In Eq. 8, we combine $\beta(x^2) = x^2 \cdot B_{odd}(x^2)$, because $\beta(x^2) \in \mathbf{Z}_q[x]/(x^n+1)$, so $\beta(x^2) = (-B_{odd}[n-1], B_{odd}[0], B_{odd}[1], \ldots B_{odd}[n-2])$. From Eq. 8, we derive Eqs. 10 and 11.

$$A(x) = A_{even}(x^2) + x \cdot A_{odd}(x^2)$$
$$\implies \mathcal{A} = \mathcal{NTT}(A)$$
$$\Leftrightarrow [\mathcal{A}_{even}, \mathcal{A}_{odd}] = [\mathcal{NTT}(A_{even}), \mathcal{NTT}(A_{odd})] \tag{9}$$
$$(8) \implies \mathcal{C} = [\mathcal{C}_{even}, \mathcal{C}_{odd}]$$
$$\text{where}\quad \mathcal{C}_{even} = \mathcal{A}_{odd} * \mathcal{NTT}(x^2 \cdot B_{odd}) + \mathcal{A}_{even} * \mathcal{B}_{even}$$
$$= \mathcal{A}_{odd} * \overrightarrow{\mathcal{B}_{odd}} + \mathcal{A}_{even} * \mathcal{B}_{even} \quad \text{with}\quad \overrightarrow{\mathcal{B}_{odd}} = \mathcal{NTT}(\beta) \tag{10}$$
$$\text{and}\quad \mathcal{C}_{odd} = \mathcal{A}_{even} * \mathcal{B}_{odd} + \mathcal{A}_{odd} * \mathcal{B}_{even} \tag{11}$$

After $\mathcal{C}_{odd}$ and $\mathcal{C}_{even}$ are calculated, the inverse $\mathcal{NTT}$ of $\mathcal{C}$ is calculated as follows:

$$C(x) = \mathcal{NTT}^{-1}(\mathcal{C}) = [\mathcal{NTT}^{-1}(\mathcal{C}_{odd}), \mathcal{NTT}^{-1}(\mathcal{C}_{even})]$$
$$= C_{even}(x^2) + x \cdot C_{odd}(x^2) \tag{12}$$

To some extent, Toom-Cook evaluates a certain number of points, while $\mathcal{NTT}$ evaluates all available points and then computes the pointwise multiplication. The inverse $\mathcal{NTT}$ operation has similar meaning to the interpolation in Toom-k. $\mathcal{NTT}$ suffers overhead in pre-processing and post-processing for all-point evaluations. However, when polynomial degree n is large enough, the computational cost of $\mathcal{NTT}$ is smaller than the cost of Toom-k. The downside of $\mathcal{NTT}$ is the NTT friendly ring $\mathcal{R}_q$.

The summary of polynomial multiplication using the incomplete $\mathcal{NTT}$, a.k.a. 1Pt$\mathcal{NTT}$, is shown in Algorithm 2.

Algorithm 2: 1Pt$\mathcal{NTT}$: Product of $A(x)$ and $B(x) \in \mathbf{Z}_q[x]/(x^n + 1)$

Input: Two polynomials $A(x)$ and $B(x)$ in $\mathbf{Z}_q[x]/(x^n + 1)$
Output: $C(x) = A(x) \times B(x)$

1 $[\mathcal{A}_{odd}, \mathcal{A}_{even}] \leftarrow \mathcal{NTT}(A(x))$
2 $[\mathcal{B}_{odd}, \mathcal{B}_{even}, \overrightarrow{\mathcal{B}_{odd}}] \leftarrow \mathcal{NTT}(B(x))$
3 **for** $i \leftarrow 0$ **to** $n - 1$ **do**
4 $\quad \mathcal{C}_{odd}^i = \mathcal{A}_{even}^i * \overrightarrow{\mathcal{B}_{odd}^i} + \mathcal{A}_{odd}^i * \mathcal{B}_{even}^i$
5 $\quad \mathcal{C}_{even}^i = \mathcal{A}_{odd}^i * \overrightarrow{\mathcal{B}_{odd}^i} + \mathcal{A}_{even}^i * \mathcal{B}_{even}^i$
6 $C(x) \leftarrow [\mathcal{NTT}^{-1}(\mathcal{C}_{even}), \mathcal{NTT}^{-1}(\mathcal{C}_{odd})]$

---

4   Toom-Cook in NTRU and Saber Implementations

Batch Schoolbook Multiplication. To compute multiplication in batch, using vector registers, we allocate 3 memory blocks for 2 inputs and 1 output for each multiplication. Inputs and the corresponding output are transposed before and after batch schoolbook, respectively. To make the transposition efficient, we only transpose matrices of the size 8×8 and remember the location of each 8×8 block in batch-schoolbook. A single 8×8 transpose requires at least 27 vector registers, thus, memory spills occur when the transpose matrix is of the size 16×16. In our experiment, utilizing batch schoolbook with a matrix of the size 16×16 yields the best throughput. Schoolbook 16×16 has 1 spill, 17×17 and 18×18 cause 5 and 14 spills and waste additional registers to store a few coefficients.

Karatsuba. ($K2$) is implemented in two versions, original Karatsuba [17], and combined two layers of Karatsuba ($K2 \times K2$), as shown in Algorithms 3 and 4. One-layer Karatsuba converts one polynomial of the length n to 3 polynomials of the length $n/2$ and introduces 0 bit-loss due to the addition and subtraction performed only in the interpolation step.

Algorithm 3: 2×Karasuba: Evaluate4(A) over points: $\{0, 1, \infty\}$

Input: $A \in \mathbf{Z}[X] : A(X) = \sum_{i=0}^{3} \alpha_i \cdot X^i$
Output: $[\mathcal{A}_0(x), \ldots \mathcal{A}_8(x)] \leftarrow$ **Evaluate4**(A)

1 $w_0 = \alpha_0; \quad w_2 = \alpha_1; \quad w_1 = \alpha_0 + \alpha_1;$
2 $w_6 = \alpha_2; \quad w_8 = \alpha_3; \quad w_7 = \alpha_2 + \alpha_3;$
3 $w_3 = \alpha_0 + \alpha_2; \quad w_5 = \alpha_1 + \alpha_3; \quad w_4 = w_3 + w_5;$
4 $[\mathcal{A}_0(x), \ldots \mathcal{A}_8(x)] \leftarrow [w_0, \ldots, w_8]$

Algorithm 4: 2×Karatsuba: Interpolate4(A) over points: $\{0, 1, \infty\}$

Input: $[\mathcal{A}_0(x), \ldots \mathcal{A}_8(x)] \in \mathbf{Z}[X]$
Output: $A(x) \leftarrow \textbf{Interpolate4}(\mathcal{A})$
1 $[\alpha_0, \ldots \alpha_8] \leftarrow [\mathcal{A}_0(x), \ldots \mathcal{A}_8(x)]$
2 $w_0 = \alpha_0; \quad w_6 = \alpha_8;$
3 $w_1 = \alpha_1 - \alpha_0 - \alpha_2; \quad w_3 = \alpha_4 - \alpha_3 - \alpha_5; \quad w_5 = \alpha_7 - \alpha_6 - \alpha_8;$
4 $w_3 = w_3 - w_1 - w_5; \quad w_2 = \alpha_3 - \alpha_0 + (\alpha_2 - \alpha_6); \quad w_4 = \alpha_5 - \alpha_8 - (\alpha_2 - \alpha_6);$
5 $A(x) \leftarrow \textbf{Recomposition}$ of $[w_0, \ldots w_6]$

Toom-3. (TC3) evaluation and interpolation adopts the optimal sequence from Bodrato et al. [6] over points $\{0, \pm 1, -2, \infty\}$. To utilize 32 registers in ARM and reduce memory load and store, the two evaluation layers of Toom-3 are combined $(TC3 \times TC3)$, as shown in Algorithm 5. Toom-3 converts 1 polynomial of the length n to 5 polynomials of the length $n/3$ and introduces 1 bit-loss due to a 1-bit shift operation in interpolation.

Algorithm 5: 2×Toom-3: Evaluate9(A) over points: $\{0, \pm 1, -2, \infty\}$

Input: $A \in \mathbf{Z}[X]$: $A(X) = \sum_{i=0}^{8} \alpha_i \cdot X^i$
Output: $[\mathcal{A}_0(x), \ldots \mathcal{A}_{24}(x)] \leftarrow \textbf{Evaluate9}(A)$
1 $w_0 = \alpha_0; \quad w_1 = (\alpha_0 + \alpha_2) + \alpha_1; \quad w_2 = (\alpha_0 + \alpha_2) - \alpha_1;$
   $w_3 = ((w_2 + \alpha_2) \ll 1) - \alpha_0; \quad w_4 = \alpha_2;$
2 $e_0 = (\alpha_0 + \alpha_6) + \alpha_3; \quad e_1 = (\alpha_1 + \alpha_7) + \alpha_4; \quad e_2 = (\alpha_2 + \alpha_8) + \alpha_5;$
   $w_{05} = e_0; \quad w_{06} = (e_0 + e_2) + e_1; \quad w_{07} = (e_0 + e_2) - e_1;$
   $w_{08} = ((w_{07} + e_2) \ll 1) - e_0; \quad w_{09} = e_2;$
3 $e_0 = (\alpha_0 + \alpha_6) - \alpha_3; \quad e_1 = (\alpha_1 + \alpha_7) - \alpha_4; \quad e_2 = (\alpha_2 + \alpha_8) - \alpha_5;$
   $w_{10} = e_0; \quad w_{11} = (e_2 + e_0) + e_1; \quad w_{12} = (e_2 + e_0) - e_1;$
   $w_{13} = ((w_{12} + e_2) \ll 1) - e_0; \quad w_{14} = e_2;$
4 $e_0 = ((2 \cdot \alpha_6 - \alpha_3) \ll 1) + \alpha_0; \quad e_1 = ((2 \cdot \alpha_7 - \alpha_4) \ll 1) + \alpha_1;$
   $e_2 = ((2 \cdot \alpha_8 - \alpha_5) \ll 1) + \alpha_2; \quad w_{15} = e_0; \quad w_{16} = (e_2 + e_0) + e_1;$
   $w_{17} = (e_2 + e_0) - e_1; \quad w_{18} = ((w_{17} + e_2) \ll 1) - e_0; \quad w_{19} = e_2;$
5 $w_{20} = \alpha_6; \quad w_{21} = (\alpha_6 + \alpha_8) + \alpha_7; \quad w_{22} = (\alpha_6 + \alpha_8) - \alpha_7;$
   $w_{23} = ((w_{22} + \alpha_8) \ll 1) - \alpha_6; \quad w_{24} = \alpha_8;$
6 $[\mathcal{A}_0(x), \ldots \mathcal{A}_{24}(x)] \leftarrow [w_0, \ldots w_{24}]$

Toom-4. (TC4) evaluation and interpolation over points $\{0, \pm 1, \pm \frac{1}{2}, 2, \infty\}$. The interpolation adopts the optimal inverse-sequence from [6], with the slight modification, as shown in Algorithms 6 and 7. Toom-4 introduces a 3 bit-loss, thus a combined Toom-4 implementation was considered but not implemented due to a 6 bit-loss and high complexity.

Algorithm 6: Toom-4: Evaluate4(A) over points: $\{0, \pm 1, \pm\frac{1}{2}, 2, \infty\}$

Input: $A \in \mathbf{Z}[X] : A(X) = \sum_{i=0}^{3} \alpha_i \cdot X^i$
Output: $[\mathcal{A}_0(x), \ldots \mathcal{A}_6(x)] \leftarrow$ **Evaluate4(A)**

1 $w_0 = \alpha_0;$ $e_0 = \alpha_0 + \alpha_2;$ $e_1 = \alpha_1 + \alpha_3;$ $w_1 = e_0 + e_1;$ $w_2 = e_0 - e_1;$
2 $e_0 = (4 \cdot \alpha_0 + \alpha_2) \ll 1;$ $e_1 = 4 \cdot \alpha_1 + \alpha_3;$ $w_3 = e_0 + e_1;$ $w_4 = e_0 - e_1;$
3 $w_5 = (\alpha_3 \ll 3) + (\alpha_2 \ll 2) + (\alpha_1 \ll 1) + \alpha_0;$ $w_6 = \alpha_3;$
4 $[\mathcal{A}_0(x), \ldots \mathcal{A}_6(x)] \leftarrow [w_0, \ldots w_6]$

Algorithm 7: Toom-4: Interpolate4(A) over points: $\{0, \pm 1, \pm\frac{1}{2}, 2, \infty\}$

Input: $[\mathcal{A}_0(x), \ldots \mathcal{A}_6(x)] \in \mathbf{Z}[X]$
Output: $A(x) \leftarrow$ **Interpolate4($\mathcal{A}$)**

1 $[w_0, \ldots w_6] \leftarrow [\mathcal{A}_0(x), \ldots \mathcal{A}_6(x)]$
2 $w_5 \mathrel{+}= w_3;$ $w_4 \mathrel{+}= w_3;$ $w_4 \ggg= 1;$ $w_2 \mathrel{+}= w_1;$ $w_2 \ggg= 1;$
3 $w_3 \mathrel{-}= w_4;$ $w_1 \mathrel{-}= w_2;$ $w_5 \mathrel{-}= w_2 \cdot 65;$ $w_2 \mathrel{-}= w_6;$ $w_2 \mathrel{-}= w_0;$
4 $w_5 \mathrel{+}= w_2 \cdot 45;$ $w_4 \mathrel{-}= w_6;$ $w_4 \ggg= 2;$ $w_3 \ggg= 1;$
5 $w_5 \mathrel{-}= w_3 \ll 2;$ $w_3 \mathrel{-}= w_1;$ $w_3 \mathrel{/}= 3;$ $w_4 \mathrel{-}= w_0 \ll 4;$
6 $w_4 \mathrel{-}= w_2 \ll 2;$ $w_4 \mathrel{/}= 3;$ $w_2 \mathrel{+}= w_4;$ $w_5 \ggg= 1;$ $w_5 \mathrel{/}= 15;$
7 $w_1 \mathrel{-}= w_5;$ $w_1 \mathrel{-}= w_3;$ $w_1 \mathrel{/}= 3;$ $w_3 \mathrel{+}= 5 \cdot w_1$ $w_5 \mathrel{-}= w_1;$
8 $A(x) \leftarrow$ **Recomposition**   of $[w_0, -w_1, w_2, w_3, -w_4, w_5, w_6]$

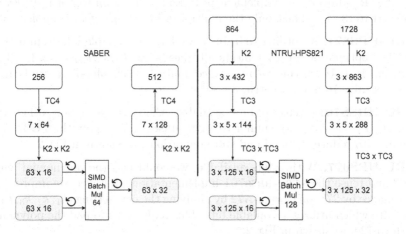

Fig. 1. The Toom-Cook implementation strategy for SABER and NTRU-HPS821

Implementation Strategy. Each vector register is 128-bit, each coefficient is a 16-bit integer. Hence, we can pack at most 8 coefficients into 1 vector register. The base case of Toom-Cook is a schoolbook multiplication, as shown in

Algorithm 1, line 4. The point-wise multiplication is either schoolbook or additional Toom-k. We use notion $(k_1, k_2, \ldots)$ as Toom-k strategy for each layer. The Toom-k strategy for the polynomial length n follows 4 simple rules:

1. Utilize available registers by processing as many coefficients as possible;
2. Schoolbook size should be close to 16;
3. The number of polynomials in batch schoolbook close to a multiple of 8;
4. The Toom-k strategy must generate a minimum number of polynomials.

4.1 Saber

We follow the optimization strategy from Mera et al.[4]. We precompute evaluation and lazy interpolation, which helps to reduce the number of evaluations and interpolations in `MatrixVectorMul` from $(2l^2, l^2)$ to $(l^2 + l, l)$, where l is (2, 3, 4) for the security levels (1, 3, 5), respectively. We also employ the Toom-k setting $(k_1, k_2, k_3) = (4, 2, 2)$ for both `InnerProd` and `MatrixVectorMul`. An example of a polynomial multiplication in Saber is shown in Fig. 1. The $\uparrow$ and $\downarrow$ are evaluation and interpolation, respectively.

4.2 NTRU

In NTRU, `poly_Rq_mul` and `poly_S3_mul` are polynomial multiplications in $(q, \Phi_1\Phi_n)$ and $(3, \Phi_n)$ respectively. Our `poly_Rq_mul` multiplication supports $(q, \Phi_1\Phi_n)$. In addition, we implement `poly_mod_3_Phi_n` on top of `poly_Rq_mul` to convert to $(3, \Phi_n)$. Thus, only the multiplication in $(q, \Phi_1\Phi_n)$ is implemented.

NTRU-HPS821. According to Table 1, we have 4 available bits from a 16-bit type. The optimal design that meets all rules is $(k_1, k_2, k_3, k_4) = (2, 3, 3, 3)$, as shown in Fig. 1. Using this setting, we compute 125 schoolbook multiplications of the size 16×16 in each batch, 3 batches in total.

NTRU-HRSS701. With 3 bits available, there is no option other than $(k_1, k_2, k_3, k_4) = (2, 3, 3, 3)$, similar to NTRU-HPS821. We apply the $TC3 \times TC3$ evaluation to reduce the load and store operations, as shown in Fig. 2.

NTRU-HPS677. With 5 bits available, we could pad the polynomial length to 702 and reuse the NTRU-HRSS701 implementation. However, we improve the performance by 27% on Cortex-A72 by applying the new setting $(k_1, k_2, k_3, k_4) = (3, 4, 2, 2)$, which utilizes 4 available bits. This requires us to pad the polynomial length to 720, as shown in Fig. 2.

5   NTT in Kyber and Saber Implementations

5.1   NTT

As mentioned in Sect. 5, NTT implementation consists of two functions. **Forward** NTT uses the Cooley-Tukey [10] and **Inverse** NTT uses the Gentleman-Sande [13] algorithms. Hence, we define the ZEROTH, FIRST, ... SEVENTH NTT

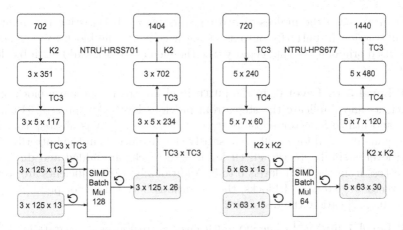

Fig. 2. Toom-Cook implementation strategy for NTRU-HPS677 and NTRU-HRSS701

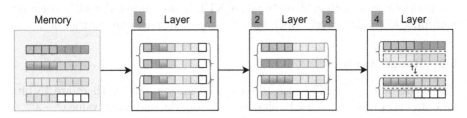

Fig. 3. Index traversals up to the NTT level FOURTH

level by the distance of indices in power of 2. For example, in the FIRST and SECOND level, the distances are 2^1 and 2^2, respectively. For simplicity, we consider 32 consecutive coefficients, with indices starting at $32i$ for $i \in [0, \ldots 7]$ as a block. The index traversals of the first 5 levels are shown in Fig. 3. Each color defines four consecutive indices.

NTT Level 0 to 4. In the ZEROTH and FIRST level, we utilize a single load and interleave instruction vld4q_s16 to load data to 4 consecutive vector registers $[r_0, r_1, r_2, r_3]$. The computation between registers $[r_0, r_1], [r_2, r_3]$ and $[r_0, r_2], [r_1, r_3]$ satisfy the distances 2^0 and 2^1 in the ZEROTH and FIRST level respectively. This feature is shown using curly brackets on the left and right of the second block in Fig. 3.

In the SECOND and THIRD level, we perform 4×4 matrix transpose on the left-half and right-half of four vector registers, with the pair of registers $[r_0, r_1]$, $[r_2, r_3]$ and $[r_0, r_2], [r_1, r_3]$ satisfying the SECOND and THIRD level respectively. See the color changes in the third block in Fig. 3.

In the FOURTH level, we perform 4 transpose instructions to arrange the left-half and right-half of two vector pairs $[r_0, r_1]$ and $[r_2, r_3]$ to satisfy the distance

2^4. Then we swap the indices of two registers $[r_1, r_2]$ by twisting the addition and subtraction in butterfly output. Doing it converts the block to its original order, used originally in the memory. See the memory block and fourth block in Fig. 3.

NTT Level 5 to Level 6. In the FIFTH level, we create one more block of 32 coefficients and duplicate the steps from previous levels. We process 64 coefficients and utilize 8 vector registers $[r_0, \ldots r_3], [r_4, \ldots r_7]$. It is obvious that the vector pairs $[r_i, r_{i+4}]$ for $i \in [0, \ldots 3]$ satisfy the distance 2^5 in the butterfly. The SIXTH level is similar to the FIFTH level. Two blocks are added and duplicate the process from the NTT levels 0 to 5. Additionally, 128 coefficients are stored in 16 vector registers as 4 blocks, the operations between vector pairs $[r_i, r_{i+8}]$ for $i \in [0, \ldots 7]$ satisfy the distance 2^6.

NTT Level 7 and n^{-1}. The SEVENTH layer is treated as a separate loop. We unroll the loop to process 128 coefficients with the distance 2^7. Additionally, the multiplication with n^{-1} in **Inverse** NTT is precomputed with a constant multiplier at the last level, which further saves multiplication instructions.

5.2   Range Analysis

The Kyber and Saber NTT use 16-bit signed integers. Thus, there are 15 bits for data and 1 sign bit. With 15 bits, we can store the maximum value of $-2^{15} \leq \beta \cdot q < 2^{15}$ before overflow. In case of Kyber $(\beta, q) = (9, 3329)$. In case of Saber, $q = (7681, 10753)$ and $\beta = (4, 3)$, respectively.

Kyber. The optimal number of Barrett reductions in Inverse NTT is 72 points, as shown in Westerbaan [26] and applied to the reference implementation. After Barrett reduction has been changed from targeting $0 \leq r < q$ to $-\frac{q-1}{2} \leq r < \frac{q-1}{2}$, coefficients grow by at most q instead of $2q$ in absolute value at the level 1. We can decrease the number of reduction points further, from 72 to 64. The indices of 64 lazy reduction points in Kyber can be seen in Table 2.

Table 2. Improved 64 points Barrett reduction in Inverse NTT of Kyber

Layer	Indexes	Total
4	$32 \to 35$, $96 \to 99$, $160 \to 163$, $224 \to 227$	16
5	$0 \to 7$, $64 \to 71$, $128 \to 135$, $192 \to 199$	32
6	$8 \to 15$, $136 \to 143$	16

Saber. In Twisted-NTT [8,21], we can compute the first 3 levels without additional reductions. We can apply range analysis and use Barrett reduction. Instead, we twist constant multipliers to the ring of the form $Z_q[x]/(x^n - 1)$ in the THIRD level, which not only reduces coefficients to the range $-q \leq r < q$, but also reduces the number of modular multiplications at subsequent levels. This approach is less efficient than regular NTT uses Barrett reduction in neon, however the performance different is negligible due to small $\beta = 3$.

5.3 Vectorized Modular Reduction

Inspired by *Fast mulmods* in [8,21], we implemented four smull_s16 multiply long and one mul_s16 multiply instructions. We use the unzip instructions to gather 16-bit low and high half-products. Unlike AVX2, ARMv8 does not have an instruction similar to vpmulhw, thus dealing with 32-bit products is unavoidable. In Algorithm 8, lines $1 \rightarrow 4$ can be simplified with 2 AVX2 instructions vpmullw, vpmulhw. Similarly, lines $6 \rightarrow 8$ can be simplified with a single high-only half-product vpmulhw. The multiplication by q^{-1} in line 5 can be incorporated into lines $1 \rightarrow 2$ to further save one multiplication. In total, we use two more multiplication instructions, as compared to AVX2 [8]. In the vectorized Barrett reduction, used in both Kyber and Saber, we use three multiplication instructions – one additional multiplication as compared to AVX2, as shown in Algorithm 9.

Algorithm 8: Vectorized multiplication modulo a 16-bit q

Input: $B = (B_L, B_H), C = (C_L, C_H), R = 2^{16}$
Output: $A = B * (CR) \bmod q$
1 $T_0 \leftarrow \text{smull\_s16}(B_L, C_L)$
2 $T_1 \leftarrow \text{smull\_s16}(B_H, C_H)$
3 $T_2 \leftarrow \text{uzp1\_s16}(T_0, T_1)$
4 $T_3 \leftarrow \text{uzp2\_s16}(T_0, T_1)$
5 $(A_L, A_H) \leftarrow \text{mul\_s16}(T_2, q^{-1})$
6 $T_1 \leftarrow \text{smull\_s16}(A_L, q)$
7 $T_2 \leftarrow \text{smull\_s16}(A_H, q)$
8 $T_0 \leftarrow \text{uzp2\_s16}(T_1, T_2)$
9 $A \leftarrow T_3 - T_0$

Algorithm 9: Vectorized central Barrett reduction

Input: $B = (B_L, B_H), \text{constant } V = (V_L, V_H), \text{Kyber}: (i, n) = (9, 10)$
Output: $A = B \bmod q$ and $-q/2 \leq A < q/2$
1 $T_0 \leftarrow \text{smull\_s16}(B_L, V_L)$
2 $T_1 \leftarrow \text{smull\_s16}(B_H, V_H)$
3 $T_0 \leftarrow \text{uzp2\_s16}(T_0, T_1)$
4 $T_1 \leftarrow \text{vadd\_n\_s16}(T_0, 1 \ll i)$
5 $T_1 \leftarrow \text{shr\_n\_s16}(T_1, n)$
6 $A \leftarrow \text{mls\_s16}(B, T_1, q)$

---

6 Results

ARMv8 Intrinsics are used for ease of implementation and to take advantage of the compiler optimizers. The optimizers know how intrinsics behave. As a result, some optimizations may be available to reduce the number of intrinsic instructions. The optimizer can expand the intrinsic and align the buffers, schedule pipeline, or make adjustments depending on the platform architecture[2]. In our implementation, we always keep vector register usage under 32 and examine assembly language code obtained during our development process. We acknowledge the compiler spills to memory and hide load/store latency in favor of pipelining multiple multiplication instructions.

Benchmarking Setup. Our benchmarking setup for ARMv8 implementations included MacBook Air with Apple M1 SoC and Raspberry Pi 4 with `Cortex-A72` @ `1.5 GHz`. For AVX2 implementations, we used a PC based on `Intel Core i7-8750H` @ `4.1 GHz`. Additionally, in Tables 6 and 8, we report benchmarking results for the newest x86-64 chip in `supercop-20210125` [5], namely `AMD EPYC 7742` @ `2.25 GHz`. There is no official clock frequency documentation for Apple M1 CPU. However, independent benchmarks strongly indicate that the clock frequency of 3.2 GHz is used[3].

We use PAPI [24] library to count cycles on Cortex-A72. In Apple M1, we rewrite the work from Dougall Johnson[4] to perform cycles count[5].

In terms of compiler, we used `clang 12.0` (default version) for Apple M1 and `clang 11.1` (the most recent stable version) for Cortex-A72 and Core i7-8750H. All benchmarks were conducted with the compiler settings `-O3 -mtune=native -fomit-frame-pointer`. We let the compiler to do its best to vectorize pure C implementations, denoted as `ref` to fairly compare them with our `neon` implementations. Thus, we did not employ `-fno-tree-vectorize` option.

The number of executions on ARMv8 Cortex-A72 and Intel i7-8750H was $1,000,000$. On Apple M1, it was $10,000,000$ to force the benchmarking process to run on the high-performance 'Firestorm' core. The benchmarking results are in kilocycles *(kc)*.

NTT Implementation. In Table 3, the speed-ups of `neon` vs. `ref` are 5.8 and 7.5 for forward and inverse NTT on Cortex-A72. On Apple M1, the corresponding speed-ups are 7.8 and 12.0. There is no official NTT-based reference implementation of Saber released yet. We analyzed cycle counts in the forward and inverse NTT transform for our NEON-based implementation without comparing it with any reference implementation.

---

[2] https://godbolt.org/z/5qefG5.
[3] https://www.anandtech.com/show/16252/mac-mini-apple-m1-tested.
[4] https://github.com/dougallj.
[5] https://github.com/GMUCERG/PQC_NEON/blob/main/neon/kyber/m1cycles.c.

Table 3. Cycle counts of the NEON-based NTT implementation on `Cortex-A72` and Apple M1

Cortex-A72	ref		neon		ref/neon		Levels
Apple M1	NTT	NTT^{-1}	NTT	NTT^{-1}	NTT	NTT^{-1}	
Cortex-A72							
saber	–	–	1,991	1,893	–	–	$0 \rightarrow 7$
kyber	8,500	12,533	1,473	1,661	5.8	7.5	$1 \rightarrow 7$
Apple M1							
saber	–	–	539	531	–	–	$0 \rightarrow 7$
kyber	3,211	5,118	413	428	7.8	12.0	$1 \rightarrow 7$

Table 4. Fast NTT-based and Toom-Cook implementations of multiplication in NTRU, Saber and Kyber measured in kilocycles – neon vs. `ref`

Cortex-A72	Level 1 *(kilocycles)*			Level 3 *(kilocycles)*		
1500 MHz	ref	neon	ref/neon	ref	neon	ref/neon
Level 1: NTRU-HRSS701 | NTRU-HPS677, Level 3: NTRU-HPS821						
poly_Rq_mul	426.8	70.1 | 55.0	6.09 | 7.78	583.9	83.5	6.99
poly_S3_mul	432.8	72.2 | 56.1	5.99 | 7.76	588.7	83.1	7.08
Saber: Toom-Cook | NTT						
InnerProd	27.7	18.1 | 22.5	1.53 | 1.23	41.4	25.0 | 31.5	1.64 | 1.31
MatrixVectorMul	55.2	40.2 | 37.0	1.37 | 1.49	125.7	81.0 | 71.3	1.55 | 1.76
Kyber						
VectorVectorMul	44.4	7.1	6.3	59.7	9.9	6.1
MatrixVectorMul	68.1	10.7	6.4	117.5	19.3	6.1

Table 5. Fast NTT-based and Toom-Cook implementations of multiplication in NTRU, Saber and Kyber measured in kilocycles – neon vs. AVX2

Apple M1	Level 1 *(kilocycles)*			Level 3 *(kilocycles)*		
INTEL I7-8750H	AVX2	neon	AVX2/neon	AVX2	neon	AVX2/neon
Level 1: NTRU-HRSS701 | NTRU-HPS677, Level 3: NTRU-HPS821						
poly_Rq_mul	6.0 | 6.0	15.7 | 11.6	0.38 | 0.52	8.7	17.2	0.51
poly_S3_mul	6.2 | 6.3	15.7 | 11.9	0.40 | 0.53	9.2	17.4	0.53
Saber: Toom-Cook | NTT						
InnerProd	2.2 | 1.8	3.2 | 6.1	0.69 | 0.29	3.5 | 2.4	4.3 | 8.5	0.80 | 0.29
MatrixVectorMul	3.9 | 2.9	6.6 | 10.1	0.59 | 0.28	8.2 | 5.6	14.0 | 18.9	0.59 | 0.30
Kyber						
VectorVectorMul	0.5	1.9	0.27	0.7	2.5	0.26
MatrixVectorMul	0.7	2.8	0.26	1.2	4.9	0.25

Table 6. Encapsulation and Decapsulation speed comparison over three security levels. ref and **neon** results for Apple M1. AVX2 results for AMD EPYC 7742. *kc*-kilocycles.

Apple M1	ref (*kc*)		neon (*kc*)		AVX2 (*kc*)		ref/neon		AVX2/neon	
AMD EPYC 7742	E	D	E	D	E	D	E	D	E	D
NTRU-HPS677	183.1	430.4	60.1	54.6	26.0	45.7	3.05	7.89	0.43	0.84
NTRU-HRSS701	152.4	439.9	22.8	60.8	20.4	47.7	6.68	7.24	0.90	0.78
LIGHTSABER	50.9	54.9	37.2	35.3	41.9	42.2	1.37	1.55	1.13	1.19
KYBER512	75.7	89.5	32.6	29.4	28.4	22.6	2.33	3.04	0.87	0.77
NTRU-HPS821	245.3	586.5	75.7	69.0	29.9	57.3	3.24	8.49	0.39	0.83
SABER	90.4	96.2	59.9	58.0	70.9	70.7	1.51	1.66	1.18	1.22
KYBER768	119.8	137.8	49.2	45.7	43.4	35.2	2.43	3.02	0.88	0.77
FIRESABER	140.9	150.8	87.9	86.7	103.3	103.7	1.60	1.74	1.18	1.20
KYBER1024	175.4	198.4	71.6	67.1	63.0	53.1	2.45	2.96	0.88	0.79

Table 7. SHAKE128 performance with dual-lane 2×KeccakF1600 neon vs. 2×ref, benchmark on Apple M1.

Input length	Output length	2× ref	neon	2×ref/neon
32	1,664	15,079	11,620	1.30
32	3,744	33,249	26,251	1.27
32	6,656	57,504	45,658	1.26

Table 8. Encapsulation and Decapsulation ranking benchmarked on Apple M1 and AMD EPYC processor. The baseline is the largest number of cycles for each security level.

Rank	neon				AVX2			
	E	↑	D	↑	E	↑	D	↑
1	ntru-hrss701	1.00	kyber512	1.00	ntru-hrss701	1.00	kyber512	1.00
2	kyber512	1.43	lightsaber	1.20	ntru-hps677	1.27	lightsaber	1.87
3	lightsaber	1.63	ntru-hps677	1.85	kyber512	1.39	ntru-hps677	2.03
4	ntru-hps677	2.64	ntru-hrss701	2.06	lightsaber	2.05	ntru-hrss701	2.11
1	kyber768	1.00	kyber768	1.00	ntru-hps821	1.00	kyber768	1.00
2	saber	1.22	saber	1.27	kyber768	1.45	saber	1.63
3	ntru-hps821	1.54	ntru-hps821	1.51	saber	2.37	ntru-hps821	2.01
1	kyber1024	1.00	kyber1024	1.00	kyber1024	1.00	kyber1024	1.00
2	firesaber	1.23	firesaber	1.29	firesaber	1.64	firesaber	1.95

NTT and Toom-Cook Multiplication. In Table 4, NTRU-HRSS701 and NTRU-HPS677 share polynomial multiplication implementation in the **ref** implementation. In the **neon** implementation of poly_Rq_mul, the NTRU-HPS677 takes 55.0 *kilocycles*, which corresponds to the speed-up of 7.78 over **ref**, as compared to 6.09 for NTRU-HRSS701. In the case of Saber, the two numbers for **neon** and **ref/neon** represent Toom-Cook and NTT-based implementations, respectively. The Toom-Cook implementation of InnerProd shows better speed across security levels 1, 3, and 5. In contrast, for MatrixVectorMul, the NTT-based implementation outperforms Toom-k implementation for all security levels. When Saber uses NTT as a replacement for the Toom-Cook implementation on Cortex-A72 and Apple M1, performance gains in encapsulation are $(-1\%, +2\%, +5\%)$ and $(-15\%, -13\%, -14\%)$. For decapsulation, they are $(-4\%, -2\%, +2\%)$ and $(-21\%, -18\%, -19\%)$, respectively. Our benchmarks show that NTT-based implementations performs better in AVX2 than in the **neon** implementation, as shown in the Saber section of Table 5. We believe that the gap is caused by the lack of an instruction of ARMv8 equivalent to vmulhw. In the case of Kyber, we consistently achieve **ref/neon** ratio greater than 6.0 in VectorVectorMul and MatrixVectorMul, as shown in Table 4.

AVX2 and NEON. In Table 6, **neon** and AVX2 implementations of Kyber are the fastest in decapsulation across all security levels. In the **neon** implementation of Kyber, the leftover bottleneck is SHAKE128/256. Although we implemented a 2×KeccakF1600 permutation function that utilizes 128-bit vector registers, the performance gain is 25% as compared to 2× reference implementation, as shown in Table 7. This speed-up translates to only a fraction of the encapsulation/decapsulation time. We expect that the speed-up will be greater when there is hardware support for SHA3. In the AVX2/neon comparison, the **neon** implementations of MatrixVectorMul, VectorVectorMul, and NTT have the performance at the levels of 25% → 27% of the performance of AVX2 (see Table 5). However, for the entire encapsulation and decapsulation, these differences are significantly smaller (see Table 6).

In the case of Saber, we selected the Toom-Cook implementation approach for **ref**, **neon**, and AVX2. The **neon** consistently outperforms AVX2. Please note that the **ref** implementations of Saber and NTRU employ similar Toom-k settings as the **neon** and AVX2 implementations. In addition, the **neon** Toom-k multiplications in InnerProd, MatrixVectorMul perform better than the NTT implementations, as shown in Table 4.

The performance of **neon** for NTRU-HPS677 and NTRU-HPS821 are close to the performance of AVX2. Additionally, when compared to the **ref** implementation, the decapsulation speed-up of **neon** is consistently greater than 7.

In Table 8, the rankings for **neon** implementations running on Apple M1 and AVX2 implementations running on the AMD EPYC 7742 core are presented. For decapsulation, the rankings are identical at all three security levels. The advantage of Kyber over Saber is higher for AVX2 than for **neon**. For encapsulation, at levels 1 and 3, NTRU-HPS is faster than Kyber and Saber only for AVX2. As a result, at level 3, NTRU is ranked no. 3 for **neon** and no. 1 for AVX2.

In Table 9, we summarize results for key generation executed on Cortex-A72 and Apple M1. The NTRU key generation was not implemented as it requires inversion. As a result, it is both time-consuming to implement and has a much longer execution time. By using **neon** instructions, the key generation for Kyber is sped up, as compared to the reference implementation, by a factor in the range 2.03–2.15 for Cortex-A72 and 2.58–2.91 for Apple M1. For Saber, the speed-ups are more moderate in the ranges 1.13–1.29 and 1.41–1.55, respectively.

Table 9. Key generation time for Saber and Kyber over three security levels measured in kilocycles (kc) - **Cortex-A72** vs. **Apple M1**

Keygen	Cortex-A72 *(kc)*			Apple M1 *(kc)*		
	ref	neon	ref/neon	ref	neon	ref/neon
LIGHTSABER	134.9	119.5	1.13	44.0	31.2	1.41
KYBER512	136.7	67.4	2.03	59.3	23.0	2.58
SABER	237.3	192.9	1.23	74.4	51.3	1.45
KYBER768	237.7	110.7	2.15	104.9	36.3	2.89
FIRESABER	370.5	286.6	1.29	119.2	77.0	1.55
KYBER1024	371.9	176.2	2.11	162.9	55.9	2.91

7   Conclusions

In conclusion, 1. The NEON-based NTT implementation is slower than the corresponding implementation using AVX2 due to the lack of a NEON instruction equivalent to **vmulhw**. 2. Performance of NTT in Saber is close to the performance of the Toom-Cook algorithm. We advise to continue using Toom-Cook on ARMv8. 3. The rankings of lattice-based PQC KEM finalists in terms of speed in software are similar for NEON-based implementations and AVX2-based implementations. The biggest change is the lower position of **ntru-hps677** and **ntru-hps821** in NEON-based implementations.

References

1. Post-Quantum Cryptography: Round 3 Submissions (2021). https://csrc.nist.gov/Projects/post-quantum-cryptography/round-3-submissions
2. Alkim, E., Alper Bilgin, Y., Cenk, M., Gérard, F.: Cortex-M4 optimizations for {R,M} LWE schemes. TCHES **2020**(3), 336–357 (2020). https://doi.org/10.46586/tches.v2020.i3.336-357
3. Avanzi, R., et al.: CRYSTALS-Kyber: algorithm specifications and supporting documentation (version 3.01). Technical report, January 2021

4. Bermudo Mera, J.M., Karmakar, A., Verbauwhede, I.: Time-memory trade-off in Toom-Cook multiplication: an application to module-lattice based cryptography. IACR Trans. Cryptographic Hardware Embed. Syst. **2020**(2), 222–244 (2020). https://doi.org/10.13154/TCHES.V2020.I2.222-244

5. Bernstein, D.J., Lange, T.: eBACS: ECRYPT Benchmarking of Cryptographic Systems (2021). https://bench.cr.yp.to

6. Bodrato, M., Zanoni, A.: Integer and polynomial multiplication: towards optimal Toom-Cook matrices. In: International Symposium on Symbolic and Algebraic Computation, ISSAC 2007, pp. 17–24 (2007). https://doi.org/10.1145/1277548.1277552

7. Botros, L., Kannwischer, M.J., Schwabe, P.: Memory-efficient high-speed implementation of Kyber on Cortex-M4. In: Buchmann, J., Nitaj, A., Rachidi, T. (eds.) AFRICACRYPT 2019. LNCS, vol. 11627, pp. 209–228. Springer, Cham (2019). https://doi.org/10.1007/978-3-030-23696-0_11

8. Chung, C.M.M., Hwang, V., Kannwischer, M.J., Seiler, G., Shih, C.J., Yang, B.Y.: NTT Multiplication for NTT-unfriendly Rings: New Speed Records for Saber and NTRU on Cortex-M4 and AVX2. TCHES, pp. 159–188, February 2021. https://doi.org/10.46586/tches.v2021.i2.159-188

9. Cook, S.A., Aanderaao, S.O.: On the minimum computation time of functions. Trans. Am. Math. Soc. **142**, 291–314 (1969)

10. Cooley, J.W., Tukey, J.W.: An algorithm for the machine calculation of complex fourier series. Math. Comput. **19**(90), 297–301 (1965)

11. Danba, O.: Optimizing NTRU Using AVX2. Master's thesis, Radboud University, Nijmegen, Netherlands, July 2019

12. Fujisaki, E., Okamoto, T.: Secure integration of asymmetric and symmetric encryption schemes. J. Cryptol. **26**(1), 80–101 (2013). 10/bxwqr4

13. Gentleman, W.M., Sande, G.: Fast fourier transforms: for fun and profit. In: Fall Joint Computer Conference, AFIPS 1966, San Francisco, CA, pp. 563–578. ACM Press, November 1966. https://doi.org/10.1145/1464291.1464352

14. Gupta, N., Jati, A., Chauhan, A.K., Chattopadhyay, A.: PQC acceleration using GPUs: FrodoKEM, NewHope, and Kyber. IEEE Trans. Parallel Distrib. Syst. **32**(3), 575–586 (2021). https://doi.org/10.1109/TPDS.2020.3025691

15. Hoang, G.L.: Optimization of the NTT Function on ARMv8-A SVE. Bachelor's thesis, Radboud University, The Netherlands, June 2018

16. Kannwischer, M.J., Rijneveld, J., Schwabe, P., Stoffelen, K.: Pqm4 - Post-quantum crypto library for the {ARM} {Cortex-M4} (2019). https://github.com/mupq/pqm4

17. Karatsuba, A., Ofman, Y.: Multiplication of many-digital numbers by automatic computers. Dokl. Akad. Nauk SSSR **145**(2), 293–294 (1962)

18. Karmakar, A., Bermudo Mera, J.M., Sinha Roy, S., Verbauwhede, I.: Saber on ARM. IACR Trans. Cryptographic Hardware Embed. Syst. **2018**(3), 243–266 (2018). https://doi.org/10.13154/tches.v2018.i3.243-266

19. Mansouri, F.: On the parallelization of integer polynomial multiplication. Master's thesis, The University of Western Ontario (2014)

20. Scott, M.: A note on the implementation of the number theoretic transform. In: O'Neill, M. (ed.) IMACC 2017. LNCS, vol. 10655, pp. 247–258. Springer, Cham (2017). https://doi.org/10.1007/978-3-319-71045-7_13

21. Seiler, G.: Faster AVX2 optimized NTT multiplication for Ring-LWE lattice cryptography. Cryptology ePrint Archive 2018/039, January 2018

22. Sinha Roy, S.: SaberX4: high-throughput software implementation of saber key encapsulation mechanism. In: 2019 IEEE 37th International Conference on Computer Design (ICCD), Abu Dhabi, United Arab Emirates, pp. 321–324. IEEE, November 2019. https://doi.org/10.1109/ICCD46524.2019.00050

23. Streit, S., De Santis, F.: Post-quantum key exchange on ARMv8-A: a new hope for NEON made simple. IEEE Trans. Comput. **67**(11), 1651–1662 (2018). 10/gff3sc

24. Terpstra, D., Jagode, H., You, H., Dongarra, J.: Collecting performance data with PAPI-C. In: Müller, M., Resch, M., Schulz, A., Nagel, W. (eds.) Tools for High Performance Computing 2009, pp. 157–173. Springer, Heidelberg (2010). https://doi.org/10.1007/978-3-642-11261-4_11

25. Toom, A.: The complexity of a scheme of functional elements realizing the multiplication of integers. Soviet Math. Doklady **3**, 714–716 (1963)

26. Westerbaan, B.: When to Barrett reduce in the inverse NTT. Cryptology ePrint Archive 2020/1377, November 2020

27. Zhou, S., et al.: Preprocess-then-NTT technique and its applications to KYBER and NEWHOPE. In: Guo, F., Huang, X., Yung, M. (eds.) Inscrypt 2018. LNCS, vol. 11449, pp. 117–137. Springer, Cham (2019). https://doi.org/10.1007/978-3-030-14234-6_7

Isogeny

CSI-RAShi: Distributed Key Generation for CSIDH

Ward Beullens[1], Lucas Disson[2], Robi Pedersen[1(✉)], and Frederik Vercauteren[1]

[1] imec-COSIC, ESAT, KU Leuven, Leuven, Belgium
{ward.beullens,robi.pedersen,frederik.vercauteren}@esat.kuleuven.be
[2] ENS, Lyon, France
lucas.disson@ens-lyon.fr

Abstract. We present an honest-majority Distributed Key Generation protocol (DKG) based on Shamir's (k, n)-threshold secret sharing in the setting of Very Hard Homogenous Spaces (VHHS). DKGs in the discrete logarithm setting use Pedersen commitments, for which there is no known analogue in the VHHS setting. As a replacement, we introduce a new primitive called *piecewise verifiable proofs*, which allow a prover to prove that a list of NP-statements is valid with respect to a common witness, and such that the different statements can be verified individually. Our protocol is robust and actively secure in the Quantum Random Oracle Model. For n participants, the total runtime of our protocol is $2 + \lambda + n(1 + 4\lambda)$ group action evaluations, where λ is the underlying security parameter, and is thus independent of the threshold k. When instantiated with CSIDH-512, this amounts to approximately $4.5 + 18n$ seconds.

Keywords: Isogeny-based cryptography · Distributed key generation · Secret sharing · Class group action · CSIDH · QROM

1 Introduction

Isogeny-based cryptography, proposed by Couveignes [9] and independently by Rostovtsev and Stolbunov [26], is a very promising approach to post-quantum cryptography. Two different types of isogeny-based Diffie-Hellman key agreement schemes exist: Supersingular Isogeny Diffie-Hellman or SIDH [12] and its "commutative" variant called CSIDH [6]. Whereas SIDH relies on random walks in isogeny graphs over $\mathbb{F}_{p^2}$, CSIDH closely follows the CRS approach and constructs a so-called very hard homogeneous space (VHHS) based on supersingular curves over $\mathbb{F}_p$.

A VHHS is a natural generalisation of a group for which the decisional Diffie-Hellman problem is hard; in particular, exponentiation in the group is

This work was supported in part by the Research Council KU Leuven grants C14/18/067 and STG/17/019, and by CyberSecurity Research Flanders with reference number VR20192203. Ward Beullens is funded by FWO fellowship 1S95620N. Date of this document: July 2, 2021

J. H. Cheon and J.-P. Tillich (Eds.): PQCrypto 2021, LNCS 12841, pp. 257–276, 2021.
https://doi.org/10.1007/978-3-030-81293-5_14

now replaced by a group action on a set. For CSIDH, the group action corresponds to the action of the ideal class group $Cl(\mathcal{O})$ on the set of supersingular elliptic curves over $\mathbb{F}_p$ whose $\mathbb{F}_p$-endomorphism ring is precisely $\mathcal{O}$.

In 2019, Beullens, Kleinjung and Vercauteren [4] computed the class group structure of the CSIDH-512 parameter set. Knowledge of the class group structure, for CSIDH-512 it is cyclic of order $N \approx 2^{256}$, allows to identify the ideal classes with integers mod N, which makes it possible to sample uniformly from the class group and represent the elements uniquely. This allowed Beullens *et al.* to instantiate a simple identification scheme that goes back to Couveignes, Rostovtsev and Stolbunov and combined with the Fiat-Shamir transform resulted in CSI-FiSh [4], which was the first practical post-quantum isogeny-based signature scheme. With the class group structure known, more cryptographic applications, including threshold signatures, threshold PKE and ring signatures are suddenly within reach [3,10,13].

This paper focuses on the threshold schemes. The idea of threshold schemes is that n participants are each given a share of a secret s, in such a way that any qualified subset of participants can reconstruct the secret or perform an action requiring the knowledge of s, such as signing a message or decrypting a ciphertext. Threshold schemes have seen a surge of interest in recent years [22], due to their usage in voting schemes and blockchain applications among others [1,20]. Secret sharing schemes were initially introduced by Shamir in the late '70s [27] and first turned into a threshold ElGamal encryption scheme by Desmedt and Frankel [14]. Later, threshold signature schemes were proposed in the discrete-logarithm (DLOG) [17–19] and in the RSA setting [15,28]. A key question in these schemes is how to generate and share the secret s among all parties without s being revealed. While initial schemes relied on a trusted party called the dealer, in the early '90s, Pedersen [23] introduced the first distributed key generation (DKG) protocol in an honest majority k-out-of-n threshold, i.e. where at least k players are honest and at most $k-1$ malicious and each subset of k players is qualified. Pedersen's protocol was improved by Gennaro et al. [18] to a robust DKG scheme, i.e. where the reconstruction of s is possible, even if malicious players try to sabotage the computation.

Motivation and Related Work. De Feo and Meyer [13] introduced threshold variants of encryption and signature schemes in the VHHS setting and instantiated their protocols using CSIDH-512. Their approach is similar to DLOG schemes and use Shamir secret sharing. However, since in the VHHS setting, players cannot individually combine partial signatures into the final signature, players have to compute their parts subsequently in a round-robin fashion. The work of De Feo and Meyer does not provide a method for the key distribution: they simply assume that key generation is done by a trusted dealer. An alternative VHHS-based threshold signing protocol called Sashimi was presented by Cozzo and Smart [10] based on replicated secret sharing. In contrast to [13], Sashimi is actively secure, which is achieved using zero-knowledge proofs. Cozzo and Smart give a protocol to generate keys, but this protocol is not robust (an attacker can sabotage the computation), and the adversary can also influence the distribution of the public keys by selectively sabotaging the DKG protocol if it doesn't like the outcome. Therefore, the question of how to robustly and securely perform a distributed key generation in the VHHS setting is still open. In this paper, we provide a robust and actively secure solution to this problem that is proven secure in the Quantum Random Oracle Model (QROM).

Our Contributions. We introduce a new primitive called *Piecewise Verifiable Proofs* (PVP), which are zero-knowledge proofs of a list of NP-statements sharing a common witness, where individual relations (pieces) can be verified independently and at low cost. We show that PVPs can be used as a practical and efficient alternative to Pedersen commitments, which can not be translated directly to the VHHS setting. This allows their use in the construction of a distributed key generation protocol (DKG) based on Shamir secret sharing in the VHHS setting. Our result is an honest-majority (k, n)-threshold scheme called CSI-RAShi[1], based on the blueprint set out by Gennaro et al. [18] that is also robust and actively secure. By using PVPs in the isogeny setting, our protocol is very efficient in comparison to current isogeny-based distributed signature schemes, such as Sashimi [10]. In particular, while standard zero-knowledge proofs would require $O(\lambda n^2)$ group action operations and naive PVP constructions still $O(\lambda n)$, our approach only needs $O(\lambda)$ group actions and instead $O(\lambda n)$ calls to a hash function, which can be evaluated much faster. Using recent results on the post-quantum security of the Fiat-Shamir transform [16,31], we prove security of the proposed PVPs, and consequently of our DKG scheme, in the QROM.

2 Background

We denote by $\mathbb{Z}_N := \mathbb{Z}/N\mathbb{Z}$ the ring of integers modulo N, where N is a composite number with prime factorization $N = \prod_{i=1}^{s} q_i^{e_i}$, such that $q_1 < \cdots < q_s$. We further call $\mathbb{Z}_N[X]_{\leq k-1}$ the set of polynomials over $\mathbb{Z}_N$ of degree $\leq k-1$.

2.1 Very Hard Homogeneous Spaces

Very hard homogeneous spaces were introduced by Couveignes [9] in order to generalize the notion of cyclic groups in which the computational and decisional Diffie-Hellman problems are hard. We give a similar definition to the original one here using the notation common in the isogeny setting.

Definition 1 (Very hard homogeneous spaces [7,9,13]). *A very hard homogeneous space is a pair* $(\mathcal{E}, \mathcal{G})$*, where* $\mathcal{G}$ *is a finite Abelian group acting freely and transitively on a finite set* $\mathcal{E}$ *by the map* $* : \mathcal{G} \times \mathcal{E} \to \mathcal{E}$*, for which there are easy (i.e. efficiently computable) and hard algorithmic problems. The easy problems include group operations and sampling in* $\mathcal{G}$*, testing elements for equality and membership in* $\mathcal{E}$ *and performing the group action computation, while the hard problems include*

---

[1] "Commutative Supersingular Isogeny Robust and Actively secure distributed Shamir secret sharing", pronounced *chirashi*, in reference to the Japanese dish *chirashi sushi*, translated as "scattered sushi".

- Vectorization: *Given $E_1, E_2 \in \mathcal{E}$, find $\mathfrak{a} \in \mathcal{G}$, such that $\mathfrak{a} * E_1 = E_2$.*
- Parallelization: *Given $E_1, E_2, F_1 \in \mathcal{E}$ with $E_2 = \mathfrak{a} * E_1$, compute $F_2 = \mathfrak{a} * F_1$.*
- Decisional Parallelization: *Distinguish with non-negligible advantage between the distributions $(\mathfrak{a} * E, \mathfrak{b} * E, \mathfrak{a}\mathfrak{b} * E)$ and $(\mathfrak{a} * E, \mathfrak{b} * E, \mathfrak{c} * E)$ where $E \in \mathcal{E}$ and $\mathfrak{a}, \mathfrak{b}, \mathfrak{c}$ are chosen at random from $\mathcal{G}$.*

Notation. In the case where $\mathcal{G}$ is cyclic of order N, and $\mathfrak{g}$ is a generator of $\mathcal{G}$, we can also define the group action $[\ ] : \mathbb{Z}_N \times \mathcal{E} \to \mathcal{E}$, such that, for $a \in \mathbb{Z}_N$, $E \in \mathcal{E}$, we have $[a]E = \mathfrak{g}^a * E$. It then holds that $[a][b]E = [a+b]E$.

2.2 Zero-Knowledge Proofs

We revisit the non-interactive version of the zero-knowledge proofs for simultaneous instances of the vectorization problem introduced in [10]. Let R^m be the relation $R^m = \{((E_i, E_i')_{i \in \{1,\dots,m\}}, s) \mid E_i' = [s]E_i \forall i \in \{1,\dots,m\}\}$. For a statement $\mathbf{X} \in \mathcal{E}^{2m}$, Algorithm 1 allows the prover to publish a proof of knowledge of s, such that $(\mathbf{X}, s) \in R^m$, which can be verified using Algorithm 2. Here, $\mathcal{H} : \{0,1\}^* \to \{0,1\}^\lambda$ denotes a hash function (modelled as a quantum-accessible random oracle) used to generate the challenge. Both the prover and the verifier need to compute $m\lambda$ group actions.

Input : m tuples $\mathbf{X} = (E_i, E_i')_{i \in \{1,\dots,m\}}$ with $E_i, E_i' \in \mathcal{E}$, the secret s.
Output: A non-interactive proof π of knowledge of s.
1 **for** $j = 1, \dots, \lambda$ **do**
2 $\quad$ $b_j \leftarrow \mathbb{Z}_N$ uniformly at random
3 $\quad$ **for** $i = 1, \dots, m$ **do** $\hat{E}_{i,j} \leftarrow [b_j]E_i$
4 $\mathbf{c} = c_1 \dots c_\lambda \leftarrow \mathcal{H}(\mathbf{X} \parallel \hat{E}_{1,1} \parallel \dots \parallel \hat{E}_{m,1} \parallel \dots \parallel \hat{E}_{1,\lambda} \parallel \dots \parallel \hat{E}_{m,t})$
5 **for** $j = 1, \dots, \lambda$ **do** $r_j \leftarrow b_j - c_j s \mod N$ **return** $\pi = (\mathbf{c}, \mathbf{r})$, *where* $\mathbf{r} = (r_1, \dots, r_\lambda)$.

Algorithm 1: Non-interactive zero-knowledge proof ZK.P

Input : m tuples $\mathbf{X} = (E_i, E_i')_{i \in \{1,\dots,m\}}$ with $E_i, E_i' \in \mathcal{E}$, a
$\qquad\qquad$ non-interactive proof $\pi = (\mathbf{c}, \mathbf{r})$.
Output: A boolean value signaling if the proof is deemed correct.
1 **for** $j = 1, \dots, \lambda$ **do**
2 $\quad$ **if** $c_j = 0$ **then** let $\widetilde{E}_{i,j} \leftarrow [r_j]E_i$ for $i = 1, \dots, m$
3 $\quad$ **if** $c_j = 1$ **then** let $\widetilde{E}_{i,j} \leftarrow [r_j]E_i'$ for $i = 1, \dots, m$
4 $\tilde{c}_1 \dots \tilde{c}_\lambda \leftarrow \mathcal{H}(\mathbf{X} \parallel \widetilde{E}_{1,1} \parallel \dots \parallel \widetilde{E}_{m,1} \parallel \dots \parallel \widetilde{E}_{1,\lambda} \parallel \dots \parallel \widetilde{E}_{m,\lambda})$
5 **return** $\tilde{c}_1 \dots \tilde{c}_\lambda == \mathbf{c}$

Algorithm 2: Non-interactive zero-knowledge verification ZK.V

Theorem 1. *The Algorithms 1 and 2 constitute a non-interactive zero-knowledge quantum proof of knowledge in the QROM for the relation R^m.*

Proof. The work of Cozzo et al. [10] proves that the sigma protocol that underlies ZK has special soundness and honest verifier zero-knowledge (HVZK). Moreover, since the group action is free, it is clear that the sigma protocol has perfect unique responses. Therefore, the work of Don et al. [16] shows that the protocol is a quantum proof of knowledge. The work of Unruh [31] shows that because the sigma protocol has completeness, unpredictable commitments and HVZK, the protocol is zero-knowledge against quantum adversaries.

3 Distributed Key Generation in the VHHS-Setting

We introduce the security definitions for distributed protocols between n players $\mathcal{P}_1, \ldots, \mathcal{P}_n$. We use Shamir secret sharing over the ring $\mathbb{Z}_N$, which is secure as long as $n < q_1$, the smallest prime factor of N [13]. We base our definitions on those introduced in [18], but have to use slightly weaker definitions, due to the difference of VHHS and the DLOG setting. As in [25], we assume a reliable broadcast channel that identifies the sender and pairwise secure communication channels between the players. Similarly to [18] we assume these channels to be partially synchronous, i.e. messages are received within some fixed time bound.

3.1 Security Definitions

We require correctness and secrecy for a Shamir secret sharing-based DKG protocol. *Correctness* requires that if there are at least k honest and at most $k-1$ malicious parties, the protocol ends with each honest $\mathcal{P}_i$ holding a tuple (E, s_i) with the same E. Moreover, there exists a polynomial $f(X) \in \mathbb{Z}_N[X]_{\leq k-1}$, such that $E = [f(0)]E_0$ and $s_i = f(i)$, except with negligible probability. Our definition implies *robustness* [18], i.e. the reconstruction of the secret should also be possible if malicious parties try to subvert the computation. Let $b_1, b_2 \leftarrow \langle B_1^{\mathcal{O}}(x) | B_2^{\mathcal{O}}(y) \rangle$ denote the joint distribution of local outputs of two interacting (groups of) oracle algorithms B_1 and B_2 after running together on inputs x and y respectively. In the definitions below, we simply refer to the adversary's local output as A.

Definition 2 (Robust correctness). *We say a Shamir DKG protocol $\Pi = \{\mathcal{P}_i\}_{i \in \{1,\ldots,n\}}$ is correct, if for any PPT adversary $\mathcal{A}$, any positive integers $k \leq n$, and any subset $I \subseteq \{1, \ldots, n\}$ with $|I| \geq k$ and $n - |I| < k$ we have that*

$$\Pr \left[\begin{array}{l} \nexists f \in \mathbb{Z}_N[x]_{\leq k-1} : \\ E_1 = \cdots = E_n = [f(0)]E_0 \\ \text{and } \forall i \in I : f(i) = s_i \end{array} \middle| A, \{(E_i, s_i)\}_{i \in I} \leftarrow \langle \mathcal{A}^{\mathcal{O}}(1^\lambda) | \{\mathcal{P}_i^{\mathcal{O}}(1^\lambda)\}_{i \in I} \rangle \right]$$

is a negligible function of the security parameter.

For *secrecy*, we require that the protocol does not reveal anything about the secret key s beyond what can be learned from the public key $E = [s]E_0$. This is formalized with a simulator-based definition. For every adversary $\mathcal{A}$, we require a simulator that, given a random $E \leftarrow \mathcal{E}$, simulates honest parties, such that its interaction with $\mathcal{A}$ results in E as the public key. The existence of such a simulator shows that the execution of the transcript can be generated from $E = [s]E_0$ alone, which means that the protocol does not reveal any information beyond what can be learned from E itself. More formally we define:

Definition 3 (Secrecy). *We say a Shamir DKG protocol* $\Pi = \{\mathcal{P}_i\}_{i \in \{1,\ldots,n\}}$ *has secrecy, if for any PPT adversary* $\mathcal{A}$*, and any index set of honest users* $I \subseteq \{1,\ldots,n\}$ *with* $|I| \geq k$ *and* $n - |I| < k$*, there exists a simulator* $\mathsf{Sim} = (\mathsf{Sim}_1, \mathsf{Sim}_2)$ *such that for any* $i_0 \in I$*, the following distributions are computationally indistinguishable*

$$\left\{ (A, E_{i_0}) \big| A, \{(E_i, s_i)\}_{i \in I} \leftarrow \langle \mathcal{A}^{\mathcal{O}}(1^\lambda) | \{\mathcal{P}_i^{\mathcal{O}}(1^\lambda)\}_{i \in I} \rangle \right\} \approx_c$$

$$\left\{ (A, E) \bigg|_{\substack{E \leftarrow \mathcal{E} \\ A \leftarrow \langle \mathcal{A}^{\mathsf{Sim}_2}(1^\lambda) | \mathsf{Sim}_1(E, 1^\lambda) \rangle}} \right\}.$$

Remark 1. The secrecy definition implies that, even in the presence of at most $k-1$ corrupted parties, the distribution of public keys is computationally indistinguishable from the uniform distribution.

3.2 Comparison to Security Definitions in DLOG Setting

Our security definition is slightly weaker than the standard security definition for DLOG-based DKG protocols introduced by Gennaro et al. [18], because there is a subtle difference in the definition of the secrecy property. Both definitions require a simulator that, given a public key E, outputs a transcript of a protocol execution that results in E as a public key. The difference is that we only require the transcript to be indistinguishable from real transcripts that result in E as public key *if E is chosen uniformly at random*, whereas the standard definition in the DLOG setting requires the transcripts to be indistinguishable for every choice of E. In the DLOG setting this slightly stronger notion can be achieved using Pedersen commitments. This technique does not seem possible in the VHHS setting, so we have to rely on the parallelization problem, which requires E to be chosen uniformly at random. The property of Gennaro et al. is used to prove that the distribution of the public key is perfectly uniform, even in the presence of up to $k-1$ adversaries. In contrast, our property only implies that the distribution of the public key is indistinguishable from the uniform distribution.

4 Piecewise Verifiable Proofs

We now introduce *non-interactive piecewise verifiable proofs* (NIPVP) based on sigma protocols with binary challenges. Instead of a single commitment however, the prover produces $n + 1$ individual commitments, that can be opened and verified independently without revealing any information about the remaining statements. Given a list of NP relations $R_0, \ldots, R_n$ that share the same witness space and a list of statements $x_0, \ldots, x_n$, a NIPVP allows a prover to prove the existence of a witness w such that $(x_i, w) \in R_i$ for all $i \in \{0, \ldots, n\}$. The proof is of the form $\pi = (\tilde{\pi}, \{\pi_i\}_{i \in \{0,\ldots,n\}})$, where we think of $\tilde{\pi}$ as the central proof and of the π_i as proof pieces that are only relevant for R_i. The piecewise verifiability property says that for any $i \in \{0, \ldots, n\}$, given a statement piece x_i and a proof piece $(\tilde{\pi}, \pi_i)$ the verifier can check the proof with respect to x_i. If these piecewise verifications succeed for all $i \in I \subseteq \{0, \ldots, n\}$, then this convinces the verifier of the existence of a witness w such that $(x_i, w) \in R_i$ for all $i \in I$. Crucially, we want the proof pieces not to leak information on the statements $\{x_i\}_{i \notin I}$. In the following definitions, we use $x_I = \{x_i\}_{i \in I}$, $\pi_I = \{\pi_i\}_{i \in I}$ and $x = \{x_i\}_{i \in \{0, \ldots, n\}}$, and we write $(x_I, w) \in R_I$ and $(x, w) \in R$ if $(x_i, w) \in R_i$ for all $i \in I$ or for all $i \in \{0, \ldots, n\}$, respectively.

Definition 4 (NIPVP in the QROM). *Let $R = R_0, \ldots, R_n$ be a list of NP relations that share the same witness space. A non-interactive piecewise verifiable proof (NIPVP) in the QROM for R consists of a pair of PPT algorithms $(P^{\mathcal{O}}, V^{\mathcal{O}})$ with quantum access to a random oracle $\mathcal{O}$ such that:*

- *$P^{\mathcal{O}}$ takes as input $x = (x_0, \cdots, x_n)$ and w such that $(x, w) \in R$ and outputs a proof $\pi = (\tilde{\pi}, \{\pi_i\}_{i \in \{0, \ldots, n\}})$.*
- *$V^{\mathcal{O}}$ takes as input a statement piece (i, x_i) and a proof piece $(\tilde{\pi}, \pi_i)$ and outputs 1 or 0, signaling that it accepts or rejects the proof, respectively.*

We require completeness, soundness and zero-knowledge for NIPVPs with respect to a quantum polynomial-time (QPT) adversary. Unlike conventional non-interactive proofs, these properties need to hold with respect to any $I \subseteq \{0, \ldots, n\}$. For the soundness property we require that, if there does not exist a w such that $(x_i, w) \in R_i$ for all $i \in I$, then a prover can not output accepting proof pieces $(\tilde{\pi}, \{\pi_i\}_{i \in I})$ (except with negligible probability). For the zero-knowledge property we require a simulator that simulates piecewise proofs given only a partial statement x_I. This implies that a set of proof pieces $(\tilde{\pi}, \{\pi_i\}_{i \in I})$ does not leak information on the witness or on $\{x_i\}_{i \notin I}$.

Definition 5 (completeness). *We say a NIPVP $(P^{\mathcal{O}}, V^{\mathcal{O}})$ for the list of relations R is complete if for any $(x, w) \in R$ and any $i \in \{0, \ldots, n\}$ we have*

$$\Pr[V^{\mathcal{O}}(i, x_i, \tilde{\pi}, \pi_i) = 1 \,|\, \pi \leftarrow P^{\mathcal{O}}(x, w)] = 1.$$

Definition 6 (soundness). *For a NIPVP $(P^{\mathcal{O}}, V^{\mathcal{O}})$ for the list of relations R, a subset $I \subseteq \{0, \cdots, n\}$ and an adversary $\mathcal{A}$, we define the soundness advantage*

$$\mathsf{Adv}_{\mathcal{A}, I}^{\mathsf{sound}} = \Pr\left[\begin{array}{c} \forall i \in I : V^{\mathcal{O}}(i, x_i, \tilde{\pi}, \pi_i) = 1 \\ \nexists w : (x_I, w) \in R_I \end{array} \middle| (x_I, \tilde{\pi}, \pi_I) \leftarrow \mathcal{A}^{\mathcal{O}}(1^{\lambda}) \right].$$

We call $(P^{\mathcal{O}}, V^{\mathcal{O}})$ sound, if for every QPT adversary $\mathcal{A}$ and all $I \subseteq \{0, \cdots, n\}$ the advantage $\mathsf{Adv}_{\mathcal{A}, I}^{\mathsf{sound}}$ is a negligible function of the security parameter.

Definition 7 (zero-knowledge). *We say a NIPVP $(P^{\mathcal{O}}, V^{\mathcal{O}})$ for the list of relations R is zero-knowledge if for any subset $I \subseteq \{0, \ldots, n\}$, there exists a simulator $\mathsf{Sim} = (\mathsf{Sim}_1, \mathsf{Sim}_2)$, such that for any QPT distinguisher $\mathcal{A}$ the advantage*

$$\mathsf{Adv}_{\mathsf{Sim}, \mathcal{A}}^{\mathsf{zk}} = \left| \Pr\left[\mathcal{A}^{P', \mathcal{O}}(1^{\lambda}) = 1\right] - \Pr\left[\mathcal{A}^{S, \mathsf{Sim}_2}(1^{\lambda}) = 1\right] \right|,$$

is a negligible function of the security parameter, where P' is an oracle that on input $(x, w) \in R$ runs $\pi := P^{\mathcal{O}}(x, w)$ and outputs $(\tilde{\pi}, \{\pi_i\}_{i \in I})$ and S is an oracle that on input $(x, w) \in R$ returns $\mathsf{Sim}_1(x_I)$ (i.e. Sim_1 does not get to see the witness or x_i for $i \notin I$.

We present the following list of relations $R = (R_0, \ldots, R_n)$, whose common witness space is $\mathbb{Z}_N[X]_{\leq k-1}$:

$$R_0 = \{(x_0 = (E_0, E_1), f(x))|[f(0)]E_0 = E_1\},$$
$$\forall i \in \{1, \ldots, n\} : R_i = \{(x_i, f(x))|f(i) = x_i\}. \tag{1}$$

Thus, a statement for R_0 consists of a pair $(E_0, E_1) \in \mathcal{E}^2$, and a statement for the remaining relations $\{R_i\}_{i \in \{1, \ldots, n\}}$ is an element of $\mathbb{Z}_N$.

Algorithms 3 and 4 implement a non-interactive proof of relation (1). They make use of a random oracle $\mathcal{H} : \{0,1\}^* \to \{0,1\}^\lambda$, and a non-interactive commitment scheme $\mathcal{C} : \{0,1\}^* \times \{0,1\}^\lambda \to \{0,1\}^{2\lambda}$, that takes as input a message $m \in \{0,1\}^*$ and λ uniformly random bits bits, where λ is the security parameter, and outputs a 2λ-bit long commitment $\mathcal{C}(m, \text{bits})$. We assume this commitment function is collapsing (see [30, Def. 13] and [29]) and quantum computationally hiding (see [30, Def. 10]).

Input : A witness polynomial $f(X) \in \mathbb{Z}_N[X]_{\leq k-1}$,
     a statement $x = ((E_0, E_1), x_1, \cdots, x_n))$.
Output: A non-interactive piecewise proof π of the relations in (1).
1 **for** $j = 1, \ldots, \lambda$ **do**
2     $b_j \leftarrow \mathbb{Z}_N[X]_{\leq k-1}$ uniformly at random
3     $\hat{E}_j \leftarrow [b_j(0)]E_0$
4 $y_0, y_0' \leftarrow \{0,1\}^\lambda$ uniformly at random
5 $\mathsf{C}_0 \leftarrow \mathcal{C}(\hat{E}_1 \| \cdots \| \hat{E}_\lambda, y_0)$
6 $\mathsf{C}_0' \leftarrow \mathcal{C}(E_0 \| E_1, y_0')$
7 **for** $i = 1, \ldots, n$ **do**
8     $y_i, y_i' \leftarrow \{0,1\}^\lambda$ uniformly at random
9     $\mathsf{C}_i \leftarrow \mathcal{C}(b_1(i) \| \cdots \| b_\lambda(i), y_i)$
10     $\mathsf{C}_i' \leftarrow \mathcal{C}(x_i, y_i')$
11 $c = c_1 \ldots c_\lambda \leftarrow \mathcal{H}(\mathsf{C}, \mathsf{C}')$, where $\mathsf{C} = (\mathsf{C}_0, \ldots, \mathsf{C}_n), \mathsf{C}' = (\mathsf{C}_0', \ldots, \mathsf{C}_n')$
12 **for** $j = 1, \ldots, \lambda$ **do** $r_j(x) \leftarrow b_j(x) - c_j f(x) \mod N$ **return**
    $\tilde{\pi} = (\mathsf{C}, \mathsf{C}', \mathbf{r})$ and $\{\pi_i = (y_i, y_i')\}_{i \in \{0, \ldots, n\}}$, where $\mathbf{r} = (r_1, \ldots, r_\lambda)$.

Algorithm 3: NIPVP proof algorithm PVP.P

Input : An index $i \in \{0, \ldots, n\}$, a statement piece x_i of the form
     $(E_0, E_1) \in \mathcal{E}^2$ if $i = 0$, or $x_i \in \mathbb{Z}_N$ if $i \neq 0$, and a proof piece
     $(\tilde{\pi}, \pi_i) = ((\mathsf{C}, \mathsf{C}', \mathbf{r}), (y_i, y_i'))$.
Output: A boolean value signaling if the proof is deemed correct
1 **if** $\mathsf{C}_i' \neq \mathcal{C}(x_i, y_i')$ **then return** 0 $c_1 \ldots c_\lambda \leftarrow \mathcal{H}(\mathsf{C}, \mathsf{C}')$
2 **if** $i == 0$ **then**
3   **for** $j = 1, \ldots, \lambda$ **do** $\tilde{E}_j \leftarrow [r_j(0)]E_{c_j}$ **return**
     $\mathsf{C}_0 == \mathcal{C}(\tilde{E}_1 \| \cdots \| \tilde{E}_\lambda, y_0)$
4 **else return** $\mathsf{C}_i == \mathcal{C}(r_1(i) + c_1 x_i \| \cdots \| r_\lambda(i) + c_\lambda x_i \| x_i, y_i)$

Algorithm 4: NIPVP piecewise verification algorithm PVP.V

Theorem 2. *Algorithms 3 and 4 constitute a complete, sound and zero-knowledge NIPVP in the QROM for the list of relations of (1) provided that the commitment scheme $\mathcal{C}$ is collapsing and quantum computationally hiding.*

We prove Theorem 2 in Appendix A.

Cost. Algorithm 3 requires the computation of λ group actions, one call to the random oracle $\mathcal{H}$ and $2(n+1)$ calls to the commitment scheme $\mathcal{C}$, while Algorithm 4 requires one call to the random oracle $\mathcal{H}$, two calls to the commitment scheme $\mathcal{C}$, and only in the case $i = 0$ it requires the computation of λ group actions.

5   Distributed Key Generation

In this section, we present CSI-RAShi, a DKG protocol based on the NIPVP of Sect. 4. The structure of our protocol is similar to the Gennaro protocol in the DLOG setting [18], which consists of 4 phases:

1. **Generating VSS.** Each party $\mathcal{P}_i$ performs a Pedersen verifiable secret sharing (VSS) protocol for a random value $z^{(i)} = f^{(i)}(0)$ and sends a share $s_{ij} = f^{(i)}(j)$ of a Shamir secret sharing of $z^{(i)}$ to each player $\mathcal{P}_j$.
2. **Verifying VSS.** Each party $\mathcal{P}_j$ verifies correctness of the received s_{ij}, otherwise it broadcasts a complaint against $\mathcal{P}_i$. At the end, the honest parties agree on a set $\mathcal{Q}$ of qualified parties who performed their VSS correctly.
3. **Compute shares.** The common secret key is implicitly defined as $\sum_{i \in \mathcal{Q}} z^{(i)}$. Each party $\mathcal{P}_j$ can compute their share $s_j = \sum_{i \in \mathcal{Q}} s_{ij}$ of it.
4. **Compute common public key.** The common public key is now $\prod_{i \in \mathcal{Q}} g^{z^{(i)}}$. Each party publishes $g^{z^{(i)}}$, which other players can verify using their shares. If it is not consistent, then the honest parties will agree on this, and they publish their shares s_{ij} such that $z^{(i)}$ can be publicly reconstructed.

The first problem that arises when trying to adapt this protocol to VHHS is that there is no analogue of the Pedersen VSS in this setting. We solve this by using NIPVPs instead: in the first phase, each party $\mathcal{P}_i$ picks a polynomial $f^{(i)}(X) \in \mathbb{Z}_N[X]_{\leq k-1}$ and a $R^{(i)} \in \mathcal{E}$, then publishes $(R^{(i)}, R'^{(i)} = [f^{(i)}(0)]R)$ as a commitment to $z^{(i)} = f^{(i)}(0)$ and sends the share $s_{ij} = f^{(i)}(j)$ to party $\mathcal{P}_j$. It also constructs a piecewise verifiable proof $\pi = (\tilde{\pi}, \{\pi_i\}_{i \in \{0,...,n\}})$ using PVP.P in order to prove that there exists a polynomial $f^{(i)}(x)$ such that:

$$R'^{(i)} = [f^{(i)}(0)]R^{(i)} \text{ and } \forall j \in \{0,\ldots,n\} : f^{(i)}(j) = s_{ij}.$$

Using piecewise verifiability, each party $\mathcal{P}_j$ uses PVP.V to verify that $R'^{(i)} = [f^{(i)}(0)]R^{(i)}$ and $f^{(i)}(j) = s_{ij}$. The zero-knowledge property guarantees that the proof does not leak any information about s_{ij} to the other parties.

A second problem is that in the last phase of the Gennaro protocol, parties can compute $\prod_{i \in \mathcal{Q}} g^{z^{(i)}}$ from the $g^{z^{(i)}}$. This is not possible in the VHHS setting, because it is not possible to compute $[\sum_{i \in \mathcal{Q}} z^{(i)}]E_0$, given $[z^{(i)}]E_0$ for all $i \in \mathcal{Q}$.

We solve this problem by using the standard zero-knowledge proofs from Sect. 2.2 and a round-robin computation: Each party computes $F_i = [z^{(i)}]F_{i-1}$, where $F_0 = E_0$, and publishes this value together with a zero-knowledge proof that there exists an $a \in \mathbb{Z}_N$ such that $F_i = [a]F_{i-1}$ and $R'^{(i)} = [a]R^{(i)}$. This proves that $\mathcal{P}_i$ honestly added his share of the secret key to F_{i-1}.

Figure 1 presents CSI-RAShi, a robust DKG protocol based on Shamir secret sharing and non-interactive piecewise verifiable zero-knowledge proofs.

Theorem 3. *If both* ZK *and* PVP *are sound, then the distributed key generation protocol of Fig. 1 satisfies the correctness requirement of Definition 2. Moreover, if additionally $(\mathcal{E}, \mathbb{Z}_N)$ constitutes a very hard homogeneous space with map $\mathbb{Z}_N \times \mathcal{E} \to \mathcal{E} : (a, E) \mapsto [a]E$ and if* ZK *and* PVP *are zero-knowledge, then the DKG protocol satisfies the secrecy requirement of Definition 3.*

We prove Theorem 3 in the full version of the paper [2].

Cost. We consider the cost of evaluating $\mathcal{H}$ and C as negligible compared to group actions. In the VSS step, each party computes $2 + n\lambda$ group actions, which can be done in parallel. The public key generation step is innately sequential and players need to verify the proofs (in parallel) before advancing. In the first round, players can however already compute the commitments for the relation $(R^{(i)}, R'^{(i)})$ as part of their proof. Thus, the first round takes $1 + 4\lambda$, while subsequent rounds take $1 + 3\lambda$ group actions. Assuming n qualified players, we get the total sequential protocol cost of $T(n, \lambda) = 2 + \lambda + n(1 + 4\lambda)$. The actual computational effort per player is $T_{\mathcal{P}}(n, \lambda) = 3(1 + n\lambda)$. Note that both costs are independent of the threshold k. If corrupt parties misbehave, the honest parties have to compute up to $n - k$ additional group actions to recover the F_i, which is a small cost compared to the total cost of the execution of the protocol.

6   Instantiation Based on Isogenies

In this section, we instantiate the VHHS with supersingular elliptic curve isogeny graphs as in the CSIDH [6] and CSI-FiSh [4] settings. In this scenario, the elements in $\mathcal{E}$ are supersingular elliptic curves defined over the finite field $\mathbb{F}_p$ with endomorphism ring $\mathcal{O} \simeq \mathbb{Z}[\sqrt{-p}]$. The group $\mathcal{G}$ is the class group $\mathrm{Cl}(\mathbb{Z}[\sqrt{-p}])$, which acts freely and transitively on elements of $\mathcal{E}$ as follows

$$\mathfrak{a} * E = E/E[\mathfrak{a}], \text{ where } E[\mathfrak{a}] = \{P \in E(\mathbb{F}_p) \mid \alpha(P) = 0 \ \forall \alpha \in \mathfrak{a}\}$$

for $\mathfrak{a} \in \mathrm{Cl}(\mathbb{Z}[\sqrt{-p}])$. For efficiency reasons one chooses $p = 4 \prod_{i=1}^n \ell_i - 1$, where $\ell_1 < \cdots < \ell_{n-1}$ are the first $n - 1$ odd primes and ℓ_n is chosen, so that p becomes prime. With this choice, the group action can be efficiently computed as consecutive evaluations of ℓ_i-isogenies by representing them as $\mathfrak{a} = \prod_{i=1}^n \mathfrak{l}_i^{e_i}$, where $e_i \in [-b, b]$, b a small integer, and where $\mathfrak{l}_i = (\ell_i, \pi - 1)$ and $\mathfrak{l}_i^{-1} = (\ell_i, \pi + 1)$.

In order to represent arbitrary ideal classes with smooth ideals, we need to know the relation lattice and the group structure of $\mathrm{Cl}(\mathbb{Z}[\sqrt{-p}])$. This has been

---

CSI-RAShi

Generating the VSS. Each $\mathcal{P}_i$ samples $f^{(i)}(x)$ and $R^{(i)}$ uniformly from $\mathbb{Z}_N[x]_{\leq k-1}$ and $\mathcal{E}$, respectively, then determines $R'^{(i)} = [f^{(i)}(0)]R^{(i)}$ and computes the full statement

$$x^{(i)} = (x_0^{(i)} = (R^{(i)}, R'^{(i)}), \{x_j^{(i)} = f^{(i)}(j)\}_{j \in \{1,\ldots,n\}}).$$

Then, it constructs a piecewise verifiable proof

$$\pi^{(i)} = (\tilde{\pi}^{(i)}, \{\pi_j^{(i)}\}_{j \in \{0,\ldots,n\}}) \leftarrow \mathsf{PVP}.P^{\mathcal{O}}(x^{(i)}, f^{(i)}(x))$$

and publishes $(x_0^{(i)}, \tilde{\pi}^{(i)}, \pi_0^{(i)})$ and sends $(x_j^{(i)}, \pi_j^{(i)})$ privately to $\mathcal{P}_j$.

Verifying the VSS. Each $\mathcal{P}_j$ verifies all the proof pieces with respect to the $R'^{(i)} = [f^{(i)}(0)]R^{(i)}$ and the $f^{(i)}(j) = s_{ij}$ part of the statement: For each $i \neq j$ it runs $\mathsf{PVP}.V^{\mathcal{O}}(0, x_0^{(i)}, \tilde{\pi}^{(i)}, \pi_0^{(i)})$ and $\mathsf{PVP}.V^{\mathcal{O}}(j, x_j^{(i)}, \tilde{\pi}^{(i)}, \pi_j^{(i)})$. If at least one of these checks fails $\mathcal{P}_j$ broadcasts a complaint against $\mathcal{P}_i$.

Any player with at least k complaints is disqualified. If $\mathcal{P}_j$ complains that $\mathcal{P}_i$'s proof does not verify, $\mathcal{P}_i$ responds by broadcasting $(x_j^{(i)}, \pi_j^{(i)})$ so that everyone can verify $\mathsf{PVP}.V^{\mathcal{O}}(j, x_j^{(i)}, \tilde{\pi}^{(i)}, \pi_j^{(i)})$. If this verification succeeds, the protocol continues as normal, otherwise $\mathcal{P}_i$ is disqualified. Since disqualifying players happens on the basis of only broadcasted information, all the honest players will agree on the same set of qualified parties $\mathcal{Q} \subset \{1, \ldots, n\}$.

Compute shares. At this point the joint secret key is implicitly defined as $s = \sum_{i \in \mathcal{Q}} f^{(i)}(0)$. Each party $\mathcal{P}_j$ derives their share of s as $s_j = \sum_{i \in \mathcal{Q}} x_j^{(i)}$.

Compute common public key.

1. In a round-robin way, the qualified players compute $F_i = [f^{(i)}(0)]F_{i-1}$, where $F_0 = E_0$. At each step, player $\mathcal{P}_i$ publishes the proof

   $$\pi'^{(i)} \leftarrow \mathsf{ZK}.P((R^{(i)}, R'^{(i)}), (F_{i-1}, F_i), f^{(i)}(0)),$$

   which is verified by all other parties.
2. If $\mathcal{P}_j$ finds that the proof by player $\mathcal{P}_i$ is wrong, it publishes $(x_j^{(i)}, \pi_j^{(i)})$. Then, every party runs $\mathsf{PVP}.V^{\mathcal{O}}(j, x_j^{(i)}, \tilde{\pi}^{(i)}, \pi_j^{(i)})$ for all the published pairs. If there are k honest players, then at least k parties can publish a tuple $(x_j^{(i)}, \pi_j^{(i)})$ for which the verification will succeed, so the honest parties can all reconstruct $f^{(i)}(0)$, compute F_i, and continue the protocol.
3. The parties return $F_{|\mathcal{Q}|}$ as their public key.

Fig. 1. CSI-RAShi, a robust DKG protocol using NIPVPs for the relations $R_0 = \{((R, R'), f(x)) | [f(0)]R = R'\}$ and $R_i = \{(x_i, f) | x_i = f(i)\}$ with witness space $\mathbb{Z}_N[x]_{\leq k-1}$.

computed for the CSIDH-512 parameter set ($n = 74$, $\ell_n = 587$) in [4], making it possible to efficiently evaluate the action of arbitrary ideal classes. The authors in [4] found that e.g. $\mathfrak{l}_1 = (3, \pi - 1)$ generates the full group. The full group order is divisible by 3 (and 37), thus for $n > 2$ (or $n > 36$) players, we need to work in a subgroup of $\#\mathrm{Cl}(\mathbb{Z}[\sqrt{-p}])$, generated by $\mathfrak{l}_1^3$ (or $\mathfrak{l}_1^{111}$). With current optimizations [21], group actions can be evaluated in about 35 ms on a commercial CPU.

Security. While the CSIDH-512 parameter set is believed to provide 128 bits of classical security, its quantum security is much lower and still an object of discussion (cf. e.g. [5, 8, 24]). Determining larger parameter sets currently seems out of reach using classical computers [4]. Luckily, the ideal class group can be computed in quantum polynomial time [11], so switching to larger parameter sets should be possible well before the CSIDH-512 parameters are broken.

Protocol Cost. Using the runtime from Sect. 5 and plugging in the standard security parameter of $\lambda = 128$ and the estimate of 35 ms per isogeny, we can express the estimated runtime as $T(n, \lambda) = (4.6 + 18.0n)$ seconds. This makes the cost of the key generation step considerably lower than e.g. the cost of the distributed signature computation in the Sashimi protocol [10], which for three players takes about five minutes per participating player.

7   Conclusion

We introduced a new primitive called *piecewise verifiable proofs* (PVP), providing an alternative to Pedersen commitments in the very hard homogeneous spaces (VHHS) setting. Using PVPs we created CSI-RAShi, a robust and actively secure distributed key generation protocol in the Quantum Random Oracle model. When instantiated with the CSIDH-512 parameter set, the execution time of CSI-RAShi with n participants takes approximately $4.5 + 18n$ seconds.

It would be of interest to further reduce this runtime, while keeping the protocol actively secure. Especially the public key computation step currently takes about twice as long as the secret sharing step and relies on a sequential round-robin structure with expensive zero-knowledge proofs. We also leave it as an open problem to prove that our protocol, or an adaptation thereof, is secure against adaptive corruptions.

In analogy to [13], the instantiation of our protocol with isogenies relies on the knowledge of the underlying class group structure and relation lattice. So far, this has only been computed for the CSIDH-512 parameter set, whose current security estimate is assumed to be below the NIST-1 level [5, 8, 24]. It would be of considerable interest to also compute the class group and relation lattice for higher parameter sets.

For future research, it would also be interesting to use piecewise verifiable proofs as building blocks in other cryptographic protocols. In particular, we expect PVPs or adaptations thereof to be a useful tool for constructing other threshold schemes, such as signatures and/or decryption algorithms or in multi-party computations.

A   Security Proof of NIPVP

A.1   Completeness

Lemma 1. *Algorithms 3 and 4 constitute a complete NIPVP in the QROM for the list of relations of (1) if the used commitment scheme is collapsing and quantum computationally hiding.*

Proof. If the protocol is followed correctly and if the input was a valid statement-witness pair $(x, w) \in R$, then the verifier will accept the proof piece with probability 1.

- In the case $i = 0$ the verifier will accept the proofs because the curves $\widetilde{E}_j$ recomputed by the verifier match the curves $\hat{E}_j$ computed by the prover: for each $j \in \{1, \ldots, \lambda\}$, if $c_j = 0$, then $r_j = b_j$ and hence $\widetilde{E}_j = [r_j(0)]E_0 = [b_j(0)]E_0 = \hat{E}_j$. If $c_j = 1$, then $r_j(0) = b_j(0) - f(0)$, so again we have $\widetilde{E}_j = [r_j(0)]E_1 = [b_j(0) - f(0)][f(0)]E_0 = [b_j(0)]E_0 = \hat{E}_j$. Thus both C_0 are equal and the verifier will accept.
- In the case $i > 0$ for each $j \in \{1, \ldots, \lambda\}$, the prover computes $b_j(i)$, and the verifier computes $r_j(i) + c_j x_j = b_j(i) - c_j f(i) + c_j x_j = b_j(i)$, if $x_i = f(i)$. So if the witness is valid, then the C_i match and the verifier will accept.   □

A.2   Soundness

Our protocol can be seen as a "weak" Fiat-Shamir transformed version of a sigma protocol, where by "weak" we mean that, to obtain a challenge we only hash the commitment (instead of hashing both the commitment and the statement). The known results on the security of the FS transform in the QROM are about the strong FS transform. Therefore, before we can prove the soundness of our protocol we first prove the following lemma, which allows us to prove the security of the weak FS transform. This lemma bootstraps the known results for the strong FS transform to prove the soundness of the weak FS transform of a sigma protocol where the first message of the prover commits to the statement.

Lemma 2. *Suppose $\Sigma = (P_1, V_1, P_2, V_2)$ is a sigma protocol for the relation R with superpolynomially sized challenge space Ch, special soundness and quantum computationally unique responses. Let $\Sigma' = (P', V')$ be the following sigma protocol:*

$$P_1'(x, w) : y \leftarrow \{0, 1\}^\lambda, C_x \leftarrow C(x, y), com \leftarrow P_1(x, w),$$
$$com' = (C_x, com)$$
$$V_1'(com') : ch \leftarrow Ch$$
$$P_2'(ch) : rsp \leftarrow P_2(ch), rsp' \leftarrow (x, y, rsp)$$
$$V_2'(x, com', ch, rsp') : accept \ if \ C_x = C(x, y) \ and \ V_2(x, com, ch, rsp) = 1$$

Then the weak Fiat-Shamir transformed version of Σ' is a quantum proof of knowledge for the same relation R, assuming that C is collapsing.

Proof. The strategy of the proof is to interpret the weak FS transform for the relation R as the strong FS transformed protocol for a different relation R'. We can then use the techniques of Don et al. [16] on the security of the strong FS transform in the QROM. We define the following relation

$$R' = \{(\mathsf{C}_x, (x, y, w)) \mid \mathsf{C}_x = \mathcal{C}(x, y) \text{ and } (x, w) \in R\},$$

and the following sigma protocol $\Sigma'' = (P'', V'')$:

$$\begin{aligned}
P_1''(\mathsf{C}_x, (x, y, w)) &: com \leftarrow P_1(x, w) \\
V_1''(com) &: ch \leftarrow \mathcal{C}h \\
P_2''(ch) &: rsp'' \leftarrow (x, y, P_2(ch)) \\
V_2''(\mathsf{C}_x, com, ch, rsp'') &: \text{accept if } \mathsf{C}_x = \mathcal{C}(x, y) \text{ and } V_2(x, com, ch, rsp) = 1
\end{aligned}$$

Observe that the adaptive proof of knowledge game against the weak FS transform of Σ' is identical to the adaptive proof of knowledge game against the strong FS transform of Σ'', so it suffices to prove that $FS(\Sigma'')$ is a quantum proof of knowledge to finish the proof. We do this by invoking the theorems of Don et al. [16, Th. 25 and Cor. 16], which say that if Σ'' has special soundness, quantum computationally unique responses and a superpolynomial challenge space, then $FS(\Sigma'')$ is a quantum proof of knowledge. Note that the challenge space $\mathcal{C}h$ is superpolynomial by assumption.

Special Soundness.[2] Suppose we are given two accepting transcripts $\mathsf{C}_x, com, ch, (x, y, rsp)$ and $\mathsf{C}_x, com, ch', (x', y', rsp')$ with $ch \neq ch'$, which means

$$\mathsf{C}_x = \mathcal{C}(x, y) = \mathcal{C}(x', y'), \text{ and}$$
$$V_2(x, com, ch, rsp) = V_2(x', com, ch', rsp') = \text{accept}.$$

Then, we can either extract a collision $\mathcal{C}(x, y) = \mathcal{C}(x', y')$ for $\mathcal{C}$ in the case $x \neq x'$, or we can invoke the special soundness of Σ to obtain a witness w such that $(x, w) \in R$, which means we can construct a witness $w' = (x, y, w)$ such that $(\mathsf{C}_x, w') \in R'$.

Quantum Computationally Unique Responses ([16, Def. 24]). We define 3 games Game_i for $i \in \{1, 2, 3\}$, played by a two-stage poly-time adversary $\mathcal{A} = (\mathcal{A}_1, \mathcal{A}_2)$:

---

[2] Our extractor is not guaranteed to output a witness, instead it is allowed to output a collision in $\mathcal{C}$. This means that the extractor for the FS transformed protocol could also output a collision for $\mathcal{C}$ instead of outputting a witness. This is not a problem, because $\mathcal{C}$ is assumed to be collapsing, which implies that an efficient adversary can only output collisions with negligible probability [29].

$$\mathsf{Game}_i^{\mathcal{A}}() : \quad (x, y, rsp), com, ch \leftarrow \mathcal{A}_1()$$

$$z \leftarrow V_2(x, com, ch, rsp) \text{ and } \mathsf{C}_x = \mathcal{C}(x, y)$$

$$\text{if } i \in \{1, 2\} \quad rsp \leftarrow \mathcal{M}(rsp)$$

$$\text{if } i \in \{1\} \quad (x, y) \leftarrow \mathcal{M}(x, y)$$

$$(com, ch) \leftarrow \mathcal{M}(com, ch)$$

$$b \leftarrow \mathcal{A}_2(x, y, rsp, com, ch)$$

Then the sigma protocol has quantum computationally unique responses if for any adversary $\mathcal{A}$, the following advantage is a negligible function of the security parameter:

$$Adv = \left| \Pr_{\mathsf{Game}_1^{\mathcal{A}}}[z = b = 1] - \Pr_{\mathsf{Game}_3^{\mathcal{A}}}[z = b = 1] \right|. \tag{2}$$

This follows immediately from the assumptions, because the assumption that $\mathcal{C}$ is collapsing implies that $\left| \Pr_{\mathsf{Game}_1^{\mathcal{A}}}[z = b = 1] - \Pr_{\mathsf{Game}_2^{\mathcal{A}}}[z = b = 1] \right|$ is negligible, and the assumption that Σ has quantum computationally unique responses implies that $\left| \Pr_{\mathsf{Game}_2^{\mathcal{A}}}[z = b = 1] - \Pr_{\mathsf{Game}_3^{\mathcal{A}}}[z = b = 1] \right|$ is negligible. $\qquad\square$

Lemma 3. *Algorithms 3 and 4 constitute a sound NIPVP in the QROM for the list of relations of (1) if the used commitment scheme is collapsing.*

Proof. We need to prove that for any $I \subseteq \{0, \dots, n\}$ and any QPT adversary $\mathcal{A}^{\mathcal{O}}$, the following advantage is negligible:

$$\mathsf{Adv}_{\mathcal{A},I}^{\mathsf{sound}}(\lambda) = \Pr \left[\begin{matrix} \forall i \in I : V^{\mathcal{O}}(i, x_i, \tilde{\pi}, \pi_i) = 1 \\ \nexists w : (x_I, w) \in R_I \end{matrix} \middle| (x_I, \pi_I) \leftarrow \mathcal{A}^{\mathcal{O}}(1^\lambda) \right].$$

If $|I| < k$, then $\mathsf{Adv}_{\mathcal{A},I}^{\mathsf{sound}} = 0$ for any $\mathcal{A}$, simply because for every x_I, there exists a $w \in \mathbb{Z}_N[x]_{\leq k-1}$ such that $(x_I, w) \in R_I$. Therefore, we can focus on the case $|I| \geq k$ for the remainder of the proof. We fix $I \subset \{0, \dots, n\}$ with $|I| \geq k$. We define the function F as follows

$$F : \{0, 1\}^\lambda \times \mathcal{X}_I \times (\{0, 1\}^\lambda)^I \times (\mathbb{Z}_N[x]_{\leq k-1})^\lambda \to (\{0, 1\}^{2\lambda})^I$$

$$(\mathbf{c}, x_I, y_I, \mathbf{r}) \mapsto \{C_i'\}_{i \in I},$$

where $C_0' = \mathcal{C}([r_1(0)]E_{c_1}|| \cdots ||[r_\lambda(0)]E_{c_\lambda}||x_0, y_0)$ (if $0 \in I$), and where $C_i' = \mathcal{C}(r_1(i) + c_1 x_i|| \cdots ||r_\lambda(i) + c_\lambda x_i||x_i, y_i)$. With this notation we have $V^{\mathcal{O}}(i, x_i, \tilde{\pi}, \pi_i) = 1$ for all $i \in I$ if and only if $F(\mathcal{O}(C), x_I, y_I, \mathbf{r}) = C_I$ and $C_i' = \mathcal{C}(x_i, y_i)$ for all $i \in I$. So the claim that the advantage $\mathsf{Adv}_{\mathcal{A},I}^{\mathsf{sound}}(\lambda)$ is negligible for every efficient adversary $\mathcal{A}$ is equivalent to the claim that the "weak" FS transform of the following sigma protocol $\Sigma' = (P_1', V_1', P_2', V_2')$ is a quantum computationally sound proof for R_I ([16, Def. 9]):

$$P_1'(x_I, w) : y_I, y_I' \leftarrow (\{0,1\}^\lambda)^I, \mathsf{C}_i' \leftarrow \mathcal{C}(x_i, y_i') \text{ for all } i \in I,$$
$$\mathbf{b} \leftarrow (\mathbb{Z}_N[x]_{\leq k-1})^\lambda, \mathsf{C}_I = F(0, x_I, y_I, \mathbf{b})$$
$$V_1'(\mathsf{C}_I, \mathsf{C}_I') : \mathbf{c} \leftarrow \{0,1\}^\lambda$$
$$P_2'(\mathbf{c}) : \mathbf{r} \leftarrow \mathbf{b} - \mathbf{c} \cdot w, rsp \leftarrow (y_I, y_I', \mathbf{r})$$
$$V_2'(rsp) : \text{ accept if } \mathsf{C}_I = F(\mathbf{c}, x_I, y_I, \mathbf{r}) \text{ and } \mathsf{C}_i' = \mathcal{C}(x_i, y_i) \text{ for all } i \in I$$

Since quantum computational soundness is implied by the quantum proof of knowledge property, it suffices to prove that the weak FS transform of Σ' is a quantum proof of knowledge. This sigma protocol takes the form of Σ' in the statement of Lemma 2, so we can conclude that our NIPVP is sound if the sigma protocol $\Sigma = (P_1, V_1, P_2, V_2)$ with

$$P_1(x_I, w) : y_I \leftarrow (\{0,1\}^\lambda)^I, \mathbf{b} \leftarrow (\mathbb{Z}_N[x]_{\leq k-1})^\lambda, \mathsf{C}_I = F(0, x_I, y_I, \mathbf{b})$$
$$V_1(\mathsf{C}_I) : \mathbf{c} \leftarrow \{0,1\}^\lambda$$
$$P_2(\mathbf{c}) : \mathbf{r} \leftarrow \mathbf{b} - \mathbf{c} \cdot w, rsp \leftarrow (\mathbf{r}, y_I)$$
$$V_2(rsp) : \text{ accept if } \mathsf{C}_I = F(\mathbf{c}, x_I, y_I, \mathbf{r})$$

has a superpolynomial challenge space, special soundness and quantum computationally unique responses.

Superpolynomial Challenge Space. The size of the challenge space is 2^λ, which is superpolynomial in λ.

Special Soundness.[3] Let $x_I, \mathsf{C}_I, \mathbf{c}, \mathbf{r}$ and $x_I, \mathsf{C}_I, \mathbf{c}'', \mathbf{r}'$ be two accepting transcripts with $\mathbf{c} \neq \mathbf{c}'$. Take $j \in \{1, \dots, \lambda\}$ such that $c_j \neq c_j'$, without loss of generality we can assume $c_j = 0$ and $c_j' = 1$. Then, if $0 \in I$ and $[r_j(0)]E_0 \neq [r'(0)]E_1$, we found a collision in $\mathcal{C}$. Similarly, if for some non-zero $i \in I$ we have $r_j(i) \neq r_j'(i) + x_i$, we also have a collision for $\mathcal{C}$. If there is no collision, we have

$$r_j(i) = r_j'(i) + x_i \text{ for all } i \in I, i > 0, \text{ and}$$
$$[r_j(0)]E_0 = [r'(0)]E_1 \quad (\text{if } 0 \in I),$$

so $r_j(x) - r_j'(x)$ is a witness for x_I.

Quantum Computationally Unique Responses. Notice that F factors as $F = G \circ H$, where H is the function that given $\mathbf{c}, x_I$ and $\mathbf{r}$ computes the input to the commitment function $\mathcal{C}$, and where G takes the output of H and the commitment randomness y_I and outputs C_I. We define 3 games Game_i for $i \in$

---

[3] Similar to the proof of Lemma 2, our special soundness extractor outputs either a witness w such that $(x, w) \in R$, or a collision for $\mathcal{C}$. Since $\mathcal{C}$ is collision resistant, this is not a problem, because the PoK extractor can only output a collision with negligible probability.

$\{1, 2, 3\}$, played by a two-stage poly-time adversary $\mathcal{A} = (\mathcal{A}_1, \mathcal{A}_2)$:

$$\mathsf{Game}_i^{\mathcal{A}}() : \quad (y_I, \mathbf{r}), (C_i, \mathbf{c}) \leftarrow \mathcal{A}_1()$$
$$z \leftarrow 1 \text{ if } C_I = F(\mathbf{c}, x_I, y_I, \mathbf{r}) \text{ and } 0 \text{ otherwise.}$$
$$\text{if } i = 3 \quad \mathbf{r} \leftarrow \mathcal{M}(\mathbf{r})$$
$$\text{if } i \in \{2, 3\} \quad (h, y_I) \leftarrow \mathcal{M}(H(\mathbf{c}, x_I, \mathbf{r}), y_I)$$
$$(C_I, \mathbf{c}) \leftarrow \mathcal{M}(C_I, \mathbf{c})$$
$$b \leftarrow \mathcal{A}_2(x, y, rsp, com, ch)$$

We need to prove that for any efficient $\mathcal{A}$ the following is a negligible function:

$$\left| \Pr_{\mathsf{Game}_1^{\mathcal{A}}}[z = b = 1] - \Pr_{\mathsf{Game}_3^{\mathcal{A}}}[z = b = 1] \right| .$$

Since G is just the parallel composition of $|I|$ instances of $\mathcal{C}$, and since we assumed that $\mathcal{C}$ is collapsing it follows that G is collapsing. Therefore we have that $\left| \Pr_{\mathsf{Game}_1^{\mathcal{A}}}[z = b = 1] - \Pr_{\mathsf{Game}_2^{\mathcal{A}}}[z = b = 1] \right|$ is negligible. Since for a fixed value of x_I and $\mathbf{c}$, the function $H(\mathbf{c}, x_I, \cdot)$ is injective (here we use that $|I| \geq k$), we get that after measuring h and $\mathbf{c}$, the register $\mathbf{r}$ is not in a superposition of basis vectors. Therefore, the measurement $\mathbf{r} \leftarrow \mathcal{M}(\mathbf{r})$ does not affect the state of the system and we have $\Pr_{\mathsf{Game}_2^{\mathcal{A}}}[z = b = 1] = \Pr_{\mathsf{Game}_3^{\mathcal{A}}}[z = b = 1]$. □

A.3   Zero-Knowledge

For a fixed $I \subseteq \{0, \ldots, n\}$, our security definition of zero-knowledge for NIPVP is similar to the standard definition of non-interactive zero-knowledge in the QROM (e.g. [31, Def. 6]), except that the simulator is only given a partial statement x_I, instead of the full statement $\mathbf{x}$. Our proof strategy is to first reduce the NIPVP soundness to the standard zero-knowledge property of a standard sigma protocol. Then, we can use the results of Unruh [31] to finish the proof.

Lemma 4. *Fix $I \subset \{0, \ldots, n\}$ and suppose $\mathsf{Sim} = (\mathsf{Sim}_1, \mathsf{Sim}_2)$ is a zero-knowledge simulator for the "weak" FS transform of the sigma protocol $\Sigma = (P_1, V_1, P_2, V_2)$ for the relation R_I.*

$$P_1(x_I, w) : y_I, y_I' \leftarrow (\{0, 1\}^\lambda)^I, C_i' \leftarrow \mathcal{C}(x_i, y_i') \text{ for all } i \in I,$$
$$\mathbf{b} \leftarrow (\mathbb{Z}_N[x]_{\leq k-1})^\lambda, C_I = F(0, x_I, y_I, \mathbf{b})$$
$$V_1(C_I, C_I') : \mathbf{c} \leftarrow \{0, 1\}^\lambda$$
$$P_2(\mathbf{c}) : \mathbf{r} \leftarrow \mathbf{b} - \mathbf{c} \cdot w, rsp \leftarrow (y_I, y_I', \mathbf{r})$$
$$V_2(rsp) : \text{accept if } C_I = F(\mathbf{c}, x_I, y_I, \mathbf{r}) \text{ and } C_i' = \mathcal{C}(x_i, y_i) \text{ for all } i \in I .$$

Then there exists a simulator $\mathsf{Sim}' = (\mathsf{Sim}_1', \mathsf{Sim}_2')$ such that for any QPT distinguisher $\mathcal{A}$, the distinguishing advantage

$$\mathsf{Adv}_{\mathsf{Sim}, \mathcal{A}}^{\mathsf{zk}} = \left| \Pr\left[\mathcal{A}^{P', \mathcal{O}}(1^\lambda) = 1 \right] - \Pr\left[\mathcal{A}^{S', \mathsf{Sim}_2'}(1^\lambda) = 1 \right] \right| ,$$

is a negligible function of the security parameter, where P' is an oracle that on input $(\mathbf{x}, w) \in R$ runs $\pi := P^{\mathcal{O}}(\mathbf{x}, w)$ and outputs $\pi_I = (\tilde{\pi}, \{\pi_i\}_{i \in I})$ and S' is an oracle that on input $(\mathbf{x}, w) \in R$ returns $\mathsf{Sim}'_1(\{x_i\}_{i \in I})$.

Proof. The simulator Sim'_2 simply forwards all its queries to Sim_2, and Sim'_1 forwards his queries to Sim_1 to obtain $C_I, y_I, y'_I, \mathbf{r}$. Then, for all $i \notin I$ the simulator Sim'_1 commits to dummy values to produce C_i and C'_i. Then Sim'_1 outputs $\tilde{\pi} = (C, C', \mathbf{r}), \{\pi_i = (y_i, y'_i)\}_{i \in I}$.

We prove the lemma with a simple hybrid argument: Let Sim'' be identical to Sim' except that it interacts with a real prover for Σ, instead of with Sim. Then, because Sim is supposed to be computationally indistinguishable from a real prover, we have that $\left| \Pr\left[\mathcal{A}^{S', \mathsf{Sim}'_2}(1^{\lambda}) = 1 \right] - \Pr\left[\mathcal{A}^{S'', \mathsf{Sim}''_2}(1^{\lambda}) = 1 \right] \right|$ is negligible. Secondly, since the only difference between an honest prover for the NIPVP protocol and Sim'' is that Sim'' commits to dummy values instead of real values for $i \notin I$, it follows from the quantum computationally hiding property of the commitment scheme that $\left| \Pr\left[\mathcal{A}^{P', \mathcal{O}}(1^{\lambda}) = 1 \right] - \Pr\left[\mathcal{A}^{S'', \mathsf{Sim}''_2}(1^{\lambda}) = 1 \right] \right|$ is negligible. □

Lemma 5. *Algorithms 3 and 4 form a zero-knowledge NIPVP in the QROM for the list of relations of (1) if the used commitment scheme is quantum computationally hiding and collapsing.*

Proof. In light of Lemma 4, if suffices to prove that for every $I \subseteq \{0, \dots, n\}$, the "weak" FS transform of the sigma protocol Σ_I is zero-knowledge. Unruh proved (Theorem 20 of [31]) that if a sigma protocol has HVZK, completeness and unpredictable commitments, then the "strong" FS transform of that sigma protocol is zero-knowledge, but the proof goes through without problems in case of a "weak" FS transform also. Therefore, it suffices to prove for each $I \subset \{0, \dots, n\}$, that Σ_I has HVZK, completeness and unpredictable commitments.

Completeness. The protocol has perfect completeness. The proof is similar to the proof of Lemma 1.

Unpredictable Commitments. We say the sigma protocol has unpredictable commitments if the commitments have superlogarithmic collision entropy. More concretely, if there exists a negligible function $\mu(\lambda)$, such that for every $(x_I, w) \in R_I$ we have

$$\Pr[(C_I, C'_I) = (C''_I, C'''_I) | (C_I, C'_I) \leftarrow P_1(x_I, w), (C''_I, C'''_I) \leftarrow P_1(x_I, w)] \leq \mu(\lambda).$$

Let $i \in I$, then since C_i and C''_i are commitments, there are two possible ways to get a collision:

- The first possibility is that both commit to the same value. But since C_i commits to λ uniformly random elements of $\mathcal{G}$ (or $\mathcal{E}$ in case $i = 0$), the probability that this happens is negligible.

- The second possibility is that both commitments commit to different values. Since we assume that $\mathcal{C}$ is collapsing (which implies collision resistance), this can also only happen with negligible probability.

Honest Verifier Zero Knowledge. The protocol has perfect HVZK. Consider the simulator that picks $y_I, y'_I, \mathbf{r}$ and $\mathbf{c}$ uniformly at random and sets $\mathsf{C}_I = F(\mathbf{c}, x_I, y_I, \mathbf{r})$ and $\mathsf{C}'_i = \mathcal{C}(x_i, y'_i)$ for all $i \in I$.

This produces the same distribution of transcripts as honest executions of the protocol, because in both cases $y_I.y'_I, \mathbf{r}$ and $\mathbf{c}$ are uniformly random, and the rest of the transcript is a function of $y_I, y'_I, \mathbf{r}$ and $\mathbf{c}$.

References

1. Adida, B.: Helios: web-based open-audit voting. In: USENIX Security Symposium, vol. 17, pp. 335–348 (2008)
2. Beullens, W., Disson, L., Pedersen, R., Vercauteren, F.: CSI-RASHi: distributed key generation for CSIDH (2020)
3. Beullens, W., Katsumata, S., Pintore, F.: Calamari and falafl: logarithmic (linkable) ring signatures from isogenies and lattices. In: Moriai, S., Wang, H. (eds.) ASIACRYPT 2020. LNCS, vol. 12492, pp. 464–492. Springer, Cham (2020). https://doi.org/10.1007/978-3-030-64834-3_16
4. Beullens, W., Kleinjung, T., Vercauteren, F.: CSI-FiSh: efficient isogeny based signatures through class group computations. In: Galbraith, S.D., Moriai, S. (eds.) ASIACRYPT 2019. LNCS, vol. 11921, pp. 227–247. Springer, Cham (2019). https://doi.org/10.1007/978-3-030-34578-5_9
5. Bonnetain, X., Schrottenloher, A.: Quantum security analysis of CSIDH. In: Canteaut, A., Ishai, Y. (eds.) EUROCRYPT 2020. LNCS, vol. 12106, pp. 493–522. Springer, Cham (2020). https://doi.org/10.1007/978-3-030-45724-2_17
6. Castryck, W., Lange, T., Martindale, C., Panny, L., Renes, J.: CSIDH: an efficient post-quantum commutative group action. In: Peyrin, T., Galbraith, S. (eds.) ASIACRYPT 2018. LNCS, vol. 11274, pp. 395–427. Springer, Cham (2018). https://doi.org/10.1007/978-3-030-03332-3_15
7. Castryck, W., Sotáková, J., Vercauteren, F.: Breaking the decisional Diffie-Hellman problem for class group actions using genus theory. IACR Cryptology ePrint Archive 2020, 151 (2020)
8. Chavez-Saab, J., Chi-Dominguez, J.-J., Jaques, S., Rodriguez-Henriquez, F.: The SQALE of CSIDH: square-root vélu quantum-resistant isogeny action with low exponents. Technical report, Cryptology ePrint Archive, Report 2020/1520 (2020). https://eprint.iacr.org
9. Couveignes, J.M.: Hard homogeneous spaces. IACR Cryptology ePrint Archive 2006, 291 (2006)
10. Cozzo, D., Smart, N.P.: Sashimi: cutting up CSI-FiSh secret keys to produce an actively secure distributed signing protocol. In: Ding, J., Tillich, J.-P. (eds.) PQCrypto 2020. LNCS, vol. 12100, pp. 169–186. Springer, Cham (2020). https://doi.org/10.1007/978-3-030-44223-1_10
11. De Feo, L., Galbraith, S.D.: SeaSign: compact isogeny signatures from class group actions. In: Ishai, Y., Rijmen, V. (eds.) EUROCRYPT 2019. LNCS, vol. 11478, pp. 759–789. Springer, Cham (2019). https://doi.org/10.1007/978-3-030-17659-4_26

12. De Feo, L., Jao, D., Plût, J.: Towards quantum-resistant cryptosystems from super singular elliptic curve isogenies. J. Math. Cryptol. **8**(3), 209–247 (2014)
13. De Feo, L., Meyer, M.: Threshold schemes from isogeny assumptions. In: Kiayias, A., Kohlweiss, M., Wallden, P., Zikas, V. (eds.) PKC 2020. LNCS, vol. 12111, pp. 187–212. Springer, Cham (2020). https://doi.org/10.1007/978-3-030-45388-6_7
14. Desmedt, Y.: Threshold cryptosystems. In: Seberry, J., Zheng, Y. (eds.) AUSCRYPT 1992. LNCS, vol. 718, pp. 1–14. Springer, Heidelberg (1993). https://doi.org/10.1007/3-540-57220-1_47
15. Desmedt, Y., Frankel, Y.: Shared generation of authenticators and signatures. In: Feigenbaum, J. (ed.) CRYPTO 1991. LNCS, vol. 576, pp. 457–469. Springer, Heidelberg (1992). https://doi.org/10.1007/3-540-46766-1_37
16. Don, J., Fehr, S., Majenz, C., Schaffner, C.: Security of the Fiat-Shamir transformation in the quantum random-oracle model. In: Boldyreva, A., Micciancio, D. (eds.) CRYPTO 2019. LNCS, vol. 11693, pp. 356–383. Springer, Cham (2019). https://doi.org/10.1007/978-3-030-26951-7_13
17. Gennaro, R., Jarecki, S., Krawczyk, H., Rabin, T.: Robust threshold DSS signatures. In: Maurer, U. (ed.) EUROCRYPT 1996. LNCS, vol. 1070, pp. 354–371. Springer, Heidelberg (1996). https://doi.org/10.1007/3-540-68339-9_31
18. Gennaro, R., Jarecki, S., Krawczyk, H., Rabin, T.: Secure distributed key generation for discrete-log based cryptosystems. J. Cryptol. **20**(1), 51–83 (2007)
19. Harn, L.: Group-oriented (t, n) threshold digital signature scheme and digital multisignature. IEE Proc. Comput. Digit. Tech. **141**(5), 307–313 (1994)
20. Kate, A.: Distributed key generation and its applications (2010)
21. Meyer, M., Reith, S.: A faster way to the CSIDH. In: Chakraborty, D., Iwata, T. (eds.) INDOCRYPT 2018. LNCS, vol. 11356, pp. 137–152. Springer, Cham (2018). https://doi.org/10.1007/978-3-030-05378-9_8
22. National Institute of Standards and Technology. Threshold cryptography (2020)
23. Pedersen, T.P.: A threshold cryptosystem without a trusted party. In: Davies, D.W. (ed.) EUROCRYPT 1991. LNCS, vol. 547, pp. 522–526. Springer, Heidelberg (1991). https://doi.org/10.1007/3-540-46416-6_47
24. Peikert, C.: He gives C-sieves on the CSIDH. In: Canteaut, A., Ishai, Y. (eds.) EUROCRYPT 2020. LNCS, vol. 12106, pp. 463–492. Springer, Cham (2020). https://doi.org/10.1007/978-3-030-45724-2_16
25. Rabin, T., Ben-Or, M.: Verifiable secret sharing and multiparty protocols with honest majority. In: Proceedings of the Twenty-First Annual ACM Symposium on Theory of Computing, pp. 73–85 (1989)
26. Rostovtsev, A., Stolbunov, A.: Public-key cryptosystem based on isogenies. IACR Cryptology ePrint Archive 2006, 145 (2006)
27. Shamir, A.: How to share a secret. Commun. ACM **22**(11), 612–613 (1979)
28. Shoup, V.: Practical threshold signatures. In: Preneel, B. (ed.) EUROCRYPT 2000. LNCS, vol. 1807, pp. 207–220. Springer, Heidelberg (2000). https://doi.org/10.1007/3-540-45539-6_15
29. Unruh, D.: Collapse-binding quantum commitments without random oracles. In: Cheon, J.H., Takagi, T. (eds.) ASIACRYPT 2016. LNCS, vol. 10032, pp. 166–195. Springer, Heidelberg (2016). https://doi.org/10.1007/978-3-662-53890-6_6
30. Unruh, D.: Computationally binding quantum commitments. In: Fischlin, M., Coron, J.-S. (eds.) EUROCRYPT 2016. LNCS, vol. 9666, pp. 497–527. Springer, Heidelberg (2016). https://doi.org/10.1007/978-3-662-49896-5_18
31. Unruh, D.: Post-quantum security of Fiat-Shamir. In: Takagi, T., Peyrin, T. (eds.) ASIACRYPT 2017. LNCS, vol. 10624, pp. 65–95. Springer, Cham (2017). https://doi.org/10.1007/978-3-319-70694-8_3

SimS: A Simplification of SiGamal

Tako Boris Fouotsa[1]([✉])[iD] and Christophe Petit[2,3][iD]

[1] Università Degli Studi Roma Tre, Rome, Italy
takoboris.fouotsa@uniroma3.it
[2] Université Libre de Bruxelles, Brussels, Belgium
[3] University of Birmingham's School of Computer Science, Birmingham, UK

Abstract. At Asiacrypt 2020, Moriya et al. introduced two new IND-CPA secure supersingular isogeny based Public Key Encryption (PKE) protocols: SiGamal and C-SiGamal. Unlike the PKEs canonically derived from SIDH and CSIDH, the new protocols provide IND-CPA security without the use of hash functions. SiGamal and C-SiGamal are however not IND-CCA secure. Moriya et al. suggested a variant of SiGamal that could be IND-CCA secure, but left its study as an open problem.

In this paper, we revisit the protocols introduced by Moriya et al. First, we show that the SiGamal variant suggested by Moriya et al. for IND-CCA security is, in fact, not IND-CCA secure. Secondly, we propose a new isogeny-based PKE protocol named SimS, obtained by simplifying SiGamal. SimS has smaller public keys and ciphertexts than (C-)SiGamal and it is more efficient. We prove that SimS is IND-CCA secure under CSIDH security assumptions and one Knowledge of Exponent-type assumption we introduce. Interestingly, SimS is also much closer to the CSIDH protocol, facilitating a comparison between SiGamal and CSIDH.

Keywords: Post-quantum cryptography · Supersingular isogenies · PKE · CSIDH · SiGamal · SimS

1 Introduction

The construction of a large scale quantum computer would make the nowadays widely used public PKE schemes insecure, namely RSA [29], ECC [21] and their derivatives. As a response to the considerable progress in constructing quantum computers, NIST launched a standardization process for post-quantum secure protocols in December 2016 [26].

Isogeny-based protocols are in general based on the assumption that given two isogenous curves E and E', it is difficult to compute an isogeny from E to E'. This hard problem was used by J. M. Couveignes [11], Rostovtsev and Stolbunov [30] to design a key exchange protocol using ordinary isogenies, and by Charles, Goren and Lauter [8] to design a cryptographic hash function using supersingular isogenies. In 2011, as a countermeasure to the subexponential quantum attack on the CRS (Couveignes-Rostovtsev-Stolbunov)

© Springer Nature Switzerland AG 2021
J. H. Cheon and J.-P. Tillich (Eds.): PQCrypto 2021, LNCS 12841, pp. 277–295, 2021.
https://doi.org/10.1007/978-3-030-81293-5_15

scheme by Childs et al. [9], Jao and De Feo designed SIDH [19] (Supersingular Isogeny Diffie-Hellman), a Key Exchange protocol based on supersingular isogenies. The submission of SIKE [20] (a Key Encapsulation Mechanism based on SIDH) to the NIST standardization process marked the starting point of a more active research in isogeny-based cryptography. Isogeny-based protocols are not the most efficient candidates for post quantum cryptography, but they provide the shortest keys and ciphertexts.

In 2018, Castryck et al. constructed CSIDH [6] (Commutative SIDH) using the $\mathbb{F}_p$-sub-graph of the supersingular isogeny graph. CSIDH key exchange is close to CRS but is an order of magnitude more efficient. PKE schemes based on isogeny problems include SIKE, SÉTA [14] and more recently SiGamal and C-SiGamal [24]. SÉTA and the PKEs canonically derived from the key exchange protocols SIDH and CSIDH are only OW-CPA secure. They require the use of hash functions and/or generic transformations such as the Fujisaki-Okamoto [16] or OAEP [1] to fulfil higher security requirements such as IND-CPA and IND-CCA security ([14, Sect. 2.4], [20, Sect. 1.4], [24, Sect. 3.3]). This motivated Moriya, Onuki and Tagaki to introduce the SiGamal [24, Sect. 5] and C-SiGamal [24, Sect. 6] PKE schemes derived from CSIDH. SiGamal and C-SiGamal provide IND-CPA security under new assumptions they introduce. The authors noticed that neither SiGamal nor C-SiGamal is IND-CCA secure. In Remark 7 of [24], they suggest a slightly modified version of SiGamal that from their point of view could be IND-CCA secure, but they left its study as open problem.

Contributions. In this paper, we prove that the variant of SiGamal suggested by Moriya et al. in Remark 7 of their paper is not IND-CCA secure by exhibiting a simple and concrete attack. We then modify SiGamal to thwart this attack, and obtain a new isogeny-based PKE scheme which we call SimS. We prove that SimS is IND-CPA secure relying on CSIDH security assumptions (Assumption 2). This is a considerable improvement on SiGamal whose IND-CPA security relies on new assumptions. We then introduce a "knowledge of Exponent" type assumption (Assumption 3) under which we prove that SimS is IND-CCA secure. This assumption may have other applications in isogeny-based cryptography.

We adapt the Magma code for SiGamal [23] to run a proof of concept implementation of SimS using the SiGamal primes p_{128} and p_{256}. For the prime p_{128}, SimS is about 1.13x faster than SiGamal and about 1.19x faster than C-SiGamal. For the prime p_{256}, we get a 1.07x speedup when compared to SiGamal and a 1.21x speedup when compared to C-SiGamal.

For the same set of parameters, SimS has smaller private keys, public keys and ciphertexts compared to SiGamal and C-SiGamal. SimS is simple, sits between SiGamal and CSIDH, helps to better understand the relation between SiGamal and CSIDH while providing IND-CCA security and being more efficient compared to SiGamal. Table 1 best summarizes our contributions.

Table 1. Comparison between CSIDHpke, SimS, SiGamal and C-SiGamal. CSIDHpke uses the csidh-512 prime, while SimS, SiGamal and C-SiGamal use the primes p_{128} and p_{256} which are SiGamal primes that provide the same security level as the csidh-512 prime.

	CSIDHpke	SimS	SiGamal	C-SiGamal
Private key	$[\mathfrak{a}]$	$[\mathfrak{a}]$	$\mathfrak{a}$	$\mathfrak{a}$
Size of plaintext	$\log_2 p$	$r - 2$	$r - 2$	$r - 2$
Size of Alice's public key	$\log_2 p$	$\log_2 p$	$2 \log_2 p$	$2 \log_2 p$
Size of ciphertexts (or Bob's public key)	$2 \log_2 p$	$2 \log_2 p$	$4 \log_2 p$	$2 \log_2 p$
Class group cost for p_{128} compared to CSIDH	x1.00	x1.30	x1.50	x1.50
Class group cost for p_{256} compared to CSIDH	x1.00	x2.31	x2.57	x2.57
Enc + Dec cost for p_{128} compared to CSIDHpke	x1.00	x1.38	x1.57	x1.65
Enc + Dec cost for p_{256} compared to CSIDHpke	x1.00	x2.62	x2.82	x3.17
Security	OW-CPA	IND-CCA	IND-CPA	IND-CPA

Outline. The remainder of this paper is organized as follows: in Sect. 2, we recall the security definitions for PKE schemes, the main ideas of the class group action and the CSIDH key exchange protocol. In Sect. 3, we present the SiGamal PKE scheme and we show that the variant suggested in [24, Remark 7] is not IND-CCA secure. Section 4 is devoted to SimS and its security arguments. In Sect. 5 we present the outcome of a proof-of-concept implementation and compare SimS to CSIDH and (C-)SiGamal in Sect. 6. We conclude the paper in Sect. 7.

2 Preliminaries

2.1 Public Key Encryption

We recall standard security definitions related to public key encryption.

Definition 1 (PKE). *A Public Key Encryption scheme $\mathcal{P}_\lambda$ is a triple of PPT algorithms (*Key Generation, Encryption, Decryption*) that satisfy the following.*

1. *Given a security parameter λ as input, the key generation algorithm* Key Generation *outputs a public key pk, a private key sk and a plaintext space $\mathcal{M}$.*
2. *Given a plaintext $\mu \in \mathcal{M}$ and a public key pk as inputs, the encryption algorithm* Encryption *outputs a ciphertext $c = $ Encryption$_{pk}(\mu)$.*
3. *Given a ciphertext c and sk as inputs, the decryption algorithm* Decryption *outputs a plain text $= $ Decryption$_{sk}(c)$.*

Definition 2 (Correctness). *A PKE scheme $\mathcal{P}_\lambda$ is correct if for any pair of keys (pk, sk) and for every plaintext $\mu \in \mathcal{M}$,*

$$\text{Decryption}_{sk}\left(\text{Encryption}_{pk}(\mu)\right) = \mu.$$

Definition 3 (IND-CPA secure). *A PKE scheme $\mathcal{P}_\lambda$ is IND-CPA secure if for every PPT adversary $\mathcal{A}$,*

$$Pr\left[b = b^* \middle| \begin{array}{l} (pk, sk) \leftarrow \mathsf{Key\ Generation}(\lambda), \mu_0, \mu_1 \leftarrow \mathcal{A}(pk, \mathcal{M}), \\ b \xleftarrow{\$} \{0, 1\}, \mathsf{c} \leftarrow \mathsf{Encryption}_{pk}(\mu_b), b^* \leftarrow \mathcal{A}(pk, \mathsf{c}) \end{array}\right] = \frac{1}{2} + \mathsf{negl}(\lambda).$$

Definition 4 (IND-CCA secure). *A PKE scheme $\mathcal{P}_\lambda$ is IND-CCA secure if for every PPT adversary $\mathcal{A}$,*

$$Pr\left[b = b^* \middle| \begin{array}{l} (pk, sk) \leftarrow \mathsf{Key\ Generation}(\lambda), \mu_0, \mu_1 \leftarrow \mathcal{A}^{O(\cdot)}(pk, \mathcal{M}), \\ b \xleftarrow{\$} \{0, 1\}, \mathsf{c} \leftarrow \mathsf{Encryption}_{pk}(\mu_b), b^* \leftarrow \mathcal{A}^{O(\cdot)}(pk, \mathsf{c}) \end{array}\right] = \frac{1}{2} + \mathsf{negl}(\lambda),$$

where $O(\cdot)$ is a decryption oracle that when given a ciphertext $\mathsf{c}' \neq \mathsf{c}$, outputs $\mathsf{Decryption}_{sk}(\mathsf{c}')$ or $\bot$ if the ciphertext c' is invalid.

2.2   Class Group Action on Supersingular Curves Defined Over $\mathbb{F}_p$

We refer to [31,32] for general mathematical background on supersingular elliptic curves and isogenies, to [6,15] for supersingular elliptic curves defined over $\mathbb{F}_p$ and their $\mathbb{F}_p$-endomorphism ring, and to [10,28] for isogenies between Montgomery curves.

Let $p \equiv 3 \mod 4$ be a prime greater than 3. The equation $By^2 = x^3 + Ax^2 + x$ where $B \in \mathbb{F}_p^*$ and $A \in \mathbb{F}_p \setminus \{\pm 2\}$ defines a Montgomery curve E over $\mathbb{F}_p$. The curve $E : By^2 = x^3 + Ax^2 + x$ is isomorphic (over $\mathbb{F}_p$) to the curve defined by the equation $y^2 = x^3 + Ax^2 + x$ (resp. $-y^2 = x^3 + Ax^2 + x$) when B is a square in $\mathbb{F}_p$ (resp. B is not a square in $\mathbb{F}_p$). The curve E is said to be supersingular if $\#E(\mathbb{F}_p) \equiv 1 \mod p$, otherwise E is said to be ordinary. If E is a supersingular curve defined over $\mathbb{F}_p$ with $p > 3$, then $\#E(\mathbb{F}_p) = p + 1$. All the elliptic curves we consider in this paper are supersingular curves defined by an equation of the form $y^2 = x^3 + Ax^2 + x$ where $A \in \mathbb{F}_p$ is called the Montgomery coefficient of the curve. In the rest rest of this section, we briefly describe the class group action used in CSIDH.

Let E be a supersingular curve defined over $\mathbb{F}_p$ and let π be the Frobenius endomorphism of E. The $\mathbb{F}_p$-endomorphism ring $\mathcal{O}$ of E is isomorphic to either $\mathbb{Z}[\pi]$ or $\mathbb{Z}[\frac{1+\pi}{2}]$ [15]. As in the ordinary case, the class group $\mathsf{cl}(\mathcal{O})$ of $\mathcal{O}$ acts freely and transitively on the set $\mathcal{Ell}_p(\mathcal{O})$ of supersingular elliptic curves defined over $\mathbb{F}_p$ and having $\mathbb{F}_p$-endomorphism ring $\mathcal{O}$. We have the following theorem.

Theorem 1. *[6, Theorem 7] Let $\mathcal{O}$ be an order in an imaginary quadratic field such that $\mathcal{Ell}_p(\mathcal{O})$ is non empty. The ideal class group $\mathsf{cl}(\mathcal{O})$ acts freely and transitively on the set $\mathcal{Ell}_p(\mathcal{O})$ via the map*

$$\begin{aligned} \mathsf{cl}(\mathcal{O}) \times \mathcal{Ell}_p(\mathcal{O}) &\to \quad \mathcal{Ell}_p(\mathcal{O}) \\ ([\mathfrak{a}], E) &\mapsto [\mathfrak{a}]E = E/E[\mathfrak{a}], \end{aligned}$$

where $\mathfrak{a}$ is an integral ideal of $\mathcal{O}$ and $E[\mathfrak{a}] = \cap_{\alpha \in \mathfrak{a}} \ker \alpha$.

From now on, we will consider the quadratic order $\mathbb{Z}[\pi]$ and the action of its class group $\mathsf{cl}(\mathbb{Z}[\pi])$ on the set $\mathcal{Ell}_p(\mathbb{Z}[\pi])$. We represent $\mathbb{F}_p$-isomorphism classes of curves in $\mathcal{Ell}_p(\mathbb{Z}[\pi])$ using the Montgomery coefficient A [4, Proposition 3].

The efficiency of the computation of an isogeny with known kernel essentially depends on the smoothness of its degree. In [6], the authors work with a prime p of the form $p = 4\ell_1 \cdots \ell_n - 1$. This implies that for $i \in \{1, \cdots, n\}$, $\left(\frac{-p}{\ell_i}\right) = 1$ and by the Kummer decomposition theorem [22], $(\ell_i) = \mathfrak{l}_i \bar{\mathfrak{l}}_i$ in $\mathsf{cl}(\mathbb{Z}[\pi])$, where $\mathfrak{l}_i = (\ell_i, \pi - 1)$ and $\bar{\mathfrak{l}}_i = (\ell_i, \pi + 1)$ are integral ideals of prime norm ℓ_i. It follows that $[\mathfrak{l}_i][\bar{\mathfrak{l}}_i] = [\ell_i] = [1]$ in $\mathsf{cl}(\mathbb{Z}[\pi])$, hence $[\mathfrak{l}_i]^{-1} = [\bar{\mathfrak{l}}_i]$. Since the primes ℓ_i are small, then the action of the ideal classes $[\mathfrak{l}_i]$ and $[\mathfrak{l}_i]^{-1}$ can be computed efficiently using Vélu formulas for Montgomery curves [10,28]. In reality, the kernel of the isogeny corresponding to the action of the prime ideal $\mathfrak{l}_i = (\ell_i, \pi - 1)$ is generated by a point $P \in E(\mathbb{F}_p)$ of order ℓ_i, while that of the isogeny corresponding to the action of $\mathfrak{l}_i^{-1} = (\ell_i, \pi + 1)$ is a point $P' \in E(\mathbb{F}_{p^2}) \backslash E(\mathbb{F}_p)$ of order ℓ_i such that $\pi(P') = -P'$. The computation of the action of an ideal class $\prod [\mathfrak{l}_i]^{e_i}$ where $(e_1, \cdots, e_n) \in \{-m, \cdots, m\}^n$ can be done efficiently by composing the actions of the ideal classes $[\mathfrak{l}_i]$ or $[\mathfrak{l}_i]^{-1}$ depending on the signs of the exponents e_i. Since the prime ideals $\mathfrak{l}_i$ are fixed, then the vector $(e_1, \cdots, e_n)$ is used to represent the ideal class $\prod [\mathfrak{l}_i]^{e_i}$. From the discussion in [6, Sect. 7.1], m is chosen to be the least positive integer such that

$$(2m + 1)^n \geq |\mathsf{cl}(\mathbb{Z}[\pi])| \approx \sqrt{p}.$$

2.3 CSIDH

CSIDH [6] stands for Commutative Supersingular Isogeny Diffie-Hellman and is a Diffie-Hellman type key exchange protocol. The base group in Diffie-Hellman protocol is replaced by the unstructured set $\mathcal{E}\ell\ell_p(\mathbb{Z}[\pi])$ and the exponentiation is replaced by the class group action of $\mathsf{cl}(\mathbb{Z}[\pi])$ on $\mathcal{E}\ell\ell_p(\mathbb{Z}[\pi])$. Concretely, CSIDH is designed as follows.

Setup. Let $p = 4\ell_1 \cdots \ell_n - 1$ be a prime where $\ell_1, \cdots, \ell_n$ are small distinct odd primes. The prime p and the supersingular elliptic curve $E_0 : y^2 = x^3 + x$ defined over $\mathbb{F}_p$ with $\mathbb{F}_p$-endomorphism $\mathbb{Z}[\pi]$ are the public parameters.

Key Generation. The private key is an n-tuple $e = (e_1, \cdots, e_n)$ of uniformly random integers sampled from a range $\{-m, \cdots, m\}$. This private key represents an ideal class $[\mathfrak{a}] = \prod [\mathfrak{l}_i]^{e_i} \in \mathsf{cl}(\mathbb{Z}[\pi])$. The public key is the Montgomery coefficient $A \in \mathbb{F}_p$ of the curve $[\mathfrak{a}]E_0 : y^2 = x^3 + Ax^2 + x$ obtained by applying the action of $[\mathfrak{a}]$ on E_0.

Key Exchange Suppose Alice and Bob have successfully computed pairs of private and public key (e, A) and (e', B) respectively. Upon receiving Bob's public key $B \in \mathbb{F}_p \backslash \{\pm 2\}$, Alice verifies that the elliptic curve $E_B : y^2 = x^3 + Bx^2 + x$ is a supersingular curve, then applies the action of the ideal class corresponding to her secret key $e = (e_1, \cdots, e_n)$ to E_B to compute the curve $[\mathfrak{a}]E_B = [\mathfrak{a}][\mathfrak{b}]E_0$. Bob does analogously with his own secret key $e' = (e'_1, \cdots, e'_n)$ and Alice's public key $A \in \mathbb{F}_p \backslash \{\pm 2\}$ to compute the curve $[\mathfrak{b}]E_A = [\mathfrak{b}][\mathfrak{a}]E_0$. The shared secret is the Montgomery coefficient S of the common secret curve $[\mathfrak{a}][\mathfrak{b}]E_0 = [\mathfrak{b}][\mathfrak{a}]E_0$.

The security of the CSIDH key exchange protocol relies on the following assumptions.

Let λ be the security parameter and let $p = 4\ell_1 \cdots \ell_n - 1$ be a prime where $\ell_1, \cdots, \ell_n$ are small distinct odd primes. Let E_0 be the supersingular elliptic curve $y^2 = x^3 + x$ defined over $\mathbb{F}_p$, let $[\mathfrak{a}]$, $[\mathfrak{b}]$ and $[\mathfrak{c}]$ be uniformly random ideal classes in $\mathsf{cl}(\mathbb{Z}[\pi])$.

Assumption 1. *The CSSICDH (Commutative Supersingular Isogeny Computational Diffie-Hellman) assumption holds if for any probabilistic polynomial time (PPT) algorithm $\mathcal{A}$,*

$$Pr[E = [\mathfrak{b}][\mathfrak{a}]E_0 \mid E = \mathcal{A}(E_0, [\mathfrak{a}]E_0, [\mathfrak{b}]E_0)] < \mathsf{negl}(\lambda).$$

Assumption 2. *The CSSIDDH (Commutative Supersingular Isogeny Decisional Diffie-Hellman) assumption holds if for any PPT algorithm $\mathcal{A}$,*

$$Pr\left[b = b^* \left| \begin{array}{l} [\mathfrak{a}], [\mathfrak{b}], [\mathfrak{c}] \leftarrow \mathsf{cl}(\mathbb{Z}[\pi]), b \xleftarrow{\$} \{0,1\}, \\ F_0 := [\mathfrak{b}][\mathfrak{a}]E_0, F_1 = [\mathfrak{c}]E_0, \\ b^* \leftarrow \mathcal{A}(E_0, [\mathfrak{a}]E_0, [\mathfrak{b}]E_0, F_b) \end{array} \right. \right] = \frac{1}{2} + \mathsf{negl}(\lambda).$$

In [7], Castryck et al. show that Assumption 2 does not hold for primes $p \equiv 1 \bmod 4$. This does not affect primes $p \equiv 3 \bmod 4$, which are used in CSIDH, SiGamal and in our proposal SimS.

An IND-CPA insecure PKE from CSIDH. A PKE scheme can be canonically derived from a key exchange protocol. For the case of CSIDH, this PKE scheme is sketched as follows. Suppose that Alice has successfully computed her key pair (e, A). In order to encrypt a message $\mathsf{m} \in \{0,1\}^{\lceil \log p \rceil}$, Bob computes a random key pair (e', B) and the binary representation S_{01} of the corresponding shared secret S. He sends $(B, \mathsf{c} = S_{01} \oplus \mathsf{m})$ to Alice as the ciphertext. For the decryption, Alice computes the shared secret S and its binary representation S_{01}, then recovers $\mathsf{m} = S_{01} \oplus \mathsf{c}$. In the comparison in Sect. 6, the term CSIDHpke will be used to refer to the previous PKE each time the precision is needed.

The above PKE scheme is not IND-CPA secure. In fact, given two distinct plaintexts m_0 and m_1, if (B, c) is a ciphertext for m_i, then $S_{01}^i = \mathsf{c} \oplus \mathsf{m}_i$ is the binary representation of the Montgomery coefficient of a supersingular curve while $S_{01}^{1-i} = \mathsf{c} \oplus \mathsf{m}_{1-i}$ is that of an ordinary curve with overwhelming probability. Hence an adversary can efficiently guess if the ciphertext (B, c) is that of m_0 or m_1. In practice, a hash function h is used to mask the supersingular property of the shared secret S, the ciphertext becomes $(B, \mathsf{c} = h(S_{01}) \oplus \mathsf{m})$.

3   Another Look at SiGamal Protocol

3.1   SiGamal Protocol and Variants

Let $p = 2^r \ell_1 \cdots \ell_n - 1$ be a prime such that $\ell_1, \cdots, \ell_n$ are small distinct odd primes. Let E_0 be the elliptic curve $y^2 = x^3 + x$ and let $P_0 \in E(\mathbb{F}_p)$ be a point of order 2^r. Recall that for every small odd prime ℓ_i dividing $p + 1$, there are two prime ideals $\mathfrak{l}_i = (\ell_i, \pi - 1)$ and $\overline{\mathfrak{l}}_i = (\ell_i, \pi + 1)$ above ℓ_i in $\mathsf{cl}(\mathbb{Z}[\pi])$. Also, the isogenies $\phi_{\mathfrak{l}_i}$ and $\phi_{\overline{\mathfrak{l}}_i}$ of domain E_0 correspond to the isogenies with kernel generated by $P_{\mathfrak{l}_i} \in E_0[\ell_i] \cap ker(\pi - 1)\backslash\{0\}$ and $P_{\overline{\mathfrak{l}}_i} \in E_0[\ell_i] \cap ker(\pi + 1)\backslash\{0\}$ respectively. The points $\mathfrak{l}_i P_0$ and $\overline{\mathfrak{l}}_i P_0$ are images of the point P_0 trough these isogenies respectively. Let $\mathfrak{a} = (\alpha)\mathfrak{l}_1^{e_1} \cdots \mathfrak{l}_n^{e_n} \in \mathsf{cl}(\mathbb{Z}[\pi])$ where α is an integer then point $\mathfrak{a}P_0$ is the image of P_0 by the composition of the isogenies $\phi_{\mathfrak{l}_i}$ if $e_i > 0$ or $\phi_{\overline{\mathfrak{l}}_i}$ if $e_i < 0$, and the multiplication by α. For a given integer k, we denote by $[k] \circ \mathfrak{b}$ the composition of the isogeny corresponding to the ideal class $\mathfrak{b}$ and the scalar multiplication by k, and the point $[k] \circ \mathfrak{b}P_0$ denotes the image of P_0 trough this isogeny.

The SiGamal PKE scheme can be summarized as follows.

Key Generation. Let $p = 2^r \ell_1 \cdots \ell_n - 1$ be a prime such that $\ell_1, \cdots, \ell_n$ are small distinct odd primes. Let E_0 be the elliptic curve $y^2 = x^3 + x$ and let $P_0 \in E(\mathbb{F}_p)$ be a point of order 2^r. Alice takes a random integral ideal $\mathfrak{a} = (\alpha)\mathfrak{l}_1^{e_1} \cdots \mathfrak{l}_n^{e_n}$ where α is a uniformly random element of $\mathbb{Z}_{2^r}^{\times}$, computes $E_1 := [\mathfrak{a}]E_0$ and $P_1 := \mathfrak{a}P_0$. Her public key is $(E_1, x(P_1))$ and her private key is $(\alpha, e_1, \cdots, e_n)$. Let $\mathbb{Z}_{2^{r-2}} = \mathbb{Z}/2^{r-2}\mathbb{Z}$ be the message space.

Encryption. Let $\mathsf{m} \in \mathbb{Z}_{2^{r-2}}$ be a plaintext, Bob embeds m in $\mathbb{Z}_{2^r}^{\times}$ via $\mathsf{m} \mapsto M = 2\mathsf{m} + 1$. Bob takes a random integral ideal class $\mathfrak{b} = (\beta)\mathfrak{l}_1^{e_1} \cdots \mathfrak{l}_n^{e_n}$ where β is a uniformly random element of $\mathbb{Z}_{2^r}^{\times}$. Next, he computes $[M]P_1$, $E_3 = [\mathfrak{b}]E_0$, $P_3 := \mathfrak{b}P_0$, $E_4 = [\mathfrak{b}]E_1$ and $P_4 := \mathfrak{b}([M]P_1)$. He sends $(E_3, x(P_3), E_4, x(P_4))$ to Alice as the ciphertext.

Decryption. Upon receiving $(E_3, x(P_3), E_4, x(P_4))$, Alice computes $\mathfrak{a}P_3$ and solves a discrete logarithm instance between P_4 and $\mathfrak{a}P_3$ using the Pohlig-Hellman algorithm [27]. Let $M \in \mathbb{Z}_{2^r}^{\times}$ be the solution of this computation. If $2^{r-1} < M$, then Alice changes M to $2^r - M$. She computes the plaintext $\mathsf{m} = (M - 1)/2$.

In C-SiGamal, a compressed version of SiGamal, one replaces the point $\mathfrak{a}\mathfrak{b}P_0$ by a distinguished point $P_{E_4} \in E_4$ of order 2^r, which then does not need to be transmitted. The scheme integrates an algorithm that canonically computes a distinguished point of order 2^r on a given supersingular curve defined over $\mathbb{F}_p$ where $p = 2^r l_1 \cdots l_n - 1$. We refer to [24] for more details on the SiGamal and C-SiGamal.

Moriya et al. prove that SiGamal and C-SiGamal are IND-CPA secure relying on two assumptions they introduce. However, they point out that SiGamal is not IND-CCA secure since one can efficiently compute a valid encryption of $3\mathsf{m} + 1$ from a valid encryption of m. Indeed, given $([\mathfrak{b}]E_0, \mathfrak{b}P_0, [\mathfrak{b}]E_1, [2\mathsf{m} + 1]\mathfrak{b}P_1)$ one easily computes $([\mathfrak{b}]E_0, \mathfrak{b}P_0, [\mathfrak{b}]E_1, [3][2\mathsf{m} + 1]\mathfrak{b}P_1) = ([\mathfrak{b}]E_0, \mathfrak{b}P_0, [\mathfrak{b}]E_1, [2(3\mathsf{m} + 1) + 1]\mathfrak{b}P_1)$. A similar argument applies for C-SiGamal as well.

As a remedy, Moriya et al. suggest to omit the curve $[\mathfrak{b}]E_1$ in the ciphertext (see [24, Remark 7]). We now show that this variant is still vulnerable to IND-CCA attacks.

3.2   An IND-CCA Attack on Moriya et al.'s Variant

In this version of SiGamal, a ciphertext for m is of the form $([\mathfrak{b}]E_0, \mathfrak{b}P_0, [2m + 1]\mathfrak{b}P_1)$ and the decryption process is identical to that of the original SiGamal. We prove the following lemma.

Lemma 1. *Let* (m, c) *be a pair of plaintext-ciphertext, and let* m' *be any other plaintext. One can compute a valid ciphertext for* m' *in polynomial time.*

Proof. Write $c = ([\mathfrak{b}]E_0, \mathfrak{b}P_0, [2m+1]\mathfrak{b}P_1)$. Since $2m+1, 2m'+1 \in \mathbb{Z}_{2^r}^{\times}$, then $\alpha = (2m+1)(2m'+1)^{-1} \in \mathbb{Z}_{2^r}^{\times}$. Since the curve $[\mathfrak{b}]E_0$ and its point $\mathfrak{b}P_0$ are available in c, then the ciphertext $c' = ([\mathfrak{b}]E_0, [\alpha]\mathfrak{b}P_0, [2m + 1]\mathfrak{b}P_1)$ can be efficiently computed at the cost of a point multiplication by α.

We now show that c' is a valid encryption of m'. To decrypt c', Alice computes $[\mathfrak{a}][\mathfrak{b}]E_0$ and $\mathfrak{a}([\alpha]\mathfrak{b}P_0) = [\alpha]\mathfrak{a}\mathfrak{b}P_0$, then she solves a discrete logarithm problem between $[2m + 1]\mathfrak{b}P_1 = [2m + 1]\mathfrak{a}\mathfrak{b}P_0$ and $[\alpha]\mathfrak{a}\mathfrak{b}P_0$. We have

$$[2m + 1]\mathfrak{a}\mathfrak{b}P_0 = [\alpha^{-1}(2m + 1)][\alpha]\mathfrak{a}\mathfrak{b}P_0.$$

Hence the solution of the discrete logarithm problem is

$$M' = \pm\alpha^{-1}(2m + 1) = \pm(2m' + 1)(2m + 1)^{-1}(2m + 1) = \pm(2m' + 1).$$

It follows that the corresponding plaintext (after changing M' to $2^r - M'$ when necessary) is $(M' - 1)/2 = m'$.

Corollary 1. *The variant of SiGamal suggested by Moriya et al. in [24, Remark 7] is not IND-CCA secure.*

4   SimS

We now introduce a new protocol that resists the previous attack. We name our protocol SimS (**Sim**plified **S**iGamal), which highlights the fact that our scheme is a simplification of SiGamal.

4.1   Overview

We observe that the attack presented in the previous section is effective because the ciphertext contains the curve $\mathfrak{b}E_0$ and its 2^r-torsion points $\mathfrak{b}P_0$.

SimS is obtained by adjusting SiGamal in such a way that when a curve is part of the ciphertext, then none of its points are, and the other way around. In order to achieve this, we replace the point $\mathfrak{a}\mathfrak{b}P_0$ in the (C)SiGamal protocol by a canonical point $P_{E_4} \in E_4 = [\mathfrak{a}][\mathfrak{b}]E_0$. More concretely, in SimS, Alice's secret key is an ideal class $[\mathfrak{a}]$, and her public key is the curve $E_1 = [\mathfrak{a}]E_0$. To encrypt a message m, Bob chooses a uniformly random ideal class $[\mathfrak{b}]$, he computes $E_3 = [\mathfrak{b}]E_0$, $E_4 = [\mathfrak{b}]E_1$ and he then canonically computes a point $P_{E_4} \in E_4(\mathbb{F}_p)$ of smooth order $2^r | p + 1$. He sends E_3 and $P_4 = [2m + 1]P_{E_4}$ to Alice. In order to recover m, Alice computes $E_4 = [\mathfrak{a}]E_3$ and P_{E_4}, then solves a discrete logarithm instance in a group of order 2^r using the Pohlig-Hellman algorithm. Figure 1 depicts the scheme.

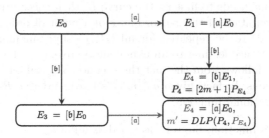

Fig. 1. SimS scheme. The elements in black are public, while those in blue are known only by Bob and those in red only by Alice. (Color figure online)

The IND-CCA attack presented in Sect. 3.2 is no more feasible in SimS since no point of the curve E_3 nor the curve E_4 are part of the ciphertexts.

4.2 The SimS Public Key Encryption Protocol

Now let us concretely describe the key generation, encryption and decryption processes. We use the Algorithm 1 to canonically compute the point $P_E \in E(\mathbb{F}_p)$ of order $2^r | p + 1$.

Before we describe the protocol, let us notice that revealing P_4 or its x-coordinate may leak too much information about the curve E_4. In fact $x(P_4)$ is the root of the 2^r division polynomial of E_4. Moreover, one could easily derive $x(P_4 + (0,0)) = \frac{1}{x(P_4)}$ by a simple inversion in $\mathbb{F}_p$, which would affect the IND-CCA security of the scheme. To avoid this, we make use of a randomizing function $f_E : \mathbb{F}_p \to \mathbb{F}_p$, indexed by supersingular curves defined over $\mathbb{F}_p$, satisfying the following conditions:

P1: f_E is bijective, f_E and its inverse $g_E = f_E^{-1}$ can be efficiently computed when E is given;

P2: for every element $x \in \mathbb{F}_p$, an adversary having no access to x and E cannot distinguish $f_E(x)$ from a random element of $\mathbb{F}_p$;

P3: for every element $x \in \mathbb{F}_p$, for every non identical rational function $R \in \mathbb{F}_p(X)$, an adversary having no access to x and E cannot compute $f_E(R(x))$ from $f_E(x)$.

Example 1. In the proof of concept implementation in Sect. 5, we use the function $f_E : x \mapsto x'$ where $\text{bin}(x') = \text{bin}(x) \oplus \text{bin}(A_E)$ and $\text{bin}(\cdot)$ takes an element in $\mathbb{F}_p$ and returns its binary representation.

Clearly, f_E is an involution, hence f_E is bijective and satisfies (P1). Proving that f_E satisfies (P2) and (P3) is less straightforward. Nevertheless, we give some intuitive arguments on why we believe that f_E satisfies (P2) and (P3). Given an element $y \in \mathbb{F}_p$, in order to distinguish whether $y = f_E(x)$ where x is the x-coordinate of a point of order 2^r on some supersingular curve E, to the best of our knowledge, one needs to first fix the curve E, then check if $\text{bin}(y) \oplus \text{bin}(A_E)$ is the bit representation of the x-coordinate of a point of order order 2^r on E. This process needs to be repeated for all $O(\sqrt{p})$ supersingular elliptic curves defined over $\mathbb{F}_p$. Hence leading to an exponential adversary. The third property (P3), intuitively, follows from the fact there is no compatibility with XOR and algebraic operations. In fact, given $a \oplus b$, it is hard to derive $R(a) \oplus b$ where R is non identical rational function.

Having such a function, SimS is designed as follows.

Key Generation: Let $p = 2^r \ell_1 \cdots \ell_n - 1$ be a prime such that $\ell_1, \cdots, \ell_n$ are small distinct odd primes and $\lambda + 2 \leq r \leq \frac{1}{2}\log p$ where λ is the security parameter. Let E_0 be the elliptic curve $y^2 = x^3 + x$. Alice takes a random ideal class $[\mathfrak{a}] \in \text{cl}(\mathbb{Z}[\pi])$, computes $E_1 := [\mathfrak{a}]E_0$. Her public key is E_1 and her private key is $[\mathfrak{a}]$. The plaintext space is the set $\mathcal{M} = \mathbb{Z}_{2^{r-2}}$.

Encryption: Let $\mathsf{m} \in \mathbb{Z}_{2^{r-2}}$ be a plaintext, Bob embeds m in $\mathbb{Z}_{2^r}^\times$ via $\mathsf{m} \mapsto 2\mathsf{m}+1$. Bob takes a random ideal class $[\mathfrak{b}] \in \text{cl}(\mathbb{Z}[\pi])$ and computes $E_3 = [\mathfrak{b}]E_0$, $E_4 = [\mathfrak{b}]E_1$ and $P_4 = [2\mathsf{m}+1]P_{E_4}$. He sends $(E_3, x' = f_{E_4}(x(P_4)))$ to Alice as the ciphertext.

Decryption: Upon receiving (E_3, x'), Alice verifies that E_3 is a supersingular curve, computes $E_4 = [\mathfrak{a}]E_3$ and P_{E_4}. If $g_{E_4}(x')$ is not the x-coordinate of a 2^r-torsion point on the curve E_4, then Alice aborts. She solves the discrete logarithm instance between $P_4 = (g_{E_4}(x'), -)$ and P_{E_4} using the Pohlig-Hellman algorithm. Let $M \in \mathbb{Z}_{2^r}^\times$ be the solution of this computation. If $2^{r-1} < M$, then Alice changes M to $2^r - M$. She computes the plaintext $(M-1)/2$.

Theorem 2. *If f_{E_4} satisfies (P1), then SimS is correct.*

Proof. Since f_{E_4} satisfies (P1), then f_{E_4} is bijective, f_{E_4} and its inverse $g_{E_4} = f_{E_4}^{-1}$ can be efficiently computed by Alice since she has access to E_4.
As in CSIDH, the Montgomery coefficients of the curves $[\mathfrak{a}][\mathfrak{b}]E_0$ and $[\mathfrak{b}][\mathfrak{a}]E_0$ are equal. Therefore Alice and Bob obtain the same distinguish point P_{E_4}. Since the points P_{E_4} and $P_4 = [2\mathsf{m}+1]P_{E_4}$ have order 2^r, then the Pohlig-Hellman algorithm can be implemented on their x-coordinates $x(P_4) = g_{E_4}(x')$ and $x(P_{E_4})$ only to recover $M \equiv \pm(2\mathsf{m}+1) \bmod 2^r$. Since $\mathsf{m} \in \mathbb{Z}_{2^{r-2}}$, then $2\mathsf{m}+1 < 2^{r-1}$.

Alice changes M to $2^r - M$ if $2^{r-1} < M$, then she computes the plaintext $(M-1)/2 = \mathsf{m}$.

Remark 1. Instantiating SimS with SIDH would lead to a PKE scheme which is not IND-CCA secure because SIDH is vulnerable to adaptive attacks [17].

4.3   Security Arguments

We prove that the IND-CPA security of SimS relies on Assumption 2. We also prove that SimS is IND-CCA secure under a Knowledge of Exponent-type assumption which we introduce.

Theorem 3. *If Assumption 2 holds and f_{E_4} satisfies (P2), then SimS is IND-CPA secure.*

Proof. We adapt the proof of [12, Theorem 1] to our setting. Let us suppose that SimS is not IND-CPA secure, then there exists a PPT adversary $\mathcal{A}$ that can successfully distinguish whether a given ciphertext (E_3, x') was encrypted from a plaintext m_0 or m_1 with a non negligible advantage γ. We will use $\mathcal{A}$ to construct a PPT CSSIDDH solver $\mathcal{A}'$ that breaks Assumption 2.

Let $(E_0, [\mathfrak{a}]E_0, [\mathfrak{b}]E_0, E)$ be a tuple given to us as a CSSIDDH instance input. Our goal is to decide if this is a **correct** tuple $([\mathfrak{a}][\mathfrak{b}]E_0 = E)$ or a **bad** tuple $([\mathfrak{a}][\mathfrak{b}]E_0 \neq E)$.

Let T be the following two-steps test.

- **Simulation.** One simulates a SimS instance using two plaintext messages $\mathsf{m}_0, \mathsf{m}_1$ chosen by the adversary $\mathcal{A}$ and $(E_0, [\mathfrak{a}]E_0, [\mathfrak{b}]E_0, E)$. Concretely, one computes P_E, secretly chooses a random bit $b \in \{0, 1\}$ and returns the ciphertext $\mathsf{c} = ([\mathfrak{b}]E_0, f_E(x([2\mathsf{m}_b + 1]P_E)))$.
- **Query** $\mathcal{A}$. One queries $\mathcal{A}$ with $([\mathfrak{a}]E_0, \mathsf{c})$ and gets a response b'. The result of the test T is 1 if $b = b'$ and 0 if $b \neq b'$.

Now we distinguish two cases.

Case 1: The Adversary $\mathcal{A}$ can detect invalid ciphertexts by returning an error message. Here we run the test T once. If the result of the query step is an error message instead of a bit, then c is an invalid ciphertext. Hence $E \neq [\mathfrak{a}][\mathfrak{b}]E_0$ and the tuple is bad. If in the query step $\mathcal{A}$ returns a bit b', then c is a valid ciphertext. Hence $[\mathfrak{a}][\mathfrak{b}]E_0 = E$, and the tuple is correct.

We therefore construct our CSSIDDH solver $\mathcal{A}'$ as follows: if the query step result is an error message, $\mathcal{A}'$ returns bad; if it is a bit, $\mathcal{A}'$ returns correct.

Case 2: The Adversary $\mathcal{A}$ cannot detect invalid ciphertexts. Here the query step result will always be a bit b'. The CSSIDDH solver $\mathcal{A}'$ repeats the test T and studies the proportion $\mathrm{Pr}_T(1)$ of 1's obtained.

Suppose that $(E_0, [\mathfrak{a}]E_0, [\mathfrak{b}]E_0, E)$ is a correct tuple, then all the ciphertexts c computed in the simulation steps are valid, hence the adversary $\mathcal{A}$ has the same advantage as in an actual attack. Therefore,

$$\mathrm{Pr}_T(1) = \frac{1}{2} + \gamma.$$

On the other hand, let suppose that $(E_0, [\mathfrak{a}]E_0, [\mathfrak{b}]E_0, E)$ is a bad tuple. Then $[\mathfrak{a}][\mathfrak{b}]E_0 \neq E$ and the ciphertext c is invalid. Since $\mathcal{A}$ does not have access to E and $x([2m_b + 1]P_E)$, and that f_E satisfies (P2), then $\mathcal{A}$ can not distinguish $x' = f_E(x([2m_b + 1]P_E))$ from a random element of $\mathbb{F}_p$. Therefore the output b' of the query step is independent of b. Hence one expects to have roughly the same number on 1's and 0's after repeating the test T several times. This implies that

$$\mathrm{Pr}_T(1) = \frac{1}{2} \pm \mathsf{ngl}(\lambda).$$

We therefore construct our CSSIDDH solver $\mathcal{A}'$ as follows: if $\mathrm{Pr}_T(1) = \frac{1}{2} \pm \mathsf{ngl}(\lambda)$, then $\mathcal{A}'$ returns bad; if not, then $\mathcal{A}'$ returns correct.   □

Compared to the IND-CPA game setting, the adversary also has access to a decryption oracle $O(\cdot)$ in the IND-CCA game setting. To prove that SimS is IND-CCA secure, it is sufficient to prove that the decryption oracle is useless. This immediately follows if we assume that no PPT adversary having access to E_0, E_1 and a valid ciphertext c, can produce a brand new valid ciphertext c' unless she encrypts c' herself. This is formalized in the following assumption.

Assumption 3. *The CSSIKoE (Commutative Supersingular Isogeny Knowledge of Exponent) assumption is stated as follows.*

Let λ be a security parameter, let $p = 2^r \ell_1 \cdots \ell_n - 1$ be a prime such that $\lambda + 2 \leq r \leq \frac{1}{2} \log p$. Let $[\mathfrak{a}]$, $[\mathfrak{b}]$ be a uniformly sampled elements of $\mathsf{cl}(\mathbb{Z}[\pi])$. Let $(f_E)_{E \in \mathsf{cl}(\mathbb{Z}[\pi])}$ be a family randomizing functions as defined in Sect. 4.2 such that each of these functions satisfies (P3).

Then for every PPT adversary $\mathcal{A}$ that takes E_0, $[\mathfrak{a}]E_0$ and $([\mathfrak{b}]E_0, f_{[\mathfrak{a}][\mathfrak{b}]E_0}(x(P)))$ where $P \in [\mathfrak{a}][\mathfrak{b}]E_0$ is a point of order 2^r as inputs, and returns a couple $([\mathfrak{b}']E_0, f_{[\mathfrak{a}][\mathfrak{b}']E_0}(x(P'))) \neq ([\mathfrak{b}]E_0, f_{[\mathfrak{a}][\mathfrak{b}]E_0}(x(P)))$ where $P' \in [\mathfrak{a}][\mathfrak{b}']E_0$ is a point of order 2^r, there exists a PPT adversary $\mathcal{A}'$ that takes the same inputs and returns $([\mathfrak{b}'], [\mathfrak{b}']E_0, f_{[\mathfrak{a}][\mathfrak{b}']E_0}(x(P'))))$.

Theorem 4. *Let us suppose that SimS is IND-CPA secure, and that Assumption 3 holds. Then SimS is IND-CCA secure.*

Proof. Let us suppose that Assumption 3 holds and SimS is not IND-CCA secure, and let us prove that SimS is not IND-CPA secure.

Since SimS is not IND-CCA secure, then there exists a PPT adversary $\mathcal{A}^{O(\cdot)} = (\mathcal{A}_1, O(\cdot))$ (where $O(\cdot)$ is the decryption oracle) that successfully determines if a given ciphertext c is that of a plaintext m_0 or m_1 with a non negligible advantage γ.

Suppose that the adversary $\mathcal{A}^{O(\cdot)}$ queries the decryption oracle $O(\cdot)$ with some valid ciphertexts $c_1 = (F_1, x_1), \cdots, c_n = (F_n, x_n)$ computed by $\mathcal{A}_1$. By Assumption 3, there exists a polynomial time algorithm $\mathcal{A}_2$ that when outputting $c_1 = (F_1, x_1), \cdots, c_n = (F_n, x_n)$ also outputs the ideal classes $[\mathfrak{b}_1], \cdots, [\mathfrak{b}_n]$ such that $F_i = [\mathfrak{b}_i]E_0$ for $i \in \{1, \cdots, n\}$. From the knowledge of the ideal classes $[\mathfrak{b}_1], \cdots, [\mathfrak{b}_n]$ and $[\mathfrak{a}]E_0$, the adversary $\mathcal{A}_2$ successfully decrypts $c_1, \cdots, c_n$.

Replacing the decryption oracle $O(\cdot)$ by $\mathcal{A}_2$, we obtain an adversary $\mathcal{A}' = (\mathcal{A}_1, \mathcal{A}_2)$ that successfully determines if a given ciphertext c is that of m_0 or m_1 with advantage γ (which is non negligible) and without making any call to the decryption oracle. This contradicts SimS's IND-CPA security.   □

Remark 2. In all this section, we have assumed that the ideal classes [$\mathfrak{a}$] and [$\mathfrak{b}$] were uniformly sampled elements of $\mathsf{cl}(\mathbb{Z}[\pi])$. Strictly speaking, in order to uniformly sample elements in $\mathsf{cl}(\mathbb{Z}[\pi])$, one needs to compute the class group structure and its generators. Computing the class group $\mathsf{cl}(\mathbb{Z}[\pi])$ requires sub-exponential time in its discriminant [3, Sect. 1]. The class group structure for the CSIDH-512 prime was computed in [3] with a lot of computational effort. As in the preliminary version of CSIDH or instantiations of CSIDH using different primes for which the class group is unknown, we assume that the many small prime ideals $\mathfrak{l}_i$ used to sampled elements in $\mathsf{cl}(\mathbb{Z}[\pi])$ (see Sect. 2.2) generate the entire class group or a sufficiently large subgroup of the class group such that the sampled ideals are close to being uniformly random. See [6, Sect. 7.1] for more details.

Remark 3. The secret vectors $(e_1, \cdots, e_n) \in [-m, m]^n$ used to sample ideals $\mathfrak{a} = \mathfrak{l}_1^{e_1} \cdots \mathfrak{l}_n^{e_n} \in \mathsf{cl}(\mathbb{Z}[\pi])$ can be seen as analogous to exponents in discrete logarithm-based protocols, and Assumption 3 is in that sense analogous to the "knowledge of exponent" assumption (see Appendix A) introduced by Damgård in the context of discrete logarithm-based cryptography [13] and also used in [18]. If ever the class group $\mathsf{cl}(\mathbb{Z}[\pi])$ were computed for the SimS primes, then the analogy would be more immediate.

5   Implementation Results

Here we present the experimentation results obtained by adapting the code of SiGamal [23]. The implementation is done using the two primes proposed by Moriya et al. for SiGamal.

SiGamal prime p_{128}. Let p_{128} be the prime $2^{130} \cdot \ell_1 \cdots \ell_{60} - 1$ where ℓ_1 through ℓ_{59} are the smallest distinct odd primes, and ℓ_{60} is 569. The bit length of p_{128} is 522. The private key bound is $m = 10$.

SiGamal prime p_{256}. Let p_{256} be the prime $2^{258} \cdot \ell_1 \cdots \ell_{43} - 1$ where ℓ_1 through ℓ_{42} are the smallest distinct odd primes, and ℓ_{43} is 307. The bit length of p_{256} is 515. The private key bound is $m = 32$.

All the costs (number of field multiplications, where 1S=0.8M and 1a=0.05M) of CSIDH presented are done with the csidh-512 prime (of 512 bits) while those of SimS, SiGamal and C-SiGamal are with p_{128} and p_{256}. The costs presented in Table 2 and Table 3 are the average costs of 20,000 rounds of key generation, encryption and decryption of each scheme.

Remark 4. In this proof of concept implementation, the class group algorithm considered does not take into account the improvements in [2,4,5].

Table 2. Cost (number of field multiplications, where 1S=0.8M and 1a=0.05M) of class group action for CSIDH with the csidh-512 prime, SimS, SiGamal and C-SiGamal with p_{128} and p_{256}.

Prime	csidh-512	p_{128}		p_{256}	
Scheme	CSIDH	SimS	(C)SiGamal	SimS	(C)SiGamal
Costs	$441,989$	$576,124$	$663,654$	$1,023,400$	$1,140,189$

Table 3. Computational costs (number of field multiplications, where $1S = 0.8M$ and $1a = 0.05M$) for C-SiGamal, SiGamal and SimS with p_{128} and p_{256}.

	p_{128}			p_{256}		
	KGen	Enc.	Dec.	KGen	Enc.	Dec.
C-SiGamal	$663,594$	$1,433,805$	$767,176$	$1,151,447$	$2,685,714$	$1,528,020$
SiGamal		$1,326,856$	$760,861$		$2,208,530$	$1,536,829$
SimS	$576,124$	$1,159,533$	$679,733$	$1,023,827$	$2,057,297$	$1,417,401$

6   Comparison with SiGamal and CSIDH

Here we compare SimS, (C-)SiGamal and CSIDH (or CSIDHpke more precisely). The comparison is done at four levels: design, security, keys and ciphertext sizes, and efficiency.

Design. At the design level, SimS sits between (C)SiGamal and CSIDH. SimS's private keys are ideal classes, as in CSIDH, while in (C)SiGamal they are integral ideals. In the class group action in (C-)SiGamal, a point has to be mapped through the isogeny as well, as opposed to CSIDH and SimS.

Securiy. Security-wise, SimS IND-CPA security relies on CSIDH assumptions, contrarily to SiGamal whose IND-CPA security relies on new assumptions. Moreover, SimS is IND-CCA secure.

Keys and ciphertext sizes. The size of SimS's ciphertexts is equal to that of C-SiGamal's ciphertexts, and is half that of SiGamal ciphertexts. The size of SimS's public keys is half that of the public keys in SiGamal and C-SiGamal. The size of the private key in (C)SiGamal, compared to that of SimS, is augmented by r bits that are used to store the integer α such that the secret ideal $\mathfrak{a}$ is in the form $\mathfrak{a} = (\alpha)\mathfrak{l}_1^{e_1} \cdots \mathfrak{l}_n^{e_n}$.

Efficiency. SimS is more efficient compared to SiGamal and C-SiGamal when using the same primes. From the results in Table 2, we have that for the prime p_{128}, the SimS class group action computation is 1.15x faster than that of (C)SiGamal and is 1.30x slower than that of CSIDH; and for the prime prime

p_{256}, it is 1.11x faster than that of (C)SiGamal and is 2.31x slower than that of CSIDH. For Encryption and decryption with the prime p_{128}, SimS is about 1.13x faster than SiGamal and about 1.19x faster than C-SiGamal. For the prime p_{256}, we get a 1.07x speedup when compared to SiGamal and a 1.21x speedup when compared to C-SiGamal.

We summarize the comparison in Table 1. Note that the encryption in CSIDHpke is essentially two CSIDH class group computations and the decryption is one class group computation.

7   Conclusion

In this paper, we revisited the protocols introduced by Moriya et al. at Asiacrypt 2020, and obtained several results. We proved that the variant of SiGamal suggested by Moriya et al. is not IND-CCA secure. We construct a new isogeny based PKE scheme SimS by simplifying SiGamal in such a way that it resists the IND-CCA attack on SiGamal and its variants. SimS is more efficient than SiGamal and it has smaller private keys, public keys and ciphertexts. We prove that SimS is IND-CPA secure relying on CSIDH assumptions. We introduce a Knowledge of Exponent assumption in the isogeny context. Relying on the later assumption, we prove that SimS is IND-CCA secure. Interestingly, SimS is also closer to CSIDH than SiGamal was, allowing for a better comparison between those two protocols.

We leave a better study of the Knowledge of Exponent assumption and further cryptographic applications of this assumption to future work.

Acknowledgements. We thank Tomoki Moriya, Hiroshi Onuki and Tsuyoshi Takagi for sharing the SiGamal magma code with us. We thank Ankan Pal for his help in running our magma code. We thank Tomoki Moriya and the anonymous reviewers for their useful feedback.

A   Knowledge of Exponent Assumption

In the context of Discrete Logarithm-based cryptography, the Knowledge of Exponent assumption is stated as follows.

Assumption 4 (Knowledge of Exponent assumption [25]). *Let $G = \langle g \rangle$ be a cyclic group of prime order q where q is of cryptographic size. Let x be a uniformly random exponent in $\{2, \cdots, q-1\}$ and let $h = g^x$. The adversary tries to compute $h_1, h_2 \in G$ such that $h_1 = g^z$ and $h_2 = h^z$ for some $z \in \{2, \cdots, q-1\}$. The knowledge of exponent assumption holds if for every polynomial time adversary $\mathcal{A}$ that when given g, q and h outputs (g^z, h^z), there exists a polynomial time adversary $\mathcal{A}'$ that for the same inputs outputs (z, g^z, h^z).*

Intuitively, this assumption states that the only efficient way to compute (g^z, h^z) is to first fix z, then to compute g^z and h^z.

In SimS, the ciphertexts are of the form $\mathsf{c} = ([\mathfrak{b}]E_0, f_{[\mathfrak{b}][\mathfrak{a}]E_0}(x([2m_0 + 1]P_{[\mathfrak{b}][\mathfrak{a}]E_0})))$. Assumption 3 states the only efficient way to compute a valid ciphertext is to first fix the ideal class $[\mathfrak{b}]$, then run the encryption algorithm of SimS to compute $\mathsf{c} = ([\mathfrak{b}]E_0, f_{[\mathfrak{b}][\mathfrak{a}]E_0}(x([2m_0 + 1]P_{[\mathfrak{b}][\mathfrak{a}]E_0})))$.

B   Generating the Distinguished Point of Order 2^r

Here we discuss how when given a supersingular curve E defined over $\mathbb{F}_p$ where $p = 2^r \ell_1 \cdots \ell_n - 1$, one can efficiently generate a distinguished point P_E of order 2^r. The algorithm used by Moriya et al. in C-SiGamal to generate such a point mainly relies on the following result.

Theorem 5. *([24, Appendix A]) Let p be a prime such that $p \equiv 3 \bmod 4$ and let E be a supersingular Montgomery curve defined over $\mathbb{F}_p$ satisfying $\mathrm{End}_{\mathbb{F}_p}(E) \cong \mathbb{Z}[\pi]$. Let $P \in E$.*
If $P \in E[\pi - 1] \setminus E[2]$, then $x(P) \in (\mathbb{F}_p^*)^2 \Longleftrightarrow P \in 2E[\pi - 1]$.
If $P \in E[\pi + 1] \setminus E[2]$, then $x(P) \notin (\mathbb{F}_p^*)^2 \Longleftrightarrow P \in 2E[\pi + 1]$.

Hence when searching for the x-coordinate of points of order 2^r in E, we need to avoid elements of $\mathbb{F}_p$ that are squares. Since $p = 2^r \ell_1 \cdots \ell_n - 1$ with $r > 1$, then $\left(\frac{-1}{p}\right) = -1$, $\left(\frac{2}{p}\right) = 1$ and $\left(\frac{\ell_i}{p}\right) = 1$ for $i \in \{1, \cdots, n\}$. Furthermore, let us suppose that $\ell_1, \cdots, \ell_{n-1}$ are the first smallest odd primes, then for every $I \subset \{0, 1, \cdots, n - 1\}$, $\left(\frac{-\prod_{i \in I} \ell_i}{p}\right) = -1$ where $\ell_0 = 2$. Moriya et al.'s Algorithm [24, Appendix A] exploits this to consecutively sample x from the sequence $-2, -3, -4, \cdots$ and when x is the x-coordinate of a point in $E(\mathbb{F}_p)$, it checks if this point has order divisible by 2^r. Corollary 2 proves that if a such x is the x-coordinate of a point in $E(\mathbb{F}_p)$ then the corresponding point has order divisible by 2^r, hence the check is not necessary.

Corollary 2. *Let p be a prime such that $p \equiv 3 \bmod 4$ and let E be a supersingular Montgomery curve defined over $\mathbb{F}_p$ satisfying $\mathrm{End}_{\mathbb{F}_p}(E) \cong \mathbb{Z}[\pi]$. Let $P \in E(\mathbb{F}_p)$ such that $x(P) \neq 0$.*
If $x(P) \notin (\mathbb{F}_p^*)^2$ then $[\ell_1 \times \cdots \times \ell_n]P$ is a point of order 2^r.

Proof. Since $E(\mathbb{F}_p) = E[\pi - 1]$ is a cyclic group, then there exist a point Q of order $p + 1 = 2^r \ell_1 \cdots \ell_n$ such that $E(\mathbb{F}_p) = \langle Q \rangle$. Set $P = [\alpha_P]Q$. Since E is in the Montgomery form, then $E(\mathbb{F}_p) \cap E[2] = \langle (0, 0) \rangle$. Since $x(P) \neq 0$, then $P \in E[\pi - 1] \setminus E[2]$. Let us suppose that $x(P) \notin (\mathbb{F}_p^*)^2$, then by Theorem 5 $P \notin 2E[\pi - 1]$, hence α_P is odd. Therefore, $\gcd(p + 1, \alpha_P) = \gcd(2^r \ell_1 \cdots \ell_n, \alpha_P) = \gcd(\ell_1 \cdots \ell_n, \alpha_P)$. This implies that $P = [\alpha_P]Q$ is a point of order

$$\frac{p + 1}{\gcd(p + 1, \alpha_P)} = 2^r \cdot \frac{\ell_1 \cdots \ell_n}{\gcd(\ell_1 \cdots \ell_n, \alpha_P)}.$$

Hence $[\ell_1 \times \cdots \times \ell_n]P$ is a point of order 2^r.

Exploiting Corollary 2 we get Algorithm 1 which improves on that used by Moriya et al. for the same purpose.

A random element $x \in \mathbb{F}_p^* \backslash (\mathbb{F}_p^*)^2$ is the x-coordinate of a point $P \in E(\mathbb{F}_p)$ with probability $\frac{1}{2}$. The probability that Algorithm outputs $\bot$ is bounded by $\left(\frac{1}{2}\right)^{\ell_{n-1}}$. For SiGamal primes p_{256} and p_{128} (see Sect. 5), ℓ_{n-1} is 191 and 281 respectively, hence the output is $\bot$ with probability 2^{-191} and 2^{-281} respectively.

Remark 5. Algorithm 1 is deterministic, hence always outputs the same point P_E when the input in unchanged.

Algorithm 1. Computing the distinguished point P_E

Require: The prime $p = 2^r \ell_1 \cdots \ell_n - 1$ and Montgomery coefficient $A \in \mathbb{F}_p$ of a supersingular curve.
Ensure: $P_E \in E(\mathbb{F}_p)$ of order 2^r.
1: Set $x \leftarrow -2$
2: **while** $x^3 + Ax^2 + x$ is not a square in $\mathbb{F}_p$ and $-x \leq \ell_{n-1} + 1$ **do**
3:     Set $x \leftarrow x - 1$
4: **if** $-x \leq \ell_{n-1} + 1$ **then**
5:     Set $P = (x, \cdot) \in E(\mathbb{F}_p)$
6:     Set $P_E = [\ell_1 \times \cdots \times \ell_n]P$
7:     **return** P_E
8: **else**
9:     **return** $\bot$.

References

1. Bellare, M., Rogaway, P.: Optimal asymmetric encryption. In: De Santis, A. (ed.) EUROCRYPT 1994. LNCS, vol. 950, pp. 92–111. Springer, Heidelberg (1995). https://doi.org/10.1007/BFb0053428
2. Bernstein, D.J., Feo, L.D., Leroux, A., Smith, B.: Faster computation of isogenies of large prime degree. Cryptology ePrint Archive, Report 2020/341 (2020). https://eprint.iacr.org/2020/341
3. Beullens, W., Kleinjung, T., Vercauteren, F.: CSI-FiSh: efficient isogeny based signatures through class group computations. In: Galbraith, S.D., Moriai, S. (eds.) ASIACRYPT 2019. LNCS, vol. 11921, pp. 227–247. Springer, Cham (2019). https://doi.org/10.1007/978-3-030-34578-5_9
4. Castryck, W., Decru, T.: CSIDH on the surface. In: Ding, J., Tillich, J.-P. (eds.) PQCrypto 2020. LNCS, vol. 12100, pp. 111–129. Springer, Cham (2020). https://doi.org/10.1007/978-3-030-44223-1_7
5. Castryck, W., Decru, T., Vercauteren, F.: Radical isogenies. In: Moriai, S., Wang, H. (eds.) ASIACRYPT 2020. LNCS, vol. 12492, pp. 493–519. Springer, Cham (2020). https://doi.org/10.1007/978-3-030-64834-3_17

6. Castryck, W., Lange, T., Martindale, C., Panny, L., Renes, J.: CSIDH: an efficient post-quantum commutative group action. In: Peyrin, T., Galbraith, S. (eds.) ASIACRYPT 2018. LNCS, vol. 11274, pp. 395–427. Springer, Cham (2018). https://doi.org/10.1007/978-3-030-03332-3_15

7. Castryck, W., Sotáková, J., Vercauteren, F.: Breaking the decisional Diffie-Hellman problem for class group actions using genus theory. In: Micciancio, D., Ristenpart, T. (eds.) CRYPTO 2020. LNCS, vol. 12171, pp. 92–120. Springer, Cham (2020). https://doi.org/10.1007/978-3-030-56880-1_4

8. Charles, D.X., Lauter, K.E., Goren, E.Z.: Cryptographic hash functions from expander graphs. J. Cryptol. 22(1), 93–113 (2009)

9. Childs, A., Jao, D., Soukharev, V.: Constructing elliptic curve isogenies in quantum subexponential time. J. Math. Cryptol. 8(1), 1–29 (2014)

10. Costello, C., Hisil, H.: A simple and compact algorithm for SIDH with arbitrary degree isogenies. In: Takagi, T., Peyrin, T. (eds.) ASIACRYPT 2017. LNCS, vol. 10625, pp. 303–329. Springer, Cham (2017). https://doi.org/10.1007/978-3-319-70697-9_11

11. Couveignes, J.M.: Hard homogeneous spaces. Cryptology ePrint Archive, Report 2006/291 (2006). https://eprint.iacr.org/2006/291

12. Cramer, R., Shoup, V.: A practical public key cryptosystem provably secure against adaptive chosen ciphertext attack. Cryptology ePrint Archive, Report 1998/006 (1998). https://eprint.iacr.org/1998/006

13. Damgård, I.: Towards practical public key systems secure against chosen ciphertext attacks. In: Feigenbaum, J. (ed.) CRYPTO 1991. LNCS, vol. 576, pp. 445–456. Springer, Heidelberg (1992). https://doi.org/10.1007/3-540-46766-1_36

14. De Saint Guilhem, C.D., Kutas, P., Petit, C., Silva, J.: SÉTA: supersingular encryption from torsion attacks. Cryptology ePrint Archive, Report 2019/1291 (2019). https://eprint.iacr.org/2019/1291

15. Delfs, C., Galbraith, S.D.: Computing isogenies between supersingular elliptic curves over $\mathbb{F}_p$. Des. Cod. Cryptogr. 78(2), 425–440 (2016)

16. Fujisaki, E., Okamoto, T.: Secure integration of asymmetric and symmetric encryption schemes. In: Wiener, M. (ed.) CRYPTO 1999. LNCS, vol. 1666, pp. 537–554. Springer, Heidelberg (1999). https://doi.org/10.1007/3-540-48405-1_34

17. Galbraith, S.D., Petit, C., Shani, B., Ti, Y.B.: On the security of supersingular isogeny cryptosystems. In: Cheon, J.H., Takagi, T. (eds.) ASIACRYPT 2016. LNCS, vol. 10031, pp. 63–91. Springer, Heidelberg (2016). https://doi.org/10.1007/978-3-662-53887-6_3

18. Hada, S., Tanaka, T.: On the existence of 3-round zero-knowledge protocols. In: Krawczyk, H. (ed.) CRYPTO 1998. LNCS, vol. 1462, pp. 408–423. Springer, Heidelberg (1998). https://doi.org/10.1007/BFb0055744

19. Jao, D., De Feo, L.: Towards quantum-resistant cryptosystems from supersingular elliptic curve isogenies. In: Yang, B.-Y. (ed.) PQCrypto 2011. LNCS, vol. 7071, pp. 19–34. Springer, Heidelberg (2011). https://doi.org/10.1007/978-3-642-25405-5_2

20. Jao, D. et al.: Supersingular isogeny key encapsulation, 1 October 2020. https://sike.org/files/SIDH-spec.pdf

21. Koblitz, N.: Elliptic curve cryptosystems. Math. Comp. 48, 203–209 (1987)

22. Kummer, E.: Zur theorie der complexen zahlen. J. für die reine und angewandte Mathematik (Crelles Journal) 35, 319–326 (1847)

23. Moriya, T.: Magma codes for sigamal, 14 August 2020. http://tomoriya.work/code.html

24. Moriya, T., Onuki, H., Takagi, T.: SiGamal: a supersingular isogeny-based PKE and its application to a PRF. In: Moriai, S., Wang, H. (eds.) ASIACRYPT 2020. LNCS, vol. 12492, pp. 551–580. Springer, Cham (2020). https://doi.org/10.1007/978-3-030-64834-3_19

25. Naor, M.: On cryptographic assumptions and challenges. In: Boneh, D. (ed.) CRYPTO 2003. LNCS, vol. 2729, pp. 96–109. Springer, Heidelberg (2003). https://doi.org/10.1007/978-3-540-45146-4_6

26. National Institute of Standards and Technology: Post-quantum Cryptography Standardization, December 2016. https://csrc.nist.gov/Projects/Post-Quantum-Cryptography/Post-Quantum-Cryptography-Standardization

27. Pohlig, S., Hellman, M.: An improved algorithm for computing logarithms over gf(p) and its cryptographic significance. IEEE Trans. Inf. Theory 24(1), 106110 (1978)

28. Renes, J.: Computing isogenies between montgomery curves using the action of (0, 0). In: Lange, T., Steinwandt, R. (eds.) Post-Quantum Cryptography, pp. 229–247. Springer International Publishing, Cham (2018)

29. Rivest, R., Shamir, A., Adleman, L.: A method for obtaining digital signatures and public-key cryptosystems. Commun. ACM 21(2), 120–126 (1978). http://people.csail.mit.edu/rivest/Rsapaper.pdf

30. Rostovtsev, A., Stolbunov, A.: Public-key cryptosystem based on isogenies. IACR Cryptol. ePrint Arch. 2006, 145 (2006)

31. Silverman, J.H.: The Arithmetic of Elliptic Curves. GTM, vol. 106. Springer, New York (2009). https://doi.org/10.1007/978-0-387-09494-6

32. Washington, L.C.: Elliptic Curves: Number Theory and Cryptography. 2 edn. Chapman & Hall/CRC, London (2008)

Memory Optimization Techniques for Computing Discrete Logarithms in Compressed SIKE

Aaron Hutchinson[1], Koray Karabina[1,2(✉)], and Geovandro Pereira[1,3]

[1] University of Waterloo, Waterloo, Canada
{a5hutchinson,koray.karabina,geovandro.pereira}@uwaterloo.ca
[2] National Research Council Canada, Waterloo, Canada
koray.karabina@nrc-cnrc.gc.ca
[3] evolutionQ Inc, Kitchener, Canada

Abstract. The supersingular isogeny-based key encapsulation (SIKE) suite stands as an attractive post- quantum cryptosystem with its relatively small public keys. Public key sizes in SIKE can further be compressed by computing pairings and solving discrete logarithms in certain subgroups of finite fields. This comes at a cost of precomputing and storing large discrete logarithm tables. In this paper, we propose several techniques to optimize memory requirements in computing discrete logarithms in SIKE, and achieve to reduce table sizes by a factor of 4. We implement our techniques and verify our theoretical findings.

Keywords: SIKE · Isogeny-based cryptography · Public key compression · Discrete logarithms

1 Introduction

The supersingular isogeny-based key encapsulation suite (SIKE) stands as an attractive post-quantum cryptosystem with its relatively small public keys. SIKE [4], a post-quantum key-encapsulaion mechanism (KEM) candidate based on the original supersingular isogeny Diffie-Hellman key exchange (SIDH) [7], was submitted to the NIST standardization process on post-quantum cryptography, and has recently advanced as one of the eight alternate candidates in public-key encryption/KEMs.

Public key sizes in SIKE can further be compressed by computing pairings and solving discrete logarithms in certain subgroups of finite fields. This comes at a cost of precomputing and storing large discrete logarithm tables. The process involves evaluating pairings over elliptic curves, and using Pohlig-Hellman algorithm to solve discrete logarithms in order-ℓ^e multiplicative subgroups of $\mathbb{F}_{p^2}^*$; [5,6,8,10]. Computing discrete logarithms is one of the main key compression bottlenecks as shown in [6,8] and the SIKE submission to NIST Round 2 [3], which make use of large precomputed tables (megabytes in some cases) for

© National Research Council of Canada 2021
J. H. Cheon and J.-P. Tillich (Eds.): PQCrypto 2021, LNCS 12841, pp. 296–315, 2021.
https://doi.org/10.1007/978-3-030-81293-5_16

speeding up such calculation. Alternatively, a recent approach is to instead of computing pairings and computing discrete logarithms over $\mathbb{F}_{p^2}^*$, project a point P onto particular subgroups $\langle R_0 \rangle, \langle S_0 \rangle \in E_0(\mathbb{F}_p)[\ell^e]$ of a curve defined over $\mathbb{F}_p$ and solve the elliptic curve discrete logarithm directly via Pohlig-Hellman [12]. This approach can also be optimized by using possibly large precomputed tables, but in that case the technique seems to loose its advantage over the previously known techniques according to [12].

We should also note that a related work allowed for completely discarding precomputed tables during the *Decapsulation* operation by eliminating the need of computing discrete logarithms [11]. On the other hand, large tables still appear in both *KeyGen* and *Encapsulation* of SIKE, and a constrained-memory device running more than just decapsulation would still benefit from reducing table sizes. A great progress has been made towards improving computation time in compressed SIKE, but they all come with a non-trivial overhead of static memory due to precomputed tables. In this paper, we propose several techniques to optimize memory requirements in computing discrete logarithms in SIKE.

1.1   The Organization and Contributions:

The contributions of this paper can be summarized as follows.

- First, we exploit signed digit representation of exponents in radix-ℓ^w and show how to compress discrete logarithm tables by a factor of 2^1.
- Second, we utilize torus-based representation of cyclotomic subgroup elements and compress tables by an additional factor 2. Unfortunately, this representation introduces extra $\mathbb{F}_p$ multiplications during the Pohlig-Hellman algorithm when computing small discrete logarithms at each leaf. We devise new algorithms to overcome this challenge and keep torus-based representations competitive (actually faster for the case where $\ell = 2$).
- Finally, we implement our techniques in C for the SIKE parameters as proposed to NIST. We verified that our factor-4 table reduction does not add computational time overhead for the case where $\ell = 2$, and add an overall 4–9% overhead to SIKE *KeyGen* for $\ell = 3$ as analyzed in Sect. 4. Our code signed-digits-based optimizations can be found on the NIST submission package of SIKE Round 3, and the torus-based optimizations were also made available online[2].

The rest of this paper is organized as follows. Appendix A serves as an overview of some well-known techniques used for computing discrete logarithms and motivates the problem of reducing table sizes. Section 2 shows how to compress discrete logarithm tables by a factor of 2. Section 3 utilizes torus-based

---

[1] This technique was originally introduced by the authors of this paper; implemented in SIKE round 3 [2]; and recently reused in [12].
[2] https://github.com/microsoft/PQCrypto-SIDH/commit/e990bc6784c68426f69ac11 ada3dd5fbfed8b714.

representations to compress tables by another factor of 2. We present our implementation results in Sect. 4 and conclude in Sect. 5. All algorithms in this work can be found in Appendix D.

1.2 Notation

We let p denote a large prime number with $p \equiv 3 \pmod 4$, $\mathbb{F}_p$ denote a field with p elements, and $\mathbb{F}_{p^2} := \mathbb{F}_p[i]/\langle i^2+1 \rangle$. For $a+bi \in \mathbb{F}_{p^2}$, we let $\overline{a+bi} = a - bi$ denote conjugation. We let $\mathbb{G}$ denote the cyclotomic subgroup of $\mathbb{F}_{p^2}^*$ of order $p+1$. We let ℓ denote a small prime number, often taken to be 2 or 3, which divides $p+1$, and we let e be the largest integer such that ℓ^e divides $p+1$. For k an integer such that ℓ^k divides $p+1$, we let $\mathbb{G}_{\ell,k}$ denote the (unique) cyclic subgroup of $\mathbb{G}$ of order ℓ^k. When ℓ and e are fixed, we let g be a fixed generator of $\mathbb{G}_{\ell,e}$ so that $\mathbb{G}_{\ell,e} = \langle g \rangle$. We let w be a small positive integer determining the size of various tables, and define $L = \ell^w$ and $m = \lceil e/w \rceil$. We let $\rho = g^{\ell^{e-w}}$ be the generator of $\mathbb{G}_{\ell,w}$. We use T to denote the table of $\mathbb{F}_{p^2}$ elements defined by $T[u][d] = g^{-d \cdot L^u}$ for $0 \le u \le m-1$ and $0 \le d < L$. Throughout the paper, additional tables T^{sgn}, CT, and T^{exp} will be defined as they are introduced. We let $\mathbf{m}$ and $\mathbf{s}$ denote the costs of multiplication and squaring in $\mathbb{F}_p$.

2   Optimization 1: Signed Digits in the Exponent

As described in Appendix A, large tables are used in SIKE for solving discrete logarithms using the Pohlig-Hellman (PH) algorithm. Here we detail a simple technique which we use to reduce table sizes by a factor of 2. The main idea is to switch to a signed representation of the digits D_k of d and use the fact that inversion in $\mathbb{G}$ has negligible cost to save from storing half of the entries in each row of the table. We give the details below.

For any $a + bi \in \mathbb{G} \subset \mathbb{F}_{p^2}$, we use the facts that $p \equiv 3 \pmod 4$ and $|\mathbb{G}| = p+1$ to derive the equality

$$1 = (a+bi)^{p+1} = (a+bi)(a+bi)^p = (a+bi)(a^p + b^p i^p) = (a+bi)(a-bi),$$

from which it immediately follows that $(a+bi)^{-1} = \overline{a+bi}$. If $\mathbb{G}_{\ell,e} = \langle g \rangle$ is an order ℓ^e subgroup of $\mathbb{G}$ and $h \in \mathbb{G}_{\ell,e}$ is the input to a DLP, we may instead represent $d = \log_g h$ in base $L = \ell^w$ using signed digits [1] as $d = \sum_{k=0}^{m-1} D'_k L^k$, where $D'_k \in [-\lceil (L-1)/2 \rceil, \lceil (L-1)/2 \rceil]$. We modify the table size by defining a new table T^{sgn} as

$$T^{\mathrm{sgn}}[k][D] = g^{-DL^k}, \text{ for } 0 \le k \le m-1, \ 1 \le D \le \lceil (L-1)/2 \rceil.$$

In addition to the upper bound on D decreasing, notice that we've also discarded the entries corresponding to $D = 0$ since they are all the identity element.

The PH algorithm then proceeds nearly identically to Appendix A: define the sequence $h_k = g^{\sum_{i=k}^{m-1} D'_i L^i}$ and determine D'_k by solving $D'_k = \log_s h_k^{L^{m-1-k}}$, where $s = g^{L^{m-1}}$. The latter equality can be solved by iterating through $T^{\mathsf{sgn}}[m-1]$ and performing two equality checks per entry:

1. If $T^{\mathsf{sgn}}[m-1][D] \overset{?}{=} h_k^{L^{m-1-k}}$ succeeds, then set $D'_k \leftarrow D$.
2. If $\overline{T^{\mathsf{sgn}}[m-1][D]} \overset{?}{=} h_k^{L^{m-1-k}}$ succeeds, then set $D'_k \leftarrow D - L$.

Using the notation from Appendix A, when a right traversal $\Delta_{j,k} \rightarrow \Delta_{j,k} \cdot g^{-D'_k L^{j+k}}$ is to be performed, there are three cases: $D'_k = 0, D'_k > 0$, or $D'_k < 0$. If $D'_k = 0$, then no action needs to be taken since $g^{-D'_k L^{j+k}} = 1$. If $D'_k > 0$, then we perform $\Delta_{j,k} \rightarrow \Delta_{j,k} \cdot T^{\mathsf{sgn}}[j+k][D'_k]$ as before. When $D'_k < 0$, then $\Delta_{j,k} \cdot g^{-D'_k L^{j+k}}$ is computed as $\Delta_{j,k} \cdot \overline{T^{\mathsf{sgn}}[j+k][-D'_k]}$.

One can easily replace the table T in SIKE with T^{sgn} with minor modifications, which reduces the table sizes by a factor of 2. The only computational overhead of this approach is that of performing a conjugation at each equality check and right traversal, the cost of which is negligible.

3   Optimization 2: Torus-Based Representation and Arithmetic in Cyclotomic Subgroups

This section details the second optimization we make, which offers an additional factor 2 compression of table sizes. In particular, we take advantage of the torus representation $a + bi \mapsto [a + 1 : b]$ of elements of $\mathbb{G}$ detailed in [14] to store elements of $\mathbb{G} \subset \mathbb{F}_{p^2}$ using only a single element of $\mathbb{F}_p$. This trade-off comes at additional computational effort introduced from the torus-based projective representation, in which checking for equality between two elements becomes a nontrivial expense. We provide the details of this projective representation in Appendix B. Computational overheads are addressed in Sects. 3.1–3.3.

Table Compression via Torus Representation. The table T^{sgn} from Sect. 2 used in generalized PH can be compressed by a factor of 2 (giving a net factor 4 compression over the original T) into a compressed table CT by applying the compression function $C(a + bi) = (a + 1)/b$ to each entry in T^{sgn} as follows, taking $C(-1) = 0$ when necessary:

$$CT[k][D] = C(T^{\mathsf{sgn}}[k][D]) = C(g^{-DL^k}), \text{ for } 0 \leq k \leq m - 2, 1 \leq D \leq \left\lceil \frac{L-1}{2} \right\rceil.$$

Despite the number of table entries appearing the same when compared to T^{sgn}, factor 2 compression is achieved since each entry of CT is a single element of $\mathbb{F}_p$ whereas T^{sgn} stores elements of $\mathbb{F}_{p^2}$. Entries of CT are interpreted as elements of $\mathbb{G}$ by taking $CT[k][D]$ to be the projective element $[CT[k][D] : 1]$.

Computational Overheads. Although the table CT has very appealing storage space over the original table T and its factor-2 compressed form T^{sgn}, the savings comes at some nontrivial computational cost. When using projective representation and CT throughout the PH algorithm, right traversals become mixed multiplications (see Table 3), left traversals become projective exponentiations by L, and the discrete logarithms in $\mathbb{G}_{\ell,w}$ computed at the leaf nodes require mixed equality checks between the DLP input and table elements of the form $[\alpha : 1]$. If a sequential search through the table is still used, the incurred cost for this DLP in $\mathbb{G}_{\ell,w}$ is at most $\lceil (L-1)/2 \rceil \mathbf{E}$ at each leaf, where $\mathbf{E}$ is the cost of an equality check; across the entire PH algorithm, this cost quickly accumulates to a significant slow down in run time. The remainder of this section is devoted to developing alternatives to an exhaustive search approach designed to mitigate the overhead incurred by projective equality checks.

In the remainder, we will let $\mathbf{E}$ and $\mathbf{L}$ denote the costs of an equality check and exponentiation by ℓ in projective coordinates.

3.1   Linear Time Algorithms

The previous subsection showed that nontrivial overhead is introduced during the DLP solved in the leaf nodes of generalized PH when using projective representation of $\mathbb{G}$ with the compressed table CT. We therefore find great interest in algorithms which can more efficiently solve the following DLP: given $\rho = g^{\ell^{e-w}}$ so that $\mathbb{G}_{\ell,w} = \langle \rho \rangle$, some $[x : y] \in \mathbb{G}_{\ell,w}$, and access to the table $CT[m-1]$, find $D \in [-\lceil (L-1)/2 \rceil, \lceil (L-1)/2 \rceil]$ such that $\rho^D = [x : y]$. This subsection will detail algorithms for solving this problem which run in time that is linear in w.

The steps of the algorithm we will define correspond to traversing an almost-full ℓ-ary tree $\mathcal{G}_{\ell,w}$ of depth-w; we describe this tree now. Intuitively, the tree $\mathcal{G}_{\ell,w}$ represents the exponentiation-by-ℓ structure of the cyclic group $\mathbb{G}_{\ell,w}$, which has order ℓ^w. Specifically, the vertex set $V = V(\mathcal{G}_{\ell,w}) = \bigcup_{j=0}^{w} V_j$ of $\mathcal{G}_{\ell,w}$ is the disjoint union of the vertex sets V_j at depth j for $j = 0, 1, \ldots, w$, where

$$V_0 = \{v_{0,0}\}, \quad V_1 = \{v_{1,i} : i = 0, \ldots, (\ell-2)\},$$

$$V_j = \{v_{j,i} : j = 2, \ldots, w, \ i = 0, \ldots, \ell^{j-1}(\ell-1) - 1\}.$$

The edge set $E = E(\mathcal{G}_{\ell,w})$ of $\mathcal{G}_{\ell,w}$ is $E = \bigcup_{j=1}^{w} E_j$, where

$$E_1 = \{vw : v = v_{0,0}, \ w \in V_1\},$$

$$E_j = \{vw : v = v_{j-1,\lfloor i/\ell \rfloor} \in V_{j-1}, \ w = v_{j,i} \in V_j, \ i \in [0, \ell^{j-1}(\ell-1))\}.$$

Note that $|V| = |\mathbb{G}_{\ell,w}| = \ell^w$ and $|E| = \ell^w - 1$. We assign integer values to each vertex in V as follows:

$$v_{0,0} = \ell^w, \tag{1}$$

$$v_{1,i} = \frac{v_{0,\lfloor i/\ell \rfloor}}{\ell} + \ell^{w-1}(i \bmod \ell) = (i+1)\ell^{w-1}, \text{ for } i \in [0, \ell-2] \tag{2}$$

$$v_{j,i} = \frac{v_{j-1,\lfloor i/\ell \rfloor}}{\ell} + \ell^{w-1}(i \bmod \ell), \text{ for } j \in [2, w], \ i \in [0, \ell^{j-1}(\ell-1)). \tag{3}$$

The vertex $v_{0,0}$ represents the identity of $\mathbb{G}_{\ell,w}$, and any two vertices are connected with an edge if and only if one of them is the ℓ-power of the other. We make this precise in Theorem 1, where we relate the vertices of $\mathcal{G}_{\ell,w}$ to the elements of $\mathbb{G}_{\ell,w}$.

Theorem 1. *Let $\mathbb{G}_{\ell,w} = \langle \rho \rangle$ and $\mathcal{G}_{\ell,w} = (V, E)$ as above. Define $g_{j,i} = \rho^{v_{j,i}}$ for all $v_{j,i} \in V$. Then*

$$\mathbb{G}_{\ell,w} = \{g_{j,i} = \rho^{v_{j,i}} : v_{j,i} \in V\}.$$

Furthermore, $g_{0,0}$ is the identity element; we have $g_{j,i}^\ell = g_{j-1,\lfloor i/\ell \rfloor}$ for $j = 1, \ldots, w$, $i = 0, \ldots, \ell^{j-1}(\ell-1)$; and the order of $g_{j,i}$ is exactly ℓ^j for $j = 0, \ldots, w$.

Proof. Clearly, $g_{0,0} = \rho^{v_{0,0}} = \rho^{\ell^w} = 1$. For $j \geq 1$, we have $g_{j,i}^\ell = (\rho^{v_{j,i}})^\ell = \rho^{v_{j-1,\lfloor i/\ell \rfloor}} = g_{j-1,\lfloor i/\ell \rfloor}$. Observing that $1 \leq v_{j,i} \leq \ell^w$ are pairwise distinct integers, and that the largest power of ℓ that divides $v_{j,i}$ is $(w-j)$ proves the rest of the claims.

Theorem 2. *Let $h \in \mathbb{G}_{\ell,w}$ be an element of order ℓ^k for some arbitrary $k \in \{1, \ldots, w\}$. Define a sequence $H = [h_0, \ldots, h_k]$ such that $h_k = h$ and $h_{j-1} = h_j^\ell$ for $j = 1, \ldots, k$. Then, there exists a unique path $P_{0,k} = v_{0,0}, v_{1,i_1}, \ldots, v_{k,i_k}$ in $\mathcal{G}_{\ell,w}$ such that $v_{j,i_j} \in V_j$ and $h_j = g_{j,i_j}$ for $j = 0, \ldots, k$.*

Proof. The proof follows by induction on k and using Theorem 1.

Theorem 3. *Let $1 \neq h \in \mathbb{G}_{\ell,w} = \langle \rho \rangle$. Given h and ρ, one can determine*

1. *k, $i_1, i_2, \ldots, i_k$, that corresponds to the path $P_{0,k} = v_{0,0}, v_{1,i_1}, \ldots, v_{j,i_k}$ as in Theorem 2;*
2. *$s_1, s_2, \ldots, s_k$ such that, $s_1 = i_1 + 1$, $s_j \in \{0, \ldots, (\ell-1)\}$, and $i_j = \ell \cdot i_{j-1} + s_k$ for $j = 2, \ldots, k$.*

Moreover, $h = \rho^d$, where $d = \ell^{w-k} \sum_{j=1}^k s_j \ell^{j-1}$.

Proof. See Appendix C.

Algorithm 1 uses the graph $\mathcal{G}_{\ell,w}$ and its properties to solve the DLP in $\mathbb{G}_{\ell,w}$. The algorithm applies to solving the DLP in any cyclic group of order ℓ^w, but is stated specifically for $\mathbb{G}_{\ell,w}$. The computational and storage complexities of Algorithm 1 are completely described in Theorem 4.

Theorem 4. *For $h \in \mathbb{G}_{\ell,w}$ let $Cost_1(h)$ denote the total cost of running Algorithm 1 with input h in terms of $\mathbf{L}$ and $\mathbf{E}$. By Theorem 1, $h = \rho^{v_{j',i'}}$ for some j' and i'.*

- *If $j' = 0$, then $Cost_1(h) = 0$.*
- *If $1 \leq j' \leq w$ and $0 \leq i' \leq \ell^{j'-1}(\ell-1) - 1$, then $Cost_1(h) = j'\mathbf{L} + \left(j' + \sum_{j=0}^{j'-1} (\lfloor i'/\ell^j \rfloor \mod \ell) \right) \mathbf{E}$.*

Consequently, the average case complexity of Algorithm 1 on a uniformly random input is exactly

$$\left(w - \frac{1}{\ell - 1} + \frac{1}{(\ell - 1)\ell^w} \right) \mathbf{L} + \left(\frac{w(\ell + 1)}{2} - \frac{\ell}{\ell - 1} + \frac{1}{\ell^{w-1}(\ell - 1)} \right) \mathbf{E},$$

and Algorithm 1 has a worst case cost of $Cost_1(\rho^{v_w, \ell^{w-1}(\ell-1)-1}) = w\mathbf{L} + (w\ell - 1)\mathbf{E}$. *Furthermore, the total storage space required by Algorithm 1 is at most* $\ell^w + w - 2$ *elements of* $\mathbb{G}_{\ell, w}$.

Proof. We skip the proof of this theorem due to space limitations, which will be available in the eprint version of this paper.

Refinements of Algorithm 1. If the cost of finding the inverse of an element in $\mathbb{G}_{\ell, w}$ is negligible, then Algorithm 1 can be improved. Intuitively, one can eliminate half of the paths $P_{0,k}$ in Theorem 3 at a cost of inverting elements in H in the beginning of the algorithm. This reduces the number of elements to be stored in Algorithm 1 by a factor of 2. One can further improve on the storage requirement and the number of equality checks by a factor of $(\ell - 1)/\ell$ because, in practice, we do not need to run the comparison $H[j] = G[j][i_j + s]$ for $s = \ell - 1$ (one out of ℓ comparisons) in Algorithm 1. Implementing these optimizations differs slightly when $\ell = 2$ and $\ell > 2$ because of the unique situation of the root vertex of $\mathcal{G}_{\ell, w}$ having only one child when $\ell = 2$. Therefore, we present these cases separately in Algorithm 2 and Algorithm 3, and Theorems 5 and 6 (for $\ell = 3$) give the time and storage complexities for these algorithms.

Theorem 5. *For* $h \in \mathbb{G}_{2,w}$, *let* $Cost_2(h)$ *denote the total cost of running Algorithm 2 with input* h *in terms of* $\mathbf{L}$ *and* $\mathbf{E}$. *By Theorem 1,* $h = \rho^{v_{j'}, i'}$ *for some* j' *and* i'.

- *If* $j' = 0$ *(so* $h = 1$*), then* $Cost_2(h) = 0$.
- *If* $1 \leq j' \leq w$ *(so* $h \neq 1$*), then* $Cost_2(h) = j'\mathbf{L} + (j' - 1)\mathbf{E}$.

Consequently, the average case complexity of Algorithm 2 on a uniformly random input is exactly

$$\left(w - 1 + \frac{1}{2^w} \right) \mathbf{L} + \left(w - 2 + \frac{1}{2^{w-1}} \right) \mathbf{E},$$

and Algorithm 2 has a worst case cost of $Cost_2(\rho^{v_w, i'}) = w\mathbf{L} + (w-1)\mathbf{E}$ *occurring at any* $i' \in [0, 2^{w-1})$. *Furthermore, the total storage space required by Algorithm 2 is at most* $2^{w-2} + w + 2$ *elements of* $\mathbb{G}_{2,w}$.

Theorem 5 can be proved in nearly the same fashion as Theorem 4, though it is much simpler since Algorithm 2 contains no nested loops and exactly one equality check is performed for each iteration of the loop with variable j (this is why the cost in Theorem 5 is independent of i').

Theorem 6. *The average case complexity of Algorithm 3 for $\ell = 3$ on a uniformly random input is exactly*

$$\left(\frac{79}{15}w - \frac{33}{10} + \frac{33}{10 \cdot 3^w}\right) \mathbf{m},$$

assuming $\mathbf{L} = 4\,\mathbf{m}$ *and* $\mathbf{E} = 1\,\mathbf{m}$. *Furthermore, the total storage space required by Algorithm 3 is at most* $3^{w-1} + w - 1$ *elements of* $\mathbb{G}_{3,w}$.

Remark 1. In Theorems 5 and 6, we assume the algorithms use only a single multiplication when checking if some element $H[j]$ is equal to some table entry $G[j][k]$ or its inverse $G[j][k]^{-1}$. If projective coordinates are used with $H[j] = [x : y]$ and $G[j][k] = [\alpha : 1]$, then both equalities can be tested at cost $1\,\mathbf{m}$ by checking $x \stackrel{?}{=} y \cdot \alpha$ and $x \stackrel{?}{=} -y \cdot \alpha$.

3.2   An Exponential Time Algorithm for $\ell = 2$

The algorithm described in the previous section has asymptotically linear time in w for $\ell = 2$, but performs relatively poorly for small values of w. In this section we describe an algorithm specific to projective coordinates and $\ell = 2$, which uses exponentially many $\mathbb{F}_p$ multiplications but performs very well for small values of w. In Sect. 3.3, we will combine both of these algorithms together to achieve an algorithm with better performance than Algorithm 2 for $\ell = 2$. We move toward describing this exponential algorithm now.

The projective points of order 2^k in $\mathbb{G}_{2,e}$ for $k \geq 1$ have a quite simple form and can be solved for explicitly. There is a single point of order 2 which is found to be $[0 : 1]$ by solving the equation $[x : 1]^2 = [1 : 0]$ for x. To find points of order 2^k for $k > 1$ we solve the equation $[x : 1]^2 = [a : 1]$ for x, which leads to the quadratic equation $x^2 - 2ax - 1 = 0$ with solution $x = a \pm \sqrt{a^2 + 1}$. We apply this formula iteratively starting with the point $[0 : 1]$ to generate all points of order 2^k for any $k \geq 1$. To study these points, we define the following recursive sequence: let $a_1 = 0$ and for $j \geq 1$ and $0 \leq i < 2^{j-1}$ define

$$a_{2^j+2i} = a_{2^{j-1}+i} + \sqrt{a_{2^{j-1}+i}^2 + 1}, \quad a_{2^j+2i+1} = a_{2^{j-1}+i} - \sqrt{a_{2^{j-1}+i}^2 + 1}. \quad (4)$$

The first 7 terms of this sequence are: $a_1 = 0$, $a_2 = 1$, $a_3 = -1$, $a_4 = 1 + \sqrt{2}$, $a_5 = 1 - \sqrt{2}$, $a_6 = -1 + \sqrt{2}$, $a_7 = -1 - \sqrt{2}$. One can use straight-forward induction on j to show that $a_{2^j+2i} = -a_{2^{j+1}-2i-1}$ and that $[a_{2^j+i} : 1]$ has order 2^{j+1} for $j \geq 0$ and $0 \leq i < 2^j$.

As may be apparent, terms in the sequence a are linear $\{-1, 0, 1\}$-combinations of a smaller set of terms. We get a hold on this sequence explicitly by defining a new sequence b as

$$b_{2^j+i} = a_{2^{j+2}+2i} - a_{2^{j+1}+i} = \sqrt{a_{2^{j+1}+i}^2 + 1}$$

for $j \geq 0$ and $0 \leq i < 2^j$. The first 3 terms of this sequence are:

$$b_1 = \sqrt{2}, \quad b_2 = \sqrt{2}\sqrt{2+\sqrt{2}}, \quad b_3 = \sqrt{2}\sqrt{2-\sqrt{2}}.$$

Notice that terms $a_1, \ldots, a_{15}$ are $\{-1, 0, 1\}$-combinations of $1, b_1, b_2,$ and b_3. As expected, the following theorem shows that we can write any term of the sequence a as a combination of terms from the sequence b.

Theorem 7. *Let $j \geq 2$ and $0 \leq i < 2^{j-1}$. Let $(\beta_{j-2} \cdots \beta_0)_2$ be the binary representation of i so that $i = \beta_{j-2}2^{j-2} + \cdots + \beta_1 2 + \beta_0$. Then*

$$a_{2^j+i} = 1 + (-1)^{\beta_{j-2}} b_1 + (-1)^{\beta_{j-3}} b_{2^1 + (\beta_{j-2})_2} + \cdots + (-1)^{\beta_0} b_{2^{j-2} + (\beta_{j-2} \cdots \beta_1)_2}$$

$$= 1 + \sum_{k=0}^{j-2} (-1)^{\beta_k} b_{2^{j-k-2} + (\beta_{j-2} \cdots \beta_{k+1})_2}.$$

Proof. The proof follows by induction on j.

Note that the theorem gives a representation of all a_k with $k \in \mathbb{N}$ as a linear combination of terms from b, since if $2^{j-1} \leq i < 2^j$ we have $a_{2^j+i} = -a_{2^j+(2^j-i-1)}$, and $0 \leq 2^j - i - 1 < 2^{j-1}$.

Algorithm 4 can be used to compute discrete logarithms by means of Theorem 7 using a table $T^{\exp}$ defined by $T^{\exp}[j][i] = b_{2^j+i}$ for $j \in [0, w-3]$ and $i \in [0, 2^j)$. Given some $[x : y]$ such that $[x : y] = [a_k : 1]$ for some a_k with $k \in [1, 2^w)$, Algorithm 4 first finds k. A precomputed conversion table Log can then be used to translate points $[a_k : 1]$ into the corresponding discrete logarithm in the desired base ρ; i.e. a table Log is defined by $Log[k] = D$ where $\rho^D = [a_k : 1]$ for $1 \leq k < 2^w$ and $D \in [-2^{w-1}, 2^{w-1}]$.

Theorem 8. *Let $Cost_4(h)$ denote the total number of $\mathbb{F}_p$ multiplications used by Algorithm 4 when ran with input h with $w \geq 2$. Then for $j' \in [2, w)$ and $i' \in [0, 2^{j'-1})$, we have*

$$Cost_4([a_{2^{j'}+i'} : 1]) = Cost_4([a_{2^{j'}+(2^{j'}-i'-1)} : 1]) = 2^{j'-2} + \lfloor i'/2 \rfloor,$$

and consequently the average number of $\mathbb{F}_p$ multiplications used by Algorithm 4 on a uniformly random input is exactly $2^{w-3} - \frac{1}{2}$. Furthermore, the total storage required by Algorithm 4 is at most $2^{w-1} - 1$ many elements of $\mathbb{F}_p$.

Proof. We skip the proof of this theorem due to space limitations, which will be available in the eprint version of this paper.

A summary of the average complexities and storage costs of the algorithms discussed so far is given in Table 1.

Table 1. Summary of algorithm computational and storage complexities. Storage is the total number of $\mathbb{F}_p$ elements stored.

	Restriction	Average Complexity	Storage
Alg. 1	$\ell = 2$	$\left(\frac{7}{2}w - 4 + \frac{4}{2^w}\right)\mathbf{m}$	$2^w + w - 2$
Alg. 2	$\ell = 2$	$\left(3w - 4 + \frac{1}{2^{w-2}}\right)\mathbf{m}$	$2^{w-2} + w + 2$
Alg. 4	$\ell = 2$	$\left(2^{w-3} - \frac{1}{2}\right)\mathbf{m}$	$2^{w-1} + 1$
Alg. 1	$\ell = 3$	$\left(\frac{28}{5}w - \frac{33}{10} + \frac{33}{10\cdot 3^w}\right)\mathbf{m}$	$3^w + w - 2$
Alg. 3	$\ell = 3$	$\left(\frac{79}{15}w - \frac{33}{10} + \frac{33}{10\cdot 3^w}\right)\mathbf{m}$	$3^{w-1} + w - 1$

3.3   A Hybrid Algorithm for $\ell = 2$

In this section we formulate a hybrid of Algorithms 2 and 4, resulting in our most efficient algorithm for computing discrete logarithms in $\mathbb{G}_{\ell,w}$ when using projective representation. Algorithm 2 performs very well asymptotically, but Algorithm 4 has much better performance for small values of w. Intuitively, the hybrid algorithm will square the input element until the order of the element is guaranteed to be small, pushing it toward the root of $\mathcal{G}_{\ell,w}$; then Algorithm 4 is ran on this small order element to compute its discrete logarithm, and finally the path which was taken through $\mathcal{G}_{\ell,w}$ is traced backwards as in Algorithm 2 to compute the full discrete logarithm.

Specifically, let $w_1, w_2 \in \mathbb{N}$ such that $w = w_1 + w_2$. The hybrid algorithm, detailed in Algorithm 5, first performs (at most) w_2 many squarings on the input element h to produce a list H of length k satisfying $H[j] = h^{2^{k-j}}$ for $j \in [0, k)$. The element $H[0]$ is then guaranteed to be in $\mathbb{G}_{2,w_1}$, and Algorithm 4 is then called with $H[0]$ as input. It could be the case that $H[0]$ is the identity element, in which case we instead call Algorithm 4 with input $H[w_1]$. Once Algorithm 4 completes and returns some logarithm d, the values ord and i_j are computed such that $d = v_{ord,i_j}$. If necessary, the list H is inverted so that the path through $\mathcal{G}_{2,w}$ lies in the region corresponding to the elements stored in the table G. The remainder of the algorithm then proceeds as in Algorithm 2 by backtracing the path through $\mathcal{G}_{2,w}$. To simplify the indexing on the computation of d in the latter part of the algorithm, a bit-shift and bit-set approach is used instead.

In the event that $H[0]$ is the identity and the number of squarings performed was no more than w_1, Algorithm 4 is instead called on h and Algorithm 5 immediately returns the proper logarithm.

To compute the value of i_j from d in Algorithm 5, the following lemma is used. The statement for $j \in \{1, 2\}$ can be easily verified by hand, after which the general proof follows easily with induction on j using the definition of $v_{j,i}$.

Lemma 1. *Let $j \in [2, w]$ and $i \in [0, 2^{j-1})$. Write*

$$i = \beta_{j-2}2^{j-2} + \beta_{j-3}2^{j-3} + \cdots + \beta_1 2 + \beta_0 \qquad \text{for } \beta_k \in \{0, 1\}.$$

Then $v_{j,i} = (2(\beta_0 2^{j-2} + \beta_1 2^{j-3} + \cdots + \beta_{j-3}2 + \beta_{j-2}) + 1)2^{w-j}$. When $j = 1$, we have $v_{1,0} = (2 \cdot 0 + 1)2^{w-1}$.

Theorem 9. *Let* $2 \leq w_1 < w$ *and let* $w_2 = w - w_1$. *Let* $Cost_5(h)$ *denote the total number of* $\mathbb{F}_p$ *multiplications used by Algorithm 5 when ran with input* h, *using* w_1 *as the parameter for Algorithm 4.*

1. *If* $j \leq w_1$ *and* $j \leq w_2$, *then* $Cost_5(\rho^{v_{j,i}}) = j\mathbf{L} + Cost_4(\rho^{v_{j,i}})$.
2. *If* $w_1 < j \leq w_2$, *then* $Cost_5(\rho^{v_{j,i}}) = j\mathbf{L} + (j - w_1)\mathbf{E} + Cost_4(\rho^{2^{j-w_1}v_{j,i}})$.
3. *If* $j > w_2$, *then* $Cost_5(\rho^{v_{j,i}}) = w_2\mathbf{L} + w_2\mathbf{E} + Cost_4(\rho^{2^{w_2}v_{j,i}})$.

When $\mathbf{L} = 2\,\mathbf{m}$ *and* $\mathbf{E} = 1\,\mathbf{m}$, *the average number of* $\mathbb{F}_p$ *multiplications used by Algorithm 5 on a uniformly random input is given by the following table:*

if $w_2 \leq 2$ and $w_2 \leq w_1$	$3w_2 + 2^{w_1-3} - \frac{1}{2} - \frac{w_2+2}{2^{w_1}} + \frac{2}{2^w}$
if $2 < w_2$ and $w_2 \leq w_1$	$3w_2 + 2^{w_1-3} - \frac{1}{2} + \frac{2^{w_2-3} - w_2 - \frac{5}{2}}{2^{w_1}} + \frac{2}{2^w}$
if $w_1 = 2$ and $2 < w_2$	$3w_2 - \frac{5}{4} + \frac{6}{2^w}$
if $2 < w_1$ and $w_1 < w_2$	$3w_2 + 2^{w_1-3} - 2^{w_1-w_2-4} - \frac{5}{16} - \frac{w_1+\frac{7}{2}}{2^{w_1}} + \frac{1}{2^{w_2}} + \frac{2}{2^w}$

Proof. We skip the proof of this theorem due to space limitations, which will be available in the eprint version of this paper.

4   Implementation Results and Comparisons

We have implemented our proposal in C language on top of the Microsoft SIDH library [9]. Our contributions were incrementally included in the SIDH library [9]. The signed-digits technique (Sect. 2) was integrated during the SIKE submission to Round 3 of the NIST process and can be found in the submitted package [2]. More recently the torus-based optimizations (Sect. 3) were included in the official Microsoft SIDH library[3].

Table 2 showcases the result of our memory optimized approach for computing discrete logarithms in $\mathbb{G}_{2,e}$ using signed-digits with torus-based representations and Algorithm 5 for leaf computations. We compare discrete logarithm computation time against previous work in terms of number of $\mathbb{F}_p$ multiplications. In this case, our approach turns out to be slightly faster in addition to the factor-4 reduction in table sizes. Despite leaf computations being more expensive than [8], savings are gained through cheaper edge traversal costs by using projective squaring and mixed multiplications (each costing $2\,\mathbf{m}$ instead of $3\,\mathbf{m}$).

Table 2 also illustrates our results for computing discrete logarithms in $\mathbb{G}_{3,e}$ using signed-digits with torus-based representations and Algorithm 3 for leaf computations. One can see that for practical values of w (i.e., tables not too large), the time overhead significantly increases ranging from $29 - 58\%$ for $w \in [2,4]$. Such large time overheads, which do not occur for $\ell = 2$, arise for two reasons: 1) left edge traversals for $\ell = 3$ consist of projective cubings that take $4\,\mathbf{m}$, which is more expensive than the cost of standard cyclotomic cubing ($3\,\mathbf{m}$); and 2) Algorithm 3 cannot exploit the extra structures that were present in the $\mathbb{G}_{2,w}$ subgroup and

---

[3] https://github.com/microsoft/PQCrypto-SIDH/commit/e990bc6784c68426f69ac11 ada3dd5fbfed8b714.

Table 2. Comparative results of the average cost (in $\mathbb{F}_p$ multiplications) and table sizes (in KiB) to compute logarithms in $\mathbb{G}_{2,e}$ and $\mathbb{G}_{3,e}$ using Pohlig-Hellman with torus-based representations, and using Algorithm 5 (or Algorithm 3) vs. previous Pohlig-Hellman with standard $\mathbb{F}_{p^2}$ representations [8,15]. We set $w_1 = w - 1$ in Algorithm 5 as it gives the best speed.

Dlog in $\mathbb{G}_{2,e}$	source	$w = 3$		$w = 4$		$w = 5$	
		time	size	time	size	time	size
$e = 216$ (SIKEp434)	Previous [8]	1944	70	1600	105	1415	342
	ours	1818	18	1542	27	1408	86
$e = 250$ (SIKEp503)	Previous [8]	2340	186	1937	279	1662	221
	ours	2184	47	1859	70	1649	56
$e = 305$ (SIKEp610)	Previous [8]	2973	268	2482	405	2126	321
	ours	2761	67	2368	102	2095	81
$e = 372$ (SIKEp751)	Previous [8]	3765	197	3126	296	2748	954
	ours	3476	49	2964	74	2688	240
Dlog in $\mathbb{G}_{3,e}$	source	$w = 2$		$w = 3$		$w = 4$	
		time	size	time	size	time	size
$e = 137$ (SIKEp434)	Previous [8]	1845	151	1407	301	1185	688
	ours	2371	34	2029	73	1868	172
$e = 159$ (SIKEp503)	Previous [8]	2208	199	1680	198	1407	895
	ours	2828	44	2397	48	2185	221
$e = 192$ (SIKEp610)	Previous [8]	2757	142	2121	284	1767	639
	ours	3496	32	2994	68	2703	158
$e = 239$ (SIKEp751)	Previous [8]	3621	429	2793	859	2337	1932
	ours	4542	95	3886	207	3507	477

were exploited in Algorithm 5. On the other hand, this is not as bad as it may seem, since according to benchmarks we ran on the compressed SIKE code, the discrete logarithm phase takes only $\approx 15\%$ of the whole *KeyGen*. Hence, the overall computational overheads would reduce to 4–9% from an end user perspective.

For integrating our results into the official SIKE suite [2], we decided to use the torus-based method only for the $\ell = 2$ to obtain a factor-4 reduction in table sizes. For $\ell = 3$, in order not to impact the runtime negatively, we use the signed-digits technique and obtain a factor-2 reduction in table sizes with no time overhead. Thus, SIKE enjoys an average factor-3 reduction in table sizes with negligible overhead in computation time. Overall cycle count benchmarks with our C code can be seen in Table 2.1 in the SIKE specification document [2], in particular in the rows named SIKEpXXX_compressed.

5 Concluding Remarks

We have proposed methods to reduce the table sizes in compressed SIKE by a factor of 4, with minimal computational overheads. For $\ell = 2$, new table sizes can range from 18 KiB to 240 KiB for all SIKE parameter sets and from 34 KiB to 477 KiB for $\ell = 3$. We have confirmed our theoretical estimates experimentally and our C implementation has been effectively integrated into the official SIKE library.

Acknowledgements. The authors would like to thank the SIKE team members for their comments on the paper and support with integrating our results into the official SIKE suite. G. Pereira is supported in part by NSERC, CryptoWorks21, Canada First Research Excellence Fund, Public Works and Government Services Canada, and by the National Research Council Canada and University of Waterloo Collaboration Center (NUCC) program 927517.

A   The Pohlig-Hellman Algorithm with width-w Windows

Given an instance $\mathbb{G}_{\ell,e}$, g, and $h \in \mathbb{G}$ of a discrete logarithm problem (DLP) in $\mathbb{G}_{\ell,e}$, *Pohlig-Hellman algorithm* (PH) [13] uses width-w windows and computes $d = \log_g h$ as follows. Let w be a positive integer with $w \mid e^4$, define $m = \lceil e/w \rceil$, and write the exponent d in base $L = \ell^w$ as $d = \sum_{i=0}^{m-1} D_i L^i$, $D_i \in [0, L)$. Define the sequence $h_k = g^{\sum_{i=k}^{m-1} D_i L^i}$, which satisfies

$$h_0 = h, \quad h_{k+1} = h_k g^{-D_k L^k}, \quad h_k^{L^{m-1-k}} = \left(g^{L^{m-1}}\right)^{D_k}, \quad k = 0, \ldots, m - 2. \quad (5)$$

Note that $D_k = \log_\rho h_k^{L^{m-1-k}} \in [0, L)$, where $\rho = g^{L^{m-1}}$ generates a group $\mathbb{G}_{\ell,w}$ of order ℓ^w. In PH, a table T of elements are precomputed and stored such that $T[k][D] = g^{-DL^k}$, for $0 \le k \le m - 1$ and $0 \le D < L$. Note that the table T consists of $m \cdot L$ elements of $\mathbb{G}_{\ell,e}$. One computes $h_0^{L^{m-1}}$, and determines D_0 by looking up the last row $T[m-1]$ of T. For $k = 1, \ldots, m-1$, first $h_k = h_{k-1}T[k-1][D_{k-1}]$ is computed (one multiplication), and then $h_k^{L^{m-1-k}}$ is computed (($m-1-k$) exponentiations by L), and D_k is determined by looking up the row $T[m-1]$. Once $D_0, \ldots, D_{m-1}$ are known, $d = \sum_{i=0}^{m-1} D_i L^i$ can be recovered.

As previously observed in the literature [8,15], the steps of the above PH algorithm can be associated with subgraph of a directed graph $\mathcal{T}_{e,w}$. The vertices of $\mathcal{T}_{e,w}$ are labeled as $\Delta_{j,k}$ for $0 \le k \le m - 1$ and $0 \le j \le m - 1 - k$, with $\Delta_{0,0}$ being the top-most vertex and $\Delta_{j,k}$ being the vertex lying at the end of the path starting at $\Delta_{0,0}$ and following j many left edges and k many right edges. The vertices $\Delta_{m-1-k,k}$ for $0 \le k \le m - 1$ are referred to as *leaves*, and $\Delta_{0,0}$ is the *root*. We make a correspondence between vertices $\Delta_{j,k}$ of $\mathcal{T}_{e,w}$ and elements of $\mathbb{G}_{\ell,e}$ by associating $\Delta_{j,k}$ with $h_k^{L^j}$, and it will be convenient to use "=" for this association: $\Delta_{j,k} = h_k^{L^j}$, for $0 \le k \le m - 1$ and $0 \le j \le m - 1 - k$ In particular, the root $\Delta_{0,0}$ is associated with the input $h_0 = h$ to the DLP, and the leaves $\Delta_{m-1-k,k}$ correspond to the elements $h_k^{L^{m-1-k}}$ used to determine D_k. The outgoing edges of non-leaf vertices $\Delta_{j,k}$ can then be interpreted as group operations in $\mathbb{G}_{\ell,e}$ as follows: *left traversal:* $\Delta_{j,k} \to \Delta_{j+1,k} = \Delta_{j,k}^L$; *right traversal:* $\Delta_{j,k} \to \Delta_{j,k+1} = \Delta_{j,k} \cdot g^{-D_k L^{j+k}}$.

Note that an edge with a positive slope in $\mathcal{T}_{e,w}$ (a *left traversal*) corresponds to exponentiation by L, and an edge with a negative slope in $\mathcal{T}_{e,w}$ (a *right*

---

[4] The case when $w \nmid e$ requires more attention as explained in [15].

traversal) corresponds to a multiplication by a group element, assuming access to the lookup table T, as previously defined.

One can notice that the computational steps in the generalized PH algorithm correspond to traversing a spanning subgraph S of $\mathcal{T}_{e,w}$, where the edge set of S consists of all the positive slope edges of $\mathcal{T}_{e,w}$, and all negative slope edges of the form $\{\Delta_{0,k}, \Delta_{0,k+1}\}$ for $k = 0, \ldots, m-1$. One can do better by assigning weights $\mathfrak{p}$ (the cost of exponentiation by ℓ^w in $\mathbb{G}_{\ell,e}$) and $\mathfrak{q}$ (the cost of multiplication in $\mathbb{G}_{\ell,e}$) to the edges of $\mathcal{T}_{e,w}$ with positive and negative slopes, respectively, and determining an *optimal strategy* (originally introduced in the context of isogeny computation [7] and then extended to discrete logarithms [8]) to minimize the cost of solving DLP. Such strategies are typically represented in *linear form* as a list of positive integers of length m. This yields a recursive algorithm to solve discrete logarithms; see Algorithm 6.3 in [15].

B   Torus-based Representations

We summarize the torus-based compressed representation of elements of $\mathbb{G}$ as detailed in [14]. Elements of $\mathbb{G}$ written in the form $a+bi$ are said to be in *standard representation*, and we must have $a^2 + b^2 = 1$ (see Sect. 2). When $b \neq 0$, one can write $a + bi = (\alpha + i)/(\alpha - i)$, where $\alpha := (a+1)/b$. Since taking $\alpha = 0$ produces $a + bi = -1 + 0i$, we can represent cyclotomic subgroup elements with a single element in $\mathbb{F}_p$ as follows:

$$\mathbb{G} = \{1\} \cup \left\{ \frac{\alpha + i}{\alpha - i} : \alpha \in \mathbb{F}_p \right\}. \tag{6}$$

Under this correspondence, we define the *compression function* $C : \mathbb{G}\backslash\{1, -1\} \to \mathbb{F}_p$ as $C(a+bi) := (a+1)/b$. Group operations respect compressed representation of elements in $\mathbb{G}$ in the following sense: If $C(a + bi) = \alpha$ and $C(c + di) = \beta$, then we have $C((a + bi)^{-1}) = -\alpha$, and

$$C((a + bi) \cdot (c + di)) = \begin{cases} (\alpha\beta - 1)/(\alpha + \beta) & \alpha + \beta \neq 0 \\ 1 & \alpha + \beta = 0 \end{cases}$$

Compressed representations inherit a *projective representation* as follows. For $x, y \in \mathbb{F}_p$ not both zero, if we define $[x : y] := \left(\frac{x+yi}{x-yi} \right)$, then we can write the identity element as $1 = [1 : 0]$ (*the point at infinity*), and for any $[x : y]$ with $y \neq 0$ we have $[x : y] = [x/y : 1]$. In other words, we can rewrite (6) as

$$\mathbb{G} = \{[1 : 0]\} \cup \{[\alpha : 1] : \alpha \in \mathbb{F}_p\} = \{[x : y] : x, y \in \mathbb{F}_p \text{ not both } 0\}. \tag{7}$$

Note that the compression function C is undefined for $1, -1 \in \mathbb{F}_p$, but these elements are represented in projective coordinates as $[1 : 0]$ and $[0 : 1]$, respectively. Passing from regular to projective representation is easy, but the reverse direction requires at least an inversion in $\mathbb{F}_p$: for $a + bi \neq -1$ and $x^2 + y^2 \neq 0$ we have

$$a + bi \longmapsto [a + 1 : b], \quad [x : y] \longmapsto \frac{x^2 - y^2}{x^2 + y^2} + \frac{2xy}{x^2 + y^2}i$$

We summarize the group operations of $\mathbb{G}$ in projective coordinates in Table 3. Each formula can be directly verified by converting to the regular representations of the involved elements using the above mappings.

Table 3. Summary of operations and their costs for elements of $\mathbb{G}$ in projective coordinates. Here, $x, y, z, t, \alpha, a, b \in \mathbb{F}_p$ with x and y not both 0, z and t not both 0, and $a^2 + b^2 = 1$.

Projective Squaring (**2 m**):	$[x : y]^2 = [(x + y)(x - y) : 2xy]$
Projective Cubing (**2 m+2 s**):	$[x : y]^3 = [x(x^2 - 3y^2) : y(3x^2 - y^2)]$
Projective Multiplication (**3 m**):	$[x : y][z : t] = [xz - yt : (x + y)(z + t) - xz - yt]$
Mixed Multiplication (**2 m**):	$[x : y][\alpha, 1] = [x\alpha - y : x + y\alpha]$
Inversion (**0 m**):	$[x : y]^{-1} = [-x : y]$
Projective Equality check (**2 m**):	$[x : y] = [z : t] \iff xt - yz = 0$
Mixed Equality check (**1 m**):	$[x : y] = [\alpha : 1] \iff x - y\alpha = 0$

C   Proofs

Below is a proof of Theorem 3.

Proof. Given $1 \neq h$, we first determine the least positive integer k such that $h^{\ell^k} = 1$, by performing k exponentiations by ℓ in $\mathcal{G}_{\ell,w}$. We also store the intermediate values $h_i = h^{\ell^{k-i}}$, $i = 0, \ldots, k$, in an array $H = [h_0 = 1, h_1, \ldots, h_k = h]$. By Theorem 2, there is a unique path $P_{0,k} = v_{0,0}, v_{1,i_1}, \ldots, v_{j,i_k}$ in $\mathcal{G}_{\ell,w}$ such that $v_{j,i_j} \in V_j$ and $h_j = g_{j,i_j}$ for $j = 0, \ldots, k$. By the proof of Theorem 2, $i_1 \in \{0, \ldots, (\ell - 2)\}$ can be determined as the integer satisfying $h_1 = g_{1,i_1}$, and we set $s_1 = i_1 + 1$. Next, we inductively assume that i_{j-1} and s_{j-1} are already known for some $2 \leq j \leq w$. By the definition of E_j, and the fact that $v_{j-1,i_{j-1}} v_{j,i_j} \in E_j$, $i_j = \ell \cdot i_{j-1} + s_j$ for some $s_j \in \{0, \ldots, (\ell - 1)\}$. Since i_{j-1} is already known, the value of s_j (and i_j) can be determined as the integer satisfying $h_j = g_{j,i_j} = g_{j,\ell \cdot i_{j-1}+s_j}$. As a result, we can recover all i_j and s_j for all $j = 1, \ldots, k$, where $s_1 = i_1 + 1$ and $i_j = \ell \cdot i_{j-1} + s_j$. To prove the last claim of our theorem, we need to show $d = v_{k,i_k}$, because $h = h_k = g_{k,i_k} = \rho^{v_{k,i_k}}$. For $k = 1$, Theorem 3 yields $d = s_1 \ell^{w-1}$, and it follows from (2) that $v_{1,i_1} = (i_1 + 1)\ell^{w-1} = s_1 \ell^{w-1} = d$, as required. In the following, we assume that $k \geq 2$. Using (1)-(3), we write

$$
\begin{aligned}
v_{k,i_k} &= \frac{v_{k-1,i_{k-1}}}{\ell} + s_k \ell^{w-1} = \frac{v_{k-2,i_{k-2}}}{\ell^2} + s_{k-1}\ell^{w-2} + s_k\ell^{w-1} \\
&= \frac{v_{1,i_1}}{\ell^{k-1}} + s_2 \ell^{w-k+1} + \cdots + s_k \ell^{w-1} = s_1 \ell^{w-k} + s_2 \ell^{w-k+1} + \cdots + s_k \ell^{w-1} \\
&= \ell^{w-k} \sum_{j=1}^{k} s_j \ell^{j-1} = d, \text{ which finishes the proof.}
\end{aligned}
$$

D   Algorithms

Algorithm 1: Discrete Logarithm Computation in $\mathbb{G}_{\ell,w}$

Parameters: ℓ (prime), $w \geq 1$, a precomputed table
$G[j][i] = g_{j,i} = \rho^{v_{j,i}} \in \mathbb{G}_{\ell,w}$ for $j \in [1,w], v_{j,i} \in V_j$.

Input   : $h \in \mathbb{G}_{\ell,w}$
Output   : $d \in [0, \ell^w)$ such that $h = \rho^d$

1   $H = [h]$
2   $k \leftarrow 0$
3   **while** $H[0] \neq 1$ **do**
4     $H.insert(0, H[0]^\ell)$
5     $k \leftarrow k + 1$
6   **end**
7   **if** $k = 0$ **then return** 0
8   $d \leftarrow 1$
9   **for** $i = 0$ **to** $\ell - 2$ **do**
10   **if** $H[1] = G[1][i]$ **then**
11      $i_j \leftarrow i$
12      $d \leftarrow (i_j + 1)$
13   **break**
14   **end**
15   **end**
16   **for** $j = 2$ **to** k **do**
17    $i_j \leftarrow \ell \cdot i_j$
18   **for** $s = 0$ **to** $(\ell - 1)$ **do**
19   **if** $H[j] = G[j][i_j + s]$ **then**
20       $d \leftarrow d + s \cdot \ell^{j-1}$
21       $i_j \leftarrow i_j + s$
22   **break**
23   **end**
24   **end**
25    $d \leftarrow \ell^{w-k} \cdot d$
26   **end**
27   **return** d

Algorithm 2: Discrete Logarithm Computation in $\mathbb{G}_{2,w}$

Parameters: $w \geq 1$, a table G such that $G[0], G[1]$ are null,
$G[2][0] = \rho^{v_{2,0}}$, and $G[j][i_j] = \rho^{v_{j,2i_j}}$ for $j \in [3,w]$,
$i_j = 0, \ldots, |V_j|/4 - 1$.

Input   : $h \in \mathbb{G}_{2,w}$
Output   : $d \in [0, 2^w)$ such that $h = \rho^d$

1   $H \leftarrow [h]$
2   $k \leftarrow 0$
3   **while** $H[0] \neq 1$ **do**
4     $H.insert(0, H[0]^2)$
5     $k \leftarrow k + 1$
6   **end**
7   **if** $k = 0$ **then return** 0
8   **if** $k = 1$ **then return** 2^{w-1}
9   $d \leftarrow 1$
10   $inv \leftarrow False$
11   **if** $H[2] \neq G[2][0]$ **then**
12    $H[i] \leftarrow H[i]^{-1}$ for $i = 2, \ldots, k$
13    $inv \leftarrow True$
14   **end**
15   $i_j \leftarrow 0$
16   **for** $j = 3$ **to** k **do**
17    $i_j \leftarrow 2 \cdot i_j$
18   **if** $H[j] \neq G[j][i_j/2]$ **then**
19      $d \leftarrow d + 2^{j-1}$
20      $i_j \leftarrow i_j + 1$
21   **end**
22   **end**
23   $d \leftarrow 2^{w-k} \cdot d$
24   **if** $inv = True$ **then**
25    $d \leftarrow 2^w - d$
26   **end**
27   **return** d

Algorithm 3: Discrete Logarithm Computation in $\mathbb{G}_{\ell,w}$ (a variant of Algorithm 1 for $\ell > 2$)

    Parameters: $\ell > 2$, $w \geq 1$, a precomputed table G such that $G[0]$ is null,
                    $G[1][i] = g_{1,i} = \rho^{v_{1,i}}$ for $i = 0, \ldots, (\ell-1)/2 - 1$,
                    $G[j][b_j(\ell-1) + s] = g_{j,b_j\ell+s} = \rho^{v_{j,b_j\ell+s}}$, for $j \in [2, w]$,
                    $b_j = 0, \ldots, \ell^{j-2}(\ell-1)/2 - 1$, $s = 0, \ldots, (\ell-1) - 1$.
    Input   : $h \in \mathbb{G}_{\ell,w}$
    Output   : $d \in [0, \ell^w)$ such that $h = \rho^d$

1 $H \leftarrow [h]$
2 $k \leftarrow 0$
3 **while** $H[0] \neq 1$ **do**
4      $H.insert(0, H[0]^\ell)$
5      $k \leftarrow k + 1$
6 **end**
7 **if** $k = 0$ **then return** 0
8 $d \leftarrow 1$
9 $inv \leftarrow False$
10 **for** $i = 0$ **to** $(\ell-1)/2 - 1$ **do**
11   **if** $H[1] = G[1][i]$ **then**
12          $i_j \leftarrow i$
13          $d \leftarrow (i_j + 1)$
14   break
15   **else if** $H[1] = G[1][i]^{-1}$ **then**
16          $i_j \leftarrow i$
17          $d \leftarrow (i_j + 1)$
18          $inv \leftarrow True$
19   break
20   **end**
21 **end**
22 **if** $inv = True$ **then** $H[i] \leftarrow H[i]^{-1}$ for $i = 2, \ldots, k$
23 **for** $j = 2$ **to** k **do**
24      $i_j \leftarrow \ell \cdot i_j$
25      $cont \leftarrow True$
26   **for** $s = 0$ **to** $(\ell-1) - 1$ **do**
27          $b \leftarrow i_j/\ell$
28   **if** $H[j] = G[j][b(\ell-1) + s]$ **then**
29             $d \leftarrow d + s \cdot \ell^{j-1}$
30             $i_j \leftarrow i_j + s$
31             $cont \leftarrow False$
32   break
33   **end**
34   **end**
35   **if** $cont = True$ **then**
36          $d \leftarrow d + (\ell-1) \cdot \ell^{j-1}$
37          $i_j \leftarrow i_j + (\ell-1)$
38   **end**
39      $d \leftarrow \ell^{w-k} \cdot d$
40 **end**
41 **if** $inv = True$ **then** $d \leftarrow \ell^w - d$
42 **return** d

Algorithm 4: 2^w Discrete Logarithm Computation

Parameters: $w \geq 2$; $\rho \in \mathbb{G}_{\ell,w}$ of order 2^w; precomputed table
$T^{\text{exp}}[j][i] = b_{2^j+i} \in \mathbb{F}_p$ for $j \in [0, w-3], i \in [0, 2^j)$; precomputed
table Log of size 2^w such that $\rho^{Log[k]} = [a_k : 1]$.

Input   : $[x : y]$ such that $[x : y] = [a_k : 1]$ for some $k \in [1, 2^w)$, or
$[x : y] = [1 : 0]$.

Output   : Digit $D \in [-2^{w-1}, 2^{w-1}]$ such that $[x : y] = \rho^D$.

1 **if** $y = 0$ **then return** $Log[0]$.
2 **if** $x = 0$ **then return** $Log[1]$.
3 **if** $x = y$ **then return** $Log[2]$.
4 **if** $x = -y$ **then return** $Log[3]$.
5 Initialize an empty list *prods*.
6 **for** $j = 2$ **to** $w - 1$ **do**
7   **for** $i = 0$ **to** $2^{j-1} - 1$ **do**
8   Let $(\beta_{j-2}, \ldots, \beta_0)$ be the bits such that
9          $i = \beta_{j-2}2^{j-2} + \cdots + \beta_1 2 + \beta_0$.
10   **if** $\beta_0 = 0$ **then**
11             $prods[2^{j-2} + i/2] \leftarrow y \cdot T^{\text{exp}}[j-2][i/2]$.
12             $sum \leftarrow y$.
13   **end**
14   **for** $k = 0$ **to** $j - 2$ **do**
15             $sum \leftarrow sum + (-1)^{\beta_{j-k-2}} prods[2^k + (\beta_{j-2} \cdots \beta_{j-k-1})_2]$.
16   **end**
17   **if** $x = sum$ **then return** $Log[2^j + i]$.
18   **if** $x = -sum$ **then return** $Log[2^{j+1} - i - 1]$.
19   **end**
20 **end**

Algorithm 5: A hybrid of Algorithms 2 and 4 for computing discrete logarithms in $\mathbb{G}_{\ell,w}$.

Parameters: $\ell = 2$, $w \geq 2$; precomputed table G such that $G[0], G[1]$ are null,
    $G[2][0] = \rho^{2^w - 2}$, $G[j][i_j] = \rho^{v_{j,2i_j}}$ for $j \in [3, w]$, $i_j \in [0, |V_j|/4)$; w_1 with
    $2 \leq w_1 < w$; precomputed table $T^{\exp}[j][i] = b_{2^j + i}$ for
    $j \in [0, w_1 - 3]$, $i \in [0, 2^j)$; precomputed table Log of size 2^{w_1} such that
    $\rho^{Log[k]} = [a_k : 1]$; $w_2 = w - w_1$.

Input : $h \in \mathbb{G}_{2,w}$.

Output : $d \in [0, 2^w)$ such that $h = \rho^d$.

1 $H \leftarrow [h]$; $k \leftarrow 0$

2 **for** $i = 1$ **to** w_2 **do**

3   **if** $H[0] \neq 1$ **then**

4      $H.insert(0, H[0]^2)$

5      $k \leftarrow k + 1$

6   **else**

7   break

8   **end**

9 **end**

10 **if** $H[0] = 1$ and $k \leq w_1$, **then** return $2^{w_2} \cdot$ Algorithm4(h)

11 **if** $H[0] \neq 1$ **then**

12    $d \leftarrow$ Algorithm4($H[0]$) $\mod 2^{w_1}$

13    $Hindex \leftarrow 0$

14 **else**

15    $d \leftarrow$ Algorithm4($H[w_1]$) $\mod 2^{w_1}$

16    $Hindex \leftarrow w_1$

17 **end**

18 $ord \leftarrow w_1 - t$, where $2^t \mid d$ and $2^{t+1} \nmid d$ with $t \geq 0$

19 $tmp \leftarrow (d/2^{w_1 - t} - 1)/2$ // tmp has at most $ord - 1$ bits

20 Let $(\beta_{ord-2} \cdots \beta_0)$ be the bits such that $tmp = \beta_{ord-2}2^{ord-2} + \cdots + \beta_1 2 + \beta_0$

21 $i_j \leftarrow \beta_0 2^{ord-2} + \cdots + \beta_{ord-3}2 + \beta_{ord-2}$; $inv \leftarrow False$

22 **if** $H[0] = -1$ **then**

23   **if** $H[1] \neq G[2][0]$ **then**

24      $H \leftarrow [H[i]^{-1} : i \in [0, k]]$; $inv \leftarrow True$

25   **end**

26 **else**

27   **if** $i_j \geq 2^{ord-2}$ **then**

28      $i_j \leftarrow 2^{ord-1} - i_j - 1$; $d \leftarrow 2^{w_1} - d$

29      $H \leftarrow [H[i]^{-1} : i \in [0, k]]$; $inv \leftarrow True$

30   **end**

31 **end**

32 $d \leftarrow 2^{w_2} d$

33 **for** $j = Hindex + 1$ **to** k **do**

34    $i_j \leftarrow 2i_j$; $d \leftarrow d/2$

35   **if** $H[j] \neq G[j - Hindex + ord + 1][i_j/2 + 1]$ **then**

36      $d \leftarrow d + 2^{w-1}$; $i_j \leftarrow i_j + 1$

37   **end**

38 **end**

39 **if** inv **then** $d \leftarrow 2^w - d$

40 return d

References

1. Avizienis, A.: Signed-digit number representations for fast parallel arithmetic. IEEE Trans. Electron. Comput. EC-10, 389–400 (1961)
2. Azarderakhsh, R., et al.: Supersingular isogeny key encapsulation. In: Submission to the 3rd Round of the NIST Post-Quantum Standardization project (2020)
3. Azarderakhsh, R., et al.: Supersingular isogeny key encapsulation. Submission to the 2nd Round of the NIST Post-Quantum Standardization project (2019)
4. Azarderakhsh, R., et al.: Supersingular Isogeny Key Encapsulation. SIKE Team (2020). https://sike.org/
5. Azarderakhsh, R., Jao, D., Kalach, K., Koziel, B., Leonardi, C.: Key compression for isogeny-based cryptosystems. In: Proceedings of the 3rd ACM International Workshop on ASIA Public-Key Cryptography, pp. 1–10 (2016)
6. Costello, C., Jao, D., Longa, P., Naehrig, M., Renes, J., Urbanik, D.: Efficient compression of SIDH public keys. In: Coron, J.-S., Nielsen, J.B. (eds.) EUROCRYPT 2017, Part I. LNCS, vol. 10210, pp. 679–706. Springer, Cham (2017). https://doi.org/10.1007/978-3-319-56620-7_24
7. De Feo, L., Jao, D., Plût, J.: Towards quantum-resistant cryptosystems from super singular elliptic curve isogenies. J. Math. Cryptology, 8(3), 209–247 (2014)
8. Gustavo, H.M., Zanon, M.A., Simplicio, G.C.C.F., Pereira, J.D., Paulo, S.L.M.B.: Faster Key Compression for Isogeny-Based Cryptosystems: IEEE Trans. Comput. 68, 688–701 (2018)
9. Longa, P.: SIDH Library. https://github.com/microsoft/PQCrypto-SIDH
10. Naehrig, M., Renes, J.: Dual isogenies and their application to public-key compression for isogeny-based cryptography. In: Galbraith, S.D., Moriai, S. (eds.) ASIACRYPT 2019, Part II. LNCS, vol. 11922, pp. 243–272. Springer, Cham (2019). https://doi.org/10.1007/978-3-030-34621-8_9
11. Pereira, G., Doliskani, J., Jao, D.: x-only point addition formula and faster compressed SIKE. J. Cryptographic Eng. 1–13 (2020). https://doi.org/10.1007/s13389-020-00245-4
12. Pereira, G., Barreto, P.: Isogeny-based key compression without pairings. In: International Conference on Practice and Theory of Public-Key Cryptography (PKC). Springer (2021)
13. Pohlig, S., Hellman, M.: An improved algorithm for computing logarithms over $GF(p)$ and its cryptographic significance. IEEE Trans. Inf. Theory 24, 106–110 (1978)
14. Rubin, K., Silverberg, A.: Compression in finite fields and torus-based cryptography. SIAM J. Comput. 37, 1401–1428 (2008)
15. Zanon, G.H.M., Simplicio, M.A., Pereira, G.C.C.F., Doliskani, J., Barreto, P.S.L.M.: Faster isogeny-based compressed key agreement. In: Lange, T., Steinwandt, R. (eds.) PQCrypto 2018. LNCS, vol. 10786, pp. 248–268. Springer, Cham (2018). https://doi.org/10.1007/978-3-319-79063-3_12

Lattice-Based Cryptography

Generating Cryptographically-Strong Random Lattice Bases and Recognizing Rotations of $\mathbb{Z}^n$

Tamar Lichter Blanks and Stephen D. Miller$^{(\boxtimes)}$

Department of Mathematics, Rutgers University, New Brunswick, USA
miller@math.rutgers.edu

Abstract. Lattice-based cryptography relies on generating random bases which are difficult to fully reduce. Given a lattice basis (such as the private basis for a cryptosystem), all other bases are related by multiplication by matrices in $GL(n,\mathbb{Z})$. We compare the strengths of various methods to sample random elements of $GL(n,\mathbb{Z})$, finding some are stronger than others with respect to the problem of recognizing rotations of the $\mathbb{Z}^n$ lattice. In particular, the standard algorithm of multiplying unipotent generators together (as implemented in Magma's `RandomSLnZ` command) generates instances of this last problem which can be efficiently broken, even in dimensions nearing 1,500. Likewise, we find that the random basis generation method in one of the NIST Post-Quantum Cryptography competition submissions (DRS) generates instances which can be efficiently broken, even at its 256-bit security settings. Other random basis generation algorithms (some older, some newer) are described which appear to be much stronger.

Keywords: Lattices · Random basis · Integral lattices · Unimodular integral matrices · DRS signature scheme

1 Introduction

In cryptography one often encounters problems which are easy to solve using a secret private basis of a lattice $\Lambda \subset \mathbb{R}^n$, but are expected to be difficult to solve using suitably-chosen public bases. Famous examples include the Shortest Vector Problem (SVP) and Closest Vector Problem (CVP).

In [17] Lenstra and Silverberg posed the challenge of whether highly-symmetric lattices have hard bases, and proved several interesting results along these lines (related to earlier work of Gentry-Szydlo [10]; see also [16,18]). One particularly beautiful question they posed is:

$$\text{can one efficiently recognize rotations of the standard } \mathbb{Z}^n \text{ lattice?} \qquad (1.1)$$

T. L. Blanks—Supported by a National Science Foundation Graduate Research Fellowship.
S. D. Miller—Supported by National Science Foundation Grants CNS-1526333 and CNS-1815562.

© Springer Nature Switzerland AG 2021
J. H. Cheon and J.-P. Tillich (Eds.): PQCrypto 2021, LNCS 12841, pp. 319–338, 2021.
https://doi.org/10.1007/978-3-030-81293-5_17

To be more precise, this problem can be stated in two different group-theoretic ways (the second being the formulation in [17, §2]). Let $\{b_1, \ldots, b_n\}$ denote a basis for Λ and let B denote the $n \times n$ matrix whose i-th row is b_i:

Problem 1a (Decision version).

Can one efficiently factor B as $B = MR$, with $M \in GL(n, \mathbb{Z})$ and $R \in O(n)$?

Problem 1b (Search version).

If so, efficiently find such matrices $M \in GL(n, \mathbb{Z})$ and $R \in O(n)$.

Alternatively, following [9] and [17, §2] we may suppose one is given a positive-definite symmetric matrix $G \in SL(n, \mathbb{Z})$ (which we think of as the Gram matrix $G = BB^t$ of Λ):

Problem 2a (Decision version).

Given a positive-definite integral matrix G, efficiently determine whether or not there is some $M \in GL(n, \mathbb{Z})$ such that $G = MM^t$.

$$(1.2)$$

Problem 2b (Search version).

If so, efficiently find such a matrix $M \in GL(n, \mathbb{Z})$.

Clearly, Problem 1 reduces to Problem 2 with $G = BB^t$. Conversely, one can orthogonally diagonalize the matrix G in Problem 2 as $G = PDP^t$ for some $P \in O(n)$ and diagonal matrix D with positive diagonal entries. Then $B = PD^{1/2}$ solves the equation $G = BB^t$, and Problem 2 therefore reduces to Problem 1 (modulo technicalities we will not delve into, such as that the entries of P, D, and B may in general be irrational).

In particular, by orthogonal diagonalization it is trivial to find a non-integral solution $M \in GL(n, \mathbb{R})$ to Problem 2. However, imposing the constraint that $M \in GL(n, \mathbb{Z})$ adds an intricate dose of number theory, since Problem 2a then becomes a class number problem: indeed, in large dimensions n there is a combinatorial explosion of possible $GL(n, \mathbb{Z})$-equivalence classes.[1]

Both Problems 1 and 2 have inefficient solutions using sufficiently strong lattice basis reduction. For example, the given information is sufficient to determine whether or not all lattice vector norms are square-roots of integers, and an SVP solver can determine the shortest nonzero norm $\lambda_1(\Lambda)$. If $\lambda_1(\Lambda) \neq 1$, the lattice Λ is definitely not a rotation of $\mathbb{Z}^n$ and Problems 1a and 2a have negative solutions. However, if one finds a vector of norm 1 and all lattice norms are

---

[1] For example, the E_8 lattice has a Gram matrix G in $SL(8, \mathbb{Z})$, but is not isometric to the $\mathbb{Z}^8$ lattice. In general the number of $GL(n, \mathbb{Z})$-equivalence classes of such integral unimodular lattices grows faster than exponentially in n [6, Chapter 16].

square-roots of integers, it is then easy to see (by subtracting multiples of this vector to obtain an orthogonal complement) that the dimension in Problems 1b and 2b reduces from n to $n-1$. It was recently shown in [13] that Problem 2a is in the class NP∩co-NP, using results of Elkies [8] on characteristic vectors of lattices (see also [11, §9.6]).

This paper primarily concerns Problem 2b, i.e., one is handed a matrix of the form MM^t and wishes to efficiently recover M. Of course permuting the columns of M does not change MM^t, nor does multiplying any subset of columns by -1; thus we look for solutions up to such signed permutations of the columns. (For this reason it is equivalent to insist that $M \in SL(n, \mathbb{Z})$.) We find that the choice of procedure to randomly generate instances of M has a drastic impact on the difficulty of the problem. We state this in terms of a probability density function $p : GL(n, \mathbb{Z}) \to \mathbb{R}_{\geq 0}$ (i.e., $\sum_{M \in GL(n, \mathbb{Z})} p(M) = 1$):

Problem 3 (Average case version of Problem 2b).

Given a random matrix $M \in GL(n, \mathbb{Z})$ drawn with respect to the probability density p, efficiently recover M from MM^t (up to signed permutations of the columns) with high probability.

In Sect. 2 we compare various methods of generating random bases of a lattice, corresponding to different probability densities p (generalizing [3, §5.1.2]; see also Sect. 4). Here one seeks distributions for which Problem 3 is hard on average, much like SIS and LWE are average-case hard instances of variants of SVP and CVP, respectively. We then perform experiments on them in Sect. 3. Some of the methods we describe, such as the long-known Algorithm 4 (see, for example, [5]), give relatively hard instances of Problem 3. However, our main finding is that a certain well-known existing method, namely generating matrices by multiplying unipotents (e.g., Magma's `RandomSLnZ` command), is cryptographically weak: we were able to recover M in instances in dimensions nearly 1500 (in some measurable ways these instances are comparable to NTRU lattices having purported 256-bit quantum cryptographic strength). That gives an example of an average-case easy distribution. In Sect. 4 we similarly find that the random basis generation method used in the DRS NIST Post-Quantum Cryptography submission [21] also gives weak instances of Problem 3: in 708 hours we could recover M generated using DRS's 256-bit security settings.

2   Choosing Random Elements of $GL(n, \mathbb{Z})$

We consider the problem of uniformly sampling matrices in a large box[2]

$$\Gamma_T := \{M = (m_{ij}) \in GL(n, \mathbb{Z}) : |m_{ij}| \leq T\}, \quad T > 0, \qquad (2.1)$$

---

[2] One can consider other shapes, such as balls; boxes are convenient for our applications and for making more concise statements. The same problem for $SL(n, \mathbb{Z})$ is of course equivalent.

inside $GL(n, \mathbb{Z})$. For large T one has $\#\Gamma_T \sim c_n T^{n^2-n}$, for some positive constant c_n.[3] We now consider a series of algorithms to sample matrices in $GL(n, \mathbb{Z})$. The most naive way to uniformly sample Γ_T is prohibitively slow:

Algorithm 1.

For each $1 \leq i, j \leq n$ sample $m_{i,j} \in \mathbb{Z} \cap [-T, T]$ at random.
Let $M = (m_{ij})$.
Discard and repeat if $\det(M) \neq \pm 1$, otherwise
return M.

Though we do not analyze it here, the determinant of such a randomly chosen matrix M is a very large integer, and highly improbable to be ± 1 as required for membership in $GL(n, \mathbb{Z})$. One minor improvement that can be made is to first check that the elements of each row (and of each column, as well) do not share a common factor, which is a necessary condition to have determinant ± 1. Nevertheless, this fails to seriously improve the extreme unlikelihood of randomly producing an integral matrix of determinant ± 1.

Problem 4.

Find a nontrivial uniform sampling algorithm which substantially speeds up Algorithm 1.

We note that some computer algebra packages include commands for generating random elements of $GL(n, \mathbb{Z})$. In addition to its command `RandomSLnZ` which we shall shortly come to in Algorithm 2, Magma's documentation includes the command `RandomUnimodularMatrix` for fairly rapidly generating matrices in $GL(n, \mathbb{Z})$ (not $SL(n, \mathbb{Z})$ as the name indicates) having "most entries" inside a prescribed interval, but provides no further explanation. Even after accounting for a typo which switches the role of the command's arguments, we found that in fact most of the entries were *outside* the prescribed interval (the documentation's claims notwithstanding). Furthermore, the lattices constructed using this command appear to be much easier to attack than those generated by the closest analog considered here (Algorithm 4). SageMath's `random_matrix` command has a `unimodular` constructor (designed for teaching purposes) which does produce matrices in $GL(n, \mathbb{Z})$ whose entries are bounded by a given size, but it is not as fast as other alternatives and its outputs must satisfy further constraints. For these reasons we did not seriously examine `RandomUnimodularMatrix` and `random_matrix`.

Because Algorithm 1 is so slow, the rest of this section considers faster algorithms which do *not* uniformly sample Γ_T, some coming closer than others.[4]

---

[3] See [12, Corollary 2.3] and [7, (1.14)] for more details on this surprisingly difficult result.

[4] Unfortunately it is prohibitively complicated here to describe particular parameter choices matching the bound in (2.1).

For $1 \leq i \neq j \leq n$ let $E_{i,j}$ denote the elementary $n \times n$ matrix whose entries are all 0 aside from a 1 in the (i,j)-th position. Here as elsewhere the abbreviation "i.i.d." stands for "independently identically distributed".

Algorithm 2 (Random products of unipotents,
such as Magma's `RandomSLNZ`).   (2.2)

Input: a size bound b and word length ℓ.
Return: a random product $\gamma_1 \cdots \gamma_\ell$, where each γ_k is chosen i.i.d. uniformly among all $n \times n$ matrices of the form $I_n + x E_{i,j}$, with $i \neq j$ and $x \in \mathbb{Z} \cap [-b, b]$.

As we shall later see, the matrices produced by Algorithm 2 have a very special form, creating a cryptographic weakness.

Algorithm 2 can be thought of as a counterpart to the LLL algorithm [15], which applies successive unipotent matrices and vector swaps to reduce lattices. Although Algorithm 2 does not literally contain vector swaps, they are nevertheless present in the background because conjugates of γ_j by permutation matrices have the same form $I_n + x E_{i,j}$ as γ_k. In that light, the following algorithm can then be thought of as an analog of BKZ reduction [23], since it utilizes block matrices of size much smaller than n. Its statement involves the embedding maps $\Phi_{k_1,\ldots,k_d} : GL(d, \mathbb{R}) \hookrightarrow GL(n, \mathbb{R})$ for size-d subsets $\{k_1, \ldots, k_d\} \subset \{1, \ldots, n\}$,

$$(\Phi_{k_1,\ldots,k_d}(h))_{i'j'} = \begin{cases} h_{ij}, & \text{if } i' = k_i \text{ and } j' = k_j \text{ for some } i, j \leq d; \\ \delta_{i'=j'}, & \text{otherwise} \end{cases} \quad (2.3)$$

where $h = (h_{ij}) \in GL(d, \mathbb{R})$.[5] The image of $\Phi_{k_1,\ldots,k_d}$ is a subgroup of $GL(n, \mathbb{R})$ isomorphic to $GL(d, \mathbb{R})$. (Of course we will only apply the map $\Phi_{k_1,\ldots,k_d}$ to elements of $GL(d, \mathbb{Z})$.)

Algorithm 3 (Random products of smaller matrices).

Input: a word length ℓ and fixed dimension $2 \leq d < n$ for which one can uniformly[a] sample $GL(d, \mathbb{Z})$ matrices in a fixed box.
Return: a random product $\gamma_1 \cdots \gamma_\ell$ in which each $\gamma_j \in GL(n, \mathbb{Z})$ is a matrix of the form $\Phi_{k_1,\ldots,k_d}(\gamma^{(d)})$, where $\gamma^{(d)}$ is a uniformly sampled random element of $GL(d, \mathbb{Z})$ in the fixed box mentioned above, and $\{k_1, \ldots, k_d\}$ is a uniformly sampled random subset of $\{1, \ldots, n\}$ containing d elements.

---

[a]More generally, one can consider non-uniform distributions as well.

We expect Algorithm 3 produces more-uniformly distributed matrices as d increases. The role of the parameter d is essentially to interpolate between Algorithm 1 (which is the case $d = n$) and Algorithm 2 (which is close to the case $d = 2$, but not exactly: $\gamma^{(2)}$ need not be unipotent).

---

[5] The role of $GL(\cdot, \cdot)$ as opposed to $SL(\cdot, \cdot)$ here is again purely cosmetic.

Next we turn to the following method, which among the algorithms we considered seems the best at rapidly creating uniformly-distributed entries of matrices in $GL(n,\mathbb{Z})$. This algorithm was originally suggested to us by Joseph Silverman in a slightly different form, in which more coprimality conditions needed to be checked. It relies on the fact that an integral $n \times n$ matrix $M = (m_{ij})$ lies in $GL(n,\mathbb{Z})$ if and only if the n determinants of $(n-1) \times (n-1)$ minors

$$
\det\begin{pmatrix} m_{22} & \cdots & m_{2n} \\ \vdots & \ddots & \vdots \\ m_{n2} & \cdots & m_{nn} \end{pmatrix}, \det\begin{pmatrix} m_{21} & m_{23} & \cdots & m_{2n} \\ \vdots & \vdots & & \ddots & \vdots \\ m_{n1} & m_{n3} & \cdots & m_{nn} \end{pmatrix}, \det\begin{pmatrix} m_{21} & \cdots & m_{2n-1} \\ \vdots & \ddots & \vdots \\ m_{n1} & \cdots & m_{nn-1} \end{pmatrix} \quad (2.4)
$$

share no common factors.

Algorithm 4 (slight modification of a suggestion of Joseph Silverman).

Uniformly sample random integers $m_{i,j} \in [-T,T]$, for $2 \le i \le n$ and $1 \le j \le n$, until the n determinants in (2.4) share no common factor. Use the euclidean algorithm to find integers $m_{11},\ldots,m_{1n}$ such that $\det((m_{ij})) = \pm 1$, the sign chosen uniformly at random. Use least-squares to find the linear combination $\sum_{i\ge 2}^{n} c_i [m_{i1} \cdots m_{in}]$ closest to $[m_{11} \cdots m_{1n}]$, and let $\widetilde{c}_i$ denote an integer nearest to c_i.
Return: the matrix M whose top row is

$$
[m_{11} \cdots m_{1n}] - \sum_{i\ge 2}^{n} \widetilde{c}_i [m_{i1} \cdots m_{in}]
$$

and whose i-th row (for $i \ge 2$) is $[m_{i1} \cdots m_{in}]$.

Remarks on Algorithm 4: The n large integers in (2.4) are unlikely to share a common factor: for example, the most probable common factor is 2, which happens only with probability $\approx 2^{-n}$. Obviously the top row of M is chosen differently than the others, and its size is different as well since it typically has entries larger than size T – this is because the euclidean algorithm can produce large coefficients (as the minors in (2.4) are themselves so enormous). Also, it is likely that the first two or three minors will already be coprime, and hence that most of the entries in $[m_{11} m_{12} \cdots m_{1n}]$ will vanish. The use of rounding and least-squares cuts down this size and further randomizes the top row, while keeping the determinant equal to one.

One could instead try a different method to find an integral combination of the bottom $n-1$ rows closer to the initial guess for the top row. One extreme possibility involves appealing to the Closest Vector Problem (CVP) itself, which is thought to be very difficult. We found Algorithm 4 gave good randomness properties in that nearly all of the matrix is equidistributed, and it is fairly fast to execute. In comparison, we will see that using Algorithm 2 requires many matrix multiplications to achieve random entries of a similar size, which are not as well distributed anyhow.

The following algorithm is folklore and has appeared in various guises in many references (for example [5], which uses Gaussian sampling and has provable hardness guarantees,[6] though not necessarily for Problem 3). As we shall see just below, it shares some similarities with Algorithm 4.

Algorithm 5 (via Hermite Normal Form).

Create a uniformly distributed $m \times n$ matrix B, with $m \geq n$ and entries uniformly chosen in $\mathbb{Z} \cap [-T, T]$.
Decompose B in a Hermite normal form $B = UM$, where $M \in GL(n, \mathbb{Z})$ and $U = (u_{ij})$ has no nonzero entries with $i < j$.
Return: M.

A surprising connection between Algorithms 4 and 5: Even though Algorithms 4 and 5 appear to be very different, they are actually extremely similar (in fact, arguably nearly identical) in practice. Algorithms for Hermite Normal Form (such as `HermiteDecomposition` in Mathematica) proceed by building the matrix M directly out of the rows of B whenever possible. For example, it is frequently the case that the first $n - 1$ rows of U agree with those of the identity matrix I_n, or at least differ only very slightly; in other words, the first $n - 1$ rows of B and M are expected to coincide or nearly coincide.[7] Also, the last row of M is an integral combination of the first n rows of B. In contrast with Algorithm 4 this last combination, however, is mainly determined by arithmetic considerations, and in particular depends on the n-th row of B; thus more random information is used than in Algorithm 4, which uses only $n^2 - n$ random integers instead of the n^2 here.[8]

To summarize, in fairly typical cases both Algorithms 4 and 5 populate the matrix M by first generating all but one row uniformly at random, and then using integral combinations to create a final row having relatively small entries. The practical distinction is essentially how this final row is created, which utilizes further random information in Algorithm 5 but not in Algorithm 4. The final row also appears to be typically smaller (that is, closer to fitting in the box defined in (2.1)) when using Algorithm 4 than when using Algorithm 5; consequently, we did not perform any experiments with Algorithm 5.

Note that the Hermite decomposition as stated above is not unique, since there are lower triangular matrices in $GL(n, \mathbb{Z})$. Thus there can be no immediate guarantee on the entry sizes of M unless this ambiguity is resolved. Algorithm 5 can be thought of as a p-adic analog of the following method of producing random rotations in $O(n)$: apply the Gram-Schmidt orthogonalization process

---

[6] It should be mentioned that provable guarantees were earlier established in [1, 2, 19] when one generates both the lattice together with a basis at random from a family. Here our emphasis is on a fixed, given lattice.

[7] In our experiments, for example, the top $n - 2$ rows agreed most of the time for $m = n \geq 10$.

[8] Note the order of magnitude of the set Γ_T from (2.1) is $T^{n^2 - n}$, naturally matching the $n^2 - n$ random integers picked in Algorithm 4.

to a matrix chosen according to a probability density function (e.g., Gaussian) which is invariant under multiplication by $O(n)$.

Remarks on an Algorithm in [22]: Igor Rivin makes the proposal in [22, §6.1] to generate matrices in $GL(n, \mathbb{Z})$ by applying complete lattice basis reduction to a basis of $\mathbb{R}^n$ chosen inside a large ball. Let $B \in GL(n, \mathbb{R})$ denote the $n \times n$ matrix whose rows consist of this basis. Complete lattice reduction produces a random element $\gamma \in GL(n, \mathbb{Z})$ of constrained size for which γB lies in a fixed fundamental domain for $GL(n, \mathbb{Z}) \backslash GL(n, \mathbb{R})$.

This procedure is extremely slow, since complete lattice reduction is impractical in large dimensions. Rivin thus considers instead using weaker lattice basis reduction methods (such as LLL [15]) to speed this up, but at the cost of less-uniform distributions. For example, the results of LLL are thought to be skewed towards certain favored outputs avoiding "dark bases" [14]. Since our interest in generating random bases is to see how long incomplete lattice reduction takes on them, the use of lattice reduction to itself make the basis itself is too slow for our purposes (hence we did not consider this algorithm in our experiments).

3   Experiments on Recognizing $\mathbb{Z}^n$

In this section we report on attempts to solve Problem 2b on instances of matrices M generated using some of the algorithms from Sect. 2 for sampling $GL(n, \mathbb{Z})$. We first note that Geissler and Smart [9] reported on attempts to solve Problem 2b on NTRU lattices using LLL [15] (as well as their own modification, for which they report up to a factor of four speedup), and concluded from lattice reduction heuristics that LLL itself is insufficient for NTRU instances with dimensions and matrix entry size far smaller than those considered in (3.2) below (see Appendix C). Nevertheless LLL performs fairly well on rotations of the $\mathbb{Z}^n$ lattice as compared to on a random lattice, which is not unexpected since the latter has shortest vector on the order of $\sqrt{n}$ (as opposed to 1 for rotations of the $\mathbb{Z}^n$ lattice). Given that LLL typically outperforms its provable guarantees, it is not surprising it is fairly effective on Problem 2b.

Our main emphasis is that LLL and BKZ perform better on certain distributions with respect to Problem 2b than on others. Instead of LLL alone, we try the following:

Procedure to test matrix generation algorithms with Problem 2b.

1. In Magma, apply LLL or Nguyen-Stehlé's L2 lattice basis reduction algorithm [20] to the Gram matrix $G = MM^t$, then

2. apply BKZ with incrementally-increasing block sizes $3, 4,$ and 5.

3. Success is measured by whether or not the output basis vectors all have norm equal to 1 (in which case they span a rotation of the $\mathbb{Z}^n$ lattice).

(3.1)

We chose to use Magma's built-in lattice basis reduction routines, partly because of slow running times with other implementations (such as fplll in SageMath) on matrices with very large integer entries. In step 2 one can of course continue further with block sizes larger than 5, but we fixed this as a stopping point in order to be systematic.

Our main finding is that Algorithm 2 in Sect. 2 (as implemented in Magma's RandomSLnZ) is insecure for generating hard instances of Problem 2b. Algorithms 3, 4, and 5 fare much better. It is not surprising that Algorithm 5 (and the nearly-equivalent Algorithm 4) give harder instances, since there are provable guarantees attached to Algorithm 5 in a different context [5]; there is a serious difference between these and Algorithm 2 described below and in Appendices A and B.

3.1 Experiments with Algorithm 2 (Magma's RandomSLnZ Command)

We begin with some comments on entropy and generating random products with a constrained number of bits. To mimic random elements of $GL(n, \mathbb{Z})$, one may desire that the product matrix has as many nonzero entries as possible per random bit. For this reason, our experiments set the parameter $b = 1$ in Algorithm 2 in order to take longer products (thereby further increasing the number of nonzero entries of the matrix), while keeping the number of random bits constant. When the product length is less than n, one expects to have rows or columns of the product matrix which are unchanged by the successive matrix multiplications. (This much less likely to be the case for the Gram matrices, however.)

Thus each random factor has at most a single nonzero off-diagonal entry, which is ± 1. It is prohibitive to pack in as many random bits as the total number of entries this way, since multiplication of large matrices is slow. As an extreme example, as part of a comparison with the last row of (C.3) we generated a random matrix in $GL(1486, \mathbb{Z})$ using products of length 55,000, again with $b = 1$. Generating the product alone took about half a day. Its row lengths were between 2^{14} and 2^{20} in size. For comparison, an NTRU matrix with similar row lengths (as in Table C.3) uses 8,173 random bits. The comparison with NTRU is made here simply because concrete bit-strengths have been asserted for NTRU lattices; this is why we took the particular values of n in (3.2) (see Appendix C for more details). One might hypothesize that having more random bits in the matrix makes solving Problem 2b more difficult, but as we shall see this in fact turns out to not always be the case: the structure of the matrix plays a very important role, and the product structure from Algorithm 2 seems to be a contributing weakness. In particular, the larger the value of the parameter b, the more unusual properties the product matrix possesses.

Successful experiments on large lattices

$n = \dim(\Lambda)$	estimated bit-hardness for corresp. NTRU (C.3)	range of vector lengths (in bits)	product length	
886	128	from 25 to 32	55,000	(3.2)
1486	256	from 14 to 20	55,000	

From the success of our trials one immediately sees the Lenstra-Silverberg Problem 2b is fairly easy for matrices M generated by Magma's `RandomSLnZ` command. (Of course it is well known to be impossible to solve Problem 2b using LLL or BKZ with small block sizes on NTRU matrices of the comparable size listed in (3.2) and (C.3), or even those much smaller.)

3.2   Experiments with Algorithm 3 (Random $GL(d, \mathbb{Z})$ Matrices)

Next we consider matrices generated by Algorithm 3 (random $GL(d, \mathbb{Z})$'s), and find that for small d they are also cryptographically weak for the Lenstra-Silverberg problem, but stronger than those generated by Algorithm 2. Furthermore, we see their strength increases with increasing d.

The tables in Appendix A list the outcomes of several experiments attacking instances of Problem 2b for matrices M generated by Algorithm 3. One sees the dramatic effect of the product length ℓ. For example, if ℓ is too short there may be rows and columns of the matrix not touched by the individual multiplications by the embedded random $d \times d$ matrices; if ℓ is too long, the matrix entries become large and lattice basis reduction becomes difficult.

3.3   Experiments with Algorithm 4

Finally, we turn to the opposite extreme of random elements of $GL(n, \mathbb{Z})$ generated by Algorithm 4, in which the bottom $n - 1$ rows are uniformly distributed among entries in the range $[-T, T]$. Here we were able to solve Problem 2b with instances having $n = 100$, even with entry sizes up to $T = 50$ (again, using the testing procedure in (3.1)). However, none of our experiments with $n \geq 110$ were successful at all, even with $T = 1$ (i.e., all entries below the top row are -1, 0, or 1). See the tables in Appendix B for more details.

4   Random Basis Generation in the DRS NIST Post-Quantum Cryptography Competition Submission

In [3, §5.1.2] some examples of methods for generating random lattice bases are described, which are closely related to Algorithms 2, 3, and 5. The authors reported their experiments on those methods resulted in similar outcomes in practice. Our experiments, however, do show a difference (as was explained in Sect. 3).

In this section we wish to make further comments about one method highlighted in [3], which is from the DRS NIST Post-Quantum competition submission [21, §2.2]. Random elements of $GL(n, \mathbb{Z})$ there are constructed as products of length $2R + 1$ of the form

$$P_1 \gamma_1 P_2 \gamma_2 P_3 \gamma_3 \cdots P_R \gamma_R P_{R+1}, \tag{4.1}$$

where $P_1, \ldots, P_{R+1}$ are chosen uniformly at random among permutation matrices in $GL(n, \mathbb{Z})$ and $\gamma_1, \ldots, \gamma_R$ are elements in $SL(n, \mathbb{Z})$ produced by the following random process. Let $A_+ = \begin{pmatrix} 1 & 1 \\ 1 & 2 \end{pmatrix}$ and $A_- = \begin{pmatrix} 1 & -1 \\ -1 & 2 \end{pmatrix}$. Then each γ_i is a block diagonal matrix with $\frac{n}{2}$ 2×2 entries chosen uniformly at random from $\{A_+, A_-\}$. This construction has some similarities with Algorithm 3 for $d = 2$, but note that here many of the $SL(2)$ matrices commute (being diagonal blocks of the same matrix). In fact, since A_+ is conjugate by $\begin{pmatrix} 1 & 0 \\ 0 & -1 \end{pmatrix}$ to A_- one may replace each γ_j with the block diagonal matrix

$$D = \operatorname{diag}(A_+, A_+, \ldots, A_+),$$

at the cost of allowing the P_i's to be signed permutation matrices. Alternatively, by rearranging the permutation matrices and applying an extra rotation on the right, Problem 2b on matrices of the form (4.1) is equivalent to it on products of the form

$$M = M_1 M_2 \cdots M_R, \tag{4.2}$$

in which each M_i is conjugate of D by a random signed permutation matrix.

Since Algorithm 3 with $d = 2$ performed relatively weakly in the experiments of Sect. 3, we suspect Problem 2b is relatively easy to solve on matrices generated using (4.1) (as compared to those, say, generated using Algorithm 4). The experiments described below bear this out. (All of our remaining comments in this section pertain solely to (4.1) in the context of Problem 2b, and not to any other aspect of [21].)

The parameters listed in [21, §3.2] assert 128-bit security for their scheme when $(n, R) = (912, 24)$, 192-bit security when $(n, R) = (1160, 24)$, and 256-bit security when $(n, R) = (1518, 24)$. Our main finding is that the testing procedure (3.1) was able to recover M chosen with the 256-bit security parameters in 708 hours of running time. We could also recover M chosen with the 192-bit security parameters in 222 hours of running time but (as we describe below) could not fully recover M with the 128-bit security parameters.

The testing procedure (3.1) also easily solves Problem 2b when n or R are smaller yet still relatively large. For example, it took roughly an hour to recover M from MM^t when $(n, R) = (180, 24)$ using BKZ with block sizes up to 26. In Fig. 1 we show the results of several experiments for the parameter choice of $n = 912$ and increasing values of R up to the recommended choice of $R = 24$ for 128-bit security. The results were strikingly successful, in that each trial for $R \leq 22$ successfully recovered M from MM^t using only LLL (without requiring BKZ). We additionally tried $R = 23$ and *nearly* recovered M using LLL this way: the longest vector in the LLL output had length $\sqrt{7}$, and subsequently applying BKZ reduction with block size 3 for less than five minutes then fully recovered M. However, we were unsuccessful in the $R = 24$ case suggested in [21].

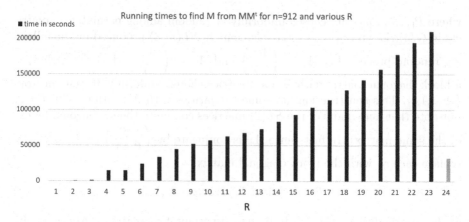

Fig. 1. We experimentally tried to solve Problem 2b on instances generated by the random basis construction from the DRS NIST submission [21, §2.2], using its suggested parameters $(n, R) = (912, 24)$ for 128-bit security. This failed with $n = 912$ and $R = 24$ itself (the gray bar on the right), but was successful for $n = 912$ and $1 \leq R \leq 23$. We were able to solve all cases for $R \leq 22$ in less than 60 hours using LLL alone, and the $R = 23$ case in slightly more time using the procedure in (3.1). We conclude that method of random basis generation in the DRS digital signature scheme is insecure with the recommended parameter setting $(n, R) = (912, 24)$, at least for Problem 2b. Times are shown for runs on a Dell PowerEdge R740xd server equipped with two Intel Xeon Silver 4114 2.2 GHz processors and 256 GB RAM.

Again, these results are *only* for Problem 2b applied to the random basis construction used in the DRS digital signature scheme [21]; nevertheless, this may indicate a weakness in the digital signature scheme as well. Somewhat counter intuitively, our experiments for fixed values of the product length parameter R sometimes fared better for *larger* values of n. For example, we were successful with $(n, R) = (912, 22)$ despite not being successful for $(n, R) = (200, 22)$, and we were successful with $(n, R) = (1160, 24)$ and $(1518, 24)$ despite not being successful for $(n, R) = (912, 24)$. Our explanation is that as n grows there may be a weakness in that it is hard to randomly fill out the full matrix M (a similar phenomenon occurs in Algorithms 2 and 3 for small ℓ). Indeed, matrices of the form (4.1) seem to have a very special form: Fig. 2 shows the entry sizes in MM^t have a banded structure.

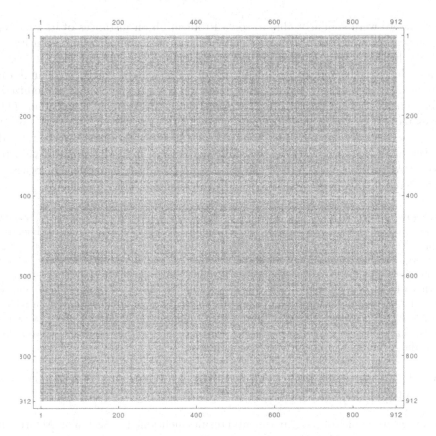

Fig. 2. Mathematica's `MatrixPlot` command displays the nonzero entries of Gram matrix MM^t as darkened pixels, where M was generated according to (4.1) with recommended parameters $n = 912$ and $R = 24$ from [21]. Similarly banded plots arise when M is generated using Algorithm 3 with $d = 2$. In contrast, Gram matrices generated by Algorithm 4 have a (provably) far more uniform structure.

5   Conclusions

We have considered the role of generating random elements in $GL(n, \mathbb{Z})$ in the difficulty of lattice problems, and have found that it can have a profound influence. Concretely, Magma's `RandomSLnZ` command (Algorithm 2) gives easy instances of Lenstra-Silverberg's "Recognizing $\mathbb{Z}^n$ Decision" Problem 2b from (1.2). We were able to successfully attack lattices of dimension up to 1,486, which are in some measurable ways comparable to NTRU lattices having claimed 256-bit quantum security. On the other hand, using the apparently stronger methods of Algorithms 3 and 4 make Problem 2b much more difficult to solve (as expected).

We would thus recommend not using Algorithm 2 in generating random bases for cryptographic applications. We also recommend not using the random basis algorithm from the NIST Post-Quantum Competition submission DRS [21], because we were similarly able to solve Problem 2b on instances of its random basis generation method with its recommend parameters for 256-bit security.

We have not fully understood the weaknesses of these algorithms. It seems plausible that the failure to quickly fill out the matrix entries in a uniform way is at least partly to blame, since many do not get sufficiently randomized. The construction of Algorithm 2 in some sense reverses the steps of an LLL basis reduction, which might explain why LLL is particularly effective against it. More generally one might expect the block sizes in Algorithm 3 to be related to the block sizes in the BKZ algorithm. It is natural from this point of view to expect Algorithms 4 and 5 to be the strongest lattice basis generation algorithms considered in this paper, consistent with the results of our experiments.

Acknowledgements. It is a pleasure to thank Huck Bennett, Leo Ducas, Nicholas Genise, Craig Gentry, Shai Halevi, Nadia Heninger, Jeff Hoffstein, Hendrik Lenstra, Amos Nevo, Phong Nguyen, Chris Peikert, Oded Regev, Ze'ev Rudnick, Alice Silverberg, Damien Stehlé, Noah Stephens-Davidowitz, and Berk Sunar for very helpful discussions. We are particularly indebted to Joe Silverman for kindly suggesting an earlier variant of Algorithm 4, which is very similar to the one we suggest here, and to Daniel J. Bernstein for important comments about the poor equidistribution provided by Algorithm 2. We are also grateful to Galen Collier of the Rutgers University Office of Advanced Research Computing for his assistance, and to the Simons Foundation for providing Rutgers University with Magma licenses.

A   Experiments with Algorithm 3 (Random $GL(d, \mathbb{Z})$ Matrices)

Below we list tables of the experimental results mentioned in Sect. 3 on Algorithm 3, performed using the testing procedure (3.1).

n	d	T	ℓ	shortest row length (in bits)	longest row length (in bits)	found M?
200	2	1	4000	6.03607	12.7988	✗
200	2	2	1500	1.29248	18.5329	✓
200	2	2	2000	7.86583	22.2151	✗
200	2	3	1000	0.5	27.0875	✗
200	2	3	2000	23.521	41.5678	✗
200	2	10	500	2.04373	38.7179	✓
200	2	10	700	7.943	49.0346	✗
200	3	1	1000	2.04373	11.3283	✓
200	3	1	1500	7.66619	17.1312	✗
200	3	1	2000	13.0661	20.8768	✗
200	3	2	500	3.27729	18.4087	✓
200	3	2	600	4.89232	24.111	✗
200	3	2	1000	13.0585	34.0625	✗
200	4	1	500	3.66096	12.2277	✓
200	4	2	300	0.5	24.2424	✓
200	4	2	400	1.79248	26.6452	✗

key: n = lattice dimension, d = size of smaller embedded matrices, T = bound on embedded matrix entries, ℓ = length of the product of smaller matrices.

n	d	T	ℓ	shortest row length (in bits)	longest row length (in bits)	found M?
500	2	1	4000	0	5.90085	✓
500	2	1	8000	3.41009	10.7467	✓
500	2	1	10000	7.08508	12.7447	✓
500	2	1	15000	12.6617	18.5326	✓
500	2	1	20000	18.0246	24.5732	×
500	2	2	4000	4.21731	18.587	✓
500	2	2	6000	12.3467	28.7882	×
500	2	2	8000	18.87	35.7267	×
500	2	2	10000	28.5508	45.8028	×
500	2	3	2000	0	19.0752	✓
500	2	3	3000	7.38752	32.9895	✓
500	2	3	4000	16.9325	40.9656	×
500	2	10	1000	0	30.3755	✓
500	2	10	2000	11.9964	61.5006	×
500	3	1	1000	0	5.39761	✓
500	3	1	2000	1.29248	9.164	✓
500	3	1	3000	2.37744	13.9903	✓
500	3	1	4000	8.43829	17.4593	✓
500	3	1	5000	14.1789	21.528	✓
500	3	1	6000	18.3878	25.2578	×
500	3	1	7000	20.5646	29.287	×
500	3	2	1000	0	15.551	✓
500	3	2	2000	3.24593	33.0945	✓
500	3	2	3000	23.5966	43.7986	×
500	3	3	1000	0	28.1575	✓
500	3	3	2000	16.6455	53.1806	×
500	3	3	3000	41.3371	83.9486	×
500	4	1	1000	0	9.85319	✓
500	4	1	2000	8.11356	18.9434	✓
500	4	1	3000	19.1019	26.9836	✓
500	4	1	4000	24.4869	35.6328	×
500	4	1	5000	26.6804	44.3982	×
500	4	1	6000	40.5944	53.3654	×
500	4	2	1000	6.29272	33.4373	✓
500	4	2	2000	33.6181	63.3469	×

key: n = lattice dimension, d = size of smaller embedded matrices, T = bound on embedded matrix entries, ℓ = length of the product of smaller matrices.

n	d	T	ℓ	shortest row length (in bits)	longest row length (in bits)	found M?
886	2	1	3000	0	3.49434	✓
886	2	1	4000	0	3.80735	✓
886	2	1	5000	0	4.40207	✓
886	2	1	6000	0	5.30459	✓
886	2	1	7000	0	6.16923	✓
886	2	1	8000	0	6.90754	✓
886	2	1	9000	1	7.58371	✓
886	2	1	10000	2.37744	8.05954	✓
886	2	1	15000	5.46942	11.2176	✓
886	2	1	20000	8.6594	14.5837	✓
886	2	1	25000	10.884	18.035	✓
886	2	1	30000	15.0082	21.0333	✓
886	2	1	35000	17.6964	24.8408	✓
886	2	1	40000	20.7706	28.3888	✓
886	2	1	45000	24.484	30.6745	✓
886	2	1	50000	25.7401	34.0742	✗

key: $n =$ lattice dimension, $d =$ size of smaller embedded matrices, $T =$ bound on embedded matrix entries, $\ell =$ length of the product of smaller matrices.

Comments

Each sequence of experiments (for fixed values of n, d, and T) eventually fails when ℓ is sufficiently large. For ℓ too small the random product will not involve all the rows and columns of the matrix, meaning that the dimension of the lattice problem is effectively reduced to a smaller value of n, so the most interesting cases are for intermediate values of ℓ (e.g., $10000 \leq \ell \leq 50000$ in this last table). There is some correlation between a successful trial and having a short vector in M (the fifth column), especially in the trials for $n = 200$. For $n = 500$ one sees more successful trials with longer shortest rows, especially as d (and to a lesser extent, T) increase. Note that each entry in these tables corresponds to a single experiment; we did not attempt to average over several experiments since we wanted to report on the range of the row lengths.

We did not take values of $d > 4$, since it is difficult to use Algorithm 1 to generate larger random elements of $GL(d, \mathbb{Z})$.

The table for $n = 886$ is in some sense an elaboration of the middle entry of (3.2), the difference being that the latter uses unipotents (instead of embedded $GL(2, \mathbb{Z})$ matrices).

B   Experiments with Algorithm 4

Below we list tables of the experiments mentioned in Sect. 3 on Algorithm 4, performed using the testing procedure (3.1).

n	T	shortest row length (in bits)	longest row length (in bits)	found M?
100	1	2.91645	4.65757	✓
100	3	4.14501	5.81034	✓
100	4	4.50141	6.20496	✓
100	10	5.64183	7.15018	✓
100	50	7.99332	9.77546	✓
100	1	2.91645	4.65757	✓
110	1	2.98864	4.54902	×
120	1	3.03304	4.77441	×
125	1	3.09491	4.93979	×
150	1	3.12396	5.09738	×
200	1	3.42899	5.32597	×
200	2	4.23584	6.42421	×
200	3	4.72766	6.82899	×
200	4	5.06529	7.41803	×

key: n = lattice dimension, T = bound on matrix entries in bottom $n-1$ rows.

Comments

In general, matrices in $GL(n,\mathbb{Z})$ with large entries have very small determinants (± 1) relative to their overall entry size, so they are already very close to singular matrices. However, the size of the rank of nearby matrices is important. The matrices produced by Algorithm 4 are perturbations of matrices having rank $n - 1$ (which is as large as possible for singular $n \times n$ matrices). In contrast, one numerically sees that matrices produced by Algorithm 2 are instead nearly rank-one matrices (i.e., up to a small overall perturbation relative to the size of the entries). We expect Algorithm 3's matrices, which are produced by taking products of random $GL(d,\mathbb{Z})$ matrices, have intermediate behavior (but have not systematically analyzed this).

A related fact is that matrices produced by Algorithm 2 frequently have a very large row or column (if b is sufficiently large) – typically coming from the first or last factor in the matrix multiplication, respectively. That serves as a possible hint to recover the spelling of the word in the random product, along the lines of the length-based attack in [4, §4]. However, we were unable to turn this into a direct, general attack. For example, it is unclear what to do when the value of $x \in \mathbb{Z} \cap [-b, b]$ is small, say in the regime that $b \leq \ell$. (The situation is clearer when b is extremely large relative to ℓ, in which case we expect a bias effect in random words similar to underlying device used in [4, §4].)

C A Reference Point for the Bit-Strength of Lattice Problems: NTRU

In this appendix we give some information about how we measured when product lengths in Algorithms 2 and 3 were sufficiently long enough to ensure Gram matrix entries have an appropriately large size. The security of lattices against LLL and BKZ is an active area in which no general consensus has been reached despite many competing suggestions (reflecting its underlying notoriously complicated difficulty).

One type of lattice for which bit strengths have been suggested are NTRU lattices. We mention this as an attempt to quantify the notion that lattice problems in high dimensions are hard, as well as to provide a point of comparison—though there are of course many differences between NTRU lattices and rotations of the $\mathbb{Z}^n$ lattice (we don't say anything about the security of NTRU itself).

NTRU matrices have the form

$$\begin{pmatrix} I_{n/2} & X \\ 0 & qI_{n/2} \end{pmatrix} \tag{C.1}$$

with n even, q an integer greater than one, and X randomly chosen from a certain distribution among all integral matrices of the form

$$X = \begin{pmatrix} x_1 & x_2\ x_3 & \cdots & x_{n/2-1}\ x_{n/2} \\ x_2 & x_3\ x_4 & \cdots & x_{n/2} & x_1 \\ \vdots & \vdots\ \vdots & \ddots & \vdots \\ x_{n/2}\ x_1\ x_2 & \cdots & x_{n/2-2}\ x_{n/2-1} \end{pmatrix}, |x_j| \leq \frac{q}{2} \tag{C.2}$$

The rows of an NTRU matrix span an "NTRU lattice" $\Lambda \subset \mathbb{R}^n$. In [24] and in earlier NIST Post-Quantum Cryptography submissions the following quantum bit security is suggested for NTRU with the following parameters:

q	$n = \dim(\Lambda)$	estimated quantum security (in bits)
2048	886	128
2048	1486	256

(C.3)

These estimates are not directly relevant to the lattice bases we examine, which have different determinants and a very different structure. Nevertheless, they are consistent with the general expectation that lattice problems in dimensions 500 or more (and especially 1,000 or more) become cryptographically difficult.

The choice of length ℓ in the experiments in (3.2) was determined as follows. The vector lengths of the rows in the NTRU matrix (C.1) are either roughly $\sqrt{\frac{\pi}{2}}\frac{q}{2}$ (for the first $n/2$ rows), or exactly q (for the last $n/2$ rows). We took ℓ large enough so that the resulting product had comparable row lengths, and made sure to use at least as many random bits as go into constructing an NTRU lattice (which is $\frac{n}{2}\log_2(q)$).

References

1. Ajtai, M.: Generating hard instances of the short basis problem. In: Wiedermann, J., van Emde Boas, P., Nielsen, M. (eds.) ICALP 1999. LNCS, vol. 1644, pp. 1–9. Springer, Heidelberg (1999). https://doi.org/10.1007/3-540-48523-6_1
2. Alwen, J., Peikert, C.: Generating shorter bases for hard random lattices. Theory Comput. Syst. **48**, 535–553 (2011)
3. Aono, Y., Espitau, T., Nguyen, P.Q.: Random Lattices: Theory And Practice, preprint. https://espitau.github.io/bin/random_lattice.pdf
4. Begelfor, E., Miller, S.D., Venkatesan, R.: Non-abelian analogs of lattice rounding. Groups Complex. Cryptol. **7**(2), 117–133 (2015)
5. Cash, D., Hofheinz, D., Kiltz, E., Peikert, C.: Bonsai trees, or how to delegate a lattice basis. In: Gilbert, H. (ed.) EUROCRYPT 2010. LNCS, vol. 6110, pp. 523–552. Springer, Heidelberg (2010). https://doi.org/10.1007/978-3-642-13190-5_27
6. Conway, J.H., Sloane, N.J.A.: Sphere Packings, Lattices, and Groups. Grundlehren der mathematischen Wissenschafter, vol. 290, 3rd edn. Springer, New York (1999). https://doi.org/10.1007/978-1-4757-6568-7
7. Duke, W., Rudnick, Z., Sarnak, P.: Density of integer points on affine homogeneous varieties. Duke Math. J. **71**, 143–179 (1993)
8. Elkies, N.D.: A characterization of the $\mathbb{Z}^n$ lattice. Math. Res. Lett. **2**, 321–326 (1995)
9. Geißler, K., Smart, N.P.: Computing the $M = UU^t$ integer matrix decomposition. In: Paterson, K.G. (eds.) Cryptography and Coding. Cryptography and Coding 2003. Lecture Notes in Computer Science, vol. 2898. Springer, Heidelberg (2003). https://doi.org/10.1007/978-3-540-40974-8_18
10. Gentry, C., Szydlo, M.: Cryptanalysis of the revised NTRU signature scheme. In: Knudsen, L.R. (ed.) EUROCRYPT 2002. LNCS, vol. 2332, pp. 299–320. Springer, Heidelberg (2002). https://doi.org/10.1007/3-540-46035-7_20. http://www.szydlo.com/ntru-revised-full02.pdf
11. Gerstein, L.: Basic Quadratic Forms. Graduate Studies in Mathematics, vol. 90. American Mathematical Society, Providence (2008)
12. Gorodnik, A., Nevo, A.: The Ergodic Theory of Lattice Subgroups. Annals of Mathematics Studies, vol. 172. Princeton University Press, Princeton (2010)
13. Hunkenschröder, C.: Deciding whether a Lattice has an Orthonormal Basis is in co-NP. arxiv:1910.03838
14. Kim, S., Venkatesh, A.: The behavior of random reduced bases. Int. Math. Res. Notices **20**, 6442–6480 (2018)
15. Arjen, K. Lenstra Jr., H.W., Lovasz, L.: Factoring polynomials with rational coefficients. Mathematische Annalen **261**, 513–534 (1982)
16. Lenstra Jr., H.W., Silverberg, A.: Revisiting the Gentry-Szydlo algorithm. In: Garay, J.A., Gennaro, R. (eds.) CRYPTO 2014. LNCS, vol. 8616, pp. 280–296. Springer, Heidelberg (2014). https://doi.org/10.1007/978-3-662-44371-2_16

17. Lenstra Jr., H.W., Silverberg, A.: Lattices with symmetry. J. Cryptol. **30**, 760–804 (2017). https://doi.org/10.1007/s00145-016-9235-7
18. Lenstra Jr., H.W., Silverberg, A.: Testing isomorphism of lattices over CM-orders. SIAM J. Comput. **48**(4), 1300–1334 (2019)
19. Micciancio, D., Peikert, C.: Trapdoors for lattices: simpler, tighter, faster, smaller. In: Pointcheval, D., Johansson, T. (eds.) EUROCRYPT 2012. LNCS, vol. 7237, pp. 700–718. Springer, Heidelberg (2012). https://doi.org/10.1007/978-3-642-29011-4_41
20. Nguyen, P.Q., Stehlé, D.: An LLL algorithm with quadratic complexity. SIAM J. Comput. **39**, 874–903 (2009)
21. Plantard, T., Sipasseuth, A., Dumondelle, C., Susilo, W.: DRS: Diagonal dominant Reduction for lattice-based Signature. NIST Post-Quantum Digital Signature Competition entry. https://csrc.nist.gov/Projects/post-quantum-cryptography/Round-1-Submissions
22. Rivin, I.: How to pick a random integer matrix? (and other questions). Math. Comp. **85**, 783–797 (2016)
23. Schnorr, C.P.: A hierarchy of polynomial time lattice basis reduction algorithms. Theor. Comput. Sci. **53**, 201–224 (1987)
24. Whyte, W., Wilson, L.: Quantum Safety In Certified Cryptographic Modules. https://icmconference.org/wp-content/uploads/A21c-Whyte.pdf

Zero-Knowledge Proofs for Committed Symmetric Boolean Functions

San Ling[1], Khoa Nguyen[1], Duong Hieu Phan[2], Hanh Tang[1(✉)], and Huaxiong Wang[1]

[1] Nanyang Technological University, Singapore, Singapore
`tang0404@e.ntu.edu.sg`
[2] LTCI, Telecom Paris, Institut Polytechnique de Paris, Paris, France

Abstract. Zero-knowledge proofs (ZKP) are a fundamental notion in modern cryptography and an essential building block for countless privacy-preserving constructions. Recent years have witnessed a rapid development in the designs of ZKP for general statements, in which, for a publicly given Boolean function $f : \{0,1\}^n \rightarrow \{0,1\}$, one's goal is to prove knowledge of a secret input $\mathbf{x} \in \{0,1\}^n$ satisfying $f(\mathbf{x}) = b$, for a given bit b. Nevertheless, in many interesting application scenarios, not only the input $\mathbf{x}$ but also the underlying function f should be kept private. The problem of designing ZKP for the setting where both $\mathbf{x}$ and f are hidden, however, has not received much attention.

This work addresses the above-mentioned problem for the class of *symmetric Boolean functions*, namely, Boolean functions f whose output value is determined solely by the Hamming weight of the n-bit input $\mathbf{x}$. Although this class might sound restrictive, it has exponential cardinality 2^{n+1} and captures a number of well-known Boolean functions, such as threshold, sorting and counting functions. Specifically, with respect to a commitment scheme secure under the Learning-Parity-with-Noise (LPN) assumption, we show how to prove in zero-knowledge that $f(\mathbf{x}) = b$, for a committed symmetric function f, a committed input $\mathbf{x}$ and a bit b. The security of our protocol relies on that of an auxiliary commitment scheme which can be instantiated under quantum-resistant assumptions (including LPN). The protocol also achieves reasonable communication cost: the variant with soundness error $2^{-\lambda}$ has proof size $c \cdot \lambda \cdot n$, where c is a relatively small constant. The protocol can potentially find appealing privacy-preserving applications in the area of post-quantum cryptography, and particularly in code-based cryptography.

1 Introduction

Zero-knowledge (ZK) proofs, introduced by Goldwasser, Micali and Rackoff [21], enable a prover to convince a verifier of the truth of a statement without leaking any other information. In the last 3 decades, ZK proofs have become a fundamental notion in complexity theory and a core building block in the design of numerous cryptographic protocols. One can separate ZK *proofs*, which provide

© Springer Nature Switzerland AG 2021
J. H. Cheon and J.-P. Tillich (Eds.): PQCrypto 2021, LNCS 12841, pp. 339–359, 2021.
https://doi.org/10.1007/978-3-030-81293-5_18

statistical soundness, and ZK *arguments*, which only guarantee computational soundness. Early feasibility results were established by Goldreich et al. [20] and Brassard et al. [8], who showed that every NP language has a ZK proof system and an argument system, respectively. Since then, numerous design approaches of ZK protocols for proving general statements have been considered, e.g., [2–4,6,9,11,18,19,24–27,30,44], based on a wide range of techniques, various computational assumptions and offering diverse levels of efficiency.

RELATED WORK AND MOTIVATION. Most of existing ZK protocols for general statements address the following setting. Let $n \in \mathbb{Z}^+$ and let $f : \{0,1\}^n \to \{0,1\}$ be an efficiently-computable function, whose description is *public*. The goal then is to prove in ZK the knowledge of a secret input $\mathbf{x} \in \{0,1\}^n$ satisfying $f(\mathbf{x}) = 1$. This setting seems general enough to capture virtually all practical applications. However, we observe that there are interesting application contexts in which not only the input $\mathbf{x}$ but also the function f need to be kept *private*.

- **Policy-based anonymous authentications.** In this setting, users of an organization can show to the public the possession of credential $\mathbf{x}$ satisfying an internal policy f. To protect users' privacy as well as organization's strategy, both $\mathbf{x}$ and f should be hidden from the public. Examples of such cryptosystems include policy-based signatures [5], functional credentials [14] and attribute-based signatures with hidden policies [16, Chapter 6].
- **Privacy-preserving access controls for encrypted databases.** Consider an encrypted database where each data item is associated with an access policy f, and is accessible only to those holding a certificate $\mathbf{x}$ such that $f(\mathbf{x}) = 1$. If the database stores sensitive information (such as health, financial or criminal records), then the policy might leak certain side-channel information, e.g., the position/specialization of the doctor accessing a health record might indicate the occurrence of some disease. A prominent example of cryptosystems simultaneously protecting data, f and $\mathbf{x}$ is "oblivious transfer with hidden access control" [10], which can be realized using ZK proofs (alongside with attribute-based [22] and predicate [28] encryption).
- **Accountable function evaluations.** Suppose that a party (e.g., a border-control agency) runs a private algorithm f on a private input $\mathbf{x}$ so that to make a decision (e.g., (dis)approval of a visa). To keep the party accountable, the used algorithm has to be committed in advance, and be revealed (e.g., to a judge) in cases of disputes. Such mechanisms were investigated in [33] and may have significant societal impact.

In all the above application scenarios, it is desirable to be equipped with ZK proofs for correct evaluation of $f(\mathbf{x})$, where both f and $\mathbf{x}$ are committed (or certified/encrypted) in advance. However, the problem of designing efficient ZK proofs in this setting is still largely open. In fact, if there is no restriction on the hidden function f, the problem is infeasible to solve, since there are a total of 2^{2^n} functions mapping $\{0,1\}^n$ to $\{0,1\}$ (consequently, at least 2^n bits are needed to encode the description of an arbitrary function). Therefore, it totally makes sense to investigate the question when f belongs to a limited class of functions. Bellare and Fuchsbauer [5], in the context of pairing-based policy-based signatures, provided such a protocol for certain relations concerning pairings. Libert et al. [35] suggested a lattice-based protocol for functions in NC1, represented by branching programs. More generally, if the considered class of function can be computed by circuits of polynomially-bounded sizes, then it may be theoretically feasible to tackle the problem via Valiant's universal circuits [31, 32,43]. To this end, one may reduce the problem to proving that $\mathsf{UC}(f', \mathbf{x}) = 1$, where f' is certain programmed code related to a circuit computing f and UC is a public universal circuit that takes as inputs f' and $\mathbf{x}$. Then, one may run a ZK protocol for public circuits. However, there are 2 issues that would render this approach inefficient. First, existing techniques for converting $f(\mathbf{x}) = 1$ to $\mathsf{UC}(f', \mathbf{x}) = 1$ incur a relatively large overhead in the circuit size[1]. Second, one would additionally have to prove that the conversion is correct, i.e., to show in ZK that f' is indeed a well-formed code corresponding to the committed f, for which no plausible solution has been known.

In this work, we study the discussed above problem when the class of function f is restricted to *symmetric Boolean functions*. An n-ary Boolean function $f : \{0,1\}^n \to \{0,1\}$ is called symmetric if, on input $\mathbf{x} \in \{0,1\}^n$, it returns an output bit depending only on $\mathsf{wt}(\mathbf{x})$ - the Hamming weight of $\mathbf{x}$. In other words, f's output remains the same when one permutes $\mathbf{x}$'s coordinates. There are exactly 2^{n+1} symmetric n-ary Boolean functions, each of which can be uniquely represented by a vector $\mathbf{v}(f) = (v_0, \ldots, v_n) \in \{0,1\}^{n+1}$, such that $f(\mathbf{x}) = v_w$ where $w = \mathsf{wt}(\mathbf{x})$. Although this class of functions seems restrictive, it does capture a number of fundamental and commonly used Boolean functions, including

- *Threshold functions:* $\mathsf{T}_k(\mathbf{x}) = 1 \iff \mathsf{wt}(\mathbf{x}) \geq k$, for some fixed k;
- *Exact-value functions:* $\mathsf{E}_k(\mathbf{x}) = 1 \iff \mathsf{wt}(\mathbf{x}) = k$, for some fixed k;
- *Parity function:* $\mathsf{PAR}(\mathbf{x}) = 1 \iff \mathsf{wt}(\mathbf{x})$ is odd;
- *Sorting function:* $\mathsf{SORT}(\mathbf{x}) = (\mathsf{T}_1(\mathbf{x}), \ldots, \mathsf{T}_n(\mathbf{x}))$;
- *Counting functions:* $\mathsf{C}_{q,r}(\mathbf{x}) = 1 \iff \mathsf{wt}(\mathbf{x}) \equiv r \pmod{q}$, for some fixed q, r.

To the best of our knowledge, the question of proving in ZK that $f(\mathbf{x}) = 1$ for committed symmetric Boolean function f and committed input $\mathbf{x}$ has not been considered in the literature. From a technical viewpoint, the question is quite non-trivial and does not seem to be solvable in an efficient manner via existing generic approaches (e.g., combinations of universal circuits and general-purpose ZK proofs). The main reason is that it requires to prove that function f does act on input $\mathbf{x}$ in a "symmetric fashion" and does produce a correct output while preserving the privacy of $(f, \mathbf{x})$ and ensuring that they are consistent with the given commitments. In terms of applications, the question is also interesting, since if we can come up with a reasonably efficient solution, it could potentially be utilized in attractive scenarios.

---

[1] The size of UC is $t \cdot \log|C|$ times larger than the size C of the original circuit for computing f, where t could be a non-small constant.

OUR RESULTS. We provide the first treatment of ZK proofs for correct evaluations of committed functions on committed inputs, with respect to the class of symmetric Boolean functions. Specifically, for f and $\mathbf{x}$ committed as $\mathbf{c}_f$ and $\mathbf{c}_x$ via the commitment scheme from [26], which is secure under the Learning-Parity-with-Noise (LPN) assumption, we design a ZK proof of knowledge for proving that the commitments $\mathbf{c}_f$ and $\mathbf{c}_x$ are well-formed and that $f(\mathbf{x}) = b$, for a given output bit $b \in \{0,1\}$. The protocol has complexity linear in n (and hence, logarithmic in the cardinality of the set all n-ary symmetric Boolean functions): the computation costs of both prover and verifier are of order $\mathcal{O}(n)$, while a proof with soundness error $2^{-\lambda}$ has size $c \cdot \lambda \cdot n$ bits, for a relatively small constant c. The protocol's security is based on that of an auxiliary commitment scheme which can be instantiated under quantum-resistant assumptions (including LPN).

POTENTIAL APPLICATIONS. Our protocol can potentially find appealing privacy-preserving applications in the area of post-quantum cryptography, and, most naturally, in code-based cryptography. In particular, it can be useful for the 3 application contexts we discussed above, when the underlying function class is exactly the class of all symmetric Boolean functions.

As a standalone scheme, our protocol readily yields an accountable function evaluation mechanism in the sense of [33]. Moreover, the protocol can be slightly modified to handle the setting when the output bit b is also committed, which could be useful when the function outputs (e.g., decisions on visa (dis)approval or job offer/rejection) are necessarily kept private for the time being.

Furthermore, the protocol could be employed as a building block in several advanced post-quantum cryptosystems. For instance, one may design a policy-based signature [5] or a policy-hiding attribute-based signature [16] by combining with the code-based accumulators from [41]. Meanwhile, by plugging the protocol into the framework of LPN-based oblivious transfers [13,15], one may enable access control to data items with hidden access policies (akin to [35]).

TECHNICAL OVERVIEW. Let f be an n-ary symmetric Boolean function represented by $\mathbf{v}(f) = (v_0, \ldots, v_n) \in \{0,1\}^{n+1}$. We commit to $\mathbf{v} = \mathbf{v}(f)$ and input $\mathbf{x} \in \{0,1\}^n$ via the LPN-based commitment scheme from [26], as $\mathbf{c}_f$ and $\mathbf{c}_x$, respectively. More precisely, we have

$$\mathbf{c}_x = \mathbf{A}_{1,x} \cdot \mathbf{x} \ \oplus \ \mathbf{A}_2 \cdot \mathbf{s}_x \ \oplus \ \mathbf{e}_x, \quad \mathbf{c}_f = \mathbf{A}_{1,f} \cdot \mathbf{v} \ \oplus \ \mathbf{A}_2 \cdot \mathbf{s}_f \ \oplus \ \mathbf{e}_f,$$

where $\mathbf{A}_{1,x}, \mathbf{A}_{1,f}, \mathbf{A}_2$ form the public commitment key; $\mathbf{s}_x, \mathbf{s}_f, \mathbf{e}_x, \mathbf{e}_f$ are the LPN randomness; and $\oplus$ denotes the addition modulo 2. Let b be a given bit. Our goal is to construct a zero-knowledge protocol for proving that:

1. $\mathbf{c}_f$ and $\mathbf{c}_x$ are well-formed commitments to $\mathbf{v} = \mathbf{v}(f)$ and $\mathbf{x}$, respectively;
2. On input $\mathbf{x}$, the symmetric Boolean function f corresponding to vector $\mathbf{v}$ does return the bit b.

We first remark that (1.) can be realized using existing techniques [26,36] for proving matrix-vector relations with some fixed-weight witness vectors, that operate in the framework of Stern's protocol [42] where the fixed-weight constraint is proved in ZK using a random permutation. A minor point[2] worth noting here is that we need to prove that vectors $\mathbf{e}_x, \mathbf{e}_f$ have non-fixed Hamming weights bounded by some given τ, for which we employ an extension trick from [36] to reduce it to the usual fixed-weight setting.

Our main technical challenge indeed lies in (2.): we need to find a method to "evaluate $f(\mathbf{x})$ in ZK." To this end, we proceed by capturing the equation $f(\mathbf{x}) = b$ by equivalent and ZK-friendly statements, i.e., those that are compatible with Stern-like ZK techniques. Specifically, we put forward the following theorem.

Theorem 1. *(informal)* Equation $f(\mathbf{x}) = b$ holds if and only if there exist vector $\mathbf{z} = (z_0, \ldots, z_n) \in \{0,1\}^{n+1}$ and bits $b_0, \ldots, b_n \in \{0,1\}$ satisfying

$$\begin{cases} \mathsf{wt}(\mathbf{x}\|\mathbf{z}) = n + 1, & (b_0, v_0, \ldots, b_n, v_n) \in \mathsf{good}(b), \\ b_0 \oplus v_0 \oplus z_0 = 1, & \forall i \in [n] : b_i \oplus v_i \oplus z_i \oplus z_{i-1} = 1. \end{cases} \tag{1}$$

In the above, $\mathsf{good}(b)$ is a well-defined (see Definition 1) subset of $\{0,1\}^{2(n+1)}$, such that $|\mathsf{good}(0)| = |\mathsf{good}(1)| = (n+1)2^n$. Furthermore, the membership of $\mathsf{good}(b)$, for $b \in \{0,1\}$, and the other conditions stated in (1) all can be proved in ZK using dedicated Stern-like permuting techniques. In other words, we can reduce problem (2.) to an equivalent and easier-to-solve problem of proving knowledge of $(\mathbf{z}, b_0, \ldots, b_n)$ satisfying (1).

Let us know discuss at a high level how the theorem is derived. We start with the observation that the value of $f(\mathbf{x})$ can be computed via the inner product $\langle \mathbf{v}(f), \mathbf{y} \rangle$, where $\mathbf{y} = (y_0, \ldots, y_n)$ is the $(n+1)$-dimensional unit vector with $y_{\mathsf{wt}(\mathbf{x})} = 1$. To take advantage of this observation, we then need to: (i) Demonstrate how the well-formed vector $\mathbf{y}$ is obtained from input $\mathbf{x}$; and (ii) The inner product evaluation does yield output bit b. While both (i) and (ii) are fairly simple from an algorithmic viewpoint, they are quite non-trivial in the ZK context. To address them simultaneously, our approach is to introduce auxiliary, intermediate witnesses $\mathbf{z}$ and $b_0, \ldots, b_n$, that are tight together with $(\mathbf{x}, \mathbf{v}, b)$ via the conditions in (1).

Once we manage to handle (2.) in ZK using Stern-like techniques, we can combine with the commitment layer in (1.) and obtain the desired protocol. We remark that, although we explicitly work with public output bit b, the protocol can easily be adjusted to handle the case when b is also committed (which could be useful for some applications.)

OTHER RELATED WORK ON CODE-BASED ZERO-KNOWLEDGE. A prominent tool for designing code-based privacy-preserving constructions is Stern's ZK protocol [42]. Variants of the protocol have been employed to build proofs of plaintext knowledge [39], ring [7,12,37,38], and group [1,17] signatures, proofs of valid openings for commitments and proofs for general relations [26]. More recently,

---

[2] In [26], the noise weight is set to be equal to τ, but then the commitment scheme has to rely on a somewhat non-standard variant of LPN. See Appendix 2.2 for more details.

Stern's techniques have been further developed to design code-based range arguments, accumulators and their applications to ring/group signatures [41] as well as group encryption [40]. The study of zero-knowledge proofs for committed symmetric Boolean functions is new to the present paper.

ORGANIZATION. In Sect. 2, we recall some background on Stern-like protocols and LPN-based commitments. Section 3 presents the technical foundations for reducing the evaluation of symmetric Boolean functions to a form compatible with Stern-like ZK proofs. The main result, stated in Theorem 1, is then used in Sect. 4, where the protocol for committed functions is described in detail.

2   Background

NOTATIONS. For integers a, b such that $a \leq b$, the set $\{a, a+1, \ldots, b\}$ is denoted by $[a, b]$. We write $[b]$ to indicate $[1, b]$. We denote column vectors by lowercase bold letters, e.g., $\mathbf{a}, \mathbf{b}$, and matrices by uppercase bold letters, e.g., $\mathbf{A}, \mathbf{B}$. The horizontal concatenation of matrices $\mathbf{A}$ and $\mathbf{B}$ is denoted by $[\mathbf{A}|\mathbf{B}]$. The concatenation of vectors $\mathbf{a}$ and $\mathbf{b}$ is denoted by $(\mathbf{a}\|\mathbf{b})$, i.e., $(\mathbf{a}\|\mathbf{b}) = [\mathbf{a}^\top|\mathbf{b}^\top]^\top$. The notation $\mathbf{I}_k$ stands for the identity matrix of order k.

Denote by $\mathsf{wt}(\mathbf{a})$ the Hamming weight of vector $\mathbf{a}$, i.e., the number of entries equal to 1 in $\mathbf{a}$. We let $\mathsf{B}(n, w)$ denote the set of all binary vectors of length n with Hamming weight w. For any $w \in [0, n]$, we denote by $\mathsf{U}(w)$ the unit vector $(u_0, \ldots, u_n)$ where $u_w = 1$ and $u_i = 0$ for all $i \in [0, n]$ satisfying $i \neq w$.

The notation $x \xleftarrow{\$} S$ means x is chosen uniformly at random from finite set S. The addition modulo 2 is denoted by $\oplus$. If b is a bit, then $\bar{b}$ denotes the bit $b \oplus 1$.

2.1   Zero-Knowledge Proofs of Knowledge and Stern-Like Protocols

Let $R = \{(x, w)\}$ be an NP relation. Informally, a zero-knowledge proof of knowledge (ZKPoK) for relation R is a two-party protocol, in which prover $\mathcal{P}$, on input a statement-witness pair (x, w), convinces verifier $\mathcal{V}$ on input statement x that $\mathcal{P}$ knows w such that $(x, w) \in R$ in a way such that no additional information about w is revealed. The protocol must satisfy the following properties:

- Completeness. If $\mathcal{P}$ is honest then $\mathcal{V}$ always accepts.
- Zero-Knowledge. There exists a PPT simulator Sim that, on input x, produces a simulated transcript that is computationally indistinguishable from an honest transcript between $\mathcal{P}$ and any (potentially cheating) verifier $\widehat{\mathcal{V}}$.
- Proof of Knowledge. From any (potentially cheating) prover $\widehat{\mathcal{P}}$, that can convince $\mathcal{V}$ with a probability larger than a threshold e (called the soundness error), a witness w' such that $(x, w') \in R$ can be efficiently extracted in a rewindable blackbox manner.

For protocols consisting of 3 moves (i.e., commitment-challenge-response), the proof-of-knowledge property is implied by *special soundness* [23], where the latter assumes that there exists a PPT extractor which takes as input a set of valid transcripts with respect to all possible values of the "challenge" to the same "commitment", and outputs w' such that $(x, w') \in R$. The ZKPoK presented in this paper is a Stern-like protocol, i.e., it follows Stern's framework [42]. In particular, it is a Σ-protocol in the generalized sense defined in [26] (where 3 valid transcripts are needed for extraction, instead of just 2). If a computationally hiding and statistically binding string commitment scheme is employed in the first move, then one obtains a computational ZKPoK with perfect completeness and soundness error $2/3$. In applications, the protocol can be repeated $t = \omega(\log \lambda)$ times to make the soundness error negligibly small in security λ.

2.2   Commitments from Learning Parity with Noise

In this paper, we commit to binary strings via the commitment scheme introduced by Jain et al. [26]. The scheme can be proven to be statistically binding and computationally hiding based on the hardness of the Learning Parity with Noise (LPN) problem. Let us recall its description.

Let κ, ℓ, s, τ be positive integers such that $\tau < \kappa$. For message space $\{0,1\}^\ell$, the commitment key is a pair of matrices $(\mathbf{A}_1, \mathbf{A}_2) \xleftarrow{\$} \{0,1\}^{\kappa \times \ell} \times \{0,1\}^{\kappa \times s}$. To commit to a message $\mathbf{x} \in \{0,1\}^\ell$, one samples an LPN secret $\mathbf{s} \xleftarrow{\$} \{0,1\}^s$, an LPN noise $\mathbf{e} \in \{0,1\}^\kappa$ satisfying $\mathsf{wt}(\mathbf{e}) \leq \tau$, and outputs commitment

$$\mathbf{c} = \mathbf{A}_1 \cdot \mathbf{x} \oplus \mathbf{A}_2 \cdot \mathbf{s} \oplus \mathbf{e}. \tag{2}$$

The opening algorithm $\mathsf{Open}(\mathbf{A}_1, \mathbf{A}_2, \mathbf{c}, \mathbf{x}, \mathbf{s}, \mathbf{e})$ then outputs 1 if $\mathsf{wt}(\mathbf{e}) \leq \tau$ and Eq. (2) holds.

We remark that, in [26], the restriction on the Hamming weight of $\mathbf{e}$ is actually $\mathsf{wt}(\mathbf{e}) = \tau$ (hence, $\mathbf{e} \in \mathsf{B}(\kappa, \tau)$), and the computational hiding property of the scheme relies on a somewhat non-standard variant of LPN called "exact LPN". The main reason is that, in their ZKPoK of a valid opening $(\mathbf{x}, \mathbf{s}, \mathbf{e})$, Jain et al. employ a Stern-like protocol, in which the constraint $\mathbf{e} \in \mathsf{B}(\kappa, \tau)$ can be easily proven in zero-knowledge using a uniformly random permutation of κ elements. The scheme we described above, however, can rely on the standard variant of LPN. To prove in zero-knowledge that $\mathsf{wt}(\mathbf{e}) \leq \tau$ (rather than the easier constraint $\mathsf{wt}(\mathbf{e}) = \tau$), we make use of a trick introduced by Ling et al. [36]. It consists of extending $\mathbf{e}$ to a vector $(\mathbf{e}\|\mathbf{e}') \in \mathsf{B}(\kappa + \tau, \tau)$ and using a uniformly random permutation of $(\kappa + \tau)$ elements to prove knowledge of the extended vector. To make Eq. (2) compatible with such extension, we can transform it to an equivalent one: $\mathbf{c} = \mathbf{A}_1 \cdot \mathbf{x} \oplus \mathbf{A}_2 \cdot \mathbf{s} \oplus [\mathbf{I}_\kappa \mid \mathbf{0}^{\kappa \times \tau}](\mathbf{e}\|\mathbf{e}')$, where $\mathbf{I}_\kappa$ is the identity matrix of order κ.

3   Techniques for Evaluating Symmetric Boolean Functions in Zero-Knowledge

Let n be a positive integer and let $f : \{0,1\}^n \to \{0,1\}$ be an n-ary symmetric Boolean function. Since the value of $f(\mathbf{x})$, for $\mathbf{x} \in \{0,1\}^n$, depends solely on wt($\mathbf{x}$), function f can be represented by vector $\mathbf{v}(f) = (v_0, \ldots, v_n) \in \{0,1\}^{n+1}$, defined as follows: v_i is the output of f on inputs of weight i, for all $i \in [0, n]$. In other words, when wt($\mathbf{x}$) = w, we have $f(\mathbf{x}) = b$ if and only if $v_w = b$.

In this section, our goal is to provide the technical foundations for proving in zero-knowledge that $f(\mathbf{x}) = b$, for hidden function f, represented by $\mathbf{v}(f)$, and hidden input $\mathbf{x}$. Specifically, we will derive necessary and sufficient conditions for $f(\mathbf{x}) = b$, which can be efficiently proved in zero-knowledge. These results are stated in Theorem 1.

Before coming to the theorem, let us define some special subsets of $\{0,1\}^{2(n+1)}$.

Definition 1. *For $b \in \{0,1\}$, define* good(b) *as the set of all vectors of the form* $\mathbf{b} = (b_{0,0}, b_{0,1}, \ldots, b_{n,0}, b_{n,1}) \in \{0,1\}^{2(n+1)}$, *for which there exists $w \in [0,n]$ such that $b_{w,0} = b_{w,1} = b$ and $b_{i,0} \neq b_{i,1}$, $\forall i \in [0,n] \setminus \{w\}$.*

We note that good(0) and good(1) are disjoint subsets of $\{0,1\}^{2(n+1)}$, and each has cardinality $(n+1)2^n$. Now, let us state the main results of this section.

Theorem 1. *Let $f : \{0,1\}^n \to \{0,1\}$ be an n-ary symmetric Boolean function represented by $\mathbf{v}(f) = (v_0, \ldots, v_n) \in \{0,1\}^{n+1}$. Let $\mathbf{x} \in \{0,1\}^n$ and $b \in \{0,1\}$. Then the following 2 statements are equivalent.*
(1) $f(\mathbf{x}) = b$.
(2) *There exist $b_0, \ldots, b_n \in \{0,1\}$ and vector $\mathbf{z} = (z_0, \ldots, z_n) \in \{0,1\}^{n+1}$ such that*
$$\begin{cases} b_0 \oplus v_0 \oplus z_0 = 1, \\ b_i \oplus v_i \oplus z_i \oplus z_{i-1} = 1 \quad \forall i \in [n] \end{cases} \tag{3}$$
and
$$\begin{cases} \text{wt}(\mathbf{x}\|\mathbf{z}) = n+1, \\ (b_0, v_0, \ldots, b_n, v_n) \in \text{good}(b). \end{cases} \tag{4}$$

Looking ahead, Theorem 1 provides us with an intriguing method to prove in zero-knowledge that $f(\mathbf{x}) = b$, for a given bit b and for secret $\mathbf{v}(f)$ and $\mathbf{x}$. Namely, we can equivalently prove in zero-knowledge the existence of bits $b_0, \ldots, b_n$ and vector $\mathbf{z} \in \{0,1\}^{n+1}$ satisfying (3) and (4). The actual protocol for doing so will be described in detail in Sect. 4. The rest of the present section is dedicated for the proof of Theorem 1. To this end, we will go through several steps.

Step 1: View $f(\mathbf{x})$ as an Inner Product. We start with a simple-yet-useful observation: $f(\mathbf{x})$ can be computed as the inner product
$$\langle \mathbf{v}(f), \mathbf{y} \rangle = v_0 \cdot y_0 \oplus \cdots \oplus v_n \cdot y_n,$$
where $\mathbf{y} = (y_0, \ldots, y_n) = \mathsf{U}(\text{wt}(\mathbf{x}))$ - the $(n+1)$-dimensional unit vector with $y_w = 1$, where $w = \text{wt}(\mathbf{x})$. Formally, we have the following lemma.

Lemma 1. *For every n-ary symmetric Boolean function f, every $\mathbf{x} \in \{0,1\}^n$ and $b \in \{0,1\}$, by setting $\mathbf{y} = (y_0, \ldots, y_n) = \mathsf{U}(\text{wt}(\mathbf{x}))$ and $\mathbf{v} = (v_0, \ldots, v_n) = \mathbf{v}(f)$, we have the equivalence: $f(\mathbf{x}) = b \iff \langle \mathbf{v}, \mathbf{y} \rangle = b$.*

Proof. Let $f(\mathbf{x}) = b$. Suppose that $w = \mathsf{wt}(\mathbf{x})$. Then, on the one hand, we know that $v_w = b$. On the other hand, since $\mathbf{y} = \mathsf{U}(w)$, we see that $y_w = 1$ and $y_i = 0$ for every $i \in [0, n] \setminus \{w\}$. Hence, $\langle \mathbf{v}, \mathbf{y} \rangle = v_w = b$.

As for the converse, since $\mathbf{y} = \mathsf{U}(\mathsf{wt}(\mathbf{x}))$, the inner product $\langle \mathbf{v}, \mathbf{y} \rangle$ extracts bit v_w from $\mathbf{v}$, where $w = \mathsf{wt}(\mathbf{x})$. This implies that $f(\mathbf{x}) = v_w = \langle \mathbf{v}, \mathbf{y} \rangle = b$.   □

By Lemma 1, to prove that $f(\mathbf{x}) = b$, we can alternatively show that $\langle \mathbf{v}, \mathbf{y} \rangle = b$. For the latter, we need to demonstrate that: (i) $\mathbf{y}$ is correctly computed, i.e., we indeed have $\mathbf{y} = \mathsf{U}(\mathsf{wt}(\mathbf{x}))$; (ii) the inner product evaluation in fact yields b. Our next 2 steps address these aspects.

Step 2: Computing $\mathbf{y} = \mathsf{U}(\mathsf{wt}(\mathbf{x}))$ from x. From an algorithmic viewpoint, it is simple to compute $\mathbf{y}$ from $\mathbf{x}$: one can just count $w = \mathsf{wt}(\mathbf{x})$ and form the corresponding unit vector $\mathbf{y}$. However, from a "zero-knowledge" point of view, proving that we do so correctly without revealing $\mathbf{x}$ nor $\mathbf{y}$ is quite non-trivial. We would need to derive certain conditions that capture $\mathbf{y} = \mathsf{U}(\mathsf{wt}(\mathbf{x}))$ and that can be demonstrated in zero-knowledge using known techniques. We therefore proceed as follows.

A necessary condition we will use is that $\mathbf{y}$ is a unit vector, i.e., $\mathsf{wt}(\mathbf{y}) = 1$. Let us assume that $y_{w'} = 1$ for some $w' \in [0, n]$ and $y_i = 0$ for all $i \in [0, n]$ satisfying $i \neq w'$. Then we need to show that this unit vector agrees with the weight of $\mathbf{x}$, i.e., $w' = \mathsf{wt}(\mathbf{x})$. To this end, we construct vector $\mathbf{z} = (z_0, \ldots, z_n) \in \{0,1\}^{n+1}$ based on $\mathbf{y}$ by flipping all entries in the right of position w'. For instance, when $\mathbf{y} = \mathsf{U}(4)$, for $n = 8$, we have

$$\mathbf{y} = (0,0,0,0,1,0,0,0), \quad \mathbf{z} = (0,0,0,0,1,1,1,1).$$

It can be seen that $\mathsf{wt}(\mathbf{z}) = n - w' + 1$. Hence, $w = w'$ if and only if $\mathsf{wt}(\mathbf{x}\|\mathbf{z}) = \mathsf{wt}(\mathbf{x}) + \mathsf{wt}(\mathbf{z}) = n + 1$.

Now, we need a sub-algorithm that computes $\mathbf{z}$, whose steps are "oblivious" and can be demonstrated in zero-knowledge. More precisely, we can assume that the computation of $\mathbf{z}$ with access pattern to entries of $\mathbf{y}$ is the same regardless of the position w' of bit 1 in $\mathbf{y}$. To this end, we define the function $\mathsf{Z}(\mathbf{y})$ which takes as input a vector $\mathbf{y} = (y_0, \ldots, y_n) \in \{0,1\}^{n+1}$ and returns the desired $\mathbf{z} = (z_0, \ldots, z_n) \in \{0,1\}^{n+1}$ by initially setting $z_0 := y_0$ and then assigning $z_i := y_i \oplus z_{i-1}$, for i running from 1 to n. The computation of $\mathsf{Z}(\mathbf{y})$ can be explained as follows. Assume that $\mathbf{y} = \mathsf{U}(w')$. We first consider z_0. Note that $z_0 = 1$ if and only if $w' = 0$. Hence,

$$(w' = 0) \implies (z_0 = y_0 = 1); \quad (w' > 0) \implies (z_0 = y_0 = 0).$$

We now consider the remaining cases of $z_1, \ldots, z_n$.

$$\begin{aligned}
(1 \leq i < w') &\implies (y_i = 0 \wedge z_{i-1} = 0) \implies (z_i = y_i \oplus z_{i-1} = 0), \\
(i = w') &\implies (y_i = 1 \wedge z_{i-1} = 0) \implies (z_i = y_i \oplus z_{i-1} = 1), \\
(i > w') &\implies (y_i = 0 \wedge z_{i-1} = 1) \implies (z_i = y_i \oplus z_{i-1} = 1).
\end{aligned}$$

The above discussions lead us to the following technical lemma.

Lemma 2. *For any* $\mathbf{x} \in \{0,1\}^n$ *and any* $\mathbf{y} = (y_0, \ldots, y_n) \in \{0,1\}^{n+1}$, *let* $\mathbf{z} = (z_0, \ldots, z_n) = \mathsf{Z}(\mathbf{y}) \in \{0,1\}^{n+1}$. *Then, we have*

$$\mathbf{y} = \mathsf{U}(\mathsf{wt}(\mathbf{x})) \iff (\mathsf{wt}(\mathbf{y}) = 1) \wedge (\mathsf{wt}(\mathbf{x}\|\mathbf{z}) = n + 1).$$

Proof. For the "$\Rightarrow$" direction, let $w = \mathsf{wt}(\mathbf{x})$. Since $\mathbf{y} = \mathsf{U}(\mathsf{wt}(\mathbf{x}))$, we know that

$$\mathbf{y} = (y_0, \ldots, y_n) \in \{0,1\}^{n+1}$$

where $y_w = 1$ and $y_i = 0$ for all $i \in [0, n]$ satisfying $i \neq w$. We claim that $\mathbf{z} = (z_0, \ldots, z_n) \in \{0,1\}^{n+1}$ has the form

$$\begin{cases} z_i = 0 & \forall i \in [0,n] \text{ satisfying } 0 \leq i < w, \\ z_i = 1 & \forall i \in [0,n] \text{ satisfying } i \geq w. \end{cases}$$

In fact, for the case of z_0, we know that $z_0 = 1$ if and only if $w = 0$. Hence, $z_0 = 1$ if and only if $y_0 = 1$. For the cases of $z_1, \ldots, z_n$, we can check the following subcases:

- If $1 \leq i < w$, then $z_{i-1} = 0$ and $y_i = 0$ implying $z_i = y_i \oplus z_{i-1} = 0$.
- If $i = w$, then $z_{i-1} = 0$ and $y_i = 1$ implying $z_i = y_i \oplus z_{i-1} = 1$.
- If $i > w$, then $z_{i-1} = 1$ and $y_i = 0$ implying $z_i = y_i \oplus z_{i-1} = 1$.

Moreover, it is obvious that $\mathsf{wt}(\mathbf{z}) = n - w + 1$. Hence $\mathsf{wt}(\mathbf{x}\|\mathbf{z}) = \mathsf{wt}(\mathbf{x}) + \mathsf{wt}(\mathbf{z}) = n + 1$. Therefore, the "$\Rightarrow$" direction is proved.

Regarding the "$\Leftarrow$" direction, as $\mathsf{wt}(\mathbf{y}) = 1$, we assume $\mathbf{y} = \mathsf{U}(w')$ for some $w' \in [0, n]$. As above, we claim that $\mathbf{z} = (z_0, \ldots, z_n) \in \{0,1\}^{n+1}$ has the form

$$\begin{cases} z_i = 0 & \forall i \in [0,n] \text{ satisfying } 0 \leq i < w', \\ z_i = 1 & \forall i \in [0,n] \text{ satisfying } i \geq w'. \end{cases}$$

It is obvious that $\mathsf{wt}(\mathbf{z}) = n - w' + 1$. Since

$$n + 1 = \mathsf{wt}(\mathbf{x}\|\mathbf{z}) = \mathsf{wt}(\mathbf{x}) + \mathsf{wt}(\mathbf{z}) = n - w' + 1 + w,$$

we see that $w' = w$. Therefore, we have $\mathbf{y} = \mathsf{U}(\mathsf{wt}(\mathbf{x}))$. $\qquad\square$

Thanks to Lemma 2, we can demonstrate the well-formedness of vector $\mathbf{y} = \mathsf{U}(\mathsf{wt}(\mathbf{x}))$ by instead showing the correct computation of $\mathbf{z} = \mathsf{Z}(\mathbf{y})$, as well as $\mathsf{wt}(\mathbf{y}) = 1$ and $\mathsf{wt}(\mathbf{x}\|\mathbf{z}) = n + 1$. That is, we need to prove the knowledge of $\mathbf{x} \in \{0,1\}^n$, $\mathbf{z} = (z_0, \ldots, z_n) \in \{0,1\}^{n+1}$ and $\mathbf{y} = (y_0, \ldots, y_n) \in \{0,1\}^{n+1}$ that satisfy the following system:

$$\begin{cases} z_0 = y_0, & \forall i \in [n] : z_i = y_i \oplus z_{i-1}, \\ \mathsf{wt}(\mathbf{x}\|\mathbf{z}) = n + 1, & \mathsf{wt}(\mathbf{y}) = 1. \end{cases} \tag{5}$$

Step 3: Computing the Inner Product $\langle \mathbf{v}, \mathbf{y} \rangle$ in Zero-Knowledge. To prove the inner-product relation $\langle \mathbf{v}, \mathbf{y} \rangle = b$ in zero-knowledge, we employ a dedicated and fairly efficient strategy. Specifically, we extend vectors $\mathbf{y} = (y_0, \ldots, y_n)$ and $\mathbf{v} = (v_0, \ldots, v_n)$ to vectors $\tilde{\mathbf{y}}$ and $\tilde{\mathbf{v}}$, respectively, where

$$\tilde{\mathbf{y}} = \mathsf{ext}(\mathbf{y}) := (y_0, 0, y_1, 0, \ldots, y_n, 0) \in \{0,1\}^{2n+2},$$

$$\tilde{\mathbf{v}} = \mathsf{enc}(\mathbf{v}) := (\overline{v_0}, v_0, \overline{v_1}, v_1, \ldots, \overline{v_n}, v_n) \in \{0,1\}^{2n+2}. \qquad (6)$$

Note that, for each $i \in [0, n]$, we have $\mathsf{wt}((\overline{v_i}, v_i)) = 1$. Note also that $\mathsf{wt}((y_w, 0)) = 1$, while $\mathsf{wt}((y_i, 0)) = 0$ for all $i \in [0, n]$ satisfying $i \neq w$. Define

$$\mathbf{b} = (b_{0,0}, b_{0,1}, \ldots, b_{n,0}, b_{n,1}) = \tilde{\mathbf{v}} \oplus \tilde{\mathbf{y}} = (\overline{v_0} \oplus y_0, v_0, \ldots, \overline{v_n} \oplus y_n, v_n). \qquad (7)$$

Note that $\mathbf{b}$ consists of $(n+1)$ blocks of length 2, where the i-th block is $(b_{i,0}, b_{i,1}) = (\overline{v_i} \oplus y_i, v_i)$. We observe that $(b_{w,0}, b_{w,1}) = (\overline{v_w}, v_w) \oplus (y_w, 0)$ is of even weight (i.e., 0 or 2), while $(b_{i,0}, b_{i,1}) = (\overline{v_i}, v_i) \oplus (y_i, 0)$ is of weight 1, for all $i \in [0, n]$ satisfying $i \neq w$. Consider the special block

$$(b_{w,0}, b_{w,1}) = (\overline{v_w} \oplus y_w, v_w) = (v_w \oplus y_w \oplus 1, v_w) = (v_w, v_w).$$

It can be seen that this block indicates the output bit $b = v_w = \langle \mathbf{v}, \mathbf{y} \rangle$ because both of its entries are equal to b. Therefore, the addition $\mathsf{enc}(\mathbf{v}) \oplus \mathsf{ext}(\mathbf{y})$ clearly captures the output of the inner product $\langle \mathbf{v}, \mathbf{y} \rangle$.

Now, looking back at Definition 1, we note that vector $\mathbf{b}$ constructed above indeed satisfies $\mathbf{b} \in \mathsf{good}(b)$. This explains the rationality of defining $\mathsf{good}(b)$.

Conversely, if $\tilde{\mathbf{v}} = \mathsf{enc}(\mathbf{v})$ of the form (6) and $\mathbf{b} = \tilde{\mathbf{v}} \oplus \mathsf{ext}(\mathbf{y}) \in \mathsf{good}(b)$, with $b_{w,0} = b_{w,1} = b$, then the sum $\tilde{\mathbf{y}} = (\tilde{y}_{0,0}, \tilde{y}_{0,1}, \ldots, \tilde{y}_{n,0}, \tilde{y}_{n,1}) = \tilde{\mathbf{v}} \oplus \mathbf{b}$ belongs to $\mathsf{B}(2n + 2, 1)$, where $\tilde{y}_{w,0} = 1$. In fact, since $\tilde{\mathbf{v}}$ is of the form (6), every 2-bit block of $\tilde{\mathbf{v}}$ has weight 1. Moreover, since $b_{w,0} = b_{w,1}$ and $b_{i,0} \neq b_{i,1}$ for all $i \in [0, n] \setminus \{w\}$, we have $\mathsf{wt}((b_{w,0}, b_{w,1}))$ is even and $\mathsf{wt}((b_{i,0}, b_{i,1})) = 1$ for all $i \in [0, n] \setminus \{w\}$. Hence, $\tilde{\mathbf{y}}$ has $(\tilde{y}_{w,0}, \tilde{y}_{w,1})$ of weight 1 and $(\tilde{y}_{i,0}, \tilde{y}_{i,1})$ of even weight for all $i \in [0, n] \setminus \{w\}$. Since $b_{i,1} = v_i \oplus 0 = v_i$ for all $i \in [0, n]$, it can be seen that $\tilde{y}_{i,1} = b_{i,1} \oplus v_i = 0$. Therefore, we have $\tilde{\mathbf{y}} \in \mathsf{B}(2n + 2, 1)$ and $\tilde{y}_{w,0} = 1$. This implies $\tilde{\mathbf{y}} = \mathsf{ext}(\mathbf{y})$ for some $\mathbf{y} \in \mathsf{B}(n + 1, 1)$. We then have the following lemma.

Lemma 3. Let $\mathbf{b} = \mathsf{enc}(\mathbf{v}) \oplus \mathsf{ext}(\mathbf{y})$. Then,

$$\big(\mathbf{y} \in \mathsf{B}(n + 1, 1)\big) \wedge \big(\langle \mathbf{v}, \mathbf{y} \rangle = b\big) \iff \mathbf{b} \in \mathsf{good}(b). \qquad (8)$$

Proof. If $\mathbf{y} \in \mathsf{B}(n + 1, 1)$ and $b = \langle \mathbf{v}, \mathbf{y} \rangle$, then assume that $y_w = 1$ for some $w \in [0, n]$. We have

$$\mathbf{b} = (b_{0,0}, b_{0,1}, \ldots, b_{n,0}, b_{n,1}) = \mathsf{enc}(\mathbf{v}) \oplus \mathsf{ext}(\mathbf{y})$$

$$= (\overline{v_0} \oplus y_0, v_0, \ldots, \overline{v_n} \oplus y_n, v_n) = (v_0 \oplus y_0 \oplus 1, v_0, \ldots, v_n \oplus y_n \oplus 1, v_n).$$

Let us view $\mathbf{b}$ as the collection of $(n + 1)$ length-2 blocks $(b_{i,0}, b_{i,1})$. Since $y_w = 1$, we see that $(b_{w,0}, b_{w,1}) = (v_w \oplus y_w \oplus 1, v_w) = (v_w, v_w)$. Note that $b = \langle \mathbf{v}, \mathbf{y} \rangle$. Since $y_w = 1$ and $y_i = 0$ for all $i \in [0, n] \setminus \{w\}$, it is obvious that $b = \langle \mathbf{v}, \mathbf{y} \rangle = v_w$ and hence $(b_{w,0}, b_{w,1}) = (v_w, v_w) = (b, b)$. For every $i \in [0, n] \setminus \{w\}$, the block $(b_{i,0}, b_{i,1}) = (v_i \oplus y_i \oplus 1, v_i) = (v_i \oplus 1, v_i)$, because $y_i = 0$. Hence, $b_{i,0} \neq b_{i,1}$. As a result, we have $\mathbf{b} \in \mathsf{good}(b)$.

As for the converse, we assume there exists $w \in [0, n]$ such that $b = b_{w,0} = b_{w,1}$ and $b_{i,0} \neq b_{i,1}$ for all $i \in [0, n] \setminus \{w\}$. Note that $\mathsf{enc}(\mathbf{v}) = (\overline{v_0}, v_0, \dots, \overline{v_n}, v_n)$ and $\mathsf{ext}(\mathbf{y}) = (y_0, 0, \dots, y_n, 0)$. Since $\mathbf{b} = \mathsf{enc}(\mathbf{v}) \oplus \mathsf{ext}(\mathbf{y})$, we see that

$$\forall i \in [0, n]: \quad b_{i,0} = v_i \oplus y_i \oplus 1; \quad b_{i,1} = v_i.$$

Hence $y_i = b_{i,0} \oplus v_i \oplus 1 = b_{i,0} \oplus b_{i,1} \oplus 1$ for all $i \in [0, n]$. Since $b_{w,0} = b_{w,1}$, we have $y_w = 1$. On the other hand, since $b_{i,0} \neq b_{i,1}$ for all $i \in [0, n] \setminus \{w\}$, we have $y_i = b_{i,0} \oplus b_{i,1} \oplus 1 = 0$. Hence $\mathbf{y} = (y_0, \dots, y_n) \in \mathsf{B}(n + 1, 1)$. Now consider the inner product $\langle \mathbf{v}, \mathbf{y} \rangle$. It is clear that $\langle \mathbf{v}, \mathbf{y} \rangle = v_w$ as $y_w = 1$. Since $b_{w,0} = b_{w,1} = b$ and $b_{w,0} = b_{w,1} = v_w$, we hence conclude that $\langle \mathbf{v}, \mathbf{y} \rangle = v_w = b$. □

Putting Pieces Together. Given the above expositione, we now can employ the results of Lemmas 1, 2 and 3 to prove our Theorem 1.

Proof (of Theorem 1). We first prove that $(1) \Rightarrow (2)$. Suppose that $f(\mathbf{x}) = b$ and let $w = \mathsf{wt}(\mathbf{x})$ and $\mathbf{y} = (y_0, \dots, y_n) = \mathsf{U}(w)$. We thus have $y_w = 1$ and $y_i = 0$ for all $i \in [0, n] \setminus \{w\}$. Define

$$\begin{aligned} \mathbf{b} &= \mathsf{enc}(\mathbf{v}) \oplus \mathsf{ext}(\mathbf{y}) = (v_0 \oplus 1, v_0, \dots, v_n \oplus 1, v_n) \oplus (y_0, 0, \dots, y_n, 0) \\ &= (v_0 \oplus y_0 \oplus 1, v_0, \dots, v_n \oplus y_n \oplus 1, v_n). \end{aligned}$$

By defining $b_i = v_i \oplus y_i \oplus 1$ for all $i \in [0, n]$, we have $\mathbf{y} = (b_0 \oplus v_0 \oplus 1, \dots, b_n \oplus v_n \oplus 1)$. Letting $\mathbf{z} = (z_0, \dots, z_n) = \mathsf{Z}(\mathbf{y})$, we see that $\mathbf{z}$ and $\mathbf{y}$ together satisfy linear system (3). By Lemma 2, $\mathsf{wt}(\mathbf{x} \| \mathbf{z}) = n + 1$. Since $f(\mathbf{x}) = b$, by Lemma 1, we have $\langle \mathbf{v}, \mathbf{y} \rangle = b$. Since $\mathbf{y}$ is a unit vector, by Lemma 3, we deduce that $\mathbf{b} \in \mathsf{good}(b)$.

We now prove that $(2) \Rightarrow (1)$. Defining

$$\mathbf{y} = (y_0, \dots, y_n) = (b_0 \oplus v_0 \oplus 1, \dots, b_n \oplus v_n \oplus 1),$$

we have $\mathbf{b} = (b_0, v_0, \dots, b_n, v_n) = \mathsf{enc}(\mathbf{v}) \oplus \mathsf{ext}(\mathbf{y})$. As $\mathbf{b} \in \mathsf{good}(b)$, Lemma 3 implies that $\mathbf{y} \in \mathsf{B}(n + 1, 1)$ and $\langle \mathbf{v}, \mathbf{y} \rangle = b$. Based on system (3), we know that $\mathbf{z} = (z_0, \dots, z_n) = \mathsf{Z}(\mathbf{y})$. Since $\mathbf{y} \in \mathsf{B}(n + 1, 1)$ and $\mathsf{wt}(\mathbf{x} \| \mathbf{z}) = n + 1$, by Lemma 2, it holds that $\mathbf{y} = \mathsf{U}(\mathsf{wt}(\mathbf{x}))$. Finally, by Lemma 1, since $\langle \mathbf{v}, \mathbf{y} \rangle = b$ and $\mathbf{y} = \mathsf{U}(\mathsf{wt}(\mathbf{x}))$, we obtain that $f(\mathbf{x}) = b$. □

4 Protocol

We are now ready to describe our ZKPoK for the correct evaluation $f(\mathbf{x}) = b$, where both $\mathbf{v}(f)$ and $\mathbf{x}$ are secret and committed via the LPN-based commitment scheme from [26] (also recalled in Appendix 2.2). We first formally state the problem in Sect. 4.1, then we present the protocol in Sect. 4.2.

4.1 Problem Statement

Let $n \in \mathbb{Z}^+$ and let $f : \{0,1\}^n \rightarrow \{0,1\}$ be a symmetric Boolean function represented by $\mathbf{v} = (v_0, \ldots, v_n) = \mathbf{v}(f) \in \{0,1\}^{n+1}$. We aim to construct a computational ZKPoK for the correct evaluation of f on input $\mathbf{x}$ while $\mathbf{x}$ and $\mathbf{v}$ are committed as $\mathbf{c}_x$ and $\mathbf{c}_f$, respectively. Specifically, for commitment parameters κ, s, τ and keys $\mathbf{A}_{1,x} \in \{0,1\}^{\kappa \times n}$, $\mathbf{A}_{1,f} \in \{0,1\}^{\kappa \times (n+1)}$, $\mathbf{A}_2 \in \{0,1\}^{\kappa \times s}$, we have:

$$\mathbf{c}_x = \mathbf{A}_{1,x} \cdot \mathbf{x} \oplus \mathbf{A}_2 \cdot \mathbf{s}_x \oplus \mathbf{e}_x \in \{0,1\}^\kappa \wedge \mathsf{wt}(\mathbf{e}_x) \le \tau, \tag{9}$$

$$\mathbf{c}_f = \mathbf{A}_{1,f} \cdot \mathbf{v} \oplus \mathbf{A}_2 \cdot \mathbf{s}_f \oplus \mathbf{e}_f \in \{0,1\}^\kappa \wedge \mathsf{wt}(\mathbf{e}_f) \le \tau, \tag{10}$$

where $\mathbf{s}_x \in \{0,1\}^s$, $\mathbf{s}_f \in \{0,1\}^s$, $\mathbf{e}_x \in \{0,1\}^\kappa$ and $\mathbf{e}_f \in \{0,1\}^\kappa$. For a given bit $b \in \{0,1\}$, we would like to prove knowledge of valid openings $(\mathbf{x}, \mathbf{s}_x, \mathbf{e}_x)$ and $(\mathbf{v}, \mathbf{s}_f, \mathbf{e}_f)$ for $\mathbf{c}_x$ and $\mathbf{c}_f$, respectively, and that $f(\mathbf{x}) = b$ holds. The protocol can be summarized as follows.

- **Common inputs:** $\mathbf{A}_{1,x}$, $\mathbf{A}_{1,f}$, $\mathbf{A}_2$, $\mathbf{c}_x$, $\mathbf{c}_f$ and b.
- **Prover's inputs:** $\mathbf{x}$, $\mathbf{s}_x$, $\mathbf{e}_x$, $\mathbf{v}$, $\mathbf{s}_f$ and $\mathbf{e}_f$.
- **Prover's goal:** Prove to $\mathcal{V}$ the knowledge of $(\mathbf{x}, \mathbf{s}_x, \mathbf{e}_x)$ and $(\mathbf{v}, \mathbf{s}_f, \mathbf{e}_f)$ satisfying (9) and (10), and $f(\mathbf{x}) = b$.

In other words, we aim to obtain a ZKPoK for relation R_{sym} defined as follows.

$$R_{\mathsf{sym}} = \{ ((\mathbf{A}_{1,x}, \mathbf{A}_{1,f}, \mathbf{A}_2, \mathbf{c}_x, \mathbf{c}_f, b), \mathbf{x}, \mathbf{s}_x, \mathbf{e}_x, \mathbf{v}(f), \mathbf{s}_f, \mathbf{e}_f) : f(\mathbf{x}) = b \wedge$$
$$\mathsf{Open}(\mathbf{A}_{1,x}, \mathbf{A}_2, \mathbf{c}_x, \mathbf{x}, \mathbf{s}_x, \mathbf{e}_x) = 1 \wedge \mathsf{Open}(\mathbf{A}_{1,f}, \mathbf{A}_2, \mathbf{c}_f, \mathbf{v}, \mathbf{s}_f, \mathbf{e}_f) = 1 \}.$$

4.2 Construction

Our ZKPoK for relation R_{sym} can be viewed as a combination of 2 sub-protocols operating in Stern's framework [42]. The first one proves the possession of tuple $(\mathbf{x}, \mathbf{s}_x, \mathbf{e}_x, \mathbf{v}(f), \mathbf{s}_f, \mathbf{e}_f)$ satisfying (9) and (10). This is a fairly standard Stern-like sub-protocol for matrix-vector relations, for which we adapt the extension trick from [36] to handle the constraints $\mathsf{wt}(\mathbf{e}_x) \le \tau$ and $\mathsf{wt}(\mathbf{e}_f) \le \tau$. To this end, we append $\mathbf{e}'_x, \mathbf{e}'_f \in \{0,1\}^\tau$ to $\mathbf{e}_x, \mathbf{e}_f$ so that the extended vectors have fixed Hamming weight: $(\mathbf{e}_x \| \mathbf{e}'_x), (\mathbf{e}_f \| \mathbf{e}'_f) \in \mathsf{B}(\kappa + \tau, \tau)$. Then, (9) and (10) are equivalently transformed into

$$\mathbf{A}_{1,x} \cdot \mathbf{x} \oplus \mathbf{A}_2 \cdot \mathbf{s}_x \oplus [\mathbf{I}_\kappa | \mathbf{0}^{\kappa \times \tau}] \cdot (\mathbf{e}_x \| \mathbf{e}'_x) = \mathbf{c}_x \wedge (\mathbf{e}_x \| \mathbf{e}'_x) \in \mathsf{B}(\kappa + \tau, \tau), \tag{11}$$

$$\mathbf{A}_{1,f} \cdot \mathbf{v} \oplus \mathbf{A}_2 \cdot \mathbf{s}_f \oplus [\mathbf{I}_\kappa | \mathbf{0}^{\kappa \times \tau}] \cdot (\mathbf{e}_f \| \mathbf{e}'_f) = \mathbf{c}_f \wedge (\mathbf{e}_f \| \mathbf{e}'_f) \in \mathsf{B}(\kappa + \tau, \tau), \tag{12}$$

which can be proved in zero-knowledge using Stern's original techniques [42].

The main difficulty lies in the second sub-protocol, which addresses the correct computation $f(\mathbf{x}) = b$, for the *same* $\mathbf{v} = \mathbf{v}(f) = (v_0, \ldots, v_n)$ and $\mathbf{x}$ in the first sub-protocol. To this end, we apply the results established in Theorem 1.

By combining the equivalent conditions for $f(\mathbf{x}) = b$ in Theorem 1 and the constraints in (11) and (12), we achieve the following system of linear equations

$$\begin{cases} \mathbf{A}_{1,x} \cdot \mathbf{x} \oplus \mathbf{A}_2 \cdot \mathbf{s}_x \oplus [\mathbf{I}_\kappa | \mathbf{0}^{\kappa \times \tau}] \cdot (\mathbf{e}_x \| \mathbf{e}'_x) = \mathbf{c}_x, \\ \mathbf{A}_{1,f} \cdot \mathbf{v} \oplus \mathbf{A}_2 \cdot \mathbf{s}_f \oplus [\mathbf{I}_\kappa | \mathbf{0}^{\kappa \times \tau}] \cdot (\mathbf{e}_f \| \mathbf{e}'_f) = \mathbf{c}_f, \\ b_0 \oplus v_0 \oplus z_0 = 1, \ \forall i \in [n] : \ b_i \oplus v_i \oplus z_i \oplus z_{i-1} = 1, \end{cases} \quad (13)$$

and the following constraints

$$\mathsf{wt}(\mathbf{e}_x \| \mathbf{e}'_x) = \mathsf{wt}(\mathbf{e}_f \| \mathbf{e}'_f) = \tau, \ \mathsf{wt}(\mathbf{x} \| \mathbf{z}) = n + 1, \ (b_0, v_0, \ldots, b_n, v_n) \in \mathsf{good}(b) \quad (14)$$

where $\mathbf{z} = (z_0, \ldots, z_n)$ and $\mathsf{good}(b)$ is as defined in Definition 1.

Let $K = 2\kappa + n + 1, L = 2(\kappa + \tau) + 4n + 3$ and $S = 2s$. From linear system (13) and constraint system (14), we define witness vectors

$$\mathbf{w} = (\mathbf{e}_x \| \mathbf{e}'_x \| \mathbf{e}_f \| \mathbf{e}'_f \| \mathbf{x} \| \mathbf{z} \| \mathbf{b}) \in \{0,1\}^L, \quad \hat{\mathbf{w}} = (\mathbf{s}_x \| \mathbf{s}_f) \in \{0,1\}^S. \quad (15)$$

Furthermore, we define public matrix $\mathbf{M} \in \{0,1\}^{K \times (L+S)}$ and public vector $\mathbf{c} = (\mathbf{c}_x \| \mathbf{c}_f \| \mathbf{1}^{n+1}) \in \{0,1\}^K$ satisfying $\mathbf{M} \cdot (\mathbf{w} \| \hat{\mathbf{w}}) = \mathbf{c}$ if and only if system (13) is satisfied. Let us explain setting of $K = 2\kappa + n + 1$. Based on (13), there are

- 2κ rows for stacking commitments $\mathbf{c}_x$ and $\mathbf{c}_f$,
- $n + 1$ rows for ensuring $b_0 \oplus v_0 \oplus z_0 = 1$ and $b_i \oplus v_i \oplus z_i \oplus z_{i-1} = 1, \ \forall i \in [n]$.

Permuting Techniques. In order to prove that the component-blocks of $\mathbf{w} = (\mathbf{e}_x \| \mathbf{e}'_x \| \mathbf{e}_f \| \mathbf{e}'_f \| \mathbf{x} \| \mathbf{z} \| \mathbf{b})$ satisfy the constraints in (14), we employ permuting techniques in the framework of Stern's protocol [34,42]. Specifically, we use a permutation Γ_ϕ, where ϕ belongs to some finite set $\mathcal{F}$, to permute the witness $\mathbf{w}$. The permuted vector $\Gamma_\phi(\mathbf{w})$ has the following property: $\mathbf{w}$ satisfies the given constraints if and only if $\Gamma_\phi(\mathbf{w})$ belongs to some set $\mathsf{VALID}(b)$ where b is the public output bit of $f(\mathbf{x})$. Moreover, $\Gamma_\phi(\mathbf{w})$ must reveal no additional information about $\mathbf{w}$. In particular, we require that $\mathcal{F}$ and $\mathsf{VALID}(b)$ satisfy the conditions stated in (16).

$$\begin{cases} \forall \phi \in \mathcal{F} : \mathbf{w} \in \mathsf{VALID}(b) \iff \Gamma_\phi(\mathbf{w}) \in \mathsf{VALID}(b), \\ \text{If } \mathbf{w} \in \mathsf{VALID}(b) \text{ and } \phi \text{ is uniform in } \mathcal{F}, \text{ then } \Gamma_\phi(\mathbf{w}) \text{ is uniform in } \mathsf{VALID}(b). \end{cases} \quad (16)$$

We first define the set $\mathsf{VALID}(b)$. Then, based on this set, we can define $\mathcal{F}$. We let $\mathsf{VALID}(b)$ be the set of all vectors $\mathbf{w}$ of the form (15) satisfying constraint system (14). That is, $\mathsf{VALID}(b)$ is the set

$$\left\{ \mathbf{w} = (\mathbf{e}_x \| \mathbf{e}'_x \| \mathbf{e}_f \| \mathbf{e}'_f \| \mathbf{x} \| \mathbf{z} \| \mathbf{b}) : \begin{array}{l} \mathbf{e}_x, \mathbf{e}_f \in \{0,1\}^\kappa, (\mathbf{e}_x \| \mathbf{e}'_x), (\mathbf{e}_f \| \mathbf{e}'_f) \in \mathsf{B}(\kappa + \tau, \tau), \\ \mathbf{x} \in \{0,1\}^n, (\mathbf{x} \| \mathbf{z}) \in \mathsf{B}(2n+1, n+1), \mathbf{b} \in \mathsf{good}(b) \end{array} \right\}.$$

At this point, we observe that R_{sym} can be reduced to the relation

$$R'_{\mathsf{sym}} = \{((\mathbf{M}, \mathbf{c}), \mathbf{w}, \hat{\mathbf{w}}) : \mathbf{M} \cdot (\mathbf{w} \| \hat{\mathbf{w}}) = \mathbf{c} \ \wedge \ \mathbf{w} \in \mathsf{VALID}(b)\}.$$

To prove that $\mathbf{w} \in \mathsf{VALID}(b)$, we pay a special attention on developing a permuting technique for handling the constraint $\mathbf{b} \in \mathsf{good}(b)$, as the constraints of $(\mathbf{e}_x \| \mathbf{e}'_x)$, $(\mathbf{e}_f \| \mathbf{e}'_f)$, $(\mathbf{x} \| \mathbf{z})$ can be proved in a routine manner.

For any $t \in \mathbb{Z}^+$, we let $\mathcal{S}_t$ denote the set of all permutations of t elements. To prove that $\mathbf{b} \in \mathsf{good}(b)$, we use a permutation $\Pi_{\varphi, p_0, \ldots, p_n} \in \mathcal{S}_{2n+2}$ to permute

$$\mathbf{b} = (b_{0,0}, b_{0,1}, \ldots, b_{n,0}, b_{n,1}) = (b_0, v_0, \ldots, b_n, v_n),$$

where, for each $i \in [0, n]$, a bit p_i is used to internally permute the block $(b_{i,0}, b_{i,1})$ to $(b_{i,p_i}, b_{i,\overline{p_i}})$, and a permutation $\pi \in \mathcal{S}_{n+1}$ is used to re-arrange the $n+1$ blocks of length 2. Then, we observe that, for every $b \in \{0, 1\}$,

$$\begin{cases} \forall \varphi \in \mathcal{S}_{n+1}, p_0, \ldots, p_n \in \{0,1\} : \ \mathbf{b} \in \mathsf{good}(b) \iff \Pi_{\varphi, p_0, \ldots, p_n}(\mathbf{b}) \in \mathsf{good}(b), \\ \text{If } \mathbf{b} \in \mathsf{good}(b) \text{ and } (\varphi, p_0, \ldots, p_n) \text{ is uniform in } \mathcal{S}_{n+1} \times \{0,1\}^{n+1}, \\ \qquad\qquad \text{then } \Pi_{\varphi, p_0, \ldots, p_n}(\mathbf{b}) \text{ is uniform in } \mathsf{good}(b). \end{cases} \quad (17)$$

Now, we are ready to define the finite set $\mathcal{F}$ associated with $\mathsf{VALID}(b)$, for any $b \in \{0, 1\}$. We let $\mathcal{F}$ be the set of all $\phi = (\pi_1, \pi_2, \pi_3, \varphi, p_0, \ldots, p_n)$, where $\pi_1, \pi_2 \in \mathcal{S}_{\kappa+\tau}$, $\pi_3 \in \mathcal{S}_{2n+1}$, $\varphi \in \mathcal{S}_{n+1}$ and $p_0, \ldots, p_n \in \{0, 1\}$. For any $\phi \in \mathcal{F}$, the action of Γ_ϕ on

$$\mathbf{u} = (\mathbf{u}_1 \| \mathbf{u}_2 \| \mathbf{u}_3 \| \mathbf{u}_4) \in \{0, 1\}^L,$$

where $\mathbf{u}_1, \mathbf{u}_2 \in \{0, 1\}^{\kappa+\tau}, \mathbf{u}_3 \in \{0, 1\}^{2n+1}, \mathbf{u}_4 \in \{0, 1\}^{2n+2}$, is defined to be

$$\Gamma_\phi(\mathbf{u}) = (\pi_1(\mathbf{u}_1) \| \pi_2(\mathbf{u}_2) \| \pi_3(\mathbf{u}_3) \| \Pi_{\varphi, p_0, \ldots, p_n}(\mathbf{u}_4)).$$

We then observe that $\mathsf{VALID}(b)$ and $\mathcal{F}$ satisfy conditions in (16).

---

1. **Commitment.** $\mathcal{P}$ samples $\mathbf{r} \xleftarrow{\$} \{0,1\}^L$, $\hat{\mathbf{r}} \xleftarrow{\$} \{0,1\}^S$, $\phi \xleftarrow{\$} \mathcal{F}$ and randomness $\zeta_1, \zeta_2, \zeta_3$ for Com. Then $\mathcal{P}$ sends $\mathrm{CMT} = (C_1, C_2, C_3)$ to $\mathcal{V}$, where

$$C_1 = \mathsf{Com}(\phi, \ \mathbf{M} \cdot (\mathbf{r} \| \hat{\mathbf{r}}); \ \zeta_1), \quad C_2 = \mathsf{Com}(\Gamma_\phi(\mathbf{r}); \ \zeta_2), \quad C_3 = \mathsf{Com}(\Gamma_\phi(\mathbf{w} \oplus \mathbf{r}); \ \zeta_3).$$

2. **Challenge.** $\mathcal{V}$ sends a challenge $Ch \xleftarrow{\$} \{1, 2, 3\}$ to $\mathcal{P}$.
3. **Response.** Depending on Ch, $\mathcal{P}$ sends RSP computed as follows:
   - $Ch = 1$: Let $\mathbf{t}_w = \Gamma_\phi(\mathbf{w})$, $\mathbf{t}_r = \Gamma_\phi(\mathbf{r})$, and RSP $= (\mathbf{t}_w, \mathbf{t}_r, \zeta_2, \zeta_3)$.
   - $Ch = 2$: Let $\phi_2 = \phi$, $\mathbf{w}_2 = \mathbf{w} \oplus \mathbf{r}$, $\hat{\mathbf{w}}_2 = \hat{\mathbf{w}} \oplus \hat{\mathbf{r}}$ and RSP $= (\phi_2, \mathbf{w}_2, \hat{\mathbf{w}}_2, \zeta_1, \zeta_3)$.
   - $Ch = 3$: Let $\phi_3 = \phi$, $\mathbf{w}_3 = \mathbf{r}$, $\hat{\mathbf{w}}_3 = \hat{\mathbf{r}}$ and RSP $= (\phi_3, \mathbf{w}_3, \hat{\mathbf{w}}_3, \zeta_1, \zeta_2)$.

Verification. Receiving RSP, $\mathcal{V}$ proceeds as follows:

   - $Ch = 1$: Check that $\mathbf{t}_w \in \mathsf{VALID}(b)$, $C_2 = \mathsf{Com}(\mathbf{t}_r; \ \zeta_2)$, $C_3 = \mathsf{Com}(\mathbf{t}_w \oplus \mathbf{t}_r; \ \zeta_3)$.
   - $Ch = 2$: Check that $C_1 = \mathsf{Com}(\phi_2, \mathbf{M} \cdot (\mathbf{w}_2 \| \hat{\mathbf{w}}_2) \oplus \mathbf{c}; \ \zeta_1)$, $C_3 = \mathsf{Com}(\Gamma_{\phi_2}(\mathbf{w}_2); \ \zeta_3)$.
   - $Ch = 3$: Check that $C_1 = \mathsf{Com}(\phi_3, \mathbf{M} \cdot (\mathbf{w}_3 \| \hat{\mathbf{w}}_3); \ \zeta_1)$, $C_2 = \mathsf{Com}(\Gamma_{\phi_3}(\mathbf{w}_3); \ \zeta_2)$.

In each case, the $\mathcal{V}$ outputs 1 if and only if all the conditions hold.

Fig. 1. A ZKPoK for the relation R'_{sym}.

The Interactive Protocol. Given the above preparations, the prover and the verifier now can perform a typical Stern-like ZKPoK for relation R'_{sym}. The protocol, presented in Fig. 1, employs an auxiliary commitment Com that is statistically binding and computationally hiding. We have the following theorem, whose proof employs standard simulation and extraction techniques for Stern-like protocols [26, 29, 34, 36]. If Com [26] is based on LPN, then so is the ZK property of the protocol. When the protocol is employed as a building block in a more advanced post-quantum cryptosystem, we additionally require the security of the commitment scheme underlying $\mathbf{c}_f$ and $\mathbf{c}_x$, which in turn relies on LPN.

Theorem 2. *Assume that* Com *is a computationally hiding and statistically binding string commitment scheme. Then, the protocol in Fig. 1 is a computational ZKPoK for relation R'_{sym} with perfect completeness and soundness error $2/3$. Consequently, there exists a computational ZKPoK for relation R_{sym} with perfect completeness and soundness error $2/3$.*

Proof. Assume that Com is computationally hiding and statistically binding. We first show that the protocol in Fig. 1 is a computational ZKPoK for relation R'_{sym}. Later on, based on relation R'_{sym}, we will show the implication of a computational ZKPoK for R_{sym}.

Computational ZKPoK for R'_{sym}. We will prove the following aspects.

1. *Perfect completeness.* It is clear that, if $\mathcal{P}$ is honest, then $\mathcal{P}$ is able to convince $\mathcal{V}$ by responding accordingly to the challenge sent from $\mathcal{V}$.
2. *Computational zero-knowledge.* Let $\hat{\mathcal{V}}$ be an arbitrary PPT verifier. Define Sim to be a PPT algorithm that, with oracle access to $\hat{\mathcal{V}}$ and with probability negligibly close to $2/3$, outputs a simulated transcript computationally close to the real transcript between $\hat{\mathcal{P}}$ and $\hat{\mathcal{V}}$. Sim starts by guessing $\overline{Ch} \in \{1, 2, 3\}$ indicating the challenge which $\hat{\mathcal{V}}$ will not choose. Based on $\overline{Ch}$, Sim simulates the transcript as follows:
   (a) *Case $\overline{Ch} = 1$.* Sim finds $\mathbf{w}' \in \{0,1\}^L$ and $\hat{\mathbf{w}}' \in \{0,1\}^S$ such that $\mathbf{M} \cdot (\mathbf{w}' \| \hat{\mathbf{w}}') = \mathbf{c}$. Then, Sim samples $\mathbf{r} \xleftarrow{\$} \{0,1\}^L, \hat{\mathbf{r}} \xleftarrow{\$} \{0,1\}^S, \phi \xleftarrow{\$} \mathcal{F}$ and randomness $\zeta_1, \zeta_2, \zeta_3$ for the commitment scheme. Sim sends commitment $\text{CMT} = (C'_1, C'_2, C'_3)$ to $\hat{\mathcal{V}}$, where
   $$C'_1 = \text{Com}(\phi, \mathbf{M} \cdot (\mathbf{r} \| \hat{\mathbf{r}}); \zeta_1), \quad C'_2 = \text{Com}(\Gamma_\phi(\mathbf{r}); \zeta_2), \quad C'_3 = \text{Com}(\Gamma_\phi(\mathbf{w}' \oplus \mathbf{r}); \zeta_3).$$

   On receiving $Ch \in \{1, 2, 3\}$ from $\hat{\mathcal{V}}$, Sim responds as follows:
   – If $Ch = 1$, Sim returns $\perp$ and aborts.
   – If $Ch = 2$, Sim sends $\text{RSP} = (\phi, \mathbf{w}' \oplus \mathbf{r}, \hat{\mathbf{w}}' \oplus \hat{\mathbf{r}}, \zeta_1, \zeta_3)$.
   – If $Ch = 3$, Sim sends $\text{RSP} = (\phi, \mathbf{r}, \hat{\mathbf{r}}, \zeta_1, \zeta_2)$.
   (b) *Case $\overline{Ch} = 2$.* Sim samples $\mathbf{w}' \xleftarrow{\$} \text{VALID}(b), \mathbf{r} \xleftarrow{\$} \{0,1\}^L, \hat{\mathbf{r}} \xleftarrow{\$} \{0,1\}^S, \phi \xleftarrow{\$} \mathcal{F}$ and randomness $\zeta_1, \zeta_2, \zeta_3$ for the commitment scheme. Sim sends commitment $\text{CMT} = (C'_1, C'_2, C'_3)$ to $\hat{\mathcal{V}}$, where
   $$C'_1 = \text{Com}(\phi, \mathbf{M} \cdot (\mathbf{r} \| \hat{\mathbf{r}}); \zeta_1), \quad C'_2 = \text{Com}(\Gamma_\phi(\mathbf{r}); \zeta_2), \quad C'_3 = \text{Com}(\Gamma_\phi(\mathbf{w}' \oplus \mathbf{r}); \zeta_3).$$

On receiving $Ch \in \{1, 2, 3\}$ from $\hat{\mathcal{V}}$, Sim responds as follows:
- If $Ch = 1$, Sim sends RSP $= (\Gamma_\phi(\mathbf{w}'), \Gamma_\phi(\mathbf{r}), \zeta_2, \zeta_3)$,
- If $Ch = 2$, Sim returns $\perp$ and aborts.
- If $Ch = 3$, Sim sends RSP $= (\phi, \mathbf{r}, \hat{\mathbf{r}}, \zeta_1, \zeta_2)$.

(c) *Case* $\overline{Ch} = 3$. In this case, the simulator Sim samples the following objects: $\mathbf{w}' \xleftarrow{\$} \mathsf{VALID}(b), \hat{\mathbf{w}}' \xleftarrow{\$} \{0, 1\}^S, \mathbf{r} \xleftarrow{\$} \{0, 1\}^L, \hat{\mathbf{r}} \xleftarrow{\$} \{0, 1\}^S, \phi \xleftarrow{\$} \mathcal{F}$, as well as randomness $\zeta_1, \zeta_2, \zeta_3$ for the commitment scheme. Sim sends commitment CMT $= (C_1', C_2', C_3')$ to $\hat{\mathcal{V}}$, where

$$C_1' = \mathsf{Com}(\phi, \mathbf{M} \cdot ((\mathbf{w}' \oplus \mathbf{r}) \| (\hat{\mathbf{w}}' \oplus \hat{\mathbf{r}})) \oplus \mathbf{c}; \zeta_1),$$
$$C_2' = \mathsf{Com}(\Gamma_\phi(\mathbf{r}); \zeta_2), \ C_3' = \mathsf{Com}(\Gamma_\phi(\mathbf{w}' \oplus \mathbf{r}); \zeta_3).$$

On receiving $Ch \in \{1, 2, 3\}$ from $\hat{\mathcal{V}}$, Sim responds as follows:
- If $Ch = 1$, Sim sends RSP $= (\Gamma_\phi(\mathbf{w}'), \Gamma_\phi(\mathbf{r}), \zeta_2, \zeta_3)$,
- If $Ch = 2$, Sim sends RSP $= (\phi, \mathbf{w}' \oplus \mathbf{r}, \hat{\mathbf{w}}' \oplus \hat{\mathbf{r}}, \zeta_1, \zeta_3)$,
- If $Ch = 3$, Sim returns $\perp$ and aborts.

We see that, for every $\overline{Ch} \in \{1, 2, 3\}$ and every $Ch \in \{1, 2, 3\}$ satisfying $\overline{Ch} \neq Ch$, the transcript (CMT, Ch, RSP) is computationally close to the real transcript between $\mathcal{P}$ and $\hat{\mathcal{V}}$. Therefore, with probability negligibly close to $2/3$, Sim can produce a simulated transcript computationally close to the real one between $\mathcal{P}$ and $\hat{\mathcal{V}}$.

3. *Proof of knowledge.* Let RSP$_1 = (\mathbf{t}_w, \mathbf{t}_r, \zeta_1, \zeta_2)$, RSP$_2 = (\phi_2, \mathbf{w}_2, \hat{\mathbf{w}}_2, \zeta_1, \zeta_3)$, RSP$_2 = (\phi_3, \mathbf{w}_3, \hat{\mathbf{w}}_3, \zeta_1, \zeta_2)$ be all accepted responses sent by $\mathcal{P}$ corresponding to all challenges $Ch \in \{1, 2, 3\}$ with the same first message CMT. Then, we have $\mathbf{t}_w \in \mathsf{VALID}(b)$ and

$$\begin{cases} C_1 = \mathsf{Com}(\phi_2, \mathbf{M} \cdot (\mathbf{w}_2 \| \hat{\mathbf{w}}_2) \oplus \mathbf{c}; \ \zeta_1) = \mathsf{Com}(\phi_3, \mathbf{M} \cdot (\mathbf{w}_3 \| \hat{\mathbf{w}}_3); \ \zeta_1), \\ C_2 = \mathsf{Com}(\mathbf{t}_r; \ \zeta_2) = \mathsf{Com}(\Gamma_{\phi_3}(\mathbf{w}_3); \ \zeta_2), \\ C_3 = \mathsf{Com}(\mathbf{t}_w \oplus \mathbf{t}_r; \ \zeta_3) = \mathsf{Com}(\Gamma_{\phi_2}(\mathbf{w}_2); \ \zeta_3). \end{cases}$$

Since Com is statistically binding, with overwhelming probability, we have:

$$\phi_2 = \phi_3, \ \mathbf{M} \cdot (\mathbf{w}_2 \| \hat{\mathbf{w}}_2) \oplus \mathbf{c} = \mathbf{M} \cdot (\mathbf{w}_3 \| \hat{\mathbf{w}}_3), \ \mathbf{t}_r = \Gamma_{\phi_3}(\mathbf{w}_3), \ \mathbf{t}_w \oplus \mathbf{t}_r = \Gamma_{\phi_2}(\mathbf{w}_2).$$

Let $\phi = \phi_2 = \phi_3$. We see the following equivalence:

$$\mathbf{t}_w \oplus \mathbf{t}_r = \Gamma_\phi(\mathbf{w}_2) \iff \mathbf{t}_w \oplus \Gamma_\phi(\mathbf{w}_3) = \Gamma_\phi(\mathbf{w}_2) \iff \mathbf{t}_w = \Gamma_\phi(\mathbf{w}_2 \oplus \mathbf{w}_3).$$

Since $\mathbf{t}_w \in \mathsf{VALID}(b)$, by condition (16), we deduce that $\mathbf{w}_2 \oplus \mathbf{w}_3 \in \mathsf{VALID}(b)$. Thus, by the equivalence

$$\mathbf{M} \cdot (\mathbf{w}_2 \| \hat{\mathbf{w}}_2) \oplus \mathbf{c} = \mathbf{M} \cdot (\mathbf{w}_3 \| \hat{\mathbf{w}}_3) \iff \mathbf{M} \cdot ((\mathbf{w}_2 \oplus \mathbf{w}_3) \| (\hat{\mathbf{w}}_2 \oplus \hat{\mathbf{w}}_3)) = \mathbf{c},$$

we conclude that $\mathbf{w} = \mathbf{w}_2 \oplus \mathbf{w}_3 \in \mathsf{VALID}(b)$ and $\hat{\mathbf{w}}$ form a valid witness pair.

Computational ZKPoK for R_{sym}. We will show that the given ZKPoK for R_{sym} immediately yields a ZKPoK for R'_{sym}. To begin with, we recall that $K = 2\kappa + n + 1, L = 2(\kappa + \tau) + 4n + 3$ and $S = 2s$.

1. *Perfect completeness.* If $\mathcal{P}$ is honest, we know that the reduction from R_{sym} to R'_{sym} is correct. Perfect completeness of the protocol for R_{sym} follows.
2. *Computational zero knowledge.* Since the construction is the same for both R'_{sym} and R_{sym}, the protocol for R_{sym} is computationally ZK.
3. *Proof of knowledge.* By the soundness property of the computational ZKPoK for R'_{sym}, we can extract a vector $\mathbf{w} \in \mathsf{VALID}(b)$ and $\hat{\mathbf{w}} \in \{0,1\}^S$ such that $\mathbf{M} \cdot (\mathbf{w} \| \hat{\mathbf{w}}) = \mathbf{c}$. Parse

$$\mathbf{w} = (\mathbf{e}_x \| \mathbf{e}'_x \| \mathbf{e}_f \| \mathbf{e}'_f \| \mathbf{x} \| \mathbf{z} \| \mathbf{b}) \in \{0,1\}^L, \quad \hat{\mathbf{w}} = (\mathbf{s}_x \| \mathbf{s}_f) \in \{0,1\}^S,$$

where we have $\mathbf{e}_x, \mathbf{e}_f \in \{0,1\}^{\kappa}$, $\mathbf{e}'_x, \mathbf{e}'_f \in \{0,1\}^{\tau}$ such that $(\mathbf{e}_x \| \mathbf{e}'_x), (\mathbf{e}_f \| \mathbf{e}'_f) \in \mathsf{B}(\kappa + \tau, \tau)$; $\mathbf{x} \in \{0,1\}^n$, $\mathbf{z} \in \{0,1\}^{n+1}$ such that $(\mathbf{x} \| \mathbf{z}) \in \mathsf{B}(2n+1, n+1)$ and $\mathbf{b} = (b_0, v_0, \ldots, b_n, v_n) \in \mathsf{good}(b)$.

From the linear equation $\mathbf{M} \cdot (\mathbf{w} \| \hat{\mathbf{w}}) = \mathbf{c}$ and $\mathbf{w} \in \mathsf{VALID}(b)$, we see that the linear system (13) and constraint system (14) are satisfied. We trivially see that $(\mathbf{x}, \mathbf{s}_x, \mathbf{e}_x)$ is a valid opening of $\mathbf{c}_x$. By setting $\mathbf{v} = (v_0, \ldots, v_n)$, we hence see that $(\mathbf{v}, \mathbf{s}_f, \mathbf{e}_f)$ is a valid opening of $\mathbf{c}_f$. Moreover, we also see that

$$b_0 \oplus v_0 \oplus z_0 = 1, \quad b_i \oplus v_i \oplus z_i \oplus z_{i-1} = 1, \quad \forall i \in [n].$$

Since $\mathbf{b} \in \mathsf{good}(b)$ and $\mathsf{wt}(\mathbf{x} \| \mathbf{z}) = n+1$, Theorem 1 implies that $b = f(\mathbf{x})$.

Thus, there exists a computational ZKPoK for R_{sym} with perfect completeness and soundness error $2/3$. $\qquad\square$

Efficiency. We evaluate the complexity of the protocol according to parameter n, i.e., the input length of function f. In terms of computation costs, both $\mathcal{P}$ and $\mathcal{V}$ only have to performs $\mathcal{O}(n)$ binary operations. The average communication cost of the protocol is $5n$ bits (which can be optimized to $\frac{7}{3}n$ bits in practice). To achieve soundness error $2^{-\lambda}$, for some security parameter λ, we can repeat the protocol $t = \lceil \frac{\lambda}{\log_2 3 - 1} \rceil$ times, yielding overall proof size of $5tn$ bits. Concretely, for 80 bits of security, the total communication cost of our protocol is around 100 KB for $n = 128$ and around 200 KB for $n = 1000$.

Acknowledgements. We thank the anonymous reviewers of PQCrypto 2021 for helpful comments. The research is supported by Singapore Ministry of Education under Research Grant MOE2019-T2-2-083 and by A*STAR, Singapore under research grant SERC A19E3b0099. Duong Hieu Phan was supported in part by the French ANR ALAMBIC (ANR16-CE39-0006).

References

1. Alamélou, Q., Blazy, O., Cauchie, S., Gaborit, P.: A code-based group signature scheme. Des. Codes Cryptogr. **82**(1–2), 469–493 (2017)
2. Ames, S., Hazay, C., Ishai, Y., Venkitasubramaniam, M.: Ligero: lightweight sublinear arguments without a trusted setup. In: ACM CCS 2017, pp. 2087–2104. ACM (2017)

3. Attema, T., Cramer, R.: Compressed ς-protocol theory and practical application to plug & play secure algorithmics. In: Micciancio, D., Ristenpart, T. (eds.) CRYPTO 2020. LNCS, vol. 12172, pp. 513–543. Springer, Cham (2020). https://doi.org/10.1007/978-3-030-56877-1_18

4. Baum, C., Bootle, J., Cerulli, A., del Pino, R., Groth, J., Lyubashevsky, V.: Sublinear lattice-based zero-knowledge arguments for arithmetic circuits. In: Shacham, H., Boldyreva, A. (eds.) CRYPTO 2018. LNCS, vol. 10992, pp. 669–699. Springer, Cham (2018). https://doi.org/10.1007/978-3-319-96881-0_23

5. Bellare, M., Fuchsbauer, G.: Policy-based signatures. In: Krawczyk, H. (ed.) PKC 2014. LNCS, vol. 8383, pp. 520–537. Springer, Heidelberg (2014). https://doi.org/10.1007/978-3-642-54631-0_30

6. Bootle, J., Cerulli, A., Chaidos, P., Groth, J., Petit, C.: Efficient zero-knowledge arguments for arithmetic circuits in the discrete log setting. In: Fischlin, M., Coron, J.-S. (eds.) EUROCRYPT 2016. LNCS, vol. 9666, pp. 327–357. Springer, Heidelberg (2016). https://doi.org/10.1007/978-3-662-49896-5_12

7. Branco, P., Mateus, P.: A code-based linkable ring signature scheme. In: Baek, J., Susilo, W., Kim, J. (eds.) ProvSec 2018. LNCS, vol. 11192, pp. 203–219. Springer, Cham (2018). https://doi.org/10.1007/978-3-030-01446-9_12

8. Brassard, G., Chaum, D., Crépeau, C.: Minimum disclosure proofs of knowledge. J. Comput. Syst. Sci. **37**(2), 156–189 (1988)

9. Bünz, B., Bootle, J., Boneh, D., Poelstra, A., Wuille, P., Maxwell, G.: Bulletproofs: short proofs for confidential transactions and more. In: IEEE SP 2018, pp. 315–334. IEEE (2018)

10. Camenisch, J., Dubovitskaya, M., Enderlein, R.R., Neven, G.: Oblivious transfer with hidden access control from attribute-based encryption. In: Visconti, I., De Prisco, R. (eds.) SCN 2012. LNCS, vol. 7485, pp. 559–579. Springer, Heidelberg (2012). https://doi.org/10.1007/978-3-642-32928-9_31

11. Cramer, R., Damgård, I.: Zero-knowledge proofs for finite field arithmetic, or: can zero-knowledge be for free? In: Krawczyk, H. (ed.) CRYPTO 1998. LNCS, vol. 1462, pp. 424–441. Springer, Heidelberg (1998). https://doi.org/10.1007/BFb0055745

12. Dallot, L., Vergnaud, D.: Provably secure code-based threshold ring signatures. In: Parker, M.G. (ed.) IMACC 2009. LNCS, vol. 5921, pp. 222–235. Springer, Heidelberg (2009). https://doi.org/10.1007/978-3-642-10868-6_13

13. David, B., Dowsley, R., Nascimento, A.C.A.: Universally composable oblivious transfer based on a variant of LPN. In: Gritzalis, D., Kiayias, A., Askoxylakis, I. (eds.) CANS 2014. LNCS, vol. 8813, pp. 143–158. Springer, Cham (2014). https://doi.org/10.1007/978-3-319-12280-9_10

14. Deuber, D., Maffei, M., Malavolta, G., Rabkin, M., Schröder, D., Simkin, M.: Functional credentials. Proc. Priv. Enhancing Technol. **2018**(2), 64–84 (2018)

15. Döttling, N., Garg, S., Hajiabadi, M., Masny, D., Wichs, D.: Two-round oblivious transfer from CDH or LPN. In: Canteaut, A., Ishai, Y. (eds.) EUROCRYPT 2020. LNCS, vol. 12106, pp. 768–797. Springer, Cham (2020). https://doi.org/10.1007/978-3-030-45724-2_26

16. El Kaafarani, A.: Traceability, linkability and policy hiding in attribute-based signature schemes. Ph.D. thesis (2015)

17. Ezerman, M.F., Lee, H.T., Ling, S., Nguyen, K., Wang, H.: Provably secure group signature schemes from code-based assumptions. IEEE Trans. Inf. Theory **66**(9), 5754–5773 (2020)

18. Gentry, C., Groth, J., Ishai, Y., Peikert, C., Sahai, A., Smith, A.: Using fully homomorphic hybrid encryption to minimize non-interative zero-knowledge proofs. J. Cryptol. **28**(4), 820–843 (2015)

19. Giacomelli, I., Madsen, J., Orlandi, C.: Zkboo: faster zero-knowledge for Boolean circuits. In: USENIX 2016, pp. 1069–1083. USENIX (2016)

20. Goldreich, O., Micali, S., Wigderson, A.: How to prove all NP statements in zero-knowledge and a methodology of cryptographic protocol design (extended abstract). In: Odlyzko, A.M. (ed.) CRYPTO 1986. LNCS, vol. 263, pp. 171–185. Springer, Heidelberg (1987). https://doi.org/10.1007/3-540-47721-7_11

21. Goldwasser, S., Micali, S., Rackoff, C.: The knowledge complexity of interactive proof-systems (extended abstract). In: STOC 1985, pp. 291–304. ACM (1985)

22. Goyal, V., Pandey, O., Sahai, A., Waters, B.: Attribute-based encryption for fine-grained access control of encrypted data. In: ACM CCS 2006, pp. 89–98. ACM (2006)

23. Groth, J.: Evaluating security of voting schemes in the universal composability framework. In: Jakobsson, M., Yung, M., Zhou, J. (eds.) ACNS 2004. LNCS, vol. 3089, pp. 46–60. Springer, Heidelberg (2004). https://doi.org/10.1007/978-3-540-24852-1_4

24. Groth, J.: On the size of pairing-based non-interactive arguments. In: Fischlin, M., Coron, J.-S. (eds.) EUROCRYPT 2016. LNCS, vol. 9666, pp. 305–326. Springer, Heidelberg (2016). https://doi.org/10.1007/978-3-662-49896-5_11

25. Ishai, Y., Kushilevitz, E., Ostrovsky, R., Sahai, A.: Zero-knowledge from secure multiparty computation. In: STOC 2007, pp. 21–30. ACM (2007)

26. Jain, A., Krenn, S., Pietrzak, K., Tentes, A.: Commitments and efficient zero-knowledge proofs from learning parity with noise. In: Wang, X., Sako, K. (eds.) ASIACRYPT 2012. LNCS, vol. 7658, pp. 663–680. Springer, Heidelberg (2012). https://doi.org/10.1007/978-3-642-34961-4_40

27. Jawurek, M., Kerschbaum, F., Orlandi, C.: Zero-knowledge using garbled circuits: how to prove non-algebraic statements efficiently. In: ACM CCS 2013, pp. 955–966. ACM (2013)

28. Katz, J., Sahai, A., Waters, B.: Predicate encryption supporting disjunctions, polynomial equations, and inner products. In: Smart, N. (ed.) EUROCRYPT 2008. LNCS, vol. 4965, pp. 146–162. Springer, Heidelberg (2008). https://doi.org/10.1007/978-3-540-78967-3_9

29. Kawachi, A., Tanaka, K., Xagawa, K.: Concurrently secure identification schemes based on the worst-case hardness of lattice problems. In: Pieprzyk, J. (ed.) ASIACRYPT 2008. LNCS, vol. 5350, pp. 372–389. Springer, Heidelberg (2008). https://doi.org/10.1007/978-3-540-89255-7_23

30. Kilian, J.: A note on efficient zero-knowledge proofs and arguments (extended abstract). In: STOC 1992, pp. 723–732. ACM (1992)

31. Kiss, Á., Schneider, T.: Valiant's universal circuit is practical. In: Fischlin, M., Coron, J.-S. (eds.) EUROCRYPT 2016. LNCS, vol. 9665, pp. 699–728. Springer, Heidelberg (2016). https://doi.org/10.1007/978-3-662-49890-3_27

32. Kolesnikov, V., Schneider, T.: A practical universal circuit construction and secure evaluation of private functions. In: Tsudik, G. (ed.) FC 2008. LNCS, vol. 5143, pp. 83–97. Springer, Heidelberg (2008). https://doi.org/10.1007/978-3-540-85230-8_7

33. Kroll, J., Huey, J., Barocas, S., Felten, E., Reidenberg, J., Robinson, D., Yu, H.: Accountable algorithms. U. Pennsylvania Law Rev. **165**(3), 633–705 (2017)

34. Libert, B., Ling, S., Mouhartem, F., Nguyen, K., Wang, H.: Signature schemes with efficient protocols and dynamic group signatures from lattice assumptions. In: Cheon, J.H., Takagi, T. (eds.) ASIACRYPT 2016. LNCS, vol. 10032, pp. 373–403. Springer, Heidelberg (2016). https://doi.org/10.1007/978-3-662-53890-6_13

35. Libert, B., Ling, S., Mouhartem, F., Nguyen, K., Wang, H.: Adaptive oblivious transfer with access control from lattice assumptions. In: Takagi, T., Peyrin, T. (eds.) ASIACRYPT 2017. LNCS, vol. 10624, pp. 533–563. Springer, Cham (2017). https://doi.org/10.1007/978-3-319-70694-8_19

36. Ling, S., Nguyen, K., Stehlé, D., Wang, H.: Improved zero-knowledge proofs of knowledge for the ISIS problem, and applications. In: Kurosawa, K., Hanaoka, G. (eds.) PKC 2013. LNCS, vol. 7778, pp. 107–124. Springer, Heidelberg (2013). https://doi.org/10.1007/978-3-642-36362-7_8

37. Aguilar Melchor, C., Cayrel, P.-L., Gaborit, P.: A new efficient threshold ring signature scheme based on coding theory. In: Buchmann, J., Ding, J. (eds.) PQCrypto 2008. LNCS, vol. 5299, pp. 1–16. Springer, Heidelberg (2008). https://doi.org/10.1007/978-3-540-88403-3_1

38. Melchor, C.A., Cayrel, P.-L., Gaborit, P., Laguillaumie, F.: A new efficient threshold ring signature scheme based on coding theory. IEEE Trans. Inf. Theory **57**(7), 4833–4842 (2011)

39. Morozov, K., Takagi, T.: Zero-knowledge protocols for the McEliece encryption. In: Susilo, W., Mu, Y., Seberry, J. (eds.) ACISP 2012. LNCS, vol. 7372, pp. 180–193. Springer, Heidelberg (2012). https://doi.org/10.1007/978-3-642-31448-3_14

40. Nguyen, K., Safavi-Naini, R., Susilo, W., Wang, H., Xu, Y., Zeng, N.: Group encryption: full dynamicity, message filtering and code-based instantiation. In: Garay, J.A. (ed.) PKC 2021. LNCS, vol. 12711, pp. 678–708. Springer, Cham (2021). https://doi.org/10.1007/978-3-030-75248-4_24

41. Nguyen, K., Tang, H., Wang, H., Zeng, N.: New code-based privacy-preserving cryptographic constructions. In: Galbraith, S.D., Moriai, S. (eds.) ASIACRYPT 2019. LNCS, vol. 11922, pp. 25–55. Springer, Cham (2019). https://doi.org/10.1007/978-3-030-34621-8_2

42. Stern, J.: A new paradigm for public key identification. IEEE Trans. Inf. Theory **42**(6), 1757–1768 (1996)

43. Valiant, L.G.: Universal circuits (preliminary report). In: STOC 1976, pp. 196–203. ACM (1976)

44. Xie, T., Zhang, J., Zhang, Y., Papamanthou, C., Song, D.: Libra: succinct zero-knowledge proofs with optimal prover computation. In: Boldyreva, A., Micciancio, D. (eds.) CRYPTO 2019. LNCS, vol. 11694, pp. 733–764. Springer, Cham (2019). https://doi.org/10.1007/978-3-030-26954-8_24

Short Identity-Based Signatures
with Tight Security from Lattices

Jiaxin Pan[1(✉)] and Benedikt Wagner[2]

[1] Department of Mathematical Sciences, NTNU - Norwegian University of Science
and Technology, Trondheim, Norway
jiaxin.pan@ntnu.no
[2] KIT - Karlsruhe Institute of Technology, Karlsruhe, Germany
udpto@student.kit.edu

Abstract. We construct a short and adaptively secure identity-based signature scheme *tightly* based on the well-known Short Integer Solution (SIS) assumption. Although identity-based signature schemes can be tightly constructed from either standard signature schemes against adaptive corruptions in the multi-user setting or a two-level hierarchical identity-based encryption scheme, neither of them is known with short signature size and tight security based on the SIS assumption. Here "short" means the signature size is independent of the message length, which is in contrast to the tree-based (tight) signatures.

Our approach consists of two steps: Firstly, we give two generic transformations (one with random oracles and the other without) from non-adaptively secure identity-based signature schemes to adaptively secure ones tightly. Our idea extends the similar transformation for digital signature schemes. Secondly, we construct a non-adaptively secure identity-based signature scheme based on the SIS assumption in the random oracle model.

Keywords: Identity-based signatures · Tight security · Short integer solution assumption · Lattices

1 Introduction

TIGHT SECURITY. In public-key cryptography, we often prove the security of a scheme by reductions. Namely, we prove that, if there is an adversary $\mathcal{A}$ that can break the security of a scheme, then we can construct a reduction $\mathcal{R}$ to solve some hard problem (for instance, the short integer solution (SIS) problem [2]). More precisely, by doing this, we establish the relation that $\varepsilon_{\mathcal{A}} \leq \ell \cdot \varepsilon_{\mathcal{R}}$ and the running time of $\mathcal{A}$ and $\mathcal{R}$ are roughly the same, where $\varepsilon_{\mathcal{A}}$ and $\varepsilon_{\mathcal{R}}$ are the success probability of $\mathcal{A}$ and $\mathcal{R}$, respectively.

B. Wagner—This work was done while the second author was doing an internship with the first author at NTNU, and it was partially supported by the Erasmus + traineeship program.

© Springer Nature Switzerland AG 2021
J. H. Cheon and J.-P. Tillich (Eds.): PQCrypto 2021, LNCS 12841, pp. 360–379, 2021.
https://doi.org/10.1007/978-3-030-81293-5_19

In particular, if the security loss ℓ is a small constant, then we call the reduction *tight* [5,7]. Recently, a relaxed notion called "almost tight" is considered [12,20], where the security loss can be dependent linearly or logarithmically on the security parameter. A cryptographic scheme with tight reductions does not need to increase the key length to compensate a security loss.

In the recent years, many tools have been developed to construct tightly secure cryptosystems [9,12,19,20,28,29,35]. However, currently, many of these techniques crucially require pairing groups and the Diffie-Hellman assumption which is known to be insure against a powerful quantum computer. The digital signature scheme in [1,8] and the identity-based encryption schemes in [10,31] are among the few exceptions which have tight post-quantum security using lattice-based techniques.

OUR GOAL: IDENTITY-BASED SIGNATURES WITH TIGHT POST-QUANTUM SECURITY. We are interested in advanced cryptographic schemes with tight post-quantum security. In this paper, we consider identity-based signature (IBS) schemes [44]. In an IBS, an honest user with identity id can sign a message μ using its secret key $\mathsf{sk}_{\mathsf{id}}$, and a signature σ can be publicly verified, given the master public key mpk and a user's identity id. We are interested in the adaptive security of IBS schemes, where an adversary aims at forging a fresh signature after adaptively learning users' secret keys and signatures. The use of identity-based cryptography can simplify the PKI requirements, and we refer [32] for more discussion about that.

There are mainly two approaches to construct IBS schemes, but neither of them directly yields an IBS scheme with tight post-quantum security. The first approach [6,16] is to transform a (standard) signature scheme into an IBS, which is often referred as the certification approach. The generic transformations in [6,16] are not tight. Recently, it has been shown that, if the underlying signature scheme is tightly secure in the multi-user setting with adaptive corruption, then the IBS scheme is tightly secure [38].

Compared to the classical unforgeability in the single-user setting (EUF-CMA) [26], the multi-user security with corruption (MU-EUF-CMA^{corr}) [3] is a stronger security notion for signature schemes, where an adversary receives verification keys of multiple users and is allowed corrupt some of them. Although EUF-CMA non-tightly implies MU-EUF-CMA^{corr}, constructing a tightly MU-EUF-CMA^{corr} secure signature scheme is highly challenging: To the best of our knowledge, [3,15,24] are the only schemes that have tight MU-EUF-CMA^{corr} security, and they are all based on the Diffie-Hellman assumption. There is a generic construction in [3], but it requires a non-interactive witness-indistinguishable proof of knowledge (NIWIPoK) system. It is unclear how to construct this particular proof system and to instantiate their generic construction in the post-quantum setting, while in the pairing setting we have the Groth-Sahai system [27] to implement it.

To give a bit more technical insights to it, in the lattice setting, one may consider to use a proof system (for instance, the one in [14]) together with the OR-proof technique [13] to construct such a NIWIPoK system. However, it requires the rewinding technique to show the PoK property, which leads to a non-tight reduction.

The second approach [32] is to transform a 2-level hierarchical IBE (HIBE) [23] tightly to an IBS scheme. However, the existing tightly secure HIBE schemes are pairing-based [35–37]. We note that in [10] Boyen and Li proposed an almost tightly secure lattice-based IBE and claimed (without a concrete scheme) that it can be turned into a 2-level HIBE. Their construction is motivated by the Katz-Wang "random-bit" technique [25], and it is rather inefficient, due to the use of lattice-based PRFs and their key-homomorphic evaluation. Lattice-based PRFs [4,30,33] often use a large modulus and have almost tightness only. In Sect. 1.2, we further sketch why the "random-bit" technique is not enough for achieving our goal.

OUR RESULTS. We propose the *first* tightly secure IBS scheme based on lattices. We prove the tight adaptive security of our IBS scheme based on the short integer solution (SIS) assumption [2] which is a quantum-safe assumption. Our proof is in the random oracle model. Different to the tree-based tight SIS-based signature scheme in [8], our signatures are short and contain only constant number of elements. Our scheme uses the Micciancio-Peikert (MP) trapdoor technique [41] and the Bonsai tree technique [11]. Moreover, our construction does not require any lattice-based PRF as in [10].

1.1 Technical Details

We achieve our results in two steps.

STEP 1: IBS WITH NON-ADAPTIVE SECURITY. We consider a (weaker) non-adaptive security of IBS schemes, where an adversary has to commit its user secret key queries and signing queries before receiving the master public key. This weaker security gives rise to a tight construction. The main reason is that in the security proof, since adversaries' user secret key queries and signing queries are committed in advance, the reduction can tightly embed the SIS instances in the forgery without any guessing.

More precisely, the overall idea of our non-adaptively secure scheme is as follows. The master public key of our scheme is a random matrix $\mathbf{A} \in \mathbb{Z}_q^{n \times m}$ with $m \geq 3n \log q$ where the SIS assumption holds, and the master secret key is a MP trapdoor [41] for $\mathbf{A}$. For generating user secret keys and signing, we associate matrices $\mathbf{F}_{\mathsf{id}} := [\mathbf{A} \mid \mathsf{H}_1(\mathsf{id})] \in \mathbb{Z}_q^{n \times (m+n\lceil \log q \rceil)}$ and $\mathbf{F}_{\mathsf{id},\mu} := [\mathbf{A} \mid \mathsf{H}_1(\mathsf{id}) \mid \mathsf{H}_2(\mathsf{id},\mu)] \in \mathbb{Z}_q^{n \times (m+2n\lceil \log q \rceil)}$ with identity id and message μ, where $\mathsf{H}_1, \mathsf{H}_2 : \{0,1\}^* \to \mathbb{Z}_q^{n \times n\lceil \log q \rceil}$ will be simulated as random oracles in the security proof.

The secret key of identity id is a MP trapdoor for $\mathbf{F}_{\mathsf{id}}$. Given the trapdoor of $\mathbf{A}$, this can be efficiently computed using trapdoor delegation, e.g. the Bonsai technique [11]. The signature for message μ under identity id is a "short" integer vector $\mathbf{z}$ in the kernel of $\mathbf{F}_{\mathsf{id},\mu}$ (namely, $\mathbf{F}_{\mathsf{id},\mu} \cdot \mathbf{z} = \mathbf{0}$).

Now we are ready to sketch our tight proof. We denote the list of all identities id for user secret key queries as $\mathcal{L}_{id}$, and the list of all identity-message pairs

(id, μ) for signing queries as $\mathcal{L}_m$. An adversary $\mathcal{A}$ has to output these two lists before receiving the master public key. The key step in our proof is that, by programming the random oracles H_1 and H_2, the reduction can embed a gadget matrix into $\mathbf{F}_{\mathsf{id}}$ (for all $\mathsf{id} \in \mathcal{L}_{id}$) and $\mathbf{F}_{\mathsf{id},\mu}$ (for all $(\mathsf{id}, \mu) \in \mathcal{L}_m$) so that efficiently inverting the SIS function for these $\mathbf{F}_{\mathsf{id}}$ and $\mathbf{F}_{\mathsf{id},\mu}$ is possible. However, for all $\mathsf{id}^* \notin \mathcal{L}_{id}$ and $(\mathsf{id}^*, \mu^*) \notin \mathcal{L}_m$, $\mathbf{F}_{\mathsf{id}^*}$ and $\mathbf{F}_{\mathsf{id}^*,\mu^*}$ are random matrices and inverting the SIS function for these random matrices is hard. Here, the reduction does not need to guess the forgery (id^*, μ^*), and thus it is tight.

STEP 2: FROM NON-ADAPTIVE TO ADAPTIVE SECURITY. For digital signature schemes, it is known that, using a chameleon hash, the non-adaptive security can be tightly transformed to adaptive security [34]. This transformation has been used in the lattice-setting as well [11,41] with the SIS-based chameleon hash function [11]. In this paper, we extend this generic transformation to the IBS setting, and thus our tightly non-adaptively secure IBS yields a tight scheme with adaptive security. Moreover, we propose a more efficient transformation in the random oracle model (cf. Sect. 3.2), since our non-adaptively secure scheme uses random oracles already. The common practice of instantiating the random oracle with a hash function such as SHA3 will be more efficient than using the chameleon hash technique. In particular, signature sizes are roughly the same, whereas the chameleon hash based on SIS requires to add a matrix to the public key. Further, the computation of this chameleon hash function is less efficient than an highly optimized evaluation of SHA3.

EXTENSION AND FUTURE WORK. We note that our approach can be extended to construct hierarchical IBS schemes. We leave this as a future work.

Further, we only analyze security in the (classical) random oracle model. Since our proof does not adaptively program the random oracle, an analysis in the quantum random oracle may be possible. As this model is more desirable for post-quantum cryptography, we think it is an interesting question for future work. We leave constructing an efficient non-adaptively secure short IBS with tight security in the standard model as an open problem. In combination with our transformation from Sect. 3, this will lead to an adaptively secure short IBS in the standard model with tight security. Finally, our techniques may be transferred to the ring setting, which may be of interest in terms of efficiency.

1.2   More on Related Work

THE KATZ-WANG "RANDOM-BIT" TECHNIQUE. The "random-bit" technique can be used to turn the non-tight Gentry-Peikert-Vaikuntanathan (GPV) IBE [22] to a tightly secure one [10,31]. However, we suppose this technique is not useful to construct a tightly secure 2-level HIBE. The high-level idea can be sketched easily. In the tight IBE, the secret key of identity id can be viewed as the GPV secret key of identity $(\mathsf{id}, b_{\mathsf{id}})$, where $b_{\mathsf{id}} \in \{0,1\}$ is a random bit associated with id, and the ciphertext of μ under id^* contains two GPV ciphertexts $(\mathsf{c}_0, \mathsf{c}_1)$ of μ under identity $(\mathsf{id}^*, 0)$ and $(\mathsf{id}^*, 1)$. In the security proof, by putting a lattice trapdoor in the b_{id}-side and embedding an LWE instance in $(1 - b_{\mathsf{id}})$-side for all identities id, we generate secret keys for identities $(\mathsf{id}, b_{\mathsf{id}})$ and randomize $c_{1-b_{\mathsf{id}^*}}$ in the challenge ciphertext. This is the key step, and it is important that b_{id^*} to be perfectly hidden, as otherwise the adversary may attack the side without any LWE instance.

One can extend this "random-bit" idea to the 2-level HIBE in the natural manner, namely, the secret key of identity $(\mathsf{id}_1, \mathsf{id}_2)$ is the secret key of identity $(\mathsf{id}_1, b_{\mathsf{id}_1}, \mathsf{id}_2, b_{\mathsf{id}_2})$ in the 2-level GPV HIBE. The encryption algorithm is adapted accordingly. Imagine that $(\mathsf{id}_1^*, \mathsf{id}_2^*)$ is the challenge identity for the 2-level HIBE. An adversary can learn the bit $b_{\mathsf{id}_1^*}$ used by the reduction, by asking a user secret key of $(\mathsf{id}_1^*, \mathsf{id}_2)$ with $\mathsf{id}_2 \neq \mathsf{id}_2^*$. The similar problem will happen, when we directly use this technique in constructing tightly secure IBS. Thus, we believe the Katz-Wang "random-bit" technique is not useful in constructing tightly secure 2-level HIBE or IBS.

OTHER TIGHTLY SECURE IBS. We note that in [45] tightly secure IBS schemes is proposed in a weaker security model, where an adversary cannot ask for the secret key of id if a signature has been asked for id. Moreover, their security relies on the factoring-based and Dlog-based assumptions, while ours is based on the quantum-safe SIS assumption.

COMPARISON WITH THE CERTIFICATION APPROACH. Finally, we compare the efficiency of our scheme with those obtained via the certification approach in Table 1. As we mentioned earlier, a digital signature scheme can be turned into an IBS non-tightly. Here we only focus on instantiating this approach with digital signature schemes based on the plain SIS assumption in the random oracle model, namely, [22,39], for a fair comparison, since our scheme is based on the same assumption. We are optimistic that our scheme can be translated into the more efficient ring setting, and we leave it as our future work.

Table 1. Comparison of our results with identity-based signature schemes obtained by applying the certification approach [32]. We use the chameleon hash function given in [11]. All sizes are in bits, where M denotes the size of an SIS matrix and z the size of an element in $\mathbb{Z}_q$.

Scheme	tight	$|\mathsf{mpk}|$	$|\sigma|$
Ours + Sect. 3.1	✓	$2M$	$(3m + 2n \log q)z$
Ours + Sect. 3.2	✓	M	$(m + 2n \log q)z + 2\omega(\log \lambda)$
GPV [22] + Cert.	✗	M	$M + 2mz$
Lyu [39] + Cert.	✗	$M + n^2 z$	$M + (n^2 + 2m)z + 2\omega(\log \lambda)$

We note that the certification approach increases the size of user secret keys and signatures. Namely, a user secret key consists of a secret key, a public key and a signature of the underlying signature scheme, and an identity-based signature contains a public key and two signatures. For schemes in [22,39], their public keys contain a matrix. This is the reason why their signature size (in terms of numbers of elements) is quadratic in n, while ours is linear. For schemes based on structured (and hence stronger) assumptions such as Dilithium [17] and Falcon

[18], the certification method will lead to a linear overhead, but it is still not tight.

2   Preliminaries

We use standard notation for sets $\mathbb{N}, \mathbb{P}, \mathbb{R}, \mathbb{Z}, \mathbb{Z}_q$ of natural numbers, primes real numbers, integers and integers modulo $q \in \mathbb{N}$, respectively. By $[n] := \{1, \ldots, n\}$ we denote the set of the first n natural numbers. We denote the security parameter by $\lambda \in \mathbb{N}$. All algorithms will get 1^λ either explicit or implicit as an input. A probabilistic algorithm $\mathcal{A}$ is said to be PPT (probabilistic polynomial time) if its running time can be bounded by a polynomial in its input size. We also make use of standard asymptotic notation for positive functions such as ω and O. A function $\nu : \mathbb{N} \to \mathbb{R}$ is negligible in its input λ if $\nu \in \lambda^{-\omega(1)}$. The term $\mathsf{negl}(\lambda)$ always denotes a negligible function. If a function ν is at least $1 - \mathsf{negl}(\lambda)$, we say that it is overwhelming.

Matrices and vectors are written in bold letters. Vectors should be understood as column vectors. The Euclidean norm of a vector $\mathbf{v}$ is denoted by $\|v\|$, and the spectral norm of a matrix $\mathbf{A}$ is denoted by $s_1(\mathbf{A})$.

If $\mathcal{D}$ is a distribution, we write $x \leftarrow \mathcal{D}$ to state that x is sampled from $\mathcal{D}$. If S is a finite set, the notation $x \xleftarrow{\$} S$ states that x is sampled uniformly random from S. The statistical distance of distributions $\mathcal{D}_1, \mathcal{D}_2$ on the support $\mathcal{X}$ is defined to be $\frac{1}{2} \sum_{x \in \mathcal{X}} |\Pr[\mathcal{D}_1 = x] - \Pr[\mathcal{D}_2 = x]|$. If the statistical distance is negligible in λ, we say the distributions are statistically close. The min-entropy is $H_\infty(\mathcal{D}_1) := -\log(\max_{x \in \mathcal{X}} \Pr[\mathcal{D}_1 = x])$.

If A is an algorithm, the notation $y \leftarrow \mathsf{A}(x)$ means that the variable y is assigned to the output of A on input x. Sometimes we make the randomness used by an algorithm explicit by writing $y \leftarrow \mathsf{A}(x; r)$ if $r \in \{0, 1\}^*$ is A's randomness. If we want to state that y is a possible output of Alg on input x, we write $y \in \mathsf{A}(x)$. We use the notation $\mathbf{T}(\mathsf{A})$ for running time. In all code-based security games, numerical values are assumed to be implicitly initialized as 0, sets and lists as $\emptyset$. If $\mathbf{G}$ is a game, we write $\mathbf{G}_\Pi^{\mathcal{A}}(1^\lambda) \Rightarrow b$ to state that the game $\mathbf{G}$ outputs the bit $b \in \{0, 1\}$ considering the adversary $\mathcal{A}$ and the scheme Π.

Definition 1 (Chameleon Hash Function). *A $\varepsilon_{\mathsf{trap}}$-chameleon hash function (CHF) is a triple of PPT algorithms $\mathsf{CHF} = (\mathsf{CHGen}, \mathsf{CHash}, \mathsf{CHColl})$, where*

- *$\mathsf{CHGen}(1^\lambda)$ takes as input the security parameter 1^λ and outputs the hash key hk and the trapdoor td. We assume that hk implicitly defines a message space $\mathcal{M}_{\mathsf{hk}}$, a randomness distribution $\mathcal{R}_{\mathsf{hk}}$ and hash value space $\mathcal{H}_{\mathsf{hk}}$.*
- *$\mathsf{CHash}(\mathsf{hk}, m; r)$ takes as input the hash key hk, a message $m \in \mathcal{M}_{\mathsf{hk}}$ and randomness $r \in \mathcal{R}_{\mathsf{hk}}$ and outputs a hash value $h \in \mathcal{H}_{\mathsf{hk}}$.*
- *$\mathsf{CHColl}(\mathsf{hk}, \mathsf{td}, m, r, \hat{m})$ takes as input the hash key hk, a message $m \in \mathcal{M}_{\mathsf{hk}}$, randomness $r \in \mathcal{R}_{\mathsf{hk}}$ and a message $\hat{m}$ and outputs a value $\hat{r} \in \mathcal{R}_{\mathsf{hk}}$.*
- *For every $(\mathsf{hk}, \mathsf{td}) \in \mathsf{CHGen}(1^\lambda)$, $m, m' \in \mathcal{M}_{\mathsf{hk}}$ the following distributions have statistical distance at most $\varepsilon_{\mathsf{trap}}$:*

$$\left\{ (r, h) \,\middle|\, \begin{array}{l} r \leftarrow \mathcal{R}_{\mathsf{hk}}, \\ h := \mathsf{CHash}(\mathsf{hk}, m; r) \end{array} \right\} \text{ and } \left\{ (r, h) \,\middle|\, \begin{array}{l} r' \leftarrow \mathcal{R}_{\mathsf{hk}}, h := \mathsf{CHash}(\mathsf{hk}, m'; r'), \\ r \leftarrow \mathsf{CHColl}(\mathsf{hk}, \mathsf{td}, m', r', m) \end{array} \right\}$$

If $\varepsilon_{\text{trap}}$ is negligible in λ, we simply say that CHF *is a chameleon hash function.*

Definition 2 (Collision Resistant CHF). *Let* CHF $=$ (CHGen, CHash, CHColl) *be a chameleon hash function. We say that* CHF *is collision resistant if for every* PPT *algorithm $\mathcal{A}$ the following advantage is negligible in λ:*

$$\text{Adv}^{\text{coll}}_{\mathcal{A},\text{CHF}}(\lambda) := \Pr\left[\begin{array}{c|c}\text{CHash}(\text{hk}, m; r) = \text{CHash}(\text{hk}, m'; r') & (\text{hk}, \text{td}) \leftarrow \text{CHGen}(1^\lambda) \\ \wedge (m, r) \neq (m', r') & (m, r, m', r') \leftarrow \mathcal{A}(\text{hk})\end{array}\right]$$

We note that chameleon hash functions based on lattice assumptions are known in the literature [11].

Definition 3 (Identity-Based Signature Scheme). *An Identity-based Signature Scheme (IBS) is defined as a tuple of* PPT *algorithms* IBS $=$ (Setup, KeyExt, Sig, Ver), *where*

- Setup(1^λ) *takes as input the security parameter λ and outputs a master public key* mpk *and a master secret key* msk*. We assume that* mpk *implicitly defines a message space $\mathcal{M} = \mathcal{M}_{\text{mpk}}$ and an identity space $\mathcal{ID} = \mathcal{ID}_{\text{mpk}}$.*
- KeyExt(msk, id) *takes as input a master secret key* msk *and an identity* id $\in \mathcal{ID}$ *and outputs a secret key* sk_{id}, *we assume that* sk_{id} *implicitly contains* id.
- Sig($\text{sk}_{\text{id}}, \mu$) *takes as input a secret key* sk_{id} *and a message $\mu \in \mathcal{M}$ and outputs a signature σ.*
- Ver(mpk, id, μ, σ) *is deterministic, takes as input a master public key* mpk, *identity* id $\in \mathcal{ID}$, *message $\mu \in \mathcal{M}$ and signature σ and outputs a bit $b \in \{0, 1\}$.*

We say that IBS *is ρ-complete, if for every* (mpk, msk) $\in$ Setup(1^λ), $\mu \in \mathcal{M}$, id $\in$ $\mathcal{ID}$ *we have*

$$\Pr\left[\text{Ver}(\text{mpk}, \text{id}, \mu, \sigma) = 1 \mid \text{sk}_{\text{id}} \leftarrow \text{KeyExt}(\text{msk}, \text{id}), \sigma \leftarrow \text{Sig}(\text{sk}_{\text{id}}, \mu)\right] \geq \rho.$$

Definition 4 (Security of IBS). *Let* IBS $=$ (Setup, KeyExt, Sig, Ver) *be an IBS and consider games* **UF-CMA**, **UF-naCMA** *given in Fig. 1. We say that* IBS *is* UF-naCMA *secure, if for every* PPT *adversary $\mathcal{A}$ the following advantage is negligible in λ:*

$$\text{Adv}^{\text{UF-naCMA}}_{\mathcal{A},\text{IBS}}(\lambda) := \Pr\left[\textbf{UF-naCMA}^{\mathcal{A}}_{\text{IBS}}(\lambda) \Rightarrow 1\right].$$

We say that IBS *is* UF-CMA *secure, if for every* PPT *adversary $\mathcal{A}$ the following advantage is negligible in λ:*

$$\text{Adv}^{\text{UF-CMA}}_{\mathcal{A},\text{IBS}}(\lambda) := \Pr\left[\textbf{UF-CMA}^{\mathcal{A}}_{\text{IBS}}(\lambda) \Rightarrow 1\right].$$

BACKGROUND ON LATTICES AND GAUSSIANS. For any m-dimensional lattice (i.e. discrete additive subgroup of $\mathbb{R}^m$) Λ and vector $\mathbf{c} \in \mathbb{R}^m$ we denote the discrete Gaussian distribution with parameter $s > 0$ over the coset $\mathbf{c} + \Lambda$ by $D_{\mathbf{c}+\Lambda,s}$. More precisely, this is the distribution proportional to $\rho_s(\mathbf{x}) := \exp(-\pi\|\mathbf{x}\|^2/s^2)$

Game $\mathbf{UF\text{-}naCMA}^{\mathcal{A}}_{\mathsf{IBS}}(\lambda)$	Game $\mathbf{UF\text{-}CMA}^{\mathcal{A}}_{\mathsf{IBS}}(\lambda)$
01 $(\mathcal{L}_{id}, \mathcal{L}_m, St) \leftarrow \mathcal{A}(1^\lambda)$	13 $(\mathsf{mpk}, \mathsf{msk}) \leftarrow \mathsf{Setup}(1^\lambda)$
02 $(\mathsf{mpk}, \mathsf{msk}) \leftarrow \mathsf{Setup}(1^\lambda)$	14 $(\mathsf{id}^*, \mu^*, \sigma^*) \leftarrow \mathcal{A}^{\mathrm{KEY}, \mathrm{SIG}, \mathsf{H}}(1^\lambda, \mathsf{mpk})$
03 **for** $\mathsf{id} \in \mathcal{L}_{id}$:	15 **if** $\mathsf{id}^* \in \mathcal{L}_{id}$: **return** 0
04 $\mathsf{sk}_{\mathsf{id}} \leftarrow \mathsf{KeyExt}(\mathsf{msk}, \mathsf{id})$	16 **if** $(\mathsf{id}^*, \mu^*) \in \mathcal{L}_m$: **return** 0
05 $\mathcal{L}_{sk} := \mathcal{L}_{sk} \cup \{\mathsf{sk}_{\mathsf{id}}\}$	17 **return** $\mathsf{Ver}(\mathsf{mpk}, \mathsf{id}^*, \mu^*, \sigma^*)$
06 **for** $(\mathsf{id}, \mu) \in \mathcal{L}_m$:	
07 $\sigma \leftarrow \mathsf{Sig}(\mathsf{sk}_{\mathsf{id}}, \mu)$	**Oracle** $\mathrm{KEY}(\mathsf{id})$
08 $\mathcal{L}_{sig} := \mathcal{L}_{sig} \cup \{\sigma\}$	18 $\mathcal{L}_{id} := \mathcal{L}_{id} \cup \{\mathsf{id}\}$
09 $(\mathsf{id}^*, \mu^*, \sigma^*) \leftarrow \mathcal{A}^{\mathsf{H}}(St, \mathsf{mpk}, \mathcal{L}_{sk}, \mathcal{L}_{sig})$	19 **return** $\mathsf{KeyExt}(\mathsf{msk}, \mathsf{id})$
10 **if** $\mathsf{id}^* \in \mathcal{L}_{id}$: **return** 0	
11 **if** $(\mathsf{id}^*, \mu^*) \in \mathcal{L}_m$: **return** 0	**Oracle** $\mathrm{SIG}(\mathsf{id}, \mu)$
12 **return** $\mathsf{Ver}(\mathsf{mpk}, \mathsf{id}^*, \mu^*, \sigma^*)$	20 $\mathcal{L}_m := \mathcal{L}_m \cup \{(\mathsf{id}, \mu)\}$
	21 $\mathsf{sk}_{\mathsf{id}} \leftarrow \mathsf{KeyExt}(\mathsf{msk}, \mathsf{id})$
	22 **return** $\sigma \leftarrow \mathsf{Sig}(\mathsf{sk}_{\mathsf{id}}, \mu)$

Fig. 1. The games **UF-naCMA** (left) and **UF-CMA** (right) for an identity-based signature scheme IBS and a random oracle H (in the standard model case, the oracle H is removed).

restricted to the coset $\mathbf{c} + \Lambda$. Let $\mathbf{A} \in \mathbb{Z}_q^{n \times m}, m > n$ be a matrix. It defines an m-dimensional q-ary lattice and lattice cosets as follows:

$$\Lambda_q^\perp(\mathbf{A}) := \{\mathbf{z} \in \mathbb{Z}^m : \mathbf{Az} = \mathbf{0} \mod q\}, \quad \Lambda_\mathbf{A}^\perp(\mathbf{u}) := \{\mathbf{z} \in \mathbb{Z}^m : \mathbf{Az} = \mathbf{u} \mod q\}.$$

We recall some standard facts about these lattices. For simplicity, throughout the paper we just deal with a prime modululs q. However, the techniques can be generalized to composite q as well [41]. The following lemma is obtained from Lemma 2.9 in [40] by setting $t = \sqrt{m} + \sqrt{n} \in \omega(\sqrt{\log m})$ and hence doubling the constant.

Lemma 1. *There is some universal constant $C_0 > 0$ such that the following holds: Let $n, m \in \mathbb{N}$ and $\mathbf{X} \in \mathbb{R}^{n \times m}$ be a random δ-subgaussian matrix with parameter s. Then we have $s_1(\mathbf{X}) \leq C_0 \cdot s \cdot (\sqrt{m} + \sqrt{n})$ except with negligible probability.*

The following facts are from [2,21,22,42,43] and can be obtained by using Lemmas 5.1, 5.2 and 5.3 in [21] and Lemma 4.4 in [42].

Lemma 2. *Let $n, m \in \mathbb{N}$, $q \in \mathbb{P}$ at least polynomial in n, $m \geq 2n \log q$. Consider any $\omega(\sqrt{\log m})$ function and $s \geq \omega(\sqrt{\log m})$. Then for all but a negligible (in n) fraction of all $\mathbf{A} \in \mathbb{Z}_q^{n \times m}$ the following distribution is statistically close to uniform over $\mathbb{Z}_q^n$: $\{\mathbf{Ae} \mid \mathbf{e} \leftarrow D_{\mathbb{Z}^m, s}\}$. Furthermore, the conditional distribution of $\mathbf{e} \leftarrow D_{\mathbb{Z}^m, s}$ given $\mathbf{u} = \mathbf{Ae} \mod q$ is exactly $D_{\Lambda_\mathbf{A}^\perp(\mathbf{u}), s}$.*

Lemma 3. *Let $n \in \mathbb{N}$, $q \in \mathbb{P}$ and $m \geq 2n \log q$. Consider any $\omega(\sqrt{\log m})$ function and $s \geq \omega(\sqrt{\log m})$. Then for all but an at most q^{-n} fraction of all $\mathbf{A} \in \mathbb{Z}_q^{n \times m}$ and any vector $\mathbf{u} \in \mathbb{Z}_q^n$, we have $\Pr\left[\|\mathbf{x}\| > s\sqrt{m} \mid \mathbf{x} \leftarrow D_{\Lambda_\mathbf{u}^\perp(\mathbf{A}), s}\right] \leq 2^{-m+1}$.*

Lemma 4. *Let $n \in \mathbb{N}$, $q \in \mathbb{P}$ and $m \geq 2n \log q$. Consider any $\omega(\sqrt{\log m})$ function and $s \geq \omega(\sqrt{\log m})$. Then for all but an at most q^{-n} fraction of all $\mathbf{A} \in \mathbb{Z}_q^{n \times m}$ and any vector $\mathbf{u} \in \mathbb{Z}_q^n$, we have $H_\infty\left(D_{\Lambda_{\mathbf{u}}^\perp(\mathbf{A}),s}\right) \geq m - 1$.*

Throughout this paper, we let $\mathbf{G}$ be the fixed gadget matrix introduced in [41]. Let $n, m, q \in \mathbb{N}, m \geq n\lceil \log q\rceil$ and $\mathbf{A} \in \mathbb{Z}_q^{n \times m}$ be a matrix. A trapdoor for $\mathbf{A}$ is a matrix $\mathbf{R} \in \mathbb{Z}^{(m-n\lceil \log q\rceil) \times n\lceil \log q\rceil}$ such that $\mathbf{A}[\mathbf{R}^t \mid \mathbf{I}_{n\lceil \log q\rceil}]^t = \mathbf{G}$. The next lemma summarizes the results in [41]. In particular, we obtained the precise statements from Sect. 5 of [41], we use the statistical instantiation of trapdoors and the constant is $C_1 = \sqrt{s_1(\Sigma_{\mathbf{G}}) + 2} \leq 3$ (see [41]).

Lemma 5. *Let C_0 be the constant from Lemma 1. There are* PPT *algorithms* GenTrap, SampleD, Invert *and* DelTrap *and constants $C_1 \leq 3$ such that for $n, q, m \in \mathbb{N}, q \geq 2, m \geq 3n \log q, w := n\lceil \log q\rceil$ and any $\omega(\sqrt{\log n})$ function the following holds with overwhelming probability over all random choices:*

- *For any $s \geq \omega(\sqrt{\log n})$ the algorithm* GenTrap$(1^n, 1^m, s, q)$ *outputs matrices $\mathbf{A} \in \mathbb{Z}_q^{n \times m}, \mathbf{R} \in \mathbb{Z}^{(m-w) \times w}$ such that $\mathbf{A}$ is statistically close to uniform, $\mathbf{R}$ is a trapdoor for $\mathbf{A}$ with entries sampled from $D_{\mathbb{Z},s}$ and $s_1(\mathbf{R}) \leq s \cdot C_0 \cdot (\sqrt{m - w} + \sqrt{w})$.*
- *For any matrix $\mathbf{A} \in \mathbb{Z}_q^{n \times m}$ with trapdoor $\mathbf{R}$, for any $\mathbf{u} \in \mathbb{Z}_q^n$ and any $s \geq C_1 \cdot \sqrt{s_1(\mathbf{R})^2 + 1} \cdot \omega(\sqrt{\log n})$, the following distribution is statistically close to $D_{\Lambda_{\mathbf{A}}^\perp(\mathbf{u}),s}$:*

$$\{\mathbf{z} \mid \mathbf{z} \leftarrow \mathsf{SampleD}(\mathbf{A}, \mathbf{R}, \mathbf{u}, s)\}$$

- *For any matrix $\mathbf{A} \in \mathbb{Z}_q^{n \times m}$ with trapdoor $\mathbf{R}$, any matrix $\mathbf{A}' \in \mathbb{Z}_q^{n \times w}$ and any $s \geq C_1 \cdot \sqrt{s_1(\mathbf{R})^2 + 1} \cdot \omega(\sqrt{\log n})$,* DelTrap$([\mathbf{A} \mid \mathbf{A}'], \mathbf{R}, s)$ *outputs a trapdoor $\mathbf{R}' \in \mathbb{Z}_q^{m \times w}$ for $[\mathbf{A} \mid \mathbf{A}']$ with distribution independent of $\mathbf{R}$ and $s_1(\mathbf{R}') \leq s \cdot C_0 \cdot (\sqrt{m} + \sqrt{w})$. Further, for $\tilde{s} \geq \omega(\sqrt{\log n})$ and under the same conditions, the following distributions are statistically close:*

$$\left\{(\mathbf{A}, \mathbf{A}', \mathbf{R}') \middle| \begin{array}{l} (\mathbf{A}, \mathbf{R}) \leftarrow \mathsf{GenTrap}(1^n, 1^m, \tilde{s}, q), \mathbf{A}' \xleftarrow{\$} \mathbb{Z}_q^{n \times w}, \\ \mathbf{R}' \leftarrow \mathsf{DelTrap}([\mathbf{A} \mid \mathbf{A}'], \mathbf{R}, s) \end{array}\right\}$$

and

$$\left\{(\mathbf{A}, \mathbf{A}', \mathbf{R}') \middle| (\mathbf{A}, \mathbf{R}) \leftarrow \mathsf{GenTrap}(1^n, 1^m, \tilde{s}, q), \mathbf{R}' \leftarrow D_{\mathbb{Z},s}^{m \times w}, \mathbf{A}' := \mathbf{A}\mathbf{R}' + \mathbf{G}\right\}$$

Definition 5. (Short Integer Solution Assumption (SIS)). *Let $\lambda \in \mathbb{N}, n = n(\lambda), m = m(\lambda), \beta = \beta(\lambda) \in \mathbb{N}$ and $q = q(n)$ be prime number. We say that the* SIS$_{n,m,q,\beta}$ *assumption holds, if for every* PPT *algorithm $\mathcal{A}$ the following advantage is negligible in λ:*

$$\mathsf{Adv}_{\mathcal{A}}^{\mathsf{SIS}_{n,m,q,\beta}}(\lambda) := \Pr\left[\mathbf{A}\mathbf{z} = 0 \wedge \mathbf{z} \neq 0 \wedge \|\mathbf{z}\| \leq \beta \mid \mathbf{A} \xleftarrow{\$} \mathbb{Z}_q^{n \times m}, \mathbf{z} \leftarrow \mathcal{A}(1^\lambda, \mathbf{A})\right].$$

The hardness of SIS for certain parameters is supported by several worst-case to average-case reductions, see [2, 22, 42].

3   Generic Constructions of Adaptively Secure IBS

In this section we will provide two transformations from non-adaptively secure identity-based signature schemes to adaptively secure ones. Let $\mathsf{IBS}' = (\mathsf{Setup}',$ $\mathsf{KeyExt}', \mathsf{Sig}', \mathsf{Ver}')$ be an identity-based signature scheme with identity space $\mathcal{ID}$ and message space $\mathcal{M}$, $\mathsf{CHF} = (\mathsf{CHGen}, \mathsf{CHash}, \mathsf{CHColl})$ a chameleon hash function, $\mathsf{H}_1 : \{0,1\}^* \to \mathcal{ID}, \mathsf{H}_2 : \{0,1\}^* \to \mathcal{M}$ random oracles and $\ell = \ell(\lambda) \in \mathbb{N}$. We define new identity-based signature schemes IBS in Fig. 2 and $\mathsf{IBS}_{\mathsf{ROM}}$ in Fig. 5. Note that the first transformation works in the standard model, whereas the second one uses random oracles. The reason why we also introduce this second transformation is that our non-adaptively secure construction from lattices uses random oracles already, so we can use the second transformation which is more efficient and without relying on additional primitives such as chameleon hash functions.

3.1   Transformation in the Standard Model

Here we will show that if IBS' is non-adaptively secure and CHF is a collision-resistant chameleon hash, then IBS, defined in Fig. 2, is adaptively secure. It is clear that if IBS' is ρ-complete, then IBS is ρ-complete as well.

Alg $\mathsf{Setup}(1^\lambda)$	**Alg** $\mathsf{Sig}(\mathsf{sk}_{\mathsf{id}}, \mu)$
01 $(\mathsf{hk}, \mathsf{td}) \leftarrow \mathsf{CHGen}(1^\lambda)$	09 **parse** $\mathsf{sk}_{\mathsf{id}} = (r, \mathsf{sk}'_{\mathsf{id}})$
02 $(\mathsf{mpk}', \mathsf{msk}') \leftarrow \mathsf{Setup}'(1^\lambda)$	10 $s \leftarrow \mathcal{R}_{\mathsf{hk}}$
03 $\mathsf{mpk} := (\mathsf{mpk}', \mathsf{hk}), \mathsf{msk} := \mathsf{msk}'$	11 $\sigma' \leftarrow \mathsf{Sig}'(\mathsf{sk}'_{\mathsf{id}}, \mathsf{CHash}(\mathsf{hk}, \mu; s))$
04 **return** $(\mathsf{mpk}, \mathsf{msk})$	12 **return** (r, s, σ')
Alg $\mathsf{KeyExt}(\mathsf{msk}, \mathsf{id})$	**Alg** $\mathsf{Ver}(\mathsf{mpk}, \mathsf{id}, \mu, \sigma)$
05 $r \leftarrow \mathcal{R}_{\mathsf{hk}}$	13 **parse** $\sigma = (r, s, \sigma')$
06 $\mathsf{id}' := \mathsf{CHash}(\mathsf{hk}, \mathsf{id}; r)$	14 $\mathsf{id}' := \mathsf{CHash}(\mathsf{hk}, \mathsf{id}; r)$
07 $\mathsf{sk}'_{\mathsf{id}} \leftarrow \mathsf{KeyExt}'(\mathsf{msk}', \mathsf{id}')$	15 $\mu' := \mathsf{CHash}(\mathsf{hk}, \mu; s)$
08 **return** $(r, \mathsf{sk}'_{\mathsf{id}})$	16 **return** $\mathsf{Ver}'(\mathsf{mpk}', \mathsf{id}', \mu', \sigma')$

Fig. 2. Our adaptively secure $\mathsf{IBS} = (\mathsf{Setup}, \mathsf{KeyExt}, \mathsf{Sig}, \mathsf{Ver})$ for a given non-adaptively secure $\mathsf{IBS}' = (\mathsf{Setup}', \mathsf{KeyExt}', \mathsf{Sig}', \mathsf{Ver}')$ and a chameleon hash function $\mathsf{CHF} = (\mathsf{CHGen}, \mathsf{CHash}, \mathsf{CHColl})$.

Theorem 1. *Let IBS' be an identity-based signature scheme and CHF be an $\varepsilon_{\mathsf{trap}}$-chameleon hash function. If IBS' is UF-naCMA secure and CHF is collision resistant, then IBS is UF-CMA secure. In particular, for every algorithm $\mathcal{A}$ making at most Q_S signing queries and Q_C secret key queries there are algorithms $\mathcal{B}_1$ and $\mathcal{B}_2$ such that*

$$\mathsf{Adv}^{\mathsf{UF\text{-}CMA}}_{\mathcal{A}, \mathsf{IBS}}(\lambda) \leq \mathsf{Adv}^{\mathsf{coll}}_{\mathcal{B}_1, \mathsf{CHF}}(\lambda) + \mathsf{Adv}^{\mathsf{UF\text{-}naCMA}}_{\mathcal{B}_2, \mathsf{IBS}'}(\lambda) + (Q_C + 2Q_S)\varepsilon_{\mathsf{trap}}.$$

and $\mathbf{T}(\mathcal{B}_1) \approx \mathbf{T}(\mathcal{A}), \mathbf{T}(\mathcal{B}_2) \approx \mathbf{T}(\mathcal{A})$.

Game $\mathbf{G}_0, \mathbf{G}_1$

01 $(\mathsf{hk}, \mathsf{td}) \leftarrow \mathsf{CHGen}(1^\lambda)$
02 $(\mathsf{mpk}', \mathsf{msk}') \leftarrow \mathsf{Setup}'(1^\lambda)$
03 $\mathsf{mpk} := (\mathsf{mpk}', \mathsf{hk}), \mathsf{msk} := \mathsf{msk}'$
04 $(\mathsf{id}^*, \mu^*, (r^*, s^*, \sigma^*)) \leftarrow \mathcal{A}^{\mathrm{KEY}, \mathrm{SIG}}(\mathsf{mpk})$
05 if $\mathsf{id}^* \in \mathcal{L}_{id}$: return 0
06 if $(\mathsf{id}^*, \mu^*) \in \mathcal{L}_m$: return 0
07 $\mathsf{id}_h^* := \mathsf{CHash}(\mathsf{hk}, \mathsf{id}^*; r^*)$
08 $\mu_h^* := \mathsf{CHash}(\mathsf{hk}, \mu^*; s^*)$
09 if $\exists (\mathsf{id}', \mathsf{id}, r) \in \mathcal{H}_{id} : \mathsf{id}_h^* = \mathsf{id}'$:
10      $\mathsf{bad}_1 = 1, \mathbf{return\ 0}$
11 if $\exists ((\mathsf{id}', \mathsf{id}, r), (\mu', \mu, s)) \in \mathcal{H}_m$:
12      $\mathsf{id}_h^* = \mathsf{id}' \wedge \mu_h^* = \mu'$:
13          $\mathsf{bad}_2 = 1, \mathbf{return\ 0}$
14 return $\mathsf{Ver}(\mathsf{mpk}, \mathsf{id}^*, \mu^*, \sigma^*)$

Oracle $\mathrm{KEY}(\mathsf{id})$

15 $\mathcal{L}_{id} := \mathcal{L}_{id} \cup \{\mathsf{id}\}$
16 $r \leftarrow \mathcal{R}_{\mathsf{hk}}, \mathsf{id}' := \mathsf{CHash}(\mathsf{hk}, \mathsf{id}; r)$
17 $\mathsf{sk}'_{\mathsf{id}} \leftarrow \mathsf{KeyExt}'(\mathsf{msk}', \mathsf{id}')$
18 $x := (\mathsf{id}', \mathsf{id}, r)$
19 $\mathcal{H}_{id} := \mathcal{H}_{id} \cup \{x\}$
20 return $(r, \mathsf{sk}'_{\mathsf{id}})$

Oracle $\mathrm{SIG}(\mathsf{id}, \mu)$

21 $\mathcal{L}_m := \mathcal{L}_m \cup \{(\mathsf{id}, \mu)\}$
22 $r \leftarrow \mathcal{R}_{\mathsf{hk}}, \mathsf{id}' := \mathsf{CHash}(\mathsf{hk}, \mathsf{id}; r)$
23 $\mathsf{sk}'_{\mathsf{id}} \leftarrow \mathsf{KeyExt}'(\mathsf{msk}', \mathsf{id}')$
24 $s \leftarrow \mathcal{R}_{\mathsf{hk}}, \mu' := \mathsf{CHash}(\mathsf{hk}, \mu; s)$
25 $\sigma' \leftarrow \mathsf{Sig}'(\mathsf{sk}'_{\mathsf{id}}, \mu')$
26 $x := ((\mathsf{id}', \mathsf{id}, r), (\mu', \mu, s))$
27 $\mathcal{H}_m := \mathcal{H}_m \cup \{x\}$
28 return (r, s, σ')

Fig. 3. Games $\mathbf{G}_0$ and $\mathbf{G}_1$ in the proof of Theorem 1. The shaded statements are only executed in $\mathbf{G}_1$.

We prove the statement via a games $\mathbf{G}_0$ and $\mathbf{G}_1$ and reductions $\mathcal{B}_1$ and $\mathcal{B}_2$. Games $\mathbf{G}_0, \mathbf{G}_1$ are formally presented in Fig. 3. In every game $i \in \{0, 1\}$, we denote the advantage of adversary $\mathcal{A}$ as $\mathsf{Adv}_i(\mathcal{A}) := \Pr\left[\mathbf{G}_i^{\mathcal{A}} \Rightarrow 1\right]$. Game $\mathbf{G}_0$ is the original game **UF-CMA**, hence we aim to bound $\mathsf{Adv}_0(\mathcal{A})$. Game $\mathbf{G}_1$ keeps track of the hashed identities and messages for all key and signing queries. That is, it holds lists $\mathcal{H}_m$ and $\mathcal{H}_{id}$ such that $(\mathsf{id}', \mathsf{id}, r) \in \mathcal{H}_{id}$ means that the adversary asked for a secret key for identity id and when answering the query, the game hashed id to id' using r, i.e. $\mathsf{id}' = \mathsf{CHash}(\mathsf{hk}, \mathsf{id}; r)$. In a similar way, a tuple $((\mathsf{id}', \mathsf{id}, r), (\mu', \mu, s))$ is in $\mathcal{H}_m$ if in some signing query, id was hashed to id and μ was hashed to μ' using randomness r, s respectively. After obtaining $\mathcal{A}$'s forgery $(\mathsf{id}^*, \mu^*, (r^*, s^*, \sigma^*))$, the game checks additional conditions and returns 0 if one of them holds. These are modeled as the events $\mathsf{bad}_1, \mathsf{bad}_2$. Setting $\mathsf{bad} := \mathsf{bad}_1 \vee \mathsf{bad}_2$ we can bound the difference of both games by

$$|\mathsf{Adv}_0(\mathcal{A}) - \mathsf{Adv}_1(\mathcal{A})| \leq \Pr[\mathsf{bad}].$$

Next, consider the definition of bad_1:

$$\mathsf{bad}_1 := (\exists (\mathsf{id}', \mathsf{id}, r) \in \mathcal{H}_{id} : \mathsf{CHash}(\mathsf{hk}, \mathsf{id}^*; r^*) = \mathsf{id}'),$$

which implies that there is a collision

$$\mathsf{CHash}(\mathsf{hk}, \mathsf{id}^*; r^*) = \mathsf{id}' = \mathsf{CHash}(\mathsf{hk}, \mathsf{id}; r).$$

This collision is non-trivial, as $\mathsf{id}^* \notin \mathcal{L}_{id}$ and hence $\mathsf{id}^* \neq \mathsf{id}$. Similarly, a non-trivial collision can be found if bad_2 occurs. Simulating $\mathbf{G}_1$ and checking which collision occurs can be done efficiently without the knowledge of the hash trap-door td, hence we have a direct reduction $\mathcal{B}_1$ that finds a collision for given hk if bad holds true. Clearly the running time of $\mathcal{B}_1$ is dominated by running $\mathcal{A}$ once. We see that

$$\Pr\left[\text{bad}\right] \leq \mathsf{Adv}^{\text{coll}}_{\mathcal{B}_1,\text{CHF}}(\lambda).$$

Finally, we bound the advantage of $\mathcal{A}$ in game $\mathbf{G}_1$ by a reduction $\mathcal{B}_2$ playing the

---

Alg $\mathcal{B}_2(1^\lambda)$
01 $(\mathsf{hk}, \mathsf{td}) \leftarrow \mathsf{CHGen}(1^\lambda)$
02 **for** $i \in [Q_S]$:
03      $s_i \leftarrow \mathcal{R}_{\mathsf{hk}}$
04      $\mu' := \mathsf{CHash}(\mathsf{hk}, 0; s_i)$
05      $r_i \leftarrow \mathcal{R}_{\mathsf{hk}}$
06      $\mathsf{id}' := \mathsf{CHash}(\mathsf{hk}, 0; r_i)$
07      $\mathcal{L}_m' := \mathcal{L}_m' \cup \{(\mathsf{id}', \mu')\}$
08 **for** $i \in [Q_C]$:
09      $\bar{r}_i \leftarrow \mathcal{R}_{\mathsf{hk}}$
10      $\mathsf{id}' := \mathsf{CHash}(\mathsf{hk}, 0; \bar{r}_i)$
11      $\mathcal{L}_{id}' := \mathcal{L}_{id}' \cup \{\mathsf{id}'\}$
12 $St := \{\mathsf{hk}, \mathsf{td}, (\bar{r}_i)_i, (s_i, r_i)_i\}$
13 **return** $(\mathcal{L}_{id}', \mathcal{L}_m', St)$

Oracle KEY(id)
14 $\mathsf{ctr}_{key} := \mathsf{ctr}_{key} + 1$
15 $i := \mathsf{ctr}_{key}$
16 $\mathcal{L}_{id} := \mathcal{L}_{id} \cup \{\mathsf{id}\}$
17 $r \leftarrow \mathsf{CHColl}(\mathsf{hk}, \mathsf{td}, 0, \bar{r}_i, \mathsf{id})$
18 $x := (\mathsf{CHash}(\mathsf{hk}, \mathsf{id}; r), \mathsf{id}, r)$
19 $\mathcal{H}_{id} := \mathcal{H}_{id} \cup \{x\}$
20 **return** (r, sk_i')

Alg $\mathcal{B}_2(St, \mathsf{mpk}', \{\mathsf{sk}_i'\}_i, \{\sigma_i'\}_i)$
21 $\mathsf{mpk} := (\mathsf{mpk}', \mathsf{hk})$
22 $(\mathsf{id}^*, \mu^*, (r^*, s^*, \sigma^*)) \leftarrow \mathcal{A}^{\text{KEY,SIG}}(\mathsf{mpk})$
23 **if** $\mathsf{id}^* \in \mathcal{L}_{id}$: **return** 0
24 **if** $(\mathsf{id}^*, \mu^*) \in \mathcal{L}_m$: **return** 0
25 $\mathsf{id}_h^* := \mathsf{CHash}(\mathsf{hk}, \mathsf{id}^*; r^*)$
26 $\mu_h^* := \mathsf{CHash}(\mathsf{hk}, \mu^*; s^*)$
27 **if** $\exists (\mathsf{id}', \mathsf{id}, r) \in \mathcal{H}_{id} : \mathsf{id}_h^* = \mathsf{id}'$:
28      $\mathsf{bad}_1 = 1, \textbf{return}\ 0$
29 **if** $\exists ((\mathsf{id}', \mathsf{id}, r), (\mu', \mu, s)) \in \mathcal{H}_m$:
30      $\mathsf{id}_h^* = \mathsf{id}' \wedge \mu_h^* = \mu'$:
31          $\mathsf{bad}_2 = 1, \textbf{return}\ 0$
32 **return** $(\mathsf{id}_h^*, \mu_h^*, \sigma^*)$

Oracle SIG(id, μ)
33 $\mathsf{ctr}_{sig} := \mathsf{ctr}_{sig} + 1, i := \mathsf{ctr}_{sig}$
34 $\mathcal{L}_m := \mathcal{L}_m \cup \{(\mathsf{id}, \mu)\}$
35 $r \leftarrow \mathsf{CHColl}(\mathsf{hk}, \mathsf{td}, 0, r_i, \mathsf{id})$
36 $s \leftarrow \mathsf{CHColl}(\mathsf{hk}, \mathsf{td}, 0, s_i, \mu)$
37 $\mathsf{id}' := \mathsf{CHash}(\mathsf{hk}, \mathsf{id}; r)$
38 $\mu' := \mathsf{CHash}(\mathsf{hk}, \mu; s)$
39 $x := ((\mathsf{id}', \mathsf{id}, r), (\mu', \mu, s))$
40 $\mathcal{H}_m := \mathcal{H}_m \cup \{x\}$
41 **return** (r, s, σ_i')

Fig. 4. Reduction $\mathcal{B}_2$ in the proof of Theorem 1 simulating game $\mathbf{G}_1$ for adversary $\mathcal{A}$ and playing the game **UF-naCMA** for the scheme IBS'.

game **UF-naCMA** for the scheme IBS'. The reduction makes use of the trap-door td and is formally presented in Fig. 4. Reduction $\mathcal{B}_2$ chooses a chameleon hash key and a trapdoor for it and then hashes Q_S many arbitrary values (in our presentation: 0) using randomness r_i, s_i to hash values id_i', μ_i'. These hash values will then be given to the UF-naCMA challenger as the (non-adaptive) signing queries. $\mathcal{B}_2$ will then get a public key mpk' and the signatures σ_i' for these queries. Afterwards, when $\mathcal{A}$ issues the i-th (adaptive) signature query for the pair (id, μ), the reduction uses its trapdoor to find randomness r and s, such that $\mathsf{CHash}(\mathsf{hk}, \mathsf{id}; r) = \mathsf{id}_i'$ and $\mathsf{CHash}(\mathsf{hk}, \mu; s) = \mu_i'$, i.e.

$$r \leftarrow \mathsf{CHColl}(\mathsf{hk}, \mathsf{td}, 0, r_i, \mathsf{id}), s \leftarrow \mathsf{CHColl}(\mathsf{hk}, \mathsf{td}, 0, s_i, \mu).$$

Then the reduction can simply return (r, s, σ_i'), which is correct, by definition of the scheme. A similar collision strategy is applied to handle the adaptive secret key queries after non-adaptively obtaining secret keys. After obtaining $\mathcal{A}$'s forgery $(\text{id}^*, \mu^*, (r^*, s^*, \sigma^*))$, $\mathcal{B}_2$ checks all the winning conditions and outputs $(\mathsf{CHash}(\mathsf{hk}, \text{id}^*; r^*), \mathsf{CHash}(\mathsf{hk}, \mu^*; s^*), \sigma^*)$. It follows from the properties of the chameleon hash function that this collision finding using the trapdoor and honest signing are statistically close. To be precise, the statistical distance between $\mathbf{G}_1$ and the game simulated by $\mathcal{B}_2$ can be bounded by $(Q_C + 2Q_S)\varepsilon_{\mathsf{trap}}$, as $\mathcal{B}_2$ applies CHColl once per secret key query and twice per signing query. Let us now argue that $\mathcal{B}_2$ wins the game **UF-naCMA**, assuming $\mathcal{A}$ wins. By definition of the verification algorithm of the scheme, if $\mathcal{A}$ outputs a valid signature (r^*, s^*, σ^*) for message μ^* and id^*, then σ^* is a valid signature for identity $\mathsf{CHash}(\mathsf{hk}, \text{id}^*; r^*)$ and message $\mathsf{CHash}(\mathsf{hk}, \mu^*; s^*)$ with respect to IBS′. Hence we only need to check freshness: For the sake of contradiction, assume the secret key of $\mathsf{CHash}(\mathsf{hk}, \text{id}^*; r^*)$ was (non-adaptively) queried by $\mathcal{B}_2$. Then there is some $i \in [Q_C]$ such that $\mathsf{CHash}(\mathsf{hk}, \text{id}^*; r^*) = \mathsf{CHash}(\mathsf{hk}, 0; \bar{r}_i)$. The way $\mathcal{B}_2$ answers signature queries tells us that $(\mathsf{CHash}(\mathsf{hk}, 0; \bar{r}_i), \text{id}, r) \in \mathcal{H}_{id}$ for the i-th key query id and some randomness r. This is exactly the definition of event bad_1, which we ruled out before. An analogous argument using bad_2 shows that $(\mathsf{CHash}(\mathsf{hk}, \text{id}^*; r^*), \mathsf{CHash}(\mathsf{hk}, \mu^*; s^*))$ was not queried by $\mathcal{B}_2$. Thus, we have

$$\mathsf{Adv}_1(\mathcal{A}) \leq \mathsf{negl}(\lambda) + \mathsf{Adv}_{\mathcal{B}_2, \mathsf{IBS}'}^{\mathsf{UF\text{-}naCMA}}(\lambda).$$

Finally, the running time of $\mathcal{B}_2$ is dominated by evaluating the polynomial time chameleon hash and running adversary $\mathcal{A}$.   □

3.2   Transformation in the Random Oracle Model

Next, we will show that if IBS′ is non-adaptively secure and $\ell \in \omega(\log \lambda)$, then $\mathsf{IBS_{ROM}}$, defined in Fig. 5, is adaptively secure. Clearly, if IBS′ is ρ-complete, then $\mathsf{IBS_{ROM}}$ is also ρ-complete.

Alg $\mathsf{KeyExt}(\mathsf{msk}, \text{id})$	**Alg** $\mathsf{Ver}(\mathsf{mpk}, \text{id}, \mu, \sigma)$
01 $r \xleftarrow{\$} \{0,1\}^\ell, \text{id}' \leftarrow \mathsf{H}_1(\text{id}, r)$	05 **parse** $\sigma = (r, s, \sigma')$
02 **return** $(r, \mathsf{KeyExt}'(\mathsf{msk}', \text{id}'))$	06 $\text{id}' \leftarrow \mathsf{H}_1(\text{id}, r)$
	07 $\mu' \leftarrow \mathsf{H}_2(\mu, s)$
Alg $\mathsf{Sig}(\mathsf{sk_{id}} = (r, \mathsf{sk}_{id}'), \mu)$	08 $v := \mathsf{Ver}'(\mathsf{mpk}', \text{id}', \mu', \sigma')$
03 $s \xleftarrow{\$} \{0,1\}^\ell, \mu' \leftarrow \mathsf{H}_2(\mu, s)$	09 **return** v
04 **return** $(r, s, \mathsf{Sig}'(\mathsf{sk}_{id}', \mu'))$	

Fig. 5. Our adaptively secure $\mathsf{IBS_{ROM}} = (\mathsf{Setup} := \mathsf{Setup}', \mathsf{KeyExt}, \mathsf{Sig}, \mathsf{Ver})$ for a non-adaptively secure $\mathsf{IBS}' = (\mathsf{Setup}', \mathsf{KeyExt}', \mathsf{Sig}', \mathsf{Ver}')$ with random oracles $\mathsf{H}_1, \mathsf{H}_2$ and a natural number $\ell = \ell(\lambda)$.

Theorem 2. *Let* IBS' *be an identity-based signature scheme,* $H_1 : \{0,1\}^* \to \mathcal{ID}, H_2 : \{0,1\}^* \to \mathcal{M}$ *be random oracles and* $\ell = \ell(\lambda) \in \omega(\log(\lambda))$. *If* IBS' *is UF-naCMA secure, then* IBS$_{ROM}$ *is UF-CMA secure. In particular, for every algorithm* $\mathcal{A}$ *making at most* Q_S *signing queries,* Q_C *secret key queries and* Q_H *hash queries (including the indirect ones induced by singing and key queries) there is an algorithm* $\mathcal{B}$ *such that* $\mathbf{T}(\mathcal{B}) \approx \mathbf{T}(\mathcal{A})$ *and*

$$\mathsf{Adv}^{\mathsf{UF\text{-}CMA}}_{\mathcal{A},\mathsf{IBS}_{ROM}}(\lambda) \leq \mathsf{Adv}^{\mathsf{UF\text{-}naCMA}}_{\mathcal{B},\mathsf{IBS}'}(\lambda) + (Q_C + 2Q_S)\frac{Q_H}{2^\ell} + \frac{Q_C}{|\mathcal{ID}|} + \frac{Q_S}{|\mathcal{ID}||\mathcal{M}|}.$$

The proof mimics the idea of Theorem 1 by replacing the chameleon hash with a random oracle. We will present it in the full version.

4 Non-adaptive Security from SIS

In this section we construct a non-adaptively secure identity-based signature scheme IBS$_{SIS}$ based on the SIS assumption. Combined with the transformation presented in the previous section, we obtain an adaptively secure one. The scheme is presented in Fig. 6. Its main parameters are SIS parameters $n \in \mathbb{N}, q \in \mathbb{P}, m \geq 3n\log q, \beta > 0$. We also need gaussian parameters $s_0, s, s', s'', \tilde{s} > \omega(\sqrt{\log m})$ (needed for regularity, Lemma 2), where the parameter $\tilde{s}$ is only used in the proof, s_0, s, s', s'' satisfy the conditions for Lemma 5 and β is large enough:

$$s \geq C_1\sqrt{s_0^2 C_0^2(\sqrt{m - n\lceil\log q\rceil} + \sqrt{n\lceil\log q\rceil})^2 + 1} \cdot \omega(\sqrt{\log n})$$

$$s' \geq C_1\sqrt{s^2 C_0^2(\sqrt{m} + \sqrt{n\lceil\log q\rceil})^2 + 1} \cdot \omega(\sqrt{\log n})$$

$$s'' \geq C_1\sqrt{s'^2 C_0^2(\sqrt{m + n\lceil\log q\rceil} + \sqrt{n\lceil\log q\rceil})^2 + 1} \cdot \omega(\sqrt{\log n})$$

$$\beta \geq (1 + 2C_0\tilde{s}(\sqrt{m} + \sqrt{n\lceil\log q\rceil}))s''\sqrt{m + 2n\lceil\log q\rceil}$$

Lemma 6. *The identity-based signature scheme* IBS$_{SIS}$ *is* ρ-*complete, where* $\rho \geq 1 - \mathsf{negl}(\lambda)$.

Proof. Consider keys (mpk $= \mathbf{A}$, msk $= \mathbf{T_A}$) $\in$ Setup(1^λ), an arbitrary identity id and message μ. Let sk$_{id} \in$ KeyExt(msk, id) and $\mathbf{z} \in$ Sig(sk$_{id}, \mu$). By definition of KeyExt we have that sk$_{id} = \mathbf{T}_{id}$ is a trapdoor for the matrix $\mathbf{F}_{id} = [\mathbf{A} \mid H_1(\mathsf{mpk}, \mathsf{id})]$, which is a prefix of $\mathbf{F}_{id,\mu} = [\mathbf{A} \mid H_1(\mathsf{mpk}, \mathsf{id}) \mid H_2(\mathsf{mpk}, \mathsf{id}, \mu)]$. Hence $\mathbf{T}_{id,\mu}$ as used in the signature scheme is a trapdoor for $\mathbf{F}_{id,\mu}$, by Lemma 5 and the conditions of parameters. The same Lemma tells us that $\mathbf{z}$ is distributed statistically close to $D_{\Lambda_q^\perp(\mathbf{F}_{id,\mu}),s''}$, which implies $\mathbf{F}_{id,\mu}\mathbf{z} = \mathbf{0}$ and with overwhelming probability (by Lemma 3) $\|\mathbf{z}\| \leq s'' \cdot \sqrt{m + 2n\lceil\log q\rceil}$, which makes Ver accept. □

```
Alg Setup(1^λ)                              Alg Sig(sk_id, μ)
01 set parameters as in the text.           09 H_1 ← H_1(mpk, id), H_2 ← H_2(mpk, id, μ)
02 (A, T_A) ← GenTrap(1^n, 1^m, s_0, q)      10 F_id,μ := [A | H_1 | H_2]
03 mpk := A ∈ Z_q^{n×m}, msk := T_A          11 T_id,μ ← DelTrap(F_id,μ, T_id, s')
04 return (mpk, msk)                         12 z ← SampleD(F_id,μ, T_id,μ, 0, s'')
                                             13 return σ := z
Alg KeyExt(msk, id)
05 H_1 ← H_1(mpk, id)                        Alg Ver(mpk, μ, z)
06 F_id := [A | H_1]                          14 H_1 ← H_1(mpk, id), H_2 ← H_2(mpk, id, μ)
07 T_id ← DelTrap(F_id, T_A, s)              15 F_id,μ := [A | H_1 | H_2]
08 return sk_id := T_id                      16 if z = 0 ∨ F_id,μ z ≠ 0 : return 0
                                             17 return ‖z‖ ≤ s'' √(m + 2n⌈log q⌉)
```

Fig. 6. The identity-based signature scheme $\mathsf{IBS_{SIS}} = (\mathsf{Setup}, \mathsf{KeyExt}, \mathsf{Sig}, \mathsf{Ver})$, where $H_1 : \{0,1\}^* \to \mathbb{Z}_q^{n \times n\lceil \log q \rceil}, H_2 : \{0,1\}^* \to \mathbb{Z}_q^{n \times n\lceil \log q \rceil}$ are random oracles.

Theorem 3. *The scheme* $\mathsf{IBS_{SIS}}$ *is an* UF-naCMA *secure identity-based signature scheme, under the* $\mathsf{SIS}_{n,m,q,\beta}$ *assumption. In particular, for every* PPT *algorithm* $\mathcal{A}$ *there is a* PPT *algorithm* $\mathcal{B}$ *such that*

$$\mathsf{Adv}^{\mathsf{UF\text{-}naCMA}}_{\mathcal{A},\mathsf{IBS_{SIS}}}(\lambda) \leq \mathsf{Adv}^{\mathsf{SIS}_{n,m,q,\beta}}_{\mathcal{B}}(\lambda) + \mathsf{negl}(\lambda)$$

and $\mathbf{T}(\mathcal{B}) \approx \mathbf{T}(\mathcal{A})$.

Proof. The proof is via a reduction $\mathcal{B}$, formally given in Fig. 7. The idea is as follows: The given SIS matrix $\mathbf{A}$ is set as the master public key $\mathsf{mpk} := \mathbf{A}$. For any identity $\mathsf{id} \in \mathcal{L}_{id}$, for which the adversary queries the secret key, $\mathcal{B}$ programs the random oracle $H_1(\mathsf{mpk}, \mathsf{id}) := \mathbf{A}\hat{\mathbf{R}}_{\mathsf{mpk,id}} + \mathbf{G}$, where $\hat{\mathbf{R}}_{\mathsf{mpk,id}} \leftarrow D^{m \times n\lceil \log q \rceil}_{\mathbb{Z},s}$ is short. Hence, $\hat{\mathbf{R}}_{\mathsf{mpk,id}}$ is a trapdoor for $\mathbf{F}_{\mathsf{id}} := [\mathbf{A} | H_1(\mathsf{mpk}, \mathsf{id})]$ and $\mathcal{B}$ can return it as $\mathsf{sk_{id}}$. Note that by definition of the non-adaptive security game, $\mathcal{A}$ did not query the random oracle before, hence programming is possible. For all other identities, the hash value will be programmed to $H_1(\mathsf{mpk}, \mathsf{id}) := \mathbf{A}\hat{\mathbf{R}}_{\mathsf{mpk,id}}$. A similar programming policy is applied for H_2: For every pair $(\mathsf{id}, \mu) \in \mathcal{L}_m$, for which the adversary wants to know a signature, the random oracle is programmed as $H_2(\mathsf{mpk}, \mathsf{id}, \mu) := \mathbf{A}\mathbf{R}_{\mathsf{mpk,id},\mu} + \mathbf{G}$ for $\mathbf{R}_{\mathsf{mpk,id},\mu} \leftarrow D^{m \times n\lceil \log q \rceil}_{\mathbb{Z},s}$. Using $\mathbf{R}_{\mathsf{mpk,id},\mu}$ as a trapdoor for $[\mathbf{A} | H_2(\mathsf{mpk}, \mathsf{id}, \mu)]$ the reduction can compute a trapdoor for $\mathbf{F}'_{\mathsf{id},\mu} := [\mathbf{A} | H_2(\mathsf{mpk}, \mathsf{id}, \mu) | H_1(\mathsf{mpk}, \mathsf{id})]$, sample from $D_{\Lambda_q^\perp(\mathbf{F}'_{\mathsf{id},\mu}),s''}$ and permute the resulting vector to get a signature as in the real scheme. Again, the random oracle value is not yet defined and can be programmed and other queries are programmed as $H_2(\mathsf{mpk}, \mathsf{id}, \mu) := \mathbf{A}\mathbf{R}_{\mathsf{mpk,id},\mu}$. In the end $\mathcal{A}$ will return a forgery $(\mathsf{id}^*, \mu^*, \mathbf{z}^*)$. We assume that $\mathcal{A}$ queried all related random oracle queries $H_1(\mathsf{mpk}, \mathsf{id}^*)$ and $H_2(\mathsf{mpk}, \mathsf{id}^*, \mu^*)$ (otherwise we can build a new adversary making the queries after running $\mathcal{A}$ and having the same success probability). If $\mathcal{A}$ is successful, then $\mathsf{id}^* \notin \mathcal{L}_{id}$ and $(\mathsf{id}^*, \mu^*) \notin \mathcal{L}_m$, which implies that

$$0 = \mathbf{F}_{\mathsf{id}^*,\mu^*} \mathbf{z}^* = [\mathbf{A} | \mathbf{A}\hat{\mathbf{R}}_{\mathsf{mpk,id}^*} | \mathbf{A}\mathbf{R}_{\mathsf{mpk,id}^*,\mu^*}] = \mathbf{A}[\mathbf{I}_m | \hat{\mathbf{R}}_{\mathsf{mpk,id}^*} | \mathbf{R}_{\mathsf{mpk,id}^*,\mu^*}]\mathbf{z}^*,$$

and hence $\mathcal{B}$ can return

$$\mathbf{z} := [\mathbf{I}_m \mid \hat{\mathbf{R}}_{\mathsf{mpk,id^*}} \mid \mathbf{R}_{\mathsf{mpk,id^*},\mu^*}]\mathbf{z}^*.$$

Alg $\mathcal{B}(\mathbf{A} \in \mathbb{Z}_q^{n \times m})$
01 $(\mathcal{L}_{id}, \mathcal{L}_m, St) \leftarrow \mathcal{A}(1^\lambda)$
02 $\mathsf{mpk} := \mathbf{A}$
03 **for** $\mathsf{id} \in \mathcal{L}_{id}$:
04 $\quad \hat{\mathbf{R}}_{\mathsf{mpk,id}} \leftarrow D_{\mathbb{Z},s}^{m \times n \lceil \log q \rceil}$
05 $\quad h[1, \mathsf{mpk}, \mathsf{id}] := \mathbf{A}\hat{\mathbf{R}}_{\mathsf{mpk,id}} + \mathbf{G}$
06 $\quad \mathsf{sk}_{\mathsf{id}} := \hat{\mathbf{R}}_{\mathsf{mpk,id}}$
07 $\quad \mathcal{L}_{sk} := \mathcal{L}_{sk} \cup \{\mathsf{sk}_{\mathsf{id}}\}$

08 **for** $(\mathsf{id}, \mu) \in \mathcal{L}_m$:
09 $\quad \mathbf{R}_{\mathsf{mpk,id},\mu} \leftarrow D_{\mathbb{Z},s}^{m \times n \lceil \log q \rceil}$
10 $\quad h[2, \mathsf{mpk}, \mathsf{id}, \mu] := \mathbf{A}\mathbf{R}_{\mathsf{mpk,id},\mu} + \mathbf{G}$
11 $\quad \mathbf{B} := \mathsf{H}_1(\mathsf{mpk}, \mathsf{id})$
12 $\quad \mathbf{C} := h[2, \mathsf{mpk}, \mathsf{id}, \mu]$
13 $\quad \mathbf{F}'_{\mathsf{id},\mu} := [\mathbf{A} \mid \mathbf{C} \mid \mathbf{B}]$
14 $\quad \mathbf{F}_{\mathsf{id},\mu} := [\mathbf{A} \mid \mathbf{B} \mid \mathbf{C}]$
15 $\quad \mathbf{T}'_{\mathsf{id},\mu} \leftarrow \mathsf{DelTrap}(\mathbf{F}'_{\mathsf{id},\mu}, \mathbf{R}_{\mathsf{mpk,id},\mu}, s')$
16 $\quad \mathbf{z} \leftarrow \mathsf{SampleD}(\mathbf{F}'_{\mathsf{id},\mu}, \mathbf{T}'_{\mathsf{id},\mu}, 0, s'')$
17 $\quad \mathbf{z}_{\mathsf{id},\mu} := [\mathbf{z}_1^t \mid \mathbf{z}_3^t \mid \mathbf{z}_2^t]^t$
18 $\quad \mathcal{L}_{sig} := \mathcal{L}_{sig} \cup \{\mathbf{z}_{\mathsf{id},\mu}\}$

19 $(\mathsf{id}^*, \mu^*, \mathbf{z}^*) \leftarrow \mathcal{A}^{\mathsf{H}_1,\mathsf{H}_2}(St, \mathsf{mpk}, \mathcal{L}_{sk}, \mathcal{L}_{sig})$

20 **if** $\mathsf{id}^* \in \mathcal{L}_{id} \vee (\mathsf{id}^*, \mu^*) \in \mathcal{L}_m$:
21 $\quad$ **return** $\bot$
22 **if** $\mathbf{z}^* > s'' \sqrt{m} \vee \mathbf{z}^* = \mathbf{0}$:
23 $\quad$ **return** $\bot$
24 $\mathbf{B} := \mathbf{A}\hat{\mathbf{R}}_{\mathsf{mpk,id^*}}, \mathbf{C} := \mathbf{A}\mathbf{R}_{\mathsf{mpk,id^*},\mu^*}$
25 $\mathbf{F}_{\mathsf{id^*},\mu^*} := [\mathbf{A} \mid \mathbf{B} \mid \mathbf{C}]$
26 **if** $\mathbf{F}_{\mathsf{id^*},\mu^*}\mathbf{z}^* \neq 0$: **return** $\bot$
27 $\mathbf{z} := [\mathbf{I}_m \mid \hat{\mathbf{R}}_{\mathsf{mpk,id^*}} \mid \mathbf{R}_{\mathsf{mpk,id^*},\mu^*}]\mathbf{z}^*$
28 **return** $\mathbf{z}$

Oracle $\mathsf{H}_1(\mathsf{mpk}, \mathsf{id})$
29 **if** $h[1, \mathsf{mpk}, \mathsf{id}] = \bot$:
30 $\quad \hat{\mathbf{R}}_{\mathsf{mpk,id}} \leftarrow D_{\mathbb{Z},\tilde{s}}^{m \times n \lceil \log q \rceil}$
31 $\quad h[1, \mathsf{mpk}, \mathsf{id}] := \mathbf{A}\hat{\mathbf{R}}_{\mathsf{mpk,id}}$
32 **return** $h[1, \mathsf{mpk}, \mathsf{id}]$

Oracle $\mathsf{H}_2(\mathsf{mpk}, \mathsf{id}, \mu)$
33 **if** $h[2, \mathsf{mpk}, \mathsf{id}, \mu] = \bot$:
34 $\quad \mathbf{R}_{\mathsf{mpk,id},\mu} \leftarrow D_{\mathbb{Z},\tilde{s}}^{m \times n \lceil \log q \rceil}$
35 $\quad h[2, \mathsf{mpk}, \mathsf{id}, \mu] := \mathbf{A}\mathbf{R}_{\mathsf{mpk,id},\mu}$
36 **return** $h[2, \mathsf{mpk}, \mathsf{id}, \mu]$

Fig. 7. Reduction $\mathcal{B}$, solving the SIS problem using an adversary $\mathcal{A}$ against the UF-naCMA security of IBS$_{\mathsf{SIS}}$.

Note that the running time of the reduction is dominated by running $\mathcal{A}$. Let us now look at the details and show that the simulation is perfect (up to negligible statistical distance) and that $\mathbf{z}$ has the correct length and is not zero. As $s, \tilde{s} > \omega(\sqrt{\log m})$ and $m \geq 2n \log q$, Lemma 2 shows that $\mathbf{AR}$ is statistically close to uniform for $\mathbf{A} \xleftarrow{\$} \mathbb{Z}_q^{n \times m}$ and $\mathbf{R} \leftarrow D_{\mathbb{Z},\kappa}^{m \times n \lceil \log q \rceil}$ for $\kappa \in \{s, \tilde{s}\}$, hence the simulation of H_1 and H_2 is statistically close to the real game. Next, the distribution of the secret keys $\mathsf{sk}_{\mathsf{id}} = \hat{\mathbf{R}}_{\mathsf{mpk,id}}$ is statistically close to the real game, which can be obtained by applying the properties of $\mathsf{DelTrap}$ from Lemma 5. Further, $\mathbf{R}_{\mathsf{mpk,id},\mu}$ is a trapdoor for $[\mathbf{A} \mid \mathbf{AR}_{\mathsf{mpk,id},\mu} + \mathbf{G}]$, which is a prefix of $\mathbf{F}'_{\mathsf{id},\mu}$ (as defined in Fig. 7) and thus the signature output by $\mathcal{B}$ are statistically close to $D_{\Lambda_q^\perp(\mathbf{F}_{\mathsf{id},\mu}),s''}$, as honest signatures are. It remains to show that $\mathbf{z}$ is a suitable solution for SIS: To see that $\mathbf{z}$ is not zero, write $\mathbf{z}^* = [\mathbf{z}_1^* \mid \mathbf{z}_2^*]^t$ where $\mathbf{z}_1^* \in \mathbb{Z}_q^m, \mathbf{z}_2^* \in \mathbb{Z}_q^{2n \lceil \log q \rceil}$ and note that

$$\mathbf{z} = \mathbf{z}_1^* + [\hat{\mathbf{R}}_{\mathsf{mpk,id^*}} \mid \mathbf{R}_{\mathsf{mpk,id^*},\mu^*}]\mathbf{z}_2^*.$$

Now, if $\mathbf{z}_2^* = 0$, then $\mathbf{z} \neq 0$ as $\mathbf{z}_1^* \neq 0$. Otherwise there is some non-zero component $z_{2,j}^* \neq 0, j \in [2n\lceil\log q\rceil]$. Denote the columns of $[\hat{\mathbf{R}}_{\mathsf{mpk},\mathsf{id}^*} \mid \mathbf{R}_{\mathsf{mpk},\mathsf{id}^*,\mu^*}]$ by $\mathbf{r}_i \in \mathbb{Z}_q^m, i \in [2n\lceil\log q\rceil]$. Then $\mathbf{z} = 0$ implies that

$$-\frac{1}{z_{2,j}^*}(\mathbf{z}_1^* + \sum_{i \neq j} z_{2,i}^* \mathbf{r}_i) = \mathbf{r}_j.$$

Further, note that the only information about $\mathbf{r}_j$ that $\mathcal{A}$ gets is a column of the hash value $\mathsf{H}_1(\mathsf{mpk}, \mathsf{id}^*) = \mathbf{A}\hat{\mathbf{R}}_{\mathsf{mpk},\mathsf{id}^*}$ (if $j \leq n\lceil\log q\rceil$) or $\mathsf{H}_2(\mathsf{mpk}, \mathsf{id}^*, \mu^*) = \mathbf{A}\mathbf{R}_{\mathsf{mpk},\mathsf{id}^*,\mu^*}$ (otherwise). Let $\mathbf{u}$ denote that column. Then from $\mathcal{A}$'s view, $\mathbf{r}_j$ is distributed as $D_{\Lambda_\mathbf{u}^\perp(\mathbf{A}),\tilde{s}}$. This distribution has a large min-entropy (with overwhelming probability over $\mathbf{A} \overset{\$}{\leftarrow} \mathbb{Z}_q^{n \times m}$) by Lemma 4, and hence the probability that $\mathbf{z} = 0$ is negligible. Finally, by Lemma 1 we have that $s_1(\hat{\mathbf{R}}_{\mathsf{mpk},\mathsf{id}^*}), s_1(\mathbf{R}_{\mathsf{mpk},\mathsf{id}^*,\mu^*}) \leq C_0 \cdot \tilde{s} \cdot (\sqrt{m} + \sqrt{n\lceil\log q\rceil})$ with overwhelming probability. Hence

$$\|\mathbf{z}\| \leq \|\mathbf{z}_1^*\| + \|[\hat{\mathbf{R}}_{\mathsf{mpk},\mathsf{id}^*} \mid \mathbf{R}_{\mathsf{mpk},\mathsf{id}^*,\mu^*}]\mathbf{z}_2^*\|$$
$$\leq (1 + 2C_0\tilde{s}(\sqrt{m} + \sqrt{n\lceil\log q\rceil}))s''\sqrt{m + 2n\lceil\log q\rceil} \leq \beta,$$

which finishes the proof. $\square$

Let us note the key and signature sizes (in bits) of our (non-adaptive) scheme :

$$|\mathsf{mpk}| = n \cdot m \cdot \lceil\log(q)\rceil, \qquad |\mathsf{msk}| = (m - n\lceil\log(q)\rceil) \cdot n \cdot \lceil\log(q)\rceil^2,$$
$$|\mathsf{sk}_{\mathsf{id}}| = m \cdot n \cdot \lceil\log(q)\rceil^2, \qquad |\sigma| = (m + 2 \cdot n \cdot \lceil\log(q)\rceil) \cdot \lceil\log(q)\rceil.$$

In order to get concrete parameters, we can use an estimation that in every delegation, it is enough (up to constants) that the gaussian width multiplies with $\sqrt{m} \cdot \omega(\sqrt{\log m})$. For the worst-case to average-case reductions [22,42] to work, we need to choose $q \geq \beta \cdot \mathsf{poly}(n)$, where $\mathsf{poly}(n)$ can grow roughly as $\sqrt{n}$. One obtains that the following example instantiation satisfies all our conditions for large enough n and $n^4 \leq q \leq n^5$ prime:

$$m := 3n\log q, \qquad\qquad s_0 := \tilde{s} := \omega(\sqrt{\log m}),$$
$$s := \hat{C} \cdot m^{1/2} \cdot \omega(\sqrt{\log m})^2, \qquad s' := \hat{C}^2 \cdot m \cdot \omega(\sqrt{\log m})^3,$$
$$s'' := \hat{C}^3 \cdot m^{3/2} \cdot \omega(\sqrt{\log m})^4, \qquad \beta := \tilde{C} \cdot n^{5/2} \cdot \log(n)^{5/2} \cdot \omega(\sqrt{\log m})^5.$$

where $\hat{C} := 4C_0C_1$ and $\tilde{C} := 48 \cdot 3^{3/2} \cdot 5^{5/2} \cdot \hat{C}^3 C_0$ are constants chosen such that the estimation is correct.

References

1. Abdalla, M., Fouque, P.-A., Lyubashevsky, V., Tibouchi, M.: Tightly-secure signatures from lossy identification schemes. In: Pointcheval, D., Johansson, T. (eds.) EUROCRYPT 2012. LNCS, vol. 7237, pp. 572–590. Springer, Heidelberg (2012). https://doi.org/10.1007/978-3-642-29011-4_34

2. Ajtai, M.: Generating hard instances of lattice problems (extended abstract). In: 28th ACM STOC, pp. 99–108. ACM Press, May 1996
3. Bader, C., Hofheinz, D., Jager, T., Kiltz, E., Li, Y.: Tightly-secure authenticated key exchange. In: Dodis, Y., Nielsen, J.B. (eds.) TCC 2015, Part I. LNCS, vol. 9014, pp. 629–658. Springer, Heidelberg (2015). https://doi.org/10.1007/978-3-662-46494-6_26
4. Banerjee, A., Peikert, C., Rosen, A.: Pseudorandom functions and lattices. In: Pointcheval, D., Johansson, T. (eds.) EUROCRYPT 2012. LNCS, vol. 7237, pp. 719–737. Springer, Heidelberg (2012). https://doi.org/10.1007/978-3-642-29011-4_42
5. Bellare, M., Boldyreva, A., Micali, S.: Public-key encryption in a multi-user setting: security proofs and improvements. In: Preneel, B. (ed.) EUROCRYPT 2000. LNCS, vol. 1807, pp. 259–274. Springer, Heidelberg (2000). https://doi.org/10.1007/3-540-45539-6_18
6. Bellare, M., Namprempre, C., Neven, G.: Security proofs for identity-based identification and signature schemes. In: Cachin, C., Camenisch, J.L. (eds.) EUROCRYPT 2004. LNCS, vol. 3027, pp. 268–286. Springer, Heidelberg (2004). https://doi.org/10.1007/978-3-540-24676-3_17
7. Bellare, M., Ristenpart, T.: Simulation without the artificial abort: simplified proof and improved concrete security for Waters' IBE scheme. In: Joux, A. (ed.) EUROCRYPT 2009. LNCS, vol. 5479, pp. 407–424. Springer, Heidelberg (Apr (2009)
8. Blazy, O., Kakvi, S.A., Kiltz, E., Pan, J.: Tightly-secure signatures from chameleon hash functions. In: Katz, J. (ed.) PKC 2015. LNCS, vol. 9020, pp. 256–279. Springer, Heidelberg (2015). https://doi.org/10.1007/978-3-662-46447-2_12
9. Blazy, O., Kiltz, E., Pan, J.: (Hierarchical) identity-based encryption from affine message authentication. In: Garay, J.A., Gennaro, R. (eds.) CRYPTO 2014, Part I. LNCS, vol. 8616, pp. 408–425. Springer, Heidelberg (2014). https://doi.org/10.1007/978-3-662-44371-2_23
10. Boyen, X., Li, Q.: Towards tightly secure lattice short signature and Id-based encryption. In: Cheon, J.H., Takagi, T. (eds.) ASIACRYPT 2016, Part II. LNCS, vol. 10032, pp. 404–434. Springer, Heidelberg (2016). https://doi.org/10.1007/978-3-662-53890-6_14
11. Cash, D., Hofheinz, D., Kiltz, E., Peikert, C.: Bonsai trees, or how to delegate a lattice basis. In: Gilbert, H. (ed.) EUROCRYPT 2010. LNCS, vol. 6110, pp. 523–552. Springer, Heidelberg (2010). https://doi.org/10.1007/978-3-642-13190-5_27
12. Chen, J., Wee, H.: Fully, (Almost) tightly secure IBE and dual system groups. In: Canetti, R., Garay, J.A. (eds.) CRYPTO 2013, Part II. LNCS, vol. 8043, pp. 435–460. Springer, Heidelberg (2013). https://doi.org/10.1007/978-3-642-40084-1_25
13. Cramer, R., Damgård, I., Schoenmakers, B.: Proofs of partial knowledge and simplified design of witness hiding protocols. In: Desmedt, Y.G. (ed.) CRYPTO 1994. LNCS, vol. 839, pp. 174–187. Springer, Heidelberg (1994). https://doi.org/10.1007/3-540-48658-5_19
14. del Pino, R., Lyubashevsky, V., Neven, G., Seiler, G.: Practical quantum-safe voting from lattices. In: Thuraisingham, B.M., Evans, D., Malkin, T., Xu, D. (eds.) ACM CCS 2017, pp. 1565–1581. ACM Press, October/November 2017
15. Diemert, D., Gellert, K., Jager, T., Lyu, L.: More efficient digital signatures with tight multi-user security. In: Garay, J.A. (ed.) PKC 2021. LNCS, vol. 12711, pp. 1–31. Springer, Cham (2021). https://doi.org/10.1007/978-3-030-75248-4_1

16. Dodis, Y., Katz, J., Xu, S., Yung, M.: Strong key-insulated signature schemes. In: Desmedt, Y.G. (ed.) PKC 2003. LNCS, vol. 2567, pp. 130–144. Springer, Heidelberg (2003). https://doi.org/10.1007/3-540-36288-6_10
17. Ducas, L., Lepoint, T., Lyubashevsky, V., Schwabe, P., Seiler, G., Stehle, D.: CRYSTALS - Dilithium: Digital signatures from module lattices. Cryptology ePrint Archive, Report 2017/633 (2017). http://eprint.iacr.org/2017/633
18. Fouque, P.A., et al.: Falcon: Fast-Fourier lattice-based compact signatures over NTRU. Submission to the NIST's Post-Quantum Cryptography Standardization Process **36** (2018)
19. Gay, R., Hofheinz, D., Kohl, L.: Kurosawa-Desmedt meets tight security. In: Katz, J., Shacham, H. (eds.) CRYPTO 2017, Part III. LNCS, vol. 10403, pp. 133–160. Springer, Cham (2017). https://doi.org/10.1007/978-3-319-63697-9_5
20. Gay, R., Hofheinz, D., Kohl, L., Pan, J.: More efficient (Almost) tightly secure structure-preserving signatures. In: Nielsen, J.B., Rijmen, V. (eds.) EUROCRYPT 2018, Part II. LNCS, vol. 10821, pp. 230–258. Springer, Cham (2018). https://doi.org/10.1007/978-3-319-78375-8_8
21. Gentry, C., Peikert, C., Vaikuntanathan, V.: Trapdoors for hard lattices and new cryptographic constructions. Cryptology ePrint Archive, Report 2007/432 (2007). http://eprint.iacr.org/2007/432
22. Gentry, C., Peikert, C., Vaikuntanathan, V.: Trapdoors for hard lattices and new cryptographic constructions. In: Ladner, R.E., Dwork, C. (eds.) 40th ACM STOC, pp. 197–206. ACM Press, May 2008
23. Gentry, C., Silverberg, A.: Hierarchical ID-based cryptography. In: Zheng, Y. (ed.) ASIACRYPT 2002. LNCS, vol. 2501, pp. 548–566. Springer, Heidelberg (2002). https://doi.org/10.1007/3-540-36178-2_34
24. Gjøsteen, K., Jager, T.: Practical and tightly-secure digital signatures and authenticated key exchange. In: Shacham, H., Boldyreva, A. (eds.) CRYPTO 2018, Part II. LNCS, vol. 10992, pp. 95–125. Springer, Cham (2018). https://doi.org/10.1007/978-3-319-96881-0_4
25. Goh, E.J., Jarecki, S., Katz, J., Wang, N.: Efficient signature schemes with tight reductions to the Diffie-Hellman problems. J. Cryptol. **20**(4), 493–514 (2007)
26. Goldwasser, S., Micali, S., Rivest, R.L.: A digital signature scheme secure against adaptive chosen-message attacks. SIAM J. Comput. **17**(2), 281–308 (1988)
27. Groth, J., Sahai, A.: Efficient non-interactive proof systems for bilinear groups. In: Smart, N. (ed.) EUROCRYPT 2008. LNCS, vol. 4965, pp. 415–432. Springer, Heidelberg (2008). https://doi.org/10.1007/978-3-540-78967-3_24
28. Hofheinz, D.: Algebraic partitioning: fully compact and (almost) tightly secure cryptography. In: Kushilevitz, E., Malkin, T. (eds.) TCC 2016, Part I. LNCS, vol. 9562, pp. 251–281. Springer, Heidelberg (2016). https://doi.org/10.1007/978-3-662-49096-9_11
29. Hofheinz, D., Jager, T.: Tightly secure signatures and public-key encryption. In: Safavi-Naini, R., Canetti, R. (eds.) CRYPTO 2012. LNCS, vol. 7417, pp. 590–607. Springer, Heidelberg (2012). https://doi.org/10.1007/978-3-642-32009-5_35
30. Jager, T., Kurek, R., Pan, J.: Simple and more efficient PRFs with tight security from LWE and matrix-DDH. In: Peyrin, T., Galbraith, S. (eds.) ASIACRYPT 2018, Part III. LNCS, vol. 11274, pp. 490–518. Springer, Cham (2018). https://doi.org/10.1007/978-3-030-03332-3_18
31. Katsumata, S., Yamada, S., Yamakawa, T.: Tighter security proofs for GPV-IBE in the quantum random oracle model. In: Peyrin, T., Galbraith, S. (eds.) ASIACRYPT 2018, Part II. LNCS, vol. 11273, pp. 253–282. Springer, Cham (2018). https://doi.org/10.1007/978-3-030-03329-3_9

32. Kiltz, E., Neven, G.: Identity-based signatures. In: Joye, M., Neven, G. (eds.) Identity-Based Cryptography. IOS Press (2009)
33. Kim, S.: Key-homomorphic pseudorandom functions from LWE with small modulus. In: Canteaut, A., Ishai, Y. (eds.) EUROCRYPT 2020, Part II. LNCS, vol. 12106, pp. 576–607. Springer, Cham (2020). https://doi.org/10.1007/978-3-030-45724-2_20
34. Krawczyk, H., Rabin, T.: Chameleon signatures. In: NDSS 2000. The Internet Society, February 2000
35. Langrehr, R., Pan, J.: Tightly secure hierarchical identity-based encryption. In: Lin, D., Sako, K. (eds.) PKC 2019, Part I. LNCS, vol. 11442, pp. 436–465. Springer, Cham (2019). https://doi.org/10.1007/978-3-030-17253-4_15
36. Langrehr, R., Pan, J.: Hierarchical identity-based encryption with tight multi-challenge security. In: Kiayias, A., Kohlweiss, M., Wallden, P., Zikas, V. (eds.) PKC 2020, Part I. LNCS, vol. 12110, pp. 153–183. Springer, Cham (2020). https://doi.org/10.1007/978-3-030-45374-9_6
37. Langrehr, R., Pan, J.: Unbounded HIBE with tight security. In: Moriai, S., Wang, H. (eds.) ASIACRYPT 2020, Part II. LNCS, vol. 12492, pp. 129–159. Springer, Cham (2020). https://doi.org/10.1007/978-3-030-64834-3_5
38. Lee, Y., Park, J.H., Lee, K., Lee, D.H.: Tight security for the generic construction of identity-based signature (in the multi-instance setting). Theor. Comput. Sci. **847**, 122–133 (2020). https://www.sciencedirect.com/science/article/pii/S0304397520305557
39. Lyubashevsky, V.: Lattice signatures without trapdoors. In: Pointcheval, D., Johansson, T. (eds.) EUROCRYPT 2012. LNCS, vol. 7237, pp. 738–755. Springer, Heidelberg (2012). https://doi.org/10.1007/978-3-642-29011-4_43
40. Micciancio, D., Peikert, C.: Trapdoors for lattices: simpler, tighter, faster, smaller. Cryptology ePrint Archive, Report 2011/501 (2011). http://eprint.iacr.org/2011/501
41. Micciancio, D., Peikert, C.: Trapdoors for lattices: simpler, tighter, faster, smaller. In: Pointcheval, D., Johansson, T. (eds.) EUROCRYPT 2012. LNCS, vol. 7237, pp. 700–718. Springer, Heidelberg (2012). https://doi.org/10.1007/978-3-642-29011-4_41
42. Micciancio, D., Regev, O.: Worst-case to average-case reductions based on Gaussian measures. In: 45th FOCS, pp. 372–381. IEEE Computer Society Press, October 2004
43. Regev, O.: On lattices, learning with errors, random linear codes, and cryptography. In: Gabow, H.N., Fagin, R. (eds.) 37th ACM STOC, pp. 84–93. ACM Press, May 2005
44. Shamir, A.: Identity-based cryptosystems and signature schemes. In: Blakley, G.R., Chaum, D. (eds.) CRYPTO 1984. LNCS, vol. 196, pp. 47–53. Springer, Heidelberg (1985). https://doi.org/10.1007/3-540-39568-7_5
45. Zhang, X., Liu, S., Gu, D., Liu, J.K.: A generic construction of tightly secure signatures in the multi-user setting. Theor. Comput. Sci. **775**, 32–52 (2019). https://www.sciencedirect.com/science/article/pii/S0304397518307333

On Removing Rejection Conditions in Practical Lattice-Based Signatures

Rouzbeh Behnia[1], Yilei Chen[2], and Daniel Masny[3(✉)]

[1] University of South Florida, Tampa, USA
[2] Tsinghua University, Beijing, China
[3] Visa Research, Palo Alto, USA
daniel.masny@rub.de

Abstract. Digital signatures following the methodology of "Fiat-Shamir with Aborts", proposed by Lyubashevsky, are capable of achieving the smallest public-key and signature sizes among all the existing lattice signature schemes based on the hardness of the Ring-SIS and Ring-LWE problems. Since its introduction, several variants and optimizations have been proposed, and two of them (i.e., Dilithium and qTESLA) entered the second round of the NIST post-quantum cryptography standardization. This method of designing signatures relies on rejection sampling during the signing process. Rejection sampling is crucial for ensuring both the correctness and security of these signature schemes.

In this paper, we investigate the possibility of removing the two rejection conditions used both in Dilithium and qTESLA. First, we show that removing one of the rejection conditions is possible, and provide a variant of Lyubashevsky's signature with comparable parameters with Dilithium and qTESLA. Second, we give evidence on the difficulty of removing the other rejection condition, by showing that two very general approaches do not yield a signature scheme with correctness or security.

1 Introduction

The emergence of quantum computers has made the development of signatures with post-quantum security a necessity. A promising source of post-quantum hardness is computational intractability assumptions on lattices. Common assumptions are the hardness of learning with errors (LWE) problem, and the short integer solution (SIS) problem, which are both related to solving the shortest vector problem in a lattice [1,28].

The origin of lattice-based signatures can be traced back to the proposal of Goldreich et al. [18] and the NTRU signature scheme [21]. They use the "trapdoor approach". Namely, they let the public verification key and the secret signing key (the trapdoor) be a "bad" basis and a "good" basis of a lattice, respectively. However, the initial schemes were broken since signatures leaked information about the secret "good" basis. By obtaining sufficiently many signatures, the secret "good" basis could be completely recovered [17,26].

Lattice signatures following the trapdoor approach were fixed by the seminal work of Gentry et al. [16]. Their trapdoor mechanism allowed to produce a

© Springer Nature Switzerland AG 2021
J. H. Cheon and J.-P. Tillich (Eds.): PQCrypto 2021, LNCS 12841, pp. 380–398, 2021.
https://doi.org/10.1007/978-3-030-81293-5_20

signature securely without leaking the signing key following the full-domain hash paradigm. When relying on the NTRU problem, this approach leads to more efficient signatures. However, this approach has been less competitive for LWE or SIS, since it led to large key and signature sizes.

A different method for constructing digital signatures is through the Fiat-Shamir [14] transformation. This technique uses a random oracle to transform an interactive identification protocol to a digital signature, which is non-interactive. The challenge of constructing a lattice based identification protocol is that the security of LWE and SIS inherently rely on the fact that a solution does not only need to have a particular algebraic structure, but it also needs to be small. Finding a large solution is easy for a SIS instance as well as in case of an LWE instance when the noise term is treated as a part of the solution. This is a significant difference compared to the realm of cyclic groups and the discrete logarithm assumption, where efficient identification protocols exist, e.g., the Schnorr identification protocol [29].

A key principle of the Schnorr identification protocol is to rerandomize a discrete logarithm problem instance and expose the rerandomized solution as an evidence of authenticity, or in case of a digital signature, as a signature. This can be efficiently done using a uniform masking term. Unfortunately, this does not translate to the lattice realm, since the verification mechanism that checks the validity of a signature needs to ensure that a solution is small. A uniform masking term would make the signature large, hence, one would need to use a small masking term, which when applied in a straightforward fashion, would expose parts of the secret key.

In his paper "Fiat-Shamir with Aborts", Lyubashevsky [23] has overcome this obstacle. One of his key findings is the idea of aborting, in case information of the secret key is leaked. This process of rejection and resampling, i.e. rejection sampling, helps to ensure correctness and security and has led to a fruitful line of signature schemes based on the LWE and SIS problems [4,5,12,13,19,22,24].

Nevertheless, this does not lead to a smooth adaptation of signatures with additional properties, such as blind signatures [7], multi signatures [6] and threshold signatures [8,9]. Moreover, there is a concern of potential side-channel attacks. Countermeasures for such attacks have been studied [25]. Nevertheless, providing less attack surface to such attacks would be preferable.

While rejection sampling has provided a solution for efficient constructing lattice based signatures, it constitutes at the same time an obstacle. Rejection based lattice signatures have in common that their rejection mechanism achieves integrity and security by ensuring two rejection conditions. The focus of this work is to investigate the necessity of these two rejection conditions for Fiat-Shamir based lattice signatures. The question we want to answer is:

How crucial are the two rejection conditions for efficiency when applying the "Fiat-Shamir" paradigm to lattices?

1.1   Contributions

We show both positive and negative results on removing the rejection conditions in Fiat-Shamir based lattice signatures. Out of the two rejection conditions used both in Dilithium and qTESLA, we show that removing one of the rejection conditions is possible. As a result, we provide a variant of Lyubashevsky's signature with one rejection condition.

The variant of Fiat-Shamir based lattice signature we propose can be instantiated with comparable parameters with Dilithium and qTESLA in terms of security, public-key and signature sizes, and rejection rate. The key difference to the previous schemes is that the secret key and masking terms are sampled uniformly random over the base ring.

The remaining rejection condition in our signature scheme is used to ensure that the first message (the commitment of the masking term) in the 3 round lattice-based ID protocol can be recovered from the rest of the transactions. We show that this rejection conditions is unlikely to be removed when the scheme uses a polynomially large modulus. First, we adopt a recent result by Guo et al. [20], which states that there is no non-interactive reconciliation mechanism for lattice based key exchange protocols [11,27]. In our case this translates to the fact that there is no reconciliation mechanism without taking additional hints about the first message. We then take a step further and consider reconciliation mechanisms that takes hints. Indeed, the reconciliation mechanisms with hints used in lattice based key exchange protocols [11,27] can be adopted in our signature scheme to remove the rejection condition and provide correctness. Unfortunately both reconciliations mechanisms are not reusable under the same initial key exchange messages [10,15] which could be considered as a public key. Since a signature scheme needs to allow polynomially many signatures per public key, both reconciliation mechanisms are not sufficient for our purposes. Even further, we show an attack against a wide ranged class of potential reconciliation mechanisms.

1.2   Technical Overview

Let us recall the idea of "Fiat-Shamir with Aborts" from a more technical perspective. We present a simplified version of Bai and Galbraith's scheme [5] based on Lyubashevsky's "Fiat-Shamir with Aborts" paradigm [24], which is followed by Dilithium and qTESLA [4,13]. In the overview we assume the base ring is $\mathbb{Z}_q$. The final scheme is instantiated on a polynomial ring.

The public key pk consists of a uniform $\mathbf{A} \in \mathbb{Z}_q^{n \times m}$ and $\mathbf{y} \approx \mathbf{s}\mathbf{A} \mod q$, where $\mathbf{s} \in \mathbb{Z}_q^{n \times n}$ is sampled from a distribution such that the norm of $\mathbf{s}$ is small (the typical choices are uniform or Gaussian with small standard deviations). Let $\lfloor \cdot \rceil_p$ be the rounding function that drops the $\log q - \log p$ least significant bits.

To sign a message m, there are two steps to follow:

1. Sample a small $\mathbf{r} \in \mathbb{Z}_q^n$, compute $H(\lfloor \mathbf{r}^t \mathbf{A} \rceil_p, \mathsf{pk}, \mathsf{m}) = \mathbf{c}$, where $\mathbf{c}$ is a small vector in $\mathbb{Z}_q^n$.

2. Compute $\mathbf{z}^t = \mathbf{r}^t + \mathbf{c}^t \mathbf{s} \in \mathbb{Z}_q^n$, then check the following two conditions. If they are satisfied, output signature $(\mathbf{z}, \mathbf{c})$; if they are not satisfied, restart from the first line.
   (a) $\mathbf{r}^t + \mathbf{c}^t \mathbf{s}$ is sufficiently small and does not leak the secret $\mathbf{s}$.
   (b) $\lfloor \mathbf{z}^t \mathbf{A} - \mathbf{c}^t \mathbf{y} \rfloor_p = \lfloor \mathbf{r}^t \mathbf{A} \rfloor_p$.

The verification algorithm accepts a signature $(\mathbf{z}, \mathbf{c})$ if and only if $\mathbf{z}$ is sufficiently small and $H(\lfloor \mathbf{z}^t \mathbf{A} - \mathbf{c}^t \mathbf{y} \rfloor_p, \mathsf{pk}, \mathsf{m}) = \mathbf{c}$.

For the security of the scheme, it is important that $\mathbf{z}$ is small, since only then would breaking the scheme lead to solving the SIS problem. But this presents a challenge, since in addition to $\mathbf{c}^t$ and $\mathbf{z}$, $\mathbf{r}$ needs to be small too. Therefore $\mathbf{r}$ might not completely hide the sensitive term $\mathbf{c}^t \mathbf{s}$ when publishing $\mathbf{z}$. A carefully tailored rejection sampling, i.e., Step 2.(a), resolves this issue.

The second rejection, i.e., Step 2.(b), seems to be important mostly for correctness. For correctness, the verification algorithm needs to be able to recover the same $\mathbf{c}$, by hashing $\lfloor \mathbf{z}^t \mathbf{A} - \mathbf{c}^t \mathbf{y} \rfloor_p$ as the signing algorithm which hashes $\lfloor \mathbf{r}^t \mathbf{A} \rfloor_p$. This is only the case when $\lfloor \mathbf{z}^t \mathbf{A} - \mathbf{c}^t \mathbf{y} \rfloor_p = \lfloor \mathbf{r}^t \mathbf{A} \rfloor_p$. We will observe that this step is crucial for security as well.

Removing Rejection condition 2.(a). In the scheme proposed in this paper, the signing algorithm samples $\mathbf{r}$ uniformly at random from $\mathbb{Z}_q^n$, instead of sampling $\mathbf{r}$ with small norm. The signing algorithm then computes $H(\lfloor \mathbf{r}^t \mathbf{A} \rfloor_p, \mathsf{pk}, \mathsf{m}) = \mathbf{c}$, $\mathbf{z}^t = \mathbf{r}^t + \mathbf{c}^t \mathbf{s}$ and rejects if $\lfloor \mathbf{z}^t \mathbf{A} - \mathbf{c}^t \mathbf{y} \rfloor_p \neq \lfloor \mathbf{r}^t \mathbf{A} \rfloor_p$. As a result, we are able to remove Step 2.(a) in the signing algorithm. Consequently, the verification algorithm no longer checks whether $\mathbf{z}$ is small.

The security of the scheme relies on the fact that the public key is indistinguishable from uniform based on the LWE assumption and for a uniform public key. Forging a signature in our scheme is related to finding a vector $\mathbf{r} \in \mathbb{Z}_q^n$, given a uniform $\mathbf{A} \in \mathbb{Z}_q^{n \times m}$ and $\mathbf{y} \in \mathbb{Z}_p^m$ such that $\lfloor \mathbf{r}^t \mathbf{A} \rfloor_p = \mathbf{y}^t$. Depending on the choice of parameters p, q, m and n, the hardness of this problem varies from trivial, computationally hard or even statistically hard (when $\mathbf{y}$ is uniformly random). The problem of finding $\mathbf{r}$, is identical to finding $\mathbf{r}$ and a sufficiently small noise term $\mathbf{e}$, which is related to the rounding function, such that $\mathbf{r}^t \mathbf{A} + \mathbf{e}^t = \tilde{\mathbf{y}}^t$, for $\tilde{\mathbf{y}} \in \mathbb{Z}_q^m$. We therefore refer to this problem as Bounded Distance Decoding. In our actual scheme, we use a more tailored problem that we denote as Adaptive BDD (ABDD). Like BDD, ABDD can be computationally or statistical hard. Our scheme also accomplishes a tight security proof and security in the quantum random oracle model (QROM) for the reasons pointed out by Unruh [30] and Kiltz, Lyubashevsky and Schaffner [22].

Let us remark that one can also choose q to be sufficiently larger than p such that the rounding function is more likely to round away the noise term affecting $\mathbf{y}$. The probability of a rejection can be made negligibly small, when choosing a super-polynomially large modulus q. But choosing a large modulus q makes the scheme inefficient.

Evidence on the difficulty of removing rejection condition 2.(b). Compared to Rejection condition (a), Rejection condition (b) seems much harder to remove without sacrificing the efficiency of the scheme. In fact, we show two general approaches of removing Rejection condition (b) fail.

In the first approach, we consider the possibility of constructing functions g and f that map $\mathbf{r}^t\mathbf{A}$ and $\mathbf{r}^t\mathbf{A}+\hat{\mathbf{e}}^t$ for any bounded error term $\hat{\mathbf{e}}$ to the same value, i.e. $g(\mathbf{r}^t\mathbf{A}) = f(\mathbf{r}^t\mathbf{A}+\hat{\mathbf{e}}^t)$, while ensuring that $g(\mathbf{r}^t\mathbf{A})$ serves as a commitment of $\mathbf{r}$, or at least preserves high min-entropy; then we can apply the hash function on $g(\mathbf{r}^t\mathbf{A})$ instead of $\lfloor \mathbf{r}^t\mathbf{A} \rfloor_p$. However, one can show such functions g, f do not exist when the modulus q is polynomially large. The result follows by the one of Guo et al. [20], which shows a similar impossibility result for the lattice-based key exchange protocols [11,27].

In the second approach, we try to adapt the reconciliation mechanism used in lattice-based key-encapsulation mechanisms [11,27]. While the reconciliation mechanisms can be adapted in our signature scheme to provide correctness, we show that they leak information about the error term $\mathbf{e}$ in the public key. More generally, we rule out the possibility of achieving security when a string of the form of $\mathbf{r}^t\mathbf{A} + \hat{\mathbf{e}}^t$, where $\hat{\mathbf{e}}$ is bounded and independent of the challenge $\mathbf{c}$, is recovered from any potential reconciliation mechanism (no matter if the mechanism is the same from the ones in [11,27] or not).

We also discuss the generalizations and limitations of these two types of negative results.

Concrete Parameters. For the variant of Fiat-Shamir lattice-based signature scheme we propose, we give a detailed analysis of the hardness of ABDD and appropriate parameter choices in Sect. 3 and Sect. 6. Even though, we are able to remove the rejection condition on $\mathbf{z}$ being small, the larger dimension m causes a significant loss of efficiency compared to Dilithium and qTESLA in the random oracle model (ROM). When considering tight security reductions, i.e. when ABDD is statistically hard, the efficiency, security and rejection rate are comparable to those of Dilithium-QROM and qTESLA-provable, for carefully chosen parameters. We give concrete parameter choices for our scheme and a comparison to Dilithium and qTESLA in Sect. 6.

2   Preliminaries

Notations. We use κ to denote the security parameter and $v \xleftarrow{\$} S$ for a uniformly random variable v over set S. $\approx_s$ and $\approx_c$ denote statistically close and computationally indistinguishable, respectively. For $i \in \mathbb{N}$, we use $[i]$ to denote $\{1,\ldots,i\}$. For a modulus $q \in \mathbb{N}$, we denote $\mathbb{Z}/q\mathbb{Z}$ by $\mathbb{Z}_q$ and represent $\mathbb{Z}_q$ by $[-\lfloor\frac{q}{2}\rfloor, \lfloor\frac{q-1}{2}\rfloor]$. Vectors are written as a bold lower-case letter (e.g. $\mathbf{v}$) and its ith component is v_i. A matrix is written as a bold capital letter (e.g. $\mathbf{A}$) and its ith column vector is $\mathbf{a}_i$. The ℓ_p-norm is $\|\mathbf{v}\|_p := (\sum v_i^p)^{1/p}$ and the infinity norm is $\|\mathbf{v}\|_\infty := \max_i\{|v_i|\}$. The length of a matrix is the norm of its longest column: $\|\mathbf{A}\|_p := \max_i \|\mathbf{a}_i\|_p$. For a random variable X, $H_\infty(X) := -\log(\max_x \Pr[X = x])$ is the min-entropy.

Standard Definitions. We use the standard definitions of lattices, cyclotomic rings, coefficient embeddings, LWE and module LWE. We refer to the full version of the paper.

3   Adaptive Bounded Distance Decoding

The security of our signature scheme requires the hardness of the adaptive bounded distance decoding problem, defined as follows.

Definition 1 (Bounded Distance Decoding (BDD)). *Let $q, l, k \in \mathbb{N}$ and ring R. Bounded distance decoding for a tolerance set $\mathcal{B} \subset R_q$, and dimension l is (t, ϵ)-hard if for any ppt algorithm $\mathcal{A}$ with running time t*

$$\Pr \left[\begin{array}{c} \exists \mathbf{e} \in \mathcal{B}^k \ s.t. \\ \mathbf{y}^t - \mathbf{z}^t \mathbf{A} = \mathbf{e}^t \end{array} \middle| \begin{array}{c} \mathbf{A} \xleftarrow{\$} R_q^{l \times k}, \mathbf{y} \xleftarrow{\$} R_q^k \\ \mathbf{z} \leftarrow \mathcal{A}(\mathbf{A}, \mathbf{y}) \end{array} \right] \leq \epsilon.$$

Definition 2 (Adaptive Bounded Distance Decoding (ABDD)). *Let $p, q, l, k \in \mathbb{N}$ and ring R. Adaptive bounded distance decoding for dimension l and challenge set $\mathcal{C} \subset R$ is (t, ϵ)-hard if for any ppt algorithm $\mathcal{A}$ with running time t*

$$\Pr \left[\mathbf{w}^t = \lfloor \mathbf{z}^t \mathbf{A} - c\mathbf{y}^t \rfloor_p \middle| \begin{array}{c} \mathbf{A} \xleftarrow{\$} R_q^{l \times k}, \mathbf{y} \xleftarrow{\$} R_q^k \\ (\mathbf{w}, \mathsf{st}) \leftarrow \mathcal{A}(\mathbf{A}, \mathbf{y}) \\ c \xleftarrow{\$} \mathcal{C} \\ \mathbf{z} \leftarrow \mathcal{A}(c, \mathsf{st}) \end{array} \right] \leq \epsilon,$$

where st *is a state of algorithm* $\mathcal{A}$.

For some parameter choices, the BDD and ABDD problems are statistically hard, meaning that with overwhelming probability, the problems are hard even for computationally unbounded adversaries. For some other parameter choices, the BDD and ABDD problems are conjectured to be computationally hard.

In both the computational and the statistical parameter regimes, we can reduce bounded distance decoding by a simple rewinding argument to adaptive bounded distance decoding. For the lemmas and proofs, we refer to the full version of this paper.

4   Proposed Scheme

In our scheme, we choose a random oracle-like hash function $H : R_p^k \times R_q^{l \times k} \times R_q^k \times \mathsf{M} \to \mathcal{C}$, that hashes a rounded vector of ring elements, the public key and a message to our challenge set $\mathcal{C}$. Further, we define a set Good that is used to determine whether a signature is safe to publish, i.e. the acceptance condition, as well as whether it satisfies correctness. We choose b_e such that $\|c\mathbf{e}\|_\infty \leq b_e$ with overwhelming probability over the choice of $\mathbf{e} \leftarrow \chi^k$ and $c \xleftarrow{\$} \mathcal{C}$.

Definition 3 (Rejection Condition, Set Good**).** *Let h denote the coefficient embedding. For parameters $p, q, d, k, b_e \in \mathbb{N}$, $q > p$ and ring $R := \mathbb{Z}[x]/(x^d + 1)$, we define the set* Good $\subset R_q^k$ *as follows.* $(h_i(x))_{i \in [k]} \in R_q^k$, *if for all $j \in [k], i \in [d]$,*

$$h_{j,i} \in \mathbb{Z}_q \setminus \bigcup_{\ell=-\lfloor p/2 \rfloor}^{\lfloor p/2 \rfloor} \left[-b_e + \left\lfloor \frac{\ell q}{p} \right\rfloor, b_e + \left\lfloor \frac{\ell q}{p} \right\rfloor \right].$$

In Fig. 1, we depict our scheme. The key generation algorithm samples the secret $\mathbf{s}$ from a uniform distribution and the error $\mathbf{e}$ from the noise distribution χ. To sign a message $\mathsf{m} \in \mathsf{M}$, we first sample a one-time masking term $\mathbf{r}$ from uniform from the same domain as the secret key, and compute $c := H(\lfloor \mathbf{r}^t \mathbf{A} \rfloor_p, \mathsf{pk}, \mathsf{m})$. The process is restarted if $\mathbf{r}^t \mathbf{A} - c \mathbf{e}^t \notin$ Good. For an eligible $\mathbf{r}$, i.e., $\mathbf{r}^t \mathbf{A} - c\mathbf{e}^t \in$ Good, the signer computes $\mathbf{z} := \mathbf{r} + c\mathbf{s}$ (mod q) and outputs the signature as $\sigma := (\mathbf{z}, c)$. The verification of our scheme checks if $c = H(\lfloor \mathbf{z}^t \mathbf{A} - c\mathbf{y}^t \rfloor_p, \mathsf{pk}, \mathsf{m})$.

The condition $\mathbf{r}^t \mathbf{A} - c\mathbf{e}^t \in$ Good implies that $\lfloor \mathbf{z}^t \mathbf{A} - c\mathbf{y}^t \rfloor_p = \lfloor \mathbf{r}^t \mathbf{A} \rfloor_p$. Hence our scheme is correct. In fact, our signature scheme is perfectly correct, though during the signing process, there might be many rejections. Nevertheless, for a acceptance probability of ρ_r, the signing process is expected to terminate in time $t \propto 1/\rho_r$. More precisely, the signing process terminates with an overwhelming probability within κ/ρ_r rejections.

We give a more formal treatment of correctness in the following.

(sk, pk) $\leftarrow$ KGen(1^κ):	$\sigma \leftarrow$ Sign(sk, m):	$\{0, 1\} \leftarrow$ Verify(pk, σ, m):
$\mathbf{s} \xleftarrow{\$} R_q^l$, $\mathbf{e} \leftarrow \chi^k$,	Repeat until $\mathbf{r}^t \mathbf{A} - c\mathbf{e}^t \in$ Good	Parse $\sigma = (\mathbf{z}, c)$
$\mathbf{A} \xleftarrow{\$} R_q^{l \times k}$	$\mathbf{r}^t \xleftarrow{\$} R_q^l$,	$\mathbf{w} := \lfloor \mathbf{z}^t \mathbf{A} - c\mathbf{y}^t \rfloor_p$
$\mathbf{y}^t := \mathbf{s}^t \mathbf{A} + \mathbf{e}^t$ (mod q)	$c := H(\lfloor \mathbf{r}^t \mathbf{A} \rfloor_p, \mathsf{pk}, \mathsf{m})$	if $c = H(\mathbf{w}, \mathsf{pk}, \mathsf{m})$
sk := $\mathbf{s}$, pk := $(\mathbf{A}, \mathbf{y})$	$\mathbf{z} := \mathbf{r} + c\mathbf{s}$ (mod q)	then Return 1
Return (pk, sk)	Return $\sigma := (\mathbf{z}, c)$	else Return 0

Fig. 1. Proposed signature scheme

We show in Appendix B that the proposed scheme is correct and EU-CMA secure under the ABDD assumption in the ROM.

5 The Difficulty of Removing the Remaining Rejection Condition

5.1 Impossibility of Extracting Consistent Values from Commitments with Errors

Suppose there are functions g, f that map $\mathbf{r}^t \mathbf{A}$ and $\mathbf{r}^t \mathbf{A} + \hat{\mathbf{e}}^t$ for any bounded error term $\hat{\mathbf{e}}$ to the same value, and make sure that $g(\mathbf{r}^t \mathbf{A})$ serves as a commitment of r, or at least preserves high min-entropy; then we can apply the hash function on $g(\mathbf{r}^t\mathbf{A})$ instead of $\lfloor \mathbf{r}^t\mathbf{A} \rceil_p$.

However, when q is polynomial, no balanced functions g, f are able to guarantee that $g(\mathbf{r}^t\mathbf{A}) = f(\mathbf{r}^t\mathbf{A} + \hat{\mathbf{e}}^t)$ with probability $1 - \mathsf{negl}$. Here a boolean function is called balanced if it outputs 0 and 1 with almost the same probability over a random input from the domain. The result follows a recent result of Guo et al. [20], which shows a similar impossibility result for the lattice-based key exchange protocols [11,27].

The following corollary is implicit from [20, Theorem 1].

Corollary 1. *Let $m, q \geq 2$, χ be a symmetric distribution over $\mathbb{Z}_q$ such that for any $a \in \mathbb{Z}_q \backslash 0$, it holds that $\Pr_{x \leftarrow \chi}[ax = 0] \leq 9/10$, and $\Pr_{x \leftarrow \chi}[ax = q/2] \leq 9/10$. Consider the joint distribution of $(\mathbf{x}, \mathbf{y})$ where $\mathbf{x} \leftarrow U(\mathbb{Z}_q^m)$, $\mathbf{y} = \mathbf{x} + \mathbf{e}$ where $\mathbf{e} \leftarrow \chi^m$. Then, for any balanced function $f, g : \mathbb{Z}_q^m \to \{0, 1\}$, it holds that*

$$\Pr_{(\mathbf{x}, \mathbf{y})}[f(\mathbf{x}) = g(\mathbf{y})] \leq 1 - \Omega(1/q^2)$$

In our application, $\mathbf{x} = \mathbf{r}^t\mathbf{A} \pmod q$. $\mathbf{x}$ is uniform over R_q since $\mathbf{A}$ is sampled uniformly random over R_q.

5.2 Evidence on the Difficulty of Adapting the Reconciliation Mechanism

We also tried to adapt the reconciliation mechanism used in lattice-based key-encapsulation mechanisms [11,27]. The reconciliation mechanisms can be adapted to our signature scheme to provide correctness when removing all rejection conditions. Nevertheless, we show that they would leak information about the error term $\mathbf{e}$ in the public key. Therefore, this attempt fails for security reason.

For clarity, we present the theorem in the form where the signature scheme is instantiated over the base ring $\mathbb{Z}_q$, or we can think of it as the coeffcient embedding of the scheme over R_q. Notice that the attack runs polynomial in noise and rounding bound B. Hence if B is superpolynomial, the attack will not be efficient. But this would require a superpolynomial modulus q.

Theorem 1. *Let SGN be a signature scheme with public key $\mathbf{A} \in \mathbb{Z}_q^{n \times m}, \mathbf{Y} = \mathbf{SA} + \mathbf{E} \in \mathbb{Z}_q^{n \times m}$, based on the Fiat-Shamir transform of an identification scheme where first message contains $\mathbf{r}^t\mathbf{A} + E(\mathbf{A}, \mathbf{r}, \mathbf{S}, \mathbf{E}) \in \mathbb{Z}_q^{1 \times m}$, second message contains $\mathbf{c} \in \{0, 1\}^n$ and third message contains $\mathbf{z} = \mathbf{r} + \mathbf{cS} \in \mathbb{Z}_q^{1 \times n}$, where E is an arbitrary randomized function with range $[-B, B]^{1 \times m}$, $2B \leq q$. Then for any reconciliation function and hint that allows to recover $\mathbf{r}^t\mathbf{A} + E(\mathbf{A}, \mathbf{r}, \mathbf{S}, \mathbf{E})$, there is a key recovery attack against SGN given $3B\kappa$ signature queries and time polynomial in κ and B.*

Proof. We describe an successful attack algorithm $\mathcal{A}$ as follows. The fact $\mathbf{z}^t\mathbf{A} - \mathbf{c}^t\mathbf{Y} = \mathbf{r}^t\mathbf{A} - \mathbf{c}^t\mathbf{E}$ allows $\mathcal{A}$ to compute

$$F(\mathbf{r},\mathbf{c})_{\mathbf{A},\mathbf{S},\mathbf{E}} := \mathbf{r}^t\mathbf{A} + E(\mathbf{A},\mathbf{S},\mathbf{E},\mathbf{r}) - (\mathbf{z}^t\mathbf{A} - \mathbf{c}^t\mathbf{Y})$$

$$= E(\mathbf{A},\mathbf{S},\mathbf{E},\mathbf{r}) + \mathbf{c}^t\mathbf{E} = \begin{pmatrix} E_1(\mathbf{A},\mathbf{S},\mathbf{E},\mathbf{r}) \\ \vdots \\ E_m(\mathbf{A},\mathbf{S},\mathbf{E},\mathbf{r}) \end{pmatrix}^t + \mathbf{c}^t\mathbf{E}$$

$\mathcal{A}$ uses an estimator to estimate the mean of several random variables. To get a good estimator for the mean μ of a random variable $X \in [-B, B]$, it computes $\mu' := \frac{1}{B\kappa}\sum x_i$, where for $i \in [B\kappa]$, $x_i \leftarrow X$. By the Hoeffding bound,

$$\Pr[|\mu' - \mu| \geq \frac{1}{3}] \leq 2e^{-\frac{2}{18}\kappa}.$$

$\mathcal{A}$ picks $B\kappa$ signatures for which $c_1 = 0$ and computes an estimate of the mean $\mu_{E_1,\mathbf{c}\backslash c_1}$ of the first entry of $F(\mathbf{r},\mathbf{c})_{\mathbf{A},\mathbf{S},\mathbf{E}}$.

$$E_1(\mathbf{A},\mathbf{S},\mathbf{E},\mathbf{r}) + \sum_i c_i\mathbf{E}_{1,i} = E_1(\mathbf{A},\mathbf{S},\mathbf{E},\mathbf{r}) + \sum_{i \neq 1} c_i\mathbf{E}_{1,i}.$$

Here, we think of $\mathbf{r},\mathbf{c}$ as the source of independence in each signature sample.

It then computes an estimation of the mean $\mu_{E_1,\mathbf{c},c_1}$ of $E_1(\mathbf{A},\mathbf{S},\mathbf{E},\mathbf{r}) + \sum_i c_i\mathbf{E}_i$ for $B\kappa$ samples with $c_1 = 1$. With overwhelming probability the estimate matches the actual mean and thus $\mathcal{A}$ recovers $\mathbf{E}_{1,1}$ correctly by computing $\mathbf{E}_{1,1} = \lfloor\mu_{E_1,\mathbf{c},c_1}\rceil - \lfloor\mu_{E_1,\mathbf{c}\backslash c_1}\rceil$. It repeats this to recover the first row of $\mathbf{E}$ which allows to recover the first row of $\mathbf{S}$ as well. Repeating this for each entry allows to recover the whole secret $\mathbf{S}$. By Chernoff bound, for each $b \in \{0,1\}$ at least $B\kappa$ out of $3B\kappa$ many random signatures will correspond to challenge $\mathbf{c}_1 = b$ except negligible probability. By a union bound over all n entries of $\mathbf{c}$, this will hold for all entries of $\mathbf{c}$. Therefore, with overwhelming probability, $3B\kappa$ random signature queries are sufficient for the attack.   □

5.3   Discussions of the Possible Generalizations and Limitations

Let us conclude this section with a summary of the possible generalizations and limitations of our negative results.

For the first negative result, we are not able to rule out the possibility that the function g depends on the public matrix $\mathbf{A}$. In [20], the authors are able to rule out such a possibility for the lattice-based key exchange. The setting in the signature scheme seems to be different. In fact, given that in our setting, using reconciliation mechanisms with hints has already provide a scheme with correctness, we do not attempt to rule out the possibility of achieving correctness.

For the second negative result, we are not able to rule out the possibility of using the reconciliation mechanism when the underlying commitment, on a string $\mathbf{r}$, is not of the form of $\mathbf{r}^t\mathbf{A}$. However, changing the structure of the commitment in the first round of the ID protocol seems to require a significant change in the lattice-based commitment protocol.

Let us also remark that it is impossible to rule out a lattice-based signature scheme with polynomial modulus without rejection sampling, given the presence of the signature scheme based on lattice trapdoor [16]. But of course, this would require significant changes to our protocol or similar rejection sampling based protocols like [4,5,12,13,19,22–24].

6   Parameter and Comparison

We provide concrete parameters for the signatures in two settings. In the first setting, the parameters are set so that the adaptive bounded distance decoding problem (ABDD, cf. Definition 2) is hard even for a computationally unbounded adversary. In the second setting, the parameters are set so that the ABDD problem is computationally hard. Compared to the first setting, the second setting gives schemes with smaller public keys and less number of repetitions, while relying on one more computational assumptions.

It is reasonable to compare our first setting with Dilithium-QROM [22] and the "provable" version of qTESLA [4], since all of them set the scheme in the "lossy" mode, so that the schemes have tight security proofs from (Ring or Module)LWE in the QROM [22]; then compare our second setting with Dilithium [13], which also requires additional computational assumptions in addition to Module LWE. We do not compare with the "heuristic" version of qTESLA [4] since there are bugs in those parameter estimations, and the qTESLA team decided to drop the "heuristic" parameters in the second round of NIST PQC standardization.

Let us recall the notations. Let $R := \mathbb{Z}[x]/(x^d + 1)$, where d is a power-of-two. Let q be the bigger modulus, p be the smaller modulus after rounding. Let $b_r := \lfloor \frac{q}{p} \rfloor - 1$. When setting the concrete parameters, we assume $b_r + 1$ is a power of 2. Then rounding a number $a \in \mathbb{Z}_q$ to $\mathbb{Z}_p$ is effectively done by dropping the $\log(b_r + 1)$ least significant bits when $a \in [0, \lfloor q/2 - 1 \rfloor]$, or dropping the $\log(b_r + 1)$ least significant bits then subtracting by 1 when $a \in [-\lfloor q/2 \rfloor, 0)$. Let $\mathbf{A} \in R_q^{l \times k}$. Let $n = d \cdot l$, $m = d \cdot k$. Let $\mathcal{C} \subseteq R$ denote the space of the challenge c.

In the following, we only state our final parameter choices, for the details of how we obtained these parameter selection, we refer to the full version of this paper.

In Table 1, we provide 6 sets of concrete parameters. Parameter sets 1 and 2 follow the q, d, l, η, w, b_e values chosen in [13] and [22], then derive m, expected repetition, LWE hardness, and the rest of the parameters. The parameter sets 3 to 6 choose the q, d, l, η, w, b_e values that are more suitable for our scheme.

In Table 2, we compare the parameters of our scheme with the parameters of Dilithium-QROM and qTESLA-provable. We only list the classical security estimation since under the commonly used LWE security estimation model [2,3], schemes with 140-bit classical security are expected to have 128-bit quantum security (similarly for the higher security level). Compared to Dilithium-QROM, we achieve smaller signatures, similar rejection rates, but bigger public

Table 1. Parameters of our scheme assuming the statistical hardness of ABDD

Parameters	1	2	3	4	5	6
$\log_2 q$	23	45	30	28	27	31
d	256	512	1024	1024	1024	512
l	3	4	1	1	1	3
k	14	8	5	4	4	9
$n = d \cdot l$	768	2048	1024	1024	1024	1536
$m = d \cdot k$	3584	4096	5120	4096	4096	4608
$\eta\ (= \|\mathbf{e}\|_\infty)$	6	7	20	10	6	3
w = the weight of c	60	46	36	36	36	46
$\log_2(b_r)$	18	20	24	21	20	21
b_e	360	322	720	360	216	138
Expected repetitions	19097	12.4	1.55	4.08	5.41	1.83
LWE security	122.8	165.1	139.4	140.2	138.1	170.0
Public key size (bytes)	10336	23072	19232	14368	13856	17888
Signature size (bytes)	2247	11589	3972.5	3716.5	3588.5	6021.8

Table 2. Comparison with Dilithium-QROM and qTESLA-provable.

Parameters	Classical security	PK size	Sign size	Exp. repetitions
Dilithium-QROM standard	140	7712	5696	4.3
qTESLA-p standard	140	14880	2592	3.45*
Ours standard-I	138.1	13856	3588.5	5.41
Ours standard-II	140.2	14368	3716.5	4.08
Ours standard-III	139.4	19232	3972.5	1.55
Dilithium-QROM high	175	9632	7098	2.2
qTESLA-p high	279	38432	5664	3.84*
Ours high	170.0	17888	6021.8	1.83

*: The expected repetition numbers reported in [4] are obtained by experiments

keys, since they use an extra public-key optimization technique. Compared to qTESLA-provable, under similar rejection rates, our public key sizes are smaller, but the signature sizes are larger.

In Table 3, we provide the concrete parameters. In each of the 6 sets of parameters, the values of q, d, l, η and w follow the same choices of from Table 1. We then choose smaller values for k, so that the computational hardnesses of the ABDD problem match the hardnesses of breaking the LWE instance in the public key.

In Table 4 we compare the parameters of our scheme with the parameters of Dilithium [13]. Compared to Dilithium, the sizes of signatures and public keys of our scheme are larger. The public key is inherently larger in our scheme since m has to be larger than n for the hardness of ABDD to hold, whereas Dilithium can choose m smaller than n and base the security of the signature on the hardness

Table 3. Parameters of our scheme assuming the computational hardness of ABDD.

Parameters	1	2	3	4	5	6
$\log_2 q$	23	45	30	28	27	31
d	256	512	1024	1024	1024	512
l	3	4	1	1	1	3
k	6	5	2	2	2	5
$n = d \cdot l$	768	2048	1024	1024	1024	1536
$m = d \cdot k$	1536	2560	2048	2048	2048	2560
$\eta\ (= \|\mathbf{e}\|_\infty)$	6	7	20	10	6	3
w = the weight of c	60	46	36	36	36	46
$\log_2(b_r)$	18	20	24	21	20	20
b_e	360	322	720	360	216	138
Expected repetitions	68.3	4.82	1.19	2.02	2.33	1.96
BKZ approx factor δ	1.0053	1.0045	1.0049	1.0042	1.0041	1.0035
BKZ block-size β	258	332	290	370	388	492
ABDD hardness	103.2	126.8	115.1	138.4	142.6	173.1
LWE security	122.8	165.1	139.4	140.2	138.1	170.0
Public key size (bytes)	4448	14432	7712	7200	6944	9952
Signature size (bytes)	2247	11589	3972.5	3716.5	3588.5	6021.8

Table 4. Comparison with Dilithium.

Parameters	Classical security	PK size	Sign size	Exp. repetitions
Dilithium standard	138	1472	2701	6.6
Ours standard-I	138.4	7200	3716.5	2.02
Ours standard-II	138.1	6944	3972.5	2.33
Dilithium high	174	1760	3366	4.3
Ours high	170.0	9952	6021.8	1.96

of SIS. Even adding the public-key optimization technique from [13] is not likely to make the public key of our scheme smaller than Dilithium.

A   Standard Definitions

A.1   Digital Signatures

The following presents syntax and security definition of a digital signature scheme.

Definition 4 (Digital Signatures). *A digital signature scheme for a messages space* M *is a triplet of ppt algorithms* (KGen, Sign, Verify) *with the following syntax*

KGen: *Takes as input 1^κ and outputs a key pair* (pk, sk).
Sign: *Takes as input* sk, *a message* m $\in$ M *and outputs a signature* σ.
Verify: *Takes as input* pk, *a message* m $\in$ M, *a signature* σ *and outputs 1 if* σ *is a valid signature under* pk *for message* m. *Otherwise, it outputs 0.*

For correctness, for any m $\in$ M, *we require that* Verify(pk, m, σ) $= 1$, *where* (pk, sk) $\leftarrow$ KGen(1^κ), $\sigma \leftarrow$ Sign(sk, m).

Definition 5 (Existential Unforgeability under Chosen Message Attacks (UF-CMA) Security). *A signature scheme* SGN *is* (t, ϵ, q_S, q_H)-UF-CMA *secure (existentially unforgeable under chosen message attacks) if for all algorithms* $\mathcal{A}$ *running in time at most* t *and making at most* q_S *queries to the signing oracle and* q_H *queries to the random oracle,*

$$\Pr\left[\begin{array}{l}\text{Verify(pk, m}^*, \sigma^*) = 1 \\ \wedge \text{ m}^* \notin \{\text{m}_i \mid i \in [q_S]\}\end{array}\Bigg| \begin{array}{l}(\text{pk, sk}) \leftarrow \text{KGen}(1^\kappa) \\ (\text{m}^*, \sigma^*) \leftarrow \mathcal{A}^{\mathcal{O}_H;\text{Sign(sk},\cdot)}(\text{pk})\end{array}\right] \leq \epsilon,$$

where for $i \in [q_S]$, *on the* i-*th query* m_i *the signing oracle* Sign(sk, $\cdot$) *returns* $\sigma_i \leftarrow$ Sign(sk, m_i) *to* $\mathcal{A}$ *and* $\mathcal{O}_H$ *denotes query access to a random oracle.*

B   Correctness and Security Analysis

Lemma 1 (Correctness and Termination). *The signature scheme in Fig. 1 is perfectly correct and has a heuristic acceptance rate of*

$$\rho_r := \left(\frac{b_r - 2b_e - 1}{b_r}\right)^{dk},$$

where $b_r := \lfloor \frac{q}{p} \rfloor - 1$.

Proof. Let $(\mathbf{z}, c)$ be the output of Sign(sk, m) for m $\in$ M and (sk, pk) $\leftarrow$ KGen(1^κ). By the acceptance condition, $\mathbf{r}^t\mathbf{A} - c\mathbf{e}^t \in$ Good always holds. By the definition of set Good, the coefficient of each entry of $\mathbf{r}^t\mathbf{A} - c\mathbf{e}^t$ have a distance larger than b_e from the rounding borders (namely, $\lfloor \frac{\ell q}{p} \rfloor$ for $\ell = -\lfloor p/2 \rfloor, ..., \lfloor p/2 \rfloor$) caused by rounding function $\lfloor \cdot \rfloor_p$. Hence, $\mathbf{r}^t\mathbf{A}$ rounds to the same value as $\mathbf{r}^t\mathbf{A} - c\mathbf{e}^t$, i.e. $\lfloor \mathbf{r}^t\mathbf{A} - c\mathbf{e}^t \rfloor_p = \lfloor \mathbf{r}^t\mathbf{A} \rfloor_p$.

By the definition of $\mathbf{z}$ and public key $(\mathbf{A}, \mathbf{y})$, $\mathbf{z}^t\mathbf{A} - c\mathbf{y}^t = \mathbf{r}^t\mathbf{A} - c\mathbf{e}^t$. Further, by the definition of c, $c = H(\lfloor \mathbf{r}^t\mathbf{A} \rfloor_p, \text{pk}, \text{m})$. Thus, the verification check $c = H(\lfloor \mathbf{z}^t\mathbf{A} - c\mathbf{y}^t \rfloor_p, \text{pk}, \text{m})$ passes and Verify returns 1.

For the acceptance rate ρ_r, we need to compute the probability over $\mathbf{r} \xleftarrow{\$} R_q^\ell$ and $c \xleftarrow{\$} \mathcal{C}$ that $\mathbf{r}^t\mathbf{A} - c\mathbf{e}^t \in$ Good. With overwhelming probability, $\|c\mathbf{e}\|_\infty \leq b_e$. The probability that a random element u in $\mathbb{Z}_q$ falls in the bad region excluded in Good is

$$\Pr_{u \xleftarrow{\$} \mathbb{Z}_q}\left[u \in \bigcup_{\ell=-\lfloor p/2 \rfloor}^{\lfloor p/2 \rfloor}\left[-b_e + \left\lfloor \frac{\ell q}{p} \right\rfloor, b_e + \left\lfloor \frac{\ell q}{p} \right\rfloor\right]\right] \leq \frac{2b_e + 1}{b_r},$$

For the claimed heuristic bound in the lemma statement, we use the heuristic that the coefficients of $\mathbf{r}^t\mathbf{A} - c\mathbf{e}^t$ fall independently in the bad region.   □

In Theorem 2 below, we prove that our signature scheme is EU-CMA in the ROM.

Theorem 2. *Let LWE be* $(t_{\mathsf{LWE}}, \epsilon_{\mathsf{LWE}})$-*hard, ABDD be* $(t_{\mathsf{ABDD}}, \epsilon_{\mathsf{ABDD}})$-*hard and* $H_\infty(\lfloor \mathbf{r}^t\mathbf{A}\rfloor_p \mid \mathbf{A}) \geq \xi$. *Then, the signature scheme in Fig. 1 is* $(t_\mathcal{A}, \epsilon_\mathcal{A}, q_S, q_H)$-*UF-CMA secure in the programmable random oracle model, where* $t_\mathcal{A} \approx t_{\mathsf{LWE}} + t_{\mathsf{ABDD}}$ *and* $\epsilon_\mathcal{A} \leq \epsilon_{\mathsf{LWE}} + q_H\epsilon_{\mathsf{ABDD}} + q_S 2^{-\kappa} + \kappa^2\rho_r^{-2}q_S^2 2^{-\xi} + 2\kappa\rho_r^{-1}q_Sq_H 2^{-\xi}$.

Proof. On a high level, we prove this theorem in two hybrids. In the first hybrid, we exploit the programmability of the random oracle to respond to signature queries without knowing the secret key. This step of faithfully simulating signatures without knowing the secret key crucially relies on the rejection sampling condition.

During the second hybrid, the public key of our signature scheme is replaced with uniform randomness. In this hybrid, there will be no secret key that allows to sign messages and, furthermore, it is infeasible for an adversary who cannot program the random oracle to forge signatures.

In the following, we define the two hybrids and show that: 1) by a statistical argument, simulated signatures are identically distributed as signatures created by the signing algorithm with access to the secret key, i.e. every algorithm has the same advantage in the UF-CMA game and hybrid 1; 2) there is no algorithm that has a different advantage in hybrid 1 and hybrid 2, unless it implicitly breaks the LWE assumption; 3) there is no algorithm that can forge a signature in hybrid 2, unless it implicitly breaks the ABDD assumption.

To summarize, this proves the theorem statement. The detailed description of the hybrids and the UF-CMA game are depicted in Fig. 2.

Game:
$\mathbf{s} \xleftarrow{\$} R_q^l, \mathbf{e} \leftarrow \chi^k, \mathbf{A} \xleftarrow{\$} R_q^{l\times k}$ \UF-CMA, hybrid 1
$\mathbf{y}^t := \mathbf{s}^t\mathbf{A} + \mathbf{e}^t \pmod{q}$ \UF-CMA, hybrid 1
$\mathbf{A} \xleftarrow{\$} R_q^{l\times k}, \mathbf{y} \xleftarrow{\$} R_q^k$ \hybrid 2
$(\mathsf{m}^*, \sigma^*) \leftarrow \mathcal{A}^{\mathcal{O}_H;\mathsf{Sign}(\mathbf{s}, \cdot)}(\mathbf{A}, \mathbf{y})$ \UF-CMA
$(\mathsf{m}^*, \sigma^*) \leftarrow \mathcal{A}^{\mathcal{O}_H;\mathsf{Sign}(\cdot)}(\mathbf{A}, \mathbf{y})$ \hybrid 1, hybrid 2

$\mathcal{O}_H(a)$:
If $H(a)$ is not defined
then $H(a) \xleftarrow{\$} \mathcal{C}$
Return $H(a)$

$\sigma \leftarrow \mathsf{Sign}(\mathbf{s}, \mathsf{m})$:
Repeat until $\mathbf{r}^t\mathbf{A} - c\mathbf{e}^t \in \mathsf{Good}$
    $\mathbf{r}^t \xleftarrow{\$} R_q^l$
    $c := H(\lfloor \mathbf{r}^t\mathbf{A}\rfloor_p, (\mathbf{A}, \mathbf{y}), \mathsf{m})$
    $\mathbf{z} := \mathbf{r} + c\mathbf{s} \pmod{q}$
Return $\sigma := (\mathbf{z}, c)$

$\sigma \leftarrow \mathsf{Sign}(\mathsf{m})$:
Repeat until $\mathbf{z}^t\mathbf{A} - c\mathbf{y}^t \in \mathsf{Good}$
    $\mathbf{z} \xleftarrow{\$} R_q^l, c \xleftarrow{\$} \mathcal{C}$
    $\mathbf{w} := \lfloor \mathbf{z}^t\mathbf{A} - c\mathbf{y}^t\rfloor_p$
    $H(\mathbf{w}, (\mathbf{A}, \mathbf{y}), \mathsf{m}) := c$
Return $\sigma := (\mathbf{z}, c)$

Fig. 2. UF-CMA security game and hybrids to prove Theorem 2

We start the formal argument with showing that any adversary that is successful in the UF-CMA game is also successful in hybrid 1.

Lemma 2. *Let there be an algorithm that* (t, ϵ, q_S, q_H) *breaks the* UF-CMA *security and* $H_\infty(\lfloor \mathbf{r}^t \mathbf{A} \rfloor_p \mid \mathbf{A}) \geq \xi$. *Then, there is also an algorithm that* $(t', \epsilon', q'_S, q'_H)$ *forges a signature in hybrid 1 for* $t' \approx t$, $\epsilon' \geq \epsilon - q_S 2^{-\kappa} - \kappa^2 \rho_r^{-2} q_S^2 2^{-\xi} - 2\kappa \rho_r^{-1} q_S q_H 2^{-\xi}$, $q'_S = q_S$, *and* $q'_H = q_H$.

Proof. The difference between the UF-CMA game and hybrid 1 is how signing queries are answered. In the UF-CMA game, one first samples $\mathbf{r} \xleftarrow{\$} R_q^l$, computes $c = H(\lfloor \mathbf{r}^t \mathbf{A} \rfloor_p, \mathsf{pk}, \mathsf{m})$, rejects if $\mathbf{r}^t \mathbf{A} - c e^t \notin \mathsf{Good}$ and then computes $\mathbf{z} = \mathbf{r} + c\mathbf{s}$.

In hybrid 1, one samples first $\mathbf{z} \xleftarrow{\$} R_q^l$, $c \xleftarrow{\$} C$, rejects if $\mathbf{z}^t \mathbf{A} - c\mathbf{y}^t \notin \mathsf{Good}$ and finally programs the random oracle H on point $(\lfloor \mathbf{z}^t \mathbf{A} - c\mathbf{y}^t \rfloor_p, (\mathbf{A}, \mathbf{y}), \mathsf{m})$ to be equal to c. In the following, we show that created signatures $(\mathbf{z}, c)$ have the same distribution.

As a first intermediate step, we want to show that the generated signatures $(\mathbf{z}, c)$ before the rejection have the same distribution in game UF-CMA and hybrid 1. This can only be the case if the reprogramming step of the oracle does not fail. Except with probability $q_S 2^{-\kappa}$, there are at most κ/ρ_r many reprogrammings per signature for all signature queries. The amount of defined points of the random oracle within hybrid 1 is upper bounded by $\kappa \rho_r^{-1} q_S + q_H$. At each reprogramming step, $\lfloor \mathbf{r}^t \mathbf{A} \rfloor_p$ has at least min-entropy ξ given $\mathbf{A}$. Hence the probability that the random oracle is already defined for partial input $\lfloor \mathbf{r}^t \mathbf{A} \rfloor_p$ is at most $(\kappa \rho_r^{-1} q_S + q_H) 2^{-\xi}$. Since there are at most $\kappa \rho_r^{-1} q_S$ reprogramming steps, the probability that reprogramming the random oracle fails in hybrid 1 is upper bounded by $q_S 2^{-\kappa} + \kappa \rho_r^{-1} q_S (\kappa \rho_r^{-1} q_S + q_H) 2^{-\xi}$. For the remaining parts of the proof, we assume that the reprogramming does not fail.

The challenge c in game UF-CMA is the output of the random oracle on input $\lfloor \mathbf{r}^t \mathbf{A} \rfloor_p, (\mathbf{A}, \mathbf{y}), \mathsf{m}$ and therefore uniformly distributed. In hybrid 1, c is sampled uniformly at random and it is programmed to be the output of the oracle on input $\lfloor \mathbf{z}^t \mathbf{A} - c\mathbf{y}^t \rfloor_p, (\mathbf{A}, \mathbf{y}), \mathsf{m}$. Under the premise that $\lfloor \mathbf{z}^t \mathbf{A} - c\mathbf{y}^t \rfloor_p = \lfloor \mathbf{r}^t \mathbf{A} \rfloor_p$, c has the same distriubtion in game UF-CMA and hybrid 1.

We focus now on showing that $\mathbf{z}$ has the same distribution. In game UF-CMA, $\mathbf{z} := \mathbf{r} + c\mathbf{s}$, where $\mathbf{r} \xleftarrow{\$} R_q^l$. In hybrid 1, $\mathbf{z} \xleftarrow{\$} R_q^l$ and we can define $\mathbf{r} := \mathbf{z} - c\mathbf{s}$. Therefore in hybrid 1, $\mathbf{r}$ is also uniform and $\mathbf{z}$ is determined by $\mathbf{r}, \mathbf{s}$ and c as in UF-CMA.

It is left to show that the premise $\lfloor \mathbf{z}^t \mathbf{A} - c\mathbf{y}^t \rfloor_p = \lfloor \mathbf{r}^t \mathbf{A} \rfloor_p$ is implied by the rejection condition and that the rejection condition does not introduce any difference between the signature disitribution in game UF-CMA and hybrid 1. The latter is easy to show. $\mathbf{r}^t \mathbf{A} - ce^t \in \mathsf{Good}$ is identical with $\mathbf{z}^t \mathbf{A} - c\mathbf{y}^t \in \mathsf{Good}$, because $\mathbf{r}^t \mathbf{A} - ce^t = \mathbf{z}^t \mathbf{A} - c\mathbf{y}^t$. Obviously, we could replace the rejection condition in the orignial scheme with the publicly verifiable condition $\mathbf{z}^t \mathbf{A} - c\mathbf{y}^t \in \mathsf{Good}$ that we need in hybrid 1. The only reason against it is a slight performance gain due to the fact that $\mathbf{r}^t \mathbf{A}$ has already been computed when evaluating the random oracle.

By the same argument as used for correctness (see Lemma 1), $\mathbf{r}^t\mathbf{A} - c\mathbf{e}^t \in$ Good implies $\lfloor \mathbf{z}^t\mathbf{A} - c\mathbf{y}^t \rfloor_p = \lfloor \mathbf{r}^t\mathbf{A} \rfloor_p$. Therefore all signatures obtained by the adversary, i.e. that pass the rejection condition, have the same distribution in hybrid 1 and game UF-CMA.

All other signatures, i.e. the once that trigger the rejection condition, remain hidden and an adversary could at most observe a reprogrammed challenge. This might be a problem, because there could be a slight bias in the random oracle since the partial input $\lfloor \mathbf{z}^t\mathbf{A} - c\mathbf{y}^t \rfloor_p$ might be biased with the output c (which disappears for not rejected signatures where $\lfloor \mathbf{z}^t\mathbf{A} - c\mathbf{y}^t \rfloor_p = \lfloor \mathbf{r}^t\mathbf{A} \rfloor_p$). But in order to detect this bias, he would need to guess $\lfloor \mathbf{z}^t\mathbf{A} - c\mathbf{y}^t \rfloor_p$ which has at least min-entropy ξ for the same reason why $\lfloor \mathbf{r}^t\mathbf{A} \rfloor_p$ has at least min-entropy ξ. The ability of an adversary to detect this bias is upper bounded by $\kappa \rho_r^{-1} q_S q_H 2^{-\xi}$. $\square$

Lemma 3. *Let there be an algorithm that (t, ϵ, q_S, q_H) forges a signature in hybrid 1 and let LWE be $(t_{\mathsf{LWE}}, \epsilon_{\mathsf{LWE}})$-secure. Then, there is also an algorithm that $(t', \epsilon', q_S', q_H')$ forges a signature in hybrid 2 for $t' \approx t + t_{\mathsf{LWE}}$, $\epsilon' \geq \epsilon - \epsilon_{\mathsf{LWE}}$, $q_S' = q_S$, and $q_H' = q_H$.*

Proof. The lemma follows from a straightforward reduction to LWE. The only difference between hybrid 1 and hybrid 2 is the distribution of the public key $(\mathbf{A}, \mathbf{y})$. In hybrid 1, it is LWE distributed, while uniform in hybrid 2. If there is an algorithm that ϵ forges in hybrid 1 and ϵ' forges in hybrid 2, then LWE can be told apart from uniform with advantage $|\epsilon - \epsilon'|$, i.e. $\epsilon_{\mathsf{LWE}} \geq |\epsilon - \epsilon'|$. $\square$

Lemma 4. *Let there be an algorithm that (t, ϵ, q_S, q_H) forges a signature in hybrid 2. Then, there is also an algorithm that $(t_{\mathsf{ABDD}}, \epsilon_{\mathsf{ABDD}})$ solves ABDD for $t_{\mathsf{ABDD}} \approx t$, $\epsilon_{\mathsf{ABDD}} \geq \frac{1}{q_H}\epsilon$.*

Proof. We prove the lemma by embedding an ABDD challenge in hybrid 2 such that if an algorithm forges successfully, it solves the ABDD problem. This is straight forward. We use the ABDD challenge $(\mathbf{A}, \mathbf{y})$ as a public key in hybrid 2. We guess a random oracle query for point $(\mathbf{w}, (\mathbf{A}, \mathbf{y}), \mathsf{m}^*)$ to request a challenge c for query $\mathbf{w}^* = \mathbf{w}$ from the ABDD challenger. We program the random oracle by setting $H(\mathbf{w}, (\mathbf{A}, \mathbf{y}), \mathsf{m}^*) = c$. With a probability of $\frac{1}{q_H}$, the forgery will be for this c and message m^* thereby a valid signature $(\mathbf{z}, c)$ contains a valid ABDD solution $\mathbf{z}$. $\square$

For applicability of Theorem 2, we need to show that $\xi \leq H_\infty(\lfloor \mathbf{r}^t\mathbf{A} \rfloor_p \mid \mathbf{A})$ is sufficiently large. Technically, it would be sufficient to show that it is hard for any efficient adversary to compute $\lfloor \mathbf{r}^t\mathbf{A} \rfloor_p$, given $\mathbf{A}$. This would be sufficient, since it only needs to be hard for an efficient adversary to guess the points where the random oracle is going to be programmed during the simulation. Though, using computational intractability is not necessary.

Instead, we use a similar approach as used by Bai and Galbraith [5, Lemma 3], relying on the fact that the public key component $\mathbf{A}$ has at least one invertible ring element. Unlike [5], we do not need to rely on a Gaussian heuristic, since in our case $\mathbf{r}$ is chosen uniformly at random, which leads to a very simple analysis.

Lemma 5. *For any* $\mathbf{A} \in R_q^{l \times k}$ *with an invertible entry* $a_{i,j} \in R_q$,

$$H_\infty(\lfloor \mathbf{r}^t \mathbf{A} \rfloor_p \mid \mathbf{A}) \geq d \log p,$$

where $\lfloor \mathbf{r}^t \mathbf{A} \rfloor_p \in \mathbb{Z}_p^m$.

Proof. Since $a_{i,j}$ is invertible,

$$H_\infty(r_i a_{i,j} \mid \mathbf{A}) = H_\infty(r_i) = d \log q.$$

The rounding function causes to lose $\log(q/p)$ entropy at each of the d coefficients of $r_i \in R_q$ with respect to the coefficient embedding. ☐

References

1. Ajtai, M.: Generating hard instances of lattice problems (extended abstract). In: STOC, pp. 99–108 (1996)
2. Albrecht, M.R., et al.: Estimate all the LWE, NTRU schemes! In: Catalano, D., De Prisco, R. (eds.) SCN 2018. LNCS, vol. 11035, pp. 351–367. Springer, Cham (2018). https://doi.org/10.1007/978-3-319-98113-0_19
3. Albrecht, M.R., Player, R., Scott, S.: On the concrete hardness of learning with errors. J. Math. Cryptol. **9**(3), 169–203 (2015)
4. Alkim, E., et al.: The lattice-based digital signature scheme qtesla. IACR Cryptology ePrint Archive, vol. 85 (2019)
5. Bai, S., Galbraith, S.D.: An improved compression technique for signatures based on learning with errors. In: Benaloh, J. (ed.) CT-RSA 2014. LNCS, vol. 8366, pp. 28–47. Springer, Cham (2014). https://doi.org/10.1007/978-3-319-04852-9_2
6. Boyd, C.: Digital multisignatures. Cryptography and Coding, pp. 241–246 (1986)
7. Chaum, D.: Blind signatures for untraceable payments. In: Chaum, D., Rivest, R.L., Sherman, A.T. (eds.) Advances in Cryptology, pp. 199–203. Springer, Boston, MA (1983). https://doi.org/10.1007/978-1-4757-0602-4_18
8. Desmedt, Y.: Society and group oriented cryptography: a new concept. In: Pomerance, C. (ed.) CRYPTO 1987. LNCS, vol. 293, pp. 120–127. Springer, Heidelberg (1988). https://doi.org/10.1007/3-540-48184-2_8
9. Desmedt, Y., Frankel, Y.: Threshold cryptosystems. In: Brassard, G. (ed.) CRYPTO 1989. LNCS, vol. 435, pp. 307–315. Springer, New York (1990). https://doi.org/10.1007/0-387-34805-0_28
10. Ding, J., Fluhrer, S., Rv, S.: Complete attack on RLWE key exchange with reused keys, without signal leakage. In: Susilo, W., Yang, G. (eds.) ACISP 2018. LNCS, vol. 10946, pp. 467–486. Springer, Cham (2018). https://doi.org/10.1007/978-3-319-93638-3_27
11. Ding, J., Xie, X., Lin, X.: A simple provably secure key exchange scheme based on the learning with errors problem. Cryptology ePrint Archive, Report 2012/688 (2012)
12. Ducas, L., Durmus, A., Lepoint, T., Lyubashevsky, V.: Lattice signatures and bimodal gaussians. In: Canetti, R., Garay, J.A. (eds.) CRYPTO 2013. LNCS, vol. 8042, pp. 40–56. Springer, Heidelberg (2013). https://doi.org/10.1007/978-3-642-40041-4_3

13. Ducas, L., et al.: Crystals-dilithium: a lattice-based digital signature scheme. IACR Trans. Cryptogr. Hardw. Embed. Syst. **2018**(1), 238–268 (2018)
14. Fiat, A., Shamir, A.: How to prove yourself: practical solutions to identification and signature problems. In: Odlyzko, A.M. (ed.) CRYPTO 1986. LNCS, vol. 263, pp. 186–194. Springer, Heidelberg (1987). https://doi.org/10.1007/3-540-47721-7_12
15. Fluhrer, S.R.: Cryptanalysis of ring-LWE based key exchange with key share reuse. IACR Cryptology ePrint Arch. vol. 85 (2016)
16. Gentry, C., Peikert, C., Vaikuntanathan, V.: Trapdoors for hard lattices and new cryptographic constructions. In: STOC, pp. 197–206 (2008)
17. Gentry, C., Szydlo, M.: Cryptanalysis of the revised NTRU signature scheme. In: Knudsen, L.R. (ed.) EUROCRYPT 2002. LNCS, vol. 2332, pp. 299–320. Springer, Heidelberg (2002). https://doi.org/10.1007/3-540-46035-7_20
18. Goldreich, O., Goldwasser, S., Halevi, S.: Public-key cryptosystems from lattice reduction problems. In: Kaliski, B.S. (ed.) CRYPTO 1997. LNCS, vol. 1294, pp. 112–131. Springer, Heidelberg (1997). https://doi.org/10.1007/BFb0052231
19. Güneysu, T., Lyubashevsky, V., Pöppelmann, T.: Practical lattice-based cryptography: a signature scheme for embedded systems. In: Prouff, E., Schaumont, P. (eds.) CHES 2012. LNCS, vol. 7428, pp. 530–547. Springer, Heidelberg (2012). https://doi.org/10.1007/978-3-642-33027-8_31
20. Guo, S., Kamath, P., Rosen, A., Sotiraki, K.: Limits on the efficiency of (Ring) LWE based non-interactive key exchange. In: Kiayias, A., Kohlweiss, M., Wallden, P., Zikas, V. (eds.) PKC 2020. LNCS, vol. 12110, pp. 374–395. Springer, Cham (2020). https://doi.org/10.1007/978-3-030-45374-9_13
21. Hoffstein, J., Howgrave-Graham, N., Pipher, J., Silverman, J.H., Whyte, W.: NTRUSign: digital signatures using the NTRU lattice. In: Joye, M. (ed.) CT-RSA 2003. LNCS, vol. 2612, pp. 122–140. Springer, Heidelberg (2003). https://doi.org/10.1007/3-540-36563-X_9
22. Kiltz, E., Lyubashevsky, V., Schaffner, C.: A concrete treatment of Fiat-Shamir signatures in the quantum random-oracle model. In: Nielsen, J.B., Rijmen, V. (eds.) EUROCRYPT 2018. LNCS, vol. 10822, pp. 552–586. Springer, Cham (2018). https://doi.org/10.1007/978-3-319-78372-7_18
23. Lyubashevsky, V.: Fiat-Shamir with aborts: applications to lattice and factoring-based signatures. In: Matsui, M. (ed.) ASIACRYPT 2009. LNCS, vol. 5912, pp. 598–616. Springer, Heidelberg (2009). https://doi.org/10.1007/978-3-642-10366-7_35
24. Lyubashevsky, V.: Lattice signatures without trapdoors. In: Pointcheval, D., Johansson, T. (eds.) EUROCRYPT 2012. LNCS, vol. 7237, pp. 738–755. Springer, Heidelberg (2012). https://doi.org/10.1007/978-3-642-29011-4_43
25. Migliore, V., Benoît Gérard, Tibouchi, M., Fouque, P.-A.: Masking dilithium - efficient implementation and side-channel evaluation. In: Applied Cryptography and Network Security - 17th International Conference, ACNS 2019, Bogota, Colombia, 5–7 June 2019, Proceedings, pp. 344–362 (2019)
26. Nguyen, P.Q., Regev, O.: Learning a parallelepiped: cryptanalysis of GGH and NTRU signatures. In: Vaudenay, S. (ed.) EUROCRYPT 2006. LNCS, vol. 4004, pp. 271–288. Springer, Heidelberg (2006). https://doi.org/10.1007/11761679_17
27. Peikert, C.: Lattice cryptography for the internet. In: Mosca, M. (ed.) PQCrypto 2014. LNCS, vol. 8772, pp. 197–219. Springer, Cham (2014). https://doi.org/10.1007/978-3-319-11659-4_12
28. Regev, O.: On lattices, learning with errors, random linear codes, and cryptography. J. ACM **56**(6), 40 (2009)

29. Schnorr, C.P.: Efficient identification and signatures for smart cards. In: Brassard, G. (ed.) CRYPTO 1989. LNCS, vol. 435, pp. 239–252. Springer, New York (1990). https://doi.org/10.1007/0-387-34805-0_22
30. Unruh, D.: Post-quantum security of Fiat-Shamir. In: Takagi, T., Peyrin, T. (eds.) ASIACRYPT 2017. LNCS, vol. 10624, pp. 65–95. Springer, Cham (2017). https://doi.org/10.1007/978-3-319-70694-8_3

Secure Hybrid Encryption in the Standard Model from Hard Learning Problems

Xavier Boyen[1], Malika Izabachène[2], and Qinyi Li[3(✉)]

[1] QUT, Brisbane, Australia
[2] Cosmian, Paris, France
[3] Griffith University, Brisbane, Australia
qinyi.li@griffith.edu.au

Abstract. We present chosen-ciphertext secure hybrid encryption systems in the standard model from the learning with errors problem and low-noise learning parity with noise problem. The systems consist of public-key key encapsulation mechanisms that are not chosen-ciphertext secure. The systems are more efficient than the existing chosen-ciphertext secure hybrid encryption systems in the standard model based on the same hard learning problems.

Keywords: Hybrid encryption · CCA security · Standard model

1 Introduction

When encrypting large messages, public-key encryption (PKE) is mostly used as a key encapsulation mechanism (KEM) with a secret-key data encapsulation mechanism (DEM) to build hybrid encryption (HE) system. In a HE system, the KEM produces secret session keys for the DEM to encrypt the actual messages. The HE paradigm was proposed in [9], and it is known that if the KEM and the DEM are both adaptive-chosen ciphertext secure (CCA secure), then the HE system is CCA secure. Since CCA-secure DEM is relatively easy to obtain, the natural step of constructing a CCA-secure HE is to build a CCA-secure KEM or PKE. For example, starting from a weakly secure (i.e., chosen-plaintext secure or even oneway) PKE system, a CCA-secure KEM can be built in the random oracle model (ROM) (or the quantum random oracle model (QROM)) by applying to the Fujisaki-Okamoto transformation [13], or its variants, e.g., [15]. On the other hand, CCA-secure KEM is not necessary for a CCA-secure HE system. One of the prominent examples is the Kurosawa-Desmedt HE system [18], which is CCA secure, but its KEM is not ([2,16] showed that the KEM meets weaker security than the CCA security). CCA-secure HE systems with weakly secure KEMs are often more efficient than the CCA-secure HE systems with CCA-secure KEMs. For instance, the Kurosawa-Desmedt system is more efficient than the Cramer-Shoup system [8]. However, to the best of our knowledge, CCA-secure HE systems with similar feature (i.e., non-CCA-secure KEMs) under the post-quantum assumptions remain unknown.

© Springer Nature Switzerland AG 2021
J. H. Cheon and J.-P. Tillich (Eds.): PQCrypto 2021, LNCS 12841, pp. 399–418, 2021.
https://doi.org/10.1007/978-3-030-81293-5_21

1.1 Our Contributions

We present a post-quantum HE system in the standard model from the learning with errors (LWE) problem. The HE system is CCA secure, but its KEM is not, which gives the first post-quantum CCA-secure HE system with non-CCA-secure KEM. Our HE system's KEM is a non-adaptive CCA-secure PKE system provided in [19]. The DEM part constitutes a message authentication code (MAC) and a weakly secure secret-key encryption (SKE) system. Due to the KEM's simplicity, the HE system is more efficient than the existing HE systems from lattices in the standard model.

Our technique extends to a CCA-secure HE system from low-noise LPN, based on the Kiltz et al.'s LPN double trapdoor [17]. However, by avoiding the generic transformations, our HE system is more efficient than the HE system obtained from [17]. Our technique also gives simple CCA-secure KEMs from LWE (and low-noise LPN). This is done by combining the non-CCA-secure KEMs with a one-time secure MAC.

It is worth mentioning that our LWE-based HE system and KEM system can be adapted straightforwardly to the ring LWE setting) to be made more space-efficient, since their basis is the trapdoor function from [19], which has ring versions (also supported by practical implementations, e.g., [5,12]). This is not known to be the case for some previous constructions (e.g., [7]). Table 1 and Table 2 summarise comparisons among post-quantum HE systems in the standard model. We compare our LWE-based HE system with two HE systems. The first one is the combination of the CCA1 PKE system in [19], Boneh-Katz transformation [6], and a chosen-plaintext secure secret-key encryption system as the DEM (we note that the MAC in the transformation is also used to authenticate the whole ciphertext, which allows avoiding a CCA-secure DEM). The other one is the combination of the CCA-secure KEM from [7] and a CCA-secure KEM (which can be built by using a chosen-plaintext secure secret-key encryption and a MAC). We also compare our LPN-based HE system with the HE system derived from applying Boneh-Katz transformation to the tag-based encryption system from [17] and a secret-key encryption system.

Table 1. Comparison among LWE-based HE systems

LWE constructions	$|\mathsf{pk}|$	$|\mathsf{ct}|$	Enc. Time	Dec. Time	Ring?
[19]+[6]+CPA-DEM	$2nm\log q$	$2nm\log q + |\mathsf{tag}| + |\mathsf{com}| + |\phi|$	$t + t_{\mathsf{com}}$	$t' + t_{\mathsf{decom}}$	YES
[7]+CCA-DEM	$3nm\log q$	$2nm\log q + |\mathsf{tag}| + \lambda + |\phi|$	$t + t_{\mathsf{sis}}$	$t' + t_{\mathsf{sis}}$	Unknown
This work	$2nm\log q$	$2m\log q + |\mathsf{tag}| + |\phi|$	t	t'	YES

The comparisons assume the HE systems using the same LWE/LPN parameters (e.g., dimensions, noise ratios) and consider the KEM part encapsulates $\lambda \leq n$-bit session keys. $|\mathsf{tag}|$ denotes the size of tags output by the MAC (either for Boneh-Katz transformation or for CCA-secure DEM). $|\mathsf{com}|$ denotes the size

Table 2. Comparison between LPN-based HE systems

LPN constructions	$|pk|$	$|ct|$	Enc. Time	Dec. Time
[17]+[6] +CPA-DEM	$n(3m+\lambda)$	$3m + \lambda + |tag| + |com| + |\phi|$	$\tau + t_{com}$	$\tau' + t_{decom}$
This work	$n(3m+\lambda)$	$3m + \lambda + |tag| + |\phi|$	τ	τ'

of commitment from the commitment scheme used by Boneh-Katz transformation. $|\phi|$ denotes the size of encryption of messages produced by the secret-key encryption systems. We use t and τ (resp. t' and τ') to denote the encryption and decryption time of our LWE-based construction (resp. LPN-based construction). t_{com} and t_{decom} denote the time used to compute the commitments and decommitments in the Boneh-Katz transformation (using the commitment scheme recommended in [6], computing the commitment and the commitment contains computing a collision-resistant hash and evaluating a universal hash function). t_{sis} denotes the time of computing the function $f(\mathbf{x}) = \mathbf{A}\mathbf{x}$ where $\mathbf{A} \in \mathbb{Z}_q^{n \times m}$ and $\mathbf{x} \in \mathbb{Z}^m$. We also consider whether the system can be adapted to the ring LWE setting. Enabling realisation over rings may help to improve the space efficiency of the systems. The comparisons show our HE systems are either more efficient or more flexible (i.e., support ring LWE). We note that our HE system and the HE system based on Boneh-Katz transformation lose a factor of the number of decryption queries, in security reduction, i.e., it is not tight, while the construction obtained from [7] loses a constant factor.

1.2   Our Approach

We provide the intuition of our approach. The ciphertext of the KEM part of our LWE-based HE system contains LWE samples $\mathbf{c}_0$, $\mathbf{c}_1$ where

$$[\mathbf{c}_0^{*\mathsf{T}}|\mathbf{c}_1^{*\mathsf{T}}] = \mathbf{s}^\mathsf{T}[\mathbf{A}|\mathbf{A}_1 + H(\mathbf{c}_0^*)\mathbf{G}] + [\mathbf{e}_0^\mathsf{T}|\mathbf{e}_1^\mathsf{T}]$$

where $\mathbf{A}$, $\mathbf{A}_1 = \mathbf{A}\mathbf{R}$ are public matrices, $\mathbf{G}$ is the gadget matrix [19], H is a collision resistant hash function with full-rank difference property (see [3]). The session key $\mathbf{k}^*$ for the DEM, a random bit string, is embedded into the LWE secret vector $\mathbf{s}$, e.g., by $\mathbf{s} = \tilde{\mathbf{s}} + \mathbf{k}^* \lfloor q/2 \rfloor$. Using the trapdoor $\mathbf{R}$, the private key, $\mathbf{k}^*$ can be recovered. The KEM is not CCA secure: Adding a small vector to $\mathbf{e}_1$ results in a correct ciphertext of $\mathbf{k}^*$. In addition to the KEM, our DEM uses a secret-key encryption (SKE) system to encrypt the actual message M and uses an authentication code (MAC) to authenticate the ciphertext:

$$\phi^* \leftarrow \mathsf{SKE.Enc}(dk, M) \quad \text{and} \quad \sigma^* \leftarrow \mathsf{MAC.Sign}(mk, \mathbf{c}_0||\mathbf{c}_1||\phi)$$

where MAC key mk and SKE key dk are derived from $\mathbf{k}^*$ via a key derivation function (KDF). In a nutshell, the construction is reminiscent of the Boneh-Katz transformation [6] that turns any selectively secure identity-based encryption into a CCA-secure PKE using a MAC and a commitment scheme. $\mathbf{c}_0^*$ constitutes LWE samples and, thus, can be seen as a statistically binding (by that the

LWE problem has unique solutions) and computationally hiding (by the LWE assumption) commitment of the session key $\mathbf{k}^*$. The intuition of security, given the ciphertext $\mathbf{c}_0^*, \mathbf{c}_1^*, \phi^*, \sigma^*$, is that (1) any decryption query with $\mathbf{c}_0 \neq \mathbf{c}_0^*$ is not helpful as the security reduction will use the technique from [3] to embed $\mathbf{c}_0^*$ into the $\mathbf{A}_1$, i.e., $\mathbf{A}_1 = \mathbf{AR} - H(\mathbf{c}_0^*)\mathbf{G}$, so it can decrypt using the trapdoor $\mathbf{R}$, and (2) if the adversary makes a decryption query with $\mathbf{c}_0 = \mathbf{c}_0^*$, since $\mathbf{c}_0^*$ uniquely determines $\mathbf{k}^*$ by the binding property of LWE, the adversary has to know $\mathbf{k}^*$ to forge the MAC or break the security of the SKE. However, $\mathbf{k}^*$ is hidden by LWE assumption.

2 Preliminaries

We use symbol "⊤" for matrix/vector transpose, e.g., $\mathbf{A}^\top$ means the transpose of $\mathbf{A}$. We denote by $x \leftarrow X$ the process of sampling x according to the distribution X. Let $x \sim X$ denote sample x satisfies distribution X. We use $U(X)$ to denote the uniform distribution over the set X. We will be using standard asymptotic notations, e.g., O, Ω, ω. Let $\lambda \in \mathbb{N}$, the function $f : \mathbb{N} \to \mathbb{R}$ is said to be negligible if $f(\lambda) = \lambda^{-\omega(1)}$ and is written as $f(\lambda) = \mathsf{negl}(\lambda)$.

Let X and Y be two random variables over some finite set S. The statistical distance between X and Y is defined as $\Delta(X, Y) = \frac{1}{2}\sum_{s \in S} |\Pr[X = s] - \Pr[Y = s]|$. Let X_λ and Y_λ be ensembles of random variables indexed by the security parameter λ. We say that X and Y are $\mathsf{negl}(\lambda)$-statistically close (or simply statistically close) if $\Delta(X_\lambda, Y_\lambda) = \mathsf{negl}(\lambda)$. We use the following lemma in our security proofs.

Lemma 1 (Special case of Lemma 4.4 of [20]). *For* $\mathbf{x} \leftarrow D_{\mathbb{Z}^m, s}$, $\Pr[\|\mathbf{x}\| > s\sqrt{m}] < 1 - 2^{-\Omega(m)}$.

Lemma 2 (Proposition 5.1 of [14]). *Let* $q \geq 2$. *For all but a* $2q^{-n}$ *fraction of all* $\mathbf{A} \in \mathbb{Z}_q^{n \times m}$ *and for any* $s \geq \omega(\sqrt{\log n})$, *the distribution of* $\mathbf{Ae} \bmod q$ *is statistically close to uniform over* $\mathbb{Z}_q^n$, *where* $\mathbf{e} \sim D_{\mathbb{Z}^m, s}$.

We will use the super-increasing vector $\mathbf{g}^\top = (1, 2, 4, \ldots, 2^{k-1})$, for $k = \lceil \log_2 q \rceil$ and extend it to form a "gadget" matrix $\mathbf{G} = diag(\mathbf{g}^\top, \ldots, \mathbf{g}^\top) \in \mathbb{Z}_q^{n \times nk}$ as in [19]. Here we use a base 2 but other choices of base can be used. We formulate the following lemma which is directly derived from the Theorem 4.1 and Theorem 5.4 and of [19].

Lemma 3. *Let* $w = n\lceil \log q \rceil$. *Let* $\mathbf{F} = [\mathbf{A} | \mathbf{AR} + \mathbf{HG}]$ *where* $\mathbf{R} \in \mathbb{Z}^{m \times w}$, $\mathbf{H} \in \mathbb{Z}_q^{n \times n}$ *is invertible in* $\mathbb{Z}_q$, *and* $\mathbf{G} \in \mathbb{Z}_q^{n \times w}$ *is the gadget matrix. Given* $\mathbf{b}^\top = \mathbf{s}^\top\mathbf{F} + \mathbf{e}^\top$ *where* $\mathbf{e}^\top = [\mathbf{e}_0^\top | \mathbf{e}_1^\top]$, *there exists an efficient algorithm* $\mathsf{Invert}(\mathbf{R}, \mathbf{F}, \mathbf{b})$ *that outputs* $\mathbf{s}$ *and* $\mathbf{e}$ *when* $\|\mathbf{e}_1^\top - \mathbf{e}_0^\top\mathbf{R}\|_\infty < q/4$.

Definition 1 ((Normal Form) Learning-With-Errors Problem). *Let* λ *be the security parameter,* $n = n(\lambda)$, $m = m(\lambda)$, $q = q(\lambda)$ *and an error distribution*

$\chi = \chi(n)$ over $\mathbb{Z}_q$. The advantage of an adversary $\mathcal{A}$ for the (normal-form) $\mathsf{NLWE}_{n,m,q,\chi}$ problem, denoted by $\mathsf{Adv}_{\mathcal{A}}^{\mathsf{NLWE}_{n,m,q,\chi}}(\lambda)$, is defined as

$$|\Pr[\mathcal{A}(\mathbf{A}, \mathbf{s}^{\mathsf{T}}\mathbf{A} + \mathbf{e}^{\mathsf{T}}) = 1] - \Pr[\mathcal{A}(\mathbf{A}, \mathbf{b}^{\mathsf{T}}) = 1]|$$

where $\mathbf{A} \leftarrow \mathbb{Z}_q^{n \times m}$, $\mathbf{s} \leftarrow \chi^n$, $\mathbf{e} \leftarrow \chi^m$. The $\mathsf{NLWE}_{n,m,q,\chi}$ problem is hard if $\mathsf{Adv}_{\mathcal{A}}^{\mathsf{NLWE}_{n,m,q,\chi}}(\lambda) \leq \mathsf{negl}(\lambda)$ for all p.p.t adversary $\mathcal{A}$.

We note the normal-form LWE problem is equivalent to the standard form of the LWE problem. A series of works have established the hardness of the LWE problem. We refer to [22,23] for details.

2.1 Definitions of Cryptographic Primitives

Public-Key Encryption (PKE). A PKE system $\mathsf{PKE} = (\mathsf{PKE.Gen}, \mathsf{PKE.Enc}, \mathsf{PKE.Dec})$ consists of three algorithms. The probabilistic key generation algorithm $\mathsf{PKE.Gen}(1^\lambda)$ takes as input a security parameter λ, returns a key pair $(\mathsf{pk}, \mathsf{sk})$. The probabilistic encryption algorithm $\mathsf{PKE.Enc}(\mathsf{pk}, M)$ returns a ciphertext ct. The deterministic decryption algorithm $\mathsf{PKE.Dec}(\mathsf{pk}, \mathsf{sk}, \mathsf{ct})$ recovers the message M, or returns $\perp$, indicating decryption fails. The correctness of PKE requires that for all $\lambda \in \mathbb{N}$, all $(\mathsf{pk}, \mathsf{sk}) \leftarrow \mathsf{PKE.Gen}(1^\lambda)$,

$$\Pr[\mathsf{PKE.Dec}(\mathsf{pk}, \mathsf{sk}, \mathsf{PKE.Enc}(\mathsf{pk}, M)) = K] \geq 1 - \mathsf{negl}(\lambda)$$

where the probability is over the randomness of $\mathsf{PKE.Gen}$ and $\mathsf{PKE.Enc}$.

Definition 2. *We say PKE is chosen-ciphertext-attack secure (CCA-secure) if for all PPT adversary $\mathcal{A}$, the advantage function*

$$\mathsf{Adv}_{\mathsf{PKE},\mathcal{A}}^{\mathsf{ind-cca}}(\lambda) = \left|\mathsf{Exp}_{\mathsf{PKE},\mathcal{A}}^{\mathsf{ind-cca}}\lambda) - 1/2\right| \leq \mathsf{negl}(\lambda)$$

where the experiment $\mathsf{Exp}_{\mathsf{PKE},\mathcal{A}}^{\mathsf{ind-cca}}\lambda)$ is defined in Fig. 1. In the experiment, the adversary is not allowed to query ct^* to the oracle $\mathcal{O}$ in step 4.

Secret-Key Encryption (SKE). A SKE system $\mathsf{SKE} = (\mathsf{SKE.Enc}, \mathsf{SKE.Dec})$ with key space $\mathcal{K}_{\mathsf{ske}}$ and ciphertext space $\mathcal{C}_{\mathsf{ske}}$ (typically $\mathcal{K}_{\mathsf{ske}} = \{0,1\}^\lambda$ for the security λ) consists of two algorithms. The deterministic encryption algorithm $\mathsf{SKE.Enc}(dk, M)$ uses a key $dk \in \mathcal{K}_{\mathsf{ske}}$ to encrypt message M into a ciphertext ϕ. The deterministic decryption algorithm $\mathsf{SKE.Dec}(dk, \phi)$ recovers message M, or return $\perp$, indicating decryption fails. We require that for all $dk \in \mathcal{K}_{\mathsf{ske}}$ and message M, $\mathsf{SKE.Dec}(dk, \mathsf{SKE.Enc}(dk, M)) \to M$.

Definition 3. *We say a secret-key encryption scheme SKE is one-time secure if for all PPT adversary $\mathcal{A}$ the advantage function*

$$\mathsf{Adv}_{\mathsf{SKE},\mathcal{A}}^{\mathsf{ot-ind}}(\lambda) = \left|\Pr[\mathsf{Exp}_{\mathsf{SKE},\mathcal{A}}^{\mathsf{ot-ind}}(\lambda) = 1] - 1/2\right| \leq \mathsf{negl}(\lambda)$$

where the experiment $\mathsf{Exp}_{\mathsf{SKE},\mathcal{A}}^{\mathsf{ot-ind}}(\lambda)$ is defined as in Fig. 2.

Experiment $\mathsf{Exp}_{\mathsf{PKE},\mathcal{A}}^{\mathsf{ind-cca}}\lambda)$:

1. $(\mathsf{pk}, \mathsf{sk}) \leftarrow \mathsf{PKE.Gen}(1^\lambda)$
2. $(M_0, M_1) \leftarrow \mathcal{A}^{\mathcal{O}}(\mathsf{pk})$
3. $b \leftarrow U(\{0,1\})$, $\mathsf{ct}^* \leftarrow \mathsf{PKE.Enc}(\mathsf{pk}, M_b)$
4. $b' \leftarrow \mathcal{A}^{\mathcal{O}}(\mathsf{pk}, \mathsf{ct}^*, \mathsf{pk})$
5. Return 1 if $b' = b$; Otherwise, return 0.

Oracle $\mathcal{O}(\mathsf{ct})$:

1. Return $\mathsf{PKE.Dec}(\mathsf{pk}, \mathsf{sk}, \mathsf{ct})$

Fig. 1. CCA security definitions for PKE

Experiment $\mathsf{Exp}_{\mathsf{SKE},\mathcal{A}}^{\mathsf{ot-ind}}(\lambda)$:

1. $M \leftarrow \mathcal{A}(1^\lambda)$
2. $dk \leftarrow \mathcal{K}_{\mathsf{ske}}$, $b \leftarrow U(\{0,1\})$, $\phi_0 \leftarrow \mathsf{SKE.Enc}(dk, M)$, $\phi_1 \leftarrow \mathcal{C}_{\mathsf{ske}}$
3. $b' \leftarrow \mathcal{A}(1^\lambda, \phi_b)$
4. Return 1 if $b' = b$; Otherwise, return 0

Fig. 2. Security experiments of SKE

Message Authentication Codes (MACs). In a MAC system MAC = (MAC.Sign, MAC.Ver) with key space $\mathcal{K}_{\mathsf{mac}}$ (typically $\mathcal{K}_{\mathsf{mac}} = \{0,1\}^\lambda$ for the security parameter λ), the algorithm $\mathsf{MAC.Sign}(K, x)$ takes as input a key $K \in \mathcal{K}_{\mathsf{mac}}$, a message x and some random coins, and returns a tag σ. The deterministic algorithm $\mathsf{MAC.Ver}(K, \sigma, x)$ returns 1 if $\sigma \leftarrow \mathsf{MAC.Sign}(K, x)$, or outputs 0, otherwise.

Definition 4. *Let λ be the security parameter. We say a mac MAC is secure with one-time strong unforgeablility if for all PPT adversary $\mathcal{A}$, the advantage function*

$$\mathsf{Adv}_{\mathsf{MAC},\mathcal{A}}^{\mathsf{ot-suf}}(\lambda) = \Pr[\mathsf{Exp}_{\mathsf{MAC},\mathcal{A}}^{\mathsf{ot-suf}}(\lambda) = 1] \leq \mathsf{negl}(\lambda)$$

where the experiment $\mathsf{Exp}_{\mathsf{MAC},\mathcal{A}}^{\mathsf{ot-suf}}(\lambda)$ is defined as in Fig. 3.

Experiment $\mathsf{Exp}_{\mathsf{MAC},\mathcal{A}}^{\mathsf{ot-suf}}(\lambda)$:

1. $mk \leftarrow \mathcal{K}_{\mathsf{mac}}$, $x \leftarrow \mathcal{A}(1^\lambda)$
2. $\sigma \leftarrow \mathsf{MAC.Sign}(mk, x)$
3. $(x', \sigma') \leftarrow \mathcal{A}(1^\lambda, \sigma)$
4. If $\mathsf{MAC.Ver}(K, x', \sigma')$ and $(x, \sigma) \neq (x', \sigma')$, return 1
5. Otherwise, return 0

Fig. 3. Security experiments of MAC

Collision Resistant Hashing. Let $H : \{0,1\}^* \to \{0,1\}^\ell$ be a hash function (where ℓ is a function of the security parameter).

Definition 5. *We say that H is collision resistant if for all p.p.t algorithms $\mathcal{A}$, the advantage,*

$$\mathsf{Adv}_{\mathcal{A}}^{\mathrm{coll}}(\lambda) = \Pr[\mathcal{A}(1^\lambda, H) \to (x, x') : \ x \neq x \ and \ H(x) = H(x')] \leq \mathsf{negl}(\lambda)$$

where $x \leftarrow \{0,1\}^*$ and λ is the security parameter.

Key Derivation Functions. Our constructions use key derivation functions (KDFs) to expand short random keys to longer pseudorandom keys for message authentication codes and secret-key encryption. Basically, a KDF is a pseudorandom number generator.

Definition 6. *Let λ be the security parameter. Let $\mathcal{K}$ be a set with size $\{0,1\}^{\geq\lambda}$. We say a key derivation function $\mathsf{KDF} : \mathcal{K} \to \{0,1\}^\ell$ is secure if the advantage function*

$$\mathsf{Adv}_{\mathsf{KDF},\mathcal{A}}^{\mathrm{ind}}(\lambda) = |\Pr[\mathcal{A}(1^\lambda, \mathsf{KDF}(k))] = 1 - \Pr[\mathcal{A}(1^\lambda, r) = 1]| \leq \mathsf{negl}(\lambda)$$

where $k \leftarrow U(\mathcal{K})$ and $r \leftarrow U(\{0,1\}^\ell)$.

3 CCA-Secure Hybrid Encryption from LWE

The system uses the following public parameters shared by all system instances.

1. We use $\mathsf{NLWE}_{n,m,q,D_{\mathbb{Z},\alpha q}}$ problem for some polynomial-size (in n) prime q. n, q, m, α are determined to ensure $\mathsf{NLWE}_{n,m,q,D_{\mathbb{Z},\alpha q}}$ problem is hard. Let $w = n\lceil \log q \rceil$ and $m \geq n \log q + \omega(\sqrt{\log n})$.
2. A full-rank difference encoding as defined in [3] $\mathsf{FRD} : \mathbb{Z}_q^n \to \mathbb{Z}_q^{n \times n}$ that for any $\mathbf{x}, \mathbf{y} \in \mathbb{Z}_q^n$ with $\mathbf{x} \neq \mathbf{y}$, $\mathsf{FRD}(\mathbf{x}) - \mathsf{FRD}(\mathbf{y})$ is invertible over $\mathbb{Z}_q^{n \times n}$. In particular, $\mathsf{FRD}(\mathbf{x})$ is invertible over $\mathbb{Z}_q^{n \times n}$ if $\mathbf{x} \neq \mathbf{0}$.
3. A collision resistance hash function $H : \{0,1\}^* \to \mathbb{Z}_q^n \setminus \{\mathbf{0}\}$ where $\mathbf{0}$ is the zero matrix in $\mathbb{Z}_q^n$, a secret-key encryption system $\mathsf{SKE} = (\mathsf{SKE.Enc}, \mathsf{SKE.Dec})$ with key space $\mathcal{K}_{\mathsf{ske}}$, message space $\mathcal{M}_{\mathsf{ske}}$, and ciphertext space $\mathcal{C}_{\mathsf{ske}}$, a secure message authentication code $\mathsf{MAC} = (\mathsf{MAC.Sign}, \mathsf{MAC.Ver})$ with key space $\mathcal{K}_{\mathsf{mac}}$. A key derivation function $\mathsf{KDF} : \{0,1\}^n \to \mathcal{K}_{\mathsf{ske}} \times \mathcal{K}_{\mathsf{mac}}$.

- $\mathsf{PKE.Gen}(1^\lambda)$:
    1. $\mathbf{A} \leftarrow U(\mathbb{Z}_q^{n \times m})$, $\mathbf{R} \leftarrow D_{\mathbb{Z},\omega(\sqrt{\log n})}^{m \times w}$
    2. $\mathbf{A}_1 \leftarrow \mathbf{AR}$.
    3. $\mathsf{pk} \leftarrow (\mathbf{A}, \mathbf{A}_1)$, $\mathsf{sk} \leftarrow \mathbf{R}$
- $\mathsf{PKE.Enc}(\mathsf{pk}, M)$:
    1. $\mathbf{k} \leftarrow U(\{0,1\}^n)$, $(dk, mk) \leftarrow \mathsf{KDF}(\mathbf{k})$
    2. $\bar{\mathbf{s}} \leftarrow D_{\mathbb{Z},\alpha q}^n$, $\mathbf{s} \leftarrow \mathbf{k}\lfloor q/2 \rfloor + \bar{\mathbf{s}}$.
    3. $\mathbf{e}_0 \leftarrow D_{\mathbb{Z},\alpha q}^m$, $\mathbf{c}_0^\mathsf{T} \leftarrow \mathbf{s}^\mathsf{T}\mathbf{A} + \mathbf{e}_0^\mathsf{T}$.
    4. $\mathbf{e}_1 \leftarrow D_{\mathbb{Z},s}^w$ where $s^2 = (\|\mathbf{e}_0\|^2 + m(\alpha q)^2) \cdot \omega(\sqrt{\log n})^2$.

5. $\mathbf{c}_1^\mathsf{T} \leftarrow \mathbf{s}^\mathsf{T}(\mathbf{A}_1 + \mathsf{FRD}(H(\mathbf{c}_0)\mathbf{G}) + \mathbf{e}_1^\mathsf{T}$.
6. $\phi \leftarrow \mathsf{SKE.Enc}(dk, M)$, $\sigma \leftarrow \mathsf{MAC.Sign}(mk, \mathbf{c}_0\|\mathbf{c}_1\|\phi)$.
7. $\mathsf{ct} \leftarrow (\mathbf{c}_0, \mathbf{c}_1, \phi, \sigma)$.

- $\mathsf{PKE.Dec}(\mathsf{pk}, \mathsf{sk}, \mathsf{ct})$:
  1. Parse $\mathsf{ct} = (\mathbf{c}_0, \mathbf{c}_1, \phi, \sigma)$; Output $\perp$ if ct doesn't parse.
  2. Recover $(\mathbf{s}, \mathbf{e}_0, \mathbf{e}_1) \leftarrow \mathsf{Invert}(\mathbf{R}, [\mathbf{A}|\mathbf{A}_1 + \mathsf{FRD}(H(\mathbf{c}_0))\mathbf{G}], [\mathbf{c}_0^\mathsf{T}|\mathbf{c}_1^\mathsf{T}])$.
  3. If $\|\mathbf{e}_0\| > \alpha q \sqrt{m}$ or $\|\mathbf{e}_1\| > \alpha q \sqrt{2mw} \cdot \omega(\sqrt{\log n})$, output $\perp$.
  4. Set $\mathbf{k}[i] \leftarrow 0$ if $\mathbf{s}[i]$ is closer to 0 or $\mathbf{k}[i] \leftarrow 1$ if $\mathbf{s}[i]$ is closer to $q/2$.
  5. Output $\perp$ and aborts if $\|\mathbf{s} - \mathbf{k}\| > \alpha q \sqrt{n}$; Else, output $\mathbf{k}$ and continue.
  6. $(dk, mk) \leftarrow \mathsf{KDF}(\mathbf{k})$.
  7. Return $M \leftarrow \mathsf{SKE.Dec}(dk, \phi)$ if $1 \leftarrow \mathsf{MAC.Ver}(mk, \mathbf{c}_0\|\mathbf{c}_1\|\phi)$, or else $\perp$.

Correctness. We show that by the chosen parameters, given an honestly generated ciphertext $\mathsf{ct} = (\mathbf{c}_0, \mathbf{c}_1, \phi, \sigma)$, the algorithm $\mathsf{Invert}(\mathbf{R}, [\mathbf{A}|\mathbf{A}_1 + \mathsf{FRD}(\mathbf{c}_0)\mathbf{G}], [\mathbf{c}_0^\mathsf{T}|\mathbf{c}_1^\mathsf{T}])$ correctly returns the $\mathbf{s}$. The rest part of correctness readily follows from the correctness of SKE and MAC. Recall that $[\mathbf{c}_0^\mathsf{T}|\mathbf{c}_1^\mathsf{T}] = \mathbf{s}^\mathsf{T}[\mathbf{A}|\mathbf{A}_1 + \mathsf{FRD}(H(\mathbf{c}_0))\mathbf{G}] + [\mathbf{e}_0^\mathsf{T}|\mathbf{e}_1^\mathsf{T}]$ where $\mathbf{e}_0 \sim D_{\mathbb{Z},\alpha q}^m$ and $\mathbf{e}_1 \sim D_{\mathbb{Z},s}^w$ where $s^2 = (\|\mathbf{e}_0\|^2 + m(\alpha q)^2) \cdot \omega(\sqrt{\log n})^2$. According to Lemma 1, with overwhelming probability, $\|\mathbf{e}_0\| \leq \alpha q \sqrt{m}$ and $\|\mathbf{e}_1\| \leq s\sqrt{w}$. So, the error term is bounded

$$\left\|\mathbf{e}_1^\mathsf{T} - \mathbf{e}_0^\mathsf{T}\mathbf{R}\right\|_\infty \leq \left\|\mathbf{e}_1^\mathsf{T} - \mathbf{e}_0^\mathsf{T}\mathbf{R}\right\| \leq \left\|\mathbf{e}_1^\mathsf{T}\right\| + \left\|\mathbf{e}_0^\mathsf{T}\mathbf{R}\right\| \quad \leq 2\alpha q \cdot O(\sqrt{w}) \cdot \omega(\sqrt{\log n}) \cdot \sqrt{3w}$$
$$= q \cdot \alpha \cdot O(w) \cdot \omega(\sqrt{\log n})$$

with overwhelming probability. For large enough $1/\alpha = O(w) \cdot \omega(\sqrt{\log n})$, the error term is smaller than $q/4$ as required by Lemma 3. With $\mathbf{s} = \mathbf{k}\lfloor q/2 \rfloor + \bar{\mathbf{s}}$, $\mathbf{k}$ can be recovered with overwhelming probability since $\|\bar{\mathbf{s}}\| \leq \alpha q \sqrt{n} < q/4$ with overwhelming probability.

3.1 Security Proof

Theorem 1. *Under the assumptions that the problem* $\mathsf{NLWE}_{n,m,q,D_{\mathbb{Z},\alpha q}}$ *is hard, MAC, SKE are secure w.r.t Definition 4 and 3, respectively, and H is collision resistant w.r.t Definition 5, the hybrid encryption system PKE is CCA secure w.r.t to Definition 2.*

Proof. Let λ be the security parameter. Let $\mathcal{A}$ be any PPT adversary who has advantage $\mathsf{Adv}_{\mathsf{PKE},\mathcal{A}}^{\mathsf{ind-cca}}(\lambda)$ against the proposed public-key (hybrid) encryption scheme. We show how to bound $\mathsf{Adv}_{\mathsf{PKE},\mathcal{A}}^{\mathsf{ind-cca}}(\lambda)$ by the hardness of the $\mathsf{NLWE}_{n,m,q,D_{\mathbb{Z},\alpha q}}$ problem, the one-time security of MAC and SKE, and the collision resistance of H.

We proceed with a sequence of security games. Figure 4 describes how pk, sk, and the challenge ciphertext ct^* are generated, and Fig. 5 describes how decryption queries are responded in the security games. We denote by E_i that some event E happens in Game i. Each security game eventually outputs a binary

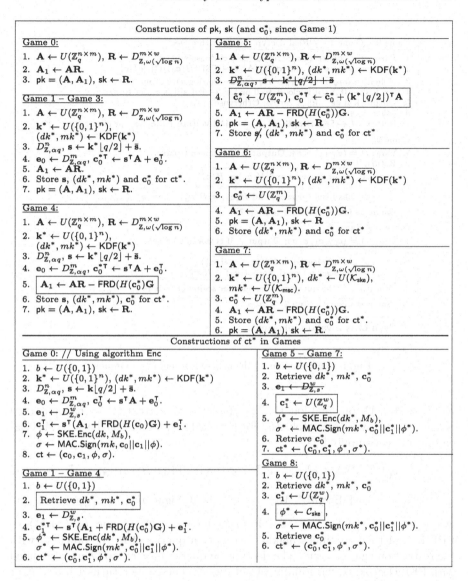

Fig. 4. Generating Keys (and $\mathbf{c}_0^*$) and ct^* in Games

value. We denote by S_i the event that Game i outputs 1 (which means that the adversary wins the chosen-ciphertext security game). Throughout the proof, we say a ciphertext is *valid* if it can be properly decrypted to some message.

Game 0. The first game, Game 0, follows the security experiment $\mathsf{Exp}_{\mathsf{PKE},\mathcal{A}}^{\mathrm{ind-cca}}(\lambda)$. That is, $\mathcal{A}$ is given a public key pk and starts making decryption queries to $\mathcal{O}$. The decryption queries are answered by $\mathsf{PKE.Dec}$. After that, $\mathcal{A}$ submits two

Descriptions of decryption oracle $\mathcal{O}$ in Games

Game 0 – Game 1: // Real decryption algorithm Dec

1. Parse $\mathsf{ct} = (\mathbf{c}_0, \mathbf{c}_1, \phi, \sigma)$; Output $\perp$ if ct doesn't parse.
2. Recover $(\mathbf{s}, \mathbf{e}_0, \mathbf{e}_1) \leftarrow \mathsf{Invert}(\mathbf{R}, [\mathbf{A}|\mathbf{A}_1 + \mathsf{FRD}(H(\mathbf{c}_0))\mathbf{G}], [\mathbf{c}_0^\mathsf{T}|\mathbf{c}_1^\mathsf{T}])$.
3. If $\|\mathbf{e}_0\| > \alpha q \sqrt{m}$ or $\|\mathbf{e}_1\| > \alpha q \sqrt{2mw} \cdot \omega(\sqrt{\log n})$, output $\perp$.
4. Set $\mathbf{k}[i] \leftarrow 0$ if $\mathbf{s}[i]$ is closer to 0 or $\mathbf{k}[i] \leftarrow 1$ if $\mathbf{s}[i]$ is closer to $q/2$.
5. Output $\mathbf{k}$ if $\|\mathbf{s} - \mathbf{k}\| \leq \alpha q \sqrt{n}$; Otherwise output $\perp$.
6. $(dk, mk) \leftarrow \mathsf{KDF}(\mathbf{k})$.
7. Return $M \leftarrow \mathsf{SKE.Dec}(dk, \phi)$ if $1 \leftarrow \mathsf{MAC.Ver}(mk, \mathbf{c}_0\|\mathbf{c}_1\|\phi)$, or else $\perp$.

Game 2:

1. Parse $\mathsf{ct} = (\mathbf{c}_0, \mathbf{c}_1, \phi, \sigma)$; Output $\perp$ if ct doesn't parse.
2. Return $\perp$ if
   - $\boxed{\mathsf{ct}^* \text{ is not released and } H(\mathbf{c}_0) = H(\mathbf{c}_0^*).}$
   - $\boxed{\mathsf{ct}^* \text{ has been released, and } H(\mathbf{c}_0) = H(\mathbf{c}_0^*) \text{ where } \mathbf{c}_0 \neq \mathbf{c}_0^*.}$
3. (Same as Game 1, step 2 to Step 7)

Game 3 – Game 7:

1. Parse $\mathsf{ct} = (\mathbf{c}_0), \mathbf{c}_1, \phi, \sigma)$; Output $\perp$ if ct doesn't parse.
2. Return $\perp$ if
   - ct^* is not released and $H(\mathbf{c}_0) = H(\mathbf{c}_0^*)$.
   - ct^* has been released, and $H(\mathbf{c}_0) = H(\mathbf{c}_0^*)$ where $\mathbf{c}_0 \neq \mathbf{c}_0^*$.
3. $\boxed{\text{Return } \perp \text{ if the query } \mathsf{ct} \text{ is made after seeing } \mathsf{ct}^* \text{ where } \mathbf{c}_0 = \mathbf{c}_0^*.{}^a}$
4. (Same as Game 1, step 2 to Step 7)

   ^{a} Even ct is a valid ciphertext.

Fig. 5. Descriptions of decryption oracle $\mathcal{O}$ in Games

messages M_0, M_1 of equal length. The challenge ciphertext $\mathsf{ct}^* = (\mathbf{c}_0^*, \mathbf{c}_1^*, \phi^*, \sigma^*)$ is constructed by $\mathsf{PKE.Enc}(\mathsf{pk}, M_b)$ for $b \leftarrow U(\{0,1\})$, and sent back to $\mathcal{A}$. Concretely, ct^* is computed as

$$\mathbf{c}_0^{*\mathsf{T}} = \mathbf{s}^{*\mathsf{T}}\mathbf{A} + \mathbf{e}_0^\mathsf{T} \quad ; \quad \mathbf{c}_1^{*\mathsf{T}} = \mathbf{s}^{*\mathsf{T}}(\mathbf{A}_1 + \mathsf{FRD}(H(\mathbf{c}_0^*))\mathbf{G}) + \mathbf{e}_1^\mathsf{T}$$

$$\phi^* = \mathsf{SKE.Enc}(dk^*, M_b) \quad ; \quad \sigma = \mathsf{MAC.Sign}(mk^*, \mathbf{c}_0^*\|\mathbf{c}_1^*\|\phi^*)$$

where $\mathbf{k}^* \leftarrow U(\{0,1\})$, $\mathbf{s} = \tilde{\mathbf{s}} + \mathbf{k}^*\lfloor q/2 \rfloor$ for $\tilde{\mathbf{s}} \leftarrow D_{\mathbb{Z},\alpha q}^n$, and $(dk^*, mk^*) \leftarrow \mathsf{KDF}(\mathbf{k}^*)$. $\mathcal{A}$ then continues making decryption queries ct to the oracle $\mathcal{O}$ with the restriction that $\mathsf{ct} \neq \mathsf{ct}^*$. The decryption queries $\mathsf{ct} \neq \mathsf{ct}^*$ to $\mathcal{O}$ are responded with $\mathsf{PKE.Dec}(\mathsf{pk}, \mathsf{sk}, \mathsf{ct})$. Finally, $\mathcal{A}$ outputs b'. The game returns 1 if $b' = b$, or 0, otherwise. By definition, we have

$$\Pr[S_0] = \Pr[\mathsf{Exp}_{\mathsf{PKE},\mathcal{A}}^{\mathrm{ind-cca}}(\lambda) = 1] \tag{1}$$

Game 1. Game 1 modifies Game 0 on the ways that pk, sk, and challenge ciphertext ct^* are generated, as specified in Fig. 4. Decryption queries in this game are responded to as in Game 0. It can be seen that the modification does not change $\mathcal{A}$'s view: the precomputed $\mathbf{k}^*$ and $\mathbf{c}_0^*$ are distributed as they are in Game 0. They are independent of pk and unavailable to $\mathcal{A}$ until ct^* gets released. So,

$$\Pr[S_1] = \Pr[S_0]. \tag{2}$$

Game 2. As detailed in Fig. 5, Game 2 is identical to Game 1 except for decryption oracle $\mathcal{O}$, the two types of decryption queries are rejected with returning $\bot$ regardless whether they are valid ciphertexts: (1) $\mathsf{ct} = (\mathbf{c}_0, \mathbf{c}_1, \phi, \sigma)$ with $H(\mathbf{c}_0) = H(\mathbf{c}_0^*)$ made before seeing ct^* (where $\mathbf{c}_0$ can be the same as or different from $\mathbf{c}_0^*$); and (2) $\mathsf{ct} = (\mathbf{c}_0, \mathbf{c}_1, \phi, \sigma)$ with $\mathbf{c}_0 \neq \mathbf{c}_0^*$ and $H(\mathbf{c}_0) = H(\mathbf{c}_0^*)$. We prove the following Lemma.

Lemma 4. *Let Q_1 (resp. Q_2) be the maximun number of decryption queries made before (resp. after) seeing ct^*. We have for some adversary $\mathcal{B}_1$ against H.*

$$| \Pr[S_2] - \Pr[S_1]| \leq \frac{Q_1}{q^m} + Q_2 \cdot \mathsf{Adv}_{H,\mathcal{B}_1}^{\mathrm{coll}}(\lambda) \tag{3}$$

Proof. Assume Q_1, Q_2 be the number of decryption queries (both are polynomials in λ) that the adversary can make in the first decryption query phase (i.e., before seeing ct^*) and the second decryption query phase (i.e., after seeing ct^*), respectively. First of all, recall that Game 2 pre-computes $\mathbf{c}_0^*$ and releases it as a part of the challenge ciphertext ct^*, after the first decryption query phase is over. Therefore, $\mathbf{c}_0^* \in \mathbb{Z}_q^m$ is independent of $\mathcal{A}$'s view during the first decryption phase, and, $\mathcal{A}$ makes type-(1) query (in the first decryption query phase) with at most Q_1/q^m.

Next, we construct an adversary $\mathcal{B}_1$ to break the collision resistance of H if the type-(2) query is very made. $calB_1$ receives the security parameter λ and a collision-resistance hash function $H : \mathbb{Z}_q^m \rightarrow \mathbb{Z}_q^n \setminus \{\mathbf{0}\}$. It runs follows the process specified in Fig. 4 (for Game 1, which is same for Game 2) to produce pk, sk and $\mathsf{ct}^* = (\mathbf{c}_0^*, \mathbf{c}_1^*, \phi^*, \sigma^*)$. It also follows Fig. 5 to respond decryption queries made before the release of ct^*. Whenever the adversary $\mathcal{A}$ makes a type-(2) decryption query $\mathsf{ct} = (\mathbf{c}_0, \mathbf{c}_1, \phi, \sigma)$, such that $\mathbf{c}_0 \neq \mathbf{c}_0^*$ and $H(\mathbf{c}_0) = H(\mathbf{c}_0^*)$, $\mathcal{B}$ aborts the Game and return $(\mathbf{c}_0, \mathbf{c}_0^*)$ as a collision for H. Since $\mathcal{A}$ can make at most Q_2 decryption queries after seeing the challenge ciphertext, we have $\mathcal{A}$ makes a type-(2) query with probability at most $Q_2 \cdot \mathsf{Adv}_{H,\mathcal{B}_1}^{\mathrm{coll}}(\lambda)$. We conclude the proof by the Difference Lemma, i.e., [24], Lemma 1.   □

Looking ahead, after Game 2, any decryption query in which $\mathbf{c}_0 = \mathbf{c}_0^*$ in the pre-challenge decryption query phase is rejected, and any decryption query with $H(\mathbf{c}_0) \neq H(\mathbf{c}_0^*)$ after the challenge ciphertext has released are rejected.

Game 3. Game 3 is identical to Game 2 except that the decryption oracle $\mathcal{O}$ is implemented slightly differently. Let $\mathsf{ct}^* = (\mathbf{c}_0^*, \mathbf{c}_1^*, \phi^*, \sigma^*)$ be the challenge ciphertext in which the session key $\mathbf{k}^* \in \{0, 1\}^n$ is encapsulated in $\mathbf{c}_0^*$ for generating dk^* and mk^*. We focus on the decryption queries of the form $\mathsf{ct} = (\mathbf{c}_0^*, \mathbf{c}_1, \phi, \sigma)$ that are issued after the challenge ciphertext ct^* is released. In Game 3, the oracle rejects (by returning $\bot$) such decryption queries. Figure 5 specifies in more details how the queries are simulated in Game 3.[1] We define

---

[1] Note that the decryption queries ct made before the release of ct^* where $H(\mathbf{c}_0) = H(\mathbf{c}_0^*)$ are already responded with $\bot$, and $\mathsf{ct} \neq \mathsf{ct}^*$ as querying ct^* is not allowed.

Valid the event that $\mathcal{A}$ submits a valid decryption query $\mathsf{ct} = (\mathbf{c}_0^*, \mathbf{c}_1, \phi, \sigma)$ $(\mathbf{c}_1,$ ϕ, and σ are arbitrary) after seeing ct^*. In Game 3, we cannot determine exactly the probability of the event Valid, i.e., $\Pr[\mathsf{Valid}_3]$. However, we can bound it considering two sub-events:

- NoBind: a session key $\mathbf{k} \neq \mathbf{k}^*$ is associated to $\mathbf{c}_0^*$, i.e. $\mathbf{c}_0^* = (\tilde{\mathbf{s}} + \mathbf{k}\lfloor q/2 \rfloor)^\mathsf{T} \mathbf{A} + \mathbf{e}_0^\mathsf{T}$ for some $\tilde{\mathbf{s}} \sim D_{\mathbb{Z},\alpha q}^n$ and $\mathbf{e}_0 \sim D_{\mathbb{Z},\alpha q}^m$.
- Forge: the session key $\mathbf{k}^*$ associated to ct^* has also been used for ct. And since the query is valid, we have that $1 \leftarrow \mathsf{MAC.Ver}(dk^*, \sigma, \mathbf{c}_0^* \| \mathbf{c}_1 \| \phi)$ where $(dk^*, mk^*) \leftarrow \mathsf{KDF}(\mathbf{k}^*)$.

Note that we have $\Pr[\mathsf{Valid}_3] \leq \Pr[\mathsf{NoBind}_3] + \Pr[\mathsf{Forge}_3]$. It is the fact that over the random choice of matrix $\mathbf{A}$ and $\mathbf{e}_0$, $\mathbf{c}_0^{*\mathsf{T}} = \mathbf{s}^\mathsf{T}\mathbf{A} + \mathbf{e}_0^\mathsf{T}$ uniquely determines $\mathbf{s}$, and, thus $\mathbf{k}^*$, (see e.g., [25], Lemma 6). Therefore, $\Pr[\mathsf{NoBind}_3]$ is negligible. Meanwhile, we can see that Game 3 and Game 2 are identical until Valid occurs. Hence, we have

$$| \Pr[S_3] - \Pr[S_2]| \leq \Pr[\mathsf{Valid}_3] \leq \Pr[\mathsf{Forge}_3] + \mathsf{negl}(\lambda) \qquad (4)$$

for some negligible function $\mathsf{negl}(\lambda)$.

Game 4. Game 4 is identical to Game 3 except it slightly modifies the construction of matrix $\mathbf{A}_1$ when defining pk, as specified in Fig. 4. Notice that the distributions of $\mathbf{A}_1$ in Game 4 $(\mathbf{A}_1 = \mathbf{AR} - \mathsf{FRD}(H(\mathbf{c}_0^*))\mathbf{G})$ and Game 3 $(\mathbf{A}_1 = \mathbf{AR})$ are both statistically close to $U(\mathbb{Z}_q^{n \times w})$. So, the distributions of pk in Game 4 and Game 3 are statistically close. The decryption oracle in Game 4 can handle the same set of decryption queries as Game 3, except for decryption query of the form $\mathsf{ct} = (\mathbf{c}_0, \mathbf{c}_1, \phi, \sigma)$ where $H(\mathbf{c}_0) = H(\mathbf{c}_0^*)$. This is because for any such decryption query, $[\mathbf{A}|\mathbf{A}_1 + \mathsf{FRD}(H(\mathbf{c}_0))\mathbf{G}] = [\mathbf{A}|\mathbf{AR} + (\mathsf{FRD}(H(\mathbf{c}_0)) - \mathsf{FRD}(\mathbf{c}_0^*))\mathbf{G}]$ where $\mathsf{FRD}(H(\mathbf{c}_0)) - \mathsf{FRD}(\mathbf{c}_0^*)$ is invertible over $\mathbb{Z}_q^{n \times n}$. Thus, the trapdoor $\mathbf{R}$ can be used, same as in Dec, to recover the encryption randomness $\mathbf{s}, \mathbf{e}_0, \mathbf{e}_1$, and, then the message. However, such a decryption query has already been handled by returning $\bot$ by the implementation of $\mathcal{O}$. Therefore, the modification introduced in Game 4 does not statistically change $\mathcal{A}$'s view, and, hence,

$$| \Pr[S_4] - \Pr[S_3]| \leq \mathsf{negl}(\lambda) \quad \text{and} \quad | \Pr[\mathsf{Forge}_4] - \Pr[\mathsf{Forge}_3]| \leq \mathsf{negl}(\lambda) \qquad (5)$$

where the function $\mathsf{negl}(\lambda)$ accounts for the negligible statistical errors.

Game 5. In Game 5, we further modify the way that pk and ct^* are generated, as specified by Fig. 4. The decryption queries in Game 5 are responded as in Game 4. In particular, we chose pk with the same distribution of pk in Game 5 is identical to that of pk in Game 4. Note that in Game 4, the ciphertext components $\mathbf{c}_0^*$, $\mathbf{c}_1^*$ are LWE samples while, in Game 5, they are distributed uniformly random. We can show $\Pr[S_4]$ and $\Pr[S_5]$, $\Pr[\mathsf{Forge}_4]$ and $\Pr[\mathsf{Forge}_5]$ are close under the LWE assumption via Lemma 5.

Lemma 5. *For Game 4 and Game 5 defined as per Fig. 4 and Fig. 5, we have*

$$|\Pr[S_5] - \Pr[S_4]| \leq \mathsf{Adv}_{\mathcal{B}_2}^{\mathsf{NLWE}_{n,m,q,D_{\mathbb{Z},\alpha q}}}(\lambda) \tag{6}$$

$$|\Pr[\mathsf{Forge}_5] - \Pr[\mathsf{Forge}_4]| \leq 2 \cdot \mathsf{Adv}_{\mathcal{B}_2'}^{\mathsf{NLWE}_{n,m,q,D_{\mathbb{Z},\alpha q}}}(\lambda) \tag{7}$$

for some adversary $\mathcal{B}_2$ and $\mathcal{B}_2'$ against the LWE problem.

Proof. We show that $|\Pr[S_5] - \Pr[S_4]|$ is negligible if $\mathsf{NLWE}_{n,m,q,D_{\mathbb{Z},\alpha q}}$ assumption holds. We do this by constructing an efficient algorithm $\mathcal{B}_2$ who interacts with the PKE adversary $\mathcal{A}$. $\mathcal{B}_2$ receives an instance of $\mathsf{LWE}_{n,m,q,D_{\mathbb{Z},\alpha q}}$ $(\mathbf{B}, \mathbf{b}^\mathsf{T}) \in (\mathbb{Z}_q^{n \times m} \times \mathbb{Z}_q^m)$. It decides that if $\mathbf{b}$ is uniformly random (independent of $\mathbf{B}$) or there exists $\mathbf{x} \sim D_{\mathbb{Z},\alpha q}^n$ and $\mathbf{y} \sim D_{\mathbb{Z},\alpha q}^m$ such that $\mathbf{b}^\mathsf{T} = \mathbf{x}^\mathsf{T}\mathbf{B} + \mathbf{y}^\mathsf{T}$. $\mathcal{B}_2$ works as follows.

- It follows Game 5 (as specified in Fig. 4) to generate pk, sk except that it sets $\mathbf{A} \leftarrow \mathbf{B}$, $\tilde{\mathbf{c}}_0^* \leftarrow \mathbf{b}$.
- It follows Game 5 (as specified in Fig. 4) to generate ct* except for $\mathbf{c}_1^*$ (note that $\mathbf{c}_0^*$ has been constructed when generating pk). To construct $\mathbf{c}_1^*$, $\mathcal{B}_2$ samples $\mathbf{v} \leftarrow D_{\mathbb{Z},\alpha q \sqrt{m} \cdot \omega(\sqrt{\log n})}^w$ and sets $\mathbf{c}_1^{*\mathsf{T}} \leftarrow \mathbf{c}_0^{*\mathsf{T}}\mathbf{R} + \mathbf{v}^\mathsf{T}$.
- It follows Game 5 (as specified in Fig. 5) for answering decryption queries.
- Finally, $\mathcal{B}_2$ outputs 1 when the security game outputs 1 (i.e., $\mathcal{A}$ outputs $b' = b$). Otherwise $\mathcal{B}_2$ outputs 0.

We analyse the reduction. First, recall that the distributions of pk in Game 4 and Game 5 are identical. Second, the same set of decryption queries are handled in Game 4 and Game 5, and the responses of decryption queries in the two games have the same distribution. Moreover, we can see that the distributions of ϕ^* and σ^* are identical in Game 4 and Game 5. Finally, if the challenge $(\mathbf{A}, \mathbf{b})$ is random, the challenge ciphertext ct* distributes as in Game 5. Hence, we have $\Pr[S_5] = \Pr[\mathcal{B}_2(\mathbf{B}, \mathbf{b}^\mathsf{T}) = 1]$.

On the other hand, if $\mathbf{b}^\mathsf{T} = \mathbf{x}^\mathsf{T}\mathbf{B} + \mathbf{y}^\mathsf{T}$, we implicitly set $\tilde{\mathbf{s}} \leftarrow \mathbf{x}$ and $\mathbf{e}_0 \leftarrow \mathbf{y}$, and we have

$$\mathbf{c}_0^{*\mathsf{T}} = \tilde{\mathbf{c}}_0^* + (\mathbf{k}^* \lfloor q/2 \rfloor)^\mathsf{T}\mathbf{A} = \tilde{\mathbf{s}}^\mathsf{T}\mathbf{A} + \mathbf{e}_0^\mathsf{T} + (\mathbf{k}^* \lfloor q/2 \rfloor)^\mathsf{T}\mathbf{A}$$
$$= \mathbf{s}^\mathsf{T}\mathbf{A} + \mathbf{e}_0^\mathsf{T}$$

where $\mathbf{s} = \tilde{\mathbf{s}} + (\mathbf{k}^* \lfloor q/2 \rfloor)$ and

$$\mathbf{c}_1^{*\mathsf{T}} = \mathbf{c}_0^{*\mathsf{T}}\mathbf{R} + \mathbf{v}^\mathsf{T} = (\mathbf{s}^\mathsf{T}\mathbf{A} + \mathbf{e}_0^\mathsf{T})\mathbf{R} + \mathbf{v}^\mathsf{T} = \mathbf{s}^\mathsf{T}(\mathbf{AR}) + (\mathbf{e}_0^\mathsf{T}\mathbf{R} + \mathbf{v}^\mathsf{T})$$
$$= \mathbf{s}^\mathsf{T}(\mathbf{A}_1 + \mathsf{FRD}(H(\mathbf{c}_0^*))\mathbf{G}) + \mathbf{e}_1^\mathsf{T}$$

By adapting Theorem 3.1 of [21] and Corollary 3.10 of [23], conditioned on $\mathbf{A}_1$, $\mathbf{e}_1$ has a distribution that is statistically close to $D_{\mathbb{Z},s}^w$, where $s^2 = (\|\mathbf{e}_0\|^2 + m(\alpha q)^2) \cdot \omega(\sqrt{\log n})^2$. Therefore, we have $\Pr[S_4] = \Pr[\mathcal{B}_2(\mathbf{B}, \mathbf{x}^\mathsf{T}\mathbf{B} + \mathbf{y}^\mathsf{T}) = 1]$, the Inequality 6 follows.

Next, we show $\Pr[\mathsf{Forge}_4]$ and $\Pr[\mathsf{Forge}_5]$ are close. Let $\mathcal{B}_2'$ be an LWE-problem solver interacting with the PKE scheme adversary $\mathcal{A}$. $\mathcal{B}_2'$ receives an instance of $\mathsf{LWE}_{n,m,q,D_{\mathbb{Z},\alpha q}}$ $(\mathbf{B}, \mathbf{b}^\mathsf{T}) \in (\mathbb{Z}_q^{n \times m} \times \mathbb{Z}_q^m)$. It needs to decide that if $\mathbf{b}$ is uniformly random (independent of $\mathbf{B}$) or there exists $\mathbf{x} \sim D_{\mathbb{Z},\alpha q}^n$ and $\mathbf{y} \sim D_{\mathbb{Z},\alpha q}^m$ such that $\mathbf{b}^\mathsf{T} = \mathbf{x}^\mathsf{T}\mathbf{B} + \mathbf{y}^\mathsf{T}$. $\mathcal{B}_2'$ works as follows:

- It follows Game 5 (as specified in Fig. 4) to generate pk, sk except that it sets $\mathbf{A} \leftarrow \mathbf{B}, \tilde{\mathbf{c}}_0^* \leftarrow \mathbf{b}$.
- It follows Game 5 (as specified in Fig. 4 to generate ct* except for $\mathbf{c}_1^*$. To construct $\mathbf{c}_1^*$, $\mathcal{B}_2$ samples $\mathbf{v} \leftarrow D_{\mathbb{Z}, \alpha q \sqrt{m} \cdot \omega(\sqrt{\log n})}^w$ and set $\mathbf{c}_1^{*\mathsf{T}} \leftarrow \mathbf{c}_0^{*\mathsf{T}} \mathbf{R} + \mathbf{v}^{\mathsf{T}}$.
- Decryption queries made before the release of ct* are answered by following the Game 5 specification (i.e., Fig. 5). For any decryption query $\mathsf{ct} = (\mathbf{c}_0^*, \mathbf{c}_1, \phi, \sigma) \neq \mathsf{ct}^*$, check if $\mathsf{MAC.Ver}(mk^*, \sigma, \mathbf{c}_0 \| \mathbf{c}_1 \| \phi) = 1$. If so, abort the experiment and output 1. Otherwise, return $\perp$ to $\mathcal{A}$. [2]
- Eventually, if $\mathcal{A}$ halts and $\mathcal{B}_2'$ has not previously aborted the experiment, $\mathcal{B}_2'$ outputs a random bit.

Notice that if the given challenge $(\mathbf{B}, \mathbf{b}^{\mathsf{T}})$ are LWE samples, $\mathcal{B}_2'$ simulates Game 4 and aborts when Forge_4 happens (i.e., $\mathsf{MAC.Ver}(mk^*, \sigma, \mathbf{c}_0^* \| \mathbf{c}_1 \| \phi) = 1$). So, $\Pr[\mathcal{B}_2'(\mathbf{B}, \mathbf{b}^{\mathsf{T}}) = 1] = \Pr[\mathcal{B}_2'(\mathbf{B}, \mathbf{b}^{\mathsf{T}}) = 1 | \neg \mathsf{Forge}_4] \cdot \Pr[\neg \mathsf{Forge}_4] + \Pr[1 \leftarrow \mathcal{B}_2' | \mathsf{Forge}_4] \cdot \Pr[\mathsf{Forge}_4] = \frac{1}{2} + \frac{1}{2} \cdot \Pr[\mathsf{Forge}_4]$. Similarly, we have $\Pr[\mathcal{B}_2'(\mathbf{B}, \mathbf{x}^{\mathsf{T}}\mathbf{B} + \mathbf{y}^{\mathsf{T}}) = 1] = \frac{1}{2} + \frac{1}{2} \cdot \Pr[\mathsf{Forge}_5]$. This leads to the Inequality 7.   □

Game 6. In Game 6, we modify the way that $\mathbf{c}_0^*$ in ct* are generated (as shown in Fig. 4). Specifically, $\mathbf{c}_0^* \leftarrow U(\mathbb{Z}_q^m)$. The other parts of ct* and decryption queries are handled as in Game 5. Notice that in both Game 5 and Game 6, $\mathbf{c}_0^*$ are uniformly random over $\mathbb{Z}_q^m$ (recall in Game 5, $\mathbf{c}_0^* \leftarrow \tilde{\mathbf{c}}_0^* + \mathbf{A}^{\mathsf{T}}(\mathbf{k}^* \lfloor q/2 \rfloor)$ for $\tilde{\mathbf{c}}_0^* \leftarrow U(\mathbb{Z}_q^m)$ and $\tilde{\mathbf{c}}_0^*$ is not used in anywhere else). Hence, the distributions of the two games are identical, and, we have

$$\Pr[S_6] = \Pr[S_5] \quad \text{and} \quad \Pr[\mathsf{Forge}_6] = \Pr[\mathsf{Forge}_5] \tag{8}$$

Game 7. In Game 7, we modify the way of generating the symmetric encryption key dk^* and the MAC key mk^*, as specified in Fig. 4. In particular, dk^* and mk^* are chosen uniformly at random from the key spaces of SKE and MAC (as opposed to computed by $\mathsf{KDF}(\mathbf{k}^*)$). The other parts are exactly the same as Game 6. Since $\mathbf{k}^*$ is independent of ct*, this change is not noticeable to the adversary by the security of KDF, as stated in the following lemma.

Lemma 6. *For Game 6 and Game 7 defined as per Fig. 4 and Fig. 5, we have*

$$|\Pr[S_7] - \Pr[S_6]| \leq \mathsf{Adv}_{\mathsf{KDF}, \mathcal{B}_3}^{\mathsf{ot-ind}}(\lambda) \tag{9}$$

$$|\Pr[\mathsf{Forge}_7] - \Pr[\mathsf{Forge}_6]| \leq 2 \cdot \mathsf{Adv}_{\mathsf{KDF}, \mathcal{B}_3'}^{\mathsf{ind}}(\lambda) \tag{10}$$

for some adversary $\mathcal{B}_3$ and $\mathcal{B}_3'$ against the LWE problem.

Proof. We first show that $\Pr[S_7]$ and $\Pr[S_6]$ are computationally close. Let $\mathcal{B}_3$ be an adversary against KDF. First, $\mathcal{B}_3$ receives a string $r \in \{0,1\}^{|\mathcal{K}_{\mathsf{ske}}| + |\mathcal{K}_{\mathsf{mac}}|}$ and it needs tell if r is random or $r = \mathsf{KDF}(\mathbf{k}^*)$ for some $\mathbf{k}^* \in \{0,1\}^n$. $\mathcal{B}_3$ proceeds with as follows

---

[2] Note that any decryption query made before the release of ct* with $H(\mathbf{c}_0) = H(\mathbf{c}_0^*)$ is excluded since Game 2.

- It follows Game 6 to generate pk, sk, c_0^* (as specified in Fig. 4) except that in step 2, it simply sets the first $|\mathcal{K}_{\mathsf{ske}}|$ bits (resp. the last $|\mathcal{K}_{\mathsf{mac}}-)$ bits of r to be dk^* (resp. mk^*). Then, it sets $\mathbf{A} \leftarrow \mathbf{B}$, $\tilde{c}_0^* \leftarrow \mathbf{b}$.
- It follows Game 7 specification to generate ct^* (as specified in Fig. 4) .
- It follows Game 7 specification (Fig. 5) to answer decryption queries.
- Finally, $\mathcal{B}_2$ outputs 1 when the security game outputs 1 (i.e., $\mathcal{A}$ outputs $b' = b$). Otherwise $\mathcal{B}_2$ outputs 0.

We can see that $\Pr[\mathcal{B}_3(1^\lambda, \mathsf{KDF}(\mathbf{k}^*)) = 1] = \Pr[S_6]$ and $\Pr[\mathcal{B}_3(1^\lambda, r)] = \Pr[S_7]$ where r is random, and thus we get the inequality 9.

Similarly, we can show that Forge_6 and Forge_7 happen with essentially the same probability provided KDF is secure. To this end, we build an efficient algorithm $\mathcal{B}_3'$ that breaks KDF. $\mathcal{B}_3'$ proceeds as follows:

- It follows Game 6 to generate pk, sk, c_0^* (as specified in Fig. 4) except that in step 2, it simply sets the first $|\mathcal{K}_{\mathsf{ske}}|$ bits (resp. the last $|\mathcal{K}_{\mathsf{mac}}|)$ bits of r to be dk^* (resp. mk^*). Then, it sets $\mathbf{A} \leftarrow \mathbf{B}$, $\tilde{c}_0^* \leftarrow \mathbf{b}$.
- It follows Game 7 to generate ct^* (as specified in Fig. 4).
- Decryption queries made before the release of ct^* are answered by following Game 7 specification. For any decryption query $\mathsf{ct} = (\mathbf{c}_0, \mathbf{c}_1, \phi, \sigma) \neq \mathsf{ct}^*$ made after the release of ct^*
  1. if $\mathbf{c}_0 \neq \mathbf{c}_0^*$ (which implies $H(\mathbf{c}_0) \neq H(\mathbf{c}_0^*)$), answer it by following Game 7 specification (Fig. 5).
  2. For $\mathbf{c}_0 = \mathbf{c}_0^*$, check if $\mathsf{MAC.Ver}(mk^*, \sigma, \mathbf{c}_0||\mathbf{c}_1||\phi) = 1$. If so, abort the experiment and output 1. Otherwise, return $\perp$ to $\mathcal{A}$.
- Finally, $\mathcal{B}_3'$ outputs 1 when the security game outputs 1 (i.e., $\mathcal{A}$ outputs $b' = b$). Otherwise $\mathcal{B}_3'$ outputs 0.

We can see that $\Pr[\mathcal{B}_3'(1^\lambda, r \leftarrow \mathsf{KDF}(\mathbf{k}^*))] = \frac{1}{2} + \frac{1}{2} \cdot \Pr[\mathsf{Forge}_6]$ and $\Pr[\mathcal{B}_3'(1^\lambda, r \leftarrow U)] = \frac{1}{2} + \frac{1}{2} \cdot \Pr[\mathsf{Forge}_7]$ for random r. This shows the inequality 10. $\square$

We note that in Game 7, since mk^* is sampled at random and independent of $\mathbf{c}_0^*$, $\mathbf{c}_1^*$ and ϕ^*, we can easily bound $\Pr[\mathsf{Forge}_7]$ by the security of MAC. We prove the following Lemma.

Lemma 7. *Let Q_2 be the maximun number of decryption queries that the adversary $\mathcal{A}$ can make after seeing ct^* in Game 7. Then we have*

$$\Pr[\mathsf{Forge}_7] \leq Q_2 \cdot \mathsf{Adv}_{\mathsf{MAC}, \mathcal{B}_4}^{\mathsf{ot-suf}}(\lambda) \tag{11}$$

for some adversary $\mathcal{B}_4$ against the unforgeability of MAC.

Proof. Let $Q_2 = Q_2(\lambda)$ be the upper bound on the number of decryption query made by $\mathcal{A}$ *after* seeing the challenge ciphertext ct^*. We constructed an efficient MAC-breaking algorithm $\mathcal{B}_4$ which works as follows:

- $\mathcal{B}_4$ chooses a random index j from $\{1, 2, ..., Q_2\}$.
- It follows Game 7 to generate pk, sk, c_0^* (as specified in Fig. 4) except for mk^* (which is possessed by the MAC challenger). Note that dk^* remains randomly chosen as in Game 7.

- For decryption queries $\mathsf{ct} = (\mathbf{c}_0, \mathbf{c}_1, \phi, \sigma) \neq \mathsf{ct}^*$ made by $\mathcal{A}$ before the release of the challenge ciphertext. we know that $H(\mathbf{c}_0) \neq H(\mathbf{c}_0^*)$. So, such decryption queries are answered in the usual way using the algorithm Invert with the gadget trapdoor as in Game 7.
- It follows Game 7 to generate ct^* (as specified in Fig. 4) except for σ^* (i.e., $\mathcal{B}_4$ generates $\mathbf{c}_1^*$, ϕ^* together with the already existed $\mathbf{c}_0^*$). To get σ^*, $\mathcal{B}_4$ sends "message" $\mathbf{c}_0^* \| \mathbf{c}_1^* \| \phi^*$ to its challenger and gets back σ^*. Then it releases $\mathsf{ct}^* = (\mathbf{c}_0^*, \mathbf{c}_1^*, \phi^*, \sigma^*)$ to $\mathcal{A}$.
- For ith after-challenge decryption query where $1 \leq i \leq j - 1$, $\mathcal{B}_4$ proceeds as specified by Game 7. For the ith after-challenge decryption query $\mathsf{ct} = (\mathbf{c}_0, \mathbf{c}_1, \phi, \sigma)$, $\mathcal{B}_4$ submits $(\mathbf{c}_0 \| \mathbf{c}_1 \| \phi)$ to its MAC challenger and halts.

It can be seen that the probability of $\mathcal{B}_4$ in outputting a valid MAC forgery is at least $\Pr[\mathsf{Forge}_7]/Q_2$ which shows $\Pr[\mathsf{Forge}_7] \leq Q_2 \cdot \mathsf{Adv}^{ot-suf}_{\mathsf{MAC},\mathcal{B}_4}(\lambda)$. $\qquad \square$

Game 8. Game 8 is identical to Game 7 except that the challenge ciphertext components ϕ^* are chosen randomly (as specified in Fig. 4). Since dk^* is independently and randomly chosen, a straightforward reduction shows that Game 6 and Game 7 are computationally indistinguishability. In particular,

$$|\Pr[S_8] - \Pr[S_7]| \leq \mathsf{Adv}^{ot-ind}_{\mathsf{SKE},\mathcal{B}_5}(\lambda). \tag{12}$$

for some adversary against SKE. Finally, we can see that in Game 8, the challenge ciphertext ct^* is independent of the bit value b. So, the adversary has no advantage in winning the game. So,

$$\Pr[S_8] = 1/2 \tag{13}$$

Combining inequalities (1) to (13) with triangle inequality, we obtain the bound

$$\mathsf{Adv}^{ind-cca}_{\mathsf{PKE},\mathcal{A}}(\lambda) \leq \frac{Q_1}{q^m} + Q_2 \cdot \mathsf{Adv}^{coll}_{H,\mathcal{B}_1}(\lambda) + \mathsf{Adv}^{\mathsf{NLWE}_{n,m,q,D_{\mathbb{Z},\alpha q}}}_{\mathcal{B}_2}(\lambda)$$

$$+ 2 \cdot \mathsf{Adv}^{\mathsf{NLWE}_{n,m,q,D_{\mathbb{Z},\alpha q}}}_{\mathcal{B}'_2}(\lambda) + \mathsf{Adv}^{ot-ind}_{\mathsf{SKE},\mathcal{B}_3}(\lambda) + 2 \cdot \mathsf{Adv}^{ot-ind}_{\mathsf{SKE},\mathcal{B}_3}(\lambda)$$

$$+ Q_2 \cdot \mathsf{Adv}^{ot-suf}_{\mathsf{MAC},\mathcal{B}_4}(\lambda) + \mathsf{Adv}^{ot-ind}_{\mathsf{SKE},\mathcal{B}_5}(\lambda) + \mathsf{negl}(\lambda)$$

where all terms are negligible based on our assumptions.

4   CCA-Secure Hybrid Encryption from Low-Noise LPN

This section shows how to combine our idea with the tag-based encryption system from low-noise learning parity with noise problem due to Kiltz et al. [17] to obtain a CCA-secure hybrid encryption system. Following Kiltz et al. [17], we denote by Ber_p be the Bernouli distribution with parameter $0 \geq p \leq 1/2$, i.e. $x \leftarrow \mathsf{Ber}_p$ is the random variable over $\{0,1\}$ with $\Pr[x = 1] = p$. The LPN problem and its variant extended Knapsack LPN problem used in our system are as defined in Sect. 2.2, [17]. They have low noise rate $p \approx 1/\sqrt{n}$. We denote by $|\mathbf{a}|$ the hamming weight of vector $\mathbf{a} \in \mathbb{Z}_2^n$.

The hybrid encryption system uses the following public parameters.

1. The security parameter λ, the dimension of LPN problem n, and parameter $m \geq 2n$. A constant c with $0 < c < 1/4$ that defines: (1) the Bernoulli parameter $p = \sqrt{c/m}$, and (2) the bound $\beta = 2\sqrt{cm}$ for checking decryption consistency, and (2) a binary linear error-correcting code with generation matrix $\hat{\mathbf{G}}_1 : \mathbb{Z}_2^{n\times m}$ which corrects up to αm errors for some $4c < \alpha < 1$. Another error-correcting code with generation matrix $\hat{\mathbf{G}}_2 \in \mathbb{Z}_2^{n\times\ell}$ (where $\mathbb{Z}_2^\ell$ for $\ell \geq \lambda$ is the session key space for the KEM part).
2. A full-rank difference encoding (see [3,17]) FRD $: \mathbb{Z}_2^n \to \mathbb{Z}_2^{n\times n}$ that for any $\mathbf{x}, \mathbf{y} \in \mathbb{Z}_2^n$ with $\mathbf{x} \neq \mathbf{y}$, FRD$(\mathbf{x}) -FRD(\mathbf{y})$ is invertible over $\mathbb{Z}_2^{n\times n}$. In particular, FRD$(\mathbf{x})$ is invertible over $\mathbb{Z}_2^{n\times n}$ if $\mathbf{x} \neq \mathbf{0}$.
3. A collision resistance hash function $H : \{0,1\} \to \mathbb{Z}_2^n \setminus \{\mathbf{0}\}$ where $\mathbf{0}$ is the zero vector of $\mathbb{Z}_2^n$, a secret-key encryption system SKE $=$ (SKE.Enc, SKE.Dec) with key space $\mathcal{K}_{\mathsf{ske}}$, message space $\mathcal{M}_{\mathsf{ske}}$, and ciphertext space $\mathcal{C}_{\mathsf{ske}}$, a secure message authentication code MAC $=$ (MAC.Sign, MAC.Ver) with key space $\mathcal{K}_{\mathsf{mac}}$. A key derivation function KDF $: \{0,1\}^\ell \to \mathcal{K}_{\mathsf{ske}} \times \mathcal{K}_{\mathsf{mac}}$.

- PKE.Gen(1^λ):
  1. $\mathbf{A} \leftarrow U(\mathbb{Z}_2^{n\times m})$, $\mathbf{A}_2 \leftarrow U(\mathbb{Z}_2^{n\times m})$, $\mathbf{U} \leftarrow U(\mathbb{Z}_2^{n\times\ell})$.
  2. $\mathbf{T} \leftarrow \mathsf{Ber}_p^{m\times m}$, $\mathbf{A}_1 \leftarrow \mathbf{AT}$.
  3. pk $\leftarrow (\mathbf{A}, \mathbf{A}_1, \mathbf{A}_2, \mathbf{U})$, sk $\leftarrow \mathbf{T}$.
- PKE.Enc(pk, M):
  1. $\mathbf{k} \leftarrow U(\{0,1\}^\ell)$, $(dk, mk) \leftarrow$ KDF$(\mathbf{k})$.
  2. $\mathbf{s} \leftarrow U(\mathbb{Z}_2^n)$, $\mathbf{T}_1, \mathbf{T}_2 \leftarrow \mathsf{Ber}_p^{m\times m}$, $\mathbf{e}_0 \leftarrow \mathsf{Ber}_p^m$.
  3. $\mathbf{e}_1^\intercal \leftarrow \mathbf{e}_0^\intercal\mathbf{T}_1$, $\mathbf{e}_2 \leftarrow \mathbf{e}_0^\intercal\mathbf{T}_2$, $\mathbf{e}_3 \leftarrow \mathsf{Ber}_p^\ell$.
  4. $[\mathbf{c}_0^\intercal|\mathbf{c}_2^\intercal|\mathbf{c}_3^\intercal] \leftarrow \mathbf{s}^\intercal[\mathbf{A}|\mathbf{A}_2|\mathbf{U}] + [\mathbf{e}_0^\intercal|\mathbf{e}_2^\intercal|\mathbf{e}_3^\intercal] + \mathbf{k}^\intercal\hat{\mathbf{G}}_2$
  5. $\mathbf{c}_1^\intercal \leftarrow \mathbf{s}^\intercal(\mathbf{A}_1 + \mathrm{FRD}(H(\mathbf{c}_0||\mathbf{c}_2||\mathbf{c}_3))\hat{\mathbf{G}}_1) + \mathbf{e}_1^\intercal$
  6. $\phi \leftarrow$ SKE.Enc(dk, M), $\sigma \leftarrow$ MAC.Sign$(mk, \mathbf{c}_0||\mathbf{c}_1||\mathbf{c}_2||\mathbf{c}_3||\phi)$.
  7. Return ct $\leftarrow (\mathbf{c}_0, \mathbf{c}_1, \mathbf{c}_2, \mathbf{c}_3, \phi, \sigma)$.
- PKE.Dec$(\mathsf{pk}, \mathsf{sk}, \mathsf{ct})$:
  1. Parse ct $= (\mathbf{c}_0, \mathbf{c}_1, \mathbf{c}_2.\mathbf{c}_3, \phi, \sigma)$; Output $\perp$ if ct doesn't parse.
  2. Let $\mathbf{H} \leftarrow \mathrm{FRD}(H(\mathbf{c}_0||\mathbf{c}_2||\mathbf{c}_3)) \in \mathbb{Z}_2^{n\times n}$; Set $\tilde{\mathbf{c}}_0^\intercal \leftarrow -\mathbf{c}_0^\intercal\mathbf{T} + \mathbf{c}_1^\intercal = (-\mathbf{e}_0^\intercal\mathbf{T} + \mathbf{e}_1^\intercal) + \mathbf{s}^\intercal\mathbf{H}\hat{\mathbf{G}}_1$; Use the error correction property of $\hat{\mathbf{G}}_1$ to reconstruct $\mathbf{s}^\intercal\mathbf{H}$ (from the error $-\mathbf{e}_0^\intercal\mathbf{T} + \mathbf{e}_1^\intercal$), and, then recover $\mathbf{s}^\intercal \leftarrow \mathbf{s}^\intercal\mathbf{H}\mathbf{H}^{-1}$.
  3. If $|\mathbf{c}_0^\intercal - \mathbf{s}^\intercal\mathbf{A}| \leq \beta$, $|\mathbf{c}_1^\intercal - \mathbf{s}^\intercal(\mathbf{A}_1 + \mathbf{H}\hat{\mathbf{G}}_1)| \leq \alpha m/2$, $|\mathbf{c}_2^\intercal - \mathbf{s}^\intercal\mathbf{A}| \leq \alpha m/2$, compute $\tilde{\mathbf{c}}_2^\intercal \leftarrow \mathbf{c}_3^\intercal - \mathbf{s}^\intercal\mathbf{U} = \mathbf{e}_3^\intercal + \mathbf{k}^\intercal\hat{\mathbf{G}}_2$ and use the error correction property of $\hat{\mathbf{G}}_2$ to recover $\mathbf{k}$ and $\mathbf{e}_3$; Otherwise, abort and return $\perp$.
  4. If $|\mathbf{e}_3| > \beta$, abort and return $\perp$; Otherwise, set $(dk, mk) \leftarrow$ KDF$(\mathbf{k})$ and continue.
  5. Output $M \leftarrow$ SKE.Dec(dk, ϕ) if $1 \leftarrow$ MAC.Ver$(mk, \mathbf{c}_0||\mathbf{c}_1||\mathbf{c}_2||\mathbf{c}_3||\phi, \sigma)$; Otherwise output $\perp$.

Discussions. The system is based on the selective-tag weak CCA-secure encryption system by Kiltz et al. [17] (KMP system), except with the following differences. First, the system uses a hash of the concatenation of ciphertext components $\mathbf{c}_0, \mathbf{c}_2, \mathbf{c}_3$ as a tag for the tag-based trapdoor function of the KMP system, while the tag is chosen uniformly random from $\mathbb{Z}_2^n$ (and then mapped into a matrix in $\mathbb{Z}_2^{n \times n}$). Second, $\mathbf{k}$ in [17] is the message being encrypted. In our case, the session key is encapsulated in the KEM part. Then, the session key is used to derive keys for the secret-key encryption and the MAC. In summary, the "public-key" part of our system is essentially the same as the KMP system, and hence, its correctness follows directly from the correctness of the KMP encryption system (refer to [17] for details), and the correctness of the secret-key encryption and the MAC systems.

The security of the above HE system follows from the security of our LWE-based HE system. There are three differences between these two systems. The first one is that the LPN-based one has an extra matrix $\mathbf{A}_2 \in \mathbb{Z}_2^{n \times m}$, which is needed for the double trapdoor technique from [17]. Due to the low noise rate of the private key $\mathbf{T}$, the public matrix $\mathbf{A}_1 = \mathbf{AT}$ is only computationally indistinguishable from random (based on the Knapsack LPN problem). So, in the security proof, $\mathbf{T}$ cannot be used for responding to decryption queries when we need to argue the distribution of $\mathbf{A}$ is computationally uniform. The matrix $\mathbf{A}_2$ helps to bring in an extra trapdoor, by setting $[\mathbf{A}|\mathbf{A}_2] = [\mathbf{A}|\mathbf{A}\hat{\mathbf{T}} + \hat{\mathbf{G}}_1]$, to bridge this gap. The second difference is we add LPN samples $\mathbf{c}_3$ for hiding the session key $\mathbf{k}$, whereas we directly encode the session key into the LWE "witness" $\mathbf{s} \in \mathbb{Z}_q^n$. We do this with the LPN-based constriction to follow the KMP construction [17]. The last one is the construction of noise terms $\mathbf{e}_1, \mathbf{e}_2$. We follow the KMP system to compute the noise terms $\mathbf{e}_1, \mathbf{e}_2$ from the noise $\mathbf{e}_0$ (whereas all LWE error terms are vectors chosen independently from some Gaussian distributions). The hardness of the leaky knapsack LPN problem is used to handle such a correlation in [17], which applies to our case as well.

The security proof of our LPN system is very similar to the security proof of our LWE-based HE system, thanks to the similarities of Kiltz et al.'s double-trapdoor and Micciancio-Peikert lattice trapdoor. Our LWE-based system crucially relies on the fact that the LWE trapdoor function's tag, $H(\mathbf{c}_0)$, is a secure commitment of the session key. Similarly, the LPN trapdoor function's "tag" $H(\mathbf{c}_0||\mathbf{c}_2||\mathbf{c}_3)$ is also an binding and hiding commitment of the session key: Given a random $\mathbf{A} \in \mathbb{Z}_2^{n \times m}$, and $\mathbf{e} \leftarrow \text{Ber}_p^m$, $\mathbf{c}_0^\mathsf{T} = \mathbf{s}^\mathsf{T}\mathbf{A} + \mathbf{e}_0^\mathsf{T}$, a noisy random linear code w.r.t $\mathbf{A}$, determines $\mathbf{s}$ w.h.p over the choice of $\mathbf{A}$ (see [11], Theorem 2.3). So, $\mathbf{c}_3^\mathsf{T} = \mathbf{s}^\mathsf{T}\mathbf{A} + \mathbf{e}_3^\mathsf{T} + \mathbf{k}^\mathsf{T}\hat{\mathbf{G}}_2$ with $\mathbf{e}_3 \leftarrow \text{Ber}_p^m$ determines $\mathbf{k}$ due to the error correction and unique decoding properties of $\hat{\mathbf{G}}_2$. The SKE and MAC in the two systems are used in the same way. Therefore, we can apply exactly the same strategy that used in proving the LWE-based construction to the LPN-based system. Due to the space limitation and high similarity with the proof of Theorem 1, we omit the security proof of the LPN-based HE system.

5   Conclusion

Based on the LWE problem and the low-noise LPN problem, we have presented two CCA-secure hybrid encryption systems in the standard model. The systems give the first post-quantum examples of CCA-secure hybrid encryption systems with non-CCA secure KEMs. Our systems are efficient. For instance, the KEM part of the LWE-based HE system is simply the lattice trapdoor function from [19], which is supported by efficient implementations (e.g., [5,12]). Our systems do not fit into the theoretic frameworks established in [1,16]. We leave providing a theoretic framework that explains our constructions as future work.

References

1. Abdalla, M., et al.: Searchable encryption revisited: consistency properties, relation to anonymous IBE, and extensions. In: Shoup, V. (ed.) CRYPTO 2005. LNCS, vol. 3621, pp. 205–222. Springer, Heidelberg (2005). https://doi.org/10.1007/11535218_13
2. Abe, M., Gennaro, R., Kurosawa, K.: Tag-KEM/DEM: a new framework for hybrid encryption. J. Cryptol. **21**(1), 97–130 (2008)
3. Agrawal, S., Boneh, D., Boyen, X.: Efficient lattice (H)IBE in the standard model. In: Gilbert, H. (ed.) EUROCRYPT 2010. LNCS, vol. 6110, pp. 553–572. Springer, Heidelberg (2010). https://doi.org/10.1007/978-3-642-13190-5_28
4. Alekhnovich, M.: More on average case vs approximation complexity. In: FOCS 2003, Proceedings, pp. 298–307 (2003)
5. Bert, P., Fouque, P.-A., Roux-Langlois, A., Sabt, M.: Practical implementation of ring-SIS/LWE based signature and IBE. In: Lange, T., Steinwandt, R. (eds.) PQCrypto 2018. LNCS, vol. 10786, pp. 271–291. Springer, Cham (2018). https://doi.org/10.1007/978-3-319-79063-3_13
6. Boneh, D., Katz, J.: Improved efficiency for CCA-secure cryptosystems built using identity-based encryption. In: Menezes, A. (ed.) CT-RSA 2005. LNCS, vol. 3376, pp. 87–103. Springer, Heidelberg (2005). https://doi.org/10.1007/978-3-540-30574-3_8
7. Boyen, X., Izabachène, M., Li, Q.: A simple and efficient CCA-secure lattice KEM in the standard model. In: Galdi, C., Kolesnikov, V. (eds.) SCN 2020. LNCS, vol. 12238, pp. 321–337. Springer, Cham (2020). https://doi.org/10.1007/978-3-030-57990-6_16
8. Cramer, R., Shoup, V.: A practical public key cryptosystem provably secure against adaptive chosen ciphertext attack. In: Krawczyk, H. (ed.) CRYPTO 1998. LNCS, vol. 1462, pp. 13–25. Springer, Heidelberg (1998). https://doi.org/10.1007/BFb0055717
9. Cramer, R., Shoup, V.: Design and analysis of practical public-key encryption schemes secure against adaptive chosen ciphertext attack. SIAM J. Comput. **33**(1), 167–226 (2003)
10. Döttling, N.: Low noise LPN: KDM secure public key encryption and sample amplification. In: Katz, J. (ed.) PKC 2015. LNCS, vol. 9020, pp. 604–626. Springer, Heidelberg (2015). https://doi.org/10.1007/978-3-662-46447-2_27
11. Döttling, N.M.: Cryptography based on the Hardness of Decoding. Ph.D. thesis, Karlsruhe Institute of Technology (2014)
12. El Bansarkhani, R.: LARA: a design concept for lattice-based encryption. In: Goldberg, I., Moore, T. (eds.) FC 2019. LNCS, vol. 11598, pp. 377–395. Springer, Cham (2019). https://doi.org/10.1007/978-3-030-32101-7_23
13. Fujisaki, E., Okamoto, T.: Secure integration of asymmetric and symmetric encryption schemes. J. Cryptol. **26**(1), 80–101 (2013)

14. Gentry, C., Peikert, C., Vaikuntanathan, V.: Trapdoors for hard lattices and new cryptographic constructions. In: STOC , pp. 197–206 (2008)

15. Hofheinz, D., Hövelmanns, K., Kiltz, E.: A modular analysis of the Fujisaki-Okamoto transformation. In: Kalai, Y., Reyzin, L. (eds.) TCC 2017. LNCS, vol. 10677, pp. 341–371. Springer, Cham (2017). https://doi.org/10.1007/978-3-319-70500-2_12

16. Hofheinz, D., Kiltz, E.: Secure hybrid encryption from weakened key encapsulation. In: Menezes, A. (ed.) CRYPTO 2007. LNCS, vol. 4622, pp. 553–571. Springer, Heidelberg (2007). https://doi.org/10.1007/978-3-540-74143-5_31

17. Kiltz, E., Masny, D., Pietrzak, K.: Simple chosen-ciphertext security from low-noise LPN. In: Krawczyk, H. (ed.) PKC 2014. LNCS, vol. 8383, pp. 1–18. Springer, Heidelberg (2014). https://doi.org/10.1007/978-3-642-54631-0_1

18. Kurosawa, K., Desmedt, Y.: A new paradigm of hybrid encryption scheme. In: Franklin, M. (ed.) CRYPTO 2004. LNCS, vol. 3152, pp. 426–442. Springer, Heidelberg (2004). https://doi.org/10.1007/978-3-540-28628-8_26

19. Micciancio, D., Peikert, C.: Trapdoors for lattices: simpler, tighter, faster, smaller. In: Pointcheval, D., Johansson, T. (eds.) EUROCRYPT 2012. LNCS, vol. 7237, pp. 700–718. Springer, Heidelberg (2012). https://doi.org/10.1007/978-3-642-29011-4_41

20. Micciancio, D., Regev, O.: Worst-case to average-case reductions based on gaussian measures. SIAM J. Comput. 37(1), 267–302 (2007)

21. Peikert, C.: An efficient and parallel Gaussian sampler for lattices. In: Rabin, T. (ed.) CRYPTO 2010. LNCS, vol. 6223, pp. 80–97. Springer, Heidelberg (2010). https://doi.org/10.1007/978-3-642-14623-7_5

22. Peikert, C., et al.: A decade of lattice cryptography. Found. Trends® Theor. Comput. Sci. 10(4), 283–424 (2016)

23. Regev, O.: On lattices, learning with errors, random linear codes, and cryptography. In: STOC 2005, pp. 84–93 (2005)

24. Shoup, V.: Sequences of games: a tool for taming complexity in security proofs. Cryptology ePrint Archive, Report 2004/332 (2004)

25. Zhang, J., Yu, Y., Fan, S., Zhang, Z.: Improved lattice-based CCA2-secure PKE in the standard model. Sci. China Inf. Sci. 63(8), 1–22 (2020). https://doi.org/10.1007/s11432-019-9861-3

Cryptanalysis

Attacks on Beyond-Birthday-Bound MACs in the Quantum Setting

Tingting Guo[1,2], Peng Wang[1,2(✉)], Lei Hu[1,2], and Dingfeng Ye[1,2]

[1] SKLOIS, Institute of Information Engineering, CAS, Beijing, China
{guotingting,wpeng,hulei,yedingfeng}@iie.ac.cn
[2] School of Cyber Security, University of Chinese Academy of Sciences,
Beijing, China

Abstract. We systematically study the security of twelve Beyond-Birthday-Bound Message Authentication Codes (BBB MACs) in the Q2 model where attackers have quantum-query access to MACs. Assuming the block size of the underlying (tweakable) block cipher is n bits, the security proofs show that they are secure at least up to $\mathcal{O}(2^{2n/3})$ queries in the classical setting. The best classical attacks need $\mathcal{O}(2^{3n/4})$ queries. We consider secret state recovery against SUM-ECBC-like and PMAC_Plus-like MACs and key recovery against PMAC_Plus-like MACs. Both attacks lead to successful forgeries. The first attack costs $\mathcal{O}(2^{n/2}n)$ quantum queries by applying Grover-meet-Simon algorithm. The second attack costs $\mathcal{O}(2^{m/2})$ quantum queries by applying Grover's algorithm, assuming the key size of (tweakable) block cipher is m bits. As far as we know, these are the first quantum attacks against BBB MACs. It is remarkable that our attacks are suitable even for some optimally secure MACs, such as mPMAC+-f, mPMAC+-p1, and mPMAC+-p2.

Keywords: Beyond-birthday-bound · Message authentication codes · Quantum attacks

1 Introduction

Quantum Attacks Against Symmetric Crypto Primitives. Recent years we have seen amount of work to exploit the quantum security of symmetric crypto primitives, such as Feistel structure [14], Even-Mansour cipher [21], FX construction [22], message authentication codes (MACs) [17], authenticated encryption schemes [17], hash functions [10,15], etc., by using quantum algorithms including Simon's algorithm [29], Grover's algorithm [12], Grover-meet-Simon algorithm [22], BHT algorithm [5], etc. All the attacks are carried on in the Q2 model, where attackers can make superposition queries to a quantum oracle of $U_F : |x, y\rangle \mapsto |x, y \oplus F(x)\rangle$, where F is the classic primitive.

Simon's Algorithm and Birthday Attacks. Common standard MACs such as CBC-MAC, CMAC, PMAC, GMAC, suffer from birthday attacks in the classic setting, and are broken by using Simon's algorithm in polynomial time [17].

© Springer Nature Switzerland AG 2021
J. H. Cheon and J.-P. Tillich (Eds.): PQCrypto 2021, LNCS 12841, pp. 421–441, 2021.
https://doi.org/10.1007/978-3-030-81293-5_22

The procedure of the attack using Simon's algorithm is as follows: first construct a periodic function $f(x)$ based on the scheme, where the period is a hidden value s such that $f(x) = f(x \oplus s)$ for all x; second use Simon's algorithm to find the period s; third use the period s to carry out forgery etc. attacks. The period s also can be retrieved from a collision of $f(x) = f(y)$ for $x \neq y$, so that $s = x \oplus y$ with high probability. Therefore $\mathcal{O}(2^{n/2})$ classic queries is enough to find the period and break the scheme, where n is usually the block size of the underling (tweakable) block ciphers. So the schemes broken by using Simon's algorithm are destined to suffer from birthday attacks.

Beyond-Birthday-Bound MACs. The crypto community made great efforts to enhance the security of MACs, by constructing beyond-birthday-bound (BBB) ones, which are secure for above $2^{n/2}$ queries. In 2010, Yasuda firstly proposed a provable BBB MAC: SUM-ECBC [32]. Later on, other BBB MACs, such as PMAC_Plus [33], 3kf9 [34], LightMAC_Plus [26], 1k-PMAC_Plus [9], Poly-MAC [20] and so on were proposed. In 2018, Datta et al. [7] reduced the number of keys and proposed BBB MACs: 2K-ECBC_Plus, 2K-PMAC_Plus, 2kf9, and so on, where 2kf9 was broken by a birthday bound attack by Shen et al. [28]. The primary proofs show that they are secure up to $2^{2n/3}$ queries (ignoring the maximum message length). All the above BBB MACs follow a generic design paradigm called Double-block Hash-then-Sum (in short DbHtS) [7], which generates double hash blocks on the message and then sum the two encrypted blocks as the output. So the computation of DbHtS consists of two chains, which were denoted as G and H, and $DbHtS(M) = G(M) \oplus H(M)$ for the message M.

In 2020, Cogliati et al. [6] proposed some variants of PMAC_Plus: mPMAC+-f, mPMAC+-p1, mPMAC+-p2, with optimal security, in other words, security up to 2^n queries. They follow a variant of DbHtS, we call it as Double-block Hash-then-Function (in short DbHtF). The computation of DbHtF also consists of two chains, denoted as G and H, but the chain results are processed by a more general function F from $2n$ bits to n bits: $DbHtF(M) = F(G(M), H(M))$. Therefore all PMAC_Plus-like MACs which follow DbHtS also follow DbHtF. The double blocks bring $2n$-bit internal state, making the classic birthday attack no longer applicable.

Classical Attacks. Due to the $2n$-bit internal state in DbHtS MACs, the output collision of a pair of messages can not benefit forgery attacks. The best classical attacks against part of DbHtS MACs proposed by Leurent et al. [23] need $\mathcal{O}(2^{3n/4})$ queries. The crucial point is to find a quadruple of messages, which leads to successful forgeries. The search for such a quadruple is reduced to a 4-xor problem with $3n$-bit outputs based on DbHtS MACs. Recently, Kim et al. [20] further proved that some of them are secure up to $2^{3n/4}$ queries. So the attack is optimal in terms of the query number. In fact, Leurent's attack is suitable for 2K-ECBC_Plus, PolyMAC, and 2K-PMAC_Plus as well.

Direct Quantum Acceleration. The k-xor problem, a generalized birthday problem [30], is a hot topic related to quantum collision finding of hash functions [10,11,15,27]. The main idea comes from BHT algorithm [5]. To solve the core 4-xor problem with $3n$-bit outputs proposed in [23], the best algorithm needs $\mathcal{O}(2^{3n/5})$ quantum queries, which is the lowest bound according to [1]. Note that $\mathcal{O}(2^{3n/5})$ is slightly better than the query complexity of classical attacks.

Motivations. Are there any better quantum attacks against BBB MACs? What about the security of BBB MACs in the quantum setting?

Grover-meet-Simon Algorithm. For BBB MACs, Simon's algorithm is invalid. We need new techniques. In 2017, Leander and May [22] combined Grover's algorithm with Simon's algorithm to attack FX construction [18,19]. The main idea is to construct a function with two inputs based on FX, say $f(u, x)$. When the first input u equals to a special value k, the function has a hidden period s such that $f(k, x) = f(k, x \oplus s)$ for all x. Their combined algorithm use Grover's algorithm to search k, by running many independent Simon's algorithms to check whether the function is periodic or not, and recover both k and s in the end. The attack only costs $\mathcal{O}(2^{m/2}(m+n))$ quantum queries to FX, which is much less than the proved security up to $2^{\frac{m+n}{2}}$ queries [18], where m is the bit length of u, which is the key length of the underlying block cipher and n is the bit length of s, which is the block size. Their work provides a new tool to study the quantum security of symmetric schemes.

Attack Strategies. With strategies 1 and 2, we utilize Grover-meet-Simon algorithm to recover some secret states of BBB MACs, which lead to successful forgery attacks.

1) Strategy 1: For SUM-ECBC-like DbHtS MACs, G and H process the message in the same way but with different keys, and they are not secure under the quantum attack using Simon's algorithm. We can use the same method C, based on G (resp. H), to construct a periodic function denoted as $g(b, x) = C^G(b, x)$ (resp. $h(b, x) = C^H(b, x)$) where $b \in \{0, 1\}$ and $x \in \{0, 1\}^n$. The periods of g and h are denoted as $1\|s_1$ and $1\|s_2$ respectively. Then use the same method C on $DbHtS = G \oplus H$, we get $C^{DbHtS}(b, x) = C^G(b, x) \oplus C^H(b, x) = g(b, x) \oplus h(b, x)$. Unfortunately s_1 is equal to s_2 usually with negligible probability, so $C^{DbHtS}(b, x)$ is not a periodic function. We construct

$$f(u, x) = C^{DbHtS}(0, x) \oplus C^{DbHtS}(1, x \oplus u)$$
$$= g(0, x) \oplus h(0, x) \oplus g(1, x \oplus u) \oplus h(1, x \oplus u).$$

We can verify that when $u = s_1$ or s_2, $f(u, x)$ is a periodic function: the period is $s_1 \oplus s_2$. Thus we can use Grover-meet-Simon algorithm to recover both s_1 and s_2.

2) Strategy 2: For PMAC_Plus-like DbHtF MACs, G and H process the message in different ways with the same keys, making Strategy 1 not applicable. But we can use the same method based on G (resp. H), to construct a function denoted as $g(u, b, x)$ (resp. $h(u, b, x)$). When u equals a special value say u^*, both $g(u^*, b, x)$ and $h(u^*, b, x)$ are periodic functions with the same period $1\|s$. If the method is applied to $DbHtF$, we get

$$f(u, b, x) = F(g(u, b, x), h(u, b, x)).$$

For $u = u^*$, $f(u^*, b, x)$ is a periodic function. So Grover-meet-Simon algorithm can be applied to recover the special value u^* and the period $1\|s$.

3) Strategy of key search: We notice that most BBB MACs have more than one key. For example, mPMAC+-f, mPMAC+-p1, and mPMAC+-p2, are respectively keyed by five independent m-bit keys. For a perfect crypto primitive, there should be no better way to recover the keys than the exhaustive search, whose complexity is $\mathcal{O}(2^{5m/2})$ for $5m$-bit keys by Grover's algorithm. We found it is sufficient to find one key in order to create any number of forgeries for DbHtF MACs. Accelerating the search by Grover's search, the attack costs $\mathcal{O}(2^{m/2})$ quantum queries. Especially, we are able to recover all keys after recovering one key for some of DbHtS MACs.

Table 1. Summary of the main results. n is the message block size, m is the length of the key of underlying (tweakable) block cipher. The number of maximum blocks of a query is in number of constant length queries.

Scheme	Key space	Provable classical security query bound	Query complexity of classical attack	Query complexity of the quantum acceleration of classical attack	Quantum secret state recovery attack (our work)		Quantum key recovery attack (our work)	
					Queries	Qubits	Queries	Qubits
SUM-ECBC [32]	2^{4m}	$\Omega(2^{3n/4})$ [20]	$\mathcal{O}(2^{3n/4})$ [23]	$\mathcal{O}(2^{3n/5})$	$\mathcal{O}(2^{n/2}n)$	$\mathcal{O}(n^2)$	$\mathcal{O}(2^m n)$	$\mathcal{O}(m+n^2)$
2K-ECBC_Plus [7]	2^{3m}	$\Omega(2^{2n/3})$ [7]	$\mathcal{O}(2^{3n/4})$	$\mathcal{O}(2^{3n/5})$	$\mathcal{O}(2^{n/2}n)$	$\mathcal{O}(n^2)$	$\mathcal{O}(2^m n)$	$\mathcal{O}(m+n^2)$
PolyMAC [20]	2^{2m+2n}	$\Omega(2^{3n/4})$ [20]	$\mathcal{O}(2^{3n/4})$	$\mathcal{O}(2^{3n/5})$	$\mathcal{O}(2^{n/2}n)$	$\mathcal{O}(n^2)$	$\mathcal{O}(2^{(n+m)/2}n)$	$\mathcal{O}(m+n^2)$
GCM-SIV2 [16]	2^{4m+2n}	$\Omega(2^{2n/3})$ [16]	$\mathcal{O}(2^{3n/4})$ [23]	$\mathcal{O}(2^{3n/5})$	$\mathcal{O}(2^{n/2}n)$	$\mathcal{O}(n^2)$	$\mathcal{O}(2^{(n+m)/2}n)$	$\mathcal{O}(m+n^2)$
PMAC_Plus [33]	2^{3m}	$\Omega(2^{3n/4})$ [20]	$\mathcal{O}(2^{3n/4})$ [23]	$\mathcal{O}(2^{3n/5})$	$\mathcal{O}(2^{n/2}n)$	$\mathcal{O}(n^2)$	$\mathcal{O}(2^{m/2})$	$\mathcal{O}(m+n)$
1k-PMAC_Plus [9]	2^{m}	$\Omega(2^{2n/3})$ [9]	$\mathcal{O}(2^{3n/4})$ [23]	$\mathcal{O}(2^{3n/5})$	$\mathcal{O}(2^{n/2}n)$	$\mathcal{O}(n^2)$	$\mathcal{O}(2^{m/2})$	$\mathcal{O}(m+n)$
2K-PMAC_Plus [7]	2^{2m}	$\Omega(2^{2n/3})$ [7]	$\mathcal{O}(2^{3n/4})$	$\mathcal{O}(2^{3n/5})$	$\mathcal{O}(2^{n/2}n)$	$\mathcal{O}(n^2)$	$\mathcal{O}(2^{m/2})$	$\mathcal{O}(m+n)$
3kf9 [34]	2^{3m}	$\Omega(2^{3n/4})$ [20]	$\mathcal{O}(\sqrt[3]{n}2^{3n/4})$ [23]	$\mathcal{O}(2^{3n/5})$	$\mathcal{O}(2^{n/2})$	$\mathcal{O}(n)$	$\mathcal{O}(2^{m/2})$	$\mathcal{O}(m+n)$
mPMAC+-f [6]	2^{5m}	$\Omega(2^{n})$ [6]	-	-	$\mathcal{O}(2^{n/2}n)$	$\mathcal{O}(n^2)$	$\mathcal{O}(2^{m/2})$	$\mathcal{O}(m+n)$
mPMAC+-p1 [6]	2^{5m}	$\Omega(2^{n})$ [6]	-	-	$\mathcal{O}(2^{n/2}n)$	$\mathcal{O}(n^2)$	$\mathcal{O}(2^{m/2})$	$\mathcal{O}(m+n)$
mPMAC+-p2 [6]	2^{5m}	$\Omega(2^{n})$ [6]	-	-	$\mathcal{O}(2^{n/2}n)$	$\mathcal{O}(n^2)$	$\mathcal{O}(2^{m/2})$	$\mathcal{O}(m+n)$
PMAC_TBC3k [25]	2^{3m}	$\Omega(2^{n})$ [25]	-	-	-	-	$\mathcal{O}(2^{m/2})$	$\mathcal{O}(m+n)$

Our Contributions. Table 1 summarizes our main results and comparisons with provable security claims, best classical attack results, and its quantum acceleration results.

1) We reduce the query complexity from $\mathcal{O}(2^{3n/5})$ by direct quantum acceleration of classic method to $\mathcal{O}(2^{n/2}n)$ by our secret state recovery attacks in the Q2 model for both DbHtS and DbHtF MACs. Especially, our attack strategies are even suitable to optimal secure MACs, including mPMAC+-f, mPMAC+-p1, mPMAC+-p2 and PMAC_TBC3k.

2) We introduce a method which is sufficient to find one key in order to create any number of forgeries for DbHtF MACs, whose complexity is $\mathcal{O}(2^{m/2})$ in the Q2 model. Although one key recovery is enough to get successful forgery, we can further recover all keys of PMAC_Plus, 3kf9, and 2K-PMAC_Plus.

2 Preliminaries

For a positive integer m, let $\{0,1\}^m$ be the set of all m-bit binary string. For two bit strings x and y, the concatenation is $x\|y$, the *bitwise exclusive-or* is $x \oplus y$. Let $|\mathcal{U}|$ be the number of the elements in set $\mathcal{U}$.

2.1   Quantum Algorithms

1) Grover's algorithm. Grover's algorithm [12] can find a target value with high probability.

Grover Problem. Let m be a positive integer, and $test : \{0,1\}^m \to \{0,1\}$ be a boolean function ($|\{u : test(u) = 1\}| = e$). Find a u such that $test(u) = 1$.

Classically, we can search an element who satisfies $test(u) = 1$ with $\mathcal{O}(\frac{2^m}{e})$ queries to $test(\cdot)$. However, the Grover's algorithm [12] can find such an element with only $\mathcal{O}(\sqrt{\frac{2^m}{e}})$ quantum queries [4]. Generally, the $test$ function can't describe the target objects precisely. So we consider Grover problem with biased $test$ function.

Grover Problem with Biased Test Function. Let m be a positive integers, $\mathcal{U}(|\mathcal{U}| = e)$ be a subset in $\{0,1\}^m$, $test : \{0,1\}^m \to \{0,1\}$ be a boolean function who satisfies

$$\begin{cases} \Pr[test(u) = 1] = 1, & u \in \mathcal{U}, \\ \Pr[test(u) = 1] \leq p_1, & u \notin \mathcal{U}. \end{cases}$$

Find a $u \in \mathcal{U}$.

Grover's algorithm can solve the problem as well with high probability. Combined with Theorem 1 in paper [3], we get the following theorem.

Theorem 1. *(Adapted from [3]) Let $m, e, \mathcal{U}, test$ be defined as in Grover problem with biased test function, and $p_0 := \frac{e}{2^m}$. Assume the quantum implementation of $test(\cdot)$ costs $\mathcal{O}(n)$ qubits. Then Grover's algorithm with $t = \lceil \frac{\pi}{4 \arcsin \sqrt{p_0}} \rceil$ quantum queries to $test(\cdot)$ and $\mathcal{O}(m + n)$ qubits will output a $u \in \mathcal{U}$ with probability at least $\frac{p_0}{p_0 + p_1}[1 - (\frac{p_1}{p_0} + \sqrt{p_0 + p_1} + 2\sqrt{1 + \frac{p_1}{p_0}} p_0)^2]^{-3}$.*

We put Grover's algorithm and the proof of Theorem 1 in the full paper [13]. When apply Theorem 1 to concrete attacks of MACs, if $e = 1, p_1 \leq \frac{1}{2^{2m}}$, then for sufficient large m the Grover's algorithm with $\mathcal{O}(2^{m/2})$ quantum queries to $test(\cdot)$ and $\mathcal{O}(m + n)$ qubits will output a $u \in \mathcal{U}$ with probability almost 1 by Theorem 1.

2) Simon's algorithm. Simon's algorithm [29] finds the period of a periodic function in polynomial time.

Periodic/Aperiodic Function. Let n, d be two positive integers, $f : \{0,1\}^n \to \{0,1\}^d$ be a boolean function. We call f as a periodic (resp. aperiodic) function if there is a unique (resp. no) $s \in \{0,1\}^n \backslash \{0^n\}$ such that $f(x) = f(x \oplus s)$ for all $x \in \{0,1\}^n$.

Simon Problem. Let n, d be two positive integers, $f : \{0,1\}^n \to \{0,1\}^d$ be a periodic function with a period s. Find s.

Classically, if f is a periodic function, we can find out the period by searching collisions with $\mathcal{O}(2^{n/2})$ queries. However, if f is given as a quantum oracle, Simon's algorithm [29] can solve it with only $\mathcal{O}(n)$ quantum queries. Let

$$\varepsilon(f) := \max_{t \in \{0,1\}^n \backslash \{0^n, s\}} \Pr_x[f(x) = f(x \oplus t)]. \tag{1}$$

This parameter quantifies the disturbance of other partial periods, i.e., $f(x) = f(x \oplus t)$ where $t \in \{0,1\}^n \backslash \{0^n, s\}$. Kaplan et al. [17] have proved the following theorem.

Theorem 2. [17] *Let n, d, f, s be defined as in Simon problem. Let $\varepsilon(f)$ be defined as in Eq. (1), and c be a positive integer. Then Simon's algorithm with cn quantum queries to f and $\mathcal{O}(n + d)$ qubits will recover s with probability at least $1 - [2(\frac{1+\varepsilon(f)}{2})^c]^n$.*

3) Grover-meet-Simon Algorithm. In 2017 Leander and May [22] combined Grover's algorithm with Simon's algorithm to analyze FX construction. Their analysis is combined with FX construction too closely. So we consider the generalization case. A general problem is described as follows:

Grover-meet-Simon Problem. Let m, n, d be three positive integers, set $\mathcal{U} \subseteq \{0,1\}^m (|\mathcal{U}| = e)$ and $f : \{0,1\}^m \times \{0,1\}^n \to \{0,1\}^d$ be a function who satisfies

$$\begin{cases} f(u, \cdot) \text{ is a period function with period } s_u, & u \in \mathcal{U}, \\ f(u, \cdot) \text{ is an aperiodic function}, & u \notin \mathcal{U}. \end{cases}$$

Set $\mathcal{U}_s := \{(u, s_u) : u \in \mathcal{U}, s_u \text{ is the period of } f(u, \cdot)\}$. Find any tuple $(u, s_u) \in \mathcal{U}_s$.

The problem consists of the Grover problem as a whole and the Simon problem partially. The main idea is to search $u \in \mathcal{U}$ by Grover's algorithm and check whether or not $u \in \mathcal{U}$ by whether $f(u, \cdot)$ is periodic or not, which can be implemented by Simon's algorithm. Bonnetain [3] has formalized the Grover-meet-Simon algorithm. He presented the success probability for $|\mathcal{U}| = 1$. Let

$$\varepsilon(f) := \max_{(u,t) \in \{0,1\}^m \times \{0,1\}^n \backslash (\mathcal{U}_s \cup \{0,1\}^m \times \{0^n\})} \Pr_x[f(u, x) = f(u, x \oplus t)] \quad (2)$$

to quantify the disturbance of $u \notin \mathcal{U}$ and other partial periods ts for $u \in \mathcal{U}$, i.e., $f(u, x) = f(u, x \oplus t)$ where $(u, t) \in \{0,1\}^m \times \{0,1\}^n \backslash (\mathcal{U}_s \cup \{0,1\}^m \times \{0^n\})$. We generalize the success probability of the algorithm for $|\mathcal{U}| \geq 1$ as follows.

Theorem 3. *Let $m, n, d, f, \mathcal{U}, \mathcal{U}_s, e$ be defined as in Grover-meet-Simon problem. Let $\varepsilon(f)$ be defined as in Eq. (2). Let c be a positive integer, $p_0 := \frac{e}{2^m}$ and $p_1 := [2 \cdot (\frac{1+\varepsilon(f)}{2})^c]^n$. Then Grover-meet-Simon algorithm with $\lceil \frac{\pi}{4 \arcsin \sqrt{p_0}} \rceil \cdot cn$ quantum queries to f and $\mathcal{O}(m + cn^2 + cdn)$ qubits outputs a tuple $(u, s_u) \in \mathcal{U}_s$ with probability at least $\frac{(1-p_1)p_0}{p_0+p_1}[1 - (\frac{p_1}{p_0} + \sqrt{p_0 + p_1} + 2\sqrt{1 + \frac{p_1}{p_0}} p_0)^2]$.*

We put Grover-meet-Simon algorithm and the proof of Theorem 3 in the full paper [13]. When apply this algorithm to a concrete attack of MACs, if $\varepsilon(f) \leq 3/4, e \leq 2, d = m = n$ and n is sufficient large, then we let $c = 16$ and Grover-meet-Simon algorithm after $\mathcal{O}(2^{n/2}n)$ quantum queries to f using $\mathcal{O}(n^2)$ qubits will output a tuple $(u, s_u) \in \mathcal{U}_s$ with probability almost 1 by Theorem 3.

2.2   Quantum Security of MACs

Message authentication code (MAC) generates a tag T for any message M with key K: $T = \mathrm{MAC}_K(M)$. Given the quantum oracle of $\mathrm{MAC}_K(\cdot)$, Boneh and Zhandry [2] defined the existential unforgeability against quantum chosen message attack (EUF-qCMA). One MAC is EUF-qCMA if no quantum attacker can output $q+1$ distinct massage-tag pairs with non-negligible probability after q quantum queries to MAC_K. Notice that we can regard any classical query as a special quantum query. So the q quantum queries contain q quantum and classical queries in all.

For all concrete MACs in this paper, we assume the bit length of message is integral multiples of n. Also, we assume the underlying (tweakable) block cipher of MACs is a (tweakable) random permutation.

3   Secret State Recovery Attack for BBB MACs

3.1   Secret State Recovery Attack for SUM-ECBC-like MACs

We focus on DbHtS MAC [7]: $DbHtS(M) = G(M) \oplus H(M)$, which is the generic paradigm of SUM-ECBC-like MACs. Strategy 1 in Sect. 1 constructs

$$f(u, x) = g(0, x) \oplus h(0, x) \oplus g(1, x \oplus u) \oplus h(1, x \oplus u),$$

where periodic function g (resp. h) based on G (resp. H) and $g(b, x)$ (resp. $h(b, x)$) with a period $1\|s_1$ (resp. $1\|s_2$). When $u = s_1$ or s_2, $f(u, x)$ has a period of $s_1 \oplus s_2$. If $\varepsilon(f) \le 3/4$, then by Theorem 3, Simon-meet-Grover algorithm can find both s_1 and s_2 with at most $\mathcal{O}(2^{n/2}n)$ quantum queries and $\mathcal{O}(n^2)$ qubits. In the following, for any concrete SUM-ECBC-like MAC, we only give the construction of function f, the estimation of $\varepsilon(f)$, and the forgery attack after recovery of s_1 and s_2. The method applies to SUM-ECBC [32], PolyMAC [20], the authentication part of GCM-SIV2 [16] and 2K-ECBC_Plus [7]. We only take SUM-ECBC and PolyMAC as examples.

1) Secret State Recovery Attack for SUM-ECBC. SUM-ECBC was designed by Yasuda in 2010 [32], which is the sum of two independent ECBC-MACs. The scheme uses a block cipher keyed by four independent keys, denoted as E_1, E_2, E_3, E_4.

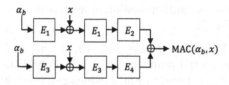

Fig. 1. SUM-ECBC with two-block message $M = (\alpha_b, x)$.

Construction of Function f. Let $b \in \{0,1\}$, $x \in \{0,1\}^n$, and α_0, α_1 are two arbitrary different fixed numbers in $\{0,1\}^n$. SUM-ECBC with message $M = (M[1], M[2]) = (\alpha_b, x)$ is shown in Fig. 1, which can be written as

$$\mathrm{MAC}(\alpha_b, x) = g(b, x) \oplus h(b, x),$$

where

$$g(b, x) = E_2(E_1(E_1(\alpha_b) \oplus x)), h(b, x) = E_4(E_3(E_3(\alpha_b) \oplus x)).$$

Obviously, g (resp. h) has a period of $1\|s_1$ where $s_1 = E_1(\alpha_0) \oplus E_1(\alpha_1)$ (resp. $1\|s_2$ where $s_2 = E_3(\alpha_0) \oplus E_3(\alpha_1)$). Given that E_1, E_3 are two independent random permutations, the probability of $s_1 = s_2$ is $1/2^n$. So in the following we assume $s_1 \neq s_2$. Let

$$f(u, x) = \mathrm{MAC}(\alpha_0, x) \oplus \mathrm{MAC}(\alpha_1, x \oplus u).$$

Then we have $\varepsilon(f) \leq \frac{1}{2}$, which has been proved in Appendix A.

Forgery Attack. After recovering s_1 and s_2, by using the property of $f(s_1, x) = f(s_1, x \oplus s_1 \oplus s_2)$ for any $x \in \{0,1\}^n$, we can make a successful forgery after 3 classic queries as follows.

1) Query $M_1 = (\alpha_0, x)$ and get tag T_1;
2) Query $M_2 = (\alpha_1, x \oplus s_1)$ and get tag T_2;
3) Query $M_3 = (\alpha_0, x \oplus s_1 \oplus s_2)$ and get tag T_3;
4) Forge $M_4 = (\alpha_1, x \oplus s_2)$ and its tag $T_1 \oplus T_2 \oplus T_3$.

In fact, we can forge any number of forgeries by repeating the above classic forgery step for different x. Now we try to break the notion of EUF-qCMA security. If $q' = \mathcal{O}(2^{n/2}n)$ denote the number of quantum queries made to find s_1 and s_2. The attacker just repeats the above classic forgery step $q' + 1$ times. So that $4q' + 4$ messages with valid tags are produced, using a total of $4q' + 3$ classical and quantum queries. Therefore, SUM-ECBC is broken by a quantum existential forgery attack. Generally, the EUF-qCMA attack is straightforward after we find the hidden periods. So we omit it in the following examples.

2) Secret State Recovery Attack for PolyMAC. By replacing the block cipher E_i in SUM-ECBC with multiplication functions $H_{k_i}(x) = k_i \cdot x$ for $i = 1, 3$, we get PolyMAC [20], where k_1, k_3 are two independent keys in $\{0,1\}^n$ and they are independent of the keys of E_2, E_4. The chain of MAC is actually Poly-Hash, which is used in the authentication of associated data in GCM-SIV2 [16], GCM [24] and HCTR [31].

Construction of Function f. Let $b \in \{0,1\}$ and $x \in \{0,1\}^n$, α_0, α_1 are two arbitrary different fixed numbers in $\{0,1\}^n$. PolyMAC with message $M = (M[1], M[2]) = (\alpha_b, x)$ is shown in Fig. 2, which can be written as

$$\mathrm{MAC}(\alpha_b, x) = g(b, x) \oplus h(b, x),$$

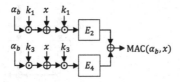

Fig. 2. PolyMAC with two-block message $M = (M[1], M[2]) = (\alpha_b, x)$.

where

$$g(b, x) = E_2(k_1^2 \alpha_b \oplus k_1 x), h(b, x) = E_4(k_3^2 \alpha_b \oplus k_3 x).$$

Obviously, g (resp. h) has a period of $1\|s_1$ where $s_1 = k_1 \alpha_0 \oplus k_1 \alpha_1$ (resp. $1\|s_2$ where $s_2 = k_3 \alpha_0 \oplus k_3 \alpha_1$). The probability of $s_1 = s_2$ is $1/2^n$ by the randomness of k_1, k_3. So in the following we assume $s_1 \neq s_2$. Let

$$f(u, x) = \mathrm{MAC}(\alpha_0, x) \oplus \mathrm{MAC}(\alpha_1, x \oplus u).$$

Similar as SUM-ECBC, we can prove $\varepsilon(f) \leq 3/4$.

3.2 Secret State Recovery Attack for PMAC_Plus-like MACs

We focus on DbHtF MAC [7]: $DbHtF(M) = F(G(M), H(M))$, which is the generic paradigm of PMAC_Plus-like MACs. Strategy 2 in Sect. 1 constructs

$$f(u, b, x) = F(g(u, b, x), h(u, b, x)),$$

where $g(u, b, x)$ (resp. $h(u, b, x)$) based on G (resp. H). When u equals a special value u^*, both $g(u^*, b, x)$ and $h(u^*, b, x)$ are periodic functions with the same period $1\|s$. Thus $f(u^*, b, x)$ is a periodic function with period $1\|s$. If $s \neq 0^n, \varepsilon(f) \leq 3/4$, we can apply Grover-meet-Simon algorithm (Theorem 3) to recover u^* and s with at most $\mathcal{O}(2^{n/2}n)$ quantum queries using $\mathcal{O}(n^2)$ qubits. If $s = 0^n$, we can apply Grover algorithm (Theorem 1) to recover u^* with at most $\mathcal{O}(2^{n/2})$ quantum queries and $\mathcal{O}(n)$ qubits. In the following, for any concrete PMAC_Plus-like MAC, we only give the construction of function f, the estimation of $\varepsilon(f)$. The method applies to PMAC_Plus [33], 1k-PMAC_Plus [8,9], 3kf9 [34] and 2K-PMAC_Plus [7], for which the function F is the sum of two cipher blocks. The method even applies to optimally secure MACs, including mPMAC+-f [6], mPMAC+-p1 [6] and mPMAC+-p2 [6], for which the function F is HtmB-f, HtmB-p1 and HtmB-p2 [6] respectively. We only take PMAC_Plus [33] and 3kf9 [34] as examples.

1) Secret State Recovery Attack for PMAC_Plus. PMAC_Plus was designed by Yasuda in 2011 [33]. The scheme uses a block cipher keyed by three independent keys, denoted as E_1, E_2, E_3.

Construction of Function f. Let $b \in \{0, 1\}, u, x \in \{0, 1\}^n$ and

$$\alpha_b := \begin{cases} 2E_1(0) \oplus 2^2 E_1(1), & \text{if } b = 0, \\ 2^2 E_1(0) \oplus 2^4 E_1(1), & \text{if } b = 1. \end{cases}$$

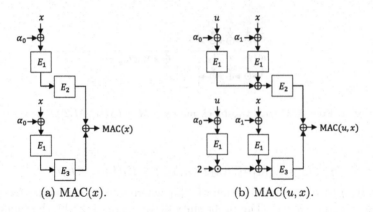

Fig. 3. PMAC_Plus with one-block message $M = (x)$ and two-block message $M = (u, x)$.

PMAC_Plus with message $M = (M[1]) = (x)$ and message $M = (M[1], M[2]) = (u, x)$ are shown as Fig. 3, which can be written as

$$\text{MAC}(M) = \begin{cases} F(g(u, 0, x), h(u, 0, x)), \text{ if } M = (x), \\ F(g(u, 1, x), h(u, 1, x)), \text{ if } M = (u, x), \end{cases}$$

where

$$g(u, b, x) = \begin{cases} E_1(x \oplus \alpha_0), & \text{if } b = 0, \\ E_1(x \oplus \alpha_1) \oplus E_1(u \oplus \alpha_0), \text{ if } b = 1, \end{cases}$$

$$h(u, b, x) = \begin{cases} E_1(x \oplus \alpha_0), & \text{if } b = 0, \\ E_1(x \oplus \alpha_1) \oplus 2E_1(u \oplus \alpha_0), \text{ if } b = 1. \end{cases}$$

$$F(x', y') = E_2(x') \oplus E_3(y').$$

where $x', y' \in \{0, 1\}^n$. We define

$$f(u, b, x) = \begin{cases} \text{MAC}(x), & \text{if } b = 0, \\ \text{MAC}(u, x), \text{ if } b = 1. \end{cases}$$

Let $u^* \in \{0, 1\}^n$ such that $E_1(u^* \oplus \alpha_0) = 0^n$. When $u = u^*$, $f(u, b, x)$ has a period $1 \| (\alpha_0 \oplus \alpha_1)$. We prove $\varepsilon(f) \leq 1/2$ in appendix B.

2) Secret State Recovery Attack for 3kf9. 3kf9 was designed by Zhang et.al. [34]. The scheme uses a block cipher keyed with three independent keys, denoted as E_1, E_2, E_3.

Construction of Function f. Let $b \in \{0, 1\}, u, x \in \{0, 1\}^n$. Then 3kf9 with message $M = (M[1]) = (x)$ and message $M = (M[1], M[2]) = (u, x)$ are shown in Fig. 4, which can be written as

$$\text{MAC}(M) = \begin{cases} F(g(u, 0, x), h(u, 0, x)), \text{ if } M = (x), \\ F(g(u, 1, x), h(u, 1, x)), \text{ if } M = (u, x), \end{cases}$$

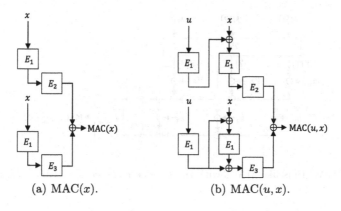

(a) MAC(x).   (b) MAC(u, x).

Fig. 4. 3kf9 with one-block message $M = (x)$ and two-block message $M = (u, x)$.

where

$$g(u, b, x) = \begin{cases} E_1(x), & \text{if } b = 0, \\ E_1(x \oplus E_1(u)), & \text{if } b = 1, \end{cases}$$

$$h(u, b, x) = \begin{cases} E_1(x), & \text{if } b = 0, \\ E_1(x \oplus E_1(u)) \oplus E_1(u), & \text{if } b = 1, \end{cases}$$

$$F(x', y') = E_2(x') \oplus E_3(y').$$

where $x', y' \in \{0, 1\}^n$. We define

$$f(u, b, x) = \begin{cases} \text{MAC}(x), & \text{if } b = 0, \\ \text{MAC}(u, x), & \text{if } b = 1. \end{cases}$$

Let $u^* \in \{0, 1\}^n$ such that $E_1(u^*) = 0^n$. It is easy to obtain that u^* is unique by permutation E_1. Then when $u = u^*$, $f(u^*, 0, x) = f(u^*, 1, x)$ holds for all $x \in \{0, 1\}^n$. It means the period is $1\|0^n$, which is trivial. So we apply Grover algorithm to recover u^* directly. We define $test : \{0, 1\}^n \to \{0, 1\}$ as

$$test(u) = \begin{cases} 1, \text{if } f(u, 0, x_i) = f(u, 1, x_i), i = 1, \dots, q, \\ 0, \text{otherwise}, \end{cases}$$

where $x_i \in \{0, 1\}^n$ and x_i are different from each other. We have proved $\max_{u \in \{0,1\}^n \setminus \{u^*\}} \Pr[test(u) = 1] \leq 2^{-2n}$ for $q = \mathcal{O}(1)$ in Appendix C.

4   Key Recovery Attack for PMAC_Plus-like MACs

We observe that PMAC_Plus-like MACs such as PMAC_Plus [33], 3kf9 [34] etc., with message $M = (M[1], M[2], M[3])$ share a common structure as in Fig. 5.

Let message $M = (M[1], M[2], M[3]) \in (\{0, 1\}^n)^3$, the tag $\text{MAC}_{k_1, k_{else}}(M) \in \{0, 1\}^n$, the independent keys $k_1 \in \{0, 1\}^m$, $k_{else} \in \{0, 1\}^l$, P_{k_1} be a permutation from $3n$ bit to $3n$ bit keyed by k_1 and $F_{k_{else}}$ be a function from $2n$ bit to n bit keyed by k_{else}, $Y = (Y[1], Y[2], Y[3]) \in (\{0, 1\}^n)^3$, public constants $A =$

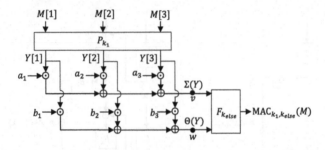

Fig. 5. PMAC_Plus-like MACs with three-block message $M = (M[1], M[2], M[3])$.

$(a_1, a_2, a_3) \in (\{0,1\}^n)^3, B = (b_1, b_2, b_3) \in (\{0,1\}^n)^3$. Then the procedure of $MAC_{k_1, k_{else}}(M)$ is as follows.

1) Given message M, compute $Y = P_{k_1}(M)$;
2) Compute linear combination processes $\Sigma(Y) := a_1 Y[1] \oplus a_2 Y[2] \oplus a_3 Y[3]$ and $\Theta(Y) := b_1 Y[1] \oplus b_2 Y[2] \oplus b_3 Y[3]$;
3) Compute $F_{k_{else}}(\Sigma(Y), \Theta(Y))$ and output it.

4.1   Partial Key Recovery Attack for PMAC_Plus-like MACs

We notice that most BBB MACs have several keys. So we consider a partial key recovery attack, and find that knowing the key k_1 is enough to create forgeries. The recovery of k_1 is as follows. Firstly we fix arbitrary values at points v and w. Secondly, we reverse the linear combination process in step 2) to get two arbitrary different solutions $C_0, C_1 \in \{0,1\}^{3n}$. Thirdly, we guess k_1 and reverse step 1) to get two messages. Finally, input the two messages into the oracle of $MAC_{k_1, k_{else}}(\cdot)$ to get two tags. If the guess is correct, then the two tags are same by colliding at both points v and w. Otherwise, the two tags may be different with overwhelming probability. That is to say, we check whether or not the guess is correct by whether or not the two tags are equal.

Accelerate the Search of k_1 by Applying Grover's Search. Let set

$$\mathcal{C} := \left\{ (C_0, C_1) \middle| \begin{array}{l} \Sigma(C_0) = \Sigma(C_1), \Theta(C_0) = \Theta(C_1), \text{ where} \\ C_j = (C_j[1], C_j[2], C_j[3]) \in (\{0,1\}^n)^3, j = 0, 1 \text{ and } C_0 \neq C_1 \end{array} \right\}$$

and function $f : \{0,1\}^m \times \{0,1\}^{3n} \to \{0,1\}^n$ as $f(k, C) = MAC_{k_1, k_{else}}(P_k^{-1}(C))$. Then we define $test : \{0,1\}^m \to \{0,1\}$ as

$$test(k) = \begin{cases} 1, & \text{if } f(k, C_0^i) = f(k, C_1^i), i = 1, \dots, q, \\ 0, & \text{otherwise,} \end{cases}$$

where $(C_0^i, C_1^i) \in \mathcal{C}$. We notice when $k = k_1$, $test(k) = 1$. Given quantum oracle of $MAC_{k_1, k_{else}}(\cdot)$, if the deviation $\max_{k \in \{0,1\}^m \setminus \{k_1\}} \Pr[test(k) = 1] \leq 2^{-2m}$ for $q = \mathcal{O}(1)$, then we can recover k_1 by Grover's algorithm (Theorem 1) with at most $\mathcal{O}(2^{m/2})$ quantum queries and $\mathcal{O}(m+n)$ qubits.

Forgery Attack. After recovering k_1, we make a successful forgery after a classical query as follows.

1) Choose an arbitrarily pair $(C_0, C_1) \in \mathcal{C}$.
2) Compute $M_0 = (P_{k_1})^{-1}(C_0)$ and $M_1 = (P_{k_1})^{-1}(C_1)$;
3) Query M_0 to $\mathrm{MAC}_{k_1, k_{else}}(\cdot)$ and get T;
4) Forge message-tag pair (M_1, T).

The EUF-qCMA attack is straightforward. So we omit it.

The method apply to PMAC_Plus [33], PMAC_TBC3k [25], mPMAC+-f [6], mPMAC+-p1 [6], mPMAC+-p2 [6], 1k-PMAC_Plus [8,9], 3kf9 [34] and 2K-PMAC_Plus [7]. In Appendix D, we take PMAC_Plus [33] and 3kf9 [34] as examples and prove the deviation $\max_{k \in \{0,1\}^m \backslash \{k_1\}} \Pr[test(k) = 1] \leq 2^{-2m}$ for $q = \mathcal{O}(1)$ for both of them.

4.2   Full Key Recovery Attack for PMAC_Plus-like MACs

Although one key recovery is enough to get successful forgery, we can further recover all keys of PMAC_Plus, 3kf9, and 2K-PMAC_Plus after knowing k_1. Their finalization functions all can be represented as the sum of two keyed permutations. That is to say, $k_{else} = (k_2, k_3)$ and for all $x, y \in \{0,1\}^n$ we have $F_{k_{else}}(x, y) = F_{k_2}(x) \oplus F'_{k_3}(y)$ where F, F' are two keyed permutations on n bits and k_2, k_3 are two m-bit keys. Our goal is to recover k_2, k_3. In fact, after recovering k_1, we are able to evaluate the inputs of $F_{k_{else}}(\cdot, \cdot)$ and get the output which is tag. That is to say, we are able to construct the quantum oracle of $F_{k_{else}}(\cdot, \cdot)$ by given the quantum oracle of $P_{k_1}^{-1}(\cdot)$ and $\mathrm{MAC}_{k_1, k_{else}}(\cdot)$. Let function $f : \{0,1\}^m \times \{0,1\}^n \times \{0,1\}^n \to \{0,1\}^n$ as $f(k, x_1, x_2) = F_k(x_1) \oplus F_k(x_2)$ for $k \in \{0,1\}^m, x_1, x_2 \in \{0,1\}^n$. Then we are able to know whether $k = k_2$ or not by whether $f(k, x_1, x_2) = F_{k_{else}}(x_1, y) \oplus F_{k_{else}}(x_2, y)$ or not. Applying Grover's algorithm we can recover k_2. Then the last unknown key k_3 can be recovered easily by Grover's algorithm as well. The whole attack costs $\mathcal{O}(2^{m/2})$ quantum queries and $\mathcal{O}(m + n)$ qubits.

5   Conclusions

In this paper, we introduce secret state recovery and key recovery for a series of BBB MACs in the Q2 model, leading to forgery attacks. Notice that PMAC_TBC3k handles message blocks with different tweakable block ciphers but not the same block cipher as other PMAC_Plus-like MACs in Sect. 3.2. So we are not able to construct a period function and the secret state recovery attack is not suitable for it. Another notice is that SUM-ECBC-like MACs handle the message with two different hash block chains and have no linear combination processes. So we can't apply key recovery attack in Sect. 4 to them. However, there is another key recovery attack. Take SUM-ECBC as an example. The complexity of the attack is $\mathcal{O}(2^m n)$ quantum queries assuming the size of message block is n bits and the size of all keys is $4m$ bits. We describe it in Appendix E.

The further question is if there is provable security in the quantum setting to show the tightness of the bound. We leave it as an open problem.

Acknowledgment. The authors thank the anonymous reviewers for many helpful comments. The work of this paper was supported by the National Natural Science Foundation of China (No. 61732021) and the National Key Research and Development Project (No. 2018YFA0704704 and No.2018YFB0803801).

A   Proof of $\varepsilon(f) \leq \frac{1}{2}$ for SUM-ECBC

In this case, $\mathcal{U}_s = \{(s_1, s_1 \oplus s_2), (s_2, s_1 \oplus s_2)\}$,

$$\varepsilon(f) = \max_{(u,t)\in\{0,1\}^n \times \{0,1\}^n \backslash (\mathcal{U}_s \cup \{0,1\}^n \times \{0^n\})} \Pr_x[f(u,x) = f(u, x \oplus t)].$$

We consider $u = s_1$ as an example and the other situation is similar. In this case $f(u,x) = f(s_1, x) = E_4(E_3(x \oplus E_3(\alpha_0)) \oplus E_4(E_3(x \oplus s_1 \oplus E_3(\alpha_1)))$. We will prove $\varepsilon(f(s_1, \cdot)) \leq \frac{1}{2}$ with overwhelming probability. Otherwise, there is $t \notin \{0^n, s_1 \oplus s_2\}$ such that $\Pr_x[f(s_1, x) = f(s_1, x \oplus t)] > 1/2$, i.e.,

$$\Pr_x \left[\begin{array}{c} E_4(E_3(x \oplus E_3(\alpha_0))) \oplus E_4(E_3(x \oplus s_1 \oplus E_3(\alpha_1))) \oplus \\ E_4(E_3(x \oplus t \oplus E_3(\alpha_0))) \oplus E_4(E_3(x \oplus t \oplus s_1 \oplus E_3(\alpha_1))) \end{array} \right] > 1/2. \quad (3)$$

When $t \notin \{0^n, s_1 \oplus s_2\}$ and $s_1 \neq s_2$, we know the four inputs of $E_4(E_3(\cdot))$ are different from each other. If E_4 is a random function and E_3 is a permutation, the Eq. (3) happens with negligible probability.

B   Proof of $\varepsilon(f) \leq \frac{1}{2}$ for PMAC_Plus

In this case, $\mathcal{U}_s = \{(u^*, 1\|\alpha_0 \oplus \alpha_1)\}$. Let $\mathcal{U}_t := \{0,1\}^n \times \{0,1\} \times \{0,1\}^n \backslash (\mathcal{U}_s \cup \{0,1\}^n \times \{0^{n+1}\})$, then

$$\varepsilon(f) = \max_{(u,t_1,t_2)\in\mathcal{U}_t} \Pr_{b,x}[f(u,b,x) = f(u, b \oplus t_1, x \oplus t_2)].$$

We consider $u = u^*$ as example and the other is similar. Firstly, we divide the scope $t_1\|t_2 \in \{0,1\}^{n+1}\backslash\{0^{n+1}, 1\|\alpha_0 \oplus \alpha_1\}$ into two parts $t_1 = 0, t_2 \neq 0^n$ and $t_1 = 1, t_2 \neq \alpha_0 \oplus \alpha_1$. We take the former as example. In fact, when $u = u^*, t_1 = 0, t_2 \neq 0^n$, the equation $f(u,b,x) = f(u, b \oplus t_1, x \oplus t_2)$ equals

$$E_2(E_1(x \oplus \alpha_b)) \oplus E_2(E_1(x \oplus t_2 \oplus \alpha_b)) \oplus E_3(E_1(x \oplus \alpha_b)) \oplus E_3(E_1(x \oplus t_2 \oplus \alpha_b)) = 0^n. \quad (4)$$

When $t_2 \neq 0^n$ and E_1 is a random permutation, we obtain both the two inputs of E_2 and the two inputs of E_3 are different respectively. Therefore, by the randomness of E_2, E_3, the Eq. (4) holds with probability at most $1/2$ with overwhelming probability.

C   Proof of $\max_{u \in \{0,1\}^n \setminus \{u^*\}} \Pr[test(u) = 1] \leq 2^{-2n}$ for 3kf9

The deviation

$$\max_{u \in \{0,1\}^n \setminus \{u^*\}} \Pr[test(u) = 1]$$

$$= \max_{u \in \{0,1\}^n \setminus \{u^*\}} \Pr[f(u, 0, x_1) = f(u, 1, x_1), \ldots, f(u, 0, x_q) = f(u, 1, x_q)].$$

Here, the equation system

$$f(u, 0, x_i) = f(u, 1, x_i), i = 1, 2, \ldots, q,$$

equals

$$E_2(y_i^1) \oplus E_2(y_i^2) \oplus E_3(y_i^3) \oplus E_3(y_i^4) = 0^n, i = 1, 2, \ldots, q,$$

where $y_i^1 = E_1(x_i), y_i^2 = E_1(x_i \oplus E_1(u)), y_i^3 = E_1(x_i), y_i^4 = E_1(x_i \oplus E_1(u)) \oplus E_1(u)$. To calculate the probability of these q equations, we consider sampling about E_2. If y_i^1, y_i^2, who are the inputs of E_2 in the i'th equation, have all appeared in the other $q-1$ equations, then we don't sample in the i'th equation. In fact, if $x_i \oplus x_j = E_1(u)$ then $y_i^1 = y_j^2, y_i^2 = y_j^1$. Therefore, we have to sample E_2 in at least $\lfloor \frac{q+1}{2} \rfloor$ equations among q. For every equation, by the randomness of E_2, it holds with probability at most $\frac{1}{2^n - 2q}$. Therefore, for any $u \in \{0,1\}^n \setminus \{u^*\}$, we have $\Pr[test(u) = 1] \leq (\frac{1}{2^n - 2q})^{\frac{q-1}{2}}$. When $q = 7$, we have $\Pr[test(u) = 1] \leq 2^{-2n}$ for $n \geq 4$.

D   Deviation Estimation in Key Recovery Attacks

D.1   Deviation Estimation for PMAC_Plus

We have introduced PMAC_Plus in Sect. 3.2. Assume the three independent keys are $(k_1, k_2, k_3) \in (\{0,1\}^m)^3$. The construction with three-block message $M = (M[1], M[2], M[3])$ is shown in Fig. 6, where $t_{k_1}^j = 2^j E_{k_1}(0^n) \oplus 2^{2j} E_{k_1}(0^{n-1} \| 1), j = 1, 2, 3$.

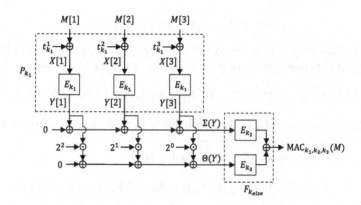

Fig. 6. PMAC_Plus with three-block message $M = (M[1], M[2], M[3])$.

Estimation of $\max_{k \in \{0,1\}^m \setminus \{k_1\}} \Pr[test(k) = 1]$. The deviation is equals to

$$\max_{k \in \{0,1\}^m \setminus \{k_1\}} \Pr[f(k, C_0^1) = f(k, C_1^1), \ldots, f(k, C_0^q) = f(k, C_1^q)].$$

Here, the equation system

$$f(k, C_0^i) = f(k, C_1^i), i = 1, 2, \ldots, q, \tag{5}$$

equals $E_{k_2}(\Sigma(Y_0^i)) \oplus E_{k_3}(\Theta(Y_0^i)) = E_{k_2}(\Sigma(Y_1^i)) \oplus E_{k_3}(\Theta(Y_1^i)), i = 1, 2, \ldots, q$, where

$$\Sigma(Y_b^i) = E_{k_1}(X_b^i[1]) \oplus E_{k_1}(X_b^i[2]) \oplus E_{k_1}(X_b^i[3]), b = 0, 1,$$
$$\Theta(Y_b^i) = 2^2 E_{k_1}(X_b^i[1]) \oplus 2 E_{k_1}(X_b^i[2]) \oplus E_{k_1}(X_b^i[3]), b = 0, 1,$$

and

$$X_b^i[1] = E_k^{-1}(C_b^i[1]) \oplus t_k^1 \oplus t_{k_1}^1,$$
$$X_b^i[2] = E_k^{-1}(C_b^i[2]) \oplus t_k^2 \oplus t_{k_1}^2,$$
$$X_b^i[3] = E_k^{-1}(C_b^i[3]) \oplus t_k^3 \oplus t_{k_1}^3.$$

We assume all $C_b^i[a], i = 1, \ldots, q, b = 0, 1, a = 1, 2, 3$ are different. This can be realized easily. Then all $X_b^i[j], i = 1, \ldots, q, b = 0, 1$ are different where $j \in \{1, 2, 3\}$.

In the following, we only consider the equations which have new sample of E_{k_1} among the q equations in (5). If $X_b^i[a], b = 0, 1, j = 1, 2, 3$, who are the inputs of E_{k_1} in the i'th equation, have all appeared in the other $q - 1$ equations, then we don't sample in the i'th equation. In fact, there may be $X_b^i[a_1] = X_{b'}^{i'}[a_2] = X_{b''}^{i''}[a_3]$, where a_1, a_2, a_3 are three different values belong to $\{1, 2, 3\}, b, b', b'' \in \{0, 1\}, i', i'' \in \{1, \ldots, q\}$. Take $X_0^i[1]$ as example, there may be $b', b'' \in \{0, 1\}, i', i'' \in \{1, \ldots, q\}$ such that $X_0^i[1] = X_{b'}^{i'}[2] = X_{b''}^{i''}[3]$. Therefore, it is easily to obtain that we have to sample E_{k_1} at least $\lfloor \frac{q+2}{3} \rfloor$ equations among q. Then we consider the probability of the i'th equation $f(k, C_0^i) = f(k, C_1^i)$ where we have new sample of E_{k_1}.

1) If

$$\Sigma(Y_0^i) = \Sigma(Y_1^i), \Theta(Y_0^i) = \Theta(Y_1^i), \tag{6}$$

then the ith equation holds. We want to know the upper bound of the probability of this case. So we only consider $\Sigma(Y_0^i) = \Sigma(Y_1^i)$. It means

$$E_{k_1}(X_0^i[1]) \oplus E_{k_1}(X_0^i[2]) \oplus E_{k_1}(X_0^i[3]) = E_{k_1}(X_1^i[1]) \oplus E_{k_1}(X_1^i[2]) \oplus E_{k_1}(X_1^i[3]).$$

By the randomness of E_{k_1}, the probability to make the above equation holds by sampling E_{k_1} is at most $\frac{1}{2^n - 6q}$.

2) When the equation set (6) doesn't holds but

$$E_{k_2}(\Sigma(Y_0^i)) \oplus E_{k_3}(\Theta(Y_0^i)) = E_{k_2}(\Sigma(Y_1^i)) \oplus E_{k_3}(\Theta(Y_1^i)), \tag{7}$$

then the ith equation holds as well. Firstly, we exclude the case that $\Sigma(Y_0^i), \Theta(Y_0^i), \Sigma(Y_1^i), \Theta(Y_1^i)$ in the i'th equation have all appeared in other $q - 1$ equations, whose probability is at most $(\frac{2q}{2^n-6q})^4$. Then we assume that in the i'th equation that at least $\Sigma(Y_0^i)$ hasn't been appeared in other $q - 1$ equations, which means $E_{k_2}(\Sigma(Y_0^i))$ is a new sample. Thus the i'th equation holds with probability at most $\frac{1}{2^n-2q}$. Overall, this case happens with probability at most $(\frac{2q}{2^n-6q})^4 + \frac{1}{2^n-2q}$.

Sum of case 1) and 2), the i'th equation holds with probability at most $\frac{1}{2^n-6q} + (\frac{2q}{2^n-6q})^4 + \frac{1}{2^n-2q} \leq \frac{q}{2^{n-3}}$ assuming $6q \leq 2^{n-1}$. Therefore, the q equations happens with probability at most $(\frac{q}{2^{n-3}})^{\frac{q-1}{3}}$. For PMAC_Plus, the key length $m \leq 2n$. Then when $q = 16$, we have $\Pr[test(k) = 1] \leq 2^{-2m}$ for $m \geq 42$ and any $k \in \{0,1\}^m \backslash \{k_1\}$.

D.2   Deviation Estimation for 3kf9

We have introduced 3kf9 in Sect. 3.2. Assume the three keys are $(k_1, k_2, k_3) \in (\{0,1\}^m)^3$. The construction with massage $M = (M[1], M[2], M[3])$ is defined as in Fig. 7.

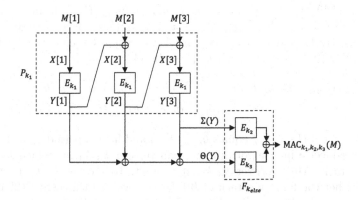

Fig. 7. 3kf9 with three-block message $M = (M[1], M[2], M[3])$.

Estimation of $\max_{k \in \{0,1\}^m \backslash \{k_1\}} \Pr[test(k) = 1]$. The deviation is equals to

$$\max_{k \in \{0,1\}^m \backslash \{k_1\}} \Pr[f(k, C_0^1) = f(k, C_1^1), \ldots, f(k, C_0^q) = f(k, C_1^q)].$$

Here, the equation system

$$f(k, C_0^i) = f(k, C_1^i), i = 1, 2, \ldots, q, \tag{8}$$

equals

$$E_{k_2}(\Sigma(Y_0^i)) \oplus E_{k_3}(\Theta(Y_0^i)) = E_{k_2}(\Sigma(Y_1^i)) \oplus E_{k_3}(\Theta(Y_1^i)), i = 1, 2, \ldots, q,$$

where
$$\Sigma(Y_b^i) = E_{k_1}(X_b^i[3]), b = 0, 1,$$
$$\Theta(Y_b^i) = E_{k_1}(X_b^i[1]) \oplus E_{k_1}(X_b^i[2]) \oplus E_{k_1}(X_b^i[3]), b = 0, 1,$$

and
$$X_b^i[1] = E_k^{-1}(C_b^i[1]),$$
$$X_b^i[2] = E_{k_1}(X_b^i[1]) \oplus C_b^i[1] \oplus E_k^{-1}(C_b^i[2]),$$
$$X_b^i[3] = E_{k_1}(X_b^i[2]) \oplus C_b^i[2] \oplus E_k^{-1}(C_b^i[3]).$$

We assume all $C_b^i[1], i = 1, \ldots, q, b = 0, 1$ are different. This can be realized easily. Then all $X_b^i[1], i = 1, \ldots, q, b = 0, 1$ are different from each other, which means we have to sample for $E_{k_1}(X_0^i[1])$ in every equation in (8). Similar as the PMAC_Plus in Appendix D.1, every equation $f(k, C_0^i) = f(k, C_1^i)$ holds with probability at most $\frac{q}{2^{n-3}}$. Therefore, the q equations happens with probability at most $(\frac{q}{2^{n-3}})^q$. For 3kf9, the key length $m \le 2n$. Then when $q = 5$, we have $\Pr[test(k) = 1] \le 2^{-2m}$ for $m \ge 24$ and any $k \in \{0, 1\}^m \setminus \{k_1\}$.

E   Key Recovery Attack for SUM-ECBC

Let $b \in \{0, 1\}, x \in \{0, 1\}^n$. Similar as introduction (Sect. 1, strategy 1), we construct $C^{\mathrm{MAC}_{k_1, k_2, k_3, k_4}}(b, x) = g_{k_1, k_2}(b, x) \oplus h_{k_3, k_4}(b, x)$ from SUM-ECBC through method C, where $g_{k_1, k_2}(b, x)$ and $h_{k_3, k_4}(b, x)$ have periods $1 \| s_1$ and $1 \| s_2$ respectively and k_1, k_2, k_3, k_4 are keys. Then we construct a function $f : \{0, 1\}^m \times \{0, 1\}^m \times \{0, 1\} \times \{0, 1\}^n \to \{0, 1\}^n$ as

$$f_{k_1, k_2, k_3, k_4}(k_3', k_4', b, x) = C^{\mathrm{MAC}_{k_1, k_2, k_3, k_4}}(b, x) \oplus h_{k_3', k_4'}(b, x)$$
$$= g_{k_1, k_2}(b, x) \oplus h_{k_3, k_4}(b, x) \oplus h_{k_3', k_4'}(b, x).$$

When $(k_3', k_4') = (k_3, k_4)$, f equals $g_{k_1, k_2}(b, x)$ and have a period $1 \| s_1$. By applying Grover-meet-Simon algorithm, we can recover k_3, k_4, s_1, which leads to a forgery attack. After recover k_3, k_4, it is easily to recover k_1, k_2 by Grover's search. Either the forgery attack or full key recover attack costs $\mathcal{O}(2^m n)$ quantum queries with $\mathcal{O}(m + n^2)$ qubits by Theorem 3 and Theorem 1.

References

1. Belovs, A., Spalek, R.: Adversary lower bound for the k-sum problem. In: Proceedings of the 4th Conference on Innovations in Theoretical Computer Science, pp. 323–328 (2013)
2. Boneh, D., Zhandry, M.: Quantum-secure message authentication codes. In: Johansson, T., Nguyen, P.Q. (eds.) EUROCRYPT 2013. LNCS, vol. 7881, pp. 592–608. Springer, Heidelberg (2013). https://doi.org/10.1007/978-3-642-38348-9_35
3. Bonnetain, X.: Tight bounds for Simon's algorithm. IACR Cryptology ePrint Archives 2020, 919 (2020). https://eprint.iacr.org/2020/919

4. Brassard, G., Hoyer, P., Mosca, M., Tapp, A.: Quantum amplitude amplification and estimation. Contemp. Math. **305**, 53–74 (2002)
5. Brassard, G., Hoyer, P., Tapp, A.: Quantum algorithm for the collision problem. arXiv preprint quant-ph/9705002 (1997)
6. Cogliati, B., Jha, A., Nandi, M.: How to build optimally secure PRFs using block ciphers. In: Moriai, S., Wang, H. (eds.) ASIACRYPT 2020. Part I. LNCS, vol. 12491, pp. 754–784. Springer, Cham (2020). https://doi.org/10.1007/978-3-030-64837-4_25
7. Datta, N., Dutta, A., Nandi, M., Paul, G.: Double-block hash-then-sum: a paradigm for constructing BBB secure PRF. IACR Trans. Symmetric Cryptol. **2018**(3), 36–92 (2018). https://doi.org/10.13154/tosc.v2018.i3.36-92
8. Datta, N., Dutta, A., Nandi, M., Paul, G., Zhang, L.: Building single-key beyond birthday bound message authentication code. Technical report, Cryptology ePrint Archive, Report 2015/958 (2015). http://eprint.iacr.org
9. Datta, N., Dutta, A., Nandi, M., Paul, G., Zhang, L.: Single key variant of PMAC_plus. IACR Trans. Symmetric Cryptol. **2017**(4), 268–305 (2017). https://doi.org/10.13154/tosc.v2017.i4.268-305
10. Dong, X., Sun, S., Shi, D., Gao, F., Wang, X., Hu, L.: Quantum collision attacks on AES-like hashing with low quantum random access memories. In: Moriai, S., Wang, H. (eds.) ASIACRYPT 2020. Part II. LNCS, vol. 12492, pp. 727–757. Springer, Cham (2020). https://doi.org/10.1007/978-3-030-64834-3_25
11. Grassi, L., Naya-Plasencia, M., Schrottenloher, A.: Quantum algorithms for the *k*-xor problem. In: Peyrin, T., Galbraith, S. (eds.) ASIACRYPT 2018. Part I. LNCS, vol. 11272, pp. 527–559. Springer, Cham (2018). https://doi.org/10.1007/978-3-030-03326-2_18
12. Grover, L.K.: A fast quantum mechanical algorithm for database search. In: 1996 Proceedings of the Twenty-Eighth Annual ACM Symposium on the Theory of Computing, pp. 212–219 (1996). https://doi.org/10.1145/237814.237866
13. Guo, T., Wang, P., Hu, L., Ye, D.: Attacks on beyond-birthday-bound macs in the quantum setting. Cryptology ePrint Archive, Report 2020/1595 (2020). https://eprint.iacr.org/2020/1595
14. Hodžić, S., Knudsen Ramkilde, L., Brasen Kidmose, A.: On quantum distinguishers for type-3 generalized feistel network based on separability. In: Ding, J., Tillich, J.-P. (eds.) PQCrypto 2020. LNCS, vol. 12100, pp. 461–480. Springer, Cham (2020). https://doi.org/10.1007/978-3-030-44223-1_25
15. Hosoyamada, A., Sasaki, Yu.: Finding hash collisions with quantum computers by using differential trails with smaller probability than birthday bound. In: Canteaut, A., Ishai, Y. (eds.) EUROCRYPT 2020. Part II. LNCS, vol. 12106, pp. 249–279. Springer, Cham (2020). https://doi.org/10.1007/978-3-030-45724-2_9
16. Iwata, T., Minematsu, K.: Stronger security variants of GCM-SIV. IACR Trans. Symmetric Cryptol. **2016**(1), 134–157 (2016). https://doi.org/10.13154/tosc.v2016.i1.134-157
17. Kaplan, M., Leurent, G., Leverrier, A., Naya-Plasencia, M.: Breaking symmetric cryptosystems using quantum period finding. In: Robshaw, M., Katz, J. (eds.) CRYPTO 2016. Part II. LNCS, vol. 9815, pp. 207–237. Springer, Heidelberg (2016). https://doi.org/10.1007/978-3-662-53008-5_8
18. Kilian, J., Rogaway, P.: How to protect DES against exhaustive key search. In: Koblitz, N. (ed.) CRYPTO 1996. LNCS, vol. 1109, pp. 252–267. Springer, Heidelberg (1996). https://doi.org/10.1007/3-540-68697-5_20

19. Kilian, J., Rogaway, P.: How to protect DES against exhaustive key search (an analysis of DESX). J. Cryptol. **14**(1), 17–35 (2000). https://doi.org/10.1007/s001450010015

20. Kim, S., Lee, B., Lee, J.: Tight security bounds for double-block hash-then-sum MACs. In: Canteaut, A., Ishai, Y. (eds.) EUROCRYPT 2020. Part I. LNCS, vol. 12105, pp. 435–465. Springer, Cham (2020). https://doi.org/10.1007/978-3-030-45721-1_16

21. Kuwakado, H., Morii, M.: Security on the quantum-type Even-Mansour cipher. In: Proceedings of the International Symposium on Information Theory and its Applications, ISITA 2012, pp. 312–316 (2012). http://ieeexplore.ieee.org/document/6400943/

22. Leander, G., May, A.: Grover meets Simon – quantumly attacking the FX-construction. In: Takagi, T., Peyrin, T. (eds.) ASIACRYPT 2017. Part II. LNCS, vol. 10625, pp. 161–178. Springer, Cham (2017). https://doi.org/10.1007/978-3-319-70697-9_6

23. Leurent, G., Nandi, M., Sibleyras, F.: Generic attacks against beyond-birthday-bound MACs. In: Shacham, H., Boldyreva, A. (eds.) CRYPTO 2018. Part I. LNCS, vol. 10991, pp. 306–336. Springer, Cham (2018). https://doi.org/10.1007/978-3-319-96884-1_11

24. McGrew, D.A., Viega, J.: The security and performance of the Galois/Counter Mode (GCM) of operation. In: Canteaut, A., Viswanathan, K. (eds.) INDOCRYPT 2004. LNCS, vol. 3348, pp. 343–355. Springer, Heidelberg (2004). https://doi.org/10.1007/978-3-540-30556-9_27

25. Naito, Y.: Full PRF-secure message authentication code based on tweakable block cipher. In: Au, M.-H., Miyaji, A. (eds.) ProvSec 2015. LNCS, vol. 9451, pp. 167–182. Springer, Cham (2015). https://doi.org/10.1007/978-3-319-26059-4_9

26. Naito, Y.: Blockcipher-based MACs: beyond the birthday bound without message length. In: Takagi, T., Peyrin, T. (eds.) ASIACRYPT 2017. Part III. LNCS, vol. 10626, pp. 446–470. Springer, Cham (2017). https://doi.org/10.1007/978-3-319-70700-6_16

27. Naya-Plasencia, M., Schrottenloher, A.: Optimal merging in quantum k-xor and k-sum algorithms. In: Canteaut, A., Ishai, Y. (eds.) EUROCRYPT 2020. Part II. LNCS, vol. 12106, pp. 311–340. Springer, Cham (2020). https://doi.org/10.1007/978-3-030-45724-2_11

28. Shen, Y., Wang, L., WengS, J.: Revisiting the security of DbHtS MACs: beyond-birthday-bound in the multi-user setting. IACR Cryptology ePrint Archives 2020, 1523 (2020). https://eprint.iacr.org/2020/1523

29. Simon, D.R.: On the power of quantum computation. SIAM J. Comput. **26**(5), 1474–1483 (1997). https://doi.org/10.1137/S0097539796298637

30. Wagner, D.: A generalized birthday problem. In: Yung, M. (ed.) CRYPTO 2002. LNCS, vol. 2442, pp. 288–304. Springer, Heidelberg (2002). https://doi.org/10.1007/3-540-45708-9_19

31. Wang, P., Feng, D., Wu, W.: HCTR: a variable-input-length enciphering mode. In: Feng, D., Lin, D., Yung, M. (eds.) CISC 2005. LNCS, vol. 3822, pp. 175–188. Springer, Heidelberg (2005). https://doi.org/10.1007/11599548_15

32. Yasuda, K.: The sum of CBC MACs is a secure PRF. In: Pieprzyk, J. (ed.) CT-RSA 2010. LNCS, vol. 5985, pp. 366–381. Springer, Heidelberg (2010). https://doi.org/10.1007/978-3-642-11925-5_25

33. Yasuda, K.: A new variant of PMAC: beyond the birthday bound. In: Rogaway, P. (ed.) CRYPTO 2011. LNCS, vol. 6841, pp. 596–609. Springer, Heidelberg (2011). https://doi.org/10.1007/978-3-642-22792-9_34

34. Zhang, L., Wu, W., Sui, H., Wang, P.: 3kf9: enhancing 3GPP-MAC beyond the birthday bound. In: Wang, X., Sako, K. (eds.) ASIACRYPT 2012. LNCS, vol. 7658, pp. 296–312. Springer, Heidelberg (2012). https://doi.org/10.1007/978-3-642-34961-4_19

An Algebraic Approach to the Rank Support Learning Problem

Magali Bardet[1,3] and Pierre Briaud[2,3(✉)]

[1] LITIS, University of Rouen Normandie, Rouen, France
magali.bardet@univ-rouen.fr
[2] Sorbonne Universités, UPMC Univ, Paris 06, France
pierre.briaud@inria.fr
[3] Inria, Team COSMIQ, Paris, France

Abstract. Rank-metric code-based cryptography relies on the hardness of decoding a random linear code in the rank metric. The Rank Support Learning problem (RSL) is a variant where an attacker has access to N decoding instances whose errors have the same support and wants to solve one of them. This problem is for instance used in the Durandal signature scheme [5]. In this paper, we propose an algebraic attack on RSL which often outperforms the previous attacks to solve this problem when the number of instances is of the order of the one used in Durandal. We build upon [8], where similar techniques are used to solve MinRank and RD. However, our analysis is simpler and overall our attack relies on very elementary assumptions compared to standard Gröbner bases attacks. In particular, our results show that key recovery attacks on Durandal are more efficient than was previously thought, especially in a parameter range where the RD attack from [8] is not the most powerful.

Keywords: Post-quantum cryptography · Rank metric code-based cryptography · Algebraic attack

1 Introduction

Rank metric code-based cryptography. In the last decade, rank metric code-based cryptography has proved to be a powerful alternative to traditional cryptography based on the Hamming metric. Compared to the situation in the Hamming metric, a few families of codes with an efficient decoding algorithm were considered in rank-based cryptography. Starting with the original GPT cryptosystem [13], a first trend was to rely on Gabidulin codes. However, their algebraic structure was successfully exploited by the Overbeck attack [25] and variants. More recent proposals [2,3,15,17] inspired by the NTRU cryptosystem [20] were based on LRPC codes. These schemes can be viewed as the rank metric analogue of the MDPC cryptosystem in the Hamming metric [22], where the trapdoor is given by a small weight dual matrix which allows efficient decoding.

The cryptosystems submitted to the NIST post-quantum Standardization Process [1,4] were of this kind. They have not passed the second round of this

© Springer Nature Switzerland AG 2021
J. H. Cheon and J.-P. Tillich (Eds.): PQCrypto 2021, LNCS 12841, pp. 442–462, 2021.
https://doi.org/10.1007/978-3-030-81293-5_23

competition, but the NIST still encourages further research on rank-based cryptography. First, they offer an interesting gain in terms of public-key size due to the underlying algebraic structure. Also, this type of cryptography is not restricted to the aforementioned encryption schemes, as shown by a proposal for signature [5] and even the IBE scheme from [14], and more progress might be made in that direction.

Decoding problems in rank metric. Codes used in rank metric cryptography are linear codes over an extension field $\mathbb{F}_{q^m}$ of degree m of $\mathbb{F}_q$. An $\mathbb{F}_{q^m}$-linear code of length n is an $\mathbb{F}_{q^m}$-linear subspace of $\mathbb{F}_{q^m}{}^n$, but codewords can also be viewed as matrices in $\mathbb{F}_q^{m \times n}$. Indeed, if $(\beta_1, \ldots, \beta_m)$ is an $\mathbb{F}_q$-basis of $\mathbb{F}_{q^m}$, the word $\boldsymbol{x} = (x_1, \ldots, x_n) \in \mathbb{F}_{q^m}^n$ corresponds to the matrix $\mathrm{Mat}(\boldsymbol{x}) = (X_{ij})_{i,j} \in \mathbb{F}_q^{m \times n}$, where $x_j = \beta_1 X_{1j} + \cdots + \beta_m X_{mj}$ for $j \in \{1..n\}$. The weight of $\boldsymbol{x}$ is then defined by using the underlying rank metric on $\mathbb{F}_q^{m \times n}$, namely $|\boldsymbol{x}|_{\mathrm{RANK}} := \mathrm{Rank}(\mathrm{Mat}(\boldsymbol{x}))$, and it is also equal to the dimension of the *support* $\mathrm{Supp}(\boldsymbol{x}) := \langle x_1, \ldots, x_n \rangle_{\mathbb{F}_q}$. Similarly to the Hamming metric, the main source of computational hardness for rank-based cryptosystems is a decoding problem. It is the decoding problem in rank metric restricted to $\mathbb{F}_{q^m}$-linear codes, namely

Problem 1 (Rank Decoding problem (RD)).
    Input: an $\mathbb{F}_{q^m}$-basis $(\boldsymbol{c}_1, \ldots, \boldsymbol{c}_k)$ of a subspace $\mathcal{C}$ of $\mathbb{F}_{q^m}{}^n$, an integer $r \in \mathbb{N}$, and a vector $\boldsymbol{y} \in \mathbb{F}_{q^m}{}^n$ such that $|\boldsymbol{y} - \boldsymbol{c}|_{\mathrm{RANK}} \leq r$ for some $\boldsymbol{c} \in \mathcal{C}$.
    Output: $\boldsymbol{c} \in \mathcal{C}$ and an *error* $\boldsymbol{e} \in \mathbb{F}_{q^m}{}^n$ such that $\boldsymbol{y} = \boldsymbol{c} + \boldsymbol{e}$ and $|\boldsymbol{e}|_{\mathrm{RANK}} \leq r$.

We also adopt the *syndrome* formulation: given $\boldsymbol{s} \in \mathbb{F}_{q^m}^{n-k}$ and $\boldsymbol{H} \in \mathbb{F}_{q^m}^{(n-k) \times n}$ a parity-check matrix of the code, find $\boldsymbol{e} \in \mathbb{F}_{q^m}^n$ such that $\boldsymbol{H}\boldsymbol{e}^{\mathsf{T}} = \boldsymbol{s}^{\mathsf{T}}$ and $|\boldsymbol{e}|_{\mathrm{RANK}} \leq r$. Without this restriction to $\mathbb{F}_{q^m}$-linear codes, the decoding of arbitrary codes in rank metric is also worthy of interest. It is equivalent to the following MinRank problem, as explained in [12].

Problem 2 (MinRank problem).
    Input: an integer $r \in \mathbb{N}$ and K matrices $\boldsymbol{M}_1, \ldots, \boldsymbol{M}_K \in \mathbb{F}_q^{m \times n}$.
    Output: field elements $x_1, x_2, \ldots, x_K \in \mathbb{F}_q$, not all zero, such that

$$\mathrm{Rank}\left(\sum_{i=1}^{K} x_i \boldsymbol{M}_i\right) \leq r.$$

This problem was originally defined and proven NP-complete in [10], and it is now ubiquitous in multivariate cryptography. However, the RD problem is not known to be NP-complete, even if there exists a randomized reduction to the decoding in the Hamming metric, which is NP-complete [18]. Still, this problem is believed to be hard and the best attacks have exponential complexity. The first attacks against RD were of combinatorial nature [6,16,19], but the recent developments in [7,8] tend to show that algebraic methods now perform better, even for small values of q.

The RSL problem. The Rank Support Learning problem is a generalization of the RD problem to several syndromes which correspond to errors with the same support.

Table 1. Complexity of our attack on parameters (m, n, k, r, N) corresponding to Durandal parameter sets given in Table 2. "Best RD" refers to the RD attack from [8] which is the best RSL attack so far. The last two columns correspond to our attack for the two values of N considered in Durandal. An underlined value is an improvement upon the RD attack.

(m, n, k, r)	Best RD	$N = k(r - 2)$	$N = k(r - 1)$
$(277, 358, 179, 7)$	130	<u>125</u>	<u>126</u>
$(281, 242, 121, 8)$	159	170	<u>128</u>
$(293, 254, 127, 8)$	152	172	<u>125</u>
$(307, 274, 137, 9)$	251	<u>187</u>	<u>159</u>

Problem 3 (Rank Support Learning (RSL)).

Input: $(\boldsymbol{H}, \boldsymbol{H}\boldsymbol{E}^{\mathsf{T}})$, where $\boldsymbol{H} \in \mathbb{F}_{q^m}^{(n-k) \times n}$ is full-rank and $\boldsymbol{E} \in \mathbb{F}_{q^m}^{N \times n}$ has all its entries lying in a subspace $\mathcal{V} \subset \mathbb{F}_{q^m}$ of dimension r for some $r \in \mathbb{N}$.

Output: The secret subspace $\mathcal{V}$.

In other words, an RSL instance of parameters (m, n, k, r, N) consists of N RD instances $\boldsymbol{H}\boldsymbol{e}_i^{\mathsf{T}} = \boldsymbol{s}_i^{\mathsf{T}}$ with common support $\mathcal{V}$ of dimension r for $i \in \{1..N\}$. The RSL problem can be seen as the rank metric analogue of the Support-Learning problem in the Hamming metric, which had already been used for cryptographic purposes [21,23]. However, the RSL problem turns out to be much more versatile for the future of rank-based cryptography. It was introduced in [14] to build an IBE scheme, broken lately in [11]. More importantly, this problem is at the heart of the security of the Durandal signature scheme [5], and solving the underlying RSL instance leads to a key recovery attack. It is readily apparent that the difficulty of RSL decreases when the number of RD instances grows. On the one hand, the RSL problem is equivalent to RD when $N = 1$, and therefore the best known attacks are exponential in the parameters (m, n, k, r). On the other hand, difficult instances must satisfy $N < kr$, as explained in [11]. So far, the only attempt to solve RSL for all values of N was the combinatorial algorithm from the original RSL paper [14], which leaves room for improvement.

Contribution. Our contribution is an algebraic attack on the RSL problem and therefore a key recovery attack on Durandal. To the best of our knowledge, it is the only attack on RSL when $N < kr$ which is not an attack on RD since [14]. Note that the Durandal current parameter sets were already broken by the algebraic attacks from [8] and have not been updated since then. Therefore, we propose new parameters in order to avoid these attacks as well as the other known attacks on Durandal (see Sect. 5), and in Table 1 we compare our attack to the best existing attack on RSL for these parameters.

Our attack is very often more efficient than the best current RSL attack, especially for a large number of errors. The improvement is also more significant for larger values of parameters (see for instance the last row in Table 1 compared to the other ones). Regarding the security of Durandal, our work greatly improves upon previous key recovery attacks and therefore it will have to be taken into account when selecting future parameters for the scheme.

The original attack from [14] is a combinatorial algorithm to look for elements of low weight in a code $\mathcal{C}_{aug} := \mathcal{C} + \langle e_1, \ldots, e_N \rangle_{\mathbb{F}_q}$ of typical dimension $km + N$ which contains many such codewords. Our approach is to attack the very same code $\mathcal{C}_{aug}$ but by using algebraic techniques. A direct adaptation would be to consider a MinRank instance with $km + N$ matrices in $\mathbb{F}_q^{m \times n}$ which represent an $\mathbb{F}_q$-basis of $\mathcal{C}_{aug}$. However, the region of parameters used in rank-based cryptography is typically $m = \Theta(n)$ and $k = \Theta(n)$, so that the number of matrices is $\Theta(n^2)$ due to the term km. This makes the cost of this approach too high to be relevant. Therefore, we propose a bilinear modeling of the problem with only N matrices in $\mathbb{F}_q^{m \times n}$ instead of $km + N$. The way this system is obtained is very reminiscent of the work of [8] to attack MinRank and RD. First, it consists of the set of all maximal minors of a matrix of linear forms over $\mathbb{F}_{q^m}$ which are then "descended" over $\mathbb{F}_q$ as in the MaxMinors modeling. Second, we adopt a similar λ-XL type strategy by multiplying the initial equations by monomials in only one of the two blocks of variables. The system is then solved by linearization at some bi-degree $(b, 1)$. To determine precisely this degree, we have to carefully count the number of independent equations at each bi-degree. In the case of MinRank, Bardet *et al.* are able to construct explicit linear relations between the augmented equations and they argue that the rest of the equations are linearly independent [8, Heuristic 2, p.19]. Their counting is valid whenever $b < r + 2$, where r is the target rank in MinRank. However, our analysis will be much tighter. Indeed, up to a minor assumption on the RSL instance that can be easily checked by linear algebra on the syndromes, we can construct an explicit basis for the rowspace of the Macaulay matrix at each bi-degree $(b, 1)$, and we do no longer have a limitation on the value of b apart from $b < q$ $(q \neq 2)$.

Also, we do not restrict ourselves to the words of lowest weight in $\mathcal{C}_{aug}$ as in [14]. The reason is that decreasing the target weight r as much as possible is always advantageous for the combinatorial attacks, but not necessarily for the algebraic attacks. Indeed, decreasing r will cause to decrease both the number of equations and variables in the system, but the ratio between the two might become unfavorable.

Notation. For a, b integers such that $a \leq b$, we denote by $\{a..b\}$ the set of integers from a to b. The notation $\#I$ stands for the cardinal of the finite set of integers I, and for a an integer, $I + a$ stands for the set $\{i + a : i \in I\}$. Also, we denote by $Pos(i, I)$ the position of the integer i in the ordered set I.

The space of matrices of size $m \times n$ over a field $\mathbb{K}$ is denoted by $\mathbb{K}^{m \times n}$. Matrices and vectors are denoted by bold lowercase letters (M, v). For $I \subset \{1..n\}$ and $J \subset \{1..m\}$, we use the notation $M_{I,J}$ for the submatrix of M formed by its rows (resp. columns) with indexes in I (resp. J). We adopt the shorthand notation $M_{*,J} = M_{\{1..m\},J}$ and $M_{I,*} = M_{I,\{1..n\}}$, where M has size $m \times n$.

2 Durandal and the RSL Problem

Assessing the hardness of RSL is needed to evaluate the security of the Durandal signature scheme [5]. This scheme is based on the Lyubashevsky framework adapted to the rank metric setting. For a 128-bit security level, the original parameters offer a signature size of less than $4\,\mathrm{kB}$ and a public key of size less than $20\,\mathrm{kB}$.

2.1 Key Pair in Durandal

Durandal is an authentication protocol turned into a signature thanks to the Fiat-Shamir transform. For the purposes of this paper, we simply describe the key pair and we refer the reader to [5, §3] for a full presentation of this protocol. First, the secret key consists of a couple of matrices $(\boldsymbol{E}_1, \boldsymbol{E}_2) \in \mathbb{F}_{q^m}^{\ell k \times n} \times \mathbb{F}_{q^m}^{\ell' k \times n}$ whose entries lie in a subspace $\mathcal{V}$ of dimension r. The public key is $(\boldsymbol{H}, \boldsymbol{S}_1 | \boldsymbol{S}_2)$ such that $\boldsymbol{H} \in \mathbb{F}_{q^m}^{(n-k) \times n}$ is a random full-rank ideal matrix[1], $\boldsymbol{S}_1 = \boldsymbol{H}\boldsymbol{E}_1^\mathsf{T} \in \mathbb{F}_{q^m}^{(n-k) \times \ell k}$ and $\boldsymbol{S}_2 = \boldsymbol{H}\boldsymbol{E}_2^\mathsf{T} \in \mathbb{F}_{q^m}^{(n-k) \times \ell' k}$, where $|$ denotes matrix concatenation. It is readily verified that the couple $(\boldsymbol{H}, \boldsymbol{S}_1 | \boldsymbol{S}_2)$ is an instance of RSL with parameters (m, n, k, r) and $N = \ell k + \ell' k$, and that solving this instance leads to a key-recovery attack. However, it is not a *random* instance. Indeed, the matrix $\boldsymbol{S}_1$ (resp. $\boldsymbol{S}_2$) can be reconstructed from only ℓ (resp. ℓ') of its columns due to the ideal structure of $\boldsymbol{H}$. However, we have not been able to fully exploit this fact, except to prove that Durandal instances satisfy our Assumption 1. Since this extra structure is only used for efficiency, we assume without loss of generality that we attack a random RSL instance satisfying Assumption 1.

2.2 Previous Cryptanalysis on RSL

The security of Durandal relies on the hardness of RD and RSL, as well as on the PSSI^+ problem, which is an *ad hoc* assumption [5, Problem 5]. In this section, we describe the prior work on RSL which was considered to design the parameters.

Attacks for large N. First, the RSL problem becomes easy when $N \geq nr$ and a polynomial attack is detailed in [14, §4.2, p.14]. This linear algebra argument is not really specific to the rank metric in the sense that it can be applied to the very same problem in the Hamming metric. A more powerful attack is given in [11] and suggests that secure instances of RSL must satisfy the stronger condition $N < kr$. When $N \geq kr$, the idea is that if the parity-check matrix $\boldsymbol{H}$ is in systematic form, then the public $\mathbb{F}_q$-linear code

$$\mathcal{C}_{synd} := \left\{ \boldsymbol{x}\boldsymbol{E}\boldsymbol{H}^\mathsf{T}, \ \boldsymbol{x} \in \mathbb{F}_q^N \right\}$$

is such that $\dim_{\mathbb{F}_q} (\mathcal{C}_{synd} \cap \mathcal{V}^{n-k}) \geq N - kr$, and therefore there exist at least q^{N-kr} words of weight r in $\mathcal{C}_{synd}$. The authors propose a bilinear modeling to

---

[1] See for instance [5, §2.2, Definition 8] for a definition.

recover one of these codewords and due to the high number of solutions, many variables can be eliminated from the system. The attack is efficient because the Gröbner basis techniques on this system are expected to take subexponential time. However, it seems difficult to adapt the argument of [11] for N even slightly below kr, because the intersection $\mathcal{C}_{synd} \cap \mathcal{V}^{n-k}$ will be trivial. Therefore, the Durandal parameter sets are chosen such that $N = (k-2)r$ or $N = (k-1)r$ and the complexity analysis is based on the original attack from [14].

Solving RSL when $N < kr$. A naive way to solve RSL when $N < kr$ is to attack one of the N RD instances. Following [24], the strategy is to look for words of weight $\leq r$ in an augmented $\mathbb{F}_{q^m}$-linear code of the form $\mathcal{C}_e = \mathcal{C} \oplus \langle e \rangle$. To tackle several errors, note that adding $e_1, \ldots, e_N$ to the code $\mathcal{C}$ in an $\mathbb{F}_{q^m}$-linear manner will lead to a deadlock, because the augmented code quickly covers the whole space $\mathbb{F}_{q^m}^n$. Therefore, the authors of [14] consider a code containing all the errors but which is simply $\mathbb{F}_q$-linear.

Let $W_U \subset \mathbb{F}_{q^m}^{n-k}$ be the $\mathbb{F}_q$-linear space generated by the s_i for $i \in \{1..N\}$ and let $\mathcal{C}_{aug}$ be the $\mathbb{F}_q$-linear code defined by

$$\mathcal{C}_{aug} := \left\{ x \in \mathbb{F}_{q^m}^n, \ H x^\mathsf{T} \in W_U \right\}.$$

If we set $\mathcal{C}' := \langle e_1, \ldots, e_N \rangle_{\mathbb{F}_q}$, then we clearly have $\mathcal{C}' \subset \mathcal{C}_{aug}$. Codewords in $\mathcal{C}'$ all have weight $\leq r$, and therefore the code $\mathcal{C}_{aug}$ typically contains q^N words of this weight. It also contains the public $\mathbb{F}_{q^m}$-linear code $\mathcal{C} = \left\{ x \in \mathbb{F}_{q^m}^n, \ H x^\mathsf{T} = 0 \right\}$. We have $\dim_{\mathbb{F}_q} \mathcal{C}_{aug} \leq \dim_{\mathbb{F}_q} \mathcal{C} + \dim_{\mathbb{F}_q} W_U \leq km + N$. In general, this inequality is an equality and we will make this assumption from now on. In particular, it implies that the errors $e_1, \ldots, e_N$ are linearly independent over $\mathbb{F}_q$. The authors propose a combinatorial algorithm [14, §4.3, Algorithm 1] to look for low weight codewords in $\mathcal{C}_{aug}$. Their attack greatly benefits from the fact that there are many words of weight r in $\mathcal{C}'$ and, a fortiori, in $\mathcal{C}_{aug}$. Indeed, the algorithm will still succeed by targeting a word of weight equal to the minimum distance of $\mathcal{C}'$. This leads to the complexity claimed in [14, Theorem 2], which is equal to $q^{min(e_-, e_+)}$, where $K = km + N$ and

$$e_- = \left(w - \left\lfloor \frac{N}{n} \right\rfloor \right) \left(\left\lfloor \frac{K}{n} \right\rfloor - \left\lfloor \frac{N}{n} \right\rfloor \right)$$

$$e_+ = \left(w - \left\lfloor \frac{N}{n} \right\rfloor - 1 \right) \left(\left\lfloor \frac{K}{n} \right\rfloor - \left\lfloor \frac{N}{n} \right\rfloor - 1 \right) + n \left(\left\lfloor \frac{K}{n} \right\rfloor - \left\lfloor \frac{N}{n} \right\rfloor - 1 \right).$$

3   The RSL-Minors Modeling

In this section, we introduce the algebraic modeling that we use to solve the RSL problem and we propose two ways to restrict the number of solutions, so that the final system has roughly one solution.

3.1 The Basic Modeling

Our system is obtained as follows. First, a public basis of the code $\mathcal{C}_{aug}$ can be obtained by considering an $\mathbb{F}_{q^m}$-basis of $\mathcal{C}$ (*i.e.* a full-rank generator matrix $G \in \mathbb{F}_{q^m}^{k \times n}$) together with elements $y_i \in \mathbb{F}_{q^m}^n$ such that $y_i H^\mathsf{T} = s_i$ for $i \in \{1..N\}$. A word of weight $w \leq r$ in $\mathcal{C}_{aug}$ is then written as

$$e := xG + \sum_{i=1}^{N} \lambda_i y_i := (\beta_1, \beta_2, \ldots, \beta_m)CR,$$

where the quantities $x \in \mathbb{F}_{q^m}^k$, $\lambda_i \in \mathbb{F}_q$ for $i \in \{1..N\}$, $C \in \mathbb{F}_q^{m \times w}$ and $R \in \mathbb{F}_q^{w \times n}$ are unknowns[2]. Since $GH^\mathsf{T} = 0$, variables can be removed by multiplying to the right by H^T, and one obtains

$$\sum_{i=1}^{N} \lambda_i s_i = (\beta_1, \ldots, \beta_m)CRH^\mathsf{T}.$$

The vector $\sum_{i=1}^{N} \lambda_i s_i$ is a linear combination over $\mathbb{F}_{q^m}$ of the rows of RH^T. This means that the following matrix

$$\Delta_H := \begin{pmatrix} \sum_{i=1}^{N} \lambda_i s_i \\ RH^\mathsf{T} \end{pmatrix} = \begin{pmatrix} \sum_{i=1}^{N} \lambda_i y_i \\ R \end{pmatrix} H^\mathsf{T} \in \mathbb{F}_{q^m}^{(w+1) \times (n-k)}$$

has rank at most w. Finally, equations are obtained by canceling all the maximal minors of Δ_H. They are labeled by all the subsets $J \subset \{1..n-k\}$ of size $w+1$.

$$\mathcal{F} = \left\{ |\Delta_H|_{*,J} = 0 \,\middle|\, J \subset \{1..n-k\}, \#J = w+1 \right\}. \tag{1}$$

The following Lemma 1 shows that the equations are bilinear in the λ_i and in the r_T variables, which are the maximal minors of R.

Lemma 1. *Let $J \subset \{1..n-k\}$ such that $\#J = w+1$. We have*

$$Q_J := |\Delta_H|_{*,J} = \sum_{i=1}^{N} \lambda_i \sum_{T \subset \{1..n\}, \#T = w} r_T \sum_{t \notin T} y_{i,t}(-1)^{1+Pos(t,T \cup \{t\})} |H|_{J,T \cup \{t\}},$$

where $r_T = |R|_{*,T}$, $T \subset \{1..n\}$, $\#T = w$. Without loss of generality, we assume that $H_{*,\{k+1..n\}} = I_{n-k}$, so that Q_J contains $N\binom{k+1+w}{w}$ monomials.

The proof can be found in Appendix A. Since the equations have coefficients in $\mathbb{F}_{q^m}$ and solutions λ_i, r_T are searched in $\mathbb{F}_q$, we *unfold* the system over $\mathbb{F}_q$. It consists in expanding each equation f over $\mathbb{F}_{q^m}$ as m equations $[f]_j$ over $\mathbb{F}_q$ for $j \in \{1..m\}$ which represent the "coordinates" of f in an $\mathbb{F}_q$-basis of $\mathbb{F}_{q^m}$.

---

[2] We adopt this notation because the matrix R (resp. C) represents a basis of the Rowspace (resp. Column space) of $\mathrm{Mat}(e)$.

Modeling 1 (RSL Minors modeling). *We consider the system over* $\mathbb{F}_q$ *obtained by unfolding the system* (1)*:*

$$\mathbf{UnFold}(\mathcal{F}) = \mathbf{UnFold}\left(\left\{f = 0 \middle| f \in \mathrm{MaxMinors}(\Delta_H)\right\}\right). \qquad (2)$$

We search for solutions λ_i, r_T*'s in* $\mathbb{F}_q$*. This system contains:*

- $m\binom{n-k}{w+1}$ *bilinear equations with coefficients in* $\mathbb{F}_q$,
- $N + \binom{n}{w}$ *unknowns:* $\boldsymbol{\lambda} = (\lambda_1, \cdots, \lambda_N)$ *and the* r_T*'s, where* $r_T = |\boldsymbol{R}|_{*,T}$ *for* $T \subset \{1..n\}$, $\#T = w$.

We now describe two ways to restrict the number of solutions to the RSL Minors system. Note that the weight $w \leq r$ in Modeling 1 is not set to a precise value, and contrary to [14], we will not necessarily target the words of lowest weight in $\mathcal{C}_{aug}$. Actually, we prefer to work in a code which is obtained by shortening $\mathcal{C}_{aug}$ and to attack a word of weight $w := r - \delta$ for some $\delta \geq 0$.

Definition 1 (Shortening a matrix code). *Let* $\mathcal{C}_{mat} \subset \mathbb{F}_q^{m \times n}$ *be a matrix code of parameters* $[m \times n, K]_q$ *and* $I \subset \{1..n\}$*. The shortening* $\mathcal{S}_I(\mathcal{C}_{mat}) \subset \mathbb{F}_q^{m \times (n-\#I)}$ *of* $\mathcal{C}_{mat}$ *is the* $[m \times (n - \#I), K' \geq K - m\#I]_q$*-code defined as follows:*

$$\mathcal{S}_I(\mathcal{C}_{mat}) := \left\{\boldsymbol{R}_{*,\{1..n\}\setminus I} \mid \boldsymbol{R} \in \mathcal{C}_{mat}, \ \boldsymbol{R}_{*,I} = 0_{*,I}\right\}.$$

Moreover, when the code $\mathcal{C}_{mat}$ *is* $\mathbb{F}_{q^m}$*-linear, this definition coincides with the usual definition of shortening on* $\mathbb{F}_{q^m}$*-linear codes.*

This operation is interesting because it allows to decrease the number of r_T variables in Modeling 1 without altering the number of equations, which would be the case if we simply target a word of lower weight but without shortening.

3.2   Shortening $\mathcal{C}_{aug}$ as Much as Possible ($\delta = 0$)

A first idea is to look for a word of weight r in a shortening of $\mathcal{C}_{aug}$ which contains roughly a unique word of this weight. Let $a \in \mathbb{N}$ be the unique integer such that $ar < N \leq (a+1)r$. From now on, we only consider $N' = ar + 1$ errors. For $i \in \{1..N'\}$, we write $\boldsymbol{e}_i = (\beta_1, \ldots, \beta_m)\boldsymbol{C}\boldsymbol{R}_i$, where the matrix $\boldsymbol{C} \in \mathbb{F}_q^{m \times r}$ is an $\mathbb{F}_q$-basis of $\mathcal{V}$ and the matrices $\boldsymbol{R}_1, \ldots, \boldsymbol{R}_{N'}$ are random in $\mathbb{F}_q^{r \times n}$. Thus, there exists roughly one linear combination of the $\boldsymbol{e}_i$ of the form

$$\underline{e} = (\beta_1, \ldots, \beta_m) \times \boldsymbol{C}\left(0_{r \times a} \ \widetilde{\boldsymbol{R}}\right),$$

where $\widetilde{\boldsymbol{R}} \in \mathbb{F}_q^{r \times (n-a)}$. A fortiori the error $\underline{e}$ lies in $\mathcal{C}_{aug}$, and its first a coordinates are zero. In other words, the shortening $\mathcal{S}_{\{1..a\}}(\mathcal{C}_{aug})$ contains about one word of weight $\leq r$. We use Modeling 1 to attack this codeword, and the product $\boldsymbol{R}\boldsymbol{H}^{\mathsf{T}}$ from the original system is replaced by $\widetilde{\boldsymbol{R}}\widetilde{\boldsymbol{H}}^{\mathsf{T}}$, where the matrix $\widetilde{\boldsymbol{H}}$ consists of the last $n - a$ columns of $\boldsymbol{H}$ (note that we still have $\widetilde{\boldsymbol{H}}_{*,\{k+1..n\}} = \boldsymbol{I}_{n-k}$). The resulting system has roughly one solution. It consists of $m\binom{n-k}{r+1}$ equations but with only N' variables λ_i and $\binom{n-a}{r}$ variables r_T. Finally, the number of non-zero terms per equation is $N'\binom{k+1+r}{r}$.

3.3 Looking for Words of Smaller Weight in $\mathcal{C}_{aug}$ ($\delta > 0$)

Let $d_{\mathcal{C}'}$ be the minimum distance of $\mathcal{C}'$ and $\delta_{max} = r - d_{\mathcal{C}'}$. When N is large enough, we have $\delta_{max} > 0$ and therefore there exist codewords of weight $w = r - \delta$ in $\mathcal{C}'$ for all $\delta \in \{1..\delta_{max}\}$. Once again, these codewords can be recovered by using Modeling 1. To estimate the number of solutions, we try to be more precise than the argument in [14, C.1, Lemma 2] based on the rank Singleton bound and we use the following proposition.

Proposition 1. *Let $r \in \mathbb{N}$ and $w \leq r$. Let $X_{\mathcal{C}',w}$ be the random variable counting the number of codewords of weight w in $\mathcal{C}'$, where the randomness comes from the choice of a support $\mathcal{V}$ of dimension r and of N errors with support $\mathcal{V}$. The expectation and the variance of $X_{\mathcal{C}',w}$ are respectively given by*

$$E[X_{\mathcal{C}',w}] = \frac{S_{w,r,n}}{q^{r \times n - N}} \text{ and}$$

$$\text{Var}[X_{\mathcal{C}',w}] = S_{w,r,n} \times (q-1) \times \left(\frac{1}{q^{r \times n - N}} - \left(\frac{1}{q^{r \times n - N}} \right)^2 \right),$$

where $S_{w,r,n}$ is the cardinal of the sphere of radius w in $\mathbb{F}_q^{r \times n}$ for the rank metric.

The proof can be found in Appendix B. When q is a constant, one obtains:

$$E[X_{\mathcal{C}',w}] = \Theta(q^{w(n+r-w)-r \times n + N}) = \Theta(q^{N-(r-w)(n-w)}) \text{ and} \quad (3)$$

$$\text{Var}[X_{\mathcal{C}',w}] = \Theta(q^{N+1-(r-w)(n-w)}) = \Theta(q^{N-(r-w)(n-w)}). \quad (4)$$

Then, the code $\mathcal{C}'$ contains a word of weight $r - \delta$ with good probability whenever $N \geq \delta(n - r + \delta)$ using Eq. (3), and we look for such a codeword in the public code $\mathcal{C}_{aug}$. Also, when there are many of them, we proceed as in Sect. 3.2 by shortening this code. For instance, if one has

$$N > \delta(n - r + \delta) + a \times (r - \delta),$$

we assume that there exists roughly one word of weight $\leq r - \delta$ in $\mathcal{S}_{\{1..a\}}(\mathcal{C}')$. Therefore, the numbers of equations and monomials at bi-degree $(1,1)$ are now $m\binom{n-k}{r-\delta+1}$ and $N'\binom{n-a}{r-\delta}$ respectively, where $N' = \delta(n - r + \delta) + a \times (r - \delta)$. The number of monomials per equation is $N'\binom{k+1+r-\delta}{r-\delta}$. In practice, we choose the value of a which leads to the best complexity (see Table 2).

4 Solving the RSL Minors Equations by Linearization

Now that we have restricted the number of solutions, we follow the approach from [8] which consists in multiplying the bilinear equations by monomials in the λ_i's and then solving by linearization at some bi-degree $(b,1)$ when there are enough equations compared to the number of monomials. In our case, the counting is much easier than in [8] and we are able to determine with certainty the number of equations which are linearly independent over $\mathbb{F}_{q^m}$.

4.1   Number of Independent Equations for the System over $\mathbb{F}_{q^m}$

In this section, we focus on the initial system (1) whose equations are in $\mathbb{F}_{q^m}$. Our results rely on the following assumption. This assumption is very easy to check by linear algebra on the syndromes and was always verified in practice. The proofs of Theorems 1 and 2 can be found in Appendix A.

Assumption 1. *Let* $\boldsymbol{S} = \left(\boldsymbol{s}_1^{\mathsf{T}} \ldots \boldsymbol{s}_N^{\mathsf{T}}\right) \in \mathbb{F}_{q^m}^{(n-k)\times N}$. *We assume that the matrix* $\boldsymbol{S}_{\{1..n-k-w\},*}$ *has rank* $n - k - w$.

Under this assumption, we show that all the equations in system (1) are linearly independent over $\mathbb{F}_{q^m}$. Note also that due to the specific structure, Assumption 1 is always satisfied in the Durandal case, see the end of Appendix A for a proof of this assertion.

Theorem 1. *The* $\binom{n-k}{w+1}$ *equations of system* (1) *are linearly independent over* $\mathbb{F}_{q^m}$ *under Assumption 1.*

As mentioned above, we are also interested in the number of independent equations over $\mathbb{F}_{q^m}$ at a higher bi-degree $(b,1)$ for $b \geq 2$. This number is not the maximal possible since linear relations between the augmented equations occur starting at $b = 2$. However, this phenomenon is perfectly under control and Theorem 2 gives the exact number of independent equations at bi-degree $(b,1)$. Contrary to [8], this counting is still exact even when $b \geq w + 2$.

Theorem 2. *Under Assumption 1 and for any* $b \geq 1$, *the* $\mathbb{F}_{q^m}$-*vector space generated by the rows of the Macaulay matrix in bi-degree* $(b,1)$ *has dimension*

$$\mathcal{N}_b := \sum_{d=2}^{n-k-w+1} \binom{n-k-d}{w-1} \sum_{j=1}^{d-1} \binom{N-j+1+b-2}{b-1}. \tag{5}$$

4.2   Solving the RSL Minors Equations by Linearization

To obtain solutions over $\mathbb{F}_q$, one can expand each of the independent equations over $\mathbb{F}_{q^m}$ as m equations over $\mathbb{F}_q$. We assume that linear relations do not occur after this process when there are less equations than the number of monomials in the resulting system. Recall also that this system has a unique solution. Therefore, the following Assumption 2 gives the number of linearly independent equations at bi-degree $(b,1)$ at hand for any $b < q$. This assumption was somehow implicit in [8] for the MaxMinors modeling, and it is also verified on our experiments in magma.

Assumption 2. *For* $b \geq 1$ *and* $b < q$, *let* $\mathcal{M}_b$ *be the number of monomials at bi-degree* $(b,1)$. *Then, the number of linearly independent equations at bi-degree* $(b,1)$ *in the augmented system* (2) *is* $m\mathcal{N}_b$ *when* $m\mathcal{N}_b < \mathcal{M}_b$, *and* $\mathcal{M}_b - 1$ *otherwise, where* $\mathcal{N}_b$ *is defined as in Theorem 2.*

Combining Assumption 2 and Theorem 2, we obtain that one can solve by linearization at bi-degree $(b, 1)$ whenever $b < q$ and $m\mathcal{N}_b \geq \mathcal{M}_b - 1$, where $\mathcal{N}_b$ is defined above and $\mathcal{M}_b := \binom{n}{w}\binom{N+b-1}{b}$.

For cryptographic applications, we are mainly interested in the $q = 2$ case, and due to the field equations we only have to consider squarefree monomials. In this particular case, we determined experimentally that there are some new reductions dues to the field equations compared to Theorem 2, see Appendix A for a description. The full proof of the number of independent equations in the $q = 2$ case will be the subject of a dedicated paper. However, note that for $b = 1 < 2 = q$ our proof is still valid.

The number of independent equations is now $m\mathcal{N}_b^{\mathbb{F}_2}$ when $m\mathcal{N}_b^{\mathbb{F}_2} < \mathcal{M}_b^{\mathbb{F}_2}$, where $\mathcal{M}_b^{\mathbb{F}_2} := \binom{n}{w}\binom{N}{b}$ and

$$\mathcal{N}_b^{\mathbb{F}_2} := \sum_{d=1}^{b} \sum_{j=1}^{n-k} \binom{j-1}{d-1}\binom{n-k-j}{w-d+1}\binom{N-j}{b-d} \quad \text{for } b \leq w + 1 \text{(heuristic)}.$$

When $q = 2$, it is favorable to consider all the equations up to bi-degree $(b, 1)$ instead of those of exact bi-degree $(b, 1)$. With $\mathcal{M}_{\leq b}^{\mathbb{F}_2} := \sum_{j=1}^{b} \mathcal{M}_j^{\mathbb{F}_2}$ and $\mathcal{N}_{\leq b}^{\mathbb{F}_2} := \sum_{j=1}^{b} \mathcal{N}_j^{\mathbb{F}_2}$, the condition to solve by linearization therefore reads

$$m\mathcal{N}_{\leq b}^{\mathbb{F}_2} \geq \mathcal{M}_{\leq b}^{\mathbb{F}_2} - 1. \tag{6}$$

The final linear system can be solved using the Strassen algorithm or the Wiedemann algorithm [26] if it is sparse enough. Note that the number of monomials per equation is equal to $N\binom{k+1+w}{w}$, so that the system is even sparser when b increases. If b is the smallest positive integer such that (6) holds, the complexity of solving this system is

$$\mathcal{O}\left(\min\left((\mathcal{N}_{\leq b}^{\mathbb{F}_2})(\mathcal{M}_{\leq b}^{\mathbb{F}_2})^{\omega-1}, N\binom{k+1+w}{w}(\mathcal{M}_{\leq b}^{\mathbb{F}_2})^2\right)\right) \tag{7}$$

field operations over $\mathbb{F}_2$, where ω is the linear algebra constant. Finally, one can use the hybrid approach [9] that performs exhaustive search in α_R variables r_T and/or α_λ variables λ_i in order to solve at a smaller bi-degree $(b, 1)$, and this strategy sometimes leads to better results (see Table 2).

5   Complexity of the Attack on New Durandal Parameters

We now present the best complexities obtained with our attack. In order to apply this attack to Durandal, we construct new parameters (m, n, k, r, N) for the scheme by taking into account the constraints mentioned in [5, §6.1] but also the recent algebraic attacks from [8]. The main ways to counteract these attacks are to increase the couple (n, k) compared to m or to increase the weight r, and the proposed parameters try to explore the two options. The missing parameters are chosen as follows. We always take $d = r$ and also $\ell' = 1$ in $N = (\ell + \ell')k$

as in [5, §6.2]. Apart from the key recovery attack, the most threatening attack against the scheme is the distinguishing attack on the PSSI$^+$ problem [5, §4.1], which basically prevents from taking too small values for m and N. In particular, in Table 2 we do not give the complexity of the RSL attack when $N < k(r-2)$ if the PSSI$^+$ attack is below 192 for this value of N.

In Table 2, Column 2 refers to the distinguishing attack on PSSI$^+$. The cost corresponds to the advantage given in [5, §4.1, Proposition 18]. The attacker is supposed to have access to 2^{64} signatures, so that the success probability must be $\leq 2^{-192}$ instead of $\leq 2^{-128}$. Column 3 refers to the RD attack from [8] which is the best key recovery attack so far. The former combinatorial attack on RSL is much less efficient, so we do not even mention it. The rest of the table corresponds to our attack. We present the two ways to decrease the number of solutions described in Sect. 3.2 ("$\delta = 0$") and Sect. 3.3 ("$\delta > 0$") and we give the value of b to solve by linearization. Sometimes, the best strategy is the hybrid approach by fixing α_R columns in R or α_λ variables λ_i. Also, the attack from Sect. 3.3 looks for a word of weight $w < r$ in $\mathcal{C}_{aug}$ and proceeds by shortening the matrices on a columns. Therefore, the couple (w, a) leading to the best complexity is also given. Finally, an underlined value represents an improvement upon the best RD attack, and a value in bold is a value below the 128-bit security level.

Table 2. Attack on 128-bit security parameter sets for Durandal. The missing parameters are chosen as in [5, §6]: we always take $d = r$ and also $\ell' = 1$ in $N = (\ell + \ell')k$. These choices only impact the PSSI$^+$ attack. Recall that the value in Column 2 must be ≥ 192 assuming that the attacker has access to 2^{64} signatures. A starred value is obtained with the Wiedemann algorithm, otherwise the Strassen algorithm is used.

$(m, n, k, r), N$	PSSI$^+$	RD [8]	$\delta = 0$	b	$(\alpha_C, \alpha_\lambda)$	$\delta > 0$	b	$w = r - \delta$	a	$(\alpha_C, \alpha_\lambda)$
$(277, 358, 179, 7)$										
$N = k(r-3)$	199	130	173	2	(0,0)	174*	3	6	60	(0,0)
$N = k(r-2)$	207	130	147	1	(0,0)	**126**	1	5	37	(0,2)
$N = k(r-1)$	213	130	145	1	(0,0)	**125**	1	5	19	(0,1)
$(281, 242, 121, 8)$										
$N = k(r-2)$	193	159	170	2	(0,0)	170*	3	7	70	(0,0)
$N = k(r-1)$	201	159	144	1	(0,0)	**128**	1	5	27	(2,3)
$(293, 254, 127, 8)$										
$N = k(r-2)$	205	152	172	2	(0,0)	172*	3	7	73	(0,0)
$N = k(r-1)$	213	152	145	1	(0,0)	**125**	1	5	28	(1,4)
$(307, 274, 137, 9)$										
$N = k(r-2)$	199	251	187	2	(0,0)	<u>187</u>*	3	8	86	(0,0)
$N = k(r-1)$	207	251	<u>159</u>	1	(0,0)	165*	2	8	103	(0,0)

First, note that our attack does not outperform the RD attack on the current Durandal parameters. However, these parameters correspond to an "overdetermined" RD instance as defined in [8, §4], and it is likely that future parameters will be chosen outside of this range. Regarding the results given in Table 2, the cost of our attack is always below the one of the best RD attack when $N = (k-1)r$, and it is very often the case for other values as well. This improvement is not associated to a particular value of N from which our attack will always be superior, but it is particularly obvious when the system can be solved at $b = 1$. Note also that the progress is significant on the set of parameters with $r = 9$, which suggests that our attack will be probably better for larger values of parameters as well. Finally, even if the cost of our attack is sometimes slightly below the 128-bit security level, the effect on Durandal remains limited. This is mainly due to the fact that the attack on PSSI$^+$ is very powerful in a scenario in which the attacker has access to 2^{64} signatures.

6   Conclusion

In this paper, we propose a new algebraic attack on RSL which improves upon the previous attacks on this problem, especially when the RD attack from [8] is not very efficient. As in [8], it relies on a bilinear modeling and avoids the use of generic Gröbner bases algorithms. However, the algebraic properties of our system allow a clearer analysis.

Acknowledgments. This work has been supported by the French ANR projects CBCRYPT (ANR-17-CE39-0007). We would like to thank Jean-Pierre Tillich for fruitful discussions.

A   Proofs of Lemma 1 and Theorems 1 And 2

Proof of Eq. (9). We use the linearity of the determinant and Laplace expansion along first row to obtain, for any $J \subset \{1..n-k\}$ of size $w + 1$:

$$Q_J = |\Delta_H|_{*,J} = \sum_{i=1}^{N} \sum_{j \in J} (-1)^{1+Pos(j,J)} \lambda_i s_{i,j} \left| RH^\mathsf{T} \right|_{*,J\setminus\{j\}} .$$

Then we use the Cauchy-Binet formula to express the determinant of a product of non-square matrices as a sum of product of determinants, and we get, with $r_T = |R|_{*,T}$:

$$Q_J = \sum_{i=1}^{N} \sum_{T \subset \{1..n\}, \#T=w} r_T \lambda_i \left(\sum_{j \in J} (-1)^{1+Pos(j,J)} s_{i,j} |H|_{J\setminus\{j\},T} \right) .$$

Without loss of generality, we assume from now on that $H_{*,\{k+1..n\}} = I_{n-k}$. Then by Laplace expansion along columns in $\{k+1..n\}$, it is clear that if $T \cap$

$\{k+1..n\} \not\subset (J+k)$, we have $|\boldsymbol{H}|_{J\setminus\{j\},T} = 0$ for any j and the monomials involving r_T do not appear in Q_J. There are at most $N\binom{k+w+1}{w}$ terms in Q_J, that can be written

$$Q_J = \sum_{i=1}^{N} \lambda_i \sum_{\substack{T=T_1\cup T_2, \#T=w, \\ T_1 \subset \{1..k+1\}, T_2 \subset (J+k)}} r_T \left(\sum_{j\in J} (-1)^{1+Pos(j,J)} s_{i,j} |\boldsymbol{H}|_{J\setminus\{j\},T} \right). \quad (8)$$

Proof of Theorem 1. We start by fixing a particular monomial ordering on $\mathcal{R}$ and we then provide, under Assumption 1, a concrete linear transformation of the equations such that the resulting equations have distinct leading monomials. This will prove that they are linearly independent.

Let $\prec$ be the grevlex monomial ordering on the variables λ_i and r_T such that

$$r_{\{t_1<\cdots<t_w\}} \prec r_{\{t_1'<\cdots<t_w'\}} \text{ iff } \qquad t_i = t_i' \text{ for all } i < j \text{ and } t_j < t_j',$$
$$r_T \prec \lambda_N \prec \lambda_{N-1} \prec \cdots \prec \lambda_1 \qquad \forall T \subset \{1..n\}, \#T = w.$$

This means that $\lambda_i r_T \prec \lambda_j r_{T'}$ iff $r_T \prec r_{T'}$ or $r_T = r_{T'}$ and $\lambda_i \prec \lambda_j$, and for instance with $w = 3$,

$$\lambda_1 r_{\{n-2,n-1,n\}} \succ \cdots \lambda_N r_{\{n-2,n-1,n\}} \succ \lambda_i r_{\{n-3,n-1,n\}} \cdots \succ \lambda_N r_{\{1,2,3\}}.$$

Lemma 2. *For any* $J \subset \{1..n-k\}$ *of size* $w+1$, *one can write*

$$Q_J = \sum_{j\in J} \sum_{i=1}^{N} (-1)^{1+Pos(j,J)} s_{i,j} \lambda_i r_{(J\setminus\{j\})+k} + \text{ (smaller terms wrt } \prec). \quad (9)$$

where the smaller monomials are $\lambda_i r_T$ *with* $T \cap \{1..k\} \neq \emptyset$, *whereas the largest monomials are* $\lambda_i r_T$ *with* $T \subset (J+k) \subset \{k+1..n\}$.

Proof. We start from (8). According to the choice of the monomial ordering, the largest monomials are the $\lambda_j r_I$ with $I \subset \{k+1..n\}$, and they come from subsets $T \subset (J+k)$ of size w. If $T \subset J+k$ and $j \in T$, then $|\boldsymbol{H}|_{J\setminus\{j\},T} = \boldsymbol{I}_{J\setminus\{j\},T-k} = 0$ whereas for $\{j\} = J \setminus (T-k)$ we have $|\boldsymbol{H}|_{J\setminus\{j\},T} = \boldsymbol{I}_{T-k,T-k} = 1$. Then,

$$Q_J = \sum_{i=1}^{N} \lambda_i \sum_{\substack{T\subset J+k \\ \#T=w, \{j\}=J\setminus T}} r_T (-1)^{1+Pos(j,J)} s_{i,j} + \text{(smaller terms)}$$

$$= \sum_{i=1}^{N} \sum_{j\in J} (-1)^{1+Pos(j,J)} s_{i,j} \lambda_i r_{(J\setminus\{j\})+k} + \text{(smaller terms)}$$

We now construct the Macaulay matrix $\mathcal{M}$ associated to the Q_J's in bi-degree $(1,1)$, which is the matrix whose columns are labeled by the monomials $\lambda_i r_T$ sorted in decreasing order w.r.t. $\prec$, whose rows correspond to the polynomials Q_J, and whose entry in row Q_J and column $\lambda_i r_T$ is the coefficient of the monomial $\lambda_i r_T$ in the polynomial Q_J.

Let $I = \{j_2 < \cdots < j_{w+1}\} \subset \{1..n-k\}$ of size w. Consider the submatrix of the Macaulay matrix formed by the rows $Q_{\{1\}\cup I}, \ldots, Q_{\{j_1\}\cup I}, \ldots, Q_{\{j_2-1\}\cup I}$. It has the shape

$$\mathcal{M}_I = \begin{array}{c} \\ Q_{\{1\}\cup I} \\ Q_{\{j_1\}\cup I} \\ Q_{\{j_2-1\}\cup I} \end{array} \begin{array}{ccccc} \cdots & \lambda_1 r_{I+k} & \cdots & \lambda_N r_{I+k} & \cdots \\ \left(\begin{array}{ccccc} 0 & s_{1,1} & \cdots & s_{N,1} & \cdots \\ 0 & s_{1,j_1} & & s_{N,j_1} & \cdots \\ 0 & s_{1,j_2-1} & & s_{N,j_2-1} & \cdots \end{array}\right) \end{array} = \left(\mathbf{0} \ S_{\{1..j_2-1\},*} \ \cdots\right).$$

We assume from now on that Assumption 1 is satisfied, say the first $n-k-w$ rows of $S = (s_1^{\mathsf{T}} \ldots s_N^{\mathsf{T}})$ are linearly independent. This implies that, up to a permutation of the s_i's, there exist an invertible lower-triangular matrix $L \in \mathbb{F}_{q^m}^{(n-k-w)\times(n-k-w)}$ and an upper-triangular matrix $U \in \mathbb{F}_{q^m}^{(n-k-w)\times N}$ such that all the entries of U on its main diagonal are ones, and that $LS_{\{1..n-k-w\},*} = U$. Then we have $L_{\{1..j_2-1\},\{1..j_2-1\}}\mathcal{M}_I = (\mathbf{0} \ U_{\{1..j_2-1\},*} \ \cdots)$, i.e.

$$L_{\{1..j_2-1\},\{1..j_2-1\}}\mathcal{M}_I = \begin{array}{ccccc} \cdots & \lambda_1 r_{I+k} & \cdots & \lambda_{j_2-1} r_{I+k} & \cdots \\ \left(\begin{array}{cccc} 0 & 1 & \cdots & u_{1,j_2-1} & \cdots \\ 0 & 0 & \ddots & u_{j_1,j_2-1} & \cdots \\ 0 & 0 & 0 & 1 & \cdots \end{array}\right) \end{array}$$

After applying those operations on all blocks, we have new equations $\tilde{Q}_{\{j_1\}\cup I}$ with leading monomials $\lambda_{j_1} r_{I+k}$ for all $1 \le j_1 < j_2$. Finally, any equation Q_J has been transformed into an equation $\tilde{Q}_J$ with leading monomial $\lambda_{j_1} r_{(J\setminus\{j_1\})+k}$ where $j_1 = \min(J)$, and they are all different, so that the equations are linearly independent.

Proof of Theorem 2. We first determine the number of linearly independent polynomials among the polynomials $\lambda_j \tilde{Q}_J$. As the leading term of $\tilde{Q}_J$ is $\lambda_{\min(J)} r_{J\setminus\{\min(J)\})+k}$, the relations between the polynomials can only come from the pairs $(\lambda_j \tilde{Q}_{\{i\}\cup I}, \lambda_i \tilde{Q}_{\{j\}\cup I})$ for all $I \subset \{1..n-k\}$ of size w and all $1 \le i < j < \min(I)$. If we order the polynomials $\lambda_i \tilde{Q}_{\{i\}\cup I}$ such that

$$\lambda_i \tilde{Q}_J \prec \lambda_{i'} \tilde{Q}_{J'} \text{ iff } (J \prec_{lex} J') \text{ or } (J = J' \text{ and } i > i')$$

where $J = \{j_1 < \cdots < j_{w+1}\} \prec_{lex} J'$ iff $j_t = j_t' \forall t > l$ and $j_l < j_l'$.

Then it is clear that when we compute a row echelon form (without row pivoting) on the Macaulay matrix in bi-degree $(2,1)$ for those polynomials in decreasing order, the only rows that can reduce to zero are the rows corresponding to the polynomials $\lambda_i \tilde{Q}_{\{j\}\cup I}$ with $I \subset \{1..n-k\}$ of size w and $1 \le i < j < \min(I)$. There are $\sum_{j_2=1}^{n-k-w+1} \binom{j_2-1}{2}\binom{n-k-j_2}{w-1} = \binom{n-k}{w+2}$ such polynomials.

On the other hand, the following Lemma 3 provides the same number of linearly independent relations between those polynomials, which shows that the vector space $\langle \lambda_j \tilde{Q}_J : 1 \le j \le N, J \subset \{1..n-k\}, \#J = w+1\rangle_{\mathbb{F}_{q^m}}$ is generated by the $\{\lambda_j \tilde{Q}_J : \min(J) \leq j \leq N, J \subset \{1..n-k\}, \#J = w+1\}$ that are linearly independent (they have distinct leading terms).

To conclude the proof of Theorem 2 for any $b \geq 1$, it is readily seen that among the polynomials $\lambda_1^{\alpha_1} \cdots \lambda_N^{\alpha_N} \tilde{Q}_{\{j_1\} \cup I}$ for $\sum_i \alpha_i = b-1$, $j_1 < \min(I)$, the ones with $\sum_{i=1}^{j_1-1} \alpha_i \neq 0$ reduce to zero (they are some multiple of a $\lambda_i \tilde{Q}_J$ with $i < \min(J)$ that reduces to zero), and the other polynomials have distinct leading terms

$$\mathrm{LT}(\lambda_{j_1}^{\alpha_{j_1}} \cdots \lambda_N^{\alpha_N} \tilde{Q}_{\{j_1\} \cup I}) = \lambda_{j_1}^{\alpha_{j_1}} \cdots \lambda_N^{\alpha_N} \mathrm{LT}(\tilde{Q}_{\{j_1\} \cup I}) = \lambda_{j_1}^{\alpha_{j_1}+1} \cdots \lambda_N^{\alpha_N} r_{I+k},$$

The total number of such polynomials is:

$$\sum_{j_2=2}^{n-k-w+1} \underbrace{\binom{n-k-j_2}{w-1}}_{\substack{\text{number of sets } I \\ \text{with } \min(I)=j_2}} \sum_{j_1=1}^{j_2-1} \underbrace{\binom{N-j_1+1+b-2}{b-1}}_{\substack{\text{number of monomials in} \\ \lambda_{j_1},...,\lambda_N \text{ of degree } b-1.}}$$

We are just left with the last lemma and its proof.

Lemma 3. *The following $\binom{n-k}{w+2}$ relations*

$$\left| \begin{pmatrix} \Delta_H \\ \sum_{i=1}^N \lambda_i s_i \end{pmatrix} \right|_{*,K} = 0 \qquad \forall K \subset \{1..n-k\}, \#K = w+2,$$

are relations between the $\lambda_j Q_J$'s (hence the $\lambda_j \tilde{Q}_J$'s), and under Assumption 1 they are linearly independent.

Proof. Those minors are zero because the first and the last rows of the matrix are equal. There are $\binom{n-k}{w+2}$ of them. Laplace expansion along the last row gives, with $K = \{k_1 < k_2 < \cdots < k_{w+2}\}$:

$$\sum_{i=1}^N \lambda_i \sum_{u=1}^{w+2} (-1)^{w+u} s_{i,k_u} Q_{K \setminus \{k_u\}} = \sum_{u=1}^{w+2} ((-1)^{w+u} \sum_{i=1}^N \lambda_i s_{i,k_u}) Q_{K \setminus \{k_u\}}$$

which corresponds to a syzygy

$$\mathcal{G}^K = \left(\underset{J \not\subset K}{\underbrace{0}}, \underset{K \setminus J = \{k\}}{\underbrace{(-1)^{w+u} \sum_{i=1}^N s_{i,k} \lambda_i}} \right)_{J \subset \{1..n-k\}, \#J = w+1} \tag{10}$$

If we order the $(Q_J)_J$ by decreasing lex ordering ($Q_J \prec_{lex} Q_{J'}$ if $J \prec_{lex} J'$), then the first non-zero position of the syzygy $\mathcal{G}^K$ is the coefficient of the largest $Q_{K \setminus \{k_u\}}$, which is Q_{K_1} with $K_1 = K \setminus \{k_1\}$. The coefficient is:

$$(-1)^{w+1} \sum_{i=1}^N s_{i,k_1} \lambda_i = (-1)^{w+1} \begin{pmatrix} s_{1,k_1} & \cdots & s_{N,k_1} \end{pmatrix} \begin{pmatrix} \lambda_1 & \cdots & \lambda_N \end{pmatrix}^{\mathsf{T}}.$$

This syzygy $\mathcal{G}^K$ shares the same leading position Q_{K_1} with exactly the syzygies $\mathcal{G}^{\{j\}\cup K_1}$ for $1 \leq j < k_1$. If Assumption 1 is satisfied, then the coefficient in position Q_{K_1} of

$$\boldsymbol{L}_{\{1..k_1\},\{1..k_1\}} \begin{pmatrix} \mathcal{G}^{\{1\}\cup K_1} \\ \vdots \\ \mathcal{G}^{\{k_1\}\cup K_1} \end{pmatrix}$$

is

$$(-1)^{w+1} \begin{pmatrix} 1 & \cdots & u_{1,k_1} & \cdots \\ & \ddots & \vdots & \cdots \\ 0 & & 1 & \cdots \end{pmatrix} \begin{pmatrix} \lambda_1 \\ \vdots \\ \lambda_N \end{pmatrix}$$

This shows that the syzygies $\mathcal{G}^{\{j\}\cup K_1}$, for $1 \leq j \leq k_1$ are linearly independent.

Particular case $q = 2$. Note that Theorems 1 and 2 are true regardless of the value of b compared to q, and regardless of the value of q. However, in Sect. 4.2, we want to find the solutions of the system over $\mathbb{F}_2$, which can be obtained by considering all polynomials over $\mathbb{F}_{2^m}$ modulo the so-called field equations[3] $\lambda_i^2 - \lambda_i$. In this section, we want to count the number of linearly independent rows in the Macaulay matrix where all monomials are reduced modulo the field equations.

It is clear that the $\binom{n-k}{w+1}$ equations Q_J in bi-degree $(1,1)$ are unchanged when reduced by the field equations (they only involve squarefree variables), so that they remain linearly independent over $\mathbb{F}_{2^m}$ modulo the field equations. For higher degree, things are different. In particular, there are drops in the leading monomials, and the leading monomial of the polynomial $\lambda_{j_1}\tilde{Q}_{\{j_1,j_2,\ldots,j_{w+1}\}}$ after reduction of the Macaulay matrix is $\lambda_{j_1}\lambda_{j_2}r_{\{j_1,j_3,\ldots,j_{w+1}\}}$ (instead of $\lambda_{j_1}^2 r_{\{j_2,j_3,\ldots\}}$ for $q > 2$). It is clear that for $J = \{j_1 < \cdots < j_{w+1}\}$, the polynomials

$$\lambda_{i_1}^{\delta_1} \cdots \lambda_{i_{b-1}}^{\delta_{b-1}} Q_J, \qquad j_1 < i_1 < \cdots < i_{b-1}, \delta_i \in \{0,1\}$$

are linearly independent, as their leading term modulo the field equation is

$$\mathrm{LT}(\lambda_{i_1}^{\delta_1} \cdots \lambda_{i_{b-1}}^{\delta_{b-1}}\tilde{Q}_J) = \lambda_{j_1}\lambda_{i_1}^{\delta_1} \cdots \lambda_{i_{b-1}}^{\delta_{b-1}} r_{\{j_2,\ldots,j_{w+1}\}}.$$

Experimentally, we have found that the leading monomial of $\lambda_{j_1} \cdots \lambda_{j_{b-1}}Q_J$ becomes $\lambda_{j_1} \cdots \lambda_{j_b}r_{J\setminus\{j_b\}}$ after reduction, and moreover for $j_1 < \cdots < j_{w+1}$, $i_d < \cdots < i_{b-1}, j_{d-1} < i_d < j_d$ the polynomials $\lambda_{j_1} \cdots \lambda_{j_{d-1}}\lambda_{i_d} \cdots \lambda_{i_{b-1}}Q_J$ reduce to zero. This gives, for $b \leq w + 1$,

$$\mathcal{N}_b^{\mathbb{F}_2} = \sum_{d=1}^{b} \sum_{j_d=1}^{n-k} \underbrace{\binom{j_d-1}{d-1}}_{\substack{\text{number of sets} \\ \{j_1 < \cdots < j_{d-1}\} \\ \text{in } \{1..j_d-1\}}} \underbrace{\binom{n-k-j_d}{w+1-d}}_{\substack{\text{number of sets} \\ \{j_{d+1} < \cdots < j_{w+1}\} \\ \text{in } \{j_d+1..n-k\}}} \underbrace{\binom{N-j_d}{b-d}}_{\substack{\text{number of sets} \\ \{i_d < \cdots < i_{b-1}\} \\ \text{in } \{j_d+1..N\}}} \qquad (b \leq w+1)$$

---

[3] We do not need the field equations for the r_T's, as they only appear in degree 1.

For $b \geq w + 2$, we experimentally see that there are some degree fall and some reduction to zero. Experimentally we have

$$\mathcal{N}_b^{\mathbb{F}_2} \leq \sum_{d=1}^{w+1} \sum_{j_d=1}^{n-k} \binom{j_d - 1}{d - 1}\binom{n - k - j_d}{w + 1 - d}\binom{N - j_d}{b - d} + \sum_{j=1}^{n-k} \binom{j - 1}{w}\binom{N - j}{b - w - 2}(b \geq w + 2)$$

$$\text{and } \mathcal{N}_b^{\mathbb{F}_2} = \sum_{d=1}^{b} (-1)^{d+1}\binom{n - k}{w + d}\binom{N}{b - d}(b \leq w + 1)$$

Proof of Assumption 1 in the Durandal case. Let's consider RSL instances which correspond to private keys in the Durandal signature scheme. As in the original parameter sets, we assume that both m and $k = n/2$ are prime. In this case, Assumption 1 is a direct consequence of the following result.

Lemma 4. *Let* $\boldsymbol{S} = \left(\boldsymbol{s}_1^{\mathsf{T}} \ldots \boldsymbol{s}_N^{\mathsf{T}}\right) \in \mathbb{F}_{q^m}^{(n-k) \times N}$ *from the Durandal RSL instance and assume that both k and m are prime (this is the case in the original parameter sets). Then, there exists an invertible matrix $\boldsymbol{U} \in \mathbb{F}_{q^m}^{k \times k}$ such that*

$$\boldsymbol{U}\boldsymbol{S} = \left(\boldsymbol{I}_k \, * \right).$$

Proof. Up to permutation of the columns of $\boldsymbol{S}$, one can assume that the k first syndromes $\boldsymbol{s}_1^{\mathsf{T}}, \ldots, \boldsymbol{s}_k^{\mathsf{T}}$ correspond to the ideal shifts of one unique σ^{T}. In this case, the left $k \times k$ block in $\boldsymbol{S}$ is equal to the ideal matrix $\mathcal{IM}(\sigma)^{\mathsf{T}}$, where the notation $\mathcal{IM}(\sigma)$ is defined in [4, Definition 2.0.1]. We also have $\sigma \neq 0$ with overwhelming probability since the double circulant ideal matrix $\boldsymbol{H}$ in Durandal is generated as random. Since P is irreducible over $\mathbb{F}_q$ and both m and k are prime, [4, Lemma 1] ensures that there exists a vector $u \in \mathbb{F}_{q^m}^k$ such that $\sigma u = 1 \mod P$. This implies $\mathcal{IM}(\sigma)\mathcal{IM}(u) = \boldsymbol{I}_k$, and the lemma follows by considering $\boldsymbol{U} := \mathcal{IM}(u)^{\mathsf{T}}$. $\qquad \square$

B   Number of Low Weight Codewords

This section contains the proof of Proposition 1 which provides formulae for the number of words of weight $\leq r$ in $\mathcal{C}'$ and, a fortiori, in $\mathcal{C}_{aug}$. Recall that $X_{\mathcal{C}',w}$ is the random variable which counts the number of codewords of weight w in $\mathcal{C}'$.

Let $\mathcal{D}$ be the $[r \times n, N]_q$-matrix code generated by the right factors $\boldsymbol{R}_i$, where $\boldsymbol{e}_i := (\beta_1, \ldots, \beta_m)\boldsymbol{C}\boldsymbol{R}_i$ for $i \in \{1..N\}$. We assume that $\mathcal{D}$ is a random $\mathbb{F}_q$-linear code (see the end of Sect. 2.1). The matrix $\boldsymbol{C}$ has rank exactly equal to r, so that $X_{\mathcal{C}',w} = X_{\mathcal{D},w}$ for all $w \leq r$. For $\boldsymbol{c} \in \mathbb{F}_q^{r \times n}$, we denote by $1_{\boldsymbol{c} \in \mathcal{D}}$ the random variable equal to 1 if $\boldsymbol{c} \in \mathcal{D}$ and 0 otherwise, so that $X_{\mathcal{D},w} = \sum_{\omega(\boldsymbol{c}) = w} 1_{\boldsymbol{c} \in \mathcal{D}}$. By linearity of expectation, one obtains:

$$\mathrm{E}[X_{\mathcal{D},w}] = \sum_{\omega(\boldsymbol{c}) = w} \mathrm{E}[1_{\boldsymbol{c} \in \mathcal{C}}] = \sum_{\omega(\boldsymbol{c}) = w} \mathcal{P}(\boldsymbol{c} \in \mathcal{D}).$$

The probability that $\boldsymbol{c} \in \mathcal{D}$ is the one to satisfy $r \times n - N$ independent parity-check equations of the form $\langle h, \boldsymbol{c} \rangle = 0$, hence $\mathcal{P}(\boldsymbol{c} \in \mathcal{D}) = \frac{1}{q^{r \times n - N}}$. The result follows by summing over all the codewords of weight w. For the variance, we start by computing the quantity

$$\mathrm{E}\big[X_{\mathcal{D},w}^2\big] = \sum_{\omega(c_1)=w.} \sum_{\omega(c_2)=w.} \mathrm{E}[1_{c_1 \in \mathcal{D}} 1_{c_2 \in \mathcal{D}}],$$

and by definition we have $\mathrm{E}[1_{c_1 \in \mathcal{D}} 1_{c_2 \in \mathcal{D}}] = \mathcal{P}(c_1 \in \mathcal{D}, c_2 \in \mathcal{D})$. The code $\mathcal{D}$ being $\mathbb{F}_q$-linear, the events $c_1 \in \mathcal{D}$ and $c_2 \in \mathcal{D}$ are not independent when $c_2 \in \langle c_1 \rangle_{\mathbb{F}_q}$. In this case, one has

$$\mathcal{P}_{c_2 \in \langle c_1 \rangle_{\mathbb{F}_q}}(c_1 \in \mathcal{D}, c_2 \in \mathcal{D}) = \mathcal{P}(c_1 \in \mathcal{D}) = \frac{1}{q^{r \times n - N}}.$$

Therefore:

$$\mathrm{E}\big[X_{\mathcal{D},w}^2\big] = \sum_{\substack{\omega(c_1)=w \\ \omega(c_2)=w}} \sum_{c_2 \in \langle c_1 \rangle_{\mathbb{F}_q}} \frac{1}{q^{r \times n - N}} + \sum_{\substack{\omega(c_1)=w \\ \omega(c_2)=w}} \sum_{c_2 \notin \langle c_1 \rangle_{\mathbb{F}_q}} \left(\frac{1}{q^{r \times n - N}}\right)^2$$

$$= \mathcal{S}_{w,r,n}(q-1)\frac{1}{q^{r \times n - N}} + \mathcal{S}_{w,r,n}\left(\mathcal{S}_{w,r,n} - (q-1)\right)\left(\frac{1}{q^{r \times n - N}}\right)^2$$

$$= \mathrm{E}[X_{\mathcal{D},w}]^2 + \mathcal{S}_{w,r,n} \times (q-1) \times \left(\frac{1}{q^{r \times n - N}} - \left(\frac{1}{q^{r \times n - N}}\right)^2\right).$$

References

1. Aguilar Melchor, C., et al.: Rank quasi cyclic (RQC). Second round submission to the NIST post-quantum cryptography call, April 2019. https://pqc-rqc.org
2. Aragon, N., et al.: LAKE - Low rAnk parity check codes Key Exchange. First round submission to the NIST post-quantum cryptography call, November 2017
3. Aragon, N., et al.: LOCKER - LOw rank parity ChecK codes EncRyption. First round submission to the NIST post-quantum cryptography call, November 2017
4. Aragon, N., et al.: ROLLO (merger of Rank-Ouroboros, LAKE and LOCKER). Second round submission to the NIST post-quantum cryptography call, March 2019. https://pqc-rollo.org
5. Aragon, N., Blazy, O., Gaborit, P., Hauteville, A., Zémor, G.: Durandal: a rank metric based signature scheme. In: Ishai, Y., Rijmen, V. (eds.) EUROCRYPT 2019. Part III. LNCS, vol. 11478, pp. 728–758. Springer, Cham (2019). https://doi.org/10.1007/978-3-030-17659-4_25
6. Aragon, N., Gaborit, P., Hauteville, A., Tillich, J.P.: A new algorithm for solving the rank syndrome decoding problem. In: 2018 IEEE International Symposium on Information Theory, ISIT 2018, Vail, CO, USA, 17–22 June 2018, pp. 2421–2425. IEEE (2018). https://doi.org/10.1109/ISIT.2018.8437464
7. Bardet, M., et al.: An algebraic attack on rank metric code-based cryptosystems. In: Canteaut, A., Ishai, Y. (eds.) EUROCRYPT 2020. LNCS, vol. 12107, pp. 64–93. Springer, Cham (2020). https://doi.org/10.1007/978-3-030-45727-3_3

8. Bardet, M., et al.: Improvements of algebraic attacks for solving the rank decoding and MinRank problems. In: Moriai, S., Wang, H. (eds.) ASIACRYPT 2020. LNCS, vol. 12491, pp. 507–536. Springer, Cham (2020). https://doi.org/10.1007/978-3-030-64837-4_17

9. Bettale, L., Faugere, J.C., Perret, L.: Hybrid approach for solving multivariate systems over finite fields. J. Math. Cryptol. **3**(3), 177–197 (2009)

10. Buss, J.F., Frandsen, G.S., Shallit, J.O.: The computational complexity of some problems of linear algebra. J. Comput. Syst. Sci. **58**(3), 572–596 (1999)

11. Debris-Alazard, T., Tillich, J.-P.: Two attacks on rank metric code-based schemes: RankSign and an IBE scheme. In: Peyrin, T., Galbraith, S. (eds.) ASIACRYPT 2018. LNCS, vol. 11272, pp. 62–92. Springer, Cham (2018). https://doi.org/10.1007/978-3-030-03326-2_3

12. Faugère, J.-C., Levy-dit-Vehel, F., Perret, L.: Cryptanalysis of MinRank. In: Wagner, D. (ed.) CRYPTO 2008. LNCS, vol. 5157, pp. 280–296. Springer, Heidelberg (2008). https://doi.org/10.1007/978-3-540-85174-5_16

13. Gabidulin, E.M., Paramonov, A.V., Tretjakov, O.V.: Ideals over a non-commutative ring and their application in cryptology. In: Davies, D.W. (ed.) EUROCRYPT 1991. LNCS, vol. 547, pp. 482–489. Springer, Heidelberg (1991). https://doi.org/10.1007/3-540-46416-6_41

14. Gaborit, P., Hauteville, A., Phan, D.H., Tillich, J.-P.: Identity-based encryption from codes with rank metric. In: Katz, J., Shacham, H. (eds.) CRYPTO 2017. LNCS, vol. 10403, pp. 194–224. Springer, Cham (2017). https://doi.org/10.1007/978-3-319-63697-9_7

15. Gaborit, P., Murat, G., Ruatta, O., Zémor, G.: Low rank parity check codes and their application to cryptography. In: Proceedings of the Workshop on Coding and Cryptography WCC'2013, Bergen, Norway (2013). www.selmer.uib.no/WCC2013/pdfs/Gaborit.pdf

16. Gaborit, P., Ruatta, O., Schrek, J.: On the complexity of the rank syndrome decoding problem. CoRR abs/1301.1026 (2013). http://arxiv.org/abs/1301.1026

17. Gaborit, P., Ruatta, O., Schrek, J., Zémor, G.: New results for rank-based cryptography. In: Pointcheval, D., Vergnaud, D. (eds.) AFRICACRYPT 2014. LNCS, vol. 8469, pp. 1–12. Springer, Cham (2014). https://doi.org/10.1007/978-3-319-06734-6_1

18. Gaborit, P., Zémor, G.: On the hardness of the decoding and the minimum distance problems for rank codes. IEEE Trans. Inf. Theory **62**(12), 7245–7252 (2016)

19. Hauteville, A., Tillich, J.P.: New algorithms for decoding in the rank metric and an attack on the LRPC cryptosystem. In: Proceedings of the IEEE International Symposium Information Theory - ISIT 2015, Hong Kong, China, pp. 2747–2751, June 2015. https://doi.org/10.1109/ISIT.2015.7282956

20. Hoffstein, J., Pipher, J., Silverman, J.H.: NTRU: a ring-based public key cryptosystem. In: Buhler, J.P. (ed.) ANTS 1998. LNCS, vol. 1423, pp. 267–288. Springer, Heidelberg (1998). https://doi.org/10.1007/BFb0054868

21. Kabatianskii, G., Krouk, E., Smeets, B.: A digital signature scheme based on random error-correcting codes. In: Darnell, M. (ed.) Cryptography and Coding 1997. LNCS, vol. 1355, pp. 161–167. Springer, Heidelberg (1997). https://doi.org/10.1007/BFb0024461

22. Misoczki, R., Tillich, J.P., Sendrier, N., Barreto, P.S.L.M.: MDPC-McEliece: new McEliece variants from moderate density parity-check codes (2012). http://eprint.iacr.org/2012/409

23. Otmani, A., Tillich, J.-P.: An efficient attack on all concrete KKS proposals. In: Yang, B.-Y. (ed.) PQCrypto 2011. LNCS, vol. 7071, pp. 98–116. Springer, Heidelberg (2011). https://doi.org/10.1007/978-3-642-25405-5_7

24. Ourivski, A.V., Johansson, T.: New technique for decoding codes in the rank metric and its cryptography applications. Probl. Inf. Transm. **38**(3), 237–246 (2002). https://doi.org/10.1023/A:1020369320078

25. Overbeck, R.: A new structural attack for GPT and variants. In: Dawson, E., Vaudenay, S. (eds.) Mycrypt 2005. LNCS, vol. 3715, pp. 50–63. Springer, Heidelberg (2005). https://doi.org/10.1007/11554868_5

26. Wiedemann, D.: Solving sparse linear equations over finite fields. IEEE Trans. Inf. Theory **32**(1), 54–62 (1986)

Quantum Indistinguishability for Public Key Encryption

Tommaso Gagliardoni[1], Juliane Krämer[2], and Patrick Struck[2(✉)]

[1] Kudelski Security, Cheseaux-sur-Lausanne, Switzerland
tommaso.gagliardoni@kudelskisecurity.com
[2] Technische Universität Darmstadt, Darmstadt, Germany
{juliane,patrick}@qpc.tu-darmstadt.de

Abstract. In this work we study the quantum security of public key encryption schemes (PKE). Boneh and Zhandry (CRYPTO'13) initiated this research area for PKE and symmetric key encryption (SKE), albeit restricted to a classical indistinguishability phase. Gagliardoni et al. (CRYPTO'16) advanced the study of quantum security by giving, for SKE, the first definition with a quantum indistinguishability phase. For PKE, on the other hand, no notion of quantum security with a quantum indistinguishability phase exists.

Our main result is a novel quantum security notion (qIND-qCPA) for PKE with a quantum indistinguishability phase, which closes the aforementioned gap. We show a distinguishing attack against code-based schemes and against LWE-based schemes with certain parameters. We also show that the canonical hybrid PKE-SKE encryption construction is qIND-qCPA-secure, even if the underlying PKE scheme by itself is not. Finally, we classify quantum-resistant PKE schemes based on the applicability of our security notion.

Our core idea follows the approach of Gagliardoni et al. by using so-called type-2 operators for encrypting the challenge message. At first glance, type-2 operators appear unnatural for PKE, as the canonical way of building them requires both the secret and the public key. However, we identify a class of PKE schemes - which we call *recoverable* - and show that for this class type-2 operators require merely the public key. Moreover, recoverable schemes allow to realise type-2 operators even if they suffer from decryption failures, which in general thwarts the reversibility mandated by type-2 operators. Our work reveals that many real-world quantum-resistant PKE schemes, including most NIST PQC candidates and the canonical hybrid construction, are indeed recoverable.

1 Introduction

The discovery of Shor's [31] and Grover's [20] quantum algorithms had a significant impact on cryptographic research. Shor's algorithm in particular has the potential to completely break most of the public key cryptosystems used nowadays. This led to the development of quantum-resistant (or post-quantum [10]) cryptography, that is, cryptography that can run on non-quantum computers

© Springer Nature Switzerland AG 2021
J. H. Cheon and J.-P. Tillich (Eds.): PQCrypto 2021, LNCS 12841, pp. 463–482, 2021.
https://doi.org/10.1007/978-3-030-81293-5_24

but should withstand attackers equipped with quantum computing power. In recent years the research efforts on quantum-resistant cryptography accelerated significantly due to the standardisation process initiated by the NIST [28].

Modern cryptography is based on the paradigm of *provable security*, which is itself given in terms of a security notion, an adversarial model, and a security proof. A widely used framework for defining security notions is the so-called *game-based security*, which is presented as a game between two or more parties. In the case of encryption schemes these parties are: a challenger, representing the user of the scheme, and an adversary, representing an attacker against the scheme. Any meaningful model for quantum-resistant schemes should entail that the adversary has quantum computing power. Based on this, we can differentiate between different models depending on the computing power of the challenger. In the literature there are mainly two of these models that are taken into account. In the first, the challenger remains fully classical, implying that any communication between adversary and challenger is also classical (including oracles provided by the challenger to the adversary), while the adversary retains local quantum computing power. This is the model most often considered in quantum-resistant cryptography, and it is also called QS1 [17] or Q1 [23]. In the second model, the challenger also has quantum computing power, which enables quantum communication between challenger and adversary. This stronger model is sometimes called "superposition-attack security" [16], QS2 [17], or Q2 [23]. We give some more motivation for this model in the full version [19].

Boneh and Zhandry [12] initiated the study of QS2 security for cryptographic primitives. For signature schemes, they give a security definition that allows the adversary to query the signing oracle on a superposition of messages. For public and symmetric key encryption (PKE and SKE) schemes, on the other hand, they prove that simply allowing the adversary to query a superposition of messages as challenge in a "natural" way gives an unachievable security notion (fqIND-CPA). This is due to entanglement between the plaintext register and the ciphertext register. They show how to exploit this entanglement to break this security notion irrespectively of the used encryption scheme. To resolve this, they propose another security notion (IND-qCPA) which allows the adversary superposition queries in the CPA phase while the challenge messages in the IND phase are restricted to be classical. This notion coincides with the traditional QS1 security notion for PKE (as the adversary can simulate the encryption in superposition using his local computing power and the public key), while for SKE, this yields a notion of QS2 security - although the restriction to a classical challenge in this case is clearly a shortcoming.

Gagliardoni et al. [18] overcame this shortcoming in the symmetric key case by showing how to model a quantum challenge query, while keeping the resulting security notion still achievable, yet stronger than IND-qCPA. At the heart of their idea lies the use of so-called *type-2 operators* (also called *minimal oracles* in [24]) rather than so-called type-1 operators when encrypting the challenge messages of the adversary. Type-1 operators are the "canonical" way of implementing a classical function $\mathcal{F}$ on a quantum superposition of input, by mapping the state $|x, y\rangle$ to $|x, y \oplus \mathcal{F}(x)\rangle$, thereby ensuring reversibility for any function $\mathcal{F}$ (reversibility being necessary when defining non-measurement quantum operations). An important property of type-1 operators is that they create entanglement between the input and output registers. This is exactly the entanglement which Boneh and Zhandry exploit to show that fqIND-CPA is unachievable. In contrast to these, type-2 operators work directly on the input register, i.e., they map the state $|x\rangle$ to $|\mathcal{F}(x)\rangle$. Only reversible functions, for instance permutations, can be implemented as type-2 operators, while it is impossible to compute, say, an arbitrary one-way function through a type-2 operator. Gagliardoni et al. observe that SKE schemes act as permutations between the plaintext space and the ciphertext space, which allows to implement the encryption algorithm as a type-2 operator. This, in turn, allows to build a solid framework for QS2 security in the case of SKE.

In [18] the authors speculate that their techniques could be extended to the public key case as well. However, defining type-2 operators for PKE schemes is much more involved than for SKE schemes. First, to achieve IND-CPA security, PKE schemes are inherently randomised and the randomness is usually erased in the process of decryption. Second, many constructions for quantum-resistant PKE schemes, in particular lattice-based and code-based schemes, suffer from a small probability of decryption failures, i.e., ciphertexts which do not decrypt correctly. Given the above, at first glance it is unclear whether type-2 operators for PKE schemes are possible at all, as these two properties seem to thwart the mandatory reversibility. Hence, QS2 security for the public key case remained an open problem so far.

1.1   Our Contribution

We present a novel QS2 security notion[1] for PKE, provide both achievability results and separation to the QS1 notion through many real-world schemes, and give a general classification of PKE with respect to our security notion.

Our core focus is to extend the results from [18] to the public key scenario. We first formalise the theory of type-2 encryption operators for PKE. For perfectly correct schemes (i.e., schemes which do not suffer from the possibility of decryption failures) we define the type-2 operator to preserve a randomness register in input and output. Even if such approach might look strange at first glance, we show that this is the most natural way of defining type-2 operators for PKE schemes. As a next step, we identify a class of PKE schemes (which we call *recoverable*) where decryption failures can always be avoided given knowledge of the randomness used during encryption, regardless of the actual failure probability of the decryption algorithm. We observe that most real-world partially correct PKE schemes (including many quantum-resistant NIST candidates) are actually of this type. Then, for schemes that are perfectly correct or recoverable, we show how to efficiently construct the type-2 encryption operator. Moreover, we show that for recoverable schemes, this can be done by knowledge of the public key

---

[1] See [19, Appendix C] for concurrent and independent work.

only! This implies, perhaps surprisingly, that the adversary can implement efficiently this type-2 operator already in the QS1 model. Such observation marks a substantial difference from the symmetric key case, where the need for type-2 operators is dictated by necessity in order to cover exotic attack models.

Using the theory of type-2 operators developed so far, we give a novel QS2 security notion for PKE, that we call *quantum ciphertext indistinguishability under quantum chosen plaintext attack* (qIND-qCPA). For a new security notion to be meaningful, two properties are required. First, it has to be achievable, and, second, it has to differ from existing security notions.

We analyse several real-world PKE schemes with respect to our new security notion qIND-qCPA. For code-based schemes, we observe that some constructions (such as ROLLO-II [8]) encrypt the message using a one-time pad operation, which allows to exploit the "Hadamard distinguisher" given in [18]. We also show, in the full version of this paper [19], that the canonical LWE-based PKE scheme [29] can be attacked for certain parameters.

However, in practice most real-world PKE schemes (including the NIST submissions) are used as Key Encapsulation Mechanisms (KEM) in combination with an SKE scheme, yielding a hybrid PKE-SKE construction. Looking at such canonical hybrid construction then, we show that its qIND-qCPA security mostly depends on the underlying SKE scheme, while the PKE scheme only needs to be secure in the QS1 sense. Hence, even the code-based PKE scheme ROLLO-II, which as a stand-alone PKE scheme is not qIND-qCPA-secure, can be used to achieve qIND-qCPA security if combined with an SKE scheme secure in the QS2 sense via the hybrid construction, which is the default way of using it in practice.

In the full version of this paper [19], we additionally discuss the difficulty of defining type-2 operators (and the related QS2 security notion) for arbitrary schemes that are neither perfectly correct nor recoverable. For this, we study the problem of their general classification and we identify a class of schemes, that we call *isometric*, that allow to overcome such difficulty. Furthermore, we provide constructions and separation results.

1.2   Related Work

The study of quantum security under adversarial queries in superposition can be traced back to works such as [11, 16, 33], which explore different settings where this additional adversarial power has an impact on security. However, for the case of signatures and encryption schemes, the first framework going beyond the traditional QS1 paradigm was given in [12]. This paradigm was further extended in [18] for symmetric key encryption schemes, and in [5] for MACs/signatures.

Regarding examples of exotic quantum attacks previously mentioned: it is currently not known whether any of these are feasible at all, but as noted in [17]: (1) if they are feasible, in some cases they do not even require a fully fledged quantum computer (for example, in the attack from [18] it would be only necessary to produce and detect a Hadamard superposition of messages); and (2) it is already known in the literature that these attacks can be devastating. For example, related-key attacks [30], and superposition attacks against Even-Mansour [26], Feistel networks [21,25], block ciphers [6,7], and HMAC constructions [22].

In concurrent and independent work, Chevalier et al. [14] propose alternative QS2 security notions for encryption schemes. Their and our notion are incomparable, as also claimed in a recent work by Carstens et al. [13]. We discuss the differences in more detail in the full version [19, Appendix C].

2   Preliminaries

In the following, we use "classical" as meaning "non-quantum". By *algorithm* or *procedure* we mean a uniform family of circuits (classical or quantum) of depth and width polynomial in the index of the family. We call such index a *security parameter*, and we denote it by λ (or 1^λ if written in unary notation). We implicitly assume that all algorithms take 1^λ as a first input, so we will often omit this. We call *negligible* a function that grows more slowly than any inverse polynomial, and *overwhelming* a function which is 1 minus a negligible function. Background on PKE is given in the full version [19].

2.1   Quantum Notation

We assume familiarity with the topic of quantum computing, but recall here the basic required notation. For an in-depth discussion we refer to [27].

A quantum system, identified by a letter A, is represented by a complex Hilbert space, which we denote by $\mathfrak{H}_A$. If A is clear from the context, we write $\mathfrak{H}$ rather than $\mathfrak{H}_A$. Pure states in a Hilbert space $\mathfrak{H}$ are representatives of equivalence classes of elements of $\mathfrak{H}$ of norm 1. Mixed states, on the other hand, are a more general representation of quantum states that takes *entanglement* with external systems into account; they are elements of the density matrix operator space over $\mathfrak{H}$, that is, Hermitian positive semi-definite linear operators of trace 1, denoted as $\mathfrak{D}(\mathfrak{H})$. We use the ket notation for pure states, e.g., $|\varphi\rangle$, while mixed states will be denoted by lowercase Greek letter, e.g., ρ. Operations on pure states from A to B are performed by applying a unitary operator $U\colon \mathfrak{H}_A \to \mathfrak{H}_B$ to the state, while the more general case of operations on mixed states is described by superoperators of the form $U\colon \mathfrak{D}(\mathfrak{H}_A) \to \mathfrak{D}(\mathfrak{H}_B)$.

The canonical way to compute a classical function $\mathcal{F}\colon \mathcal{X} \to \mathcal{Y}$ on a superposition of possible inputs $\sum_{x\in\mathcal{X}} \alpha_x |x\rangle$ is through the so-called *type-1 operator for $\mathcal{F}$* described by

$$U_{\mathcal{F}}^{(1)}\colon \sum_{x,y}\alpha_{x,y}|x,y\rangle \mapsto \sum_{x,y}\alpha_{x,y}|x,y\oplus\mathcal{F}(x)\rangle .$$

This can always be implemented efficiently whenever $\mathcal{F}$ is efficient [27]. By linearity, it is sufficient to specify just the behaviour on the basis elements, i.e.,

$$U_{\mathcal{F}}^{(1)}\colon |x,y\rangle \mapsto |x,y\oplus\mathcal{F}(x)\rangle .$$

If $\mathcal{F}$ is invertible, then there is another non-equivalent possible way to compute $\mathcal{F}$ in superposition. This is done through the so-called *type-2 operators*, which are defined as the unitary

$$U_{\mathcal{F}}^{(2)} : |x\rangle \mapsto |\mathcal{F}(x)\rangle \ .$$

See Fig. 1 for an illustration of these different operators. Kashefi et al. [24] first introduced type-2 operators using the term *minimal oracles* instead. They show that these operators are strictly stronger by giving a problem which can be solved exponentially faster with type-2 operators than with type-1 operators. They also observe that the adjoint of the type-2 operator corresponds to the type-2 operator of the inverse function $\mathcal{F}^{-1}$, which is (usually) not the case for type-1 operators. Besides that, type-2 operators have been used by Gagliardoni et al. [18] to define quantum security for secret key encryption schemes.

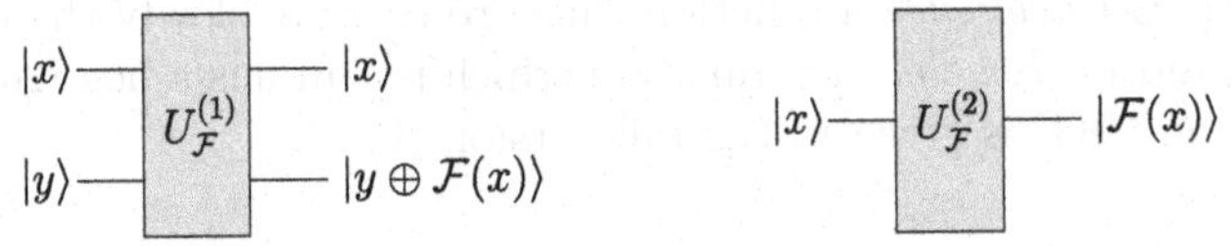

Fig. 1. Type-1 operator (left) and type-2 operator (right) for a function $\mathcal{F}$.

3   Quantum Indistinguishability for PKE Schemes

In this section we extend the QS2 security notion of qIND-qCPA introduced for SKE schemes in [18] to the public key case. This is much more complex than the symmetric case, for the following reasons:

1. PKE schemes are randomised to achieve ciphertext indistinguishability and adversaries must not learn the used randomness, even in the one-time case;
2. when derandomising the encryption procedure and considering the randomness as additional input, there might be collisions (different randomnesses leading to the same ciphertext), hence ensuring reversibility of type-2 operators is not straightforward;
3. many existing schemes, such as lattice- or code-based NIST candidates, suffer from a small decryption failure probability.

In particular, as we will see, there are two main consequences: (1) the inverse of type-2 encryption operators is not generally a type-2 decryption operator; and (2), most interestingly, many type-2 encryption operators can be built efficiently by using only knowledge of the public key. The last point is crucial: it shows that in the PKE case, type-2 encryption operators are much more natural than in the SKE case, and for certain schemes they are actually already covered in the usual notion of QS1 "post-quantum" security. We will also show that some of these schemes are very relevant, such as the LWE-based scheme used as a blueprint for many NIST submissions. In this section we will do the following:

1. First, we revisit and define formally type-1 operators for PKE, and we show the difference between type-1 encryption and decryption (cf. Sect. 3.1).
2. We define type-2 encryption operators for perfectly correct PKE schemes, and we show that they can be efficiently implemented with knowledge of secret and public key (cf. Sect. 3.2).
3. We define what we call *recoverable* PKE schemes, i.e., schemes that admit an efficient procedure to recover the message given randomness, ciphertext and public key, without the secret key. We show that for such schemes the 'canonical' type-2 encryption operator can be built by only using the public key, *even* if the scheme is not perfectly correct (cf. Sect. 3.3).
4. We define the qIND-qCPA security notion for any PKE scheme where one can efficiently build the type-2 encryption operator. This includes in particular perfectly correct and recoverable schemes (cf. Sect. 3.4).
5. Finally, we discuss how to extend these results to the *chosen ciphertext attack* (CCA) scenario (cf. Sect. 3.5).

3.1 Type-1 Operators for PKE

Recall that, for an arbitrary function $f : \mathcal{X} \to \mathcal{Y}$, the corresponding type-1 operator is the "canonical" way of computing f on a superposition of input through the unitary operator $U_f : \mathcal{H}_\mathcal{X} \otimes \mathcal{H}_\mathcal{Y} \to \mathcal{H}_\mathcal{X} \otimes \mathcal{H}_\mathcal{Y}$ defined by: $U_f : |x, y\rangle \mapsto |x, y \oplus f(x)\rangle$. Realising U_f is always efficient if f is efficiently computable.

Traditionally, when looking at (deterministic) encryption schemes, the type-1 operator for encryption has been defined as:

$$U_{\mathtt{Enc}} : |m, y\rangle \mapsto |m, y \oplus \mathtt{Enc}(m)\rangle .$$

This is the approach used in, e.g., [12] and [18]. However, in our case of PKE schemes (which are generally randomised), we have to consider that encryption can be performed locally by the quantum adversary, who therefore has full control not only on the randomness used for encryption (i.e., it is necessary to explicitly derandomise the encryption procedure[2]), but also on the public key used (i.e., it is theoretically possible to compute encryption for a superposition of different public keys). Therefore, the most general definition of a type-1 encryption operator would look like:

$$U_{\mathtt{Enc}} : |\mathsf{pk}, r, m, y\rangle \mapsto |\mathsf{pk}, r, m, y \oplus \mathtt{Enc}_{\mathsf{pk}}(m; r)\rangle .$$

We argue that this is indeed the most general and correct way to model the local computational power of a quantum adversary, even in the QS1 case. However, for ease of exposition (and also because it would go beyond the traditional meaning of ciphertext indistinguishability), in the present work we do not consider superpositions of public keys, as we assume that the (classical) public key to be attacked is given to the adversary at the beginning of the security game. Hence, we drop the register containing the public key and consider it a parameter of the unitary. This leads us to the following definition.

---

[2] This is implicitly considered in [12] and [18], but not explicitly formalised.

Definition 1 (Type-1 Encryption for PKE). *Let* $\Sigma = (\mathsf{KGen}, \mathsf{Enc}, \mathsf{Dec})$ *be a PKE scheme and let* $(\mathsf{pk}, \mathsf{sk}) \leftarrow \mathsf{KGen}$. *The* type-1 encryption operator *for* pk *is the unitary defined by:*

$$U_{\mathsf{Enc}_{\mathsf{pk}}}^{(1)} : |r, m, y\rangle \mapsto |r, m, y \oplus \mathsf{Enc}_{\mathsf{pk}}(m; r)\rangle \ .$$

Usually the public key is clear from the context, so we will omit that dependency and just write $U_{\mathsf{Enc}}^{(1)}$. As usual, when there is no ambiguity, we identify the corresponding superoperator acting on mixed states rather than pure states with the same symbol $U_{\mathsf{Enc}}^{(1)} : \mathfrak{D}(\mathfrak{H}_{\mathcal{R}} \otimes \mathfrak{H}_{\mathcal{M}} \otimes \mathfrak{H}_{\mathcal{C}}) \to \mathfrak{D}(\mathfrak{H}_{\mathcal{R}} \otimes \mathfrak{H}_{\mathcal{M}} \otimes \mathfrak{H}_{\mathcal{C}})$. By letting the randomness be an input, Definition 1 allows to encrypt using a superposition of randomnesses, which is fine in the case of the adversary generating ciphertexts himself. Note also that the case of different randomnesses for each message in superposition can be realised by using a single classical randomness and a QS2-secure pseudorandom function [34], as shown by Boneh and Zhandry [12].

The type-1 decryption operator is defined analogously to Definition 1, but with an important difference: the decryption algorithm does not take the randomness used for encryption as input.

Definition 2 (Type-1 Decryption for PKE). *Let* $\Sigma = (\mathsf{KGen}, \mathsf{Enc}, \mathsf{Dec})$ *be a PKE scheme and let* $(\mathsf{pk}, \mathsf{sk}) \leftarrow \mathsf{KGen}$. *The* type-1 decryption operator *for* sk *is the unitary defined by:*

$$U_{\mathsf{Dec}_{\mathsf{sk}}}^{(1)} : |c, z\rangle \mapsto |c, z \oplus \mathsf{Dec}_{\mathsf{sk}}(c)\rangle \ .$$

As usual we denote it by $U_{\mathsf{Dec}}^{(1)}$, leaving the secret key understood, and when there is no ambiguity with the same symbol we denote the superoperator acting on mixed states also by $U_{\mathsf{Dec}}^{(1)} : \mathfrak{D}(\mathfrak{H}_{\mathcal{C}} \otimes \mathfrak{H}_{\mathcal{M}}) \to \mathfrak{D}(\mathfrak{H}_{\mathcal{C}} \otimes \mathfrak{H}_{\mathcal{M}})$.

Notice the difference in type-1 encryption and decryption acting on different spaces: this is not surprising, as it is already known that the adjoint of a type-1 encryption operator is not, generally, a type-1 decryption operator. Notice also how both operators are efficiently computable, because Enc and Dec are efficient algorithms. The difference is that realising $U_{\mathsf{Dec}}^{(1)}$ requires knowledge of the secret key sk, while for realising $U_{\mathsf{Enc}}^{(1)}$ it is sufficient to know the public key pk.

3.2   Type-2 Encryption for PKE

When defining type-2 encryption for PKE schemes, we have to remember that defining these operators only makes sense for functions which are reversible. If a PKE scheme is perfectly correct, then encryption is always reversible if seen as a function of the *plaintext*, but not necessarily as a function of the *randomness*. That is because it might be the case that for a given message different randomnesses lead to the same ciphertext. In the context of security games, message and randomness have very different roles anyway, as one is generally chosen by the adversary, while the other is generally chosen by the challenger.

Ultimately, what we want is to define a type of unitary which generalises the case of arbitrary permutations from plaintext to ciphertext spaces (the same approach as considered in [18]). In order to avoid the issue raised by randomness collisions, we will keep the auxiliary randomness register both in input and output of the circuit. This ensures reversibility of the operator, because given a certain ciphertext and a certain randomness, there is only one possible plaintext which was mapped to that ciphertext (otherwise we would have a decryption failure, and for now we are only considering perfectly correct schemes). So, if the sizes of the plaintext space and the ciphertext space coincide, i.e., there is no ciphertext expansion and thus $\dim(\mathfrak{H}_\mathcal{M}) = \dim(\mathfrak{H}_\mathcal{C})$, then we can define the corresponding type-2 encryption operator as:

$$U^{(2)}_{\mathsf{Enc}} : |r, m\rangle \mapsto |r, \mathsf{Enc}_{\mathsf{pk}}(m; r)\rangle \,,$$

where, as usual, the public key pk is implicit in the definition of $U^{(2)}_{\mathsf{Enc}}$, i.e., it is a parameter of the unitary operator in question.

In the more general case of message expansion, i.e., $\dim(\mathfrak{H}_\mathcal{M}) < \dim(\mathfrak{H}_\mathcal{C})$, we use the same approach as in [18]: we introduce an auxiliary register in a complementary space $\mathfrak{H}_{\mathcal{C}-\mathcal{M}}$[3] that ensures reversibility of the operation, and which is initialised to $|0\dots0\rangle$ during an honest execution to yield a correct encryption. So we consider a family of unitary superoperators of the form:

$$U : \mathfrak{D}(\mathfrak{H}_\mathcal{R} \otimes \mathfrak{H}_\mathcal{M} \otimes \mathfrak{H}_{\mathcal{C}-\mathcal{M}}) \to \mathfrak{D}(\mathfrak{H}_\mathcal{R} \otimes \mathfrak{H}_\mathcal{C}), \text{ such that}$$
$$U : |r, m, y\rangle\langle r, m, y| \mapsto \psi,$$

and we define a type-2 encryption operator to be any arbitrary, efficiently computable (purified) representative of the above family such that:

$$U^{(2)}_{\mathsf{Enc}} : |r, m, 0\dots0\rangle \mapsto |r, \mathsf{Enc}_{\mathsf{pk}}(m; r)\rangle\,. \tag{1}$$

The choice of the particular representative is irrelevant in our exposition as long as it respects (1) above and it is efficiently computable. However, as already discussed in [18], it might be the case that realising this operator requires knowledge of the secret key, not only of the public key. This finally leads to the following.

Definition 3 (Type-2 Encryption for PKE). *Let $\Sigma = (\mathsf{KGen}, \mathsf{Enc}, \mathsf{Dec})$ be a perfectly correct PKE scheme, and let $(\mathsf{pk}, \mathsf{sk}) \leftarrow \mathsf{KGen}$. A type-2 encryption operator for Σ is an efficiently computable unitary in the family defined by:*

$$U^{(2)}_{(\mathsf{Enc},\mathsf{pk},\mathsf{sk})} : |r, m, 0\dots0\rangle \mapsto |r, \mathsf{Enc}_{\mathsf{pk}}(m; r)\rangle\,.$$

It will be usually denoted by just $U^{(2)}_{\mathsf{Enc}}$ when there is no ambiguity.

---

[3] We denote by $\mathfrak{H}_{\mathcal{C}-\mathcal{M}}$ a Hilbert space such that $\mathfrak{H}_\mathcal{M} \otimes \mathfrak{H}_{\mathcal{C}-\mathcal{M}}$ is isomorphic to $\mathfrak{H}_\mathcal{C}$. Notice that the opposite case, i.e., $\dim(\mathfrak{H}_\mathcal{M}) > \dim(\mathfrak{H}_\mathcal{C})$, cannot happen because it would lead to collisions on the ciphertexts and thus introduce decryption failures. Also notice that, as in [18], the case of adversarially-controlled ancilla qubits is left as an open problem.

It is always possible to find and efficiently sample and implement at least one valid representative for $U_{\text{Enc}}^{(2)}$ given the secret and public keys, by using a conversion circuit of type-1 encryption and decryption operators in a similar way as presented in [18]. We call this the *canonical* type-2 operator.

Theorem 4 (Efficient Realisation of Type-2 Encryption). *Let Σ be a perfectly correct PKE scheme with $\Sigma = (\text{KGen}, \text{Enc}, \text{Dec})$, and let $(\text{pk}, \text{sk}) \leftarrow \text{KGen}$. Then there exists an efficient procedure which takes pk and sk as input, and outputs a polynomial-size quantum circuit realising $U_{\text{Enc}}^{(2)}$.*

Proof. The explicit circuit of the procedure is shown in Fig. 2. It uses type-1 encryption and decryption operators as underlying components, which are both efficient with knowledge of the respective keys. □

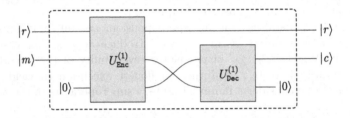

Fig. 2. Canonical type-2 encryption operator for perfectly correct PKE schemes.

Notice that realising this canonical type-2 operator requires knowledge of the secret key, even if it is just an encryption operator, but that is fine because as previously mentioned type-2 operators usually require this additional knowledge. We have to make a distinction between the encryption *unitary* as defined above (a quantum gate modelling local computation of encryption by a party with knowledge of the relevant keys) and the encryption *oracle* (modelling the interaction of the adversary with such party, usually the challenger). By letting the randomness be an input, Definition 3 allows to encrypt using a superposition of randomnesses, which is fine in the case of a party generating ciphertexts himself. In our security notion, however, the (honest) challenger will always produce ciphertexts using a (secret) classical randomness not controlled by the adversary $\mathcal{A}$. In the security game, the challenger cannot send the randomness register back to $\mathcal{A}$, because knowledge of the randomness used would trivially break security, even in a classical scenario. But at the same time if the challenger withholds the randomness register, from $\mathcal{A}$'s perspective this would be equivalent to tracing it out, and if the type-2 encryption operator introduces entanglement between ciphertext and randomness output registers, then tracing out the randomness would disturb the ciphertext state.

Luckily, a simple observation solves this dilemma: as we have already discussed, in our oracle case the randomness is chosen by the (honest) challenger during the challenge query, so we can safely model it as classical.[4] Looking at Definition 3, this means that the output state is always separable as $|r\rangle\langle r| \otimes \psi$. Therefore, in our oracle definition the randomness register can be discarded after applying the type-2 encryption without disturbing the ciphertext state. This leads to the following.

Definition 5 (Type-2 Encryption Oracle). *Let* $\Sigma = (\mathsf{KGen}, \mathsf{Enc}, \mathsf{Dec})$ *be a PKE scheme and let* $(\mathsf{pk}, \mathsf{sk}) \leftarrow \mathsf{KGen}$. *The* type-2 encryption oracle $O_{\mathsf{Enc}}^{(2)}$ *for* pk *is defined by the following procedure:*

Oracle $O_{\mathsf{Enc}}^{(2)}(\varphi)$ *on input* $\varphi \in \mathfrak{D}(\mathfrak{H}_{\mathcal{M}})$

$\quad 1: \quad r \xleftarrow{\$} \mathcal{R}$

$\quad 2: \quad |r\rangle\langle r| \otimes \psi := U_{\mathsf{Enc}}^{(2)} \left(|r\rangle\langle r| \otimes \varphi \otimes |0\ldots0\rangle\langle0\ldots0| \right)$

$\quad 3: \quad$ *trace out* $|r\rangle\langle r|$

$\quad 4: \quad$ **return** ψ

3.3 Recoverable PKE Schemes

Now we introduce a special case of PKE schemes where it is possible to decrypt a ciphertext *without* knowledge of the secret key, but having access to the randomness used for the encryption instead. These schemes might not be perfectly correct, so the decryption procedure might fail on some ciphertext, yet still the recovery procedure will 'decrypt' correctly if the right randomness is provided. We will see in Sect. 4 that many PKE schemes are actually of this type.

Definition 6 (Recoverable PKE Scheme). *Let* $\Sigma = (\mathsf{KGen}, \mathsf{Enc}, \mathsf{Dec})$ *be a (not necessarily perfectly correct) PKE scheme. We call* Σ *a recoverable PKE scheme if there exists an efficient algorithm* $\mathsf{Rec} : \mathcal{P} \times \mathcal{R} \times \mathcal{C} \rightarrow \mathcal{M}$ *such that, for any* $\mathsf{pk} \in \mathcal{P}, r \in \mathcal{R}, m \in \mathcal{M}$, *it holds that*

$$\mathsf{Rec}(\mathsf{pk}, r, \mathsf{Enc}_{\mathsf{pk}}(m; r)) = m.$$

Notice how the recovery procedure will always allow to avoid decryption failures even for schemes which are not perfectly correct. We will sometimes write a recoverable scheme $\Sigma = (\mathsf{KGen}, \mathsf{Enc}, \mathsf{Dec})$ with recovery algorithm Rec directly as $\Sigma = (\mathsf{KGen}, \mathsf{Enc}, \mathsf{Dec}, \mathsf{Rec})$. Given pk, it is of course possible to define a type-1 operator for Rec in the canonical way.

Definition 7 (Type-1 Recovery for PKE). *Let* $\Sigma = (\mathsf{KGen}, \mathsf{Enc}, \mathsf{Dec}, \mathsf{Rec})$ *be a recoverable PKE scheme, and let* $(\mathsf{pk}, \mathsf{sk}) \leftarrow \mathsf{KGen}$. *The* type-1 recovery *operator for* pk *is the unitary defined by:*

$$U_{\mathsf{Rec}_{\mathsf{pk}}}^{(1)} : |r, c, z\rangle \mapsto |r, c, z \oplus \mathsf{Rec}_{\mathsf{pk}}(r, c)\rangle.$$

---

[4] Even if considering challengers that use superpositions of randomnesses, we show in the full version [19] that the difference is irrelevant, and that we can always restrict ourselves to the case of a classical randomness register.

As usual we will denote this operator by $U_{\text{Rec}}^{(1)}$ when there is no ambiguity in the choice of pk, and with the same symbol we denote the superoperator acting on mixed states, i.e., $U_{\text{Rec}}^{(1)} : \mathfrak{D}(\mathfrak{H}_{\mathcal{R}} \otimes \mathfrak{H}_{\mathcal{C}} \otimes \mathfrak{H}_{\mathcal{M}}) \to (\mathfrak{H}_{\mathcal{R}} \otimes \mathfrak{H}_{\mathcal{C}} \otimes \mathfrak{H}_{\mathcal{M}})$.

Now, the crucial observation is the following: for recoverable PKE schemes, the canonical type-2 encryption operator can be efficiently implemented using only the public key.

Theorem 8 (Type-2 Encryption Operator for Recoverable Schemes).
Let $\Sigma = (\mathsf{KGen}, \mathsf{Enc}, \mathsf{Dec}, \mathsf{Rec})$ be a recoverable PKE, and let $(\mathsf{pk}, \mathsf{sk}) \leftarrow \mathsf{KGen}$. Then there exists an efficient procedure which only takes pk as input, and outputs a polynomial-size quantum circuit realising the canonical operator $U_{\text{Enc}}^{(2)}$.

Proof. The explicit circuit of the procedure is shown in Fig. 3. It uses type-1 encryption and recovery operators as underlying components, which are both efficient with knowledge of the public key only. Realisation of both these components is independent of the fact whether the scheme has full correctness or not, as the decryption algorithm itself is never used.   □

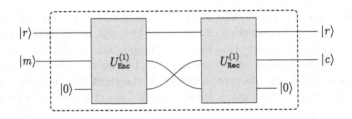

Fig. 3. Canonical type-2 encryption operator for recoverable PKE schemes.

In particular, for recoverable PKE schemes the type-2 encryption operator can be realised locally by a quantum adversary (or a reduction), without need of additional oracle access. This, together with the fact that most real-world PKE schemes are recoverable (as we will see in Sect. 4) shows that type-2 encryption operators are very natural, and unlike in the symmetric key case considered in [18] they also appear implicitly in QS1 security notions for such schemes.

3.4   The qIND-qCPA Security Notion

We are now ready to define the notion of *quantum ciphertext indistinguishability under quantum chosen plaintext attack* (qIND-qCPA) for PKE schemes which admit an efficient construction of the canonical type-2 encryption operator $U_{\text{Enc}}^{(2)}$. This includes in particular perfectly correct schemes and recoverable schemes.[5]

---

[5] As we will see, these cover all the interesting cases in practice, although there might be other classes of schemes which allow an efficient construction of $U_{\text{Enc}}^{(2)}$; we address the general case in the full version [19].

We follow the approach in [18] and we define a game where a polynomially bounded quantum adversary plays against an external challenger. We have to define the challenge phase and the learning (quantum CPA) phases (pre- and post-challenge), using the theory of type-2 operators we have devised so far.

For the challenge query it is pretty straightforward: as in the original qIND security definition for symmetric key encryption, we assume that the challenger $\mathcal{C}$ generates a keypair and sends the public key pk to the adversary $\mathcal{A}$. Then $\mathcal{A}$ sends two plaintext quantum states (possibly mixed) φ_0, φ_1 to $\mathcal{C}$, who will flip a random bit $b \leftarrow \{0,1\}$, discard (trace out) φ_{1-b}, and encrypt the other message with the type-2 encryption oracle $\psi \leftarrow O_{\text{Enc}}^{(2)}(\varphi_b)$. Finally, ψ is sent back to $\mathcal{A}$, who will have to guess b in order to win the game.

Justifying the use of a type-2 encryption during the challenge phase requires arguments different from the symmetric key case. In the classical IND-CPA game for PKE, the challenger does not even need to know the secret key, as it is not needed for encryption, and we saw already that the secret key is sometimes necessary to implement the canonical type-2 encryption operator. However, in the QS2 case the challenger can produce ciphertext-encoding quantum states with very different structure depending on whether he knows the secret key or not, thereby leading to different attack models. Type-2 encryption operators in particular are more general in this respect, and allow us to aim for a stronger security notion. Moreover we also saw how certain schemes, like the recoverable ones, allow to build the type-2 operator using only the public key. Thus it makes sense for a QS2 security notion to include the use of type-2 operators during the challenge phase.

The other question we have to address, which was left unspecified in [18], is about the learning (qCPA) phase. Shall the adversary be able to perform only type-1 encryption operations, or type-2 as well? In the QS1 case the answer is obvious: it depends on the scheme, e.g., for recoverable schemes both type-1 and type-2 operations are allowed, but in the general case only type-1 operations should. Instead, in the QS2 case that we are considering, the answer is less straightforward. For recoverable schemes again there is no difference, as the adversary can implement both types of operators locally. But for general schemes there might be a difference, and there might exist non-recoverable PKE schemes which become insecure when giving oracle access to a type-2 encryption operator during the learning phase.[6]

In our definition of qIND-qCPA we opt for giving to the adversary as much power as possible, hence explicitly giving access to a type-2 encryption oracle when dealing with non-recoverable schemes, both in the learning and challenge

---

[6] For example, one could combine a suitable separating SKE scheme with the canonical hybrid construction (cf. Sect. 4.2), so that the separation property is 'inherited' by the resulting PKE scheme. We are not aware of an explicit example of such SKE scheme and we leave this as an open problem. We stress that such a counterexample is not found in [13], as the authors there "excluded [...] notations that [...] combine quantum learning queries with quantum challenge queries of different query models.".

phases. The reason for this choice is twofold. First, this allows us to aim for potentially stronger security notions. Second, remember that, classically, CPA attacks model not only the case where the adversary can compute ciphertexts himself (as in the case of PKE), but also scenarios where the adversary can "trick" an honest encryptor in providing certain ciphertexts (as in the case of IND-CPA security for symmetric key encryption). In the quantum PKE setting, there is a difference whether these ciphertexts are computed locally by the adversary or obtained by the challenger through "trickery" (including scenarios already considered in [18], such as quantum side-channel attacks, quantum obfuscation, etc.), because the challenger has knowledge of the secret key, and is therefore capable of generating type-2 ciphertexts even if the scheme is non-recoverable. So, giving the adversary access to the type-2 encryption oracle seems to be the "safe" choice.

These considerations finally lead to the following.

Experiment 9. The qIND-qCPA *experiment* qIND-qCPA$(\Sigma, \mathcal{A}, \lambda)$ for a PKE scheme $\Sigma = (\mathtt{KGen}, \mathtt{Enc}, \mathtt{Dec})$ is defined as follows:

1: $\mathcal{C}$ runs $(\mathtt{pk}, \mathtt{sk}) \leftarrow \mathtt{KGen}$ and implements $O_{\mathtt{Enc}}^{(2)}$
2: $\mathcal{A}^{O_{\mathtt{Enc}}^{(2)}}(\mathtt{pk}) \rightarrow (\varphi_0, \varphi_1, \sigma_{state})$
3: $\mathcal{C}$ receives φ_0, φ_1 and does the following:
    - flips $b \xleftarrow{\$} \{0, 1\}$
    - traces out φ_{1-b}
    - calls $\psi \leftarrow O_{\mathtt{Enc}}^{(2)}(\varphi_b)$
    - sends ψ to $\mathcal{A}$
4: $\mathcal{A}^{O_{\mathtt{Enc}}^{(2)}}(\sigma_{state}, \psi) \rightarrow b' \in \{0, 1\}$
5: **if** $b = b'$ **then return** *win*; **else return** *rej*.

Security is defined as negligible advantage over guessing.

Definition 10 (qIND-qCPASecurity). *A public key encryption scheme Σ has quantum ciphertext indistinguishability under quantum chosen plaintext attack, or is qIND-qCPA-secure, iff for any QPT adversary $\mathcal{A}$ it holds:*

$$\left| \Pr\left[\mathsf{qIND\text{-}qCPA}(\Sigma, \mathcal{A}, \lambda) \rightarrow win \right] - \frac{1}{2} \right| \leq \mathrm{negl}(\lambda).$$

It is easy to show that the above notion is at least as strong as the QS1 notion of IND-qCPA for PKE introduced in [12]. Before we show this, let us first recall some game-based notation [9,32]. Let G be a game (or experiment) instantiated with a cryptographic scheme Σ and $\mathcal{A}$ be an adversary. We write $\mathbf{Adv}_{\Sigma}^{G}(\mathcal{A})$ to denote the advantage of $\mathcal{A}$ in game G instantiated with Σ, e.g., $\mathbf{Adv}_{\Sigma}^{\mathsf{qIND\text{-}qCPA}}(\mathcal{A})$ for the qIND-qCPA advantage against Σ. If the scheme is clear from the context, we simply write $\mathbf{Adv}^{G}(\mathcal{A})$.

Theorem 11 (qIND-qCPA $\Rightarrow$ IND-qCPA). *Let $\Sigma = (\mathtt{KGen}, \mathtt{Enc}, \mathtt{Dec})$ be a PKE scheme. For any adversary $\mathcal{A}$, it holds that*

$$\mathbf{Adv}^{\mathrm{IND\text{-}qCPA}}(\mathcal{A}) \leq \mathbf{Adv}^{\mathrm{qIND\text{-}qCPA}}(\mathcal{A}).$$

Proof. We show that any adversary $\mathcal{A}$ wins the qIND-qCPA game with at least the same probability of winning the IND-qCPA game [12]. The differences with Experiment 9 are:

1. In the IND-qCPA game $\mathcal{A}$ does not get oracle access to $O_{\text{Enc}}^{(2)}$. Hence, when switching to qIND-qCPA, the winning probability cannot decrease, because the power of the adversary is augmented by the type-2 oracle.
2. In the IND-qCPA game $\mathcal{A}$ is restricted to classical challenge messages m_0, m_1. When switching to qIND-qCPA, the adversary will simply use quantum states $|m_0\rangle, |m_1\rangle$ as challenge plaintexts instead, and will measure the quantum ciphertext received by the challenger.

Notice in fact that, since the randomness r in the qIND-qCPA challenge query is classical, the type-2 operator $U_{\text{Enc}}^{(2)}$ will produce a ciphertext state which is just a classical ciphertext encoded as a basis state $|c = \text{Enc}_{\text{pk}}(m; r)\rangle$. In other words, quantum plaintexts are *more generic* than classical plaintexts (or, to put it differently, classical plaintexts are a very special case of quantum plaintexts), and hence again the power of the adversary is not diminished when switching to the qIND-qCPA game. $\square$

3.5   The CCA Case

We leave the case of extending our exposition to the quantum chosen ciphertext attack case (with the relevant notions of qIND-qCCA1 and qIND-qCCA2) as future work, but we want anyway to sketch here the general strategy.

The first task is to formalise a type-2 operator for decryption. Unlike in the symmetric key setting considered in [18], this is not necessarily going to be the adjoint of the type-2 encryption operator, and in particular it might not require a randomness register as input; this has to be expected given that there is already an asymmetry in the definition of type-1 encryption and decryption operators in the public key setting. Then, in the qIND-qCCA1 case, we just extend the qIND-qCPA experiment by also providing the adversary with oracle access to the type-1 and type-2 decryption operators.

Extending the framework to the qIND-qCCA2 case is not straightforward, mainly due to no-cloning and the destructive nature of quantum measurement. In fact, this case was left as an open problem already in [18] for the symmetric key setting. Fortunately, the technique presented in [4] shows how to overcome this difficulty, by using a real-VS-ideal approach which makes it possible to differentiate the behaviour of the adversary when replaying the challenge ciphertext to the decryption oracle, hence effectively detecting a challenge replay attack. The approach in [4] (and its extension to the public key case presented in [3]) is given in the context of *quantum encryption schemes* (a scenario which falls under the QS3 domain in [17]), but it is easy to generalise to the QS2 notions we are considering here.

4 Security Analysis for Real-World PKE Schemes

We analyse the qIND-qCPA security of several real-world public key encryption schemes. We start with the code-based PKE scheme ROLLO-II in Sect. 4.1. These results can be analogously applied to the canonical LWE-based PKE scheme. In Sect. 4.2 we study the qIND-qCPA security of the hybrid encryption scheme.

$\text{KGen}(\lambda; r)$	$\text{Enc}(\text{pk}, m; r)$	$\text{KGen}(\lambda)$	$\text{Enc}_{\text{pk}}(m; r)$
$x, y := r$	$e_1, e_1 := r$	$(\text{pk}, \text{sk}) \leftarrow \text{KGen}^P(\lambda)$	**parse** r **as** (r_1, r_2, r_3)
$h := x^{-1}y \bmod P$	$E := \text{Supp}(e_1, e_2)$	**return** (pk, sk)	$k := \text{KGen}^S(\lambda; r_1)$
$\text{sk} := (x, y)$	$c_1 := m \oplus O(E)$		$c_1 := \text{Enc}_k^S(m; r_2)$
$\text{pk} := h$	$c_2 := e_1 + e_2 h \bmod P$		$c_2 := \text{Enc}_{\text{pk}}^P(k; r_3)$
return (pk, sk)	**return** $c := (c_1, c_2)$		**return** (c_1, c_2)

Fig. 4. Left: Pseudocode of the code-based public key encryption scheme ROLLO-II. Right: Hybrid encryption scheme $\Sigma = (\text{KGen}, \text{Enc}, \text{Dec})$ built from a PKE scheme $\Sigma^P = (\text{KGen}^P, \text{Enc}^P, \text{Dec}^P)$ and an SKE scheme $\Sigma^S = (\text{KGen}^S, \text{Enc}^S, \text{Dec}^S)$. For the randomness r used by KGen and Enc, let $x := r$ denote that x is deterministically derived from r. Decryption algorithms are omitted.

4.1 Results for Code-Based PKE ROLLO-II

The encryption scheme ROLLO-II [8] is a code-based public key encryption scheme based on rank metric codes. The scheme in a generic, simplified form is displayed in Fig. 4, where O is a random oracle, Supp describes the support of vectors, and P is a polynomial from the underlying code problem.

We first notice that ROLLO-II is recoverable, and hence admits a qIND-qCPA security definition (the proof is found in the full version [19].) We also point out that, by the same arguments, the code-based PKE schemes which underlie the NIST proposals BigQuake [15], HQC [1], and RQC [2] are recoverable as well.

Lemma 12. *The scheme ROLLO-II, shown in Fig. 4, is recoverable.*

We note that ROLLO-II is not qIND-qCPA-secure. In the full version [19] we give an explicit attack against the qIND-qCPA security of ROLLO-II. The attack is a Hadamard distinguisher that exploits the fact that the message is essentially encrypted using a one-time pad (ciphertext part c_1 in Fig. 4).

Theorem 13. *Let Σ be the scheme ROLLO-II shown in Fig. 4. Then there exists an efficient adversary $\mathcal{A}$ that wins* qIND-qCPA$(\Sigma, \mathcal{A})$ *with probability* $\geq \frac{3}{4}$.

A similar attack applies to the canonical LWE-based PKE scheme which we give in the full version [19]. The attack allows to perfectly distinguish the ciphertexts, yet is restricted to certain parameters. We conjecture that it can be adapted to the general case.

4.2 Results for Hybrid Encryption

The canonical hybrid PKE-SKE encryption scheme combines a public key encryption and a symmetric key encryption scheme into a public key encryption scheme. That is, a message is encrypted using a fresh one-time key of the symmetric encryption scheme. The one-time key is then encrypted using the public key encryption scheme, whereupon the encrypted one-time key is attached to the ciphertext. To decrypt, one first recovers the symmetric one-time key, and then uses it to decrypt the ciphertext containing the message. The canonical hybrid encryption scheme is shown in Fig. 4. For additional background on symmetric key encryption schemes and the security notion used in this section, we refer to the full version [19], where we show that the canonical hybrid encryption scheme is recoverable: Given the randomness, the used one-time key can be obtained, which allows to decrypt the ciphertext part containing the message. We stress that this holds even if the underlying PKE scheme is not recoverable.

Lemma 14. *The canonical hybrid encryption scheme is recoverable.*

It turns out that the QS2 security depends on the underlying SKE scheme, while the underlying PKE scheme merely requires QS1 security. This is formalised in the theorem below. The proof appears in the full version [19].

Theorem 15 (QS2 Security of Hybrid Encryption). *Let* $\Sigma = (\mathrm{KGen}, \mathrm{Enc}, \mathrm{Dec})$ *be the hybrid encryption scheme built from an SKE scheme* $\Sigma^S = (\mathrm{KGen}^S, \mathrm{Enc}^S, \mathrm{Dec}^S)$ *and a PKE scheme* $\Sigma^P = (\mathrm{KGen}^P, \mathrm{Enc}^P, \mathrm{Dec}^P)$, *as shown in Fig. 4. For any adversary* $\mathcal{A}$ *against* Σ, *there exist adversaries* $\mathcal{B}$ *and* $\mathcal{C}$ *against* Σ^P *and* Σ^S, *respectively, such that*

$$\mathbf{Adv}_{\Sigma}^{\mathrm{qIND\text{-}qCPA}}(\mathcal{A}) \leq \mathbf{Adv}_{\Sigma^P}^{\mathrm{IND\text{-}qCPA}}(\mathcal{B}) + \mathbf{Adv}_{\Sigma^S}^{\mathrm{qIND}}(\mathcal{C}).$$

Theorem 15 reveals that to achieve our qIND-qCPA security notion, we can instantiate the hybrid encryption scheme with a PKE that merely achieves QS1 security. This positive result includes, e.g., the use of ROLLO-II as a KEM, despite it not being qIND-qCPA-secure when used as a stand-alone PKE scheme.

   In the following theorem we show that Theorem 15 is strict. If the underlying SKE is not qIND-secure, then the resulting hybrid scheme is not qIND-qCPA-secure, irrespectively of the underlying PKE scheme. The proof is given in the full version [19]. Examples for SKE schemes which are not qIND-secure are given in [18].

Theorem 16. *Let* $\Sigma = (\mathrm{KGen}, \mathrm{Enc}, \mathrm{Dec})$ *be the hybrid encryption scheme built from an SKE scheme* $\Sigma^S = (\mathrm{KGen}^S, \mathrm{Enc}^S, \mathrm{Dec}^S)$ *and a PKE scheme* $\Sigma^P = (\mathrm{KGen}^P, \mathrm{Enc}^P, \mathrm{Dec}^P)$, *as shown in Fig. 4. Assume that there exists an adversary* $\mathcal{A}$ *which has some non-negligible advantage* ε *against the qIND security of* Σ^S. *Then there exists an adversary* $\mathcal{B}$ *against* Σ *such that*

$$\mathbf{Adv}_{\Sigma}^{\mathrm{qIND\text{-}qCPA}}(\mathcal{B}) \geq \varepsilon.$$

Acknowledgements. The authors are very grateful to the anonymous reviewers for spotting a flaw in a previous version of this manuscript. The authors also thank Cecilia Boschini and Marc Fischlin for helpful discussions regarding the correctness of public key encryption schemes and Andreas Hülsing for general discussions on the content of this work. TG acknowledges support by the EU H2020 Project FENTEC (Grant Agreement #780108). JK and PS acknowledge funding by the Deutsche Forschungsgemeinschaft (DFG) – SFB 1119 – 236615297.

References

1. Aguilar Melchor, C., et al.: HQC. Technical report, National Institute of Standards and Technology (2019). https://csrc.nist.gov/projects/post-quantum-cryptography/round-2-submissions
2. Aguilar Melchor, C., et al.: RQC. Technical report, National Institute of Standards and Technology (2019). https://csrc.nist.gov/projects/post-quantum-cryptography/round-2-submissions
3. Alagic, G., Gagliardoni, T., Majenz, C.: Can you sign a quantum state. IACR Cryptology ePrint Archive, 2018:1164 (2018)
4. Alagic, G., Gagliardoni, T., Majenz, C.: Unforgeable quantum encryption. In: Nielsen, J.B., Rijmen, V. (eds.) EUROCRYPT 2018, Part III. LNCS, vol. 10822, pp. 489–519. Springer, Cham (2018). https://doi.org/10.1007/978-3-319-78372-7_16
5. Alagic, G., Majenz, C., Russell, A., Song, F.: Quantum-access-secure message authentication via blind-unforgeability. In: Canteaut, A., Ishai, Y. (eds.) EUROCRYPT 2020, Part III. LNCS, vol. 12107, pp. 788–817. Springer, Cham (2020). https://doi.org/10.1007/978-3-030-45727-3_27
6. Alagic, G., Russell, A.: Quantum-secure symmetric-key cryptography based on hidden shifts. In: Coron, J.-S., Nielsen, J.B. (eds.) EUROCRYPT 2017, Part III. LNCS, vol. 10212, pp. 65–93. Springer, Cham (2017). https://doi.org/10.1007/978-3-319-56617-7_3
7. Anand, M.V., Targhi, E.E., Tabia, G.N., Unruh, D.: Post-quantum security of the CBC, CFB, OFB, CTR, and XTS modes of operation. In: Takagi, T. (ed.) PQCrypto 2016. LNCS, vol. 9606, pp. 44–63. Springer, Cham (2016). https://doi.org/10.1007/978-3-319-29360-8_4
8. Aragon, N., et al.: ROLLO. Technical report, National Institute of Standards and Technology (2019). https://csrc.nist.gov/projects/post-quantum-cryptography/round-2-submissions
9. Bellare, M., Rogaway, P.: The security of triple encryption and a framework for code-based game-playing proofs. In: Vaudenay, S. (ed.) EUROCRYPT 2006. LNCS, vol. 4004, pp. 409–426. Springer, Heidelberg (2006). https://doi.org/10.1007/11761679_25
10. Bernstein, D.J., Buchmann, J., Dahmen, E.: Post-quantum cryptography (2009)
11. Boneh, D., Dagdelen, Ö., Fischlin, M., Lehmann, A., Schaffner, C., Zhandry, M.: Random oracles in a quantum world. In: Lee, D.H., Wang, X. (eds.) ASIACRYPT 2011. LNCS, vol. 7073, pp. 41–69. Springer, Heidelberg (2011). https://doi.org/10.1007/978-3-642-25385-0_3
12. Boneh, D., Zhandry, M.: Secure signatures and chosen ciphertext security in a quantum computing world. In: Canetti, R., Garay, J.A. (eds.) CRYPTO 2013, Part II. LNCS, vol. 8043, pp. 361–379. Springer, Heidelberg (2013). https://doi.org/10.1007/978-3-642-40084-1_21

13. Carstens, T.V., Ebrahimi, E., Tabia, G., Unruh, D.: On quantum indistinguishability under chosen plaintext attack. Cryptology ePrint Archive, Report 2020/596 (2020). https://eprint.iacr.org/2020/596

14. Chevalier, C., Ebrahimi, E., Vu, Q.-H.: On the security notions for encryption in a quantum world. IACR Cryptology ePrint Archive, 2020/237 (2020)

15. Couvreur, A., et al.: BIG QUAKE. Technical report, National Institute of Standards and Technology (2017). https://csrc.nist.gov/projects/post-quantum-cryptography/round-1-submissions

16. Damgård, I., Funder, J., Nielsen, J.B., Salvail, L.: Superposition attacks on cryptographic protocols. In: Padró, C. (ed.) ICITS 2013. LNCS, vol. 8317, pp. 142–161. Springer, Cham (2014). https://doi.org/10.1007/978-3-319-04268-8_9

17. Gagliardoni, T.: Quantum security of cryptographic primitives. Ph.D. thesis, Darmstadt University of Technology, Germany (2017)

18. Gagliardoni, T., Hülsing, A., Schaffner, C.: Semantic security and indistinguishability in the quantum world. In: Robshaw, M., Katz, J. (eds.) CRYPTO 2016, Part III. LNCS, vol. 9816, pp. 60–89. Springer, Heidelberg (2016). https://doi.org/10.1007/978-3-662-53015-3_3

19. Gagliardoni, T., Krämer, J., Struck, P.: Quantum indistinguishability for public key encryption. Cryptology ePrint Archive, Report 2020/266 (2020). https://eprint.iacr.org/2020/266

20. Grover, L.K.: A fast quantum mechanical algorithm for database search. In: 28th ACM STOC, pp. 212–219. ACM Press, May 1996

21. Ito, G., Hosoyamada, A., Matsumoto, R., Sasaki, Yu., Iwata, T.: Quantum chosen-ciphertext attacks against feistel ciphers. In: Matsui, M. (ed.) CT-RSA 2019. LNCS, vol. 11405, pp. 391–411. Springer, Cham (2019). https://doi.org/10.1007/978-3-030-12612-4_20

22. Kaplan, M., Leurent, G., Leverrier, A., Naya-Plasencia, M.: Breaking symmetric cryptosystems using quantum period finding. In: Robshaw, M., Katz, J. (eds.) CRYPTO 2016, Part II. LNCS, vol. 9815, pp. 207–237. Springer, Heidelberg (2016). https://doi.org/10.1007/978-3-662-53008-5_8

23. Kaplan, M., Leurent, G., Leverrier, A., Naya-Plasencia, M.: Quantum differential and linear cryptanalysis. IACR Trans. Symm. Cryptol. 2016(1), 71–94 (2016). http://tosc.iacr.org/index.php/ToSC/article/view/536)

24. Kashefi, E., Kent, A., Vedral, V., Banaszek, K.: Comparison of quantum oracles. Phys. Rev. A 65(5), 050304 (2002)

25. Kuwakado, H., Morii, M.: Quantum distinguisher between the 3-round feistel cipher and the random permutation. In: Proceedings of IEEE International Symposium on Information Theory, ISIT 2010, Austin, Texas, USA, 13–18 June 2010, pp. 2682–2685 (2010)

26. Kuwakado, H., Morii, M.: Security on the quantum-type even-mansour cipher. In: Proceedings of the International Symposium on Information Theory and its Applications, ISITA 2012, Honolulu, HI, USA, 28–31 October 2012, pp. 312–316 (2012)

27. Nielsen, M.A., Chuang, I.L.: Quantum Computation and Quantum Information: 10th Anniversary Edition, 10th edn. Cambridge University Press, New York (2011)

28. National Institute of Standards and Technology. Post-quantum cryptography standardization process (2017)

29. Regev, O.: On lattices, learning with errors, random linear codes, and cryptography. In: Gabow, H.N., Fagin, R. (eds.) 37th ACM STOC, pp. 84–93. ACM Press, May 2005

30. Rötteler, M., Steinwandt, R.: A note on quantum related-key attacks. Inf. Process. Lett. **115**(1), 40–44 (2015)
31. Shor, P.W.: Algorithms for quantum computation: discrete logarithms and factoring. In: 35th FOCS, pp. 124–134. IEEE Computer Society Press, November 1994
32. Shoup, V.: Sequences of games: a tool for taming complexity in security proofs. Cryptology ePrint Archive, Report 2004/332 (2004). http://eprint.iacr.org/2004/332
33. Watrous, J.: Zero-knowledge against quantum attacks. SIAM J. Comput. **39**(1), 25–58 (2009)
34. Zhandry, M.: How to construct quantum random functions. In: 53rd FOCS, pp. 679–687. IEEE Computer Society Press, October 2012

A Practical Adaptive Key Recovery Attack on the LGM (GSW-like) Cryptosystem

Prastudy Fauzi[1]([✉]), Martha Norberg Hovd[1,2], and Håvard Raddum[1]

[1] Simula UiB, Bergen, Norway
prastudy@simula.no
[2] University of Bergen, Bergen, Norway

Abstract. We present an adaptive key recovery attack on the leveled homomorphic encryption scheme suggested by Li, Galbraith and Ma (Provsec 2016), which itself is a modification of the GSW cryptosystem designed to resist key recovery attacks by using a different linear combination of secret keys for each decryption. We were able to efficiently recover the secret key for a realistic choice of parameters using a statistical attack. In particular, this means that the Li, Galbraith and Ma strategy does not prevent adaptive key recovery attacks.

Keywords: Key recovery · Somewhat homomorphic encryption · GSW · Statistical attack

1 Introduction

Fully homomorphic encryption (FHE) is a powerful primitive which allows for meaningful computations to be performed on encrypted data, without the need for decryption. An FHE scheme allows for ciphertexts to be evaluated over any circuit without risking an erroneous decryption of the resulting ciphertext, i.e., $\text{Dec}(C(\text{Enc}(m))) \neq C(m)$ for some circuit C. There are other flavours of homomorphic encryption as well: leveled homomorphic encryption (LHE) and somewhat homomorphic encryption (SHE), which both allow for a *limited amount* of operations to be performed on a ciphertext before there is a risk of decryption failure. A key difference between LHE and SHE is that the key generation of LHE schemes takes an extra parameter as input, which specifies the depth of the deepest circuit the scheme is able to homomorphically evaluate.

Many F/L/SHE schemes rely on a quantum secure assumption, such as the hardness of learning with errors (LWE) and ring learning with errors (RLWE), to provide security against key recovery attacks and/or message recovery. In fact, these schemes are typically shown to achieve IND-CPA security, meaning an adversary with access only to the public key and parameters is provably unable to distinguish between the encryptions of any two messages. However, most existing F/L/SHE schemes are known to be susceptible to *adaptive* key recovery attacks [8,10]. In these attacks an adversary has temporary access to

© Springer Nature Switzerland AG 2021
J. H. Cheon and J.-P. Tillich (Eds.): PQCrypto 2021, LNCS 12841, pp. 483–498, 2021.
https://doi.org/10.1007/978-3-030-81293-5_25

484 P. Fauzi et al.

a decryption oracle, and is able to recover the secret key based on information leaked from the decryption queries.

For example, schemes based on LWE or RLWE (such as GSW [11]) can leak one bit of the secret key from a small number of decryption queries. These schemes have public keys of the form $(\mathbf{A}, \mathbf{As} + \mathbf{e})$ with secret key $\mathbf{s}$, a matrix $\mathbf{A}$, and noise $\mathbf{e}$. Key recovery attacks either compute $\mathbf{s}$ directly, or first compute the noise $\mathbf{e}$ and use this to derive $\mathbf{s}$. Chenal and Tang used this approach to attack several (R)LWE schemes, one of which was GSW [8].

Li, Galbraith and Ma (LGM, [13]) proposed a technique to circumvent such key recovery attacks: instead of decrypting using a single secret key $\mathbf{s}$, they suggested changing secret keys for every decryption, so any information leaked from two different decryption queries would be unrelated, which should make it impossible for an adversary to recover any secret key. They constructed an LHE scheme based on GSW they claimed achieved IND-CCA1 security, though they were unable to provide a formal proof.[1]

Concretely, they start with the dual version of GSW, where the public key is of the form $(\mathbf{A}, \mathbf{As})$, but the secret key $\mathbf{s}$ must have small norm; security now depends on the hardness of the inhomogeneous short integer solution (ISIS) problem, which is also assumed to be quantum secure. Instead of having one secret key $\mathbf{s}$, they generate t distinct secret keys: $\mathbf{s}_1, \ldots, \mathbf{s}_t$. During decryption a random linear combination of the secret keys, $\mathbf{s}' = \sum_{i=1}^{t} \lambda_i \mathbf{s}_i$, is used, where the λ_i's are redrawn from a distribution for each decryption. The message space is $\mathbb{Z}_2$, so a decryption query leaks, at best, one bit of $\mathbf{s}'$: an unknown linear combination of secret keys unlikely to ever be reused, since the λ_is that generate it are redrawn for every decryption. The technique successfully thwarts the known adaptive key recovery attacks on GSW and similar schemes, and Li et al. therefore argue that their scheme achieves IND-CCA1 security, though they are unable to prove it.

In this paper we show that the LGM scheme is still susceptible to an adaptive key recovery attack, as we are able to recover a secret key using a statistical attack. We go even further to claim that the general approach of using a random linear combination of secret keys for each decryption query is susceptible to statistical adaptive key recovery attacks. To the best of our knowledge, the LGM scheme is currently the only concrete leveled homomorphic encryption scheme attempting to achieve IND-CCA1 security, which has proven a difficult security notion to achieve for SHE or LHE schemes.[2]

2 Preliminaries

Vectors are denoted by bold, lower case letters, and are assumed to be in column form. Logarithms are always base 2. For a real number x, let $\lfloor x \rceil = \lfloor x + \frac{1}{2} \rfloor$ be the

---

[1] The original paper was published in ProvSec 2016 [14] however, the ePrint version [13] of the paper contains major changes. In particular, the scheme we mount the adaptive key recovery attack on in this article is found in the ePrint version.

[2] There are suggestions for generic constructions achieving IND-CCA1 security (e.g., [7]), but there are no concrete instantiations of these constructions.

closest integer to x. For any integers x and q, let $x \mod q$ denote the modular reduction centered around zero. For a vector $\mathbf{v}$, let $\|\mathbf{v}\|$ be its Euclidean norm. Unless stated otherwise, we refer to somewhat, leveled, and fully homomorphic encryption schemes as simply *homomorphic encryption schemes*.

The gadget vector $\mathbf{g}$ is defined as the column vector $(1, 2, \ldots, 2^{l-1})^T$, and the gadget matrix is defined as $\mathbf{G} = \mathbf{I}_n \otimes \mathbf{g} \in \mathbb{Z}_q^{n \times nl}$ (i.e., $\mathbf{G}$ is a matrix with $\mathbf{g}$ on the diagonal), for $l = \lfloor \log(q) \rfloor + 1$.

Define $\mathbf{G}^{-1} : \mathbb{Z}_q^{n \times n'} \rightarrow \{0, 1\}^{nl \times n'}$ to be the operation such that for any matrix $\mathbf{M} \in \mathbb{Z}_q^{n \times n'}$, we have that $\mathbf{G} \cdot \mathbf{G}^{-1}(\mathbf{M}) = \mathbf{M}$.

IND-CCA1. An encryption scheme $\mathcal{E} = (\text{Setup}, \text{KeyGen}, \text{Enc}, \text{Dec})$ achieves the security notion *indistinguishability under (non-adaptive) chosen ciphertext attack* (IND-CCA1) if any probabilistic polynomial time adversary $\mathbb{A}$ has at most a $1/2 + \text{negl}$ chance of winning the following game against a challenger $\mathcal{C}$:

- $\mathcal{C}$ derives the parameters using *params* $\leftarrow$ Setup(1^κ), draws a key pair $(pk, sk) \leftarrow$ KeyGen(*params*), and sends pk and the parameters to $\mathbb{A}$.
- $\mathbb{A}$ sends ciphertexts c to her decryption oracle $\mathcal{O}_{\text{Dec}}$, which returns Dec(c).
- $\mathbb{A}$ sends two messages of equal length (m_0, m_1) to $\mathcal{C}$.
- $\mathcal{C}$ returns $c \leftarrow$ Enc(pk, m_b) to $\mathbb{A}$, for a randomly chosen bit $b \in \{0, 1\}$.
- $\mathbb{A}$ outputs the bit b^*, and wins if $b^* = b$.

The notion of IND-CPA security is defined in a similar way, but here $\mathbb{A}$ does not have access to a decryption oracle.

An adaptive key recovery attack is stronger than an IND-CCA1 attack, as recovering the secret key enables an adversary to decrypt *all* ciphertexts, not just distinguish between the encryptions of two chosen messages.

LWE. The *Learning With Errors* (LWE) distribution is defined as follows: for a fixed vector $\mathbf{s}$ drawn uniformly at random from $\mathbb{Z}_q^n$, sample a vector $\mathbf{a}$ uniformly at random from $\mathbb{Z}_q^n$ and an error e from some noise distribution χ, and output $(\mathbf{a}, b = \mathbf{a} \cdot \mathbf{s}^T + e \mod q)$. The search problem of LWE is to find $\mathbf{s}$ given m samples of the LWE distribution, where $\mathbf{s}$ is fixed for all the samples.

ISIS. Given a modulus q, a matrix $\mathbf{B} \in \mathbb{Z}_q^{n \times m}$, and a vector $\mathbf{u}$, the *Inhomogeneous Short Integer Solution* (ISIS) problem is to find a vector $\mathbf{e}$ drawn from a distribution χ with bound B such that $\mathbf{B}\mathbf{e} = \mathbf{u} \mod q$, if such a vector exists. It is required that $m > n$ to prevent an adversary simply finding $\mathbf{e}$ using Gaussian elimination [5,13].

2.1 Distributions

For integers $a \leq b$, let $[a, b]$ denote the set of integers x such that $a \leq x \leq b$. A distribution over values $S = [a, b]$ for integers $a \leq b$ is *discrete uniform* if all $n = b - a + 1$ values $x \in S$ can occur with equal probability $1/n$. Such a distribution has mean $\frac{a+b}{2}$ and variance $\frac{n^2-1}{12}$.

A distribution over values $\mathbb{R}$ is *Gaussian* with mean μ and variance σ^2 if it follows the probability density function

$$g(x) = \frac{1}{\sigma\sqrt{2\pi}} e^{\frac{(x-\mu)^2}{2\sigma^2}} .$$

A random variable following a Gaussian distribution is also said to be *normally distributed*. The value σ is also known as the *standard deviation*.

We provide, without proof, some known properties of Gaussian distributions.

Lemma 1. *Let $(X_i)_{i=1}^n$ be normally distributed independent random variables with mean μ_i and variance σ_i^2 for $i \in \{1, 2, \ldots, n\}$. Let $(a_i)_{i=1}^n$ be real numbers. Then $X = \sum_{i=1}^n a_i X_i$ is also normally distributed, with mean $\sum_{i=1}^n a_i \mu_i$ and variance $\sum_{i=1}^n a_i^2 \sigma_i^2$.*

Lemma 2. *Let X be a random variable following a Gaussian distribution with mean μ and variance σ^2. Then $Pr[\|X - \mu\| \geq t\sigma] = \mathbf{erf}(t/\sqrt{2})$, where $\mathbf{erf}(x) = \frac{2}{\sqrt{\pi}} \int_0^x e^{-t^2} dt$ is the error function. In particular, $Pr[\|X - \mu\| \geq 5\sigma] \leq 2^{-20}$.*

Theorem 1 (Central limit theorem for sample). *Let $X_1, \ldots, X_n$ be independent random variables from a distribution with mean μ and variance σ^2. Let $X = 1/n \cdot \sum_{i=1}^n X_i$. Then if n approaches infinity, $X - \mu$ converges to a Gaussian distribution with mean 0 and variance σ^2/n.*

Informally, by taking a large enough sample size n, $X - \mu$ has mean ϵ_μ and variance $\sigma^2/n + \epsilon_\sigma$, where $\epsilon_\mu, \epsilon_\sigma$ may both be made arbitrarily small.

Discrete Gaussian Distribution. The *discrete Gaussian distribution* may be viewed as a Gaussian distribution where the values are restricted to a countable set, say $\mathbb{Z}$. To preserve the desirable properties of Gaussian distributions mentioned above, one should not simply sample a Gaussian and round to the closest integer. Instead, we adapt the definition of Gaussian distributions over $S \subseteq \mathbb{Z}$ presented by Micciancio and Walter [16]. For the more general definition over $S \subseteq \mathbb{Z}^n$, we refer to [1,13].

Definition 1. *Let S be a subset of $\mathbb{Z}$. For $c \in \mathbb{R}$ and a parameter $\sigma > 0 \in \mathbb{R}$, define $\rho_{\sigma,c}(x) = e^{-\pi \frac{(x-c)^2}{\sigma^2}}$ and $\rho_{\sigma,c}(S) = \sum_{x \in S} \rho_{\sigma,c}(x)$. The discrete Gaussian distribution over S with center c and standard deviation σ is defined as*

$$\forall x \in S : D_{S,\sigma,c}(x) = \frac{\rho_{\sigma,c}(x)}{\rho_{\sigma,c}(S)}.$$

We also state Theorem 7 (one dimensional leftover hash lemma) of [13], as it is central for the derivation of parameters for the LGM scheme. Li et al. present it as a special case of Theorem 2 of Agrawal et al. [2].

Theorem 2. *Let $\sigma, \epsilon \in \mathbb{R}$ be such that $\epsilon > 0$ and $\sigma > C$ for some absolute constant C (see [2]). Let $t, \sigma' \in \mathbb{R}$ be such that $t \geq 10 \log(8t^{1.5}\sigma)$ and $\sigma' \geq 4t \log(1/\epsilon)$. Then the statistical difference between the following two distributions is bounded by 2ϵ.*

- *Choose a length t vector $\mathbf{x} \in \mathbb{Z}^t$ with entries chosen from the discrete Gaussian distribution on $\mathbb{Z}^t$ with parameter σ and a length t vector $\mathbf{z} \in \mathbb{Z}^t$ with entries chosen from a discrete Gaussian distribution on $\mathbb{Z}^t$ with parameter σ' and compute the output $\mathbf{x}^T \mathbf{z}$.*
- *Choose and output an element from the discrete Gaussian distribution on $\mathbb{Z}$ with parameter $\sigma\sigma'$.*

3   The LGM Scheme

The leveled homomorphic encryption scheme LGM [13] is also known as DMGSW since it uses a multi-key and dual version of GSW. We present it using mostly the original notation, but denote the secret keys as $\mathbf{s}_i = (\mathbf{r}_i \,\|\, -\mathbf{e}_i^T)^T$, as opposed to $\mathbf{e}_i = (\mathbf{I}_i \,\|\, -\mathbf{t}_i^T)^T$. Note also that we omit the details of homomorphic addition and multiplication, as they are not relevant for our attack.

Setup($1^\kappa, 1^L$): Let $n = n(\kappa, L)$ and $m = m(\kappa, L)$ be parameters $n < m$ that depend on the security parameter κ and number of levels L. Choose a modulus q and bounded noise distribution $\chi = \chi(\kappa, L)$ on $\mathbb{Z}$ with bound B such that it achieves at least 2^κ security against known attacks. Choose the number of secret keys $t = O(\log n)$. Let $l = \lfloor \log q \rfloor + 1$ and $N = (t + m)l$. Output $params = (n, q, \chi, m, t, l, N)$.

KeyGen($params$): Uniformly sample $\mathbf{B} \in \mathbb{Z}_q^{n \times m}$. For $i \in [1, t]$, sample $\mathbf{e}_i$ from χ^m, set $\mathbf{u}_i = \mathbf{B}\mathbf{e}_i$ and set $\mathbf{s}_i = (\mathbf{r}_i \,\|\, -\mathbf{e}_i^T)^T$, where $\mathbf{r}_i$ is the i-th row of the $t \times t$ identity matrix. Return the public key $\mathbf{A} = [\mathbf{u}_1 \,\|\, \ldots \,\|\, \mathbf{u}_t \,\|\, \mathbf{B}] \in \mathbb{Z}_q^{n \times (t+m)}$ and the secret key $\mathbf{s} = (\mathbf{s}_1, \ldots, \mathbf{s}_t)$.

Enc($\mathbf{A}, \mu \in \mathbb{Z}_2$): Let $\mathbf{G}$ be the $(t+m) \times N$ gadget matrix. Sample $\mathbf{R} \leftarrow \mathbb{Z}_q^{n \times N}$ and $\mathbf{X} \leftarrow \chi^{(t+m) \times N}$. Output $\mathbf{C} = \mu \cdot \mathbf{G} + \mathbf{A}^T \mathbf{R} + \mathbf{X} \in \mathbb{Z}_q^{(t+m) \times N}$.

Dec($\mathbf{s}, \mathbf{C}$): Sample $(\lambda_1, \ldots, \lambda_t) \in \mathbb{Z}_q^t \setminus \{0\}^t$ until the generated $\mathbf{s}' = \sum_{i=1}^t \lambda_i \mathbf{s}_i$ has small norm. Let $i \in [1, t], j, I = (i-1)l + j$ be integers such that $\lambda_i \neq 0$, $2^{j-1} \in (q/4, q/2]$ and $I \in [1, tl]$. Compute $u = \langle \mathbf{C}_I, \mathbf{s}' \rangle \mod q$, where $\mathbf{C}_I$ is the Ith column of the ciphertext matrix $\mathbf{C}$. Finally, output $\|\lfloor u/2^{j-1} \rceil\| \in \{0, 1\}$.

Correct decryption of honestly generated ciphertexts follows from the following observations: first, note that $\mathbf{A}\mathbf{s}_i = 0$ for all i by construction, which ensures that $\mathbf{A}\mathbf{s}' \equiv 0 \mod q$. Then, due to $\mathbf{s}'$ being small and the choice of I, $u = \mu \mathbf{G}^T \mathbf{s}' + \mathbf{X}^T \mathbf{s}' = \mu 2^{j-1} + E$ for some small E. It is clear that the rounded division with 2^{j-1} will result in the message μ.

Li et al. mainly focus on the case where the λ_is are drawn uniformly at random from $\{0, 1\}$, but they also discuss other possible distributions to sample from, such as a larger uniform distribution or a discrete Gaussian distribution. We consider the security of the scheme in all these cases.

Deducing a message from a ciphertext boils down to solving the LWE-like instance $\mathbf{B}^T\mathbf{R} + \mathbf{X}$, whilst security against (non-adaptive) key recovery attacks is based on the ISIS problem.

The intuition behind LGM's claimed IND-CCA1 security is that since a new secret key is being used to decrypt every time the oracle is called, an adversary will be unable to deduce anything meaningful about either the summands of the key or the key itself, as she gets at most one bit of information from each decryption query, since the message space is $\mathbb{Z}_2$. Li et al. argued that any information leaked from one decryption query cannot be combined with information from another query, since the secret keys are different every time.

3.1 Parameter Derivation

The authors do not suggest a concrete parameter setting for the LGM scheme; we therefore derive a realistic choice for parameters based on the information and bounds provided in [13], which we also state here.

- The parameters m, n, q and the bound B must all be chosen so that the instantiated cases of LWE and ISIS problems are hard to solve.
- The inequality $tB + mB^2 < q/8$ must be satisfied in order to prevent an erroneous decryption of a fresh (i.e., unevaluated) ciphertext.
- Li et al. suggest setting $B = 6\sigma$.
- If the distribution of the values of $\langle \mathbf{C}_I, \mathbf{s}' \rangle \mod q = \langle \mathbf{C}_I, \sum_{i=1}^{t} \lambda_i \mathbf{s}_i \rangle \mod q$ resembles a uniform distribution over $\mathbb{Z}_q$, it must be indistinguishable from a uniform distribution over $\mathbb{Z}_q$. By the leftover hash lemma, we must have $t \geq \log(q) + 3\kappa$ where κ is the security parameter of the scheme for the two distributions to be indistinguishable.
- If the distribution of the values of $\langle \mathbf{C}_I, \mathbf{s}' \rangle \mod q = \langle \mathbf{C}_I, \sum_{i=1}^{t} \lambda_i \mathbf{s}_i \rangle \mod q$ resembles a discrete Gaussian distribution over $\mathbb{Z}_q$, t and σ must satisfy the bounds of Theorem 2, i.e., $t \geq 10\log(8t^{1.5}\sigma)$ and $\sigma \geq C$. This ensures that statistical difference of the distribution of values of $\langle \mathbf{C}_I, \mathbf{s}' \rangle \mod q$ and a discrete Gaussian with parameter $\sigma\sigma'$ is bounded by 2ϵ.

We stress that the distribution mentioned in the two final points arise naturally during decryption, and that the properties of the distribution depends on $\mathbf{C}_I$, so both points must be taken into account. We start from the final point to derive $\sigma \leq C$, for $C \geq 18K\eta_\epsilon(\mathbb{Z})$, where $K > 1$ is some universal constant and $\eta_\epsilon(\mathbb{Z}) \leq \sqrt{\ln(\epsilon/44 + 2/\epsilon)/\pi}$ is the smoothing parameter of the integers [2,18]. Setting $\epsilon = 0.005$ to provide a statistical difference of 0.01 according to Theorem 2 and assuming $K \approx 1$, we derive $\sigma \geq 25$, so we choose $\sigma = 25$. Using the other bounds, we get $t = 400$, $m = 525$, $B = 150$ and $q = 94,980,001$, which ensures a 120-bit security against currently known attacks on LWE and ISIS [3,5].[3]

---

[3] Seeing as we do not use n in our attack, we do not set it explicitly. We do note, though, that it affects the hardness of the LWE instance, and is implicitly set by the requirement $m > n$. We assume $m \approx n$.

4   The Key Recovery Attack

First note that any non-zero linear combination of the secret vectors can be used to decrypt. Hence, to perform a successful key recovery attack we will only need to recover any single $\mathbf{s}_i = (\mathbf{r}_i \parallel -\mathbf{e}_i^T)^T$. We present our attack to recover the entire secret key $\{\mathbf{s}_1, \ldots, \mathbf{s}_t\}$, by recovering the coefficients at a particular index across the t secrets $\mathbf{s}_i$, index by index. However, for the concrete experiments, we recover just one secret key.

We first assume the suggested variant of LGM where the values λ_i are chosen uniformly at random from $\mathbb{Z}_2$, and present the basic attack for this case. Afterwards we show that the attack generalises to the cases $\lambda_i \in [0, b-1]$ and $\lambda_i \in [-b, b]$, where b is some (very) small constant. This constraint on λ_i is necessary to ensure that $\|\mathbf{s}' = \sum \lambda_i \mathbf{s}_i\|$ is small, as is required by the scheme. We also discuss the security of the scheme for the case where the λ_is are sampled from a discrete Gaussian distribution.

$\lambda_i \in \{\mathbf{0, 1}\}$. Recall that decryption works by first choosing $\lambda_1, \ldots, \lambda_t$ uniformly at random from $\{0, 1\}$ and then generating a one-time decryption key $\mathbf{s}'$ as

$$\mathbf{s}' = \lambda_1 \mathbf{s}_1 + \ldots + \lambda_t \mathbf{s}_t = (\lambda_1, \ldots, \lambda_t, \sum_{i=1}^{t} \lambda_i e_{i,1}, \ldots, \sum_{i=1}^{t} \lambda_i e_{i,m}).$$

Next, a column $\mathbf{C}_I$ of the ciphertext matrix $\mathbf{C}$ is chosen, where I corresponds to some index k that satisfies $\lambda_k = 1$. Then $u = \langle \mathbf{C}_I, \mathbf{s}' \rangle \mod q$ is computed, and the decryption oracle returns $\|\lfloor u/2^{j-1} \rceil\|$, for the unique (and known) value j for which $q/4 < 2^{j-1} \le q/2$.

In the following we focus on recovering the first component of each $\mathbf{e}_i$, namely the $e_{1,1}, e_{2,1}, \ldots, e_{t,1}$ that are linearly combined in position $t+1$ of $\mathbf{s}'$. The same attack can be carried out to recover all the other m positions with an easy adaptation. We construct our chosen ciphertexts from column vectors $c_{a,i}$ with some integer a in position i for $1 \le i \le t$, a 1 in position $t+1$ and 0 elsewhere:

$$c_{a,i} = (\underbrace{0, \ldots, a, \ldots, 0}_{\text{length } t, \, a \text{ in pos. } i}, \underbrace{1, 0, \ldots, 0}_{\text{length } m})^T.$$

Let D_α be the ciphertext matrix where for all i the column corresponding to λ_i is $c_{\alpha, i}$, and let $R_{a,i}$ be the ciphertext matrix where every column is $c_{a,i}$:

$$D_\alpha = \begin{bmatrix} \alpha & 0 & \cdots & 0 \\ 0 & \alpha & \cdots & 0 \\ 0 & 0 & \cdots & \alpha \\ 1 & 1 & \cdots & 1 \\ & \mathbf{0}_{(m-1) \times t} & & \end{bmatrix}, \quad R_{a,i} = \begin{bmatrix} & \mathbf{0}_{(i-1) \times t} & & \\ a & a & \cdots & a \\ & \mathbf{0}_{(t-i) \times t} & & \\ 1 & 1 & \cdots & 1 \\ & \mathbf{0}_{(m-1) \times t} & & \end{bmatrix}.$$

Asking for the decryption of D_α will result in the following expression for $u = u(D_\alpha)$, no matter which index k corresponds to the chosen column $\mathbf{C}_I$:

$$u(D_\alpha) = \langle c_{\alpha, i}, \mathbf{s}' \rangle = \alpha + \sum_{i=1}^{t} \lambda_i e_{i,1}.$$

This is because it is a requirement that $\lambda_k = 1$ for the chosen index I. The output of the decryption query will depend on the size of α, as well as the value of $\sum_{i=1}^{t} \lambda_i e_{i,1}$. In the attack we will only use values of α that are close to 2^{j-2}. In particular, we will always have $0 < \alpha + \sum_{i=1}^{t} \lambda_i e_{i,1} < q$, and thus will never have to consider any reductions modulo q. If $\alpha + \sum_{i=1}^{t} \lambda_i e_{i,1} < 2^{j-2}$ the decryption oracle will return 0, and if $\alpha + \sum_{i=1}^{t} \lambda_i e_{i,1} \geq 2^{j-2}$ it will return 1. Define the value $E = \sum_{i=1}^{t} \lambda_i e_{i,1}$. Asking for the decryption of D_α many times will make E a stochastic variable that takes its value according to a discrete Gaussian distribution over the interval $[E_{\min}, E_{\max}]$, where $E_{\min}$ and $E_{\max}$ are the minimum and maximum values E can take, respectively. Denoting the expected value of E by $\mathbb{E}(E)$, we get $\mathbb{E}(E) = 1/2 \sum_{i=1}^{t} e_{i,1}$. Approximately half of the time E will take a value that is smaller than $\mathbb{E}(E)$ and approximately half of the time the value of E will be greater than $\mathbb{E}(E)$.

Similarly, asking for the decryption of $R_{a,i}$ will give the following expression for $u = u(R_{a,i})$:

$$u(R_{a,i}) = \langle c_{a,i}, \mathbf{s}' \rangle = \lambda_i a + \lambda_i e_{i,1} + \sum_{k \neq i} \lambda_k e_{k,1}.$$

In this case we do not know if λ_i is 0 or 1. If $\lambda_i = 0$, the result is $u(R_{a,i}) = \sum_{k \neq i} \lambda_k e_{k,1} \ll 2^{j-2}$, and so the decryption will output 0. If $\lambda_i = 1$ the output of the decryption query will depend on the size of a and the value of the sum $\sum_{k \neq i} \lambda_k e_{k,1}$. Define E_i to be $E_i = \sum_{k \neq i} \lambda_k e_{k,1}$. In the same way as above, asking for decryptions of $R_{a,i}$ multiple times will make E_i be normally distributed over some interval, with an expected value $\mathbb{E}(E_i) = 1/2 \sum_{k \neq i} e_{k,1}$.

The main idea of the attack is to ask for many decryptions of D_α and $R_{a,i}$, and count how often the decryption oracle returns 1. Asking for sufficiently many decryptions makes the randomness of the unknown and varying λ_i's even out to their expected values. Counting how often the decryption oracle returns 1 for various values of α and a allows us to extract information about the size of $e_{i,1}$, and accurately estimate its value.

Attack Procedure. For a more detailed explanation of how the attack works, we start with the following definition.

Definition 2. *Let $h(\alpha)$ be the number of times the decryption oracle returns 1 when asked for a number of decryptions of D_α, and let $h_i(a)$ be the number of times the decryption oracle returns 1 when asked for a number of decryptions of $R_{a,i}$.*

The number of times we ask for the decryption of the same ciphertext is denoted by T, and its exact value will be determined later. By doing a binary search, find the integer α_0 such that $h(\alpha_0) < T/2 \leq h(\alpha_0 + 1)$. Next, make an interpolated value α_{est} that we estimate would give exactly $T/2$ decryptions returning 1 if we were allowed to ask for decryptions of D_α for $\alpha \in \mathbb{R}$:

$$\alpha_{est} = \frac{h(\alpha_0 + 1) - T/2}{h(\alpha_0 + 1) - h(\alpha_0)}\alpha_0 + \frac{T/2 - h(\alpha_0)}{h(\alpha_0 + 1) - h(\alpha_0)}(\alpha_0 + 1).$$

Note that the value α_{est} is a real value, and it is our best estimate for the equation $\alpha_{est} + 1/2 \sum_{i=1}^{t} e_{i,1} = 2^{j-2}$ to hold. To be precise, we get the equation

$$\alpha_{est} + 1/2 \sum_{i=1}^{t} e_{i,1} = 2^{j-2} + \epsilon, \tag{1}$$

where $|\epsilon|$ becomes small when the sample size T grows large.

Next, we repeat the process and ask for decryptions of $R_{a,i}$ for $i = 1, \ldots, t$. Note that $\lambda_i = 0$ half of the time in these decryptions, which always causes the oracle to return the value 0. So the values $h_i(a)$ will be approximately half of $h(a)$. This is compensated for by finding the value a_0 such that $2h_i(a_0) < T/2 \leq 2h_i(a_0 + 1)$. Knowing that $\lambda_i = 1$ whenever we get a 1-decryption, we do the same interpolation as above and find an estimate $a_{est} \in \mathbb{R}$ such that

$$a_{est} + e_{i,1} + 1/2 \sum_{k \neq i} e_{k,1} = 2^{j-2} + \epsilon_i, \tag{2}$$

where $|\epsilon_i|$ is small. Subtracting (2) from (1) and rearranging we get

$$e_{i,1} = 2(\alpha_{est} - a_{est}) + 2(\epsilon_i - \epsilon). \tag{3}$$

Rounding the right-hand side value recovers the correct $e_{i,1}$, provided that T is large enough to make $|\epsilon_i| < 1/8$ and $|\epsilon| < 1/8$.

The attack can be repeated to recover all the $e_{i,x}$ for $x = 2, 3, \ldots, m$ by setting the 1 in $c_{a,i}$ to be in position $t + x$. One can also focus on fully recovering only one of the vectors $\mathbf{e}_i$ by recovering $e_{i,x}$ for some fixed i and $x = 1, 2, \ldots, m$. Note that the recovery of an entry of any $\mathbf{e}_i$-vector is independent of the recovery of any other entry. This is what enables us to recover a single $\mathbf{e}_i$-vector in its entirety, which can be used as a decryption key.

For the attack to work with high probability, we need $T \in O(t \cdot \sigma^2)$. In particular, we have the following:

Lemma 3. *If* $T \geq 800 \cdot t \cdot \sigma^2$ *then in Eq. (1) we have that* $Pr[|\epsilon| \geq 1/8] \leq 2^{-20}$ *and in Eq. (2) we have that* $Pr[|\epsilon_i| \geq 1/8] \leq 2^{-20}$.

Proof. Since λ_i is taken from the uniform distribution over $\{0, 1\}$ it has mean $1/2$ and variance $1/4$. Moreover, $e_{i,1}$ is taken from a Gaussian distribution with mean 0 and variance σ^2. Then $\lambda_i \cdot e_{i,1}$ is taken from a Gaussian distribution with mean $1/2 \cdot \sum e_{i,1}$ and variance $1/2 \cdot \sigma^2$. Hence $\epsilon = \sum_{i=1}^{t} \lambda_i \cdot e_{i,1} - \mathbb{E}(E)$ is a sum of Gaussians, which by Lemma 1 is also a Gaussian with mean 0 and variance $t/2 \cdot \sigma^2$. However, if we take an average of T samples of such a function, then by the central limit theorem for sample means we get a Gaussian X with mean 0 and variance $\frac{t}{2T} \cdot \sigma^2$. If $T \geq 800 \cdot t \cdot \sigma^2$ then X has standard deviation $\leq 1/40$, in which case $Pr[|\epsilon| \geq 1/8] \leq 2^{-20}$ by Lemma 2. Similarly, $Pr[|\epsilon_i| \geq 1/8] \leq 2^{-20}$. $\square$

Remark 1. We cannot get a smaller lower bound for T using Lemma 8.1 of [1] since there is no guarantee that the Gaussian X in the above proof is integral.

The running time will then be $O(Tm) = O(t\sigma^2 m)$. We have that t can only be polynomially large in the security parameter to have efficient encryption. Also, $\|\mathbf{s}'\|$ must be small in order for the underlying ISIS problem to be hard. Therefore, the attack runs in polynomial time.

4.1 Generalisation of the Attack

The above attack assumes that the values λ_i were sampled uniformly at random from $\{0,1\}$. We now investigate whether the attack can be prevented by choosing the λ_i from a larger set. The two generalisations we consider are $\lambda_i \in \{0,1,\ldots,b-1\}$, or $\lambda_i \in \{-b,\ldots,b\}$. As before, we can take $T \in O(t \cdot \sigma^2)$. We show that the attack can be generalised to work in both cases.

$\lambda_i \in \{\mathbf{0,1},\ldots,\mathbf{b-1}\}$. The attack can be adapted to work when the λ_i are sampled uniformly at random from $\{0,1,\ldots,b-1\}$. We again focus on recovering the coefficients $e_{i,1}$, the other $e_{i,x}$'s are recovered by repeating the attack with the same adaptation as above. This also means that we may choose to recover a single $\mathbf{e}_i$-vector here as well.

When the decryption oracle is given the ciphertext matrix D_α, it will compute $u(D_\alpha) = \lambda_k\alpha + \sum_{i=1}^{t}\lambda_i e_{i,1}$, where $\lambda_k \neq 0$. When $\alpha \approx 2^{j-2}/(b-1)$, the decryption oracle will return 0 whenever $\lambda_k < b-1$, since $\lambda_k\alpha + \sum_{i=1}^{t}\lambda_i e_{i,1} < 2^{j-2}$ in this case. Only when $\lambda_k = b-1$ can we get decryptions that return 1. We know that $\lambda_k \neq 0$ when decrypting D_α, so the probability that $\lambda_k = b-1$ is $1/(b-1)$.

As before, we scale the numbers $h(\alpha)$ with $b-1$ to do a binary search and find the value α_0 such that $(b-1)h(\alpha_0) < T/2 \leq (b-1)h(\alpha_0+1)$. We then use this to estimate the α_{est} for which we would expect $(b-1)h(\alpha_{est}) = T/2$ if we were allowed to ask for decryptions of D_α where $\alpha \in \mathbb{R}$.

When $\lambda_i \in \{0,1,\ldots,b-1\}$, the expected value of $\sum_{i=1}^{t}\lambda_i e_{i,1}$ is $\frac{b-1}{2}\sum_{i=1}^{t}e_{i,1}$. The α_{est} we find therefore gives the equation

$$(b-1)\alpha_{est} + \frac{b-1}{2}\sum_{i=1}^{t}e_{i,1} = 2^{j-2} + \epsilon, \tag{4}$$

where $|\epsilon|$ is small for large T.

In the same fashion we can ask for decryptions of $R_{a,i}$ where $a \approx 2^{j-2}/(b-1)$ and count the number of 1-decryptions we get. When decrypting $R_{a,i}$ we may have $\lambda_i = 0$, so the probability that $\lambda_i = b-1$ (which is necessary for the decryption oracle to return 1) is $1/b$. We therefore scale the values of $h_i(a)$ by b, and find an interpolated value for a_{est} based on the value a_0 for which $bh_i(a_0) < T/2 \leq bh_i(a_0+1)$. This yields the equation

$$(b-1)a_{est} + (b-1)e_{i,1} + \frac{b-1}{2}\sum_{k\neq i}^{t}e_{k,1} = 2^{j-2} + \epsilon_i, \tag{5}$$

where $|\epsilon_i|$ is small. Subtracting (5) from (4) gives

$$e_{i,1} = 2(\alpha_{est} - a_{est} + \frac{\epsilon_i - \epsilon}{b - 1}),$$

and rounding this value recovers the correct $e_{i,1}$, provided $|\epsilon_i| < (b-1)/8$ and $|\epsilon| < (b-1)/8$.

The proof of the following lemma is almost identical to Lemma 3 and is thus omitted. In fact, the upper bound for $Pr[|\epsilon_i| \geq (b-1)/8]$ and $Pr[|\epsilon| \geq (b-1)/8]$ will be even smaller than 2^{-20} for $b > 2$.

Lemma 4. If $T \geq 800 \cdot t \cdot \sigma^2$ then in Eq. (4) we have that $Pr[|\epsilon| \geq 1/8] \leq 2^{-20}$ and in Eq. (5) we have that $Pr[|\epsilon_i| \geq 1/8] \leq 2^{-20}$.

$\lambda \in \{-\mathbf{b}, \ldots, \mathbf{b}\}$. We start by asking for T decryptions of D_α, where $\alpha \approx 2^{j-2}/b$, and count how often the decryption oracle returns 1. Recall that the decryption outputs the absolute value of $\lfloor u/2^{j-1} \rceil$, so there are now two cases where the decryption oracle can return 1, namely when $\lambda_i = b$ or $\lambda_i = -b$. There are $2b+1$ numbers in $\{-b, \ldots, b\}$, but 0 cannot be chosen for λ_k when decrypting D_α, so the probability of having λ_k equal to $-b$ or b is $2/2b = 1/b$. We scale the numbers $h(\alpha)$ by a factor b to compensate for this. We then interpolate like before to find the value α_{est} such that we would expect $h(\alpha_{est}) = T/2$ if we were allowed to ask for decryptions of $D_{\alpha_{est}}$ for $\alpha \in \mathbb{R}$. When the set of values that λ_i can take is symmetric around 0, the expected value of $\sum \lambda_i e_{i,1}$ is 0. The equation we get for α_{est} is then simplified to

$$b\alpha_{est} = 2^{j-2} + \epsilon, \tag{6}$$

where $|\epsilon|$ is small. Note that we do not need to distinguish between the cases $\lambda_k = -b$ and $\lambda_k = b$, as this is incorporated in the probability $2/2b$ for having the possibility of 1-decryption. So the α_{est} we find covers both the cases $-b\alpha < -2^{j-2}$ and $b\alpha > 2^{j-2}$, which both result in 1-decryptions.

When decrypting $R_{a,i}$ we can have $\lambda_i = 0$, so the probability of $\lambda_i = -b$ or $\lambda_i = b$ is then $2/(2b+1)$. We ask T times for decryptions of $R_{a,i}$, and as before find the value a_{est} that is the best estimate for $\frac{2b+1}{2}h_i(a_{est}) = T/2$. We then get the equation

$$ba_{est} + be_{i,1} = 2^{j-2} + \epsilon_i, \tag{7}$$

where $|\epsilon_i|$ is small. Subtracting (7) from (6) gives us

$$e_{i,1} = \alpha_{est} - a_{est} + \frac{\epsilon_i - \epsilon}{b}.$$

Rounding this value to the nearest integer recovers the correct $e_{i,1}$, provided T is large enough to make $|\epsilon_i| < b/4$ and $|\epsilon| < b/4$.

The proof of the following lemma is almost identical to Lemma 3 and is thus omitted. In fact, the upper bound for $Pr[|\epsilon_i| \geq b/4]$ and $Pr[|\epsilon| \geq b/4]$ will be even smaller than 2^{-20}.

Lemma 5. *If* $T \geq 800 \cdot t \cdot \sigma^2$ *then in Eq.* (6) *we have that* $Pr[|\epsilon| \geq 1/8] \leq 2^{-20}$ *and in Eq.* (7) *we have that* $Pr[|\epsilon_i| \geq 1/8] \leq 2^{-20}$.

4.2   Implementation of the Attack

We have implemented the attack and verified that it works as explained. The code for the attack was written in C, and can be found at [17]. The secret e_i-vectors were sampled using the DGS library [4].

For testing the attack we have used a Dell server with 75 CPU cores (AMD Epyc 7451). We ran the attack twice, using the parameter sets deduced in Sect. 3.1. For the first attack we used $t = 190, m = 525, b = 2$, and $\sigma = 25$, which gives the sample size $T = 95,000,000$ according to Lemma 3. For the second attack we used $t = 400, m = 525, b = 2$, and $\sigma = 25$, for which Lemma 3 gives the sample size $T = 200,000,000$. In both attacks we drew the λ_i's uniformly from $\{0,1\}$ and aimed to recover all the 525 coefficients of $\mathbf{e}_2$[4].

In the attack on the $t = 190$ case, 519 of the 525 coefficients were recovered correctly. The six coefficients that were wrong all had a difference 1 with the correct value. In the attack on the $t = 400$ case, all 525 coefficients of $\mathbf{e}_2$ were recovered correctly.

The run time for the first attack was approximately 12 h, and for the second attack approximately 48 h, both using 75 CPU cores in parallel. However, the code can be optimised in several ways to reduce the run time. In particular, it is possible to abort early and not do all T decryptions when it is clear that $h(\alpha)$ or $h_i(a)$ will be much greater or smaller than $T/2$. We did not implement this optimisation, and computed all T decryptions every time.

Our attack does not necessarily recover a secret key flawlessly, as demonstrated above with the $t = 190$ case, where 6 out of 525 estimated coefficients were either -1 or 1 off from their true value. In these cases, we need a second phase to recover the entire secret key. It is straightforward to check whether such a second phase is necessary, as we may simply check if $\mathbf{A}\tilde{\mathbf{s}}_i = 0$, for an estimated secret key $\tilde{\mathbf{s}}_i = (\mathbf{r}_i, -\tilde{\mathbf{e}}_i)^T$, where $\tilde{\mathbf{e}}_i$ is the estimate of $\mathbf{e}_i$ we get by running the attack. If $\mathbf{A}\tilde{\mathbf{s}}_i \neq 0$, there is at least one wrong entry of $\tilde{\mathbf{e}}_i$, implying $\mathbf{e}_i = \tilde{\mathbf{e}}_i + \epsilon$, where ϵ is a non-zero vector sampled from a Gaussian distribution with mean 0 and a very small standard deviation. Recall that the public key is $\mathbf{A} = [\mathbf{u}_1 \parallel \dots \parallel \mathbf{u}_t \parallel \mathbf{B}]$, where $\mathbf{u}_i = \mathbf{B}\mathbf{e}_i$, so we can calculate $\mathbf{B}\epsilon = \mathbf{B}\tilde{\mathbf{e}}_i - \mathbf{u}_i$. Now, $\mathbf{B}\epsilon$ may be described as n highly unbalanced instantiations of the knapsack problem: only approximately 1% of the coefficients of ϵ are either -1 or 1. These instantiations are much simpler to solve than the standard knapsack problem: one estimation for the time complexity for the $\mathbf{B}\epsilon$ case is $\tilde{O}(2^{0.03n})$ [6], another is $\tilde{O}(2^{0.0473n})$ [12], though the first algorithm does not guarantee finding the solution. Even though the memory requirement is higher in either case, the (potential) second phase of the attack does not contribute in any substantial way to the cost of the key recovery attack, and ensures that the secret key is completely recovered.

---

[4] We chose $\mathbf{e}_2$ arbitrarily; the attack works to recover any $\mathbf{e}_i$, $i \in \{1, \dots, t\}$.

4.3 λ_i Drawn from a Non-uniform Distribution

Whilst the authors of LGM mainly focus on the $\lambda_i \in \{0,1\}$ case, they also discuss other distributions it would be possible to sample from, e.g., other uniform distributions, or a discrete Gaussian distribution. As shown above, sampling λ_i from other uniform distributions does not prevent our attack, however, a line of argument in the LGM paper suggests that a particular choice of a discrete Gaussian distribution might.[5]

The argument is as follows: if the values of $\langle \mathbf{C}_I, \sum_{i=1}^{t} \mathbf{s}_i \rangle$ resemble samples from a discrete Gaussian distribution, and the standard deviation σ' of the λ-distribution satisfies the condition of Theorem 2, the theorem itself is applicable to the distribution of the values of $\langle \mathbf{C}_I, \sum_{i=1}^{t} \lambda_i \mathbf{s}_i \rangle$. Then, seeing as $\langle \mathbf{C}_I, \sum_{i=1}^{t} \lambda_i \mathbf{s}_i \rangle$ is statistically close to a 'regular' discrete Gaussian distribution with standard deviation $\sigma\sigma'$ by Theorem 2, the result from the decryption oracle cannot leak any information about the secret key.

A rough estimate for the parameters required to achieve 120-bit security in these cases is: $t = 400, \sigma = 25, B = 150, \sigma' = 12,231, m = 940$, and q is a 40-bit number. These parameters prevent any practical use of the system, especially given the fact that the scheme encrypts a single bit at a time.

But that aside, could the scheme with this λ-distribution be regarded as a theoretical construct to demonstrate that IND-CCA1 security is achievable for homomorphic encryption schemes? We argue that the answer is no. Even if the λ-distribution is chosen according to Theorem 2, the theorem only guarantees that the distribution over $\langle \mathbf{C}_I, \sum_{i=1}^{t} \lambda_i \mathbf{s}_i \rangle$ is statistically close to a discrete Gaussian distribution *if* the matrix column $\mathbf{C}_I$ is such that the values of $\langle \mathbf{C}_I, \sum_{i=1}^{t} \mathbf{s}_i \rangle$ appear to be drawn from a discrete Gaussian distribution themselves.

We stress that the choice of $\mathbf{C}_I$ is *entirely* up to the adversary in an IND-CCA1 game, as she can simply submit a ciphertext matrix where every column is $\mathbf{C}_I$. It is therefore feasible for her to submit a $\mathbf{C}_I$ such that the values of $\langle \mathbf{C}_I, \sum_{i=1}^{t} \mathbf{s}_i \rangle$ do not appear to be drawn from a discrete Gaussian distribution, meaning Theorem 2 does not apply. It is therefore not possible to positively conclude that no useful information is leaked by a decryption query, even if it merely results in an adversary obtaining a non-negligible advantage in the IND-CCA1 game, and not a complete recovery of the secret key. Furthermore, the adversary can adapt her choice of $\mathbf{C}_I$, whilst the choice of the distribution from which the λ_is are drawn is fixed when the system is generated. The λ-distribution therefore cannot be constructed to fit both the situation where $\mathbf{C}_I$ is designed to provide values of $\langle \mathbf{C}_I, \sum_{i=1}^{t} \mathbf{s}_i \rangle$ seemingly drawn from a discrete Gaussian distribution and when it is designed to *not* provide such values.

4.4 Thwarting the Attack

We discuss some possible ideas to prevent the key recovery attack described above, and argue that they will not work.

---

[5] See discussion in Sect. 7 of [13].

Decryption Oracle Uses the Same $(\lambda_1, \ldots, \lambda_t)$ **for the Same Ciphertext.**
One can ensure that an attacker that queries the same ciphertext C (say, $C = D_\alpha$
as defined previously) multiple times will have the same set of λ-values chosen
in every decryption. It will then be impossible to do the attack we presented, as
it relies on having random and independent λ-values chosen for each query. This
can be done by setting $(\lambda_1, \ldots, \lambda_t) = \mathsf{PRF}(C)$ for some pseudo-random function
PRF that returns a vector of small values.

To circumvent this measure, the attacker can add a few 1's to the large part
of the top t rows of D_α or $R_{a,i}$ that are defined to be 0. The number of 0's in this
part of D_α or $R_{a,i}$ is $t(t-1)$. So if the attacker intends to ask for T decryptions
of the same matrix, she can make the matrices unique by adding up to ρ 1's in
all possible ways in the top t rows. The computation in the decryption will still
be approximately the same. The largest number ρ of 1's that must be added in
this way is the smallest integer that satisfies

$$\sum_{i=0}^{\rho} \binom{t(t-1)}{i} \geq T.$$

For the parameters used in our attack ($t = 190, T = 200.000.000$) this is satisfied
already for $\rho = 2$.

When adding two 1's to D_α or $R_{a,i}$, the estimates in Eq. (1) and Eq. (2) will
be disturbed by an extra 1 in approximately $(2/t) \cdot (1/2) = 1/t$ of the queries
(the chosen column contains an extra 1 with probability $2/t$, and the λ_j-value it
meets in the inner product will also be 1 with probability $1/2$). This error can be
compensated for in the estimation of α_{est} and a_{est} by adding an extra term to the
equations in Eq. (1) and Eq. (2), but both values will be the same and anyway
cancel out in Eq. (3). Hence the attacker can overcome such a countermeasure.

**Repeat Multiple Decryptions and Return a Value only if They Are
Consistent.** Alternatively, one can define a new decryption function which runs
the original decryption function ℓ times and return bit b only if all ℓ evaluations
return b, and abort (i.e., return $\bot$) if they are not all equal. However, note that
we now have 3 return values $(0, 1, \bot)$ instead of 2, and can compute the expected
value of each return value for every α similar to before.

For instance, consider querying D_α to the new decryption oracle, where α is
a value such that the original decryption oracle would return 0 with probability
p, and 1 with probability $1 - p$. Then the new decryption oracle aborts with
probability $1 - (p^\ell + (1-p)^\ell)$, which achieves maximum at $p = 1/2$. Hence to
detect an optimal α_{est} as in Eq. (1), one asks for T decryptions of $D_{\alpha_{est}}$ and
makes sure $\approx (1 - 2^{1-\ell}) \cdot T$ of them abort. Note that the attack strategy fails if ℓ
is sufficiently large (e.g., $\ell \in \Theta(\kappa)$), but a large choice of ℓ also severely restricts
the LGM scheme's level of homomorphism, since a noisy ciphertext obtained
from a homomorphic evaluation would also fail (i.e., return $\bot$ or the wrong bit)
with non-negligible probability in the new decryption function.

Ciphertext Checks. A plausible strategy to thwart our attack would be to add a ciphertext check during decryption, to ensure that the ciphertext to be decrypted has been honestly generated. Using a ciphertext check, Loftus et al. [15] constructed an SHE scheme that provably achieved IND-CCA1 security, although the underlying hardness assumption was later shown to be insecure; see discussion in [13] and the references therein. If such a ciphertext check is added to the decryption procedure, maliciously generated ciphertexts may simply be rejected by the decryption oracle, which will make it impossible to mount our attack. As illustrated by the previous idea, it is far from clear how to successfully add an efficient ciphertext check to the LGM scheme.

We argue that in general any such ciphertext check that uses the same secret key value both to check ciphertexts are well-formed and to decrypt will naturally give some information about the secret key. One can instead have two secret key values as in the CCA1-secure group homomorphic encryption scheme CS-lite [9], where the first value is used only for checking ciphertexts are well-formed, while the second value ensures indistinguishability even if the first value is revealed. We leave as an open problem how such a method can work with LGM or other homomorphic encryption schemes.

5 Conclusion

We have shown that the LGM scheme is susceptible to an adaptive key recovery attack, disproving the authors' claim that the scheme achieves IND-CCA1 security. The attack is practical for λ_i's drawn uniformly from $\{0, 1\}$, and is still practical and efficient for λ_i's drawn uniformly from a larger set of integers. We have also argued that the scheme is not secure even if the λ_i's are drawn from a discrete Gaussian distribution. In short, none of the distributions suggested by Li et al. ensures the IND-CCA1 security of the LGM scheme.

A plausible strategy to thwart our attack would be to add a ciphertext check during decryption, but we do not know if the strategy can be applied to the LGM scheme, and we know of no other strategies that may be applicable to the scheme to achieve IND-CCA1 security. We therefore do not know how to tweak the LGM scheme to be resistant to our proposed statistical attack.

References

1. Agrawal, S., Boneh, D., Boyen, X.: Efficient lattice (H)IBE in the standard model. In: Gilbert, H. (ed.) EUROCRYPT 2010. LNCS, vol. 6110, pp. 553–572. Springer, Heidelberg (2010). https://doi.org/10.1007/978-3-642-13190-5_28
2. Agrawal, S., Gentry, C., Halevi, S., Sahai, A.: Discrete Gaussian leftover hash lemma over infinite domains. In: Sako, K., Sarkar, P. (eds.) ASIACRYPT 2013, Part I. LNCS, vol. 8269, pp. 97–116. Springer, Heidelberg (2013). https://doi.org/10.1007/978-3-642-42033-7_6
3. Albrecht, M.R., Player, R., Scott, S.: On the concrete hardness of learning with errors. Cryptology ePrint Archive, Report 2015/046 (2015). http://eprint.iacr.org/2015/046

4. Albrecht, M.R., Walter, M.: DGS, discrete Gaussians over the Integers (2018). https://bitbucket.org/malb/dgs
5. Bai, S., Galbraith, S.D., Li, L., Sheffield, D.: Improved combinatorial algorithms for the inhomogeneous short integer solution problem. J. Cryptol. **32**(1), 35–83 (2019). https://doi.org/10.1007/s00145-018-9304-1
6. Becker, A., Coron, J.S., Joux, A.: Improved generic algorithms for hard knapsacks. In: Paterson, K.G. (ed.) EUROCRYPT 2011. LNCS, vol. 6632, pp. 364–385. Springer, Heidelberg (2011). https://doi.org/10.1007/978-3-642-20465-4_21
7. Canetti, R., Raghuraman, S., Richelson, S., Vaikuntanathan, V.: Chosen-ciphertext secure fully homomorphic encryption. In: Fehr, S. (ed.) PKC 2017, Part II. LNCS, vol. 10175, pp. 213–240. Springer, Heidelberg (2017). https://doi.org/10.1007/978-3-662-54388-7_8
8. Chenal, M., Tang, Q.: On key recovery attacks against existing somewhat homomorphic encryption schemes. In: Aranha, D.F., Menezes, A. (eds.) LATINCRYPT 2014. LNCS, vol. 8895, pp. 239–258. Springer, Heidelberg (2015). https://doi.org/10.1007/978-3-319-16295-9_13
9. Cramer, R., Shoup, V.: A practical public key cryptosystem provably secure against adaptive chosen ciphertext attack. In: Krawczyk, H. (ed.) CRYPTO'98. LNCS, vol. 1462, pp. 13–25. Springer, Heidelberg (1998). https://doi.org/10.1007/BFb0055717
10. Dahab, R., Galbraith, S., Morais, E.: Adaptive key recovery attacks on NTRU-based somewhat homomorphic encryption schemes. In: Lehmann, A., Wolf, S. (eds.) ICITS 15. LNCS, vol. 9063, pp. 283–296. Springer, Heidelberg (2015). https://doi.org/10.1007/978-3-319-17470-9_17
11. Gentry, C., Sahai, A., Waters, B.: Homomorphic encryption from learning with errors: conceptually-simpler, asymptotically-faster, attribute-based. In: Canetti, R., Garay, J.A. (eds.) CRYPTO 2013, Part I. LNCS, vol. 8042, pp. 75–92. Springer, Heidelberg (2013). https://doi.org/10.1007/978-3-642-40041-4_5
12. Howgrave-Graham, N., Joux, A.: New generic algorithms for hard knapsacks. In: Gilbert, H. (ed.) EUROCRYPT 2010. LNCS, vol. 6110, pp. 235–256. Springer, Heidelberg (2010). https://doi.org/10.1007/978-3-642-13190-5_12
13. Li, Z., Galbraith, S.D., Ma, C.: Preventing adaptive key recovery attacks on the gentry-sahai-waters leveled homomorphic encryption scheme. Cryptology ePrint Archive, Report 2016/1146 (2016). http://eprint.iacr.org/2016/1146
14. Li, Z., Galbraith, S.D., Ma, C.: Preventing adaptive key recovery attacks on the GSW levelled homomorphic encryption scheme. In: Chen, L., Han, J. (eds.) ProvSec 2016. LNCS, vol. 10005, pp. 373–383. Springer, Heidelberg (2016). https://doi.org/10.1007/978-3-319-47422-9_22
15. Loftus, J., May, A., Smart, N.P., Vercauteren, F.: On CCA-secure somewhat homomorphic encryption. In: Miri, A., Vaudenay, S. (eds.) SAC 2011. LNCS, vol. 7118, pp. 55–72. Springer, Heidelberg (2012). https://doi.org/10.1007/978-3-642-28496-0_4
16. Micciancio, D., Walter, M.: Gaussian sampling over the integers: efficient, generic, constant-time. In: Katz, J., Shacham, H. (eds.) CRYPTO 2017, Part II. LNCS, vol. 10402, pp. 455–485. Springer, Heidelberg (2017). https://doi.org/10.1007/978-3-319-63715-0_16
17. Raddum, H., Fauzi, P.: LGM-attack (2021). https://github.com/Simula-UiB/LGM-attack
18. Zheng, Z., Xu, G., Zhao, C.: Discrete Gaussian measures and new bounds of the smoothing parameter for lattices. Cryptology ePrint Archive, Report 2018/786 (2018). https://eprint.iacr.org/2018/786

Author Index

Bardet, Magali 442
Barenghi, Alessandro 23
Behnia, Rouzbeh 380
Bert, Pauline 195
Beullens, Ward 257
Biasse, Jean-François 23
Blanks, Tamar Lichter 319
Bombar, Maxime 3
Boyen, Xavier 399
Briaud, Pierre 442

Castryck, Wouter 133
Chailloux, André 44
Chen, Yilei 380
Couvreur, Alain 3

Debris-Alazard, Thomas 44
Disson, Lucas 257
Dooms, Ann 133

Eaton, Edward 154
Eberhart, Gautier 195
Eisenbarth, Thomas 177
Emerencia, Carlo 133
Etinski, Simona 44

Fauzi, Prastudy 483
Fouotsa, Tako Boris 277
Furue, Hiroki 65

Gagliardoni, Tommaso 463
Gaj, Kris 234
Gellersen, Tim 177
Gonzalez, Ruben 215
Guo, Tingting 421

Hovd, Martha Norberg 483
Hu, Lei 421
Hülsing, Andreas 215
Hutchinson, Aaron 296

Izabachène, Malika 399

Kannwischer, Matthias J. 215
Karabina, Koray 296
Kirshanova, Elena 117
Krämer, Juliane 215, 463

Lange, Tanja 215
Lemmens, Alexander 133
Li, Qinyi 399
Ling, San 339

Masny, Daniel 380
May, Alexander 117
Miller, Stephen D. 319

Nakamura, Shuhei 65
Nguyen, Duc Tri 234
Nguyen, Khoa 339

Øygarden, Morten 98

Pan, Jiaxin 360
Pedersen, Robi 257
Pereira, Geovandro 296
Persichetti, Edoardo 23
Petit, Christophe 277
Phan, Duong Hieu 339
Prabel, Lucas 195

Raddum, Håvard 483
Roux-Langlois, Adeline 195

Sabt, Mohamed 195
Santini, Paolo 23
Seker, Okan 177
Smith-Tone, Daniel 79, 98
Stebila, Douglas 154
Stöttinger, Marc 215
Struck, Patrick 463

Takagi, Tsuyoshi 65
Tang, Hanh 339

van Hoof, Iggy   117
Verbel, Javier   98
Vercauteren, Frederik   257

Wagner, Benedikt   360
Waitz, Elisabeth   215

Wang, Huaxiong   339
Wang, Peng   421
Wiggers, Thom   215

Yang, Bo-Yin   215
Ye, Dingfeng   421